GERMANY: THE LONG ROAD WEST

Heinrich August Winkler

Germany: The Long Road West

Volume 2: 1933–1990

Translated by
ALEXANDER J. SAGER

OXFORD
UNIVERSITY PRESS

This book has been printed digitally and produced in a standard specification
in order to ensure its continuing availability

OXFORD
UNIVERSITY PRESS

Great Clarendon Street, Oxford OX2 6DP
United Kingdom

Oxford University Press is a department of the University of Oxford.
It furthers the University's objective of excellence in research, scholarship,
and education by publishing worldwide.

Oxford is a registered trade mark of Oxford University Press in the UK
and in certain other countries

© Verlag C.H. Beck oHG, Munich, 2000

British Library Cataloguing in Publication Data
Data available

Library of Congress Cataloging in Publication Data
Data available

ISBN 978-0-19-926598-5

Preface

At the end of my work on this second and final volume of the history of Germany in the nineteenth and twentieth centuries, I owe no small debts of gratitude. First and foremost to my wife, my co-thinker in all the most important sections; then to Ernst-Peter Wieckenberg, former chief reader at C. H. Beck, who counterchecked each separate chapter with uniform thoroughness. I thank Ms Gretchen Klein, who transformed the greater part of the handwritten draft into a press-ready manuscript, and Ms Monika Rossteuscher, who prepared the manuscript for parts of the final chapter. My assistants Daniel Bussenius, Teresa Löwe, Sebastian Ullrich, and Stephanie Zloch helped me over the course of several years with sources and secondary literature, chapter headings, proofreading, and the compilation of the index. I thank them for all they contributed to this volume.

H.A.W.

Berlin
July 2000

The publication of this work was supported by grants from the Goethe-Institut and from the Ebelin and Gerd Bucerius ZEIT Foundation.

Contents

Abbreviations

AAP	*Akten zur Auswärtigen Politik der Bundesrepublik Deutschland* (see Ch. 2 n. 6, Ch. 4 n. 7)
ABC weapons	Atomic, biological, and chemical weapons
ABM	Anti-ballistic missiles
ADAP	*Akten zur deutschen auswärtigen Politik* (see Ch. 1 n. 17, Ch. 3 n. 3)
AdG	*Archiv der Gegenwart*
ADGB	Allgemeiner Deutscher Gewerkschaftsbund (General German Trade Union Association)
ADN	Allgemeiner Deutscher Nachrichtendienst
AdR	*Akten der Reichskanzlei* (see Ch. 1 n. 7)
AfNS	Amt für Nationale Sicherheit
ANSA	Agenzia nazionale stampa associata
APO	Ausserparlamentarische Opposition (Extra-Parliamentary Opposition)
APZ	*Aus Politik und Zeitgeschichte*
ARD	Arbeitsgemeinschaft der öffentlich-rechtlichen Rundfunkanstalten der Bundesrepublik Deutschland
AWACS	Airborne Early Warning and Control Systems
Bafög	Bundesausbildungsförderungsgesetz
BBC	British Broadcasting Corporation
BGBl.	*Bundesgesetzblatt*
BGH	Bundesgerichtshof
BHE	Bund der Heimatvertriebenen und Entrechteten (League of Expellees and Those Deprived of Rights)
BK	Bekennende Kirche (Confessing Church)
BRD	Bundesrepublik Deutschland (see FRG)
BVerfGE	*Entscheidungen des Bundesverfassungsgerichts* (see Ch. 3 n. 16, Ch. 4 n. 15, Ch. 5 nn. 15, 17)
BVP	Bayerische Volkspartei (Bavarian People's Party)
CARE	Cooperation for American Remittance to Europe
CC	central committee
CDU	Christlich-Demokratische Union (Christian Democratic Union)
CEH	*Central European History*

CFE	Conventional Armed Forces in Europe
CFSP	Common Foreign and Security Policy
CIA	Central Intelligence Agency
COMECON	Council for Mutual Economic Assistance
Cominform	Communist Information Bureau
Comintern	Communist International
CPSU	Communist Party of the Soviet Union
CSCE	Conference on Security and Cooperation in Europe
CSSR	Czechoslovak Socialist Republic
CSU	Christlich-Soziale Union (Christian Social Union)
DA	Demokratischer Aufbruch (Democratic Awakening)
DA	*Deutschland Archiv*
DAF	Deutsche Arbeitsfront (German Labour Front)
DC	Glaubensbewegung Deutsche Christen (German Christian Faith Movement)
DDR	Deutsche Demokratische Republik (see GDR)
DKP	Deutsche Kommunistische Partei (German Communist Party)
DM	Deutsche Mark (Deutschmark)
DNVP	Deutschnationale Volkspartei (German National People's Party)
DP	Deutsche Partei (German Party)
DSU	Deutsche Soziale Union (German Social Union)
DTV	DTV
DVP	Deutsche Volkspartei (German People's Party)
EA	*Europa-Archiv*
EC	European Community
ECU	European Currency Unit
EDC	European Defence Community
EEC	European Economic Community
EKD	Evangelische Kirche in Deutschland (Evangelical Church in Germany)
FAZ	*Frankfurter Allgemeine Zeitung*
FDGB	Freier Deutscher Gewerkschaftsbund (Free German Trade Union Association)
FDJ	Freie Deutsche Jugend (Free German Youth)
FDP	Freie Demokratische Partei (Free Democratic Party)
FR	*Frankfurter Rundschau*
FRG	Federal Republic of Germany

GATT	General Agreeement on Tariffs and Trade
GDR	German Democratic Republic
Gestapo	Geheime Staatspolizei (Secret State Police)
GG	*Geschichte und Gesellschaft*
GI	Popular term for an American Soldier ('Government Issue', i.e., the standard equipment of the soldier)
Grafög	Graduiertenförderungsgesetz
GSG	Grenzschutzgruppe (Federal Border Guard)
GVP	Gesamtdeutsche Volkspartrei (All-German People's Party)
GWU	*Geschichte in Wissenschaft und Unterricht*
HIAG	Hilfsgemeinschaft auf Gegenseitigkeit (Mutual Assistance Community, of former soldiers of the Waffen SS)
HZ	*Historische Zeitschrift*
IM	Inoffizieller Mitarbeiter (Unofficial Collaborator of the Ministry for State Security)
IMG	Internationaler Militärgerichtshof (International or Nuremberg Military Tribunal; *IMG*: see Ch. 1 n. 18)
IMT	International Military Tribunal
INF	Intermediate Range Nuclear Forces
infas	Institut für angewandte Sozialwissenschaft
Jusos	Junge Sozialisten (Young Socialists)
KdF	Kraft durch Freude (Strength through Joy)
KGB	Komitet Gosudarstvennoy Bezopasnosti (Soviet Secret Service)
KPD	Kommunistische Partei Deutschlands (Communist Party of Germany)
KZ	Konzentrationslager (concentration camp)
KZSS	*Kölner Zeitschrift für Soziologie und Sozialpsychologie*
LDPD	Liberaldemokratische Partei Deutschlands (Liberal Democratic Party of Germany)
LPG	Landwirtschaftliche Produktionsgenossenschaft (Agricultural Production Cooperative)
MBFR	Mutual Balanced Force Reduction
MfS	Ministerium für Statssicherheit (Ministry for State Security)
MLF	Multilateral Force
Nasi	Popular name for AfNS
NATO	North Atlantic Treaty Organization
NBC	National Broadcasting Company
ND	*Neues Deutschland*

NDPD	Nationaldemokratische Partei Deutschlands (National Democratic Party of Germany)
NG	*Neue Gesellschaft* or *Neue Gesellschaft/Frankfurter Hefte*
NMT	Nuremberg Military Tribunal
NÖSPL	Neue Ökonomische System der Planung und Leitung (New Economic System of Planning and Leadership)
NPD	Nationaldemokratische Partei Deutschlands (National-Democratic Party of Germany)
NSBO	Nationalsozialistische Betriebszellen-Organisation
NSDAP	Nationalsozialistische Deutsche Arbeiterpartei (National Socialist German Workers' Party)
NSRB	Nationalsozialitischer Rechtswahrerbund (National Socialist Jurists' Association)
NVA	Nationale Volksarmee (National People's Army)
OKW	Oberkommando der Wehrmacht (Supreme Command of the Wehrmacht)
OPEC	Organization of Petroleum Exporting Countries
PDS	Partei des Demokratischen Sozialismus (Party of Democratic Socialism)
PLO	Palestinian Liberation Organization
PUWP	Polish United Workers' Party
RAF	Rote Armee Fraktion (Red Army Fraction)
RF-SS	Reichsführer SS
RGBl.	*Reichsgesetzblatt*
SA	Sturmabteilungen (Storm Troopers)
SALT	Strategic Arms Limitation Talks
SD	Sicherheitsdienst (Security Service)
SDI	Strategic Defence Initiative
SDP	Sozialdemokratische Partei in der DDR (Social Democratic Party in the GDR)
SDS	Sozialistischer Deutscher Studentenbund (Socialist German Student Federation)
SED	Sozialistische Einheitspartei Deutschlands (Socialist Unity Party of Germany)
SMAD	Soviet Military Administration in Germany
Sopade	The name of the SPD in exile after 1933
SOZ	Soviet Occupied Zone
SPD	Sozialdemokratische Partei Deutschlands (Social Democratic Party of Germany)

SRP	Sozialistische Reichspartei (Socialist Reich Party)
SS	Schutzstaffel (Security Force)
START	Strategic Arms Reduction Talks
Sten. Ber.	*Stenographischer Bericht der Verhandlungen des Deutschen Reichstages* or *Stenographischer Bericht der Verhandlungen des Deutschen Bundestages*
SZ	*Süddeutsche Zeitung*
TASS	Telegrafnoe Agentstvo Sovetskogo Soyuza (Telegraph Agency of the Soviet Union)
taz	*Die Tageszeitung*
VEB	Volkseigener Betrieb (Publicly Owned Enterprise)
VfZ	*Vierteljahrshefte für Zeitgeschichte*
WEU	West European Union
ZDF	Zweites Deutsches Fernsehen
ZfG	*Zeitschrift für Geschichtswissenschaft*

Introduction

The first volume of this history of Germany in the nineteenth and twentieth centuries traced developments from the end of the old empire to the collapse of the Weimar Republic. The second volume begins with Hitler's accession to power and concludes with the reunification and its consequences. Like the first volume, it is not meant to be a 'total history', but a 'problem history' centred around the relationship between democracy and nation in Germany.

The National Socialist era is not the subject of the first chapter only. The years 1933–45 had such an impact on later decades that the history of divided Germany is, for long stretches, a history of attempts to come to terms with the 'German catastrophe'. This book's main focus is on politics and political culture. Reflections on Germany and the Germans loom large. Like the first volume, this study is as much discourse history as an account of events and processes.

From the 1970s onward, the discursive terrain of the former Federal Republic came to be dominated increasingly by the left, which gained intellectual ascendancy after the change of government in Bonn in 1969. Since that time the left's challengers have grown ever fewer. The spirit blows where it will, but from the right it evidently saw fit to blow no more. The only way the intellectual right was conspicuous was by its absence. In the later phase of the former Federal Republic, therefore, my criticism is primarily directed leftwards. Sometimes this criticism is self-criticism; the author was himself a participant in some of the discourses examined in this book.

The value standards that undergird this history are those of western democracy. My definition of liberty is not the relativist one that determined how the Weimar constitution was interpreted and that, some time ago now, rose again in certain quarters in the form of a postmodernist, pseudo-liberal latitudinarianism. Rather, it is the value-based definition that informs the Basic Law—the German constitution, in which the experiences of the country's political and constitutional history have been assimilated and transcended, 'sublated' in the Hegelian sense. What transpired in the GDR I do not, therefore, evaluate in a 'system-immanent' manner. That would be tantamount to an elevated kind of positivism. But this does not mean that the historian may judge the people who lived in the GDR and who were compelled to come to an arrangement with it as if they had thought and acted under the same conditions of freedom as the Germans in the Federal Republic.

The Germans must critically examine their *entire* history. This was a premise of this two-volume German history of the last two centuries, and it is also one of its lessons. The fact that they did not experience what we might call 'western normality' before the year 1990 does not give the Germans a claim to perpetual anomaly. They cannot shirk the responsibility of pondering their contribution to the European project, but they will not be successful in their efforts without first coming to clarity about their national identity.

The closer this study comes to the present, the more difficult it becomes to draw a line between historical and political judgements. To do without judgements is not an option, however. I hope that readers who find themselves disagreeing with some of my evaluations will nonetheless keep reading, for they might come to their own conclusions.

1

The German Catastrophe 1933–1945

NATIONAL SOCIALISM AS A POLITICAL RELIGION

The man who stood at the apex of the German Reich government on 30 January 1933 believed himself chosen by providence to be the redeemer of the Germans, indeed of the whole Germanic race. He wanted to save the Germans not merely from the disgrace of the Treaty of Versailles, from Marxism, liberalism, and parliamentary rule, but also, and above all, from what he considered the single evil force behind all these phenomena: international Jewry. In Hitler's view, the Jew employed multiple masks to disguise his insidious machinations. Marxism was only one of these, albeit the most successful one thus far, having brought the entire working class under Jewish control. According to this logic, only a political movement and a leader willing to wage the most uncompromising kind of war against Jewry could succeed in liberating the workers from the influence of international Marxism and winning them over to the cause of the nation.

Hitler knew himself to be the leader of such a movement. In *Mein Kampf*,[*] written during his imprisonment in Landsberg in 1924, he had put his convictions into words meant as apocalyptically as they sounded: 'If the Jew, with the help of his Marxist credo, succeeds in gaining the victory over the peoples of the world, then his crown will be humanity's dance of death, and this planet will go spinning through the ether as empty of mankind as it was millions of years ago. Eternal Nature avenges the transgression of her commands. Thus I am convinced that I act according to the will of the Creator: *by fending off the Jew, I fight for the Cause of the Lord.*'

Such sacral phraseology reveals very clearly what the 'Führer' intended his National Socialist movement to be: a worldly *ecclesia militans*, outside of which there could be no salvation, a totalitarian political religion. 'Totalitarian' was the term Italian liberal, democratic, and socialist critics had used to characterize Mussolini's regime, even before the Duce himself spoke of the 'wild, totalitarian will' (*feroce volontà totalitaria*) of his movement for the first time in June 1925. A regime in which political life was defined in terms of a struggle of friend against enemy; that violently repressed any manifestation of opposition and intimidated all dissidence by means of an omnipresent secret police; that eliminated every

---

[*] Hitler, *My Struggle*.

kind of separation of powers for the sake of a one-party monopoly; and that fostered through ideology, propaganda, and terror the acclamatory mass approval it needed to legitimate its dominance, both domestically and abroad—such a regime, as Mussolini's Italy was by the 1930s at the latest, certainly merits the name of 'totalitarian'. In this sense not only fascist Italy, but also the Soviet Union was a totalitarian state, a new kind of dictatorship differing measurably from authoritarian systems such as the military dictatorships of Europe and Latin America. The main innovations of the new system were the mobilization of the masses and the doctrine of the 'new man', by means of which the movement sought control over the totality of the individual person. In Germany, such a system was not yet in place in the weeks immediately following 30 January 1933. But for anyone who had paid attention to the public declamations Hitler had made during the 'years of struggle', it was obvious that the regime he sought to establish would be at least as 'totalitarian' as that of Mussolini.

German National Socialism had much in common with Italian Fascism: radical nationalism, anti-Marxism, and anti-liberalism, the militarization of the domestic political scene, the cults of youth, manhood, and violence, and the central role of the charismatic leader. Both movements traced their origins to the consequences of the First World War and the human trauma they had generated. The National Socialists ascribed the German defeat to the 'stab in the back' perpetrated by the 'November criminals' against the German army. In like fashion the Italian Fascists blamed the weakness of the liberals and the internationally-oriented left for the 'mutilated victory', the frustration of Italy's ambitious plans of annexation by the western allies. Both parties were able to manipulate widespread anxieties and fears, above all the fear of a 'red' revolution after the example of the Russian Bolsheviks. Both took advantage of the schism in the Marxist workers' movement in the wake of the war and the October Revolution.

The similarities shared by Mussolini's and Hitler's movements were so pronounced that many contemporaries, especially on the left, were unable to see in National Socialism anything more than the German version of 'Fascism'. Fascism it certainly was, to the extent that the term is used to define the new type of militant mass movement on the extreme right, a type non-existent in Europe before the First World War. Yet National Socialism was more than 'German Fascism'. To a far greater extent than Italian Fascism it was a political religion that laid claim to the entirety of the human being (in this sense it was rather more like its antipode, Bolshevism). It was in all ways more extreme and more totalitarian than its Roman prototype. In addition, National Socialism was possessed of a quasi-mythological enemy of a kind lacking in Mussolini's movement and regime. The lethal hatred of the Jews, the very centre of Hitler's 'world view', was unknown in Fascist Italy.[1]

According to his own view, as expressed in *Mein Kampf*, Hitler became a dedicated anti-Semite between 1908 and 1913, his 'Vienna years of apprenticeship and suffering'. All non-Jewish peoples in the capital city of the multi-ethnic Austrian empire could find their lowest common denominator, whenever they sought one, by distinguishing themselves sharply from the Jews. In the late Habsburg empire, anti-Semitism was far more widespread than in Wilhelmine Germany, and had greater popular resonance. This was due not least to the efforts of Karl Lueger, the leader of the Christian Social party and longtime mayor of Vienna, whom the young Hitler greatly admired.

During his Vienna years, while he was living in a dormitory for men in Vienna-Brigittenau and earning his money by reproducing paintings, Hitler read a great deal of anti-Semitic literature by obscure authors. One of these was the former priest Josef Adolf Lanz, whose pen-name was Jörg Lanz von Liebenfels. Nonetheless, Hitler was not yet a 'practising' anti-Semite, but rather a Pan-German in the sense of Georg von Schönerer's Pan-German party, which opposed the Habsburg empire and promulgated the unity of Germany and Austria. Although he freely vented his hatred of social democracy and affected to despise the proletariat, into which milieu he—son of an impoverished official from Braunau on the Inn—was at great pains not to sink, Hitler still maintained personal contact with Jews. It is possible that he had already developed anti-Semitic prejudices by this time, but if so, they were not yet conspicuously radical.

Such is also the case during Hitler's early years at Munich, beginning in May 1913, and during the years he fought as a volunteer in a Bavarian infantry regiment on the western front during the First World War. There is no evidence of explicit anti-Semitism at this time. The earliest testimony comes from the year 1919. Hitler's transformation into an implacable enemy of the Jews occurred, it seems, at the same time he resolved to become a politician. Only by clearly identifying an enemy could he discern a role for himself and give meaning to his life in post-war Germany. The country owed its military defeat to Marxism, and behind Marxism was the Jew—as soon as he had 'recognized' this, Hitler knew why 'Providence' had permitted him, the 'obscure private', to survive the war.

In September 1919 Hitler was working as an 'intermediary' for the political department of the army's Munich district command and had just joined a small, right-wing extremist group, the German Workers' Party (*Deutsche Arbeiterpartei*), founded eight months before. By this time his anti-Semitic world view was firmly in place:

Everything that causes a man to strive for the heights, be it religion, socialism, democracy—all these things are simply means to his [the Jew's, H.A.W.] ends, tools to help him satiate his lust for money and power. His machinations bring about the racial tuberculosis of nations and peoples. The upshot is clear: what begins as purely emotional anti-Semitism will find its final expression in the form of programs [*sic!*]. A rational anti-Semitism, on the other hand, must strive, methodically and legally, to oppose and eliminate the privileges of the Jews, which they possess in contrast to the other foreigners who live among us (alien laws and statutes). The final goal, however, from which it may not swerve, must be the elimination of the Jews altogether. Only a government of national power can accomplish this goal. A government of national impotence must fail.

The 'positive' side of the struggle against the Jews was the struggle for the racially pure greater German Reich of the future, in comparison to which earlier German empires, from the medieval empire to the Reich of Bismarck, would necessarily pale. Hitler spelled this out in *Mein Kampf*: 'The borders of 1914 mean absolutely nothing for the future of the German Nation. They provided no protection in the past, and they can provide no strength for the future.'

Germany will either be a World Power, or it will cease to be at all. In order to become a World Power, however, it will need to be of such size as to give it the significance it requires at the present time and to provide life for its citizens. Herein we National Socialists draw a definitive line under the foreign policy of our pre-war period. We will pick up where history left off six centuries ago. We will stop the eternal Germanic migrations to the south and west and direct our gaze to the lands towards the east. We will conclude, once and for all, the colonialist and commercial policies of the pre-war period and initiate the territorial policy of the future.

The east was 'Russia and the subject states on its borders'. In Hitler's view, fate itself had delivered Russia over to the Bolsheviks and thereby provided a sign to Germany: the Bolshevik takeover meant the replacement of an originally Germanic ruling class with Jews, who would not be able to keep such a powerful empire together for long: 'The giant empire in the east is on the verge of collapse. And the end of the Jewish reign in Russia spells the end of Russia as a state. We have been chosen by fate to bear witness to a catastrophe that will provide the strongest possible confirmation of the truth of the racial theory of the *Volk*.'

As leader of the National Socialist German Workers' Party (*Nationalsozial-istische Deutsche Arbeiterpartei* or NSDAP; he had announced the renaming of the German Workers' Party in February 1920), Hitler was, first and foremost, an anti-Semitic agitator. What made him successful in Munich would not yet work in the rest of Germany, however. After 1929, as the NSDAP prepared to take power by 'legal' means, campaigns against the Jews took a back seat to declarations against the Weimar 'system', against Marxism, Bolshevism, and the 'enslavement' of the German people by means of the Young Plan and the international 'bondage of interest payments'. Nationalist slogans had a far greater appeal to the wider populace than anti-Semitic rhetoric, and at any rate the radical Jew-haters were already within the National Socialist camp. In his main campaign speeches at the end of the Weimar era, Hitler also took pains not to emphasize the foreign policy programme outlined in *Mein Kampf* (as well as in his unpublished 'second book' of 1928). Declamations on the necessity of a war for *Lebensraum* ('living space') in eastern Europe, in the territory of the Bolshevist arch-enemy, was not the kind of issue that would have attracted new voters to the party. Hitler's public speeches between 1930 and 1933 were calculated to hide his central convictions, and this was one of the main reasons National Socialism was able to attract mass support.

In linking nationalism and socialism, Hitler's movement differed from all other mass movements on the right in late imperial Germany, including the German Fatherland party of 1917. The NSDAP was no party of notabilities. It owed its electoral successes more to the demagogic talents of its leader and the activism of his followers than to the financial support of right-leaning industrialists and bankers. The 'socialism' of the movement long kept many bourgeois voters at a fearful distance, especially those in the independent middle classes. As late as December 1932, the newly founded *Kampfbund*, a militant party organization tailored to the interests of tradesmen and small business owners, found it necessary to assure these groups that the aim of National Socialist economic and social policy was the 'de-proletarization' of the German worker: 'The goal of the socialist idea is to make owners out of those who own nothing. In this matter Adolf Hitler's socialism stands in the sharpest possible contrast to the sham-socialism of the Marxists, whose purpose is expropriation.' To 'national' workers and employees, as well as students and young academics, 'national Socialism' had a different appeal. Under the party banner, these groups could distance themselves from both international Marxism and the nationalist 'reaction', adopting a 'third' stance, a seemingly future-oriented position beyond proletarian class struggle and bourgeois concern for vested rights and interests.

Nationalism was what connected—or at least appeared to connect—the NSDAP with bourgeois Germany. No political party considered the Versailles Treaty justified, and none rejected the project of a 'Greater Germany'. In their demand for equal rights for Germany and unification with Austria, the National Socialists certainly spoke more radically than any other group. But in the substance of the matter, the revision of the post-war international order, there was broad national consensus, on a superficial level at any rate. Austrian Pan-German and disciple of Schönerer as he was, Hitler had no difficulty adding to the demand for his homeland's unification with the German Reich a declared belief in the Prussian tradition, Frederick the Great, and Bismarck. This was of great help to him politically. The fact that he had been raised in a Catholic household also did him no harm. Younger, non-Marxist, non-religious Germans considered the confessional divisions as historically outmoded as the idea of class struggle. Many people believed Hitler could reconcile what had always seemed to be incompatible antagonisms: not only nationalism and socialism, but also Evangelical and Catholic Germany. In this belief lay Hitler's great opportunity.

The magic words of this grand synthesis were 'community of the *Volk*' (*Volksgemeinschaft*) and 'Reich'. The word *Volksgemeinschaft* was probably first employed by Friedrich Schleiermacher and is found in the marginal notes to a manuscript from the year 1809. In the following decades the concept was introduced into jurisprudence through the work of the legal scholar Friedrich Carl von Savigny, and in 1887 into sociology by the sociologist Ferdinand

Tönnies (in his book *Gemeinschaft und Gesellschaft*)*. By the time of the First World War, political movements of all colours—conservatives and liberals, trade union officials and social-democratic reformers—were talking about the *Volksgemeinschaft*. Only confirmed Marxists avoided the word.

The term could have different meanings, depending on who employed it. It could be used to promote the peaceful resolution of social conflicts in a free nation. It could be part of an appeal to an authoritarian order, in which decisions about the good or the bad of the community were imposed from 'above'. But the rhetoric of the National Socialists was the most radical. They used the concept to call for the destruction of Marxism, since any appeal to class struggle implied the negation of the *Volksgemeinschaft*. Furthermore, they interpreted the concept in terms of their racial theories. Only 'Aryan' Germans had a place in the National Socialist community; Jews, Gypsies, and members of other 'inferior' races did not. The overt racializing of the nation distinguished the NSDAP from all other parties in the Weimar Republic.

The 'Reich' had, in the years before 1933, increasingly become the watchword of the militant right in its battle against the republic. To speak of the 'Reich' was to invoke the past and the future simultaneously. The association of the imperial idea with hopes of redemption and salvation lay deep in German history. Such associations were especially prominent in the discourse of the 'Third Empire' (*Drittes Reich*) during the Weimar Republic. This term first became a political slogan after the publication of the book by the same name in 1923 by Arthur Moeller van den Bruck, one of the pioneers of the 'conservative revolution'. Following the First Empire, the Holy Roman Empire of the German Nation, and the Second, 'Little German' (*kleindeutsch*) Empire created by Bismarck (which Moeller considered an imperfect, 'intermediate Empire'), the Third Empire would again be pan-German (*grossdeutsch*) in nature, that is, it would include Austria. Moeller called National Socialism the 'champion of the Final Empire' (*Endreich*): 'It is always being prophesied. And it is never fulfilled. It is perfection itself, to be reached only through imperfection . . . There is only One Empire, just as there is only One Church. Everything else of the same name is a mere state, or community, or sect. There is only The Empire.'

Elsewhere in his book Moeller explicitly denied the existence of a 'thousand-year Empire'. The 'Empire of Reality' (*Wirklichkeitsreich*), he wrote, the empire a nation realizes within its own territory, was the only one there was. Nonetheless, the eschatological aura of the book's title was a calculated effect. The idea of a 'Third Empire' could be traced back to the twelfth-century Italian theologian Joachim of Fiore, who had prophesied that the first two ages of the world, the order of God the Father and the order of Jesus Christ the Son, would be followed by a third, thousand-year age of spiritualization and perfection presided over by the Holy Spirit. The vision of a thousand-year empire had its origins in

---

* Tönnies, *Community and Society*.

chapter 20 of the Book of Revelation. Joachim of Fiore's interpretation of this prophecy was passed on to the chiliastic movements of the ensuing eras. The flagellants of the thirteenth and fourteenth centuries, the Bohemian Taborites of the fifteenth, and the Anabaptists of the sixteenth century were all inspired by the dream of a millennial epoch between the defeat of the Antichrist and the Last Judgment, a period in which the devil would no longer have any power over mankind. Even Hegel's *Geschichtsphilosophie** reflects traces of the Joachite doctrine of the three empires of the Father, Son, and Holy Spirit. (According to Hegel, the Germanic tribes in the Roman empire represent the first, the Christian Middle Ages the second, and the post-Reformation period the third empire or third epoch in the Germanic world.)

Soon after the publication of Moeller's book, the National Socialists took up the slogan of the 'Third Reich', which seemed to embody the essence of their aims. The leader of the NSDAP first learned of the concept through Gregor Strasser's brother Otto (who broke with Hitler in June 1930, ostensibly because the latter had renounced the 'socialism' of the 1920 party platform). Only much later did it occur to Hitler that there were problems with the idea of the 'Third Reich'. It seemed to invite speculation about a further, 'fourth' empire, as well as imply a lack of continuity in German imperial history. In June 1939 the main party office announced that it was the Führer's will that the term 'Third Reich' no longer be used. By that time, however, the concept had already done its work. It was one of the reasons many Germans looked upon Hitler as their saviour.

Hitler tried more than once to press the myth of the 'thousand years' into the service of his rule. 'Just as the world does not live by wars, peoples do not live by revolutions,' he declared on 4 September 1934 at the NSDAP national congress in Nuremberg following the bloody elimination of the SA leadership.

In both cases, the most that can be achieved is the creation of conditions for new life. Woe, however, if the act of destruction does not occur in the service of a better and higher idea, but obeys only the nihilistic impulse to destroy, thus bringing about eternal hatred instead of a new and better creation . . . True revolutions are only conceivable as the consummation of a new mission, a mission assigned its historical task in this way by the will of the people . . . We all know whom the nation has chosen for this task! Woe to him who does not know it, or forgets it! Revolutions have always been rare among the German people. It is with us that the nervous era of the nineteenth century has finally come to an end. In the next thousand years, there will be no more revolutions in Germany.

On 10 February 1933 Hitler opened the parliamentary electoral campaign with a speech in the Berlin Sportpalast. Accusations against the 'parties of decline, of November, of revolution', which had been destroying, corroding, and breaking up the German people for fourteen years, were followed by an appeal for the

* Hegel, *Philosophy of History.*

Germans to grant the new government four years before passing judgement on it. The final words of the speech were modelled on the Bible and the Evangelical version of the 'Our Father'. Hitler tried in this way to represent his own will to power in terms of service to the 'Reich' and as the fulfilment of a divinely appointed task.

For I cannot detach myself from the belief in my people, cannot renounce the conviction that this nation will one day rise up again, cannot separate myself from the love of this my people, and I am firmly convinced that the hour will indeed come one day when the millions who hate us will stand behind us and with us will welcome the collectively created, hard-won, bitterly-earned new German Empire of greatness and honour and power and glory and justice. Amen!

What Hitler planned to do if the Germans obeyed this call he had explained in some detail—albeit not completely—in a secret speech to the commanders of the army and navy in the apartment of General von Hammerstein-Equord on 3 February 1933, one week before the Sportpalast address:

Extirpation of Marxism root and branch . . . Strictest authoritarian government. Removal of the cancer of democracy! . . . Building up of army most important prerequisite for the attainment of goal: regaining of political power. General conscription must come again . . . How should political power be used, when it has been won? Cannot yet be said. Perhaps acquisition of new export opportunities, perhaps—and probably better—conquest of new living space in the east and its ruthless Germanization.[2]

FROM THE REICHSTAG FIRE TO THE ENABLING ACT

The electoral campaign, which took place against the background of a 'national uplifting' (*nationale Erhebung*), was overshadowed by numerous acts of National Socialist terror. The victims were mainly Communists and Social Democrats. Herman Goering, the acting interior minister of Prussia, told the police on 17 February to make ruthless use of their firearms if necessary. Five days later he deployed units of the SA, SS, and Stahlhelm as volunteer police forces in order to combat the supposedly increasing violence from the left more effectively. Five days after that, on 27 February, the Reichstag building went up in flames.

Scholars still debate today whether the Dutch anarcho-syndicalist Marinus van der Lubbe was the sole arsonist or whether he had National Socialist accomplices. The prevalent opinion is that he acted alone. Nonetheless Hitler, Goering, and Joseph Goebbels, the national director of propaganda (*Reichspropagandaleiter*), immediately came out with the false declaration that the Communists were responsible for the crime. The burning of the Reichstag, they claimed, was intended as a 'signal for bloody rebellion and for civil war'. In the night of 27–8 February Goering ordered the Communist and Social Democratic press to be banned (the latter for a period of two weeks), the KPD offices to be closed, and all Communist delegates and party functionaries to be taken into 'preventive detention'. On 28 February the cabinet passed an 'emergency measure for the protection of the people and the state', which suspended the most important basic rights 'until further notice', created new ways of taking action against the individual states, and introduced the death penalty for a number of terrorist acts, including arson. The decree, based on Article 48 of the constitution, did nothing less than liquidate the rule of law in Germany.

Apart from Communist functionaries, some the first victims of the new reality were well-known intellectuals. Among those taken into 'preventive detention' on 28 February were Carl von Ossietzky, publisher of *Die Weltbühne*, the writers Erich Mühsam and Ludwig Renn, the 'roving reporter' Egon Erwin Kisch, the sexologist Max Hodann, and the lawyer Hans Litten. Three days later, on the basis of a denunciation, the police struck successfully against the top level of the KPD, arresting party leader Ernst Thälmann and several of his closest associates—including Werner Hirsch, editor of the *Rote Fahne*—in an illegal quarter in Berlin-Charlottenburg on 3 March.

Terror and propaganda did not fail to have their effect. The Hitler government emerged victorious from the parliamentary elections on 5 March 1933. The two formations composing the cabinet achieved 51.9% of the vote: 43.9% for the NSDAP, massively financed by the whole of heavy industry for the first time, and 8% for the *Kampffront Schwarz–Weiss–Rot*, a union of DNVP, Stahlhelm, and non-aligned conservative politicians, among them Papen. The Communists, harder hit than all other parties by the persecution, suffered heavy losses, while those of the Social Democrats were comparatively modest (4.6% and 2.1%, respectively). The two Catholic parties did well: 11.2% for the Centre party, 2.7% for the Bavarian People's party (BVP). The two liberal parties remained splinter groups, although the more 'left' did worse than the right: the German People's party (DVP) took 1.1%, the German State party 0.9% of the vote. Besides the gains of the NSDAP (+10.8%), the most dramatic thing about the election was the increased turnout (+10.2%). There was no mistaking the connection between the two. The National Socialists attracted a far greater number of newly mobilized and first-time voters than any other party.

Hitler's electoral victory was followed by what the National Socialists called the 'national revolution'. One of its most significant results was the *Gleichschaltung* or 'coordination' of the individual provinces: the replacement of their governments—whether purely bourgeois or partly composed of Social Democrats—with cabinets led by National Socialists. The 'coordination' was a product of the combined pressure from 'above', from Interior Minister Frick, and 'below', from the storm columns of the SA and SS. The transition took longest in Bavaria, the bastion of German federalism. Not until 16 March did the National Socialists rule in Munich.

The 'coordination' of the *Länder* was accompanied by the conquest of power in cities and municipalities. The SA and SS occupied city halls, arrested 'Marxist' (i.e. Social Democratic) city councilors in many places, and forced mayors and chief mayors they considered unacceptable to resign. Employment offices and hospitals were subject to the same excesses.

Many of the arrested political adversaries were turned over to the police, but many were not. The SA and SS often took the 'execution of the sentence' into their own hands. Shortly after the Reichstag elections, the first 'wild' concentration camps appeared in Berlin and its environs, which the National Socialists used ruthlessly to settle their accounts with the 'Bolsheviks'. The first official concentration camps followed in March 1933, beginning with Bavarian Dachau. Not only Communists, but increasingly Social Democrats and other political enemies of the regime were sent to these facilities, which were controlled by the SA and SS. The number of Communists taken into 'preventive detention' throughout March and sent to a 'KZ' (from *Konzentrationslager*) was estimated by Rudolf Diels, then chief of the Berlin political police, to be 20,000 for Prussia alone.* At the end of July 1933, by which time the SA terror had subsided, official statistics recorded some 27,000 'preventive detainees' in the whole of the country, about 15,000 of them in Prussia. However, these figures did not include the inmates in the 'wild' camps, several of which still existed at this time. The number of those murdered in the torture chambers of the SA and SS in the first months of the Third Reich was also never recorded.

The 'national revolution' also included countless pogroms. In Breslau the SA staged a putsch against Jewish lawyers and judges. In many places Jewish doctors in the civil service were declared dismissed, and Jewish theatres, cabarets, jewellers, clothing stores, banks, and warehouses were stormed. On 10 March protest from the German Nationalists compelled Hitler to order his followers to stop 'the harassment of individual persons, the blocking of automobiles or disturbances of business life'. 'You must, my Comrades,' ran the text of the appeal, 'see to it that the national revolution cannot be compared in history with the revolution of the knapsack Spartacists in the year 1918. As for the rest, do not let yourselves be deterred for a second from our watchword. It is: The extermination of Marxism.'

The 'wild' activities of the SA, SS, and the small business-oriented *Kampfbund* gradually diminished in the second half of March. The conservative bourgeoisie, which had been disturbed by the attacks, returned to calm. It was assisted in this by an unconstitutional decree from the Reich president, which Hitler announced by radio on 12 March: from the next day onward, the black–white–red flag and the swastika flag were 'to be hoisted together until the final settlement of the Reich colours'. The explanation was balm for the German Nationalists and all who had remained monarchists in their hearts: 'These banners are bound together by the glorious history of the German Empire and the powerful rebirth

* [Translator's note: 'KZ' is pronounced *kah-tsétt* in German.]

of the German Nation. United, they are to embody the power of the state and the inner solidarity of all national circles of the German people.'

Hindenburg's flag decree was the prelude to the 'day of Potsdam'. On 21 March the ceremonial opening of the newly elected Reichstag took place in the garrison church of Prussia's unofficial capital. 'Marxists' did not participate. The Communist delegates had been arrested or gone underground, and the Social Democratic fraction—in the absence of nine members in 'preventive detention'—had decided the day before not to attend.

The celebrations were designed to underscore Hitler's commitment to unite 'old greatness' with 'young power'. With the lively participation of the two large Christian churches, Weimar was finally borne to its grave. In the Evangelical service held in the Church of St Nicholas, Otto Dibelius, general superintendent of the Kurmark, gave his sermon on the same passage in the Letter to the Romans that Ernst von Dryander had used for his address in the Berlin cathedral on 4 August 1914: 'If God is for us, who can be against us?' When President von Hindenburg went down alone into the crypt of the grave of Frederick the Great in the garrison church to hold silent converse with the king, many Germans were overcome by the same patriotic feelings the *Fridericus* films from Alfred Hugenberg's 'Ufa' had been inspiring for years. Nonetheless, 21 March 1933 did not resurrect old Prussia. The new lords of Germany simply availed themselves of its cult in order to lend their lordships the semblance of a higher legitimation than the one they had received from the voters on 5 March.

On 23 March the Reichstag convened at its new location, the Kroll Opera at the Platz der Republik in Berlin, in order to deliberate on the draft (nominally proposed by the NSDAP and DNVP) of a 'Law to Alleviate the Sufferings of the People and the Country' (*Gesetz zur Behebung der Not von Volk und Reich*). Also known as the Enabling Act (*Ermächtigungsgesetz*), this law gave the government unrestricted powers for four years to pass laws that were not in accordance with the constitution. The only 'restrictions' were that the laws were not to have as their object the institutions of the Reichstag or the Reichsrat as such nor affect the powers of the Reich president. Henceforth, the Reichstag and Reichsrat had no further right to participate in the legislative process. This was also the case when it came to concluding treaties with foreign states, as the text of the bill explicitly stated. All that was now required for the government's laws to enter into effect was the signature of the president and an announcement in the *Reich Law Bulletin*.

In order to secure the two-thirds majority necessary for constitutional amendment, the government violated the constitution prior to the law's passage: the Communist seats were treated as non-existent, reducing the 'lawful number of members' of the Reichstag by eighty-one. Then, on 23 March, the Reichstag changed its procedure. Delegates absent without excuse could be excluded from the negotiations for up to sixty days of the session; excluded delegates were nonetheless still considered 'present'. Thus even if it had boycotted the session en masse, the SPD could not have prevented the fulfilment of the two requirements for a constitutional amendment: two-thirds of the 'lawful members' had to be present, and two thirds of those present had to vote for the change.

Hitler won the support of the Centre (and the Bavarian People's party) by including in his inaugural speech several statements by the Centre leader, Monsignor Kaas, concerning the relationship between the Church and the State and by making additional verbal promises to the Catholic party's negotiators (who then waited in vain on 23 March for the written confirmation). The negative votes of the ninety-three SPD delegates present, which Otto Wels defended in an impressive speech, were anticipated. The smaller bourgeois parties voted for the bill, including the five delegates of the German State party, Hermann Dietrich, Reinhold Maier, Theodor Heuss, Ernst Lemmer, and Heinrich Landahl. The necessary majority was obtained easily, with 444 to 94 votes. As it turned out, the unconstitutional manipulation of the Reichstag membership was not even necessary.

The consent of the bourgeois parties was the result of deception, self-deception, and blackmail. The Centre's vote can be seen in terms of the rightward course the party had taken ever since Monsignor Kaas was elected party leader in December 1928. For Kaas, the rights of the Catholic Church were more important than the rights of the parliament, and he prevailed with this attitude against a resistant minority around Brüning, which bowed to the demands of party discipline for the plenary vote on 23 March 1933. What led the delegates of the German State party to abandon the principles of the rule of law was the belief that the legal dictatorship desired by the majority was still a lesser evil than the illegal dictatorship a rejection of the law threatened to produce. Only the Social Democrats withstood the massive pressure, thus rescuing not only their own honour, but also the honour of the first German republic. The fact that not a single delegate from the ranks of the Catholic and liberal parliamentarians voted with them makes clear, once again, why Weimar had failed. The founding party of the state had lost its bourgeois partners, without whom democracy could not prevail against its enemies.

The National Socialists would not have relinquished power even if the Enabling Act had failed to clear the hurdle of the two-thirds majority. But its passage made the erection of the dictatorship a great deal easier. The semblance of legality fostered a semblance of legitimacy and guaranteed the regime the loyalty of the majority. The loyalty of the government bureaucracy was particularly important. The tactics of legality, a significant precondition of Hitler's accession to power, had not yet fully served their purpose on 30 January 1933. They proved themselves yet again on 23 March 1933, where they were used for the de facto abolition of the Weimar constitution. Henceforth, Hitler could make the elimination of the Reichstag seem like a task the Reichstag itself had commissioned him to fulfil.[3]

DISCRIMINATION AND REPRESSION: THE ERECTION
OF A DICTATORSHIP

The government's first large-scale campaign after the Enabling Act was the boycott of Jewish businesses on 1 April 1933. The National Socialist leadership intended this event both as an outlet for the pressure from 'below', from the ranks of its supporters, and as a response to the sharp criticism the German March pogroms had occasioned from Jewish organizations, as well as liberal and socialist newspapers, throughout the world. The task of leading the offensive against this 'global persecution' (*Weltgreuelhetze*) was assigned to Julius Streicher, Franconian district leader of the NSDAP and publisher of the anti-Semitic polemical newspaper *Der Stürmer*. The real force behind the scenes was Joseph Goebbels, who had assumed leadership of the new Reich Ministry for Public Enlightenment and Propaganda (*Reichsministerium für Volksaufklärung und Propaganda*) on 14 March. Goebbels was satisfied with the way the one-day boycott with the slogan 'Germans! Defend yourselves! Don't buy from Jews!' came off. 'The effects of our boycott can already be measurably felt,' he wrote in his journal on 2 April. 'Those abroad are gradually coming to their senses. The world will learn that it is not a good idea to let the Jewish emigrants teach it how things are in Germany.'

The propaganda minister spoke too soon. On 22 April the German envoy in Norway, Ernst von Weizsäcker, in many ways a typical representative of the 'old elite', commented: 'The anti-Jewish campaign is a very difficult thing for foreign countries to comprehend, for they themselves have not experienced this Jewish flood. The fact exists that our position in the world has suffered because of this and that the effects are now being felt, politically and in other ways.' Germans continued to buy from Jews even after the boycott campaign. But the warning was unmistakable. The possibility of their expulsion from the business life of the country now hung like a sword of Damocles over the Jewish community. The regime reserved for itself the right to determine the date and the extent of the next measures against the economic influence of the Jews—that was the message of 1 April 1933.[4]

The elimination of the Jews from the economy was preceded by their removal from the civil service. On 7 April 1933 the government promulgated a Law for the Restoration of the Professional Civil Service (*Gesetz zur Wiederherstellung des Berufsbeamtentums*). It was directed against all officials whom the ruling National Socialists considered unreliable: against so-called *Parteibuchbeamte* ('civil servants with party membership books') of the Weimar Republic, especially those who belonged to or were connected with a leftist group, and also against 'non-Aryan' officials. The law compelled them to retire, excepting only former front soldiers, fathers or sons of the fallen, and those who had attained the status of civil servant before 1 August 1914. These exceptions were adopted at the initiative of President von Hindenburg, who had himself been petitioned by the National Federation of Jewish Front Soldiers (*Reichsbund jüdischer Frontsoldaten*) to speak to Hitler on its behalf.

The new law ended the phase of 'spontaneous' purges of the civil service by local NSDAP activists and initiated an 'orderly' and comprehensive purge by the state. Among those affected were hundreds of university teachers. The Universities of Berlin and Frankfurt lost nearly a third of their teaching staff, Heidelberg a quarter, and Breslau more than a fifth. Several Nobel prize winners were among the victims, including the physicists Albert Einstein and Gustav Hertz and the chemist Fritz Haber. Those dismissed for racial or political reasons—or both—included the philosophers Theodor Adorno, Max Horkheimer, and Helmuth Plessner; the jurists Hermann Heller, Hans Kelsen, and Hugo Sinzheimer; the sociologists Karl Mannheim and Emil Lederer; the economists Moritz Julius Bonn and Wilhelm Röpke; the psychologist Erich Fromm; the theologian Paul Tillich; and countless others. Most of them left Germany. Whole research institutes like the Frankfurt Institute for Social Research and specializations like Freudian psychoanalysis were wiped out.

The purge of the academic staff was accompanied by the purge of the student body. On 28 April 1933, in the course of a general restriction of admissions, the number of 'non-Aryan' students was reduced to 1.5 per cent so as to conform approximately to the proportion of Jews in the population. Students who had belonged to the KPD or were considered Communist sympizers were forced to abandon their studies. Rectors unacceptable to the government were replaced by regime-friendly ones. On 20 April 1933, Hitler's forty-fourth birthday, Martin Heidegger was elected rector of Freiburg University. He joined the NSDAP on 1 May. In his inaugural address on 27 May he committed the teachers and students of the university to a triad of engagements in 'labour service, military service, and knowledge service'.

In their war against everything they felt to be 'un-German', 'decadent', and 'corrosive', the National Socialists took aim at the living and the dead. On 10 May 1933, public book-burnings took place in the capital and university cities throughout the country. Members of the National Socialist German Student Association threw writings by leftist, pacifist, liberal, and Jewish authors into the flames, including works of Heinrich Heine, Karl Marx, Karl Kautsky, Sigmund Freud, Alfred Kerr, Heinrich Mann, Erich Kästner, Lion Feuchtwanger, Erich Maria Remarque, Arnold Zweig, Theodor Wolff, Bertolt Brecht, Kurt Tucholsky, and Carl von Ossietzky. Most of the campaign's living victims had already left Germany. One of them, Carl von Ossietzky, had been arrested on 28 February. Another, Erich Kästner, stood by unrecognized as the ceremonial burning took place on the square in front of the Friedrich-Wilhelms-Universität in Berlin.

The book-burning marked the beginning of campaigns against all forms of 'degenerate art' in literature and music, painting and architecture. Radio, film, theatre, and press were purged and 'coordinated' within a few months in 1933. With regard to the newspapers, the regime showed a certain sense of nuance. The fact that an internationally well-known paper like the *Frankfurter Zeitung* cultivated a more dispassionate style in its reportage and commentary than the *Völkischer Beobachter*, even expressing criticism within narrow limits, lay within the well-understood interests of the Third Reich. A facade of professional tastefulness and calculated diversity in the press was useful not only for foreign policy reasons, but also for the regime's image within Germany, at least for the moment. What mattered was that, whenever important issues were at stake, the linguistic rulings of the propaganda ministry were followed in a manner that accorded with Goebbels's wishes.

On 7 April, the day the Law for the Restoration of the Professional Civil Service was passed, the government also placed the relationship between the Reich and the individual German states on a new legal basis. A first 'coordination' law on 31 March had changed the composition of the provincial parliaments to reflect the outcome of the Reichstag elections on 5 March (ignoring the Communist votes, of course) and empowered the governments of the *Länder* to promulgate laws and even constitutional amendments independently of their parliaments. The Second Law for the Coordination of the States with the Reich (*Zweites Gesetz zur Gleichschaltung der Länder mit dem Reich*) of 7 April created the institution of the Reich governor (*Reichsstatthalter*), who represented the highest authority in the *Land* from that moment forward. In most cases Hitler conferred these offices on the NSDAP district leaders. He himself became the Reich governor of Prussia, where a new parliament had been elected on 5 March. On 11 April he appointed a new Prussian prime minister. It was Hermann Goering, who also held the offices of president of the Reichstag and Reich minister without portfolio.[5]

ORGANIZED LABOUR: DESTRUCTION, COORDINATION, REALIGNMENT

National Socialism's most important political enemy, 'Marxism', had been permanently weakened by the passage of the Enabling Act, but it had by no means been completely eliminated. That was only true of the Communists. Since, after the Reichstag fire, the members of the KPD could no longer legally engage in political activities, and with its functionaries arrested, abroad, or underground, the withdrawal of the Communist seats in parliament on 31 March was almost entirely symbolic in significance.

But the SPD continued to exist as an organization. To be sure, three Social Democratic politicians the National Socialists counted among the 'November criminals'—Philipp Scheidemann, Wilhelm Dittmann, and Arthur Crispien—had already left Germany before the Reichstag fire, at the direction of the party leadership. They were followed in March by, among others, Otto

Braun, former Prussian interior minister Albert Grzesinski, and Rudolf Hilferding. Others, including Julius Leber, a Reichstag delegate from Lübeck, were in prison when the Reichstag convened to pass the Enabling Act. The Cologne delegate and former national interior minister Wilhelm Sollmann was in a prison hospital after an assault by men from the SA and SS.

For a period of time after 23 March, however, the party leadership still believed that the regime would honour Social Democratic moderation and lift the ban Goering had imposed on all Social Democratic newspapers after the Reichstag fire, provided the party distanced itself clearly enough from the 'anti-German hounding' abroad. And in fact, in consultation with Goering, well-known Social Democrats like Otto Wels travelled to neighbouring countries in order to inform their friends about developments in Germany and to correct several false reports. Wels even resigned from the 'Office', the executive committee of the Socialist Workers' International, on 30 March. This was an act of protest against a declaration by the Second International on 27 March denouncing terror and anti-Semitism in Hitler's Germany without prior consultation with the SPD. But despite such good behaviour, the ban on the Social Democratic press continued.

While the SPD was manoeuvring cautiously, the General German Trade Union Association adapted to the new situation step by step after February 1933. By this time, the Free Trade Unions had been emphasizing their 'national' orientation and distancing themselves from the Social Democratic party for several years, especially since the autumn of 1932. The ADGB strengthened this course in the spring of 1933 until it could no longer be distinguished from an opportunistic truckling with Nazism. On 13 April the leaders of the Free Trade Unions met for the first time with the main functionaries of the National Socialist *Betriebszellen-Organisation* (NSBO) to discuss the formation of a common union. Given the nature of the political situation, the leadership of such an organization could only have been National Socialist or at least regime-friendly. Two days later, the ADGB national executive made a public announcement hailing the government's decision to establish 1 May as 'National Labour Holiday'. On 19 April followed—despite the fact that Theodor Leipart, the national chairman, had assured party head Otto Wels that it would not happen—the national committee's appeal to the union members 'to everywhere celebrate the holiday proclaimed by the government, in full consciousness of their pioneering efforts on behalf of the May idea, for the honour of creative labour, and for the integration of the labour force into the state on terms of equality'.

The 'National Labour Holiday' came off as Hitler and Goebbels had planned. The national committee ordered the buildings of the Free Trade Unions to be hung with the black, white, and red. At the main demonstration on the Tempelhofer Feld, Karl Schrader, head of the Textile Workers' Association, even marched under a swastika flag with members of his union. Hitler's speech was broadcast by all radio stations in the country. It was a skilful appeal to the self-esteem of the workers and in keeping with the maxim 'Honour labour and value the worker!' The National Socialists, the chancellor said, wanted to eradicate the 'terrible prejudice' that manual labour was inferior. The duty of 'labour service' (*Arbeitsdienst*) would inculcate in the German people the realization that manual work was not disgraceful. 'We do not intend to defeat Marxism only on the outside. We are resolved to remove its very preconditions . . . Headworkers and handworkers must never stand against each other.' Hitler promised job-creation measures, including the 'gigantic task' of road construction. He emphasized his desire for peace and concluded, as he so often did, with a sacral touch: 'Lord, we shall not forsake Thee! Now bless our battle for our liberty and with it our German people and Fatherland!'

After the 'National Labour Holiday' came 2 May, the day the government had long planned with military precision for a strike against the Free Trade Unions. Throughout the country the SA and SS took over union buildings, the editorial offices of union newspapers, and the bank of the workers, employees, and civil servants, along with its branches. Leipart and other union leaders were taken into 'preventive detention', which in most cases lasted about two weeks. Leipart and his deputy Peter Grassman were not released until June. Less prominent officials were ordered to continue working under the new leadership, the NSBO.

The two other politically oriented labour unions, the Christian-national and the liberal, submitted unconditionally to Hitler on 4 May, wishing to avoid the fate of the Free Trade Unions. Two days later Robert Ley, Gregor Strasser's successor as national leader of the NSDAP, announced the founding of the German Labour Front (*Deutsche Arbeitsfront* or DAF). Its first congress took place in Berlin on 10 May under the auspices of Hitler, who designated himself as 'honest broker' between the different strata of the German people. Ley was appointed head of the DAF. Walter Schuhmann, head of the NSBO, assumed leadership of the workers' organizations. Thus did the Third Reich acquire its labour organization. Independent workers' organizations did not exist after 4 May 1933. Labour contract agreements were now also a thing of the past. According to a law of 19 May, contract guidelines were to be set by labour trustees appointed by the chancellor.

In contrast to the unions, the employers' associations were able to maintain their organizational independence. They had to get rid of top officials who were Jews or political undesirables, but in doing so they assured themselves a high degree of corporate continuity. In June 1933 the National Association of German Industry and the Association of German Employers' Associations united to form the Reich Estate of German Industry (*Reichsstand der deutschen Industrie*). The term 'estate' (*Stand*) corresponded to the language of the National Socialist *Mittelstand* ideologues. In substance, however, these ideologues suffered serious defeats in the summer of 1933, failing to subjugate big business. On orders from Rudolf Hess, Hitler's representative, they had to stop their campaigns against the 'Jewish' department stores and the 'Marxist' consumer associations. For the

National Socialist leadership, successes in the 'labour battle' were what counted. The destruction of the department stores and consumer cooperatives would have cost the jobs of many workers and salaried employees, thus it was out of the question. It made no difference that the *Mittelstand* functionaries of the NSDAP pointed to statements from the 1920 party platform and to campaign promises. Now that the party was in power, it had other priorities.

The situation of the agricultural associations was completely different. The National Land League, which had contributed greatly to Hitler's rise in January 1933, was absorbed into the newly created Reich Nutrition Estate (*Reichsnährstand*) in July 1933. This organization was directed by Richard Walther Darré, leader of the agrarian-political apparatus of the NSDAP, who had also succeeded Hugenberg as minister of nutrition and agriculture the month before. Darré's increase in power occurred at the expense of the East Elbian manorial lords, who had exercised a decisive influence over the policies of the National Land League and the German National People's party for many years. The transfer of power from the big agriculturalists to peasant farming was part of Hitler's strategy to create as much autarky as possible in preparation for a war over *Lebensraum*, which was to make Germany self-sufficient in all aspects of the economy. Seen in this way, the realignment of the agricultural interest organizations was as 'logical' as the decision not to push for radical changes in the system of industrial associations.[6]

THE ELIMINATION OF THE SOCIAL DEMOCRATS

The breaking up of the Free Trade Unions had immediate effects on the Social Democratic party. Put on guard by the events on 2 May, the party executive decided two days later that its three full-time members—party head Otto Wels, the former editor-in-chief of the *Vorwärts*, Friedrich Stampfer, and the main treasurer, Siegfried Crummenerl—should leave the country and continue the struggle against Hitler from abroad. The three men departed right away for Saarbrücken, the first way station of exile. This was the beginning of a political separation within the SPD, with the executive in exile under Wels, and party in Germany led (though in an unofficial capacity) by Paul Löbe, former president of the Reichstag.

Open conflict between the two Social Democratic 'camps' broke out on 17 May. The Reichstag had been convened on this day so that Hitler could declare the government's position on the Geneva disarmament conference. The chancellor desired a strong demonstration of national unity in order to counter the country's international isolation. The SPD executive in Saarbrücken urged the Reichstag fraction to make a different kind of demonstration: through non-participation. Only a minority of the fraction under the delegate Kurt Schumacher supported this position. The majority succumbed to the threats of Interior Minister Frick, who openly declared before the SPD parliamentary advisory committee that imprisoned party members would be killed if the fraction did not endorse the Reichstag's statement of support for the government's position.

Hitler's speech on 17 May 1933 was the most moderate and conciliatory he ever gave. There was no mention of Jews or Marxists. He did not speak of the 'diktat', but rather of the 'peace treaty' of Versailles, professed an understanding for the security interests of the neighbouring countries, especially the French and the Poles, and made a declaration in favour of peace the likes of which none of his predecessors could have delivered. 'No new European war would be able to replace the dissatisfying conditions of today with better ones', said the chancellor. He only desired equal rights for Germany, no more and no less. Even a concealed threat sounded defensive: 'As a people constantly defamed, it would be difficult for us to continue to belong to the League of Nations.' This was greeted with storms of applause from the National Socialists, the German Nationalists, and the Bavarian People's party.

After the governmental address Goering, the Reichstag president, read the resolution of approval put forward by the NSDAP, DNVP, Centre, and BVP and asked the delegates who wished to endorse the statement to rise from their seats. The minutes record the response of the assembly. 'All members of the Reichstag rise. The assembly sings the Deutschlandlied.' Goering declared that the result of the vote proved that the German people were one when their fate hung in the balance. Then he expressly noted — 'so that it is recorded in the minutes' — 'that all parties have accepted the resolution'. This sentence was followed by more storms of applause.

The applause was intended primarily for the Social Democrats, whom the right had not thought capable of so much 'patriotism'. A hint of the historic parliamentary session on 4 August 1914 was in the air. For a brief moment it seemed as though the Social Democrats had been accepted into the *Volksgemein-schaft*, and there may even have been SPD delegates who sincerely believed that their endorsement of Hitler's 'peace address' would help bring about an end to the repression and allow the party to exist legally within the Third Reich.

But Hitler's state was not Wilhelmine Germany. The total state, unlike the authoritarian, could not suffer an autonomous worker's movement and a parliamentary opposition. The SPD had raised Hitler's standing abroad. This was the only use its legality possessed for the regime, and after the desired effect had been achieved, the end of the breathing space once again granted to the SPD on 17 May was already in sight.

The vote for Hitler provoked a rupture between the 'Reich SPD' and the Second International. On 18 May the SAI Office condemned the behaviour of the Social Democratic parliamentary delegates: it did not express the true convictions of the German working class and contradicted the principles of the International. Otto Wels, who had resigned from the Office on 30 March, retracted his resignation on 17 May. For the leader of the SPD, there was no longer any doubt that a battle for the party had commenced, one that the executive could win only with the help of the International. On 21 May the party executive decided to move from Saarbrücken to Prague. The choice of the Czechoslovak capital was strategic: the densely forested mountains to the west and north offered easy passage into Bavaria, Saxony, and Silesia, an important consideration for the kind of illegal operations the exiled party leaders now saw as their only option.

There were a few further attempts to come to an understanding between Berlin and Prague, but the rift could not be healed. On 18 June the first edition of the *Neue Vorwärts* appeared in Karlsbad, containing an announcement entitled 'Zerbrecht die Ketten!'* from the exiled party leadership. It was the sharpest Social Democratic attack against the Hitler regime to date. 'The defeated of today will be the victors of tomorrow,' the text read.

It is our task to tell the truth to the world, and also to open up Germany to this truth . . . We sound the call to battle, which will restore to the German people its honour and its *liberty*, and to the *working class* its rights, which, achieved with such great toil, have only been lost for a short time . . . *On new paths to the old socialist goal! Break the chains! Forward!*

The next day, the 'Löbe SPD' convened in the Prussian parliament building for a national conference. Löbe accused the exiled party leaders of retracting the offer of loyal cooperation contained in Wels's speech on the Enabling Act. Ernst Heilmann, former floor leader in the Prussian parliament, gave classic expression to the majority line: 'We must continue to spin the thread of legality for as long as it can be spun.' The task of conducting party business was given to a six-member directory entirely 'Aryan' in composition. The new executive, to which Löbe himself belonged, immediately made it clear that it had sole authority to speak for the party. 'German comrades in exile can make no declarations for the party. The party expressly disclaims any responsibility for all of their statements.'

But the repudiation of the 'Praguers' no longer did the SPD any good. On 21 June Interior Minister Frick, alleging 'high treasonous activities against Germany' instigated by the exiled party executive, ordered a comprehensive political ban of the SPD. The decree went into effect on 22 June. That same day a massive wave of arrests led to the detention of numerous SPD officials and parliamentary delegates, as well as four members of the new directory, including Löbe. One member, Erich Rinner, managed to escape, since he was already on the way to Prague. The sixth member did not survive 22 June. Johannes Stelling, former prime minister of Mecklenburg-Strelitz, was savagely murdered by the SA in the course of the 'bloody week of Köpenick'. On 6 July the secret police arrested the Reichstag delegate Kurt Schumacher, a sharp critic

* 'Break the chains!'

of the 'Löbe course', in Berlin. He was sent to his first concentration camp in August, on the Heuberg in the vicinity of Stuttgart. He would not be released for ten years.[7]

THE DISSOLUTION OF THE WEIMAR PARTY SYSTEM

The elimination of the SPD was the prelude to the destruction of the entire party system. On 21 June, the same day the SPD was outlawed, the interior minister ordered the ban of the *Deutschnationale Kampfringe*, the paramilitary organization of the German National Front (the name of the German National People's party after the middle of May). The official reason, infiltration by 'large numbers of Communist and other elements hostile to the state', sounded bizarre. Alfred Hugenberg, the leader of the German National Front, initially hoped that Hindenburg would intervene. When he did not, Hugenberg submitted his resignation from the offices of minister of economics and agriculture to the Reich president on 26 June. Hitler attempted to dissuade his 'partner' of 30 January from leaving the government, but continued to insist on the dissolution of the German National Front. On 27 June Hugenberg resigned as economics and agricultural minister in the Reich and in Prussia. The self-dissolution of the German National Front took place on the same day. Hugenberg's two representatives worked out a 'friendship agreement' with the NSDAP, which provided for the German National parliamentarians to be admitted into the National Socialist party fractions. German conservatism thus lost its political arm, capitulating to the revolutionary movement it had resolved to tame.

The left wing of liberalism left the political stage one day after the conservatives. The German State party dissolved itself on 28 June, pre-empting action from the state. The final decision was made after the party's seats in the Prussian parliament were terminated, which the government justified by claiming that the State party had got into parliament by means of an electoral arrangement (a list connection) with the SPD and was therefore subject to the same political ban.

The demise of the liberal right wing was even less heroic. On 1 April the party executive and national committee of the German People's party announced that the DVP had 'waged the war against Weimar as one of the sources of downfall . . . for more than a decade, and with great sacrifice'; now 'a powerful national popular movement has succeeded in clearing away the obstacle to German convalescence.' On 23 April the head of the DVP, Eduard Dingeldey, exhorted the members of his party to 'join in the work of building up the nation, which has commenced under the leadership of Adolf Hitler'. Within a few weeks the party of Gustav Stresemann had completely collapsed. The final dissolution came on 4 July by order of Dingeldey, whose explanation hit the mark: '[P]arties in the old sense are not compatible with the current nature of the National

Socialist State.' Hitler expressed his gratitude by promising Dingeldey on 12 July that DVP members and voters would not 'be subject to any professional and civil demotion' due to their party activities.

The end of political Catholicism was decided in Rome. In April 1933 Vice Chancellor von Papen undertook negotiations with the Vatican over a concordat, whereby Monsignor Kaas, head of the Centre party (a purely nominal function after the beginning of May) played an important role for the Church as papal house prelate. The curia, in exchange for the assurance that the Church itself would preserve a certain freedom of action, abandoned the political, social, and professional organizations of German Catholicism. On 5 July, three days after the drafting of the concordat, the Centre party terminated its existence. The Bavarian People's party had done the same on the previous day.

The policy of conscious re-Catholicization, with which the Centre had sought to combat the creeping erosion of the Catholic milieu after the late 1920s, was brought to an end by the party's submission to ecclesiatic realpolitik in 1933. At the same time, many Catholics were also consciously turning toward National Socialism, beginning with the March elections. The Christian religion, the valorization of order and authority, the antagonism to atheist Marxism, the idea of the Reich—in the eyes of many Catholics, clergy and lay alike, National Socialism and Catholicism had more in common than they had previously been willing to admit.

The young publicist Oskar Köhler, a spokesman for the youth organization *Neudeutschland*, spoke for a powerful current within German Catholicism (though not for all German Catholics) when, in summer 1934, he positively contrasted the Reich of Adolf Hitler with Weimar democracy:

Germany as a republic was unthinkable as bearer of the Reich . . . The German people, as authority among the western nations, must fulfil the task of the Reich—and this authority is only conceivable as a person. A government dependent on and liable to be brought down by a parliament can never be an authority of the Reich . . . Since there is one, comprehensive goal, there must also be one man who can lead us to it. The natural principle of the One is a reflection of the supernatural. To the one God corresponds the one, highest Leader.

On 14 July 1933 (the anniversary of the storming of the Bastille) the Hitler government passed a law permitting only one political party in Germany, the NSDAP, and sanctioning with imprisonment anybody who undertook 'to preserve the organization of another political party or to found a new political party'. It had taken the National Socialists less than half a year to become a monopoly party. They still shared power—with the Reichswehr, the high levels of the bureaucracy, and big industry. Nonetheless, the destruction of the party system was an important milestone in the NSDAP seizure of the state, a process that had begun the day Hitler was appointed chancellor.[8]

CHURCHES, UNIVERSITIES, AND CULTURAL LIFE
AFTER 1933

As a totalitarian political religion, National Socialism could not, in principle, tolerate competition from any other religion that contradicted its message. In practice, it was forced to come to terms with the fact that the vast majority of Germans belonged to a Christian church. Of these, at least a strong minority were 'practising' Christians. The NSDAP leadership thus had a strong interest in preventing the rise of an opposition from within the churches. The Reich concordat, signed on 20 July 1933 in the Vatican and in force in Germany as of 10 September 1933, was a means to this end. The Catholic Church was permitted to conduct its internal affairs without interference from the state. It was granted assurances in matters pertaining to the confessional schools, religious instruction, and social organizations, including youth groups. The most important thing the curia gave up in exchange was political activity on the part of the clergy. The concordat was both a public relations success and a political victory for the Third Reich. With the Catholic Church politically neutralized, the National Socialists would find it much easier to suppress the cultural and philosophical influence of Catholicism within the Reich.

In Protestant Germany, National Socialism had already conquered strong bastions before 30 January 1933, though more so among the flock than within the church leadership, which was still strongly German Nationalist in outlook. The National Socialist 'German Christian Faith Movement' (*Glaubensbewegung Deutsche Christen* or DC), which promoted a 'affirmative, race-appropriate faith in Christ', sought to prove that Christ was an 'Aryan', and occasionally referred to itself as the 'SA of Jesus Christ' or the 'SA of the Church', had already received a third of the seats in the Prussian church elections of November 1932. Before the general church elections in July 1933, Hitler, nominally still a Catholic, gave a radio address from Bayreuth (where he was attending the Wagner festival) in support of the 'German Christians'. The appeal was not without effect: the DC gained a two-thirds majority. The National Socialists then tried to take power within the Evangelical church itself, and at first seemed to succeed. During the German National Synod in Wittenberg at the end of September, the East Prussian military district pastor Ludwig Müller, a 'German Christian' and Hitler's personal adviser in church affairs, was elected to the office of Reich bishop of the newly created German Evangelical Church.

But Wittenberg also witnessed the first appearance of a counter-movement, the 'Emergency Pastoral League' (*Pfarrernotbund*) around the Dahlem pastor Martin Niemöller, a former submarine commander and free corps soldier; the Berlin theology lecturer Dietrich Bonhoeffer; and Otto Dibelius, whom the 'German Christians' had removed from the superintendency of the Kurmark in

June 1933. Within a few weeks the Emergency Pastoral League gave rise to the Confessing Church (*Bekennende Kirche* or BK), which counted about a third of German pastors as members by the end of 1933.

The Confessing Church did not consider itself a political opposition, not even when it broke with the DC-controlled church leadership at the Barmen Confessional Synod in May 1934. It only spoke out against the politicization of the Gospel, against political pressure within the church, and against the 'Aryan paragraph', which the 'German Christians' were promoting in order to remove Christians of Jewish background from all church offices. The BK resistance was not a declaration against the general politics of the National Socialist leadership, nor did it entail solidarity with Jews who had not converted to Christianity.

From the 'German Christian' point of view, however, even this limited opposition was political, since it contradicted the National Socialist claim to the entirety of the human person. In principle Hitler thought no differently. But he was also a student of realpolitik, and as such he considered other goals more important than the conquest of the Evangelical church from within. The unexpected strength of the countervailing forces prompted him to 'realign' the situation in the autumn of 1934. Bishops deposed by the 'German Christians' were allowed to return to their offices. The 'Reich bishop' preserved his title, but no longer had any real influence in the church.

Although the battle over the church was broken off, the struggle against the church and for the hearts and minds of Protestants and Catholics continued. The leadership of the campaign was assumed by Alfred Rosenberg, editor-in-chief of the *Völkischer Beobachter* and the Führer's official representative 'for the entire intellectual and philosophical education of the NSDAP'. For dedicated Lutherans and Catholics, Rosenberg was *the* embodiment of National Socialist 'neo-paganism'. His book *Der Mythus des 20. Jahrhunderts** was placed on the index of forbidden books by papal decree in February 1934. For Hitler himself, the most important thing was the removal of youth from the influence of the church and of religious households. In this respect the battle over the church was *not* a failure. At the end of December 1933 the 1.2 million members of the Evangelical youth organizations were absorbed into the Hitler Youth. Their education in National Socialism could begin.

The fact that Hitler seemed to have removed himself from the battle over the church was favourable to his image in religious circles. In addition, he could count on the sympathies of all those who, though rejecting the fanaticism of the 'German Christians', supported the project of a German national church that would overcome confessional divides. One of the most eloquent advocates of this goal on the Evangelical side was Wilhelm Stapel, one of the most widely read authors of the 'conservative revolution'. He supported the Third Reich for

---

* Rosenberg, *The Myth of the Twentieth Century*.

different reasons than the Catholic ideologues of the Reich, but the intended effect was the same on both sides: the ideological elevation of Hitler's rule.

'A real state, and thus the Hitler state, too, desires the "unified spirit of the nation"' wrote Stapel in his 1933 book *Die Kirche Christi und der Staat Hitlers.**

[T]his means nothing other than the unified moral power and force of the people. To an authentic people and state belongs, to speak with Ernst Moritz Arndt, a 'common spirit'. This *moral* common spirit desires to know that it is the 'will of God', and therefore it tends toward a national religion and a national church. The Hitler state would be complete if a positive-Christian national church stood at its side . . . The Reformation is incomplete so long as it does not give rise to a real and authentic reformed confession for all. Whether we wish it or no, the will to a unified church will grow out of the unified Evangelical church. But this unity can only be a *unity of faith*. Therefore, *one* confession must be found for *one* church.

In the universities, too, there were large numbers of conservatives like Stapel. For them, 30 January 1933 brought no fundamental change, whether in teaching or in research programmes. The 'nationally' minded were not harassed, as long as they refrained from criticizing National Socialism and the leadership of the Reich. Nor were the professors compelled to embrace anti-Semitism. In the new situation, however, many did voluntarily what had been frowned upon before 1933, giving vent at the lectern to their antipathy for the Jews. In 1936 the Munich historian Karl Alexander von Müller, an early Hitler partisan, initiated 'research on the Jewish question' in his capacity as president of the Bavarian Academy of Sciences. Prominent scholars and publicists participated. Wilhelm Stapel dedicated himself to *Die literarische Vorherrschaft der Juden in Deutschland, 1918–1933.*[†] The Tübingen philosopher Max Wundt wrote on the theme *Nathan der Weise oder Aufklärung und Judentum.*[‡] The Evangelical theologian Gerhard Kittel, also a professor in Tübingen, discussed the *Entstehung des Judentums und die Entstehung der Judenfrage.*[§] The Munich constitutional and church scholar Johannes Heckel, who, in the last year of the Weimar Republic, had wanted to prevent Hitler's rise to power by a declaration of a state of national emergency, now occupied himself with the *Einbruch des jüdischen Geistes in das deutsche Staats- und Kirchenrecht durch Friedrich Julius Stahl.*[¶]

Like Heckel, Carl Schmitt was originally a proponent of emergency 'exceptionalism' and an adversary of National Socialism. Shortly after 30 January 1933, however, he advised the new government on the *Reichsstatthalter* bill of 7 April 1933, and commented on the law after its passage. His official membership in the NSDAP dates from 1 May 1933. During that same year Schmitt,

---

* Stapel, *The Church of Christ and the State of Hitler.*
[†] Stapel, *The Literary Dominance of the Jews in Germany, 1918–1933.*
[‡] Wundt, *Nathan the Wise or Enlightenment and Jewry.*
[§] Kittel, *The Rise of the Jews and the Origins of the Jewish Question.*
[¶] Heckel, *Friedrich Julius Stahl and the Penetration of the Jewish Spirit into German Constitutional and Church Law.*

now a professor at the Friedrich-Wilhelms-Universität in Berlin, took over the direction of the party organization of university professors (the *Reichsgruppe Hochschullehrer*) within the National Socialist Jurists' Association (*National-sozialitischer Rechtswahrerbund* or NSRB, literally the 'League of Law Protectors'). In October 1936 he organized a conference with the theme 'Jewry in the Legal Profession'. In his concluding address he quoted Hitler's statement 'By fending off the Jew, I fight for the Cause of the Lord.' Schmitt required every citation from the works of a Jew—if their use could not be altogether avoided—to include a reference to the author's Jewish background, and he expressed his hope that 'the mere use of the word "Jewish" . . . would give rise to a healthy exorcism.'

As in the two churches, it was primarily the younger generation of university teachers who went over to National Socialism. Most of them were influenced by the 'free youth' (*bündisch*) movement and the ideas of the 'conservative revolution'. To be affiliated with these milieus did not necessarily mean to become a National Socialist. After National Socialism was in power, however, it took strong convictions not to take this step. Only a minority of young academics possessed the requisite mental and moral resources in 1933.

What was true in academics was also true in all other areas of cultural life. The expulsion of Jews and leftists of all stripes was accompanied by an increasing cultural 'self-alignment' with the policies and spirit of Germany's new masters. In September 1933 Goebbels was able to set up the new ministry of culture, the *Reichskulturkammer*. This mammoth office was divided into numerous special chambers, each responsible for organizing the 'cultural workers' (so-called *Kulturschaffende*) of a particular field, thus subjecting them to the political and ideological control of the regime. Membership in one of the chambers, whether for literature, the press, radio, theatre, music, or the fine arts, was necessary if one wished to participate in German cultural life. The statistical and documentary identification of the desirables went hand-in-hand with the exclusion of the undesirables. The latter were not only forced out of the universities, but also, after 23 August 1933, lost their German citizenship if they chose to leave the country and criticize the situation in Germany from abroad. Their property was confiscated. Those affected included, in addition to many leftist politicians, the theatre critic Alfred Kerr, the writer Lion Feuchtwanger, and the publicists Kurt Tucholsky and Leopold Schwarzschild.[9]

OUTLINES OF THE '*VOLKSGEMEINSCHAFT*'

The urban intelligentsia, which had mostly been driven out of Germany by the autumn of 1933, found, in the National Socialist world view, its diametric opposite in the down-to-earth farmers. The peasantry's preservation and consol-idation was the purpose of a law governing the legal status of farms, the so-called *Reichserbhofgesetz*, passed on 29 September 1933. This law bore the stamp of the foremost representative of 'blood and soil' (*Blut und Boden*) mythology, Richard Walther Darré, agriculture minister and director of the Reich Nutrition Estate. It did not affect either very large or very small farms, but was designed with the medium-sized family enterprise in mind, which accounted for about one-third of farms in the country. The heir of the family farm, usually the youngest son, *had* to become a farmer. His property could only be mortgaged within certain limits and could no longer—as was frequently the case in southern Germany—be divided among the members of the family.

The unavoidable consequence was increased migration from the land. This result contradicted the agro-romantic rhetoric of the NSDAP, but nonetheless served a higher goal of the party leadership. The new industrial reserve army provided workers for the armaments industry, which paid much higher wages than agriculture. The resulting shortage of agricultural labour was met by the Voluntary Labour Service (*Freiwillige Arbeitsdienst*, created in 1931), the prototype of the Reich Labour Service (*Reichsarbeitsdienst*), in which, after June 1935, all Germans between 18 and 25 years of age, women as well as men, were supposed to serve for half a year. The Labour Service, in turn, fulfilled the promise Hitler had made in his speech on 1 May 1933 that 'headworkers' would have to perform physical labour at least once in their lives.

The psychological valorization of labour was the counterpart to what went on in reality, the elimination of workers' rights. On 20 January 1934 the Reich government decreed a law for the ordering of national labour, the 'Magna Carta' of industrial relations in the Third Reich. The law commissioned the 'company leader' (*Führer des Betriebs*) with the task of providing for the well-being of the workforce (termed the *Gefolgschaft*, literally 'retinue') and of making decisions in all company affairs with it in mind. The company leader was advised by a 'council of trust' (*Vetrauensrat*) elected from a list, with the company leader and a representative from the German Labour Front deciding all candidates in advance. The 'council of trust' bore no resemblance to the shop council (*Betriebsrat*) of the Weimar Republic. The beneficiaries of the new system were the business owners, who felt themselves to be 'masters of the house' once again—that is, as long as they did not come into conflict with the DAF. Still, there was little dissatisfaction among the workers. The credit for the fall in unemployment was commonly ascribed to the policies of the Third Reich and its Führer. The loss of political and trade union liberty was compensated by an increase in job security.

The same was true in the case of most women workers. Although the National Socialists declared war on 'double incomes' both before and after their rise to power, they did so only in words. Their rhetoric about woman's place being 'in house and home', that is, taking care of husband and children, had virtually no effect in reality. Women's participation in the labour force not only did not decrease during the Third Reich, it rose. The only women who were systematically removed from their positions were civil servants and academics, and here the National Socialists were able to continue where a law on the legal status of female civil servants from 30 May 1932 had left off. In addition, supported by a national law against overcrowding in German universities and schools from 25 April 1933, the regime lowered the proportion of women in the student body to the historic low of 11.2% in the summer of 1939. The progress Germany had made toward the emancipation of women, both in law and in reality, was largely reversed after 1933. National Socialism *was* radically anti-emancipatory, despite what a number of historians and sociologists have claimed about how the Third Reich, whether it intended to or not, contributed to the comprehensive modernization of German society.

One year after their 'seizure of power', the *Volksgemeinschaft* of the National Socialists began to take on definite shape. The *Volksgemeinschaft* sought to eliminate all differences in the ways Protestants and Catholics, city and country dwellers, and 'workers of the mind and fist' thought and felt. It was dominated by men, organized into professional-corporative bodies, chambers, and the German Labour Front, all subservient to the *Führerprinzip*, the 'leader principle'. The businessman had become the 'company leader', the workforce the 'retinue'. The elected representatives of the agricultural organizations had been replaced by local and district 'peasant leaders', *Ortsbauernführer* and *Kreisbauernführer*, appointed by the Reich Nutrition Estate. The universities were placed under the leadership of the rector, appointed by the ministry of culture. In the press, a law from 4 October 1933 made the editor-in-chief responsible for all statements made by his employees. Moreover, there was a gigantic number of minor and medium-level leaders of the NSDAP, the 'block leader' (*Blockwart*), 'cell leader' (*Zellenleiter*), 'local chapter leader' (*Ortsgruppenleiter*), 'district leader' (*Kreisleiter*), and 'region leader' (*Gauleiter*), not to mention the functionaries of the party subdivisions and affiliated organizations like the National Socialist Women's Association (*NS-Frauenschaft*), the National Socialist People's Welfare Association (*NS-Volkswohlfahrt*), and the National Socialist Motor Corps (*Nationalsozialistisches Kraftfahrerkorps*), to name just a few. They were all dependent on the will of the *one* 'Führer'. And, at the same time, they could feel they were sharing in his rule.

If anyone was so bold as to express criticism of the leadership or of Hitler himself, he or she could expect to be denounced and—depending on the seriousness of the situation—sent to a concentration camp. In its efforts to control the Germans, the regime did not have to depend only on its paid informers and the relatively small number of secret police (of which there were 43 in Essen and Wuppertal, 28 in Duisburg, and 22 in Würzburg in 1937, to name only four examples); there were also countless patriotic citizens (the term used was *Volksgenosse* or *Volksgenossin*) who believed they were helping the Führer by reporting 'enemies of the people' (*Volksschädlinge*) to the authorities.

Even in the first year of the National Socialist regime, the belief in Hitler and his historical mission was the most important element binding the *Volksgemeinschaft* together. The Führer cult could not be permitted to lose its efficacy, for the Third Reich was inconceivable without it. This absolutely correct insight formed the basis of the regime's daily propaganda, which was coordinated by Goebbels, and which virtually no German could escape for long.[10]

THE FÜHRER MYTH AND POLYCRATIC RULE

Nothing strengthened the belief in Hitler in the year 1933 as much as the chancellor's successes, and these were many and rapid. In the economy the first signs of a recovery were already in evidence by the late summer of 1932. The upswing first manifested itself in terms of falling unemployment during the next year, and this the regime interpreted as a success of its 'labour battle' (*Arbeitsschlacht*). On the domestic political front, too, a majority of Germans considered the elimination of the party system, especially the destruction of 'Marxism' and 'Bolshevism', to be a success. Within a few months the National Socialists had asserted a total propaganda monopoly and stripped their political adversaries of all ability to articulate themselves legally.

In foreign policy, on the other hand, the Third Reich could not claim a positive balance of successes in the autumn of 1933. Hitler's chancellorship had isolated the country, a fact demonstrated very clearly by the Geneva disarmament conference. The military parity fundamentally granted to Germany in December 1932 receded ever further into the future. When, in October 1933, Britain proposed a control system that threatened to put a stop to the secret German rearmament, Hitler decided to break off negotiations and withdraw from the League of Nations.

The rejection of the Versailles system was extraordinarily popular, and since this was the case, Hitler succeeded in turning a foreign policy defeat into a domestic political victory. On 12 November 1933 the Germans had the chance to register their feelings about the withdrawal from the League of Nations and, at the same time, to vote for a new Reichstag. Of the valid referendum votes 95.1% were positive, which amounted to 89.9% of eligible voters. In the Reichstag elections 92.1% of the valid votes—87.8% of the population—went to the NSDAP list.

Thus the acclamation was greater for the plebiscite than for the Reichstag elections. The regime had cause to interpret both results as an impressive confirmation of its policies. For, as intimidating as the terror and propaganda were, it was still possible at this point to vote negatively or in a deliberately invalid manner—or, at least in the large cities, to avoid the ballot box—without great personal risk. In former leftist strongholds or in neighbourhoods where many Jews lived, the negative votes in the referendum and invalid votes in the election often reached double digits. The rejectionist leader was Lübeck with 22.1% and 21.8%, respectively. For the National Socialist leadership, this kind of data was no cause for alarm; if the government and the NSDAP had done significantly better, the world would have called the credibility of the votes into question.

Two months later Germany was able to mitigate its isolation with the help of an unexpected partner. On 26 January 1934 the German Reich concluded a non-aggression pact with Poland. During the Weimar Republic the eastern neighbour had been almost uniformly regarded as a threat. Not only its borders, but its very national existence were considered by many Germans to be incompatible with the interests of Germany. Now, both sides committed themselves to avoiding violence against each other in all circumstances. This about-face was easier for Hitler, an Austrian by birth, than for the Prussian-influenced, traditionally anti-Polish foreign office. For the chancellor, another enemy was far more important: the Soviet Union. In his view, anti-Communist and anti-Russian Poland could play the role of junior partner in a foreign policy directed against Moscow—at least for the time being. Before 1933 such a prospect would have been completely out of the question.

On 30 January 1934, four days after the German–Polish treaty was signed, the National Socialists celebrated the first anniversary of their so-called 'seizure of power'. The Reich government took this opportunity to have its law for the restructuring of the Reich passed by the newly elected Reichstag. This law abolished the parliaments of the *Länder* and transferred their authority to the national government. From this point forward the governments of the individual German states were subject to the Reich government, and the Reich governor came under the authority of the Reich interior minister. This seemed to represent an epochal shift, the final victory of the unitary over the particularist forces. At least this is how Interior Minister Wilhelm Frick wanted the Germans to view it. 'The centuries-old dream has been fulfilled. Germany is a weak federal state no longer, but a strong unitary national state.'

But Frick's triumph was premature. The more powerful Reich governors had no intention of subordinating themselves to the Berlin ministries, and their opposition was far from ineffective. Although Hitler agreed with his interior minister 'in principle', he had no desire to alienate his 'old fighters'. As a result, the members of the Reich government were constantly countermanded and left in the lurch by the chancellor. Frick protested in a letter to the Reich chancellery on April 1934: in the interests of a 'central and unitary leadership of the Reich by the Herr Chancellor and the special ministers at his side', it was not possible 'to propagate differences of opinion between a Reich special minister and a Reich governor'.

Hitler's response was the opposite of a decision. Through Heinrich Lammers, state secretary of the Reich chancellery, he told Frick on 27 June 1934 that it was also his view that, in general, it was not possible to propagate differences of opinion between a Reich special minister and a Reich governor over the justifiability or practicability of a state law that he, Hitler, had decided. 'However, in the view of the Herr Reich Chancellor, an exception must apply for cases involving questions of particular political importance. Such an arrangement is, according to the Reich Chancellor, in keeping with his position as leader.'

This incident was typical not only for Hitler, but also for the entire structure of his regime. Hitler was fixated on his ultimate goals. In matters of internal political organization, however, he did not have a clear plan and preferred to avoid decisions. Thus he repeatedly contravened developments that, in and of themselves, lay within the 'logic' of National Socialism—the systematic centralization Frick was demanding, for example, which fitted in with the 'leader principle'. And yet, in a certain sense, this inconsistency itself possessed a certain logic. Hitler's policies were conceived more in terms of 'movement' than of 'order', and continual dynamism was not compatible with the consolidation of stable structures. In addition, the rivalry among his followers also had its good side. *He* had to be called on to arbitrate, and he remained the master of the game even when he did not decide.

The much-discussed 'polycratic' nature of the National Socialist regime was not confined to the antagonisms between the Reich ministries and the Reich governors. There were also frequent conflicts between the Reich economics ministry and the German Labour Front, between the Reich economics ministry and the Reich Nutrition Estate, between the Reich Nutrition Estate and the German Labour Front, and between the foreign office and the NSDAP foreign policy office under Alfred Rosenberg (a conflict yet another competitor, the 'Ribbentrop Bureau', joined in 1936). The basic question of whether the state was subordinate to the party or the party to the state was never definitively answered during the Third Reich, not even by the 'law for the unity of party and state' of 1 December 1933, in consequence of which Rudolf Hess, the representative of the Führer, and Ernst Röhm, chief of the SA, were appointed members of the government. According to the historian Martin Broszat, the deeper cause of the never-resolved relationship lay in the fact that neither the state nor the party 'possessed sovereign power, but only power derived from and subject to the charismatic leader'. Broszat's analysis hits the mark: 'Since, however, the absolute leader could only assert his authority by means of either the power of the party or the power of the state and thus himself remained dependent on both, we can speak of a tripartite entity—party/state/absolute leader—as the basic structure of the NS-system.'[11]

THE MURDERS ON 30 JUNE 1934: PREHISTORY AND CONSEQUENCES

In June 1933 Ernst Röhm, chief of the SA, wrote a policy article for the *Nationalsozialistische Monatshefte* that left no doubt about the political ideas and expectations of the paramilitary arm of the NSDAP. The central passages were as follows:

If the philistine souls believe it is enough that the state apparatus has been given a makeover, that the 'national' revolution has already been going on too long, then we, for once, gladly agree with them. Indeed, it is high time that the national revolution be brought to an end and the National Socialist revolution begin! Whether it suits them or not, we shall continue to wage our war. *With* them, if they finally come to realize what it's all about. *Without* them, if they do not want it. And *against* them, if it should prove necessary!

After the Stahlhelm was integrated into the SA at the beginning of July, Röhm led an organization of at least 1.5 million members. Nonetheless, he still spoke for the 'old fighters', who believed that Hitler's rise to the chancellorship on 30 January 1933 was their doing. They were dissatisfied with the pace of change in the country and demanded a second revolution, one that would give them, the 'brown battalions', access to the levers of power in state and society. But Hitler knew very well that he could not achieve his long-term goals against the resistance of the army, bureaucracy, and business community. On 6 July 1933 the chancellor responded to Röhm's challenge in a speech to the Reich governors assembled in Berlin.

The revolution is not, and must not be allowed to become, a permanent condition. Now that the current of revolution has been liberated, it must be guided into the secure bed of evolution . . . The party has now become the state. All power lies in the hands of the Reich authority. The central emphasis of German life must not be shifted into separate areas once again, much less separate organizations.

This public reprimand had as little effect on the SA chief as his appointment to the position of Reich minister without portfolio on 4 December 1933, a move Hitler hoped would curb the SA. Röhm now demanded that the SA also play the main role in the *Wiederwehrhaftmachung*, the restoration of the country's military capacity, as well as form the core of a future militia. On 1 February 1934 he sent Defence Minister Blomberg a memorandum in which the Reichswehr was relegated to the status of a mere training organization. Röhm's intentions were clear: the army and the SA should exchange military-political roles.

Blomberg had no difficulty in convincing Hitler to take the side of the military. On 28 February, speaking before the leaders of the Reichswehr, SA, and SS, Hitler rejected Röhm's militia plans in no uncertain terms. He was resolved, he said, 'to set up a people's army, erected on the basis of the Reichswehr, thoroughly trained and armed with the most modern weapons'. This new army would have to be ready for all defensive operations within five years, and for offensive operations within ten years. The SA was expected to act in accordance with the chancellor's wishes. During the transitional period he would employ it for tasks of border defence and pre-military training. 'For the rest, the Wehrmacht must be the sole armed force of the nation.' The army honoured Hitler's support in a way that could not but please the leader of the NSDAP. That same day, 28 February 1933, Blomberg decreed that the Reichswehr would adopt the Aryan paragraph of the Law for the Restoration of the Professional Civil Service.

In the weeks that followed, Röhm did not openly question the new guidelines of his Führer. However, his speeches—including an address to the Diplomatic Corps on 18 April—remained as 'revolutionary' as ever, and clashes between the SA and the Reichswehr increased. For the first time since Hitler assumed the chancellorship, the public gained the impression of a weakness in the Reich leadership, a mood Goebbels sought to counteract with a campaign against 'killjoys and criticasters' in May 1934. The continuing troubles disturbed conservative circles around the vice chancellor, Franz von Papen, and prompted them to work towards a resolution of the power question in a manner favourable to themselves. One solution that recommended itself to the conservatives was the restoration of the monarchy after the death of Hindenburg, an event the aged president's deteriorating health seemed to make likely in the near future.

Papen's speech at the University of Marburg on 17 June 1934 was intended as a signal for the formation of a conservative front against the radical forces within National Socialism. The text was written by the publicist Edgar Jung, one of the vice chancellor's closest associates. It was the sharpest public critique since Otto Wels's speech against the Enabling Act of the terrorist methods of the NSDAP, the primitive nature of its propaganda, and the Byzantine cult around Hitler. It was an appeal to the principles of humanity, liberty, and equality before the law, values that the vice chancellor claimed were not of liberal, but of Christian-Germanic origin. The attack on the proponents of a 'second revolution' was obvious.

No people can tolerate a perpetual rebellion from below if it wishes to maintain itself in the face of history. At some point the movement must come to an end, and at some point a firm social structure must come into being, held together by an incorruptible system of justice and an uncontested state authority. Germany must not become a train steaming off into the blue, destination unknown . . . It is time to gather together in fraternal love and respect for our *Volksgenossen*, to leave off disturbing the work of serious men, and to silence the doctrinaire fanatics.

The applause of the Marburg audience was overwhelming, and the speech's resonance in the rest of Germany would have been no less powerful if Goebbels had not quickly banned its broadcast and publication. And although Papen complained twice to Hitler in person (on 18 and 19 June) and once by letter, arranged a common meeting with Hindenburg, and finally threatened to resign, the ban was not withdrawn. On 25 June Edgar Jung was arrested by the Gestapo. By this time, however, Hitler had come to realize that he was in the middle of a two-front domestic-political war and that his only chance lay in defeating both Röhm's 'revolutionary' SA and the monarchist 'reaction' at the same time. If he turned against only the Papen circle and the old elites, the resulting SA victory could have become very dangerous for Hitler. If he proceeded only against the SA, his 'bourgeois' allies would have been strengthened, which he also could not want. Papen's Marburg speech now gave him the opportunity to conduct a surprise strike against both sides and to resolve the internal crisis in a radical manner.

The events at the end of June and beginning of July 1934 became fixed in the imaginations of both contemporaries and posterity as the 'Röhm revolt' (the Nazi term) or the 'Röhm putsch'. The SA chief did not rebel or attempt a coup. At the beginning of June, after a long conversation with Hitler, Röhm left on a cure and ordered general 'leave' for the SA during the month of July. This made it much easier for Hitler, with the cooperation of the Reichswehr and the SS (which was formally still a part of the SA at this time), to launch a massive strike against his long-time friend and comrade-in-arms. On 30 June Röhm and other high SA leaders were arrested in Bad Wiessee in Bavaria. Hitler himself was present. The detainees were transported to the prison in Munich-Stadelheim and, with the exception of Röhm, summarily shot that same day. Hitler had the deposed SA chief shot on 1 July.

SA officials were not the only victims of the so-called 'Röhm putsch'. Hitler, Goering, and the SS under their *Reichsführer*, Heinrich Himmler, availed themselves of the opportunity to liquidate opponents from diverse political camps. Among those murdered on 30 June were Gustav Ritter von Kahr, former general state commissar of Bavaria; Ministerial Director Erich Klausener, president of Catholic Action and close associate of Papen; Papen's collaborators Herbert von Bose and Edgar Jung; Gregor Strasser, former Reich organization leader of the NSDAP; the former chancellor, General Kurt von Schleicher, along with his associate, General Ferdinand von Bredow. Hitler accused the former chancellor of high treason and treason to country in cooperation with Röhm, and General von Bredow of foreign policy assistance to Schleicher—groundless charges in both cases. The number of identifiable victims is known: eighty-five people were murdered, fifty of them members of the SA.

Thus, along with the SA leadership, Hitler had also got rid of conservative adversaries. Papen, the momentary figurehead of the conservative front (though all-in-all he played a fairly passive role), got off lightly. Goering held him for two days under house arrest, and a short time later Hitler obliged him with a statement in defence of his honour. On 7 August Papen left the office of vice chancellor and, at the Führer's request, took up the post of German ambassador extraordinary in Vienna. The Austrian National Socialists had attempted to take over the government there a short time before, on 25 July, and had murdered the Austrian chancellor, Engelbert Dollfuss. Although the coup was thwarted, it prompted an international crisis. Mussolini, whom Hitler had met for the first time in mid-June in Venice, ordered Italian troops to march to the Brenner Pass in order to warn Germany against the annexation of Austria. Papen's mission was to work for a restoration of Germany's image in Austria. This effectively foreclosed the possibility that incidents like the Marburg speech would be repeated.

On 3 July 1934 the Reich government passed a law retrospectively justifying the actions undertaken on 30 June, 1 and 2 July 1934 for the 'suppression of attacks of high treason and treason to country' as legitimate in the 'emergency defence of the state'. Hitler explained his rationale to the Reichstag on 13 July. 'If anyone reproaches me for not employing the regular courts in the condemnations, then I can only respond by saying that, in this hour, I was responsible for the fate of the German nation and was therefore the supreme judge of the German people!'

The task of supplying Hitler's murderous campaign with a semblance of natural-law legitimacy—and thus of liquidating the idea of an independent judiciary—was reserved for Carl Schmitt. In an article entitled 'Der Führer schützt das Recht,'* Schmitt appropriated Hitler's idea of the 'supreme judge'. 'The true Führer is always also a judge,' he wrote.

Judgeship flows from Leadership [*Aus dem Führertum fliesst das Richtertum*]. Whoever separates the two, or sets one against the other, turns the judge into a counter-leader or into the tool of a counter-leader and seeks to overturn the state with the help of the judiciary . . . In truth, the Führer's deed was an authentic judicial act. It is not subject to justice, but rather is itself highest Justice . . . The Führer's capacity as judge flows from the same source of law from which all law arises, among every people. It is in the greatest emergency that the highest Law proves itself and the highest degree of the Law's avenging justice is made manifest.

The 'healthy instincts of the *Volk*' came to the same conclusion as the law professor. The strike against the notorious troublemakers at the head of the SA was celebrated by many Germans as a deed of liberation. 'The manner in which the Röhm revolt was liquidated has greatly increased the good feelings the people have for the Führer,' proclaimed one testimony from Ingolstadt. A government observer reported similar feelings in Marktredwitz, a poor region in the eastern marches of Bavaria. 'Through his decisive action, the Führer has made massive gains among the broad masses, especially with those who have been undecided about the movement. He is not only admired, he is idolized.' A Berlin agent of the SPD leadership in exile expressed himself with somewhat more reserve: 'The position of the workers with regard to the regime must, as before, be described as one of benevolent neutrality. There has not yet been any visible change, even after the recent events.'

The beneficiaries of the SA crisis were, apart from Hitler himself, the Reichs-wehr and the SS. The army leadership, in order to secure a monopoly on the armed forces, had made itself accomplice to a crime. It was even prepared to accept the murder of two generals. From this moment forward the Reichswehr was morally vulnerable and susceptible to blackmail. The SS, in recognition of services rendered during the elimination of the SA leadership, was elevated by Hitler to the status of an independent organization within the NSDAP on 20 July 1934. Heinrich Himmler, the *Reichsführer SS*, from April 1934 head of the

---

* Schmitt, 'The Führer Protects the Law'.

'Political Police' in all of Germany, thus advanced another rung in the hierarchy of the Third Reich. His *Schutzstaffeln* could now commence their development into a state within a state.[12]

On 2 August 1934 Reich President Paul von Hindenburg died at his estate Neudeck, where he had been since the beginning of June. He was 86 years old. The second head of state in the Weimar Republic had mistrusted the NSDAP leader until the very last days of January 1933. After Hitler became chancellor, however, Hindenburg's reservations quickly disappeared. On only two occasions was a moderating influence from the president in evidence after that time: in the softening of the anti-Jewish regulations of the Law for the Restoration of the Professional Civil Service from April 1933, and in the summer of that year during the battle over the church. Hindenburg remained to the end the unpolitical professional soldier, for whom authority was more important than all else. He believed that Hitler's chancellorship had finally put Germany on the path to the internal tranquility he had long hoped for. After the suppression of the putative 'Röhm putsch', Hindenburg, who had found the homosexual SA chief deeply repellent, sent congratulatory telegrams to Hitler and Goering. Everything he learned of these events in the remaining days of his life increased his appreciation of the chancellor.

Nonetheless, at the time of his death, Hindenburg had not arrived at the goal of his political wishes. As a young Prussian officer he had witnessed the proclamation of the emperorship on 18 January 1871 in Versailles. In May 1934 he signed his 'last wish', an appeal for the restoration of the Hohenzollern monarchy. The 'last wish' was addressed to the 'Herr Chancellor' and was to be put in Hitler's hands after the president's death. By the time Papen, on behalf of Oskar von Hindenburg, gave the document to the chancellor on 14 August in Berchtesgaden, Hitler was already long familiar with its contents. On the next day he had Hindenburg's 'testament' published, which he had also received from the former vice chancellor. This document contained words of the highest recognition for 'my Chancellor Adolf Hitler and his movement', but nothing that hinted at Hindenburg's 'last wish'.

Hitler acted according to his own interests. He rejected a restoration of the monarchy as incompatible with his own view of himself as Führer. Hindenburg's death provided him with the opportunity of further expanding his leadership. Already on 1 August, one day before the president's death, the government proclaimed the unification of the offices of Reich chancellor and Reich president. This move not only contradicted Hindenburg's 'last wish'; it also violated the Enabling Act, which had left the authority of the president untouched. What is more, during the same cabinet session, Defence Minister von Blomberg announced that he would have the soldiers of the Wehrmacht take an oath of loyalty to the 'Führer and Reich Chancellor' immediately after Hindenburg's death on 2 August 1934.

Throughout the entire Reich the soldiers were compelled to swear the new oath, which was backed by no law and which contained no reference to an obligation to the people, country, or constitution of Germany. The new loyalty was to one man alone. 'I swear by God this holy oath that I will give unconditional obedience to the Führer of the German Reich and people, Adolf Hitler, the Supreme Commander of the Army, and that, as a courageous soldier, I will be prepared at all times to offer my life in fulfilment of this oath.'

On 2 August 1934 Hitler's personal power became such as had not been seen since the age of absolutism. The 'seizure of power' had reached its institutional conclusion. The only thing that remained was to receive the acclamation of the *Volk*. On 19 August 1934, four days after the publication of Hindenburg's testament, the Germans had the chance to express their opinion about the Law on the Head of State of the German Reich of 1 August, which transferred 'the powers of the Reich president to the Führer and Reich Chancellor, Adolf Hitler'. As expected, a large majority approved. Of the valid votes 89.9% were positive, representing 84.3% of the electorate.

At first glance this result was a resounding success. But the contrast with the referendum on 12 November 1933 was sobering. The number of those expressing their rejection of the regime through non-participation or an invalid or negative vote had increased. The government's supporters had shrunk in number, from 89.9% to 84.3% of the electorate. The proportion of negative votes was particularly high in the urban districts of Hamburg (20.4%), Aachen (18.6%), and Berlin (18.5%). All the districts in the capital reported negative vote percentages in the double digits, with formerly 'red Wedding' at the top of the list with 19.7%.

Germany's departure from the League of Nations was clearly much more popular than the unification of the two top government offices. Hitler's prestige was not seriously affected by this disaffection of a minority. Measured according to the regime's own expectations, however, the outcome of the second plebiscite was indeed the 'failure' Goebbels spoke about in his journal entry on 22 August. The propaganda minister's conclusions were also those of his leader: 'Speak and go to the people more . . . More firmness against enemies of the state.'[13]

THE GERMANS UNDER THE SWASTIKA

Among the 'enemies of the state', the remaining supporters of social democracy were in all likelihood still the largest group in the summer of 1934. At the beginning of the year the SPD executive in Prague had endeavored to redefine the party's basic stance in terms of a radical departure from the reformist practice the Social Democrats had hitherto been committed to. The 'Prague manifesto', drafted by Rudolf Hilferding and passed on 20 January 1934, proclaimed 'revolutionary struggle' against the 'total fascist state' and declared the setting up of a revolutionary organization to be a requirement of this struggle.

The victory of the total state poses the question of its defeat with cruel clarity. The answer is total revolution—moral, intellectual, political, and social revolution! . . . The battle to bring down the dictatorship cannot be waged other than in a revolutionary way. Whether Social Democrat, Communist, or member of the numerous splinter groups, the enemy of dictatorship was transformed in the struggle, and by dint of the very conditions of that struggle, into this same social revolutionary. The unification of the working class is a necessity imposed by history itself.

For the sake of its own credibility, the Social Democratic party had to round off its revolutionary vision with a self-critical assessment of its unrevolutionary policies during the revolution of 1918–19. This was no great challenge for Hilferding, a former Independent Social Democrat. Already on 23 September 1933 he had written in a letter to Karl Kautsky, another former Independent, saying that, ever since 1923, the politics of the Social Democrats had been more or less constrained by the political situation and could not have been much different. 'At this point in time, a different policy could hardly have produced a different result. In 1914, however, and even more so between 1918 and the Kapp putsch, the policy was malleable, and the worst mistakes were made at this time.' Four months later, this was the official viewpoint of the SPD. The Prague manifesto contains the following evaluation of 1918–19: 'The most serious historical mistake of the German worker's movement, disoriented as it was by the war, was that it adopted the old state apparatus virtually unchanged.'

The target audience of the appeal from Prague was, first and foremost, the mentioned 'numerous splinter groups' between the SPD and KPD that were working towards the reunification of the badly divided workers' movement, groups like *Neu Beginnen* around the former Communist Walter Loewenheim ('Miles') and Richard Löwenthal, and the Socialist Workers' Party (*Sozialistische Arbeiterpartei*), formed at the beginning of October 1931 in protest against the toleration policy of the SPD. And indeed, thanks to its strong leftward shift, which was certainly more than merely tactical, the *Sopade*—the name the exile-SPD gave to itself—was able to gain a temporary leadership role among the forces of the non-Communist left. But the Communists had no intention of adopting Social Democratic ideas about leftist unity. Instead, well into the year 1934 they held fast to the ultra-leftist general guideline of the 1928 Sixth World Congress of the Comintern, a policy that obligated them to wage a ruthless war against social democracy.

Only in June 1934 did the Communist International change course. It directed the Communist Party of France to agree to the Socialists' offer of a unitary anti-fascist front, which the Socialist party executive made conditional upon a non-aggression agreement between the two parties. There were foreign policy reasons for the about-face. Stalin had begun to take the threat of Hitler's anti-Bolshevism seriously. The logical consequence was a rapprochement with the west. In September 1934 the Soviet Union joined the League of Nations, and in May 1935 it concluded mutual assistance pacts with France and Czechoslovakia. In the summer of 1935 the Seventh World Congress of the Comintern committed the member parties to the new policy of the unitary anti-fascist front and, concomitantly, to cooperation with social democracy. One year later, after a leftist electoral victory in France, the first popular front government was formed under the Socialist leader, Léon Blum. Although the Communists did not provide any ministers, they enabled the cabinet of Socialists and bourgeois Radical Socialists to achieve a majority in the National Assembly.

By this time, the *Sopade* in Prague had already altered its leftward course again. The main reason was the party's disappointment with the behaviour of the German proletariat. According to reports from its agents in the Reich, Hitler was enjoying widespread approval even among the working class. On 13 January 1935, the date set by the Treaty of Versailles, the population of Saarland voted by the overwhelming majority of 91% for return to the Reich. Only a small minority of 9% followed the appeal of the SPD and KPD to preserve the status quo under the League of Nations so that at least this part of Germany could be kept from the rule of the National Socialists. After the Saar referendum, Wels and Hilferding gave up their hopes for independent action by the German workers and went over to cooperating with exiled bourgeois politicians like former Reich chancellor Joseph Wirth of the Centre party and the *volkskonservativ* politician Gottfried Treviranus, himself closely connected to another political refugee, Heinrich Brüning.

To be sure, the party executive in Prague exile did not represent the whole SPD emigration. After the end of 1935 Rudolf Breitscheid, Willi Münzenberg, the former leader of the Communist press concern, and Heinrich Mann worked together in Paris to establish a popular front in Germany that could overcome the opposition between Social Democrats and Communists. Hilferding, for his part, believed that anything beyond a non-aggression agreement between the two wings of the labour movement was illusionary and dangerous. At the end of December 1935, shortly before the beginning of Stalin's 'Great Terror', the mass elimination of supposed 'enemies of the party' between 1936 and 1938, Hilferding refused to sign a protest Münzenberg had initiated, with Breitscheid's support, against the execution of the German Communist Rudolf Claus in Berlin. He could not protest 'with murderers against murder', as he put it in a letter to his party colleague, the former Reichstag delegate Paul Hertz.[14]

The differences of opinion among the SPD émigrés had no effect on the German working class. Only a minority totally rejected National Socialism, and an even smaller number was prepared to offer resistance, for example by disseminating illegal political literature or by painting anti-regime slogans on buildings or bridges. Communist resistance groups, especially active in this regard, were the first to be infiltrated by the Gestapo. This helped keep other oppositional forces away from the Communists. By the end of 1934 some 2,000 Communists had been killed. The number of those arrested was about 60,000 in 1933–4, and another 15,000 in 1935.

The Social Democrats were generally far more cautious than the Communists. They cultivated their solidarity in gatherings, consumer cooperatives, or—as during the anti-socialist law under Bismarck—during the funerals of their comrades. The especially courageous among them maintained contact with the *Sopade* and circulated its literature, which was typically disguised behind non-political titles like those of classical drama or cookbooks.

The year 1935 saw an increase in the number of 'Marxists' arrested and the number of successful attacks against illegal groups of Social Democrats and trade unionists. The regime conducted mass trials against its adversaries; 400 Social Democrats were prosecuted on one occasion, 626 trade unionists on another, and 232 Social Democrats on yet a third, in Cologne. The group *Neu Beginnen* was almost completely broken up by 1938. Nearly all the sentences involved prison terms of many years. With the exception of small groups of conspirators, organized labour resistance had been eliminated in Germany by the time the Second World War began in 1939.

Churchgoing Christians and Christian organizations resisting National Socialist 'coordination' continued to be perceived as a threat to the regime. In the years 1936–7 a wave of morality trials, accompanied by press campaigns against the Roman church, was directed against members of the Catholic clergy and Catholic orders. During this same period, schools were ordered to remove crucifixes from their buildings. This was met with so much criticism and resistance from the faithful, however, that the National Socialists saw themselves forced to withdraw the ban.

Criticism and resistance also continued among the Protestants of the Confessing church. Martin Niemöller, pastor of St Anne's in Berlin-Dahlem, repeatedly accused Hitler from the pulpit of having broken his promises to the Evangelical church. He was arrested by the Gestapo on 1 July 1937. The verdict of the Berlin special court on 2 March 1938—seven months in prison, which were considered already served during Niemöller's period in custody, as well as a 2,000 mark fine—was tantamount to a moral acquittal, a view made especially clear in the text of the judges' opinion. Hitler did not accept the ruling. Niemöller, designated a 'prisoner of the Führer', was transported directly from the court building in Moabit to the Sachsenhausen concentration camp near Oranienburg. In July 1941 he was moved to the camp in Dachau, where he remained until the end of the war.

Niemöller was a privileged prisoner, protected to a certain extent by his position in the church and by the worldwide protests his arrests generated. Most of the regime's political prisoners had to deal with incomparably harsher conditions in the concentration camps. Communists and Social Democrats, especially, paid for their opposition to National Socialism before or after 1933. Humiliation, beatings and torture, and the shooting of 'fleeing' inmates were quotidian occurrences. The former SPD Reichstag delegate Kurt Schumacher, a disabled veteran (he had lost an arm), was forced to carry heavy stones in Dachau in 1935. It took a four-week hunger strike to stop the camp management from trying to work him to death. He was not released until March 1943. Two of his colleagues from the SPD fraction got out earlier, Julius Leber in 1937 and Carlo Mierendorff in 1938. Ernst Heilmann, SPD floor leader in the Prussian parliament and Reichstag delegate during the Weimar period, was subject to especially sadistic treatment as a Jew. At the beginning of April 1940 Himmler, after 1936 'Chief of the German Police', had him murdered in Buchenwald. Ernst Thälmann, the long-time head of the KPD and a prisoner since 1933, died in the same camp; Hitler ordered him shot on 18 August 1944.

There had been about 27,000 political prisoners in all of Germany at the end of July 1933. By June 1935 the concentration camps had fewer than 4,000 inmates. This was an indication that National Socialist rule had stabilized. By 1937 only four concentration camps remained in the entire Reich: Dachau, Sachsenhausen, Buchenwald, and Lichtenburg. They were managed by the SS, which stationed a 'Death's Head' group (*Totenkopfverband*) of 1,000 to 1,500 men at each camp. After 1934 the 'political' prisoners were joined by further categories of inmates: so-called 'elements deleterious to the people' (*volksschädigende Elemente*) like 'asocial' and 'work-shy types', homosexuals, Jehovah's Witnesses, former émigrés who had temporarily or permanently returned to Germany, and Jews, who were numbered among one or more of these groups. Such 'elements' were not covered under the penal system of current German law, but they also had no place in the *Volksgemeinschaft* of National Socialism. The National Socialist solution to this dilemma was to send them to the concentration camps.

These camps were the most patent expression of the National Socialist *Massnahmestaat* ('measure state'), which had arisen along side the still-existing *Normenstaat* ('principled norm state') and restricted its reach more and more. At the same time, the camps formed the backbone of the SS economic empire. Forced labour proved so lucrative that it created a demand for more prisoners. The year 1938 provided several opportunities to satisfy this need. The annexations of Austria and the Sudetenland increased the number of the regime's enemies, thus producing more political prisoners. Tens of thousands of Jews were sent to the camps after the pogroms of 9 November. The quarries where the prisoners worked produced most of the stone that went into the monumental buildings the Nazis erected in Nuremberg, Munich, and Berlin under the direction of Hitler's chief architect, Albert Speer. For reasons of practicality, new camps were frequently built in the vicinity of granite quarries, for example near Flossenburg in the Upper Palatinate and, after the *Anschluss* of Austria, in Mauthausen near Linz.

Between resistance with the goal of bringing down the Hitler regime and unreserved support for National Socialism lay a broad spectrum of attitudes and positions. Very common was a mixture of admiration for the Führer and contempt for the 'little Hitlers' in one's immediate environs. This ambivalence was endemic in the NSDAP itself, party membership being, for many, a matter of professional necessity (there were 18.5 million members by the end of the war). Many *Volkgenossen*, while supporting the regime's policies in most cases, disapproved of its measures in certain areas, for example with regard to the schools and churches. The disapproval of some was so strong that they avoided the 'Hitler greeting' and the hoisting of the swastika banner as much as possible and joined either no National Socialist organizations at all or else, if absolutely necessary, only 'harmless' groups like the NS People's Welfare Association. Though this was not resistance *per se*, it did represent an aloofness from, non-participation in, and, to a certain extent, rejection of the National Socialist system. In private, when one could be certain that nobody would overhear what was not meant to be overheard, doubt and critique of Hitler could be expressed and jokes told about him, Goering, or Goebbels. For the great majority of Germans, however, the Führer was sacrosanct. To a great degree, his successes and popularity compensated for the objectionable aspects of daily life in the 'Third Reich'.[15]

Among the German masses, Hitler's popularity continually increased during the years before the war. This was not the case among many intellectuals of the 'right'. Some who had applauded the 1933 'seizure of power' turned away in the following years from open support of National Socialism, disgusted with the plebeian character of the 'movement' and disappointed with the mediocrity of its 'intellectual' representatives. This was true of the poet Gottfried Benn, the sociologist Hans Freyer, and the philosophers Arnold Gehlen and, to a certain extent, Martin Heidegger, whom radical National Socialists attacked as 'philosophically unreliable'.

The case of the constitutional scholar Carl Schmitt was different. He did not lose his faith in National Socialism; rather, National Socialism lost faith in him. At the end of 1936, shortly after he had embraced anti-Semitism in the most blatant manner, the SS journal *Das Schwarze Korps* exposed his earlier connections to Jews and political Catholicism and his opposition to National Socialism in the period before 1933. Schmitt lost all his political offices, except for his membership in the Prussian State Council, which he owed to Goering. He also retained his professorship. Even after falling out of favour, however, Schmitt continued to assist the Third Reich. His 1939 book *Völkerrechtliche Grossraumordnung mit Interventionsverbot für raumfremde Mächte** attempted to provide the German expansion with a semblance of legality by arguing that it was the historical task of the Reich to establish, as the title suggests, German hegemony over a new large-scale territorial order.

The intellectuals who neither left Germany in 1933 nor embraced National Socialism found themselves in a state of 'inner emigration'. This was a place where some of the most famous German authors met: Ernst Jünger, Ricarda Huch, Reinhold Schneider, Ernst Wiechert, and Werner Bergengruen, and others. As

---

* Schmitt, *International Law of the Greater Territorial Order, with a Prohibition of Intervention by Foreign Powers.*

long as they did not express openly political views, they could continue to publish. Even disguised criticism of National Socialism sometimes made it past the censors, for example Bergengruen's 1935 novel *Der Grosstyrann und das Gericht** and Jünger's *Auf den Marmorklippen*† of 1939. The literature of the 'inner emigration' was read, but the party press completely ignored it. The official tone was set by authors whose 'line' was more congenial to the regime: Hans Friedrich Blunck, for example, a writer of northern German mythic prose and sometime president of the 'Reich Literature Chamber' (*Reichsschrifttumskammer*); Hans Grimm, author of the colonial novel *Volk ohne Raum*;‡ and Werner Beumelburg, a writer of novels idealizing the 'war experience' of the years 1914–18.

The 'inner emigration' was made up of writers from the middle and older generations. Younger intellectuals tended to regard National Socialism as a force for the comprehensive renewal of the German nation—or sought make it into such a force. In the mid-1930s, important levers of power in the SS, its security service, the SD, and the Gestapo, were tended by young academics who had completed their studies during the *Systemzeit* ('system period'), that is, the Weimar Republic. A good example was the jurist Werner Best (born in 1903), the son of a Mainz civil servant, who served the Gestapo in the capacity of organizer, chief of personnel, legal adviser, and ideologue.

The 'war experience' of the young National Socialist technocrats was the civil-war-like conflict in Germany between 1918 and 1920 and in 1930–3 and especially the battles for Upper Silesia and during the Ruhr occupation of 1923. The young Nazi intellectuals were decisively influenced by *völkisch* nationalism and intent on using the methods of the totalitarian state to build a racially homogenous *Volksgemeinschaft*. The elimination of 'Bolshevists', 'Marxists', and other enemies of the state was their area of responsibility, and they had made a good deal of progress in it since 1933. The elimination of the Jews, however, was as yet a largely unsolved task. The young academics of the SS, SD, and Gestapo knew this, and they worked towards a solution.[16]

DISPOSSESSION, ISOLATION, AND PERSECUTION OF THE JEWS

Theoretically speaking, a forced emigration from Germany could have been a Nazi 'solution to the Jewish question', and a plan of this kind was indeed in the works during the first year of the Third Reich. In August 1933 the Reich economics ministry concluded the 'Haavara agreement' with Zionist representatives from Germany and Palestine. This made it easier for Jewish emigrants to transfer a

---

* Bergengruen, *The Great Tyrant and the Court* (tr. as *A Matter of Conscience*).
† Jünger, *On the Marble Cliffs*.
‡ Grimm, *A People without Space*.

part of their assets indirectly to Palestine (another part was appropriated by the German Reich, which could also now sell more goods to Palestine). The Haavara agreement provided some material assistance to most of the 60,000 Jews who emigrated to Palestine between 1933 and 1939. Nonetheless, it took a great deal of wealth to make use of this option, and only a certain number of German Jews could afford to do so. And among these, only a minority considered the situation in Germany so threatening at this juncture as to necessitate emigration. Between 1933 and 1937 some 129,000 of a total of 525,000 Jews left Germany, most for western Europe.

The spring of 1935 saw another increase in anti-Semitic pressure from 'below'. It was driven primarily by the National Socialist small and medium-sized business community, which sought to get rid of undesirable competition through spontaneous campaigns like attacks against Jewish shops. The economic damage was considerable, and the negative echo from abroad was so massive that the regime—mainly at the instigation of the 'bourgeois' economics minister, Hjalmar Schacht—decided in August to channel the protest.

The result was the 'Nuremberg laws', passed by the Reichstag on 15 September 1935 in Nuremberg, where at the same time and place the NSDAP party congress was being held. The 'Reich Flag Law' (*Reichsflaggengesetz*) abolished the March 1933 pairing of the swastika flag with the imperial black, white, and red banner; from now on, the National Socialist symbol would be the sole national flag. The 'Law for the Protection of German Blood and German Honour' (*Gesetz zum Schutz des deutschen Blutes und der deutschen Ehre*) outlawed marriages and extramarital sexual relations between Jews and citizens of German or 'related' (*artsverwandt*) blood. Moreover, it forbade Jews from employing 'Aryan' female domestic servants younger than 45 years of age and from flying the swastika flag. The 'Reich Citizenship Law' (*Reichsbürgergesetz*) defined the concept of 'citizen' and created the legal category of the 'Reich citizen' (*Reichsbürger*) for 'Aryan' Germans. Only 'Reich citizens' possessed full political rights, including the right to vote. Mere 'citizens' were reduced to the status of tolerated guests.

Of the four drafts of the Citizenship Law presented to him, Hitler selected the 'mildest' version, but eliminated the restrictive clause according to which the law applied only to 'full Jews' (*Volljuden*). Accordingly, it was left for the implementation process to distinguish among the 'full Jew', the 'mixed breed of first and second degree' (*Mischling ersten und zweiten Grades*), the 'person accepted as' or 'considered' a Jew (*Geltungsjude*), and the 'person of German blood' (*Deutschblütiger*)—and to decide what consequences were to follow for those not of purely 'German blood'. Hitler reserved for himself the role of supreme arbiter in borderline cases.

The 'Nuremberg laws' abolished Jewish emancipation and reduced German identity to a question of biology. This was a clear declaration of war on German culture as a whole. But it met with no inconsiderable approval. The legal pathway to a restriction of Jewish influence was more acceptable to most Germans than uncontrolled attacks on the Jews. One official report from Berlin stated that, after years of conflict between Germandom and Jewry, 'things have now finally been straightened out'; this 'has given rise to great satisfaction and enthusiasm among the people everywhere'. In Koblenz there was 'contentment', since the blood protection law 'would bring about the desired isolation of the Jews more than the unpleasant activities by isolated individuals'. The agents of the Social Democrats, in contrast, spoke of a rejection of the Jewish laws among the working class and bourgeoisie, an attitude to be found even 'well into the circles of the National Socialists'. According to this source, however, the replacement of the imperial flag with the swastika was criticized at least as much as the elimination of Jewish rights. In the official reports, too, the Reich Flag Law was the least popular of the 'Nuremberg laws'.

After the passage of the 'Nuremberg laws', Germany entered a phase of superficial calm. The year 1936 saw the Olympic games in Garmisch-Partenkirchen and Berlin, and the National Socialist leadership made an effort to project a friendly image of Germany to the world. When a Jewish medical student, David Frankfurter, shot the leader of the NSDAP in Switzerland, Wilhelm Gustloff, on 5 February, the regime banned all anti-Semitic demonstrations and campaigns. The Olympic winter games began the next day in Garmisch-Partenkirchen.

Two and a half years later, another assassination prompted the largest wave of pogroms Germany had seen since the murders of Jews in the years 1348–50, during the Black Death. On 7 November 1938 Herschel Grynszpan, the son on a Jewish family that had been deported from Germany to the Polish border, shot and seriously wounded Ernst vom Rath, a diplomatic official at the German embassy in Paris. The attack took place during a period of increased anti-Semitic violence, including arson attacks against synagogues in Munich and Nuremberg, and sharpened discriminatory measures against Jews, like those banning Jewish doctors and lawyers from the practice of their profession. Ernst vom Rath died of his wounds on the afternoon of 9 November. Within a few hours, synagogues were in flames throughout the whole country; 267 were destroyed and some 7,500 Jewish businesses laid waste. At least 91 Jews were killed. Hundreds committed suicide or died as a result of abuse in the concentration camps, where tens of thousands of wealthy Jews had been brought with a view to forcing them to emigrate.

It was Goebbels, after consultation with Hitler, who had given the signal for the pogroms of what became known as the 'night of broken glass' (*Kristallnacht* or *Reichskristallnacht*). The violence was the work of the SA and SS, along with countless party members. Except in rare cases, the population as a whole neither participated in the violence and vandalism nor expressed support for the perpetrators. 'In the faces, too, there was only very rarely any indication of what their owners were thinking,' reported one source from Munich. 'Here and there there was gloating, but occasionally also expressions of revulsion.' In the small town of Heilbrunn near Bad Tölz, some people 'approved of the actions against the Jews, others looked on passively, and still others feel compassion, even if they do not express it publicly.' According to the SPD agents, the 'excesses were sharply condemned by a majority of the German people.'

Goebbels ordered the pogroms stopped on 10 November. Jewry, as the Reich Ministry for Public Enlightenment and Propaganda declared, would be given the final answer by means of the legislative process. The first decrees came on 12 November. The German Jews were forced to pay an 'atonement' of 1 billion marks to the German Reich, repair damage to their businesses out of their own pockets, and sign their insurance claims over to the state. An 'Ordinance on the Elimination of Jews from Economic Life' (*Verordnung über die Ausschaltung der Juden aus dem Wirtschaftsleben*) excluded Jews from the operation of individual retail shops, mail-order firms, sales agencies, as well as the independent operation of a trade. They were ordered to sell their landed property, businesses, stocks, jewels, and works of art by 1 January 1939. The proceeds of these sales was so low that the 'Aryanization' (*Arisierung*) was tantamount to expropriation. In effect, it was a colossal redistribution of assets from the Jews to their non-Jewish competitors, the effects of which are still felt today.

The Aryanization, which had begun long before 9 November 1938, was accompanied by measures designed purely to harass. Jews were no longer allowed to patronize swimming pools, cinemas, theatres, concerts, and museums. They were forbidden to sit in train compartments used by 'Aryans'. They were no longer allowed to possess gold, silver, gems, and radios. Telephone connections and driver's licences were taken away from them. Ordinances could now be passed relocating Jews to 'Jewish houses' and forcing them to do labour. German schools were closed to them, and welfare offices would no longer serve them. The social isolation of the Jews found especially defamatory expression in a legislative requirement that went into effect on 1 January 1939: Jews without a 'typically Jewish' first name had to add the name 'Israel' or 'Sara' to it.

A decision about what to do with the 214,000 Jews living, according to a May 1939 census, in 'Greater Germany' had not yet been made by this time. The 'Reich Central Office for Jewish Emigration' (*Reichszentrale für jüdische Auswanderung*), set up in February 1939 under Reinhard Heydrich, chief of the security police, succeeded in reducing the number of Jews in Germany by some 30,000 by the start of the Second World War. But since no other nation was prepared to take in a large number of poor German Jews, a quick and comprehensive solution to the German 'Jewish question' was not to be expected by way of forced emigration.

But there could be no doubt about the will of the Nazi leadership to get rid of the Jews. Hitler was firmly resolved 'to get the Jews out of Germany', as he told the Polish foreign minister, Józef Beck, in Berchtesgaden on 5 January. 'They would still be permitted to take a portion of their assets with them . . . However, the longer they delayed their emigration, the less they would be able to take.' Three and a half weeks later, on 30 January 1939, the sixth anniversary of the so-called 'seizure of power', Hitler announced in the Reichstag that he would once again, as so often in his life, speak as a prophet. 'If international finance Jewry inside and outside Europe should once again succeed in pushing the nations into a world war, then the result will not be the Bolshevization of the earth and thus the victory of Jewry, but the destruction of the Jewish race in Europe.'[17]

THE ROAD TO WAR: REARMAMENT
AND THE ANNEXATION OF AUSTRIA

One of the most important stages on the road to the Second World War was reached when general conscription was reintroduced in Germany on 16 March 1935. This was a clear violation of the Treaty of Versailles, which restricted Germany to a professional army of 100,000 and a navy of 15,000 men. The new Wehrmacht was designed to have a peacetime strength of 36 divisions and 550,000 men. Since the victorious powers, which still included Fascist Italy at this point, contented themselves with merely formal protest, Hitler was able to deal the fatal blow to the systems of Versailles and Locarno only one year later. On 7 March 1936 he ordered the occupation of the demilitarized zone of the Rhineland. Once again the western powers took no action.

The success of these surprise moves massively increased Hitler's popularity in Germany. The Führer seized the moment and used a plebiscite to confirm his power. The hastily scheduled Reichstag elections on 29 March 1936 (in which Jews were not allowed to participate and local ballot committees greatly 'improved' deficient results) produced 98.8% in favour of the 'list of the Führer'. Hitler now seemed to be convinced of his own infallibility. He had become a 'believer in his own cult', as the British historian Ian Kershaw writes. At the 'Party Congress of Honour' (*Parteitag der Ehre*) in September 1936, he posed as the saviour of the nation and spoke of the mystical union between himself and the *Volk*. 'This is the miracle of our age—that you found me! [storms of applause] That among so many millions, you found me! And that I found you. That is Germany's great fortune!'

The September 1936 congress gave Hitler the welcome opportunity to present himself to Germany and the world once again as their saviour from Bolshevism. The immediate cause of his apocalyptic warnings was the Spanish civil war (which had not been started by the Communists, but by the nationalists under General Franco, who by that time were receiving massive assistance from units of all the different forces in the Wehrmacht).

Hitler numbered the battles in Spain among the 'omens of an evil time to come':

What we have been preaching for years about the great threat to the world at the end of this second millennium of our Christian history is becoming frightful reality. Everywhere the tunneling work of the Bolshevist wire-pullers is beginning to prove effective. In a time when bourgeois statesmen speak of non-intervention, an international Jewish revolutionary headquarters, using all radio stations and with a thousand channels of finance and propaganda, is working for the revolutionization of this continent, starting from Moscow.

The conclusions Hitler drew seemed logical: just as National Socialism had dealt with 'this global persecution' internally, so too would it 'ward off all external attacks with the most brutal resolve.' For this reason, Germany would rearm.

By the time of the 'Party Congress of Honour', Hitler had already presented his secret timetable for the war. '1. The German army must be prepared for action within four years. 2. The German economy must be able to wage war within four years.' These were the two fundamental points in Hitler's memorandum on the Four Year Plan of August 1936. By the time of the Nuremberg party congress, at which the plan was announced, the German economy had reached virtual full employment. The regime no longer had any need for successes in the 'labour battle' in order to secure the loyalty of the masses. On the international stage, the sovereignty of the Reich had been fully restored. All the conditions were now in place for the Nazis to commence working toward their actual, expansive goals—that is, to begin systematic preparations for a great war.

In order to be ready for the kind of war Hitler envisioned, Germany first had to attain the greatest possible autarky by the year 1940. This was necessary in order to enable the Reich to wage a war for new *Lebensraum*, which would then bring absolute autarky. If the regime's ambitious goal could not be achieved through private industry, then the state would have to intervene. Such were the guidelines Hitler gave to his plenipotentiary for the implementation of the Four Year Plan, Hermann Goering.

Goering's agency became a counterpole to the Reich economics ministry and Goering himself the adversary of Hjalmar Schacht, who occupied three top positions simultaneously: president of the Reichsbank (from March 1933), Reich economics minister (from July 1934), and plenipotentiary-general for the war economy (from May 1935). The Four Year Plan was the beginning of National Socialist state capitalism. The regime's influence on the economy now took on a new quality. In July 1937 an iron ore mining and foundry complex, the *A. G. für Erzbergbau und Eisenhütten Hermann Goering*, was established in Salzgitter. This operation was the nucleus of the 'Hermann Goering Works' (*Reichswerke Hermann Goering*) founded one year later, a mammoth concern employing 600,000 workers by 1940 and uniting all levels of production. Schacht, all but deprived of his power, submitted his resignation as economics minister and plenipotentiary-general for the war economy to Hitler in August 1937. Hitler accepted his resignation on 26 November 1937. Schacht retained the post of Reichsbank president until January 1939.

In a secret meeting on 5 November 1937, three weeks before Schacht stood down as economics minister, Hitler gave an overview of his entire military-strategic programme to a group of his top officials. Present were Reich War Minister Werner von Blomberg; Foreign Minister Konstantin von Neurath; the supreme commanders of the three branches of the armed forces, Werner von Fritsch for the army, Erich Raeder for the navy, and Hermann Goering for the air force; and Colonel Friedrich Hossbach, a Wehrmacht adjutant. According to a report written five days later by Hossbach, Hitler was convinced that Germany's need for territory could only be satisfied by the use of force. It was expedient that the raw materials Germany required for its world empire, which was to be ruled over by a solid racial core, lay in areas directly peripheral to the Reich, not overseas. It was his, Hitler's, 'irrevocable decision to solve the German territorial question by 1943–5 at the latest'. However, it was possible that action would have to be taken even earlier, in the event of civil war in France or France's involvement in a war with a third power. In order to improve its military-strategic position, Germany's first goal in any case of military involvement would have to be the subjugation of 'Czechia' and Austria. This was necessary in order to eliminate any threat from the flanks in the case of action in the west.

The plan Hitler expounded on 5 November 1937 was basically nothing other than a shortened version of the *Lebensraum* programme he had worked out in *Mein Kampf.* As early as 3 February 1933 he had made it unambiguously clear to the military leadership that he intended to adhere firmly to these goals as chancellor of the Reich. His timetable was in place by August 1936. During the 5 November meeting, therefore, his audience can have had little cause for surprise. What several of them—namely Neurath, Blomberg, and Fritsch—objected to was, on the one hand, Hitler's assumption that Britain and France would take no action against a German attack on Czecholslovakia, and, on the other, his hope that the Spanish civil war would soon lead to an Anglo-French war against Fascist Italy. The foreign minister's reservations seem to have been particularly serious. They were, in effect, no longer distinguishable from criticism of the Führer. There is much to suggest that Neurath's behaviour on that day set the ball in motion for his own dismissal at the beginning of February 1938.[18]

We have no evidence that Hitler also decided at this point to separate himself from Blomberg and Fritsch. The fact that they were no longer in office three months later has to do with two unforeseen scandals. These gave Hitler the chance to undertake a large-scale reshuffle, perfectly suited to conceal highly embarrassing events. The first involved the war minister's second marriage. On 21 January 1938 Hitler, who, together with Goering, had been a witness at the wedding of Blomberg and Margarethe Gruhn, learned that the bride was a former pornographic model and prostitute.

Among the conceivable successors to the compromised Blomberg was the supreme commander of the army, Colonel General Baron Werner von Fritsch. However, a police file on Fritsch—which Hitler tried and failed to have destroyed in 1936—recorded a statement by a professional criminal to the effect that the army commander had been blackmailed about a homosexual affair. As a military court determined in March 1938, this accusation was false, the result of a confusion of names. Initially, however, the information produced by the Gestapo under Himmler's orders seemed to inculpate Fritsch. The result was that he, in addition to the war minister, lost his office—both on account of 'health problems', as the official announcement put it.

There was no minister of war after 4 February 1938. The duties of this office were assumed by the newly created 'Supreme Command of the Wehrmacht' (*Oberkommando der Wehrmacht* or OKW). Hitler occupied the top post. Directly under him was the new 'Chief of the OKW', artillery general Wilhelm Keitel, who was equal to a Reich minister in rank. Colonel General Walter von Brauchitsch was appointed as Fritsch's successor. Goering, the commander of the air force (Luftwaffe), was appointed Field Marshal, thus making him the highest-rank German soldier. In addition to numerous other rearrangements in the military, justified as deliberate measures to build up a younger general staff, there were two new appointments to top ministerial posts. Foreign Minister von Neurath was replaced by Joachim Ribbentrop, from 1934 Hitler's foreign policy adviser in his capacity as leader of the 'Ribbentrop Bureau' and from 1936 German ambassador to London. It was also announced that Walther Funk, hitherto state secretary of the propaganda ministry, would be taking over the leadership of the Reich economics ministry from Hjalmar Schacht.

The outcome of the Blomberg and Fritsch affairs proved extremely germane to Hitler's plans. The Wehrmacht now finally had a unified leadership, one in which the 'Prussian' army lost its special position and Hitler's power increased even further. The reshuffle of the top posts in the foreign office and economics ministry also gave greater influence to the National Socialists in diplomacy and economics at the expense of the 'old elites'. Taken together, the changes on 4 February 1938 gave both contemporaries and later historians the impression of long-term planning. In fact, what happened in early 1938 demonstrates once again Hitler's improvisational genius. He was able, in masterly fashion, to turn to his benefit events that took him as much by surprise as the rest of the world.

The domestic-political coup of 4 February 1938 was followed by the first strike across Germany's borders. In a meeting on the Obersalzberg near Berchtesgaden on 12 February, Hitler confronted the Austrian chancellor, Kurt von Schuschnigg, with a series of ultimative demands, including the appointment of the National Socialist Artur Seyss-Inquart to the position of interior minister and the alignment of Austrian foreign and economic policy with that of the German Reich. The Vienna government, hoping in this way to preserve at least a formal independence, submitted.

This was a deceptive hope. When, on 9 March, Schuschnigg exhorted the Austrians to vote for 'a free and German, independent and social, Christian and united Austria' in the plebiscite scheduled four days later, Hitler forced the government to call off the vote. Schuschnigg resigned on 11 March, whereupon Seyss-Inquart announced he would remain in office as minister of security. While Austrian National Socialists rose to seize power throughout the country, Hitler gave the order for the Wehrmacht to enter Austria the next day, on 12 March. The agreement of Mussolini, who had hitherto played the role of protector of the Alpine state, was secured late in the evening on 11 March. Hitler signed a law for the 'Reunification of Austria with the German Reich' on 13 March in Linz.

Two days later he spoke to a jubilant crowd from the balcony of the Hofburg in Vienna. Austria, on whose borders the 'storms of the east' had broken for centuries, would have a new mission. 'It is in keeping with the commandment that once brought the settlers of the old German Reich to this land. The oldest Eastern March of the German people must, from now on, be the newest bulwark of the German Nation and thus of the German Reich.' Hitler concluded with the 'greatest notice of orders executed [*grösste Vollzugsmeldung*]' in his life: 'As Führer and Chancellor of the German Nation and the Reich, I report before history the entry of my homeland into the German Reich.'

The resonance from the 'old Reich' was overwhelming. The general mood of the country was aptly characterized in April by the Swabian president, who said that in March the German people experienced 'a high point in their history, the birth of the greater and ethnic German Reich [*gross- und volksdeutschen Reiches*] and with it the fulfilment of the old longing of all Germans, the "German miracle".' 'The Führer's "greatest notice of orders executed in his life" set off an elemental spring storm of enthusiasm.' From the reports of its agents in the Reich, the SPD in Prague exile concluded 'that the national euphoria . . . is authentic and that only a more far-seeing minority remains staunch in its criticism and refuses to have anything to do with it.' In Austria the Catholic bishops and even a prominent Social Democrat, former state chancellor Karl Renner, campaigned for a positive vote in the plebiscite on 10 April. In both Austria and the 'old Reich', 99 per cent of the population voted for the 'reunification' and the 'list of our Führer Adolf Hitler'—the only list in the election for the new, 'Greater German' Reichstag.

By April 1938, the secret ballot was a thing of the past. In many places invalid votes were changed to positives and negative votes invalidated. Nonetheless, there could be no cause for doubt about the popularity of the *Anschluss* or of the man who had brought it about. By this time even many people who had mistrusted Hitler had come to regard him as the statesman who perfected the work of Bismarck by overcoming the break of 1866 and taking up the legacy of the 'old', first German empire, destroyed in 1806. In any case, proponents of 'Little Germany' were virtually non-existent by 1938. The hour of the Protestant National Liberals had long since passed, and the dissolution of the Habsburg empire had rendered obsolete the insight from the latter days of the Frankfurt parliament that Austria barred the way to a German national state. Ever since 1918, the only thing keeping Germany and Austria apart was the will of the victorious powers. The fact that Britain and France now once again bowed to Hitler's presentation of a fait accompli was an especial cause for celebration, not least among those Germans who had been expecting a strong reaction. Their Führer had swept aside the peace treaties of Versailles and St Germain, realized the claim of Germans and Austrians to national self-determination, and defied the whole world yet again. Such was the predominant opinion among those who gave Hitler their votes on 10 April 1938.[19]

THE BREAKING UP OF CZECHOSLOVAKIA

The governments in Paris and London would not have been able to win their nations over to the idea of fighting for the independence of Austria despite the fact that a majority of Austrians obviously did not want to be independent. By the spring of 1938, however, it was clear that the list of Hitler's territorial demands was not even close to being exhausted. His next goal would be the territories in Czechoslovakia inhabited by the Sudeten Germans. This had come out in a speech before the Reichstag on 20 February 1938. Hitler spoke of Germany's right to protect the '10 million Germans' in 'two states lying on our borders', Germans who had been united 'to the whole of the German people in a constitutional bond before 1866'. One of these two states, Austria, was now a part of Germany. The second, Czechoslovakia, was allied to France and, since 1935, to the Soviet Union. Consequently, German threats to Prague would immediately lead to a serious international crisis.

'Objectively' speaking, Czechoslovakia was a multi-ethnic state. Subjectively, however, the Czechs considered themselves to be the dominant national group, even though they represented 46 per cent and thus only a relative minority of the population. Their attitude was reflected in the 1920 law declaring Czech and Slovak the official languages of the state. The 3.5 million Germans, the second-strongest nationality with 28% of the population, had become citizens of the Czechoslovak republic against their will. Despite their formally equal civil status, they had cause to feel themselves treated as second-class citizens. Konrad Henlein's Sudeten German Party (*Sudetendeutsche Partei*), which obtained two-thirds of the German seats in the Prague parliament in the elections of 1935, increasingly became the mouthpiece of their disaffection. Henlein openly declared his support for National Socialism in 1937. He could not yet demand the incorporation of the Sudeten territories into the German Reich, since this would have led to the banning of his party. What he could do, however, was what Hitler committed him to at a meeting on 28 March 1938, immediately after the annexation of Austria: make impossible demands of the government in Prague. From that moment on, this was the policy of the Sudeten German party.

The crisis between Berlin and Prague came to a dramatic head at the end of May 1938. On May 20, mistakenly fearing an imminent German attack, the

Czech side mobilized. The British government informed Hitler that it would stand by France if the latter decided to come to the assistance of its Czech ally. At the same time, however, Britain told the Quai D'Orsay not to count on its military engagement. On 30 May Hitler informed the Wehrmacht of his 'irrevocable decision' 'to break up Czechoslovakia by force in the near future'. He set 1 October 1938 as the date the Wehrmacht was to be ready to march into Czechoslovakia and take possession of Bohemia and Moravia.

Faced with the acute threat of a great European war, which could turn into another world war, leading military commanders, diplomats, and conservatives rebelled against Hitler for the first time in the summer of 1938. The chief of the general staff, General Ludwig Beck, supported by his own memoranda on the military situation, appealed to the commander-in-chief of the army to give the signal among the generals for a collective refusal to obey orders. But Brauchitsch could not bring himself to do this, whereupon Beck resigned from his post on 18 August. His successor, General Franz Halder, gave sporadic support to plans for a coup. Among the many involved were General Erwin von Witzleben, commander of the Berlin district; Colonel General Count Walter von Brockdorff-Ahlefeldt, chief of defence; Admiral Canaris and his associate Count Fritz Dietlof von der Schulenburg, vice president of the Berlin police; Hans von Dohnanyi, a high official in the judiciary; and Theodor Kordt, an official in the London embassy. The commander-in-chief of the Wehrmacht, Colonel General Walther von Brauchitsch, was not informed of the plot. Without his cooperation it was bound to fail. Another precondition was an intransigent attitude on the part of Britain. Only if London staunchly opposed Hitler did the conservative resistance see a chance of bringing down the dictator. A restoration of the monarchy under one of the sons of Crown Prince William seemed to many to be the best and most traditionalist alternative.

Beck and the other conservatives in no way excluded the possibility of war as a means of increasing German influence in central Europe. However, Germany would have to have a realistic chance of winning such a war, and that meant, in their view, a limited number of war goals, the smallest possible number of adversaries, and a carefully chosen moment for the commencement of aggressions. They wished to avoid conflict with Britain at virtually any price. In this respect they agreed not only with the state secretary of the foreign office, Ernst von Weizsäcker, and Reichsbank president Hjalmar Schacht, but even with Goering. The rebellious conservatives wanted to pursue an expansive great power policy in the Wilhelmine style. Hitler's brinkmanship, they believed, was putting Germany's future at risk.

For the conservative government in London, the conservative opposition in Berlin was not a very attractive alternative to Hitler. On 7 September, Foreign Secretary Halifax met with Kordt, who, with Weizsäcker's approval, urged him to take a tough line with Hitler. But neither the chief of the foreign office nor the British prime minister, Neville Chamberlain, saw any benefit in a pact with Prussian politicians and military officials, whose foreign policy goals, which included demands for German colonies, they regarded as even more dangerous than those of the Führer. In the view of the ruling Tories, Hitler had done a good thing in turning Germany into a bulwark against Bolshevism, and it lay in their interest and the interest of Europe that this achievement not be destabilized by an openly reactionary regime.

A continuation of the 'appeasement' policy vis-à-vis National Socialist Germany, begun by Britain in June 1935 with a German–British naval treaty, seemed desirable for other reasons as well. The British population was not psychologically prepared for a long war. The same was true of all branches of the British military, despite an increase in armament. A European war with British participation would have exacerbated the anti-colonial independence movements in Asia and Africa and spelled great danger to the British empire. Economically, too, there were promising developments towards a German–British balancing of interests. To break with this policy by taking a hostile line towards Hitler was very risky for London. A war would then be extremely likely, but the chances of a successful coup in Germany extremely uncertain.

Lord Runciman was sent to Prague in August 1938 in an attempt to arbitrate, but with no success. Henlein, in close cooperation with Hitler, rejected all concessions from Czechoslovak president Edvard Beneš, even after every demand of the Sudeten German party had been met. At the NSDAP 'Greater Germany' party congress, which began in Nuremberg on 6 September 1938, the tone of Hitler's attacks against the Czechoslovak leadership was harsher than ever before. In his concluding address on 12 September, he accused the Prague government of 'terrorist blackmail' and 'criminal aims', stressed Germany's massive military efforts, insisted that the only thing he was interested in was the Sudeten Germans' right to self-determination, and pronounced a threat: 'If the democracies, however, harbour the belief that they . . . must do all they can to shield the repression of the Sudeten Germans, then there will be serious consequences! . . . The Germans in Czechoslovakia are neither defenceless, nor have they been abandoned. Let this be taken into consideration.'

Towards the end of his speech, Hitler sought to give his policy a great historical profile. He drew a parallel between Germany under his leadership and Italy under Mussolini and appealed to the special historical status of the 'old German Reich', to which Bohemia and Moravia had belonged at one time. In this context, Hitler's return of the old imperial insignia, including crown, orb, sceptre, and sword, from Vienna, city of the Habsburg emperors, to Nuremberg, city of the NSDAP Reich congresses, was given a contemporary significance.

When we consider the incredible provocation that, in these past months, even a little state has seen fit to offer Germany, then the only explanation we can find is the general lack of willingness to recognize in the German Reich a state that is more than a peaceable parvenu . . . The Roman empire is beginning to breathe again. Germany, however, though historically infinitely younger, is also no new-born on the international scene. I have had the insignia of the old German Reich brought to Nuremberg in order to remind not only our own people, but the whole world that, a half a millennium before the discovery of the New World, there was already a massive Germanic-German Reich in existence . . . The German *Volk* is now awake and has given itself its own thousand-year crown . . . The new Italian-Roman empire and the new Germanic-German Reich are, in truth, ancient phenomena. One does not have to love them. But no power on earth will now be able to get rid of them.

The outbreak of a great war seemed imminent after the Nuremberg party congress. On 14 September Chamberlain announced his intention of meeting with Hitler, and the meeting took place the next day in the Berghof on the Obersalzberg. Hitler attempted to intimidate Chamberlain in the same way he had done with Schuschnigg seven months before. But the leader of the nation Hitler had always regarded as his ideal maritime partner did not behave like the Austrian chancellor. Chamberlain answered Hitler's threats of war by asking why he, the Reich chancellor, had even desired to meet with him, given that he was already resolved to employ force. Under these circumstances it was probably better that he, Chamberlain, leave again immediately.

Hitler yielded. If Chamberlain would recognize the right of the Sudeten Germans to self-determination, then the details of its practical realization could be worked out subsequently. The British prime minister promised to discuss Sudeten German self-determination and the possibility of ceding areas of greater than 50 per cent German population with his cabinet. Hitler himself promised not to use force against Czechoslovakia in the intervening period.

The British cabinet backed Chamberlain, as did the French government under the bourgeois Radical Socialist Édouard Daladier (whose cabinet was still being tolerated by the Socialists at this juncture). On 21 September Prague, under massive pressure from London and Paris, bowed to the inevitable, agreeing to the British proposal to cede its purely German territories to Germany and to allow referenda under international supervision in the contested areas.

Chamberlain met with Hitler again on 22 September, this time in Bad Godesberg. The negotiations did not proceed as the prime minister had expected, however. Hitler insisted that the Wehrmacht immediately march into Czechoslovakia and that the territorial claims of Hungary and Poland, which he had encouraged, be satisfied. Chamberlain could not assent to such demands without exposing himself to the accusation that he had surrendered to threats. In the late evening of 23 September, while the talks were still going on, the report came that Czechoslovakia had mobilized. Despite the seeming hopelessness of the situation, Chamberlain declared himself willing to communicate the German demands to the Prague government. Hitler set the date of 28 September at 2.00 in the afternoon for unconditional acceptance.

When, on 26 September, he received report that the Czechoslovak government had rejected his conditions, the world again seemed to teeter on the brink of war. Britain had mobilized its navy the day before, and France had called in reserves. On 26 September the British government announced it would support France in case of a military attack against Czechoslovakia. Hitler, speaking in the Berlin Sportpalast that same evening, called upon Beneš to choose between peace and war, and stated that the Sudetenland was Germany's last territorial demand in Europe. 'We don't want any Czechs.' His fanatical speech was greeted with frenetic applause. But the mood in the arena was not the mood of the German people. According to the official reports, the population as a whole showed virtually no war enthusiasm, but a uniform desire for peace.

On the next day, 27 September, Hitler ordered the readying of forces for a first assault and the mobilization of nineteen divisions. The German conspirators now had to expect that the war would begin the next day. But the order to attack did not come. On 28 September, before the expiration of the German ultimatum, Mussolini, at Chamberlain's request, made an offer of Italian arbitration. Hitler could not have rejected the offer of the 'Duce', with whom he had established the 'Berlin–Rome axis' in October 1936, without appearing as a warmonger before the whole world, including his own people.

On 29 September, Hitler, Mussolini, Chamberlain, and Daladier met in Munich. The result of their negotiations came very close to Hitler's Godesberg demands. Czechoslovakia was compelled to clear out of all purely German areas between 1 and 10 October, during which time the Wehrmacht would occupy them in stages. A referendum was planned for the ethnically mixed areas, with option rights for Germans and Czechs living outside of their new national borders. Great Britain and France guaranteed the integrity of Czechoslovakia's remaining state territory in the case of an unprovoked attack. Germany and Italy expressed their intention of joining this guarantee after the settlement of the question of the Hungarian and Polish minorities.

Hitler was both the winner and the loser of the Munich conference. He had, yet again, conquered a German-settled territory for Germany without having to strike a blow. This was further grist for the propaganda mills in praise of his genius as a statesman. But he had wanted far more than the annexation of the Sudetenland. What he had wanted was to launch the Wehrmacht towards Prague, completely destroy the Czechoslovak state, and take possession of Bohemia and Moravia. Mussolini's intervention had kept him from achieving these goals. He would also not have reached them without war, one probably of European dimensions. Germany was not prepared for such a war in the autumn of 1938. On the afternoon of 26 September, as he stood at the window of the Reich chancellery and saw how indifferent and dejected the Berlin citizens looked as they watched a motorized division marching by, the Führer was himself forced to conclude: 'I cannot yet wage a war with this people.' The applause Chamberlain and Daladier received from the inhabitants of Munich was yet further evidence of the German population's love of peace. From this point of view, of course, the Munich agreement was indeed a highly respectable intermediate result.

For Czechoslovakia the agreement was pure disaster. The country had been sacrificed on the altar of 'appeasement', mainly because the western powers were neither militarily not psychologically prepared for a showdown with National Socialist Germany and because their governments harboured the illusion that Hitler's expansionist desires would now be satisfied and European peace secured. After Munich, however, the dissolution of the rest of Czechoslovakia was only a question of time. On 2 October Polish troops occupied the area around Teschen (Cieszyn). President Beneš resigned three days later. On 2 November Czechoslovakia was compelled to submit to the (first) Vienna arbitration by Germany and Italy, which awarded Hungary a part of Slovak territory with a primarily Hungarian population. On 19 November Prague passed laws creating the legal framework for the de facto autonomy of Slovakia and Carpatho-Ukraine.

The Soviet Union, after France Czechoslovakia's most important ally, had not been invited to the Munich agreement. The outcome of the autumn 1938 European crisis led the Communist power to conclude that the capitalist nations could easily overcome the antagonism between democracy and fascism and join forces against it. Opposition to the revolutionary power in the east was, in truth, one of the factors uniting the participants of the Munich conference. But British and French anti-Bolshevism was defensive, not offensive, at least as far as governmental policy was concerned. The great powers that pursued an offensive strategy against the Soviet Union were National Socialist Germany and Japan, which had concluded the Anti-Comintern Pact in November 1936, and Italy, which joined a year later.

Accordingly, Stalin had cause to feel threatened. But he, too, represented a threat to others. He wanted to respond to a German assault against Czechoslovakia by attacking Poland, and, through the agency of the Comintern, he supported the Czechoslovak Communists in their plan to bring about the proletarian revolution by transforming a national defensive war into a central European civil war. Thus the fact that Hitler's anti-Bolshevism found an audience in the western democracies was, in part, a result of Stalin's own policies: the great purges in the Soviet Union, the civil war propaganda, and the Comintern's revolutionary agitation west of the Soviet borders.[20]

The course of future German policy was set out in late 1938 in two secret addresses. On 8 November Heinrich Himmler, the Reichsführer SS, announced to the top echelons of his organization that the Führer would 'create a great Germanic empire . . . the greatest empire ever established by this humanity and ever seen by the world'. For Himmler, the choice was between 'the great Germanic empire or nothingness'. Hitler himself, speaking confidentially to selected representatives of the German press two days later, said that the regime's peace propaganda, which reasons of foreign policy had forced on him, but which obviously had 'its questionable side', was obsolete. It had become necessary 'to gradually realign the psychology of the German people and to slowly make it clear to them that there are things that, if they cannot be achieved by peaceful means, must be brought about by means of force'.

It was not only Hitler's peace propaganda that now revealed itself to have been 'questionable'. The re-education programme to prepare the Germans for war also had to consider the fact that, despite the Hitler Youth, Labour Service, and general conscription, daily German life in the late 1930s was shaped by the regime's civil achievements: increasing security in the workplace, a series of social improvements, primarily for women and families, and the leisure activities of 'Strength through Joy' (*Kraft durch Freude* or KdF), the most popular programme of the German Labour Front. The expectations of countless millions had nothing to do with conquests in war, but with KdF cruises to Norway or in the Mediterranean or with the purchase of a new Volkswagen, in which one could travel the 'Streets of the Führer', the new Autobahn networks, and discover the new, now larger Germany.

In 1938 the number of unemployed was 400,000 or 1.9 per cent of the dependent workforce. To what extent the decrease in unemployment was due to the rearmament economy; how much higher personal incomes would have been without the massive military expenditures; what the true value of the mark would have been given conditions of free conversion and free-market regulation of prices, wages, and rents instead of state controls—one could only speculate about such things. What mattered was not jeopardizing what had been achieved.

Most Germans also did not believe that the Führer was intent on war. On 10 November, the same day Hitler gave his secret address to the press, the president of Lower Franconia reported: 'The reputation of the Führer has grown even further, and even the very last are now beginning to adopt a positive attitude towards the new state. It is generally recognized that the foreign policy leadership has never been so excellent, purposeful, and successful as in the last few years.' In the eyes of the faithful, the Munich agreement proved that Hitler was able to master even the most serious international crises without war. If the official reports are to be believed, the vast majority of Germans felt this way at the end of 1938.

By the time of Hitler's and Himmler's secret speeches, the next stages of Germany's massive expansion had already been set out. On 21 October Hitler gave the order 'to take care of left-over Czechia' (*Rest-Tschechei*) and to occupy the Memelland (annexed by Lithuania in 1923, autonomous after 1924). On 24 November he added to these instructions the order to prepare for the occupation of the Free City of Danzig, which the Treaty of Versailles had placed under the protection of the League of Nations.

The Danzig question brought Poland into the sights of Germany's expansive power politics. On 24 October Foreign Minister von Ribbentrop proposed an arrangement to the Polish ambassador, Józef Lipski. Its signal points were the return of Danzig to the German Reich, extra-territorial connections between East Prussia and the Reich proper, a free Polish harbour in Danzig territory, also including extra-territorial links to Poland, a twenty-five-year extension of the 1934 non-aggression treaty, and Poland's accession to the Anti-Comintern Pact. If Poland had agreed to the German suggestions, the most it could have expected would have been an uncertain future as a junior partner in Germany's war against the Soviet Union, which doubtless would not have been long delayed. Such a prospect seemed little short of open self-immolation. When, on 5 January 1939, Hitler proposed a slightly altered version of this plan to Jósef Beck, the Polish foreign minister, at a meeting in Berchtesgaden, the latter did not definitively reject it, but left no doubt that Polish public opinion could not be made to accept the disappearance of Free Danzig.

On 10 February Hitler explained to troop commanders what drove him to place his bets on war and only on war. The successes of 1938, he said, were only way stations along the road to a much more ambitious goal.

When the collapse came in 1918, the numerically strongest people in Europe lost its political position and, with it, all possibility of asserting its most important and most natural life-interests with all means and under all circumstances. Really, we are talking about the strongest people not only in Europe, but . . . practically in the world. [It was necessary to] represent the interests of our people as if the fate of our race in the coming centuries were placed in our hand today, and today only . . . We cannot release ourselves from the obligation to act as if our actions today will shape the entire German future exclusively . . . We must make up for the neglect of three centuries . . . Ever since the Peace of Westphalia, our people has been traveling a path that led us away from world power and increasingly into immiseration and political impotence.

Germany's renewal, begun in 1933, did not represent the end of its path, but only the beginning. And the Führer was convinced of yet another thing: 'The next war will be an ideological war, that is, a conscious ethnic and racial war.'

Hitler's speech made clear what separated his agenda from that of the old 'Wilhelmine' elite. The latter wanted to return to the pre-First World War era, Hitler to the era before the Thirty Years War. The old elite thought in terms of the nation and believed themselves to be representing German interests; Hitler thought in terms of race and was convinced he was in possession of the only correct world view, National Socialism. When he spoke of 'world power', he was using a concept his audience could understand. But for the man who stood at the head of the 'strongest people' in the world, it was not enough to lead one world power among several. The Reich was to become the strongest world empire. Germany was to rule the world, in effect. This was the context in which Hitler, in January 1939, ordered the construction of a great navy and, in March, enjoined preliminary work for the foundation of a Reich colonial office.

On 12 February, two days after his secret policy speech, Hitler received the Slovak politician Vojtech Tuka, who in 1929 had been sentenced to a long prison term for high treason. Hitler assured Tuka of his sympathies for the Slovak independence movement. His decision to solve the problem of 'left-over

Czechia' as soon as possible had been made. With the help of Slovak separatists, he brought about a declaration of Slovak independence on 14 March.

Hitler summoned the Czech president, Emil Hácha, to Berlin that evening in order to compel the unconditional surrender of his state. In the early morning Hácha and foreign minister František Chvalkovský signed an 'agreement' stating that the Czechoslovak president had declared that, 'in order to bring about a final pacification', he was 'placing the fate of the Czech people and country confidently into the hands of the Führer of the German Reich'. The Wehrmacht began its march into 'left-over Czechia' immediately thereafter. On 16 March, speaking in the Hradschin in Prague, Hitler announced the founding of the 'Protectorate of Bohemia and Moravia'. That same day, by formal request of the Slovak president Jozef Tiso, he assumed the protection of Slovakia.[21]

THE UNLEASHING OF THE SECOND WORLD WAR

'Prague' was a watershed in more than one sense. Hitler's third attack on national borders also crossed the boundary of German national identity. In turning 'left-over Czechia' into a 'Protectorate of Bohemia and Moravia', the German Reich ceased to be a nation state among other nation states. The concept of the 'Reich' now took on a new—and simultaneously very old—quality. As the Austrian-born legal historian Karl Gottfried Hugelmann (who taught in Münster after 1935), a staunch advocate of a 'Greater Germany', put it in his 1940 book *Volk und Staat im Wandel deutschen Schicksals*:* if 'greatness, power, and dignity' were the 'essential characteristics' of the German Reich in the Middle Ages, then this dignity was henceforth founded 'on the consciousness of a mission'. The 'incorporation' of the Czech people into Greater Germany was, in terms of the 'Reich' idea, legitimate and sensible. It was, in fact, clear 'that, with the incorporation of the Protectorate of Bohemia and Moravia into the Greater German Reich, the latter's character as an empire . . . emerges even more strongly'.

In his 1939 *Völkerrechtliche Grossraumordnung*, written immediately after the protectorate was established (it was an expanded version of a lecture held at the University of Kiel on 1 April), Carl Schmitt emphasized the point that in the German language, 'the great, historically powerful polities—the empires of the Persians, the Macedonians, and the Romans, the empires of the Germanic peoples as well as those of their adversaries—were always called *Reich* in a specific sense.' The German Reich in the middle of Europe lay 'between the universalism of the powers of the liberal-democratic, melting-pot west and the

* Hugelmann, *People and State and the Transformations of German Destiny.*

universalism of the Bolshevist, world-revolutionary east' and was 'forced to defend on both fronts the sacredness of a non-universalist, *Volk*-oriented way of life, respecting race and nationality'. According to international law, the concept of 'empire' was that of

a large-scale territorial order controlled by specific ideological beliefs and principles, excluding the intervention of foreign powers and having as its guarantor and protector a people that has proven itself equal to the task. . . Our idea of the *Reich*, which is that of an ethnically-oriented, large-scale territorial order sustained by a *Volk*, is the new concept of order in a new international law.

National Socialist jurists associated with Himmler immediately attacked Schmitt, calling his attempt to create a German counterpart to the 1823 American Monroe doctrine half-hearted and without ideological content. In August 1939 Werner Best, the personnel and organizational leader of the SD, argued that, according to the *völkisch* world view, international law could not even be considered authentic law. 'Every *Volk* has only the purpose of self-preservation and self-development and knows only standards that are commensurate with this purpose. In its behaviour towards other peoples, no people can permit itself to be bound to rules that claim validity without regard to its life-purposes.' Thus Hitler's Reich could not only lay claim to a higher law than other states and peoples in its 'own' territorial sphere of control, its *Grossraum*; it was *the* Reich, and there existed no law any other state or people could assert against it.

Outside of Germany the 1938 'ideas of March' marked a turning point. The violation of the Munich agreement was so brutal that only the staunch right advocated further appeasement. Among the left, the forces of the centre, and conservative realists, the politics of accommodation lost all credibility. Even Chamberlain, in a speech in Birmingham on 16 March, expressed his outrage at Hitler's 'coup'. Although he himself still entertained illusions about the Führer, British public opinion made a continuation of his government's policy impossible.

In the week following the occupation of 'left-over Czechia', Hitler did everything possible to strengthen the hand of the anti-appeasement camp. On 21 March he renewed the October 1938 German proposals to Poland in a form that was tantamount to an ultimatum. On that same day, Ribbentrop demanded the immediate return of the Memelland from Lithuania. The government in Kaunas submitted. The first German troops entered the Memelland on the morning of 23 March. After the occupation of Klaipeda/Memel, a naval squadron brought Hitler into the capital, where he announced to an enthusiastic crowd the return of the former East Prussian territory to the German Reich.

Meanwhile, the international situation had changed rapidly, and in Germany's favour. On 21 March Prime Minister Chamberlain proposed to Poland a 'consultative pact', to be joined by France and the Soviet Union. Warsaw agreed two days later. On 26 March Poland definitively rejected the German proposals.

On 31 March Chamberlain declared that Poland's territorial integrity would be guaranteed in the case of direct or indirect aggression. Hitler reacted by ordering the Wehrmacht high command on 3 April to have the troops ready for the invasion of Poland anytime after 1 September 1939. In a speech to the Reichstag on 28 April he announced the termination of the 1934 German–Polish non-aggression treaty and the 1935 naval treaty with Great Britain.

Hitler's Reichstag speech was a polemical and rhetorically effective response to the American president Franklin Delano Roosevelt, who, on 14 April, had requested from Hitler and Mussolini a guarantee not to attack thirty-one countries (which he listed by name), at least within the next twenty-five years. If Germany and Italy were to make a similar request of the United States, Hitler said, Roosevelt would surely respond by invoking the Monroe doctrine (according to which European powers were not to interfere in the affairs of North, Central, and South America). 'This is exactly the kind of doctrine we Germans are now claiming for Europe, in any case for the territory and the affairs of the Greater German Reich.' Hitler had outlined a kind of 'German Monroe doctrine' already in October 1930, invoking a 'Germany for the Germans'. His extension of the idea to cover all of Europe was inspired by Carl Schmitt's Kiel speech of 1 April 1939. High-ranking National Socialist jurists had apparently communicated the idea to the Führer, who thereafter considered it his own.

The other great flanking power, the Soviet Union, also returned to the European stage in spring 1939. On 10 March, a few days before the German occupation of 'left-over Czechia', Stalin announced at the eighteenth congress of the CPSU that the Soviet Union had 'no intention of pulling others' chestnuts out of the fire'. This could only mean that Britain and France, which had concluded the Munich agreement with Hitler six months earlier without any consultation with him, Stalin, were not to count on Russian help in a confrontation with National Socialist Germany. On 17 April Merekalov, the Soviet ambassador in Berlin, informed State Secretary Weizsäcker that his government was interested in improving its relations with Germany. An even clearer signal came from Moscow on 4 May when Stalin replaced his relatively 'west-oriented' foreign minister, Maxim Litvinov, whom the National Socialist press persistently referred to as 'Jew Finkelstein', with Vyacheslav Molotov, head of the Council of People's Commissars (this was the first time a member of the Politburo took over the foreign office).

The least that could be gleaned from the words and deeds of the Soviet leadership between March and May 1939 was an openness to both sides. The USSR was not committed to joining the western powers against National Socialism. In certain circumstances, it was even prepared to come to an arrangement with the 'fascist' arch-enemy in Berlin. And in fact, the Soviet Union negotiated with both of the two western powers and with Germany between April and August 1939. By 24 July it looked as though an agreement with London and Paris was in the offing. In Moscow the three parties initialled a mutual assistance pact that was also to include Poland, the Baltic countries, Finland, Romania, Greece, Turkey, and Belgium. But the military convention was delayed by Polish resistance to allowing Soviet troops to march through Poland in the case of war with Germany. When the military discussions commenced in Moscow on 12 August, the British delegation was able to record only that Poland would probably accept Soviet support.

Hitler was able to offer Stalin more, and this was decisive. On 23 August the world learned to its amazement and shock that Ribbentrop and Molotov had signed a German–Soviet non-aggression treaty in Moscow. For a period of ten years the two powers promised to refrain from aggressive acts against each other, from assisting a third power involved in a war with the treaty partner, and from participating in any coalition directly or indirectly involved in hostilities against the same.

The international public did not learn about the secret addendum to the treaty. This provided for the partition of Poland and the Baltic countries, including Finland, into German and Soviet spheres of influence, separated by the northern border of Lithuania and a line marked by the courses of the Narew, Vistula, and San rivers. In south-eastern Europe, Germany recognized the Soviet interest in Bessarabia, which belonged to Romania. Unresolved was the question of 'whether the interests of both sides make the preservation of an independent Polish state seem desirable, and how this state should be demarcated'. This matter, as the text meaningfully stated, could only be cleared up in the course of further political developments.

The pact was practically an invitation for Hitler to invade Poland. Stalin was unconcerned. He not only acquired a large amount of territory, something the west had not been in a position to offer; he also gained time to rearm and to prepare for the eventuality that Hitler would return to his goal of expanding German *Lebensraum* at the expense of the Soviet Union. In the meantime, he would have the opportunity to watch the capitalist powers attack and weaken each other. It is not certain that he could have avoided war in the autumn of 1939 if he had come to an understanding with France and Britain.

Ideologically speaking, the cooperation with Hitler's Germany was difficult to rationalize. According to the party line, formulated in December 1933 by Georgi Dimitro, general secretary of the Comintern, and 'officially' adopted at the Seventh World Congress in August 1935, 'Fascism in power' was 'the open, terrorist dictatorship of the most reactionary, chauvinistic, and imperial elements of finance capital'. To undertake an alliance with such a system meant abandoning fundamental Communist principles. This was the accusation many Communists in the west levelled against the Hitler–Stalin pact, at least at first. But if one believed that there could be no contradiction between the well-understood interests of the international working class and the Soviet Union, then the German–Soviet agreement of 23 August 1939 could be justified as service to the world proletariat and the world revolution. One needed only the proper dialectical perspective.[22]

Hitler also had a very difficult time explaining to his confused and in many cases enraged followers that the alliance with Germany's absolute ideological enemy was not only permitted, but necessary. He had repeatedly portrayed Germany as the power whose task it was to stop the advance of the evil that Bolshevism represented. At the September 1934 Nuremberg party congress, for example, he had gone far back in history to underscore this German mission. 'Just as . . . earlier the waves of peoples and races from the east broke apart on Germany, once again our people has become the breakwater in a flood that would have buried Europe, its welfare and culture.' The following year, on 26 November 1935, he told the American journalist Hugh Baillie, the president of the United Press, that 'Germany is the bulwark of the west against Bolshevism and will fight propaganda with propaganda, terror with terror, and force with force in order to fend it off.' During the 'Party Congress of Labour' in September 1937, he spoke of 'Jewish world Bolshevism' as 'an absolutely foreign body' in the 'community of European cultural nations' and the 'claim of an uncivilized, Jewish-Bolshevist international guild of criminals to rule over the old European cultural country of Germany from Moscow' as a 'shameless provocation'.

Now, two years later, Hitler concluded a pact with 'Satan' in order to drive out the 'devil', as he himself put it. The removal of Litvinov (as well as Trotsky and other Jewish Bolsheviks, as later became clear) served as evidence that the Soviet Union under Stalin was now willing to break with internationalism and interventionism and move towards a kind of national socialism. Talk of 'Jewish Bolshevism' and Germany's war against it was suddenly no longer permissible. Countless propaganda texts with the old message became so much waste paper overnight, and anti-Bolshevist propaganda films were taken out of circulation.

On 25 August Hitler made an offer to the British ambassador, Sir Neville Meyrick Henderson: the German Reich would use its power to secure the preservation of the British empire if Britain would not stand in the way of Germany's solution to the German–Polish problem. After the conclusion of the German–Soviet non-aggression pact, Hitler believed Germany's position so strong that he seriously expected his offer to be accepted. Accordingly, he scheduled the war to begin the next day at 4.30 in the morning. Later on 25 August, however, he learned that Mussolini, with whom he had signed a mutual assistance agreement, the 'pact of steel', on 22 May, intended to keep Italy out of the war with Poland. He was also informed that a British–Polish mutual assistance pact was in the offing. With these developments, what Hitler believed impossible suddenly seemed possible—a two-front war, just like in 1914. Disconcerted, the Führer, at Brauchitsch's suggestion, withdrew his orders to the army that same day.

During this breathing space, State Secretary von Weizsäcker and Theodor Kordt at the London embassy frantically attempted to preserve the peace.

Goering, too, tried to avert war at the last minute, with the help of Swedish arbitration. But neither Halder nor Brauchitsch had any intention of standing in the way of an invasion of Poland. Hitler himself was committed to war. Although he still hoped to keep Britain and France from intervening, he had nothing more solid than hope. Great Britain could not accept his proposals without abrogating its promises to Poland. And his proposals to Poland were nothing more than a historical alibi. On 31 August Mussolini suggested that London permit the return of Danzig to the German Reich in order to prepare the way for a conference of great powers. But this, too, was pure fantasy. That same day, at 12.40 in the afternoon, Hitler gave the final order for the start of the war against Poland. It was to begin on 1 September 1939 at 4.45 in the morning. The SS was ordered to create an 'incident' on the German–Polish border in order to provide a pretext for the invasion.

Unlike twenty-five years before, there was no war enthusiasm in Germany in the summer of 1939. 'The will to peace is stronger than the will to war,' observed the *Landrat* of Ebermannstadt in Upper Franconia. 'Therefore, the great majority of the population is only willing to support a solution to the Danzig question if it can be brought off both rapidly and without bloodshed, like the other annexations in the east . . . An enthusiasm like that in 1914 cannot be counted upon today.' A month later, the same official summarized the public mood in the following words: 'As far as the public is concerned, the answer to the question of how to solve the problem of "Danzig and the corridor" is still the same: annexation by the Reich? Yes. Through war? No.' On 31 August, the day before the war, the official noted down what was being reported in other parts of Germany: 'Public confidence in the Führer is now being subject to a trial by fire, certainly the harshest yet. The greater part of the *Volksgenossen* expects him to prevent the war, even by renouncing Danzig and the corridor, if there is no other way.'

In his Reichstag address on 1 September 1939 Hitler invoked Frederick the Great, the historical idol to whom he felt closest. Hitler called the Prussian king as witness that Germany could defy even a great coalition, if it should come to that.

One word I have never learned, and that is 'capitulation'. If anyone says that we are perhaps heading into a difficult time, then I would ask him to consider that the Prussian king once stood against one of the greatest coalitions with a ridiculously small state and, after three battles, was finally successful, because he had a faithful and strong heart. A heart that we, too, need in this time. But as to the rest of the world, I would like to assure them that there will never again be another November 1918 in the history of Germany!

On 1 September, after the German attack on Poland had begun, the British and French governments demanded that Germany immediately stop all hostile actions and withdraw its troops from Polish territory. The note from London was followed the next day by an ultimatum, demanding compliance by 3 September at 11 a.m. Since no German answer was forthcoming by this time, Britain was now at war with Germany. The French ultimatum was handed to Ribbentrop at 12.20 in the afternoon that same day. It expired at 5.00 that evening. Germany was now at war with France too.

Hitler, who had not expected such prompt replies from the western democracies, decided to escape by advancing, as it were. After 3 September he again had a clear enemy: the Jews. Now, however, it was no longer Jewry in its 'Bolshevist' form, but in its 'democratic', 'plutocratic', 'capitalist' guise. In a dialectic move that nearly matched Stalin's achievements, Hitler blamed the Jews for the European war he had created. In an appeal on 3 September, written before France's entrance into the war, Hitler declared that the British people as a whole were not to be held responsible for the war. 'Rather, it is that Jewish-plutocratic and democratic ruling class, believing all peoples of the world its obedient slaves, who hates our new Reich, since it sees in it the example of a new social labour that it fears might also infect its own country.'

To 'National Socialist men and women' Hitler made the following claim on 3 September: 'Our Jewish-democratic world enemy has succeeded in harrying the English people into war against Germany. The reasons are every bit as mendacious and threadbare like [*sic*] the reasons in 1914.'* Party members were exhorted in the following manner: 'Within a few short weeks, the National Socialist readiness for war must be transformed into a spirit of unity, sworn together in life or death. Then the capitalist warmongers in England and its satellites will discover in a short time what it means to attack the largest people's state of Europe without the slightest provocation.'

Hitler's language on 3 September 1939 strongly recalled a particular version of the 'ideas of 1914': the juxtaposition of social or, indeed, 'socialist' Germany and capitalist, 'plutocratic' England. Such rhetoric probably found a certain resonance among the German working class, thanks to now full employment, the expansion of the welfare state, and the popular leisure programmes offered through the German Labour Front. And the support of the workers was important if Hitler wished to avoid a repetition of 'November 1918'. Unlike in Wilhelmine Germany, of course, the appeal to anti-Jewish resentment now came not from various societal or political groups, but directly from above, as 'official' discourse. Regardless of the details of its reception and resonance among the German population, anti-Semitism was in power in Germany after 1933. This was one of the crucial differences between the outbreaks of war in 1914 and 1939, as well as between the wars themselves.

Another difference can be seen in a decree Hitler signed in October 1939 and backdated to 1 September 1939, the first day of the war. It ran thus:

* [Translator's note: in the German, Hitler's text has *als* ('as') instead of the correct *wie* ('like'). In order to reproduce the mistake in English, the opposite must be done.]

Reich Leader Bouhler and Dr Brandt, MD, are hereby given the responsibility of expanding the authority of certain doctors, to be designated by name, such that merciful death can be granted to patients who, as far as it is humanly possible to judge and after a critical review of their condition, are considered terminally ill.—Adolf Hitler

Hitler had now become master over life and death. 'His' war was to give him the opportunity of realizing the ultimate consequences of his social Darwinist ideology, not only on the international stage, but also within German society. With the attention of the German people fixed on the two-front war, it would be easier to take the step from 'prevention of genetically impaired offspring', which a law of 14 July 1933 permitted, to the 'destruction of life unworthy of living', from eugenics through sterilization to euthanasia. It was true that certain voices had called for such measures much earlier, for example the penologist Karl Binding and the psychiatrist Alfred Hoche in their 1920 book *Die Freigabe der Vernichtung lebensunwerten Lebens*,* which radicalized scientific theories developed during the Wilhelmine era. And already during the lean years of the First World War, mentally ill patients had been deliberately undernourished, leading to a considerable increase in the mortality rate in sanatoriums. But in broad circles of society, and especially in the Christian churches, the 'mercy killing' of the mentally ill was still considered murder. Under the pressure of war, Hitler hoped that he could bring about the civilizational breach he desired. It lay within the logic of the totalitarian state to clear away, when necessary, inconvenient norms from the bourgeois tradition of the rule of law. In National Socialist Germany this logic could only be fully asserted after the war had begun.[23]

FROM THE POLAND CAMPAIGN TO 'OPERATION BARBAROSSA'

'War enthusiasm' was not required for Germany to wage Hitler's war. It was sufficient that the soldiers did what they believed was their patriotic duty and that most of them, like the great majority of the German people, continued to believe in the Führer. There were still those who staunchly opposed Hitler and the war, but they could not refuse military service without jeopardizing their lives. On 8 September the president of Lower Bavaria concluded from the reports he had received on the public mood 'that the populace doesn't want war, but nonetheless, despite the lack of a war enthusiasm like in 1914, will calmly and optimistically support the unavoidable, confident in the Führer, even in a situation of war.' At the end of September, after Poland had been defeated and divided between Germany and the Soviet Union, the district leader of

---

* Binding and Hoche, *Permitting the Destruction of Unworthy Life*.

the Gendarmerie in Upper Franconian Ebermannstadt reported 'joyous, duty-conscious optimism. The people know their fate to be in good hands and believe in a successful outcome to the war that has been forced on the Reich.'

The fate of the Polish people was of no concern to German 'popular opinion'. The German victory was followed by the fifth partition of Poland. Germany annexed a large territory in the west and north, the Soviet Union an area in the east. The part left over, the so-called 'General Government' (*Generalgouvernement*), to which Warsaw belonged, became a kind of lateral province of the Reich.

'Special Action Groups' (*Einsatzgruppen*) of the SS were active in Poland already in September. They staged mass executions of Jews and members of the Polish intelligentsia, including priests, teachers, lawyers, doctors, and landowners. Some 88,000 Poles, Jews, and Gypsies were deported to the General Government by the end of 1939. The goal was to make room for the settlement of German east Europeans (called *Volksdeutsche*), especially Baltic Germans from Estonia and Kurland and Volhynian Germans from Ukraine, in the Warthegau, in the Reichsgau of Danzig-West Prussia, in the new East Prussian district of Zichenau, and in now expanded Upper Silesia. It was Hitler's will that the territory of the future German Reich should be inhabited only by Germans. He commissioned the Reichsführer SS, Heinrich Himmler, with this task, appointing him to the position of 'Reich Commissar for the Strengthening of Germandom' (*Reichkommissar für die Festigung des deutschen Volkstums*) on 7 October 1939.

German scholars offered their services to assist the political leadership in this 'population supplantation' (*Umvolkung*). Research groups like the *Volksdeutsche Forschungsgemeinschaften*, founded in 1931, played a key role in researching and planning the operations. The *Nord- und Ostdeutsche Forschungsgemeinschaft*, led by the historian Albert Brackmann, was especially industrious. One of the active members of this group was the young Königsberg historian Theodor Schieder, who was later to become one the most prominent German historians of the Federal Republic and head of the German Historians' Association in 1967–72.

On 7 October 1939 Schieder submitted an 'Aufzeichnung über Siedlungs- und Volkstumsfragen in den wiedergewonnenen Ostprivinzen'.* He noted that the 'restitution of German property and ethnicity' in the new Reich territories represented the 'rectification of an obvious political injustice', the territorial losses of 1919. Indeed, it was a 'rectification from *Volk* to *Volk*'. To accomplish this purpose, he believed, 'population transfers on the largest scale' were necessary. The expected wave of Polish emigrants from Posen-West Prussia was, optimally, to be directed 'overseas'. Schieder considered an increase of uprooted Polish emigrants in 'left-over Poland' possible only after 'the removal of Jewry from the Polish cities' and a comprehensive intensification of Polish agriculture. The

---

* Schieder, 'Report on Settlement and Ethnicity Questions in the Regained Eastern Provinces'.

memorandum left open the question of where the expelled Jews should go. That they *had* to be expelled was clear, however:

The de-Jewification of left-over Poland and the construction of a healthy ethnic order demand the engagement of German resources and forces. There is the accompanying danger that a new Polish ruling elite may develop out of the new middle class. If these things are left to themselves, it is to be feared that the corrosion of the Polish ethnic body might turn into a new source of dangerous unrest.

This report, the product of deliberations among a circle of scholars led by the Breslau historian Hermann Aubin, quoted a passage from Hitler's Reichstag speech on the previous day. The most important task of Germany's Polish policy was 'a new ethnographic order, that is, a resettlement of the nationalities so that, when the development has been concluded, there will be clearer lines of separation than is the case today.'

The consequences of all this for the Poles in the General Government were summarized by Heinrich Himmler in May 1940 in a memorandum, expressly authorized by Hitler, on the 'Behandlung der Fremdvölkischen im Osten'.* All Poles who were not of 'good blood' and thus 'Germanizable' would never again rise above the status of a Helot people. For the non-German peoples of the east, no education would be permitted beyond that provided in a four-year state school. 'The goal of this state school will be limited to the following: simple mathematics with the numerical upper limit of 500; the writing of one's name; instruction that obedience to the Germans, as well as honesty, hard work, and good behaviour, are commands of God. I do not consider reading necessary.' Parents of children of 'good blood' were either to go to Germany and become loyal citizens or give up their children. 'They will then probably have no more children, thus extinguishing the threat that such people of good blood could form a dangerous ruling elite, equal to us, among this eastern people of lower order.' The great majority of Poles, who could not be 'Germanized', had only one prospect: they were to 'be available as a leaderless, labouring people, providing Germany with migrant labour every year and workers for special assignments (streets, quarries, construction).'

These instructions were carried out. The Poles were treated as lesser human beings, as *Untermenschen*. The greater part of their leadership elite was destroyed. German rule in Poland was that of a colonial power that looked upon its subjects as creatures of inferior race. In contrast to the German overseas colonies of the Wilhelmine era, ruled by officers and civil servants, the real power in German-occupied Poland was in the hands of irregular bodies: the NSDAP, which appointed Hans Frank as 'General Governor', and the SS, which executed Hitler's racial policies. This disempowerment of the classical bureaucracy was intentional. The kind of thinking that shaped the higher bureaucracy, guided as

---

* Himmler, 'Treatment of Racial Aliens in the East'.

it was by a traditional system of norms, regulations, and competencies, was to be given no opportunity to constrain the dynamics of racial revolution.

After October 1939 there was also no more military administration in Poland. The Wehrmacht, after clearing the way for the 'new ethnographic order' with its military victories, left the implementation in the hands of the SS, SD, and special police forces. Nonetheless, a clear line of separation between a 'clean' Wehrmacht and a 'criminal' SS no longer existed, even in September 1939. Certain regular troop units also committed crimes against the civilian population. The division of labour between military and politics during the war was an extension of the complicity the Wehrmacht had assumed in the suppression of the 'Röhm putsch' in summer 1934. The war against Poland was no longer a 'normal' European war, but the first racial war in Europe. As such it represented, along with the ensuing occupation, the shape of things to come in the Slavic east.[24]

The European west did not yet see war in 1939. Britain sent troops to France in September. France shifted several units to the vicinity of its eastern borders. But although assaults against Germany might have relieved Poland, none came. In April 1940 Hitler struck in the north. German troops occupied Denmark and commenced the occupation of Norway, which, after heavy fighting, was concluded on 10 June. The Norway campaign came just in time to pre-empt a British invasion. Denmark and Norway, both neutral powers, were made subject to German rule. Denmark's government was formally kept in place until the summer of 1943, but was beholden to orders from a 'Reich plenipotentiary' (this office was held by the envoy Cecil von Renthe-Fink until the beginning of 1942, then by Werner Best, former organizer of the Gestapo). Norway was placed under a German 'Reich commissar', Josef Terboven, former *Gauleiter* of Essen.

The western campaign began on 10 May 1940. Three new countries were attacked, the Netherlands, Belgium, and Luxembourg. German troops were entering northern France by 20 May. Fascist Italy declared war on Great Britain and France on 10 June. Paris fell to the Germans without a battle on 14 June. The German conditions for an armistice were handed to a French delegation in Compiègne on 21 June. Hitler himself was present. The parties met in the same rail coach in which the Germans had signed the armistice on 11 November 1918. The first signing of the document took place on 22 June, and the ceasefire went into effect in the night of 24–5 June. It placed France's entire Atlantic coast, as well as the east and north of the country, including Paris, under German occupation. The former Reich territory of Alsace-Lorraine received a German administration. Though not yet official, its annexation was a fact. The new *État français* under Marshal Pétain was relocated to Vichy in unoccupied France. Another French government, the resistance forces of Brigadier General Charles de Gaulle's *France libre*, escaped to England and raised its voice from London.

Hitler was never so popular in Germany as in the summer of 1940, after the disgrace of 1918 had been extinguished and the First World War seemed finally won. 'Today all well-meaning *Volksgenossen* recognize without reservation, and with joy and gratitude, the superhuman greatness of the Führer and his work,' the president of Swabia reported on 9 July. The district leader of Augsburg-Stadt had this to say a day later: 'It can now be said that the whole nation is filled with a faithful confidence in the Führer, the likes and degree of which have perhaps never been seen.' Academic Germany showed no less enthusiasm than the many nameless *Volksgenossen*. Even a former 'reasoned republican' like Friedrich Meinecke, who had strong reservations against Hitler and National Socialism, admitted in a letter to another German historian, Siegfried A. Kaehler, on 4 July 1940:

For me, too, joy, admiration, and pride in this army must dominate for the time being. And to have regained Strasbourg! How could one's heart not throb? Building up such an army of millions from the ground up in four years and training it for such accomplishments—an astonishing achievement, probably the greatest positive accomplishment of the 3rd Reich.

When, in the spring of 1940, it commenced a campaign to gain European support for a leadership role of the Reich (and, at times, a similar role for Italy), the National Socialist government could depend on the support of many, if not most, German historians. In the journal *Das Reich*, published by Goebbels from the end of May 1940, the historian Peter Richard Rohden declared (on 21 July 1940) that Germany and Italy had a particular mission: 'Within the Germanic-Roman territory, only Italy and Germany represent an authentically imperial idea of order, resting not upon suppression and exploitation, but upon justice and liberty—Italy as heir of the *pax Romana*, Germany as heir of the *Sacrum Imperium*.' In a 1941 article in the *Historische Zeitschrift*, Heinrich Ritter von Srbik, an 'all-German' Austrian historian committed to the *grossdeutsch* idea, celebrated the Third Reich for having 'once again taken up the old task of the First and Second Empires' to 'establish a new and more salutary order for *Mitteleuropa* and this part of the world', one 'without imperialism, and no longer on the basis of an idea of humanity as a whole, but based on its own idea of the *Volk* and of socially exemplary cultural work'.

That same year Karl Richard Ganzer, who was to assume provisional leadership of the 'Reich Institute for the History of the New Germany' (*Reichsinstitut für Geschichte des neuen Deutschlands*) shortly thereafter, published a book entitled *Das Reich als europäische Ordnungsmacht*.* The central message was contained in one bold-faced sentence:

The German core, by virtue of its higher political potency, organizes around itself as formative centre a political community made up of a group of spaces different in nature, which, racially speaking, might be completely autonomous. In this community, German leadership and the autonomy of the other races are balanced in an organic hierarchy.[25]

For Hitler, of course, this 'autonomy of the other races' was not something he felt bound to respect, even in the European west. Even before the war, in May

---

* Ganzer, *The Reich as a European Force for Order*.

1937, he had dreamed of the 'future liquidation of the Peace of Westphalia'. After a conversation with Hitler, Goebbels noted in his journal on 7 November 1939: 'The strike against the western powers will not be long delayed. Perhaps the Führer will succeed in annulling the Peace of Westphalia more rapidly than we all imagine. This would be the crowning achievement of his historical life.' Hitler returned to this theme ten days later. 'The Führer speaks about our war aims,' Goebbels wrote on 17 November.

When one has made a start, then it is necessary to settle the open questions. He has in mind the total liquidation of the Peace of Westphalia, which was concluded in Münster and which he wishes to do away with in Münster. This would be our great goal. Once it is accomplished, then we can close our eyes and rest.

To abolish the 1648 Peace of Münster and Osnabrück: this was Hitler's shorthand for a total redrawing of the European map with the Reich as permanent hegemon over the continent. In this context the restitution of the Holy Roman Empire's old western border would probably have been only a minimal requirement. In *one* of his territorial demands in the autumn of 1939, Hitler went much further. When (according to Goebbels's testimony) he began to partition French provinces on 3 November, he designated Burgundy for settlement by the South Tyroleans—who, in keeping with a German–Italian agreement of 23 June 1939, were to decide by the end of the year whether they wished to emigrate to Germany or to remain in Italy as Italian citizens without special rights. After the victory over France, the regime took the first steps toward the realization of this plan. On 10 July 1940 Heinrich Himmler travelled to Burgundy for a tour of inspection. His task was to determine how the territory could be Germanized through settlement of German peasant families. According to documents presented at the end of December 1940, it would take one million Germans to fulfil the settlement needs of nine French *départements*.

The Germanization of Burgundy was part of the 'Greater Germanic policy' proclaimed by Hitler in spring 1940. On 9 April, the day Germany invaded Denmark and Norway, he told his closest associates the following: 'Just as the Bismarck Empire arose from the year 1866, so too will the Greater Germanic Empire arise from this day.' Before the war Hitler had used the term 'Germanization' to describe the conquest of *Lebensraum* in the east. Ever since the German–Soviet non-aggression agreement of 23 August 1939, however, Russia no longer played a role in his visions of the Reich of the future. The 'Greater Germanic Reich' was to unite Germanic peoples like the Danes, Norwegians, Dutch, and Flemish into a single polity under German leadership—a racially pure community, but no longer a nation state.

With this vision, Hitler was resurrecting the old, pre-national idea of *Germania magna*, which had been invoked by the German humanists around 1500 and again, in the early nineteenth century, by Ernst Moritz Arndt. The difference was, of course, that in 1940 such a project was necessarily 'post-national' in nature. The only significant European powers that could have survived in the face of a 'Greater Germanic Reich' were Italy and—if it was prepared to come to an agreement with Germany—Britain. These were the outlines of Hitler's new European order west of the Russian border at the point of his greatest military triumphs thus far.[26]

Hitler's plan was one thing, reality another. His most faithful vassals in the occupied Germanic or partly Germanic countries—Vidkun Quisling in Norway, Anton Mussert in the Netherlands, and the Walloon Léon Degrelle in Belgium—enjoyed very little support among their populations. The result was that German rule never developed into anything more than a foreign occupation, regardless of whether it was exercised by Reich commissars like Terboven in Norway and Seyss-Inquart in Holland, Reich plenipotentiaries like Renthe-Fink and Best in Denmark, or military commanders like General von Falkenhausen in Belgium.

Moreover, in the course of 1940, the aura generated by the German military successes began to fade. Britain, led after 10 May 1940 by Winston Churchill, Chamberlain's staunchest adversary in the Conservative party, had no interest in the peace agreement Hitler was hoping for again after the collapse of France. Churchill was impressed neither by Hitler's warning that Great Britain would lose its world empire if it continued the war against Germany, nor by the bombing runs of Hermann Goering's Luftwaffe. Since Germany was not able to gain control of the skies above southern England, the planned invasion by ground troops had to be postponed. In the meantime, the economic and military assistance Britain received from the American president Franklin Delano Roosevelt began to have a strong effect. For the time being at least, Germany's most powerful enemy could not be conquered.

The realization that Germany could neither bring Britain 'peacefully' to its side nor defeat it militarily caused Hitler to rethink his strategy in summer 1940. His original foreign policy goal, a war against Russia for German *Lebensraum*, provisionally 'repressed' after August 1939, now re-emerged into the consciousness of the Führer. In an address to the commanders of the three branches of the German military on 21 July 1940, he spoke of destroying the Soviet Union in a rapid surprise attack. He justified this course with the assumption that one of the main reasons Britain was continuing the war was because it hoped for an alliance with Moscow and for American participation in the war. Ten days later, on 31 July, the 'destruction of Russia's life-force' had advanced to the status of a goal to be achieved in the immediate future by means of a 'lightning war' (*Blitzkrieg*). The eastern campaign was to begin in May 1941, since practical and especially climatic considerations made an earlier start impossible.

The historian Andreas Hillgruber writes that Great Britain's resistance, effectively shored up by the United States, caused a 'reversal in Hitler's thinking':

For the defeat of France and the hoped-for 'settlement' with Great Britain was to clear Hitler's back, thus providing him with a strategic basis from which to launch an attack against the east when he deemed the moment best. Now, what had been his main goal, the conquest of the east, simultaneously became a means to deal with the Anglo-Saxon maritime powers, who were not prepared to accept his lordship over the western parts of continental Europe.

The schedule Hitler proposed on 31 July 1940 was not yet irrevocable, however. In the autumn, he gave his attention to Ribbentrop's idea of an anti-British 'continental bloc', to which the Soviet Union was to be won over. Such an agreement might function as an intermediate solution. And indeed, Hungary, Romania, Slovakia, and Bulgaria joined the three-powers pact that the anti-Comintern partners, Germany, Italy, and Japan, had concluded on 27 September 1940. But the Soviet Union refused. Molotov, the Soviet foreign minister, was in Berlin on 12 and 13 November. After this visit, which made the incompatible interests of the two sides very clear, Hitler decided once and for all that there was no alternative to an eastern campaign in spring 1941. On 18 December 1940 he issued orders with the symbolic title 'Barbarossa Case', which invoked the glory of the medieval German empire: 'The German armed forces must be prepared to defeat the Soviet Union in a rapid campaign even before the conclusion of the war against England.'

A quarter of a year later, on 3 March 1941, Hitler directed the Reichsführer SS, Heinrich Himmler, to undertake *'special assignments* preparatory to the *political administration'* in the future area of operations, assignments 'that the final confrontation between two diametrically opposed political systems' made necessary. Speaking before about 200 higher officers shortly thereafter, on 30 March, Hitler (according to notes made by Halder) declared Bolshevism 'asocial and criminal' and Communism an 'enormous threat'.

We must move away from the idea of soldierly camaraderie. The Communist is no comrade, neither before nor afterwards. We are talking about a war of eradication . . . War against Russia: destruction of the Russian commissars and the Russian intelligentsia. War must be waged against the poison of corrosion. This is no matter for the military tribunals . . . This war will differ greatly from the war in the west. In the east, harshness is mild for the future.

Hitler's notorious 'commissar order' was given its first draft the next day, on 31 March 1941, and its final form on 12 May. The main thrust was that 'Political officers and leaders (commissars) are to be eliminated.'

Hitler's language in spring 1941 was once again that of the 'years of struggle' before 1933. From the very beginning, the war against the Soviet Union was to be an ideological and civil war, one in which everything was at stake. The period was now over in which he could fight against *only* the democratic or plutocratic version of 'international Jewry'. The war against the USSR returned the struggle against 'Jewish Bolshevism' to centre stage, a struggle he had been forced to abandon after the German–Soviet non-aggression pact was concluded. Most of the officers Hitler committed to the new policy and the new methods on 30 March

1941 understood and agreed with him. At least there was no criticism. And although Hitler, according to Halder's report, did not attack the Jews in so many words, those present could have been under no illusion about who and what he was talking about.

General Erich Hoepner, for one, who belonged to the military resistance against Hitler and who would be expelled from the Wehrmacht in January 1942 for disobeying an order to hold out, drew the conclusions Hitler wished to be drawn. 'The war against Russia is the necessary consequence of the struggle for existence that has been forced on us, a struggle for, in particular, the economic autonomy of Greater Germany and the European territory it controls.' Thus ran Hoepner's deployment order on 2 May 1941.

It is the old struggle of the Germanic peoples against Slavdom, the defence of European culture against Muscovian-Asiatic inundation, the fending off of Jewish Bolshevism. This struggle must have as its goal the destruction of present-day Russia and must therefore be waged with unprecedented harshness. Every military act must, in its conception and execution, be directed by the iron will to mercilessly and utterly wipe out the enemy. In particular, this means no quarter for the leaders of the current Russian-Bolshevist system.

It was primarily because of Mussolini that the 'Barbarossa Case' timetable, which provided for the eastern campaign to begin on 15 May 1941, could not be carried out. Fascist Italy had attacked Greece at the end of October, but suffered serious defeats, as earlier against the British in the Mediterranean. Hitler had rushed to the aid of his ally, at first by sending an Africa corps under General Rommel. At the end of March 1941, however, before the Führer could intervene in Greece, the Axis-friendly government of Yugoslavia was brought down by a military coup. The new government under the king Peter II (still in his minority) concluded a treaty of friendship and non-aggression with the Soviet Union at the beginning of April. Hitler decided right after the Belgrade coup to attack both Yugoslavia and Greece. The Yugoslav army was driven to surrender on 17 April, Greece's army on 21 April. Four weeks later the British were driven out of Crete.

Hitler was victorious, but the Balkan blitzkrieg had cost him valuable time. The attack against the Soviet Union had to be postponed to 22 June 1941. Another famous campaign against Russia had also begun on a 22 June: that of Napoleon in the year 1812. In his proclamation from the Imperial Headquarters in Wilkowyszki, Napoleon had justified his invasion by citing Russian–British collusion in violation of existing treaties. It was no different 129 years later. In his 'Proclamation to the German People', Hitler spoke of a putative 'coalition meanwhile formed between England and Soviet Russia' and numerous border violations by Soviet armed forces. 'This has brought us to the hour when it is necessary for us to take steps against this plot devised by the Jewish Anglo-Saxon warmongers and equally the Jewish rulers of the Bolshevist centre in Moscow.'

What Hitler did *not* say was that he was pre-empting a Soviet attack on Germany. He had no evidence of such an intention on the part of Stalin in

1941, and to this day no solid proof of one has ever been discovered. It is true that in mid-May 1941 Marshal Timoshenko, commissar of defence, and Georgi Zhukov, chief of the general staff, tried to persuade the Soviet dictator to launch a preventive strike against Germany. But they did not succeed. Stalin wanted to respond to a German attack with a massive counter-strike. The fact that the forces concentrated on the western borders of the Soviet Union were designed for offence, not for defence, is to be seen in this light.

Most Germans were shocked by the turn of events. But the military successes of the Wehrmacht impressed them soon enough. Among the first to applaud the invasion were Evangelical and Catholic churchmen. The *Geistlicher Vertrauensrat*, a special council of the German Evangelical Church led by the bishop of Hanover, August Marahrens, thanked Hitler on 30 June for calling to arms 'our people and the people of Europe to a decisive battle against the mortal enemy of all order and the entirety of western Christian culture'. The Catholic bishops simply exhorted the members of their flock to 'the faithful fulfilment of duty, courageous perseverance, self-sacrificing engagement and struggle in the service of our people'. Many church leaders went further in the months that followed. The bishop of Eichstätt, Michael Rackl, hailed the Russian campaign as a 'crusade, a holy war for homeland and people, for faith and Church, for Christ and His most holy cross'. The archbishop of Paderborn, Lorenz Jaeger, spoke of a struggle 'for the preservation of Christianity in our Fatherland, for the salvation of the Church from the dangers of anti-Christian Bolshevism'. The bishop of Augsburg, Joseph Kumpfmüller, compared the Bolshevist danger to the Turkish threat of previous centuries and prayed openly for a 'rapid, complete victory over the enemies of our faith'.

The most radical appeal to a just war against the godless Bolshevists came from the bishop of Münster, Count Clemens August von Galen. In a letter to his flock of 14 September 1941, he wrote that the termination of the 'Russian pact' by the 'Führer and Reich Chancellor' on 22 June represented 'liberation from a serious concern and relief from a heavy burden'. He quoted Hitler's statement about the 'Jewish-Bolshevist power-centre' in Moscow.

Our thoughts are with our courageous soldiers night and day. Night and day do our prayers rise to heaven that God's succour may continue to be with them in the future, helping them to successfully defend our people and country against the Bolshevist threat. And helping them to liberate the Russian people, too, which has been contaminated with the plague of Bolshevism for almost twenty-five years and has been nearly destroyed.

Bolshevism, he said, was not merely a physical danger that could be driven back and overcome through external means.

It is also and above all a teaching, a system of doctrine, derived and developed out of a naturalism inimical to Revelation and out of socialist materialism. Ignoring national borders and war fronts, it seeks, by means of its insidious and generally clandestine propaganda, to lay hold of and seduce even those peoples who politically defend themselves against the military potency of Bolshevism. After all, the Führer explicitly stressed on 22 June that, for over two hundred years, the lords of Moscow have been continually trying to set fire to Germany and all of Europe in an ideological sense, too.

Hitler also received moral support from German historians. In his *Deutsches Mittelater,** a collection of essays published in 1941, Hermann Heimpel, who taught at the newly created 'Reich University' in Strasbourg after November of that year, emphasized that 'medieval empire and imperial *auctoritas*, which also extended over the independent peoples of the west, repeatedly drew its inner legitimacy from the armed mission in the east.' No less symbolic was Heimpel's reference to the medieval belief that the Antichrist would not come to power as long as the Roman empire, which had been transferred to the Franks and thus to the Germans, continued to exist. The empire, as 'God's call', was still the agent of a mission within salvation history. 'The two last possible forms, the diametrical extremes of the missionary Reich, are the World Revolution and the Kingdom of God.'

Heimpel's was not a marginal voice. Other historians of repute also defended what they saw as the historical task of the German Reich. After the summer of 1941, in keeping with instructions from Ribbentrop's foreign office and Goebbels's propaganda ministry, this task was redefined as a *European* one. In the orientation courses for non-German volunteers in the SS, Herbert Grundmann and Fritz Rörig, two well-known scholars of the medieval period, explained why only 'the Reich' could lead the 'European crusade against Bolshevism', a mission outlined by the foreign office in a policy article published in the *Deutsche diplomatische-politische Information* on 27 June 1941. In a 1942 pamphlet intended only for internal use, Erich Maschke, an expert on the history of the Teutonic Order, wrote that the Germans alone had 'drawn the eastern territory to Europe, organically, without breaks, without symptoms of poisoning, from the Narva and St Petersburg to the Black Sea, connecting it with Europe, its fate and its culture.' From these realities emerged now the 'task for the present and the future'. For Reinhard Wittram, a historian of the modern period teaching at the 'Reich University' in Posen, the German was the 'soldier of Europe' who realized a 'new order' and restored 'wholeness' to Europe. He accomplished this in the struggle against the 'demon' in the east, against the 'counter-force calling everything into question that has granted this part of the earth its historical prestige'.

The German academics who lent their pens and voices to the regime did not, in general, do so out of opportunism. They did not write and speak against their better judgement. Rather, they offered to the leadership of the Greater Germanic Reich what they believed to be their knowledge and what they knew to be their beliefs. They did not agree with Hitler in everything, but in most things. For his part, the Führer had read and appropriated much of what German historians and other authors had written about German and world history.

* Heimpel, *The German Middle Ages*.

The German cultural heritage within which Hitler lived and which he put into practice was nothing more than a parody of the German cultural heritage. Nonetheless, large portions of educated Germany recognized themselves in it. This was more true of younger Germans than of those who had grown up before 1914, many of whom never managed to overcome their reservations against the vulgarity of the 'upstart'. There was an elective affinity between Hitler and the younger Germans, who believed themselves to embody the German spirit. This affinity outlasted the invasion of the Soviet Union. Indeed, it was never so strong as at the moment when Hitler seemed about to triumph in the final battle against Bolshevism.[27]

THE WAR FOR *LEBENSRAUM* AND THE MURDER OF THE EUROPEAN JEWS

In the letter to his flock on 14 September 1941 justifying the war against Bolshevism, Clemens August von Galen also directed sharp criticism at National Socialism. The bishop pointed out the danger 'that, behind the backs of the victorious army, false teachings and errors are tolerated and followed, which, no less than Russian Communism, represent naturalism and materialism, doctrines taught and spread also in Germany.' This was an attack on the policy, ordered by Hitler, of killing the mentally ill. Galen had criticized this practice twice before, once in an addendum to a pastoral letter by the Catholic bishops of 6 July and again in a sermon on 3 August 1941. He called 'horrifying' the 'practice of a teaching that claims it is permissible to deliberately take the lives of "unproductive people", of the poor, innocent mentally ill; a teaching that basically opens the way to the violent killing of all people labelled as "unproductive": the terminally ill, those disabled by work and war, and those weakened by age!" '.

Galen's high public standing and the stir caused by his public protest against the 'euthanasia campaign' made it impossible for the regime to simply arrest him and send him to a concentration camp. By the summer of 1941, Hitler's decree, officially dating from 1 September 1939, had terminated over 70,000 lives. The killing was first done by lethal injection, then, after January 1940, by gas. It was stopped on 24 August 1941, after popular unrest had reached a point Hitler considered politically dangerous. But the interruption did not mean the end of the 'destruction of life unworthy of living'. Hitler's order only applied to the murder centres in the 'old Reich', in Grafeneck in Württemberg, Hadamar near Limburg, and Brandenburg on the Havel, all of which were well known by that point. The murders continued in decentralized form and by other methods, including deliberate starvation, mass shootings by the SS in the new Reichsgau of Danzig-West Prussia, and dynamite. One particular group of patients were killed without exception and without the individual case review typically undertaken: mentally ill Jews.

At about this same time, in the summer of 1941, a 'solution' to the entire 'Jewish question' began to take on more definite outlines. After the occupation and partition of Poland, Berlin first considered a 'territorial' solution within Poland itself. Hitler and Himmler envisioned a special 'Jewish district' to be set up in Lublin, the easternmost district of the General Government. However, the first deportations, which took place in December 1939 and involved nearly 90,000 people, were so chaotic that General Governor Hans Frank did all he could to prevent further transports and the establishment of a Jewish reservation east of the Vistula. And he was initially successful.

Frank's efforts were aided by a new proposal for the 'territorial' solution to the 'Jewish question' in the early summer of 1940. This plan, which found Himmler's approval, involved transporting the Jews overseas. At the beginning of June 1940, on the eve of victory over France, Franz Rademacher, the head of the Jewish desk in the foreign office, took up an idea that the German anti-Semite Paul de Lagarde had first thrown into the debate in 1885. The Jews—or, as Rademacher specified, the 'western Jews'—were to be taken to the French colony of Madagascar. After Hitler and Himmler agreed to the idea, the Reich Security Main Office presented its own Madagascar plan, according to which the island off the east coast of Africa would be turned into a large-scale ghetto under German supremacy.

Madagascar's climate and lack of infrastructure, however, would have quickly led to a physical partial solution to the 'Jewish question', that is, to mass mortality. But these were not the only reasons the Madagascar plan was not an 'authentic' alternative to the killing of the Jews. Since the deportation of the Jewish millions was to be accomplished by British and French ships, it would not work unless a peace treaty could be concluded with Great Britain. Germany's inability to compel such a treaty meant that the 'Madagascar plan' became a dead letter after the autumn of 1940.

While the Nazi leadership was thinking over the Lublin and the Madagascar versions of a 'territorial' solution to the 'Jewish question', the Jews in the Warthegau and the General Government were being amassed in ghettos and isolated from the rest of the population. The living conditions in the ghettos were so bad that mass mortality began shortly after their organization, costing the lives of some 500,000 Jews, according to the historian Raul Hilberg. The ghettos were originally conceived as a provisional measure, as a way station either to the eastern part of the General Government or overseas. After the Lublin and Madagascar projects proved chimerical, the German offices attempted in several places—in Lodz, for one—to keep the ghetto Jews alive through work in the manufacture of armaments. Other German authorities, including those in Warsaw, intended to simply let them starve. In April 1941 the proponents of 'productivity' were able to win out over the advocates of 'starvation'. But only for a short time. A new episode in the National Socialist Jewish policy began on 22 June 1941 with the invasion of the Soviet Union. In retrospect, the fate of the

Jews in the German sphere of influence was sealed the moment Hitler resolved upon the destruction of 'Jewish Bolshevism'.

Hitler's decision to invade the Soviet Union in spring 1941 was made in December 1940. At about this same time, the Führer declared his intention of bringing 'the Jewish question to a final solution after the war, in the part of Europe ruled or controlled by Germany'. As chief of the security police and the SD (the security service of the SS), Reinhard Heydrich (according to a report by Theodor Dannecker, who headed the Gestapo's Jewish desk in Paris) was given the 'task of presenting a final solution project' 'by the Führer through the RF-SS, or through the Reich Marshal', that is, through Himmler or Goering. By the time Dannecker wrote his report on 21 January 1941, Hitler and Goering had already seen the 'project in its main outlines'. The further planning was to deal with 'both the studies preliminary to a total deportation of the Jews as well as the detailed planning of a settlement campaign in the territory, which is yet to be determined'.

By March 1941 at the latest, Heydrich's thoughts were concentrated on the Soviet Union, especially on a remote and particularly inhospitable area: the coast of the Arctic Ocean. On 23 September 1941 Heydrich told Goebbels that the Jews should be transported to the camps the Bolshevists had set up. They could not have survived there for long. That many would die on the way was a prospect Heydrich and his colleagues had already factored in. Plans to destroy the greater part of the Jews fit for work through forced labour in road construction and swamp drainage were ripening in the Reich Security Main Office probably in the spring of 1941.[28]

A 'final solution to the Jewish question' was one of the main aims of the war against the USSR, but it was not the only one. On 15 July 1941, about three weeks after the eastern campaign had begun, Himmler, in his capacity as 'Reich Commissar for the Strengthening of Germandom', presented the first version of the 'General Plan East' (*Generalplan Ost*), a scheme of gigantic population transfers and 'supplantations' in the eastern territories. The plan's details were worked out in the ensuing months. It provided for the Germanization of the entire General Government, along with Galicia, the Baltic countries, White Ruthenia, and parts of Ukraine, within a period of thirty years at the most. Of the populations currently living in these areas, 31 million were to be expelled to western Siberia, leaving 14 million 'of good race' (*Gutrassige*) behind.

As Hitler told his inner circle on 16 July 1941, the war was to make the 'formation of a military power west of the Urals' impossible from then on. His first concern was 'to cut the giant cake into manageable slices, in order to be able, first, to control it, second, to administer it, and third, to exploit it'. The Crimea, the Baltic, and old-Austrian Galicia would be made into Reich territories, along with the Volga colony (i.e. the settlement area of the Volga Germans) and the area around Baku with its rich oil fields on the Caspian Sea. Germany's true aims were not to be announced to the whole world. 'Thus, it should not be clear that this represents the initiation of a final arrangement! Despite this, however, we will and can take all necessary measures—shootings, evacuations, etc.' A quarter of a year later, on 17 October 1941, Hitler, speaking in his headquarters, summarized his goals in the east in one sentence: 'There is only one task: to undertake Germanization by bringing in the Germans and by treating the native inhabitants as Indians.'

From the beginning, the war for *Lebensraum* in the east had another purpose, one having to do with social politics. In *Mein Kampf* Hitler had called for the 'acquisition of new land' in order to overcome the unhealthy consequences of industrialization, preserve a 'healthy peasantry' for Germany, and 'more or less end dependence on foreign countries for the alimentation of the population'. In October 1941 Himmler wanted to prevent an 'increase in the average age in the skilled trades in the Old Reich' by 'making skilled trades in the Old Reich, as it were, the mother companies of the young shops in the newly acquired areas of the east, thereby securing a constant circulation of fresh blood between the old and young shops'. In August of the following year Himmler, returning from a trip to Kiev, summed up his social-political ideas in the remark that 'one can only solve the social question by killing the others so as to obtain their fields.' With this comment, the Reichsführer SS was describing the reality of German rule in the east. The mass shootings and hangings were now supplemented by a policy of mass starvation. The Wehrmacht, too, employed this method against Soviet prisoners of war and the native civilians. In both cases the victims were numbered in the millions.

From the first day of the eastern campaign, the mass murder of the Jews was primarily the job of the four newly created 'Special Action Groups' of the SS. Each was assigned to an area corresponding to one of the three main army divisions, Army Group North, Centre, and South (Special Actions Groups C and D shared the territory of Army Group South). Hitler's conflation of Jews with Bolshevist party members and partisans spelled, at first, the death of most adult male Jews within the Special Action Groups' areas of operation. After the end of July, the SS and its squads increasingly began to kill all Jews they encountered, including women and children. This policy was connected with a new regulation of official competencies. On 16–17 July Hitler had transferred the 'police security of the newly occupied eastern areas' to the 'Reichsführer SS and chief of the German police', Heinrich Himmler. This put the police solution to the 'Jewish question' in Himmler's hands. On 14–15 August 1941, speaking to Otto Bradfisch, leader of Special Action Commando 8, in Minsk, Himmler referred to the 'Führer's order concerning the shooting of all Jews'. The order was followed. In the area of Group A alone, which included the Baltic countries and parts of northern Russia, some 125,000 Jews and 5,000 non-Jews were liquidated between 22 June and 15 October 1941. Approximately 500,000 Jews were murdered in the first five months of the eastern campaign. The genocide had begun.

Anti-communists from the local populations often participated in the mass shootings, especially in Lithuania, eastern Galicia, and Ukraine. Wehrmacht soldiers were also not infrequently involved. In the autumn of 1941 two German general field marshals exhorted their troops to look upon their war against the Soviet Union not as a conventional war, but as an ideological and racial struggle. Walther von Reichenau spoke as Hitler's mouthpiece when he declared on 10 October that the 'soldier in the east' was the 'agent of an inexorable racial idea', one who 'must have a *complete* understanding for the necessity of the harsh but just atonement of Jewish sub-humanity'. Erich von Manstein used almost the same words in November: 'The Jewish-Bolshevist system must be exterminated once and for all. Never again must it be permitted to invade our European living space. The soldier must comprehend the necessity of the harsh atonement of Jewry, the spiritual agent of the Bolshevist terror.'

The nominal head of the German political administration in the occupied areas of the Soviet Union was Alfred Rosenberg, appointed Reich minister for the occupied eastern territories on 17 November 1941. The real power lay in the hands of two NSDAP functionaries: Hinrich Lohse, *Gauleiter* of Schleswig-Holstein, as Reich commissar for the *Ostland*, consisting of the three Baltic states of Lithuania, Latvia, and Estonia (which Stalin had annexed in July and August 1940), as well as of White Russia; and Erich Koch, *Gauleiter* of East Prussia, as Reich commissar for Ukraine (which had been reduced in size). Koch saw Ukraine purely in terms of exploitation and looked upon its inhabitants as a slave people whose only purpose was to work for their German masters. Rosenberg himself considered this policy disastrous, since it made cooperation with native anti-Bolshevist forces impossible. But his objections had no effect. Martin Bormann, the powerful leader of the party chancellery, sided with Koch, and was supported by Hitler.

When it came to the Jews, however, Rosenberg also abandoned practical considerations. When the general commissar for White Ruthenia, Wilhelm Kube, former *Gauleiter* of Brandenburg, protested in October 1941 against the mass killing of Jews, including many skilled tradesmen, and asked the minister of the east if it was true that all Jews were to be liquidated 'without regard to age and gender and economic interests' (for example, the interests of the Wehrmacht in armaments workers), Rosenberg sent the following reply: 'Economic considerations are basically to be ignored in the resolution of the question. Moreover, it is requested that all further questions that should arise be settled directly with the Higher SS and Police Leader.'[29]

Although the extermination of the Jews had begun in the summer of 1941, much was still unresolved. The mass murder was temporarily restricted to groups of eastern Jews. The primary method was shooting. To kill many millions of people within a short time in this way was technically impossible, dangerous for the 'morale' of the active participants, and hardly to be kept secret from the international public. Thus the 'overall draft for the execution of the desired final solution of the Jewish question', which Goering, as coordinator of all not purely military activities in the eastern campaign, requested from Heydrich on 31 July 1941, was still going to be necessary.

Moreover, in the first part of summer 1941, Hitler, as far as the timetable of the 'final solution to the Jewish question' was concerned, was still making a deliberate distinction between eastern and western Jews. In a speech to the Reichstag on 30 January 1941, he had referred to his 'comment' of 30 January 1939 (which he incorrectly dated to 1 September 1939, the day the war began) that 'if Jewry were to plunge the world into general war, the role of Jewry would be finished in Europe.' He apparently thought of the German and west European Jews as hostages whom the United States could not ignore. If the USA were to completely go over to the camp of Germany's enemies, however, he, Hitler, would no longer need to show any consideration for the Jews in Germany and western Europe—much less once he had won the war. However things turned out, in the long term the Jews in Germany's sphere of influence had no chance of survival.

In mid-August 1941 an event occurred that cast doubt on Hitler's overall strategic and political planning. On 14 August the American and British governments announced the formation of the Atlantic Charter, concluded by Roosevelt and Churchill two days previously. This agreement committed the two powers to a set of common aims, including the 'final destruction of the Nazi tyranny'. The Führer could now no longer count on the British making an arrangement with Germany after the defeat of the Soviet Union. *One* of the results of his rethinking was the end of the blitzkrieg strategy, which had sought to capture Moscow as quickly as possible. Hitler now shifted the focus to the conquest of material resources in the south of the Soviet Union with the goal of obtaining for the Reich the means to conduct a longer war.

The other consequence of the new situation had to do with the Jews. In view of American entrance into the war in the immediate future and an Allied invasion on the Atlantic coast, Hitler now began to contrive the destruction of *all* European Jews *during* the war. Extermination of the European Jews as a response to the transformation of the European into a world war: Hitler's actions reflected the categories in which he thought.

On 18 August 1941 Hitler approved his propaganda minister's idea to compel all Jews in the Reich to wear 'a large visible badge' identifying them as Jews. The yellow Jewish star was introduced on 1 September. During that same talk with Goebbels, Hitler spoke of the 'Jewish problem' in general, and in a way that made it clear he was now thinking of solving the 'Jewish question' by means of physical liquidation on a European scale while the war lasted.

The Führer is of the belief that his earlier prophecy in the Reichstag—that, if Jewry succeeded in provoking another world war, it would end with the destruction of the Jews—is being borne out. It has been coming true in these last weeks and months with an almost eerie certainty. In the east the Jews must pay the price. They have already paid in part in Germany and will have to pay more in the future. North America is their last resort. And they will one day have to pay the price there too, sooner or later.

On 16 November the 'Reich Minister for Public Enlightenment and Propaganda' published a column in his weekly, *Das Reich*, informing the German people and the international public that Hitler had been deadly serious in his prophecy. Under the title 'Die Juden sind schuld!'* (which he had used once before in an August 1932 article in the *Angriff*), Goebbels wrote:

We are witnessing the fulfilment of this prophecy, and the fate that is now catching up with the Jews is certainly hard, but more than deserved. Compassion, much less regret, is completely inappropriate. World Jewry erred in estimating the forces available to it for this war, and now it is gradually experiencing the destruction it had planned for us and would have carried out without a second thought if it had possessed the ability. It is now perishing according to its own law: 'An eye for an eye, a tooth for a tooth!'

In August 1932 the slogan 'The Jews are Guilty!' had served to console Hitler's 'old fighters' after the Reichstag elections on 31 July, when the great electoral victory of the NSDAP had still not been enough to bring them to power and enable them to annul judicial decisions against SA terrorism. At that time the declaration that the Jews would 'not escape the punishment they deserved' was meant as an appeal not to give up hope, since the day of victory would one day come—and, with it, vengeance against the guilty, the Jews. Nine years later, in November 1941, the hope of a quick victory against the Soviet Union had long since evaporated. Leningrad had not been taken. The early winter frustrated the conquest of Moscow. The 'weather god', as Goebbels noted on 14 November, 'has thwarted us once again.' The guilty party in the autumn of 1941 was the same as in the summer of 1932: the Jews—who, however, would not escape just atonement this time, either. On both occasions, the increase in aggression had the same cause, the frustration of ambitious goals unfulfilled.

Goebbels's announcement that Hitler's 'prophecy' concerning the 'destruction of the Jewish race in Europe' had already entered the phase of 'fulfilment' was impossible to misunderstand or ignore. *Das Reich* had a circulation of one million in the autumn of 1941. Whoever read or heard about the 16 November article learned that masses of Jews were being killed in the east and that the regime was resolved to continue this process to the bitter end. 'In this historic struggle, every Jew is our enemy,' continued the column, 'regardless of whether he is vegetating in a Polish ghetto or carrying on his parasitic existence in Berlin or Hamburg or blowing the trumpet of war in New York or Washington . . . The Jews are the enemy's emissaries among us. Whoever stands by them is going over to the enemy in time of war.'

The article was, first and foremost, a warning to the apparently many Germans who sympathized with the Jews. All who showed such compassion were

---

* Goebbels, 'The Jews are Guilty!'

threatened with the harshest repercussions. 'If someone is wearing the Jewish star, he is marked as an enemy of the people. Anyone who still consorts with him privately belongs to him and must be evaluated and treated just like a Jew.' It is uncertain whether Goebbels also intended his column as a kind of final warning to the American Jews, whom he accused of trying to push the United States into war with Germany. It seems quite possible. After all, the 'world war' Hitler thought was imminent in mid-August was, in November 1941, not yet a reality.

The American public knew from continual reports in the *New York Times* that Jews were being deported from the Reich into the eastern territories from the middle of October 1941 onward. The deportations were Hitler's response to Roosevelt's orders on 11 September 1941 for the American navy to fire at Axis ships in the American sphere of interest. As long as formal peace still existed between the Reich and the USA, however, Hitler did not wish to proceed with the liquidation of the German Jews. On 30 November the unauthorized shooting of some 5,000 Jews from Reich territory near Kaunas gave him cause to have Himmler order Heydrich: 'Transport of Jews from Berlin! No liquidation.' (The order arrived late at its destination, Riga, where 1,000 German Jews had been killed that same day; but it was obeyed in the other Jewish deportations from Germany.) Whereas Goebbels's column on 16 November spoke of the war guilt of 'world Jewry' and threatened the destruction of all Jews, two weeks later Hitler seemed prepared to delay the order for the annihilation of the German and west European Jews until there could no longer be any possible doubt about the shift from a European conflict to a world war.

The Japanese attack on the American fleet at Pearl Harbor on 7 December 1941 ended Hitler's policy of handling the 'Jewish question' in light of tactical consideration for the United States. Germany and Italy declared war on the USA on 11 December, thus uniting the European and Pacific wars into a world war. Japan was a strong ally for Germany, much stronger than Italy, and this fact was enough to make war with the United States seem necessary to Hitler. But his relief at the news from Hawaii most likely had an additional cause: he could finally do with the Jews what he had long planned.

Hitler's final decision to kill all the Jews within the German sphere of influence while the war lasted must date from the time immediately following Pearl Harbor. 'We know the power that stands behind Roosevelt,' he declared to the Reichstag on 11 December 1941. 'It is the eternal Jew, who now believes that the hour has come for him to do with us what happened in Soviet Russia, which we all were forced to watch in horror.' Hitler spoke to the Reich and district leaders the next day. 'As for the Jewish question, the Führer is resolved to settle the matter once and for all,' Goebbels wrote in his journal.

He has foretold to the Jews that if they should once again bring about a world war, they would witness their own destruction. That was not meant rhetorically. The world war is here, and the destruction of the Jews must be the necessary consequence. We are not here for the purpose of sympathizing with the Jews, but only with our own German people. If the German people have sacrificed some 160,000 soldiers in the eastern campaign, then the instigators of this bloody conflict will have to pay for it with their lives.

Hans Frank, who was also present at the 12 December gathering, told the General Government administration on 16 December that the Jews would not be deported into the *Ostland* or Ukraine, but killed within the General Government itself.

In Berlin we were told: why are you making all this trouble? We can't do anything with them in the *Ostland* or the Reich Commissariat, either. Liquidate them yourselves! . . . For us too the Jews are exceptionally harmful, devouring our food like animals . . . We cannot shoot these 3.5 million Jews, we cannot poison them, but we will be able to take measures that will lead somehow to successful destruction; and this in connection with the procedures which are to be discussed in the Reich.

Two days later Himmler, after a talk with Hitler, wrote: 'Jewish question./ to be exterminated as partisans.' The meaning of this laconic remark is not difficult to decode. Now that the USA had entered the war, all Jews Germany could get hold of were to be liquidated, just as hundreds of thousands had already been killed in the Soviet Union.

The discussion Frank mentioned took place on 20 January 1942 in the Haus am Grossen Wannsee 56–58 in Berlin. It was led by Reinhard Heydrich. It had originally been planned for 9 December 1941, but then postponed for an indefinite period because of the new international situation. Present were representatives from the SS, the foreign office, the ministry of justice, the ministry of the Eastern Territories, the office of the Four Year Plan, the General Government, and the Reich chancellery, including four state secretaries, an undersecretary, and a ministerial director. The subject of the discussion was the 'Final Solution to the Jewish Question'. According to the minutes, written by Adolf Eichmann, leader of the Jewish desk in the Reich Security Main Office, Heydrich spoke in coded form about what the 'evacuation of the Jews to the East' was to be:

In the course of the final solution and under appropriate direction, the Jews are to be utilized for work in the East in a suitable manner. In large labour columns, separated by sexes, Jews capable of working will be dispatched to these regions to build roads, and in the process a large number of them will undoubtedly drop out by way of natural attrition. Any final remainder will have to be given suitable treatment because they unquestionably represent the most resistant segments and therefore constitute a natural elite that, if allowed to go free, would turn into a germ cell of renewed Jewish revival. (Witness the experience of history.) In the course of the practical implementation of the final solution, Europe will be combed through from West to East.

The 'Wannsee conference' marked the beginning of large-scale 'combing out' operations with the goal of making German-occupied or German-controlled Europe 'Jew-free'. From this point forward, forced labour in road construction no longer played an important role in the destruction of the Jews, since the military situation in the east was no longer conducive to this kind of German colonization. The 'final solution', now conceived in terms of industrial mass annihilation, took place mainly on Polish territory. From the autumn of 1941, experts of 'Operation T-4' (named after Tiergartenstrasse 4 in Berlin, where the main planning centre for the murder of the mentally ill was located) assisted in the technical preparations for the mass murder. They were experienced in the use of poison gas and mobile gas chambers or 'gas vans'. In October 1941 the SS began the construction of the first 'pure' extermination camp, Belzec near Lublin. This is clear evidence that the decision to physically destroy at least the eastern Jews had been made by this time. Belzec was followed by Sobibór and Treblinka. The already existing camps of Auschwitz and Majdanek, on the other hand, were not 'pure' extermination facilities, but concentration camps with affiliated business enterprises. The gassing began on 8 December 1941 in the Chelmno camp in the German village of Kulmhof, located in the Warthegau. It was the 'first murder factory in the history of mankind', as the Dutch historian L. J. Hartog wrote. The first victims were Polish Jews no longer able to work, as well as Gypsies.

At the time of the Wannsee conference, the machinery of mass murder was just being developed. It became ever more 'efficient' throughout the course of 1942. The gas vans were replaced by the large-scale gas chambers of Auschwitz, Belzec, Sobibór, Treblinka, and Majdanek. Zyklon B, a hydrocyanic acid gas, replaced carbon monoxide. In Auschwitz-Birkenau, 'annihilation through work' took place until the end, in a branch of IG Farben, among other companies; other Jews, as well as Gypsies and Soviet prisoners of war, were gassed immediately upon delivery. In Auschwitz alone, which has become the symbol of this German crime against humanity, some 1.5 million human beings were murdered by the time the facility was dismantled in November 1944, when Himmler declared the 'Jewish question' practically solved. The total number of Jews killed by German orders during the Second World War is estimated at between 5 and 6 million.

The Jews were exterminated without any written orders from Hitler himself. The German reaction to the campaign against the mentally ill militated against this kind of command process. Instead, Hitler expressed his will on the 'Jewish question' in such a way that the subordinate leaders, from the Reichsführer SS to the Higher SS and Police Leaders down to the heads of the Special Action Groups and Special Action Commandos, were forced to assume that the most radical version of the orders was the one that best corresponded to the desires of the Führer. This is *one* of the reasons for the increasing radicalization of the process of Jewish annihilation.

Another reason can be seen in the results of previous measures, taken without any thought to the consequences. The settlement of ethnic Germans in the Warthegau, along with the deportations of Jews from the Reich and the Protectorate of Bohemia and Moravia into the General Government, created a logistical and demographic pressure that could not be relieved by further deportations into formerly Soviet territory. The border areas were already spoken for in the 'General Plan East', and the Arctic coast remained inaccessible to the German military. A 'territorial solution to the Jewish question' east of Poland was therefore no longer possible. Such a solution would also have led to the destruction of the Jews, but over a longer period of time. After this option disappeared, the only remaining 'final solution' was the one actually implemented. The practical constraints and compulsions that made the mass murder seem inevitable—above all the food situation, increasingly critical from the end of 1941 onward—was the result of decisions for which, in the final analysis, Hitler was always responsible. The long-debated question of whether the extermination of the Jews was 'intentional', in accordance with Hitler's plans and wishes, or 'functional', the result of the inner logic of the National Socialist war and racial policy, cannot be answered to the exclusion of either 'school'. Both came together.

Ten days after the Wannsee conference, on 30 January 1942, the ninth anniversary of his 'seizure of power', Hitler, speaking in the Berlin Sportpalast, once again reminded his audience of his prophecy concerning the destruction of the Jews.

We well understand that the war can only end in one of two ways: either the Aryan peoples will be exterminated, or Jewry will vanish out of Europe . . . This time, and for the first time, the authentic old Jewish law of 'an eye for an eye, a tooth for a tooth' will be applied. And the further these struggles spread, the more—let world Jewry hear it clearly!—the more anti-Semitism will spread. It will find nourishment in every prison camp, in every family enlightened about why it ultimately had to make its sacrifice. And the hour will come when the most evil enemy of the world throughout all time will be finished, at least for a millennium.

In the thousand-year period between the defeat of the Antichrist and the Last Judgment, the devil would have no more power over humanity: Hitler, without referring to the Bible, was paraphrasing the twentieth chapter of the Book of Revelation in order to convince the Germans of the greatness of their mission in history, indeed, in salvation history. And not only the Germans. Hitler was no less convinced than Goebbels that Europe, and the 'Aryan' race as a whole, had every reason to thank Germany for its liberation from the Jewish world danger. On 24 February 1943, three weeks after the Sixth Army surrendered in the 'cauldron' of Stalingrad, the Führer, in a proclamation for the celebration of the founding of the NSDAP, said that the present war would

come to an end not with the destruction of Aryan humanity, but with the extermination of European Jewry. Beyond that, however, our movement's way of thinking will be adopted even by our enemies and—thanks to this war—become the common property of all peoples. State after state, even while fighting against us, will be increasingly forced to apply National Socialist arguments to conduct the war they themselves unleashed. And thus the very war itself will spread the knowledge of the accursed criminal activities of the Jews to all peoples.

In a column in *Das Reich* on 9 May 1943, Goebbels wrote that the present war was a racial war.

If the Axis powers lose, then there will no longer be a dike to save Europe from the Jewish-Bolshevist deluge... No prophetic word of the Führer is coming true with such an uncanny certainty as this, that if Jewry succeeds in provoking a second world war, it will not end with the destruction of Aryan humanity, but with the annihilation of the Jewish race. This process is of world-historical significance, and since it will probably have unforeseeable consequences, it also requires time. But it can no longer be stopped.

It is undeniable that the anti-Semitic rhetoric of the National Socialists found a certain resonance in the German-occupied zones of Europe. The racial laws in Fascist Italy (1938), Vichy France (1940–1), and Romania under General Antonescu (1940) were all voluntary 'achievements', not measures imposed by Germany on resistant regimes. And in the Jewish deportations, the SS and Gestapo found willing collaborators not only in most of Germany's south-east European satellites, but also in the *État français*. Nonetheless, the Nazi anti-Jewish campaigns were only 'popular' in a few traditionally anti-Semitic countries in eastern central Europe, most notably in the areas that had become Soviet shortly before, in the wake of the Hitler–Stalin pact, and that were conquered by the Wehrmacht in 1941.

Nazi anti-Bolshevism found more support abroad. The claim that the 'Greater German Reich' was defending Europe or the 'Occident' (the latter term was used more and more, and with conscious pathos, after 1943) against Bolshevism was a central part of large-scale campaigns by the foreign office and the propaganda ministry. The SS and the Waffen-SS also used this language in their efforts to recruit non-German volunteers. But mass support beyond the German borders was not to be gained with such 'European' propaganda. Germany exploited the countries under its control in a way that made European solidarity with it impossible.

Within Germany, too, anti-Bolshevism was more important than anti-Semitism for the legitimation of the regime. The leadership knew that the German people would not have supported the goal of murdering the European Jews. Therefore, despite all selective references to the 'disappearance', 'destruction', or 'extermination' of the Jewish race, the process itself, along with the methodology of the murder, was kept secret. It is an open question whether Hitler's closest followers shared his apocalyptic vision of a final struggle between the 'Aryan' and Jewish races. It was in no way necessary that they did so in order to be fanatical anti-Semites. In fact, it was not even necessary that a given subordinate personally hate the Jews in order to carry out Hitler's orders for their destruction. As long as the charismatic Führer was considered politically infallible, it was *a priori* impossible that anything he desired in Germany's name could be wrong. A 'compulsion to obey orders' seems not to have existed in this case. As far as we know, none of the German policemen in the east who refused to fire on unarmed Jewish men, women, and children was ever punished. For the majority, 'orders were orders', irrespective of the individual's personal feelings about the Jews. The social pressure of camaraderie was, as a rule, stronger than individual conscience.

For all that, however, antipathy to the Jews was certainly not inconsiderable. It had long been part of the conservative tradition in Germany, and not only there. It had been part of the Christian tradition for even longer. Even if it reached a murderous level only in a minority, it nonetheless enabled many people to cooperate or turn a blind eye when Hitler undertook to put his credo into practice. Both churches protested against the killing of the mentally ill. Against the murder of the Jews, however, about which far more came out than the regime desired, only a few clergy spoke out. One of them was the Catholic Bernhard Lichtenberg, dean of St Hedwig's Cathedral in Berlin, who paid for his courage with imprisonment and death. The treatment meted out to the Evangelical bishop of Württemberg, Theophil Wurm, was mild in comparison. Though himself a professed anti-Semite in the tradition of Adolf Stoecker, Wurm protested against the extermination of the Jews in several sermons and letters in 1943. He even wrote to Hitler and Goebbels on the matter. In March 1944 he was banned from speaking and writing.

The slaughter of millions of Jews required not only an army of subalterns following orders. It also required the participation of the elites: the military, whose successes in battle cleared the way for the extermination camps; the captains of industry, who joined in and profited from the policy of killing through forced labour; the banks, who transformed the wedding rings and gold fillings of murdered Jews into assets for the Reich and provided credit for the construction of extermination camps; scientists and technicians, who prepared the machinery of mass murder; jurists, who lent a sheen of legality and processual regularity to the dispossession and persecution of the Jews; historians and economists, who prepared the way for the 'solution to the Jewish question' by placing their knowledge at the service of the regime. The murder of the Jews was not the occult project of German history, implicit and inevitable from the beginning. But German history can indeed explain why there was so little resistance when the man in whom the majority of Germans still believed set about the realization of his own project, the project of radical anti-Semitism.[30]

THE RESISTANCE TO HITLER

Organized resistance to Hitler and his regime, in order to be effective, had to be close to the centres of power. This paradoxical reality was in place as soon as National Socialism enjoyed broad support among the population, thus by the summer of 1933 at the latest. Close to power, but not identical with power's inmost core: this condition did not apply to the workers' movement, among whose divided ranks the first resistance from 'below' developed. It did apply to certain groups within the higher officers' corps and bureaucracy that had kept—or regained—their distance from National Socialist ideology. The first was true of the older, the second of some of the younger members of Hitler's conservative (in the widest sense of the term) opponents.

In addition to those who wielded actual power, there were those who possessed special authority and specialized knowledge, for example Ludwig Beck, former chief of the army general staff, and Carl Goerdeler, former mayor of Leipzig; theologians of both great confessions like the Protestant Dietrich Bonhoeffer and the Catholic Jesuit Alfred Delp; former Social Democratic politicians like Julius Leber, Carlo Mierendorff, and Theodor Haubach; former labour union leaders like Wilhelm Leuschner and Jakob Kaiser, the former from the ranks of the Free Trade Unions, the latter from those of the Christian labour organizations. The active officers, diplomats, and civil servants who decided to resist needed the knowledge of the experts and connections to the most important groups in society. The advisers and planners were compelled to cooperate with the oppositional forces within the military and civil state apparatus if they wanted to accomplish anything.

Politically speaking, the practical cooperation between Hitler's adversaries was tantamount to a coalition. It embraced Social Democrats at one end and German Nationalists at the other. The right wing included advocates of authoritarian rule and staunch monarchists; on the left were proponents of a unified labour union and those who wanted to nationalize key industries. What brought these disparate groups together was the belief that arbitrary rule had to be replaced by the rule of law. Still, all were agreed that there could be no 'return to Weimar'. Those who, like the conservatives, had rejected the first German democracy during its short life continued to do so after 1933. And even the former defenders of the republic could not countenance the restitution of a system that had failed not least because of the flaws within its own constitution.

The 'Kreisau circle' around the jurist Count Helmuth James von Moltke attempted to synthesize the antithetical traditions within the resistance. In Silesian Kreisau, Moltke's estate, and in the Berlin apartment of his friend Count Peter Yorck von Wartenburg, an official on the Economic Staff East of the Army High Command, conservatives and socialists contemplated a post-war Germany in which the opposition between 'right' and 'left' would be overcome. The society they discussed was centred more on the 'small communities' of family, home town, municipality, profession, and work life than on political parties and other mass organizations. In the post-war order as they saw it, self-government and federalism were to counterbalance the Reich as the highest authority of the German people. Direct elections were to take place for all representative offices below the county (*Kreis*) level (with fathers of families receiving an additional vote for each child below voting age). Above the county level, elections would be indirect. In such a system, the parliaments of the individual *Länder* would be elected by the municipal and county assemblies, and the Reichstag by the *Länder* parliaments. In foreign policy, the Kreisau circle—led by their spokesman in international matters, Adam von Trott zu Solz, a member of the intelligence department of the foreign office—opposed traditional nationalism and supported a unified Europe (though Trott himself at times advocated keeping the Sudetenland and parts of West Prussia in Germany).

In contrast to the Kreisau group, the older conservatives—men like Carl Goerdeler, considered prospective chancellor, Ulrich von Hassell, former ambassador to Rome and prospective foreign minister, and Johannes Popitz, the Prussian finance minister—were great-power politicians in the Wilhelmine style. With the exception of the General Government and the official 'Protectorate' over Bohemia and Moravia, all of Hitler's conquests up to 1940 were to remain in German possession. Much like the scholarly partisans of National Socialism, these men believed the Reich to represent the primary force for European order. Although they rejected Hitler's particular way of subjugating the east, this did not stop them from seeing the positive side of the war against the Soviet Union (until the end of 1941 and beginning of 1942, that is). The elimination of Bolshevism and the consolidation of German hegemony were ideas that well fitted their vision of a new European order.

In terms of domestic politics, the older conservatives were far more resolute in their rejection of western democracy than the Kreisau circle. Popitz wanted a strongly centralized state. In his draft of a provisional constitution at the beginning of 1940, the Prussian finance minister gave the head of state dictatorial powers. Only in the final version were the people to be granted the right to exercise political influence, and then only through a professional-corporative representative body.

Goerdeler, too, wanted a largely independent executive without effective parliamentary control. The government would be able to decree measures with the force of law anytime it chose, and a two-thirds majority in the Reichstag would be necessary to annul them or bring down the government. A simple majority would be sufficient if both the Reichstag and the 'House of the Estates' (*Reichsständehaus*), a first chamber of representatives from the professional associations, churches, and universities, sought the resignation of the government and proposed a new one in its place. Half of the members of the Reichstag were to be elected from the district parliaments (*Gautage*), the other half directly by the people. Male heads of households with at least three children would receive an additional vote. Laws could only be passed upon the approval of the House of the Estates. The Reich would initially be headed by a 'general governor' (*Generalstatthalter*), later perhaps by a hereditary monarch.

Goerdeler's reservations against democracy were those of the conservative tradition. But that was not their only source. One did not have to be a conservative to conclude from the Weimar experience that the majority could err and should therefore not be allowed to rule unrestricted. Although Hitler had not attained the chancellorship by free elections, he owed his political ascent to the voters, who had made his party the strongest in Germany by far. His continuing popularity justified a suspicion of the judgement of the masses, and many Social Democrats joined the conservatives in thinking so. Nonetheless, an authoritarian system of the kind that Popitz or—in attenuated form—Goerdeler envisioned could only have held itself in power by military force. Hitler's conservative adversaries thought that the people would be content with far fewer political rights than they had possessed before 1933. This was an illusion.

The conservatives working to overthrow Hitler were also not necessarily staunch opponents of anti-Semitism. Antipathy to the Jews also belonged to the tradition of German conservatism, and the belief that the Jewish influence on the economy and culture had to be reduced was a part of the conservative credo both before and after 1933. Accordingly, many conservatives thought that the Nuremberg laws were at least partially justified as a defence against Jewish presumption. Goerdeler was one of these. While he wished, in a memorandum written at the beginning of 1941, to abolish a series of discriminatory measures against Jews and to make ghetto conditions in the occupied east more 'humane', he also thought that if a Jewish state could be set up 'in parts of either Canada or South America under definitely viable conditions' with international cooperation, then the Jews should automatically be deported there. There were only a few exceptions: Jews who had participated in the First World War, those who could prove that their families had been naturalized before 1871, those who could prove baptism, and the Christian offspring of 'mixed marriages' concluded before the National Socialist 'seizure of power'. Goerdeler's statement that these rules would 'completely' obviate the need for the Nuremberg laws was hardly an exaggeration. Nor did his comment that it was a 'truism' 'that the Jewish people belong to another race' represent a departure from the conservative world view.

Goerdeler's memorandum was written before the beginning of the systematic annihilation of the Jews. The members of the resistance movement were unanimous in their condemnation of this crime. In another memorandum of 1944 Goerdeler spoke of the 'enormity of the planned and bestially executed elimination of the Jews'. A young officer of the legendary Potsdam infantry regiment no. 9, Axel von dem Bussche, after witnessing a mass shooting of Jews in Ukraine in the autumn of 1942, decided that the policy's author had to be assassinated, and volunteered his own person towards that end. In cooperation with like-minded officers, including Count Claus Schenk von Stauffenberg, colonel in the general staff, he conspired to blow Hitler up while modelling a new army uniform for him. Before the plot could be carried out, however, Axel von dem Bussche was seriously wounded on the front and could play no further active role in the conspiracy. Another young officer, Ewald Heinrich von Kleist-Schmenzin, sought to kill Hitler in the same way in early February 1944. But the uniform presentation was cancelled at short notice, thwarting the plan.

Bussche and Kleist were not the only officers who tried to blow Hitler up in suicide missions. Rudolf-Christoph von Gersdorff, like Stauffenberg a colonel in the general staff and a member of the old Prussian nobility, began preparations for such an attack during the summer of 1942. By 21 March 1943, 'Heroes' Memorial Day', the plot was ripe. Gersdorff planned to set off two English limpet mines at a presentation of captured enemy war materiel to the Führer in the Zeughaus in Berlin during the main holiday celebrations. But Hitler rushed through the exhibition so hurriedly that the attack could not take place. Gersdorff barely managed to prevent the explosion of the one mine he had already ignited. The 'providence' Hitler had so often invoked seemed to be on his side once again.

The main motivator of Gersdorff's failed attack was Colonel Henning von Tresckow, First General Staff Officer of Army Group Centre. Tresckow was a key figure in the military resistance. He had exact information about the crimes committed by the SS in the east. He signed and passed on orders for the execution of partisans, real or supposed, Jewish or non-Jewish, along with their families, including the women and children. Tresckow apparently considered extreme harshness in the battle against partisans to be a military necessity, and the war against Bolshevism was also his war, at least at first. In the course of the conflict, he came to believe that the regime directing it was fundamentally criminal, and so he decided to work towards its overthrow.

Colonel Count Claus Schenk von Stauffenberg, the man behind the plot to kill Hitler with a bomb in the 'Wolf's Lair', the Führer Headquarters near Rastenburg, on 20 July 1944, came from a Swabian Catholic noble family. Like his older brother Berthold, Claus von Stauffenberg had been a member of the circle around the poet Stefan George and shared the latter's dream of a nobility of the spirit, a 'new Reich', and an 'inward Germany'. At first, the brothers believed that National Socialism represented an opportunity to establish a *Volksgemeinschaft* that could unite a fragmented Germany. Even the racial idea seemed healthy to them. They were, to be sure, against the Nazi race policy, but only because they considered it a dangerous exaggeration of an otherwise correct principle. Claus von Stauffenberg's view of Hitler vacillated between contempt and admiration. According to the testimony of his Wuppertal bookseller, he felt 'release' when the troops first marched to war. 'After all, war had been his craft for centuries,' the same source reports him as saying. In mid-September 1939 he wrote from Poland to his wife that the country was bleak, mere sand and dust. 'The populace is an incredible rabble; very many Jews and very many mongrels. The kind of people only comfortable under the rod. The thousands of prisoners will be very good for our agriculture. In Germany they can surely be used very well, being hard-working, willing, and undemanding.'

When, in 1941 or at the beginning of 1942, Helmuth von Moltke put out feelers about the possibility of Stauffenberg's participation in the resistance, the answer was no: Germany first had to win the war, and the 'brown plague' could not be taken care of during a struggle against Bolshevism, only afterwards. It was only during the course of 1942 that Stauffenberg changed his mind, realizing that Germany could not win the war, but thinking that defeat was still avoidable in the east.

Stauffenberg's bomb exploded after he had left the Führer Headquarters near Rastenburg for Berlin. What the conspirators of the Bendlerblock, the headquarters of the Wehrmacht high command, did on 20 July 1944 to overthrow the National Socialist regime was doomed to failure, for their presupposition was false: Hitler was not dead, but had survived the attack with light wounds.

That evening, Stauffenberg and his co-conspirators Friedrich Olbricht, Albrecht Ritter Mertz von Quirnheim, and Werner von Haeften were shot in the courtyard of the Bendlerblock on the orders of General Fromm, commander of the replacement army. Colonel General Ludwig Beck, who was to be head of state after a successful coup, was already dead by this time. Pressed by Fromm, he had first tried to shoot himself, then, after failing, was shot by a sergeant. The next day Henning von Tresckow committed suicide on the eastern front near Polish Ostrów, simulating an enemy hand grenade attack. His decision was predicated on the fear that he could be tortured into revealing the identities of other conspirators.

Hitler's vengeance against the direct and indirect participants in the plot was terrible. At their trial, however, he could not stop the accused from openly declaring, one after another, their responsibility for their actions and defying the outraged president, Roland Freisler. Count Ulrich Wilhelm Schwerin von Schwanenfeld, who worked in the office of the quarter master general, told the court that 'the many murders in Poland' were one of the motives for his involvement in the conspiracy. Count Peter Yorck stated: 'The important thing is what ties all these issues together, the totalizing claim of the state on the citizen to the exclusion of his religious and moral obligations to God.' Hans-Bernd von Haeften, an official in the foreign office and older brother of Werner von Haeften, also spoke for his friends when he said: 'According to what I see as the world-historical role of the Führer, I take him to be a great executioner of evil.'

Among those whom Freisler condemned to death, the first eight, among them Field Marshal Erwin von Witzleben, General Erich Hoepner, and Yorck, were hanged in the prison at Berlin-Plötzensee immediately after sentencing on 8 August. Others had to wait for their sentences to be carried out. Julius Leber, seized by the Gestapo on 5 July because of his contacts with the outlawed KPD, was condemned to death on 20 October and executed on 5 January 1945. Goerdeler's sentence was pronounced on 8 September and carried out on 2 February 1945. Moltke was condemned and executed in January 1945. Bonhoeffer, who had been imprisoned at the beginning of April 1943, was transported to the concentration camp at Flossenburg in February 1945, where he was killed by the SS on 9 April after a summary court martial. The total number of executions in connection with the plot on 20 July 1944 was about 200.

If Hitler had been killed by Stauffenberg's bomb, the conspirators would still not necessarily have been successful. They had little popular support. According to the official reports, most Germans were outraged at the attack, and their joy was correspondingly great at hearing that the Führer suffered only minor wounds. The president of the Nuremberg court of appeals observed that the assassination attempt was 'also rejected by people who are not declared National Socialists, not only due to repugnance at the crime itself, but also because they believe that the Führer alone can master the situation and that his death would result in chaos and civil war.'

The prospect of chaos and civil war was not unrealistic. Power struggles would probably have broken out among the leading National Socialists. Even Himmler was 'embroiled' in the plot through his contacts with Popitz. Moreover, there was no evidence that the Wehrmacht as a whole would have gone over to the side of the plotters. On the contrary: Stauffenberg and his friends would certainly have been accused of stabbing the troops on the front in the back. The National Socialist claim that the attack was the work of a small reactionary coterie fell on fertile ground. It was true that the 'cult of the Führer' had suffered severely from the reverses in the Russian war during the winter of 1941–2 and especially after the defeat at Stalingrad at the end of January 1943. But it was not yet at an end. In fact, it experienced a brief renaissance after the failed attack on 20 July 1944, since many people now thought that Hitler really was in league with 'providence' and that only he could save Germany.

Hitler was more popular than the men of 20 July 1944, and they could be in no doubt about the fact. It was also highly uncertain that they would have been able to convince the German people of the necessity of tyrannicide after the fact, by exposing Nazi crimes. After January 1943, when Roosevelt and Churchill, meeting in Casablanca, had agreed to demand unconditional surrender from the Axis powers, the conspirators could not even be certain that the Allies would grant Hitler's enemies a better peace settlement than Nazi Germany. And yet, for the core group of the resistance at least, the prospects of success were not the deciding factor in the summer of 1944. Their prime concern was different. They wanted to show the world and the coming generations that Hitler was not Germany, that a different, better Germany did exist.

A different Germany *did* stand before Freisler's seat of judgment. Its best representatives were acting in accordance with a tradition shaped by Christianity or humanism, Kantian philosophy or Prussiandom. This tradition recognized one authority higher than the state and the man who led it—the individual conscience. Because the conspirators followed their conscience, 20 July 1944 came to be one of the great days in the history of modern Germany. Two further days in the annals of the anti-Hitler resistance can claim a similar moral status: 8 November 1939, the day the Württemberg carpenter Johann Georg Elser tried to kill Hitler with a self-made bomb during an event at the Munich Bürgerbräukeller; and 18 February 1943, when Hans and Sophie Scholl, the founders of the opposition student group *Weisse Rose* ('White Rose'), passed out hundreds of fliers against Hitler's unscrupulous war leadership (the German army had surrendered at Stalingrad on 2 February) in the courtyard of the University of Munich.

Elser, a simple man acting alone; the Scholl siblings; their fellow students Christoph Probst, Alexander Schmorell, and Willi Graf; their academic mentor Kurt Huber: like the men of 20 July 1944, all were executed. If, after the collapse, the German people had something to give them heart as they looked back over the years between 1933 and 1944, it was because these people and others like them had stood up against Hitler. Otherwise there would have been very little indeed.[31]

THE FINAL DAYS OF THE FÜHRER CULT

On 1 September 1939, the first day of the war, Hitler had announced in the Reichstag that there would be no repeat of November 1918. On this point he really did show himself to be a prophet. No strikes or mutinies took place in Germany during the Second World War, not to mention a revolution. The ubiquity of terror was not the only or even most important reason. The main reason was the ruthless exploitation of the occupied territories, which kept Germany from experiencing the kind of famine it had seen during the First World War. Another important factor was the ruthless exploitation of millions of foreign civil labourers, prisoners of war, and concentration camp inmates. This new sub-proletariat was itself divided into a racial hierarchy: 'eastern workers' received far more brutal treatment than 'western workers', and the Jews the most inhuman treatment of all. For them, forced labour was to be only a way station along the road to destruction.

The forced and slave labour also prevented the war from being as 'total' for the Germans as it might have been, to judge by Goebbels's notorious speech in the Berlin Sportpalast on 18 February 1943. Compulsory service for women was not introduced; it contradicted Hitler's petty bourgeois view of the German woman. The German people were to remain loyal to their Führer, and this aim placed limits on the exploitation of German labour. Hitler saw to it personally that these limits were respected.

Despite everything the Nazis did to shore up the 'home front', however, the belief in the final victory, the *Endsieg*, began to crumble, and with it the cult of the Führer. Occasional revivals, like after 20 July 1944, did not affect the general trend. Mussolini's Fascist system had broken apart in Italy in July 1943. The Red Army was advancing unstoppably from the east. The Allies landed in Normandy on 6 July 1944. In Germany itself, hardly a day or a night passed after 1942 without an enemy air attack on the larger cities and towns. The bombs struck not only transport routes, factories, houses, and people, but also, when it was clear that the war was coming to an end, the morale of the survivors. Staunch National Socialists, especially the very young, responded with the defiant will to endure, but they were in the minority. The attitude of the majority in the last months of the war was probably similar to that of an inhabitant of Berchtesgaden, who, according to an SD report in March 1945, said: 'If anyone had suspected in 1933 that events would take such a turn, Hitler would never have been elected.'

He would also not have been elected if the Germans had known about what he was planning to do after the war: relegate Christianity to the dustbin of history. This task, which he failed to accomplish, was Hitler's 'secret', not the destruction of the Jews, which he openly advocated and in which he largely succeeded. 'The dogma of Christianity crumbles in the face of science,' he opined on 14 October 1941 in Himmler's presence. 'The best way . . . to gain liberation from Christianity is by letting it fade away.'

In his monologues in the Führer Headquarters, Hitler returned again and again to the idea that Christ was an Aryan and that it was Paul, the Jew, who had put primitive Christianity on the path toward Bolshevism. 'By turning the Aryan protest movement against the Jews in Palestine into a supra-national Christian religion, Paul, the Jew, destroyed the Roman empire,' he said on 21 October 1941.

With his Christianity, Paul confronted the Roman idea of the state with the idea of a kingdom higher than the state. Paul proclaimed the equality of all men and one God, and his success perforce spelled the eclipse of Roman state authority . . . Rome became Bolshevist, and this Bolshevism had exactly the same effect on Rome as it later did on Russia, as we have seen . . . Saul turned into Paul and Mordecai into Karl Marx. [Mordecai was the family name of Marx's grandfather, H.A.W.] If we stamp out this plague, we will accomplish a deed for humanity, the magnitude of which our men out there cannot yet imagine.

Three years later, on 30 November 1944, Hitler expressed his belief in the Jewish nature of Christianity in the following way:

Jesus fought against the ruinous materialism of his age and therefore against the Jews . . . Paul recognized that the correct utilization of a foundational idea among the Gentiles would provide much greater power than the promise of material rewards to the Jew. And so Saul/Paul cleverly falsified the Christian teaching: the declaration of war against the deification of money and the declaration of war against Jewish self-interest turned into the foundational idea of the racially inferior, the oppressed, the poor in money and property against the ruling class, against the higher race, against the oppressors. The religion of Paul and what from that moment onward was put across as Christianity was nothing other than Communism.

Hitler's hatred of the Jews was not simply a function of 'racism'. The 'Negroes', whom he despised most of all, were not to be extirpated, but only reduced to a subservient status. He had the 'alien' Gypsies murdered primarily because of their 'asocial' character. The Japanese and Chinese, on the other hand, enjoyed his increasing respect. The racist Hitler was conscious of the fact that, strictly speaking, the Jews were not a race. 'The Jewish race is, above all, a community of the spirit,' he dictated (presuming the documentation is correct) on 3 February 1945 to Martin Bormann, director of the party chancellery. 'Spiritual race is of a tougher and more enduring kind than natural race. The Jew remains a Jew, wherever he goes. He is, in his nature, a creature that cannot be assimilated. And it is this quality of non-assimilability that characterizes his race and offers us sad proof of the superiority of "spirit" over flesh!'

The physical destruction of the Jews did not mean that the Jewish 'spirit' was defeated once and for all. Since this spirit had entered into Christianity, the 'Nordic race' would still face difficult struggles after the 'Jewish question' was solved. Accordingly, it was Hitler's plan that the military *Endsieg* would be followed by an unprecedented cultural revolution. Its goal was to rectify a historical mistake made nearly 2,000 years before, when the Jewish spirit in Christian form set about conquering Europe and breaking the back of the Aryan race by driving out its masterful nature and shackling it to the alien, Jewish commandment of 'Thou shalt not kill'.

Nineteenth-century German anti-Semites like Paul de Lagarde had written on Paul's supposed falsification of Jesus's teachings. Hitler thought their conclusions through to the radical end. The 'final solution to the Jewish question' was the necessary precondition for the elimination of the influence the Jews and Jewish Christianity had exercised, and continued to exercise, over European and world history. Only thereafter would true Aryan nature, liberated from all inhibitions of a morality of compassion, develop fully and enable the Aryan race to assert itself successfully in the struggle for existence. To achieve this goal, or come as close to it as possible, was the mission of the man who saw himself as 'merely an executor of the will of history'.

At the same time, Hitler knew that the great majority of Germans were not yet prepared to take up the struggle against Christianity and the traditional values of the west. He therefore did not speak openly about what he looked upon as not only a historical necessity, but as *the* great ideological challenge of the post-war period. His support within Germany and, for a period, from beyond the German borders was predicated above all on his war against militantly anti-Christian Bolshevism. He concealed his own opposition to Christianity under religious rhetoric, a tactic that was as successful as his professed commitment to legality before 1933 and his pacifist posturing in the years following. By the spring of 1945, when there could be little doubt about the imminent end of his regime, many people who had believed in him now saw themselves as his victims. The reports of SD officials reflect a broad-based opinion in the final weeks of the Third Reich: 'The Führer was sent to us by God, not to rescue Germany, but to destroy Germany. Providence has decided to annihilate the German people, and has appointed Hitler its executor.'

By the time Hitler committed suicide in the 'Führer bunker' in Berlin on 30 April 1945, his cult was all but a thing of the past. The false report of his death on 1 May—'our Führer Adolf Hitler fell this afternoon at his command post in the Reich Chancellery, fighting to the last breath against Bolshevism and for Germany'—was met with little mourning. By this time the Allies had already occupied large parts of Germany. When their troops approached, the Germans got rid of the Führer portraits, swastika flags, Nazi uniforms and party emblems, and other symbols of the Third Reich as quickly and completely as possible.

The belief in the charisma of the Führer, more than any other single factor, had made it possible for Hitler to rule over Germany for twelve years. The late realization that this rule had become a catastrophe for Germany broke the spell Hitler had cast over a majority of the German people. After the unconditional surrender on 8 May 1945, there were few true believers left. Germany was now a country of former National Socialists.[32]

THE GERMAN CATASTROPHE: INTERPRETATIONS

Hitler's former supporters and those who had sympathized with his conservative allies were not the only ones who considered themselves his victims in 1945. Even a liberal émigré like the economist Wilhelm Röpke, who had gone to Turkey in 1933 and had been teaching in Geneva since 1937, confirmed this German self-assessment. In his much-read 1945 book *Die deutsche Frage*,* the native Hanoverian did speak of negative factors in German history, which he connected to Luther, Frederick the Great, and Bismarck—to Prussia, in a word, as 'Germany's evil spirit'. But Röpke's actual message was comforting:

Today, it should be clear to everyone that the Germans were the first victims of the barbarian invasion that poured upon them from below; that they were the first to be overwhelmed with terror and mass hypnosis; and that everything the occupied countries then had to endure afterwards was done to the Germans first, including the worst of all fates: being made or seduced into becoming the tools of further conquest and oppression.

'Victims,' of course, would have experienced the end of oppressive rule as a 'liberation'. But such was not the common perception during the downfall of the Third Reich in the spring of 1945. The word 'collapse' (*Zusammenbruch*) conveyed the feelings of most Germans much more accurately, since it described not only the country's political and economic conditions, but also the hopes most Germans had placed in Hitler. The ruins of the cities, the suffering of those who had been evacuated or driven from their homes by the bomb attacks, the misery of the refugees and expellees, and, finally, the spread of detailed information on the concentration camps and the murder of the Jews—all these things spoke

* Röpke, *The German Question*.

against Hitler and against any relapse into Nazism. Still, it was one thing to distance oneself from Hitler and his fanatical henchmen; it was quite another to contemplate the German traditions that lay behind Hitler's movement and meditate upon one's individual responsibility for what had happened in and through Germany after 1933.

In the so-called *Stuttgarter Schuldbekenntnis* ('Stuttgart confession of guilt') of October 1945, the Provisional Council of the German Evangelical church, led by the Württemberg bishop Theophil Wurm and the church president of Hesse-Nassau, Martin Niemöller, a former concentration camp inmate, spoke of a 'solidarity of guilt' between the church and the people. This idea met with widespread opposition, even within the church itself. One sentence in particular was seen as an inappropriate confirmation of the Allied arguments about the 'collective guilt' of the German people: 'Through us, endless suffering has been brought down upon many peoples and countries.' And far too much for conservative Protestants was the confession's self-accusation: '[W]e reproach ourselves for not witnessing more courageously, for not praying more faithfully, for not believing more joyously, and for not loving more ardently.'

The philosopher Karl Jaspers provoked similar reactions in 1946 with *Die Schuldfrage*,* the published version of a lecture from the 1945–6 winter semester. Jaspers, whom the Nazi regime had forbidden to teach or publish after 1937–8, spoke of a 'moral collective guilt' in the sense of the German people's responsibility for the political situation in their country in the years 1933–45. 'We all bear responsibility for the fact that the spiritual-intellectual conditions of German life contained the possibility of such a regime.' Jaspers's use of the term 'collective guilt' was enough to bring him many accusations of compliance with the Allied forces. In fact, he argued against sole German responsibility for Nazism and saw the Allies as partially complicit in Hitler's rise. Quoting Röpke, he spoke of the Germans as Hitler's 'first victims' and asserted that German anti-Semitism was 'at no time a people's movement'. But these aspects of his analysis did not lessen the rage of the philosopher's critics.

Friedrich Meinecke's book *Die deutsche Katastrophe*,[†] which also came out in 1946, was not as controversial. The old Berlin historian (he was born in 1862) lamented the 'continuity of mechanized soldiership and drill mentality from the days of Frederick William I'. He spoke of 'dark aspects' of Bismarck's founding of the German Reich, which, in his view, was both 'an achievement of historical dimensions' and 'the decisive deviation from liberal, west European ideas'. He called the German Fatherland party and the *Dolchstosslegende*, the legend of the 'stab in the back', the 'fatal turning point in the development of the German bourgeoisie'.

---

* Jaspers, *The Question of German Guilt*.
† Meinecke, *The German Catastrophe*.

But when it came to the Jews, Meinecke's thoughts reflected the same old anti-Semitic prejudices. He had the following to say about the late nineteenth century: 'The Jews, who, once the economic climate is in their favour, are in the habit of enjoying it without thought to the consequences, had created a good deal of bad will since their full emancipation.' Meinecke even showed a certain understanding for the anti-Semitism of the Weimar Republic. 'Many Jews were among those who raised the chalice of opportunistic power to their lips far too quickly and greedily. They now appeared to all anti-Semites as the beneficiaries of the German defeat and revolution.'

Despite all his criticism of 'Prussian militarism', Meinecke did not succeed in placing National Socialism in the larger context of German history. The deciding factor in Hitler's appointment to the chancellorship was 'nothing general, but pure chance: the weakness of Hindenburg', he wrote, in sovereign disregard of the Reich president's social environment and the political forces influencing him. On the character profile of Hitler himself, Meinecke quoted what Otto Hinze had once said to him: 'This person does not really even belong to our race. There is something totally alien about him, something like a primordial and otherwise extinct race, still completely amoral in nature.'

The lesson the historian drew from the 'German catastrophe' was a replacement of politics by culture or, in his words, an 'internalization of our existence'. Meinecke, who at the beginning of the twentieth century had praised the German path from cosmopolitanism to nationalism as historical progress, was now exhorting his countrymen to move in the opposite direction. 'The achievement of the Bismarck era has now been shattered, and we ourselves are to blame. We must now climb over its ruins and seek the path back to the age of Goethe.' To this end, 'Goethe communities' (*Goethegemeinden*) were to be established in all German cities, and on every Sunday, if possible in a church, ceremonies were to be held, accompanied 'by great German music, Bach, Mozart, Beethoven, Schubert, Brahms, and so forth . . . If we then look upwards to the highest spheres of the Eternal and Divine, we will hear in response: "Ye shall have hope." '

The intellectual challenge to which Meinecke proved unequal was mastered by Thomas Mann. The writer, who had been living in the United States since 1939, shared his thoughts on 'Germany and the Germans' at the end of May 1945 in the Library of Congress in Washington. He spoke in English.* His talk, designed as a 'piece of German self-criticism', was in fact much more. It exposed the deep layers within German consciousness, layers that had taken on concrete form in National Socialism. As such, it contributed toward overcoming the alleged antagonism between politics and culture.

---

* [Translator's note: the text appearing in the German editions contains somewhat more detail and nuance than Mann's original English address. I translated the former, though following closely the formulations of the latter. The bibliographical reference to the original English address can be found in the endnotes.]

Mann went much further back into history than Meinecke had gone. His analysis began with the Middle Ages, many aspects of which still influenced Germany—or, indeed, lived on—in the twentieth century. Just as Luther, who 'had a good deal of the medieval man about him in his way of thinking and the shape of his soul', had wrestled with the Devil all his life, so too did Goethe's *Faust*.

The hero of our greatest literary work, Goethe's *Faust*, is a man who stands at the dividing line between the Middle Ages and Humanism, a man of God who, out of a presumptuous urge for knowledge, surrenders to magic, to the Devil. Wherever arrogance of the intellect mates with spiritual archaism and bondage of the soul, there is the Devil's domain. And the Devil, Luther's Devil, Faust's Devil, strikes me as a very German figure, and the pact with him, the Satanic covenant, to win all treasures and power on earth for a time at the cost of the soul's salvation, strikes me as something uncannily typical of German nature.

Luther, the conservative revolutionary, said Mann, had conserved Christianity. Like the later uprising against Napoleon, his Reformation was a '*nationalistic* movement for liberty'.

The German concept of liberty was only ever directed outward; it meant the right to be German, only German, and nothing else and nothing beyond that. It was a concept of protest, of self-centred defence against everything that sought to limit and restrict *völkisch* egotism, to tame it and to direct it toward service to the community, service to humanity. Obdurate individualism outwardly, in its relations to the world, to Europe, to civilization, this German concept of liberty tolerated within itself a disconcerting lack of freedom, a disturbing degree of immaturity and dull servility. It was a militant slave mentality, and National Socialism went so far in its exaggeration of this incongruity between the external and internal need for freedom as to think of world enslavement by a people themselves enslaved at home.

That the German desire for freedom amounted to an internal deficit of freedom and, ultimately, to an attempt on the freedom of all others, had, in Mann's view, a deeper cause: 'Germany has never had a revolution and has never learned to combine the concept of the national with the concept of liberty.' Even Goethe's disavowing attitude toward 'political Protestantism, the populist rabble-democracy', had affected the intellectually influential part of the nation, the bourgeoisie: '[it] served only as a confirmation and a deepening of the Lutheran dualism of spiritual and political liberty, with the result that the German concept of culture was prevented from taking up the political element.'

This meditation upon German history led Mann to a conjecture that went far beyond the history of his country. It was possible that the world was

not the sole creation of God, but a cooperative work with somebody else. One would like to ascribe to God the merciful fact that good can come from evil. But that evil so often comes from good is obviously the contribution of the other fellow. Germans might well ask why all their good, in particular, so often turns to evil, becomes evil in their hands. Take, for example, their fundamental universalism and cosmopolitanism, their inner boundlessness, which may be regarded as a spiritual accessory of their ancient super-national realm, the Holy Roman Empire of the German Nation. This is a highly valuable, positive trait, which, however, was transformed into evil by a sort of dialectic inversion. The Germans yielded to the temptation of basing upon their innate cosmopolitanism a claim to European hegemony, even to world domination, whereby this trait became its exact opposite, namely the most presumptive and menacing nationalism and imperialism. At the same time, they noticed that they were too late again with their nationalism, because it had outlived its time. Therefore they substituted something newer, more modern, for it, the racial idol, which promptly led them to monstrous crimes and plunged them into the depths of distress.

Even the 'perhaps most notable quality of the Germans', their 'inwardness', had, as Mann saw it, done them more harm than good. The 'great historical deed of German inwardness', Luther's Reformation, was a deed of liberation, but it also brought about the religious schism of the Occident and the disaster of the Thirty Years War. German Romanticism, another expression of German inwardness, imparted 'deep and vitalizing impulses' to European thought, especially philosophy and historiography, as well as to European art, above all poetry and music. But the Germans became 'the people of the romantic counter-revolution against the philosophical intellectualism and rationalism of enlightenment—a revolt of music against literature, of mysticism against clarity.'

The history of German inwardness was Mann's real theme. It was, as he said towards the end of his talk,

a melancholy story—I call it that, instead of 'tragic', because misfortune should not boast. This story should convince us of one thing: that there are *not* two Germanies, a good one and a bad one, but only one, whose best turned into evil through devilish cunning. Wicked Germany is merely good Germany gone astray, good Germany in misfortune, in guilt, and ruin . . . Not a word of all that I have just told you about Germany or tried to indicate to you, came out of alien, cool, objective knowledge. It is all within me. I have been through it all.

Thomas Mann had to travel a long road before arriving at this view of German history. During the First World War he had employed his pen in the defence of the authoritarian German state. After 1918 he became an advocate of the German republic. By 1939 he had recognized the Führer of the German Reich to be 'brother Hitler': a failed artist who was trying to imitate the mythic world of Richard Wagner, and butchering it in the process. When, a few short weeks after the end of the Second World War, Thomas Mann sought to explain the German catastrophe in terms of German inwardness gone astray, he had been working on his novel *Doktor Faustus* for two years. It is no coincidence that the story's protagonist, the composer Adrian Leverkühn, who makes a pact with the devil for the sake of his art and is finally taken to hell, is a German. He stood for a Germany that thought itself more 'profound' than the rest of the world and 'whose best turned into evil through devilish cunning'.

The end of the Third Reich on 8 May 1945 also spelled the end of what Thomas Mann called the 'Unholy German Empire of the Prussian Nation', which, he said, could only ever be an 'empire of war'. The downfall of Prussia, which Hitler's regime had reduced to a shadowy existence, was sealed by the Allied Control Council on 25 February 1947 in law no. 46. This ordinance decreed the dissolution of the state of Prussia, which 'has always been the representative of militarism and reaction in Germany' and which, in reality, no longer even existed.

Whatever else remained to be said of Prussia, of Weimar Prussia, for example, or the Prussia of 20 July 1944, the fact remains that without the cult of Prussia and the cult of Frederick the Great, the Austrian Adolf Hitler could not have ruled over Germany and could not have led the Germans into war. By the end, the mythology of Prussia was as used up as the much older mythology of the Reich, which had survived the downfall of the Holy Roman Empire of the German Nation in 1806 by 139 years. Nothing had alienated the Germans from the west as much as their claim to universalism, which they connected to the Reich—the claim be more than the other European nations and their nation states. The role of the Reich in the Second World War was still seen by many historically and theologically educated Germans in terms of the *catechon*, the power holding back the rule of the Antichrist, who proclaimed himself as god, and had now taken on the form of Bolshevism. That the leader of the Reich himself fitted the Antichrist image no less than Stalin was something the Germans realized only when the end of his rule was near. By the time the war came to an end, it was not only their Reich that was gone. It was uncertain that the Germans would ever have a national state again.

In *Mythus des Staates*,* his last book before his death in American exile in April 1945, shortly before the end of the war, the German philosopher Ernst Cassirer interpreted Hitler's career as a triumph of myth over reason and this triumph as the consequence of a profound crisis.

Politics always means living on volcanic soil. We must be prepared for abrupt convulsions and eruptions. In all critical moments of societal life, the forces of reason, which stand against the reawakening of old mythic ideas, are no longer sure of themselves. In such moments, myth sees its hour come round again. For it has not really been defeated and suppressed. It is always there, hidden in the darkness, biding its time, waiting for its opportunity. Its hour comes as soon as the other cohesive forces in societal life, for one reason or another, lose their power and are no longer able to fight against the demonic forces.

The German myths Hitler used and abused were completely destroyed by him. Herein lay the liberating effect of his fall, something the Germans came to realize only in the course of time. And in learning to grasp the 'collapse' as a liberation, they came to understand that Germany was itself responsible for the fate that had overtaken it.[33]

---

* Cassirer, *The Myth of the State*.

2

Democracy and Dictatorship 1945–1961

THE CAESURA OF 1945

The year 1945 was a more profound watershed in world history than 1918. The First World War led to the dissolution of three multinational empires, the Habsburg, the Ottoman, and, in part, the Russian empire. The successor states in eastern central and south-eastern Europe, originally set up as democracies, nearly all turned into authoritarian dictatorships in the 1920s and 1930s. The first of the two world wars also gave rise to the totalitarian movements, which came to power first in Russia in communist form, then in Italy and Germany as fascist regimes. The United States of America and Bolshevist Russia, the two flanking powers that had entered the European political stage in the epochal year of 1917, influenced the developments in Europe, but remained part of the periphery during the inter-war period. The fact that they became partners during the Second World War and divided the continent between them at its end was the work of the man who had seen himself as Europe's last chance.

By the time Hitler's Reich collapsed, European world dominance was also at an end. The European overseas empires were living on borrowed time after 1945. By making war on Britain, France, the Netherlands, and Belgium, Hitler had inadvertently helped the colonial peoples in their wars of liberation in Asia and Africa. The unleashing of the Second World War was Germany's second bid for hegemony over Europe in the twentieth century. This connects the Second World War with the First and gives a certain historical justification to the common view that the years between 1914 and 1945 represented another 'Thirty Years War'. The unprecedented nature of Hitler's regime and its crimes should not blind us to the continuity of the German will to fundamentally reshape the balance of world power in favour of the Reich, which finally paid the price of this politics with its downfall.

The year 1945 represents the end of *one* of the two forms of totalitarian rule, the fascist or National Socialist. The *other*, communist form, emerged from the war stronger than before. The Soviet Union was able to expand its sphere of influence well into the centre of Europe. After the Yalta conference in February 1945, when Roosevelt and Churchill tacitly agreed to a division of Europe into eastern and western spheres of interest, the western Allies were unable to prevent Stalin from annexing the Baltic states and gaining control of Poland, Czechoslovakia, Hungary, Romania, and Bulgaria. At the Potsdam conference in July and August 1945, the USA and Great Britain accepted a solution placing the territories east of the Oder and Neisse rivers under Polish administration, and northern East Prussia under Soviet control. In the case of the area surrounding Königsberg, the proviso that the arrangement would only be final at the conclusion of a peace treaty was undermined by the British–American statement that they would support the Soviet claims to this territory in the negotiations.

According to the Treaty of Potsdam, all Germans still living in the eastern territories—those who had not already fled before the Red Army—were to be transferred to Germany 'in an orderly and humane way'. This clause also applied to the Sudeten and Hungarian Germans, also forced to abandon their homelands in 1945. The brutal expulsion of undesirable natives, a practice begun by the Nazis, was now directed at the Germans—a violation of human rights that seems not to have caused pangs of conscience for the western actors. Of all the eastern territories colonized by Germans from the Middle Ages onward, the only part that remained German was to the west of the Oder and Neisse. The western border of the Soviet sphere, as of Soviet-occupied Germany, now ran along the Elbe, Werra, and Fulda rivers.

Germany was divided into four zones of occupation and the former Reich capital, Berlin, into four sectors. This partition marks one of the biggest differences between the outcomes of the two world wars. Unlike in 1918, there was no longer any German government in 1945. Sovereignty over the country was transferred to the four occupying powers (USA, Soviet Union, Great Britain, and France), who established the Allied Control Council as a common executive on 30 August 1945. The surviving leaders of the Third Reich were tried in the International Military Tribunal in Nuremberg beginning in November 1945. The 'war crimes', 'crimes against peace', and 'crimes against humanity' prosecuted by the Nuremberg court were all new legal entities, as was the concept of the 'criminal organization'. Their legal basis was a Control Council law of 20 December 1945, itself derived from the Potsdam treaty's stipulations on the prosecution of war criminals. Thus the breakthrough to a new international law was purchased at the price of a violation of the legal principle *nulla poena sine lege*, 'no punishment without law', according to which a court can only condemn an act on the basis of a law that already existed at the time the act was committed. The legality of the Nuremberg proceedings also suffered from the fact that one of the powers sitting in judgment, the Soviet Union, had itself committed war crimes, crimes against peace, and crimes against humanity. Nonetheless, the magnitude of the deeds condemned in Nuremberg was so great that justice would have suffered far more if they had gone unpunished.

The judgments against the main perpetrators were handed down on 1 October 1946. Twelve of the highest functionaries of the Third Reich, including

Goering, Ribbentrop, Rosenberg, and Keitel, were condemned to death by hanging. Others, like Hitler's deputy Rudolf Hess and Albert Speer, minister of armaments, were sentenced to long prison terms. Goering escaped the execution of his sentence by committing suicide on 16 October. Papen and Schacht, who had smoothed Hitler's path to the Reich chancellorship but had committed none of the crimes prosecuted at Nuremberg, were acquitted.

The 'de-Nazification' of the millions of members of National Socialist organizations, a policy also decided at Potsdam, proceeded differently in the four occupation zones, but more or less schematically in all of them. The Soviet methods were the most rigorous and, at the same time, the most arbitrary. The detained National Socialists—those not deported to the Soviet Union—were put in 'special camps' along with troublesome bourgeois democrats, Social Democrats, and even oppositional Communists. Of the more than 120,000 prisoners of these camps, which were not dismantled until 1950, some 42,000 are thought to have died. The former concentration camp at Buchenwald was used for this purpose. When, on 1 August 1949, Thomas Mann spoke in the German National Theatre at Weimar on the occasion of Goethe's 200th birthday, he refused to discuss this continuity of terror, to the disappointment of many of his admirers.

The counterpart of repression was the selective distribution of privilege. The bureaucracy, police, judiciary, and schools were all thoroughly 'cleansed' and trustworthy Communists expedited, whenever possible, to the most important levers of power. Hastily trained 'people's judges' and 'new teachers' replaced their politically compromised predecessors. Criteria like professionalism and efficiency played no role in this personnel change. De-Nazification and Communist cadre politics were two sides of the same coin.

The counterpole to the Soviet Occupied Zone (SOZ; *Sowjetische Besatzungszone* or SBZ in German) was that of France. The French treated former Nazi officials with comparative leniency. From the start they used the biographies of 'party comrades' as a means of forcing their loyalty. But there were arrests, imprisonments, and dismissals here, too. They formed the first phase of the de-Nazification in all four zones, continuing into 1946. The second phase, which began in March 1946 in the American zone, and in the British and French zones half a year later, was characterized by trial-like proceedings before tribunals known as *Spruchkammern*. Germans whose 'questionnaires' had given cause for attention were divided into five categories: 'major offenders', 'offenders', 'lesser offenders', 'fellow travellers', and 'exonerated'. The Americans were the most strict, classifying only a tiny minority as 'exonerated' and initially forbidding 'fellow travellers' the practice of their professions. The British did not enforce such a policy, declaring more than half of those they questioned 'exonerated'.

As the antagonism between the east and the west grew, the Americans also became more lenient with former Nazis. Hitler had been a national hero for years, his party a mass movement. To treat his former followers in all severity was to risk creating a reservoir of social discontent and political radicalism. A policy of forbearance, coupled with political 're-education', seemed to promise better results: a rapid habituation of the Germans to democracy and resistance to extremist rhetoric, both rightist and leftist. All in all, de-Nazification proved to be a failure. After 1949 most former Nazis not prosecuted as criminals were able to return to their former jobs and positions. 'Fellow travellers', 'lesser offenders', and even 'offenders' could, after a few years, look forward to a day when they would no longer be confronted with their political biographies.

The Soviet Union did not treat 'little' Nazis much differently. They could re-educate themselves and become good 'anti-fascists'. In any case the most important part of de-Nazification, in the view of the Soviet Military Administration in Germany (or SMAD), was not the punishment of the individual National Socialists, but structural changes. This meant breaking the power of the societal classes that, according to the Marxist-Leninist interpretation of history, had helped fascism to power. The 'land reform' of September 1945 was part of this programme. It literally cut the ground from beneath the feet of the East Elbian Junkers. Some 7,000 large landowners were expropriated without compensation. The declared aim was to put 'Junker lands into peasant hands'. Among the 500,000 people who obtained land in this way, 83,000 were 'resettlers' (*Umsiedler*), that is, Germans who had been driven out of their homes in the eastern territories. The expropriation was in no way limited to former supporters of National Socialism; opponents of the Hitler regime were also affected. Nor was the reform, as radical as it was, specifically communist in nature. Bourgeois reformers had been calling for changes in the property relations of the East Elbian agricultural system for decades, pushing for policies favourable to smaller and medium-sized farms. Their ideas had not included expropriation without compensation, of course. But the popularity of the 'land reform' was little affected. The feeling that the redistribution of the Junker estates was just and overdue was shared by a large portion of the bourgeoisie.

The same cannot be said of the 'industry reform', which commenced shortly thereafter, in October 1945. It was not only aimed at 'war criminals' and 'Nazis', but at big business as a whole. Nearly 10,000 firms had been nationalized without compensation by the spring of 1948. Some 40 per cent of industrial production was now in the hands of the state. This did not include the so-called 'Soviet Stock Companies' (*Sowjetische Aktiengesellschaften* or SAGs) in heavy industry, run directly by the occupying power itself. Banks, large and small, had been nationalized already in July 1945. By the autumn of that year, there could be no further doubt about the intentions of the SMAD: the capitalist system was to be systematically taken apart and replaced by a socialist society.

In the western zones, the societal interventions of the occupying powers were comparatively limited in scope. Land reforms were planned but never carried out. Several large companies and banks that had played an important role under the

Nazi regime—IG Farben, the iron and steel businesses in the British zone, the Commerzbank, the Dresdner Bank, and the Deutsche Bank—were confiscated and placed under the direction of trustees. The British, after expropriating the twelve largest coal and steel concerns without compensation in December 1945, turned them into twenty-eight separate and independent companies. The Labour party, in power in London from July 1945, advocated the nationalization of large companies, as the German Social Democrats and trade unions were demanding. But Lucius B. Clay, the American military governor, was against this move, and his counsels prevailed. The official policy was that nationalization was such a major issue that it could not be decided by a single country or in a single zone, but should be postponed until a later German legislative authority could deal with it.

The importance of the year 1945 in German social history can only be measured when one takes into consideration the situation in Germany after the First World War. None of the 'old power elites' had been completely destroyed in the revolution of 1918–19. The Junkers, though initially losing political influence, were able to maintain the social basis of their power. Heavy industry managed to resist the nationalization movement. The shake-up of the bureaucracy did not go very deep, and the judiciary was not touched at all. The military was forced to comply with the restrictions imposed on it by the Treaty of Versailles, but essentially remained in the republic what it had been during the Wilhelmine era: a 'state within a state' and a major player on the domestic political scene, one that could advance to executive power in a state of emergency.

After the Second World War, the Potsdam agreement, which called for the 'demilitarization' of Germany, saw to it that the country had no military forces at all for years. The great East Elbian landowners were destroyed as a class. Heavy industry was expropriated in the east; in the west it was first broken up, then, after the founding of the Federal Republic of Germany, subject to co-determination by the employees. The result was that none of the old elites, most of whom had strongly opposed democracy in Germany before 1933, was able to play the same or a similar role in German society after 1945.

There was, however, a strong continuity in the civil administration of the western zones. American and British attempts to break up the German bureaucracy and replace it with a civil service of the Anglo-Saxon type met with no success. No judge was condemned for involvement in the judicial terror of the Third Reich. A number of university professors who had particularly compromised themselves between 1933 and 1945, including Martin Heidegger and Carl Schmitt, lost their posts. But many who, in retrospect, seemed hardly less culpable were able, after a short period of involuntary leave, to pick up where they had left off in 1945. The political screening of the bureaucracy had a disciplinary effect similar to the sobering impact of the 'collapse'. Open hostility to democracy was now discredited, both in the civil administration and the judicial system.

There was no real *Stunde Null* or 'zero hour' after the fall of the Hitler regime, and yet this term exactly describes the general feeling of Germans at the time. The future of Germany had never been as unforeseeable, and chaos never as omnipresent, as in the spring of 1945. The personal experience of the victors' brutality was much worse in the Soviet zone, especially for German women. But lawlessness was everywhere in the first weeks after the war's end. Post-collapse German society was highly mobile in all zones. Millions of 'displaced persons', expellees from the east, and refugees from the bombed-out cities were on the move, looking for a new home. Hungry city-dwellers undertook foraging expeditions to the countryside, where they bartered for the necessities of life. Many 'better situated' people, having lost their salaries, pensions, and other forms of steady income, were reduced to performing menial tasks, at least for the time being. The *Trümmerfrauen*, or 'rubble women', became the symbol of a radical reversal of gender roles.

The Allied bombs, the expulsions, and the internal collapse changed German society far more than the first ten years of the Third Reich had done. Social change was accompanied by a moral revolution. Traditional values were deeply shaken by the experience of starvation, homelessness, and the daily battle for survival. Even church leaders expressed understanding when members of their flock did not respect the difference between 'mine' and 'thine' as much as in the past. The end of all security profoundly impressed itself upon the consciousness of those who lived through it. And yet the changes of 1945 were not to last. Post-collapse Germany was a society in a state of emergency. This state did not produce a new order, but rather a deep longing to return to some kind of 'normality' as quickly as possible.

In the landscape of ruin that was post-war Germany, the least probable of all outcomes was that another politician like Adolf Hitler would be able to manipulate the desires and longings of the Germans for his own ends. It was too glaringly obvious that the leader of the Third Reich had unleashed the Second World War and bore the main responsibility for its results. This time, legends of German innocence and of 'stabs in the back' had no chance of finding mass appeal. This is one of the main differences between the two post-war Germanies in the twentieth century.[1]

THE COLD WAR AND THE ROOTS OF THE GERMAN PARTITION

The weakness and errors of his democratic enemies was not the least of the reasons for Hitler's success. The surviving Weimar politicians were in agreement on this point. Those from the bourgeois camp generally saw the fragmentation of the party system as a main cause of the first German republic's demise. Consequently, they sought a concentration of political forces, whether under a

Christian or a liberal label. The former supporters of the Centre party quickly came to the conclusion that National Socialism had taught staunch Christians of both confessions a valuable lesson—namely, that what they had in common far outweighed what separated them. Therefore, after the end of the dictatorship, there could be no more talk of restoring the old denomination-based parties like the Catholic Centre or, on the Evangelical side, the Christian-Social People's Service. The goal now was to establish a large Christian party.

The fruit of this insight was the Christian-Democratic Union (*Christlich-Demokratische Union* or CDU), founded in the spring of 1945 in Berlin, Cologne, and Frankfurt. Within a short time Konrad Adenauer became the new party's leading voice. Restored to his position as mayor of Cologne by the Americans in March 1945, Adenauer was dismissed again in October by the British. In March 1946 a party congress elected him CDU leader in the British zone. This was the beginning of a political career that was to shape the early Federal Republic of Germany more than any other.

Liberals joined forces in 1945 under a number of different names: the Liberal Democratic Party of Germany (*Liberaldemokratische Partei Deutschlands* or LDPD) in Berlin and the Soviet zone; the Democratic People's Party (*Demokratische Volkspartei*) in Württemberg-Baden; and the Free Democratic Party (*Freie Demokratische Partei*) in Bavaria. The representatives of the liberal parties came together in 1948, electing Theodor Heuss as their leader. A publicist from Württemberg, Heuss had been one of Friedrich Naumann's closest associates, as well as a Reichstag delegate for the German Democratic and, later, the German State party. The old opposition between left and right had now been overcome, at least on the surface. It lived on inside the FDP; the Hesse party, under its leader Martin Euler, was as clearly 'National Liberal' in outlook as the Württemberg Baden party under Reinhold Maier was 'Democratic'.

Openly 'rightist' parties had no chance of being tolerated by the occupying powers in the years immediately after the end of the war. But moderately conservative parties did exist on the regional level. One of these was the Lower Saxony State Party (*Niedersächsische Landespartei* or NLP), which took up the legacy of the 'Guelf' parties of the Wilhelmine era and Weimar Republic. In 1946 it renamed itself the German Party (*Deutsche Partei* or DP), thus ceasing to be a purely regional organization. The other, far more important conservative group was the CDU's sister party, the Christian Social Union (*Christlich-Soziale Union* or CSU). It placed great emphasis on organizational independence, just as the Bavarian People's Party (BVP) had done vis-à-vis the Centre between 1919 and 1933. But the CSU also stressed a federalist perspective. In fact it was compelled to do so, since otherwise it would have had great difficulty in maintaining itself in competition with another BVP successor, the staunchly particularist Bavaria Party (*Bayernpartei*).

The largest democratic party of the Weimar Republic, the SPD (*Sozialdemokratische Partei Deutschlands*), had lost many of its leaders between 1933 and 1945. Otto Wels died in June 1939 in Paris exile. Rudolf Hilferding took his own life in Paris in 1941 after the French police had arrested him in the unoccupied south and handed him over to the Gestapo. Rudolf Breitscheid, also seized in France and given to the Gestapo, died in the Buchenwald concentration camp in August 1944, allegedly during a bomb attack. Ernst Heilmann was murdered in the same camp in April 1940. Carlo Mierendorff, a member of the 'young right' before 1933, was killed in an air attack in December 1943. Two of his friends in the resistance, Julius Leber and Theodor Haubach, were executed in Berlin-Plötzensee in January 1945. Among those who survived was Erich Ollenhauer, head of the SPD youth organization between 1928 and 1933, and member of the party executive after 1933 during all the stations of its exile (Prague, Paris, and London).

The refounding of the SPD began with the former Reichstag delegate Kurt Schumacher, who had been released from Dachau in March 1943 after an almost ten-year ordeal. On 19 April 1945, nine days after the Americans occupied Hanover, Schumacher called a first preparatory meeting. The founding of a local Social Democratic party followed on 6 May, two days before the unconditional surrender of the German Reich. The Hanover organization was the birthplace of the SPD in the British and American zones, and the 'Schumacher office' was its provisional headquarters. The wounded veteran of the First World War (his right arm had been amputated in 1915, and his left leg would follow more than three decades later, in 1948) possessed more authority and charisma than any other surviving Social Democrat. He was the man of the hour for the SPD in 1945.

Schumacher drew three lessons from the downfall of the Weimar Republic. First, the Social Democrats were never again to let any doubts arise concerning their national sentiments. Secondly, it was imperative that they gain the support of the middle classes. Thirdly, they had to draw a very clear distinction between themselves and the German Communists beholden to Moscow. In his 'Political Guidelines for the SPD in its Relationship to the Other Political Factors' of August 1945, Schumacher wrote that '[t]he Communist party is indissolubly joined to one, and only one, of the victorious powers, to nationalist and imperialist Russia and to its foreign policy aims.' His staunch anti-communism made him the opponent not only of Otto Grotewohl, the head of the SPD central committee in the Soviet zone, but of many Social Democrats throughout the whole country who, like the Communists, regarded the split in the Marxist workers' movement as one of the main reasons for the rise and triumph of National Socialism.

The KPD (*Kommunistische Partei Deutschlands*) was the first political party to officially establish itself in post-war Germany. Its avant-garde, the 'Ulbricht group' (named after Walter Ulbricht, the secretary of the politburo of the KPD in exile), was flown from Moscow to Germany in April 1945, where it did what it could to aid the Soviet army in setting up a new system. The refounding of the KPD took place on 11 June 1945 in Berlin, one day after the Soviet occupying authority became the first to officially permit the formation of political organizations. The founding manifesto of the KPD was markedly national and 'reformist' in its language. The German Communists advocated 'completely unhampered development of free trade and private business initiative on the basis of private property'. The document continued:

It is our view that the forced imposition of the Soviet system on Germany would be the wrong path, for it does not fit the current conditions for development in Germany. Rather, it is our belief that, in the present situation, the decisive interests of the German people prescribe a different path for Germany, that is, the founding of an anti-fascist, democratic regime in a parliamentary-democratic republic with all democratic rights and liberties for the people.

That sounded like a reformulation of the language used in the Potsdam treaty concerning the 'reshaping of German political life on a democratic basis'. But the long-term plans of the Communists were quite different. On 24 April 1944, while still in exile in Moscow, Walter Ulbricht, the 'strong man' of the KPD, member of the party since 1919 and of its central committee since 1923, had directed the party to put its ultimate goals on hold during the 'period of the founding of a new democracy'. At the same time, however, the conditions for the achievement of those goals were to be put in place. Unification with the SPD was to happen when the Communists were organizationally strong enough to assume the leadership of a unified workers' party. For the time being, they were, in Ulbricht's words, to lend a helping hand in the 'creation of a Social Democratic party that will cooperate with us'.

As the year 1945 proceeded, Social Democrats in the Soviet zone grew ever more doubtful about the sincerity of the Communist rhetoric. The impulse to unite the parties weakened accordingly. In mid-January 1946 the SPD central committee under Grotewohl decided to allow fusion only on the condition that a national party congress pass the corresponding resolution. By this time, however, the occupying power was exerting so much pressure on all levels that, on 10 February, the committee abruptly reversed itself and agreed to unification with the KPD. The Socialist Unity Party of Germany (*Sozialistische Einheitspartei Deutschlands* or SED) was created on 20 and 22 April 1946 at a joint party congress at the Admiralspalast in Berlin. A ballot of Social Democratic party members could only take place in the city's western sectors; 82% rejected the merger, and 62% supported further cooperation with the KPD. In the eastern sector and the Soviet zone, anyone who openly declared allegiance to the principles of social democracy could expect severe punishment.

The SED was a product of large-scale intimidation and opportunistic conformism. By the spring of 1946, freedom of decision was already so restricted in the Soviet zone that the term 'forced unification' comes very close to the truth. The elimination of an independent Social Democratic party was followed by the gradual assimilation of the bourgeois parties to the SED agenda. The LDPD under Wilhelm Külz and Eugen Schiffer, both former Reich ministers from the German Democratic Party, was pressured to join the 'People's Congress Movement' (*Volkskongressbewegung*) at the end of 1947. The main goal of this movement was to lend the Soviet Union's Germany policy a semblance of broad popular support. When the CDU refused to participate, its two leaders (Jakob Kaiser, a former Christian labour union leader and resistance fighter, and Ernst Lemmer, a former Reichstag delegate for the DDP) were summarily dismissed by the SMAD in December 1947. The new party head, Otto Nuschke (also a former DDP delegate to the Reichstag), proved more manageable.

The developments in the Soviet zone strengthened Kurt Schumacher's position in the western SPD. Until then, it had not gone uncontested. There is much to suggest that the Communists would also have made great gains in the west if it had not been for Schumacher's passionate political engagement and moral authority, which won him the allegiance of most Social Democrats. By rejecting unification with the KPD, Schumacher placed liberty above unity, both the 'unity of the working class' and the unity of the nation. Germany's later alliance with the Euro-Atlantic west was something Schumacher rejected, at least in the form it occurred. Without him, however, this policy would probably not have been possible.

To his battle against the Communists, which had begun before 1933, Schumacher now added the fight against the Union parties, which he saw as the political spearhead of a clerical and capitalist restoration. He was just as aggressive against the latter as against the former, and in both cases his rhetoric was emphatically nationalist, as the very first manifesto from the 'Schumacher office' in August 1945 made clear: 'The Reich must remain a political and national whole!' In invoking the idea of the Reich, Schumacher was fighting against what he regarded as the 'separatist aspirations' of politicians like Konrad Adenauer. And in fact the SPD leader, a West Prussian of Evangelical background (he was from Kulm), did indeed have a much closer relationship to Bismarck's Reich than the Catholic leader from Cologne. The prospect that Germany would no longer be a 'Reich' or a national state in the foreseeable future was something Schumacher was unable to accept. Adenauer, on the other hand, spoke repeatedly, and with seemingly little sentiment, about what he saw as the simple truth already in the summer and autumn of 1945: 'The Russian-occupied part is lost to Germany for an incalculable period of time.'

As far as their economic policy was concerned, the Social Democrats had hardly evolved since Weimar. They considered a planned economy superior to a market system and advocated the nationalization of key branches of industry. In the early CDU, too, there were those who supported the nationalization of mining as well as a considerable degree of 'economic planning and dirigism'.

The August 1947 'Ahlen platform' of the CDU in the British zone included both points. It also defined the goal of the economy as the 'satisfaction of needs'. Jakob Kaiser, who promoted 'Christian socialism', assigned Germany the task of building bridges between east and west in both economics and foreign policy and of paving a 'third way' between communism and capitalism.

The CDU's economic vision began to change in the spring of 1948 with the political rise of a man who stood for radically different ideas and—despite the fact he did not belong to the party—was able to convince the CDU of their soundness. This man was Ludwig Erhard. Born in Franconian Fürth in 1897, Erhard had earned a doctorate in economics from the University of Frankfurt in 1925. In March of 1948 he became director of economics on the economic council of the Unified Economic Area, the so-called 'Bizone', created by a merger between the British and American zones the year before. Erhard's 'Social Market Economy' (*Soziale Marktwirtschaft*; the term comes from his associate, Alfred Müller-Armack) broke with the policy of state control, giving the market over to the free play of supply and demand. Unlike 'Manchester liberalism', however, the state would not be released from all economic responsibility. It would guarantee competition by breaking up monopolies and cartels, and it would foster social balance through a number of other flanking measures.[2]

Erhard's programme would not have been successful if the relations between the four occupying powers, as well as the international situation in general, had not radically changed since the end of the war. French resistance had prevented the creation of centralized administrations, such as the Potsdam treaty called for. The Soviet Union had obstructed another of that agreement's provisions, a common reparations policy. Moscow wanted to maintain Germany at a very low level of industrialization in order to squeeze as much in reparations as possible from its zone in the shortest possible time. It aimed for a level of production that would guarantee the country's self-sufficiency, but nothing more. In order to accommodate the Soviet Union, a decision by the Allied Control Council on 28 March 1946 restricted industrial activity, but it went so far that German production did not even come close to covering the costs of the necessary imports, above all of food.

In contrast to Soviet indifference, the USA and Great Britain found it necessary to pump massive subsidies into their zones. Thus the American and British taxpayers were the ones who ultimately compensated for the Soviets' refusal to allow German re-industrialization and to coordinate their reparations policy with the other occupying powers. If Washington and London had adopted a different policy, and if millions of Americans, in response to a campaign by the Cooperation for American Remittance to Europe (CARE), had not sent packages of food, the scarcity in Germany might well have turned into widespread starvation.

The Bizone, which went into effect on 1 January 1947, was the product of Anglo-American rethinking. French and Soviet resistance made it impossible to treat Germany as the single economic entity intended by the Potsdam treaty. The ruthless elimination of all non-Communist forces in the countries within the Soviet sphere further increased the distance between the erstwhile allies. Clearly, Stalin was interested in one thing above all: to weaken the US position in Europe. If he succeeded in driving the Americans from the continent, there would be no other power able to stand in the way of Soviet hegemony in Europe.

The British realized earlier than the Americans that the Soviet challenge required a clear response from the west. In the spring and summer of 1946, at a conference of the foreign ministers of the 'Big Four' in Paris, the British representative, Ernest Bevin of the Labour party, made a point of taking a conciliatory approach to demands of Paris. If France would not countenance German unity, then, for the sake of a unified western front, that goal would have to be abandoned. James F. Byrnes, the American Secretary of State, went over to Bevin's position when it became clear that his Soviet interlocutor, Molotov, would remain inflexible. On 6 September 1946, Byrnes gave a speech in Stuttgart in which he announced that the USA would keep its troops in Germany as long as other powers saw fit to do so. German industrial production would be increased even if the country's economy was not going to be unified. This speech caused a sensation. The die was now cast for the formation of a western German state. Since the Allies were not able to agree on the country's future, Germany would have to be divided.

Byrnes's Stuttgart address was followed on 12 March 1947 by the promulgation of the 'Truman doctrine'. The American president Harry S. Truman used the Greek civil war (in which the Communists received more indirect and covert than open support from Moscow) as an opportunity to promise the help of the United States to all peoples wishing to preserve their liberty. Three months later, on 5 June 1947, General George C. Marshall, Byrnes's successor in the State Department, announced in a speech at Harvard University that America would give Europe large-scale economic assistance. The Marshall Plan, passed by Congress on 3 April 1948, was designed to help Europe help itself. It satisfied America's moral need to be the champion of freedom as well as its material interest in restoring tight economic links with Europe.

The European Recovery Program was a great success for the United States and for the participating European countries. It was clear from the beginning that western Germany would be one of these. The states in the Soviet sphere of influence, though they too had been approached by the USA, were kept from joining by Moscow's veto. From the Kremlin's point of view, the world was now divided into 'two main camps', an 'imperialist and anti-democratic camp' under the leadership of the USA, and an 'anti-imperialist and democratic camp' led by the USSR. This doctrine was promulgated at Stalin's behest by Andrei Zhdanov, secretary of the central committee, in September 1947, at the founding of the Cominform (successor to the Comintern, disbanded in May 1943). It was binding policy for all Communist parties thereafter.

The Marshall Plan made the United States the political leader of Europe. This was a role it had refrained from adopting after the First World War. Its leaders were now fully cognizant of the consequences of the old isolationism. One of these was that Hitler's expansionist policies had not met with any effective resistance for a long time. Now, however, America was not willing to stand idly by as the Soviets expanded the reach of their power. The policy of 'containment' was an attempt to learn from history. As we now know, the lesson was successful.

The American decision to massively subsidize European reconstruction went hand-in-hand with a reorientation of western security policy. On 17 March 1948 Great Britain, France, the Netherlands, Belgium, and Luxembourg concluded the Brussels Treaty in the city of the same name. The resulting 'Western Union' was the first European post-war alliance directed no longer against Germany, but against the policies of the Soviet Union. In response, Stalin removed the Soviet military governor, Marshal Sokolovsky, from the Allied Control Council on 20 March 1948. The Four Powers' alliance was at an end.

The next step along the way to the partition of Germany was the currency reform in the three western zones. The introduction of the Deutschmark (*Deutsche Mark* or DM) on 20 June 1948 ended the command economy, whose policies had been concealing the true weakness of the Reichsmark. A system of ration cards for food and other goods also put an end to the black market, the economic symbol of the early post-war period. Moreover, the checkpoints on the border between the French zone and the Bizone disappeared, along with the passes necessary to cross them.

The lifting of controls on most prices was the courageous act of Ludwig Erhard, the director of economics. The Social Democrats, who criticized the decision, had themselves prepared the ground for it when, in July 1947, after the formation of the Bizone's economic council (a quasi-parliamentary representative assembly elected from the parliaments of the states in the Unified Economic Area), they preferred the role of opposition and left the five main administrations in the hands of the bourgeois parties. Since prices rose much faster than wages, Erhard's policy was initially unpopular. Within a year, however, it was clear to most Germans in the three western zones that the currency reform was the biggest change since the 'collapse' and represented, all in all, a change for the better.

Two days after the western currency reform, the Soviets instituted a currency reform of their own in the part of Germany they controlled and in Berlin. Ernst Reuter, the elected mayor of the greater Berlin area (he had, however, not been confirmed by the Soviet commander of the city), a Social Democrat, and at this time city councillor for public transportation and utilities, warned against the inclusion of Berlin in the eastern reform in the weeks prior to the reform: 'Whoever possesses the currency possesses the power.' The three western commanders of the city followed this advice. On 24 June they prevented the municipal authorities from following Soviet orders and introduced the Deutschmark (stamped with a 'B') in the western sectors. The *Ost-Mark* was also accepted as a valid method of payment. The SMAD, however, made the possession of DM in the Soviet sector a punishable offence.

The real Soviet response to the western currency reform was the blockade of Berlin's western sectors. On 4 August 1948, traffic along the roads, railways, and waterways between the western zones and the western part of Berlin was cut off. The transport of goods between the eastern and western parts of the city was blocked in November. Stalin's goal was clear: the prospect of mass starvation (more than two million people were affected) would compel the western powers to abandon west Berlin, abolish the currency reform, and give up their plans for a west German state. But the west did not yield. It supplied west Berlin from the air over a period of nine months. Technically, politically, and morally, the Berlin airlift was an achievement few would have thought possible in the summer of 1948.

The administrative partition of Berlin occurred during the blockade and airlift. On 6 September 1948, Communist demonstrators forcefully broke up an assembly of freely elected city councilors. Two different city governments were in place by November, one for the three western sectors and one for the eastern sector. The west held elections on 5 December. The SPD was victorious, gaining 64.5 per cent of the vote. Ernst Reuter was elected mayor two days later.

Stalin began to relent at the beginning of 1949. In March, American and Soviet diplomats met secretly in Canada. The result was the end of the Soviet blockade of West Berlin and of the counter-blockade of the Soviet zone by the west. The west's tenaciousness had paid off. The inhabitants of West Berlin had not caved in to Soviet pressure. Both factors contributed towards making those Germans who lived under conditions of political liberty increasingly feel part of the west.

As long as they did not have their own state, however, they would not be able to join the western powers' new defensive alliance. On 4 April 1949 the USA, Canada, the five states of the 'Western Union', Iceland, Norway, Denmark, Italy, and Portugal, joined together in the North Atlantic Treaty Organization (NATO). The basic principle of the NATO agreement was an obligation to mutual assistance in case of an attack on one or more member states by a foreign power in Europe or North America. The alliance was a response to the Soviet transformation of Poland, Hungary, Bulgaria, Romania, and Czechoslovakia into satellite states, to the massive pressure Stalin was putting on the national-Communist Yugoslavia of Marshal Tito, and, not least, to the Berlin blockade. Through the Atlantic alliance, America—which was still the only great power that possessed nuclear weapons in spring 1949—tied its fate completely and utterly to the fate of Europe. Stalin's chances of reversing this development were now much slimmer, though there is no evidence he ever thought of abandoning this aim.[3]

THE FOUNDING OF THE REPUBLIC: THE DRAFTING OF THE BASIC LAW

The decision to establish a federal west German state with strong *Länder* and a weak central government was made in London between February and June 1948 at a conference of the three western powers with the 'Benelux' countries. France, in particular, insisted on a strongly federalized state, not because it corresponded to French ideas of political organization, but because Paris wanted to prevent any future concentration of power east of the Rhine. On 1 July 1948 the London recommendations, titled the 'Frankfurt Documents', were sent to the heads of the west German *Länder*, who discussed them between 8 and 10 July on the Rittersturz near Koblenz.

There was widespread agreement about the fundamentals. First, since all the west German leaders were still committed to German unity, the temporary nature of any west German state would have to be emphasized. For this reason the provisional *Grundgesetz* or 'Basic Law' was to be drafted not by a constituent assembly elected by the people, but by a 'Parliamentary Council' elected by the parliaments of the individual *Länder*. These parliaments would also approve the constitution; it would not be subject to a referendum. Secondly, the adoption of the constitution would be preceded by a statute making the rights of the occupying powers obligatory. (The prime ministers ultimately failed to gain acceptance for this provision.) A further conference, held in the hunting lodge of Niederwald on 21–2 July, was necessary before remaining doubts about the legitimacy of the west German project could be cleared away. As Ernst Reuter from Berlin told those who feared a west German federal state would in fact seal the partition of Germany: 'We are of the opinion that the political and economic consolidation of the west is also an elementary prerequisite for our own recovery and for the return of the east to the common motherland.'

In August 1948 a group of experts appointed by the prime ministers, meeting in Herrenchiemsee, drew up the fundamentals of a German constitution. They managed to agree on a number of important points. The future federal state was to have a purely representative head of state, a two-chamber system, and a government that could assert itself against negative parliamentary majorities. It was to be a representative, not a plebiscitary, democracy. Its federalism was to be secured by a general assumption of *Länder* rights and competences. All these postulates were guided by the desire to learn from the mistakes of Weimar. This was also true of the proposal to curtail the basic rights of those who would use them to 'fight against the liberal and democratic order'. This rationale sounded like a distant echo of positions taken by Carl Schmitt in his book *Legalität* *und Legitimität** of summer 1932: 'It goes without saying that any democracy neglectful in this regard runs the risk of becoming suicidal.'

The results of the Herrenchiemsee convention were taken up by the Parliamentary Council, which convened its constituent assembly on 1 September 1948 in the courtyard of the Koenig Museum in Bonn. The group consisted of sixty-five politicians elected by the parliaments of their *Länder*; Berlin was represented by delegates in an advisory capacity. Konrad Adenauer, head of the CDU in the British zone, was elected president of the assembly. The Social Democrat Carlo Schmid, the justice minister of Württemberg-Hohenzollern, became the head of the main committee.

Schmid, the Council's most brilliant orator, wrote the most eloquent statement of the lessons from Weimar. On 8 September he exhorted the democratic parties to have the 'courage to be intolerant of those . . . who seek to use democracy in order to kill it.' The next day Walter Menzel, Schmid's party colleague, agreed 'that we must not permit democracy to be destroyed yet again.' Josef Schwalber, a CSU delegate, said that the Weimar constitution, which had been praised by its adherents as the best and most democratic in the world, was so democratic 'that it granted the same, if not more, rights to the enemies of the state than to the friends of the constitution. It was so liberal that it offered the enemies of freedom and democracy a platform from which they could, by legal means, destroy both.'

The fathers and mothers of the Weimar constitution would have seen the kinds of normative standards postulated by Schmid, Menzel, and Schwalber as a relapse into authoritarianism. In its 1919 interpretation, democracy meant sovereignty of the people. The creators of the Weimar state did not believe that the will of the majority should be subjected to constitutional restrictions. Three decades later, the Parliamentary Council in Bonn found itself in a radically different situation than the constituent German national assembly in Weimar. It could look back on the history of a failed parliamentary democracy and a totalitarian dictatorship overthrown by external force. At the same time, it saw the rise of a new dictatorship in the east, in the Soviet-occupied zone. In the light of this background and these circumstances, the political leaders of west Germany decided to work towards a type of democracy different from the one that had run aground after 1930.

Although the name of Carl Schmitt was rarely mentioned in the west German constitutional deliberations of 1948–9, it was omnipresent. In many ways the Bonn politicians turned Schmitt's Weimar positions upside down. They chose a thoroughly representative democracy over a plebiscitary system, a symbolic-representative head of state over any kind of presidential dictatorship, and made the courts the 'guardian of the constitution', not the president. Nonetheless, in their opposition to Weimar-style moral relativism, the fathers and mothers of

---

* Schmitt, *Legality and Legitimacy*.

the Basic Law were very much followers of Schmitt. Except in one way: they thought in categories of natural law and did not look upon the 'decision' as an end in itself. They were not decisionists, but normativists.

The possibility of the forfeiture of basic rights; the outlawing of anti-constitutional parties by the Federal Constitutional Court (*Bundesverfassungs-gericht*); the 'perpetuity clause' of Article 79, Paragraph 3, which forbade any change of the constitution affecting the division of the state into federal *Länder*, the participation of the *Länder* in the legislative process, or the fundamentals set down in the articles on basic rights: these were a few of the precautions the Parliamentary Council took in order to ensure that the Federal Republic of Germany would be a value-oriented and well-fortified democracy. The Weimar experience imposed obligations on the legislature and restrictions on the popular will that made the new west German Basic Law unique among democratic constitutions. The provision protecting majorities from themselves by placing certain basic rights beyond their reach reflected the hard-learned lesson that majorities could err as fundamentally as the Germans had in 1932, when they voted for parties that paraded their hostility to democracy for all to see.

The view that only a functional parliamentary system could create belief in democratic legitimacy was another fruit of the Weimar experience. Therefore, the Parliamentary Council saw to it that parliamentary majorities could no longer shift their responsibility onto the head of state and would only be able to bring down a government by means of a 'constructive vote of no confidence', that is, by electing a successor. The Weimar constitution had permitted the Reich president, elected directly by the people, to claim a higher legitimacy than parliament, divided as it was into different parties. The Bonn constitution strengthened the government responsible to parliament, especially the chancellor, who was elected by that body. This change was designed to counteract two sources of danger: the opportunistic tendencies of the parties and the 'Bonapartist' tendencies of the head of state.

The second German democracy was to differ from the first in another respect, too. The legislature, executive, and judiciary were directly bound to uphold the basic rights, permanently and without qualification. In contrast to the Weimar Republic, in which they possessed merely programmatic significance, the basic rights were made the immediate law of the land. Furthermore, the Basic Law could henceforth only be changed by a law explicitly altering or supplementing its text. Deviations decided by two-thirds majority but not formally modifying the wording of the document were now no longer possible, as they had been under the Weimar system. However, in rejecting plebiscitary forms of democracy, such as popular initiatives and referendums, the west German leaders were not only thinking of Weimar; they were also guided by the fear that the Communists might use such instruments demagogically for their own ends.

Most of the Parliamentary Council's basic decisions were supported by a broad, supra-party consensus. But the distribution of authority between the

Federation (*Bund*) and the Federal States (*Länder*) was deeply controversial from the beginning. The Allies, under the influence of France, pressed for as much federalism as possible. German groups, too, favoured decentralization, above all the Bavarian CSU. The SPD and FDP were the most strongly unitarian. The sharpest differences emerged over the distribution and administration of government revenue. At the end of November 1948 the military governors gave the Parliamentary Council a document containing their demands, especially those concerning the relationship between the Federation and the Federal States. The Council's main committee, headed by Carlo Schmid, responded in February 1949, presenting the Allies with a draft constitution designed to garner a broad majority in the plenum assembly. This text met with massive criticism by the military governors, who found it too centralizing. They demanded greater federalism, including in government finance. The CSU agreed. The Bavaria Party—though not represented in the Parliamentary Council—rejected the draft constitution in its entirety.

The toughest resistance to the ideas of the Allies came from the Social Democrats. In spring 1949 their leader, Kurt Schumacher, who did not belong to the Parliamentary Council, seized the opportunity of giving his party a sharper national image. He demanded that the Federation not be made dependent on the States. To do so would be to endanger its chances of survival. This was not merely a partisan position; it was also plausible in substance. Konrad Adenauer did not think much differently, though he expressed himself with greater reservation.

On 20 April the expanded executive of the SPD, at Schumacher's urging, announced in Hanover that the party would reject the Basic Law if its demands were not adopted. This caused a sensation. No German party had yet treated the Allies with such self-confidence. In fact, Schumacher had learned from unofficial British sources that the Allies were prepared to give in. On 22 April the military governors gave the head of the Parliamentary Council a note to this effect. Adenauer felt that the Allies had gone behind his back. But he, too, could be well satisfied with the result. The sections of the Basic Law dealing with government finance were changed to fit German ideas more than most observers would have thought possible before 22 April 1949.

Unlike in 1919, there was no battle over the national flag in 1949. All parties in the Parliamentary Council agreed on the colours black, red, and gold. The name of the new state was also quickly settled. A small minority, represented by Hans-Christoph Seebohm of the German Party (*Deutsche Partei*) and Jakob Kaiser of the Berlin CDU, wanted to retain the word 'Reich'. Carlo Schmid reprimanded them in the principles committee on 6 October 1948: 'To the ears of our neighbours, the word "Reich" simply has an aggressive sound. These people interpret the word as a claim to hegemony.' There was a broad consensus for the name *Bundesrepublik Deutschland* (Federal Republic of Germany or FRG), proposed by the 'Ellwang circle' of the CDU in April 1948. This title did justice to both the federalist convictions of the Union and the republican credo of the SPD. Moreover, it contained a claim to the sole legal succession of the German Reich and the hope for a unified and democratic German state. The name 'Federal Republic of Germany' represented the sum of all the things an overwhelming majority of the Parliamentary Council were in agreement about.

On 8 May 1949, the fourth anniversary of the German surrender, the Council voted 53 to 12 for the new Basic Law. The votes against came from the CSU, the two members of the newly founded Centre Party (*Zentrumspartei*), the German Party, and the KPD. The parliaments of the *Länder* ratified the constitution between 18 and 21 May, with one exception. The Bavarian parliament rejected it, 101 to 63 votes, as too centralizing. Bavaria did not wish to exclude itself from the new state, however. At the behest of the government, the parliament voted to recognize the Basic Law if two-thirds of the other *Länder* adopted it.

The new constitution was ceremoniously proclaimed on 23 May 1949. This event was preceded by the approval of the military governors on 12 May, which was itself made conditional on the provisions of the occupation statute of 10 May codifying the comprehensive rights and privileges of the Allies, as well as on the recognition of West Berlin as the twelfth federal state. The latter proviso was *not* met. West Berlin became a unique kind of *Bundesland*: the House of Representatives adopted the new federal law without modification, to the extent that it did not conflict with the city's special status. Berlin was represented in an advisory capacity in both the Federal Parliament (*Bundestag*) and Federal Council (*Bundesrat*). Its representatives in the Bundestag were not elected by the people, but appointed by the House of Representatives. The three western Allies maintained their role as the highest executive authority.

On 10 May the Parliamentary Council voted, by 33 to 29 votes, to make its home city of Bonn the provisional federal capital. Frankfurt am Main also received a good deal of support. One of the reasons Bonn was chosen over Frankfurt was that the city on the Rhine more strongly emphasized the provisional nature of the new state than the city where the German national assembly had met in 1848. Berlin received only three votes, from the three representatives of the KPD.

The transitional character of the new constitution and the fiduciary role of the Parliamentary Council were also emphasized in the preamble to the Basic Law. The German people in the states of Baden, Bavaria, Bremen, Hamburg, Hesse, Lower Saxony, North Rhine-Westphalia, Rhineland-Palatinate, Schleswig-Holstein, Württemberg-Baden, and Württemberg-Hohenzollern were giving a new order to their political life 'for a transitional period', it read. 'They have also acted on behalf of those Germans to whom participation was denied. The entire German people are called upon to achieve in free self-determination the unity and freedom of Germany.'

Accordingly, Article 146 stipulated that the Basic Law would cease to be valid on the day 'in which a constitution adopted by a free decision of the German people comes into force'. Article 23, which provided that the Basic Law would 'be put into force in other parts of Germany on their accession', was not designed as an alternative to Article 146. Rather, as applied to the *Länder* under Soviet control, it was supposed to function as a bridging mechanism until the ratification of a new constitution for unified Germany. But it also opened up the possibility of another part of Germany acceding to the new state, at least theoretically: the Saarland, which had been incorporated into the French economic area in December 1946 and thus cut off from the rest of the French-occupied zone. The Saarland still belonged to Germany in terms of international law. In the German view the bond was constitutional. But since the special status of the territory was accepted by both the USA and Britain, and since Paris had reason to believe that both powers would legalize the status quo in a peace treaty, the most the Germans could do in 1949 was hope that their stance would ultimately prevail.

The voting law used in the first Bundestag elections combined individual candidacies with party lists. Its effect was that of a modified system of proportional representation. A 5-per cent clause (which the military governors decided should apply only to one *Land* at a time, not to the whole electoral area) was to prevent excessive fragmentation of the party system. The Federal Assembly (*Bundesversammlung*), responsible for choosing the federal president, consisted, according to the Basic Law, of the representatives of the Bundestag and an equal number of representatives from the individual state parliaments. An absolute majority was necessary in the first two ballots; a simple majority would suffice in a third. All the other details were codified in the 'Electoral Law for the First Federal Parliament and for the First Election of the Federal Assembly of the Federal Republic of Germany', promulgated by the prime ministers on 15 June 1949. The date for the Bundestag election was set that same day: 14 August 1949.

The electoral campaign was dominated by the question 'planned economy or social market economy?' This made the election a referendum on the policies of Ludwig Erhard, who ran for office in the district of Ulm for the CDU. The bourgeois parties supporting him emerged victorious. The CDU and CSU gained 31.0% of the vote, the FDP 11.9%, and the DP, which achieved double-digit results in four north German *Länder*, 4%. The SPD obtained 29.2%, the KPD 5.7%, and 18.2% went to numerous small groups of widely different political persuasions. Adenauer, a staunch opponent of a Grand Coalition (in contrast to left-leaning Union politicians like Jakob Kaiser or Karl Arnold, prime minister of North Rhine-Westphalia), set the course for the formation of a completely bourgeois cabinet by committing his party to the election of a federal president from the liberal camp. On 12 September Theodor Heuss, the 65-year-old head of the FDP, defeated the Social Democratic candidate, Kurt Schumacher, in the second ballot of the Bundesversammlung.

The Bundesrat and the Bundestag had convened for the first time five days before, on 7 September 1949. The Bundestag commenced its affairs with an act of great symbolic force. In keeping with parliamentary tradition, the first session was called to order by the most senior representative. This was the 'Weimar' politician Paul Löbe. Born on 14 December 1875, Löbe, formerly long-standing president of the Reichstag, now represented Berlin for the Social Democrats. The first historical decision was made in the chamber on the Rhine on 15 September: Konrad Adenauer, Löbe's junior by three weeks, was elected federal chancellor (*Bundeskanzler*) by a majority of one vote. After the formation of his cabinet, which consisted of members of the CDU/CSU, FDP, and DP, the numbers looked somewhat less precarious for the new government: it would be able to count on the votes of 208 out of 402 representatives.

The Occupation Statute entered into effect on 20 September, one day after Adenauer's inaugural address. The three military governors of the western Allies were transformed into a 'High Commission', with a main office on the Petersberg above Bonn and a catalogue of rights and powers so long as to make it the veritable 'supreme government' of the new country. No German law could enter into effect without first being countersigned by the High Commission. The Federal Republic of Germany was indeed a nation, but it was by no means a sovereign one when first established.[4]

STALIN'S GERMANY POLICY AND THE FOUNDING OF THE GDR

During the founding of the west German state, Stalin was pursuing a double strategy with regard to Germany. After the war alliance came to a definitive end in 1947, his main goal was to drive the Soviets' main adversary, the 'imperialist' United States, out of Europe. Once there were no more American troops in Germany, the USA would no longer have the basis of an effective military presence on the continent, and Soviet hegemony would be assured. In the short term, therefore, everything depended on the Soviet Union gaining as much influence as possible over Germany as a whole. A united Germany dependent on Moscow in its foreign policy accorded more with Stalin's view of Soviet interests than a separate Communist state in the territory of the Soviet Occupied Zone. It was true that the Soviets were making structural changes in order to give the Communists all possible advantage in the coming power struggle. Nonetheless, Stalin did not want his German vassal to become a 'people's democracy', an openly Communist satellite regime like those in place in Poland, Hungary, and Czechoslovakia by 1948—at least not while he still thought he had a chance to bring all of Germany under Soviet control.

On the other hand, however, the Soviet ruler was also prepared in case his policy of preventing a western German state failed. Everything taking place in the SOZ also made sense in terms of clearing the way for a Communist takeover east of the Elbe, Werra, and Fulda. By spring 1948 at the latest, Sergei Tulpanov, the

Soviet military governor in Germany, and Walter Ulbricht, deputy head of the SED, had set their sights on this latter goal—well before Stalin had given up hope for an all-Germany solution. On 18 December 1948 Stalin told Wilhelm Pieck (representative of the former KPD and co-leader of the SED, along with Otto Grotewohl, a former Social Democrat) that the German Communists should 'disguise' themselves and pursue a 'cautious' and 'opportunist' policy instead of waging 'war too openly'. Stalin entertained no doubts about the goal, 'socialism'. However, as he put it, this goal was best pursued in a 'zigzag course', not by 'direct intervention'.

Another characteristic piece of Stalinesque dialectics was his May 1948 directive that the SMAD create another party with the task of offering a political home to former members of the NSDAP and former professional soldiers. The Soviet leader even provided the name: the National Democratic Party of Germany (*Nationaldemokratische Partei Deutschlands*). Led by Lothar Bolz, a former member of the KPD, the NDPD spread nationalist propaganda with the blessing of the Soviets. It was even permitted to use such slogans as 'Against Marxism—for democracy!' in recruiting new membership. Along with the Democratic Peasants' Party of Germany (*Demokratische Bauernpartei Deutschlands*), founded at about the same time and headed by Ernst Goldenbaum, another former Communist, the NDPD was supposed to weaken the 'old' bourgeois parties, the CDU and LDPD, and strengthen the SED.

Both new organizations were immediately included in the 'People's Congress Movement' (*Volkskongressbewegung*) and its executive organ, the German People's Council (*Deutscher Volksrat*), which declared itself the 'appointed representative for all of Germany' in June 1948. A quarter of a year later, in October 1948, the People's Council unanimously adopted a first draft constitution. This document borrowed heavily from the Weimar constitution of 1919, especially in the part dealing with basic rights. A revised second draft, presented on 19 March 1949, was approved by the newly elected Third People's Congress on 30 May. The Council justified its claim to represent all of Germany by pointing to the 100 west German Communist sympathizers among its membership of 400. The draft constitution, therefore, was nothing more than a preparation for the possibility that the Soviet Union might find itself compelled to respond in kind to the founding of a west German state.

This situation occurred approximately one year later. On 27 September 1949, three weeks after the formation of the Bundestag and Bundesrat in Bonn, Stalin granted a SED delegation permission to establish the German Democratic Republic (*Deutsche Demokratische Republik*). The People's Congress Movement was succeeded on 4 October by the National Front of Democratic Germany (*Nationale Front des Demokratischen Deutschland*), which embraced all parties and mass organizations. On 7 October the German People's Congress named itself the Provisional People's Chamber (*Provisorische Volkskammer*) and adopted the constitution approved by the Third People's Congress at the end of May. On the face of it, this document guaranteed bourgeois liberties, including property rights, as well as the trade unions' right to strike. But the appearance was deceptive. Article 6 defined such acts as 'incitement to the boycott of democratic institutions and organizations, incitement to the murder of democratic politicians, the propagation of religious, racial, and national hatred, and the incitement to war' as punishable offences. These definitions cleared the way for the elimination of dissent.

The GDR constitution made no provision for the separation of powers. Nominally, the Volkskammer was the 'highest authority in the Republic', which excluded the possibility of an independent judiciary from the outset. But even this body had no real power. As the main representative assembly of the GDR, the Volkskammer was completely lacking in any kind of democratic legitimacy. It was simply the Third German People's Congress, elected according to the 'bloc system' in May 1949, in new clothing. The distribution of seats among the parties and mass organizations was set before the election in a way that guaranteed the absolute dominance of the SED and made opposition from the bloc parties all but impossible: 77.5 per cent of the representatives belonged to the SED or to groups directly dependent on it; only 22.5 per cent were members of the CDU and LDPD.

The adoption of the constitution on 11 October 1949 was followed by the election of Wilhelm Pieck, a founding member of the Spartacus Group and the KPD, to the presidency of the GDR. Otto Grotewohl was elected prime minister the next day. His deputies, Walter Ulbricht (SED), Otto Nuschke (CDU), and Hermann Kastner (LDPD), were elected by the Volkskammer on the same day. The SED provided the heads of the three key ministries of the interior, justice, and 'people's education' (*Volksbildung*), as well as three further cabinet ministers from a total of fourteen. The remaining posts were staffed by the bloc parties.

Thus, numerically speaking, the 'bourgeois' politicians seemed to have a small advantage. This was nothing more than a facade. The real power had long been in the hands of the SED. The idea of a non-Bolshevist 'special German path to socialism', which Central Committee Secretary Anton Ackermann had proclaimed in the name of the party in February 1946, had been repudiated as a 'false, rotten, and dangerous theory' by the same man in September 1948, also at the behest of the party. The transformation of the SED into a 'new kind of party' along Soviet lines followed in January 1949 at the first party congress. By the time the GDR was established, the SED had become a Marxist-Leninist cadre party with no remaining ties to the traditions of social democracy—declaring, in fact, relentless war on 'social democratism'. The communist party calling itself the SED propagated 'democratic centralism', the total subjugation of all party subdivisions to their leaders, absolute party discipline, and the 'leadership role' of the Soviet Union. The GDR began its life as a totalitarian party dictatorship, and although the new state contained features that did not seem to fit this definition, they were, in fact, the result of a calculated effort to conceal the true aims of the Soviets and the SED.

The Parliamentary Council had looked at the recent history of Germany and learned 'anti-totalitarian' lessons from it. For the German People's Council, the only acceptable moral was an 'anti-fascist' one. Anti-fascism became the foundation myth of the GDR. It served as the justification for the founding of a new dictatorship, one that posed as the only true democratic government on German soil and as a guarantee against a relapse into barbarism. To speak of the Communist role in the rise of National Socialism would have been considered a kind of 'incitement to boycott'. The same was true of any reference to the fact that Stalin had had many more Communists killed than Hitler. Furthermore, a discussion of Stalin's role in unleashing the Second World War would have been regarded as 'propagation of national hatred', if not 'incitement to war'.

The GDR constitution spoke of Germany as an 'indivisible democratic republic'. This claim transcended the limits of the SOZ and embraced, in principle, all four occupation zones. In this sense, connections to the Weimar constitution had an eminently practical purpose. According to the official Soviet view, the GDR had not yet entered the phase of the 'building up of socialism' by the autumn of 1949; it was still in a period of transition, dedicated primarily to the anti-fascist revolution of society. The Soviet Union also continued to avoid calling the GDR a 'people's democracy'. If the reunification of the four occupation zones had proved feasible in a manner more congenial to Soviet interests than the status quo, the GDR regime would not have been sacrosanct. Thus the Federal Republic of Germany, the second German democracy, was not the only 'provisional' German government. That was also true, though in a different way, for the second dictatorship on German soil, the German Democratic Republic.[5]

THE CONTROVERSY OVER THE WESTERN ALLIANCE: THE FEDERAL REPUBLIC UP TO 1953

In 1956, when the Federal Republic had just turned seven years old, Fritz René Altmann published *Bonn ist nicht Weimar.** In this book the Swiss publicist recognized that one of the most basic differences between the first and second German democracies was to be seen in an astonishing role reversal between 'left' and 'right'. During the Weimar Republic the left had been internationalist, the right nationalist in outlook. In the new Bonn republic, the moderate forces of the centre right, represented by Konrad Adenauer's bourgeois coalition, pursued a politics of supra-national integration, while the moderate left, represented by

---

* Altmann, *Bonn is not Weimar*.

the Social Democrats under Kurt Schumacher and Erich Ollenhauer, assumed the nationalist role and styled themselves the party of German unity.

Accordingly, Adenauer did not have to contend with an anti-democratic 'national opposition', as there had been in Weimar, but with a simultaneously democratic, anti-communist, *and* national opposition on the left. If things had been otherwise, the FRG's western alliance would hardly have been possible. As it turned out, however, the nationalist politics of the Social Democrats were a veritable prerequisite for the success of Adenauer's trans-national policy. Needless to say, this dialectic was hardly a matter of conscious intention on the part of the actors at the time.

Adenauer's primary goal for the foreseeable future was to make the FRG a sovereign state firmly allied with the west as rapidly as possible. With this aim in mind, he pursued a kind of *Erfüllungspolitik* or 'fulfilment policy' with regard to the western powers in order to build up their confidence in the new West German nation. On 22 November 1949 he concluded the Petersberg Agreement with the High Commission. While this did not bring an immediate end—very much desired on the German side—to the dismantling of heavy industrial plant for reparations and de-militarization purposes, the Allies promised to restrict themselves to the remaining purely military facilities and to conclude as quickly as possible (in fact, they took until the middle of 1951). For his part, Adenauer permitted West Germany to join the International Ruhr Authority, in which, according to the Ruhr Statute of December 1948, the three western powers and the Benelux states exercised control over the mining and distribution of coal and steel from the Rhenish-Westphalian industrial area. Although this agreement rescued the largest German steelworks and tens of thousands of jobs, Schumacher was highly dissatisfied. In a dramatic extended Bundestag session on 24–5 November 1949, he yelled out a comment that went down in the annals of the Federal Republic, calling Adenauer the 'chancellor of the Allies'.

The following year Adenauer gave the opposition another opportunity to cast doubt on his 'national' values. At the end of March 1950, at the behest of French foreign minister Robert Schuman (a Christian Democrat from Lorraine), the ministers of the European Council (founded in 1949) invited West Germany and the Saar territory to become associated members. For the Social Democrats, this was an attempt to separate the Saarland from Germany once and for all. In their view it would also weaken Germany's claim to the territories east of the Oder and Neisse rivers. Similar arguments were raised inside the Union by Jakob Kaiser (CDU), federal minister 'for all-German affairs', as well as by two liberal members of the cabinet, vice chancellor and FDP leader Franz Blücher and his party colleague, Thomas Dehler, the minister of justice. For his part, Adenauer saw membership in the European Council as an opportunity to move closer to national sovereignty. He ultimately prevailed. On 15 June the Bundestag voted to make Germany an associate member of the European Council. The associate status reflected the rights and privileges of the Allies, and was transformed into full membership in May 1951. The Saarland remained an associate member.

On 9 May 1950 Paris presented the Federal Republic with a second, far more ambitious project: the so-called 'Schuman plan', drafted by Jean Monnet, the leader of the French 'Planning Office'. According to this project, France, West Germany, Italy, and the Benelux states would form a common market for coal and steel for a period of fifty years, thus clearing the way for a comprehensive economic and political unification of western Europe. The domestic-political fronts were the same as during the debate over European Council membership: the governmental coalition supported, the opposition rejected Monnet's plan. As a staunch European, Adenauer was in favour of it, since it promised to irrevocably link the FRG to the west. The 'nationalist' Schumacher, on the other hand, considered the restrictions on German sovereignty in coal and steel production to represent an unacceptable disadvantage for the new republic.

On 18 April 1951 the foreign ministers of the six participating nations, including Adenauer, who had taken over the leadership of the new foreign office a month before, met in Paris to sign the treaty founding the European Coal and Steel Community. The Bundestag ratified the treaty on 11 January 1952, against the votes of the Social Democrats. The International Ruhr Authority and the Ruhr Statute were now things of the past. The course was set towards an expansion of the European Coal and Steel Community into a European Economic Community (EEC).

The debates over the European Council and the European Coal and Steel Community were mild compared to the long and bitter controversy over the rearmament of West Germany. For Adenauer, there was never any doubt that the West German partnership with the west would have a military component. He had confederates on the other side of the Atlantic. In the autumn of 1949 the American army began thinking about West German forces as a way of counterbalancing the overwhelming numerical superiority of Soviet troops in Europe and as a western response to the paramilitary forces of the GDR, the so-called 'Garrisoned People's Police' (*Kasernierte Volkspolizei*), set up in spring 1948.

These deliberations entered an acute phase in the summer of 1950. On 25 June highly armed Communist North Korea attacked the southern part of the divided country. A wave of fear swept America and Europe; many people saw the events in the far east as a prelude to a third world war. Walter Ulbricht did everything in his power to stoke this fear. On 3 August he announced over Berlin radio:

Korea shows us that a marionette regime like the one in South Korea—or we can also say the one in Bonn—will sooner or later be swept away by the will of the people . . . But since the nations wish to preserve peace, the majority of every people will resist all acts of aggression on the part of the imperialist powers. And the struggle will be taken up by the patriotic forces of the people, and they will fight with all their power to liquidate the nests of war provocation. This is what is happening in South Korea at the present moment.

A rhetorical challenge from East Berlin was not necessary to set Konrad Adenauer thinking about the practical lessons of the Korean War. On 17 August he proposed to the High Commission that the FRG be empowered to establish a voluntary army of 150,000 troops. In response to a question from High Commissioner John McCloy, Adenauer agreed to a suggestion by Winston Churchill, now the leader of the opposition in Britain. On 11 August, speaking before the European Council in Strasbourg, Churchill had made the case for a European army, which was to include a German contingent. On 30 August the German chancellor had a 'security memorandum' summarizing his ideas handed to McCloy immediately prior to the latter's departure for Washington.

The cabinet did not have a chance to debate the chancellor's memo. On 31 August the ministers, with one exception, emphatically confirmed Adenauer's assessment of the situation and his proposals for a West German military contribution. The only one who disagreed was Gustav Heinemann, minister of the interior, the leading representative of the Evangelical minority in the Union, and head of the Synod of the Evangelical Church in Germany. Heinemann was strongly against any German rearmament, and on 9 October 1950 he resigned his government office.

The Protestant background of this protest was no coincidence. The Evangelical tie to the German Reich of 1871 was stronger than that of German Catholics. As a Catholic from the Rhineland, Adenauer had to face the suspicion of many Protestants that the main reason he was not strongly invested in the reunification of Germany was that it would shift the confessional balance against the Catholics and decrease the electoral strength of the CDU. Before 1933 pious Evangelicals were mostly to be found on the right, in the camp of the 'national opposition'. Now a part of them, so as to remain 'national', moved to the left. Heinemann himself was not a German Nationalist during the Weimar Republic; he was a Democrat, and as such an exception. His confederate Martin Niemöller, church president of Hesse-Nassau and director of the foreign office of the German Evangelical church, had travelled a long road from a First World War submarine commander to free corps fighter after 1918 to active opponent of Hitler. After 1945 he became a 'practical' pacifist. During all these shifts, however, he preserved his 'national' convictions. Even though he now committed himself to democracy, the western world and its political ideas remained basically alien to him, all the changes of government in Germany notwithstanding. 'The present-day West German form of government was conceived in Rome and born in Washington,' he told an American journalist at the end of 1949.

Heinemann and Niemöller spoke for a part of German Protestants. Other Evangelical leaders found their political home in the CDU. The most important of these was Otto Dibelius, the head of the Council of the Evangelical Church in

Germany and bishop of Berlin and Brandenburg. Dibelius had been a member of the German Nationalist party before 1933. Hermann Ehlers, the founder of the Evangelical Working Group of the CDU/CSU and president of the Bundestag, had joined the DNVP in 1931; in 1933 he had become active in the Christian-Social People's Service and thereafter, like Dibelius, in the Confessing Church. In the early 1950s Ehlers quickly became Heinemann's main opponent. The theologian Eugen Gerstenmaier, Bundestag representative for the CDU after 1949 and Ehler's successor as president of the parliament after the latter's untimely death in October 1954, hailed from the 'Kreisau circle' around Count Helmuth James von Moltke and had been condemned to a long prison term after 20 July 1944. If Heinemann and Niemöller stood for a 'leftward swing' among Protestants, Ehlers and Gerstenmaier represented an Evangelical turn towards 'conservative democracy'.

The rearming of Germany, opposed by the left Protestants, was also unpopular in the country as a whole at first. After the Third Reich and the Second World War, the German people had had enough of all things military. Moreover, they were afraid that new armed forces would increase the risk of war and further divide the Germans in the west from those in the east. The rejectionist attitude, characterized by the slogan *Ohne mich!* ('Not with me!'), was especially widespread among Social Democrats and unionized labour. While the head of the SPD, Kurt Schumacher, was not against rearmament in principle, he tied his vote for German participation in a European armed force to conditions the western powers were unable to fulfil—above all, to the acceptance of the FRG as a fully equal partner in the project.

Like Heinemann and Niemöller, Schumacher doubted Adenauer's commitment to German unity and rejected the military-political plans of the government. In terms of its organization, however, the opposition to the 're-militarization' remained split. The bourgeois camp was represented by the Emergency Community for Peace in Europe (*Notgemeinschaft für den Frieden Europas*), established in November 1951, and the All-German People's Party (*Gesamtdeutsche Volkspartei* or GVP), founded a year later. Both these groups were initiated by Heinemann, and neither enjoyed mass support. The Social Democratic wing was much stronger. After Schumacher's death in August 1952 and the election of Erich Ollenhauer as his successor a month later, the SPD drew even closer to the positions of the left-Protestant pacifists. By this time, however, the *Ohne mich!* attitude was already on the retreat.

By the autumn of 1950 the debate over the rearming of West Germany was also a debate over the formation of a European Defence Community (EDC). The French government, led by René Pleven, put forward this project (which, like the coal and steel union, originated with Jean Monnet) in October. The integration of separate national forces was to commence on the lowest possible level. For West Germany, this was the battalion. Bonn protested and, supported by the United States, succeeded in convincing Paris in December 1950 to begin the integration with the corps, that is, above the division level. In September 1951, while the EDC negotiations were being conducted, deliberations began over a general treaty to place the relations between the FRG and the three western powers on a new basis. All the while, the organizational preparations for the rearmament of Germany were proceeding apace, coordinated from the end of October 1950 by the 'Blank office', the nucleus of what was to become the ministry of defence. This office was named after its head, the CDU representative Theodor Blank. This politician was also one of the founders of the German Trade Union Association (*Deutscher Gewerkschaftsbund*, established in October 1949), a new unified union replacing the ideologically-oriented organizations of the Weimar Republic. In choosing Blank, Adenauer was attempting to gain the support of the workers, among whom resistance to the 're-militarization' was particularly strong.[6]

Stalin could not afford to look on the new developments in western Europe with complacency. A West Germany militarily allied to its western neighbours and the USA would jeopardize his plans to bring continental Europe under Soviet control. At first he delegated 'all-German' counter-measures to his vassals in East Berlin. The first campaign was initiated with such slogans as *Deutsche an einen Tisch!* ('Germans to one table!'). In November 1950 Otto Grotewohl, the prime minister of the GDR, sent a letter to Adenauer proposing a *Gesamtdeutscher Rat* ('All-German Council') with equal representation from both parts of divided Germany; its task would be to prepare for free elections throughout the whole country. Adenauer, speaking at a press conference on 15 January 1951, demanded free elections as a first step towards reunification. On 15 September of that year, the Volkskammer of the GDR appealed to the Bundestag to participate in deliberations for all-German elections and a peace treaty. The Bundestag responded on 27 September by proposing a procedure for free, all-German elections. One of the provisions was supervision by the United Nations, the successor to the League of Nations in June of 1945.

Moscow got directly involved about six months later. On 10 March 1952 the Soviet government sent a memorandum to the governments of France, the United Kingdom, and the United States suggesting that a peace treaty be drafted with direct German participation. The Four Powers would therefore have to 'examine the conditions under which a unified German government, which is what the German people desire, might be brought into existence as rapidly as possible'. According to the 'Political Guidelines' contained in the memorandum's draft of the peace treaty, Germany was to be given the opportunity of 'developing as an independent, democratic, peace-loving state'. 'Democratic parties and organizations' were to be guaranteed a free hand in the reunified country. Organizations 'opposed to democracy and the cause of peace and its preservation', on the other hand, would be banned. Germany would obligate itself 'to eschew membership in any kind of coalition or military alliance directed against any state that participated with its forces in the war against

Germany'. The territory of the country was to be 'fixed by the borders resolved upon at the Potsdam Conference of the great powers.' The 'Military Guidelines' permitted Germany 'to possess sufficient forces (land, air, and naval) for its own self-defence'.

The Soviet initiative on 10 March 1952 is one of the most debated events in the history of divided Germany. The basic question has remained the same over the years: did the west in general, and West Germany in particular, miss the historical opportunity of reunifying in peace and liberty? The most controversial issues are Stalin's intentions and the role of Konrad Adenauer. It is clear that the chancellor urged the western powers not to get involved in negotiations with the Soviets. Adenauer saw the Soviet move as an attempt to drive a wedge between the West Germans and the western Allies, thus undermining the policy of western integration. And in fact, the West Germans were the main addressees of the memorandum, formally directed at the Allies though it was.

If the Germans in the FRG had gone for the nationalist bait Stalin was throwing at them, he would have already achieved a considerable success. The negotiations over an integrated west European defence system would have stalled, and possibly failed entirely. Adenauer would not have survived such a blow politically. Precisely this was Stalin's near-term goal. The USA would have had a much tougher time dealing with a 'nationally' minded government in Bonn; the Soviets would have found it much easier. Ultimately, if the Germans had turned their backs on the western military project, the American position in western Europe as a whole would have been seriously compromised, and this was precisely what Stalin was trying to achieve.

Stalin was clearly not expecting a positive response from Washington, London, and Paris. He would not have to worry about negotiations that could compel him to abandon the GDR. Nonetheless, we can imagine a situation in which he might have accepted such an outcome. If, for the sake of reunification, a 'national' and 'peaceable' German government had been willing to go a long way towards meeting Soviet demands, Stalin himself would have granted it concessions. In his view, a neutral, Soviet-friendly unified Germany was greatly to be preferred to the status quo. It would have been within Soviet state interests to give up the SED's monopoly on power within the GDR. The abandonment of advanced positions would not have been permanent. What mattered was rendering American intervention impossible, securing the societal 'achievements' of the GDR, and shaping the 'democratic' order in Germany in such a way that the Communists would not be prevented from seizing power at some point in the future.

Adenauer entertained no doubts about the longer-term calculations of the Soviet dictator. 'The content of the note, at least, in no way surprised me,' he said on 27 April 1952 during a 'tea' with leading journalists. 'For a long time, my whole policy has proceeded from the assumption that it is the goal of Soviet Russia to destroy the integration of western Europe by neutralizing Germany . . . and, in such a way, to get the USA out of Europe and bring Germany, the Federal Republic, and, with them, Europe under his control.'

The term 'free elections' did not appear in the March note of the Soviets. The western powers emphasized it all the more in their responses later that month. An investigating committee (already appointed by the plenum assembly of the United Nations by this time) would have to ascertain whether 'the Federal Republic, the Soviet zone, and Berlin' already fulfilled the conditions of free elections. Additionally, the western powers demanded that a future united German government be at liberty to join alliances that accorded with the principles of the UN. The German borders could only be settled in a peace treaty. German national armed forces of the kind the Soviets envisioned would mean, in the view of the western powers, a step backward. The politics of European unification would not represent a threat to the interests of any external nation; rather, they were the true path to peace. Thus the identically worded memoranda of the Allied powers on 25 March.

In its rejoinder on 9 April, the Soviet Union now also spoke of the 'matter of holding free, all-German elections' discussed by the Four Powers. The issue would have to be looked into, not by a UN commission, but by one appointed by the Four Powers themselves. As far as the alliance problem and the finality of the German borders were concerned, Moscow repeated the position it had outlined in the first note. The diplomatic exchange lasted until September 1952, but no new matter of significance arose. On 23 September, the Allies suggested that a Four Powers conference be convened immediately to discuss free elections. The Soviets did not respond.

The 1952 exchange did not lead to any negotiations. The western powers and the FRG thought that, at this juncture, a Four Powers conference over Germany would have delayed, and thus endangered, the EDC project without contributing anything to the resolution of the German question, since the positions of the two sides were irreconcilable. None of the western powers desired German unification if it meant a neutral Germany. Such a solution threatened to clear the way for ultimate Soviet hegemony on the Continent. And for France, at least, the restoration of a German national state, under whatever conditions, was still a nightmare.

In West Germany, Gustav Heinemann and his Emergency Community for Peace in Europe saw the Soviet memoranda as the big opportunity to gain immediate reunification, as long as the government renounced the goals of rearmament and western integration. Speaking for the SPD, Kurt Schumacher demanded that the Soviet offer be explored in depth. Jakob Kaiser, the federal minister for all-German affairs, expressed himself similarly. But Adenauer stuck to his guns, insisting that the Soviets were merely engaging in disruptive tactics. Only after the western treaties were concluded would negotiations with Moscow over a peaceable and free unification be possible.

The chancellor had his way, but paid a high price. He unintentionally fostered the myth of the 'missed opportunity' of 1952. In addition to Heinemann, the publicist Paul Sethe, co-editor of the *Frankfurter Allgemeine Zeitung* in 1949–55, was especially active in propagating this idea. In his 1956 book *Zwischen Bonn und Moskau,** which found great resonance, Sethe argued that the reunification would have been possible had the FRG been firmly committed to it. On 23–4 January 1958, in a dramatic extended Bundestag session dedicated to the prospect of a nuclear-armed federal army, Heinemann (who had joined the SPD with many of his followers in 1957 after the dissolution of the All-German People's party) and Thomas Dehler, former minister of justice and former head of the FDP, sharply attacked Adenauer's treatment of the 1952 Stalin notes. The public effect of this critique was great, and all the greater for the neglect of Adenauer and the Union to respond quickly.

For the most part, the question of Stalin's long-term plans in 1952 was, and is, not something the defenders of the 'missed opportunity' argument discuss in great detail. They also tend to neglect the probable geostrategic effects of German neutrality. The problem of the German eastern border played virtually no role in the debate at the time. None of the parties in West Germany, with the exception of the KPD and the GVP, had prepared their voters for the possibility that the eastern territories might be lost forever. All of them were courting the votes of the more than 4.5 million expellees from the areas east of the Oder and Neisse rivers who were living in the FRG and Berlin. By this time the League of Expellees and Those Deprived of Rights (*Bund der Heimatvertriebenen und Entrechteten* or BHE), a refugee party founded in 1950, had become a powerful player in domestic politics. If Germany had been reunified in 1952, there would have been some 7.7 million expellees living in the territory of Germany, such as it was established in 1945. (This number includes those from the German settlement areas outside the 1937 borders of the German Reich.) The total population of Germany at this time was 70 million.

When, in a 1955 survey, representative West Germans were asked whether Adenauer should accept a hypothetical Soviet offer of German unification and free elections in exchange for the permanent renunciation of Silesia, Pomerania, and East Prussia, two thirds (67%) responded in the negative, only one-tenth (10%) in the positive. We must conclude, therefore, that a reunification within the 1945 borders would have run a great risk of provoking a radical nationalist reaction—the kind of reaction that, after 1918, had already destroyed one German democracy. If we consider both the probable internal and external effects of a reunification on the basis of the 1952 Soviet proposals, the claim of the 'missed opportunity' of that year collapses like a house of cards. Germany was not yet mature enough for a reunification within the 1945 borders. The western powers could not have paid the price Stalin was demanding for German

---

* Sethe, *Between Bonn and Moscow.*

reunification: the renunciation of the political and military integration of western Europe and its inclusion in the north Atlantic defence community. Adenauer's rejection of the Soviet advances was, in terms of domestic German politics, not without its own risks. But, all things considered, there was no realistic alternative.[7]

The Soviet notes had no effect on the policy of western integration. On 26 May 1952 the general treaty, now officially known as the 'Germany Treaty', was signed in Bonn by the foreign ministers of the USA, Great Britain, and France. The next day, the treaty establishing the European Defence Community was signed in Paris by the foreign ministers of France, the FRG, Italy, the Netherlands, Belgium, and Luxembourg. The Germany Treaty brought the occupation governments to an end and gave West Germany 'full authority in domestic and foreign affairs, except as provided in the present Convention'. This did not mean that the country had regained full sovereignty, however. The treaty still guaranteed certain rights and privileges to the Allies 'with regard to . . . Berlin and Germany as a whole, including the reunification of Germany and a peace settlement'. The Allies also enjoyed the right to station their troops in the FRG and to take measures for their security in the event of a domestic or international emergency. The final settlement of Germany's borders was to be postponed until a peace treaty could be concluded. Until that time, the treaty partners resolved to work towards a 'common aim': 'a unified Germany enjoying a liberal-democratic constitution, like that of the Federal Republic, and integrated within the European Community'.

The so-called 'binding clause' in Article 7, Paragraph 3 of the Germany Treaty caused a great deal of debate in West Germany. Written by Robert R. Bowie, the legal adviser of the American High Commissioner, it had been expressly adopted and approved by Adenauer. According to the original version, a reunited Germany would automatically enter into the rights and obligations imposed by the Germany Treaty and the treaties establishing an integrated European community. Critics from the ranks of the coalition thought this clause put the goal of German unity at risk; the Soviet Union, they argued, could never approve such a condition. In response to such objections, the clause was rewritten in somewhat attenuated language immediately prior to the signing. But its thrust remained clear: the new rights and privileges of the FRG would also be granted to a reunified Germany, provided the latter adopted the obligations of the May 1952 treaties. The FRG, in turn, promised to refrain from any agreements that violated the treaty.

This modification satisfied the critics of the CDU and FDP, but not those of the SPD, many of whom were against the treaty as a whole. In an interview on 15 May 1952, Schumacher rejected it so forcefully that his sensationalist rhetoric caused his own party considerable embarrassment: 'Whoever agrees to this treaty ceases to be a German!' Three months later, on 20 August 1952, the SPD leader died at the age of 56. Kurt Schumacher had shaped his party and, with it, the new Federal Republic of Germany, albeit in an oppositional role. It is possible that, without him, West Germany would not have even come about in the first place. His successful campaign against the unification of Social Democrats and Communists helped form the political foundation on which the new nation stood. In this way, he had made possible the very policies he fought against—though as a democrat, with parliamentary tools—after 1949.

On 19 March 1953, after passionate debate, the Bundestag passed the Germany Treaty and the treaties establishing the EDC at third reading. Two months later, on 15 May, the Bundesrat approved the ratification laws for the western treaties. This did not yet secure them as the law of the land, however. The Federal Constitutional Court (*Bundesverfassungsgericht*), which had been constituted on 28 September 1951 in Karlsruhe, was still examining a request for judicial review brought forward by the opposition on 11 May. The 'guardians of the constitution' would now have to decide whether Germany's military contribution to the western defence system violated the Basic Law, as the SPD argued. Until that decision was made, Theodor Heuss, the federal president, did not wish to sign the treaties (he had asked the court to review this matter the year before, but had then withdrawn his petition at Adenauer's urging).

The outcome of the treaties was unresolved for yet another reason: the EDC was also extremely controversial in France. The supporters of General Charles de Gaulle, head of the former government in exile in London and first premier of post-war France, were not the only ones who rejected a restriction of French sovereignty in favour of a supra-national organization in which the Germans were partners. The colonial war France was waging with increasing losses in Indochina put wind in the sails of the nationalist opposition at home. Moreover, Stalin's death on 5 March 1953 gave many in the west hope that his successors, led by Georgi Malenkov, would adopt a less aggressive course. France now felt less threatened by the Soviet Union, and its interest in an integrated west European military force diminished correspondingly. In spring 1953 the fate of the European Defence Community was more uncertain than ever.[8]

THE EXPANSION OF THE DICTATORSHIP AND THE BUILDING OF SOCIALISM: THE GDR UP TO 1953

While the Federal Republic was moving ever closer to the western democracies, the GDR was modeling itself on the example of the Communist dictatorship that had been developed in the Soviet Union over the course of more than three decades. By the time the GDR was founded in October 1949, the non-Communist parties had been largely, though not entirely, made subject to the control of the SED. At the beginning of 1950 the Communists started to come down hard on 'bourgeois' politicians who rebelled against the 'bloc' system. The most prominent of these, Hugo Hickmann, deputy head of the eastern CDU, was stripped of his public duties and thrown out of his party at the end of January. On 8 February the regime took the next step in its fight against oppositional tendencies and in its effort to enforce conformity. A Ministry for State Security (*Ministerium für Staatssicherheit*, also known as the MfS or Stasi) was added to the government. It was headed by Wilhelm Zaisser, former agent of Soviet military intelligence, member of the KPD from 1919, and chief of staff in the International Brigade (under the name 'General Gomez') during the Spanish Civil War.

At the end of April 1950 the 'Waldheim trials' commenced, in which the remaining inmates of the Soviet 'special camps' (shut down shortly beforehand) were prosecuted. The 3,300 accused included not only former National Socialists and war criminals, but political 'enemies' of all stripes, 157 of whom had belonged to the SPD before 1933, 55 to the KPD. There were death sentences for 31, and 24 were executed on 4 November 1950. The only ones who had a defender were those prosecuted in a series of ten show trials. There was no presentation of evidence to speak of. The purpose of the trials was deterrence and intimidation, and this purpose could only be accomplished by using the judicial system in terms of its 'class mission' and as an instrument of terror.

In order to do justice to its revolutionary claims and meet the expectations of the Bolshevist mother party in the Soviet Union, the SED also found it necessary to use terror against 'party enemies' within its own ranks. Regular 'purges' were a first step. During the 'party examination' of 1950–1, the SED threw out some 150,000 of its members for 'lack of reliability' or for non-conformity to the party line. Among the victims was Paul Merker, a long-time Communist and member of the politburo. Merker had deviated from Stalin's 'anti-Zionist' policy (directed against the state of Israel and Jewish communists) by demanding that the SED redress National Socialist injustices against the Jews. He was expelled from the party in August 1950 on account of past connections to an alleged 'American agent', Noel Field. In December 1952 Merker was himself arrested as an 'agent'.

In 1953 the SED was preparing to follow the example of other communist states and conduct a show trial against Merker and other former high functionaries accused of cooperating with, or not being sufficiently on guard against, 'imperialist agents'. The changes at the head of the Soviet Communist party after Stalin's death in March 1953 put an end to this plan. Show trials were now no longer seen as an appropriate form of 'socialist lawfulness'. Nonetheless, Merker was not released from prison until 1956.

The first elections to the Volkskammer were held in October 1950, one year after the GDR was founded. The only candidates on the ballot were those on the unified list of the National Front of Democratic Germany. This meant that the percentage of the vote that went to individual parties and mass organizations—the Free German Trade Union Association (*Freier Deutscher Gewerkschaftsbund* or FDGB) being by far the largest of these, with 4.7 million members—was set from the beginning. The outcome was typical of a 'people's democracy'. With a turnout of 98 per cent of the electorate, 99.7 per cent voted for the unified list. The legislative agenda was set by the leading party. In terms of economic policy, this meant that the level of production in 1955 was to be double that of 1936. The economic methods used would be those developed by the Soviets. This was the essence of the first five year plan of the GDR, drafted by the third party congress of the SED in July 1950 and explicated by Walter Ulbricht. On 25 July Ulbricht was elected general secretary by the new central committee. Only two former Social Democrats remained in the politburo.

According to the official terminology, the policies proposed and pursued by the SED in 1950 did *not* represent the 'building of socialism'. In Stalin's view the GDR was still involved in the process of anti-fascist and democratic revolution and was not to declare this phase complete as long as the Soviet Union wished to maintain German reunification as an option. The 1952 diplomatic exchange changed all that. Reunification was now no longer a Soviet aim, strategic or tactical. Therefore, at its second party conference in July 1952, the SED was able to proclaim what Ulbricht had wanted to pursue much earlier, the methodical *Aufbau des Sozialismus*, 'building of socialism'.

By the time of its inauguration, the GDR could no longer be considered a 'capitalist' society. Private ownership of industry had been largely eliminated by 1949, if not entirely so. The number of Publicly Owned Enterprises (*Volkseigene Betriebe* or VEBs) rose from 1,764 in the middle of that year to 5,000 in 1950. Between 1950 and 1951 the percentage of gross industrial production from state-owned and cooperatively organized businesses climbed from 73.1 per cent to 79.2 per cent. In addition, most of the Soviet joint-stock companies were placed under German management. By the time the second party conference announced the 'building of socialism', state companies already controlled the economy of the GDR. July 1952 marks a caesura in only one way: after this date the SED, following the Soviet model, concentrated its efforts on accelerating the building up of heavy industry. It did this despite the lack of raw materials and without regard to the appropriateness of the sites chosen. The consequences were, on the one hand, neglect of consumer goods production and a resulting decrease in the living standard, and, on the other hand, the inability of the country's new industrial sector to compete effectively on the international market. 'The "building of socialism" in the GDR', as the historian Hermann Weber writes, 'did not mean the realization of new ideas, but adoption of the obsolete Stalinist system.'

The dissolution of the five *Länder*—Saxony, Saxony-Anhalt, Thuringia, Mecklenburg, Brandenburg—and their replacement by fourteen districts (*Bezirke*) was also part of the 'building of socialism', such as the SED conceived it. This centralization was to permit more effective planning and taxation as well as to counteract forms of regional consciousness that went back to the Middle Ages. Still older were the Christian traditions espoused by a considerable proportion of the population, if not the majority. About four-fifths of the citizens of the GDR belonged to the Evangelical church in 1950, at least nominally. The SED took aim at the ties of church and religion, especially among young people, who were to be systematically re-educated. This was the task it set for the Free German Youth (*Freie Deutsche Jugend* or FDJ) in its campaign against the Young Community (*Junge Gemeinde*) of the Evangelical church. This battle came to a head in spring 1953 with the arrest of 50 priests and laymen and the expulsion of 300 student members of the Young Community from their schools.

The restructuring of the education system went forward at the same time. The primary and secondary schools were assigned the task of preparing students for the 'building of socialism', both ideologically and in the development of polytechnic knowledge and skills. At the universities, Sovietology, the fundamentals of Marxism-Leninism, and Russian language were obligatory subjects. There were still many 'bourgeois' professors, including some who had been members of the NSDAP before 1945. However, in the ideologically most important subjects—philosophy, history, education, law, and economics—reliable Marxist-Leninists replaced traditional scholars and teachers at an increasing rate. Criticism of the SED was dangerous for teachers and students alike, and anyone who engaged in it risked more than just his or her university education.

The most visible result of the 'building of socialism' was the increase in the number of those who fled the country. In the first half of 1952 some 70,000 people left the GDR; the figure was 111,000 for the second half of the year. The number rose dramatically with the new year: 180,000 people turned their backs on the GDR in the first five months of 1953. Economically speaking, flight was an especially dangerous form of protest against the declining living standard and political repression. Stalin's successors in Moscow—Malenkov, head of the party and government; Beria, head of security; and Molotov, the foreign minister—were so alarmed at the crisis in the GDR that they decided the state could only be saved through a drastic change of course, that is, by renouncing the methodical 'building of socialism'. In spring 1953 Beria seems to have seriously contemplated abandoning the GDR in favour of a neutral unified Germany.

The SED believed that a 10 per cent increase in industrial production levels would allow the country to overcome its economic difficulties. This policy, promulgated in May 1953, immediately provoked great unrest in the factories and led to a further increase in emigration. Shortly thereafter, the GDR leaders were summoned to Moscow and confronted with demands for a 'new course'. Among other things, the party was ordered to be more flexible, especially with the churches and the small business class.

On 9 June 1953 the 'new course' was passed in the politburo. The government (called the *Ministerrat* or Council of Ministers) transformed it into concrete measures two days later. The party leadership spoke in a self-critical manner, citing 'mistakes' it had made during the 'building of socialism'. It promised to develop the consumer goods industry, loosen restrictions on travel between the two parts of Germany, and create legal certainty. Recent price increases were rescinded. The May production increases were maintained, however.

For the workers, the 'new course' was a slap in the face. While other social strata were promised relief, the working class, which was supposed to be *the* ruling class in the GDR, was subject to increased exploitation. Protest demonstrations began on 11–12 June, and strikes broke out in some places. On 16 June construction workers in the Stalinallee in East Berlin proceeded to the Leipziger Strasse, where the building that housed the government ministries (the former Reich aviation ministry building) was located. They demanded not only the repeal of the new production decrees, but also the resignation of the government and free elections. The politburo announced that the obligatory production increases had been incorrect and were therefore null and void. But this would no longer satisfy the demonstrators. On 17 June hundreds of thousands of people took to the streets in Berlin and in many large cities of the GDR. The strike of the Berlin construction workers turned into a general workers' uprising throughout the country. Social protest grew into a political movement for free elections and German unity. Farmers took part in the demonstrations in many places, often long into July. This was the first mass uprising against a communist government since 1945.

Since the GDR did not possess the means to deal with the situation, the Soviets intervened. Soviet tanks were deployed in Berlin on the first day of the unrest. Between 60 and 80 demonstrators were killed throughout the country, 18 of them summarily executed by the Soviet army. On the side of the regime, between 10 and 15 members of the security and police force died in the conflict. The story that several Soviet soldiers were executed for refusal to obey orders is probably untrue. Between 10,000 and 20,000 protestors were arrested by the Soviets, some 13,000 more by the GDR authorities.

In the weeks before the rebellion, Walter Ulbricht's days as leader of the GDR had seemed to be numbered. But things turned out differently. On 26 June 1953 Beria was overthrown in Moscow, and he was shot in December. With the death of the head of Soviet security, Ulbricht's enemies in the party lost their most important ally. They grew correspondingly weaker, while the SED general secretary was able to consolidate his position. At the end of July the two most important members of the anti-Ulbricht faction, Wilhelm Zaisser, the security minister, and Rudolf Herrnstadt, editor-in-chief of *Neues Deutschland*, the central mouthpiece of the SED, were removed from their positions. They and other 'oppositional' members of the central committee were thrown out of the party in January 1954. In the ensuing months the SED and FDGB were subject to large-scale 'purges'.

One of the most important lessons the SED learned from the uprising on 17 June 1953 involved the development of a comprehensive network of informers and spies. An army of formal and informal collaborators was assigned the task of making sure that nothing escaped the 'party of the working class' that might represent a risk. The 'new course' in the economy was maintained, leading to a gradual rise in the standard of living. But the SED failed to stem the flight of its citizens from the country. For the greater part of the population, the events of summer 1953 left traumatic memories. Rebellion against the Communist dictatorship had provoked first a bloodbath, then a worsening of repression. Widespread hopes that the west would come to the aid of the demonstrators were disappointed. Among those who continued to oppose the regime but did not want to leave the GDR, there was consensus on one point: they had no desire to repeat the experiences of 17 June 1953.[9]

ADENAUER'S SUCCESSES: THE ECONOMIC MIRACLE AND THE PARIS TREATIES

In West Germany the events of June 1953 confirmed the image the parties and most of the population had of the 'eastern zone' and its occupying power. No attempt was made to intervene, neither by the West German government nor—despite all the 'rollback' rhetoric—the new Republican administration in Washington under President Dwight D. Eisenhower and his Secretary of State, John Foster Dulles. On 3 July 1953 the Bundestag resolved to honour the rebels in the GDR by declaring 17 June a national holiday, the 'Day of German Unity' (*Tag der deutschen Einheit*). The corresponding law went into effect on 4 August.

The new national holiday was not one of triumphal celebration, of course, but of defeat and loss. It memorialized the failure of the striking workers and protesting farmers of the GDR in their first battle for liberty and unity. But they *had* fought, and for the Bundestag, it was important that Germans in both parts of the divided country be continually reminded on 17 June that the goal of national unity and liberty, codified in the preamble to the Basic Law, was still obligatory. It would remain the guiding principle of *the* German state, which, as a democracy, was both entitled and compelled to consider itself responsible for the Germans living under dictatorial rule in the GDR, and to act accordingly. This, at least, was how the West German political parties viewed the task of their state—with the exception of the KPD. The West German Communists adopted the interpretation of the SED, according to which the uprising on 17 June 1953 was 'a putsch organized by provocateurs working inside and outside the state'.

While the democratic parties made a common pledge to honour the rebels, they nonetheless interpreted their actions very differently. For Konrad Adenauer, the events in the GDR confirmed his policies. 'Reunification and European cohabitation are necessary parts of one and the same policy,' he told the

Bundestag on 1 July. During the same debate, the Berlin SPD delegate Willy Brandt emphasized the role of the striking workers. They had 'proven themselves not only as partners in the struggle for unity and liberty, but as the avant-garde in the battle'. Ten days later, the youth organization of the Free Democrats used 17 June as an occasion to celebrate their 'fidelity to the Reich' at the Lübeck–Eichholz checkpoint. A year later 20,000 FDP supporters came together at the Hermann memorial in the Teutoberg forest 'to honour in nocturnal celebration the nation's fallen soldiers and to pledge our fidelity to an indivisible German Reich'. An illustrated pamphlet on the event was entitled 'The Reich will come!' (*Das Reich wird kommen!*)

Of a more non-partisan quality were the activities of 'Germany Indivisble' (*Kuratorium Unteilbares Deutschland*), founded in mid-June 1954 at the instigation of Jakob Kaiser, minister for all-German affairs (the organization's name was proposed by President Heuss). This group coordinated commemorative events in major West German cities every year on 17 June. It organized memorial bonfires on the evening of 16 June at the border between Lübeck and Hof. One of its donation collection campaigns involved selling millions of badges with an image of the Brandenburg Gate.

In the words of the historian Edgar Wolfrum, 'Germany Indivisible' celebrated the 'cult of the German national state'—a national state in the borders of 1937. In the 1950s and early 1960s the organization, with subdivisions on the regional and district level, represented something like the ruling opinion of West Germany's 'political class'. *One* politician showed conspicuous reservation, however: the chancellor. It was true that on 22 June 1953 Adenauer gave a speech in front of the Schöneberg city hall in which, by means of a pathos-laden oath, he reiterated his commitment to the goal of Germany's reunification in peace and liberty. Nevertheless, the kinds of ambitions his party colleagues Jakob Kaiser and Johann Gradl, as well as Social Democrats like Herbert Wehner, pursued with 'Germany Indivisible' were, to Adenauer's mind, too strongly reminiscent of Bismarck's Reich and not sufficiently European in character. And so he kept his distance. If his westernizing policies required a flanking rhetoric of nationalism, he wanted to be the one to determine both its volume and its vocabulary.

It was not difficult to predict that the outcome of the 17 June 1953 uprising in the GDR would benefit the Bonn coalition more than the opposition in the upcoming elections. Adenauer, who had persevered in emphasizing the Soviet threat even after the death of Stalin, saw his views confirmed by the intervention of the Red Army. Moreover, by the summer of 1953, the rearmament policy was not nearly as controversial as it had been in the previous years. In April 1951 Adenauer had managed to separate the labour unions from the ranks of the rearmament opponents by sponsoring a bill requiring equal representation of workers on the boards of coal and steel companies. Fear of a third world war also receded after UN troops under American command had driven the communist invaders from the north out of the southern part of the Korean peninsula. On

27 June 1953 an armistice was concluded at Panmunjom establishing the 38th parallel as the border between North and South Korea.

The effects of the 'Korea boom' outlasted the Korean War. The conflict in the far east had increased the worldwide demand for weapons, most of which were produced in the United States, Britain, and France. The satisfaction of this demand created shortfalls in other areas, most notably in the kinds of investment goods exported by West Germany. This connection between the Korean War and the German economy is eloquently analysed by the modern German historian Hans-Peter Schwarz.

West Germany . . . which was still strictly forbidden to produce any kind of armament, was now, aided by the international demand, able to concentrate on the reconstruction of its peacetime industry and recapture lost markets. That is, the Korean War made all things possible during these years: not only German sovereignty and a German army, but also, at least in part, the economic miracle.

What people at the time called the 'economic miracle' (*Wirtschaftswunder*) was the beginning of an unprecedented period of prosperity, the longest in the history of the German economy. The unemployment figures in West Germany decreased continually after 1950, while the number of employed steadily rose. Economic growth allowed the progressive integration of the refugees from the east into West German society and financed the programme of financial compensation (*Lastenausgleich*) that accelerated this process. The steadily strong economy weakened the kind of rightist radicalism the expellees and their organizations would have been susceptible to under economically less favourable circumstances. The effect on the left was similar: economic prosperity, the development of worker co-determination in the factories, and the negative example so manifest in the GDR during this period combined to undermine whatever support the Communists still enjoyed among the West German working class.

The social consequences of the 1950s 'economic miracle' were much more significant than all the changes that had taken place during the Weimar Republic and the Third Reich. The proportion of self-employed and agricultural workers decreased, while the percentage of non-independent workers rose, above all in the service sector. This transformation also meant a shift in importance from wage labour to salaried employment. The triumphal march of television and the increasing motorization of society helped break up what remained of the formerly segregated 'socio-moral milieus' of traditional German society. By the middle of the 1950s there was very little left of a proletarian class consciousness. The pre-industrial elites, still strong in Weimar Germany, were also gone by this time. Confessional differences had lost their old sharpness. The much-discussed idea of a 'levelled middle-class society', put forward by the sociologist Helmut Schelsky in 1956, was a rhetorical exaggeration, at least as far as the distribution of wealth was concerned. Still, the term did express something important. Never before had the values of a middle-class *juste milieu* reigned as supreme in German society as in the Federal Republic during the age of Adenauer.[10]

In the campaign for the 1953 federal elections, Adenauer was able to appeal to the widespread feeling that under his leadership the Germans in the west were making progress again, and not only in a materialist sense. The chancellor enjoyed a high reputation in western Europe and the United States. He was considered a reliable friend of the western world, far more reliable than the Social Democratic opposition under Schumacher's successor Erich Ollenhauer. In Washington, London, and Paris, it was believed that the Social Democrats might succumb to the temptations of a seesaw policy between west and east. Even the Jewish World League and Israel respected Adenauer as the representative of a new Germany. He had given his support to programmes of financial compensation for the surviving victims of Nazi crimes and to the Israeli state. This won him personal trust and respect, feelings that were gradually transferred to West Germany as a whole.

The chancellor's first official visit to the United States in April 1953 was a huge success. President Eisenhower received him at the White House with the highest honours. A military band played the 'Deutschlandlied' at a wreath-laying ceremony in Arlington National Cemetery. (The 'Deutschlandlied' had been made the Federal Republic's national anthem in May 1952, after a correspondence between the chancellor and the federal president; the government explicitly promised that only the third stanza, invoking 'unity and right and freedom for the German fatherland', would be sung at official events.)

On 6 September 1953, five months after his triumphal visit overseas, Adenauer emerged comfortably victorious from the second federal elections. The parties of the Union gained 45.2% of the vote, 14.2% more than in 1949. The Social Democrats achieved 28.8%, a loss of .3%. The Free Democrats also suffered losses, falling from 11.9% to 9.5%. The All-German Bloc/BHE, the party of the expellees, was also successful, taking 5.9% in its first election. The German party was one of the losers, down from 4.0% to 3.3%. Although a 5 per cent clause was in effect throughout the country by this time, the DP was able to secure ten Bundestag seats by means of direct mandates they had gained through agreements with the CDU at the district level.

Heinemann's All-German People's party failed to meet this goal, managing only 1.2% of the vote. One of the reasons for the debacle was that the GVP had made a pre-election alliance with the League of Germans, led by former Reich chancellor Joseph Wirth. Though Heinemann did not know it at the time, this organization was a 'fifth column' of the GDR and Soviet Union and was being financed by East Berlin. The openly communist KPD also failed to reach the 5% mark, gaining only 2.2%, 3.5% less than in 1949. At the time of the election, the Federal Constitutional Court was still reviewing a ban on the KPD, lodged by the government in November 1951. Another organization, the radical right-wing Socialist Reich Party (*Sozialistische Reichspartei* or SRP), whose interdiction the

Adenauer government had also sought in November 1951, was already illegal by election time. The court declared it unconstitutional and ordered its dissolution in October 1952.

The election outcome contained a great opportunity for Adenauer: if he took the BHE into the coalition, his government would have the two-thirds majority necessary to amend the constitution. The Constitutional Court had not yet pronounced on the constitutionality of the West German military contribution, and since it was by no means certain that the decision would go the way of the government, it made sense to bring the expellee party on board. However, the BHE was led by two politicians with National Socialist backgrounds: Waldemar Kraft, the party head, a former member of the General SS, and Theodor Oberländer, the 'strong man' of the party, who had participated in Hitler's 'march to the Feldherrnhalle' in 1923, had become a party member in May 1933 and later a SA *Obersturmführer*, and had been discharged from the Wehrmacht in 1943 for his criticism of the policies against the 'eastern peoples'. But Adenauer, for the sake of his higher goals, disregarded Kraft's and Oberländer's political biographies and brought both of them into his cabinet, Oberländer as minister of expellees, Kraft as minister for special assignments.

Before the elections, Adenauer had agreed to a Four Powers conference on Germany, a meeting that Churchill, who became British prime minister again in 1951, was especially eager to convene. Between 25 January and 18 February 1954 the foreign ministers of the 'Big Four', Dulles, Molotov, Eden, and Bidault, met in Berlin. From the beginning, it was highly improbable that there would be any kind of breakthrough. The west, in conjunction with the West German parliament and government, demanded free elections throughout Germany before the German question could be resolved. The Soviet side proposed that the Bundestag and Volkskammer form a provisional unified German government before the elections. These were then made conditional on a number of provisions that, for the west, cast doubt on Moscow's idea of 'free' elections. Moreover, Molotov demanded that unified Germany be neutral or that both German states participate in a system of collective security.

Both solutions were calculated to hamper the integration of western Europe and push the United States out of Europe. The Soviet foreign minister will not have expected the west to take up either one of them. In fact, the only purpose of the Berlin conference was to justify decisions long since taken. Moscow was resolved to hold on to the GDR. The western powers intended to persevere in the integration of western Europe, including West Germany. Both sides knew that the German question could not be resolved under such circumstances. But both found it expedient to show 'their' Germans that the other side was to blame for the negative outcome of the conference.

On 26 February 1954, one week after the end of the Berlin conference, the Bundestag approved the 'first military supplement' to the Basic Law with the votes of the coalition. This did not yet clear the way for rearmament, however, which could only commence in the agreed way after France had approved the European Defence Community treaty. In spring 1954 the prospect that *Assemblée Nationale* would do this was increasingly unlikely. On 7 May the fortress of Dien Bien Phu fell into the hands of the Vietnamese Communists under Ho Chi Minh. Five weeks later, on 12 June, the Laniel government collapsed in Paris. On 20 July, at the east Asia conference in Geneva, the new French prime minister, the Radical Socialist Pierre Mendès-France, concluded an armistice in Indochina and agreed to the provisional partition of Vietnam. After the ignominious defeat in Indochina, the EDC had no chance. The French parliament and public sphere had come to be dominated by forces that rejected any compromise of French military sovereignty. On 30 August 1954, by means of petition on a point of order, a large majority in the French National Assembly voted against the EDC. The military integration of western Europe had failed. The question of West German armed forces was wide open once again.

For Adenauer, who had identified himself so thoroughly with the European Defence Community, 30 August 1954 was a serious defeat. In the second volume of his memoirs, published in 1966, he was still speaking about it as a 'dark day for Europe'. However, just a few weeks after the debacle, it turned out that the French decision brought the chancellor a good deal closer to another of his goals, full German sovereignty. The USA and Great Britain had long been thinking very seriously about a national alternative to the supra-national arrangements for West German security. This alternative was direct West German membership in NATO. As far as European integration was concerned, this would be a step backwards. In terms of German national equality, however, it represented an advance. France, which up to this point had always rejected the idea of national German armed forces and, given the choice, would have continued to do so, could now, after 30 August 1954, no longer avoid the logic of its own decision. The rejection of the EDC made the integration of West Germany in the Atlantic alliance inevitable.

Meeting in London at the end of September and beginning of October 1954, the six EDC states, Great Britain, the USA, and Canada drafted the outlines of the new security system. They were put into the legal language of the Paris treaties between 19 and 23 October. In order to allow France a certain degree of control over the armed forces of its eastern neighbour and, at the same time, satisfy the wishes of the staunch advocates of European integration, the Brussels Pact of 1948 between Great Britain, France, and the Benelux nations was expanded to include West Germany and Italy and renamed the West European Union (WEU). Much more important was the invitation for Germany to join NATO. Bonn's military contribution to the Atlantic alliance was to be a contingent of twelve divisions. The question of the level at which the integration of German forces would begin remained unresolved in Paris. This decision fell to the NATO commanders in Europe, who commenced with the army corps and the air fleets.

The Germany Treaty of 1952 was subject to a partial revision by the three western powers in Paris. The new version granted West Germany 'the full powers of a sovereign state over its internal and external affairs'. The controversial *Bindungsklausel*, which would have committed a reunified Germany to the western treaties, was quietly eliminated. (After the Berlin conference, further 'attractive' offers with regard to German unity were hardly to be expected from Moscow.) The language declaring the end of the occupation statute and regime was kept, as were the privileges of the three western powers 'in regard to Berlin and Germany as a whole'. The Allied rights under conditions of internal and external emergency were to be valid until the German legislature came up with a suitable solution for such situations. German military equality as a member of NATO and WEU was subject to one restriction: the FRG promised to forgo the manufacture of atomic, biological, and chemical weapons (the so-called 'ABC' weapons) on its own soil, as well as a number of other heavy weapons like guided missiles, warships beyond a particular size, and strategic bombers. It was Adenauer himself who, at the nine powers conference in London on 1 October, had cleared the way for the 'NATO solution' with this improvised condition—the only 'solitary decision' he ever made, as he later wrote.

The most controversial issue in German domestic politics was the provisional solution given in Paris to the Saarland question. Until the conclusion of a peace treaty, the territory was to have an autonomous status inside the West European Union, and its monetary and customs policies were to remain connected with those of France. The population of the Saar was granted the right to hold a referendum on the statute. Paris was not alone in believing that the outcome would be positive; Adenauer, too, thought this likely. But he was willing to subordinate the German claim to the Saar to his higher goals: the sovereignty of the FRG, its permanent integration into the west, and the political unification of western Europe.

Before the Bundestag commenced the ratification of the Paris treaties, the Soviet Union made a final attempt to set West German public opinion against western integration. On 15 January 1955 TASS, the Soviet news agency, announced Moscow's willingness to allow free elections in all of Germany within the year, thus permitting the formation of a unified Germany as a great power, provided that the Bundestag reject the Paris treaties. A diplomatic campaign like that in spring of 1952 did not take place, however—an indication that the Kremlin neither believed in the chances of its own initiative nor, in all likelihood, had any real interest in negotiations with the west. On 25 January the Soviet Union officially ended the state of war with Germany. On 8 February Molotov, who retained the post of foreign minister in the new government of Nikolai Aleksandrovich Bulganin (which came to power that same day), once again emphasized the Soviet position: if the Paris treaties were ratified, the reunification of Germany would no longer be possible.

The enticements and threats from Moscow were not without effect. Speaking for the SPD, Erich Ollenhauer wrote in a letter to Adenauer on 23 January 1955 that the Paris treaties could not be ratified until a serious attempt had been made to convene a Four Powers conference for the purpose of negotiating German unification under conditions of political liberty. As in the years before, well-known Protestants like Heinemann, Niemöller, and the Berlin theologian Helmut Gollwitzer raised their voices against Adenauer's policies. On 29 January 1955 Social Democrats and nationalist Protestants met together in the restored Paulskirche in Frankfurt and presented a 'German manifesto' to the public. But this call to form a popular movement against rearmament and the western treaties met with far less resonance than the earlier campaigns against the 're-militarization'. The Bundestag passed the Paris treaties by a large majority on 27 February 1955. The vote on the Saarland statute, however, split the coalition. Together with the BHE, a majority of Free Democrats, led in parliament by Thomas Dehler, former minister of justice, voted against the statute. It was passed nonetheless. The Bundesrat ratified the treaties on 8 March.

The new Germany Treaty and the other Paris treaties entered into effect on 5 May 1955. The Federal Republic of Germany was now a sovereign power in all areas except those stipulated in the agreements. Theodor Blank, up to this point the security commissioner, became the first federal defence minister on 6 May. On 7 May Germany joined the WEU, and on 9 May NATO. Adenauer relinquished the office of foreign minister to the CDU/CSU parliamentary leader, Heinrich von Brentano, on 7 June.

The chancellor had attained the goal he had been striving for so persistently since 1949: to make the Federal Republic an equal partner in the alliance of free western powers. Already at the beginning of October 1954, after his return from the nine powers conference in London, he had spoken to the CDU executive about sending an appropriate ambassador to Moscow after the ratification of the treaties. 'Then we will have regained the status a great power must have. We can then rightly say that we are once again a great power.' To the extent that this term was applied to Great Britain and France, it was certainly true of West Germany.

Two of the chancellor's other aims were still far off. The failure of the EDC had plunged the political integration of western Europe into crisis, and it was doubtful whether the kind of supra-nationalism Adenauer desired was going to be possible. Up to this point, the restoration of German unity had *not* been one of his immediate goals. But he was firmly convinced that reunification would one day become reality if the west demonstrated to the Soviet Union sufficient firmness and resolve.

The Germany he had in mind would not be an independent national state pursuing a seesaw policy between east and west. He did not desire this kind of Germany. 'It was necessary, then as before, that Europe unite,' he wrote in the section of his memoirs dealing with the failure of the European defence project.

'It was necessary that the Federal Republic, that Germany remain firmly allied to the free west after reunification.' This remained the guiding principle of the chancellor's policy even after 1955. Adenauer thought in long time periods, and the setbacks he experienced could not shake his belief that history would prove him right.[11]

THE NAZI PAST AND CONSERVATISM IN THE EARLY FRG

On 8 May 1949, four years after the unconditional surrender of the German Reich, Theodor Heuss told the Parliamentary Council that, basically, 8 May 1945 would remain 'the most tragic and questionable paradox for us . . . since we were rescued and destroyed at the same time.' In the first years of the new nation, too, West Germans' relationship to their own recent past remained ambivalent. On the one hand they condemned Hitler and his rule. On the other hand they felt that only a few men in the top echelons of the party and the SS were really guilty. Those below the highest level who had done wrong could expect to meet with understanding and, to the extent they had committed punishable offences, with leniency. The two laws providing for immunity from prosecution, of 31 December 1949 and 17 July 1954, were both passed by the Bundestag with overwhelming majorities.

The contradiction between denial and apologetics was seldom as clear as on 11 May 1951, when two very different pieces of legislation entered into force: one redressing National Socialist injustices against members of the civil service, and another implementing Article 131 of the Basic Law. The 'clientele' of the first law were those who had been persecuted for political or racial reasons. That of the second was mostly former National Socialists who had been removed from the civil service after 1945 and whose former positions were now restored.

Countless Germans in leadership positions throughout society had cooperated with Hitler, of course, and many were accused of serious war crimes. All efforts of the Allies to call them to account met with broad resistance, both before and after 1949. The attitude was 'my country, right or wrong'. The only 'warranted' condemnations were those handed down against the most important war criminals by the International Military Tribunal in Nuremberg in October 1946. The industrialist and diplomats prosecuted in the ensuing Allied trials already enjoyed broad sympathy among the population. The secretary of the foreign office between 1938 and 1943, Ernst von Weizsäcker, condemned to seven years in prison at the 'Wilhelmstrasse trial' in April 1949, was long considered innocent by this time, and was even thought of by some as a member of the 'resistance'. In October 1950, after massive pressure from politicians, church leaders, and publicists, John McCloy, the American High Commissioner, allowed him to be released from the prison at Landsberg.

Even former members of the armed forces of the Reich who had been condemned for war crimes could count on the solidarity of large sections of German
public opinion, especially from the churches. Allied trials against former German
soldiers and, at the same time, western demands for military support—soldiers'
organizations were not alone in finding these two things incompatible. The
campaigns were successful. In 1952–3 Field Marshals Kesselring, Mackensen,
and Manstein were released from prison in Werl. At the end of June 1953 the
chancellor paid a visit to the remaining inmates in that facility, among them
General Nikolaus von Falkenhorst and SS-General Kurt Meyer, known as 'Tank
Meyer' (*Panzer-Meyer*). The nominal purpose of Adenauer's visit was to enquire
about the prison conditions in Werl. A few days later he received Erich von
Manstein in his office at the Schaumburg Palace in Bonn. The effect of these
pointed gestures on the outcome of the 1953 federal elections cannot be precisely
calculated, but even at the time they were believed to have helped the Union
parties in no small measure.

The loudest voices invoking the 'honour of the German soldier' or calling for
the rehabilitation of former Nazis were those from the BHE (whose party name
included those 'deprived of their (political) rights,' *die Entrechteten*), the DP,
and the FDP. Beginning in 1951 the FDP of North Rhine-Westphalia became
practically infiltrated by formerly high-ranking National Socialists. Some of the
more prominent were Werner Naumann, state secretary of the Reich propaganda
ministry; his associate, Wolfgang Diewerge, standard bearer of the SS; Karl
Kaufmann, *Gauleiter* in Hamburg; the Mühlheim industrialist Hugo Stinnes,
Jun.; Ernst Achenbach, a *Landtag* representative who, from the Paris embassy,
had played an important role in the deportation of French Jews during the war;
and Werner Best, former SS *Obergruppenführer*, legal adviser to the Gestapo,
and German plenipotentiary in Denmark. Working in Achenbach's law office in
Essen, Best became the driving force behind a large-scale campaign for a general
political amnesty.

Friedrich Middelhauve, head of the North Rhine-Westphalian FDP, was the
most important ally of this right-wing faction, though he himself was politically
'untainted'. When he was elected deputy party head at the national party congress
in Bad Ems in November 1952, the conspirators seemed to be close to their
goal of turning the FDP into the nucleus of a 'National Gathering'. Shortly
thereafter, however, in mid-January 1953, the British military police arrested
Naumann and seven of his party associates, including Kaufmann. Although the
West German public was outraged at this interference, it ended up causing
the FDP harm. Their losses in the second federal election were due to the
unfavorable political light the activities of the NRW party organization had shed
on them.

The coalition parties were not the only ones who courted the vote of former
Nazis (called *Ehemalige*, 'erstwhiles') in the early days of the Federal Republic.
The Social Democrats did, too. This was part of the reason SPD politicians

constantly invoked the honour of the German soldier, which Hitler's war had not stained, and emphasized the difference between the Wehrmacht, which was 'clean', and the 'criminal SS'. In fact, the general view held that only the General SS (*Allgemeine SS*) was 'criminal', not the Waffen SS. The so-called 'Mutual Assistance Community' (*Hilfsgemeinschaft auf Gegenseitigkeit* or HIAG) of former soldiers of the Waffen SS was considered a non-political interest group and was courted by all political parties.

On 4 October 1951, at the urging of Herbert Wehner (a leading former Communist who had joined the SPD in 1946 and been elected to the Bundestag in 1949), Kurt Schumacher met with two former high Waffen SS officers, one of whom was the founder of the HIAG, Otto Krumm, a retired major-general. When members of 'The Federation', an international Jewish socialist organization, protested, the SPD leader responded (30 October) by saying that the Waffen SS could not be compared to the groups involved in the exterminations and persecutions. It had always considered itself 'as a kind of fourth Wehrmacht department'. Of the 900,000 surviving members of the Waffen SS, many had been forcibly drafted.

Most of these 900,000 men have practically become pariahs . . . It seems to us a matter of human and civil necessity to break up this ring and to help the great mass of former Waffen SS soldiers to make something of their lives and become good citizens . . . A compact complex of some 900,000 men without human and societal prospects is, taken together with their families, numerically not a good thing for a young democracy, rent with the greatest class and ideological tensions. We should grant these men, who have committed no crime, the opportunity of making their way in what for them is a new world.

In the first half of the 1950s the political climate in West Germany was much more nationalist than the actual policies of the parties and the government. As late as 1955, the old imperial colours of black, white, and red still spoke to more citizens of the FRG than the official black, red, and gold. According to one survey the respective numbers were 43% to 38%. In response to a question about Germany's best period in the twentieth century, 45% of respondents came out for the Wilhelmine Reich before 1914, 42% for the years 1933–9, 7% for the Weimar Republic, and only 2% for the present. In July 1952, when asked their opinion about leading men in the Third Reich, 42% expressed themselves positively about Hjalmar Schacht; 37% had a good opinion of Goering; no less than 24% of West Germans still thought favourably of Hitler. In a survey in June 1951, 40% of representative Germans judged the 'men of 20 July' positively, 30% negatively; 11% were undecided, did not wish to express a view, or else knew nothing about the failed assassination attempt in the 'Wolf's Den'.

Theodor Heuss was thus faced with a difficult task when, on 19 July 1954, the eve of the tenth anniversary of that event, he gave a speech in the Auditorium

Maximum of the Free University in Berlin on the historical, political, and moral importance of Stauffenberg and his fellow conspirators. The president was well aware of the fact that broad circles of West German society still considered the men of 20 July guilty of treason. He argued at length against the claim that Hitler's adversaries among the officers corps had no right to break their oath to the Führer, but were sworn to unconditional obedience. He gave the express assurance that it was not his intention to inculpate those who, after 20 July 1944, had continued to fight up to the 'final catastrophe' and who 'died believing, and were justified in believing, that their struggle would save Germany from the worst'.

Heuss said this in order to awaken understanding for his true message, which was 'to bear witness and to express gratitude'. The 'witness' he wished to bear concerned not only the inner motivations of the 20 July conspirators,

> but also embraces the historical right to their thoughts and sentiments. Our gratitude, however, knows that the failure of their undertaking in no way lessens the honour of the symbolic character of their sacrifice. Here, at a time when baseness and petty, cowardly, brutal power-seeking had soiled and stained the German name, a pure desire could be seen—the desire to remove, even at the price of one's own life, murderous evil from the state and, if possible, to rescue the Fatherland from destruction.

The president concluded his address with these words: 'The disgrace into which Hitler plunged us Germans was washed from the soiled German name by their blood. The legacy is still living, the pledge not yet redeemed.'

This speech by the West German head of state, printed and disseminated in large numbers at schools and universities that year after a unanimous resolution by the Bundestag, represented the attempt to initiate a positive German tradition. Heuss, a liberal, was not the first to try this. He was preceded by the conservative historian Hans Rothfels, whom the Nazis had forced into early retirement. In 1948, while still in exile in the United States, Rothfels had presented the first positive evaluation of the German resistance. Heuss's interpretation was such that conservative Germany could see its own image both in the German resistance *and* in the new West German state. In order to achieve this, however, many important details had to be passed over: that most of the men of 20 July 1944 had not been democrats, that most of them had initially supported Hitler's policies, and that Hitler's war had long been their war, too. The anti-Hitler resistance seemed basically a resistance of elites, and Heuss did not mention that they were the same elites who had fought against the Weimar Republic in the years before 1933. He also treated the Wehrmacht leniently, criticizing only the fact that when Generals Schleicher and Bredow were murdered in the summer of 1934, when the army 'was still a force to be reckoned with', it had been silent.

It was not difficult to understand the reason for Heuss's reserve. The main outlines of the rearmament had been decided by 1954, and the building up of

German armed forces required the cooperation of officers who had not resisted Hitler ten years before, but had remained faithful to him. Germany's first federal president certainly had no intention of causing what would later come to be called 'repression of the past'. In fact he sought the opposite, historical enlightenment, and his efforts were part of the reason that 'rightist' attacks on the German resistance came to be seen for what they were: attacks on the Federal Republic of Germany itself. After the president's state address in Berlin on 19 July 1954, at the latest, the 'national opposition' to the second German democracy lost all moral legitimacy.

There was, to be sure, another side to this success. Those Germans who, before 1933, had belonged to the conservative wing of the 'nationalist opposition' against the first German democracy and had supported the German Nationalist party or the Stahlhelm, had no cause to feel that the president was exhorting them to retrospective self-criticism. In fact, whether he intended it or not, Heuss encouraged Germans to think immediately of 20 July 1944 when they heard the words 'Prussia' or 'Prussian nobility'. He did not encourage them to dwell on the extent to which the conservative forces had been responsible for the destruction of the Weimar Republic, Hitler's rise to power, and the consolidation of his rule. The attempted assassination of Hitler threatened to turn into moral alibi, and not only for the old elite. Those who heard or read the president's speech could come away believing that Stauffenberg and his friends, through their act of self-sacrifice, had redeemed the Germans and released them from national shame over the crimes of the Nazis. Even if Heuss did not intend this conclusion, the final words of his speech nonetheless suggest it.[12]

Heuss's attempt to reconcile conservatives to democracy was aided by the fact that by this time most conservative intellectuals had cut their ties to nationalism and had turned to 'Europe' or, as it was now often called, the 'Occident' (*das Abendland*). A work by the sociologist Hans Freyer, one of the leaders of the 'conservative revolution' before 1933, was symptomatic of the new trend. In 1954 he published *Eine Weltgeschichte Europas*,* which concluded with an exhortation not to doubt of the vitality of the European peoples. Freyer saw the period of the world wars as a 'transformer, converting the world history of Europe into a world history of the entire earth'. The main question was whether Europe

only wants to continue to inhabit this new earth, or actively participate in it; whether it will be but a memory and a leftover on it, or an important and necessary member. Accordingly, what does it mean to believe in the future of Europe? It means believing that its energy is in no way spent, the scope of its influence in no way exhausted. It means believing that its spirit, its power of invention, its assiduousness, its appreciation for culture and tradition, and also its colourfulness and restlessness will be indispensable within the larger dimensions of future world history, not only for the administration of traditional places of culture, but for the building of the new earth.

* Freyer, *A World History of Europe*.

In 1955 the historian Ludwig Dehio, whose book *Gleichgewicht oder Hege-monie** had caused a stir in 1948, wrote an essay arguing passionately that German unity be subordinated to the goal of western European liberty. The 'defeat of German and the containment of Russian totalitarianism' had succeeded only because of the cooperative efforts of the Anglo-Saxons, above all the Americans. From this Dehio drew the following conclusion: 'Our reunification in liberty, the preservation of occidental humanity in Germany, also presupposes a firm connection to the Anglo-Saxons, and every loosening places it at risk, if not immediately, then in the long run.' For this reason it was necessary to give the occidental vision of liberty priority over the separate national goal of unity in the hierarchy of values.

The path leading in a straight line to the national goal can only attain it at the risk of liberty, even if a rapid triumph serves as lure. . . If unity is worthless without liberty, and if the latter can only be preserved through cooperative effort, then for us not to elect solidarity would mean taking the second step before the first. . . We might find this painful self-restraint easier if we give our flight from our recent history a goal, use our experiences to fight our inclinations, and finally, if we restore the half-buried legacy of our occidental nature to its rightful honors in order to ennoble our national drives.

In the mid-1950s, Catholic conservatives went much further than the Protes-tant Dehio (who had been discriminated against for racial reasons during the National Socialist period). In 1956, for example, the right-Catholic journal *Neues Abendland*, whose views critics were in the habit of calling 'Carolingian', emphatically rejected the restoration of a *kleindeutsch* national state (and with it Berlin as capital). The editor in chief, Emil Franzel, formerly a publicist partisan first of the Sudeten German Social Democrats, then of the National Socialists around Konrad Heinlein, wrote that 'the desire to pull back and concentrate on the Little German agenda of reunification and freedom of alliance' was tanta-mount to 'nihilism and shirking the task incumbent upon us'. The rejectionist *ohne mich!* attitude of the German neutralists was 'insubordination in the face of history, and that also means to the Lord of History'.

In the same issue of *Neues Abendland*, Paul Wilhelm Wenger, the Bonn editor of the *Rheinischer Merkur* (though he was born in Württemberg), referred to federalism as the fate of Germany and Europe.

To compress Germany into a single unitarian mass is to blow it to pieces, along with Europe. . . The oft-derided *German Confederation* from 1815 to 1866, as a central European defence community, was also a German and European solution for peace. The misfortune of Germany and Europe, which is still with us today, began the moment this alliance was broken up by the fratricidal Austro-Prussian war. The inner federalization of Germany is the precondition for the only possible solution to the German question: the federalist interweaving of Germany with all of its neighbours.

---

* Dehio, *Balance or Hegemony* (tr. as *The Precarious Balance: Four Centuries of the European Power Struggle*).

Wenger quoted Friedrich von Gentz's dictum from the year 1806: 'Europe has fallen because of Germany, and through Germany it must rise again.' At the beginning of the issue, Franzel placed a quote by Constantin Frantz, the *Grossdeutschland* advocate and adversary of Bismarck, from the year 1879 elevating federalism to a universal principle. Both Wenger and Franzel considered the national-political developments after 1789, as a whole, to have been the wrong path, one that Germany and Europe could leave behind only by returning to the idea of the 'Christian west'. By this they meant not only western Europe within the borders of the Carolingian empire; they also included eastern central and south-eastern Europe, despite the fact that these lands were ruled by the Communists at the present. Catholic Poland and the Danube basin merited their special attention.

Wenger described his visions in more detail in his 1959 book *Wer gewinnt Deutschland?** The rupture of 1866 was to be healed by a central European federation, he wrote. Germany was to think of itself not so much as a political entity, but as a trans-national linguistic and cultural community. Europe as a whole was to form a network of regional federations, including a Prussian–Czech–Polish coal and steel community, and, as a supra-national league, take up the legacy of the Holy Roman Empire. This was all summed up in a suggestive Latin formula: *Translatio imperii ad Europam Foederatam.*

This Catholic utopia of absorbing Germany into Europe was anything but a conservative consensus in late 1950s West Germany. When Wenger presented his arguments to the north Baden CDU district congress in Tauberbischofs-heim on 20 April 1958, he received a standing ovation in the hall, but sharp criticism from the all-German sectors of the public. The harshest reactions came from newspapers and journals close to the Evangelical wing of the CDU, above all the weekly *Christ und Welt,* co-founded by the Bundestag president, Eugen Gerstenmaier. Wenger was accused of being 'incendiary'. Gerstenmaier himself termed Wenger's speech 'heresy'. The state secretary for all-German affairs, Franz Thedieck, responded in the official government *Bulletin* that Bismarck's Reich had been the only possible solution to the German question at the time and therefore the best solution. 'By now, after the space of nearly a century, in guilt and in destiny, the parts that Bismarck brought together have grown into such an organism that even the federalist association of one area to a neighbouring country, in whatev-er manner it were conducted, would be felt as a loss of substance and an amputation.'

The official reprimand from Bonn did not prevent another opponent of the 'Little Germany' solution from expressing sentiments similar to those of Wenger a few short months later. On 28 September 1958, at the awarding of the peace prize of the German Bookseller's Association in the Frankfurt Paulskirche

---

* Wenger, *Who Will Win Germany?*

(President Heuss was also in attendance), the philosopher Karl Jaspers repudiated the work of the founder of the Reich.

We had a Prussian Little Germany, the Bismarck state, which wrongly called itself the second empire, following in the footsteps of the first, medieval empire . . . Today, under new world powers, with the state of the world completely transformed, the Bismarck state is entirely a thing of the past. If we continue to live in such a way as if it could become reality once again, then we are allowing the ghosts of the past to feed on the blood of the present, preventing us from understanding the real dangers and the great opportunities of the future.

In view of the 'racial consciousness of the coloured peoples against the whites,' what really mattered was the 'urgently needed confederation of the occidental states'.

The deeper, apolitical German self-consciousness cannot be made identical with the political consciousness of any single German state . . . The re-establishment of our ancient German self-consciousness resides in the community of our prepolitical substance—in language, in the spirit, in the *Heimat*.* From this substance arises the particular task of each, today in Federal Republic, too.

Jaspers's speech, held in the meeting place of the national assembly of 1848, caused less of a stir than Wenger's in Tauberbischofsheim, where in July of 1866, during the German war, the Prussians had defeated Austria's Württemberg allies. Another reason for the difference was that the philosopher, unlike the publicist, was not as susceptible to the charge of being a mouthpiece or prompter for Adenauer. Moreover, his rejection of the reunification in the Paulskirche address was not nearly as radical as it would be two years later, in a television interview with Theo Koch on 10 August 1960, the controversy over which lasted for weeks. Nonetheless, even the earlier speech offered at least as much material for criticism as Wenger's. It was true that Jaspers lamented that the Germans in the east, who were the same as those in the west, had been stripped of their political liberty by the occupying power. By declaring the nation of 1871 historically defunct, however, he cut the ground from beneath the idea of national solidarity. Neither Wenger's call for the regionalization of Germany nor that of Jaspers for German particularism could be reconciled with the self-image of the West German state, such as it was expressed in the preamble to the Basic Law.

One did not have to be a German nationalist in order to disagree with Jaspers and Wenger. By 1958, in any case, there was no longer any significant difference of opinion about the priority of liberty over unity, and no political party was still seriously contesting the integration of Europe. The fact that conservatives were the first to make 'Europe' their cause after 1945 remained important in

---

* [Translator's note: the word *Heimat* can mean 'home town' or 'homeland'. In the latter sense, applied to Germany, it can signify the country as a whole and/or the individual German *Land* (Saxony, Bavaria, etc.) of one's origin.]

domestic politics, however. The pro-European conservatism of the 1950s was so successful because, in contrast to German nationalism, it did not seem historically discredited. In fact, the east–west conflict seemed to provide it with additional legitimacy.

This kind of conservatism offered a new ideological identity to many former supporters of National Socialism. It provided a new context for their anti-communism and for the kind of 'European' rhetoric common in Germany during the Second World War. Consequently, in the view of most of the 'erstwhiles', their efforts on behalf of the National Socialist cause had not been completely wrong, but only partially so. The hatred and destruction of the Jews had definitely been a mistake, as well as the persecution of dissenters. The war against Bolshevism, on the other hand, was not something a former Hitler supporter—newly or re-converted to conservatism—needed to feel any shame about. The Soviet Union was still a totalitarian state, and it had not renounced the world revolution. It was necessary and legitimate to join the old democracies in the struggle against this power. The oft-invoked 'anti-totalitarian consensus' in West Germany was a product of experiences both past and present. It also allowed Germans to judge the particular totalitarianism they had served more mildly than other kinds. In this regard 1950s West Germany was the 'Thermidor' of a revolution that had left behind its Jacobin stage and turned conservative.[13]

In January 1983, at a scholarly conference convened in Berlin on the occasion of the fiftieth anniversary of the National Socialist rise to power, the philosopher Hermann Lübbe posed the question of why, 'under the protection of publicly restored normative normality, the German attitude towards National Socialism was more placid in temporal proximity to it than in later years of our post-war history.' His answer was the following: 'This certain placidity was the necessary socio-psychological and political medium for the transformation of our post-war population into the citizenry of the Federal Republic of Germany.' The fact that Hitler's rule had enjoyed strong support among the population for so long placed the young Federal Republic in a paradoxical situation. 'The new German state had to be erected against the ideology and politics of National Socialism, the catastrophe of which had also spelled the downfall of the Reich. It could hardly be erected against the majority of the people.'

Lübbe did not wish to call this attitude 'repression', but rather 'communicative silence'. Many Germans who had 'gone along' with the National Socialists knew what many others had done, said, or written in the years between 1933 and 1945. This 'silence' prevailed both with respect to certain chapters of one's own biography as well as to the corresponding sections in the biography of one's 'neighbour'. Private discretion went hand-in-hand with the public condemnation of the Nazi regime by the new state and most of the media as well as with the beginnings of scholarly investigation into the recent past. In this sense, it is inaccurate to speak of a 'general repression' of the

National Socialist past, at least as far as the first two decades of the FRG are concerned.

That said, we certainly can speak of a refusal on the part of a large number of Germans to come to terms with their own personal histories. Since many post-war careers depended on keeping certain past acts and statements from becoming known, sooner or later such refusal generally turned into individual repression. Since this was both a mass phenomenon and one accepted in society as a whole, it was respected by even those politicians and publicists who were themselves 'untainted'. The upshot was a contradictory attitude toward National Socialism. To openly declare one's support for the Third Reich was to violate a West German taboo; but it was no less of a taboo to ask searching questions about the personal acts and culpabilities of the survivors on the second, third, or fourth level along the chain of command.

There was always public controversy whenever high positions in the new state were given to people who had had important posts under the Nazis. This was the case with Theodor Oberländer, who resigned from the office of expellee minister in April 1960 after the GDR had—falsely—accused him in a show trial of having taken part in the murder of Jews during the occupation of Lemberg in 1941. Hans Globke, on the other hand, despite the fact that he had written a 'scholarly' commentary on the Nuremberg laws while working in the Reich interior ministry as a *Korreferent* for Jewish questions, remained in his position as state secretary in the chancellor's office until the end of Adenauer's government in 1963, despite massive public protest. Globke was able to prove that he had helped many Jews and that his commentary had done as much as possible to accommodate 'mixed breeds'. Adenauer had appointed Globke in 1953 not for the sake of reconciling the 'erstwhiles' to the new state, but because he had thought him particularly qualified for the job. Even harsh attacks from the SPD were unable to persuade the chancellor that Globke's dismissal was in the interests of the state.

After the mid-1950s the West German attitude towards National Socialism gradually began to change. The tendency to gloss over the realities of the Third Reich and to ignore 'dark spots' in the biographies of prominent figures began to draw more criticism. In the summer of 1955 an FDP politician, Leonhard Schlüter, who had formerly been active on the radical right and, as a publisher, printed works of former Nazis, was made minister of culture in Lower Saxony. This appointment caused protests among students and professors in Göttingen (among the latter were also some who, like the historian Hermann Heimpel, had written and acted in a way congenial to National Socialism before 1945). The German Trade Union Association, the Central Council of the Jews in Germany (*Zentralrat der Juden in Deutschland*), and the SPD of Lower Saxony demanded Schlüter's resignation. Outrage was so strong throughout the country that Schlüter managed to last only a few days in office. This was the first time student protests succeeded in bringing down a government minister considered unacceptably 'rightist', and the event was discussed and acclaimed far beyond the borders of the FRG.

Three years after the 'Schlüter affair', in what became known as the *Ulmer Einsatzgruppenprozess*, several former members of a 'special action squad' active on the eastern front were put on trial in Ulm for the murder of thousands of Jewish men, women, and children. For the first time, the German public was confronted with detailed accounts of the immeasurable cruelty with which the Germans, along with their local henchmen, had commenced the extermination of the Jews. The shock was profound, and it had practical consequences. In December 1958 the Central Office of the State Judicial Administrations for the Investigation of National Socialist Crimes (*Zentrale Stelle der Landesjustizverwaltungen zur Aufklärung nationalsozialistischer Verbrechen*) was established in Ludwigsburg. Thus began, thirteen years after the end of the Third Reich, the systematic investigation and prosecution of Nazi crimes by West German courts. The Germans would no longer be able to repress the most horrific chapter in their recent history. And yet the consequences of the 'communicative silence' had still not been fully worked through, not by a long shot. A younger generation began to ask the very questions many of their elders were still seeking to avoid.

At the beginning of the new decade, Walter Dirks, a writer on the Catholic left, published an article in the *Frankfurter Hefte* entitled 'Der restaurative Charakter der Epoche'.* 'Restorations are attempts to restore the earlier status quo after a revolution or a period of upheaval,' Dirks wrote in the 1950 essay. He defined 'restoration' as 'an event, a process, a condition, a climate. It has many subjects, all probably interconnected, although they certainly do not necessarily all cooperate.' The 'great leap into restoration' took place at the moment of the currency reform. 'This currency reform was an act of restoration. Since, contrary to the German proposals, the sweeping programme of financial compensation was not linked to it, it fixed the privilege of material assets and prevented the expellees from being able to start over again on a level playing field.' In order to strike at the heart of the restoration, the author demanded an 'authentic right to co-determination'. For the rest, 'lots of daily hard work within the reality of restoration, without illusions' was going to be necessary.

At first glance Dirks's definition seemed to have a lot going for it. In the first years of the FRG, the longing for normality was both overwhelmingly powerful and, after the cataclysms of war and collapse, all too understandable. Immediately after the end of the war, calls for a radical reform of property relations enjoyed some support among the workers. But developments in the Soviet Zone soon acted as a deterrent, even with respect to the socialization of large industrial operations. By the time of the first federal elections, at the latest,

---

* Dirks, 'The Restoration-Like Character of Our Age'.

it was clear that the majority of West Germans did not want a 'socialist', but a 'bourgeois' policy.

The 1949 electoral outcome led to the reinstitution of much that had been completely or partially abolished by the Allies, including the traditional bureaucracy, the system of chambers under public law, and the examination for a master craftsman's diploma in the skilled trades (the so-called *Grosse Befähigungsnachweis* or 'Great Certificate of Qualifications'). Though this was often called 'restoration', it was democratically legitimated. The restoration of the monarchy or dictatorship was never under debate. The only things 'restored' in this sense were what the Nazis had abolished: the rule of law, federalism, and pluralism. And this had already taken place before the founding of the FRG. It would also be permissible to speak of the 'restoration' of parliamentary democracy, except for the fact that the new Basic Law differed so much from the Weimar constitution.

The currency was, in reality, not the kind of 'leap into restoration' Dirks made it out to be. Quite the contrary: the 'Social Market Economy', which commenced with the currency reform, turned out to be a revolutionary innovation. It broke with the traditions of economic planning and *dirigisme* to which many critics of the 'restoration' felt themselves beholden and provided more scope for economic competition than had ever been the case in Germany. At the same time, the economic democratization that the workers had been demanding ever since the Weimar days made continual progress. Worker co-determination on the boards of the coal and steel companies, secured by legislation in May 1951, made West Germany into the pioneer of the 'constitutional factory'.

All in all, what West Germany experienced after 1949 can better be described as 'conservative modernization' than 'restoration'. It was true that the consciousness and language of many Germans at the time lagged behind the pace of social and political change. The same was true of the 'occidental' rhetoric of many intellectuals. In substance, however, the integration of Europe was a profoundly progressive phenomenon.

In 1952 one of the sharpest critics of the 'restoration', Eugen Kogon—a leftist Catholic, former inmate in the concentration camp at Buchenwald, author of the much-read *Der SS-Staat*,* and co-editor of the *Frankfurter Hefte* with Walter Dirks after 1946—wrote that a 'unified Europe of democratic liberty' was the historical prerequisite for comprehensive renewal, a renewal necessary in order to overcome the 'period of restoration'. For this reason he appealed to the socialists to tolerate the cooperation of 'reactionary forces' in the project. The Federal Republic had indeed begun to open to the political culture of the west. The fact that this occurred under the aegis of a conservative like Adenauer made it difficult for other conservatives to cling to their anti-western sentiments.[14]

---

* Kogon, *The SS State*.

THE ZENITH OF THE ADENAUER ERA 1955–1957

When, on 9 May 1955, the Federal Republic of Germany became a member of NATO, all observers assumed that the USSR would not be long in responding. They were right. On 14 May the Soviet Union, Poland, the GDR, Czechoslovakia, Hungary, Romania, Bulgaria, and Albania concluded their own military alliance, the Warsaw Pact. The member states were forbidden to join any other alliances, and there was no possibility of withdrawal. The unified command of Warsaw Pact armed forces was located in Moscow, and a Soviet, Marshal Konev, was appointed commander-in-chief. Moscow now possessed another instrument of control over its allies in eastern central and south-eastern Europe, and one not purely military in nature.

During the time the eastern alliance was being concluded in Warsaw, deliberations over a 'treaty of state' with Austria, the third successor to Hitler's 'Great German Reich', were being held in Vienna. This *Staatsvertrag* was signed on 15 May in the Belvedere Palace by the foreign ministers of the USA, the Soviet Union, Great Britain, France, and Austria. The 1919 ban on German–Austrian union, the so-called *Anschlussverbot*, was renewed. In exchange, Austria regained its national independence, and the occupation statute was lifted. The treaty entered into effect on 27 July, and the last Allied troops left the country on 19 September. Finally, on 26 October, the Austrian federal parliament, the National Council (*Nationalrat*), committed itself to 'perpetual neutrality' after the example of Switzerland. This fulfilled the most important requirement of the Soviets before withdrawing their forces.

On 14 May, one day before the signing of the treaty, Molotov, the Soviet foreign minister, informed his western colleagues that the Soviet Union was prepared to hold a summit. Two months later, between 18 and 23 July 1955, the 'Big Four' met in Geneva. Since Germany was one of the main issues, delegations from the FRG and the GDR were allowed to participate as 'observers'. As was to be expected, the differences remained irreconcilable. The USSR demanded a collective security system replacing both military alliances as the precondition for reunification. The west initially insisted on reunification through free elections as the first step towards negotiations over a new European peacetime order. Then, in the course of the conference, they revealed their willingness to cooperate with the Soviet Union in matters of arms reductions and détente. This was tantamount to an acceptance of the partition of Germany. Adenauer had good reason to be worried about the 'spirit of Geneva'. Up to this point, the western powers had been supporting the West German position that the creation of a European security system had to be firmly linked to German reunification. After Geneva, Bonn could no longer be so sure about western backing in this matter.

On its return trip from Geneva, the Soviet Delegation made a stopover in East Berlin. It was led by prime minister Bulganin, a Soviet marshal, and Nikita Sergeyevich Khrushchev, the leader of the Soviet Communist party since 1953. Khrushchev, who had been forced by reasons of protocol to take a back seat to Bulganin in Geneva, took the sojourn in the 'capital of the GDR' as the opportunity to send a message to the world. In the future, he declared in a speech on the Marx-Engels-Platz (formerly the Schlossplatz), the solution to the German question would be a matter for the two German states, which were to be considered separate political entities in terms of international law. The GDR was to preserve its 'socialist achievements'. Khrushchev did not speak of the reunification of Germany, as he had done in Geneva. All the rhetoric from Bonn and its western allies notwithstanding, the partition of Germany had become a fixture in the relationship between east and west.

After another two-month period, the Soviet Union and the Federal Republic of Germany conducted direct and official negotiations for the first time. Adenauer had received an invitation to Moscow on 7 June. The purpose of the visit was to discuss the initiation of diplomatic and trade relations, along with other related questions. On 9 September the German chancellor arrived in the Soviet capital at the head of a large delegation. Adenauer was unable to get the Soviets to rescind the 'two-state theory' Khrushchev had promulgated in East Berlin. Nonetheless, he returned to Bonn on 13 September with a major success celebrated throughout the whole of Germany: the Soviet Union agreed to allow the surviving German prisoners of war and detained civilians to return home. In exchange, the chancellor agreed to establish diplomatic relations with the Soviet Union. From now on, there would be two German embassies in Moscow, one for the FRG and one for the GDR.

On the return flight to West Germany, Wilhelm Grewe, director of the political department of the foreign office, formulated a doctrine that would later be named after the state secretary of the foreign office, Walter Hall-stein. The purpose of the 'Hallstein doctrine' was twofold: to prevent other nations from recognizing the GDR, and to preserve the West German 'claim to sole representation' of the German people. On 22 September 1955 Adenauer presented this doctrine to the Bundestag in his report on the Moscow trip. He wished to note unequivocally, he said, 'that the federal government would consider it an unfriendly act for any state with which it maintained an official relationship to initiate a diplomatic relationship with the GDR, since such an act would have the effect of deepening the division of Germany.' In order to lend credibility to the threat, the government refused to take up official relations with the Communist 'satellite states' that had already recognized the GDR.

Another important event in the autumn of 1955 could not be credited to the chancellor. On 23 October, 67.7 per cent of the citizens of the Saar rejected the 'Europeanization' of their territory (with 97.5 per cent of the population participating). Adenauer had been prepared to agree to a special status for the Saarland, for the sake of European integration and a good relationship with France. He had not initially expected the Saar population to respond as it did. Basically they were voting for integration with West Germany, and France accepted their decision. On 1 January 1957 the Saarland, in keeping with a treaty worked out by Bonn and Paris a year before, became a *Land* in the Federal Republic. Economic integration followed in July 1959. This marked the first time the jurisdiction of the Basic Law was extended according to Article 23. From this moment onward a procedure was in place, and tested in practice, for the reunification of Germany—provided the 'Big Four' agreed to it.

Despite Adenauer's fears, the Saar vote did not result in a setback for the policy of western integration. In October 1956 the foreign ministers of the European Coal and Steel Community's six members nations agreed to the formation of a European Atomic Community and a European Economic Community. The 'Treaties of Rome' were signed in March 1957. Progressive dismantling of tariffs and trade restrictions were to bring about a 'Common Market' over a period of twelve years. At the same time, the economic policies of the member states would be harmonized with each other. The treaties went into effect on 1 January 1958. They caused virtually no controversy in West Germany, in contrast to the western military integration. Even the Social Democrats voted in their favour.

In the meantime, the German military contribution took on more concrete form. The first volunteers were called up on 2 January 1956, on the basis of a law of July 1955. A special committee (the *Personalgutachterausschuss*) was in place to check the personal histories of all candidates for officer positions higher than colonel (*Oberst*); persons considered 'tainted' were not admitted. The necessary changes to the Basic Law, the so-called *Wehrverfassung* or 'defence constitution amendment' of March 1956, were brought about with the help of the SPD, which took the opportunity to push for a new Bundestag office: that of the 'commissioner for the armed forces' (*Wehrbeauftragte*), an intermediary to whom the soldiers could turn if they felt their basic rights were being violated.

All males 19 years old or older could be conscripted into service in the armed forces, in the already existing Federal Border Guard (*Bundesgrenzschutz*), or in a civil defence corps yet to be created. The right to refuse military service under arms for reasons of conscience, anchored in Article 4 of the Basic Law, was thus preserved. The supreme command authority was structured in such a way as to prevent the Bundeswehr (the name was introduced by the Bundestag) from becoming a 'state within a state' like the Reichswehr in Weimar. In the first German democracy, the Reich president had been the commander-in-chief of the entire army. In the FRG, the defence minister would have the supreme command in peacetime; if the country were attacked, it would be transferred to the chancellor. Parliamentary control of the military and the primacy of politics would be preserved in all cases.

The year 1957 brought another election. The governmental camp had changed since the last elections in 1953. The BHE had split in July 1955, the FDP in February 1956. In both cases, the majority went over to the opposition while the ministerial wing remained loyal to the government. But the parliamentary majority of the Adenauer government was never in question. The Union was considered the guarantor of external security. The shock the Soviet Union caused in November 1956 when it violently repressed popular unrest in Hungary resonated for a long time thereafter and helped the staunchly anti-communist chancellor and his party with the third federal election in West Germany.

For its part the SPD, beginning in spring 1957, distinguished itself in its staunch opposition to a project that was being pushed above all by the new defence minister (appointed in October 1956), the CSU politician Franz Josef Strauss: West German carrier systems for atomic weapons (the warheads themselves were to remain under American control). In coming out against this plan, the Social Democrats found themselves in agreement with eighteen well-known atomic physicists, including Nobel Prize winners Max Born, Otto Hahn, Werner Heisenberg, and Max von Laue, who published the so-called 'Göttingen manifesto' in April 1957 warning the population about the dangers of nuclear war and demanding that West Germany renounce the plan to obtain nuclear weapons. Among the population itself, the SPD campaign did not have the desired effect, at least not in the long term. While the government's strategic plans were anything but popular, the German majority clearly mistrusted a movement that spoke first and foremost to principled pacifists and might quickly escape the control of the SPD.

In matters of social security, too, the CDU and CSU were able to claim that the Germans were in good hands with the present government. On 21 January 1957 the Bundestag passed two laws revising the pension systems of workers and employees. The centrepiece of the reform, which sailed through parliament with huge majorities, was the introduction of the 'dynamic' pension, linked to gross income. This measure, which broke with the principle of capital coverage through payment contributions (in place since the Bismarck era), gave retired Germans a share in the benefits of increasing economic prosperity by tying their pensions to the general development of incomes. The Bundestag itself, with the help of a 'social advisory council', was to decide every year to what extent pensions would go up.

The Social Democrats, staunch supporters of the dynamic pension, voted for the laws. The FDP rejected them. Nonetheless, the Union parties could count on gaining the credit. Adenauer had actively promoted the legislation. And since it was backdated to 1 January upon entering into effect, the incomes of millions of pensioners went up immediately and considerably. The long-term effects have been well described by Hans-Peter Schwarz:

The reform was a force for integration. People who wanted something turned into people who wanted to preserve something. The positive aspects of the political system and the economic system had been equally confirmed. Bourgeois democracy had proven its ability to bring about generous social reform . . . The rhetoric of class struggle and the demands for redistribution were now less well received than before.

With its 1957 electoral slogan 'No experiments!' the party of Konrad Adenauer pithily expressed the basic mood in the Federal Republic of Germany, a mood that grew even stronger after the pension reform. 'More apartments, fewer barracks!', one of the slogans of the SPD, was far less effective. But the Social Democrats, too, had reason to hope for gains at the polls. Two parties that had run candidates in 1953 did not do so in 1957, and everything pointed to the SPD benefiting more from their absence than the Union. After a persistent string of electoral defeats, Gustav Heinemann's All-German People's party had disbanded in May 1957, exhorting its members to join the SPD. The Social Democrats thus gained a number of prominent Protestants, including Heinemann himself, as well as a number of promising younger GVP members, including Johannes Rau, Erhard Eppler, and Jürgen Schmude, all of whose political careers might otherwise have come to an end with the death of their party. Another new SPD recruit was Heinemann's Catholic confederate, Helene Wessel, who had sat in the Prussian parliament from 1928 to 1933 (for the Centre party), on the Parliamentary Council in 1948–9, and in the Bundestag from 1949 to 1953.

The other party that did not participate in the 1957 election was the KPD, which had been banned and disbanded by the Federal Constitutional Court on 17 August 1956 for subversive activities and openly anti-constitutional aims. The decision's reasoning, worked out with great care and precision, was as constitutionally unassailable as the one of 23 October 1952 against the extremist right-wing SRP. Politically speaking, of course, the Communists had long since ceased to represent any threat to the domestic order of the new state. Since their party was looked on as the long arm of the SED and the Soviet Union and did all it could to live up to this reputation, it had lost continually at the polls. Already by 1953 it had come away with a mere 2.2% of the vote.

The third federal election ended with a landslide victory for the Union and a personal triumph for Adenauer. With 50.2% the CDU and CSU achieved not only an absolute majority of Bundestag seats, but also of votes. No German party in history had ever done this well in a free election on the national level. With an increase of 7% over 1953, the CDU and CSU also improved their performance much more than the SPD, which gained only 3%, climbing from 28.8% to 31.8%. The FDP's 7.7% was well below the 1953 result of 9.5%.

None of the other parties cleared the 5% hurdle. The German party, which had united with August Martin Euler's right-liberal Free People's Party (*Freie Volkspartei*), an offshoot of the FDP, in January 1957, managed only 3.3%. Nonetheless, on the basis of district-level agreements with the Lower Saxon

CDU, it was able to secure fifteen seats in the Bundestag. The BHE fell short by only a small margin, receiving 4.6%. But the decrease of 1.3% meant that the integration of the expellees had made further progress. By this time, most of them no longer believed it necessary to have their own party, and many had left Theodor Oberländer's and Waldemar Kraft's former party for the CDU and CSU.

The new cabinet was in place six weeks after the election. The third Adenauer government was a coalition between the CDU/CSU and the DP. Four of the most important ministers remained at their posts. Heinrich von Brentano (CDU) as foreign minister, Franz Josef Strauss (CSU) as minister of defence, Gerhard Schröder (CDU) as interior minister, and Ludwig Erhard (CDU) as minister of economics. Adenauer also kept Oberländer, who had joined the CDU in 1956, as expellee minister. Fritz Schäffer (CDU), whose hard 'fiscalist' policies had alienated many politicians, had to surrender his office as finance minister to Franz Etzel (CDU) and assumed control of the ministry of justice. The ministry of transport, as in all the West German governments since 1949, was once again headed by a DP politician, Hans-Christoph Seebohm.

The distribution of power in the third West German parliament was clear: 287 seats were controlled by the coalition, 210 by the SPD and FDP opposition. The Adenauer era was at its zenith. Dispassionate observers, even within the governmental camp, were aware that the 1957 electoral victory would not be easy to repeat. But in the meantime, there could be no doubt about the fact that the kind of conservative democracy Adenauer represented enjoyed broad support among the West German population.[15]

CRISIS IN THE EASTERN BLOC AND CONSOLIDATION OF SED RULE

As long as the western integration of the FRG had not been completed, the GDR attempted to mobilize the West Germans against the 'Adenauer regime' with national rhetoric. At the same time, it sought to justify its own new armed forces, 'comrades-in-arms' of the Soviet army, in historical terms. In October 1953, the 140th anniversary of the Battle of the Nations near Leipzig provided a welcome opportunity to appeal to patriotic sentiments and, simultaneously, to remind the country that Germans and Russians had joined together in those days to defeat a foreign occupying power from the west. That same year Albert Norden, who would soon become the leader of the National Council of the National Front, published a book entitled *Das Banner von 1813*.* He invoked 'the shades of Stein and Gneisenau, of Scharnhorst and Clausewitz, of Arndt and Fichte, *the men who*

---

* Norden, *The Banner of 1813*.

saved Germany because they believed in their people and fought together with Russia.' At the beginning of 1954, a book entitled *Kampf um Freiheit** was put out by an institution called 'Publishers of the Nation'(*Verlag der Nation*). It contained texts by Klopstock, Fichte, Arndt, Jahn, Schenkendorf, Körner, Clausewitz, Kleist, and many others. A few of the pieces came from new editions printed during the Third Reich. The excerpt from Jahn's *Deutsches Volkstum*[†] came from an edition published at the beginning of the war, in 1940.

Norden's book on 1813 and the book on the 'national uprising' were typical examples of the 'national turn' the central committee had made in October 1951. The new view of history replaced the so-called 'misery theory' (*Miseretheorie*), the classical expression of which was Alexander Abusch's 1946 book *Der Irrweg einer Nation.*[‡] According to this theory, the historical developments from Luther to Frederick the Great to Bismarck to Hitler were one long process of decline, a process made possible because 'reactionary' forces were always superior to the forces of 'progress'. The 'national turn', on the other hand, sought to define the great traditions of the German people and use them as a source of national self-confidence. The German-Russian struggle against Napoleon was one of these traditions, made especially pertinent by the struggle against the FRG's military integration with the west.

Even after West Germany's accession to NATO and the creation of the Warsaw Pact, the SED did not stop using 'national' traditions to polemic effect against the FRG and continued to blame the west, especially Adenauer, for the partition of Germany. After 1956, however, the 'patriotism' of the GDR began to take on more of a 'socialist' cast. West Germany was systematically compared to the Third Reich. The GDR itself was celebrated as the negation, embodied in a state, of all things that had led to 'Hitler-fascism' and had permitted Hitler to come to power. The positive traditions of German history were the progressive forces, above all the working class since the days of Marx and Engels. Its revolutionary avant-garde was the German Communist party after its founding in December 1918. The fact that this party was defeated in its struggle against 'Hitler-fascism' in 1933 was in no small measure the doing of the 'rightist' Social Democrats, who had betrayed the 'revolution', thus allowing the return of the reactionary 'monopoly bourgeoisie', and had otherwise done virtually all it could to prevent the formation of an anti-fascist unitary front. This view was the official party line for GDR historians after 1958, the fortieth anniversary of the revolution of 1918–19.

After West Germany became a member of NATO in May 1955, it was a matter of course that the GDR would become one of the founding members of the Warsaw Pact. The East German armed forces, however, which had been developed from the 'Garrisoned People's Police', did not join the alliance at first.

---

* *Struggle for Freedom.*
† Jahn, *German Folk Culture.*
‡ Abusch, *A Nation Astray.*

In September 1955, shortly after Adenauer's visit to Moscow and the creation of diplomatic relations between the Soviet Union and the FRG, the Soviet Union and the GDR signed a treaty codifying their own relationship. This agreement dissolved the office of High Commissioner and granted 'full sovereignty' to the GDR. On 28 January 1956, ten days after the Volkskammer passed a law creating a National People's Army (*Nationale Volksarmee* or NVA) and a ministry for national defence, the East German armed forces were integrated into the Warsaw Pact. The NVA consisted of voluntary cadre formations with an initial strength of 120,000 troops. Under orders from Moscow, the GDR did not introduce compulsory military service at this time.

The year 1956 witnessed a series of profound shocks in the eastern bloc. In February, at the twentieth congress of the Communist party, Khrushchev held a 'secret address' condemning the crimes of Stalin. The SED was slow to fall in line with the 'de-Stalinization'. In the 4 March edition of *Neues Deutschland*, Ulbricht wrote that

after Lenin's death, Stalin no doubt rendered great service to the building of socialism and to the struggle against the enemies of the party . . . But later, when Stalin placed himself above the party and began to foster a cult of personality, the Soviet Communist party and state suffered a great deal of harm. Stalin cannot be considered among the greats of Marxism.

Karl Schirdewan, secretary of the central committee, only allowed the delegates of the third party congress of the SED access to parts of Khrushchev's 'secret address' (already known in the west by that time). Former party leaders, forced out of the politburo and other offices in 1953 and 1954, were subsequently rehabilitated, men like Anton Ackermann and Franz Dahlem. Some 11,000 persons were granted amnesty and about 21,000 released from prison. Among these was Max Fechner, former justice minister and member of the SPD who had been arrested and expelled from the party in July 1953 for approving the right to strike, and Paul Merker, in prison since 1952.

The year 1956 occasioned profound ruptures of a different kind in two other 'socialist' countries, Poland and Hungary. In June the workers in Poznań rebelled against the rigid productivity requirements in the factories. Although the uprising was brutally suppressed, further mass demonstrations broke out in Czestochowa and Warsaw in October. In order to prevent an escalation, the politburo, without consulting Moscow, decided to change the political leadership and attempt a new political beginning. On 19–20 October Wladyslaw Gomulka was restored to his former office. (Former general secretary of the Polish United Workers' party, Gomulka had been arrested in autumn 1948 for allegedly national-communist, 'Titoist' leanings, imprisoned for several years, and not rehabilitated until August 1956.) Thus began a relative liberalization of politics in Poland, unwillingly tolerated by Moscow. Forced rural collectivization was halted and peasant agriculture restored; consumer goods production received priority in the development of industry; the relationship between the party and the Catholic Church grew less tense, and leading state security officials were dismissed and prosecuted.

The Hungarian situation turned out much differently. At the end of October 1956 the Communist government collapsed under the pressure of a massive popular uprising. The new prime minister, the reformer Imre Nagy, who had been persecuted under Stalin, negotiated a removal of the Soviet troops. They actually did withdraw on 30 October. But when Nagy's coalition government, which included former members of the 'anti-fascist' parties banned in 1948, decided that Hungary would withdraw from the Warsaw Pact, the Soviets sent their soldiers back. The 'counter-revolutionary' uprising, which was in fact a revolution, was put down with extreme brutality. Several thousand rebels lost their lives; 200,000 fled via Austria to the west, and 2,000 Hungarians were condemned to death. Nagy and two of his closest associates were prosecuted in a secret trial and executed in June 1958. The new party leader, János Kádár, had also been a reformer, but had gone over to the Soviets during the uprising. He remained loyal to Moscow, and was eventually able to secure enough of a free hand in domestic policy to implement a cautious liberalization.

The west sympathized with the cause of the Hungarian rebels, but it had little more than sympathy to offer in the autumn of 1956. At the height of the Hungarian crisis, Britain and France were fighting with Israel against Egypt in an effort to reverse the nationalization of the Suez Canal. For a few days the world seemed to teeter on the brink of a third world war. Khrushchev threatened to use nuclear weapons against western Europe. This prompted Eisenhower to put massive pressure on Paris and London. On 6 November all parties in the conflict agreed to an armistice.

The Soviet Union emerged from the double crisis in 1956 as the victor. It was able to 'restore order' in Hungary while the west looked on in moral outrage. At the same time, it could style itself the protector of the 'Third World' in the struggle against 'imperialism'. The losers were Hungary and the European colonial powers. The interaction between Moscow and Washington made it suddenly very clear that there was no longer a 'Big Four', but only two world powers, the United States and the Soviet Union.

The USA possessed nuclear weapons in 1945; the Soviets had them by 1949. Washington tested the first hydrogen bomb in 1952; Moscow followed with its own a year later. The Soviets successfully tested a multi-stage intercontinental missile at the end of 1957. It followed this up a few weeks later with a spectacular technological coup. 'Sputnik', the first man-made satellite, was launched into orbit on 4 October 1957. The military-strategic implications were obvious. The conquest of space had begun, and the Soviet Union was ahead of the United States. The launch caused profound shock, 'Sputnik shock', throughout the western world. For the leaders of the communist states, 'socialism' had now finally proven its superiority to 'capitalism' in every respect.

In the GDR, the new self-image of the party and state leadership first manifested itself in more rigorous persecution of dissenting voices. In November and December 1956, immediately following the suppression of the Hungarian 'counter-revolution', the philosopher Wolfgang Harich and other reformist intellectuals—including Gustav Just and Heinz Zöger, the two editors-in-chief of the newspaper *Sonntag*, and Walter Janka, director of the Aufbau publishing house—were arrested as 'enemies of the state'. They were condemned to long prison terms the following year. The Leipzig philosopher Ernst Bloch, whom the SED believed to be the main intellectual force behind the Harich group, was forcibly retired from his position in March 1957. Then, at the 33rd plenum of the central committee of the SED in mid-October 1957, Ulbricht declared war on 'revisionism' within the party ranks. One of those accused by name, State Security Minister Ernst Wollweber, was replaced by his state secretary, Erich Mielke, in November. (Twenty-six years before, on 9 August 1931, Mielke, acting on secret party orders, had shot two Berlin policemen.) In February 1958 Wollweber was expelled from the central committee; Karl Schirdewan and Fred Oelssner, both central committee secretaries, were thrown out of the politburo.

Those punished, according to Ulbricht, were all guilty of 'factionalism', a punishment Communist parties had been compelled to deal with harshly since the days of Lenin. In fact, Schirdewan, Oelssner, and Wollweber had been pushing for a consistent 'de-Stalinization' and, since Ulbricht rejected such a policy, they wanted him replaced as First Secretary. They were apparently supported by Khrushchev in this matter. Nonetheless, they no more questioned the 'leading role of the SED' than did Harich and his friends. None of Ulbricht's adversaries within the party sought any kind of radical break with Marxism-Leninism.

Ulbricht, who came from Leipzig and was a carpenter by trade, turned 65 on 30 June 1958. He was often mockingly called the 'German Lenin'. After the expulsion of his enemies, however, his position was stronger than ever. He profited from the fact that he had managed to postpone a meaningful 'de-Stalinization' until Khrushchev, the originator of the policy, was himself forced to stop the process of renewal in the face of the Polish and Hungarian crises and go on the offensive against 'revisionism'. The improved economic situation after the implementation of the GDR's second five-year plan in March 1956 also helped Ulbricht. According to the official numbers, industrial production climbed 8 per cent in 1957 and 12 per cent in the first half of 1958, with the consumer goods industry showing the strongest growth. Food ration cards were eliminated in 1958. Prices subsequently climbed, but wages were also raised. The number of refugees began to decrease. In 1958, 205,000 people left East Germany, down from 260,000 the year before. The number decreased by about 60,000 again in 1959. By 31 December of that year, the number of new arrivals from the GDR registered in the emergency shelters of West Berlin and other parts of West Germany was about 144,000.

It was clear that the GDR had gone through a certain process of consolidation. Even refugees, responding to West German enquiries, said that institutions like clinics, convalescent homes, and cultural institutions were 'achievements' worth preserving. 'The political dictatorship with the hierarchical leadership did not represent the whole system,' wrote Hermann Weber.

Very important for many people were the opportunities for professional advancement in all sorts of fields and the existence of spheres of personal freedom. In those days, the situation most certainly did not resemble the typical western clichés, according to which a handful of fanatical communists was oppressing a staunchly anti-communist population committed to the west. Even if the majority did not identify with the GDR, many began to come to some sort of an arrangement with it.

This relative stabilization convinced Ulbricht that the time had come for new exertions in the 'building of socialism'. At the fifth party congress of the SED in July 1958, he announced that the GDR economy was to develop in such a way that 'our working population's per-capita consumption of all important foodstuffs and consumer goods reaches and surpasses the per-capita consumption of the entire population of West Germany.' This would 'clearly prove the superiority of the socialist society of the GDR to the rule of the imperialist forces in the Bonn state'. 'Catch up and surpass!' (*Einholen und überholen*) was the pithy slogan for this ambitious goal, which was to be met as early as 1961.

The 'struggle for the victory of socialism' proclaimed by the fifth party congress was not restricted to the economy. It was also important to move forward with the 'socialist revolution in the area of ideology and culture' and the 'socialist education' of the population. With this view in mind, the Volkskammer passed a law for the 'socialist development of the education system' in December 1959. According to this legislation, a system of secondary schools providing a general polytechnic education in ten grades was to be phased in over the course of the next five years. This reform increased the average age at which pupils finished school from 14 to 16. The struggle between the social systems was brought into the schools: the more education was made to serve scientific and technical progress, the better the chances were that the GDR would catch up with and surpass West Germany. For this reason the natural sciences, mathematics, engineering, and economics were given more emphasis in the curriculum than before.

'Socialist education' did not begin only at school, but in kindergarten and, according to the wishes of the SED, with the parents. Of the 'ten commandments of socialist morality' proclaimed by Ulbricht at the fifth SED congress, the eighth ran: 'Thou shalt raise thy children in the spirit of peace and socialism to be well-rounded, firm of character, and strong of body.' The 'Young Pioneers' (*Junge Pioniere*), from 6 to 14 years old, and the Free German Youth were instructed to dedicate themselves to the same task. The end of the eighth grade, which for most pupils coincided with the completion of their fourteenth year, was the time of the *Jugendweihe*, a 'youth dedication' introduced in November 1954. This was an initiation ceremony originating in the freethinker movement and designed as a counterpart to, and replacement for, the Catholic and Protestant confirmation.

Upon leaving school and entering work life, the socialist man or woman was supposed to be a 'head and hand worker' in one person, according to the definition of Karl Marx. In April 1959 a writers' conference in Bitterfeld called for an end to the separation between production and culture. The workers were exhorted to 'take up the pen!' (*Greif zur Feder, Kumpel!*) The 'Bitterfeld way' was intended to empower the workers to storm the 'bastions of culture'. For the writers it meant the path into the factories, where they would become acquainted with daily life of the workers. This kind of experience was seen as a prerequisite for the effective representation of real life in the sense of 'socialist realism'.

On 1 October 1959 the GDR took two further steps in the direction of Sovietization. An emblem featuring a hammer and compass within a garland of wheat was added to the black, red, and gold national flag, hitherto indistinguishable from that of the FRG. The second measure betrayed the Soviet model even more blatantly: the GDR transformed its five-year plan into a seven-year plan. This decision—formally made by the Volkskammer, as in the case of the flag—could also be interpreted as a tacit admission that the economic goals proclaimed by the SED in March 1956 were not going to be met by 1961.

But the party not only held firmly to the 'building of socialism', it pushed the programme even harder. In the autumn of 1959 it decided to force the remaining independent farmers to join the Agricultural Production Cooperatives (*Landwirtschaftliche Produktionsgenossenschaften* or LPG), thus finishing the process of agricultural collectivization. About 40 per cent of arable land had been collectivized between 1952–9. Within a single quarter-year, the first three months of 1960, this proportion was doubled. One year later the state and the cooperatives, termed the 'socialist sector', were responsible for nearly 90 per cent of gross agricultural output.

This 'success' was achieved by the application of massive pressure, and its price was high. Many farmers preferred to flee to the west rather than join an LPG. Many fields were abandoned and many quotas went unmet, such that shortages in meat, milk, and butter soon occurred. The crisis in agriculture was accompanied by serious problems in the skilled trades. In 1958 private companies were responsible for 93 per cent of branch production. By 1961 the figure had fallen to 65 per cent. The cooperatives had taken over a third of trades output. During the same period, private ownership in retail trade fell to under 10 per cent. As in agriculture, the collectivization of the 'old middle class' swelled the number of refugees from the system. By 31 December 1960 West German statistics had registered 200,000. This was 55,000 more than the previous year.

The escape route was almost always through Berlin. To travel from the eastern to the western part of the city by urban rail, subway, bicycle, or foot was as easy as it was safe. Crossing the heavily guarded border zones, on the other hand, was extremely risky. But this was not the only reason West Berlin had long been a thorn in the side of the GDR and the Soviet Union. The radio and television programmes emitted by West German stations could be picked up throughout much of the GDR. West Berlin was a 'window on the west', allowing the East Germans to compare the anti-western propaganda of 'their' regime with reality. It was also a listening post for numerous western intelligence services. In the view of Moscow and East Berlin, the core of the 'West Berlin problem' was the presence of the three western powers in their sectors. Nonetheless, this state of things could not be altered as long as the western Allies insisted on their rights as victors in the Second World War—*and* as long as these rights were respected by the Soviets.

This second condition was seriously called into question for the first time in a speech by Walter Ulbricht on 27 October 1958. Berlin, though occupied by four powers, had always been a 'part of the Soviet occupation zone', the SED leader declared. The Allied commander had never had supreme authority in the city. 'The whole of Berlin lies within the territory of the German Democratic Republic. All of Berlin belongs to the jurisdiction of the German Democratic Republic.' At this time, it was not yet clear whether Khrushchev shared Ulbricht's view or what the consequences would be for the Kremlin if he did. But one thing was clear: Ulbricht's initiative had made Berlin, and with it the German question, a focus of world interest once again.[16]

THE BERLIN ULTIMATUM AND THE GERMAN QUESTION IN 1958

The third Adenauer government was not yet in place when, on 17 October 1957, the first important post-election foreign policy decision was made: the Federal Republic broke off diplomatic relations with Yugoslavia four days after Belgrade took up diplomatic relations with the GDR. It was the first time Bonn employed the 'Hallstein doctrine', according to which the FRG would regard the recognition of the GDR by a third party as an unfriendly act. Its legal position was clear: the FRG considered itself the legal successor of the German Reich; it was the only democratically legitimated German state; it alone was able to represent the interests of all Germans, including those living in the GDR. Indeed, it was compelled to do so.

The breaking off of diplomatic relations with Yugoslavia was followed on 25 March 1958 with another gesture in the 'policy of strength'. The Bundestag resolved, within the framework of the NATO treaty, to equip the Bundeswehr with nuclear missiles, whose warheads would remain under American control. This decision was preceded by contentious debates. One of the most intense took place in the night of 23–4 January 1958. Former interior minister Gustav

Heinemann, now an SPD delegate, and former minister of justice Thomas Dehler, now a delegate for the FDP, declared that Adenauer had never really wanted the reunification of Germany. The SPD, supported by the labour unions and numerous intellectuals, organized a campaign under the slogan 'Fight against atomic death!' (*Kampf dem Atomtod*). The mass demonstrations reached their climax in April 1958.

Adenauer entertained no illusions about the fact that the reunification now seemed very far away. On 19 March 1958 he asked the Soviet ambassador, to the latter's great surprise, if his government would be prepared to grant the GDR the status of Austria. Although a neutral German state between the Elbe and Oder rivers would not have solved the problem of unity, it would have solved the problem of liberty, and the latter was, for Adenauer, at the core of the German question.

Adenauer's initiative was not least a reaction to certain projects that were being floated at the time, projects the chancellor looked upon as dangerous for the security of the Federal Republic and the west as a whole, or at least as worse than the current status quo. One of these was the idea of a 'German confederation' based on the principle of parity between the FRG and the GDR, both to be nonaligned or *blockfrei* states. This scheme, first circulated by Ulbricht at the end of 1956, enjoyed the official support of the Soviet Union after August 1957. A second was the plan of Adam Rapacki, the Polish foreign minister, in October 1957 to create a militarily diluted, nuclear weapon-free zone between Poland, the GDR, and the FRG. Various ideas concerning the military 'disengagement' of both blocs were also being circulated and discussed in the west at this time. In early 1957 Hugh Gaitskell, the leader of the British Labour party, began campaigning for the withdrawal of both blocs from central Europe and supporting the cause of German reunification within the framework of a European security system. In a number of prestigious radio addresses in November and December 1957, the Reith Lectures, the historian George F. Kennan, the first American diplomat to push for a rigorous 'containment' of Soviet expansionism, came out for a neutral, reunified Germany and for the withdrawal of Soviet and American troops from the European continent. For Adenauer, all of these projects were so many alarm signals, and they motivated him to search for realistic responses to what he considered illusionary mental games.

Debate over the German question entered a new phase in the autumn of 1958. Ulbricht's 27 October speech demanding GDR sovereignty over all of Berlin was the prelude to a large-scale eastern offensive seeking to change the status quo in Germany. On 10 November Khrushchev, speaking in the Moscow sports arena, declared that only the GDR had fulfilled the stipulations of the Potsdam agreement calling for the eradication of militarism, the elimination of fascism, and the liquidation of the monopolies. Berlin's four-power status was all that was left of the treaty, and it was being used by the western powers to conduct subversive activities against the countries of the Warsaw Pact from West Berlin.

The time had come for the Potsdam signatories to give up what remained of their occupation regime. Consequently, the Soviet Union would 'transfer to the sovereign GDR those functions in Berlin still being exercised by Soviet offices'. If the western powers were interested in questions having to do with Berlin, they should take up relations with the GDR itself.

On 27 November, despite western protests, the Soviets followed up Khrushchev's Moscow address with a note to the governments in Washington, London, and Paris. This communiqué became known as Khrushchev's 'Berlin ultimatum'. The Americans, the British, and the French were given six months to agree to the transformation of Berlin into a demilitarized 'Free City'. If they refused to withdraw their troops and end the 'occupation regime', the Soviet Union and the GDR would act independently. The London protocols of 12 September and 14 November 1944, on which the western presence in Berlin was based, were considered by the Soviet Union to be invalid.

This was the first time since the Berlin blockade that the Soviet Union had thrown down a direct challenge to the west. In part, Khrushchev's threats were a response to West Germany's nuclear weapons systems and, as such, a reaction to shifts in western power he felt to represent a danger to Soviet interests. But even if the First Secretary of the Soviet Communist party was more concerned about strengthening his own camp than in extending the sphere of Soviet control, he could only achieve his goal by weakening the west militarily, politically, and psychologically. Thus success in the Berlin question would have tilted the balance of power in favour of the Soviet Union. On 10 January 1959 Khrushchev let it be known that he intended to use four-way negotiations over Germany to leverage a congenial solution to the Berlin problem. In memoranda to the Federal Republic, the GDR, and all states that had participated in the war against Germany, the Soviet prime minister proposed a peace conference and circulated the draft of a peace treaty. According to this document, both German states were to refrain from joining military alliances, withdraw from the current ones, and give up all claims to territories east of the Oder and Neisse rivers. West Berlin was to have a special status for the time being, remaining a demilitarized 'Free City' until the political unity of Germany was restored.

At first Khrushchev's plan seemed to work; the west definitely seemed somewhat intimidated at the beginning of 1959. Harold Macmillan, the Conservative British prime minister, was not only afraid of a third world war, but also a Labour victory in the upcoming elections for the House of Commons. Accordingly, during a visit to Moscow at the end of February, he demonstrated a willingness to accommodate the Soviet Union, not least in the matter of recognizing the GDR. Even Secretary of State John Foster Dulles, a close ally of Adenauer, occasionally wavered in his staunch anti-communism. On 26 November 1958 he spoke on behalf of the so-called 'agent' theory, according to which the United States would not resist if the Soviet Union were to order the documents of all American convoys to Berlin to be inspected by the GDR police (who would thus be acting as Soviet 'agents'). On 13 January 1959 Dulles even aired doubts concerning the wisdom of the formula 'reunification through free elections' at a press conference.

The French leader, on the other hand, remained completely unshakeable. General Charles de Gaulle had returned to the head of the Paris government on 1 June 1958, after a rebellion of the French military in Algiers. (He had held this office before, between September 1944 and November 1946.) On 21 December 1958 he was elected president of the new Fifth Republic, with a constitution virtually tailor-made to suit him. Ever since Adenauer's first meeting with de Gaulle in the latter's private residence at Colombey-les-deux-Églises in Lorraine in mid-September 1958, the two men enjoyed an excellent personal relationship. They were in complete agreement about the goals Khrushchev was pursuing with his 'Berlin ultimatum'.

On the domestic front, Adenauer was very worried about the effect the ultimatum was having on the Social Democrats. In its March 1959 'Germany plan', the SPD—though without actually using the word—took up Ulbricht's idea of a German confederation. Bodies representing both sides equally, first an 'all-German conference', then an elected 'all-German council', would harmonize the West and East German systems of social security and prepare for free elections to a German national assembly. The status of West Berlin was to be left unaltered until the German question was solved. To the chancellor's mind, the withdrawal of the two German states from their military alliances and the creation of a collective European security system, such as the 'Germany plan' called for, struck not only at the very existence of the FRG, but at the higher interests of the entire west. For Khrushchev, the SPD 'Germany plan' was interesting for one reason only: it could be seen as a sign that the west was 'softening'. Its authors' illusions of a 'third way' between capitalism and communism did not impress the authors of Kremlin power politics in the slightest.

Unorthodox ideas were also discussed within the chancellor's narrow circle at the beginning of 1959. The 'Globke plan', named after the state secretary of the chancellor's office, proposed that the FRG and the GDR recognize each other according to international law; that Berlin be transformed into a Free City under the auspices of the United Nations; that free elections be held within the year, allowing the participation of parties previously banned by both states; and that, after a referendum on the reunification, elections to an all-German parliament take place within five years. Unlike the SPD Germany plan, the Globke plan contained nothing about German neutrality. It was never published, and it is not even certain that Adenauer was in agreement with all the points contained in the draft he used as a basis for talks with Dulles. The Soviets, for their part, would probably have seen more disadvantages than advantages in the Globke plan, if negotiations had ever taken place on its basis.

The plan that did lead to talks was the 'Herter plan', named after Christian Herter, the successor to John Foster Dulles. (Ill with cancer, Dulles left office on

15 April 1959 and died on 24 May.) The first round of a conference between the foreign ministers of the USA, the Soviet Union, Great Britain, and France took place in Geneva between 11 May and 20 June. Delegations from West Germany and the GDR, led by their respective foreign ministers, Heinrich von Brentano and Lothar Bolz, were present in an advisory capacity, sitting at two 'little tables'. Herter pushed for the reunification of Berlin *before* the reunification of Germany. Gromyko, the Soviet foreign minister, was not willing to discuss the matter. Nonetheless, by the end of the conference it was clear that the west was prepared to disconnect the Berlin from the German question. Its promise to support the FRG in its campaign for German reunification through free elections was now finally subordinated to the western interest in détente.

The second round, which took place between 13 July and 5 August, produced no tangible results, other than an agreement between Eisenhower and Khrushchev to hold a summit. This meeting, held at Camp David on 26–7 September 1959, concluded with a communiqué in which both sides agreed that new negotiations were to take place on the Berlin question in order to find a solution satisfying all parties and conducive to the preservation of peace. This sounded like a lifting of the Berlin ultimatum of 27 November 1958. In fact, Khrushchev did not rescind his demands, but only modified their time limit. The Berlin question remained on the international agenda, and, after Camp David, Khrushchev was more certain than ever that the west wanted to avoid a conflict over the former German Reich capital. Even Eisenhower, speaking at a press conference after the meeting with the Soviet leader, called the situation in Berlin 'abnormal'.[17]

THE SPD'S CHANGE OF COURSE: GODESBERG AND THE FOREIGN POLICY TURN

For Adenauer 1959 was a bad year in other areas than foreign policy. Domestically, too, he had no luck. The second term of the first president, Theodor Heuss, expired in July (he had been re-elected in 1954), and the constitution did not permit a third. After Ludwig Erhard, the economics minister, refused to run as his successor, Adenauer offered himself as the Union parties' candidate on 7 April. In seeking the highest office in the government, he seems to have been guided by the belief that he could play a role in Germany similar to that of Charles de Gaulle in the French republic. This assumption had no basis in the Basic Law of the West German state.

It was also unclear at this time who Adenauer's successor as chancellor would be. When Ludwig Erhard emerged as a candidate at the end of April, Adenauer, vacationing in Italian Cadenabbia, let it be known that he would sooner renounce his candidacy for the presidency than agree to an Erhard chancellorship. He considered Erhard politically completely unsuited to the office and, in particular, not sufficiently committed to European integration. When the chancellor and

CDU leader failed to convince his colleagues, he withdrew his candidacy on 5 June. The Union parties then chose Heinrich Lübke, then minister of agriculture. On 1 July 1959 Lübke defeated the SPD candidate Carlo Schmid in the Bundesversammlung vote, held in Berlin. Adenauer remained chancellor, Erhard economics minister and vice chancellor. But the presidency crisis did serious harm to the public image of the 'old man'. Adenauer, now 83 years old, had not only committed foolish tactical errors; he had also shown a lack of respect for a fundamental institutional decision of the Parliamentary Council, whose president he had been in 1948–9. Neither the German public, not his party, nor he himself could depend any longer on his—hitherto mostly infallible—political instinct.

While Adenauer's star was sinking, that of a much younger politician, a Social Democrat, was on the rise. Willy Brandt (his real name was Herbert Frahm) was born in Lübeck in 1913 to an unmarried woman. He joined the SPD in 1930, the leftist Socialist Workers' Party the year following. He emigrated to Norway in 1933 and was stripped of his citizenship by the Nazis in 1938. 'Willy Brandt' was originally a pseudonym he assumed as a writer in exile, but he changed it to his official name when his citizenship was restored in 1948. His political career in post-war Germany began that same year when he assumed leadership of the SPD executive in Berlin, a position that put him in close contact with the legendary Ernst Reuter. The latter, mayor of West Berlin from 1948 until his death on 29 September 1953 (in 1950 the title of the office was changed to *Regierender Bürgermeister*, 'Governing Mayor'), was one of a group of Social Democratic mayors, the so-called *Bürgermeisterfraktion*, who were much more open to Adenauer's western policy than the party majority under Schumacher and Ollenhauer (Max Brauer, the mayor of Hamburg, and Wilhelm Kaisen, mayor and senate president of Bremen, were others in this group). Brandt's thinking was similar to Reuter's. While he rejected the EDC, he approved of West Germany's NATO membership. He also rejected the SPD's 1959 'Germany plan'.

Brandt was elected president of the Berlin House of Representatives in 1955, 'Governing Mayor' of Berlin in 1957, and head of the Berlin SPD in 1958. Under his leadership the Social Democrats won the elections to the Berlin House of Representatives on 7 December 1958—just a few days after Khrushchev's ultimatum—with 52.6 per cent of the vote. This was an increase of 8 per cent over the previous elections in December 1954.

The success was due to Brandt's sharp, rhetorically effective rejection of the threats from Moscow. His main campaign slogan was 'Berlin remains free!' (*Berlin bleibt frei!*). One week after the election, Brandt made his first big international appearance. Speaking in English to the NATO council in Paris on 14 December 1958, he described the situation in Berlin under the Soviet pressure and the resolve of the city's inhabitants to remain as firm as they had done ten years before during the blockade. From this day onward Willy Brandt was seen, both in Germany and abroad, as the main representative of a younger, dynamic, and staunchly pro-western German Social Democratic party.

It took a year for the party as a whole to adopt Brandt's image and the principles he stood for. The 'Godesberg Program', the result of a special party congress in November 1959, represented the victory of the 'modernizers' over the 'traditionalists'. It replaced both the Heidelberg Platform of 1925, which was beholden to the spirit of Marxism, and the Dortmund Action Platform of 1952, which had still been calling for the socialization of the raw materials industry.

The Godesberg platform outlined a democratic socialism rooted in Christian ethics, humanism, and classical philosophy, a socialism that neither promulgated 'absolute truths' nor sought to be a 'replacement religion'. The society the Social Democrats aspired to create would allow 'every individual the freedom to develop his or her own personality and, in service to the community, to have a role in its political, economic, and cultural life'. The party declared its allegiance 'to the free market, wherever competition rules'. Public property was relegated to the status of one among various means of legitimate public control, as a way of protecting citizens from the dominance of large business conglomerates. Referring to the origins of the socialist movement in the protests of wage-earners against the capitalist system, the new platform stated explicitly: 'The Social Democratic Party has developed from a party of the working class into a party of the people.' Its membership would be open to anyone 'committed to the basic values and demands of democratic socialism'. Socialism was thus no longer a necessary product of the historical process, as with Marx and Engels. It had become a question of will.

The Godesberg platform described a process of societal opening that had yet to be actually realized. Emancipation from Marxism was necessary in order for the SPD to draw the votes of the middle classes. But ideological housecleaning was not alone sufficient to achieve this goal. It was true that the platform very clearly rejected communism as 'suppressing liberty and raping human rights'. Nonetheless, only a few months before, in its 'Germany plan' of March 1959, the SPD had been giving the impression that it was still contemplating a social system midway between those of the FRG and the GDR. If the Social Democrats wanted to allay the suspicions this kind of thinking had provoked, they would have to take a further step, one well overdue: they would have to commit themselves to foreign policy continuity and endorse Adenauer's western policy.

This step was taken on 30 June 1960 by Herbert Wehner. Speaking for the party before the Bundestag, Wehner announced that the European and Atlantic treaty system to which the Federal Republic belonged represented 'the basis and framework for all the aims of German foreign and reunification policy'. The Social Democratic party neither demanded nor intended to seek the country's withdrawal from its treaty and alliance obligations. It was, however, of the opinion that a European security system was the best way for a reunified Germany to contribute to the security of Europe and the world. The SPD supported the defence of democracy in both word and deed and approved of the national defences. In accordance with the unanimous resolution of the Bundestag on 1 October 1959, the Social Democrats looked forward to the restoration of the political unity of Germany by means of a free and direct expression of the will of the entire German people in its currently divided two parts.

Wehner's concluding remarks had the quality of a personal credo. What the times called for was not

self-destruction, but cooperation within the framework of a democratic whole, albeit as adversaries on the concrete issues of domestic politics. Such differences give life to democracy. The kind of hostility sought and shown by some, however, ultimately kills democracy, however innocuous it may seem at the start. Divided Germany . . . cannot suffer Christian Democrats and Social Democrats who are implacable enemies.

Wehner's speech was a tactical masterstroke. Prior to 1959 the former Communist had not been among those pushing for a break with Marxism and a thoroughly 'reformist' party platform. In Godesberg, however, he placed himself at the head of the reform movement, and it was in large part due to his efforts that the new platform gained a broad majority. In matters of foreign policy, too, Wehner had long been one of the defenders of the 'old' course, which placed reunification above western integration. He was the 'father' of the March 1959 'Germany plan', and it was very confusing to both his friends and his enemies that he, of all people, should perform such an about-face less than one year later and endorse the policy Brandt was pushing. Nonetheless, Wehner now possessed the kind of authority necessary to commit the SPD to the new course. And even if his primary motivation was the will to power, after 30 June 1960 there was no returning to the earlier 'neutralist' policies. The 'westerners' in the party, led by Willy Brandt and the Bundestag delegates Fritz Erler and Karl Mommer, could now finally speak for the whole SPD. The new watchword, 'common ground' (*Gemeinsamkeit*), was to clear the path of the Social Democrats towards governmental power.

The ideological watershed at Godesberg and the foreign policy shift provoked by Wehner were the two sides of the same coin. Both decisions proceeded from the realization that, after more than a decade of Union hegemony, there was no consensus for a radical break with the prevailing social order in West Germany, but only room for its further development. Since a SPD majority was still in the distant future, the party had to make itself acceptable as a coalition partner—that is, open to an alliance with either the Union or the Free Democrats. The Godesberg congress and Wehner's speech on 30 June 1960 could be seen as tickets of admission into such a coalition.

Before they could claim a share in the government, however, the Social Democrats had to come up with an alternative to Adenauer or his CDU successor. They had to choose a candidate who could credibly claim to represent the political centre. The party head, Erich Ollenhauer, was too much a man of the political machine to have much of a chance. For a time, the party leadership contemplated running Carlo Schmid, but the eloquent aesthete—son of a Swabian father and a French mother—had no power base within the SPD and never seriously considered running. Fritz Erler, an astute thinker and splendid debater, was held by many to be the best option. But he had great doubts in his own ability to win over the masses. The man he trusted in this regard and personally supported as candidate was the mayor of Berlin, Willy Brandt, who had become increasingly popular after Khrushchev had given his ultimatum. By the time he gave his 'historic' speech on 30 June 1960, Wehner thought so too. The decision was made on 11 July 1960 at a meeting between the SPD party executive and a seven-person election commission. On 24 August the Social Democrats officially announced that they would be running Willy Brandt for the chancellorship.

Brandt, 46 years old at the time, had numerous qualifications for the office. He was a charismatic speaker, appealing not only to the party faithful, but also to Germans of bourgeois background, especially young people, as well as to intellectuals. Like Adenauer he was pro-western, but he also stood for a German symbol, the former Reich capital, now under threat from the east. As mayor of Berlin, Brandt was in a better position to appeal to nationalist sentiment than the old chancellor from Cologne. To be sure, conservative nationalists found aspects of his biography objectionable: he had emigrated from Germany, and had worked for the fall of the Hitler regime from his exile in Norway and Sweden. Fifteen years after the end of the war, it was still easy to mobilize rightist resentments against Brandt. The outcome of the fourth federal election, which was to be held a year after the SPD candidate was announced in the summer of 1960, seemed completely open.[18]

THE BUILDING OF THE BERLIN WALL
AND THE BEGINNING OF A NEW ERA

For a time it seemed the Berlin question would be the subject of another summit meeting in May of 1960, this time in Paris. But Khrushchev changed his mind. The downing of a U2 American reconnaissance plane by Soviet defences near Sverdlovsk on 1 May gave him the opportunity to pull off an unexpected coup. Having already arrived in Paris, the Soviet leader dramatically called off the meeting before the negotiations were underway. Shortly afterwards he announced that the next conference would have to wait six or eight months, with the status of Berlin remaining unaltered in the meantime. Khrushchev's plan was to await the outcome of the next American presidential election in November and then take up the Berlin issue and other open questions between the east and the west with Eisenhower's successor.

No western leader was as relieved as Adenauer at the failure of the Paris summit. He had noted with increasing worry that the two Anglo-Saxon powers still lacked the necessary resolve on the Berlin question and that the conference had not been adequately prepared. The hard Soviet line also helped the chancellor on the domestic front. The foreign policy shift of the SPD in June 1930 was in large part due to the man who called off the Paris summit and stoked the widespread fear of war.

At the same time, it did not seem out of the question that Khrushchev's plan would succeed and that the Soviets would benefit from the changing of the guard in the White House. The new American president, John F. Kennedy, had gone badly awry in his first sally into foreign policy, the CIA-supported invasion of Fidel Castro's communist Cuba by Cuban exiles. In April 1961, under pressure from Soviet threats, Kennedy called off American support for the attack, which then failed in the Bay of Pigs on the southern coast of Cuba.

Kennedy had not yet recovered from this debacle when he met with the Soviet prime minister for the first time at the beginning of June 1961 in Vienna. What Khrushchev had to say on the subject of Berlin sounded so threatening that Kennedy no longer excluded the possibility of a great war. Khrushchev presented a new Berlin ultimatum, now with a time limit of six months. If a solution in accordance with the Soviet demands was not forthcoming by December 1961, the USSR would conclude a separate peace treaty with the GDR and cede to it the authority over the travel routes to a 'Free City' of West Berlin. When Kennedy asked if this would mean that the western powers would be blocked from the city, Khrushchev responded in the affirmative.

The American president answered him in a radio and television address on 25 July. Kennedy announced a rapid and comprehensive increase in conventional forces from 875,000 to a million troops. This sounded more warlike than it was intended. In the same address Kennedy listed the 'three essentials' the Americans were resolved to uphold with regard to the former capital of the German Reich: the right of the western Allies to a presence in Berlin, their right to free access to the city, and the right to self-determination of the two million citizens of its western sector. Kennedy was silent concerning East Berlin and its citizens. Khrushchev could, and was supposed to, conclude from this that the United States would not stand in his way if he decided the time had come to seal off East Berlin and the GDR from the western part of the city.

A move of this kind was indeed to be expected. The flood of refugees into West Berlin had increased dramatically since 1960, above all in consequence of the forced collectivization of agriculture. Some 30,000 people left the GDR in April 1961 alone. There was a panicked quality to the exodus, and the party and state leadership increasingly had the feeling that it would lead to the economic collapse of the GDR. At a Moscow meeting of the Warsaw Pact in March 1961,

Ulbricht—who, after the death of Wilhelm Pieck in September 1960, had assumed leadership of the newly constituted 'State Council' (*Staatsrat*) and thus become head of state—demanded that West Berlin be sealed off immediately. His call was denied at that time. The decision to close the border between East and West Berlin seems to have been made in Moscow in July 1961, probably before Kennedy's speech. On 5 August, at another meeting of the party leaders of the Warsaw Pact states, the SED politburo received official permission to take the necessary steps at the border to the FRG.

As late as 15 June 1961, on the occasion of an international press conference, Ulbricht was still insisting that 'nobody intends to put up a wall.' But this was exactly what the SED had been planning since mid-June, under the authority of Erich Honecker, the central committee secretary for matters of security. By the time Moscow gave the go-ahead, the top-secret plan was just days away from being carried out. On 12 August Ulbricht ordered that West Berlin be cordoned off on the following day at one o'clock in the morning. Combat groups, police forces, and the army began to carry out their orders in the early morning hours. The border between East and West Berlin was sealed off first with barbed wire, then with a wall. From that moment on, anyone who ventured into the zone between the two parts of the city, or between the GDR and West Berlin, was risking his or her life. Within the month GDR 'border security' had orders to use firearms if necessary. These orders were formally confirmed to the 'border command' of the National People's Army on 6 October 1961.

In an official statement on 13 August 1961 the GDR government declared that the closing of the border was a response to West Germany's 'sharpening of the revanchist policy' and its 'systematic wooing away of citizens of the German Democratic Republic'. In reality the building of the Berlin wall exposed the bankruptcy of a system that depended on force and could avoid collapse only by compelling its inhabitants to remain within its territory. And it was not only the GDR that sought refuge in this desperate measure. When, that same day, the nations of the Warsaw Pact justified the actions of their German comrades, the entire system of Soviet 'socialism' revealed its true character to all the world. Still, the USSR had no choice. As a world power, it could not stand idly by as its German outpost crumbled. To do so would have meant abandoning the whole of its European sphere of control.

The Berlin wall represented little risk for Khrushchev. It violated none of what the west considered its fundamental interests, such as they were embodied in Kennedy's 'three essentials'. In fact, in allowing the wall to be built, the Soviet leader was accepting much less than he had demanded in his Berlin ultimatum on 27 November 1958. The action taken on 13 August 1961 was not an act of aggression against the west, but only against the Germans in the GDR. One of the reasons for Khrushchev's moderation in Europe was the relationship between the Soviet Union and Mao Zedong's People's Republic of China, which had been growing steadily worse since 1958. The western Allies honoured this moderation by restricting themselves to verbal protest against the Berlin wall. For the rest, Kennedy sought to strengthen the morale of West Berlin through demonstrative gestures. On 19 August Vice President Lyndon B. Johnson and General Lucius D. Clay, the 'father of the Berlin airlift', flew to Berlin. A contingent of 1,500 troops was sent by road to strengthen the American garrison in the city.[19]

The day the wall went up, 13 August 1961, represented the deepest break in German history since the founding of the new states in 1949, if not since the unconditional surrender of the German Reich on 8 May 1945. Compared with the Germans in the west, those in the east, within the Soviet-occupied zone and, later, in the GDR, were the real losers of the war. But only after their literal imprisonment within the borders of their state did their lack of liberty become an inescapable fate.

It seemed to make sense to blame the policy of western integration for this development. But this was erroneous. In the 1950s, Germany could only have been reunified at the price of Soviet hegemony in Europe. Nonetheless, there was no question that the building of the Berlin wall literally cemented the German partition, and that the call for reunification now threatened to become merely a hollow formula. After mid-August 1961 it seemed as though Germany would never again be a unified nation, despite the fact that both German states continued, for the time being, to insist on the existence of only *one* Germany. It was clear for all to see that there would be wide disagreement over the practical consequences of this shared belief.[20]

3

Two States, One Nation 1961–1973

THE 'SPIEGEL AFFAIR' AND WEST GERMAN POLITICAL CULTURE

Adenauer's reaction to the building of the Berlin wall exasperated many Germans, including many of his own supporters. The chancellor not only did not interrupt his election campaign, he intensified the polemics against his domestic opponents. At a CDU electoral rally in Regensburg on 14 August, he called the Social Democratic candidate 'Mr Brandt, alias Frahm', a reference to his opponent's illegitimate birth as well as to his exile in Scandinavia during the war. Two days later Adenauer received the Soviet ambassador, Andrei Smirnov, for an interview. Afterwards, in a communiqué his interlocutor had written beforehand, Adenauer announced that the West German government would undertake no action that could have a detrimental effect on its relationship with the Soviet Union and on the international situation. He waited until 22 August to pay a visit to the divided city—too late, in the opinion of not just those who lived in Berlin. Meanwhile, Willy Brandt continued to gain in political stature. After 13 August 1961 the mayor of Berlin had the opportunity to play a national role that transcended party politics, and he seized his chance during the electoral campaign.

The outcome of the fourth federal election was clear by the evening of 17 September 1961. With 45.3% of the vote, the Union parties remained the strongest political force in the country. But they had lost 4.9% in comparison with 1957. The SPD managed 36.2%, 4.4% better than at the previous election. The opposition FDP did proportionally even better, gaining an additional 5.1% of the vote for a total of 12.8%. No other party made it past the 5% clause.

Supporters of an all-party government or a 'Grand Coalition' were to be found in both the SPD and the Union in the early autumn of 1961. Their thinking was guided first and foremost by the dangerous situation in and around Berlin, which they felt could be best dealt with by a government with a broad parliamentary basis. In the CDU/CSU, however, the proponents of a new bourgeois coalition were stronger. The same was true of the FDP. But the liberals wanted Erhard as chancellor, not Adenauer. When Erich Mende, the federal leader of the FDP, made an announcement to this effect at a press conference on 18 September, it was obvious that the coalition negotiations were going to be difficult. (Mende, a former National Liberal originally from Silesia, had been elected party head in January 1960. He was also a holder of the Knight's Cross.) Immediately prior to this disclosure, the CDU executive had asked its leader—at the latter's urging—to be chancellor once again. What was not announced at the time was that Adenauer, now 85, promised to resign in the middle of the legislative period and give his successor a chance to get used to the job before the next election in 1965.

The negotiations were indeed long and complicated. Adenauer conferred with Ollenhauer, Brandt, and Wehner, the leading trio of the SPD. Both the Union and the Social Democrats held talks with the FDP. The process ended with the 'turnaround' of the FDP; they accepted Adenauer as transitional chancellor. Mende could have replaced Heinrich von Brentano as foreign minister (whom the liberals rejected as too rigid); in order to save face, however, Mende refused a cabinet position under Adenauer. Brentano was succeeded by Gerhard Schröder (CDU), hitherto interior minister. The Free Democrats assumed control of five departments: justice, finance, the treasury, expellees, and foreign aid. Finally, on 7 November 1961, nearly two months after the election, Adenauer was elected federal chancellor of the FRG for the fourth time. He received only eight more votes than necessary, his worst result since 1949.

In retrospect, the last years of the Adenauer era seem like a long series of external and internal crises. After the building of the Berlin wall, the Soviet Union repeatedly attacked the alleged abuse of the Allied air routes to Berlin by West German politicians. Khrushchev went so far as to order a massive interruption of air traffic in February 1962, which provoked sharp protest from Washington. Then, on 17 August 1962, something occurred that caused many Germans to lose faith in the United States. An 18-year-old construction worker named Peter Fechter was shot by GDR border troops while attempting to escape over the wall to West Germany near the Allied 'Checkpoint Charlie'. Seriously wounded, he fell in the border zone on the western side of the wall. American soldiers who witnessed the drama refused to intervene, saying it was not 'their problem'. Fechter then bled to death. This event made a greater impression on the Berliners and the Germans than the more than thirty other deaths caused by the border forces of the GDR since 13 August 1961. Willy Brandt, the Berlin mayor, had a difficult time calming the outraged populace and preventing even worse things from happening.

In Adenauer's view, the main problem between Bonn and the leader of the western world was that President Kennedy did not respond to Soviet pressure on Berlin with the requisite degree of toughness. In fact, in April 1962, the USA demanded—it was almost an ultimatum—that West Germany agree to an international office regulating ground and air travel between West Berlin and the FRG, an agency in which the GDR was to have a voice. The chancellor was horrified. While he managed to get the State Department to withdraw its paper on the Berlin and German question, his position was weakened by the fact that in West Germany, too, there were proponents of a 'more flexible' policy with regard to Berlin—above all the foreign minister, Gerhard Schröder, who was said to have remarked that a 'straightening of the front' was unavoidable in Berlin (a comment immediately denied by Schröder himself, of course). In May 1962 the chancellor believed that the time had come to demonstrate his own 'mobility'. He proposed to Smirnov a project he had been thinking about for a long time: a ten-year 'truce' over the question of Berlin and Germany. If Moscow would agree to a liberalization of the GDR, it would be easier to reach agreement later on the difficult questions.

The Kremlin rejected the chancellor's plan. Khrushchev had settled on a strategy of global confrontation, a decision probably made soon after the Berlin wall went up, but by spring 1962 at the latest. This shift was a kind of offensive retreat: if the Soviet Union succeeded in relegating the United States to second fiddle, it would strengthen its position with regard to another dangerous rival, communist China, consolidate the 'socialist camp', and greatly increase Moscow's influence in Europe and the 'Third World'.

In order to force the United States into accepting this new international order, the Soviets decided to station intermediate-range missiles in Cuba—in America's 'front yard', so to speak. But Kennedy was not prepared to submit to this kind of pressure. On 22 October 1962 he demanded the withdrawal of the Soviet missiles already in place and ordered a 'quarantine' of the Caribbean island. For the space of a week, the world teetered on the brink of a third world war and atomic inferno. Then Khrushchev backed down. On 28 October he signalled his willingness to dismantle the seventy-two launching pads in Cuba and transport the missiles back to the Soviet Union.

Peace was preserved—and with it, as became evident shortly, the liberty of West Berlin. The Soviet Union did not stop putting pressure on the city or demanding it be made into a 'demilitarized Free City'. After about the new year, however, Moscow no longer threatened to conclude a unilateral peace treaty with the GDR and to annul the rights of the western Allies with regard to Berlin. The lesson Kennedy had taught Khrushchev in Cuba began to take effect in Europe. The political scientist and publicist Richard Löwenthal, who taught at the Free University of Berlin from 1961 until his retirement in 1974, expressed the 'dialectic' relationship between the Berlin and Cuba crisis in the following way:

The result of the wall was the consolidation of the Soviet status quo in central Europe. The result of the missile crisis was the consolidation of the west's international position, including its position in West Berlin. The shift to international détente, first begun by Kennedy and Khrushchev, proceeded on this basis, which changed the framing conditions for West Germany's eastern policy once and for all.[1]

The Cuban missile crisis, the most serious international confrontation since 1945, took place at the same time as the most serious domestic crisis in the history of the young Federal Republic, the so-called '*Spiegel* affair'. Both events represented turning points. The former turned out to be the peripeteia in the 'Cold War'; the latter became the catalyst in a change from a conservative to a liberal view of the state.

On 26 and 27 October 1962 police stormed and searched the offices of the Hamburg news magazine *Der Spiegel*, arresting the publisher, Rudolf Augstein. Conrad Ahlers, one of the magazine's editors, was arrested in Spain (where he was vacationing) by local police after a telephone call from Defence Minister Strauss to the military attaché of the German embassy in Madrid, Achim Oster. Ahlers returned voluntarily to Germany, where he was immediately placed under arrest. Further arrests ensued, including that of Hans Detlev Becker, *Spiegel* publishing director; the attorney Josef Augstein, brother of the publisher; the editor Hans Schmelz; and two military men, Colonel Adolf Wicht of the Federal Intelligence Service and Colonel Alfred Martin of the Bundeswehr.

The cloak-and-dagger operation had been set off by an article entitled 'Bedingt abwehrbereit'* about the NATO manoeuvre 'Fallex 62', published by the *Spiegel* on 10 October 1962. The story contained explosive material about the catastrophic consequences NATO experts believed a nuclear attack by the Soviet Union would have, as well as detailed information about German–American differences over the waging of nuclear war. Nearly everything covered in the article's analysis had already been published in sources inside and outside the country. The federal prosecutor's office and the defence department never succeeded in proving that the magazine deliberately betrayed state secrets or engaged in blackmail. In May 1965 the Federal Supreme Court called off the main proceedings against Conrad Ahlers and Rudolf Augstein due to insufficient evidence. All the other plaintiffs were acquitted. The *Spiegel* lodged a formal complaint that the arrests and searches had violated the constitution. This claim was rejected by the Federal Constitutional Court in August 1966, with four votes to four.

From the beginning, the dominant view of the West German public was that the affair represented not an 'abyss of treason', as Adenauer claimed to the Bundestag on 7 November 1962, but rather the most serious attack on the freedom of the press since the founding of the Federal Republic. There was a great deal of evidence for this interpretation. The defence minister had for many years been an object of withering criticism in the *Spiegel*, for his policies as well as for his numerous affairs. Students and professors protested in the streets of all the university cities after the arrests, demanding that freedom of the press and opinion be restored and that Strauss be sacked. When, after 103 days in custody, Rudolf Augstein was finally released on 7 February 1963 (the last of those arrested), he had already long since become the hero of a critical public and of a whole generation of young academics.

* Ahlers, 'Conditionally Prepared for Defence'.

Franz Josef Strauss (who had also become head of the CSU in March 1961) had only himself to blame that the whole world outside of Bavaria considered him the villain in the *Spiegel* drama. He was the one politically responsible for the fact that the man with the actual authority in the matter, Justice Minister Wolfgang Stammberger, only learned of the affair from the press. (Stammberger and Augstein were both members of the FDP.) Strauss was the one who ordered the arrest of Conrad Ahlers in Malaga, Spain. Nonetheless, he sought to create the impression, before the public and (at first) the Bundestag, that he had had nothing to do with the whole business, in particular with Ahlers's arrest. This pose meant that the state secretaries of the defence and justice ministries, Volkmar Hopf and Walter Strauss, became the scapegoats.

During a question and answer session on 9 November 1962, it became clear that Franz Josef Strauss had lied to the Bundestag. This had no negative effect on his performance in the Bavarian elections on 25 November. With 47.5% of the vote, the CSU did even better (+1.9%) than in the previous elections on 23 November 1958. Nonetheless, his position had become untenable in the rest of the country. The five FDP ministers resigned on 19 November out of protest against Stammberger's treatment, and Mende let it be known in no uncertain terms that there would be no new coalition with the Union if Strauss held on to his post. Four CDU department heads, including Paul Lücke, minister of housing construction, also refused to participate in a cabinet with Strauss. The SPD demanded his resignation as defence minister and an all-party government to deal with the crisis.

With Adenauer's blessing, Lücke, a staunch proponent of a majority voting system, held the first confidential talks with Herbert Wehner on 26 November. (A majority system would have meant the parliamentary demise of the Free Democrats.) The subject of their discussion was the possibility of a short-term Grand Coalition government under Adenauer and without Strauss as well as the introduction of a majority voting system. The rapprochement with the SPD leadership, quite willing to enter a coalition with the Union, was already quite advanced by the time Strauss finally agreed on 30 November to resign from his office. This gave Adenauer the opportunity to negotiate with both the SPD and the FDP. On 4 December he conducted official coalition talks with the SPD leaders—party chief Erich Ollenhauer, his deputy Fritz Erler, and Herbert Wehner—for the first time. The main point of disagreement was the majority voting system, against which influential members of the CDU also had strong reservations.

A day later, prominent SPD and FDP politicians, including Brandt and Mende, met to exchange views. The liberals were relieved that the Social Democrats had no intention of seeking a change in the voting law for the next election. When the SPD parliamentary fraction met, also on 5 December, it was deeply divided not only over the question of the voting system, but also over the prospect of another Adenauer chancellorship. The leader of the government took this as an opportunity to reject further talks with the SPD. That evening he told his party that there would be no Grand Coalition.

At that point, everything pointed to a reconstitution of the very coalition that had broken apart on 19 November as a result of the *Spiegel* affair. The new cabinet included a number of younger CDU politicians, among them Rainer Barzel, a lawyer originally from East Prussia, who succeeded Ernst Lemmer as minister of all-German affairs. Kai-Uwe von Hassel (CDU) left his post as prime minister of Schleswig-Holstein to become the new defence minister. The new government was in place by 13 December 1962. Strauss was sent off with a 'Great Ceremonial Tattoo', on which occasion Adenauer heaped such praise on him that it seemed obvious his political career was not over.

Adenauer had successfully asserted his authority once again. But his reputation had suffered dramatically. Although the FDP was the Union's coalition partner once again, the smaller party, which had played a prominent role as defender of the freedom of the press and opinion in the wake of the *Spiegel* affair, now acted with more liberal self-confidence than in the past. The SPD remained in the opposition, but had been recognized by the other parties as capable of entering government. From now on there would be more political options than the one the citizens of West Germany had chosen again in December 1962.

The most important longer-term consequence of the *Spiegel* affair had to do with West German political culture. The second German democracy experienced a powerful liberalization in the autumn of 1962. Or, to put it another way, it turned its back on the authoritarian traditions that had survived through the 1950s. Two letters to the *Frankfurter Allgemeine Zeitung* cast a glaring light on the irreconcilable ideological differences that clashed during this period. On 10 November the paper published a letter to the editor from the Freiburg historian Gerhard Ritter, author of a large work entitled *Staatskunst and Kriegshandwerk** and a biography of Carl Goerdeler, among other things. Ritter, who was born in 1888, justified the conduct of the government and the federal prosecutor on all points. The 'theatrical thundering of the political literati and political partisans' was 'scandalous'.

Ritter cloaked his own views in a series of rhetorical questions.

So is there no such thing as a public conscience anymore, one aware of our shared responsibility for our state, one for whom its external security is so self-evident that the good of the state is even more important than the interruption of vacations in Spain? Has our eternal fixation on the horrors of the Hitler dictatorship made us so blind to the reality surrounding us that we are more willing to tolerate every abuse, however gross, of our constitutionally guaranteed personal rights than this or that unseemliness (or impropriety) on the part of our criminal prosecution authorities? Or do we in West Germany already live under another kind of terror, that of the news magazines, which

---

* Ritter, *The Art of the State and the Craft of War* (tr. as *The Sword and the Scepter: The Problem of Militarism in Germany*).

hold their poisoned arrows ready for anyone who does not fear them? That too is a possibility! But if this be the case, then it is certainly a very pitiful kind of democratic liberty.

Three days later, on 13 November 1962, the *FAZ* printed a reply to Ritter's letter. The author was Karl Dietrich Bracher (born in 1922), a historian of contemporary Germany and political scientist teaching in Bonn (his first major scholarly work was a monumental study, the *Auflösung der Weimarer Republik,**** published in 1955). Bracher called Ritter's letter an 'alarming document'. Its language and reasoning had 'all the signs of an ideology of the state in which the only valid politics is from the top down, in which the reasons of state are seen exclusively in terms of external security, which is granted an almost unconditional priority over domestic liberty and the rule of law.' By calling the public outrage against the government actions a 'monstrous cloud of journalistic dust' and in defining himself as a guardian of 'patriotic sentiment' against 'our garrulous democracy', Ritter was 'doing nothing more than rationalizing the disastrous tradition of the authoritarian state in Germany at the expense of democracy—a democracy in which we have only just taken our first steps.'

For Bracher, the affair had caused 'inestimable damage' to the efforts towards political education in West German society, as well as in schools and universities.

It is visual instruction of a kind that creates cynicism and resignation rather than understanding for the nature and problems of democracy . . . The danger is not the 'eternal fixation on the horrors of the Hitler dictatorship', but the persistence of an authoritarian ideology of the state, one that degrades the citizen to the status of a subject and subordinates the principles of democracy to military defence and the defence of the order. For all that, however, the affair has had a positive side: it has uncovered these dangers and tendencies and catalyzed a broad discussion, one that will hopefully continue.

The discussion did continue, and not in the direction taken by Ritter. After the *Spiegel* affair, statements like those of the Freiburg historian sounded anachronistic, whereas those of the Bonn political scientist became representative for the political thinking of the younger generation. It was clear to all that the Adenauer era was nearing its close. Although the first chancellor of the FRG was still in office, the times had passed him by, at least in terms of domestic politics and society. West Germany had become more western than the father of westernization had foreseen or intended.[2]

THE END OF THE ADENAUER ERA

The early 1960s placed the Federal Republic before a foreign policy dilemma. The close relationship it sought with France of the Fifth Republic was increasingly

---

* Bracher, *The Dissolution of the Weimar Republic.*

hard to reconcile with its continuing dependence on the United States. After the end of the Algerian war of independence in March 1962, President Charles de Gaulle began to give French politics an even more strongly nationalist profile. Already in January 1962, France had resolved to restrict the project of a European 'political union'—in the works as of the previous year—to a consultation between individual governments and to prevent the European Economic Community from becoming a supra-national political organization. In April Paris rejected Belgium's and the Netherlands' demand to involve Britain in future negotiations over political cooperation. At the beginning of July, de Gaulle and Adenauer met in Paris to discuss the possibilities of closer cooperation between the two countries. The French leader was especially emphatic about the matter of western European defence.

These talks were held at the beginning of an official visit of the chancellor in France. Its major events were a German–French military parade and a church service in the cathedral of Reims, the former coronation city of the French kings. Two months later, in September 1962, de Gaulle came to West Germany. His visit was a triumph, not least because of a number of addresses in which the French general, speaking in German, declared his deep respect for the 'great German people'.

The jubilation for de Gaulle temporarily masked the fact that the kind of Franco-German détente the two leaders had in mind was in no way a common goal of the 'political class' in West Germany. The main division was between 'Gaullists' and 'Atlanticists'. The first group supported de Gaulle's attempt to make western Europe less dependent on America, especially in matters of defence, and to exclude Great Britain from the European Economic Community for the time being, not least because of its 'special relationship' with the USA. (London had applied for accession in August 1961.) The 'German Gaullists', for their part, very much supported a federal European state and were not willing to accept de Gaulle's vision of a 'Europe of states'. (The general used the words *Europe des états*, not *Europe des patries* or 'Europe of fatherlands', as he was often quoted in Germany.) The main 'German Gaullists' were two CSU politicians, Franz Josef Strauss and Karl Theodor Freiherr von und zu Gutenberg.

The 'Atlanticists', led by Gerhard Schröder and Ludwig Erhard, considered the United States the most important partner in all respects and wanted to see Great Britain in the EEC as quickly as possible. For Adenauer, as for de Gaulle, 'Europe' meant first and foremost the Continent, not the island on the other side of the English Channel. Nonetheless, the chancellor entertained no illusions about the necessity of the American atomic shield. The great majority of SPD leaders were Atlanticists. This did not prevent Willy Brandt from showing a great deal of sympathy and understanding for de Gaulle's policies, however.

The conflict between the 'Atlanticists' and 'German Gaullists' came to a head around the beginning of the new year. Soon after the visit of the French president, negotiations began over the precise form the agreement between France and Germany should take. For Bonn, it was important that the French–German consultations be institutionalized in a way that avoided offending or worrying the other members of the EEC, the United States, or NATO. Meanwhile, the negotiations over Great Britain's accession to the EEC had entered a critical phase. Also, in December 1962, President Kennedy and Prime Minister Macmillan, meeting in the Bahamas, worked out an agreement to equip British submarines with American Polaris missiles and integrate them and other British carrier systems into NATO's nuclear 'Multilateral Force' (MLF). For de Gaulle, this represented a deliberate challenge to France. At a press conference on 14 January 1963 he confirmed his resolve to make France a nuclear power by setting up an atomic *force de frappe*. He also vetoed British accession to the EEC.

The Franco-German treaty was scheduled to be signed eight days later in Paris. After the general's declaration, however, it took on a new quality. It could now be interpreted as West German support for de Gaulle's plans. Right at this time, the foreign office successfully asserted its—constitutionally justified—view in the cabinet that the agreement had to be ratified as an official treaty. Thus, the final decision lay with the Bundestag and the Bundesrat. This gained time for Bonn. The French submitted, with the result that de Gaulle and Adenauer were able to sign the 'Elysée treaty' as planned on 22 January 1963. Among other things, it provided for a minimum of two meetings between the respective heads of state and government per year, four meetings of the foreign and defence ministers, mutual consultations in all important matters of foreign policy, and close cooperation in the areas of educational policy and youth exchange programmes.

On 25 January 1963, three days after the signing of the treaty, the government of West Germany made it clear that it had no intention of supporting de Gaulle's anti-British policy. At the urging of Foreign Minister Schröder, Bonn announced its support for Great Britain's accession to the European Economic Community. It was unable to prevent the negotiations with London from being terminated three days later as a result of the French veto. On 26 February, however, Adenauer told the Bundestag that in a number of other questions, too, he was not absolutely beholden to the French general. He stressed the importance of NATO for the security of the country, demanded a voice in the planning and deployment of atomic weapons, and announced that the Federal Republic was willing to participate in a multilateral nuclear force.

The parliamentary debates over the Elysée treaty were preceded by protests from the Soviet Union, objections by the United States, controversies within the coalition, and negotiations between the government and the opposition. After the beginning of April, a way out of the dilemma emerged and found Adenauer's acceptance: a preamble to the treaty in which the Federal Republic, in accordance with American views, declared its support for partnership with the USA, integration in the Atlantic alliance, European unification through the EEC, Britain's accession to the latter, and negotiations over an international reduction of tariffs (the so-called 'Kennedy round' of the General Agreement on Tariffs and Trade, or GATT).

The rejection of de Gaulle's aims could hardly have been more clear. This preamble significantly reduced the importance of the treaty. But it did assure its passage. The Bundestag ratified it almost unanimously on 16 May 1963, the French National Assembly just less than a month later, on 14 June. It entered into force on 2 July 1963.

The treaty preamble was not the only serious disappointment West Germany caused the president of France in spring 1963. A second bitter pill de Gaulle had to swallow was closely connected with the Elysée treaty; it was also a reaction to Adenauer's idiosyncratic dealings with the general that had led to the treaty in the first place. On 5 March, against the chancellor's wish, the CDU/CSU parliamentary fraction granted its head, Heinrich von Brentano, the power he had requested to propose a candidate for Adenauer's succession in the upcoming fall elections. On 23 April, in accordance with Brentano's wishes, the fraction chose Ludwig Erhard, the vice chancellor and economics minister, by a large majority. Adenauer, who still considered the 'father of the economic miracle' politically incompetent, had tried to the last to stop him from being elected. He felt insulted by the manner in which his party colleagues had gone about preparing the way for his successor. For de Gaulle, the decision was a serious setback. He now had to face the prospect of a chancellor inimical to the Franco-German treaty and who had never left any doubt that the relationship with Washington and London was more important to him than the one with Paris.[3]

The decision for Erhard came at a time when, as Hans-Peter Schwarz has put it, 'a profound and, as it became clear, relatively long-term climate change in world politics' was getting underway.

The great détente of the late 1960s and 1970s began to take shape already in these last months of the Adenauer era . . . At the time great pressure was being put on Berlin, opinions were divided on the question of whether and how long positions in favour of German unity should be maintained, even under the threat of war. From now on, the question was just the opposite: would it be possible to maintain the present course over the long term, even in a phase of détente between east and west? Was not everything pointing in the direction of flexible policies in response to changed conditions, even in Germany?

A speech given by John F. Kennedy at the American University in Washington on 10 June 1963 became the signal for the new era. Three-quarters of a year after the Cuban missile crisis, the most dangerous confrontation between east and west since 1945, the American leader outlined a 'strategy of peace'. Peace was a process, he said, a way of solving problems. This was also true in the relationship between the United States and the Soviet Union. Despite their opposition, the two powers had many traits in common, and none was stronger than the abhorrence of war. Americans considered communism repugnant, since it negated personal freedom and dignity. But they hoped for constructive changes within the Communist bloc, and therefore they would have to conduct their affairs in such a way that it was in the Communists' interest to agree on a genuine peace. 'For we can seek a relaxation of tension without relaxing our guard . . . We do not want a war. We do not now expect a war . . . We shall be prepared if others wish it. We shall be alert to try to stop it.' Kennedy did not revoke the missionary motto of his predecessor Woodrow Wilson in 1917 to 'make the world safe for democracy'. But he gave it a new, more realistic interpretation: '[I]f we cannot end now our differences, at least we can help make the world safe for diversity.'

Kennedy paid an official visit to West Germany on 23–6 June 1963. He was hailed with an enthusiasm that surpassed even that of Charles de Gaulle's visit a year before. In programmatic speeches at the Frankfurt Paulskirche and the Free University of Berlin, the American president made the case for his 'grand design', an Atlantic partnership with two columns, the United States and Europe. He assured his listeners that any assault on the Federal Republic would be treated as an assault on the United States. At the same time, he exhorted the Germans to have patience in their efforts to achieve reunification, which would come neither quickly nor easily. They should not think in slogans, but face the realities of the situation in order to change them. This was the only way to make life easier for those on the other side, beyond the wall. The greatest applause was reserved for a statement Kennedy made to a cheering crowd before the Schöneberg city hall in the presence of Adenauer, Brandt, and Lucius D. Clay (the president's 'ambassador extraordinary' in Berlin) on the last day of his visit: 'All free men, wherever they may live, are citizens of Berlin, and, therefore, as a free man, I take pride in the words *Ich bin ein Berliner!*'

The first to interpret Kennedy's 'strategy of peace' in terms of the German question were Berlin politicians and publicists from the ranks of the Social Democrats and their sympathizers. Already in October 1962 Mayor Willy Brandt had given a speech at Harvard University calling for an 'active, peaceful, and democratic policy of coexistence' and, to this purpose, 'as many real points of contact and as much meaningful communication' with the Communist east as possible. Kennedy's promotion of a self-assured western policy of détente moved Brandt to take a further step, which he did in an address to the Evangelical Academy in Tutzing on 16 July 1963. 'The German question can only be solved with the Soviet Union, not against it,' he told his audience.

We cannot surrender our right, but we have to get used to the idea that, in order to realize it, a new relationship between the east and west is going to be necessary, and that means a new relationship between Germany and the Soviet Union. This will take time, but we can say that the time would not seem so long and oppressive if we knew that the lives of our people over there, and our connections with them, would be made easier.

In a speech the evening before at the same place, Egon Bahr, director of the Berlin press and information office and one of Brandt's closest associates, had outlined the new policy and summarized it in the phrase *Wandel durch Annäherung*, 'change through rapprochement'. Bahr interpreted the American 'strategy of peace' not as an attempt to get rid of Communist rule, but to change it.

The change the USA wishes to bring about in the east–west relationship will help overcome the status quo by leaving it unchanged for the time being. That sounds paradoxical, but it opens up new prospects, while the policy of pressure and counter-pressure followed up to this point has only led to the rigidification of the status quo . . . The zone must be transformed with the approval of the Soviets. If this can be brought about, we will have taken a big step toward reunification.

Bahr's conclusion was a result of the compelling inner logic of his analysis. Put negatively, his argument was that 'an increase in tension strengthens Ulbricht and deepens the divide.' The positive side of this insight was summarized in the following way: 'I see only the narrow path of relief for the people, in such homeopathic doses that there will be no threat of a revolutionary backlash, which would necessarily cause the Soviets to intervene out of their own interests.'

The Berlin publicist Peter Bender argued in a similar fashion and with equal dialectic sophistication. In his 1964 book *Offensive Entspannung. Möglichkeit für Deutschland,* he came to the following conclusion:

We must recognize the status quo, for that is the only way to ameliorate its consequences. The only way left to go on the political offensive in Germany is through détente. Only a limited stabilization of the GDR will allow us to bring the superiority of the FRG to bear . . . Those who stick to the realities can only imagine a long-term process, in which détente, balancing, and alignment go hand-in-hand with a very hard confrontation between the two states in Germany. If a reunification comes about, it will not be given to us as a gift, but will only be won by diplomatic, political, and ideological struggle . . . Anyone who wants to return to how things were even in 1961 has to keep in mind that the SED can and will permit trips to the west only to the extent that the danger of flight decreases. And it is only possible to eliminate or reduce the danger of flight by eliminating or reducing the *causes* of flight. The only way to make the wall 'permeable' is by bringing the standard of living on both sides closer together.

It was anything but coincidence that the voices calling for a revision of the relationship between the two Germanies initially came almost exclusively from West Berlin. Nowhere else were the effects of the wall felt as intensely, nor the clash between the old slogans and the new reality as harsh. Without negotiations with the GDR—still referred to in the west as the 'Soviet zone'—it was not going to be possible to make life easier for the people in the eastern part of Germany and Berlin and to preserve the links between them and their fellow Germans in the west. Daily experience taught this lesson on the banks of the Spree sooner than it could be learned along the Rhine. Those advocating 'change

* Bender, *Offensive Détente: An Opportunity for Germany.*

through rapprochement' still held fast to the goal of reunification, but it was no longer one to be achieved rapidly. A reunified nation state was a hope for the future, but something had to be done for national solidarity *now*. Otherwise there might well be nothing left to unify later. Brandt, Bahr, and Bender were united in this conviction.

Since détente between west and east was a prerequisite for the possibility of humanitarian relief in divided Germany, the Federal Republic was to undertake nothing that would stand in its way. This was another point of consensus among members of the 'Berlin school'. It found the support of three important news weeklies based in Hamburg, *Der Spiegel, Die Zeit,* and *Der Stern,* as well as two daily newspapers read throughout Germany, *Der Frankfurter Rundschau* and *Die Süddeutsche Zeitung.* West Germany's claim to sole representation of the Germans as the only democratically legitimate successor to the Reich; the doctrine of non-recognition derived from this claim; the insistence on the temporary nature of the Oder–Neisse line: according to the pragmatists, these positions would have to be judged according to whether they helped or hindered the amelioration of the human situation in post-wall Germany.

From the late 1950s the relationship between West Germany and the Anglo-Saxon powers had been strained by the FRG's official state policy—not the policy of reunification as such, but rather the government's view that there could be no détente without reunification, or at least as long as the communist government was still in place in the GDR. The open German question was the cause of the 'separate German conflict with the east' to which Richard Löwenthal referred in 1974. But it took the beginnings of worldwide east–west de-escalation in 1963 to put wind in the sails of those in Germany who saw détente as the opportunity to end, or at least mitigate, this separate conflict. When he promulgated his 'strategy of peace' in the early summer of 1963, Kennedy knew he would find more support among Brandt's Social Democrats than from the Christian Democratic chancellor.

On 5 August 1963, in the presence of U Thant, secretary general of the UN, the foreign ministers of the USA, Great Britain, and the Soviet Union signed an international nuclear test-ban treaty in Moscow. The controversy surrounding this agreement soon demonstrated that Adenauer's uncompromising Germany policy had now become untenable on the domestic front as well. The treaty, which could be signed by all states, forbade nuclear tests in the atmosphere, in space, or under water. Washington not only expected West Germany to sign, but also to accept that the GDR would do the same.

Adenauer and several other leading members of the Union—including Heinrich von Brentano, the leader of the Bundestag fraction, Heinrich Krone, minister for special assignments, and Franz Josef Strauss, head of the CSU—regarded the American wishes as tantamount to an international recognition of the GDR and initially called for the treaty to be rejected. Foreign Minister Schröder argued against this interpretation. He was joined by the coalition partner, the Free

Democrats, by the Social Democratic opposition, and not least by the Evangelical wing of his own CDU. Thanks to its strong support, Schröder's more flexible attitude soon prevailed, and the FRG's ambassadors signed the treaty in Washington, London, and Moscow on 19 August. At the same time, the Bonn government announced that its accession to the treaty implied no recognition of states or governments hitherto unrecognized. A similar announcement followed from Washington on 11 September: the treaty did not alter the American position with regard to the GDR. By 1979, 106 countries had joined the agreement. France and the People's Republic of China were not among them.[4]

The Adenauer era came to a definitive end on 15 October 1963. After fourteen years, a period as long as the Weimar Republic, the first chancellor of the Federal Republic of Germany stepped down from his office, unwillingly making way for Ludwig Erhard, elected chancellor the next day (279 votes for, 180 against, and 24 abstentions). When Bundestag president Eugen Gerstenmaier concluded his tribute—which went far back in history and suggested comparisons with Bismarck—with the statement that Konrad Adenauer had done great service for his country, the whole house gave the departing chancellor a standing ovation. The tortuous battle over the succession, the decline in Adenauer's authority in the previous years, the demagogic attacks on his political opponents: all this seemed forgotten for the moment.

Adenauer himself, in his farewell address, thanked not only those who had cooperated with him during his tenure in office, but also the Social Democratic opposition—about whom he had once claimed, in the electoral campaign of 1957, that their victory would be linked to the 'downfall of Germany'. He spoke with pride in what had been achieved, though he also admitted: 'We have come no closer to reunification.' His true feelings, which did not emerge in his speech, were confided to the journalist Walter Henkels a few hours later: 'I do not go with a happy heart.'

Adenauer was not only worried about the international situation, the seriousness of which Erhard, in his opinion, was simply incapable of grasping. The former economics minister was also a liberal, and this was something the old gentleman (now 87) saw as a danger to the country and to his party, of which he was still head. Although Erhard—an Evangelical, though not exactly 'devout', Franconian—professed support for Christian values, he interpreted them in a different, less stringent way than his Catholic predecessor from Cologne. For Adenauer, the traditions of the Christian west were under increasing threat from materialism, secularization, and the decline of morals. Erhard saw the future more optimistically. Adenauer deeply mistrusted the political judgement of the German people. His successor, an unpolitical man himself, did not. Thus the first chancellor perceived the transition to the second as a dramatic shift, far more dramatic than the citizens of the Federal Republic as a whole.

In October 1951, in the third year of the Adenauer era, the Allensbach Institute for Opinion Research had conducted its first survey of representative

West German opinion on the best period for Germany during the twentieth century. At that time, 45% of those asked identified the Wilhelmine empire before 1914 as Germany's best period, and 42% said the Third Reich before 1939. Only 2% spoke for the present. Two months after Adenauer's resignation, the respective numbers were 16%, 10%, and 63%. Nearly two-thirds of West Germans now believed that the present deserved the title of the best of times.

More than anything else, it was the sustained growth of the economy that was responsible for the fact that, fourteen years after the founding of the FRG, an overwhelming majority of its citizens supported the democracy of the Basic Law and rejected dictatorship in any form. A conservative democracy, led by a 'Tory democrat', Konrad Adenauer, had given the western model its now indisputable legitimacy in the German west. The change in leadership had still to be absorbed and dealt with, and with it the beginnings of a new form of democracy, one less 'controlled' and placing greater demands on the individual citizen. Nonetheless, for the first time in German history, the elites were bound to an order in which the power of the state resided in the people. The Federal Republic of Germany had become a stable western-style democracy, and the link to the west had ceased to be a matter of controversy by the time the chancellor who had once forced it through against massive resistance handed over the reins of power.

The polarization caused by the battle over western integration had been overcome in a democratic manner and thus became a force for political integration. There were now *two* great popular democratic parties, each recognizing the political legitimacy of the other. The Union had reconciled conservative Germans to democracy. The Social Democrats had reconciled the workers to a socially domesticated form of capitalism. Radical alternatives had lost their powers of attraction once and for all, the 'right' after the experiences of National Socialism, the 'left' in the course of the example set by the eastern bloc, especially the GDR.

By the time Adenauer stepped down as chancellor, German society had almost completely shed its 'Wilhelmine' character. The building of the wall had contributed to the nationalist disillusionment, the '*Spiegel* affair' to the liberalization of the idea of the state. The expellees and those who had come to West Germany from the GDR were now socially and politically integrated. Agriculture, one of the pillars of the traditional order, had still employed 25% of the West German workforce in 1950; by 1960, that number had shrunk to 14%, and to 11% by 1965. According to confessional statistics, the FRG was still a 'Christian' country in 1961: 51.1% of the population belonged to the Evangelical, 44.1% to the Roman Catholic Church. But the ties of church and religion had loosened during the 1950s as a consequence of increasing mobility and prosperity. The 'conservative modernization' of the Adenauer era was so successful that its own basis began to erode away.

The deficiencies were nonetheless plain to see. In many areas, a phenomenon that would later be termed 'reform bottleneck' (*Reformstau*) could be observed: a lack of innovation in the education system, criminal law, and the penal system, as well as insufficient progress on equal rights for women and children born out of wedlock. Moreover, the Germans' relationship to their Nazi past was still dogged by contradiction: while the period was subject to increased scholarly and juridical scrutiny, personal guilt, to the extent that it was not 'litigable', continued to be disregarded.

The Federal Republic also lacked credibility in one other area: the German question. Again and again, Adenauer had claimed the reunification of Germany in peace and liberty as his primary goal. But it was not, and it could not be, since the antagonism of the two world powers stood in the way of a solution to the German problem. It was, and remained, legitimate to grant higher priority to West German liberty than to German national unity. In fact, it was absolutely necessary to do so. But the old formulas of the FRG's Germany policy required urgent review. They contradicted both its politics *and* its obligations to the Germans in the GDR.[5]

THE GDR AFTER THE WALL

After 13 August 1961 the Germans in the GDR had no choice but to come to some sort of arrangement with 'their' state, even if they continued to reject it. Most of them could no longer leave the country without risking their lives. Initially it looked as though the party and government leaders would aid them in their attempt to come to terms with the system. The building of the wall had stabilized it for the time being. If the SED wished to reform the GDR, it could now do so with less risk than before.

There were hopeful signs in many areas. At the twenty-second party congress of the CPSU in October 1961, Khrushchev initiated a new phase of de-Stalinization with further revelations about Stalin's system of terror. Unlike in 1956, after the twentieth CPSU congress, the GDR now adopted the new line without any reservation. Ulbricht himself now spoke of the 'crimes' committed under Stalin's leadership. The deceased dictator lost the last remnants of his status as an eponym and cult figure. Stalinstadt an der Oder, founded in 1950 as the settlement colony of the Eastern Iron Combine, was rebaptized 'Eisenhüttenstadt' in November 1961. The Stalinallee in East Berlin was renamed the 'Karl-Marx-Allee', and the monument to Stalin was torn down in the 'capital of the GDR'.

The party's cultural policy also seemed to become more liberal. Works of western authors like Max Frisch and Ingeborg Bachmann were published in licensed editions. In 1963 the writer Christa Wolf was able to publish *Der geteilte Himmel*,* a novel dealing with the taboo subject of flight from the GDR (though the book's intention, of course, was to help preserve the state). The songwriter Wolf Biermann was permitted to criticize East Germany during public concerts.

---

* Wolf, *Divided Heaven*.

In a 'youth comminiqué' of September 1963 the SED went so far as to warn against 'dismissing the awkward questions of young people as bothersome or rebellious, since such practices push young people into hypocrisy'.

The greatest changes were in economic policy. In June 1963 the government, acting on decisions made by the sixth party congress of the SED in January that year, promulgated the 'New Economic System of Planning and Leadership' (*Neues Ökonomisches System der Planung und Leitung* or NÖSPL). The most significant features of the new system were, on the one hand, the new 'economic levers' (prices, taxes, interest payments, profits, bonuses, wages), which, combined correctly, were designed to guarantee profits. On the other hand, the economy would be de-centralized by allowing individual companies and factories more latitude. It was clear that the SED derived these policies from the Soviet economist Yevsei G. Liberman's ideas about the economic benefits of 'material interest' on the part of workers and businesses—ideas that, in practice, meant attempting to make the socialist planned economy internationally competitive using the selective incorporation of capitalist techniques.

The NÖSPL had a visibly positive effect on the economy. According to official records, worker productivity increased 7% in 1964 and 6% in 1965. The national income rose 5% in both years. The economic reform led to far-reaching speculation in the west. In adopting the methods of modern management, the GDR seemed to be on its way to placing economic and social concerns above those of politics. According to many observers, this signalled not only a modernization of Marxist-Leninist ideology, but a profound transformation in the system. As the West Berlin political scientist Peter Christian Ludz put it in 1964: 'The interdependence of ideological and societal transformation points to the commonality of certain norms and ideals between the party and society. This commonality is an indication that the totalitarian system itself is changing—into an authoritarian system.'

Ludz would later go even further. In his 1968 book *Parteielite im Wandel*,* he argued that the GDR had developed from a totalitarian regime towards a system of 'consultative authoritarianism', the primary interest of which was to function smoothly. From this perspective, the new stratum of technocratic experts represented a kind of 'institutionalized counter-elite', which, in contrast to the ruling 'strategic clique' of old functionaries, had recognized the necessity of more societal participation. An even bolder analysis was proposed in 1966 by Ernst Richert, a West Berlin publicist. Richert saw the same forces of scientific and technical progress at work in the west and east, forces that were bringing forth a new society in a process of silent revolution.

The ideologies of both sides are exhausted. They were useful in the initial phases of both bourgeois and eastern-socialist society. Exhausted, too, are the norms and institutions

---

* Ludz, *The Changing Party Elite in East Germany*.

that began this process, as well as the strata or groups that sustained them. Thanks to their success, both must now hand over overall control to the material forces technology itself has unleashed.

The question of whether the two 'social systems and their societal attitudes' would draw closer to each other was one Richert wished to leave open for the time being. In the long term, however, he believed that everything pointed towards the 'convergence' of capitalism and communism. This was a belief shared by many western sociologists in the 1960s. And in fact, the course taken by the Soviet Union and its communist satellites after Stalin's death can no longer be described in the static terms of a totalitarian system. Totalitarian mass terror was a thing of the past. Communist rule had become more stable and businesslike.

This was especially true of the period after the fall of the impulsive Khrushchev and the introduction of a 'collective leadership' under Leonid Ilyich Brezhnev in October 1964. 'Khrushchev wanted to play the role of the dynamic leader in a phase in which the totalitarian dynamic of the Communist regime was petering out,' wrote Richard Löwenthal at the beginning of 1965.

When Khrushchev came to power, he was resolved to restore the institutions of the regime and renew its dynamic faith. In the end, this faith was defeated by the growing rigidity of the restored institutions . . . The formal continuity of the party regime remains unbroken, but the erosion of the ideological dynamic is now very advanced. The new men are, objectively and subjectively, unable to continue the revolution. They must content themselves with administering over its results.

The argument that the totalitarian dynamic had exhausted itself while the totalitarian institutions prevailed described the reality of the mid-1960s far better than the assumption that societal and material factors would compel the communist regimes to become more liberal and democratic, thus 'converging' with the west. As closer observation revealed, there could be no question of increasing participation on the part of the subjects of communist rule. The post-Stalin reforms were aimed not at a higher degree of political participation, but at increased economic efficiency. The modernization was designed not to overcome, but to solidify the power monopoly of the party.

But not even the economic modernization produced the desired result. This was true of all the members of the Warsaw Pact, including the GDR. It was unable to achieve the productivity and living standard of West Germany. Already in December 1964 the SED central committee, at the urging of the new Soviet leaders, revised the NÖSPL to accord with guidelines from Moscow. Once again, politics had priority over the economy. In July 1965 Ulbricht blamed Erich Apel, the director of the state planning commission, for problems that were really the result of insufficient raw materials shipments from the Soviet Union. Apel was found dead in his office on 3 December 1965. Whether he shot himself or was shot by others has never been cleared up.

Twelve days later began the eleventh congress of the SED central committee. The 'second phase' of the 'New Economic System', as it was now called, essentially meant a return to centralization. The state planning commission under Apel's successor Gerhard Schürer was forced to surrender many of its powers to existing or newly created ministries. The Publicly Owned Enterprises were again made more subject to the central authority of the *Vereinigungen Volkseigener Betriebe*. Of the original NÖSPL, little was left that could justify hopes for reform.

In the area of culture, too, the eleventh congress—which its critics called the *Kahlschlag-Plenum*, the 'demolition plenum'—restored earlier practices. In his report on 15 December Erich Honecker, the secretary for security and on most questions even more of a hardliner than Ulbricht, attacked 'manifestations of immorality and a lifestyle alien to socialism' in films, television programmes, literary works, and journals. He lambasted Wolf Biermann, whom 'the enemy' was 'systematically making into the standard-bearer of a so-called literary opposition in the GDR, into the mouthpiece of the "rebellious youth"'.

It is time to take steps against the spread of alien and harmful ideas and unartistic rubbish, which also reveals strongly pornographic features . . . We are not curmudgeons and obviously support the realistic depiction of all sides of human existence in literature and art. But this does not mean we will permit the newest effusions of shamelessness and brutality from the capitalist west to be smuggled in for the purpose of infecting our youth.

After Honecker's attack, Biermann was banned from giving public concerts, a measure also designed to intimidate other critics of the regime. One of the most vocal of these, the physicist Robert Havemann, a friend of the songwriter, had already been dealt with. In March 1964 the party leaders of Humboldt University in Berlin threw him out of the SED and stripped him of his academic position. The reason given was that the physicist had not considered it beneath his dignity to use West German organs of publication and had thus given support to the plans of the militarists and revanchists against the GDR. In addition to its attacks on writers and artists, the eleventh congress aimed sharp criticism at the FDJ. The youth organization had 'neglected the Marxist-Leninist education of the young.' The liberal youth policy introduced in the September 1963 'youth communiqué' was now also at an end.

The educational reforms were permanent. The law of 25 February 1965 establishing a unified socialist education system proclaimed the 'socialist personality' as its goal and promised all citizens an 'equal right to education'. The reform was centred on a ten-year programme of study at a secondary school (*Oberschule*) offering a general polytechnic curriculum and more practical training than before. More comprehensive instruction in Marxism-Leninism went hand-in-hand with a more intensive programme in mathematics. The students of socialist East Germany would be superior to those of the capitalist west, not only in terms of ideology, but in all areas important to societal and technical progress. Such, at least, was the goal.

The law's aims applied not only to the *Oberschule*, but also to the two-year *Erweiterte Oberschule* ('Expanded Secondary School'), designed to continue where the latter left off, as well as to schools offering professional training and continuing education, engineering and technical colleges, universities, and even, within the intrinsic limits, pre-school education. These efforts were successful in at least one area that can be measured: the number of students receiving more than eight years of education climbed from 16 per cent in 1951 to 85 per cent by 1970. This change was noted with interest in West Germany, too.

Even during the period of comparative liberalization, the SED never relaxed in its ideological battle against the other German state. At the introduction of general conscription on 24 January 1964, Colonel General Heinz Hoffmann (appointed minister for national defence in July 1960) pointed to the Treaty of Potsdam, whose primary aim it was 'to prevent German militarism from ever causing another war'. Two months later, on 25 May 1962, the National Council of the National Front published a 'National Document' with the title *Die geschichtliche Aufgabe der DDR und die Zukunft Deutschlands.** According to this text, the victory of socialism in the GDR lay in the national interest of the entire German people and was 'the decisive prerequisite for a solution to our national question'. The GDR, 'already an entire historical period ahead' of West German society, was not in a position to delay the 'completion of the building of socialism' until the 'peace-loving forces in West Germany, led by the working class', had 'achieved victory'. In the meantime, it was imperative to establish a 'German confederation' in a spirit of 'peaceable coexistence' for the purpose of securing peace until the reunification of Germany.

This call was repeated in the first party platform of the SED, proclaimed by the sixth party congress in January 1963. Here, too, the party left no doubt about the ultimate 'socialist' goal of its 'nationalist' policy. The GDR was, according to the platform,

in all areas of politics and society the national and social alternative to the imperialism ruling in West Germany. Its historical task is the comprehensive realization of socialism in the first workers' and peasants' state; this will allow the working class to assume leadership of all of Germany, the monopoly bourgeoisie to be stripped of power in West Germany, too, and the national question to be solved peacefully and in a socially progressive way.

The 'party of the working class' could not expect to find broad support for its nationalist claims among the citizens of the FRG, at least for the time being. But the rhetoric of its platform was directed primarily at its own citizens. They were the ones who had to be convinced that the country's leaders still held firmly to the goal of reunification even after the building of the 'anti-fascist barrier'. It is even quite likely that the SED believed its own rhetoric. It still considered itself to be in possession of the only teaching that recognized the systematic progress

---

* *The Historical Task of the GDR and the Future of Germany.*

of history and thus knew history's ultimate outcome. Since socialism would be victorious throughout the whole world, it was a matter of historic necessity that it also triumph in the part of Germany still provisionally ruled by capitalism. When this victory was achieved, the national question, too, would be solved, in a Marxist-Leninist way.[6]

ERHARD'S FAILURE AND THE FORMATION OF A GRAND COALITION

The relationship between the Federal Republic and the GDR was one of the first problems that the new government in Bonn, Ludwig Erhard's Christian-Liberal cabinet, had to deal with at the end of 1963. On 5 December Alexander Abusch, deputy head of the GDR ministers' council, proposed to Willy Brandt, the mayor of Berlin, that an agreement over travel permits be negotiated by letter. The goal was to allow citizens of West Berlin to visit relatives in the 'capital of the GDR' during the Christmas season. This was the kind of thing the Berlin senate had been urgently demanding. Up to that time, the GDR had been permitting citizens of the FRG proper and foreigners to visit the eastern part of the former Reich capital, but not the inhabitants of West Berlin.

The new government was divided on this issue. The head of the FDP, Erich Mende, vice chancellor and minister of all-German affairs after 17 October, supported Brandt's position. Foreign Minister Schröder was one of the warning voices, believing that an arrangement with the GDR would endanger the non-recognition policy. Chancellor Erhard was undecided, but let the Berlin senate have its way in the end. The first travel permit agreement was signed by State Secretary Erich Wendt for the GDR and Senate Councillor Horst Korber for West Berlin on 17 December 1963. Between 19 December 1963 and 5 January 1964 the citizens of West Berlin were permitted to visit members of their immediate family in the eastern part of the city. A 'safeguard clause' in the protocol noted that the two sides were unable to agree on common terms for particular locations, agencies, and offices. This meant that the document could not be construed as containing either a recognition of the GDR or a view of West Berlin as an 'independent political entity'.

The agreement was nonetheless a success for the GDR. It had shown itself to be 'humanitarian', making for favourable press in the west. It was now very doubtful whether West Germany would be able to maintain its strictly rejectionist attitude towards all kinds of official contact with the GDR (except for those through the fiduciary office for inter-zone commerce). And not least, after 17 December 1963 the GDR possessed a tool to put pressure on West Berlin and, if necessary, divide it against the Bonn government. The first travel agreement was followed by three more, the last in 1966 for the Easter and Pentecost holidays. Thereafter, however, the GDR was no longer willing to accept the 'safeguard clause'. No humanitarian ameliorations without formal recognition: this was the message from East Berlin. The GDR knew that, by this time, West German public opinion had more understanding for this view than during winter 1963–4.

By the time the Berlin Social Democrats managed to cajole the Erhard government into going along with their 'policy of small steps', the pioneer of western détente was no longer alive. On 22 November 1963 President John F. Kennedy was murdered in Dallas (to this day, it is not known who besides Lee Harvey Oswald was behind the assassination). The new president, Lyndon B. Johnson, inherited an international crisis zone from his predecessor—Vietnam, where the communist north under Ho Chi Minh and the authoritarian south under Ngo Dinh Diem had been in open war from 1960 onwards. The northern Vietcong had one distinct advantage: they had many partisans in the south who fought against the dictatorial Saigon government.

In the beginning, Kennedy had supported the corrupt but staunchly anti-communist Ngo Dinh Diem with American 'military advisers'. After Diem's fall and murder at the beginning of November 1963, this policy was continued under his successors, an officers' junta. The American rationale was a belief that if the whole of Vietnam fell into the hands of the communists, one South-East Asian country after another would go 'red'. Johnson, a firm advocate of this 'domino theory', expanded American military engagement in the summer of 1964. At this point the conflict turned into war between the small state of North Vietnam and the United States, a world power. Khrushchev was brought down in the Soviet Union shortly thereafter, in October 1964. As head of the Soviet Communist party, he had turned into a predictable partner for the USA. But the last months of his rule were overshadowed by the rupture between the Soviets and Mao Zedong's China. In mid-July 1964, in an article in the *Red Flag*, Mao had Khrushchev accused of espousing a 'counterfeit communism'. (This probably accelerated the latter's fall.) Once again, the question of whether détente would survive the new international situation was, at the end of 1964, completely open.

The year following the change in leadership in Moscow brought a series of foreign policy setbacks for Bonn. Khrushchev had planned an official visit to the Federal Republic, but his successors, party chief Brezhnev and prime minister Kosygin, had no interest in keeping this engagement. Negotiations with Czecholslovakia over trade missions failed in March 1965 because of the 'Berlin clause', the FRG's insistence that West Berlin be included in the agreement. It was obvious that the Kremlin was behind the Czechoslovak response. In 1963–4 the FRG had signed treaties with Poland, Romania, Hungary, and Bulgaria. The new Soviet leaders now decided to veto further agreements of this kind, wishing to support neither their own allies' efforts at independence nor the policy of Gerhard Schröder, all of whose efforts on behalf of better relations with the communist states of eastern central and south-eastern Europe were also guided by the desire to isolate the GDR.

The next foreign policy defeat was the result of a decision the Bonn government made primarily for moral reasons. In May 1965 the Arab states, with the exceptions of Libya, Morocco, and Tunisia, broke off diplomatic relations with the Federal Republic after it established diplomatic relations with Israel. In the case of Egypt, it was almost the FRG that made the move first, in March, in response to a visit by Walter Ulbricht to Egypt. But since President Nasser did not formally recognize the GDR, Schröder, Defence Minister von Hassel, and the Free Democratic members of the government, who supported a flexible interpretation of the 'Hallstein doctrine', decided it did not apply in this case. Erhard and a majority of the Union ministers accepted this view. The new relationship with Israel was also intended as a response to the challenge from Egypt.

These diplomatic problems with eastern Europe and the Middle East were not as serious as a crisis in the government's western policy. Once Adenauer had left the government, he became more and more vocal in his support for the 'Gaullists', with the result that their conflict with the 'Atlanticists' grew more vehement. In concrete terms, Adenauer and Strauss, the leaders of the two Union parties, saw little of interest in the détente *à la française* that de Gaulle had been pursuing after the failure of his German policy. But they did share his aspiration to make Europe more 'European', that is, less dependent on the United States. As such, they were anything but anxious for a rapid accession of Britain to the EDC.

When, at the end of 1964 and the beginning of 1965, President Johnson dropped the plan of a multilateral nuclear strike force (MLF) within NATO, a project supported by the German 'Atlanticists', the German 'Gaullists' initially stood to gain. Shortly thereafter, however, the French president did something to alienate his German followers: on 30 June 1965, France withdrew its representative from the EEC ministers' council. By means of an 'empty chair policy', de Gaulle sought to frustrate the progress of the EEC commission (led by Walter Hallstein since 1958). The commission had proposed financing the common agricultural market through revenues it would raise itself, instead of through contributions by the individual member states. It also wished to expand the authority of the European Parliament and replace the consensus with the majority principle in decisions made by the Ministers' Council after the beginning of 1966, when a new phase of integration was scheduled to commence. De Gaulle's obstructionism brought European integration to a halt and Germany into deep conflict with its western neighbour.

Nonetheless, Erhard had no reason to worry that his government's many foreign policy problems would harm his chances in the upcoming federal elections. The economy was doing very well. With an unemployment rate of only 0.7 per cent in 1965 (147,000 unemployed), West Germany was not only in a state of full employment; it was actually suffering a considerable labour shortage. After the building of the Berlin wall cut off the supply of skilled labour from

East Germany, the need for 'guest workers' (*Gastarbeiter*), above all from southern Europe and Turkey, had risen continually. Their number rose above a million in June 1965. It seemed as though the 'economic miracle' would never end.

Once again, the Social Democrats ran Willy Brandt as their main candidate. He had assumed the leadership of the party in mid-February 1964, succeeding Erich Ollenhauer, who had died on 14 December 1963. The Social Democrats decided not to run an aggressive, confrontational campaign. They sought rather to smooth over domestic differences and reconcile conflicts. They emphasized the priority of 'community tasks' like health care, education, and environmental planning. Apart from Brandt's advocacy for humanitarian relief in divided Germany, foreign policy played no role. Brandt campaigned with a 'governmental team' at his side that included, among others, Fritz Erler, Herbert Wehner, Gustav Heinemann, Carlo Schmid, the Hamburg interior minister Helmut Schmidt, and the Berlin senator Karl Schiller. The main electoral slogan was *Sicher ist sicher* ('safe is safe')—which could, of course, also be misinterpreted as a call to leave things as they were.

As the surveys had predicted, Erhard emerged victorious on the evening of 19 September 1965. The CDU/CSU gained 2.3% more of the vote than in 1961, for a total of 47.6%. The SPD did proportionally somewhat better with a 3.1% increase, reaching 39.3% of the vote. The FDP managed 9.5%, a loss of 3.3%. Together, the Union and the Free Democrats controlled a majority of 92 seats, which seemed to indicate that another Christian–liberal coalition could be expected.

The Social Democrats performed better in this election—the fifth since the founding of the FRG—than they had ever done in the history of their party. However, the man who had made the greatest single contribution to that success took the steps that seemed appropriate to him after the returns were in. On 22 September Willy Brandy announced that he would remain party head and mayor of Berlin; that is, he would not be going to Bonn to assume leadership of the parliamentary opposition. He excluded the possibility of running for chancellor in the future. He did not say that his decision was influenced by the press and rumour campaigns waged against him over his illegitimate birth and emigration, as before in 1961. But he admitted as much to the party leaders on 25 September. 'The fact remains that the smear campaign of 1961 had been transformed into comprehensive subliminal propaganda. The fact remains that, this time too, I was defamed in the most atrocious manner in many publications.'[7]

Despite the clear election result, it proved difficult to form a government. President Heinrich Lübke, whom the SPD had helped re-elect on 1 July 1964, would have preferred a Grand Coalition, but in any case wanted—as did Adenauer and Strauss—to prevent Gerhard Schröder from returning as foreign minister. The CSU rejected Erich Mende's bid to become minister for all-German affairs again, and insisted that the FDP offer some kind of apology to

Strauss, who had not yet got over his fall in November 1962 or forgiven the FDP for their role in the '*Spiegel* affair'.

In the end both Schröder and Mende retained their posts. Strauss did not enter the cabinet, but he did manage to secure a statement according to which both coalition partners considered as no longer valid any reservations against leading members of the other party with regard to their fitness for government office. Erhard first submitted to the CSU resistance to Mende, then revoked his decision when the FDP protested. In exchange, the CSU received five ministries instead of the four planned. On 20 October Erhard was re-elected to the chancellorship. But the difficulties in forming the government had weakened his authority considerably, above all in the ranks of his own CDU.

In his inaugural address on 10 November, Erhard ventured a new look at the national situation, one that drew fire immediately. 'The post-war period is at an end!' With this statement, the chancellor was seeking to bring about a shift in perspective. Since more than half of the population had no personal memories of the years 1933–45, the war and the post-war period, he believed, could no longer provide the main points of reference for the work of the Bundestag and Bundesrat.

But the past was in no way a closed chapter. On 25 March 1965 the Bundestag had voted by a large majority to extend the statute of limitations on Nazi crimes of violence. On 19 August, after more than twenty months of proceedings that aroused the passions of the German public, the Frankfurt court handed down its judgments against a number of former guards at the Auschwitz extermination camp. And even if the West Germans had long outgrown the immediate post-war years, the Germans in the GDR had to wonder if the chancellor had meant to include them in his assessment.

Another of Erhard's controversial and easily misunderstood ideas was that of the 'ordered society' (*formierte Gesellschaft**). What he meant by this expression, which had been coined by Rüdiger Altmann, one of his advisers, was a 'modern, performance-oriented society'. While such a society was not free of conflicting interests, they no longer represented 'factors in the dissolution of their unity', but were becoming, more and more, the 'motor of a permanent balancing of interests under the aegis of the common prosperity'. This sounded ambiguous. In any case, it did not exclude the possibility that the chancellor would, if necessary, subject social pluralism to discipline from 'above'. This interpretation seemed to fit in with Erhard's appeal for the West Germans to work one more hour per week instead of calling for a shorter working week. The 'father of the economic miracle' was worried about the shortage of German labour and the growing number of foreign workers. He had to convince the population of the necessity of a drastic austerity programme, which had been adopted by the cabinet on 29 October and put in the form of a law to secure the budget. The call for

* [Translator's note: *formieren* is a military term meaning 'to form up', 'to draw up in formation'.]

a longer working week, however, seemed to cast doubt on Erhard's grasp of practical reality—an ironic situation for someone who saw himself as the 'people's chancellor'.

In the foreign policy section of his address, which bore Schröder's stamp, Erhard emphasized the significance of NATO and the Franco-German treaty. He declared his allegiance to the Germans' right to self-determination, to reunification, and to the FRG's exclusive right to speak for all Germans. He appealed to the 'valid legal standpoint', according to which Germany persisted within its borders as of 31 December 1937 and the final borders could only be settled in a final peace treaty to be worked out with a freely elected, all-German government. Nonetheless, the chancellor also wished 'to further develop relations with the states in eastern and south-eastern Europe, to promote commerce, to strengthen cultural contacts, and to foster mutual understanding.' West Germany wished more détente, not less.

This sounded very general and, as for what it had to say about the eastern neighbours, was far behind the thinking of the Council of the Evangelical Church in Germany. In a document of 15 October 1965 entitled *Die Lage der Vertriebenen und das Verhältnis des deutschen Volks zu seinen östlichen Nachbarn,** published by the council's chamber for public responsibility, the authors called for a thorough reassessment and reformulation of the basis of the FRG's eastern policy, including the question of the future eastern border. It was not sufficient 'to rigidly and one-sidedly insist on the German legal standpoint'. What was needed was 'to create an atmosphere, both among the German people and for the outside world, in which acts of reconciliation with our eastern neighbours become possible, even if it is one step at a time.' On 5 December, during the Second Vatican Council in Rome, the Catholic bishops, responding to a letter of 18 November from the Polish bishops, also came out in support of mutual forgiveness and, in the spirit of Christian charity, efforts 'to overcome all the unfortunate consequences of the war in a way that is just and satisfying to all sides'.

Finally, on 25 March 1966, the Erhard government took a small step in the direction the churches were pointing. In a 'Note on Disarmament and Maintaining the Peace', which went out to nearly all the nations in the world except the GDR, the Federal Republic made suggestions for disarmament, securing the peace, and détente. To the states of eastern Europe it offered formal declarations renouncing violence and proposed the exchange of military observers for manoeuvres. Nonetheless, the text also reiterated the claims that Germany continued to exist within the 1937 borders and had the right to freely decide its own fate. Thus it was hardly surprising that the communist states of Europe rejected the West German 'peace note'.

---

* *The Situation of the Expellees and the Relationship between the German People and their Eastern Neighbours.*

In the first half of 1966, however, a real east–west dialogue seemed to be getting started between the SPD and the SED. On 18 March the Social Democratic party executive responded to an 'open letter' that the First Secretary of the SED, Walter Ulbricht, had directed on 7 February to the delegates of the SPD congress planned for June in Dortmund. In their reply, the Social Democrats rejected the idea of cooperation between the two parties, for which none of the prerequisites had been met, and refused to participate in 'people's front' manoeuvres. Instead, they suggested that both parties work towards creating a forum in which representatives of both sides could openly discuss their views on the German problem. This thought was taken up by the SED, which proposed an exchange of speakers on 26 March. The SPD agreed on 14 April.

After preparatory talks, it was agreed on 26 May that SPD representatives would speak in Karl-Marx-Stadt (formerly Chemnitz) on 14 July, and spokesmen for the SED on 21 July in Hanover. But there was a legal obstacle: Ulbricht and the other members of the SED delegation were subject to arrest and prosecution in West Germany, not least because of the deaths at the Berlin wall. In order to get past this—by no means purely theoretical—hurdle, the Bundestag passed a law on 23 June temporarily releasing Germans residing outside the territory governed by the Basic Law from the jurisdiction of the Federal Republic if, after all aspects of the matter had been considered, it was deemed to promote important public interests. (Fifty members of the CDU/CSU and two from the FDP voted against the law.)

The SED spoke of a 'handcuff law', which was exactly the reverse of its intent. But discrimination against the GDR was just enough of a pretext to justify the SED's decision to cancel the exchange, which it did on 29 June—after an intervention from Moscow. In his memoirs, Willy Brandt writes that before this announcement the Soviet ambassador in East Berlin, Piotr Abrasimov, said to him in what only seemed to be jest: 'Who knows what is being discussed there behind closed doors?' The speech Brandt had intended for Karl-Marx-Stadt was given instead over the air:

It is not for the sake of argument, but for the sake of human beings that we ask: Can something be done, and, if so, what? What can be done to make people's lives easier and to keep a divided nation's sense of solidarity alive, despite everything? Any progress along this path towards the easing of tensions is a German contribution towards a more secure peace.

Throughout 1966 the official foreign policy of the West German government was characterized by tense relations with two allies, the United States and France. At the end of January, the EEC Ministers' Council succeeded in bringing de Gaulle's 'empty chair policy' (the refusal to cooperate in any committee of the organization) to an end with the 'Luxemburg compromise': the council and commission agreed to consultations before making important decisions and left open the question of the veto. Shortly afterwards, however, the French general dealt a severe blow to the whole west: on 21 February he announced that France would be withdrawing from the NATO military forces on 1 July 1966. His main reason was that the danger of war in Europe had decreased. In fact, the military integration of western European was incompatible with de Gaulle's vision of France as a great power with independent nuclear capabilities, thanks to the *force de frappe*. Still, he did not terminate the country's membership in the NATO agreement.

The Erhard government could do nothing but state that it would stick to the policy of Atlantic integration and do everything it could to preserve the alliance. That was, in essence, the 'Atlanticist' position. The German 'Gaullists', including Adenauer, thought differently. They were not convinced that the Americans would uphold their nuclear guarantee in an emergency situation. Consequently, they saw the *force de frappe* as an additional shield and as a kind of reinsurance vis-à-vis the United States. They were not alone in this kind of thinking.

In another area, too, Charles de Gaulle pursued national interests without any regard to France's eastern neighbour. At the end of 1966, the Ministers' Council of the EEC capitulated in the face of France's tenacious resistance to common agricultural reform. The policy of 'transfers' from a common agrarian fund, paid for by contributions from all member states, above all Germany, remained in place. Thus was a system 'saved' that shielded the agricultural sectors of all the member states—especially that of France, which was still strongly rural in character—from the world market and led to massive overproduction of crops.

The relations between Bonn and Washington also came under severe strain in 1966. Erhard visited the United States at the end of September. De Gaulle's withdrawal from NATO and his spectacular visit to the Soviet Union at the end of June and beginning of July had made the relationship with America even more important for West Germany than before. But President Johnson did not do what Erhard had hoped, whether on the question of nuclear co-determination or with regard to postponing the 'offset payments' the FRG owed in connection with the American troops stationed in West Germany. The foreign exchange offset was a matter of vital significance for the chancellor. Without the cooperation of the US, he saw no way to present a balanced budget for 1967. When he returned empty-handed, it was clear to all informed observers that the 'people's chancellor' was a leader without luck.

The budget difficulties were a consequence of tax cuts and increased state spending during the previous years. Thus the government was itself partly to blame for the overheated economy, which could easily turn into recession. The risk of inflation could no longer be overlooked. The cost of living had risen 4.5% between May 1965 and May 1966. Wage increases of 7–8% were projected in August 1966. The federal bank had raised the minimum lending rate from 3.5% to 5% in May, but the only immediate effects were a reduction in domestic demand and an increase in exports. Taken together, the economic indicators seemed to point towards a crisis.

While fear spread, the cabinet in Bonn worked on the state finances. The budget it passed on 29 September contained drastic spending cuts, but insufficient revenue. The coalition partners were divided on the latter point. The Union parties were prepared to raise taxes if necessary. The FDP was not, and committed itself to a categorical rejection of tax hikes on 19 September. (The finance ministry had announced the day before that tax revenues would fall about a billion marks short of the projections.)

By this time, the budget crisis had widened into a crisis of the chancellorship. It did Erhard no good that he was now also head of the CDU (as of 23 March, when Adenauer retired to the position of 'honorary head'); the 'people's chancellor' was as much a stranger to his party as before. When Rainer Barzel, head of the CDU/CSU Bundestag fraction, stated on 4 October that Ludwig Erhard was and would remain chancellor, virtually no leading politician of the Union still believed in the political future of a man who had revealed himself to be a political incompetent. Three days later Franz Josef Strauss, speaking to the executive of the Bavarian CSU, talked in an indirect manner about the necessity of bringing Erhard down. Most of his listeners were not yet prepared to heed his message; with regional elections looming (20 November), the risks involved in a change of government in Bonn seemed too great.

The crisis came to a dramatic head on 27 October when the four Free Democratic members of the cabinet—vice chancellor Erich Mende, finance minister Rolf Dahlgrün, Ewald Bucher, minister of housing construction, and Walter Scheel, minister for economic cooperation—resigned from their posts. The day before, the FDP had announced that it rejected the (allegedly) settled intentions of the CDU/CSU to raise taxes; in a public response, Barzel called this statement a declaration of war from the FDP. That same day, the cabinet passed a resolution that tax increases would only be used as an *ultima ratio*—that is, only if spending cuts and the reduction of tax privileges and loopholes proved insufficient to cover the budget deficit (which had now grown to 4 billion marks). But this came too late to save the coalition. The Erhard cabinet was now a minority government. On 28 October four Union politicians were put in charge of the vacant ministries.

The Free Democrats were united in their rejection of tax hikes. They also believed this stance would stand them in good stead in the upcoming elections in Hesse and Bavaria. But they were divided on the course of action to follow now that the bourgeois coalition had collapsed. One group, probably the majority, supported a new alliance with the Union under a different chancellor. Another group, led by Walter Scheel, a 47-year-old politician from North Rhine-Westphalia, wanted to form a coalition with the SPD and move the FDP in a social-liberal direction.

The Social Democrats now faced the pleasant prospect of being able to choose between two partners. On 31 October they petitioned the Bundestag to call on the chancellor to subject his government to a vote of confidence. The appropriate response to this move would have been for Erhard to resign voluntarily. The chancellor was not yet prepared to do this, however, despite pressure from prominent Union politicians behind the scenes. Speaking before the CDU/CSU fraction on 2 November, he declared that the formation of a new majority government would not fail because of him. That same day the SPD presented an eight-point programme for future coalition negotiations. It was so 'statesmanlike' that even a politician like Franz Josef Strauss was able to regard it as a basis for talks, as he stated on 4 November.

Elections took place in Hesse on 6 November. The CDU and FDP suffered modest losses (−2.4% and −1.1%, respectively), while the SPD, which had been ruling in Wiesbaden with an absolute majority since 1962, made minimal gains (0.2%). The real sensation, however, was the success of a radical right-wing organization, the National Democratic Party of Germany (*Nationaldemokratische Partei Deutschlands* or NPD), founded two years previously. It achieved 7.9 per cent of the vote and eight seats straight off. For many observers in Germany and abroad, the truism 'Bonn is not Weimar' seemed in danger of being proved wrong. The rise of a nationalist protest party in the wake of growing fears of war and political instability reminded many of the period after 1930.

It did not exactly help dispel the mood of crisis when, two days after the Hesse elections, the Bundestag pronounced what was tantamount to a vote of no confidence in the chancellor for the first time in the history of the Federal Republic: 255 representatives from the SPD and FDP voted to accept the Social Democratic petition that Erhard submit to a vote of confidence; 246 members of the CDU/CSU voted against it. The chancellor immediately stated that he would not submit to the vote, a position backed up by the Basic Law.

After two more days, on 10 November, the CDU/CSU Bundestag fraction nominated its candidate for Erhard's succession, Kurt Georg Kiesinger, the prime minister of Baden-Württemberg (established in 1952). Kiesinger, a Catholic lawyer born in 1904 in Elbingen on the Swabian Alb, had been a member of the Bundestag between 1949 and 1958, where he had gained a reputation as a knowledgeable and eloquent debater in matters of foreign policy. He was elected prime minister of Baden-Württemberg in 1958. After 1964 he headed a CDU/FDP coalition. His candidacy for the chancellorship was supported by the CSU and by his fellow Swabian Eugen Gerstenmaier, who renounced his own candidacy to help Kiesinger. Nonetheless, it took him three ballots to defeat the other men in the running, Walter Hallstein, Rainer Barzel, and Gerhard Schröder. His victory did not commit him to a particular coalition, either with the FDP or with the SPD.

One chapter in Kiesinger's biography was highly controversial. He was among the *Märzgefallene*,* those who had joined the NSDAP in spring 1933. However, as a law tutor and lawyer practising in Berlin, Kiesinger never joined the National

---

* Translator's note: the term means 'those who fell in March'.

Socialist Jurists Association, and he also refused to take over a judgeship in the Prussian Supreme Court. Between 1940 and 1945 he worked in the 'Radio Political Department' of the foreign office, occasionally as an intermediary with the propaganda ministry, and then as deputy department director. On 9 November 1966, the day before his nomination as CDU/CSU candidate for the chancellorship, Conrad Ahlers of *Der Spiegel* published the minutes of a meeting in the Reich Security Office, dated 7 November 1944, in which Kiesinger was denounced for 'demonstrably hampering the anti-Jewish campaign' as well as for possibly being an agent of 'political tendencies' that 'might be contrary to the foreign policy of the Führer'.

Negotiations between the parties officially got under way on 15 November. During the ensuing three days, each of the three potential partners spoke with the other two. By 20 November, the day of the Bavarian elections, a decision had not yet been made. The CSU emerged from this contest as the clear winner with 48.1% of the vote and 110 of 204 seats, a gain of 0.6%. The SPD received 35.8% (+0.5%), the FDP 5.9% (−0.8%), and the NPD 7.4% (again running for the first time). It was a peculiarity of the Bavarian electoral system that a party, in order to get into the parliament, had to manage at least 10% of the vote in one of the seven governmental districts. The NPD succeeded. The FDP did not, unlike in 1962, and thus it clearly lost the election, despite the relatively small losses throughout Bavaria as a whole.

The Bavarian election had an impact on Bonn. It weakened the negotiating position of the Free Democrats and strengthened the hand of the CSU. Strauss left no doubt about his desire to return to the cabinet. Reservations against him, on account of the '*Spiegel*' affair', were possibly stronger in the FDP than in the SPD. The latter was divided over the coalition question. On 22 November a majority of the fraction came out in support of an alliance with the FDP. Willy Brandt, too, was tending in this direction. A strong minority was led by Brandt's deputy, Herbert Wehner, and the acting fraction head, Helmut Schmidt (representing Fritz Erler, who was seriously ill). Both men were staunch supporters of a Grand Coalition; they considered a social–liberal partnership wishful thinking. It would have had only two seats more than the absolute majority necessary for electing a chancellor. In view of the tensions within the FDP, this represented a major risk and would have made governing very difficult.

The Union and the SPD achieved broad agreement in their talks on 24 November. SPD/FDP negotiations, which took place the next day, were also very productive. Those between the FDP and the CDU/CSU, also on 25 November, made no progress. The Free Democrats stuck to their rejection of tax increases. When Mende publicly announced the likelihood of a social–liberal alliance, Kiesinger decided to make the SPD a formal coalition offer the next day. He knew he had the fraction majority, the honorary head of the CDU, Konrad Adenauer, and President Heinrich Lübke on his side. In the SPD, too, the advocates of a Grand Coalition prevailed in the party and fraction leadership on 25 November. Willy Brandt had come to realize the inevitability of this solution to the government crisis.

There was still strong resistance to cooperation with the Union parties among the SPD 'base', as well as among its young members and intellectual sympathizers. At a conference of SPD officials in Bonn on 26 November, a majority voted against a Grand Coalition. The writer Günter Grass, who had campaigned for the SPD the year before, wrote a letter to Willy Brandt warning him that the 'youth of our country' would 'turn away from the state and its constitution'; they would 'scatter to the left and right as soon as this miserable marriage takes place.'

Nonetheless, in the night of 26–7 November, a narrow two-thirds majority of the SPD Bundestag fraction voted in favour of a Grand Coalition between the SPD and the CDU/CSU. The formal agreement was signed on 27 November. Erhard resigned from the chancellorship on 30 November. On 1 December the Bundestag elected Kurt Georg Kiesinger the third chancellor of the Federal Republic of Germany. The vote count was 340 to 109, with 23 abstentions—a very weak result, given that the government parties controlled 447 and the opposition FDP only 49 seats. Kiesinger's government was far from enjoying the undivided support even of its own coalition.

The new cabinet numbered eleven ministers each from the CDU (including the chancellor) and the SPD, as well as three from the CSU. The most notable among the Social Democrats were Willy Brandt as vice chancellor and foreign minister; Gustav Heinemann as minister of justice; Karl Schiller as economics minister; Georg Leber, former head of a union (the *Industriegewerkschaft Bau, Steine, Erden*) as minister of transportation; Herbert Wehner as minister for all-German affairs; and Carlo Schmid as head of the—comparatively insignificant—Bundesrat ministry. The most important Union office-holders were Paul Lücke as interior minister, Gerhard Schröder as defence minister, Hans Katzer as minister of labour, and Bruno Heck as minister of family and youth. CSU head Franz Josef Strauss, after four years away from the federal government, returned as minister of finance. The man whose arrest he had ordered in Spain in October 1962 was now often present at the cabinet table in Bonn; Conrad Ahlers served the Grand Coalition as deputy director of the government press and information office.

The date 1 December 1966 marks a major turning point for West Germany as a whole, as well as for the Social Democrats as a party. The SPD returned to the national government for the first time since 27 March 1930. The Grand Coalition of those days had been destroyed by a crisis in state finance; now, it was up to another Grand Coalition to lead the state out of another such crisis. After seventeen years of parliamentary—and not infrequently extra-parliamentary—opposition, the Social Democrats, in the view of Herbert Wehner, their political strategist, now had one main task to accomplish before they would be in a position to successfully contest the chancellorship: to demonstrate, in a practical sense, their own political maturity as the junior partner of the more experienced Union. That was a realistic assessment. It was also one that had yet to find broad acceptance among the functionaries, members, and voters of the SPD.

The cabinet of the Grand Coalition was, in a sense, the attempt at a historic compromise. It embraced both former members of the NSDAP—including, besides Kiesinger, Gerhard Schröder of the CDU (who, however, had left the party in 1941) and the Social Democrat Karl Schiller—as well as a former high official of the Communist party, Herbert Wehner. The former émigré Willy Brandt had belonged to the Socialist Workers' party; Gerhard Schröder had been involved in the SA. The cabinet members came from oppositional camps that had fought repeatedly and bitterly since 1945. Their cooperation opened up the prospect of an end to the financial crisis as well as of other overdue reforms, some of which could only be realized by the two-thirds majority necessary to amend the constitution. But the pact also contained potential risks. Once the parliamentary opposition had been reduced to the small Free Democratic party, it could be expected that the extra-parliamentary opposition would become stronger, both from the left and from the right. The Grand Coalition could only be justified as a temporary solution to an extraordinary parliamentary impasse. Otherwise the domestic crisis threatened to turn into a crisis of legitimacy for parliamentary democracy in general.

Both the Christian and the Social Democrats were aware of this danger. Accordingly, they agreed to introduce majority voting into the West German political system in order to make coalitions superfluous in the future. Kiesinger emphasized this intention in his inaugural address on 13 December 1966, calling it the 'firm desire of the partners of the Grand Coalition that this alliance be only temporary, until the end of the legislative period.' These words were greeted with applause from both government parties. The focus of the speech was on state finances, and Kiesinger was not sparing in his criticism of the previous cabinet. He did not exclude the possibility of tax increases and, at the same time, announced an anti-cyclical economic policy. This part of the address bore the stamp of the new economics minister, Karl Schiller, a staunch proponent of the British economist John Maynard Keynes, as was evident especially in the use of such terms as 'overall control', 'promotion of growth', and 'expansive and stability-oriented economic policy'.

The foreign policy part of Kiesinger's speech was characterized by continuity. The chancellor rejected the 'false alternative of a choice' between America and France, affirmed the government's desire to work together with the Soviet Union, and emphasized the importance of reconciliation with Poland and an understanding with Czechoslovakia. Nonetheless, he explicitly reiterated the legal positions of the FRG. He expressed himself cautiously with regard to the GDR, but in a way that revealed the influence of Willy Brandt:

We wish to ease tensions, not make them worse; overcome rifts, not deepen them. Therefore, we want to promote human, economic, and intellectual relations with our countrymen in the other part of Germany with all our energy. If this should involve contact between offices in the Federal Republic and those in the other part of Germany, that does not mean the recognition of a second German state. We will handle these contacts on a case by case basis and in a way that does not allow world opinion to get the impression that we are retreating from our legal standpoint.

Kiesinger's inaugural speech was not only considerably shorter than Erhard's on 10 November 1965, it was also much more precise in content and sober in tone. The reason the 'people's chancellor' had failed was because he had lacked Adenauer's clear view for the challenges of foreign and domestic policy, as well as for the relations of power within both fields. His example was a lesson for his successors. Kiesinger, as chancellor of a Grand Coalition, had to seek balance and compromise between political camps of roughly equal strength and with greater political differences than the coalition parties up to that juncture. He was practically condemned to pursue a 'diagonal' policy, but at the same time had to avoid creating the impression of a politics without a distinctive character. His inaugural address succeeded in this balancing act. It remained to be seen if, along with the cabinet and coalition as a whole, he could translate it into practical successes.[8]

THE SELF-IMAGE OF WEST GERMANY AND 1968

Five years after the building of the Berlin wall, the way West Germans perceived themselves, their state, and the German question began to undergo noticeable changes. In 1966 Franz Josef Strauss became the first West German politician to question the policy of reunification. In a book entitled *Entwurf für Europa*,* the basic thesis of which he had laid out in an interview in *Die Zeit* on 8 April of that year, the CSU leader, taking up ideas of Charles de Gaulle, argued for a 'Europeanization of the German question'.

I do not believe in the restoration of a German national state, not even within the borders of the four occupation zones . . . Only when German reunification is no longer viewed in terms of a restoration of the nation state will we be able to come closer to its realization. It would be simply unrealistic to expect our European neighbours to promote the rise of an independent economic and political power with the potential of our people, 72 million strong . . . Therefore, a situation must be created in Europe that allows the absorption of unified German potential in a way that does not permit its inevitable dominance to put a strain on the coexistence of the European nations. This will ultimately only be possible by dismantling national sovereignty within a federative framework.

The inner counterpart to the 'Europeanization of the German question' was the departure from the idea that the Federal Republic was only a provisional

---

* Strauss, *Outline for Europe.*

political entity, a 'provisorium'. In summer 1967 an essay entitled 'Das perfekte Provisorium'* by the publicist Burghard Freudenfeld, which appeared in the Catholic journal *Hochland*, catalysed lively debate. The main argument was that the identification of the FRG with the German Reich, within whatever borders, made it impossible for West Germany to identify with itself. 'This state should not be thought of as a core state, awaiting completion through the addition of its missing parts; rather, it is a partial state, awaiting the fulfilment of its particular nature. That is, it is not lacking in a legitimate part of its area of jurisdiction, but in the quality of a nation state. It is a substantive, not a geographic, torso.' Freudenfeld considered this state of affairs dangerous and wanted to give up the idea of the FRG as provisional, which he believed hampered the development of a true West German political identity or 'state consciousness' (*Staatsbewusstsein*), as he called it. 'One cannot live within surrogates without lasting damage. To live a public lie is no less dangerous for communities than for individuals.'

This article drew criticism from the ranks of the Union and the Social Democrats, and this criticism also found its way into *Hochland*. Bundestag president Eugen Gerstenmaier, deputy national leader of the CDU, reversed Freudenfeld's thesis and wrote that it was unfortunate that the Parliamentary Council had only founded a 'provisional state' in 1948–9. It should rather have 'identified the larger and liberal part of Germany, the core German state, with the German Reich, and called the German lands and provinces occupied by the Soviet Union by their true name, that is, German territories whose inhabitants are prevented by a foreign occupying power from exercising their rights as citizens of the Reich.'

Gerstenmaier did admit that the longer reunification took, the more it was to be expected 'that what seems self-evident to the older ones among us will become questionable to the younger generations on both sides.' Nonetheless, he considered it the task of a 'national education' to keep young people conscious of the fact

that all of Germany is our fatherland, not only the Federal Republic or Ulbricht's sphere of control . . . The world is endless, and the human being needs a place to call home . . . This need for internal and external shelter gives rise to a people's free affirmation of its history, that is, of the nation and the country in which we were born. All that surrounds us; everything that has come down to us in language and culture; the destiny we have lived and suffered together with those around us; our own will to live, which recognizes and affirms the necessity of communal self-assertion; our common way of life, perhaps not ideal, but shaped by us—all of this is Fatherland.

Helmut Schmidt (leader of the SPD parliamentary fraction since the death of Fritz Erler in February 1967) disagreed with both Freudenfeld *and* Gerstenmaier. Neither of them, he wrote, distinguished clearly enough between the *Staatsvolk*,

---

* Freudenfeld, 'The Perfect Provisorium'.

the people who make up the state, and the nation, or between 'state consciousness' (*Staatsbewusstsein*) and 'national consciousness' (*Nationalbewusstsein*). In fact, they tended to conflate these concepts. But the real danger, as Schmidt saw it, lay in the consequences implicit in Freudenfeld's view. The renunciation of 'a national consciousness born of history' and an 'exclusive intensification of Federal Republican state consciousness' created the impression of a 'contrivance', 'as if German history only began in the year 1945 or 1949, and as if one could unproblematically escape the Germans' entanglement in their own past and their responsibility for the whole nation.'

Neither the Germans in the GDR nor those in the FRG could steal away from their common history by propagating their own respective national sentiments.

We must constantly remind ourselves of our shared responsibility for the political fate of our countrymen in the GDR. This is an obligation imposed on us by the fact that, although all Germans lost the war together, it is the Germans in the GDR who are paying for it virtually alone, in our stead, and at an incomparably high price . . . To strengthen the state consciousness of the FRG is a necessary and legitimate undertaking. But it would be a dangerous perversion of our nation's history to seek to reduce our national consciousness to the jurisdiction of this state consciousness. Therefore, I resist this flight into the idyll of a West German [*bundesdeutschen*] nation.

The liberal opposition, for its part, agreed with Freudenfeld almost without reservation. In another *Hochland* article Walter Scheel (head of the FDP as of the Freiburg party congress in January 1968) rejected the idea of changing the FRG's provisional status by amending the Basic Law. But he viewed this status far differently than the Parliamentary Council. For Scheel, the goal was to

overturn the annexationist-missionary interpretation of the state's provisory nature. We must learn to view the Federal Republic as provisional with regard to Europe. In the German–German perspective, this means that we are no longer permitted to interpret the provisional nature of the Federal Republic as an act of aggression against the GDR, but as a challenge to all Germans, anticipated in the constitution.

In the remarks that followed, however, it became evident that 'all Germans' meant, for Scheel, only the citizens of West Germany. It was they who were called to 'make democracy permeable' and 'to add an organ for plebiscitary processes to our representative system'.

The sociologist M. Rainer Lepsius argued in a way similar to Scheel. 'If we wish to heighten the Federal Republic's internal legitimacy in the mind of its citizenry, then what we need is not a stronger national sentiment, but a more concrete democratic consciousness,' he wrote, once again in *Hochland*.

In Germany we are in the difficult situation of not being able to compensate for the functional weaknesses of the political system by appealing to a trans-political national mindset . . . The Federal Republic must constitute its identity politically, which means, in the context of German history, in opposition to fascism . . . Because it did not want to identify itself geographically with the territory of the western zones of occupation, it has knowingly placed itself in a position in which its own existence is illegitimate. The FRG denies the existence of the GDR, thus endangering its own political identity in order to uphold the substance of the German national state. The FRG ceased to be a substantive torso a long time ago. It is also, to my mind, not a 'perfect provisorium'. Rather, it is a European state with an identity kept undefined.

The 1967–8 debate in *Hochland* showed clearly that the West German 'political class' was changing the way it thought. The conservative position, represented in Eugen Gerstenmaier's recourse to the idea of the Reich, met with little public resonance. Walter Scheel, on the other hand, the representative of reformed liberalism, found support among the anti-nationalist and internationalist left for his rejection of 'annexationism' and his European reinterpretation of the provisional nature of the West German state. The Social Democrat Helmut Schmidt expressed a normative standpoint based in German history: the core of the German question lay in the unjust allotment of the consequences of the war; since the Germans in the GDR were the real victims of the partition of Germany, the Germans in the FRG owed them national solidarity.

Schmidt was not only speaking for his party, but expressed how most Germans probably felt at the time, both in the west and in the east. But this relative consensus was beginning to come apart. The contributions of two political scientists, whom we can perhaps best describe as 'liberal-conservative', showed clearly that Freudenfeld—also a liberal-conservative—was not alone in his thinking. In 1967 Hans Buchheim exhorted the citizens of West Germany to identify 'our national consciousness unreservedly with this state'. In 1970, in what was the first large-scale discussion of West German foreign policy, Waldemar Besson declared that it was necessary for the FRG to be recognized as permanent by its citizens, and this presumed 'the development of a West German patriotism'.

The left-liberal counterpart to the revisionism of the centre-right was Peter Bender's 1968 book *Zehn Gründe für die Anerkennung der DDR*.* 'The political unity of Germany cannot be achieved in the foreseeable future, and the GDR will be asserting itself internationally as a second German state more and more.' Thus ran Bender's first argument. 'For the FRG, therefore, it seems a matter of urgent necessity not to let its hand be forced to grant what cannot be avoided, but rather to take up the inevitable in its own policy in a timely fashion.' In the tenth and final reason, Bender advocated the Europeanization of the German question. He meant something different by this than Franz Josef Strauss, but he agreed with the CSU leader in calling for an end to viewing the German question in terms of the nation state. 'The partition of Europe can only be overcome if we accept the GDR as an equal partner in the process of rapprochement between east and west. The further this process develops, the greater will be the opportunities to bridge the abyss between East and West Germany, too.'

* Bender, *Ten Reasons to Recognize the GDR*.

For both the liberal-conservative and the left-liberal revisionists, the question of political liberty for the Germans in the GDR had become a matter of mere hope. 'West German patriotism' of the kind called for by Besson no longer implied a national obligation to solidarity. Proponents of unconditional recognition of the GDR placed their hopes in the liberalizing effects of such a policy. Nonetheless, they laid themselves open to the criticism that the Federal Republic, after recognizing the GRD, would be less able to exert pressure on the latter to bring about the desired reforms. The restitution of a German national state could not, for the foreseeable future, be a practical political aim—this was something all the critics of the FRG's traditional Germany policy agreed on, and they were correct. In terms of practical politics, however, the decisive question was whether the Germans in the FRG and the GDR still thought—or should think—of themselves as one nation. As a rule, the revisionists preferred to shy away from this question.[9]

This incipient departure from the goal of a German nation state in the political discourse of the mid-1960s was accompanied by changes in the West Germans' interpretation of their own history. In 1961 the Hamburg historian Fritz Fischer published *Griff nach der Weltmacht*.* This book, an examination of the July crisis in 1914 and the war aims of imperial Germany between 1914 and 1918, had a liberating effect, overturning the standard German nationalist view of history, according to which the German Reich bore no specific responsibility for the First World War. After intensive debate at the twenty-sixth conference of German historians, which took place in October 1964 in West Berlin, Fischer's thesis was generally accepted. The same conference also broached the role of the workers' and soldiers' councils in the revolution of 1918–19 for the first time. The result shook the traditionally dominant view, which held that the only choice at the time was between Bolshevism and the policies actually pursued by the people's commissars around Friedrich Ebert. Two years later, in 1966, a number of mostly younger historians presented a collection of essays dealing critically with the domestic and foreign policy views of the conservative opposition to Hitler. They not only rejected the prevailing opinion among German historians, but also undermined one of the founding myths of the FRG: the legitimation of the new state through the spirit of 20 July 1944, which was seen exclusively in terms of this purpose.

In a 1965 book entitled *Gesellschaft und Demokratie in Deutschland*,[†] the sociologist Ralf Dahrendorf, son of a Social Democratic resistance fighter and himself the spokesman of a reformed liberalism, described the failed conservative plot against Hitler as the 'tragic end of the social revolution' initiated by the Nazi regime in Germany.

---

* Fischer, *Grab for World Power* (tr. as *Germany's Aims in the First World War*).
† Dahrendorf, *Society and Democracy in Germany*.

Only after 20 July 1944 was the return to the imperial Reich closed off for German society once and for all . . . The failure of the conspiracy and the ensuing persecutions mark the end of a German political elite. With it ended at least the reality of the idea many see symbolized in the name 'Prussia'. Prussian discipline, uprightness, morality, but also Prussian illiberality; the honest directness, but also the authoritarianism of the Prussian tradition; the humanity, but also the political immaturity of the many in the political practice of the Prussian past—all this had its final culmination on 20 July 1944. It was above all moral values and, frequently, their reality in the German past that were invoked against the despotism of National Socialist rule. And in fact, the old regime did represent a morally better world. But its rebellion failed and the brutal path into modernity took its course.

In 1967, two years after Dahrendorf's book, two psychoanalysts, Alexander and Margarete Mitscherlich, published a polemic entitled *Die Unfähigkeit zu trauern.** They, too, spoke of the destruction of tradition through National Socialism. But since the process of grieving (in the sense described by Sigmund Freud) had hardly even begun, this destruction could not be seen even in terms of an unintended modernization. The Germans, in the Mitscherlichs' diagnosis, had entertained a narcissistic relationship with Hitler. They reacted to the fall of their idol in an infantile manner, that is, by shifting all blame onto the all-powerful Führer. The collective denial of collectively incurred guilt had an exonerating effect, and prevented a serious melancholy from developing after 1945. But real liberation could only be achieved through grief, an effort unavoidably linked to the pain of memory.

The grieving process is not aimed at simple restitution. Rather, it brings us gradually to the point where we learn to accept the definitive alteration of reality brought about by the loss of the object of desire. In this process, we can also re-experience and recognize the ambivalence of the relationship. As a result, at the end of the grieving process, the individual emerges transformed, that is, more mature and with a greater ability to handle reality.[10]

By the time the Mitscherlichs' book appeared, its central argument applied only to a minority of Germans, those who were old enough to have participated in the Third Reich as responsible, thinking individuals and who later refused to engage in a self-critical assessment of their own behaviour between 1933 and 1945. Younger Germans, those unborn or too young at that time, had no cause to feel that the charge of 'repressing' the past applied to them.

They could, however, raise this charge against the generation of their parents and teachers. The analysis of Alexander and Margarete Mitscherlich found fertile ground among the German student movement, which began to take shape in the mid-1960s. In the 1964–5 winter semester, in response to a student initiative, the University of Tübingen held the first lecture series dealing with the relationship between National Socialism and higher education. Other universities followed

---

* Mitscherlich and Mitscherlich, *The Inability to Mourn.*

suit, and in 1966 the Germanists' conference in Munich dedicated itself to the theme of German studies as 'German science' in the era of National Socialism. Then, in 1967, Wolfgang Fritz Haug, publisher of the leftist theory journal *Das Argument*, wrote a book accusing universities and scholars of 'helpless anti-fascism'. Haug's main thesis was that the professors were at best superficially self-critical and had still not recognized the societal preconditions and social function of fascism. What they missed and were blocking out was the Marxist philosopher Max Horkheimer's insight in 1939, which Haug quoted: 'Whoever does not wish to speak of capitalism should be silent about fascism.'

Das Argument became a forum for the kind of thinking that went on in and around the Socialist German Student Federation (*Sozialistischer Deutscher Studentenbund* or SDS). The former student organization of the SPD had fought against the Godesberg reform, thus provoking counter-measures from the party. In May 1960 the SPD promoted the founding of a competing student organization, the Social Democratic University Federation (*Sozialdemokratischer Hochschulbund* or SHB). Two months later it broke off relations with the SDS. In November 1961 party members who had remained in the SDS, as well as in the *Sozialistische Fördergesellschaft*, a group supporting it, were thrown out of the SPD. The most notable of these was the political scientist Wolfgang Abendroth. The SDS's power of attraction for the young was not affected by these moves. Now more than ever it was seen as the avant-garde of neo-Marxist thinking in West Germany and as the mouthpiece of 'Critical Theory', represented in different forms by Theodor W. Adorno and Max Horkheimer, the fathers of the 'Frankfurt School', now returned from American exile; Herbert Marcuse, also from the old Frankfurt Institute for Social Research, now teaching in Berkeley; and the much younger Jürgen Habermas. The SDS's claim that it put 'Critical Theory' into practice was only supported by Marcuse, however. Adorno, Horkheimer, and Habermas denied the leftist student organization the right to appeal to them in its actions.

In his *Einleitung zur Kritik der Hegelischen Rechtsphilosophie** of 1843–4, Karl Marx had written: 'It is not enough for thought to strive for realization; reality must itself strive towards thought.' Nothing contributed to the success of the SDS as much as the state of things it inveighed against, which seemed to justify its criticism. The West German state considered itself the legal successor to the German Reich; the SDS pointed to the continuity of the capitalist means of production out of which 'German fascism' had arisen in the 1920s and 1930s. The West German state considered itself an anti-totalitarian community; the SDS saw the term 'totalitarian' as an unacceptable conflation of 'red' and 'brown', as an attack on the anti-fascism of the left, and as an attempt to historically legitimate all forms of anti-communism, including the fascist variety. The West German state was the declared ally of the United States; the SDS accused it of

---

* Marx, *Critique of Hegel's Philosophy of Right: An Introduction.*

complicity in America's imperialist war against the Vietnamese people, which was fighting for its national and societal liberation under the leadership of Ho Chi Minh.[11]

The Vietnam War polarized all western countries, first and foremost the United States itself. The methods it employed in its battle against the Vietcong, including napalm bombs and chemical defoliants, led to worldwide protest. The left saw the armed supporters of Ho Chi Minh as anti-colonial freedom fighters. That was partially true. They enjoyed widespread support among the peasant population, and it was also undeniable that the all-Vietnamese elections provided for in the 1954 Geneva armistice had been thwarted by the US-supported government in Saigon. In this view, America had stepped into the shoes of colonial France, which had been defeated militarily. It was fighting against a Third World country that sought independence, and in so doing it undermined its own claim to be the champion of freedom and democracy.

Opposition to the US war in South-East Asia united student protest movements from Berkeley to Paris to Berlin. Another thing they had in common was the anti-authoritarian rebellion against the lifestyle of the older generation, against the professors' control of the universities, against the 'establishment' and what only seemed to be its tolerance, but what was in reality 'repressive tolerance'. There were additional grounds for protest in West Germany. The most important was the 'repression of the past' and what was deemed to be its cause: the continuity of the societal relations of power, defined as a 'restoration'. Another factor was the virtual disappearance of a parliamentary opposition from the left after the formation of the Grand Coalition in late 1966. The student movement and its 'hard core', the SDS, seized this opportunity to represent itself as an 'Extra-Parliamentary Opposition' (*Ausserparlamentarische Opposition* or APO) and to level the same charges against the SPD that the extreme left had used repeatedly against it, ever since 1914: 'treason' against its principles.

One of the goals of the Grand Coalition seemed especially calculated to provoke the opposition of the extra-parliamentary 'New Left': the emergency laws (*Notstandsgesetze*). The Germany Treaty of 5 May 1955 stipulated that until the Federal Republic passed the necessary legislation, the Allies would retain the right to intervene in order to protect the security of their troops in the event of an internal or external emergency. While preliminary steps had long been taken, only after the formation of the Grand Coalition did the government have—at least in theory—the two-thirds majority necessary to amend the constitution. The Social Democrats used their new status as government party to push through a sophisticated set of rules designed to guarantee maximum parliamentary and judicial control of the executive during emergency situations. In this way, their programme differed from the more 'authoritarian' ideas of the former interior minister, Gerhard Schröder.

This is not how the APO saw the situation. It considered the emergency laws—which it polemically termed the 'NS laws'—as preparing the way for an authoritarian state, if not for outright fascism, as influential 'New Left' theorists maintained. A group calling itself 'Democracy in Crisis' (*Kuratorium Notstand der Demokratie*) was set up, and its campaigns united students with trade unionists, writers, artists, clergy, and professors. On 11 April 1968, just a few weeks before the laws were slated for passage, an event occurred that shocked not only the students, but the public as a whole: Rudi Dutschke, the most prominent, intelligent, eloquent, and politically astute of the student activists, was shot and critically wounded on the Kurfürstendamm in Berlin. His assailant was Josef Bachmann, a painter with a criminal record, who felt himself goaded to the deed by the anti-leftist rhetoric of the *Bild-Zeitung*. Though Dutschke survived, his serious brain injuries never completely healed and would eventually, in December 1979, claim his life.

Rudi Dutschke was not the first martyr of the Extra-Parliamentary Opposition. On 2 June 1967 Benno Ohnesorg, a student participating in the large demonstrations organized by SDS against the state visit of Reza Pahlavi, the shah of Iran, had been shot in the head by Karl-Heinz Kurras, a Berlin policeman. Dutschke's murder set off demonstrations and violent riots in many large cities and university towns. In Berlin, Hamburg, Munich, and Frankfurt, outraged supporters of the SDS tried to prevent the delivery of newspapers published by Axel Cäsar Springer, one of which was the *Bild-Zeitung*. Four weeks later, on 11 May, 'Democracy in Crisis' organized a march converging on the centre of Bonn from different directions. Between 30,000 and 70,000 people participated. The labour unions held demonstrations against the emergency laws on the same day, but in Dortmund, so as not to be seen together with the intellectual left. The protest was of no avail. On 30 May 1968 the Bundestag passed the new emergency legislation (the so-called *Notstandverfassung*) by 384 to 100 votes and 1 abstention. The package included laws restricting privacy of correspondence as well as confidentiality of telecommunication and postal communication.

The campaign against the emergency laws was the climax of the '1968 movement'. The process of dissolution set in shortly thereafter. The failure to stop the legislation had a sobering effect on many Germans, especially those who had previously not been politically active. Many now withdrew from extra-parliamentary activities. Episodes of uncontrolled violence, for example during the 'battle of the Tegeler Weg' deliberately provoked by the Berlin SDS on 4 November 1968, also helped discredit and isolate the 'revolutionary avant-garde' of the student movement.

In preparation for the 1969 federal elections, the SPD once again began to emphasize its differences with the CDU/CSU. This 'strategy of limited conflict', as Horst Ehmke, state secretary in the justice ministry, called it, made the party a good deal more attractive to students and young academics. The SDS fell apart, to be formally dissolved in March 1970. Many of its former members were now active in rival communist sects, which went down in the history of the radical left as 'K groups'. A small minority chose a different path. In the night of 2–3 April 1968, one week before Rudi Dutschke was shot, Andreas Baader, Gudrun Ensslin and a few others set fire to two department stores in Frankfurt in protest against what they called *Konsumterror*, 'consumption terrorism'. This was the opening move of what was soon to become the West German terrorist underground.

The effects of the student movement were contradictory and, to a great extent, unintentional. The activists of the APO were bitter opponents of what they called 'US imperialism'; however, by adopting 'sit-ins', 'go-ins', and other forms of protest from the American student movement, they helped further westernize and 'Americanize' West German society. They fought against pluralism, believing it to be an ideology to disguise capitalist class rule, but helped make Germany more pluralist than ever before after 1968. They attacked the parliamentary system with radical leftist-democratic rhetoric, but their practice showed that their own model amounted to the manipulation of an 'unenlightened' majority by an 'enlightened' minority. They drove forward the critical reappraisal of the National Socialist past and, at the same time, stretched the term 'fascism' so far that it could be applied to the 'late capitalist' West German state as easily as to the Third Reich. Their dissent was often extremely intolerant, and yet what later came to be seen as the characteristic 'protest culture' of West Germany is unthinkable without the '68 movement. The SDS theorists stood for a dogmatic Marxism that, in the course of propagation, degenerated into a crude and doctrinaire credo, into 'vulgar' Marxism. Simultaneously, however, they provoked an overdue critical reassessment of the works of Marx and Engels.

Many of what appear in retrospect as the achievements of the 'sixty-eighters' were *also* the result of criticism against them. The student movement drew energy from the utopian belief in a society free from relations of power; nonetheless, many of the reforms they actually did bring about—especially in the universities—proved lasting only to the extent that they, too, were amenable to reform. The APO proved what it sought to deny: the reformability of the democratic system. And it would hardly have been in a position to break apart so many ossified societal structures and force traditional authorities to legitimate themselves in such an unprecedented way if the liberalization of West Germany had not already commenced long before the year 1968.

Unlike France, West Germany did not have to deal with a real crisis of the state in 1968. In May of that year, rebellion broke out not only among the Paris students, but also the workers, who called for a general strike. Some constructed barricades in the Latin Quarter while others took over factories. Together, the new and old left brought France to the brink of revolution. The Fifth Republic was shaken to its very foundations. On 29 May, at the climax of the unrest, General de Gaulle left the country, joining the commander of the French Fifth Army, General Massu, in Baden-Baden. He even briefly considered resigning. Not until the dissolution of the National Assembly and de Gaulle's televised announcement of new elections on 30 May—he called it an 'appeal to the people'—could the protest be diverted into constitutional channels and the state crisis overcome.

Students and workers did not join forces in West Germany. The workers possessed a degree of co-determination, both within the factories and on higher levels, that made them unresponsive to the idea of 'self-administration' (the call for *autogestion* found great resonance in 1968 France, though the voters would ignore it). Moreover, unlike in France, the German parliamentary left had a share in the government. While the Grand Coalition provoked the radicalization of the fringes, it did not lead to a polarization of society. This, too, made 'May 1968' far less radical in West Germany than in its western neighbour.

Nonetheless, the events and experiences of 1968 had a lasting impact on both sides of the Rhine, both on political culture and on daily life in society as a whole. 'Individualistic and socialistic at the same time, the New Left rebelled against alienation in the sphere of production and in the sphere of the everyday,' writes the historian Ingrid Gilcher-Holtey.

In the struggle against alienation, it violated taboos, norms, and traditional values. It defied rules in order to provoke and delegitimate the sanctioning authorities . . . Different subcultures arose, and although they long continued the euphoric spirit that initially characterized the New Left as a whole, their political programmes gave way more and more to the cult of individual affect. In this way, the new beginning of 1968 led, for many, to the development of new lifestyles, to the individualization of existential opportunities and risks, but also to a retreat from politics into the private sphere.

One of the factors that aided the credibility of the West German New Left in the second half of the 1960s was the increasing visibility of the extremist right-wing National Democrats. For the APO, the NPD was clear proof that the fascist threat was not only still present, but growing. And in fact the rightist party—which strove to present more of a German nationalist than a National Socialist image—did perform very well in regional parliamentary elections in 1967–8: 5.8% of the vote in Schleswig-Holstein and 6.9% in the Rhineland-Palatinate (23 April 1967); 7% in Lower Saxony (4 June); 8.8% in Bremen (1 October); and 9.8% in Baden-Württemberg (28 April 1968).

The elections to the parliament in Stuttgart took place two weeks after the leftist rioting that followed the shooting of Rudi Dutschke. The connection between the violence and the election outcome was obvious. The NPD benefited as much from widespread fears of a radical and militant left as the latter profited from the fear of fascism. Each extreme contributed to the rise of the other.

At least until the spring of 1968. In the second half of the year, it became evident that the NPD, too, had passed its zenith. The party's performance in municipal and communal elections after October suffered marked decline in several *Bundesländer*. The economy had recovered by this time, and that had an effect on the general mood of the country and thus on the ballot box. If the economy continued to develop in a favourable direction, the widespread fear that the extreme right would gain access to the federal parliament of West Germany in the September 1969 elections might not be realized after all.[12]

THE DOMESTIC AND FOREIGN POLICY OF THE GRAND COALITION

When the Grand Coalition assumed control of the government in December 1966, its biggest challenge was dealing with the recession. While the gross domestic product decreased only a small amount from 1966 to 1967, even a small setback caused great worry after the many years of high economic growth. What most disturbed the public was the rise in joblessness. In 1966 the number of those seeking work was 161,100. By 1967 it had risen to 459,000, an increase of 185%. The unemployment rate rose from 0.7% to 2.1%, the highest since 1959.

On 5 January 1967 the board of the central bank lowered the minimum lending rate from 5% to 4.5%, a step greatly desired by the government. Two weeks later, on 20 January, Kiesinger presented to the Bundestag the draft of a balanced federal budget for 1967. The dismantling of tax privileges and comprehensive reductions in state spending allowed the deficit of 4.6 billion marks to be eliminated. As a counterpoint to the savings programme, the Bundestag passed two government bills on 23 February. One allowed 850 million marks of immediate spending in areas in urgent need of investment: transportation infrastructure, the postal system, and scientific research and development. The second empowered the finance minister to take out loans of 2.5 billion marks for investment purposes.

Another investment programme of 5.3 billion marks followed on 6 September; 2.8 billion were granted to the *Bundesländer*, 500 million to the municipalities. This Keynesian anti-cyclical economic policy was the common project of Schiller and Strauss; when it came to the battle against recession, the Social Democratic economics minister and the Christian Social minister of finance had the same view. The central bank supported the government by gradually lowering the minimum lending rate. It reached 3% on 12 May 1967, the lowest rate since 1961.

Schiller's 'Magna Carta', however, was a 'Law for the Promotion of Economic Stability and Growth', which entered into effect on 14 June 1967. Although it remained within the framework of the market economy, this law committed the government to securing price stability, full employment, and the balance of foreign trade, along with an appropriate and constant level of economic growth. It also stipulated a yearly report (to be presented in January) in which the government was to inform the Bundestag and Bundesrat about the general state of the economy as well as its economic and fiscal aims. An amendment to the constitution permitted the budgetary policies of the federal and state governments to be coordinated in a way that maintained the overall balance of the national economy. Shortly thereafter, on 6 July, the cabinet passed a bill outlining medium-term financial policy for the years 1967–71 (nicknamed *Mifrifi* for *mittelfristige Finanzplanung*). The parliament made it law on 6 September.

In order to reach his ambitious economic goals, Schiller also wanted to get the parties that decided workers' contracts involved. A programme of 'Concerted Action' was designed to bring company management, workers, and the state together in a way that guaranteed a 'controlled upswing' and 'social symmetry'. Since the government did not want to interfere with free collective bargaining, the main purpose of the programme's round-table discussions was atmospheric or psychological. Nonetheless, when the economy showed definite signs of improvement in the latter half of 1968, they helped create the impression that the Grand Coalition's economic policy was working. In real terms, the gross domestic product rose 7.3% in 1968 and 8.2% in 1969. Joblessness fell during the same period from 323,000 to 178,000, and the number of open positions rose to 747,000. The recession had given way to a new boom. There were even fresh signs of an overheating economy, for example the inflation rate, which rose from 1.5% in 1968 to 2.7% the next year. This provoked another series of counter-measures from the federal bank, which raised the minimum lending rate to 4% on 18 April, to 5% on 19 June, and to 6% on 11 September 1969.

By the time the last year of the legislative period began, the Grand Coalition had won the battle against inflation. Of the planned large-scale structural reforms in state finance, however, only the medium-term fiscal plan of August 1967 had been completed. Finally, in April and May 1969, after many years of preparation, the Bundestag and Bundesrat approved the fiscal reform package. It included a series of constitutional amendments, the most important of which had to do with the newly introduced 'joint tasks' of the Federation and the *Länder*: the expansion and founding of technical colleges, the regional economic infrastructure, structural improvements in the agrarian sector, and the coast guard. In the area of educational planning and research, the federal and state governments were now able to conclude agreements regulating their cooperation and the distribution of costs.

Although these budget and fiscal reforms did not turn West Germany into a centralized state, the federal structure did develop beyond what it had been in the year 1949—towards what became known as 'cooperative federalism' after Kiesinger's first inaugural address. The economic stability law, the medium-term fiscal plan, and the budgetary coordination between the federal and state levels gave the national executive more power. But its new responsibilities were not ones that could have been exercised by the legislative branch. Thus, contrary to the claims of the liberal press and the APO, it is idle to speak of a 'self-elimination' of the parliament. The Grand Coalition made the democratic system more resistant to crisis. This was one of its signal achievements.

The finance reform was followed by a reform of the criminal law. On 9 May 1969 the Bundestag passed by a large majority two laws that broke with the traditional principle of the punishment of guilt. The new main purpose of a criminal sentence was to reintegrate the perpetrator into society to the greatest extent possible. This reform powerfully liberalized West German society. The old-style penal institution, the *Zuchthaus*, was abolished. Prison sentences were standardized, and the courts were given greater freedom to parole offenders. Many minor offences were recategorized as 'violations of the public order' (*Ordnungswidrigkeiten*). Blasphemy, adultery, and homosexuality between adults were no longer considered punishable. Another change in criminal law came on 26 June: the Bundestag abolished the statute of limitations on genocidal crimes and extended that of crimes involving life sentences from twenty to thirty years. This reform put a temporary end to the legislative debate—not over the past as such, but over the question of how long Nazi crimes should be pursued by the courts. (Ten years later, in July 1979, the Bundestag would abolish the statute of limitations on murder, making this offence punishable even after the time limit set in 1969.)

One reform Kiesinger had particularly emphasized in his 1966 inaugural address did not come off: that of the electoral law. The main reason was that the Social Democrats progressively lost interest in a majority system. At their Nuremberg party congress in March 1968 they postponed a decision on the issue until their next regular congress in 1970—that is, until after the end of the fifth legislative period. This dilatory behaviour, which looked very much like a rejection, was a response to a clear leftward shift on the part of the liberals under Walter Scheel, elected head of the FDP at the Freiburg congress at the end of January 1969. This change suggested that a social–liberal coalition would be possible in the future. The SPD's abandonment of the majority voting system was a sign of good will toward the Free Democrats, whose party would not have survived such a reform.

The most ardent proponent of voting law reform in the Union, interior minister Paul Lücke, resigned his post on 26 March after the reorientation of the SPD. On 2 April Ernst Benda, a CDU Bundestag representative from Berlin and Lücke's parliamentary state secretary, was appointed to succeed his former boss. (The position of 'parliamentary state secretary', essentially an adviser to a federal minister, was another innovation of the Grand Coalition and introduced in April 1967.)

The most difficult tasks the Grand Coalition had to face proved to be in foreign policy. Here, too, there were points of agreement between the Union and the Social Democrats, as well as between the chancellor and the foreign minister. Kiesinger and Brandt both stressed the importance of good relations with both America and France and resisted being used by either power against the other. Both were conscious of the risks of international isolation—risks that, under Erhard's chancellorship, had arisen from the policy of making a 'real' east–west détente dependent on German reunification, whereas Johnson and de Gaulle, despite the differences in their views on the subject, were agreed on not letting Bonn disrupt their own policies on eastern Europe.

A major policy speech by the American president on 7 October 1966 made it clear that Washington did not consider the war in Vietnam a reason to pursue a confrontational policy with European communists as well. On the contrary: Johnson expressly called for 'reconciliation with the east' and the 'shift from the narrow concept of coexistence to the broader vision of peaceful engagement'. Charles de Gaulle, for his part, became suspect to the 'German Gaullists' in the wake of his visit to the Soviet Union in July 1966, which the general called 'eternal France's visit to an eternal Russia'. He also challenged the German 'Atlanticists' with the sharp words he directed against US foreign policy and warfare in Vietnam during a speech in the Cambodian capital Pnom Penh on 1 September 1966. Nonetheless, since both Paris and Washington wanted to improve their relations with the Soviet Union, Bonn was compelled to review its own stance. If it wished to avoid 'encirclement', it had no choice but to settle, or at least tone down, what Richard Löwenthal would call the 'special German conflict with the east' a few years later (1974) in the context of a discussion of the general east–west confrontation.

The coalition partners agreed in theory: West Germany had to move in a new direction with its eastern policy. But the willingness of the SPD to go much further than the Union led to problems in practice. The CDU and CSU wanted to preserve the 'Hallstein doctrine' as much as possible, whereas the SPD saw it as a shackle. The Union resisted granting the GDR the status of a state, while more and more Social Democrats thought it necessary to recognize East Germany as much as the international legal status of divided Germany permitted. In the search for further positive solutions to the problem, a 'qualified, codified, and temporally limited side-by-side existence' was necessary as a 'modus vivendi' for the two German territories: this was how Willy Brandt put it at the Dortmund party congress of the SPD at the beginning of June 1966.

Prior to his rise to the chancellorship, Kiesinger had not distinguished himself as a hardliner on questions of eastern policy; he had a—deserved—reputation for flexibility. He was also elected head of the CDU on 24 May 1967 at the Brunswick party congress. Ludwig Erhard had to accept the title of 'honorary head', succeeding Adenauer, who had died on 19 April at his house in Rhöndorf at the age of 91.

With his position within his party now much stronger, Kiesinger could afford to do something that would have been unthinkable before. On 13 June 1967 he responded to a letter from Willi Stoph, the East German prime minister (Stoph had succeeded to this office in 1964 after Otto Grotewohl's death). In substance, however, the correspondence produced no result. Stoph demanded direct negotiations for the purpose of normalizing relations and the recognition of the existing borders. Kiesinger proposed strengthening the inner solidarity of the German people by empowering representatives from both sides to conduct talks on further economic cooperation, cultural exchange, and ways of bringing relief to Germans in their daily lives.

On 17 June 1967, on the occasion of the official commemoration of the Day of German Unity, Kiesinger outlined the historical perspective from which he viewed the GDR and the unresolved German question. For one side to demand from the other complete subjection to its own viewpoint was not a promising tactic, he told the leaders in East Berlin; it created the impression that dialogue and cooperation were to be avoided.

We, on the other hand, hold it to be a tried and true method to first look for common ground, bracketing out the great divisive issues for the moment... Détente should not come down to resigned acceptance, much less to a fixing of the status quo. Wherever a policy of status quo among a people with incompatible existential interests is misconstrued as a permanent peace solution, there arises a source of sickness that can become an epidemic at any moment. For this reason, in our search for détente, we must look for ways to treat the source of the sickness with patient therapy, ultimately leading to its removal.

Kiesinger then gave voice to an insight no previous chancellor had ever expressed in so many words:

Germany, a reunited Germany, is a country of pivotal size. It is too large not to play a role in the balance of powers, and it is too small to hold in balance the powers that surround it. Therefore, it is truly very difficult to imagine that, if the present political structure in Europe continues, all of Germany could simply join one or the other side. For this very reason, the growth and merging of the two divided Germanies is something that can only be seen as part of the process of overcoming the east–west conflict in all of Europe.

As far as the relationship to the GDR was concerned—he avoided its official name, but also the terms 'Soviet zone' or 'the zone'—Kiesinger rejected 'the political and legal recognition of a second German state, that is, the acceptance of the German partition as fact'.

What is possible between us and those responsible for the other part of Germany, however, are talks and agreements to alleviate the suffering caused by the forced split and improve human, economic, and intellectual relations between the Germans; to prevent the German people from growing further apart from year to year. Such an easing of inner tensions, or inner detoxification, would fit in with our great plan for a future European peacetime order, and could serve it usefully.

Much of what the chancellor had to say on 17 June 1967 had long been nothing new to the Social Democrats, unlike Kiesinger's own party. But even in the Union, the proponents of a realistic policy towards the east had gained ground in the meantime. According to the so-called *Geburtsfehlertheorie* (literally 'congenital defect theory'), for example, developed in the foreign office under Schröder, the 'Hallstein doctrine' would not apply to states that had established diplomatic relations with East Germany at the very beginning. This interpretation was first applied to Romania, with which the FRG established full diplomatic relations on 31 January 1967. Ever since 1960—first under Communist party secretary Georghiu-Dej, then under his successor Ceausescu—Romania had been pursuing a strongly 'nationalist' line and on several occasions had stressed its independence from Moscow. For this reason, Moscow reacted strongly to the cooperation between Bonn and Bucharest. The Warsaw Pact states, meeting in the Polish capital without Romania and calling themselves the 'socialist camp', replied to the Grand Coalition's eastern policy with a resounding 'nyet!': they would entertain diplomatic relations with West Germany only if it gave up nuclear weapons, recognized the GDR and the existing European borders, and abandoned the claim to sole representation of the German people.

The consequences were no less clear than the message. During the time it was in power, the Grand Coalition was unable to conclude diplomatic relations with any other member of the Warsaw Pact. Its only achievement in this regard was the successful conclusion of economic negotiations with Czechoslovakia. As for the 'Hallstein doctrine', it was abandoned in all but name on 31 January 1968 when Bonn normalized relations with Belgrade (which had been broken off in 1957 after Yugoslavia had recognized the GDR). The *Geburtsfehlertheorie* could not be applied in this case; Yugoslavia had recognized West Germany first, then the GDR. Kiesinger, however, after returning from a visit to Asia in November 1967, had become convinced that softening the 'Hallstein doctrine' would not necessarily lead to a whole wave of 'Third World' states suddenly recognizing East Germany.

But then, in May 1969, that was exactly what happened: Cambodia, Iraq, and Sudan all recognized the GDR. In the case of Iraq and Sudan, diplomatic contact had not existed since May 1965. Not so with Cambodia, with whom the FRG entertained normal relations. After bitter controversy within the Grand Coalition—Kiesinger and the Union advocating a 'hard' line, Brandt and the SPD a 'soft' approach—the government responded on 4 June by 'freezing' diplomatic relations with Pnom Penh. This was a compromise that left doubt about whether the coalition was even still capable of meaningful foreign policy in 1969, with elections just around the corner. The FDP ridiculed what they called the government's 'cambodiating'. Cambodia itself gave Bonn a resounding slap in the face, calling its ambassador home on 11 June.

Recognition by these 'Third World' states enhanced the status of the GDR. The Bonn government responded to the new situation on 30 May with a new doctrine, designed to rationalize its current policy: every recognition of the GDR would be looked on as an unfriendly act; the attitude the West German government would adopt would depend on the particular circumstances in each case. This was now a formal renunciation of the original automatism of the 'Hallstein policy' (i.e. the termination of diplomatic relations upon recognition of the GDR). Nonetheless, the new policy did not succeed in blocking further East German diplomatic successes. In June two Arab states, Syria and South Yemen, recognized the GDR. Bonn had diplomatic relations only with the latter. On 2 July the government decided to suspend them and call the ambassador back to Germany. The FRG's embassy in Aden was closed on 27 October.

In terms of its relationship to the western world, the change from the Christian-liberal to the Grand Coalition was, all in all, good for West Germany. The new government's self-confident attitude towards the United States surprised everyone at first. On 1 February 1967, Foreign Minister Brandt announced that West Germany would sign the non-proliferation treaty currently under negotiation in Geneva between the USA, Great Britain, and the Soviet Union only if it did not discriminate against non-nuclear countries.

The chancellor went even further. On 27 February he complained before the Union press association that the United States and West Germany no longer discussed matters of common policy, but only controversial issues. It was now important to determine 'to what extent American interests agree with ours, German and European interests, and to what extent they do not or no longer agree.' At the zenith of the Cold War these interests had generally been identical, Kiesinger said, but now 'a kind of atomic "complicity"' had developed between Washington and Moscow. As Conrad Ahlers, the government's deputy chief of press, explained a few days later, the chancellor's critical remarks had mostly been in response to the lack of consultations over the non-proliferation treaty.

Kiesinger's undiplomatic language, which recalled that of de Gaulle, was in fact only partly justified and not least guided by domestic and tactical considerations. The chancellor felt he had to conform to a certain extent with Konrad Adenauer and Franz Josef Strauss, both of whom vehemently rejected the non-proliferation agreement. Adenauer denounced it as a 'Morgenthau Plan squared' (an allusion to Roosevelt's finance minister, Henry Morgenthau, who in 1944 had proposed changing Germany into an agrarian country). The CSU chief was calling the agreement a 'Versailles of curious proportions' as late as June 1968.

Although Kiesinger was more sceptical than Brandt, he believed that the international situation made an actual rejection of the non-proliferation treaty impossible. Like his foreign minister, he was mainly concerned with linking West Germany's interest in unrestricted use of atomic energy for peaceful purposes with the similar interests of other non-nuclear powers like Japan. And in the ensuing months, this policy would prove successful.

Bonn's blunt commentary achieved the desired result very quickly. In March 1967 the United States began to send detailed reports on the progress of the Geneva negotiations. Moreover, it was prepared to accommodate West Germany in the controversy over the payments for American troops stationed in the country. The Grand Coalition's self-assured pursuit of West Germany's own interests proved to have a salutary and not a negative effect on its relations with America.

Meanwhile, the French president did not cease his attempts to woo Bonn. In talks conducted with Kiesinger in Paris in mid-January 1967, de Gaulle declared his support for a reunified Germany, within the 1945 borders and without nuclear weapons. He continued to favour a German-French union and left no doubt that its centre could only be in Paris. He continued to reject British accession to the European Economic Union (a prospect even Franz Josef Strauss, previously a staunch 'German Gaullist', now supported). Increased cooperation with France in matters of eastern and Germany policy was something Kiesinger and Brandt could accept, but not an exclusive alliance with France. They pressed for Britain's acceptance into the EEC. At the same time, they conscientiously avoided placing themselves at the front of a European anti-de Gaulle movement. This was a difficult balancing act, but it succeeded for the moment. Under the Grand Coalition, relations between Paris and Bonn were initially better than they had been under Erhard.

There was no disagreement between the two countries with regard to the fusion of the European Communities, negotiated in 1965. On 1 July 1967 the European Economic Community, the European Community for Coal and Steel, and the European Atomic Energy Community were combined into a single 'European Community' (EC). Henceforth there would be one European Commission and one European Ministers' Council, located in Brussels (the European Parliament and the European Court of Justice had been responsible for all three bodies since the beginning of 1958). One of the first major decisions of the European Council was a non-decision: on 14 December 1967, owing to the French position, the council failed to reach consensus about the accession of Great Britain, Ireland, Denmark, and Norway. But even Paris now no longer raised fundamental objections to an expansion of the EC, and so the British petition remained on the agenda.

In the Atlantic alliance, the change of government in Bonn meant an increase in influence. In December 1966 the Federal Republic became a permanent member of the Nuclear Planning Group. This was in compensation for the failed MLF project. It also represented a degree of co-determination in matters atomic. On 9 May 1967 the defence ministers of the NATO countries—excluding France—voted to retire the old concept of defence in favour of a new one. The principle of 'massive retaliation' was now officially replaced by that of a 'graduated, flexible response'. The Grand Coalition government supported this new direction, thereby abandoning the position of the former cabinet whereby any attack from the east, even with conventional weapons, would have to be answered atomically.

NATO's political reorientation was far more important. On 14 December 1967 the foreign ministers of the member states released the 'Harmel report', named after the Belgian foreign minister, Pierre Harmel. Though it contained a clear message for the east, the language of the text was so balanced that both coalition parties in Bonn could endorse it. It gave NATO two functions. The first, the maintenance of sufficient military strength and political solidarity to discourage aggression and other forms of pressure, was not new. The second, the striving for détente, was. These tasks were meant to complement, not contradict one another. The authors of the report also expressly committed themselves to the ongoing review of policies 'designed to achieve a just and stable order in Europe, to overcome the division of Germany, and to foster European security'.

Some six months later, on 25 June 1968, the 'Reykjavik signal' went out. Meeting in the capital of Iceland, the NATO council, following the guidelines of the Harmel report, called for the gradual building up of a lasting European peacetime order. The Warsaw Pact was offered negotiations over a mutual and balanced reduction of troops. Foreign Minister Brandt had good reason to be satisfied with this communiqué: he had played an important role in its drafting.

Up to this point, little had changed in the bilateral relations between Bonn and Moscow. Talks and memoranda on a renunciation of armed force had not brought tangible results. The Kremlin even insisted on maintaining the 'enemy states clauses' in the 1945 Charter of the United Nations, deriving from them a right to intervene in West Germany. On 5 July 1968, acting unilaterally and violating the agreed-upon confidentiality, the Soviet Union published a part of the documents pertaining to this matter and accused West Germany of continuing to pursue revanchist aims. This was tantamount to ending negotiations. The GDR, acting in accordance with Moscow, did what it could to thwart the eastern policy efforts of the Grand Coalition. In April 1968 the East German interior ministry banned members and leading officials of the West German government from using the transit routes to West Berlin. In June measures were passed making passports and visas, obligatory in inter-German travel, also necessary for travel between West Berlin and the rest of the FRG and imposing fees for the use of East German roads and waterways.

Then, on 9 August, it suddenly looked as if the GDR was reconsidering its position with regard to Bonn. In his capacity as GDR president, Ulbricht presented the Volkskammer with proposals for the normalization of relations between the two countries. Thereupon the Volkskammer passed a resolution empowering the government to negotiate a treaty in accordance with international law as soon as two conditions had been met: West Germany would have to abandon the 'Hallstein doctrine' and its claim ('presumption', in the words of the resolution) to sole representation of the German people. The interesting thing about Ulbricht's initiative was not the old demand for international recognition, however, but the comment that the economics ministers of the two countries could, in the meantime, begin negotiations on matters of common interest. In its first response, the Bonn government rejected the GDR's prerequisites. But it did not exclude the possibility that Ulbricht's proposals, despite reiterating the old accusations, also contained 'new nuances'. 'If this is confirmed, then the federal government will certainly not react negatively.'

No negotiations resulted. On 21 August 1968 troops of the Warsaw Pact occupied the Socialist Republic of Czechoslovakia and put an end to the 'Prague Spring'. Led by Alexander Dubček, the First Secretary of the Communist Party of Czechoslovakia, Czech and Slovak reformers had been working to overcome Leninist-style party dictatorship and institute 'socialism with a human face'. In the Soviet view, however, they had crossed the line and put the solidarity of the 'socialist camp' at risk. On 15 July 1968 the members of the Warsaw Pact, with the exception of Romania, gave the Prague leadership an ultimatum, which they based on the 'Brezhnev doctrine', as it was called in the west: membership in the Warsaw Pact meant a renunciation of unconditional national sovereignty. This was tantamount to giving the Pact a right to intervene. Initially, Walter Ulbricht saw Dubček as a politician with ideas similar to his own. By the summer of 1968, however, he was one of the hardliners, and the GDR participated in the intervention (although the National People's Army only secured reinforcements and the hinterland and did not cross the border into the CSSR).

The suppression of the 'Prague Spring', which was unanimously condemned by all the parties in the Bundestag, put an end to the Grand Coalition eastern policy for the time being. Since Moscow blamed the West German 'imperialists' for the crisis in Czechoslovakia, many politicians and observers prepared themselves for a lengthy 'ice age' in the relations between east and west, especially between the FRG and the Soviet Union. Nonetheless, despite this turn, the Social Democrats and liberals refused to believe the détente policy had suffered a permanent defeat. They turned out to be correct.

On 10 January 1969 the Soviet ambassador, Semen Zarapkin, told Willy Brandt that his country wanted to improve relations with West Germany and favoured the resumption of the negotiations broken off in July 1968. On 23 February Zarapkin informed Kiesinger that the GDR would be prepared to discuss the matter of transit permits if the West German presidential election, scheduled for 5 March, was not held in Berlin. Bonn rejected this offer on the next day, but the east made a new gesture of conciliation shortly later. On 17 March, meeting in the Hungarian capital for their yearly convention, the Warsaw Pact states proposed a European security conference between themselves, the NATO countries, and the neutral powers.

Three years before, at its Bucharest conference, the Warsaw Pact had spoken of a European security system that would take the place of the existing alliances. That was no longer the case in 1969. While the Budapest announcement reiterated the demand that West Germany recognize the existing borders and the 'existence of the GDR', it was no longer a matter of conditions to be met before negotiations, but prerequisites for a future system of European security—as the Warsaw Pact interpreted it. And the 'recognition of the existence of the GDR' was a more modest demand than recognition according to international law. It looked as though the Soviet Union was prepared to meet West Germany halfway.

There were at least two reasons for these changes. First, the situation in Czechoslovakia was externally stable again. Backed up by a strong contingent of Soviet troops, Communists loyal to Moscow now had the country under control, and the reformers had been systematically removed from the party, the ministries, the universities, and the scientific institutes. It was once again quiet on the 'western front'. On the 'eastern front', however—and this is the second reason—there was shooting. On 2 March 1969 the tensions between the Soviet Union and China resulted in their first military conflict, which occurred along the Ussuri river border. This dramatic shift in the Far East conflict made the Kremlin anxious to relax tensions in the west, and the forceful suppression of the Czechoslovakian reform considerably lessened the risks of such a policy.

There were also changes in the western leadership. After 20 January 1969 the USA was led by a Republican, Richard Nixon, who had gained a reputation for staunch anti-communism as California senator and vice president under Eisenhower. Since that time, however, Nixon had become one thing above all: a devotee of realpolitik. Under the influence of his security adviser, Henry A. Kissinger (a historian originally from Fürth in German Franconia whose family had fled the Jewish persecution under the National Socialists and settled in America), Nixon sought to bring the Vietnam War to a rapid end. Over 31,000 Americans had fallen in that country by the time Nixon came to the White House, and more than half a million GIs were still stationed there. In order to bring about a peace that would be in keeping with American honour, Nixon and Kissinger worked to normalize relations with communist China. For this reason—though it was not the only one—they were also interested in continuing the search for détente in Europe.

Of course, as Nixon made clear on 10–11 April 1969 at the twentieth anniversary convention of the NATO council, the prerequisites for détente would be determined by the United States and not each of the western allies acting separately. The West German foreign minister welcomed the American desire for an easing of tensions, but his ideas were more concrete than Nixon's. Backed up by his Italian colleague, the Socialist Pietro Nenni, Brandt declared that the west should take up the Warsaw Pact's proposal for a European security conference in a constructive manner and open up public debate on certain aspects of European security. This policy prevailed. It became, as Brandt wrote in 1989, 'the march route for the western alliance—without great élan, but none the less'.

On 28 April 1969, two and a half weeks after the meeting in Washington, the man who had taken his country out of the NATO military structure and caused its worst crisis to date finally left the political stage. After the failure of a referendum on senate and regional reform, which he had made into a plebiscite on his government policy as a whole, Charles de Gaulle resigned from office. This came at a time when relations between Paris and Bonn were at a new low. The cause was a currency crisis in November 1968. Under the joint aegis of Schiller and Strauss, West Germany had resisted pressure from the USA, Britain, and France to make up for the weakness of their currencies through a revaluation of the German mark. France, whose currency was the weakest of the three, was the real loser in this matter.

At the news of de Gaulle's resignation, the primary sentiment in West Germany was relief. There were no 'German Gaullists' left by the spring of 1969. With his shift to a policy of détente, the general had often irritated his disciples east of the

Rhine more than his opponents. France had to pay a high price for the 'greatness' to which, in de Gaulle's view, it was predestined. The ambitious nuclear weapons programme of the *force de frappe* had contributed in no small measure to the weakness of the franc. German gloating was considerable, occasionally downright chauvinist in autumn 1968. 'The Germans are now number 1 in Europe!' ran the headline of the *Bild-Zeitung* on 23 November, after Bonn had successfully asserted itself in the currency crisis. But the economic strength of West Germany had another side. At the end of 1968, a danger the Grand Coalition seemed to have exorcised loomed once again: the FRG threatened to slide into crisis with its most important allies.[13]

THE ROAD TO A SOCIAL–LIBERAL COALITION

The first days of the Grand Coalition in 1966–7 were accompanied by heated protests from intellectuals and publicists. Rudolf Augstein, the publisher of *Der Spiegel*, called it the 'declared intention' of the governing alliance 'to discourage oppositional forces by changing the voting law and then to eliminate them from federal politics'. The philosopher Karl Jaspers lamented the 'decline of a democracy'. Harold Rasch, a scholar of constitutional law, went so far as to speak of a 'surreptitious *coup d'état*', the result of which was a 'de facto abolition of the constitution'.

The indisputable legislative and foreign policy successes of the Kiesinger—Brandt government soon took the wind out of the critics' sails. Nonetheless, there persisted a widespread unease concerning new decision-making bodies not provided for in the Basic Law. The 'Kressbonn circle' was one of these. It was named after Kiesinger's vacation home on the Bodensee, where the leading politicians of the two coalition parties first met in August 1967 to work out solutions to the most pressing matters. In the daily work of government the two fraction leaders, Rainer Barzel for the CDU/CSU and Helmut Schmidt for the SPD, saw to it that the partnership of convenience functioned as smoothly as possible. The result was a tacit transformation of the constitution. The Bundestag plenum and opposition lost importance. The chancellor could no longer invoke his *Richtlinienkompetenz,* his authority in matters of general policy; his role was reduced to that of an 'ambulatory mediation committee', as Conrad Ahlers put it. In this respect criticism was justified. Despite their efficiency, the decision-making processes of the Grand Coalition were not transparent. There was no longer any effective parliamentary control of the executive. If the Grand Coalition continued in power for a longer period of time, representative democracy threatened to become a mere facade.

In spring 1969 it began to look increasingly likely that the alliance would not survive the federal elections slated for that autumn. Foreign policy differences could no longer be overlooked. The Social Democrats wanted to go further towards accommodating the Soviet Union and the other Warsaw Pact states, especially the GDR, than the alliance with the Union permitted. Although not all of the domestic reforms had yet made it into law, the end was in sight. And finally the third party, the FDP, ever since its Freiburg congress in January 1968, had acquired such a 'progressive' image in matters of Germany policy, eastern policy, and domestic reform that it now had more in common with the SPD than with the Union.

In September 1968 the Free Democrats refused to go along with a Bundestag resolution on Germany policy that repeated—as the CDU was demanding—the FRG's claim to sole representation of the Germans (which the SPD was prepared to accept). In January 1969 the liberals presented the draft of a basic treaty between the two German states. It included, among other things, language about a mutual renunciation of force, extensive freedom to travel, and the release of political prisoners. While the government rejected both the substance and the timing of the draft, Herbert Wehner, minister for all-German affairs, let it be known several times at the end of April that he sympathized with the idea of a German–German treaty.

The practical feasibility of a SPD–FDP alliance was put to the test on 5 March 1969 in the presidential election. The vote was held early, after Heinrich Lübke, increasingly unequal to the mental challenges of his office, announced in October 1968 that he would resign on 30 June 1969, thus allowing the election of his successor to take place before the campaign season got under way. The Union parties put forward Gerhard Schröder as their candidate; the Social Democrats ran Gustav Heinemann, the minister of justice. Schröder was a conservative; this decreased his chances of gaining the votes of the Free Democrats, most of whom were much more amenable to Heinemann's views. By 4 March, however, when the liberal delegates under Walter Scheel met in Berlin for talks, nothing had been decided.

The party right under former FDP head Erich Mende wanted to vote for Schröder, but they remained in the minority. Like Scheel, most of the active supporters of Heinemann came from North Rhine-Westphalia, which had been governed since December 1966 by a social–liberal coalition under Social Democratic prime minister Heinz Kühn. Willi Weyer, interior minister and head of the FDP in North Rhine-Westphalia, brought forward an important argument for supporting Heinemann. Three leading Social Democrats—Herbert Wehner, Willy Brandt, and Heinz Kühn—had given him the go-ahead to announce that a majority voting system would be 'dropped once and for all if Gustav Heinemann is elected president tomorrow with the help of the FDP'. In the final ballot, 77 out of the 82 FDP delegates present voted for Heinemann, 5 against him. Schröder's candidacy, on the other hand, would have the resolute support of another party, the NPD.

Despite sustained efforts on the part of the GDR to disrupt traffic to Berlin, the fifth federal assembly convened in the Ostpreussenhalle at the exhibition centre of the Berlin radio tower on 5 March 1969. Of the 1,036 delegates, 482 belonged to the CDU/CSU, 449 to the SPD, 83 to the FDP, and 22 to the NPD. With 1,023 members of the assembly taking part in the vote, the decision was not made until the third ballot, which only required a relative majority: 512 votes went to Heinemann, 506 to Schröder.

If Schröder had won with the help of the right-wing radicals, the republic would have been shaken to its very foundations, the new president's reputation and authority seriously compromised. Heinemann's election, as he himself put it in an interview with the *Stuttgarter Zeitung* a few days later, represented 'a dose of leadership change'. While this was an unfortunate choice of words for a man soon to enter an office that required him to be non-partisan, it was basically correct. The FDP had allowed the election of a Social Democratic president, and this gave an indication about the composition of the next West German government—provided that the election outcome permitted a SPD–FDP coalition.

Heinemann's election sent a signal in several ways. He stood for an opening of the Social Democratic movement toward the bourgeoisie. He proved that pious Protestants were welcome in the SPD, even ones who had previously belonged to the CDU. The rebellious students found him to be an uncomfortable interlocutor, but that actually lent him credibility in their eyes. In radio and television addresses on 14 April 1968, after the attack on Rudi Dutschke, Heinemann had called upon the students to exercise 'self-control'. At the same time, however, he asked 'us all' 'what we ourselves might have contributed in the past towards making anti-communism into something that resorts to murder, and demonstrators lose themselves in acts of violence and arson'. Four weeks later, on 10 May 1968, he defended the federal emergency legislation before the Bundestag with the following argument:

Whoever agitates against clear emergency provisions in the constitution might as well simply say: I am for new, extra-parliamentary emergency measures only by the government, measures that no citizen will learn about until the crisis comes! . . . I ask: how do these opponents out of principle actually intend to defend their rights, if everything comes down to unwritten emergency action?

As difficult as this logic was to gainsay, the Extra-Parliamentary Opposition found it hard to accept.

On 1 July 1969, three weeks before his seventieth birthday, Heinemann assumed the office to which he had been elected. His inaugural speech was an appeal to the citizens of West Germany to reconsider their views. The real *Ernstfall*, the extraordinary situation that had to be prepared for, was not war, but peace. While he declared his support for the Bundeswehr, he said that the army was not an end in itself. He pointed out that, in addition to the east–west conflict, there was also a conflict between the north and the south, and he thanked his predecessor Heinrich Lübke for his persistence on this point. The centrepiece of the address was the proposition that liberal democracy 'must finally become the life-element of our society'.

Some people are still stuck on the authoritarian state. That was our misfortune for long enough and ended up leading us into the disaster of the Third Reich . . . Not less, but rather more democracy—that is what is needed, that is the great aim to which we, and especially the young, must dedicate ourselves. Some fatherlands are difficult. One of them is Germany. But it is *our* fatherland.

For many conservatives, much of what Heinemann had to say could not but seem a provocation. And in truth, his inaugural was the most political speech ever held by a federal president upon entering office. At the same time, it was probably the most impressive testimony to the sense of optimism and new beginning in West German social and intellectual life at the end of the 1960s. Adenauer's former interior minister confirmed the end of the Adenauer era. His appeal to 'the politically mature and involved citizen' expressed a different, more active understanding of democracy than the one that had shaped the 1950s and was still very much alive. Heinemann himself was basically a bourgeois democrat, and he made frequent reference to the liberal traditions of German history, from the peasant wars of the sixteenth century to the Hambach Festival of 1832, the 1848 revolution, and especially the Baden uprising in 1849, in which several of his ancestors had fought. Part of his purpose in this was to counteract the GDR's use of the revolutionary tradition. In June 1974, at the opening of the Rastatt memorial for the historical German liberation movements, Heinemann would accuse East Germany of revising these traditions into developmental stages leading up to the coercive communist state.

In a television address on 17 January 1971, Heinemann spoke of 1871 as achieving 'an external unity without complete inner liberty on the part of the citizens'. 'A hundred years of German empire—this doesn't mean simply one Versailles, but two, in 1871 as well as in 1919. And it also means Auschwitz, Stalingrad, and the unconditional surrender of 1945.' Nonetheless, German history after 1871 also included the liberal, Catholic, and Social Democratic opponents of Bismarck and their political heirs, the parties that had upheld the Weimar Republic. They, and they alone, stood for the Germany that, in Heinemann's view, had a future.

The third president of the FRG was politicizing history, and he well knew it. His accounts were often tendentious, and sometimes his pedagogical efforts came across as crude didacticism. This drew justified criticism along with partisan polemics. All in all, however, the attempt to confront the national-conservative view of German history, still widespread and regarded in many quarters as the 'official' version, with a critical historical understanding based on the values of liberty and democracy was overdue. In Heinemann, the 'difficult fatherland' of Germany found not only a patriotic spokesman, but one whose concept of patriotism was anything but intellectually facile and shallow.

On 3 July 1969, two days after Heinemann's inaugural speech, the last session of the fifth German Bundestag took place. The 'hot phase' of the electoral campaign began thereafter. The CDU placed its bets on Kiesinger's popularity and campaigned under the slogan 'It's a matter of the right chancellor.' The SPD promised: 'We'll create modern Germany.' The FDP, which sought to distinguish itself from the other parties by using three full stops (periods) in its name ('F.D.P.') also announced a thoroughgoing renewal of the state and society, summarizing its platform in the slogan 'We'll get rid of the old hats' (*Wir schaffen die alten Zöpfe ab*).

The coalition partners fought during the summer months primarily over the question of revaluing the mark. Finance Minister Strauss, the export branches, and agriculture continued to reject such a move, while Economics Minister Schiller and most economists supported it. The opponents emphasized the disadvantages for the export economy and the farmers. The advocates highlighted one consequence of the undervalued currency that could be felt by all: the rise in prices, especially for imported goods, and the resultant increase in the cost of living. The subject of revaluation made the headlines again shortly before the election. On 25 September the government, at the suggestion of the federal bank, ordered the temporary closing of the West German foreign exchange markets. This was intended to pre-empt a speculative influx of foreign currency set off by the expectation of the mark's revaluation after the election.

The sixth German Bundestag was elected on 28 September 1969. With 46.1%, the Union parties remained the strongest single political force in the country, but lost 1.5% from 1965. The SPD did better than it ever had before, 42.7%, a 3.4% increase. The FDP fell from 9.5% to 5.8% (−3.7%), its worst performance to date and dangerously close to the 5% hurdle. With 4.3%, the NPD came just short of the chance to participate in the national parliament. There was a new leftist party on the scene, the German Communist Party (*Deutsche Kommunistische Partei* or DKP), founded in October 1968, but it did not contest the election. Unlike the KPD, banned in 1956, the new party promised 'to bring about the socialist order of society and state within the framework of the Basic Law'. The West German government had accepted the new party, thinking that the de facto revision of the Communist ban would help it in its relationship with the Soviet Union.

The message sent by the German voters could be interpreted in a number of ways. It was obvious that right-wing radicalism had weakened and that confidence in the democratic parties had strengthened once again. The Grand Coalition had not only successfully dealt with an economic crisis, it had also brought about many overdue reforms. Clearly, the political system of the Basic Law was much more than a 'fair weather democracy'; it had passed its first serious test.

The election outcome was not a referendum against the Grand Coalition. The Union's losses were too trivial, the SPD's gains too high to permit this interpretation. If the NPD voters had known that their preferred party would not make the 5 per cent barrier, many of them would probably have voted for the CDU/CSU, in which case an absolute Union majority would have been likely. There was also no clear mandate for a social–liberal coalition; otherwise the FDP's leftward shift would not have cost it so many voters, nearly 40 per cent of its 1965 strength.

Still, there was no getting around the fact that, numerically speaking at least, the election outcome allowed a 'leadership change', the formation of a social–liberal West German government. Walter Scheel, the head of the FDP, had spoken in favour of such an alliance a few days before the vote (on 25 September) in a ZDF television programme with the heads of the four parties represented in the Bundestag. Still, it had to be assumed that not all the FDP delegates would vote for a Social Democratic chancellor. With all 224 votes from his own party and all 30 from the FDP, an SPD candidate would have 12 more than the CDU/CSU, which controlled 242 seats, and 5 more than the necessary absolute or 'chancellor majority'.

Herbert Wehner and Helmut Schmidt considered this margin insufficient and the Free Democrats unreliable. The evening of the election, Wehner disparagingly referred to the FDP as 'that old swing party'.* But Karl Schiller, to whose popularity the SPD owed no small part of its electoral success, rejected another coalition with the Union. The battle over revaluation had affected his relationship with the Christian-Social finance minister, Franz Josef Strauss, so negatively that meaningful cooperation no longer seemed possible.

The decisive factor was the attitude of the party head, and Willy Brandt was resolved to risk a social–liberal coalition. His main reasons had to do with his views on eastern policy and the German–German relationship, in which areas the Grand Coalition had achieved little. He saw a chance of overcoming the stagnation with the FDP, but no longer with the Union. Speaking with Walter Scheel by telephone on the evening of the election, Brandt set the course he wished to pursue. Kiesinger, whom President Nixon had already congratulated as the victor of 28 September, now had to reckon with the prospect of going down in history as the loser.

On the day after the election, in response to the government's wish, the federal bank freed the foreign exchange rate. Prior to the intervention, the dollar had been worth 4 marks; immediately afterward the relationship was quoted at 1 to 3.84, a revaluation of 4 per cent for the German mark.

The negotiations between the SPD and the FDP went quickly. By 3 October Brandt and Scheel were able to inform President Heinemann of their intention of forming a coalition. Agreement was especially easy in foreign and Germany policy. In economic matters, the SPD accepted the FDP's wish that the system of worker co-determination not be extended. The liberals received two key

---

* [Translator's note: German *Pendlerpartei* has a more pejorative connotation than English 'swing party'.]

ministries: the foreign office went to Walter Scheel, who also became vice chancellor, and the interior ministry was given to the delegate Hans-Dietrich Genscher. (Originally from Halle, Genscher had fled the GDR in 1952.) The third FDP cabinet member was the minister of agriculture, Josef Ertl from Bavaria, a member of the liberal right wing who had initially been staunchly against a coalition with the Social Democrats.

The remaining eleven posts went to the SPD, along with the position of head of the chancellor's office, ranked as a federal minister for special assignments. This charge was awarded to Horst Ehmke, a scholar of constitutional law at the University of Freiburg (he was originally from Danzig) who had taken over as minister of justice after Heinemann's election to the presidency in March 1969. Brandt gave one of the ministries, education and science, to a non-aligned professor of technical mechanics, Hans Leussink. Karl Schiller continued as economics minister, Georg Leber as minister of transportation, and Lauritz Lauritzen as minister of housing construction. Alex Möller, general director of Karlsruhe Life Insurance and head of the SPD in Baden-Württemberg, took over the finance ministry; Helmut Schmidt, hitherto leader of the parliamentary fraction, the ministry of defence; the jurist Gerhard Jahn the ministry of justice; and Walter Arendt, head of the miners' union, the labour ministry. The new minister for German–German relations (the name 'all-German affairs' was dropped) was Egon Franke from Lower Saxony (his predecessor in this office, Herbert Wehner, took over as SPD fraction head). The minister of development—the official title was 'minister for economic cooperation'—was the Swabian Erhard Eppler, who had assumed this post already in October 1968 when the then incumbent, Hans-Jürgen Wischnewski, left to become the managing director of the federal SPD.

The Bundestag elected Willy Brandt chancellor of the Federal Republic of Germany on 21 October 1969. He received 251 out of 495 votes; 235 delegates voted against him, 5 abstained, and 4 submitted invalid vote cards. One of the 496 delegates entitled to vote did not participate. The number who voted for Brandt was two more than the necessary absolute majority and three less than the number of seats the new social–liberal coalition controlled. All things considered, this was a satisfying result, and in any case it was sufficient. For the first time since the fall of Reich chancellor Herman Müller on 27 March 1930, there was a Social Democratic head of government in Germany once again.[14]

THE GDR IN THE SECOND HALF OF THE 1960s

In the second half of the 1960s the GDR consolidated its independent statehood and dismantled what remained of its previous adherence to the idea of a single German national state. The SED responded to the Grand Coalition's first steps toward a new eastern policy by taking a harder line with West

Germany. Accordingly, at the beginning of February 1967, the State Secretariat for All-German Affairs was rebaptized the State Secretariat for West German Affairs. That same month the Warsaw Pact states, meeting in the Polish capital, formulated a kind of 'Hallstein doctrine' in reverse, called the 'Ulbricht doctrine' in the west. No member of the alliance was permitted to recognize the FRG as long as the latter refused to accept the existing borders and the existence of two German states. This was intended to prevent the example of Romania, which had taken up diplomatic relations with the Federal Republic at the end of January, from spreading. Shortly thereafter, on 20 February 1967, the Volkskammer passed a law introducing a new 'GDR citizenship'. The revocation of the project of a German confederation followed in April, at the seventh party congress of the SED; the plan was all-German in nature and thus irreconcilable with the new policy.

The counterpart to this elimination of all-German commonalities was the attempt to create for the GDR an especially prominent position within the circle of socialist states. On 12 September 1967 Ulbricht gave a speech entitled 'The meaning of Karl Marx's *Das Kapital* for the creation of the developed socialist system in the GDR'. Ulbricht's point of departure was the seventh party congress's 'strategic goal' of 'shaping the developed societal system of socialism, thus perfecting socialism'. His main argument was that 'socialism is not a short-term, transitional phase in the development of society, but rather a relatively autonomous socio-economic formation within the historical epoch of the shift from capitalism to communism on a global scale.'

This represented not only a correction of Marx and Lenin, it also challenged the Soviet Union, which ever since 1936 had been claiming to be already on the way from socialism to communism and, consequently, an entire historical period ahead of the other socialist countries. Ulbricht was interpreting this Soviet self-assessment as incorrect, albeit in an indirect manner. But if the two societies, the Soviet and the East German, both found themselves in the same socio-economic formation—that of socialism—it meant that the Soviet Union no longer enjoyed a qualitative lead. In May 1968 Ulbricht, on the occasion of the 150th anniversary of Karl Marx's birthday, described the socialism of the GDR as 'socialism in a modern, industrially highly developed country'. This implied a claim to paradigmatic status for the East German model.

The GDR was given a new criminal code and a new constitution in 1968. The revised criminal code, introduced on 12 January, made several innovations that were also a part of the West German reforms the following year: the *Zuchthaus* was abolished, probation and rehabilitation given increased emphasis, the law governing sexual offences liberalized, and the paragraph on blasphemy eliminated. The legislative treatment of political crimes was completely different; the list of punishable offenses was expanded and the punishments intensified. The catalogue now included 'crimes against the sovereignty of the GDR, peace, humanity, and human rights'; the 'gathering of intelligence'; 'sabotage';

'trafficking in human beings in a manner hostile to the state'; and 'agitation against the state'. The last offence, as Christoph Klessmann has written, was defined so broadly 'that any oppositional activity could be subsumed under it'. Several offences were still punishable by execution. The new code spoke of the 'independence of the judges', who were subject only to the constitution and the law. But the addendum that they were 'responsible to the people's representatives for the fulfilment of the duties assumed upon their election' made it all quite clear: the GDR had no intention of subjecting itself to the standards of bourgeois 'rule of law'.

The 'people's deliberation' (*Volksaussprache*) over the draft of a new, 'socialist' constitution began in February 1968. A few new ideas were taken up and put into the final version: the basic rights of freedom of conscience, worship, and religious belief, as well as the immunity of the Volkskammer representatives. A referendum took place on 6 April, when 94.5 per cent of the delegates voted for the constitution. Its first article reflected reality far more accurately than the 1949 version, which had read: 'Germany is an indivisible democratic republic, the foundations of which are the German *Länder.*' The new constitution began with the observation: 'The German Democratic Republic is a socialist state of the German nation. It is the political organization of the working people in town and countryside who are jointly implementing socialism under the leadership of the working class and its Marxist-Leninist party.' The basic rights were also to be interpreted in the light of this definition of the state and its goals, for example the freedom of speech guaranteed by Article 27:

Every citizen of the German Democratic Republic has the right, in accordance with the spirit and the aims of this Constitution, to express his opinion freely and publicly. This right is not limited by any service or employment relationship. Nobody may be placed at a disadvantage for using this right.

In the summer and autumn of 1968, the many GDR citizens who sympathized with the 'Prague Spring', especially young people, had a chance to find out what this right was worth in actual practice. The protests began after the Warsaw Pact intervention on 21 August. Slogans were painted on the streets and the walls of buildings, distributed in leaflets and signature petitions. Parallels were drawn again and again to the year 1938, when Wehrmacht troops had marched into Czechoslovakia. By 29 August the interior ministry had counted 1,112 cases of 'agitation threatening to the state' and 'libel against the state'. The Ministry for State Security registered over 2,000 'hostile acts' by 20 November. The protesters included workers, secondary school students, university students, and intellectuals, including members of the SED.

The exact number of those sentenced to prison terms and expelled from the universities is not known. The infringement of SED party discipline, on the other hand, can be quantified. According to an official report of 12 December 1968 there were 3,358 cases of 'unclear thinking', 'ambiguous behaviour', and 'acts harmful to the party' in 2,500 party organizations. The disciplinary consequences are summarized as follows:

Up to this point, 522 party sanctions have been resolved, including 223 expulsions, 55 cancellations, 109 serious reprimands, and 135 reprimands. In 297 cases, members and candidates were given warnings and expressions of disapproval. In 2,017 cases, political-ideological conferences and clarifications were concluded in the party organizations without leading to disciplinary measures.

The year 1968 left deep marks in the GDR. The vision of a 'socialism with a human face' had inspired a whole generation. The 'fraternal assistance' that the Warsaw Pact states provided to the orthodox minority in the Czechoslovak Communist party destroyed this hope. From that moment on, it was no longer possible to believe in the reformability of a Communist party dictatorship. Those who rejected the existing system could now only look to its collapse, its revolutionary destruction, or to a gradual lessening of repression as a consequence of international détente.

The effects of '1968' were thus much different in the GDR from in West Germany. In the latter the student protest movement, generally speaking, transformed itself from a radical opposition to the 'system' into a movement seeking to transform that system from within, not least within the Social Democratic party. In the GDR, there was broad sympathy in spring 1968 for the Prague reforms and for the hope of similar developments within East Germany itself. By the autumn, agreement was widespread that communist systems under the aegis of Moscow were incapable of fundamental reforms. What remained in both the west and the east was the citizens' own experience of revolt. In the west the protests were partially successful; in the east they failed. The 'cult of 1968' was a purely western phenomenon.

The East German state celebrated the twentieth anniversary of its founding in 1969. In January a committee set up for this purpose described the GDR as 'the state of peace and liberty, humanity and social justice legitimated by the centuries-long history of our people'. The authors drew a line from the peasant wars to the uprisings of 1813 and 1848, the revolutionary workers' movement and the anti-fascist resistance, all the way up to their own state. 'All the great, progressive ideas ever brought forward by the German people, the legacy of all the struggles for an empire of peace and social security, human dignity and fraternity, find their fulfilment in the GDR.'

For Ulbricht, this was apparently still not enough. In a speech on 22 March 1969 the First Secretary of the SED and GDR president described the 'socialist human community' (*sozialistische Menschengemeinschaft*), which he had proclaimed in April 1967 at the seventh party congress, in greater detail. The 'socialist human community' arising in the GDR went, in Ulbricht's vision, far beyond the old humanist ideal.

It signifies not only readiness to help, goodness, fraternity, and love of one's fellow man. It embraces both the development of the individual socialist personalities as well as of the many towards socialist communities in the process of common labour, learning, and participation in the planning and leadership of societal development... It has spread around in the world that the 'German miracle' that has taken place in our republic is not simply an 'economic miracle', but above all consists of the great transformation of the people.

To judge by the harmonizing rhetoric of the 'socialist human community', the GDR had already all but created the ideal classless society—and with it the 'new man', who, according to Marxist-Leninist doctrine, would only be realized with communism. Intimations of the National Socialist 'community of the *Volk*' were not intentional, but at the same time difficult to miss. Social security as compensation for the lack of political liberty: this was in both cases a mechanism of rule designed to guarantee mass loyalty to the regime. The disadvantages of this rhetoric were obvious. It could easily lead to the party underestimating the difficulty of the tasks ahead. For the time being, however, the idea of the 'socialist human community' was mainly needed to replace another concept. Since the SED had not yet given up the idea of the 'German nation', which reappeared in the 1968 constitution, it could not refer to the GDR as an actual 'nation'. The new term was designed to fill this gap by reinforcing East Germans' feeling of togetherness.

Three months after Ulbricht's speech on the 'socialist human community', the Evangelical Church in Germany (EKD), one of the last remaining all-German institutions, fell apart. The church leadership held its last conference in the GDR on 10 June 1969. The purpose of the meeting was twofold. On the one hand, the statutes of the new Federation of the Evangelical Church in the GDR were to be signed. Unlike its predecessor, this organization was not a regional body within the framework of the EKD, but autonomous. The other task was the appointment of ten delegates for the new federation's constitutive synod, to be held in September. In breaking away from the EKD (a move prepared by Albrecht Schönherr, bishop of Berlin-Brandenburg, and the church jurist Manfred Stolpe, leader of the administrative office of the Evangelical Church leadership in the GDR and designated secretary of the new federation), the church did what the state expected and had been massively pressing it to do. In the view of its advocates, organizational independence seemed necessary in order to improve relations with the state in the interests of the church. The formation of a new federation, however, was not something the SED wanted, and official recognition came only in 1971.

If Ulbricht had had his way, he would have written to President Heinemann in the summer of 1969, while the West German electoral campaign was still going on, and proposed negotiations over measures to secure the peace; a 'national peace initiative', he thought, could clear the way 'for good neighbourly relations between both sovereign German states'. But the Soviets were unwilling to surrender the initiative in dealing with the FRG, and they promised only to take the interests of the GDR into consideration. On 12 September, about two weeks before the West Germans went to the polls, Moscow proposed in an aide-memoire to West Germany that talks be resumed on a non-aggression agreement. On 22 September, six days before the election, Foreign Minister Brandt confirmed reception of the note in talks with his Soviet colleague, Gromyko, in New York City. The substantive response would come from the new West German government, Brandt said. He himself had no doubt that it would respond positively. That, at least, would be his own recommendation.[15]

THE BEGINNINGS OF THE BRANDT GOVERNMENT AND THE NEW *OSTPOLITIK*

Willy Brandt was able to do much more than give the new government policy suggestions; the Basic Law allowed him to determine the basic outlines of policy. One of his cabinet's first decisions had to do with the currency. The controls on the mark had been lifted on 29 September; on 24 October the government decided to increase its value by 8.5%, and the measure went into effect on 27 October. That same day (the negotiations went long into the night), the Ministers' Council of the European Community dealt with the question of how German agriculture might be spared the disadvantages resulting from the revaluation. (Since German agricultural prices were linked to the EC unit of account, their value in marks sank in proportion to the revaluation.) On 12 November the council passed a compromise that had essentially been worked out in the early morning hours of 28 October: for a period of four years, the government could provide West German farmers with full compensation for the losses incurred through the currency policy (estimated at 1.7 billion marks). It received grants from the EC agrarian fund for this purpose.

Brandt gave his first inaugural speech as chancellor on 28 October 1969. Like Heinemann's, it became a manifesto for a new age in German politics. 'We want to risk more democracy' was the core of Brandt's domestic platform. The reforms were to be led by changes in education and apprenticeship training, science, and research. A long-term (fifteen to twenty year) plan for education would coordinate the four main areas of the educational system—primary and secondary schools, higher education, vocational and occupational training, and adult education—in a clear and rational manner. Further goals were a national educational budget for a period of five to fifteen years and a university reform law (*Hochschulrahmengesetz*) that, among other things, would aim to 'overcome obsolete hierarchical structures'. Brandt summarized the education part of his address with a memorable sentence suggestively modifying the old Prussian adage that the army was the school of the nation: 'The school of the nation is the school.'

In the economic part, Brandt identified his government's most important goals as 'stabilization without stagnation', the strengthening of competition, and the targeted creation of wealth. In the area of legal policy he emphasized the reform of marriage law, the completion of the criminal law reform, and the further reform of the penal system. Reforms in public administration and the civil service were also urgently necessary, especially the introduction of a promotion policy based on merit. As his first legislative project, the chancellor promised the presentation of a bill lowering the voting age from 21 to 18 and the age of eligibility for political office from 25 to 21.

When he turned to matters of foreign policy and the German–German relationship, Brandt knew that not only the whole country was paying attention, but the whole world as well. Now, twenty years after the founding of the FRG and the GDR, it was imperative to prevent the German nation from growing further apart, he said. Accordingly, the attempt would be made 'to reach togetherness by means of a carefully arranged existence side-by-side'. Referring to the efforts of the Grand Coalition, Brandt offered the East German government

new negotiations on both sides, without discrimination on the government level, for the purpose of arriving at a cooperation to be codified in treaty form. There can be no question of official recognition of the GDR by the government of the FRG. Even if two states exist in Germany, they are not foreign countries to each other. Their mutual relations can only be of a special kind.

To the 'socialist states' in general, but expressly including the GDR, Brandt spoke in favour of a non-aggression treaty, a reduction in military confrontation, and a European security conference. With Czechoslovakia, his government was prepared to conclude agreements 'that go beyond the past'. The People's Republic of Poland could expect a 'proposal for the start of talks, in response to the elucidations of Wladyslaw Gomulka from 17 May of this year'. (The First Secretary of the Polish United Workers' party had stated on this day that there were no legal obstacles to a final recognition of the existing Polish border by the FRG; Poland would be ready at any time to conclude an official treaty.)

For the head of the CDU/CSU fraction, Rainer Barzel, Brandt's brief remarks on the matter of Poland were too vague. 'The parliament would have liked to hear something about that,' he called out to the chancellor. Brandt replied that he had 'said what is necessary today within the framework of an inaugural address' and concluded with words that drew 'sustained, lively applause from the government parties,' but also protests from the opposition. 'We are not at the end of our democracy. We are really just beginning. We want to be and become a people of good neighbours, both within the country and for the outside world.'

The importance Brandt ascribed to education drew a great deal of public praise, and his policy was indeed in keeping with the times. In 1964 the pedagogue Georg Picht had complained about the low numbers (according to international standards) of secondary school graduates, university students, and teachers as well as the small public budgets for education. He spoke of a 'German educational catastrophe'. After 1965 the sociologist Ralf Dahrendorf (who would be elected to the Bundestag for the FDP in 1969 and temporarily hold the office of parliamentary state secretary in the foreign office in the Brandt–Scheel government) called for 'education as a civil right', one that must also benefit traditionally disadvantaged groups like children of rural and working-class families, girls, and Catholics.

Students and university assistants highlighted another problem. The full professors (*Ordinarien*) still had all the authority in the universities, even though a great number of teaching duties had long since become the responsibility of others—non-full professors, outside lecturers, and assistants. By the end of the 1960s many educational reformers, the Federal University Assistants' Conference (*Bundesassistentenkonferenz*, founded in 1967), and the Extra-Parliamentary Opposition, were demanding a voice for all groups of the teaching staff, as well as for students and non-academic personnel. The idea of *Drittelparität*, 'parity of thirds', was especially popular among the so-called 'functional groups'. Professors, academic and non-academic staff, and students would each have one-third of the seats in the bodies of university self-governance. 'Democratization of the university' was the slogan that encapsulated these demands.

Since university policy was primarily determined by the individual *Bundesländer*, these were the actual addressees of the call for the 'group university' (*Gruppenuniversität*). To a greater or lesser extent, the states ruled by Social Democratic governments instituted *Drittelparität* in university governance. In practice, however, the new model fostered democratization less than the feudal-ization of the university. Many university presidents claimed a status equal to that of the democratically legitimated parliaments and governments. Members of the middle levels pressed for life tenure, which was then widely awarded, much to the detriment of the generation that followed. Performance and test standards—above all in the social sciences—were lowered and redefined in such a way as to permit a purely 'Marxist' course of study.

On 29 May 1973 the Federal Constitutional Court handed down a judgment awarding the permanent professorate decisive authority in university governance in questions of teaching and research. This ruling affected not only the specific legislation under scrutiny, a preliminary bill towards a university-wide law in Lower Saxony; all university laws in the *Bundesländer* that conflicted with this principle had to be changed, and the federal university reform law of January 1976 was also designed in conformity with it. The *Gruppenuniversität* continued to exist, albeit in greatly modified form. The amount of co-determination by the 'functional groups' was different in each *Bundesland*. The result was not a return to the university of the *Ordinarien*, but nonetheless a distinct turning away from the utopian vision of the 'New Left'. The situation in the universities had shown that, after a certain point, a rigorous 'democratization of society' necessarily came into conflict with the democracy of the Basic Law. Publicly financed institutions, appealing to *their* interpretation of democracy, had removed themselves from the control of the democratically legitimated authorities to such an extent that, in extreme cases, they alone decided what their societal mission would be. The consequence was corrective and regulatory intervention by the state, leading to the bureaucratization of the university. This did not increase the productivity of higher education in Germany, nor did it help the institutions of learning to reform themselves.

Much less controversial was the promotion of individual education in secondary and post-secondary schools and the fostering of up-and-coming academics. The legislative foundations for these reforms were laid in September 1971 in two laws, one providing financial assistance to students (the *Bundesausbildungsförderungsgesetz* or *Bafög*) and the other postgraduate support (the *Graduiertenförderungsgesetz* or *Grafög*). The first was designed to give children from financially disadvantaged families better access to higher education; the second gave highly qualified graduates the chance to earn their doctorates or undertake research studies. Another popular measure was the 'First Outline Plan for the Construction of Institutions of Higher Learning', worked out in a common planning committee in July 1971: the Federation and State governments each committed themselves to raising half of a 16 billion mark sum by 1975 in order to keep up with the expected growth in the student population. A total of 665,000 university students was expected for the year 1974/5, 45 per cent more than in 1969.

The social–liberal university reforms were not the only response to the student protests. Changes were also made in the legal system. In May 1970 the Bundestag, with the votes of the coalition, passed the Third Law for the Liberalization of the Penal Code, which liberalized the right to political demonstration. This legislation was flanked by a law guaranteeing amnesty in minor offences connected with demonstrations. Both the coalition and the opposition were courting the votes of the younger generation when, in July 1970, they voted by a two-thirds majority to lower the voting age to 18 and the age of eligibility for political office to 21, the official age of majority (itself lowered to 18 in March 1974).

The government's economic and fiscal policies between 1969 and 1973 were not guided by reform legislation, but by repeated efforts to adapt to the current situation. In January 1970, in order to avoid an overheated economy, the government passed a stability law for the domestic economy capping the federal budget at 2.7 billion marks and mandating savings of 2.5 billion marks between the federal and state levels for purposes of dealing with economic fluctuations. A refundable increase was introduced on wage, income, and corporation taxes in July 1970 (it was paid back after July 1972). When prices still continued to rise during the first months of 1971, the government decontrolled the exchange rate once again and passed another stability law mandating spending cuts on the federal and state levels, providing for further savings, and limiting public debt.

This was the last victory—or at least apparent victory—of Alex Möller, the Social Democratic minister of finance. After the cabinet ministers tenaciously refused to curb reform plans for the sake of savings, Möller resigned on 13 May 1971. Brandt, not particularly savvy in economic and finance matters, did nothing to stop him, appointing as his successor Karl Schiller, the economics minister, a notorious adversary and personal rival of Möller. Schiller assumed the new post in addition to his old one, thus becoming a 'super minister'. In view of his pronounced love of the spotlight, this was a risky decision.

Brandt's main interest was foreign policy, and in this area the social–liberal cabinet set a new course immediately. On 15 November 1969, three weeks after Brandt's inaugural, the new West German government and the Soviet Union agreed to start talks over a non-aggression treaty. A week later, on 21–2 November, Bonn and Warsaw agreed to negotiate over their mutual relations. Another week later, on 28 November, the West German ambassadors signed the nuclear non-proliferation treaty in Washington, Moscow, and London.

At a conference in The Hague between the heads of state and government in the EC countries at the beginning of December, Brandt proposed that the EC expand and work towards closer cooperation in matters of economic, monetary, and foreign policy. The Gaullist successor of Charles de Gaulle, President Georges Pompidou, broke with the general's policy. In accord with the other participants, he approved the preparation of accession talks with Great Britain, Denmark, Norway, and Ireland, as well as the drafting of a multi-stage plan for an economic and monetary union.

Two days after the summit in The Hague, on 4 December, the NATO council convened in Brussels. It proposed to the Warsaw Pact states negotiations over a balanced mutual reduction of troops in Europe and gave full support to Bonn's initiatives with Moscow and Warsaw. On 16 December the three western powers proposed talks with the Soviet Union over Berlin and travel routes to the city. Four days later President Heinemann answered a letter from Ulbricht in which the latter had suggested negotiating over the draft (included in the letter) of a treaty on 'relations of equal rights' based on the familiar maximalist demands, including international recognition of the GDR and Berlin as an 'autonomous political entity'. Heinemann wrote back, telling Ulbricht that he had directed the letter and the draft treaty to the appropriate constitutional authority, the government. This was an act of politeness, but also a political signal: the GRD could expect the West German government to take up his letter.

Brandt responded on 22 January 1970, though not to Ulbricht as head of state, but, as protocol required, to the head the government, Willi Stoph. The chancellor proposed talks on an exchange of non-aggression statements. The talks were to be guided by the principle of 'non-discrimination' and open for the discussion of all matters on the agenda between the two states. Stoph wrote back on 11 February, suggesting that a meeting be arranged soon.

Brandt assented and drove to Erfurt on 19 March 1970, once the technical details had been resolved. It was the first meeting between the two German heads of government since the founding of their respective states, and the way it went differed from what the GDR leadership had foreseen. A large number of people gathered in front of the meeting place, the hotel Erfurter Hof, chanting 'Willy Brandt!' in unison. When he appeared briefly, the crowd broke into ovations. This event made a deep impression on Germans on both sides of the wall. The rulers of the GDR did not forget it either, and did all they could to prevent similar demonstrations of all-German sentiment in the future.

The meeting accomplished nothing of actual substance. The two sides exchanged points of view and agreed to another meeting. Since the first was held in the western part of the east, the next was to take place in the eastern part of the west. In the town of Kassel, on 21 May, Brandt delivered a twenty-point programme for a treaty agreement 'between the two states in Germany'. This second meeting also produced no tangible result. The GDR insisted on official international recognition, and the FRG persisted in the view that there was still only *one* German nation and that the relations between the two states could not be treated as such between two sovereign subjects of international law.

The significance of the talks between Willy Brandt and Willi Stoph had nothing to do with their content, but with the simple fact they took place at all. A spectacular event like a pair of meetings on the highest government level was probably necessary to make it clear that both German states were going to consider the existence of two states in Germany as the basis of their subsequent relationship. After a quarter-century of Cold War, the two Germanies, despite the difference in their legal positions, despite the irreconcilable antinomy of their political systems, were now on the road to mutual recognition. The mode of this recognition was still controversial, and it was not merely a German problem, but also a global one. For this reason, Erfurt and Kassel could only be the first way stations on the long road toward an easing of tensions in central Europe.

The success of the social–liberal government's 'new *Ostpolitik*' depended in large measure on the two superpowers. Washington had already indicated a positive attitude in December 1969 when it supported Brandt's and Scheel's initiatives with regard to the Soviet Union and Poland. For the America of Nixon and Kissinger, the West German willingness to 'put aside the special German conflict with the east' and join the détente between east and west was a significant step forward—provided the new government did not go too far, that is. The United States itself wanted to control the direction and the extent of the détente, allowing no doubts to arise concerning where, exactly, the leadership of the western alliance lay. A positive reaction from the eastern alliance was certain. Ever since spring 1969, Moscow had given to understand that it was interested in scaling back tensions. This policy was guided by sober calculation. The dramatic worsening of the conflict with communist China along the Ussuri river had convinced Brezhnev that the western flank of the Soviet empire had to be relieved.

This was the background to the first round of negotiations between Egon Bahr and Foreign Minister Gromyko, which began in January 1970 in the Soviet capital. Bahr had accompanied Brandt from Berlin to Bonn in 1966, where he had assumed leadership of the foreign office's new 'planning staff'. He became state secretary in the chancellor's office when the new government was formed in October 1969, and at this time he was also given access to a top-secret 'channel' to the Kremlin, set up by the KGB. Bahr's biggest challenge in Moscow was to hold fast to the German claim to self-determination and reunification in a form the Soviet Union could accept. Since Gromyko strictly refused to countenance such language in a treaty, the result could only be a one-sided statement on the part of the West German government, the so-called 'Letter on German Unity'. But the Soviet Union did acknowledge receipt of the statement, and all future German governments would be able to refer to it.

Another problem lay in the coordination and scheduling of the individual 'eastern treaties' (Ostverträge). Bonn's position was clear: the treaties planned with the Soviet Union and Poland could only enter into force after an agreement had been reached on Berlin. A Berlin agreement was also a prerequisite to a comprehensive accord between West and East Germany.

The treaty with Prague did not seem quite so pressing. Unlike with Poland, the FRG had no border dispute with the CSSR, so there was nothing that needed to be resolved before subsequent treaties could take effect. Legal complexities arising from the 1938 Munich treaty were a second reason to put off talks with Czechoslovakia, and in his memoirs Brandt discussed yet a third: the 'after-effects of August 1968, which crippled Prague's politics for a long time', and which were still to be felt when a treaty was finally signed in December 1973.

Bahr finally achieved a breakthrough in Moscow on 22 May 1970. Gromyko accepted what he had been refusing to accept all along: a letter from the West German government delineating its position on the question of the German people's right to self-determination. Even the publication of the strategically important and strictly confidential 'Bahr paper' by the magazine Quick in June 1970, a disruptive manoeuvre (a clear betrayal of state secrets, in fact) on the part of opposition supporters in secure state positions, came too late to affect Bahr's success.

Strictly speaking, Bahr's talks were only preliminary, a basis for official negotiations. These were conducted in Moscow at the end of July and beginning of August by a delegation under Foreign Minister Scheel to which Bahr belonged. The final draft of the 'Letter on German Unity' contained the explicit statement that 'this treaty does not stand in contradiction to the political goal of the Federal Republic of Germany, to work for a state of peace in Europe in which the German nation will be able to regain its unity through free self-determination.'

Scheel and Bahr were able to preserve the option of a peaceful revision of the German–German borders by successfully substituting the phrase 'inviolability of the borders' for the Soviet formulation, which had used the word 'inalterability'.* This change established a direct connection—the West German negotiators were insistent on this point—between respect for the existing borders and the renunciation of the threat and use of force. When the treaty was initialled on 7 August, Scheel formally declared that it could not enter into effect until the Four Powers had come to an agreement on Berlin. The Treaty on Non-Aggression and Cooperation, or Treaty of Moscow, was approved by the social–liberal cabinet on 11 August. Brandt and Scheel signed it in the Kremlin the next day. The new West German government had cleared its first hurdle in the new *Ostpolitik*.

The second eastern treaty was the Warsaw Treaty between the Federal Republic of Germany and the People's Republic of Poland. It was always more controversial than the Moscow Treaty. Many Germans, especially the expellees, still rejected any kind of recognition of the Oder–Neisse line. The year 1967, according to opinion surveys conducted in November, was the first in which a relative majority of West Germans—46%—supported accepting this border as permanent; 35% refused to do so. By March 1970 the respective numbers were 58% and 25%. This meant that Brandt and Scheel could expect opposition from a strong minority when they signed the Warsaw Treaty in the Polish capital on 7 December 1970. The text committed both sides to recognizing the Oder–Neisse line as Poland's western border. It emphasized the 'inviolability of its existing borders, now and in future' and declared that no side had territorial claims against the other, nor would raise any in the future.

Prior to the signing of the Moscow Treaty, the FRG and the western powers had exchanged memoranda—and communicated them to the Soviet Union—according to which the agreement would not affect the rights of the Four Powers with regard to Germany as a whole or Berlin in particular, since a peace treaty was still outstanding. The same was done with the Warsaw Treaty. In this exchange of notes, concerning which the Polish government was informed on 20 November, all participants stated that the West German government could only act in the name of the FRG and that the treaty did not touch on the rights and responsibilities of the Four Powers. This formally postponed a final agreement on the German–Polish border until a peace settlement could be reached. For its part, the Polish government stated that it was prepared, for 'humanitarian' reasons, to allow a certain number of individuals of unquestionably German background to emigrate to West Germany. (It took a great deal of effort before this promise was actually fulfilled.)

In a television address from Warsaw, Brandt assured his countrymen that the treaty, which laid 'the basis for the normalization of mutual relations', did not 'surrender anything that has not already long been forfeited', not by the leaders of the FRG, 'but by a criminal regime, National Socialism'. But it was a personal gesture on the part of the chancellor that claimed more attention, both in West

---

* [Translator's note: the respective German terms were *Unverletzlichkeit* and *Unveränderbarkeit*.]

Germany and abroad, than all the speeches and diplomatic announcements. At a wreath-laying ceremony commemorating the victims of the Warsaw ghetto uprising in spring 1943, the German chancellor fell to his knees before the memorial to the fallen and murdered Jews. The pictures of this event went around the world.

The German response to what became known as Brandt's *Warschauer Kniefall* or 'Warsaw kneeling' was mixed. Right of centre it was seen as excessive, if not as an expression of German self-abasement. On the left there was a groundswell of respect, sympathy, and admiration for the chancellor, who took upon himself a guilt that was not his own. Brandt himself would later write in his memoirs that he had 'planned nothing', but had felt the need 'to express the special nature of the commemoration at the ghetto monument. At the abyss of German history and with the burden of the murdered millions on my shoulders, I did what people do when language fails.'

The third of the eastern treaties (which depended on the first two entering into effect) dealt with Berlin and thus required the participation of the Four Powers. The western ambassadors in the FRG and the Soviet ambassador in the GDR began their talks on 26 March 1970 in the building of the Allied Control Council in the American sector (the former location of the *Kammergericht*, the supreme court of Prussia). By the end of the year, questions of status were on the agenda, and no rapprochement could be reached. Then, in spring 1971, about a year after the start of negotiations, the four ambassadors 'agreed to disagree', and the status issue was put aside for the sake of more practical questions. Egon Bahr played a very active background role in this process.

The Quadripartite Agreement on Berlin was signed on 3 September 1971 ('Berlin' did not appear in the title, since in the Soviet view the treaty only concerned West Berlin). Although it was a general treaty, requiring further agreements between the FRG and the GDR, it did guarantee freedom of travel between the Federal Republic and West Berlin and made it easier for citizens of the latter to visit East Berlin and the GDR. In a declaration included in the text of the treaty, the western powers stated that the ties between Berlin's western sectors and the FRG were to be 'maintained and developed', though they recognized that 'these sectors continue not to be a constituent part of the Federal Republic of Germany and not to be governed by it.'

Both the Basic Law and the West Berlin constitution contained language that conflicted with this declaration, but these points were suspended. The FRG was given consular authority to represent West Berlin and its citizens. International agreements entered into by the Federal Republic could be extended to the citizens of West Berlin *if* the inclusion was explicitly mentioned as such. The treaty was to enter into force on 3 June 1972—*after* the ratification of the Moscow and Warsaw treaties and the conclusion of the additional German–German accords, including the agreements on transit traffic to and from Berlin and the travel and visiting rights of citizens of West Berlin.

The Berlin agreement, while disappointing to those in both west and east who had wanted more, satisfied the realists in all camps. West Berlin was not, as Khrushchev had called it, an 'autonomous political entity'. But it was not incorrect for the Soviet Union to refer to it as an 'entity with a special political status'. The increased 'ties' (*Bindungen*) between West Berlin and the FRG were now officially recognized by the Soviets—despite the fact that Moscow and the GDR insisted on using the weaker word 'connections' (*Verbindungen*). On the other hand, the constitutional organs of the FRG would now have to refrain from acts of sovereignty in the city. The Bundesversammlung, Bundestag, and the federal government could no longer convene in West Berlin (Bundestag committees and the party fractions still could).

The treaty guaranteed West Berlin's survival. 'Berlin crises' were no longer a threat in the foreseeable future. The government's tactic of making the ratification of the Moscow and Warsaw treaties dependent on the Berlin situation had paid off. Of course, the package deal also had a counterpart in the east, now codified in official form: the Berlin agreement would enter into force only after the two eastern treaties were ratified.[16]

THE GDR BETWEEN ULBRICHT AND HONECKER

The thaw between Bonn and Moscow could not but exercise a strong influence on the relations between West and East Germany and on the relationship between East and West Germans. This was understood in the Kremlin, but it was interpreted 'dialectically'. For the Soviets, the biggest danger was that improved relations—first between the USSR and West Germany, then between the latter and the GDR—would lead to a softening of the ideological opposition between 'socialist' Germany and its 'capitalist' rival. Since development in this direction would, sooner or later, undermine the GDR's *raison d'être*, it could not be allowed to happen. This made it necessary to complement the German–German normalization with a campaign intensifying the ideological conflict between the two states. The GDR was to be helped in this by the other members of the Warsaw Pact, for if West German 'imperialism' was no longer seen as threatening, then the cohesion of the whole 'socialist camp' was at risk.

The First Secretary of the SED, at the behest of Moscow, but also very much in accordance with his own wishes, had been conspicuously friendly towards the West German Social Democrats in September 1969, right before the Bundestag elections and also for a period of time thereafter. Compared with the CDU and the CSU (especially the latter), the SPD was now regarded as relatively progressive and peaceable. Cooperation with the new social–liberal government seemed expedient to Ulbricht, especially for economic reasons: he was looking to further modernize the GDR, and saw cooperation as a means to this end. The ambitious goal of the fifth party congress of 1958, which had been to 'catch up with and surpass' West Germany in all areas by 1961, was now revised in an astonishing manner. On 23 February 1960 Ulbricht announced a new catchphrase, 'surpass without catching up' (*Überholen ohne einzuholen*). This slogan, as he explained, meant

that it cannot be a question of gradually closing in on the present highest level. Such behaviour would not secure us the necessary increase in labour productivity. The argument 'surpass without catching up' is oriented, rather, towards working out and achieving, independently of the highest current scientific-technical level—indeed bypassing it, so to speak—the practical mastery of completely new principles of industry and labour, new technological procedures, and the necessary new machine systems and instruments of production. In this way, we will determine the new highest scientific-technical level.

While Ulbricht was making the case for tactical cooperation with the Social Democrats, other members of the politburo, led by Erich Honecker, were pushing for greater distance vis-à-vis the west. In October 1969 Ulbricht again managed to assert his position. Then, before the second German–German meeting in Kassel in May 1970, Brezhnev pushed for a 'tough response' to Brandt's slogan concerning the 'easing of human relations'; the chancellor was to be given the opportunity to 'think things over', meaning that dialogue was to be stopped. When, at the beginning of July, Ulbricht relieved Honecker—now his most dangerous party opponent and a man totally faithful to Moscow—of his position as Second Secretary, Brezhnev intervened and compelled the 'crown prince' to be reinstalled.

This dealt a serious blow to the First Secretary's authority. Ulbricht's ideological high-handedness and his showcasing of the GDR's special brand of particularly 'developed' socialism had been a serious provocation to the Soviet leaders for a long time. After summer 1970 Brezhnev placed all his hopes in Honecker, on whom he impressed, at the end of July, the necessity of avoiding any kind of 'process of rapprochement between the GDR + the FRG'. Brandt sought the 'social-democratization of the GDR', he said, and the economically powerful FRG was attempting

to gain influence in the GDR, to swallow the GDR, one way or another. We, the SU, the soc[ialist] countries, will secure the outcome of the victory. We will not permit—a development [through] which our position in the GDR be weakened, put at risk, [we will] not permit the *Anschluss* [of the] GDR with W[est] G[ermany]. On the contrary—the distance, the trench between GDR + FRG will become even deeper.

On 20 August 1970, eight days after the signing of the Moscow treaty, the CPSU general secretary spoke even plainer language to Honecker and other members of a SED delegation. Brezhnev criticized Ulbricht (who was not present) for the slogan *Überholen ohne einzuholen*; after all, the capitalist west had nothing that needed to be overtaken. Socialism was a societal form 'of another, higher kind'. 'The GDR is not only your cause, it is our common cause. For us, the GDR is something that must not be shaken . . . Germany no longer exists. That is a good thing. There is the socialist GDR and the capitalist Federal Republic. That's the way it is . . . Without the SU there is no GDR.'

Although Honecker pressed Brezhnev to permit Ulbricht to be ousted in the summer of 1970, the Soviet leader did not do so. In his view, the important thing was that the real power in the politburo be transferred to Honecker and his supporters. Ulbricht, whom Brezhnev believed had accomplished several things of note, was to be brought to the point where, after a certain period of time, he himself would ask to be allowed to concentrate entirely on the office of president. Brezhnev's basic concern was that Ulbricht no longer be permitted to undertake anything at odds with Moscow's position.

In the ensuing months there was 'cold war' between Ulbricht and the politburo faction around Honecker, which also included Willi Stoph and Günter Mittag, the central committee secretary responsible for economic issues. This group even managed to prevent the publication of Ulbricht's concluding words at the fourteenth plenum of the central committee in December—the First Secretary's worst humiliation to date. He himself, now 77 years of age and debilitated by illness, had considered retirement from party office shortly beforehand. But Brezhnev, pointing to the disturbances in Poland, had asked him to postpone this decision.

When, in January 1971, it seemed as if Ulbricht might be able to consolidate his position once again, thirteen of the twenty politburo members and candidates, led by Honecker, sent a petition to the Soviet leader, asking that he bring about Ulbricht's retirement. No response came. The decision was finally made in April, in a talk between Brezhnev and Ulbricht during the twenty-fourth congress of the CPSU in Moscow. Ulbricht would give up his party office, but retain his state post. On 3 May, during the sixteenth plenum of the SED central committee, Ulbricht asked—to the surprise of the public—to be relieved of his duties as First Secretary 'for reasons of age'; he requested that Erich Honecker be elected as his successor. The CC granted this 'wish'. Ulbricht remained head of the state council, and he was also allowed—as he had requested from Brezhnev—to occupy an 'office' that did not even appear in the SED statute: 'honorary head' of the SED.

Ulbricht's more or less unwilling departure meant the end of an era in the history of the East German state. The 'first man' of the SED had shaped the 'first German workers' and peasants' state' from the first moment of its existence. He was a Stalinist during the time of Stalin and remained a staunch 'Marxist-Leninist' to the end. After the wall was built, he sometimes lost sight of the true limits of his own and his state's abilities, and the liberties he took with regard to Moscow were highly irritating to the Soviets. On 21 August 1970, during talks between an SED delegation and the CPSU politburo, he went so far as to presume to teach Brezhnev and the other Soviet comrades a lesson. The GDR, he said, in order to master the scientific-technical revolution, wished to work closely with the Soviet Union. But then he added by way of admonition: 'In this cooperation, we desire to develop as a true German state. We are not Byelorussia. We are not a Soviet state. So real cooperation.'

Ulbricht did not want to be the representative of a Soviet satellite, but of *the* socialist country that had become the Soviets' most important ally. Although he had gone about the modernization of the GDR in an undogmatic manner, he had always seen to it that the economic reforms did not call into question the party's monopoly on power, but strengthened it. Nobody in the Kremlin ever got the impression that the GDR might follow a path similar to that of Czechoslovakia prior to August 1968. When Ulbricht first spoke of a 'process of formation of a socialist nation' in the GDR on 17 December 1970, he did so in accordance with Brezhnev's wishes, who had called on him two months earlier (21 October) to work out basic principles for 'the forging of socialist patriotism and, ultimately, for the formation of the socialist nation in the GDR'. And in doing so, Ulbricht did not act in a way counter to his own convictions or against the interests of his country, as he understood them. Already on 19 January of the same year, he had described the GDR as a 'socialist German national state' and the FRG as a 'capitalist NATO-state'. In his opinion, what divided the two German states was so profoundly important that it made *re*unification impossible. His decision to describe his country as a 'nation state' and its citizens as a new kind of nation represented the attempt to make his life-work irreversible by destroying the bridges that led into the common German past.

His successor, Erich Honecker, was born in Neunkirchen in Saarland in 1912. He grew up in Wiebelskirchen, learned the roofing trade, and was active in the communist movement from his early youth. In 1937 a National Socialist court condemned him to ten years in prison for 'preparing to commit high treason'; he worked off the sentence in Brandenburg-Görden. He deserted in early 1945 when assigned to outside duties, but returned voluntarily and was liberated by the Red Army at the end of April. The first stage of his post-war political career was his appointment as head of the Free German Youth in 1946, a post he occupied until 1955. He became a member of the politburo and secretary for security in the central committee in 1958.

Ulbricht's ideological self-empowerment in the second half of the 1960s was displeasing to Honecker. He did everything he could to create seamless agreement between the SED and the CPSU, thus becoming Brezhnev's confidant. After he took power in May 1971, he began to act in a less doctrinaire way, especially towards young people, writers, and artists. Western 'beat' music, rejected in 1965 as an expression of capitalist philistinism, was permitted again, and 'blue jeans', too, could now be sold in the GDR. Beards, long hair, and short skirts were no longer considered contrary to the spirit of socialism. The reception of West German television programmes, transmitted in colour from 1967, was no longer sanctioned by the regime after 1973, and the same was true of the West German mark, the GDR's unofficial 'second currency'. Honecker, the 'inconspicuous accountant-type with the crooked spectacles' (in the description of historian

Stefan Wolle), was an even worse speaker than Ulbricht. Still, those who listened to the speeches of the new First Secretary usually found their wooden officialism to be an improvement over the belligerent falsetto tirades of his predecessor. Honecker seemed more 'dispassionate' than Ulbricht—though he was certainly also more bureaucratic.

At the eighth party congress in July 1971, the SED finally retired Ulbricht's ambitious programme of fundamental economic modernization, the 'economic system of socialism', as it had been called since the seventh congress in April 1967. The CC report, read by Honecker, described the economy as 'a means to an end, a means to the continually improved satisfaction of the growing material and cultural needs of working people'. Especially urgent and important was 'providing the people with everyday products, with consumer goods, spare parts, and services'. Consequently, in the new five year plan for the years 1971–5, the 'main task' was to 'further raise the people's material and cultural standard of living'.

Ulbricht's vision of the 'socialist human community' was no longer employed at the eighth congress, since, as the new chief ideologue of the party, Kurt Hager, explained in October 1971, it 'obscures class differences, which indeed still persist, and overestimates the degree to which the classes and strata actually have been brought together'. Ulbricht's theory that socialism was a relatively autonomous societal entity suffered the same fate. This claim, according to Hager, obscured 'the fact that socialism is the first, lower phase of the communist societal formation'. The correct concept was that of a 'developed socialist society', which had been first achieved by the Soviet Union.

As far as the terms 'nation' and 'nation state' were concerned, the eighth congress had no revisions to make, since Ulbricht himself, in December 1970, had adopted Brezhnev's new terminological ruling concerning the development of a 'socialist nation' in the GDR. 'With the foundation of the workers' and peasants' power and the building up of socialist society, a new type of nation, the socialist nation, is being developed,' the CC report continued.

In contrast to the FRG, where the bourgeois nation persists and the national question is determined by the irreconcilable class antagonism between the bourgeoisie and the working masses—which antagonism, of this we are convinced, will find a solution in the course of the world-historical process of transition from capitalism to socialism—we in the German Democratic Republic, in the socialist German state, are developing the socialist nation.

Honecker took a further step on 6 January 1972. In an address before members of the National People's Army on the island of Rügen, he declared that 'our republic and the FRG' were both behaving towards each other as towards a third state. 'That is, the FRG is a foreign country. Even more: it is an imperialist foreign power.' This radical rejection of common German ties and affiliations was also expressed in another series of linguistic revisions. 'Radio Germany' (the

Deutschlandsender) became the 'Voice of the GDR' (*Stimme der DDR*) in 1971; the 'German Academy of Sciences' was changed to the 'Academy of Sciences of the GDR' in 1972; the national anthem 'Arisen from the Ruins' (*Auferstanden aus Ruinen*), with text by Johannes R. Becher and music by Hans Eisler, could still be played, but without singing. The line 'Germany, united Fatherland' (*Deutschland einig Vaterland*) violated the new dogma, according to which a single German nation no longer existed.

The 'two nation' doctrine was the SED's answer—preformulated by the CPSU—to the SPD's idea of the two states of one nation. In 1970–1, one hundred years after the founding of Bismarck's Reich, the idea of the German nation state and the German nation was put to its final rest in East Germany. In the future, the GDR would have to identify itself exclusively in terms of ideology, as an 'ideological state'. From records of the German past, it could only take what fitted in with the current ideological programmes. In this regard the 1968 constitution, which described the GDR as the 'socialist state of the German nation', was obsolete only three years after its promulgation. It was now only a question of time before it was revised to accord with the SED's latest decisions.

Honecker's loosening of restrictions in state policy towards youth was not intended as a signal for the general liberalization of society. 'He was a man of the state security system,' writes Stefan Wolle,

and his rise to power was accompanied by the rise of Erich Mielke to the highest body of state authority. For the Ministry for State Security, this meant an increase in political importance and an opportunity for unhampered expansion in personnel and technology, towards the goal of 'blanket coverage'. With Honecker began a new wave in the militarization of society, especially in the education system, from kindergarten to university . . . A new rhetoric of class struggle replaced the official party claptrap about the harmonious 'socialist human community'. The subliminally propagated pride in the GDR was suppressed in the media in favour of a strong emphasis on the dominant role of the Soviet Union. In an ideological sense, too, therefore, all the signs pointed toward the ossification of the system.

The kind of class struggle Honecker was pushing required the liquidation of private property, to the extent that there was still any left. The last great wave of nationalization took place in 1972. Its goal was the elimination of the commercial-industrial middle class; only small workshops would be—and were—left. Businesses in which the state had a share (*halbstaatlich*), private industrial and construction firms, and larger production cooperatives engaged in industrial activities were all changed to Publicly Owned Enterprises (*Volkseigene Betriebe*, VEBs). The owners received minimal compensation and, if the workforce agreed, were allowed to continue as managers in the new VEBs.

The elimination of what remained of private enterprise did not improve the country's economy. Quite the opposite: supply problems grew worse. However, as in the agricultural sector, where compulsory industrialization was also intensified, the post-Ulbricht SED was not primarily concerned with increasing productivity and efficiency. The main goal was to bring the East German economy into line with the Soviet example. The closer it came to this goal, the further it distanced itself from the societal system of West Germany. But this was precisely the aim of the SED under Honecker at the beginning of the 1970s.[17]

BRANDT IN CRISIS: THE EASTERN TREATIES AND THE VOTE OF NO CONFIDENCE

While Brezhnev was compelling the GDR to separate itself from West Germany, he himself was pursuing a policy of virtual rapprochement with Willy Brandt. Between 16 and 18 September 1971, two weeks after the signing of the Berlin agreement, the general secretary of the CPSU welcomed the German chancellor to an exchange of views in Oreanda on the Crimean peninsula. The two leaders developed a remarkable relationship of personal trust during the sixteen hours of their talks. The political outcome was a certain degree of agreement on the continuation of military de-escalation. Brandt placed special emphasis on the western project of troop reduction on the Continent (the Mutual Balanced Force Reduction or MBFR).

These intensive consultations in no way contradicted the FRG's duties to its allies. In the light of the recent past, however, they caused a sensation and gave rise, in certain quarters, to the belief that, after the end of the 'special German conflict with the east', a new special relationship between Bonn and Moscow in the style of Rapallo (or what was associated with this name) might be worked out. In the capitals of the west, above all in Washington, such fears were usually expressed on the quiet, but they were certainly no secret. While Henry Kissinger had a personal appreciation for Egon Bahr, he also mistrusted him, believing him to be a German nationalist or even a neutralist. Nixon had strong reservations about Willy Brandt. The Union parties in Bonn entertained close contacts with the chancellor's conservative critics on the other side of the Atlantic and did all they could to strengthen their suspicions concerning Bahr and Brandt.

When, on 20 October 1971, Bundestag President Kai-Uwe von Hassel announced that the Nobel committee of the Norwegian parliament had decided to award the Nobel Peace Prize to Willy Brandt, the opposition joined in the ovations. Three Germans had already received this award: Foreign Minister Gustav Stresemann in 1926 (together with his French colleague Aristide Briand), the historian and publicist Ludwig Quidde in 1927 (together with the French pedagogue and socialist politician Ferdinand Buisson), and the publicist Carl von Ossietzky in 1935 (when he was a prisoner in the Papenburg-Esterwegen concentration camp). But the obligatory applause for Brandt, who accepted the award in Oslo on 10 December, had no effect on the domestic battle over the *Ostpolitik*. On 24 January 1972 the CDU unanimously voted to reject the treaties, accusing the government of granting unilateral concessions to the other side on the decisive questions.

The first reading of the eastern treaties took place in the Bundestag between 23 and 25 February 1972. Rainer Barzel (head of the CDU since 4 October 1971 and Union candidate for the chancellorship after 10 December) did not wish to vote for them 'in their current form', but did not discount the possibility of his fraction's endorsement if the Soviet Union was prepared to make concessions regarding its attitude on the European Community, the Germans' right to self-determination, and freedom of movement in Germany, as well as recognize the temporary nature of the treaties.

At this juncture the numeric strength of the opposition was greater than it had been when the social–liberal government was formed in October 1969. In October 1970 the FDP delegates Erich Mende, Heinz Starke, and Siegfried Zoglmann, all members of the party right, went over to the CDU/CSU fraction. The Social Democrat Klaus-Peter Schulz did the same thing a year later—though, as a delegate from Berlin, he did not have full voting rights. On 29 January 1972 Herbert Hupka, SPD delegate, head of the organization of Silesian expellees (the *Landsmannschaft Schlesien*) and vice president of the national expellee federation (the *Bund der Vertriebenen*), left the party for the CDU. This left the government coalition with only 250 full votes, the opposition with 246. The fate of the eastern treaties, and with them the government, hung on two votes.

But the party defections had not yet come to an end. Two 'rightist' FDP delegates, the industry-friendly politician Gerhard Kienbaum and Knut von Kühlmann-Stumm, were also considered potential 'turncoats', as was Günther Müller, an SPD delegate from Munich then at odds with the far left-leaning SPD in the Bavarian capital. On 23 April the CDU achieved a stunning victory in Baden-Württemberg. With 52.9% of the vote, it gained 8.7% more than in 1968 (not least because of the NPD's support) and now commanded an absolute majority of the votes and seats.

That same evening FDP delegate Wilhelm Helms announced that he was leaving the party. The farmer from Lower Saxony knew he would not obtain a place on the party list for the next Bundestag election, which made his decision easier. Barzel, believing he could count on the support of Kienbaum and Kühlmann-Stumm, decided he could now call for a constructive vote of no confidence in the chancellor. For the coalition seemed to have lost its majority.

Two days later, on 25 April 1972, the CDU/CSU fraction brought forward the motion to this effect, requesting that the Bundestag pronounce a vote of no confidence in Willy Brandt and elect the delegate Rainer Barzel as chancellor. The Bundestag voted on the motion, the first of its kind in the history of the FRG, on 27 April. Most of those present believed the government would be brought down. Vice chancellor Scheel was one of them. The speech prepared for him by Karl-Hermann Flach, FDP general secretary, was part valediction, part accusation. Scheel intimated that some of the party defections might have had something to do with the prospect of material advantages: 'Securing one's personal future in politics is not a matter of conscience . . .'* Brandt, in contrast, was optimistic: 'We'll continue to govern, even after this vote.' He was right. When President von Hassel announced the outcome of the ballot, the SPD and FDP was jubilant, the Union chagrined and silent: Barzel had managed only 247 votes, two too few to bring Brandt down.

Kienbaum and Kühlmann-Stumm insisted, and credibly so, that they had voted for Barzel. As for Helms, it is not known whether he did the same or abstained. This means that at least two and possibly three CDU/CSU delegates did not vote for Barzel. Twenty-eight years later, at the end of November 2000, *Der Spiegel* reported that the federal prosecutor had discovered the identity of a high-ranking East German spy: Leo Wagner, CDU delegate and former CDU/CSU whip, was registered as a Stasi 'Unofficial Collaborator' under the name 'Löwe' between 1976 and 1983. In 1972 Wagner, who was deeply in debt, received 50,000 West German marks from an initially unknown source. Later, a friend of Wagner's claimed to have given him a 'loan' of this amount. But there is a good deal of evidence for believing that the money came from the Ministry for State Security in East Berlin and was aimed at thwarting the Union's no-confidence motion.

As for another Union parliamentarian, CDU delegate Julius Steiner from Baden-Württemberg, it has long been known that he did not vote for Barzel and received money for his deviation from the party line. It is a proven fact that Karl Wienand, managing director of the SPD fraction, with the knowledge of Herbert Wehner, the fraction leader, worked on Steiner. Steiner himself confessed in spring 1973 to having received 50,000 marks from Wienand. The latter denied it, even before a parliamentary committee investigating the matter between June 1973 and March 1974—with no great success. Wehner, for his part, in a television interview years later (5 January 1980), hinted that Steiner had received money and that he and Wienand had known about it.

What is certain is that Steiner, a sometime double-agent between east and west, accepted 50,000 West German marks from the Ministry for State Security in East Berlin to vote against Barzel and for Brandt. If his own confession is accurate, he either received two payments of the same amount or got the Stasi money through Wienand. We may never know whether Wienand—whom the Stasi registered under the name 'Streit' in 1970 on account of contacts with an East German agent—knew about Steiner's covert activities and thus possessed the means to pressure him. In any case, money and material rewards played a decisive role in the Bundestag vote on 27 April 1972, and it was the Social

---

* [Translator's note: according to the Basic Law (Art. 38, Para. 1), delegates of the Bundestag were 'only bound to their conscience'.]

Democrats who demonstrated the most flagrant lack of scruples in this regard. For Wehner, Wienand, and probably also for Alfred Nau, the party treasurer, the ends—preservation of power and the success of the *Ostpolitik*—justified means that were illegal and reprehensible. The harm to West German political culture was wilfully ignored or considered an acceptable price to pay. And that day was not the last time the GDR exercised a profound effect on the inner development of West Germany.

The no-confidence vote was proceeded by demonstrations in numerous cities against the opposition's plan and in support of the social–liberal government. The Union failure brought a wave of support for Willy Brandt. During budget negotiations on 28 April, the day following the unsuccessful motion, the Bundestag voted on the chancellor's budget at its second reading. It failed, with 247 votes on each side, whereupon the parliament called off the budget talks for an indefinite period.

In the days that followed, the heads of the government and the opposition negotiated over a way out of the crisis. As far as the eastern treaties were concerned, the solution was reached on 9 May in a Bundestag resolution presenting the basic principles and goals of the FRG's foreign and Germany policy. The Soviet ambassador, Valentin Falin, had a hand in the drafting, which meant that the document's principal addressee, Moscow, was also its co-author.

The resolution emphasized, as Barzel wished, that the treaties were aimed at reaching a *modus vivendi* with the eastern neighbours, were not intended to pre-empt a peace agreement, and did 'not create a legal basis for the current borders'. It also stressed the rights and responsibilities of the Four Powers with regard to Germany as a whole and Berlin in particular, the FRG's membership in the Atlantic alliance, and its desire for further European integration. The Soviet government stated that it was prepared to accept the resolution as an official state document of the FRG, consider it a supplemental instrument in the interpretation of the treaties, and would direct it to the Supreme Soviet before ratification began. It could hardly have done more to enable the Bonn opposition to endorse the treaties.

On the domestic front, the resolution was addressed primarily to the expellees, of whose interests the Union considered itself the representative. If *they* were prepared to accept the treaties and invest the opposition with the additional qualifications, then there was no danger of a radicalization of sectors of the conservative constituency. Within the CDU, a strong group led by party and fraction chief Barzel and Richard von Weizsäcker, the fraction's spokesman on Germany policy, believed that the way was now clear for an endorsement of the treaties. Other delegates, including Gerhard Schröder, Bruno Heck, and most of the expellee politicians, continued to reject them, as did the entire CSU under Franz Josef Strauss.

Tough negotiations within the fraction led to a compromise: the Union would abstain from the vote, thus allowing the treaties to pass without creating the impression it had 'caved in'. This was the course favoured by Barzel and the majority, and at the vote, on 17 May, most Union delegates stuck to it, thus securing the passage of both accords (10 voted against the Moscow treaty, 17 against the Warsaw treaty). The common resolution on the treaties was passed almost unanimously, with 491 positive votes and 5 abstentions.

Two days later, on 19 May, the treaties were passed by the Bundesrat, with the states governed by the Union—the majority—abstaining. The ratification laws were signed by President Heinemann on 23 May. The Moscow and Warsaw treaties entered into force on 3 June 1972. (They had already been ratified by the Soviet Union and Poland.) The Federal Republic and Poland took up official diplomatic relations that same day.

The final protocol of the Quadripartite Agreement of 3 September 1971 was also signed on 3 June 1972, in West Berlin, by the foreign ministers of the USA, the Soviet Union, Great Britain, and France. It, too, was now in effect. The next day, two German–German arrangements and a treaty, initialled on 11 December 1971, took effect as part of the implementation process of the Berlin agreement. The first concerned an easing of restrictions and other improvements in cross-border travel and visits. Among other things, it stipulated that West Berliners could visit the eastern part of the city and the GDR thirty days per year. The second arrangement dealt with the 'question of the enclaves through the exchange of territory'. This primarily affected the enclave of Steinstücken, which belonged to the West Berlin district of Zehlendorf but was completely surrounded by GDR territory. A corridor was now created to connect it to the west. The treaty concerned the traffic of goods and persons between West Berlin and the rest of the FRG. The most significant improvements were in the payment system and the efficiency of the checkpoint procedure for transit traffic. Fees for the transit visa would now be paid in lump sum by the West German state (the so-called *Transitpauschale*), and the control process would be more rapid and take place directly at the vehicle.

This was not yet the end of social–liberal *Ostpolitik*. One transit treaty, signed on 26 May 1972, did not take effect until 17 October. After 15 June state secretaries Egon Bahr and Michael Kohl negotiated over a treaty on the basic principles governing the relations between the two German states. Talks with Czechoslovakia had not yet begun. Nonetheless, the Brandt government had met most difficult challenges. In relations with the Soviet Union and Poland, there was now a degree of normality that would have seemed inconceivable a short time before. The West Berlin situation, too, though certainly not 'normal', was more so than it had been. The FRG had gained new foreign policy options without estranging itself from the west. In fact, the new *Ostpolitik* had made the country even more 'western'. Ever since it had gone over to an activist détente policy, West Germany differed less from its western allies than it had before the leadership change of 1969.[18]

FROM PARLIAMENTARY STALEMATE TO EARLY ELECTIONS

The battle over the eastern treaties eclipsed everything else that happened in West Germany, or with West German participation, in the first half of 1972. This was also true of Bonn's policy towards the west. Brandt had supported Great Britain's accession to the European Community because he was unable to imagine Europe without Britain. The French president, Pompidou, pursued the same goal, but for different reasons: for him, Britain would help counterbalance an increasingly powerful West Germany. On 22 January 1972 Great Britain, Ireland, Denmark, and Norway signed their accession agreements with the EC. However, by the time the expansion actually took place on 1 January 1973, only three of these countries became EC members: a majority of the Norwegian population had decided against accession in September 1972.

On 29 January 1972 a decision was made that influenced the course of German domestic politics and society for years to come: the chancellor and the leaders of the *Bundesländer* signed the 'Principles for the Membership of Civil Servants in Extremist Organizations'. This agreement, which became known as the *Radikalenerlass* ('Anti-Radical Decree'), created no new law; it was aimed at the uniform application and enforcement of existing regulations. The measure came in response to politically radical university graduates seeking entrance into the civil service, especially public education, or who already occupied posts. Some of these were actively involved in communist organizations. In 1971 the federal interior ministry counted 392 extreme leftist organizations, including the communist 'K groups', with a total membership of 67,000. In the light of this situation, the federal and state leaders considered it necessary to emphasize the stipulations of civil service law. Employment in the civil service required 'that the applicant guarantee that he will, at all times, defend the fundamental liberal-democratic order of the Basic Law. If well-founded doubts in this matter exist, they will, as a rule, justify a rejection.'

To require that civil servants be loyal to the constitutional order was legitimate and necessary, as was the enforcement of the requirement. But there was good reason to criticize the means employed to this end. The *Regelanfrage*, the systematic enquiry conducted by the offices for the defence of the constitution in the *Länder*, was now employed prior to the filling of every position. This reflected bureaucratic ideas about effective supervision, but it was contrary to the principle of proportionality. Those affected, along with their sympathizers, spoke of being 'banned from their professions'. Their critique also found an echo outside of West Germany. And in truth, the surveillance practice that developed under the Anti-Radical Decree did not accord with the social–liberal government's ideas about the rule of law. Consequently, the Social and Free Democrats were also the first parties to change their policy in view of the—unintended—effects of the January 1972 decision. This happened first on the individual state level. Later, on 17 January 1979, the Schmidt government would pass new principles for the examination of loyalty to the constitution. Enquiry at the office for the defence of the constitution would then no longer be permitted as a matter of routine, but only when justified by actual evidence.

The measure against the radicals had been preceded by a decision within the SPD to clarify the party's ideological position towards the left. In the so-called *Abgrenzungsbeschluss* of 14 November 1970, the Social Democratic executive declared that the party affirmed the 'peaceful coexistence' of states with different social orders, but firmly rejected an 'ideological coexistence' with the communists. German social democracy accepted the communist challenge, the text stated. (It was written by Richard Löwenthal.) At all the crossroads of German history, both before and after 1945, the SPD had opted for democracy and against collaboration with the proponents of communist dictatorship.

Liberal democracy on the one hand, communist party dictatorship on the other: no peace policy, no policy of détente can overcome this opposition of systems, and none may overlook it. The kind of peace to which we aspire will not merely protect life; it must also guarantee our people the right to freely determine the forms of its political and social life, now and in the future. The communist system of the GDR is still not an acceptable alternative to our liberal order. Social democracy dedicates itself anew to the task of defending this order, without compromise, against all the false teachings of communism.

The 'Löwenthal paper' was designed primarily as a response to the 'Young Socialists' (*Jungsozialisten* or *Jusos*), who considered the anti-communism of the party obsolete, both internationally and domestically, and who had formed 'action leagues' at many universities with groups further to the left, including the *Marxistischer Studentenbund Spartakus*, the student organization of the DKP. After 1968 the SPD had opened itself to the 'rebellious youth'—which, in terms of its social provenance, was anything but proletarian—and now had to deal with the paradoxical consequences of its own unintended 'embourgeoisement': a redogmatization of the party by young academics appealing to Marx. There was a noticeable shift to the left within the party, proceeding from the university towns but not restricted to them. If this trend continued, the SPD ran the risk of losing the centrist constituencies it had so recently won. The ideological clarification of November 1970 was directed against this development.

The *Jusos* were doctrinaire scions of the '68 movement, but they were peaceful. Another offspring was not: organized terrorism. Among its initiators was Andreas Baader, an unemployed secondary school dropout, and Gudrun Ensslin, daughter of a pastor from a small Swabian village and trained as a teacher. In April 1968 the two set fire to two Frankfurt department stores. Sentenced to three years in prison, they were released early (June 1969) to await an appeal hearing. Baader and Ensslin used their newly won liberty to build up an underground terrorist organization, which they called the 'Red Army Fraction' (*Rote Armee Fraktion* or RAF). Baader was arrested again in April 1970. On 14 May Ulrike Meinhof, a journalist, executed an operation she had organized to storm the German Central Institute for Social Issues and liberate Baader from custody. An employee of the institute was critically wounded in the gunfire. In the early summer of 1970 the founders of the RAF fled via the East German airport of Schönefeld to Syria, where they received military training from the 'People's Front for the Liberation of Palestine'.

The training bore fruit. In May 1972 the RAF, with a 'hard core' of some twenty-five people, staged a series of attacks, including an assault on the headquarters of the fifth American army corps in Frankfurt and another on the American army's European headquarters in Heidelberg. Four American soldiers were killed and many wounded. Between these two operations came an attack against the Springer building in Hamburg, in which seventeen people were wounded. On 1 June the police finally succeeded in capturing three main leaders of the 'Baader–Meinhof Group', Baader himself, Holger Meins, and Jan-Carl Raspe. Gudrun Ensslin's arrest followed on 7 June, and Ulrike Meinhof's on 15 June. The terrorism from the left had been dealt a blow, but it was not destroyed. By this time the imprisoned leaders had a large number of armed followers, men and women determined to go even further along the paths of violence.

West Germany was one of the two European countries in which a leftist terrorist underground developed in the wake of the '68 movement and came to present a serious challenge to state and society for years to come. The other country was Italy. Both had seen the rise of fascism during the inter-war period, and in both cases the terrorist left justified its violence by claiming that, underneath the democratic facade, fascists were still in power. Theoreticians of the New Left had provided grist for the mills of this belief by identifying the 'late capitalist' state of the present as a 'corporative' and authoritarian system essentially the same as fascism, if comparatively modern in appearance. In this view, any and all kinds of government-regulated interaction between employers' associations and labour unions, from Mussolini's *stato corporativo* to Karl Schiller's 'Concerted Action', were seen as 'corporative' and therefore fascist or proto-fascist. Those who talked about the substantial continuity of 'bourgeois rule' in this way did not necessarily draw the same conclusions as the RAF, but they did often have a certain understanding for the latter's armed struggle. This widespread outlook created an atmosphere favourable to the rise of terrorism—a terrorism that, while seeing itself as anti-fascist, had much in common with historical fascism in its mentality and in its methods.

The most brutal act of terror in 1972 was not perpetrated by the RAF, however, but by 'Black September', a secret group linked to the Palestine Liberation Organization. It used the twentieth Olympic summer games in Munich for an operation designed to compel the release of more than 200 Arab prisoners in Israel. On 5 September eight members of the organization stormed the quarters of the Israeli athletes, killed two, and took nine hostage.

After the Israeli government refused to comply, the terrorists demanded to be flown with their hostages to an Arab country. The German authorities, pretending to acquiesce, readied a Lufthansa plane for a flight to Cairo from the military airport of Fürstenfeldbruck. Then, just before take-off, the Bavarian police attempted to free the hostages, but ended up provoking a bloodbath in which all eight of the Israeli hostages and five of their captors were killed. The three surviving terrorists remained only a short time in German custody. On 29 October a Lufthansa aircraft was hijacked en route from Damascus to Frankfurt, and its captors demanded the release of the three imprisoned Arabs. The West German government acceded, allowing them to travel to Zagreb, where a plane was waiting to take them to Syria. The rule of law had lost a battle in the struggle against international terrorism.

A completely different kind of battle saw the defeat of Karl Schiller, the minister of economics and finance, in the summer of 1972. In a cabinet meeting on 29 June, Schiller failed in his attempt to stop the foreign exchange controls that Karl Klasen, the president of the federal bank, was calling for to stop the rush of foreign capital into West Germany. This influx was caused by the decline of the dollar, itself a result of the expensive war in Vietnam. On 15 August the USA unilaterally abandoned the obligation to exchange the dollar for gold, thus destroying the foundation of the global monetary system set up at Bretton Woods in July 1944. Four months later, on 17–18 December 1971, the ten most important economies agreed in Washington to a new system of exchange rates devaluating the dollar and revaluating the western European currencies. For the West German mark, this meant a rise in value of 4.6 per cent against gold and 13.6 per cent against the dollar. The EC states introduced the so-called 'currency snake' in March 1972: from then on, the exchange rates of their currencies were to fluctuate by a maximum of 2.25 per cent. Nonetheless, since the payment and trade deficit of the United States persisted, speculative capital continued to flow into Europe. This was the reason for Klasen's initiative and the cause of Schiller's defeat.

Since the 'superminister' saw himself abandoned by all of his cabinet colleagues, he decided to resign. He wrote to the chancellor on 2 July, asking to be allowed to step down on 7 July, immediately following the end of Franco-German talks and the conclusion of a trade agreement with the Soviet Union. The battle over foreign exchange was not the only reason for Schiller's departure. He pointed to his colleagues' refusal to follow his fiscal directives and, furthermore, made an accusation that also touched the chancellor himself. He, Schiller, was not prepared 'to support a policy that creates the impression that the government is living according to the maxim *après nous le déluge!*' Schiller also might have mentioned his continuing conflicts with Helmut Schmidt, the ambitious minister of defence; Erhard Eppler, minister of foreign aid and an advocate of drastic tax increases; or Horst Ehmke, minister of the chancellor's office. The latter now advised Brandt not to insist that Schiller remain. The Social Democratic ministers were weary of the 'superminister' and his lectures, and they believed that he was no longer as popular in the country as he had been in 1969.

Brandt followed Ehmke's advice, asking President Heinemann to accept Schiller's resignation and to appoint Helmut Schmidt—Schiller's harshest critic—to both of his posts, the ministries of economics and finance. Georg Leber became minister of defence, and his duties as transport and postal minister were given to Lauritz Lauritzen, who exercised them along with his office as minister of housing construction. By 7 July, the day of Schiller's resignation, the cabinet reshuffle was complete.

By this time, the deadlock between the governing parties and the opposition, first revealed on 28 April in the vote on the chancellor's budget, was fully manifest. Kienbaum and von Kühlmann-Stumm, the two 'rightist' FDP delegates, had left the Bundestag in May. Their successors supported the government. That same month, the SPD ejected its delegate Günther Müller from the party for refusing to leave 'Social Democracy 72' (*Soziale Demokratie 72*), an organization he had founded. Müller would formally join the CSU in September, but counted as a member of the opposition immediately after his exclusion from the SPD, if not even earlier. This meant that each side controlled 248 seats. Since Schiller, upon leaving office, no longer participated in parliament sessions, the opposition now had a numerical advantage: it could count on one more vote than the government, at least in theory. Neither side, however, controlled a 'chancellor majority' of 249 seats.

The situation was untenable and could only be rectified by holding new elections. The Union would have preferred to accomplish this by forcing the chancellor to resign, but it did not possess the means to do so. In June the chancellor, in consultation with Scheel, decided to place his bets on the rejection of a vote of confidence, the *Vertrauensfrage*, which it planned to bring before the parliament after the summer break. In this case the president, according to Article 68 of the Basic Law, could dissolve parliament at the request of the chancellor, provided that the Bundestag could not unite a majority behind another chancellor.

Brandt asked for a vote of confidence on 20 September. It took place on 22 September (Article 68 stipulated a period of forty-eight hours between the request and the vote). In order to guarantee a rejection, the members of the government did not participate. There were 248 votes for, 233 against, and 1 abstention. Immediately thereafter, Brandt asked the president to dissolve parliament and set new elections for 19 November 1972. The opposition did not attempt to elect a new chancellor. When asked by Heinemann if he agreed to the chancellor's request, Barzel responded in the affirmative, whereupon the sixth German Bundestag was dissolved. This marks the first time in the history of the FRG that a legislative period was ended prematurely.

On 25 September, three days after the dissolution of the parliament, Chancellor Brandt and Foreign Minister Scheel held a press conference. The emphasis was on foreign policy in the weeks and months to come. Scheel announced a visit to Beijing from 10 to 14 October and the beginning of normal diplomatic relations with the People's Republic of China. Brandt dealt primarily with the current negotiations over a Basic Treaty between the FRG and the GDR. At this point, it was not clear whether these negotiations would be concluded by the time of the elections. On 10 October, the day Scheel flew to Beijing, Brezhnev and Bahr consulted for several hours in the Kremlin. Thereafter, the GDR showed greater flexibility on several matters, and the negotiations were wrapped up on 6 November. The cabinet approved the results the next day. The day after that, on 8 November, state secretaries Egon Bahr and Michael Kohl initialled the treaty in Bonn and presented it—along with the supplementary protocol, protocol notes, exchanges of correspondence, and a (written) 'oral agreement concerning political arrangements'—to the public.

The official title of the accord was 'Treaty on the Basis of Relations between the Federal Republic of Germany and the German Democratic Republic' (*Vertrag über die Grundlagen der Beziehungen zwischen der Bundesrepublik Deutschland und der Deutschen Demokratischen Republik*). It obligated both sides to work towards good-neighbourly relations with each other on the basis of equal rights, let themselves be guided by the goals and principles of the United Nations, resolve their disputes exclusively by peaceful means, and refrain from threats or use of force. Both countries emphasized the 'inviolability of the borders existing between them, now and in the future', and each assured the other of the 'unqualified respect for its territorial integrity'. They declared that neither state could 'represent the other internationally or act in its name', recognized 'that the sovereign authority of each of the two states is restricted to its territory', and respected the 'independence and autonomy of each of the two states in its internal and foreign affairs'.

'Practical and humanitarian concerns' were also mentioned, but in a relatively non-committal way. The signatories stated that they would work them out 'in the course of normalizing their relations'. In the spirit of the treaty's title, more specific accords were to be worked out in numerous areas: the economy, culture, sport, even environmental protection. Each partner would establish 'permanent representation' in the other's capital, but not formal 'embassies', as the East German leaders had always demanded, desiring the GDR to be treated as a fully separate and autonomous country. Bahr did not succeed in having any mention of German unity included in the text. Instead the preamble, reflecting the 'agree to disagree' philosophy of the signatories, spoke of 'different views . . . on the fundamental questions, including the national question'. Nonetheless, both sides did agree to formally notify the Four Powers that their rights and obligations were not affected by the treaty. The Four Powers, in turn, reiterated this standpoint in a joint statement on 9 November, and recommended that the two German states be invited to join the United Nations.

Although neither the treaty nor the statement of the Four Powers contained any mention of a 'peace treaty' or of 'Germany as a whole', a reservation in the sense of international law was implicit. The Basic Treaty was drafted and signed within the framework of continuing Allied rights and obligations. The relations between the two states were 'of a special kind', as Brandt had put it in his inaugural speech on 28 October 1969. They had force in terms of national law, but not international law. The treaty did not make the two Germanies into 'foreign' countries for each other. It was an accord between two *German* states—of which only the FRG, of course, insisted on its dissimilarity to other international treaties, whereas the GDR sought to erase this difference.

The new *Ostpolitik* played a huge role in the election campaign right from the start. After 8 November it became clear that the seventh Bundestag election was also going to be a referendum on the Basic Treaty, which had been initialled but not yet ratified. The coalition praised the accord as a step forward for Germany and as a contribution towards securing the peace in Europe. The opposition let it be known that they would not approve the treaty 'in its current form'. During a television discussion between the heads of the four Bundestag parties on 15 November, Rainer Barzel clothed his rejection in the form of a conditional sentence in the negative: in the event of a Union victory at the polls, he would not sign the treaty unless the GDR immediately stopped shooting at those attempting to escape over the border.

By 1972 the majority of the West German public felt that unrealizable demands of the kind Barzel was making did not help the situation of the Germans, whether in the GDR or in West Germany. In a statement written by Hans Mommsen in April, prior to the key decisions in the parliament, a group of some 200 prominent historians and political scientists, ranging from the Marxist Wolfgang Abendroth to the conservative Hans Rothfels, came out in support of the social–liberal *Ostpolitik*. This group included Karl Dietrich Bracher, Theodor Eschenburg, Fritz Fischer, Ernst Fraenkel, Hermann Heimpel, Eugen Kogon, Reinhart Koselleck, Richard Löwenthal, Golo Mann, Thomas Nipperdey, and Reinhard Wittram. As in 1965 and 1969, intellectuals, writers, and artists engaged in campaign initiatives for Willy Brandt, this time even more energetically and with broader public support. Once again, Günter Grass was the most famous author who, in countless events, promoted the cause of the Social Democrats and their *Ostpolitik*. Within the party itself, the backing for Brandt had never been stronger. Even the Young Socialists worked for Brandt and Scheel, despite their domestic-political differences with the SPD mainstream.

The Social Democrats' campaign slogan, 'Germans, we can be proud of our country!', originated with the chancellor himself. It reflected widespread sentiment among the population. West Germany had gained in international importance and prestige in the wake of the new *Ostpolitik*. It was doing well economically. This gave the coalition cause to hope that the voters would reward the government parties at the polls. The Union, on the other hand, came out with an advertisement campaign in which two former adversaries, Ludwig Erhard, the 'father of the economic miracle', and Karl Schiller, the former Social Democratic minister of economics, made common cause against the government's economic and fiscal policy and promoted the Union's version of the 'Social Market Economy'.

In the evening of 19 November 1972 it became clear that the SPD had achieved the best result in the party's history: 45.8% of the vote. This made it the strongest party, also for the first time, and represented an increase of 3.1% over 1969. The CDU and CSU together managed 44.9%, a loss of 1.2%. The liberals were also among the winners, gaining 8.4%, an improvement of 2.6%. The message from the voters was clear: the social–liberal coalition had a mandate to continue its policies, and the Union was to remain on the opposition benches.[19]

THE BASIC TREATY: A GERMAN–GERMAN WATERSHED

The election day of 19 November 1972 was the greatest triumph in the life of Willy Brandt, the first Social Democratic chancellor of the Federal Republic. Immediately thereafter, his political star began to sink. A throat operation forced him to give up smoking and left him unable to speak for a significant period. He was bedridden during the coalition negotiations and the formation of the cabinet, participating as best he could through written correspondence. He suffered another episode of late-autumnal depression, worse and longer than the bouts that had plagued him in earlier years. The new *Ostpolitik* had been his single focus since 1969. Now that it had largely been achieved, he lacked a new goal to challenge the charismatic politician in him. The day-to-day government routine held no fascination for Willy Brandt. These things made it difficult for him to recover from his exhaustion and regain his old vibrancy.

The seventh German Bundestag convened for its constitutive session on 13 December 1972. A woman was elected president of the parliament for the first time: the Social Democrat Annemarie Renger, for many years a close associate of Kurt Schumacher. The next day, Willy Brandt was elected chancellor for the second time, receiving 269 out of 493 votes.

His new cabinet, presented on 15 December, included thirteen Social Democrats and five liberals. The 'superministry' was split. Helmut Schmidt continued as head of finance, retaining authority over several departments in the economics ministry, including those for currency and credit. The FDP politician Hans Fridrichs became minister of economics. Other new faces in the cabinet were those of Katharina Focke (SPD) as minister of youth, family, and health; Hans-Jochen Vogel (SPD), the former mayor of Munich, now minister for environmental planning, construction, and urban development; and the law professor Werner

Maihofer (FDP), minister for special assignments. This was also Egon Bahr's new title, though he continued to work in the office of the chancellor. Horst Ehmke left the chancellor's office for the newly created ministry for research and technology; he also directed the postal ministry. The Social Democrat Klaus von Dohnanyi, who had taken over as minister of education and science after the resignation of the non-aligned Hans Leussink in March 1972, continued in this office, as did all the remaining members of the cabinet.

On 19 September, the new parliament did what its predecessor had lacked a majority to accomplish: it passed the 1972 federal budget. This put an end to the conditions—regulated by Article 112 of the Basic Law—permitting extra-budgetary spending. From now on, government spending in excess of the budget required the consent of the finance minister, who could grant it only in case of unforeseen and pressing need. The new government thus began its term with a return to budgetary normality.

Brandt gave his second inaugural address on 18 January 1973. It was entirely guided by a 'desire for continuity'. Following a draft by his adviser Klaus Harpprecht for long stretches of his speech, the chancellor spoke of a 'new kind of citizen' that had emerged after the end of the dictatorship, a citizen seeking 'to achieve his liberty also within the network of social and economic interdependencies'. The 'productive unrest from the ranks of the young and the insight of the older generation' flowed into 'what has become a new centre—the social and liberal centre . . . We have drawn closer to the Anglo-Saxon *citoyen* [*sic*], and perhaps we can say that the Federal Republic of Germany has become more "western"—even during a time dominated by the so-called *Ostpolitik*.'

As in October 1969, Brandt gave top priority to reforms in education and science. Referring to developments at many universities, he warned against intolerance and politicization: 'The institutions of teaching and research must not be transformed into political battlefields.' In the area of social policy, he announced that worker co-determination, which was part of the 'substance of the democratization process in our society', would be extended. After all, despite all their differences, the coalition parties were now both working from the 'principle of equal rights and balance between employees and shareholders'.

The first foreign policy aim Brandt mentioned was the European Union. He declared his support for the Atlantic alliance and for a European peace policy. As for the Basic Treaty, signed by Bahr and Kohl in East Berlin on 21 December, the chancellor stressed the government's resolve to

carry it out in a politically and legally rigorous manner and implement it in the interests of the people of both states . . . We have always rejected the governmental and social system of the GDR, and we continue to do so . . . Irrespective of these antagonisms, however, both governments have decided by treaty to stand up to their responsibilities and to renounce the use of force. Both must place peace higher than all differences. For us, this means that the preservation of peace has priority over the national question. This is a service the German people renders to the peoples of Europe.

Despite a number of pathos-laden and nebulous passages, which almost recalled late-period Ludwig Erhard, the January 1973 inaugural speech was, in general, more cautious in tone and less ambitious in aim than Brandt's first in October 1969. The chancellor emphasized the 'endurance' that the new reforms would require; he pointed to the 'new lines of intersection between progressive and conservative interests', lines that the 'vital spirit of citizenship' would be sensitive enough to recognize. The balanced character of the address was hardly going to satisfy the younger members of the chancellor's party. But the coalition of the 'new centre' stood for what its parties agreed on, not for the utopian hopes of the left—though they, too, had played a part in the SPD's electoral triumph.

The opposition also intended to maintain continuity, at least in matters of Germany policy. The rejection of the Basic Treaty after Bahr and Kohl initialled it on 8 November 1972 was reiterated. On 2 February 1973 the Bundesrat, with a majority of Union-governed *Länder*, approved a motion calling for the treaty's rejection. That same day, it also voted unanimously for West German membership in the United Nations. However, accession to the UN was predicated on the ratification of the Basic Treaty and the simultaneous accession of the GDR, a link explicitly established by the Four Powers in their statement on 9 November 1972. In any case, the Soviets would have used their security council veto to block West German membership in the event that the GDR did not join at the same time. Thus the attitude of the CDU and CSU was nothing less than self-contradictory.

On 9 May the Bundestag commenced the final debate over the ratification law for the Basic Treaty, and Rainer Barzel stepped down from the leadership of the Union fraction. The day before, a narrow fraction majority—including all the CSU members—had rejected his motion that the Union should vote for West German membership in the UN. His resignation was a reaction to this failure.

The position of the party and fraction leader had been weakened by the outcome of the elections on 19 November 1972. On 28 January 1973 the prime minister of Rhineland-Palatinate, Helmut Kohl, renewed his candidacy for the post of party head. (He had been defeated by Barzel at the CDU congress in Saarbrücken in November 1971.) On 17 May the CDU/CSU Bundestag fraction chose as its new head the delegate Karl Carstens, former state secretary of the chancellor's office under Kiesinger in 1968–9. The day before, Barzel had announced he would also not be running for the party leadership. On 12 June a special party congress in Bonn elected Helmut Kohl as his successor. Not until eleven years later did the public learn that Barzel's retirement from the party and fraction leadership had been made much easier for him by a contract as consultant for the Flick company.

The leadership crisis in the CDU had no effect on the ratification of the Basic Treaty. The parliament passed the ratification law in third reading on 11 May by 268 to 217 votes. Four of the positive votes, as well as all of the negative ones, came from the opposition. The ballot over the FRG's accession to the UN

Charter divided the Union into two camps. All 121 of the rejectionist votes were Union, but 99 of the 364 positive votes were from the CDU. This did not yet mean that the Basic Treaty was the law of the land, however. On 22 May, three days before the ratification debate in the Bundestag, the Bavarian government petitioned the Federal Constitutional Court to review the treaty's compatibility with the Basic Law. At the same time, it brought forward a motion to have the court order the president to delay the signing of the document until the review could be concluded.

This shifted the fight over the Basic Treaty from Bonn to Karlsruhe and transformed a political into a legal question. On 25 May the Bundesrat, in which the Unionist governments had a majority, decided against raising an objection to the treaty and voted to pass the law for West Germany's accession to the UN. On 18 June the Constitutional Court rejected the motion to delay the treaty's entrance into force. Two days later in Bonn, Egon Bahr and Michael Kohl exchanged notes in which each government notified its counterpart that the ratification process had been concluded. The Basic Treaty and its ancillary agreements entered into effect on 21 June 1973.

The Constitutional Court handed down its decision on the Bavarian government's judicial review suit on 31 July 1973. The Basic Treaty was declared to be compatible with the Basic Law. At the same time, however, and in accordance with precedent, it emphasized that the German Reich continued to exist and that the Federal Republic was identical to it as a state—though only 'party identical' (*teilidentisch*) in a geographic sense. Therefore, the constitutional organs were not to give up the restoration of state unity as a political goal. Rather, they were obliged to work towards this goal and to refrain from doing anything that would hamper it. As a part of Germany, the GDR was not a foreign country. Thus the borders between the two German states were 'similar' to the borders between the *Länder* of the FRG. GDR citizens who came under the protection of the FRG and its constitution were to be treated as citizens of the FRG. In summary, the court described the treaty as possessing a 'double character': 'According to its character, it is an international treaty; according to its specific content, it is a treaty dealing above all with relations *inter se*.'

This ruling codified the nation state solution to the German question in a more binding and restricted sense than that of the Parliamentary Council in 1949. The Bavarian government and the Union could look upon this as a success. But it was not without irony that the court's decision was provoked by a CSU government—the same party whose leader, Franz Josef Strauss, had been the first German politician to clearly reject a German national state, if only within the borders of the four occupied zones.

One of the Basic Treaty's effects had already made itself felt before the agreement actually entered into force. The GDR was able to take up diplomatic relations with twenty new states in December 1972. Thirteen more followed in January 1973, including NATO members like Italy and the Netherlands. The

USA formally recognized the GDR in 1974. By 1978 East Germany maintained official relations with 123 countries.

The GDR and the FRG became the 133rd and 134th members of United Nations on 18 September 1973. The dual statehood of Germany was now recognized internationally, in the west as well as in the east. From now on, neither state could exert pressure on a third in the matter of diplomatic relations with its rival. At the same time, both were now less dependent on the good behaviour of other states. Both gained foreign policy options, and both, it seemed, bade final farewell to the provisional nature of their respective foundings in the year 1949. How would they now shape their mutual relations? This was the question on everyone's minds after the Basic Treaty took effect in late June 1973.[20]

4

Rapprochement and Estrangement
1973–1989

WILLY BRANDT'S RESIGNATION

On 18 May 1973, a week after the Bundestag passed the ratification laws for the Basic Treaty, Leonid Brezhnev arrived in Bonn at the head of a large delegation. The Soviet leader was mainly interested in increasing economic, industrial, and technical cooperation with West Germany. The respective agreements, as well as another on cultural relations, were signed on 19 May. Brandt and Brezhnev talked about the Conference on Security and Cooperation in Europe, which began at the end of June in Helsinki (and concluded there two years later), as well as negotiations soon to begin in Vienna over mutual balanced troop reductions. The subject of 'Berlin' was discussed by Gromyko and Bahr.

According to the final communiqué, the 'strict following and full application' of the Berlin agreement was 'an important prerequisite for lasting détente in the centre of Europe and for an improvement in the relations between the states, especially between the Federal Republic of Germany and the Soviet Union.' For Brandt, this formulation represented progress. But the actual practice did not bear out his optimism. The Soviet Union continued to treat West Berlin as a special political entity, refusing, for example, to include federal institutes located in the western part of the city in a treaty on scientific-technical cooperation. In justification of their behaviour, the Soviets pointed to Bonn's plan to build a federal environmental agency in Berlin. Moscow considered this a provocation. But the real reason for the hardline attitude was obvious: the Kremlin was following the wishes of the GDR.

In their view, the GDR leaders had more than met both Bonn and Moscow halfway in the Basic Treaty. After its signing, East Berlin's main concern was to assume control of relations with the other German state. That is, it had to be made clear to Bonn that any improvements it wished to make in its relations with the GDR would have to be worked out directly, not via the Soviet Union. As the SED saw things, the best means of exerting pressure towards this end were humanitarian issues like reuniting divided families and purchasing the freedom of political prisoners—problems that for many years had been worked out between the West German ministry for all-German affairs (ministry for German–German relations after 1969) and the East Berlin attorney Wolfgang Vogel.

After the Basic Treaty was signed in December 1972, nothing further happened at the 'lawyer level'. Bahr's new plan, which the GDR agreed to at first, involved setting obligatory quotas for people wishing to emigrate from East Germany to the west. But it did not come about. Some 2,000 GDR citizens were affected, who, having received permission to do so at the end of December 1972, were subsequently forbidden to leave the country. These were the so-called 'emergency cases'. SPD fraction leader Herbert Wehner, an expert on German–German travel problems ever since his days as minister for all-German affairs, made himself into their advocate. Erich Honecker had known Wehner in the period after 1933, during which both had fought as communists against the annexation of the Saar territory. In February 1973 he sent Wehner a message to the effect that he, Honecker, would like to speak with him about preparations for a German–German summit. The invitation was renewed in April. Wehner travelled to the GDR on 30 May. Brandt, Schmidt, and Scheel were in the know about the trip, as was the fraction leader of the FDP, Wolfgang Mischnick. Like Wehner, Mischnick was from Dresden. He was in the GDR for personal reasons at this time, and Wehner had requested that he, too, speak with Honecker.

Wehner met delegates from the Volkskammer for dinner on the evening of his arrival in East Berlin. During the meal, he spoke disparagingly of a party colleague, Annemarie Renger, the president of the Bundestag. He also made another, highly instructive remark. After the Warsaw Pact states invaded Czechoslovakia on 21 August 1968, as Wehner told his dinner companions, he had presented the following assessment of the situation to the cabinet: 'He had seen all this coming and had been expecting it, for Warsaw Pact states, too, must use all means of power at their disposal if their substance is at risk. Basically, the Dubček supporters in the FRG had bet on the wrong horse.'

The next day, the meeting between Honecker and Wehner took place near Wandlitz in the Schorfheide; Mischnick arrived somewhat later. When Honecker criticized the passages in Brandt's inaugural speech that dealt with the unity of the German nation and the 'special relationship' between the two German states, Wehner, according to Honecker's report, said that

he did not approve of these words of Willy Brandt and considered them a mistake. However, because of his loyalty to the chancellor, he had to say that Brandt, in using such language, was seeking the best, albeit with illusiory intentions. To him it was clear, as he explained, that the treaty system that had been created dealt with all problems and that any attempt to alter the existing realities would be reckless.

Wehner, without being authorized to do so, was accommodating the GDR far more than his government could countenance. It seemed wrong and dangerous to him that, even after the Basic Treaty was in place, Brandt and Bahr continued to orient their eastern and Germany policies entirely towards Moscow and not towards East Berlin; and that other Social Democrats, like Klaus Schultz, the mayor of Berlin, and Annemarie Renger, were again calling for full voting powers on the part of Berlin delegates to the Bundestag. For the SPD fraction leader, this demand placed an even greater political strain on the Berlin agreement than Brandt and Bahr with their plan to set up the environmental agency in West Berlin. Wehner believed the German–German relations to be in trouble and was seeking to help overcome the crisis through his talks with the GDR.

Humanitarian issues were certainly an important motivation for Wehner in his 'parallel foreign policy', not just pretext. And he was, in fact, able to register one success in this area: after his meeting with Honecker, the previous practices for reuniting divided families and purchasing the freedom of political prisoners got started again. In the long term, however, the former Communist-turned-Social Democrat was clearly after far more than humanitarian relief and an improved relationship between Bonn and East Berlin. He wanted to help bring the divided German working class together again. Towards this aim, he was prepared to give up everything the SED could not accept, or what he thought they could not accept. The idea of one German nation, so persistently maintained in the west, was one of these things.

Wehner paid a high price for his vision of a national unity mediated through class solidarity. He not only renounced legal positions of the FRG, but also part of the moral stance of the western world. He let the 'other side' know that, in the interests of east–west and especially of German–German stability, he had full understanding even for the violent suppression of freedom movements within the territory of the Warsaw Pact. The dialectician Wehner was attempting a dialectic shift: to replace the old special conflict between the FRG and the east with a new special consensus, thus completing the move from a 'conservative' to a specifically 'social democratic' foreign and Germany policy.

Wehner was, in fact, doing exactly what he said he had not wished to do—be disloyal to Willy Brandt. Neither the chancellor nor other Social Democrats learned at that time what Wehner had said about them during his visit in the GDR. They also did not find out what kinds of statements from his interlocutors he had accepted without critique or contradiction. The true extent of his rapprochement with Honecker in the Schorfheide became clear only a good while after his death on 19 January 1990, when the archives of the GDR were opened after the reunification.

After his GDR visit, at the end of September, Wehner travelled to Moscow as part of a Bundestag delegation. It was the first time he had seen the city since he had lived there during the Hitler and Stalin period, between 1935 and 1942, before the Comintern sent him to Sweden (where he broke with communism). Comments he made to Mischnick before the departure flight seem to indicate that he was anxious about the trip and the memories it involved. Immediately upon arrival in Moscow, on 24 September, he criticized the Bonn government's

Berlin policy in a television interview. In the days following, Wehner made mocking and even contemptuous remarks to journalists about Willy Brandt. The 'number one' was 'lost in reverie' and 'limp', the listeners were informed. The chancellor 'likes a lukewarm bath—like in a bubble bath'. *Der Spiegel* quoted another sentence that caused a big stir in West Germany: 'What the government needs is a head.' This, however, was not directed at Willy Brandt; Wehner was complaining about the lack of an independent, highly positioned contact person with the east.

Brandt was in the United States when he heard about Wehner's attacks. The occasion of this trip was the FRG's accession to the United Nations. The chancellor gave a speech to the general assembly on 26 September. The news agency report reached him the next day at a stopover during his flight from Chicago to Aspen, Colorado, where he was to receive an award from the Aspen Institute. Brandt returned earlier than planned to Bonn, resolved to demand Wehner's replacement as fraction head. This would have been the correct response to Wehner's challenge and a unique opportunity to demonstrate to the party and to the public that the chancellor still possessed the kind of leadership strength that many saw him as lacking after the end of 1972. But it did not come to an open rupture. Wehner demonstrated remorse, and his support in the party and fraction was still considerable. Brandt steered away from open conflict and, in so doing, confirmed the very image Wehner had painted of him.

The autumn of 1973 was completely overshadowed by a new armed conflict in the Middle East, the Yom Kippur War, which broke out on 6 October, and by its immediate consequence, the 17 October decision of the oil-producing Arab countries to respond to the Israel-friendly policies of the western states by cutting off oil exports. On 4 November the Arab states decided to cut back oil production by 25 per cent until Israel had evacuated the territories it had occupied during the 1967 Six Day War and restored the rights of the Palestinian people. The West German government and parliament reacted by passing an energy security law, which took force on 10 November and permitted restrictions on oil and natural gas consumption. On 19 November the economics minister, Hans Friderichs, ordered driving bans for the ensuing four Sundays and speed limit restrictions on highways and secondary roads for a period of six months. Owing to measures of this kind, the 'oil price shock' made a deep impression on the collective consciousness of the West German citizens.

A crisis in transatlantic relations was one of the consequences of the Yom Kippur War and the oil crisis. On 13 October the nine governments of the European Community called upon the warring countries in the Middle East to stop fighting. On 6 November they declared that Israel should comply with the UN security council resolutions and withdraw from the territories it had occupied in 1967. Both demands were in keeping with the policy of 'European Political Cooperation' agreed to in 1970, but they also revealed western Europe's material interest in cheap oil exports from the Arab countries.

The United States, which supported Israel, soon made it clear that it was not prepared to accept further such demonstrations of 'European identity'. In the months following, the members of the EC were repeatedly and emphatically reminded that their liberty and security did not, ultimately, derive from themselves, but from America. Moreover, they were told that the EC pursued merely regional interests, whereas America's concerns were global.

The other events of 1973 garnered far less attention than the Middle East war and the oil crisis. On 11 December chancellor Brandt and Prime Minister Strougal, together with their foreign ministers, Scheel and Chnoupek, signed the last of the eastern treaties. The Prague Treaty ended the prolonged controversy over the international interpretation of the 1938 Munich Agreement. Both sides declared that this agreement, signed under Hitler's extortionist pressure, was to be considered 'by this treaty as null and void with regard to their mutual relations'. This language was less than what Prague had long been demanding: that the Munich Agreement be considered invalid *ex tunc*, that is, from the beginning. It accommodated the FRG's position that the new treaty not affect certain legal outcomes of the Munich Agreement, like the nationality of the Sudeten Germans, nor provide a justification for material claims against the FRG by Czechoslovakia. This was expressly set down in Article II. Prague and Bonn took up diplomatic relations later that same day, and Bulgaria and Hungary followed the example of their alliance partner on 21 December.

Despite these successes, the West German government was not satisfied with the state of its *Ostpolitik* at the end of the year. In a letter to Brezhnev on 30 December, Brandt wrote that West German–Soviet relations still left much to be desired. He mentioned the continuing fight over the inclusion of West Berlin in a number of agreements. The chancellor's biggest worry, however, had to do with the way German–German relations were developing. 'We have the impression that the GDR, now that it has joined the United Nations, has virtually no interest in making any effort to reach a normalization with the Federal Republic.'

As an example, Brandt mentioned the GDR's measure of 15 November doubling the minimum amount of money that visitors to East Germany were required to exchange. This increase hit pensioners especially hard and cut the number of visitors from the FRG and West Berlin in half. 'The Soviet side may not be aware', wrote Brandt, 'of how negative the impression is that these and other measures of the GDR have made on our public. The resulting situation compels me to draw your attention to the possibility that such negative developments could seriously endanger my government's efforts to expand the policy of détente.' He asked Brezhnev to work on the GDR to remedy the situation.

The chancellor's letter had no effect. When the FRG established the environmental agency in West Berlin at the beginning of 1974, the GDR, violating the transit agreement, began to obstruct traffic between the FRG and West Berlin.

After July it refused to allow employees of the new agency to travel to and from the city. As in earlier years, it had the full support of the Soviet Union.[1]

The setbacks in his *Ostpolitik* were not the only blows to the chancellor's prestige. Between June 1973 and March 1974 a parliamentary committee attempted to shed light on the Steiner–Wienand affair. Although it did not succeed in producing any clear results (the partisan nature of its composition was not the least of reasons for this), there remained the persistent suspicion that Brandt had survived the Union's motion of no confidence on 27 April 1972 because of money payments to at least one member of the opposition. This was greatly disturbing to many of the chancellor's supporters.

Another factor was the impression of government helplessness in the face of the air traffic controllers. For six months, from the end of May to the end of November 1973—the height of the vacation travel season—the air traffic controllers caused chaos in the airports of West Germany in an effort to underscore their salary demands. The weakness of the government leadership seemed confirmed when, on 13 February 1974, after a series of warning strikes culminating in a country-wide strike, the public employers granted the employees in the civil service an 11 per cent wage and salary increase. Earlier, Brandt had sharply rejected the demands of the union for civil service, transport, and traffic, which were indeed excessive. Consequently, the government's retreat could only be interpreted as a surrender. 'The loss of state authority . . . cannot be justified in any way,' the journalist Rolf Zundel wrote on 15 February 1974 in *Die Zeit*. 'And it weighs more heavily than the blemished image of the current government.'

Brandt was losing authority not only as chancellor, but also as head of the SPD. The Hanover party congress in April 1973 had strengthened him politically. In the long run, however, the persistent demands of the Young Socialists for 'system-altering reforms' like the ban on the profession of broker (passed in Hanover) overtaxed his desire and ability to integrate the young rebels. Speaking to the party executive on 9 September 1973, Brandt cautioned against 'self-destructive tendencies', 'self-mutilation', and the risk of splitting the party.

At their national congress in Munich in January 1974, the Young Socialists committed themselves to pursuing a socialist 'double strategy' inside and outside the SPD. The party executive responded with a sharply worded reprimand. Brandt again went public with a ten-point declaration approved by the SPD leadership, the so-called 'April theses', on 2 April. 'A double strategy against one's own party cannot be permitted,' he said. 'The majority opinion of the party must be the basis of its public work.' The centrepiece of the address was the following statement: 'In a democracy, there can be no majority without the centre. Whoever renounces the centre loses the power to govern. Social Democratic resolve means asserting the centre.'

Brandt had gone on the offensive again. He seemed more aggressive than in previous months, and his optimism began to rub off on his party. On 19 April he left for an official visit to two Arab countries, Algeria and Egypt. On

25 April, the day after his return, the public learned through the federal prosecutor's office about an event whose consequences could not at first be foreseen: Günter Guillaume, a close associate of Brandt's in the chancellor's office, had been arrested under the suspicion that he was an East German spy.

Guillaume was a full-time employee in the East Berlin Ministry for State Security. His rank was that of an 'officer on special duty', and he was also an officer in the National People's Army. Disguised as a refugee, he had come to the FRG with his wife Christel in 1956 and begun his intelligence activities. He joined the SPD in Frankfurt in 1957, and was soon entrusted with a series of assignments and offices. In 1970 the successful official began to work for the chancellor's office, where—as the press and information office told the government—he was responsible for scheduling the chancellor's party meetings and maintaining written correspondence with party organizations. A great deal more emerged shortly afterwards. In the summer of 1973 Guillaume had accompanied Brandt on the latter's summer vacation, during which he had had access to top secret NATO documents. He was also familiar with Brandt's private life, having been with him on many trips. In this connection, the tabloids wrote with relish concerning a number of 'affairs'.

The Federal Office for the Defence of the Constitution had had its eye on Guillaume ever since May 1973. At the end of that month the agency's president, Günther Nollau, informed the minister of the interior, Genscher, albeit in a very general way. Genscher informed Brandt. After consulting with Nollau, Genscher advised Brandt to take Guillaume with him to Norway, as planned. The two advisers were pursuing different goals. Genscher did not take the suspicions very seriously. Nollau wanted to use the chancellor as bait to catch Guillaume spying. Since Brandt heard nothing more for a long while, he came to the conclusion that the suspicions were unfounded, and forgot about them. It was not until 1 March 1974 that he learned from Nollau that Guillaume was to be arrested within two to three weeks.

Many people were guilty of negligence in the Guillaume affair: Horst Ehmke, former head of the chancellor's office, who had hired Guillaume despite his lack of qualifications; Ehmke's successor Horst Grabert, who, after Brandt had informed him about the suspicions against his employee, took no security measures; Nollau, who consciously downplayed the case against Guillaume; Genscher, who approvingly passed along Nollau's irresponsible recommendation that Guillaume be taken to Norway and himself did nothing to prevent the betrayal of military and state secrets; and Brandt himself, whose actions in the matter were ill-considered from the start.

In retrospect, after Guillaume's arrest, the chancellor was very self-critical. According to his journal, the idea of resigning came to him already on 29 April. Nonetheless, he first decided it would be best to fight it out, and his closest advisers agreed with him. Things changed on 4 May. In Bad Münstereifel, at the conference centre of the Friedrich Ebert Foundation, Herbert Wehner told him what he had learned the day before from Nollau, his fellow Saxon, concerning the chancellor's 'private life'. Wehner did not call directly for his resignation, but left Brandt in no doubt that he thought this the best course of action, if not the only realistic solution to the problem.

For Brandt, the die had been cast, and he decided to step down from his government post. Even close political friends were unable to change his mind, men like Holger Börner, the managing director of the SPD, and Karl Ravens, the parliamentary state secretary in the chancellor's office. On 5 May Brandt communicated his decision to the SPD leaders, who were meeting in Münstereifel at the time. He named as his successor Helmut Schmidt, who in previous months had accused him of weak leadership, but was now exhorting him to hold on. On 6 May Brandt asked President Heinemann to release him from his duties as chancellor. His official reason: 'I assume political responsibility for the negligence in connection with the Guillaume espionage affair.' Brandt's resignation caused a worldwide sensation.

Brandt's letter to Heinemann did not mention the culpability of others. Hans-Dietrich Genscher was more responsible than the chancellor for the way the case had developed, but he could not resign without plunging the social–liberal coalition into a serious crisis. The reason was that a successor to Heinemann—who had declined a second term for reasons of age—was to be elected on 15 May. The coalition's candidate for the presidency was Walter Scheel, and the candidate for the posts of foreign minister and FDP leader was Genscher.

Brandt's decision to resign was not compulsory or inevitable, at least theoretically speaking. If, in the wake of the November 1972 elections, he had had more luck and shown a more aggressive spirit, his chancellorship would probably have been able to survive the exposure and arrest of his subordinate. In the autumn of 1973, after Wehner's Moscow attacks, a politically strong Willy Brandt would have confronted the SPD with the choice between himself and the fraction leader. As things stood at the time, he would have emerged victorious and then not have been dependent on Wehner's opinion, ill or otherwise, in May 1974. Nonetheless, given the way things had developed from autumn 1972 onward, resignation was, in fact, Brandt's only option. It was the only way he could preserve his personal reputation and hang on to the office of party head.

The face of West Germany had changed more during the chancellorship of Willy Brandt than under his two predecessors, Kiesinger and Erhard. The historian Manfred Görtemaker rightly spoke of a 'refounding of the republic' after 1968. The Weimar Republic had also experienced a 'refounding', albeit in another direction and with other results. Hindenburg's re-election to the Reich presidency in the year 1925 initiated a conservative transformation of the first German democracy, a process that eventually led to the republic's dissolution. Brandt's election to the chancellorship in 1969 was the beginning of a social–liberal renewal and consolidation of the second German democracy.

It was true that the internal reforms of the Brandt era did not go as far as many voters had wanted, and they did not all survive. Nonetheless, they demonstrated that the democratic system had the ability both to adapt to changes in society and to drive forward the process of change. This ability had been largely denied by the Extra-Parliamentary Opposition.

It was in the area of foreign policy that Brandt had the most profound and lasting impact. The western integration, the work of Adenauer, was the secure foundation upon which Brandt opened West Germany to the east between 1969 and 1973. The FRG became—to the extent that it could—a 'normal' western state. In overcoming what Richard Löwenthal called (in 1974, the year of Brandt's resignation) the 'special conflict between the Federal Republic and the Soviet Union and the Soviet bloc', West Germany finally warded off the danger that had plagued Bonn ever since the second half of the 1950s: international isolation.

Willy Brandt's biography played a crucial role in the success of his foreign policy. Nobody could harbour any doubt about the fact that he had always been an active opponent of Hitler. This was as important for his chancellorship as the simultaneously 'nationalist' and 'western' image he had gained as mayor of Berlin. The international trust he had earned as foreign minister and chancellor strengthened the democratic self-confidence of West Germany. And although he only led the country for five short years, his place in history has long been secured beyond all partisan battles. He was the most important chancellor since Konrad Adenauer.[2]

IDENTITY THROUGH IDEOLOGY: THE GDR AS 'SOCIALIST NATION'

Brandt's resignation was the unintentional outcome of the efforts of the GDR. Günter Guillaume and his wife Christel, who brought down the first Social Democratic German chancellor, had commenced their espionage activities in 1956, the same year in which the Federal Constitutional Court, responding to government petition, had banned the German Communist party. Already during the Weimar Republic, the KPD's illegal organizations had developed the methods Guillaume's employer, the East German Ministry for State Security, was using to wage war against the 'class enemy' in West Germany: 'subversion' (*Zersetzung*) through the spread of falsified information (for example, the claim that President Heinrich Lübke was an 'architect of concentration camps'); targeted provocations (like feigned anti-Semitic machinations); covert support for the terrorist activities of third parties (in this case the RAF), and comprehensive espionage.

Not all spies were full-time agents like Guillaume. Between 1950 and 1990, 20,000 to 30,000 West German citizens worked as 'Unofficial Collaborators' (*Inoffizielle Mitarbeiter* or IM) for the Ministry for State Security. Many were former citizens of the GDR who had migrated to West Germany for the purpose of spying. But most were 'native' to the FRG. The main motivation for intelligence activities on behalf of the GDR was sympathy with the other, 'anti-fascist' German state, especially after the leftward shift at the universities in the second half of the 1960s. The British historian Patrick Major has described the antagonism between communism and anti-communism in divided Germany as 'Germany's Cold Civil War'. Guillaume's infiltration into the chancellor's office in Bonn was the GDR's most spectacular success during this conflict. But Brandt's fall was a miscalculation on the part of the SED and its secret service, for the simple fact that Moscow and East Berlin believed they had more to lose under Brandt's probable successor, Helmut Schmidt, than under Brandt himself. In this way, success and failure were closely united. On balance, the outcome of Günter and Christel Guillaume's covert activities was a defeat for the GDR.

Nonetheless, regardless of who the leader of West Germany was, after the signing of the Basic Treaty the SED was more intent than ever on stoking the ideological conflict between the two states. The party feared the creeping social-democratization of its own populace. At the end of January 1973 Kurt Hager, the SED's chief ideologist, rejected the idea of a continuing German 'cultural nation'. In mid-March, he spoke of an 'unbridgeable opposition' between the 'socialist nation in the GDR' and the 'capitalist nation persisting in the FRG'. Two months later, at the end of May 1973, Hager coined the term 'real existing socialism' (*realexistierender Sozialismus*), to which he said there was no alternative. This concept was intended to separate the SED from both the 'democratic socialism' of the SPD and the utopian socialism of the West German New Left.

The 1968 constitution of the GDR was revised by the Volkskammer on 27 September 1974. The GDR was now no longer a 'socialist state of the German nation', but a 'socialist state of the workers and peasants'. Six years before, the 'creation and maintenance of normal relations and cooperation between the two German states on the basis of equality' had been a 'national concern for the German Democratic Republic'. This statement was now eliminated, along with the next sentence: 'The German Democratic Republic and its citizens strive, moreover, to overcome the division of Germany imposed upon the German nation by imperialism, and support the step-by-step rapprochement of the two German states until the time of their unification on the basis of democracy and socialism.' The new language more strongly emphasized the links to the Soviet Union and the other members of the Warsaw Pact: 'The German Democratic Republic is forever and irrevocably allied with the Union of Soviet Socialist Republics.' 'The German Democratic Republic is an inseparable part of the socialist state community. Faithful to the principles of the Socialist International, it contributes to their strength, cultivates and develops friendship, all-round cooperation, and mutual support with all states in the socialist community.'

It was the job of philosophers and historians to provide the new doctrine of two German states with its theoretical and historical underpinnings. In a 1974 article in the *Einheit*, the SED's theoretical journal, the philosopher Alfred Kosing and the historian Walter Schmidt maintained that the division and destruction of the unity of the German nation had been the work of imperialism. At the same time, they stressed that the formation of the socialist nation in the GDR was the 'inevitable [*gesetzmässig*] outcome of the societal revolutions brought about under the leadership of the working class after 1945.'

The content and character of a nation, according to the two authors, was not primarily determined 'by certain ethnic, linguistic, or socio-psychological factors, but by the particular economic bases of the given society, its class relations, and the historical roles of its classes, especially the particular class ruling and leading the society and the nation.' Even 'bourgeois authors of the FRG' could not get around the 'bi-nationalization' of the 'populations of the GDR and the FRG'. The development of the new, socialist national consciousness in the GDR had been going on for nearly three decades, 'not only as a process of progressive separation from the imperialist FRG, but above all in increasing commonality and cooperation with the countries of the socialist state community under the leadership of the Soviet Union'. The outcome: 'At the same time as the inevitable [*gesetzmässig*] process of rapprochement among the socialist nations, new values have arisen and continue to arise, values that determine thought and give the socialist national consciousness of the GDR its internationalist character.'

Kosing and Schmidt quoted Erich Honecker in their interpretation of the historic process. They might have done the same with Walter Ulbricht, had it fitted the party line. Already in December 1970, and in Honecker's presence, the former First Secretary of the SED and head of the state council had spoken of the formation of a socialist nation in the GDR. Soon after his death on 1 August 1973, however, Ulbricht became an 'unperson' with no place in the official collective memory of the state. Nonetheless, the argument concerning the irresolvable antagonism between the new socialist and the old capitalist German nation survived him. It was not *his* argument, after all, but that of the Soviet Communist party, the leader of the 'socialist state community'. In developing an identity as a 'socialist nation', the SED and its theoreticians were complying with the wishes of Moscow. But the GDR also needed this ideological identity more than any other nation of the Warsaw Pact, since it lacked a true national identity of its own.[3]

THE DOMESTIC AND FOREIGN POLICY
OF THE SCHMIDT GOVERNMENT 1974–1976

On 15 May 1974, nine days after Willy Brandt stepped down as chancellor, the federal assembly elected Walter Scheel, hitherto foreign minister, to succeed

Gustav Heinemann as president of the Federal Republic of Germany. As the social–liberal candidate, Scheel received 530 votes, his Union opponent, Richard von Weizsäcker, 498. It was the first time since 12 September 1949 that the federal assembly did not meet in Berlin, but in Bonn. This was in accordance with the 1971 Quadripartite Agreement, which forbade the highest constitutional bodies of the FRG from performing sovereign acts in the western part of the former Reich capital.

Walter Scheel was born in 1919 in Solingen. After graduating from secondary school, he was trained in banking. He achieved the rank of First Lieutenant in the German air force during the Second World War, and after 1945 worked in private business, among other things as manager of a factory making steel products. In 1946 he joined the political party whose leader he would become in 1968: the FDP. As foreign minister in the social–liberal coalition, Scheel played an important role in the *Ostpolitik* that posterity has tended to connect with the names of Brandt and Bahr.

In his inaugural speech on 1 July 1974, the fourth president of the FRG made a few remarks about the 'provisional' nature of the current German situation. These comments sounded almost 'dialectical', but nonetheless—or perhaps for that very reason—found broad agreement.

A quarter-century has cleared up a good number of things. But one thing is not provisional: the political forces in this country will not, in the future, stop aspiring to a state of peace in Europe that will allow the German people, based on their right to self-determination, to regain their unity. If we want to achieve this goal, then we need the Federal Republic of Germany as a state, in the full sense of the word. Even if we must think about the realization of the right to self-determination in historical dimensions, for that very reason we will need an instrument designed to last. This instrument is our state, the Federal Republic of Germany.

The address in celebration of the twenty-fifth anniversary of the Basic Law on 24 May 1974 was held by the still-incumbent president. Heinemann reminded his audience of the Parliamentary Council's wish to give a new order to political life 'for a transitional period'. It was 'sad and disappointing' that this transitional period had come to last a quarter-century, and that the Basic Law's exhortation 'to achieve in free self-determination the unity and freedom of Germany' had not yet been fulfilled. Nonetheless Heinemann, the 'citizens' president', as he liked to be called, also saw cause for pride and joy. The constitution had not remained a mere paper document.

Its values and political order have penetrated our thinking. It is the first German constitution to enjoy the agreement of the vast majority of our people . . . That the Basic Law would strike roots in our consciousness was by no means automatic, for it was not the first time a democracy had been introduced after a lost war and after the example of foreign countries. This, the negative legacy of democracy, is now a thing of the past. When the Basic Law took force twenty five years ago, it was one of the great moments in our history. For the first time, we are offered the chance of realizing a liberal and social democracy under the rule of law.

Heinemann would not have been Heinemann if he had not also mentioned the difference between intentions and reality.

This order is not a plan for salvation, but, like all earthly activity, only the work of imperfect human beings. Moreover, to celebrate it does not mean that we ought to be silent about the gap that yawns between what the constitution says and the actual reality of the constitution. It is in the very nature of a liberal-democratic order not to claim that any particular set of conditions is in harmony with the ideal. Rather, it holds all conditions to be in need of continual improvement. But this means that they are also truly capable of improvement, and thus liberal democracy imposes on us the never-ending duty of persevering in our efforts to bring reality closer to the ideal of the constitution. The mere administration of current reality, without seeking to improve it—this would be the death of all politics. The unity of democracy, the rule of law, and the social state needs continual effort and attention.

By the time of this speech, Willy Brandt's successor had already been in office for a week. Helmut Schmidt was elected the fifth chancellor of the FRG on 16 May 1974 (267 to 225 votes in the Bundestag). He presented his cabinet the next day. Seven out of the fifteen ministers retained their posts. Hans-Dietrich Genscher, the new vice chancellor, left the interior ministry for the foreign office. His successor as interior minister was the legal philosopher Werner Maihofer (FDP), previously a minister for special assignments. Hans-Jochen Vogel (SPD) became minister of justice, leaving the ministry for environmental planning, construction, and urban development to Karl Ravens. The new finance minister was the economist Hans Apel, former parliamentary state secretary in the foreign office (since 1972) and a personal friend of the chancellor's. Hans Matthöfer took over research, Helmut Rohde education, and Kurt Gscheidle transport and the postal service.

All the new faces in the cabinet were Social Democrats. Matthöfer and Gscheidle came from the unions, Rohde from the SPD's 'Working Group for Workers' Questions' (*Arbeitsgemeinschaft für Arbeitnehmerfragen*). Horst Ehmke, Klaus von Dohnanyi, and Egon Bahr, three intellectual 'stars' of the Brandt cabinet, were no longer present. Bahr would soon return as successor to Erhard Eppler, the minister of development, who resigned on 4 July 1974 in protest over the reduction of his budget.

Helmut Schmidt was born on 23 December 1918 in Hamburg. He graduated from secondary school in 1937 and participated in the Second World War, achieving the rank of First Lieutenant and battery commander. He joined the SPD in 1946, finished his education in 1949 with a degree in economics, and was elected to the Bundestag in 1953, where, as a well-informed and trenchant debater, he soon acquired the sobriquet 'Schmidt-Schnauze' ('Schmidt the mouth'). From 1961 to 1965 he was minister of the interior (called *Innensenator*) in Hamburg, in 1967–9 head of the SPD fraction in the Bundestag, in 1969–72 federal minister of defence. Between 1972 and 1974 he was minister of finance (also assuming control of the economics ministry between July and December 1972, after Karl Schiller's resignation). He was a practising Protestant.

The new chancellor's conception of politics was more sober than that of his predecessor. The political visionary was succeeded by a pragmatist and ethicist of social responsibility who oriented his public life on Kant's understanding of duty and Karl Popper's critique of utopian thinking. Whereas Brandt's main sphere of activity had been foreign affairs, Schmidt was profoundly knowledgeable in virtually all aspects of government, especially in economics and finance, but hardly less so in foreign and security policy. As party leader, Brandt had taken 'centrist' positions in an effort to balance the factions; Schmidt, deputy head of the SPD from 1968, was the leading spokesman of the party right. As such, he criticized not only the 'New Left', but also Brandt's attitude toward the 'sixty-eighters', which Schmidt believed to be more accommodating than was good for the party. Accordingly, it required no great leap of imagination to predict that the events of early 1974 were going to exacerbate tensions between the chancellor and the party head. The personalities of the two men, as well as their particular political tasks, were simply too different for it to be otherwise.

The inaugural address Schmidt gave on 17 May 1974 was built on Brandt's of 18 January 1973. The new chancellor deliberately played down his goals, seeking only to give a 'provisional appraisal'. The most important reforms the government would undertake before the end of the legislative period were in tax policy, the child allowance system, worker co-determination, property law, environmental protection, and professional education. As for foreign policy, Schmidt stressed that global balance and west European security depended on the political presence of the United States on the continent.

European–American relations are determined by common security interests. The government, along with its allies, is resolved to continue and to support a policy of arms control and reduction, so as to decrease the risks of political and military pressure. In this connection, it looks upon the Warsaw Pact's increasing armament activities not without anxiety.

This last sentence prompted calls from the Union that the insight 'comes too late'.

For this reason, Schmidt continued, the government also hoped that the American–Soviet negotiations over a limitation of nuclear-strategic weapons systems (the 'Strategic Arms Limitation Talks' or SALT) would be successful. For its part, the Federal German government would continue its efforts on behalf of a mutual balanced force reduction at the MBFR negotiations in Vienna. The Conference on Security and Cooperation in Europe was also important, since it was helping to 'build confidence'. (Having begun talks in July 1973 in

Helsinki, the CSCE was now meeting in Geneva.) While he wished to improve relations with the GDR, Schmidt admonished the East Berlin leadership: 'The treaty partners must both commit to the spirit of the treaties.' The recent 'serious espionage case' was not compatible with this spirit and put considerable strain on relations. The chancellor concluded his speech with a quote from the first president of the FRG, Theodor Heuss: 'Democracy means temporary rule. Within two and a half years, the social–liberal alliance will subject itself to the decision of the citizens. In the meantime, there is much to do.'

Although only sixteen months had passed since Brandt's second inaugural, a great deal more than an interval of time lay between the two addresses. Brandt had sought to give new meaning to the social–liberal coalition. His successor stressed that social–liberal politics continued to be 'the right and necessary thing for our country', but immediately continued: 'In a time of increasing global problems, and with realism and sobriety as our guides, we shall concentrate on what is most important, on what is necessary now, and leave other things aside.' The time of great reforms was at an end, the emotions of new beginnings evaporated. The SPD and FDP were no longer a 'new centre', united in a common philosophy, but a partnership of convenience working towards the solution of pressing problems. The parliamentary opposition was not the least important factor holding them together. As long as it continued to fight the new *Ostpolitik*, the Union would not be a viable partner, for the FDP or for the SPD.

The 'increasing global problems' Schmidt mentioned in his address were primarily economic. The autumn 1973 'oil shock' continued to affect the world economy. In West Germany, decreasing domestic demand in the late summer of 1974 was followed by a sharp decrease in foreign demand. The year 1975 saw the country's worst recession since the Second World War. The gross domestic product fell 1.6 per cent in real terms, and the number of unemployed grew from 580,000 to nearly 1.1 million. Consumer prices increased. If we set the price level in 1976 at 100, the respective numbers for retail prices in the three previous years are 85.7 in 1973, 91.9 in 1974, and 96.9 in 1975.

The global economic crisis was also a structural crisis. West German jobs depended a great deal more on exports than in 1960. At that time, one in seven West German workers was employed within the export economy. Now it was one in five. This meant that there were good reasons to doubt the efficacy of the old Keynesian recipes to stimulate domestic demand. The Schmidt government sought to get at the problem with a combination of economic stimulation and budget consolidation, as well as by following what the political scientist Wolfgang Jäger has called a 'middle way between supply-oriented and demand-oriented economic policy'. An income tax reform (1 August 1974), the main purpose of which was to distribute the tax burden more equitably, helped stimulate demand by reducing taxes by 22 billion marks. A programme of investment promotion followed in 1975, benefiting the construction industry most of all. It was flanked by austerity measures affecting all departments of government. When the economy improved in 1976, the government intensified its consolidation efforts by reducing state borrowing. Despite the improved economy, however, the number of unemployed did not fall below 1 million until 1977, and the unemployment rate sank only slowly: from 4.7 per cent in 1975 to 4.3 per cent in 1978.

In politics, too, there had been fundamental changes in the world situation since the beginning of 1973. The United States and communist North Vietnam signed an armistice agreement in Paris on 27 January 1973. The last American soldiers had left the war-torn South-East Asian country within two months. This pullback, negotiated in a long series of secret talks, was a diplomatic triumph for Henry Kissinger and his boss, President Richard Nixon (who stepped down the next year in order to escape impeachment proceedings in the wake of the 'Watergate' affair; he was the first American president to resign from office). Nonetheless, the end of the Vietnam War was a traumatic experience for the United States, and continued to be so for years to come. The most powerful country in the world had been unable to militarily defeat a small 'Third World' country, and its failure amounted to a political and moral defeat. It was made even more painful by the fact that North Vietnam and the Vietcong violated the armistice and took Saigon in April 1975.

The two communist great powers were the political beneficiaries of the Vietnam War. In October 1971 the People's Republic of China was admitted into the United Nations, taking the place of the 'Republic of China'—that is, Taiwan—as a permanent member of the security council. During Nixon's visit to Beijing in February 1972, the USA and the People's Republic of China put their relations on course to normality (though full diplomatic relations would wait until 1979, owing to continuing disagreement over Taiwan). This meant that the USA now recognized China as a world power. The latter, in exchange, promised restraint in regard to the Vietnam War.

The rapprochement between Washington and Beijing was inconvenient for the Soviet Union. But for Brezhnev to hamper America's efforts towards a ceasefire in Vietnam may have made the situation worse. For the time being, the outcome of the war benefited the Soviets: the capitalist arch-enemy had suffered a loss of face throughout the whole world, above all in Europe. And here, on the old continent, the Soviet Union saw an opportunity to strengthen its military-strategic position. The area it chose was one concerning which there were no agreements or even negotiations with the west: intermediate-range missiles.

The Mutual Balanced Force Reduction negotiations, which covered troop strength and conventional weapons, had been going on in Vienna between the seven states of the Warsaw Pact and twelve NATO members (excluding France and Ireland) ever since October 1973. There were no tangible results so far. The SALT negotiations between the USA and the Soviet Union, seeking a reduction in missile defence systems and a ban on new land-based intercontinental and submarine-launched missiles, had been going on since 1969. The SALT I treaty was signed by Nixon and Brezhnev in May 1972 in Moscow. The Soviet intermediate-range missiles were not the subject of either of the above talks. Since they were aimed at European targets, they naturally caused great concern in western Europe.

Chancellor Schmidt brought the subject up with the Soviet leader for the first time at the end of October 1974, during an official visit to Moscow. He was direct and forceful. He also urged the United States to include the 'Eurostrategic' weapons in the SALT II negotiations, which had commenced in November 1972. As he writes in his book *Menschen und Mächte*,* he received oral confirmation from Nixon's successor, Gerald Ford, in mid-May 1975 when the two men met for a confidential talk during a meeting of the NATO council in Brussels. Nothing was written down, however.

Two and a half months later, the Conference on Security and Cooperation in Europe convened for the last time. The CSCE was, in a certain sense, the culmination of Willy Brandt's *Ostpolitik*. On the one hand the meeting, which brought together thirty-five European and two North American states (the USA and Canada), would have been inconceivable without the eastern treaties. The cooperation of the two Germanies was a precondition for the CSCE, and it was the foreign policy of the social–liberal coalition that made this cooperation possible. On the other hand, the eastern treaties would have remained a fragment if they had not been embedded in a pan-European project. They pointed beyond their own particular purpose. Détente in Europe was only to be realized in and around Germany. In this part of Europe, it could only be secured for the long term if the east and west could agree to place their whole relationship on a new basis.

After two years of negotiations, the final conference of the CSCE met in Helsinki between 30 July and 1 August. Among the participants was Gerald Ford, the American president; Leonid Brezhnev, the Soviet party leader; Valéry Giscard d'Estaing, the president of France; Harold Wilson, the British prime minister; Helmut Schmidt, the chancellor of West Germany; and Erich Honecker, head of the SED central committee. Schmidt took the opportunity to hold numerous bilateral summit talks. He and Honecker agreed that neither side should attempt to test the limits of the Quadripartite Agreement with regard to Berlin. With Eduard Gierek, head of the Polish United Workers' party, he worked out an agreement that was signed in Warsaw by Foreign Minister Genscher in October 1975 and ratified by the Bundestag and Bundesrat in February and March 1976: Poland received 1 billion marks worth of financial credit and a lump payment of 1.3 billion marks for the pension claims of Polish citizens. In return, Poland promised that within four years it would grant 120,000 to 125,000 citizens of German extraction permission to leave the country.

* Schmidt, *People and Powers* (tr. as *Men and Powers: A Political Retrospective*).

The Final Act of Helsinki, the designated purpose of the conference, consisted of three so-called 'baskets'. 'Basket 1' contained a statement of ten principles guiding mutual relations among participating states and a document on confidence-building measures in military matters, including the timely announcement of manoeuvres and the exchange of observers for manoeuvres. 'Basket 2' dealt with cooperation in economic, scientific, technological, and environmental matters. 'Basket 3' contained a statement on questions of security and cooperation in the Mediterranean region and another on cooperation in humanitarian and other areas. Subsequent conferences after 1977 were to investigate whether and to what extent the declarations of intention had been realized.

Both the west and the east, the members of NATO as well as those of the Warsaw Pact, were the winners in Helsinki. The final document emphasized the inviolability of the existing borders and the principle of non-intervention in the internal affairs of the signatories. For the Soviet Union, this meant the west's recognition of its hegemonic status in eastern Europe. The west, however, had successfully lobbied for the inclusion of statements on the right to national self-determination and 'respect for human rights and fundamental freedoms, including freedom of thought, conscience, religion or belief' ('Basket 1'), as well as for language on 'human contacts' and the 'improvement in the circulation of, access to, and the exchange of information' ('Basket 3). This could be construed as implying a kind of right to moral intervention: violations of human rights could now be criticized, and the criticism could not be rejected as interference in the internal affairs of another state. This, at least, was the *western* view, and civil rights activists in the 'socialist states' could now hope that it would have a political effect.

The FRG, too, could now point to this language on human rights in its dealings with the GDR. For its part, the GDR now had a second confirmation of the inviolability of its western border (the first being in the Basic Treaty). But inviolability did not mean inalterability. 'Basket 1' included (at the urging of the FRG) a statement by the signatories that 'their frontiers, in accordance with international law, can be changed by peaceful means and by agreement.' Thus the Final Act did not go beyond the FRG's eastern treaties on the question of border security. In matters of human rights, on the other hand, Helsinki was a great step forward—as long as the west insisted upon the east's declarations of intention and provided that the east was really interested in détente. If these preconditions were fulfilled, the Helsinki conference could go down in history as the final end of the 'Cold War'. If they were not fulfilled, it would simply mean the beginning of a new phase in the conflict.

The meeting in the Finnish capital offered the opportunity not only for numerous east–west talks, but also for meetings among alliance partners. Helmut Schmidt managed to convince the initially hesitant American president of the merits of a world economic summit—initially the idea of the new French president. Schmidt and Giscard d'Estaing had become acquainted when they were both finance ministers, and were now personal friends. When Giscard, a liberal, was elected president of France in May 1974 (Georges Pompidou had died in February), a new era began in German–French relations. Generally, Giscard and Schmidt saw things similarly. The same was true of the first meeting between the heads of state and government of the six leading industrial countries—the USA, Great Britain, France, West Germany, Italy, and Japan—in mid-November 1975 in Château de Rambouillet near Paris.

The result was a statement of commitment to common goals of economic policy: the fight against unemployment and inflation, the creation of strong economic growth, and the maintenance of global free trade. Regardless of what the 'Group of Six' (which became the 'Group of Seven' when Canada joined at the third round in London in May 1977) actually did with their declarations of intention, the world economic summits strengthened the domestic position of the German chancellor, whose economic expertise and political judgement gained the respect of the world. And more: the Schmidt–Giscard 'tandem' soon acquired an international authority that was able to compensate in some degree for the weakness of American leadership in the period after the end of the Vietnam War and the 'Watergate' affair.

Foreign affairs and international economic policy were the areas in which Schmidt was able to demonstrate his abilities most effectively. In most other matters, it became increasingly difficult for the coalition to work out compromises, reach majorities in the Bundesrat, or assert itself against the opposition before the Federal Constitutional Court. The university reform law passed by the Bundestag in December 1975 represented a difficult compromise between the Federation and the *Länder* controlled by the Union. The result of the arduous negotiations was something like the lowest common denominator in the controversies over access to higher education, enrolment limits, curriculum reform, and personnel structure. If, in its decision on a university law in Lower Saxony in May 1973, the Federal Constitutional Court had not prevented the outvoting of the full-time professorate in matters of teaching and research, the federal legislation would most likely either never have come off in the first place, or else emerged from the legislative process as a shell without real legal substance.

The social–liberal coalition suffered a serious defeat in the legal battle over the regulation of abortion. On 26 April 1974, in the fifth law of the criminal code reform, the Bundestag had revised Paragraph 218 of the Criminal Code to allow for the so-called *Fristenlösung*: a woman would not be subject to punishment for terminating pregnancy within three months of conception if she first received counselling. In response to a suit brought by the Union *Länder*, the Federal Constitutional Court rejected this solution as unconstitutional on 25 February 1975 and proposed that the legislature adopt the 'indication model'. One year later, on 12 February 1976, the parliament passed a new version of Paragraph 218 in accordance with this ruling: an abortion would not be subject to punishment only in the case of a medicinal, eugenic, ethical, or social indication. The concept of social or emergency indication was politically controversial from the start. It could be interpreted narrowly or broadly, and it was, with result that in the future, the practice of abortion was handled differently in different parts of the country.

The law on worker co-determination passed by the Bundestag on 18 March 1976 could be seen as a victory for the SPD and FDP. It entered into force on 1 July of the same year. On no other issue had the two parties been so far apart at the beginning of their cooperation. The position of the SPD was clear: workers should have just as many seats as employers on the boards of all industrial enterprises. This meant extending the practice used in the coal and steel community after May 1951 to the other industries. The Free Democrats had fought against equal co-determination for decades. Although their 'Freiburg theses' of October 1971 accepted the principle of parity between owners of capital and workers, they considered employees in management positions as members of the workforce and insisted they receive a third of workers' seats.

The 1976 law contained both the principle of parity between employers and employees *and* the recognition that employees in management represented a special group with the right to their own representation on the company board. On the boards of enterprises with more than 2,000 employees, the 'workers' bench' consisted of wage workers, salaried employees, and employees in management in proportion to their respective shares of the total workforce (they had to have at least one seat). However, this proportional representation only applied to the board seats not controlled by the unions. All workers' representatives, including those proposed by the unions, were elected by the workers (who could choose between direct voting or commissioning a panel of delegates for the purpose). In the case of a tied vote on the company board, the head, who was chosen by the employers, could repeat the ballot and lodge a second vote.

The new law satisfied neither the unions nor the employers. For the unions, it offered less than their goal of full parity. For the employers, it represented an attack on private property and contract autonomy. For these reasons the employers' organizations, along with nine companies, lodged a constitutional complaint against the law with the Karlsruhe court at the end of June 1977. This, in turn, caused the German Trade Union Association to stop participating in the 'Concerted Action' talks. The court handed down its ruling on 1 March 1979: the law was constitutional; it violated neither the guarantee of property, nor freedom of contract, nor freedom of economic activity, nor freedom of coalition. That was the final word on the matter. Worker co-determination, more comprehensively regulated in the FRG than anywhere else in the world, had run the judicial gauntlet. The social–liberal coalition had proceeded from the view that it was possible to balance the principles of the free market with the concern for economic democracy, and this view was confirmed in Karlsruhe.

During the Brandt era, the social–liberal coalition generally found it easy to agree on legal reforms in a narrower sense. Under the second Social Democratic chancellor, however, the main focus was not on the further liberalization of current law, but on defending society against terrorism. On 10 November 1974 Günter von Drenkmann, president of the Supreme Court of Justice, was shot in his Berlin home. A group calling itself the 'Red Army/Build-up Organization' (*Rote Armee/Aufbauorganisation*) declared itself responsible for the deed. On 21 February 1975 the head of the Berlin CDU, Peter Lorenz, was kidnapped by members of the '2 June Movement' (*Bewegung 2. Juni*) and only released after an *ad hoc* crisis committee, led by the chancellor, had acceded to the group's demands: five terrorists were released from various institutions and flown to the People's Republic of Yemen. On 24 April 1975 the 'Holger Meins Commando' occupied the West German embassy in Stockholm and shot two German diplomats, Andreas von Mirbach, a military attaché, and Heinz Hillegaard, an embassy official.

This time Bonn did not give in. An expanded crisis committee (the so-called *Grosser Krisenstab*, consisting of the chancellor, the pertinent federal ministers, the Bundestag party and fraction leaders, and the prime ministers of the *Länder*) rejected the terrorists' demand for the release of twenty-six imprisoned RAF members, including Andreas Baader and Ulrike Meinhof. The terrorists then detonated explosive charges in the embassy. Two members of the band were killed, the rest captured.

Speaking in the Bundestag on 25 April, Helmut Schmidt declared that the government would have failed in its duty 'to protect the lives and liberty of all its citizens' if it had capitulated to the demands of the terrorists and released the 'anarchist bandits'. Their return to the Federal Republic would have spelled the 'end of all security'.

Ulrike Meinhof committed suicide in her prison cell in Stuttgart-Stammheim on 9 May 1976. RAF supporters responded with attacks against German institutions abroad, including buildings of the Goethe Institute. The Bundestag answered this escalation on 24 June 1976 with an Anti-Terror Law. It extended the criminal code and criminal procedure in several areas, allowing for more effective action against terrorist organizations, broadening the investigative authority of the chief federal prosecutor, and increasing the supervision of the interaction between the legal defence and persons arrested under suspicion of forming a criminal organization. The background of the latter measure was that defence attorneys had been acting as messengers between incarcerated terrorists and their underground organizations. From a civil rights perspective, the objections against this kind of supervision were obvious. But there were even more fundamental rights at stake. The state under the rule of law would have jeopardized its authority if it had not proceeded against the aiding and abetting of crime with all due resolve.

The fact that 1976 was an election year also influenced the behaviour of the government. The SPD and FDP could not afford to give the impression that they were less committed than the CDU/CSU to fighting the terrorism from the left. The Union candidate for chancellor was Helmut Kohl, head of the CDU and prime minister of Rhineland-Palatinate. It might have been Franz-Josef Strauss, if *Der Spiegel* had not printed on 10 March 1975 a speech that the CSU head had made to his party in Sonthofen in November 1974. The key statement was that it was simply impossible for the Union 'to create too much in the way of general confrontation'. In Strauss's view, this confrontation strategy meant equating social democracy with socialism and lack of freedom and propagating the notion that Social Democratic policy would lead to Soviet hegemony over western Europe. It was impossible to win over the political centre with this kind of rhetoric. This was the reason that the CDU, acting on its own, chose Kohl as candidate on 12 May 1975. The CSU gave in only reluctantly, publicly announcing that it still considered Strauss the best candidate.

Helmut Kohl was seen as a reformer within his party. Although he had rejected the eastern treaties, he subsequently emphasized that they were now the law of the land. In a special Bundestag session on 25 July 1975, the CDU/CSU, under Kohl's authority, called upon the government to not sign the Final Act of Helsinki, alleging that to do so would make it more difficult for the entire German people to exercise their right to self-determination and serve to reinforce a worldwide delusion concerning the real global security situation. At the same time, Kohl was maintaining contacts—via CDU treasurer Walther Leisler Kiep—with the director of the western affairs department of the SED central committee, Herbert Häber. On 26 June 1975 Häber received a message from Kohl that 'the GDR would be pleasantly surprised at how reasonable the policies of a CDU government would be.'

The CDU's campaign slogan was 'freedom instead of socialism', that of the CSU 'freedom or socialism'. Both variations aimed at confrontation and polarization. Not all CDU politicians were convinced this strategy would work. In Kiep's opinion, the party would 'not succeed in making Schmidt out to be a socialist', as he told Häber on 25 June 1975. 'He is anything but.'

The elections were held on 3 October 1976. The CDU/CSU gained 48.6% of total valid votes, an increase of 2.8% from 1972. With 243 seats, the Union came close to the absolute majority, which was 249 seats. The 42.6% of the SPD represented a loss of 2.3%, the Free Democrats' 7.9% a loss of 0.5%. Together, the SPD and FDP controlled ten more seats than the Union. Since both government parties had based their election campaigns on a renewal of their coalition, it was clear that Helmut Schmidt would once again be chancellor. Both sides, the coalition and the opposition, had made the election into a referendum on the question 'Kohl or Schmidt?' The outcome was close, but unambiguous: the majority of West Germans did not want new leadership.[4]

THE GDR AFTER HELSINKI

The East German political leadership knew from the beginning that the Final Act of Helsinki contained not only opportunities, but also considerable risks. The security ministry spoke of 'intensified forms of class struggle after Helsinki' and called for new tactics against 'critical persons'. These would now, as a rule, be deported and stripped of their citizenship; imprisonment and condemnation would be reserved for very serious or exceptional cases. Deportation and expatriation were to be preceded by 'measures of disintegration' (*Massnahmen der Zersetzung*), the most important of which were described by the MfS in its 'Guideline No. 1/76' of January 1976:

Methodically discrediting the public reputation, esteem and prestige on the basis of true, verifiable and discrediting facts combined with false but plausible information impossible to refute and therefore also discrediting; methodically organizing professional and public failures for the purpose of undermining the self-confidence of individuals; purposefully undermining convictions in connection with particular ideals, models, etc. and creating self-doubt; creating distrust and mutual suspicion within groups, groupings, and organizations.

Among the 'effective means and methods of disintegration' listed were anonymous letters, compromising photographs, and the calculated dissemination of rumours.

By far the most prominent and popular East German to be stripped of his citizenship was the songwriter Wolf Biermann, an outspoken critic of the system and, at the same time, a staunch socialist. In November 1976, with the permission of the state authorities, Biermann left for a concert tour in West Germany. After a televised performance in Cologne, his GDR citizenship was withdrawn, thus preventing his return. This move drew the protests of numerous intellectuals and artists, including the writers Jurek Becker, Volker Braun, Franz Fühmann, Stephan Hermlin, Stefan Heym, Sarah Kirsch, Günter Kunert, Heiner Müller, Rolf Schneider, and Christa Wolf. Several of those who demonstrated solidarity with Biermann were thrown out of the party. Others received warnings, and still others were forced to leave East Germany. One of the latter group was the writer Jürgen Fuchs, a close friend of Biermann.

The SED's political message was obvious: it had no intention of changing the GDR system to fit the Helsinki document. Those who sought to avail themselves of the right to free expression could still expect a harsh reaction from the party and the state. The sanctions were not as brutal as they had been under Stalin, but no less effective. Biermann's expatriation spelled the end of the comparatively relaxed cultural policy Honecker had announced after his election as First Secretary of the SED and then proceeded to introduce. Anyone who had looked forward to a liberalization of 'real existing socialism' after 'Helsinki' were rapidly disabused of their hopes. The opposite happened.

A quarter of a year before Biermann's expulsion, another event in the GDR had led to extremely bad press throughout the rest of the world: on 18 August 1976 Oskar Brüsewitz, an Evangelical minister, burned himself to death in front of St Michael's church in Zeitz. His action was intended as a protest against the repressive communist system, but also against what Brüsewitz considered the church's subjugation to the dictatorship. In July 1971 the Eisenach synod of the Federation of Evangelical Churches in the GDR had come up with the slogan 'The Church: not in addition to, not against, but within socialism'. This expression of ecclesiastic realpolitik was highly controversial within the church itself. It permitted many interpretations and, in practice, amounted to a balancing act between self-assertion and conformism. Brüsewitz's suicide did not change this policy, but it did help the SED eventually realize that a certain amount of autonomy for the church benefited more than harmed the stability of the country. A 'church *within* socialism' was less than a 'church *for* socialism', such as theologians close to the state had been demanding. Nonetheless, it provided an adequate basis for 'peaceful coexistence' between the atheistic party and the Evangelical church.

The SED held its ninth official party congress in May 1976. One of the things it did on this occasion was adopt a new platform to replace the one from 1963. The new language emphasized the general applicability of the Soviet model far more strongly than had been the case in the latter part of Ulbricht's regime. Communism was now the unequivocal 'goal' once more, and the 'developed socialist society' was reduced to 'one of the historical steps along the way to communism'.

Nonetheless the demands of the day, such as they were formulated in the platform, were clearly separated from the party's final goals. The relations with 'capitalist West Germany' were to be 'developed on the basis of the principles of peaceful coexistence and the norms of international law as relations between sovereign states with different societal orders'. As for the 'socialist nation' arising in the GDR, the platform stated that its characteristic features were shaped by the working class. 'The socialist nation is a community of classes and strata tied together in friendship, free of all antagonistic contradictions, and led by the working class and its Marxist-Leninist party.' The SED also announced that it would be working to raise the material and cultural living standard of the population, stressing the 'unity between economic and social policy'. The most important aims were the construction of new housing, a stable supply of consumer goods, and the forty-hour working week.

These promises were more than the party was able to deliver. While the supply of durable consumer goods like automobiles, refrigerators, and televisions had improved markedly under Honecker, the price had been mounting debt to western nations. The rhetoric of 'unity between economic and social policy' concealed the fact that East Germany was living beyond its means. Its trade balance with western countries remained passive. From 1966 to 1970 the negative balance had amounted to 2.2 West German marks; between 1971 and 1975 it grew to almost 13 billion. Employment increased, especially among women, 77.5 per cent of whom were working by the year 1975. But this did little to alter the GDR's productivity compared to its western neighbour. In 1970 East Germany was 32.2 per cent as productive as the FRG. By 1975 the figure was only 33 per cent.

After the ninth party congress, Erich Honecker bore the same title as Ulbricht between 1950 and 1953: the General Secretary of the Central Committee of the SED. On 29 October 1976 (shortly after a Volkskammer election at which 99.86 per cent of the valid votes had gone to the candidates proposed by the National Front), Honecker also assumed the office of the head of the State Council (i.e. president of the GDR), which had gone to Willi Stoph after Ulbricht's death in August 1973. Stoph now went back to his earlier post as head of the government (the Ministers' Council). His predecessor in this office, Horst Sindermann, was elected president of the Volkskammer. Honecker was now the 'first man' of the GDR, even according to international protocol. And since the country he represented now entertained diplomatic relations with almost all the countries in the world, his status meant more than it did when Ulbricht was the First Secretary of the SED and head of the GDR State Council.[5]

THE 'GERMAN AUTUMN' OF 1977

On 19 November 1976, seven weeks after the federal elections, the CSU, meeting in Wildbad Kreuth, made a decision that hit Bonn like a bombshell: in order to help gain an absolute Union majority in 1980, the party would form its own separate fraction in the eighth Bundestag. The calculation of the CSU head, Franz Josef Strauss, was obvious: if the CSU entered the running outside of Bavaria, it would be able to draw the support of conservative voters who considered the CDU too leftist. This was turning an old slogan from the workers' movement on its head. Instead of 'united we are stronger', the new Union motto would now be 'divided we are stronger'.

A few days later, during a meeting of the Bavarian leadership of the Young Union at the Wienerwald restaurant in Munich, Strauss gave his opinion on the leader of the CDU. He considered Helmut Kohl to be completely unfit for the chancellorship.

He is totally incompetent. He lacks the necessary intellectual, political, and character qualities. He is lacking in everything...And you can rest assured about one thing:

Helmut Kohl will never become chancellor. At ninety years of age he will write in his memoirs: 'I was a candidate for the chancellorship for forty years. Lessons and experiences from a painful era.' Maybe the last chapter will be written in Siberia or somewhere.

The 'Wienerwald speech' appeared in *Der Spiegel* on 29 November.

The CDU considered the Kreuth initiative a ludicrous idea. On 22 November it ordered the CSU to see to it that unity was quickly restored, otherwise the CDU would announce the founding of its own regional organization in Bavaria. This threat had the desired effect. The two conservative parties returned to their common fraction on 12 December. The CDU did have to make one concession, however: a commission with an equal number of representatives from each party would work out the Union strategy for the 1980 federal elections.

The interval between the election and the constitution of the eighth German Bundestag was even rockier for the government coalition than for the opposition. The thorniest problem in the coalition negotiations between the SPD and the FDP turned out to be the liquidity gap in the retirement insurance programme. The two delegations finally agreed to a solution, but it violated a campaign promise. It had been announced that retirement pensions would be raised on 1 July 1977, using before-tax wages as a basis of calculation, as before. Because of the finance problems, however, the rise was to be delayed for six months. Medical insurance payments by the pension insurers would also be reduced from 17 to 11 per cent, and pensions would be calculated according to the net wage from 1979 onwards.

Practically the whole country was outraged. The opposition condemned the measures as 'pension fraud', and the liberal press accused the coalition partners of a 'breach of trust' and a 'government botch-up'. Several members of the SPD Bundestag fraction threatened to vote against the coalition agreement. This barrage of criticism forced the government leaders to retreat: as promised, pensions would be raised by 9.9% on 1 July 1977, in accordance with the increase in gross wages; a retiree contribution to health insurance would not be introduced (for the time being), and new retirement pensions would continue to be calculated according to the gross wage—with the intention of switching active retirement accounts from the pre-tax to a post-tax basis after 1 January 1979. (And in fact, the twenty-first retirement pension law of 1 July 1978 set a 4.5% pension increase for the year 1979. In 1981 the retirement contribution would increase by 0.5%. Retirees would have to make a health insurance payment from 1982 onwards, calculated according to their individual income situation.)

The Bundestag elected Helmut Schmidt to his second term as chancellor on 15 December 1976. He received 250 votes, one more than was necessary. Immediately thereafter Walter Arendt, the minister of labour, announced he was leaving the cabinet. In so doing, he made himself into the scapegoat of the retirement debacle. His successor was the SPD delegate Herbert Ehrenberg, like Arendt a union man. Marie Schlei, an SPD delegate and parliamentary state secretary in the chancellor's office since 1974, replaced Egon Bahr as minister of foreign aid; Bahr became managing director of the federal SPD. Antje Huber, a member of the SPD Bundestag fraction since 1969, succeeded Katharina Focke as minister of family affairs. All other posts remained with the incumbents.

Schmidt gave his inaugural address on 16 December. He began by apologizing for the 'retirement issue', which had led to a 'serious disturbance and strained trust in the social–liberal coalition and in the government'. This was followed by what many saw as a lacklustre litany of domestic-political resolutions. The SPD–FDP wanted to tackle a number of projects, correct mistakes in the Anti-Radical Decree, fulfil the FRG's duties as an alliance partner, and make the peace more secure. The government emphasized its commitment to 'liberality, since it is the nucleus of democracy, and solidarity, since it makes justice possible'. There was no mention of new horizons or new challenges. The chancellor was mostly concerned with winning back confidence in his government, and bold visions for the future could easily have been seen as an attempt to evade unpleasant realities.

Considering the events of the previous few years, it was understandable that Schmidt's speech would concentrate primarily on problems of domestic security. One of his main points was that the fight against terrorist violence depended more and more on international cooperation. Two weeks later began what was to go down in the annals of West German history as the 'year of terror'.

On 7 April 1977 the chief federal prosecutor, Siegfried Buback, was murdered in Karlsruhe by members of an 'Ulrike Meinhof Commando–Red Army Fraction'. His chauffeur also died in the attack, and a judicial security guard succumbed to injuries six days later. Speaking at the official ceremony for Buback and the other victims in the Evangelical town church in Karlsruhe on 13 April, Chancellor Schmidt told his audience that the shots fired at the federal prosecutor were also aimed at the rule of law in general.

The murderers want to create a general feeling of powerlessness . . . Ultimately, what they are attempting do is cause the institutions of government to abandon the principles of liberalism and the rule of law. They are hoping that their violence will provoke violence in response, an undifferentiated, uncontrolled, merely emotional violence, which will then allow them to denounce our country as a fascist dictatorship. But these hopes will not be fulfilled, for the liberal society we live in is something only we ourselves can give up. The rule of law is invulnerable as long as it continues to dwell within us. And it does dwell within us, at this very moment, and now more than ever.

The next victim was Jürgen Ponto, head of the board of directors of the Dresdner Bank. He was murdered on 30 July 1977 in the course of an attempted kidnapping at his house in Oberursel near Frankfurt. On 5 September came an attack on Hanns Martin Schleyer, head of the Federal Union of German Employers' Associations and Federal Association of German Industry, in Cologne. Schleyer's driver and all three policemen accompanying him were killed on the spot, while he himself was kidnapped. The next day, a 'Siegfried Hausner Commando RAF' demanded the release of eleven imprisoned terrorists in exchange for Schleyer, 100,000 marks for each of the liberated prisoners, and the immediate calling off of all search operations.

Schleyer's kidnapping marked the beginning of the most serious domestic crisis the FRG had ever experienced. Over the course of the next six weeks, the most important decisions were made by two bodies formed specifically for the purpose: a smaller one (known as the *Kleine Lage**) meeting daily and consisting of the chancellor, the foreign, interior, and justice ministers, the state minister and state secretary of the chancellor's office, the government's press officer, the federal prosecutor, and the head of the federal criminal office; and a 'Large Political Discussion Circle' (*Grosser Politischer Beratungskreis*) meeting once or twice a week and bringing the *Kleine Lage* together with the heads of the Bundestag parties and fractions and the prime ministers of the *Länder* in which terrorists were currently imprisoned.

The chancellor, as he declared on 15 September, was resolved to take the fight against terrorism to the very limit of what the rule of law permitted. In order to gain time and allow covert search operations to work as quickly as possible, the government ordered a news blackout. It was respected by nearly all the media. On 28 September the government introduced a 'contact prevention' bill (*Kontaktsperregesetz*) in the parliament, the purpose of which was to cut off all interaction between imprisoned terrorists as well as with the outside world—including contact with their lawyers. This measure did indeed push the limits of what law would allow. Given the seriousness of the terrorist challenge, however, it was not inappropriate. Rushed through the legislative process, it entered into effect on 2 October and was immediately brought to bear on the terrorists whom Schleyer's kidnappers were seeking to liberate.

Eleven day's later, Bonn's delaying tactics were thwarted by a new act of terror. Four Arab hijackers, calling themselves the 'Martyr Halimeh Commando', seized control of the 'Landshut', a Lufthansa Boeing 737 in flight from Palma de Mallorca to Frankfurt. There were eighty-six passengers and five crew members aboard. The aircraft was redirected to Dubai via Rome and Cyprus, then flown from Dubai to Aden. There, before continuing on to Mogadishu, the capital of Somalia, the hijackers shot the captain, Jürgen Schumann. Their goal was to force the release of the same terrorists whom the 'Siegfried Hausner' band were seeking to liberate, as well as several of their comrades imprisoned in Turkey.

The chancellor and the other German leaders found themselves in a tragic dilemma. They could not permit themselves to give in to the demands of either group. To have done so would have meant surrendering to international terrorism and abandoning the rule of law. The security of West Germany and

---

* [Translator's note: *Lage* simply means 'current situation'; *Kleine Lage* = the 'small' body meeting to deal with the 'current situation'.]

its citizens had to take precedence over the right of Hanns Martin Schleyer and the other hostages to life and freedom from physical harm. It was also clear that the West German government had to make an attempt to free the hostages in Mogadishu, even if this meant certain death for Schleyer. If the attempt failed, Schmidt knew it would mean his resignation.

On 16 October the Federal Constitutional Court rejected the Schleyer family's petition that the government be compelled by interim injunction to meet the terrorists' demands. Shortly after midnight two days later, on 18 October, a special commando of the Federal Border Guard (the 'GSG 9') succeeded in liberating the hostages at the airport of Mogadishu. The state minister of the chancellor's office, Hans-Jürgen Wischnewski, had managed to negotiate permission for the operation from Siad Barre, the president of Somalia. Three of the kidnappers were killed, one—a woman—seriously injured. None of the hostages or members of the commando squad were harmed. Seven minutes after the beginning of the rescue, Wischnewski was able to report to the chancellor by telephone: 'The job is done.'

A few hours after the good news from Mogadishu, a report came from Stuttgart that inmates Andreas Baader, Gudrun Ensslin, and Jan-Carl Raspe had committed suicide in the Stammheim prison, and that another of the terrorists, Irmgard Möller, had suffered critical injuries in the attempt to take her own life. All four of them had sought to create the impression that their deaths were the result of a politically motivated murder. This version was accepted by some members of the extreme left, both inside and outside West Germany. In several European cities outside of Germany, the events of Stuttgart-Stammheim led to anti-German demonstrations as well as to attacks on institutions of the FRG and branches of German companies.

On the evening of 18 October President Walter Scheel gave a television and radio address calling on Schleyer's kidnappers to release their captive and put an end to the 'senseless escalation of violence and death'. The appeal was in vain. The next day, the terrorists responded with the declaration that they had

ended Hanns Martin Schleyer's miserable and corruptive existence after 43 days . . . Andreas, Gudrun, Jan, Irmgard and we are not surprised by the imperialists' fascist dramaturgy for the destruction of the liberation movements. We will never forgive Schmidt and the imperialists supporting him for the blood that has been shed. The struggle has just begun. Freedom through armed anti-imperialist struggle!

Schleyer's body was found late on 19 October where the kidnappers said it would be: in the trunk of a car parked in the Rue Charles Péguy in Mulhouse, Alsace.

Speaking to the Bundestag the next day, the chancellor gave an account of what had transpired since 5 September. The 'act of liberation in Somalia' had given 'an example for the meaning of our fundamental values', he told the assembly. It had also set an example 'for the cooperation among the peoples and nations of the world and for the common fight to overcome the scourge of international terrorism, which despises life and destroys communities.' In describing the role of Somalia and its president Siad Barre, the chancellor used a biblical parable: 'Our black brother was the compassionate Samaritan, rescuing the whites, who had fallen among thieves, out of their misery.'

A passage towards the end of this speech was directed primarily at German youth. There existed no political principle, Schmidt said, that could ethically justify the lapse from humanity into barbarism. Democracy was not simply a matter of creating majorities.

Its ultimate reason for existence lies in the humanization of politics, that is, in the humanization of the unavoidable exercise of power. By tracing its origin to the dignity of the human being and forbidding not only the state, but also the individual from dealing arbitrarily with human life and dignity, the democratic constitution places limits on the actions of all of us.

These words were applauded by all the fractions in the parliament.

The chancellor's final words were very personal in tone. They were concerned with the responsibility of one who had to make decisions for and about other people.

Anyone who knows that, one way or another, despite his best efforts, he is going to be burdened with failure and culpability regardless of what he does—such a person will not try to claim that he did everything he could, and everything was correct. He will not try to shift guilt and failure onto other people. For he knows that these others are caught up in the same inevitable dilemma. But he will be able to say that we decided to do this thing and that thing, and we decided not to do these other things, for this or that reason. We must take responsibility for all these things . . . We will stand up to this responsibility in the future as well. May God help us!

In the memory of the extra-parliamentary left, the 'German autumn' of 1977 lived on as the climax of a collective hysteria suspecting everyone on the 'left' of sympathizing with terrorism. Such suspicions did indeed exist, above all on the part of the CSU head, Franz Josef Strauss, and conservative CDU politicians like Karl Carstens—suspicions directed at writers like Heinrich Böll and Günter Grass, leftist theologians like Helmut Gollwitzer, and even Social Democrats like Willy Brandt and Helmut Schmidt himself. But there were indeed sympathizers on the left, people who approved of the motives of the terrorists, if not of their actions. After the murder of Siegfried Buback, a student in Göttingen, writing under the name 'Mescalero', distributed a pamphlet in which he declared his 'secret delight' at the deed. He was not only speaking for himself, but also for no small number of up and coming academics in his generation.

The extra-parliamentary left was right to warn about increasing political intolerance and the danger of *ad hoc* legislation against terrorism leading to a permanent curtailment of the rule of law. Of course, such criticism would have been more persuasive if it had been accompanied by a degree of self-critique. The extra-parliamentary left had every reason to enquire into its own role in creating an intellectual climate in which accusations of fascism against the government could thrive. But this kind of self-scrutiny did not take place, not even after the autumn of 1977.

Instead, the extreme left persisted in its undifferentiated mistrust of the 'system', which it even believed capable of murdering the inmates at Stammheim. This sentiment was accompanied by a view rationalizing the terror of the RAF and its successors in terms of the continuing legacy of the Nazi past. The Schleyer case was 'understandable' in this light, too: West Germany's most important industrial official had once been a member of the SS and had played an important role in the economic exploitation of the Protectorate of Bohemia and Moravia. On the other hand, however, Schleyer's murder did much to permanently discredit violent brands of 'anti-fascism'. While the autumn of 1977 did not mark the end of leftist terrorism, it was its apogee. The terrorists' plan—to provoke the state into responding with 'fascist' counter-measures, thus injecting new energy into the struggle against the ruling 'late capitalist' system—had not come to fruition. The autumn 1977 crisis left a weakened leftist fundamental opposition in its wake and a West German democracy with new self-confidence after its triumph against terrorist violence.[6]

CONFLICTS ON THE LEFT: NUCLEAR ENERGY AND THE NATO DOUBLE-TRACK DECISION

The chancellor had to deal with an empty cabinet post during the crisis provoked by Hanns Martin Schleyer's kidnapping. Hans Friderichs had stepped down as economics minister on 7 October in order to replace the murdered Jürgen Ponto as board spokesman for the Dresdner Bank. The new economics minister was the FDP delegate Otto Graf Lambsdorff (who was also party treasurer in North Rhine-Westphalia between 1968 and 1978). Four months later, on 2 February 1978, there was another resignation from the Schmidt government: Georg Leber (SPD) stepped down from his post as defence minister, thus taking responsibility for illegal wire-tapping operations by the Military Counter-Espionage Service and failures in connection with an espionage case.

The day after Leber's resignation, Schmidt announced that he would reshuffle the whole cabinet. The changes were announced on 16 February. Finance Minister Hans Apel became the new minister of defence; Schmidt gave his old post to Hans Matthöfer, who turned over the ministry of research and technology to his parliamentary state secretary, the delegate Volker Hauff. Hauff, born in 1940, was one of four younger SPD delegates Schmidt brought into the cabinet: Jürgen Schmude, born in 1936, replaced Helmut Rohde as minister of education; Dieter Haack, born in 1934, succeeded Karl Ravens as minister of construction; Rainer Offergeld, born in 1937, took over the ministry of foreign aid from Marie

Schlei. The rejuvenation of the cabinet, coming just a few months before the middle of the legislative session, was intended to demonstrate leadership strength and dynamism and thus pre-empt any impression of a government crisis.

The very same day the new ministers gave their oaths of office, however, the Schmidt government barely managed to avoid a serious defeat. With 245 to 244 votes, the narrowest possible majority, the parliament passed an anti-terror law containing criminal prosecution measures dealing with domestic security: mandatory glass barriers to isolate imprisoned violent terrorists; an easing of restrictions on building searches; provisions for the setting up of checkpoints and for the identification of persons, and other measures. The opposition voted against the bill because it did not go far enough for them. Four leftist delegates rejected it because they thought it went too far. It was clear that further legislation of this kind was going to spell trouble for the coalition.

Another problem for inner security in the second half of the 1970s was the public resistance to nuclear energy. At the beginning of October 1973, the Brandt government had stated the necessity of building almost 100 new large power plants; nuclear power was to account for about half of the additional capacity. Then, after the oil crisis began shortly thereafter, atomic power came to be seen more than ever as the energy source of the future, at least by the political and business leaders of West Germany. But what seemed a necessity to the elites filled a large number of people with a virtually apocalyptic fear. The building of a nuclear power plant at Wyhl in Baden provoked violent uprisings in 1975. The situation was even worse in November 1976 at Brokdorf in Schleswig-Holstein, where armed and masked communist groups participated in the demonstrations. The Hamburg newspaper *Die Zeit* spoke of 'civil war in the Wilst marsh'. In spring 1980, a public challenge was begun near Gorleben in the Wendland of Lower Saxony, where deep drilling was supposed to test the possibilities of permanent nuclear waste disposal.

The widespread public protest against nuclear energy was an expression of the increasing scepticism with regard to the controllability of technological progress and increasing concern about the preservation of the natural environment. In 1972 the 'Club of Rome', a loose association of scholars, politicians, and economic leaders, presented a report, 'The Limits of Growth'. This was a dismal prognosis of what would happen if world population, the pollution of the environment, the production of foodstuffs, and the exploitation of natural resources were to continue increasing at the current rates. In the wake of this report, fear of humanity's gradual self-destruction spread in all industrial nations, but it was probably nowhere as strong as in West Germany. The FRG became the country with the strongest environmental movement. At the same time, the support or rejection of atomic energy turned into a question of faith for a great number of its citizens.

The conflict also began to split the two government parties in late 1976, beginning with the 'battle of Brokdorf'. In the SPD, advocates of the peaceful use of nuclear energy, including the chancellor, were opposed by a group of staunch critics. The most prominent of these was Erhard Eppler, former minister of foreign aid, whose popular 1975 book with the deliberately dramatic title *Ende oder Wende. Von der Machbarkeit des Notwendigen** took up where the 'Club of Rome' had left off. At the SPD's Hamburg congress in November 1977 Schmidt was able to work out a compromise that left the options open both for the development of nuclear energy and for its eventual phasing out. (Coal was given basic priority, however.) But this agreement simply postponed the conflict. One year later, on 14 December 1978, a group of six anti-nuclear liberals was planning to vote against a motion recommending that the government of North Rhine-Westphalia continue construction of a 'fast-breeder' reactor in Kalkar. It took Foreign Minister Genscher's threat of resignation and Schmidt's threat of a vote of confidence motion before the delegates would change their minds.

The question of nuclear power was nothing less than existential for the Social Democrats, closely tied to their future as a large popular party. A total rejection of the technology would have caused great conflict with the unions at the end of the 1970s. Unconditional backing for it would have cut off the possibility of gaining the support of the anti-nuclear movement, driven primarily by the younger generation. The party head, Willy Brandt, tended more in Eppler's than in Schmidt's direction in this conflict. Already in September 1977 he was warning the SPD executive about the risk of the anti-nuclear movement founding its own 'green' party. His advice: the SPD should 'become a green party itself, to some extent'.

For Helmut Schmidt, the idea of 'integrating' even a part of the ecological fundamentalists into the SPD was ridiculous and dangerous. Concessions to the 'green' view of politics, which he felt to be profoundly irrational, would, he believed, undermine Social Democratic credibility both in West Germany and abroad. On 17 December 1978 OPEC, the Organization of Petroleum Exporting Countries, raised the price of oil for the coming year by an average of 10 per cent. The resulting oil shock, the second since 1973, was seen both inside and outside the SPD as an argument against the abandonment of nuclear energy. This helped the chancellor and those who thought like him. But Schmidt, as well as the party as a whole, paid a price for prevailing over Eppler. In January 1980 the 'Greens', meeting in Karlsruhe, established their party on the federal level. While the Green party (*Grüne Partei*) would draw support from the disgruntled constituents of all the 'established' parties, it was the SPD that would come to feel their competition most acutely of all.

The Greens were a motley crew at first, their membership ranging from the far left to the far right. They included former activists from the 'K groups', led by Thomas Ebermann in Hamburg; Rudi Dutschke, hero of the Berlin student revolt; Joschka Fischer, leader of the Frankfurt alternative scene (the

---

* Eppler, *Destruction or Change: The Imperatives and their Feasibility.*

so-called *Spontis*); the former CDU Bundestag delegate Herbert Gruhl, author of the 1975 best-seller *Ein Planet wird geplündert** and head of the Federation for the Environment and Conservation (*Bund für Umwelt und Naturschutz*) for several years; Baldur Springmann, a conservative 'organic farmer' from Schleswig-Holstein; and the Bavarian August Haussleiter, founding member of the CSU in 1946 and in 1950 of the right-wing 'German Community' (*Deutsche Gemeinschaft*), which he united with the Action Community of Independent Germans in 1965 (*Aktionsgemeinschaft Unabhängiger Deutscher*), a group that oscillated between left and right.

The Greens met in Saarbrücken in March 1980 to hammer out a party platform. While the left did not yet have a majority, they were more united than the conservatives and agitated more successfully for their point of view. The agreement on four basic party principles, 'ecological, social, grass-roots democratic, and non-violent', was a compromise that proved advantageous for the left. 'Grass-roots democracy' meant the rotation of party positions, separation between party and delegate offices, and a system approaching the 'imperative mandate', that is, guidance and control of the parliamentary delegates by the active party members. The principle of non-violence did not exclude the use of 'violence against things' and calculated violations of the law. Once the eco-pacifist left had secured its dominance, the Greens were a party that sought a fundamental reform of the 'system' in the tradition of 1968. It had massive reservations about representative democracy and the state monopoly of force. It also believed in the abolition of the Warsaw Pact and NATO and in a 'social defence' using non-military means.

The Extra-Parliamentary Opposition had been anti-capitalist in outlook. Many Greens went further and considered industrial society as a whole to be a 'historical error of humankind', as Richard Löwenthal, the SPD theoretician, observed critically at the end of 1981. The Green party collected minorities who felt that the two great popular parties of the centre no longer had anything to say to them. It appealed particularly to young academics, many of whom had been attracted to the SPD by the reform emotionalism of Willy Brandt but then alienated by the sober pragmatism of Helmut Schmidt. The Greens did much to sharpen the environmental consciousness of the 'established' parties. They forced the risks of nuclear power to be taken seriously, at least in the SPD. They promoted equal rights for women as well as tolerance for same-sex relationships and other 'alternative' lifestyles. Nonetheless, as long as they saw themselves as a fundamentalist opposition to the 'system', rejecting significant aspects of the rule of law and the FRG's western alliances, and as the avant-garde of the peace movement, demanding unilateral disarmament of the west and the abolition of all armed forces, it was out of the question for Social Democrats to consider them a partner at any level, much less a coalition partner at the federal level.

---

* Gruhl, *The Plundering of a Planet.*

The SPD thought of itself as a party of peace, but not as a pacifist party. It actively supported the Atlantic alliance. In an October 1976 interview with *Der Spiegel*, Chancellor Schmidt explained his and his party's position in the following words: 'The preservation of the military balance of power in Europe is an existential requirement for our democratic order. That sounds like a headline, but it's deadly serious.' As long as the Social Democratic party stood behind Schmidt and remained committed to the west, it was going to be impossible for it to integrate ecological pacifism politically.

Not that the leader of the western world was making it very easy for the SPD to stick to its commitment. The United States had a new president at the beginning of 1977: Jimmy Carter, a Democrat and former governor of the southern state of Georgia. The relationship between Schmidt and Carter was tense from the start. The latter had little experience in foreign policy. Under the influence of Zbigniew Brzezinski, his national security adviser, he pursued a public campaign for human rights that Schmidt considered naïve and dangerous. On 12 July 1977, immediately before the German chancellor was scheduled to visit the United States, Carter declared at a press conference that he had approved funding for the construction of a neutron bomb. He would make a final decision on the matter when the Department of Defense had investigated its impact on the arms control efforts.

The radiation released by a neutron bomb destroyed human life in a wide radius while leaving buildings largely intact. In a polemical article in *Vorwärts*, Egon Bahr, the managing director of the federal SPD, called the new weapon a 'symbol of the perversion of thought'. The chancellor, on the other hand, wanted to use it as a tactical tool in the disarmament negotiations. But he also considered Bahr's article in the Social Democratic weekly embarrassing for another reason: it could easily create anti-American sentiment and damage the government's foreign policy.

Schmidt set out his own position on matters of weapons and disarmament on 28 October in a speech at the London Institute for Strategic Studies. He cautioned against a reduction in the strategic arms of the two superpowers *without* a simultaneous reduction of the disparities in Europe. The security of the USA's European partners would be compromised, he said, if nothing were done to address the Soviet superiority in the areas of conventional and tactical nuclear weapons. Unilateral reductions were not acceptable to any partner. The chancellor preferred mutual reductions to NATO's deployment of new weapons, but considered the latter unavoidable if no agreement could be reached about reducing total arsenal strengths in the east and west. 'The alliance must be prepared to make sufficient and appropriate means available for the current strategy and to pre-empt all developments that might undermine our strategy, which continues to be correct.'

Schmidt's London speech seemed to have the effect he had been unable to achieve in his talks with Carter: a process of rethinking began in Washington. At the end of November 1977 the American president proposed that once the USA had made the decision to build the neutron bomb, the western European allies agree not to deploy it only if the Soviet Union were prepared to give up deploying the 'Eurostrategic' SS-20 missiles. Schmidt had a hard time convincing the SPD Bundestag fraction to support this idea, but he finally received enough backing to assent to Carter's proposal in February 1978.

But his efforts were in vain, since Carter changed his mind again. At a press conference on 7 April he announced that he had decided to postpone the decision on the production of the neutron bomb indefinitely. Once again, the western response to the Soviet medium-range missiles was completely up in the air. Carter was not willing to include them in the SALT II negotiations; the verbal promise Ford had made to Schmidt in May 1975 was not binding on his successor. The production of the SS-20 could therefore continue unhindered—which did not stop Brezhnev from claiming, during a visit to West Germany in May 1978, that western Europe had absolutely nothing to fear from the Soviet Union.

Then, in autumn 1978, the chancellor's warning finally produced the desired effect: Carter proposed a western four-power conference to discuss matters of foreign and security policy. It took place on 5–6 January on the island of Guadeloupe in the French Antilles. The participants were President Carter, President Giscard d'Estaing, Prime Minister Callaghan, and Chancellor Schmidt, the only representative of a state without nuclear weapons, but now recognized as one of the western 'Big Four'.

Carter first suggested the unilateral deployment of American medium-range missiles in western Europe. Callaghan proposed making deployment dependent on the outcome of negotiations with the Soviets. Giscard wanted a time limit on the negotiations. If they ended up leading nowhere, Schmidt wanted the American systems deployed not only in the FRG, since otherwise the Soviet propaganda would be directed entirely at his country. Carter accepted all these strictures. As Schmidt would later write, the Guadeloupe conference was the 'birth of the later so-called double-track decision'.

Schmidt warned his interlocutors that the 'double-track' decision would not be greeted with unanimous approval, whether in Europe as a whole or in his own party. That was an understatement. In an article in the Social Democratic journal *Die Neue Gesellschaft* in February 1979, Herbert Wehner, head of the SPD Bundestag fraction, wrote that it was not in accordance with the 'real situation of the FRG to argue for using the putative necessity of additional weapons systems and thereby to run the risk of having such additional weapons deployed in the Federal Republic instead of throwing the weight of the alliance behind arms limitation and arms reduction.' Later that same month, Wehner stated that the Soviet arms were 'defensive, not aggression'.

Schmidt invited the Social Democratic party leaders to a discussion at the chancellor's office on 19 May 1979. Wehner spoke little at this meeting, as did Brandt, who, according to Horst Ehmke, said concerning medium-range missiles that he 'understood little of the subject and that Helmut Schmidt was the expert'. Egon Bahr, for his part, announced that 'he would have nothing to do with the modernization [of the American missiles]. That would mean an end to the *Ostpolitik*, without which we cannot win the next elections.' Ultimately, however, the interlocutors did agree to the possibility of deploying the new systems—under the condition that negotiations should have absolute priority.

Bahr's disagreement with the chancellor's position was a result of the long-term goal he had been pursuing ever since the days of the Grand Coalition: the creation of a European security system to replace both NATO and the Warsaw Pact. Brandt and Wehner, as different as they were, both agreed with Bahr on at least one point: they considered the *Ostpolitik* and the German–German relationship more important than the FRG's alliance obligations. This rift in the SPD's security policy for West Germany—between the chancellor and his defence minister, Hans Apel, on the one hand, and the party majority, represented by Brandt, Wehner, and Bahr, on the other—could no longer be ignored after the Guadeloupe summit. The division could be downplayed as long as there was hope that negotiations would be successful (the optimal solution being the so-called *Nullösung* or 'double zero option', namely, that both sides would give up deploying medium-range missiles). If they failed, however, the conflict would emerge openly.

By the time of this meeting in the chancellor's office, the federal elections Bahr was referring to were no longer very far away. There was some reason to think that the Free Democrats were not as committed to the social–liberal coalition as they had been in 1976. This was revealed during the presidential election, which took place later in May 1979. Since the CDU/CSU controlled an absolute majority in the Bundesversammlung and since the incumbent, Walter Scheel, did not plan on running again, everything pointed to the election of a Union candidate. The strongest fraction presented Karl Carstens (president of the Bundestag since 1976) on 5 March. The FDP did not wish to support either the conservative Carstens or the token candidate the SPD was planning on running. On 23 May 1979, the thirtieth anniversary of the Basic Law, Carstens was elected fifth president of the FRG in the first ballot, receiving 528 votes against 431 for the SPD candidate, Annemarie Renger. The FDP electors all abstained, which, as Wolfgang Jäger put it, 'could only be interpreted as an attempt on the part of the FDP to distance itself from the alliance with the Social Democrats'.

In fact, an actual break in the coalition was less likely in the summer of 1979 than it had been two years before, when the two parties had clashed so strongly on economic and tax policy matters. Once they had turned away from budget consolidation in September 1977 and opted to stimulate demand by increasing state debt, economic policy ceased to have a polarizing effect. In internal affairs, Gerhart Rudolf Baum of the FDP demonstrated a clear left-liberal orientation that was also received well in the SPD. (Baum's predecessor in the ministry of the interior, Werner Maihofer, had resigned in the wake of belatedly discovered failures connected with the Schleyer kidnapping case.) In foreign and security policy, finally, Hans Dietrich Genscher was a dependable partner for the Social Democratic chancellor and defence minister.

This was also true of the missile question, which was much less controversial among Free than among Social Democrats. On 13 August 1979, the eighteenth anniversary of the building of the Berlin wall, the FDP executive produced its own sophisticated 'double-track' plan. It embraced the deployment of American medium-range missiles, the 'Pershing II' and 'cruise missiles', while at the same time offering to negotiate the phasing-out or complete elimination of medium-range nuclear missiles (the 'double zero option'). The party's Bundestag fraction soon adopted this position.

The Social Democrats did not come out with their decision until several months later. On 6 December the federal party congress in Berlin adopted a security policy motion from the executive allowing new medium-range missiles under the condition that they not be deployed if disarmament talks led to satisfying results. The goal of the negotiations was 'to render superfluous the deployment of additional medium-range weapons in western Europe by reducing those of the Soviet Union and agreeing to common limits in both eastern and western Europe as a whole'.

There was a clear majority behind this position. After all, it emphasized negotiations and declared their goal to be the double zero option. But perhaps the most important reason for Helmut Schmidt's tactical victory was the fact that, by this time, it had been clear for five months who he would be defending his office against in the coming year's elections. On 2 July 1979 the CDU/CSU Bundestag fraction chose Franz Josef Strauss, prime minister of the Free State of Bavaria since November 1978, as its common candidate for the chancellorship. Even Schmidt's critics within the SPD had no desire to harm his re-election chances—much less force him to step down—by causing him major problems at the party congress. If the executive's motion had been denied, or if a competing one calling for the rejection of all medium-range missiles in Europe had been accepted (a motion defended by Gerhard Schröder, head of the Young Socialists), the result would have been Schmidt's resignation. The result of the ballot was thus hardly a surprise.

On 12 December 1979, five days after the end of the SPD congress, the foreign and defence ministers of the fourteen members of the NATO military structure met for a special conference in Brussels in order to officially adopt the 'double-track' decision. In terms of armaments, it would replace the technically obsolete Pershing Ia with 108 Pershing II missiles and 464 ground-stationed cruise missiles. At the same time, the United States would remove 1,000 nuclear warheads from Europe. Initially the new systems would be deployed only in three countries: West Germany, Great Britain, and Italy. Belgium and the Netherlands would make their decisions later. In terms of negotiations, the NATO countries supported the USA's plan of starting talks with the Soviet Union on the limitation of Eurostrategic weapons as soon as possible.

The double-track decision was designed as a lever, using arms control efforts to achieve 'a more stable overall nuclear balance at lower levels of nuclear weapons on both sides'. A 'Special Consultative Group', which included the FRG, was formed for the purpose of protecting European interests. By working closely with the United States, it would be able to exert indirect but continuous influence on the negotiations between Washington and Moscow. The time limit NATO set for negotiations was the year the new American weapons were supposed to be ready: 1983.

Thus the west responded to the Soviet challenge by announcing what its response would be if its rival continued to be inflexible in the matter of medium-range missiles. The double-track controversy did not come to an end with the Brussels conference. It was only just beginning. It was already clear by mid-December 1979 that the struggle to restore the disrupted European balance of power would go far beyond matters military. Ultimately the Soviets were using their missiles to put massive *political* pressure on western Europe. West Germany was especially exposed to such pressure, not only for geographic reasons, but also because Germany was divided and because the two German states belonged to different alliance systems.[7]

THE END OF DÉTENTE? THE INVASION
OF AFGHANISTAN AND THE CRISIS IN POLAND

The USSR invaded Afghanistan just after Christmas 1979, two weeks after the NATO meeting in Brussels. The south-central Asian country had lapsed into civil war after a communist *coup d'état* the previous year. The main reason for the invasion, which rapidly brought about a regime change in Kabul, was to stem the tide of militant Islamism that had been on the rise since the Iranian revolution in spring 1979. Moscow feared the consequences of this movement in the central Asian Soviet republics. By controlling Afghanistan, it would also be brought closer to the Persian Gulf, the oil-rich region upon which the industrial nations of the west depended so heavily.

In Washington's view, the invasion in the Hindu Kush meant the end of détente. Carter's first reaction was to recall the American ambassador to Moscow. On 3 January 1980 he asked the Senate to postpone the ratification debate over the SALT II treaty, which he and Leonid Brezhnev had signed in Vienna on 18 June 1979. Later that same day the Soviet chargé d'affaires in Washington informed the State Department that his government rejected the American offer of negotiations on the Eurostrategic weapons. Three days later Carter declared a limited economic embargo against the Soviet Union, drastically curtailing grain shipments and stopping the export of high technology. Other sanctions would be forthcoming. On 23 January the president, addressing Congress, promulgated what became known as the 'Carter doctrine': any attempt by an outside force to gain control of the Persian Gulf region would be regarded as an assault on the vital interests of the United States and would be repelled by any means necessary, including military force.

In addition to causing a serious crisis in east–west affairs, the Soviet intervention in Afghanistan put pressure on the relations between the USA and its most important allies on the Continent. The White House considered détente an indivisible quantity; Paris and Bonn, on the other hand, wished to pursue further dialogue in Europe even if the two superpowers came into sharp conflict in other pats of the world. In a common statement on 5 February 1980, Valéry Giscard d'Estaing and Helmut Schmidt declared that détente would 'not be able to stand another blow of this kind'—which implied that they still considered the situation salvageable, despite the events in Afghanistan. Carter himself, along with his security adviser, Brzezinski, felt it necessary to 'punish' the Soviets. On 20 March 1980 the German chancellor reminded the American secretary of state, Cyrus Vance, 'that there were 16 million Germans under Soviet control in the GDR, as well as 2 million in West Berlin. Whoever talks about punishing the Soviet Union must know that it is fairly easy for the Soviets to punish the Germans in return.'

West Germany cooperated with one of the American sanctions with great reluctance: the boycott of the upcoming Olympic summer games in Moscow, which the United States declared without any prior consultation with its allies. The FRG's National Olympic Committee joined the boycott on 15 May 1980. But this did not do much to improve Schmidt's relationship with the American president. After heated exchanges with Carter, Schmidt publicly criticized American foreign policy in a speech in New York on 6 March. In a letter of 12 June, Carter reprimanded the chancellor for a proposal the latter had made on 11 April at a conference of the Hamburg SPD: namely, that the east and west postpone deployment of medium-range missiles for a certain number of years and use the time for negotiations. Carter's letter immediately found its way into print, which Schmidt correctly interpreted as a deliberate attempt to embarrass him. On the eve of the sixth world economic summit, which was meeting in Venice on 12–13 June 1980, Schmidt reacted with great vehemence to Carter's and Brzezinski's doubts about his commitment to the western alliance. The American president felt compelled to publicly assure the chancellor of his trust and stress their mutual understanding on the missile policy.

Then, at the end of June, Schmidt left for a long-planned trip to Moscow. He not only had the blessing of the United States, but also an informal mandate from the most important western nations to see if the Soviet leadership was prepared to start unconditional negotiations on Eurostrategic weapons. Schmidt now achieved what his talks with the Soviets the previous year (in June with

Kosygin and Gromyko in Moscow, in November with Gromyko in Bonn) had failed to bring about. After consultation with other members of the politburo, Brezhnev (after 1977 also head of the executive of the Supreme Soviet and thus the head of state) agreed to bilateral talks with the USA regarding a limitation of Soviet medium-range missiles and the nuclear 'Forward Based Systems' of the United States. He even agreed to hold the talks before the SALT II treaty was ratified and before the comprehensive SALT III negotiations over all longer-range tactical atomic weapons got under way.

The steadfastness of the west, above all of Helmut Schmidt, had finally paid off. On 3 July Carter expressed his 'respect and admiration' for the German chancellor—praise the latter found very useful during the 1980 election campaign. But Schmidt's diplomatic coup did not yet mean a real substantive breakthrough. On 17 October American and Soviet delegations met in Geneva to discuss a reduction of their European medium-range missiles. However, after Carter was defeated by Ronald Reagan, a conservative Republican, in the presidential elections on 4 November 1980, the talks were broken off (17 November). It would be more than a year (30 November 1981) before the two superpowers returned to the negotiating table.

If things had gone his way, Schmidt would have visited another Warsaw Pact state before the West German elections: the GDR itself. A summit meeting with Erich Honecker had long been planned for the end of August 1980. But the chancellor cancelled shortly before it took place, on 22 August. The reason was a political strike in Poland, which Bonn felt could easily get out of control and cause a serious international crisis. A Soviet intervention in Poland would have been that 'other blow' that, according to Giscard's and Schmidt's declaration after the Afghanistan invasion, would have put an end to détente.

The Polish strike was catalysed by price increases on certain kinds of meat and sausage on 1 July. The movement's centre was a strike committee organized at the Lenin Shipyard under Lech Walesa, which grew to include other branches of industry within a few days. On 18 August this committee handed the *wojewod* of Gdańsk a list of twenty-one demands, the most important of which were the right to set up trade unions independent of the party and state-run businesses, the right to strike, freedom of expression, and freedom of the press. On 20 August sixty-four prominent Polish intellectuals (including the Catholic publicist Tadeusz Mazowiecki and the historians Bronislaw Geremek and Wladyslaw Bartoszewski) demanded that the government accept the Gdańsk committee as a partner in negotiations.

In the days that followed, strikes and factory takeovers spread from the Baltic coast throughout the whole country. After a period of indecision, the government agreed to negotiate, and made decisive concessions on 31 August in Gdańsk: it allowed the founding of 'new, self-governing unions . . . which are authentic representatives of the working class'; it promised to restrict censorship and allow freedom of expression, pluralism in the media, and the release of opposition intellectuals arrested on 20 August and afterward. This was a breakthrough. On 17 September the Independent Trade Union 'Solidarity' (*Solidarnooć*) was founded in Gdańsk at a meeting of workers' representatives from all of Poland. The leader was Lech Walesa. The new union was officially registered on 24 October 1980.

A non-party union in a communist state was a contradiction in terms. Lenin had seen the unions in purely instrumental terms, as 'transmission belts' between the party and the working masses. The twenty-one Gdańsk demands of 18 August 1980 were thus nothing less than a declaration of war against the 'democratic centralism' that communist parties had been compelled to observe ever since 6 August 1920, when the Comintern had set twenty-one conditions for a party's acceptance into the Communist International. The Comintern itself had been formally dissolved in May 1943, but the doctrine of 'democratic centralism' persisted, and with it the dogma of party control of the unions. Consequently, the events in Poland in summer 1980 were revolutionary—or, as orthodox Marxist-Leninists saw things, counter-revolutionary—in character.

This split in the power structure could not last very long. Sooner or later the contradiction between the liberal nature of the new trade union and the dictatorial nature of the government would provoke a showdown. How the Soviets would react was unclear throughout 1980. But what was very clear, even at that time, was one of the deeper causes of the Polish struggle for freedom: John Paul II, the new Polish pope in Rome. The elevation of Karol Wojtyla, the cardinal of Cracow, to the papacy in October 1978 gave the Polish workers a new self-confidence in their confrontation with the state and the party.

When John Paul II returned to his homeland for the first time in June 1979, he mobilized the masses to a degree that put the fear of God into the regime. This was not the first 'papal revolution' to challenge the secular authorities. Nine centuries before, Gregory VII's bull *Dictatus Papae* (1075) had claimed the power to depose princes. John Paul II did not go this far. But he showed the ruling Communists very clearly that he had more support in Poland—still a very Catholic country—than they did. Within the Catholic Church itself, the second papal revolution in history was a conservative revolution. Politically, however, it was a force for liberalization, and it played a crucial role in undermining and eventually bringing down the communist system.

In cancelling his meeting with Honecker on 22 August, Helmut Schmidt showed consideration for the FRG's allies; a demonstration of German–German détente at the height of the Polish crisis would not have gone over well in the west. But he will also have been aware that his visit might have had an unintended effect: the spread of the Polish unrest to the GDR. Furthermore, it could easily have ended in a failure or a debacle. If the Warsaw Pact states intervened in Poland, he would have been forced to leave the GDR immediately, which would in turn have been disastrous for the government's *Ostpolitik*, its German–German policy, and above all for the Germans living in the GDR. Cancelling the meeting was a political setback, but it was less serious in comparison.

Finally, Schmidt's political reputation would have suffered if the meeting with Honecker had had a negative outcome. The most important thing before the elections was to preserve as much of his 'chancellor bonus' as possible. It was already quite significant. Schmidt was widely considered the most effective crisis manager among all the western leaders. He was one of the most dominant figures at the world economic summits, if not the most dominant. Together with his friend Giscard d'Estaing, he had considerably advanced the cause of European unity. The European Monetary System (adopted in 1978) and the European Currency Unit, the 'ECU', had entered into effect in March 1979. The first direct elections to the European Parliament had taken place in June of the same year. Schmidt had dealt with the American president with the same self-assurance that characterized his relationship with the general secretary of the Soviet Communist party. And many people believed that it was due to him that the West German economy seemed able to handle the second wave of oil price increases of 1978–80 relatively well.

The Social Democratic chancellor was much more popular than his party. Many of its members disagreed with his inflexible attitude with regard to the military balance of power. But compared with the CDU/CSU candidate, Franz Josef Strauss, Schmidt was clearly much the lesser evil, even to the SPD far left. In autumn 1979 Strauss and Edmund Stoiber, general secretary of the CSU, had kicked off an anti-SPD campaign, the main claim of which was that 'National Socialists, too, were first and foremost socialists'. The Union's 1980 campaign slogan was 'Against the SPD state—stop socialism!' As long as Helmut Schmidt was chancellor, there was little chance that such rhetoric would appeal to centrist voters. For its part, the SPD also placed its bets on the choice between 'Schmidt or Strauss!' The FDP did not act much differently, at least in the final stages of the campaign, representing Schmidt as closer to their party than to his own.

The elections were held on 5 October 1980. The Union's 44.5% of the vote once again made it the strongest political force in the country, but with a loss of 4.1% compared with 1976. The SPD did slightly better, up to 42.9% from 42.6%. The FDP greatly improved its performance, gaining 10.6% of the vote, up from 7.9% four years before. The Green party received 1.5% in its first federal election, all other parties 0.5%. The SPD–FDP majority was impressive: 271 seats to the Union's 226. There could be no doubt about the reason for the coalition success: the election had indeed turned into a referendum against Franz Josef Strauss, and the FDP, which gained many former CDU voters, profited even more than the SPD. With this outcome, it was not difficult to see that, for now, at least, the liberals had no alternative to continuing their alliance with the Social Democrats.[8]

INDEPENDENCE AND DISSSOCIATION: HONECKER AND WEST GERMANY

The 'capitalist' nations were not the only ones to be hard hit by the drastic price increases on oil after 1973. The 'socialist' states clearly had an even harder time adjusting to the forced reduction in fossil fuel consumption. While the Soviet Union had massive untapped oil and gas reserves in Siberia, it lacked both the capital and the technology necessary for their large-scale exploitation. Greater cooperation with the west could solve this problem, but the Soviet missiles in Europe and the expansionist policy in central Asia stood in the way of such cooperation.

The global energy crisis caused East Germany massive problems in the second half of the 1970s. Growth rates sharply decreased in the gross domestic product, in the consumer goods industries, and in investments. Since Honecker's doctrine on the 'unity of economic and social policy' could not be touched, the only recourse was increased debt to the 'non-socialist world'. Productivity rapidly sank, which then made the GDR even less competitive compared to West Germany.

The GDR requested increased crude oil imports from the Soviet Union at a price in accordance with the Council for Mutual Economic Assistance (COMECON), the economic community of the 'socialist' nations. This would have been far below the market price, and Moscow refused (December 1976). Acute payment difficulties resulted, leading Gerhard Schürer, head of the State Planning Commission, and Günter Mittag, CC secretary of the economy, to petition Honecker in March 1977 for an increase in exports to the non-socialist world and a reduction in imports. Honecker refused. The badly needed reform of the economy and state finances did not happen. The country's solvency was secured by new loans.

Demands for political change were interpreted as attacks on socialism and were met with the power of the state. Most of the victims were critical intellectuals, who did not stop demanding the democratization of the GDR even after the expatriation of Wolf Biermann in November 1976. The physicist Robert Havemann, a close friend of Biermann's and a staunch advocate of democratic socialism, was put under house arrest in November 1976 and not released until 1979 (after the conditions of his detention were further restricted in 1978). Rudolf Bahro, former deputy editor-in-chief of the FDJ student newspaper *Forum* and later department manager in a VEB, was condemned to an eight-year prison term in 1978; in his book *Die Alternative. Zur Kritik des realexistierenden Sozialismus,** published in West Germany the year before, he had compared the

---

* Bahro, *The Alternative: A Critique of Real Existing Socialism* (tr. as *The Alternative in Eastern Europe*).

politburo with the Roman Catholic inquisition and called the SED 'the political police'. Continuous protest in the west then led to his deportation to the FRG in 1979. In January 1978 *Der Spiegel* printed the manifesto of a 'League of Democratic Communists' (*Bund der demokratischen Kommunisten*). The author was Hermann von Berg, an economics professor from Berlin and former 'IM' active in the area of German–German relations. Berg spent time in detention, was subject to interrogation for weeks on end, then finally allowed to leave for the west in 1986 after Willy Brandt intervened on his behalf.

There were two reasons the SED found it useful to allow 'incorrigible' critics and enemies of the GDR system to go to West Germany. The first was that it reduced the internal pressure for reform, which had increased measurably after the end of the Helsinki conference in the summer of 1975. Secondly, this form of human traffic had long since become a welcome, indeed indispensable, source of foreign currency. On 3 July 1980 Egon Franke, minister for German–German relations, informed the West German public that 'special efforts' on the part of the government had been instrumental in the early release of 13,000 political prisoners in the GDR since 1964. Furthermore, during the same period, the successive governments had managed to bring more than 30,000 East Germans to the west under the programme of uniting families (*Familienzusammenführung*). Altogether West Germany purchased the freedom of 33,755 political prisoners between the years 1964 and 1989, paying 3.4 billion DM. The historian Stefan Wolle has compared this 'traffic in countrymen' with the traffic in soldiers during the period of absolutism. His harsh but apposite verdict: 'This human traffic was one of the most lucrative areas on the balance sheet of the SED state, and a kind of political hazardous waste disposal to boot.'

The churches were a different matter. They proved quite 'corrigible' in the latter half of the 1970s, and under certain conditions even useful. The SED found them particularly valuable in one area above all, that of 'peace policy'. On 6 March 1978 Erich Honecker met with the executive council of the Federation of Evangelical Churches in the GDR, led by Albrecht Schönherr, bishop of Berlin-Brandenburg. The NATO modernization controversy was just beginning at this time. Honecker duly celebrated 'the churches in their conscious commitment to peace, based on the Christian values of respect for life and service to one's neighbour'. He emphasized the 'great importance of the churches' contribution towards the end of the arms race, towards the ban on weapons of mass destruction, above all the neutron bomb'. And he expressed an expectation that none of the church delegates gainsaid: 'For us, and certainly for you, too, it is disturbing that, despite the progress in détente, the imperialist side constantly pushes the arms race.'

What the East German head of state failed to mention on this occasion was that the Soviet Union had taken the initiative in the arms race. He also did not discuss a recent addition to the school curriculum, a subject called 'Socialist military education' (*Sozialistische Wehrerziehung*), about which he informed Schönherr only three months later (1 June). In 1979 the 'socialist camp' further intensified its propaganda offensive against the modernization plans of the Atlantic league. Speaking in East Berlin on 6 October during the GDR's thirtieth anniversary celebrations, Brezhnev stated that in the case of war, the deployment of American medium-range missiles on West German soil would 'increase the risk of a counter-strike against the FRG by many times'. Honecker endorsed this view. In Sofia on 1 November, he warned that the relations between the GDR and FRG would suffer if NATO went ahead with the deployment.

Then, on 13 December 1979, the day after NATO made its decision in Brussels, the language from East Berlin was suddenly very different. Honecker made it known at the eleventh conference of the SED central committee that the West German chancellor would be visiting the GDR early in the new year. This announcement was preceded by a long telephone conversation between Honecker and Schmidt on 28 November; a letter from the latter, given to Honecker on 3 December by Günter Gaus, the West German government's Permanent Representative in the GDR; and contacts mediated by the East Berlin attorney Wolfgang Vogel, the GDR's agent in the purchased release of political prisoners and related matters.

Then, at the end of January 1980, four weeks after the Soviet invasion of Afghanistan, Honecker decided to postpone Schmidt's visit, which had been scheduled for 27 February. Still, there was little doubt that he had a great interest in a German–German summit in the near future. He was pursuing a double strategy with Bonn: strong ideological and propagandistic opposition on the one hand, close economic cooperation on the other. The GDR had now become so dependent on West Germany that this policy, as paradoxical as it seemed, possessed a definite inner logic. East Germany was able to profit from the 'swing', the interest-free overdraft provision in inter-German trade that, ever since 1969, was set every year at 25 per cent of the previous year's deliveries and services. This saved the GDR some 50 million DM in yearly interest payments. The credit limit was raised from 660 million to 850 million DM per year in November 1974. In exchange for this favourable policy, the GDR exempted retired West Germans from the required currency exchange before visits to the east. The October 1949 agreement on inter-zone commerce, which considered all of Germany a single economic unit, was still in effect. It permitted the GDR to benefit from the progress of the Common Market without having to share in its costs. While this was hardly in keeping with the doctrine of 'two German nations', it certainly was economically advantageous.

The cooperation in transport and communications also proved economically beneficial for East Germany. The building of a motorway between Berlin and Hamburg, decided in November 1978, was a major breakthrough. West Germany would contribute 1.2 billion DM. On 19 February 1980 Schmidt and Honecker made an agreement by telephone to begin several further projects to improve travel to and from Berlin. Two months later, on 17 April, Günter Mittag, the CC secretary of economics, came to Bonn in order to discuss unresolved matters with the chancellor and other West German officials. Agreements to expand the motorway over the Wartha-Herleshausen checkpoint and the canal between the Ems and the Elbe rivers, as well as a rail project, were among the most important of those signed on 30 April. The FRG contributed a total of 500 million DM. One week later, on 8 May 1980, Schmidt and Honecker met in Belgrade during the funeral ceremonies for Marshal Tito, attended by leaders of states and governments from the whole world. It was the first time the two German leaders had met since the Helsinki conference in 1975.

For the 'hardliners' in the SED, Honecker's and Mittag's German–German policy was increasingly suspect. Two members of the politburo close to the Kremlin, Willi Stoph, head of government, and his deputy Werner Krolikowski, told their Soviet confidants that Mittag, in his talk with Schmidt, had 'behaved not as the representative of a strongly united community of socialist states and its unified foreign policy, but as party to a German–German flirtation.' They alerted their allies to the dangers of the transit project, which was 'a big injection of money for the GDR'; indeed, it was 'one of the FRG's biggest capital investments in the GDR' and would create 'new political and economic dependencies'. Stoph and Krolikowski spoke of the 'conspiratorial nature of this contact with the enemy'. This made the tenor of their criticism perfectly clear: they were accusing Honecker's group of cooperating secretly with the imperialist class enemy under an umbrella of official support for the strategy of the socialist nations.

This assessment was not entirely incorrect. In a certain sense, both German states were playing a 'double game' in the shadow of the east–west confrontation during the early 1980s. Honecker, despite his loyalty to the eastern alliance and its leader, did not want to damage the special relations with Bonn, since without them the GDR's economically ruinous 'unity of economic and social policy' could not be maintained. Schmidt, it can be argued, was acting on behalf of the western alliance and its interests more credibly than the United States itself. Nonetheless, he was unable to overlook for a moment the fact that a turning away from détente would affect the Germans more than any other people. During the 1980 election campaign, he referred to the East Germans as 16 million 'hostages' who were unable 'to make their own decisions' and to whom the West German government was beholden in its *Ostpolitik*. On 5 October, the evening of the election, he wrote to Honecker that the new government would 'actively continue its efforts to extend bilateral relations and work out agreements advantageous to the people of both states'. The chancellor's next words were more an exhortation and expression of hope than a description of the actual state of affairs: the two German states, 'in view of the dangerous crisis points in the world, can make an important contribution to the stability of the international situation'.

At this juncture the attention of the leaders in East Berlin was entirely focused on the situation in Poland. On 2 October, four weeks after Eduard Gierek was replaced as head of the Polish United Workers' party (PUWP) by Stanislaw Kania, who was considered a liberal, Erich Mielke, the security minister, addressed the Polish crisis during a routine meeting. The events were dangerous, he said, since they were a product of 'the concentrated efforts of counter-revolutionary forces right in the middle of our community of states, with all of the attendant risks for the GDR . . . What is happening in Poland is a crucial question for us in the GDR, too, a question of life or death. Therefore, supreme vigilance is in order.'

Already by the end of September 1980 the CC department of international relations under Herman Axen had drawn a comparison between the 'programmes and concrete demands of the antisocialist forces in Poland in 1980 and the CSSR in 1968'. It had come to the conclusion that the two were 'largely similar in nature and aims'. 'Common to both counter-revolutionary movements is the fact that they do not openly declare an alternative to socialism, but mask their antisocialist goals by claiming they wish to improve socialism.' At the end of October Joachim Herrmann, CC secretary for agitation and propaganda, told his Soviet interlocutor, Mikhail V. Zimyanin, that the situation in Poland was 'even worse than 1968 in the CSSR, worse than under Dubček', and that counter-revolution was on the march. In the light of this evaluation, the SED's response was a foregone conclusion. On 20 November Honecker told the departing Polish ambassador, Stefan Olszowski, a member of the hardliner fraction of the PUWP politburo, that in case of emergency the Polish party should not refrain from shedding blood. 'It is a last resort. But even this last resort must be used if it becomes necessary to defend the workers' and peasants' power. That was our experience in 1953, and the events in Hungary in 1956 and in Czechoslovakia in 1968 teach the same lesson.'

One week later, on 26 November, Honecker sent an urgent message to Brezhnev asking that the Warsaw Pact states be convened in order to discuss 'collective relief action to help our Polish friends overcome the crisis'. Any hesitation would be 'tantamount to death—the death of socialist Poland. Yesterday such common measures would perhaps have been premature. Today they are necessary. But tomorrow they might be too late.' The leaders of the Bulgarian and Czechoslovak Communist parties, Todor Zhivkov and Gustav Husák, joined Honecker in this request.

The meeting took place in Moscow on 5 December 1980. However, informal talks the evening before had already led to the decision not to intervene militarily in Poland for the time being, but to push for a 'Polish' solution to the crisis instead, if necessary through a declaration of martial law. This policy was clearly influenced by the Hungarian and Romanian leaders, János Kádár and Nicolae Ceausescu, who rejected intervention, as well as by political reservations on the part of the Kremlin, who were loath to put even more pressure on east–west relations after the invasion of Afghanistan.

Nonetheless, a Warsaw Pact invasion was still considered a last resort, and preparations were intensified. The operation was given the following veiled title: 'Preparation and execution of a common training measure of the United Armed Forces of the member states of the Warsaw Treaty on the territory of the People's Republic of Poland'. (This language was employed by the East German Ministry of National Defence in an order of 6 December 1980.) Four days later Honecker, in his capacity as head of the National Defence Council, signed an order empowering the defence minister, General Heinz Hoffmann, to get the National People's Army ready to mobilize. (The order would remain in effect until April 1982.) Hoffmann reported back that same day that all preparations had been concluded.

The Polish crisis also affected the relations between East and West Germany. The SED could not demand a stern response to ideological laxness in Poland if it was unwilling to demonstrate ideological stringency in its relation to Bonn. On 9 October, four days after the West German elections, the GDR ordered a large increase in the amount of currency visitors from 'non-socialist' countries were required to exchange upon entering East Germany. The new rate was 25 DM per visitor per day, up from 13 DM (6.50 DM for single-day visits to East Berlin). This also applied to the retired, who had been exempted from compulsory exchange in 1974, and to young people older than 14.

The new policy took effect on 13 October 1980. That same day, Erich Honecker gave a speech in Gera dealing with what he called 'the contradictory nature of FRG politics'. West Germany could not, he said, 'actively support the western alliance, boycott the Olympic Games in Moscow out of solidarity with the USA, present itself as the inventor of and driving force behind the Brussels missile decision, all the while pretending that the only thing it had to talk to the GDR about was easing travel restrictions.' Relations between the GDR and the FRG would

only move forward when the existence of two sovereign, independent states with different social systems is unconditionally recognized. Any effort to revise the European post-war order will adversely affect the normalization of the relations between the two German states. Indeed, it could put the whole process at risk.

What followed became known as Honecker's four 'Gera demands': West German recognition of GDR citizenship; normal embassies to replace the 'permanent representatives' in East Berlin and Bonn; a definitive ruling on the border issue along the Elbe (that is, the border was to run down the middle of the river the whole way); and the dissolution of the Central Documentation Office of the State Judicial Administrations (*Zentrale Erfassungsstelle der Landesjustizverwaltungen*) in Salzgitter, which kept track of criminal acts on the part of GDR agencies and institutions. The first two demands alone were constitutionally impossible for the FRG, as Honecker well knew. Along with the currency exchange increase, therefore, the Gera speech put an end to the improvement of German–German relations for the time being.

The speech did not convince Honecker's adversaries within the SED. On 13 November 1980 Erich Mielke, in conversation with Willi Stoph, criticized the general secretary: 'with regard to the FRG it is evident that he [Honecker, H.A.W.] presents a tough public image while privately making excuses to the FRG for his public behaviour . . . EH [Erich Honecker, H.A.W.] is taking us and our Soviet friends for a ride.' One month later, on 16 December, in a note for his Soviet connections, Werner Krolikowski wrote that Honecker was pursuing an 'irresponsible, two-faced, zigzag policy' with regard to West Germany. The Gera speech with its correct demands, he continued, had been followed [on 3 November, H.A.W.] by a meeting with the West German Permanent Representative in the GDR, Günter Gaus, during which Honecker 'gave the go-ahead for a continuation of the special German–German relationship'.

EH's approach to the FRG is erroneous. We propose that the Soviet side carefully analyse EH's foreign policy actions with regard to the FRG and speak with him about his mistakes, so that the basis for a fundamentally clear foreign policy with regard to the FRG can be worked out and presented to the tenth party congress [in April 1981, H.A.W.] for a resolution.

Despite this criticism, Honecker did not yet have to fear for his position. Mielke told Stoph one of the reasons: 'everybody is afraid of EH'. As far as the Soviet leaders were concerned, while Honecker's German–German idiosyncrasies were occasionally worrisome, they had no cause to suspect that he would attempt to escape their control. For the moment, the SED leader could assume that his 'zigzag policy' with regard to West Germany was not in jeopardy.[9]

RECESSION, THE PEACE MOVEMENT, AND THE CRISIS OF THE PARTY SYSTEM

On 5 November 1980, one month after the elections to the ninth German Bundestag, Helmut Schmidt was re-elected to the chancellorship. He received 266 votes, 5 fewer than the combined total of the SPD and FDP. The new cabinet differed very little from the old; the only changes were among the Social Democrats. Volker Hauff left the ministry of research for the ministry of transportation, taking over from Kurt Gscheidle, who had been heading that office together with the postal ministry (which he retained). Andreas von Bülow, hitherto parliamentary state secretary in the chancellor's office, became the new minister of research. Two other personnel decisions had greater significance: Klaus Bölling, government spokesman and close confidant of Schmidt, replaced Günter Gaus as the FRG's 'permanent representative' in the GDR (Gaus had been going along with the ideas of the SED leadership more frequently and to a greater degree than the chancellor thought justifiable). Bölling was replaced in Bonn by Kurt Becker, editor in chief of the Hamburg newspaper *Die Zeit* and a political independent. Manfred Lahnstein, state secretary of the finance ministry, became the new state secretary in the chancellor's office. His predecessor, Manfred Schüler, took over the Bank for Reconstruction in Frankfurt.

Schmidt's inaugural address on 24 November 1980 was lacking in bold outlines and rousing language. The chancellor did no more nor less than simply enumerate the projects the coalition partners had agreed upon in the course of difficult negotiations. And in fact, little more was possible at this point, since the Social Democrats and liberals had come close to the end of their list of common goals. Even the mutual antagonism to Franz Josef Strauss would not hold them together much longer. After the Union parties had failed with and because of Strauss in the elections, it was not to be expected that he would run again in 1984. The most probable candidate was Helmut Kohl, the CDU head, who had come very close to gaining an absolute majority four years previously. A CDU/CSU coalition with the FDP was inconceivable under Strauss; it took far less political imagination to envision one under Kohl.

Before the elections, very few people were aware that the West German economic situation had become a good deal worse again. Only in retrospect did it become clear that the after-effects of the 1978–9 oil shock were far from over. Between October 1980 and October 1981 the number of unemployed increased by some 400,000 to a total of 1.37 million. Production fell 0.5% throughout 1981 while consumer prices increased by 7%. In 1980, 6,300 companies went out of business; the next year the figure was 8,500.

The recession gave rise to a general mood of crisis, and this atmosphere in turn created anxieties that manifested themselves more and more in aggression. Non-Germans living in Germany were often the targets. The official West German population figure in 1981 was 61.7 million people. Of these, about 4.6 million (7.5%) were foreigners, about one-third of them (1.5 million) from Turkey. In addition to gainfully employed non-Germans and their families, there were about 100,000 political refugees seeking asylum, half of them from Turkey, half from other Asian countries and Africa. The Turks were accused of taking jobs away from Germans, even though most of them had been living and working in Germany for many years. The asylum seekers were often accused of being more 'economic refugees' or 'sham refugees' than anything else, and of abusing the German social system. This kind of language was used not only by armchair and alehouse politicians, but also by real ones in conservative circles. According to opinion polls, such prejudices were more common among the less educated. At the end of 1981 the Institute for Applied Social Science (*Institut für Angewandte Sozialwissenschaft* or *infas*) in Bonn published a study that reported finding at least latent forms of xenophobia among more than half of West German citizens.

Xenophobia was a phenomenon on the 'right'. Social anxieties were expressed differently on the left: against atomic energy, large technological projects, and the armed forces' deployment of new kinds of weapons. In February 1981 there was another mass demonstration against continued construction of the nuclear plant in Brokdorf. Serious riots broke out at the end of January 1982 over the building of the west runway at the Frankfurt airport. Violence was employed only by a militant minority, but its members were present almost everywhere there was cause for protest. The occasions seemed interchangeable: police operations to clear squatters out of buildings (in the Berlin 'problem zone' of Kreuzberg, in the Hafenstrasse in Hamburg, even in the 'Schwarzwaldhof' in idyllic Freiburg) mobilized as much protest as the army's public swearing-in ceremonies (beginning in Bremen in 1980) or the public appearances of American politicians. A visit by US Secretary of State Alexander Haig, a former general, on 13 and 14 September 1981 was accompanied by major rioting in West Berlin. The next day members of a resurrected RAF staged an attack against the American general Frederick James Kroesen (who emerged with only minor wounds).

Anti-American sentiments had been a key feature of the extra-parliamentary left ever since the Vietnam War at the latest. They were given a powerful new motivation by NATO's double-track decision in December 1979 and by Ronald Reagan's election to the US presidency in November 1980. Reagan, governor of California and a former actor, had gained prominence as a conservative Republican and staunch anti-communist, but had not yet shown a clear direction in foreign policy matters. When Helmut Schmidt met him during a farewell visit to Jimmy Carter at the end of November, the president-elect promised to devote great energy to bringing the disarmament talks to a successful conclusion. On 22 May 1981, in a joint statement with Schmidt during the latter's first official visit to the new president, Reagan declared his support for *both* parts of the double-track decision, for negotiations as well as armaments. On 18 November 1981, a few days before Brezhnev was scheduled to visit West Germany, Reagan announced that he had proposed to the Soviet leader negotiations (to be conducted in Geneva at the end of the month) over a substantial reduction of strategic arms (Strategic Arms Reduction Talks or START) and a double zero solution in the case of medium-range missiles. That is, NATO would withdraw plans to station its Pershing II and cruise missiles in Europe if the Soviet Union would agree to scrap its SS 20 missiles, along with the earlier models SS 4 and SS 5.

Reagan's moderate language did not persuade the German peace movement or its international affiliates. That was partly his own fault, since he continually lapsed into his old anti-communist rhetoric—most notably during a speech in Orlando, Florida, on 8 March 1983, when he called the Soviet Union an 'empire of evil'. For the peace movement, such episodes confirmed their view that the American president had no intention of pursuing arms reduction seriously. The 'Strategic Defence Initiative' (SDI), announced by Reagan on 23 March 1983, was yet more grist for the mills of the pacifists. An anti-missile defence system to be developed over the course of several years, the SDI (also dubbed 'Star Wars') was designed to eliminate the threat of a Soviet nuclear counter-strike. It would also have given the Americans a kind of protection their Western European allies could not enjoy. The Reagan administration wanted to win the arms race, and it was convinced that economic, political, and moral superiority would assure the victory of the United States.

The West German peace movement of the 1980s received its first concrete political platform on 16 November 1980 in the co-called 'Krefeld Appeal'. Very few people knew at the time who the real authors of this initiative against NATO modernization were: the GDR's Ministry for State Security. The Stasi 'enlightenment' department, led by Markus Wolf, used organizations like the German Peace Union (*Deutsche Friedensunion*), a communist cover group, and the German Communist party to launch the campaign. Since the goal was to appeal to as many non-communists as possible, the Krefeld Appeal used language that spoke to people from all levels of West German society. Among the first signatories were two prominent members of the Greens, Petra Kelly, one of the party's founders, and Gert Bastian, a former Bundeswehr general. According to the initiators, 4.7 million people had signed the manifesto by autumn 1983.

An especially large number of signatures were gathered at the congress of the German Evangelical church in Hamburg in June 1981 and in Hanover in June 1983. Hans Apel, the defence minister, was booed down in Hamburg when he tried to defend the double-track decision. Even the chancellor himself had a hard time of it, being confronted with the charge that his security policy violated the Sermon on the Mount. Another Social Democrat, Erhard Eppler, president of the congress, received standing ovations for his criticism of the NATO policy. German Protestantism, such as it presented itself at its congresses, had a markedly anti-western, very German face. It did not seem troubled about its alienation from the democracies of the west, nor even about the proximity of its demands to those of the Warsaw Pact. In appealing to the individual conscience, it rejected all dialogue or engagement with those who thought differently. Its protest was totally inward-looking and fundamentalist.

For the chancellor, the conspicuous rapprochement between his own party and the peace movement was especially threatening. In December 1980, 150 SPD delegates signed the 'Bielefeld declaration', which called the double-track policy a 'disastrous decision'. At two party assemblies, on 16 and 17 May, Schmidt publicly threatened to resign as chancellor if the Social Democrats withdrew their support for the NATO decision.

This warning was directed not only at the Young Socialists and at Eppler and his allies (like Oskar Lafontaine, mayor of Saarbrücken), but also at the head of the SPD. Willy Brandt did not take the political risks represented by the Soviet missiles nearly as seriously as did Schmidt. While he publicly supported the chancellor, he constantly made it known that he looked upon the arms race with increasing concern and, as head of the SPD, had a great interest in not letting the Greens dominate the peace movement. At the beginning of July 1981, returning from a visit to Moscow, where he had met with Brezhnev (now very ill), Brandt reported: 'They want to negotiate. And you can say what you want about Brezhnev, but the man trembles when the discussion turns to world peace. Subjectively there's no doubt about that.'

At the end of September, Schmidt tried to prevent Eppler from speaking at a peace demonstration planned for the 10 October in Bonn, arguing that such activities restricted the government's freedom of action. But he failed to convince the party executive. With Brandt's encouragement Eppler attended the event, the largest of its kind up to that point, with some 250,000 participants. More than 50 SPD Bundestag delegates were present.[10]

The SPD's coalition partner also made things difficult for the chancellor in 1981. Basically the FDP agreed with the SPD that the 1982 budget should not be financed by increasing the debt, but mainly by savings and spending cuts. Opinions differed as to the methods to be used and the programmes to be affected, however. The liberals wanted to reduce social services more than the Social Democrats were willing to countenance. The latter, for their part, wanted to introduce a supplement to the wage and income tax as a way of financing a new employment programme.

On 20 August 1981, right at the end of the parliament's summer break, Hans-Dietrich Genscher, the FDP head, vice chancellor, and foreign minister, addressed his party colleagues in what immediately became known as the *Wendebrief* ('turning point letter'). Genscher believed that West Germany had come to a 'parting of the ways'; he compared the decisions facing the country to those of the period of reconstruction after the Second World War. The 'attitude of entitlement' had to be broken, and additional changes in the corpus of social legislation were unavoidable. 'Despite the two coalition parties' fundamentally different positions on important economic and social issues', Genscher did still think it possible to reach an understanding with the Social Democrats. At the same time, this very observation made it clear that he did not exclude the possibility of a rapid end to the coalition and a new alliance with the Union parties.

After bitter negotiations, the SPD and FDP reached a compromise at the end of September. Each side gave up its maximalist demands, the SPD the tax supplement, the FDP its call for 'unpaid sick days' (with which it had wanted to lower the costs of the programme of paid sick leave, introduced by the Grand Coalition in July 1969). At the SPD Bundestag fraction meeting on 8 September 1981, however, Brandt made it clear that he had no intention of making further concessions to the FDP and considered the relationship between the Social Democrats and the labour unions more important than the survival of the coalition. Schmidt, seeking to underscore the seriousness of the situation, reminded those present about the end of the Weimar Republic's final parliamentary majority government, the Grand Coalition under the Social Democratic Reich chancellor Herman Müller, on 27 March 1930. When he criticized the 'thoughtless' behaviour of the Social Democrats at that time, Brandt responded that it was not the Social Democrats, but the liberals of the German People's party who had wanted to abandon the coalition in spring 1930. Both Schmidt and Brandt knew full well that they were not really arguing about an event that lay more than a half-century in the past. Their disagreement was really about what governmental power meant for the SPD, and what SPD participation in government meant for the Federal Republic as a whole.

At the beginning of the 1980s, unlike in 1930, an end to the governing coalition did not put the entire parliamentary system at risk. A different coalition was possible. And yet, even in retrospect, it is no exaggeration to say that, three decades after its founding, the second German democracy was in a crisis. The recession was one of the factors, but it was not the main one. The core of the problem had to do with the role and the self-image of the political parties, especially their relationship to the idea of justice and to the legal system.

The Weimar constitution had mentioned the parties only in a negative sense. Article 130 had called civil servants 'servants of the population as a whole, not of a party'. The Basic Law, influenced as it was by the Weimar experience, ascribed a positive role to the parties in Article 21, but one that was not free of restrictions: 'Political parties participate in the formation of the political will of the people. They may be freely established. Their internal organization must conform to democratic principles. They must publicly account for their assets and for the sources and use of their funds.'

In practice, the parties no longer merely 'participated' in forming the will of the people; they guided the process. Together with the large societal and religious organizations, for example, they decided on the composition of the boards of the public radio and television companies, thus having a decisive say in their management. Whenever parties exercised governmental power over a longer term, they tended to look upon positions in the civil service, down to that of school principal, as theirs to award. In this way, as sociologists Erwin K. and Ute Scheuch have described it, there developed 'feudal systems of insider relationships' trading 'privileges for fealty' from the federal all the way down to the municipal level of government. And as far as the 'inner order' of the parties was concerned, the 'iron law of oligarchy' identified by Robert Michels (a student of Max Weber) in his classic 1911 book *Zur Soziologie des Parteiwesens in der modernen Demokratie** was still in effect in the FRG: now more than ever, the real power lay in the hands of the party functionaries, men and women who literally lived for politics and from politics.

But the real trouble area was the parties' financial behaviour. Even before the first Bundestag election in 1949, a number of business organizations had joined together in the 'Pyrmont agreement' in order to financially support the parties

---

* Michels, *On the Sociology of the Party System in Modern Democracy* (tr. as *Political Parties: A Sociological Study of the Oligarchical Tendencies of Modern Democracy*).

who stood behind Ludwig Erhard's economic policies. Of a 2 million DM total, about two-thirds was given to the CDU. In 1954, with the active participation of Konrad Adenauer, his friend Robert Pferdmenges, a Cologne banker, and Fritz Berg, president of the Association of German Industry, industrialists and bankers founded the 'Civic Association of 1954' (*Staatsbürgerliche Vereinigung 1954 e. V*),* which provided the CDU, CSU, FDP, and other bourgeois parties with donations. Between 1969 and 1980 they received some 214 million marks in this way.

With a revision of the income and corporation tax code in December 1954, donations to parties 'for the promotion of political goals' were granted a favourable tax status. The state thus gave up revenue in favour of donors and their beneficiaries. This practice violated the Basic Law, a fact generally known after 1958 at the latest. On 24 June of that year, the Federal Constitutional Court declared the progressive deduction of party donations to be unconstitutional; in uniquely benefiting parties that appealed to wealthy constituents, it violated the principle of equality before the law, such as it was described in Article 3 of the Basic Law.

This ruling brought a sharp decrease in direct party donations. Indirect donations continued, however, mediated through the 'Civic Associations' on the federal and regional level and other similar organizations, often registered as 'charitable'. Since these monies were looked upon either as contributions to professional associations (in which case they were treated as publicity expenses) or as charitable donations, they were tax-deductible. The parties compensated for the decrease in direct donations by continually raising the amount they were entitled to from the federal budget.

Then, on 19 July 1966, the Constitutional Court intervened once again. The state-supported system of party finance (in place since 1959), which granted the parties federal funds for their promotion of political education, was declared unconstitutional. Only after this ruling did the Bundestag finally pass the law governing political parties that was called for in the Basic Law. It was passed by the Grand Coalition on 28 June 1967. Now there was a binding legal framework for the public defrayment of campaign expenses and the regulation of party donations.

As a way of eliminating the influence of 'big money' on politics, the parties' finance reports were required, with donations beyond certain figures, to identify the names of their donors and the amounts given. These figures were 20,000 DM per calendar year in the case of a 'natural' person and 200,000 per calendar year in the case of a 'juristic' person, that is, a corporate body. Other sources of income likewise had to be identified in full. The party accounts were subject to examination by inspectors, who were in turn required to be disinterested and conscientious in the performance of their duties.

---

* *e. V*. stands for *eingetragener Verein* ('registered society') and often designates a charity.

It was an open secret in Bonn that the requirements of the 1967 party law were systematically circumvented by means of what came to be known as 'indirect' or 'roundabout financing' (*Umwegfinanzierung*). The parliamentary fractions and partisan foundations—the CDU's Konrad Adenauer Foundation, the SPD's Friedrich Ebert Foundation, the FDP's Friedrich Naumann Foundation, and the Hanns Seidel Foundation of the CSU—were all involved. These organizations, themselves financed mainly through the federal budget, played a large role in the political training of party officials after 1966, when the Federal Constitutional Court prohibited the parties from using public funds for this purpose.

'Indirect financing' was also used by the 'European Business Consulting Company' (*Europäische Unternehmensberatungs-Anstalt*) in Liechtenstein. This entity provided receipts for the 'payment' of fictional or meaningless reports commissioned by companies and paid for as 'company expenses'. In reality, the payments were donations to the CDU. The Social Democrats used two methods: receipts for advertisements in party publications, paid for at inflated prices and often never actually appearing; and front organizations like the Israeli Fritz Naphtali Foundation and a 'shell company' in Zurich called the 'Institute for International Relations' (*Institut für Internationale Beziehungen*), which apparently laundered money for the SPD's Friedrich Ebert Foundation.

The FDP was serviced through a cartel of 'charitable' groups like the 'International Business Club in Bonn' (*Internationaler Wirtschaftsclub e. V., Bonn*) and the 'Economic Policy Association in Cologne' (*Wirtschaftspolitische Vereinigung e. V., Köln*), which 'laundered' tax-deductible funds in accounts in Miami, London, and Geneva. The CDU also maintained illicit foreign accounts, a practice begun already under Adenauer: monies from the 'Civic Association' were placed in Swiss banks, a fact that did not emerge until the beginning of the year 2000. And finally there was strong reason to suspect the workings of massive bribery operations: in the 1957 electoral campaign, the CDU was alleged to have received 50 million marks from the purchase of the HS 30 tank from the Hispano Suiza company at a price inflated by 200 million marks. The matter was never fully cleared up.

This system of quotidian illegality turned into a major political scandal in 1981. The cause was an investigation by the federal prosecutor going back to the year 1977 and implicating a member of the federal government, Otto Graf Lambsdorff, the economics minister. Lambsdorff was accused of tax evasion through covert party finance in his capacity as treasurer of the FDP in North Rhine-Westphalia between 1968 and 1977. The CDU treasurer Walther Leisler Kiep and the former SPD treasurer Alfred Nau were also investigated.

Since all the parties represented in the Bundestag were affected, the obvious thing to do was to circumvent criminal punishment by means of a general amnesty. For the Social Democrats, nothing less than their party's participation in government was at stake, since Genscher stated that the FDP would not accept

Lambsdorff's dismissal. In mid-December 1981 the fraction leaders agreed to a bill drawn up by the SPD delegate Fritz-Joachim Gnädinger (a former federal prosecutor) granting exemption from punishment for all offences connected with illegal party finance, including embezzlement, misappropriation, and fraud, under conditions easy to meet. The party leaders—Kohl, Brandt, Genscher, and Strauss—also planned a public admission of guilt.

That never happened. The amnesty, which would have shaken the very foundations of the rule of law, was rejected by the SPD Bundestag fraction and by Jürgen Schmude, the new SPD minister of justice. (Schmude, a jurist, was 44 years old at the time. Hitherto he had been minister for education and research. He replaced Hans-Jochen Vogel as justice minister on 22 January 1981 when Vogel was elected mayor of Berlin.)

Gnädinger's bill thus had to be withdrawn for the time being. But the party finance scandal not only continued, it received 'a new pungency' at around this time, as Wolfgang Jäger writes in *Die Ära Schmidt*,* a study of domestic politics under the second Social Democratic chancellor. A few days before the failure of the amnesty plan, it became known that the federal prosecutor was also investigating the Flick conglomerate and its personally liable shareholder Eberhard von Brauchitsch. In 1975 the company had sold a part of its Diamler-Benz shares, valued at 2.1 billion marks, to the Deutsche Bank, receiving 1.9 billion in proceeds. It applied for tax-free status for the reinvested amount, 1.5 billion, using Paragraph 6b of the income tax code, which had originated in the year 1964 under Ludwig Erhard. According to this paragraph, the state could grant tax-free status to profits reinvested 'in ways particularly productive for the economy'. This language allowed the state authorities considerable discretionary powers.

Brauchitsch was able to obtain official tax exemptions for a number of Flick's investment projects, including its purchase of shares in the Gerling insurance company in 1981. Cabinet members from both coalition parties—Hans Friderichs, the economics minister, his successor Lambsdorff, Hans Apel and his successor in the finance ministry, Hans Matthöfer—were involved in the process. At the end of February 1982, suspicions that the state's behaviour might have had something to do with money payments from the Flick company (the relevant legal terms were 'granting of undue advantage' and 'acceptance of undue advantage') led the federal prosecutor to open investigations against Friderichs; Lambsdorff; Matthöfer; Manfred Lahnstein, former secretary of state in the finance ministry and later head of the chancellor's office; Horst-Ludwig Riemer (FDP), economics minister of North Rhine-Westphalia; Rudolf Eberle (CDU), economics minister of Baden-Württemberg; and, from Flick itself, company president Friedrich Karl Flick as well as the two senior managers, Eberhard von Brauchitsch and Manfred Nemitz.

* Jäger, *The Schmidt Era*.

This was the beginning of the so-called 'Flick affair', which would drag on for years and shake the credibility of all parties except the Greens. Although the true dimensions of the scandal would not emerge for a long time, it was clear at the beginning of 1982 that the SPD's rejection of the common amnesty project had caused further damage to the already strained relationship between the two coalition partners. Since the FDP had more to lose from state prosecution than any other party, it seemed likely that the liberals would look for ways to give effective expression to their disappointment and bitterness.[11]

MARTIAL LAW IN POLAND AND REACTIONS IN WEST GERMANY

While the West German public was dealing with party finance scandals, in Poland the conflict between the Communist party and the Independent Labour union 'Solidarity' was coming to a head. At the end of March 1981 negotiations between Solidarity representatives and the new Jaruzelski government (in place since February) narrowly managed to avert a general strike. The threat of martial law was not without effect. Lech Walesa's intellectual advisers, led by Bronislaw Geremek and Tadeusz Mazowiecki, urged him to steer clear of a decisive showdown with the state, believing it could provoke a Soviet intervention. But this only postponed an inevitable confrontation.

On 5 June the leaders of the Polish United Workers' party received a letter from the central committee of the Soviet Communist party criticizing their 'endless concessions to the anti-socialist forces' and accusing them of gradually retreating 'under pressure from the inner counter-revolution'. This had brought the situation in Poland to a 'critical juncture'. In the middle of the next month, the PUWP's ninth congress re-elected Stanislaw Kania to the position of First Secretary. In his closing speech Kania warned about the risks of 'anarchy' and 'counter-revolution'.

Worsening food shortages provoked massive demonstrations throughout the country at the end of July and beginning of August. This caused the Soviets to increase the pressure on the Polish government. On 8 August Marshal Kulikov, commander-in-chief of the Warsaw Pact, met with Jaruzelski. Kania and Jaruzelski travelled to the Crimea on 14 August to meet with Brezhnev. The Soviet leader exhorted his Polish comrades to do everything in their power to prevent their country from going over to the capitalists. He also approved increased arms shipments to Poland and a postponement of Polish debt payments to the USSR. At the third plenum of the PUWP central committee on 2 and 3 September, Kania refuted the assumption by the 'enemies' that 'the government would definitely not declare a state of emergency in Poland.' On the contrary: it would use all means necessary to defend socialism. Here he was probably alluding to the agreement he and Jaruzelski had reached with Brezhnev on the Crimea.

The first delegate congress of the 'Independent, Self-Governing Labour Union of Solidarity' convened in Gdańsk on 9 September. The 896 delegates represented about 9.5 million members. The radicals had a majority, leading (among other things) to an appeal to the workers of eastern Europe to join them in the fight for free labour unions. This prompted Geremek, one of the moderate leaders, to remark that Solidarity had crossed over a certain border in the self-imposed discipline it had practised up to that point; 'a situation has arisen in which the security of the country is threatened to a certain degree'. The politburo accused Solidarity of compiling a platform of 'bizarre ideas and tendencies' and repeated in barely coded form its threat to declare a state of emergency or martial law. During the congress's second session, which took place at the end of September and beginning of October, Walesa was re-elected president. This was a victory for the moderates.

After the middle of October, it became more and more clear that the Communist party leadership wanted to use force. On 16 October, during the fourth plenum of the central committee, Kania announced that special powers were being conferred on the government. Local strikes against the food supply crisis, which had now reached catastrophic dimensions, were the immediate background to this decision, though Solidarity was attempting to stop them. On 18 October the CC described the situation as an 'acute threat to the existence of the nation as well as danger to the state'. This meant that 'the highest organs of the People's Republic of Poland, in the case of extreme necessity, must make use of their constitutional powers in order to protect the vital interests of the nation and the state.' That same day Prime Minister Wojciech Jaruzelski succeeded Stanislaw Kania as First Secretary of the PUWP. It is not absolutely clear when the decision to concentrate power in the hands of the general was taken (probably in August on the Crimea). But it is virtually certain Brezhnev knew of and approved it.

Talks on 4 November between Jaruzelski, Walesa, and Archbishop Józef Glemp, the primate of the Catholic Church in Poland, and between a Solidarity delegation and the government on 17 November produced no improvement in the situation. Demonstrations continued throughout the country. While a few strikes were called off, others went on, and new ones started after the negotiations came to an end. At the sixth plenum of the CC on 27 and 28 November Jaruzelski announced that a law would be introduced dealing with the state of emergency. Against Walesa's advice, Solidarity responded on 3 December with a sharply worded statement: if the Sejm (the Polish parliament) granted extraordinary powers to the government, a day-long protest strike would be called; if a state of emergency were declared, the strike would be of unlimited duration. On 8 December Archbishop Glemp called upon the Sejm, Jaruzelski, and Walesa to demonstrate moderation and a willingness to compromise. The parliament showed signs of compliance, breaking off deliberations over the emergency bill. For a short time it looked as though the crisis would be put aside without the use of force.

It was at this juncture that Helmut Schmidt, on 11 December, finally made his long-planned visit to the GDR. (Mid-December had been agreed upon by Schmidt and Honecker on 30 October.) The two leaders met in the Hubertusstock lodge on the Werbellinsee in Uckermark-Schorfheide on the evening of the chancellor's arrival. Their conversation, which lasted four hours, touched on all the controversial issues: missiles; German–German commerce; the compulsory exchange; humanitarian questions; and Honecker's 'Gera demands' regarding GDR citizenship, the Elbe border, the Salzgitter record office, and the status of envoys. The border question was the only one for which the chancellor thought a solution might be possible. After the elections in Lower Saxony that March, he said, the FRG could modify its official position, according to which the border ran along the eastern bank in certain places (and not through the middle of the river the whole way, as the GDR claimed). As far as the citizenship question was concerned, Honecker had softened his language somewhat, now using the term 'respect' instead of 'recognition'.

Schmidt openly admitted that he assumed that 'a reunification will not take place, at least not during this century.' But he still thought reasonable, neighbourly relations between the two German states possible, and his visit was intended as a contribution in that direction. 'He did not use the term "normality"; the situation at the border, at the very least, was not normal, he said.' The conversation touched on the Polish situation only in passing. When Schmidt asked for his view, Honecker replied: 'There is no country on earth that can long survive without working.'

The talks continued on the morning of 12 December at the State Council lodge on the Grosser Döllnsee, both delegations now meeting in full. Schmidt attempted to place the relations between the two Germanies in historical context. It was not, he said, the first time in history that several German states existed at the same time (express agreement from Honecker). 'If we look back over German history during the last thousand years or the last centuries, we see that all this is not so terribly new. Nonetheless, Germans on both sides have to want to get along, and to get along well.' The two countries could and should make a contribution to the improvement or de-escalation of the world situation. Both of them played down their roles far too much.

In reality both of us, in our respective alliance and economic systems, wield a great weight, and we also have a right to throw this weight onto the scales. For if a third world war does indeed come, it will take place in the central area of Europe, where the destruction would also be the greatest. We are obligated to bring our weight to bear, in the name of humanity.

The chancellor appealed for a kind of concerted action on the part of East and West Germany, with each country pushing its alliance leader towards the path of compromise and understanding. But Honecker was both unwilling and unable to take up this appeal. If he had done so, his party adversaries would once again have accused him of collaborating with the class enemy and denounced him in Moscow. He therefore restricted himself to the repetition of well-known positions, including a new critique of the NATO double-track decision.

Meaningful willingness to compromise was thus not forthcoming from the GDR on any point. And, in view of the situation, it was not to be expected. State Secretary Klaus Bölling, leader of the FRG's 'permanent representation' in East Berlin and a member of the West German delegation, later admitted:

Perhaps it was not until the meeting on the Grosser Döllnsee that a number of us realized for the first time what a nonsensical idea it was that we could gradually move the East German leaders towards our positions, perhaps in such a subtle manner that they would not even realize it, and, at the same time, to pass over their views in silence. We harboured no such illusions with any other communist-led state. But with the GDR, we thought for a long time that we could afford this self-delusion.

In the early morning hours of 13 December the Bonn delegation was rudely awakened by news from Warsaw: General Jaruzelski had declared martial law in Poland. The parliamentary deliberations over the emergency bill had been a ruse; their interruption had been intended to deceive both the Poles and the world community about the true intentions of the Polish government, and it had worked. In the dead of night, the police arrested all the Solidarity activists it could find and put the movement's intellectual sympathizers, above all Walesa's advisers, in internment camps. Altogether more than 5,000 people were arrested, according to western estimates. Poland was now a communist military dictatorship.

Helmut Schmidt's shock was not unmixed with relief. The declaration of martial law was a 'Polish' solution to the crisis and, as such, a lesser evil than the intervention of the Warsaw Pact. If the Soviets had led foreign troops into the country, as they had during the 'Prague Spring' in August 1968, it would have meant the end of east–west détente. The involvement of the GDR's National People's Army would have killed German–German cooperation for the foreseeable future. In a telephone conversation with Jaruzelski on 16 December, Honecker claimed that Schmidt had told him that it was 'about time they started putting things in order in Poland'. (When a transcript of this conversation came to light in October 1993, Schmidt immediately denied he had made such a remark.) During a television interview on 13 December, after the conclusion of his talks in East Germany, the chancellor said the following about the events in Poland: 'Herr Honecker was as shocked as I was that this was necessary.'

This unfortunate phrasing provoked massive criticism at home. Before he could deal with that, however, the chancellor had to complete the last part of his visit, a trip to Güstrow in Mecklenburg, where he planned to show his reverence for the work of the sculptor Ernst Barlach. Art was only part of Schmidt's motivation. He did not wish his visit to have the appearance of a top-level diplomatic event in which the GDR population played no role. For its part, the East German leadership feared nothing so much as a repetition of the spontaneous popular demonstrations Willy Brandt had inspired in Erfurt in March 1970. Accordingly, the security ministry had seen to it that Schmidt would not come into contact with Güstrow's real inhabitants, but only with a massive contingent of police and a group of people carefully selected to cheer Honecker. Thousands of citizens had had to promise in writing that they would not emerge from their homes during the chancellor's visit to their city.

The eerie pictures from Mecklenburg showed very clearly that the relationship between East and West Germany was anything but 'normal'. In the light of what was going on in Poland, Schmidt's and Honecker's visit to Güstrow cathedral seemed like a demonstration of German–German indifference. As a whole, the chancellor's trip to the GDR produced virtually no substantive results. It had to be looked upon as a mistake, at least at the time, since it was clear before he left that the Polish crisis would probably end in violence. The SED leadership knew by 4 December that martial law would shortly be declared. Consequently, when Franz Josef Strauss said on 14 December that Schmidt had 'walked into a trap' in East Germany, it was not an unfair assessment of the situation.

Once Schmidt had gone, however, he was unable to do what Strauss said he should have done: break off his visit on 13 December. Had he done so, it would have created an 'ice age' in the relationship between the two countries, causing considerable harm to the Germans in the GDR. The chancellor had mentioned the 16 million 'hostages' in the GDR several times throughout the year 1980; on 13 December 1981 he himself became, for the duration of several hours, a hostage of his own efforts to aid his East German countrymen.

The chancellor's trip and the Polish situation were the subject of debates in the Bundestag several days later, on 18 December. Schmidt did everything he could to correct the impression that he approved of Jaruzelski's actions. The developments in Poland and the declaration of martial law filled him with great concern, he said. 'I am completely on the side of the workers, with all my heart. We all hope with all our hearts that martial law will be brought to an end in Poland as quickly as possible.' But something else Schmidt said was highly equivocal: 'Germans still must not set themselves up as judges of the Poles, even now!' This remark provoked a response from the leader of the opposition, Helmut Kohl: 'If we are now speaking of Poland and assuring the Poles of our sympathy, then we are not Poland's judges; rather, we wish to be Poland's friends!'

After the debate the delegates unanimously passed (with one abstention) a motion that had been worked out between the party fractions and the government. It declared the parliament's 'solidarity with the sorely afflicted Polish people at this fateful hour and with their struggle for human dignity, for the rule of law, and for democracy'. The 'Polish military government' was called upon to release all political prisoners, restore accustomed liberties, and return to dialogue with the reformist and patriotic forces among the Polish people in the spirit of the

Helsinki Final Act. The West German government was called upon to suspend economic assistance to Poland for the duration of the repression.

The citizens of West Germany expressed their solidarity with the Poles mainly by sending them millions of care packages throughout the winter of 1981–2. As far as actual protest was concerned, West Germany was more reserved than its western neighbours and the United States. Many people, including Helmut Schmidt, believed that Jaruzelski's coup had pre-empted an armed intervention by the Warsaw Pact. This view cannot be proven. It is true that Moscow had been exerting massive pressure on the Polish leadership. But two factors militated against intervention: Soviet fear of international confrontation, and the fact that the eastern alliance was not united. At the beginning of December, Hungary and Romania had prevented the Warsaw Pact from issuing the official intervention Jaruzelski had been seeking with the support of the Soviets and the GDR.

Regardless of what was going on between Moscow, Warsaw, and East Berlin in the second half of 1981, however, large portions of the West German left had already distanced themselves from the Poles' latest struggle for liberty. The fact that the Solidarity movement was nationalist and Catholic in character, not leftist and socialist, limited its leftist appeal from the outset. In the course of 1981 the union's activities were perceived as increasingly disruptive, causing chaos not only in Poland, but also threatening European stability and even world peace. Because of the German partition, the FRG was more strongly affected by any crisis in east–west relations than any other member of the western alliance. Both the ideological and the specifically German reservations against Solidarity were part of the reason the leftist military dictatorship of the 'tragic patriot' Jaruzelski provoked virtually no large-scale demonstrations in West Germany—in contrast to the right-wing dictatorship set up by the anti-Marxist General Pinochet in Chile in the year 1973.

Nazi crimes were also occasionally pressed into service in order to justify the lack of West German engagement on behalf of the persecuted workers and intellectuals in Poland. When, in a February 1982 interview with *Die Zeit*, Willy Brandt was asked about French criticism of his lenient assessment of the Polish situation, he explained his position as follows:

It is certainly no surprise that a German is, and probably has to be, more reserved than others when it comes to talking about camps in Poland. For if he were to speak of them, it would automatically provoke the question of what other kinds of camps there have been in Poland. This particular awkwardness, a product of our history, is no problem for the French.

According to journal notes by Markus Wolf, director of the 'enlightenment' department of the East German security ministry, Herbert Wehner, the SPD fraction leader, had been urging the GDR to take 'decisive measures against Poland' as early as August 1981 (Wehner's contact was the lawyer Wolfgang Vogel, who visited him at his vacation home in Öland). 'The sooner, the better . . . Poland dangerous "magnet of incitement" [*Ermunterungssog*]. Internal violence is unavoidable, unfortunately. It's a half-minute to midnight.'

Egon Bahr, the architect of the Social Democratic *Ostpolitik*, was interviewed at the end of October and beginning of November 1981 by a pair of authors working on a book about his views on Germany in the world. Bahr took this occasion to set out his ideas concerning 'mutual security' (*gemeinsame Sicherheit*), a kind of thinking the Soviet Union and East Germany were, he said, still as far from as the United States and West Germany. Nonetheless, Bahr was convinced that

mutual security is the only kind that exists . . . together with the enemy, together in our alliances, together with our respective leading powers. Security for an individual country, in isolation, is no longer available. We can only have it in common with others. Applied to our situation: as the Federal Republic, I can only achieve security together with the GDR. Since otherwise, well, that's a solution to the German question, too: we're united in our downfall.

According to his interviewers, Bahr was saying here that Poland's right 'to a self-determined historical future must, if necessary, be sacrificed to this view and this kind of security. And if Poland's membership in the Warsaw Pact should be called into question, then, in the interest of the stability for which you are arguing, that could be prevented by force of arms. Indeed, it would have to be.'

Bahr agreed with this interpretation.

But of course. We said earlier that the self-determination of the nation must be subordinated to the preservation of peace. That is true for Poland, too. The Poles' national ambitions must also be subordinated to the interests of the preservation of peace. I ask this of the Federal Republic, and I can ask it of the United States. Only underneath this supreme goal should the nations, the states, have the chance to develop themselves individually. But then they should definitely have that chance.

By the time Bahr's security policy credo appeared in print in March 1982, Poland had been under martial law for three months. The Soviet Union had not intervened. Though he was cooperating with Moscow, it was a Polish leader and general who had used force of arms to prevent a development the hardliners believed was threatening all the states of the Warsaw Pact.

For the publicist Günter Gaus, former director of the FRG's permanent representation in the GDR and also a champion of the *Ostpolitik*, the 'Polish' solution was an argument against all those who looked upon the détente policy as definitively in the past. 'In Poland, where it could get much worse any day,' Gaus wrote in *Die Zeit* on 22 January 1982,

the Soviet Union has up to now found reason enough—even after 13 December 1982—to refrain from bringing about the peace of the graveyard . . . What is being demonstrated in Poland at the moment is not the failure of an ideology-free (not value-free) *Ostpolitik*. Rather, we are seeing the confirmation of the maxim that only the recognition of the status quo in Europe—the first, unavoidable step towards détente—will make it possible to overcome the status quo, which will then surely not fail to happen. Détente is a difficult art, for it can only work with a strong partner . . . Recognition of the current status quo in Europe does not proceed from the mistaken assumption that there could be a standstill in politics. But it does mean turning away from a verbal radicalism that calls for a dangerous pace of change and a kind of change that aims for the defeat of the other side. in order to survive, western Europe needs a stable eastern Europe, and vice versa.

In order to demonstrate the epochal importance of the détente policy, Gaus reached far back into the past. 'European détente represents, as it were, the difficult task of pre-empting religious war by means of the 1555 Religious Peace of Augsburg. The edict of toleration of that time also sounded pretty shabby: *cuius regio, eius religio.*'

This was a highly idiosyncratic interpretation of history. The Religious Peace of Augsburg, which empowered the Holy Roman Empire's secular estates and the self-governing imperial knights to determine the confession of their subjects, could hardly be called an 'edict of toleration'. In twentieth-century terms, the Yalta conference was more faithful to the principle of Augsburg than the policy of détente. The 1555 treaty postponed a religious and civil war, which finally came in 1618. Gaus apparently saw Europe on the brink of such a war in 1981–2. In his view the suppression of the Polish struggle for liberty, in addition to being comparatively benign, was necessary for the prevention of such a war. The lenience of the Soviet Union was, in turn, proof that the renunciation of rebellion was a prerequisite for sensible change. This was the essence of the lesson Gaus wanted the Poles—and not only them—to learn from their experiences.

Peter Bender, one of the intellectual pioneers of the new *Ostpolitik* in the 1960s, was, by spring 1982, far more sceptical than Gaus about the chances of peaceful change in the communist east.

There was a revolution in Poland, not in terms of forms, but in terms of importance and dimension. Bonn had not planned for the situation. The social-liberal proponents of *Ostpolitik* have been so fixated on evolutionary change and so fearful of revolution that they did not know how to deal with it. Yet their policies inadvertently promote revolutionary change as well . . . The Polish example is not the first to force us to ask whether evolutionary change is even possible in eastern Europe to the extent it is necessary—necessary to ward off economic and political disasters.

The developments in Poland made Bender inclined to answer this question negatively.

If that is true, then the *Ostpolitik* lesson of 13 December is that we should prepare ourselves for revolutionary movements in the Soviet sphere in the future. Up to now things have happened in intervals of twelve years: from 1956 to 1968 and from 1968 to 1980. Nobody knows how long the deterrent effect will last this time. But all the experts are agreed: the economic difficulties will increase considerably throughout all of eastern Europe, and the contradiction between the wholly obsolete system and the new, more serious economic and political demands will develop great explosive power. This means we should probably expect unrest in the future.

After 13 December 1981 the defenders of *Ostpolitik*, led by Helmut Schmidt, had good reason to distance themselves from the shrill polemics coming out of Ronald Reagan's America and from Washington's call for severe trade and credit sanctions against Poland, which could only increase the country's misery and dependence on the Soviet Union. A moderate tone with Warsaw and Moscow did not necessarily mean acceptance of the political repression in Poland. The West German government sought to put pressure on the Jaruzelski regime on a number of different levels, including through its relationship to the GDR.

In a telephone conversation on 12 January 1982, Schmidt warned Honecker that the longer the state of war lasted in Warsaw, the more east–west relations as a whole would be damaged.

My urgent recommendation is to support the release of a large number of prisoners. As to us in Bonn: with regard to our western partners and friends, but also publicly . . . we are taking General Jaruzelski at his word when he publicly stated then, on 13 December and afterwards, that he wanted to resume [the] reforms etc., go back to that. I cannot judge how much time he still needs and how free he is. But we are very much waiting here for certain signals in this direction. That is, release of the prisoners, lifting of the martial law or the state of war or, to use plain language, resumption of dialogue with the church and the union.

West Germany was not at liberty to carelessly put at risk everything the eastern treaties had achieved in divided Germany. This rule guided Helmut Schmidt's behaviour during the Polish crisis. It was for him no less a part of the FRG's political identity than membership in the western alliance. In his 1987 book *Menschen und Mächte* he wrote of the 'terrible, irresolvably tragic dilemma' of 'knowing oneself morally obligated to intervene but politically incapable of doing anything meaningful'. With regard to other Social Democrats, there was little evidence left of this kind of moral dilemma by the early 1980s. For Wehner, Bahr, and Gaus, international stability had come to represent the only legitimate interest. This meant that the desire for freedom became illegitimate the moment it came into conflict with the stability of the post-war order. The Poles were the first to be confronted with the logic of this Social Democratic security mindset. But if Bender was correct in thinking that communist regimes might be incapable of reform, it stood to reason that the Poles would not long be alone in this experience.[12]

HELMUT SCHMIDT'S LAST YEAR AS CHANCELLOR

A chancellor posed a 'real' question of confidence in his administration for the first time in West German history on 5 February 1982. When Willy Brandt did this on 22 September 1972, he was seeking to demonstrate his administration's lack of the requisite parliamentary support and thus the necessity of new elections.

Helmut Schmidt's move was designed to show his political strength. Since the SPD and FDP had just agreed to a plan to promote employment, a breakdown in the coalition was not to be expected. Still, after the fights over the budget and the amnesty bill, Schmidt wanted to force the Free Democrats to show their colours. He also wanted to discipline the left wing of his own party, which opposed the chancellor above all on security policy. His plan worked: the Bundestag declared its confidence in his government by 269 votes to 224. This did not make 5 February into a day of triumph for the chancellor, however. The mere fact that he had posed the question of confidence was a sign of the coalition's fragility. Schmidt could not afford to repeat this test of strength anytime in the near future.

He passed a different kind of test in April, obtaining clear majorities for his positions on the most controversial matters of security and energy policy at the SPD congress in Munich. Nonetheless, about a third of the delegates came out in support of Erhard Eppler's and Oskar Lafontaine's call for a permanent and total moratorium on the deployment of medium-range missiles, which amounted to a rejection of the NATO double-track decision. The SPD's 'Munich declaration' paired statements of support both for the western alliance and for a 'security partnership with the states of the east'.

Only economic policy revealed a 'leftist' profile. The congress approved a state employment programme financed partly by a short-term tax supplement on higher incomes and a 'labour market tax'. It also called for the abolition of unjustified advantages for tax shelter companies and increased taxation of property value increases. As the Social Democrats well knew, these kinds of demand would not work in a coalition with the FDP.

The Munich congress was followed by a cabinet reshuffle after the resignation of Antje Huber, the Social Democratic minister of the family. She was replaced by Anke Fuchs. Hans Matthöfer, who wanted to resign from the finance ministry for reasons of health, was succeeded by Manfred Lahnstein, hitherto head of the chancellor's office. Matthöfer took over the postal ministry after the departure of Kurt Gscheidle. Heinz Westphal succeeded Herbert Ehrenberg as minister of labour. Klaus Bölling handed over leadership of the FRG's permanent representation in the GDR to Hans-Otto Bräutigam, a non-aligned career diplomat, and resumed his old position as the government's chief of press. Hans-Jürgen Wischnewski also went back to his earlier job as state minister in the chancellor's office, where he had been from 1976 to 1979. Schmidt was obviously seeking to surround himself with colleagues whose experience he trusted. This prompted the Berlin correspondent for *Die Zeit*, Rolf Zundel, to speak of an 'astounding tendency to nostalgia'. The chancellor did little to contradict this impression. The *Neue Zürcher Zeitung* described his new team as 'the last stand', and most of the commentators at the time felt similarly.

In foreign policy the government did not achieve much in the first half of 1982. Schmidt's visit to the United States at the beginning of January was dominated by conflicting views on the Polish crisis. The Reagan administration had wanted the European allies to join in economic sanctions against Poland and the Soviet Union, declared by the United States without any prior consultation; the EC foreign ministers rejected this demand on 4 January. Ever since Schmidt's visit to Honecker, the American press had been portraying him as the leader of a country fascinated with the east and no longer capable of 'seeing the world with clear eyes' (the *New York Times* on 28 December) or even on its way to becoming the 'Finlandized vassal of a totalitarian empire' (the *Wall Street Journal* on 4 January). Reagan, in a personal conversation with the chancellor on 6 January, regretted that Schmidt had been handled unfairly in the American papers, and the joint statement following their talk revealed no differences in position. But all the participants knew that these differences continued undiminished.

This foreign policy disagreement was accompanied by a long-term battle over monetary policy. Reagan's America was pursuing a combination of deficit spending and a high interest rate policy that attracted capital from all over the world. In response, the European central banks found it necessary to raise their own interest rates, and this had a negative effect on the already crisis-ridden European economies. At the end of February 1982 Schmidt and François Mitterrand (the new French president as of May 1981) protested against the economic and financial policies of the United States, but it brought no result.

They were more successful that summer when, together with Margaret Thatcher, they took action against the United States' attempt to use a weapons export ban to stop a planned German–British–French–Soviet natural gas pipeline from Siberia to western Europe. Reagan lifted the ban in December 1982, after Schmidt had left the chancellorship. But the monetary policy differences remained serious.

The United States and the Soviet Union resumed negotiations over intermediate-range nuclear forces (INF) in Geneva on 30 November 1981. For Helmut Schmidt, no other foreign policy issue had such important domestic consequences. In May of that year he had for the first time publicly made his continued chancellorship dependent on his party's support for the NATO double-track policy. He received this support again at the Munich SPD congress in April 1982, though with the understanding that the decision about deploying the American missiles was yet to be actually made. Since the Geneva talks seemed to yield no result, the peace movement grew in strength and with it the resolve of many Social Democrats to oppose western participation in the arms race in all circumstances.

On 16 July 1982, during what became known as the 'walk in the woods', the two main negotiators in Geneva, Paul H. Nitze for the USA and Yuli Kvitsinsky for the USSR, finally managed to reach a compromise: each side was to restrict itself to seventy-five 'systems'. This would have meant the withdrawal of Soviet missiles already in place and reduced the number of units the Americans planned to deploy. Schmidt and Genscher would have accepted this solution.

Unfortunately, the allies did not learn of it until later, in autumn 1982, and then only unofficially through reports in American newspapers. By this time, Washington and Moscow had already rejected the Nitze–Kvitsinsky agreement. It became ever more probable that NATO would deploy its new arms on the scale decided in December 1979.

The lack of progress on the Eurostrategic front did not stop the United States and the USSR from starting negotiations on a different kind of disarmament in the summer of 1982: the Strategic Arms Reduction Talks (START), which commenced on 29 June 1982, also in Geneva. Here it was not only a matter of limiting arms, as in the SALT talks, but of reducing nuclear arsenals. Nonetheless, as far as the security of the continent was concerned, the INF negotiations were far more important. The failure of the Nitze–Kvitsinsky compromise made it clear that Reagan's Washington and Brezhnev's Moscow were pursuing different goals from those of the Schmidt government in Bonn. The two most powerful states in the world had no interest in strategic balance, however defined. It was military and political dominance they were after.[13]

FROM SCHMIDT TO KOHL: THE 1982 WATERSHED

The fragility of the SPD–FDP coalition was increasingly evident throughout the summer of 1982. Both parties suffered serious setbacks in the Hamburg election on 6 June. The Social Democrats lost 8.3% of the vote, falling from 51.5% to 43.2%. The Free Democrats sank from 6.6% to 4.9%. While this was only a 1.7% loss, it brought them below the 5% hurdle and cost the FDP its place in parliament. A few days later the Hesse FDP, after consulting with the party leadership in Bonn, decided to abandon the SPD after the Hesse elections on 26 September and form a governing coalition with the CDU.

The news from Hamburg and Wiesbaden put pressure on the federal government coalition just when difficult negotiations for the 1983 federal budget were getting under way. By 30 June, however, the two sides managed to reach an agreement, contrary to the expectations of many. It bore more of a liberal than a Social Democratic stamp: the SPD agreed to introduce partial self-financing for hospital treatment and stays at spas, as well as health insurance contributions by the retired.

It was not easy for the chancellor to bring the SPD Bundestag fraction into line behind the government. He admitted that the parts of the agreement dealing with the battle against unemployment were not satisfactory. But he did not blame the FDP. Instead, he described a Social Democratic dilemma:

Whoever wants to do more must cut deeper into social services than I suggested doing in the compromise package. Of the two possibilities, the one, namely financing through more debt, will be blocked by me. I cannot countenance that. It is you who are blocking the second possibility. Whoever wants to do more in terms of state spending for employment programmes must cut deeper than this into social services. Much deeper.

Two weeks later, on 15 July, the readers of the Hamburg magazine *Stern* had the chance to read what one of Schmidt's opponents in the SPD thought of the coalition compromise. Oskar Lafontaine, head of the SPD in Saarland and mayor of Saarbrücken (he was educated as a physicist), asked his readers a rhetorical question: 'What has the 1983 budget agreement between the SPD and the FDP actually changed in Bonn?' His answer: 'Helmut Schmidt goes on to talk about sense of duty, predictability, plausibility, steadfastness. Those are secondary virtues. To be exact: you can run a concentration camp with them. They are secondary virtues, the kind you have recourse to when you haven't dealt internally with what's really at stake: namely the preservation of life.'

Lafontaine had no doubt about the direction his party had to take: 'The SPD must leave the Bonn government. As things are, the party will only be able to regenerate itself in the role of opposition. Only then will we find a new concept of society, one that meets the requirements of the future.' This programme of 'regeneration' included a clear rejection of the NATO double-track policy:

All this talk about the necessity of weapons modernization is eyewash. There is such a large number of nuclear weapons that it's no longer even possible to lose. Instead we are losing control of weapons technology, and we are at the point of sliding involuntarily into an atomic holocaust. That's the reason Willy Brandt is correct. Unfortunately, this goal is impossible with Helmut Schmidt. He has no idea what's happening among young people.

Lafontaine's personal attacks were doubly wounding to the chancellor, since, apart from the 'Seeheim circle' on the party right, only weak protest was to be heard from the SPD as a whole. Aggressive language from the unions was even more dangerous, since they had usually supported Schmidt in the past. At the end of July Ernst Breit, head of the German Trade Union Association, announced a campaign against the political implementation of the budget compromise. Karl-Heinz Janzen, who sat on the board of the engineering union IG Metall, warned in the August edition of the Social Democratic journal *Die Neue Gesellschaft* that the 30 June decisions could lead to a 'deep rupture in the historically good relationship between the SPD and the unions'.

By August the liberals were also now unmistakably on the attack. In an interview with Radio Hesse on 15 August, the leader of the FDP, Foreign Minister Hans-Dietrich Genscher, spoke of the 'great task' of bringing about a 'turn to reason, to responsibility, to a greater freedom for the individual to shape his life and future'. He sharply criticized the SPD, particularly the prime minister of Hesse, Holger Börner, for allegedly 'socialist' tendencies, then talked about 'new majorities' and projects that would 'find their own majorities'. Two weeks later, in an interview with the *Bild-Zeitung*, Graf Lambsdorff, the minister of economics, described the Hesse election as a referendum on leadership change in Bonn. 'The voters in Hesse will decide what they think of the FDP joining another coalition. That would be an important thing for us in Bonn to know.'

During a meeting of the SPD fraction on 22 June, Helmut Schmidt had made a remarkable pronouncement: 'It is my firm conviction that we cannot be the ones who take upon ourselves the risk and culpability of failure.' This was the lesson he drew from the collapse of the Grand Coalition under Hermann Müller in March 1930, an event he had also referred to numerous times in the past (and would again at the fraction meeting on 30 June). Once the intentions of the FDP leadership were clear, Schmidt tenaciously stuck to this lesson, determined to make it as obvious as possible that an end of the coalition would be the liberals' doing. During a cabinet meeting on 1 September the chancellor castigated Lambsdorff and demanded that he submit his economic views to him in written form. Notice of this reprimand immediately went via Bölling to the press.

Then, before Lambsdorff could respond, Schmidt confronted the FDP in public. On the morning of 9 September, during the annual 'state of the nation' address in the Bundestag, the chancellor exhorted Helmut Kohl, the CDU/CSU fraction leader, to call for a constructive vote of no confidence. He prefaced this part of his speech by noting that, in what he was about to say, he did not claim to speak for the government as a whole, but was simply availing himself of the rights granted to the chancellor by the Basic Law. In words indirectly intended for Genscher, too, Schmidt turned to Kohl: 'If there is a majority in parliament for different kinds of policies, then by all means! That's the reason the Basic Law has Article 67. Make use of Article 67! Bring forward a petition for a constructive vote of no confidence, Herr Dr Kohl! Let us vote on it next week! . . . The citizens have a right to have this cleared up, Herr Dr Kohl!'

If the Bundestag was going to elect Kohl as his successor in a secret ballot, then, Schmidt said, he would have to compel new elections, for two reasons:

First: because a chancellor needs not only fundamental legality, but also—beyond all covert preparation for a constructive vote of no confidence—a historical legitimation which only the voters can grant. And secondly: because you have to tell the people ahead of time what you actually intend to do differently . . . If a historical era in the development of our state is going to be terminated, then let it take place in the open and with a clear decision on the part of those who want it, with reasons worthy of our state's history, not trivial and artificial arguments.

The SPD delegates gave the chancellor a standing ovation, thanking him for a 'liberating' speech. And indeed, it did have a clarifying effect. The Free Democrats could no longer keep manoeuvring between the two large popular parties, undermining the authority of a government in which they were participants. They had to make a decision.

As for Helmut Schmidt, his decision was now made. He had stuck to his party, whose service on behalf of the 'freedom and justice in Germany' he described in eloquent terms. Even more important, he emphasized the SPD's contribution to the cause of parliamentary democracy. It was this tradition that was in jeopardy if the coalition crisis persisted and the government continued to lose its ability to act.

In calling for new elections after a constructive vote of no confidence, Schmidt was calling upon the people to decide the outcome of the power struggle in Bonn. However, since the Bundestag did not have the right to dissolve itself (it could only be dissolved by the president after rejecting a vote of confidence in the chancellor), this proposal created constitutional problems. Nonetheless the idea of democratic legitimacy, such as it had been developing since 1949, made an *appel au peuple* seem indispensable.

Kohl's and Genscher's words after the chancellor's speech gave no clue as to how they would react to his challenge. The memorandum Schmidt had demanded from Lambsdorff, on the other hand, could be interpreted as the FDP's response. (It was given to the chancellor that evening.) It was a coherent manifesto for economic liberalism, for supply-oriented and against demand-oriented economic policy, for the promotion of private investment and the 'adjustment of the social security systems to the changes in the possibilities for growth and a longer-term consolidation of their finances'. This was the kind of thing Social Democrats often termed 'social dismantling' (*Sozialabbau*), 'redistribution from bottom to top', and a 'dog-eat-dog society' (*Ellbogengesellschaft* or 'elbow society' in German).

Lambsdorff defended his policies against accusations that it represented 'social demontage' or was 'socially unbalanced' or even 'unsocial'. 'In reality', he argued, it served 'the recovery and renewal of the economic foundations of our social system'. The economics minister knew that he would be hearing these charges not only from the Social Democrats, but also from labour-oriented groups within the Union, if not from the CDU and CSU leaders themselves. Politically speaking, that is, his views were largely unworkable.

Such practical considerations did not affect the strategic purpose of the memorandum. Lambsdorff was seeking to end the coalition with the Social Democrats; that was the reason he talked about the 'important crossroads' at which West Germany now stood. Since he presented it on the same day the chancellor gave his state of the nation address, it was clear that Lambsdorff's paper would be interpreted as a liberal rejoinder to Schmidt's Social Democratic credo, seeking like the latter to bring philosophical closure to the era of social–liberal cooperation. And that was exactly how it was intended.

At the cabinet meeting of 15 September the chancellor noted that his economics minister's ideas were at odds with the government's policy, and he asked Lambsdorff if his paper was intended as a 'letter of farewell'. Lambsdorff insisted that he had merely wanted to propose solutions to the specific questions at hand. But he could not undo his public statements to the contrary. Schmidt gave him two days' time to clear things up. But the chancellor made his own decision that same day: he would dismiss the four FDP ministers after his formal ultimatum expired on 17 September and transfer their posts to SPD cabinet members.

Since Kohl had not taken up his suggestion of 9 September, Schmidt now tried another tactic to bring about new elections. In cooperation with the opposition, which would have to renounce the option of a constructive vote of no confidence in this case, the chancellor would pose the question of confidence as leader of a minority cabinet and, through his party's abstention from the ballot, secure its rejection. The Bundestag could then be dissolved and new elections scheduled for November, towards the end of the sixty-day period required by the Basic Law. On the advice of Klaus Bölling, Schmidt would not blame the crisis on Lambsdorff, who after all had always pursued his aims openly and honestly, but rather on Genscher, the foreign minister and FDP head, who was to be represented as having worked behind the scenes for a long time to bring about the end of the coalition.

But Genscher knew the chancellor's intentions and, on 17 September, asked him for permission to resign. He was soon joined by the three other liberal ministers, Lambsdorff, Baum, and Ertl. Thereupon Schmidt proposed to the president that the vacancies be filled by means of dual appointments until the new elections could be held. He himself would head the foreign office; Finance Minister Lahnstein would take economics, Justice Minister Schmude the interior, and Education Minister Engholm the ministry of agriculture. (Engholm, originally from Schleswig-Holstein, had succeeded Jürgen Schmude in education in January 1981 when the latter succeeded Hans-Jochen Vogel as minister of justice.)

The dismissal of the four FDP ministers and the appointment of the SPD double ministers brought the social–liberal coalition, formed thirteen years previously in October 1969, to an end. Strictly speaking, the term 'social–liberal' had been inappropriate ever since the middle of the 1970s, when serious rifts had first begun to appear between the two parties. Under the chancellorship of Helmut Schmidt, their cooperation yielded very few new impulses to reform.

On the other hand, no other Social Democrat could have held the coalition together as long as Helmut Schmidt, for whom the state was always more important than the party. The demise of his administration was caused not by one, but by two parties. The Social Democrats had been distancing themselves more and more from their chancellor's policy on weapons modernization. The economic and finance platforms of the Munich congress in April had damaged relations with the liberals. In both areas, the FDP now had more in common with the Union than with the Social Democrats. This reality found expression in the FDP's Wiesbaden coalition statement and the public comments by Lambsdorff and Genscher. Furthermore, the FDP had reason to hope that the amnesty for illegal party finance activities, torpedoed by Social Democrats in December 1981, could be passed with the help of the CDU/CSU. That big industrial donors also wanted leadership change was self-evident.

On 17 September Helmut Schmidt stepped up to the podium of the Bundestag for the first time as chancellor of a SPD minority government. Part of what he had to say was an attempt to sum up the political era that had just come to a close.

If a historical epoch in the development of our democratic community is now . . . coming to an end; if the future of this development is now uncertain, nonetheless I wish on this occasion to once again emphasize my pride in what the social–liberal coalition has accomplished. I am proud of how we worked our way through the reform deficit left to us in 1969; I am proud of how we built up the social welfare state; and I am proud of the peace policy we pursued together with our neighbours in the east. I am proud of these common accomplishments, and I will defend them with great energy.

The main purpose of the chancellor's address, however, was an attempt to reach an understanding with the opposition about a way out of the immediate political crisis, and in this Schmidt did not succeed. At this juncture, with the coalition formally terminated, a constructive vote of no confidence had much better chances than before. If Kohl and Genscher chose not to exercise this option, they would allow Helmut Schmidt, who was very popular, to campaign with the advantages of an incumbent. Consequently, it was in their interest to reach an agreement as rapidly as possible and then use Article 67 to petition for a constructive vote of no confidence. Before that could happen, however, Genscher had to convince his own party and fraction of the necessity of coalition negotiations with the Union. At the fraction meeting in the afternoon of 17 September, 33 FDP delegates voted for talks, 18 against them, and 1 abstained. The vote was even closer in the federal party executive that evening: 18 members supported Genscher's line, 15 rejected it. The FDP faced a difficult test.

While the Union and the Free Democrats negotiated over a new coalition, the electoral campaign was coming to an end in Hesse. Schmidt was cheered wherever he went, finding large audiences for his accusations of treason against Genscher and the FDP. The election results on 26 September caused a sensation. The CDU received 45.6% of the vote, 0.4% less than four years previously. The SPD's 42.8% represented a loss of 1.5%, but that was a far better outcome than opinion surveys had been predicting that summer. The FDP was the big loser, falling from 6.6% to 3.1% and therefore now out of the parliament. The winners were the Greens, who gained 8% of the vote.

The chancellor had succeeded in 'punishing' the liberals in Hesse. To this extent his masterful crisis management was already bearing tangible fruit. Still, who would the Social Democrats work with in the future if they themselves did not have a majority and the Free Democrats were no longer in the Hesse parliament? Willy Brandt, commenting on the Green party's success in a television programme on the evening of the election, referred to 'the majority on this side of the Union', an indication of what *he* was thinking about future coalition possibilities. For Schmidt, cooperation with the eco-pacifists was out of the question, for reasons of foreign as well as domestic policy. The two men clashed fiercely on the subject at a meeting of the SPD executive on 27 September. But the only alternative to 'red–green' was 'red–black' (or 'black–red'), a constellation Schmidt himself remembered fondly from his time as fraction leader during the Grand Coalition. As long as Helmut Kohl was head of the Union, however, a return to this kind of alliance was inconceivable. Kohl had committed himself to a 'bourgeois' coalition.

Despite his party's losses, Kohl was still one of the winners of the Hesse election; its outcome weakened his most dangerous adversary. Franz Josef Strauss, who still wanted to avoid a coalition with the FDP, had been pushing for new elections without a prior change in the chancellorship, believing an absolute CDU/CSU majority now within reach. After 26 September this position was no longer tenable. It was true that for Genscher and Lambsdorff, Kohl prospective partners, the Hesse election had totally failed their hopes as a signal for a new coalition in Bonn. Since there was now no way back for them, however, their only interest was in a speedy conclusion to the coalition talks with the Union. And so it happened: by the evening of the next day, 27 September, the agreement was substantially in the bag. There was even an informal understanding about the date of the new federal elections: 6 March 1983.

The FDP made its official decisions on 28 September. Of the 54 liberal delegates in the Bundestag (including the one from Berlin), 34 voted for and 18 against a constructive vote of no confidence—that is, the replacement of Helmut Schmidt by Helmut Kohl. There were 2 abstentions. In the federal party executive the 'social liberals', who rejected Genscher's plan, were a good deal stronger; the motion to leave the coalition decision to an extraordinary party congress failed by only one vote. Of the 35 members of the executive, 19 voted for the constructive vote of no confidence, 16 against it.

Later that same evening, the Union and liberal fractions brought forward a motion that the Bundestag pronounce its lack of confidence in Helmut Schmidt and elect Helmut Kohl as his successor. This motion was the only item on the agenda for the 118th session of the ninth German Bundestag on the morning of 1 October 1982. Schmidt was the first to speak. He reminded the parliament what Genscher had said during the 1980 electoral campaign: 'Voting FDP guarantees that Schmidt remains chancellor.' Addressing the new majority, he concluded: 'The change in leadership you are striving for compromises the credibility of our democratic institutions.' Then, after restating the main lines of his policy in twelve points, Schmidt turned to his own party. In his final words, he thanked the Germans in the Federal and German Democratic Republics for the trust they had shown in the SPD's policy of peace and good neighbourly relations. 'We will not disappoint it in the future, either. Everybody can and everybody must count on our dependability.'

On the Union side, former party head Rainer Barzel was given the task of vindicating the use of Article 67. He emphasized the legitimacy of a constructive vote of no confidence: 'The German people vote for parliamentary representatives; they do not vote for the chancellor on election day . . . So when we vote for a chancellor today, we are making legitimate use of Article 67 of the Basic Law.' Turning to the Social Democrats, Barzel called out: 'Now go! For you have transformed the thriving community you took control of into a crisis-ridden country. That is now the situation.'

The speeches of the FDP delegates drew particular attention. Fraction leader Wolfgang Mischnick, who had loyally defended the SPD–FDP coalition to the end, was the only speaker who criticized the appeal to the Basic Law to justify the dissolution of the parliament and new elections. He first paid tribute to the coalition's achievements, then justified its termination by stating 'that in many questions we have, objectively speaking, nothing more in common'. 'More individual responsibility' and the need to 'renounce the entitlement mentality': these were the key ideas Mischnick cited in his attempt to explain the reason for the shift in leadership.

Former interior minister Gerhart Rudolf Baum, speaking for the minority, saw no 'substantive reason' for the end of the coalition and stated: 'The procedure that has led to the motion to vote Chancellor Helmut Schmidt out of office can, we fear, cause a change in the political culture of this country.' Hildegard Hamm-Brücher, also in the minority group, refused to vote against the chancellor in whom she had pronounced her confidence only a few months before.

I find that neither deserves this—Helmut Schmidt, to be brought down without the vote of the people, and you, Helmut Kohl, to get to the chancellor's office without the people's vote. Doubtless each of these mutually dependent procedures conforms to the constitution. Nonetheless for me they have the odium of violated democratic decency . . . As it were they damage the moral-ethical integrity of shifts in power.

The Bundestag president, Richard Stücklen (CSU), announced the result of the ballot at 3.10 in the afternoon. Of the 495 votes given (all of which were valid), 256 were for the change in the chancellorship, 235 against, with 4 delegates abstaining. This was the first successful constructive vote of no confidence in the history of the FRG. Among the first to congratulate Helmut Kohl, the new chancellor, was the man who had just been voted out of office.

After the FDP congress in Berlin in November 1982, at which Hans-Dietrich Genscher was re-elected head of the FDP by a narrow majority, four delegates who had opposed the end of the coalition and the constructive vote of no confidence left the party: Ingrid Matthäus-Maier, Friedrich Hölscher, Andreas von Schoeler, and Helga Schuchardt. Matthäus-Maier and Schoeler turned in their seats that December and joined the SPD, as did Günter Verheugen, who had resigned his post as general secretary of the FDP under protest on 29 September. Another prominent liberal, William Borm, former honorary president of the Bundestag (he was also a former political prisoner, and it would later emerge that he had been working for the GDR ministry of security since 1957–8), founded a party of 'Liberal Democrats' (*Liberale Demokraten*) at the end of November, but had no success.

Helmut Schmidt's fall from power did not harm his reputation—quite the opposite. Even his political adversaries expressed admiration for the brilliance he had demonstrated in bringing the coalition crisis to an end in autumn 1982. No chancellor before him had possessed such expertise and sound judgement in so many areas of policy. If he had a political weakness, it was his habit of making others feel his intellectual superiority, irrespective of person or office.

The great fundamental decisions that shaped the course of West German politics and society had, of course, already been made before Schmidt became chancellor in May 1974: the 'Social Market Economy', the alliance with the west, the opening towards the east. Unlike Konrad Adenauer and Willy Brandt, Helmut Schmidt would not go down in history as a political pioneer, but as a statesman who defended and consolidated what had already been achieved. He helped West Germany deal with the consequences of terrorism and world economic crisis; he played a decisive part in blocking the Soviet attempt to use its missiles to gain political power over western Europe; and, together with Valéry Giscard-d'Estaing, he laid the foundations for the European monetary union.

The fifth chancellor of the FRG was a dedicated 'pragmatist'. During his last state of the nation address on 9 September 1982, he set out his political philosophy in a way that sounded like a political testament:

Political action is not the automatic result of one's morals, ethics, or theology. Pragmatic political action is the rational employment of means to a morally justified end, and these means also cannot be immoral. Political pragmatism does not lose sight of its goal in the daily press of business; nor, in focusing on the goal and in talking about the goal, does it overlook what can be accomplished today, and every day. I often think that politics as a whole must be the application of firm moral-ethical principles to very mutable circumstances. Which also means that there can be no pragmatic and practical action without commitment to duty, to moral principles and fundamental values.

As the eight-year chancellorship of Helmut Schmidt was coming to an end, there were developments in West Germany that required urgent attention. The 'spiritual-moral renewal' that Helmut Kohl often talked about was needed in one area in particular, though Schmidt's successor would have been the last to think of it: the scandalous practices of party finance, which were incompatible with the rule of law. Apart from that, there was a general need to review vested rights and privileges that had originated in earlier, economically better days. The social welfare state had to be restructured or it would lose its financial base; on this point the liberal critique was basically correct. The tax system contained numerous unfair privileges and 'loopholes' that benefited higher income groups and burdened the nation as a whole; the Social Democrats were right in calling attention to this state of affairs.

Simple justice dictated that both of these reforms had to be undertaken simultaneously, and the SPD and FDP were neither willing nor able to do it. Whether the new Christian–liberal coalition would do better was, in the autumn of 1982, as uncertain as the future as a whole.[14]

LEGITIMATING THE CHANGE: THE 1983 ELECTIONS

The sixth chancellor of the Federal Republic of Germany was sworn into office by Bundestag president Richard Stücklen in the late afternoon of 1 October 1982. Helmut Kohl pronounced the oath as required by Article 56 of the constitution, along with the voluntary religious affirmation that all of his predecessors had also spoken: 'I swear that I will dedicate my efforts to the well-being of the German people, promote their welfare, protect them from harm, uphold and defend the Basic Law and the laws of the Federation, perform my duties conscientiously, and do justice to all. So help me God.'

Helmut Kohl was born in Ludwigshafen on the Rhine on 3 April 1930. He completed a doctoral degree in history, and was active in the CDU from early youth. In many ways he was the opposite of his predecessor. Helmut Schmidt was an astute analyst, an expert in many fields, and a brilliant speaker. Kohl, a 'generalist', was guided by his instincts and personal experiences. As Jürgen Busche, one of his biographers, writes, Kohl's speaking revealed 'a lack of intellectual self-control in the formulation of sentences and choice of images, to an extent hitherto inconceivable in the realm of public speaking'. His awkwardness as an orator was one of the main reasons he was perpetually underestimated and long disdained by intellectuals. Nobody, however, could deny that he possessed a highly developed instinct for the acquisition and preservation of political power. He had already been head of the CDU for nine years by the time he became chancellor. Though not yet in full control of his party, he was far advanced toward this end. This meant that from the very start of his chancellorship he had a power base of the kind Helmut Schmidt was never able to count on.

As Kohl saw things, the party of Konrad Adenauer was the real founder of the Federal Republic, and this gave it a greater right to rule than that enjoyed by any other party. Like Adenauer, he was absolutely convinced that the alliance with the west was irreversible and the political unification of Europe was necessary. At the same time he was a true child of the Rhineland and, as such, a German patriot in the unbroken tradition of the 1832 Hambach Festival. Unlike Adenauer, he felt a deep connection to Berlin, which he always considered the capital of Germany.

Since he looked upon every bit of power that came his way as his and his party's due, the same was true of the means required to preserve that power. Only much later, after the end of his chancellorship, would it emerge how far he went in this quest. The oath of office, which he had occasion to reiterate several times, did not prevent him from breaking laws he himself had signed. By accepting donations that were never recorded in the CDU reports—a practice that went on for many years—he violated the Basic Law and the law governing the activities of the political parties. He used these donations as he saw fit, often to create networks of personal dependence that shored up his own position. He saw nothing objectionable in the support of a large company like Flick during his quest for the chancellorship. Once he was chancellor, he accepted illegal funds in order to stay in office. He did not perceive the damage this behaviour caused to the political culture of his country. He lacked respect for the norms and institutions of the rule of law, a respect he was obligated as chancellor to demand, and did demand, from the citizens of West Germany.

Kohl presented his cabinet on 4 October, three days after his election. Three of the four FDP ministers returned to the posts they had occupied up to 17 September: vice chancellor and foreign minister Hans-Dietrich Genscher, economics minister Otto Graf Lambsdorff, and minister of agriculture Josef Ertl. The fourth cabinet liberal was new: Hans A. Engelhard, a lawyer from Munich, as minister of justice. Friedrich Zimmermann, up to this point regional head of the CSU, succeeded Gerhart Rudolf Baum as interior minister. Zimmermann was by far the most controversial German politician. In July 1960 he had been convicted of negligent perjury in connection with a Munich bank scandal, a sentence reversed in 1961 when a medical statement certified that he had been in a state of reduced physical and mental health. Even after his acquittal, however, Zimmermann could not shake his nickname 'Old Schwurhand'.*

The other members of the cabinet were: Gerhard Stoltenberg (CDU), finance minister; Norbert Blüm (CDU), minister of labour and social affairs; Manfred Wörner (CDU), defence minister; Heiner Geissler, CDU general secretary and minister of youth, family, and health; Werner Dollinger (CSU), transport minister; Christian Schwarz-Schilling (CDU), minister of the postal service and telecommunications; Oscar Schneider (CSU), minister of construction; Rainer Barzel (CDU), minister of German–German relations; Heinz Riesenhuber (CDU), minister of research and technology; Dorothee Wilms (CDU), minister of education and science; and Jürgen Warnke (CSU), minister of economic cooperation.

The new chancellor gave his inaugural address in the Bundestag on 13 October. He began by painting a dismal picture of the country's economic and financial situation, then went on to set out his guidelines for a 'politics of renewal'. On the one hand, additional federal revenue generated by the increase in the value-added tax on 1 July 1983 (passed by the previous administration) would be given back to citizens and businesses. On the other hand, the next pension adjustment would be shifted forward six months to 1 July 1983. 'We will preserve the

---

* [Translator's note: literally 'Old Oathhand'; the name is a pun on German author Karl May's western adventure novel *Old Surehand*.]

social welfare state by consolidating its economic foundations,' Kohl announced, in one of the key statements in the new government's social policy platform. Another one was the following: 'The question of the future is not how much more the state can do for its citizens. The question of the future is how freedom, dynamism, and personal responsibility can flourish anew. This is the idea on which the coalition of the centre is based.'

In the foreign policy part of his speech the chancellor said something that 'caused consternation among the SPD': 'The alliance is at the centre of the identity of the German state' (*Das Bündnis ist der Kernpunkt deutscher Staatsräson*). He went on to talk about the necessity of 'creating peace with ever fewer weapons', declared his administration's support for the NATO double-track decision, and assured his audience that 'an active peace policy with regard to the states of central and eastern Europe' continued to be one of the tasks of German foreign policy'. In this connection he called the Final Act of Helsinki—which the Union parties had rejected in 1975—'an opportunity, a charter for the coexistence of the states in Europe'. Through the eastern treaties a *modus vivendi* had been worked out with the east. 'We will stand by these treaties and we will use them as instruments of an active foreign policy.'

On the German–German situation Kohl had, among other things, the following to say: 'The nation state of the Germans is shattered. The German nation has remained, and it will continue to exist.' The chancellor did not use the word 'reunification' in his address, but he did quote from the 1970 'Letter on German Unity', according to which it was the goal of German politics to 'work for a state of peace in Europe in which the German nation will be able to regain its unity through free self-determination'. The promises of domestic renewal were thus flanked by assurances that the new administration would maintain continuity in foreign and Germany policy and clear away any doubts about West Germany's dependability as a member of the Atlantic alliance. This was Kohl's message to the Germans and the rest of the world on 13 October 1982.

As the Union and FDP had agreed, the date for the new Bundestag elections would be 6 March 1983. But there was an obstacle: the constitutional objections of the president, Karl Carstens, a scholar of national and international law and former professor at the University of Cologne. In a conversation with the chancellor on 10 November 1982, Carstens insisted that he would have to talk with the coalition partners and be convinced 'that the government did not have a majority in central matters of foreign and domestic policy' before he would dissolve parliament.

The president's reservations against an 'inauthentic' vote of no confidence had not yet been cleared up when Kohl brought forward the relevant motion under Article 68 of the Basic Law on 13 December. The motion was distributed in print the following day. On 16 December the Bundestag passed the federal budget, once again demonstrating that the administration had a majority. The vote of no confidence was on the agenda for 17 December. It had to take place on this day in order to keep to the schedule that had been agreed upon. According to Article 68, the president had twenty one days to decide whether to dissolve parliament. If he did so on 7 January, the last possible day, new elections would have to be held within sixty days. The last possible date was then 6 March 1983. There would be just two months left for campaigning. It would also take this amount of time to meet the requirements of the federal election laws.

In the debate preceding the vote of no confidence Kohl said that the coalition needed 'the decision of the people as a basis for the necessary, long-term and broadly conceived policy of renewal'. All the parties in the Bundestag, as well as the great majority of the citizens, wanted new elections. The Social Democrats would have preferred another path, as party head Willy Brandt pointed out: 'the chancellor's resignation, constitutionally completely unproblematic'. He accused Kohl—and rightly so, from a constitutional standpoint—of using the scheduled election date as a way of putting pressure on the president. At the same time, he made it clear that the SPD also insisted on holding elections on 6 March. Two politicians raised serious constitutional objections to an inauthentic vote of no confidence: Hansheinrich Schmidt of the FDP, and the former liberal, now independent delegate Helga Schuchardt. But this did not affect the outcome of the ballot. With most of the Union and liberal delegates abstaining (in keeping with a coalition agreement) and the Social Democrats voting against it, Kohl's motion for a vote of confidence failed to gain a majority (the final tally was 218 to 8, with 248 abstentions).

On 6 January 1983 President Carstens signed two directives, the first dissolving the ninth German Bundestag, the second scheduling new elections for 6 March 1983. The following day he explained his decisions to the population in an address broadcast on radio and television. His main arguments were the following. There was no majority in parliament that stood to benefit from new elections while harming the interests of a minority; both the coalition and the opposition wanted them. Moreover, the head of the Union fraction had stated that in the absence of new elections his fraction would no longer support the government. Carstens also mentioned a statement from the FDP speaker that the 'confidence bonus' the new government had enjoyed while setting up its new platform was now exhausted. He, the president, was therefore convinced 'that the government no longer had a viable parliamentary majority behind its policies. In this critical situation, unique in the history of the Federal Republic of Germany, the request for new elections, which all the parties have made, seems to me to be politically justified.'

The president was the highest state authority, but in this case his was not the final say. That belonged to the Federal Constitutional Court, which had to pronounce on a suit brought forward by four Bundestag delegates asserting that the premature dissolution of parliament had violated their rights. The court rejected this claim on 16 February. Using arguments like those of Carstens, it granted the president, Bundestag, and chancellor the authority to put an 'open constitutional norm' like that of Article 68 into concrete form. While this decision caused some controversy in the press, it also finally guaranteed that new elections would indeed be held on 6 March 1983.

Since the Bundestag was not authorized to dissolve itself, using an inauthentic vote of confidence for this purpose was an emergency expedient. Unlike in September 1972, when parliamentary stalemate had prompted Willy Brandt to use such tactics for the first time, in December 1982 the Kohl administration did control a majority. But there was general agreement on one point: in the light of how the 'chancellor democracy' had developed since 1949, a constructive vote of no confidence was not sufficient to give long-term public legitimacy to a change in national leadership. 'A democratic republic needs both legality and legitimacy,' wrote Theo Sommer, editor-in-chief at the liberal weekly *Die Zeit*, on 12 November 1983. 'A legality that does not enjoy legitimacy is as destructive as a legitimacy that turns its back on legality. But legality suffers no harm if Helmut Kohl uses Article 68 as a detour to new elections.'

By the end of October, it was clear that Helmut Kohl's Social Democratic challenger was not going to be Helmut Schmidt. The party leadership was urging him to run, but he decided against it, for reasons of health as well as politics. He had to have a pacemaker implanted in autumn 1981, and even a year later his health was still weak. But he also knew that on central questions like the NATO double-track decision and nuclear energy the SPD was moving away from policies he considered correct. He addressed this openly at the fraction meeting on 26 October. After Schmidt declined to run, Brandt asked general secretary Peter Glotz to broach the subject with two potential candidates, Johannes Rau and Hans-Jochen Vogel. Rau was prime minister of North Rhine-Westphalia, an office he had held since 1978; Vogel had been elected mayor of Berlin at the end of January 1981, but had had to cede the office to Richard von Weizsäcker in June of the same year after early elections to the Berlin House of Representatives.

Since Rau did not wish to run, the SPD executive nominated Vogel on 29 October. Three weeks later, on 19 November, the decision was ratified by a 'little party congress' in Kiel. Vogel summarized his election platform as follows: 'We want to preserve existing jobs and create new ones; secure the peace abroad and do everything in our power to bring the arms race to an end; make peace with nature and preserve the environment; assert the liberality and the defendability of our law-based state and uphold social tranquility.'

Earlier, when he was mayor of Munich between 1960 and 1972, Vogel had been one of the SPD 'right' and the staunchest opponent of the 'Young Socialists' within the party. By now, however, he had become the classic 'centrist', striving to bring oppositional forces within the party together and respected by all; a bridge-builder, seeking to give both Schmidt's and Eppler's factions the feeling that he understood them and was equally close to both of them. Hans Apel, who was generally critical of him, found words of recognition for the energy with which Vogel made 'the debased fraction and the shack [SPD party headquarters, H.A.W.] get a move on'. Apel nonetheless considered Vogel's leadership style bureaucratic and authoritarian and thought he lacked important qualities as a candidate for the chancellorship.

Political objectives are not to be heard from him. In my first speech after the changeover I said about Genscher that he confused politics with meteorology. He simply has no interest in shaping policy and, if necessary, sailing against a hard wind. He follows the weather, gives the weather report, and adapts to it. But isn't Vogel exactly the same? Either he lacks political vision and therefore objectives, or he follows the majority, not wanting to fight. Politically it amounts to the same thing.

The Social Democratic campaign slogan was 'In the German interest'. The message was clear: the Kohl–Genscher government was prepared to subordinate German to American interests; it took the military part of the NATO policy more seriously than the diplomatic part; it was not going to stand up to the virulently anti-communist American president. Having moved closer to the peace movement after the end of Schmidt's chancellorship, the SPD conducted a 'missile campaign' in spring 1983. 'A vote for Kohl automatically means new missiles,' as one electoral advertisement read.

Kohl's campaign received help from one side that was highly unwelcome to the Social Democrats. On 20 January 1983 François Mitterrand, France's Socialist president, addressing the last plenary session of the ninth German parliament on the occasion of the twentieth anniversary of the signing of the Franco-German treaty, came out strongly in favour of a rigorous implementation of the NATO double-track policy. For the rest, the chancellor trusted in the Union slogan 'For Germany to go forward, vote for the upswing!' (*Aufwärts mit Deutschland—jetzt den Aufschwung wählen*) and in admonitory statements by his party's general secretary, Heiner Geissler, such as: 'Whoever votes SPD on 6 March puts his own job at risk.'

The outcome of the election was a triumph for the Union and a serious defeat for the Social Democrats. Together the CDU and CSU won 48.8% of the vote, 4.3% more than in October 1980. The SPD lost 4.7%, falling from 42.9% to 38.2%, its weakest performance since 1961. The FDP managed 7%, a loss of 3.6%. The Greens gained 5.6%, surmounting the 5 per cent barrier for the first time on the federal level. (In 1980 they had obtained 1.5%.) Both the Union and the Greens profited from the losses of the SPD, whose leftward shift cost it more centrist voters than it made up on the left. The FDP had alienated many 'social–liberal' voters, but still done much better than had been predicted in the period immediately following the coalition change. Six months onward, the shift in leadership had been indisputably legitimated by the citizens of West Germany.

Kohl presented his second cabinet on 30 March. Owing to their losses, the FDP now had to make do with three positions, the ministry of agriculture going to the CSU delegate Ignaz Kiechle. The other newcomer was Heinrich Windelen (CDU) for German–German relations; his predecessor Rainer Barzel had been elected president of the Bundestag the day before. The chancellor gave his second inaugural address on 4 May. It was a detailed summary of the goals each ministry had set itself for the next legislative period. Bold visions were there none. The will to 'spiritual renewal' now exhausted itself in formulaic pledges to such things as a 'society with a human face', which would distinguish itself through the 'spirit of human fellowship' and 'civic spirit in practice'.[15]

REPUBLIC FOR SALE: THE PARTY FINANCE SCANDAL AND THE FLICK AFFAIR

On 19 May 1983, about two weeks after Kohl's second inaugural, the tenth German Bundestag set up a committee to look into the Flick party finance affair. This move had been preceded by federal investigations and several thoroughly researched leading articles in *Der Spiegel*. The press, the investigating committee, and court proceedings gave the public its first detailed glimpse into the ways a large German company could influence the political process.

The money from Flick was mostly illegal, originating from alleged donations to the Steyler Missionary Society in St Augustin near Bonn, which functioned as a money-laundering outfit for the company. Payments recorded by Rudolf Diehl, Flick's head accountant, under the names 'Dr Friderichs', 'Graf Lambsdorff', 'FJS' (Franz Josef Strauss), or 'Matthöfer' did not mean, or at least did not necessarily mean, that funds had been given to the politicians themselves. Rather, what Flick was doing was 'cultivating the Bonn landscape', as head manager Eberhard von Brauchitsch wrote in a note for Friedrich Karl Flick on 2 April 1979.

The illegal payments, mostly in cash and handed to the recipient in a sealed envelope, were designed to create a favourable attitude on the part of politicians and their parties for the political wishes of the donor. In the case of the SPD, funds for 'landscape cultivation' generally went through Alfred Nau, SPD treasurer from 1946 to 1975 and chairman of the Friedrich Ebert Foundation board of directors until his death in May 1983. The heads of the CDU and CSU, Kohl and Strauss, received funds directly and used them as they saw fit, sometimes transferring them to their party treasurers, sometimes setting up 'special accounts'. In addition to these cash payments, there were the moneys that came to the parties by way of 'charitable' organizations like the Civic Association, as well as legal donations. Between 1969 and 1980 Flick donated a total of 26 million DM to the parties represented in the Bundestag: 15 million to the CDU/CSU, 6.5 million to the FDP, and 4.5 million to the SPD. The goal was always the same: to create a 'climate' in which politicians would find it difficult to ignore the company's wishes.

The revelations of the early 1980s gave rise to the general impression that political decisions could be bought in Bonn. *Die gekaufte Republik** was the subtitle of a 1983 book on the Flick affair by two writers from *Der Spiegel*, Hans Werner Kilz and Joachim Preuss. And indeed, politicians who accepted support from large companies increasingly lost the ability to act in ways contrary to the interests of their donors. Under the mantle of democracy and the rule of law, networks of dependence had been created that were irreconcilable with the constitutional principle that the power of the state comes from the people.

On 29 November 1983 the federal prosecutor brought charges against former economics Minister Hans Friderichs (FDP), the North Rhine-Westphalian economics minister Horst-Ludwig Riemer (FDP), and two managers from Flick, Eberhard von Brauchitsch and Manfred Nemitz. Economics Minister Lambsdorff (FDP) was also indicted once his parliamentary immunity was lifted at the beginning of December. Two suspects were no longer alive to be prosecuted: Heinz Herbert Karry, FDP federal treasurer and economics minister of Hesse, who had been murdered by terrorists of the 'Revolutionary Cells' on 11 May 1981; and Alfred Nau, former SPD treasurer, who had died on 18 May 1983.

Nau took many secrets with him to the grave. One of them concerned the provenance of a 7.6 million mark 'collective donation' he had arranged, which appeared in the SPD report for the year 1982. There were—and still are—speculations that some of this money came from Flick. But since Nau knew how to keep quiet, the matter remained as unsolved as the details of the events in 1972, when payments to the CDU delegate Julius Steiner had helped bring down the vote of no confidence in Willy Brandt. When the parliamentary committee prematurely broke off the evidentiary phase of its Flick investigations in March 1985, the CDU/CSU, SPD, and FDP all approved. Even the Social Democrats had only a limited interest in getting to the bottom of the donation scandals.

In May 1984, before criminal proceedings began, the Union and FDP leaders made another attempt to pass an amnesty law. It failed after only a few days, brought down by a massive reaction in the media as well as by resistance within parts of the FDP itself. Facing criminal prosecution, Otto Graf Lambsdorff resigned from his post as economics minister on 27 June 1984. Bundestag president Rainer Barzel stepped down four months later, on 25 October. *Der Spiegel* was able to show that in 1973 the Flick company had eased Barzel's departure from the leadership of the CDU party and fraction by offering him a highly paid consulting contract with a Frankfurt law firm. Confronted with this revelation during interrogations in the Bundestag, Barzel was unable to refute it.

In early 1986 Kohl, the beneficiary of Barzel's dismissal, also got into serious difficulties on account of illegal party donations. During hearings in the

---

* Kilz and Preuss, *The Purchased Republic* (full German: *Flick. Die gekaufte Republik*).

parliament in Mainz in July 1985 he told the investigating committee that he had not been familiar with the Civic Association's role in obtaining donations for the CDU when he was prime minister of Rhineland-Palatinate. This assertion contradicted statements he had made to the Bundestag committee. Moreover, Kohl had not reported cash payments from Flick in December 1977 and March 1979 in the order of 55,000 DM. On 29 January 1986 Otto Schily, a Green party delegate, accused Kohl of perjury. In a television debate with Schily in mid-February, Heiner Geissler, the CDU general secretary, tried to defend Kohl: it was possible that the chancellor had had a 'blackout' while making his statement.

The investigations begun in the wake of Schily's accusations were halted in March 1986. Not until much later, in February 2000, did the public learn the reason. According to the *Süddeutsche Zeitung* Uwe Lüthje, plenipotentiary of the CDU treasury between 1971 and 1992, told a small group that he, party treasurer Walther Leisler Kiep, and financial adviser Horst Weyrauch had perjured themselves during questioning by the federal prosecutor in order to exonerate Kohl and allow him to remain chancellor.

The 'Flick trial' against Lambsdorff, Friderichs, and Brauchitsch began in August 1985 before the district court in Bonn. The charges were corruption, tax evasion, and abetment of tax evasion. In February 1987 Lambsdorff and Friderichs were convicted of tax evasion and sentenced to pay large fines; they were acquitted of corruption. Brauchitsch received a gaol term, which was then commuted to probation after he paid a fine of 550,000 DM. This did not conclude the legal action. Proceedings against Kiep and Lüthje began in 1990 before the district court in Düsseldorf, the charges being continued abetment of tax evasion. Kiep was sentenced to a fine of 675,000 DM in May 1991, though the statute of limitations caused the Federal Supreme Court to reverse this decision in September 1992. In 1993, in the last open case in connection with the Flick affair, proceedings against Kiep were called off after the imposition of a small fine for what was adjudged the defendant's 'small guilt'.

The legislative branch also took fresh action on party finance in the 1980s. A commission of experts appointed by President Carstens to look into the subject in March 1982 presented its report in April of the following year. Based on these findings, the Bundestag passed a law restructuring party finance on 1 December 1983 against the votes of the Green party. To Article 21 of the Basic Law was added the provision that the parties report not only where their funds came from, but account for all their assets. The party law was also changed. The amount parties received from the state to fund their electoral campaigns was raised; the stipulations against illegal donations were made more stringent; donations from political foundations and charitable organizations were banned; and the deductibility of large donations was expanded: up to 5% of the income of the donor, or up to 2% of a company's total turnover, wages, and salaries would be deductible as 'special expenditures' provided the donor appeared in the party report. Since this latter provision favoured 'capital friendly' parties, the law provided for 'equality of opportunity' by granting additional state funds to parties less favoured with donations, measured by the percentage of the vote they received.

The Green party's resistance did not end after this law was passed. It filed a suit with the Federal Constitutional Court on 18 April 1984. The decision, handed down on 14 July 1986, placed a uniform ceiling of 100,000 DM on tax-deductible contributions to political parties. While this restricted the progressive effect of their deductibility, it did set a surprisingly generous upper limit to donations. The new regulations, passed on 9 December 1988—once again in the face of Green resistance—expanded state campaign financing by adding 'basic sums' (*Sockelbeträge*) for parties that received more then 2 per cent of the vote; reworked the 'equality of opportunity' provision; and raised the limit beyond which 'large donations' were subject to publication from 20,000 to 40,000 DM.

Karlsruhe was compelled to issue its opinion on these changes, too. On 23 May the Greens filed another suit, and the judgment came on 9 April 1992. It was much different from the 1986 decision. The 'equality of opportunity' and 'basic sum' provisions were declared unconstitutional, as were the 60,000 DM upper limit on tax-deductible party donations, the deductibility of donations by 'juristic persons', and the new minimum publication limit of 40,000 DM. On the other hand, the principle of state financing for the parties beyond the reimbursement of their campaign expenses was, for the first time, declared to be in keeping with the constitution. However, the total amount of state funds a party received was not allowed to exceed the amount it earned for itself.

In response, the Bundestag passed the 'Sixth Law to Amend the Party Law and Other Laws' on 28 January 1994, reworking the fundamentals and the extent of state financing to accord with the latest decision from Karlsruhe. The relationship between state and private party funding was adjusted. Electoral performance was now the only factor governing how much money a party received from the federal budget. The upper limit for deductibility was set at 3,000 DM, at 6,000 DM for married couples assessed jointly. (A commission had recommended even lower limits, 2,000 and 4,000, respectively.)

In the course of its efforts to limit the political influence of big business, the state found itself continually compelled to increase the percentage of federal money in party finance. And regardless of what the Bundestag did, anyone determined to circumvent party law found ways of doing so. Around the turn of the millennium it emerged that, even after the party finance reform, Kohl had continued to accept illegal donations and use illegal accounts; that he placed a higher value on an alleged promise not to identify his donors than on his oath of office, which bound him to respect the constitution and other laws of the country; that in 1983, before the new party finance regulations went into effect, the Hesse CDU had transferred millions of marks to Switzerland in order to avoid reporting them as assets; that later, under party head Manfred Kanther, interior minister from 1993 to 1998, it had used these illegal funds to finance campaigns; and that the federal CDU, like its counterpart in Hesse, had used a fictional foundation in Liechtenstein to cover up its illegal activities.

With regard to at least one party, therefore, the Flick affair and the party finance scandal did little to change business as usual. The Christian Democratic Union, long West Germany's premier political party, persisted in its disregard for the constitution and the laws of the land. The fact that violations of party law are punished only by fines, together with the lenient sentences handed down between 1987 and 1993, prevented the scandal from having any salutary effect.

The abuses had begun during the Adenauer era. But it was only after the end of the Kohl era that the true extent of the political and moral damage they had caused could be measured. Large democratic parties are an unavoidable and necessary part of any democracy; the CDU's behaviour did not change this fact. When they allow themselves to become instruments of leaders who believe themselves to be above the law, however, political parties can cause serious harm to a democratic political culture. The citizens of West Germany did not fully realize this until after they had dismissed their sixth chancellor after sixteen years in power.[16]

FOREIGN POLICY AND GERMAN–GERMAN RELATIONS AT THE BEGINNING OF THE KOHL ERA

The March 1983 elections did not turn out to be a referendum against 'automatic' arms modernization, as the Social Democrats had been hoping. Since the INF talks in Geneva seemed to be making no progress, it became ever more likely that the deployment of American medium-range missiles would indeed go forward in autumn 1983, after the deadline NATO had set in December 1979 expired. On 19 November 1983, during an extraordinary party congress in Cologne, the SPD voted against the deployment by an overwhelming majority. Only 14 out of 400 voting delegates continued to support the former chancellor's policy.

Among the spokesmen of the rejectionist policy was Willy Brandt. Already on 22 October in Bonn, at the largest peace movement demonstration to date, the SPD leader had made it clear that he believed the 'deployment of Pershing II' was more important to the Reagan administration than the 'removal of SS 20'. On 22 November, during the Bundestag debate over the implementation of the NATO policy, Brandt placed himself among 'the great majority of people' who demanded 'deployment of new negotiations instead of new arms' (*Nachverhandeln statt Nachrüsten*). In the ensuing ballot, 286 Union and liberal delegates voted for, 225 delegates against missile deployment. The Soviet Union broke off the INF negotiations the next day, the START talks on 8 March.

The deployment of Pershing II and cruise missiles on West German territory began at the beginning of January 1984. The peace movement had failed to reach its goal. Demoralized, it began to fall apart in the autumn of that same year.

A few weeks after the Bundestag elections, on 28 May 1983, ten Social Democratic university professors came out with a sharp public critique of the new SPD foreign policy line. Written by two political scientists, Karl Kaiser and Gesine Schwan, and a historian, Heinrich August Winkler, the manifesto stated that it was 'not surprising' that talk of 'German uncertainties' was once again being heard beyond the borders of the FRG.

Unlike under Helmut Schmidt, in its 1983 election campaign the SPD no longer openly mentioned the purpose of the Soviet missile policy: in the short term, to put pressure on the people of western Europe; in the medium term, to separate them from the USA; and in the long term, to alter the conditions in Europe in a way that favours Soviet hegemony...A policy of confrontation cannot move the Soviets to disarm. But it is an illusion to believe that one-sided concessions or trust-building measures can alone lead to this goal. As history shows, the Soviets will not yield if the west is not firm and united.

Six months later, a similar warning came from Helmut Schmidt. Speaking at the SPD 'missile congress' in Cologne on 19 November 1983, the former chancellor reminded his audience of a party resolution of 14 November 1970, which had declared that no peace policy could overlook the difference between liberal democracy and communist dictatorship. Schmidt mentioned a foreign observer's comment that 'Germany is, as it has always been, a changeable, protean, unpredictable country, especially dangerous when unhappy'. He then quoted from Heine's 'Deutschland. Ein Wintermärchen':

> Franzosen und Russen gehört das Land,
> Das Meer gehört den Briten,
> Wir aber besitzen im Luftreich des Traums
> Die Herrschaft unbestritten.
>
> Hier üben wir die Hegemonie,
> Hier sind wir unzerstückelt;
> Die andern Völker haben sich
> Auf platter Erde entwickelt.*

In another reference to comments by foreign observers, Schmidt noted that 'the arguments of the peace movement give unconscious expression to something deeper. In reality, what is being voiced is anxiety, the anxiety provoked by the partition of the country and the lack of a national identity... Today, this

---

* The French and the Russians control the land, | The sea belongs to the British. | We, however, rule uncontested | The airy kingdom of dreams. || Here we have the hegemony, | Here we are undivided. | The other nations have developed | Upon the flat earth.

anxiety is being expressed as fear of missiles.' While he considered this fear 'very understandable', he cautioned:

Whoever makes fear out to be greater than hope is putting his soul in danger. He is also compromising his ability to act in a responsible manner. I place my hopes and confidence in our ability to continue the policy of détente in Europe. The basis of this policy is mutual security. I place my hopes in détente ultimately leading to a European peace order in which both parts of our nation can come together again.

The foreign policy realignment of the SPD had begun in autumn 1982. As long as Helmut Schmidt was chancellor, he had succeeded only in delaying what now forcefully asserted itself in his party's platform: the desire for a world without an arms race, without blocs, without an east–west conflict. In his first inaugural address on 28 October 1969, Willy Brandt had spoken of the Germans' wish to be 'good neighbours'; after 1982, the Social Democrats gradually distanced themselves from the idea that neighbours might be something other than good. Concepts like 'security partnership' and 'mutual security', which shaped SPD foreign policy during the 1980s, were based on a fundamentally correct premise: NATO could not make peace more secure in Europe without reaching some sort of agreement with the Warsaw Pact. Nonetheless, such language could also be interpreted another way: in the sense that Germany should be 'equidistant' from both superpowers.

In the light of these new ideas, the traditional one of a fundamental conflict between the systems, still defended by Helmut Schmidt at the Cologne congress, began to fade in the minds of many Social Democrats. Originally the détente policy and the *Ostpolitik* had been connected with *two* goals: securing the peace *and* fostering human rights where people continued to suffer repression. In the Social Democratic discourse of the 1980s, the former aim was emphasized so much that the latter was virtually eclipsed. The 'second phase of the *Ostpolitik*', first mentioned by the SPD delegate Karsten Voigt in January 1980, was to bring about a gradual retreat from the arms race. While this was fine as far as armaments policy was concerned, it did not suffice as the sum total of a foreign policy. The struggle for liberty in the nations of the Warsaw Pact played no role in the new SPD security thinking. In an address to the 'Seeheim circle' of the party right wing in September 1983, Karl Kaiser, director of the German Society for Foreign Policy (*Deutsche Gesellschaft für Auswärtige Politik*) and one of the authors of the aforementioned manifesto, criticized the Social Democrats for 'cutting eastern Europe out of their human rights discussion'. This earned him a public reprimand from Egon Bahr, the SPD disarmament expert, who accused Kaiser in *Vorwärts* (October 1983) of 'giving ideology the same priority as the preservation of the peace'.

What Bahr called 'ideology', Peter Glotz, his successor as SPD managing director, called the 'anticommunism of identity anxiety' (*Antikommunismus aus Identitätsangst*) in March 1984. The Social Democrats of the 1980s did not

actually deny their opposition to the communist system. But they rarely articulated it. For the party's intellectual leaders, a thinking person's anticommunism
was a contradiction in terms. This view had a great deal to do with intellectual
developments that had been taking place since 1968. In 1971 the journal *Der
Monat* ceased publication. Edited by Melvin J. Lasky, an American journalist
living in Berlin, it had been a major voice in anti-totalitarian discourse ever
since 1948. The aforementioned November 1970 (and February 1971) SPD
resolution quoted by Schmidt, written by Richard Löwenthal, a staff writer at
Der Monat, was never officially revoked. By the mid-1980s, however, only a
minority of Social Democrats supported it.

If the SPD never officially broke with anticommunism, it also never officially
renounced its support for NATO. Certain members of the party were indeed
pushing in this direction. In his 1983 book *Angst vor den Freunden** Oskar
Lafontaine, head of the Saarland SPD, wrote that the party's 'sudden swing
towards Adenauer's policy of western integration', including accession to NATO,
contradicted democratic socialism, which was a non-aligned (*blockfrei*) ideology.
In the light of this premise, Lafontaine's call for the Federal Republic to withdraw
from NATO military integration was only a step along the way to non-alignment.
The party as a whole was unable and unwilling to go this far. Membership in
the Atlantic alliance was not up for debate. But its consequences were. With its
rejection of NATO's modernization policy, the SPD called the very coherence
of the alliance into doubt. If it had succeeded in preventing the double-track
decision, it would have been a serious defeat for the west and a triumph for the east.

The rejection of Helmut Schmidt's position was the beginning of a politics
of 'as if', a hypothetical foreign policy that indicated what the Social Democrats
would do if they were in control in Bonn. The origins of this 'parallel foreign
policy' lay in the latter part of the Schmidt era: Willy Brandt's and Egon Bahr's
shuttle diplomacy had given their eastern interlocutors the impression of a party
that by no means unconditionally supported its chancellor.

After the October 1982 change in leadership the SPD began making disarmament agreements with the SED that went far beyond the German–German level.
On 14 March Erich Honecker and Hans-Jochen Vogel, the SPD fraction leader,
agreed to the formation of a joint SPD–SED task force to make preparations
for a chemical weapon-free zone in Europe. The resulting framework agreement
was signed in June 1985. Three months later, in September 1985, Honecker
and Brandt, continuing an initiative by Swedish prime minister Olof Palme,
agreed to hold talks on a European corridor free of nuclear arms. An SPD–SED
task force presented guidelines for this project on 21 June 1986. The long-term
aim of all Social Democratic disarmament initiatives was a 'structural inability
to attack' on the part of both sides. Both the east and the west were to have
defensive military capabilities only.

* Lafontaine, *Fear of Friends*.

The quasi-treaties that the SPD concluded with the SED were intended as a contrast to the arms race between the superpowers. They were part of the 'Europeanization of Europe', a project outlined by the Berlin publicist Peter Bender in 1981. According to Bender, east–west relations were no longer determined by ideological struggles, but only by conflicts of political interest. The rivalry between the United States and the Soviet Union, while it threatened Europe, also contained an opportunity. The countries of the old world could, and were compelled to, rediscover what they had in common and develop a new political structure: a pan-European defence community that would eventually replace the two military alliances. After this goal had been reached at some point in the future, the FRG and the GDR would also be able to reunite, or at least work out some sort of federation. What Bender was talking about here was basically another version of a model sketched by Egon Bahr in 1968, during the Grand Coalition, and then shelved as not very promising at the time.

It was undeniable that Washington and Moscow were interested in power and hegemony, not balance, in the early 1980s. But the 'age of ideology' was far from over, the antinomy between pluralist democracy and communist party dictatorship still very much alive. Europe, divided as it was, had no chance of developing into a third power. Divided Germany was as little able as Europe to de-couple from the east–west conflict. The most that Europeans and Germans could do was to limit the damage the superpowers had caused in their confrontational policy. But when the chips were down, West Germany would have to stand with the alliance that guaranteed its liberty and security, and that was NATO. The GDR also had no choice but to obey the Soviet Union, without which it would not even have existed.

Bender did not speak for the SPD, but he still agreed with Egon Bahr on all essential points. Willy Brandt's thinking was not dissimilar. During the debate over armaments in the Bundestag on 22 November 1983, the SPD party head stated his support for the 'Europeanization of Europe' and called for 'all forms of cooperation between east and west that are possible, if not absolutely necessary'. The German Social Democrats of the post-Schmidt era were not immune to self-delusion, often forgetting the possibility of war, perceiving reality selectively, and overestimating their own importance. Although they were not in power, towards the leaders of the Warsaw Pact states they behaved as if they were the true representatives of their country. This was nothing more than political wishful thinking, and it gave many observers on both sides reason to question whether the SPD was still a party of the west.[17]

The real West German government, in sticking to the NATO double-track policy, could rightly claim that it had cleared up any remaining foreign policy uncertainties and contributed to a strengthened NATO. 'In terms of the alliance, the Federal Republic of Germany was beginning to appear in an uncertain light,' Helmut Kohl declared at the beginning of his second inaugural address on 4 May 1983. Cries of 'nonsense!' came from the ranks of the Social Democrats. The chancellor continued: 'Our foreign and alliance policy puts us where we need to be: on the side of freedom, on the side of our friends.' This brought 'more laughter from the SPD and the Greens', but also 'applause from the CDU/CSU and the FDP'.

Fealty to NATO did not mean that the Kohl–Genscher government broke with the kind of *Ostpolitik* and German–German policy the Schmidt–Genscher government had pursued. When President Carstens met Erich Honecker in Moscow at Leonid Brezhnev's funeral on 14 November (the Soviet leader had died four days before at the age of 76), he not only brought him greetings from the chancellor, but also confirmed the invitation to Honecker (first extended by Helmut Schmidt) to visit the FRG and emphasized Kohl's desire for 'continuity and dialogue'. Honecker's visit was supposed to take place in 1983, but was cancelled at the end of April after a serious incident (the death of a transit passenger in the course of interrogations by GDR border authorities) caused a major setback in the relations between the two countries. Despite this crisis another, altogether spectacular chapter in the history of German–German relations soon began: the GDR received its first billion mark loan from West Germany, and it was set up by a politician who had just used the word 'murder' in connection with the border incident: the Bavarian prime minister Franz Josef Strauss.

After the Soviet Union had cut back its crude oil imports in autumn 1981, the GDR, which lacked the foreign currency to pay for them, was in serious economic difficulties. A systematic transition from heating oil to native brown coal had begun at the start of that year, allowing more Soviet crude, refined in the GDR, to be re-exported to the west in order to increase foreign exchange reserves. Besides causing great harm to the environment, the shift from oil to coal was one of the reasons for the increase in East Germany's western debt. On 30 March 1983 Werner Krolikowski, a member of the politburo and SED central committee, saw the 'solvency of the GDR in jeopardy'.

Strauss's intervention in May and June 1983 helped prevent the East German state from going bankrupt. What were his motivations? He may have been guided by the desire to rid himself of the image of the merciless anticommunist and to prove his fitness for the office of foreign minister. The first loan for over 1 billion DM was arranged between Strauss and Alexander Schalck-Golodkowski, director of the office of 'Commercial Coordination', on 29 June 1983. It was guaranteed by the FRG, and East Germany was not officially bound to do anything in return. Strauss and the West German government settled for the informal promise that the border controls would make an effort to be more polite and friendly.

In his memoirs Strauss explained his actions in terms of his 'experiences of recent history'.

In 1953, 1956, 1968, 1980–1, whether in the GDR, in Hungary, in Czechoslovakia or, most recently in Poland—never did the west intervene in an uprising in one of the eastern bloc states. Because of the risks of being pulled into a war, we were and still are unable to support popular uprisings in the states of the Warsaw Pact. Therefore, it makes no sense to exacerbate the situation there to such an extent that the people cannot bear it and things explode.

A Social Democrat might have acted and spoken the same way as Franz Josef Strauss. The new coalition government worked very deliberately to stabilize the GDR in order to prevent developments there from getting out of control. The fear that a major war might be started by a civil conflict was real, and it was felt by politicians of all parties. It was a very German fear, tied to the history of the country—to memories of Weimar, and even, perhaps, to the 'primordial catastrophe' of the Thirty Years War. One of the effects of this fear was to cause those who felt it to give the existing order, unjust though it was, priority over the idea of liberty. In this regard there was no essential difference between Bahr and Strauss. Both men were pursuing a European security policy in the German interest, or what they took to be the German interest. Both believed that, in doing so, they were also acting in the true interest of those Germans and Europeans who could not express themselves freely. And Strauss was just as convinced as Bahr that the age of ideology was over. At least he maintained as much at his first meeting with Erich Honecker on 24 July 1983 at the Hubertusstock lodge: 'In this century ideology is moving into the background, and practical-pragmatic questions are moving into the foreground.'

The loan from the FRG restored East Germany's credit-worthiness even in the west and, together with other loans from the capitalist states, permitted the continuation of the 'unity of economic and social policy' first promulgated in 1976. Although the GDR was unable to pay for this programme itself, Honecker nonetheless thought it still absolutely necessary. This meant that even after the deployment of the American missiles, he could have no real interest in a deterioration of German–German relations, despite his warnings about a 'new ice age' in a letter to the chancellor on 5 October 1983. In his response on 24 October, Kohl made reference to another phrase in the same letter. Honecker had spoken of a 'coalition of reason', which would prevent humanity from sliding into nuclear catastrophe. The FRG government, Kohl wrote, wished to do its part to preserve and stabilize the balance of power. He asked Honecker to use all the influence he had with the Soviet Union 'to see to it that the constructive western proposals are thoroughly reviewed and not rejected out of hand'.

The chancellor went even further in his next letter on 14 December. 'Our two states', he told Honecker,

form a community of responsibility towards Europe and the German people. Both can make an important contribution to stability and peace in Europe, especially during times of crisis in east-west relations, if they approach each other in good will and cooperate in moving forward what is possible at this moment...A maximum of dialogue and cooperation will help the process of détente in Europe. This is especially important when the international situation has become more difficult.

The idea that the two Germanies formed a special 'community of responsibility' (*Verantwortungsgemeinschaft*) went back to the Göttingen historian Rudolf von Thadden, who had coined the phrase in 1981 in a statement written in connection with a public hearing by the Bundestag committee for German–German relations. Helmut Schmidt had adopted it before Kohl, and Honecker himself would used it in a conversation with Hans-Jochen Vogel on 14 March 1984.

By the time the new Bonn administration had been in power for a year, a remarkable degree of agreement had developed between Honecker and Kohl. During a long telephone conversation between the two leaders on 19 December 1983, Kohl said something that Honecker had not heard from any West German chancellor:

And you can be assured especially of one thing, which I believe is very important: you are speaking here with a man who will undertake nothing for the purpose of putting you in a bad position—I will not specify that further—nothing to put you in a bad position. It's my interest to develop what has been built up with great effort and can only be moved forward with endless difficulty and in small steps, to move that forward—that's the task I have set myself.

Towards the end of the conversation Honecker told Kohl that he, too, thought the two German states had an obligation to do what they could to limit the damage caused by the escalation of the east–west conflict. He was working from the assumption 'that real interests develop the relations between the states. We ourselves do have a special responsibility in this. As you rightly say: from the point of view of peace and from the point of view of history.'

Kohl did not use the word 'reunification', whether in his exchanges with Honecker or in public. It was true that he constantly invoked the unity of the nation. Even during the 1983 electoral campaign, however, he added that he was firmly convinced that unity would not mean a 'return to the nation state of a past age'. During Kohl's tenure the chancellor's 'state of the nation' address, held every year beginning in 1968, was once again called the 'state of the nation in divided Germany', a designation the social–liberal governments had dropped between 1971 and 1982. However, like all his predecessors since Adenauer, Kohl stressed again and again that the German question was fundamentally a question of human rights and liberty. The German people's claim to self-determination and political unity was maintained. Nonetheless, the main goal of the present moment was 'to make the consequences of the partition more bearable for the German people and to preserve the unity of the nation'. This sentence appeared in a Bundestag resolution on the state of the nation and German–German relations, passed by the coalition parties and the Social Democrats on 9 February 1984.

Four days later, on 13 February 1984, Kohl and Honecker met in person for the first time, in Moscow. The occasion was the funeral of Brezhnev's successor Yuri Vladimirovich Andropov, who had died on 9 February at 69 years of age. One of the things they discussed was Honecker's long-planned visit to West Germany, which was finally to take place in 1984. This time, however, the new general secretary of the Soviet Communist party, Konstantin Ustinovich Chernenko (who was 72 when he took office), vetoed the plan. The Moscow politburo mistrusted the German–German 'special relationship' and forced Honecker to cancel his visit on 4 September.

The proximate cause of Chernenko's intervention was a second 'billion mark credit' (in reality it was 950 million) granted to the GDR by West German banks on 25 July, Strauss once again playing the role of middleman. But the cancellation of the visit did no serious damage. On 5 December 1984 Wolfgang Schäuble, director of the chancellor's office and—as of 15 November—minister for special assignments, went to East Berlin, where he discussed the state and future of German–German relations with foreign minister Oskar Fischer, Alexander Schalck-Golodkowski, CC secretary Herbert Häber, and the lawyer Wolfgang Vogel. There had been noticeable improvements in several areas: the processing of transit passengers, family visits across the borders, the length of the visits, and the exchange amount required from retired persons. It was now easier for the West German government to purchase the freedom of political prisoners. Some automatic firing systems and minefields along the German–German border had even been removed. Nonetheless, Schäuble made it clear that this was not sufficient. He demanded a general lowering of the exchange amount, the further easing of travel, postal, and telecommunication restrictions, and above all a retraction of the border guards' orders to shoot those attempting to flee the GDR. (There had been another such incident at the Berlin wall four days before, on 1 December, resulting in the death of a refugee.) Schäuble's words to Fischer on this subject were correctly noted in the minutes on the East German side: 'The inhumane shootings at the wall, which have cost another life, are condemned in the sharpest language. The FRG has noted the changes made at the barriers and the improvement of the transit processing system. But it must be demanded that all use of force cease.'

Kohl and Honecker met for the second time on 12 March 1985 at yet another state funeral in Moscow, this time Chernenko's, who had died on 10 March at 73 years of age. He was replaced the following day by the 54-year-old Mikhail Sergeyevich Gorbachev. At the time, very few people suspected that the generational change within Soviet leadership would be followed by a dramatic transformation in world politics. Already under Chernenko the foreign ministers of the two superpowers, Andrei Gromyko and George Schulz, had agreed to restart talks on a reduction of medium-range missiles, strategic nuclear arms, and on defensive and space weaponry in Geneva on 12 March 1985. Gorbachev, however, a member of the politburo since 1980, made it clear in his inaugural speech to the central committee of the Soviet Communist party that improvement of relations with the west was going to be one of his biggest goals.

The meeting between the two German leaders went better than Kohl's first meeting with Gorbachev, in which differences in security policy played a major role. The SED general secretary demonstrated his willingness to be more generous in allowing GDR citizens to travel west in matters of family emergency and the West German government to purchase the freedom of prisoners (the so called 'F cases'). While he did not commit himself to specific figures, transit traffic did increase strongly in the period following the meeting. Honecker's and Kohl's 'Moscow declaration' caused a true sensation. Among other things, it proclaimed that 'the inviolability of the borders and respect for the territorial integrity and sovereignty of all European states within their current borders' was 'a fundamental prerequisite for peace'. There was also agreement on another point: 'War must never again arise from German soil. German soil must give rise to peace.'

Kohl had used this kind of language before. Nonetheless the GDR could interpret the 'Moscow declaration' as yet another step along the way to recognition by the Federal Republic, and this brought the chancellor criticism from the Union's 'Stahlhelm faction'. In reality, unlike the billion DM loans, Kohl's statement with Honecker was only a symbolic price to pay for an improvement of the situation for the Germans in the east. Measured by the now modest expectations in Bonn, it was a realistic calculation.[18]

THE GDR AND THE GERMAN NATION AT THE BEGINNING OF THE 1980s

Whatever contribution the GDR may have made towards bringing hundreds of thousands of people onto West German streets against the deployment of American missiles, the peace movement was not restricted to western Europe. In East Germany, too, independent peace and environmental groups began to form at the end of the 1970s, protesting against the arms race in the west *and* in the east. A great stir was caused in autumn 1981 by Robert Havemann, the GDR's most prominent civil rights activist, when he sent an open letter to Leonid Brezhnev. The most explosive passage had a provocatively all-German and nationalist sound:

Now, 36 years after the end of the war, it has become a matter of urgent necessity to conclude the peace treaties and pull all occupying troops out of both parts of Germany . . . How we Germans will then solve our national question is something that must be left to us, but nobody need fear the result any more than a nuclear war.

Among the first signatories of this letter in the GDR were the Evangelical minister Rainer Eppelmann, the physicist Gerd Poppe, and the writer Sascha Anderson (who would later be identified as an Unofficial Collaborator of the Stasi). In West Germany and West Berlin it was signed by former Berlin mayor

Heinrich Albertz (SPD); the Evangelical theologian Helmut Gollwitzer; the Tübingen classicist and rhetoric professor Walter Jens; former First Mayor of Hamburg Hans Ulrich Klose (SPD); the former Evangelical bishop of Berlin-Brandenburg Kurt Scharf; the Berlin lawyer Otto Schily, active in the Green party; the SPD Bundestag delegate Gert Weisskirchen; and the writers Martin Walser, Peter-Paul Zahn, and Gerhard Zwerenz.

Havemann's letter was followed in January 1982 by the Jena 'appeal for disarmament' and the 'Berlin appeal'. The latter, written by Havemann and Eppelmann, called for 'peace without arms' (*Frieden schaffen ohne Waffen*) and described divided Germany as the 'deployment zone of the two great nuclear powers'. Its first eighty signatories included the pastor Hans-Jochen Tschiche, the writer Lutz Rathenow, and the physicist Gerd Poppe, who had also signed the open letter. Most of the participants came from the Berlin peace movement and church youth groups. Eppelmann was arrested on 9 February, but released three days later in response to church protest. Havemann died on 9 April 1982. Despite the efforts of the Stasi, a large number of demonstrators managed to take part in the funeral ceremony in Grünheide on 17 April.

The Evangelical element was manifest not only in these highly visible campaigns at the end of 1981 and beginning of 1982. In many parts of East Germany Evangelical pastors spread a cloak of protection over peace and environmental organizations. They gave moral support to the *Bausoldaten* ('construction soldiers'), members of a quasi-military programme started in 1964 for those who refused conventional military service. The *Bausoldaten* paid a heavy price for their refusal, being subject to many professional and social disadvantages. Church circles also frequently expressed sympathy for Solidarity and protested against martial law in Poland. Roland Jahn, initiator of the Jena 'peace community', was arrested at a pro-Solidarity demonstration in that city on 1 September 1982. He was sentenced to three years in prison in January 1983, but released in February on account of the large public outcry. Since he continued his activities, he was rearrested on 7 June and deported to West Germany in handcuffs the next day. There, in September of the following year, he was fined for taking part in the sit-in against the deployment of American missiles in the Swabian town of Mutlangen.

Another organization, 'Swords to Ploughshares' (*Schwerter zu Pflugscharen*), which spread from Saxony to the entire country in 1981–2, originated in the church itself. The movement took its name from Old Testament prophecy. Its original image, printed on a bookmark made out of fleece material, was first introduced in November 1980 on the occasion of the first 'peace decade'. It then spread in the form of a patch, rapidly becoming the symbol of the East German peace movement as a whole. The state responded with counter-measures, which reached their climax in March 1982. Bearers of the patch who refused to remove it were expelled from secondary schools and universities and, if additional reasons were presented, arrested. Thereafter the churches sounded the retreat. At its synod in Halle in September 1982 the Federation of the Evangelical Church in the GDR decided 'for the sake of peace' to drop the symbol that had so annoyed the state authorities.

In dealing with the church and the church-supported eco-pacifists, the SED had more trouble in the 1980s than before. One of the reasons was that the East German leadership regarded the churches as partners in its battle against NATO and thus shied away from open conflict with them. Another was that it was courting the West German Greens, who protested against the persecution of dissidents and any violation of human rights in the Warsaw Pact states much more loudly than the Social Democrats. This dilemma made it difficult for the regime to deal with activists like Jahn and Eppelmann. But it also led to a shift in tactics. Rather than destroying oppositional groups by force, in many cases the state now preferred to infiltrate and subvert them from within, using Unofficial Collaborators.

There was another reason the SED could not afford an open battle with the church at this time. Both the centenary of Karl Marx's death and the fifth centenary of the birth of Martin Luther would take place in 1983. Preparations for both events had long since begun, and both were to be celebrated on a grand scale. This would show the world, and especially West Germany, that the GDR had moved beyond a narrow view of historical progress and knew how to pay proper tribute to the great reformer and to the great figures of German history in general.

In June 1980 Erich Honecker himself had become head of the 'Martin Luther Committee for the Preparation of the Celebrations in 1983'. On 6 October 1983, five weeks before the quincentennial of Luther's birth, *Das Neue Deutschland* published an 'interview' Honecker had given to the *Lutherische Monatshefte*, a West German journal. There was now virtually nothing left of the old polemic contrast between the 'progressive' Müntzer and the 'reactionary' Luther. Luther's name, as Honecker explained, was tied to the first revolution on German soil, the early bourgeois revolution.

Luther inspired revolutionary impulses that went far beyond the German states of those days . . . Luther had a positive effect on the development of schools and popular education, marriage and family . . . When he stood before the Imperial Diet in Worms and, in the principal questions, followed his conscience rather than the official doctrines, Luther found himself in full agreement with the main current of his era.

It was true, Honecker said, that Luther had been unable to resolve the 'contradiction between his role as initiator of a great revolutionary movement and his inability to recognize the laws of societal development to which that movement was subject'. That was the 'tragic' aspect of his historical role. 'We certainly recognize the contradictions in his personality and his oeuvre. To a great extent they reflect the immaturity and contradictions of the German bourgeoisie of that period and the rising intelligentsia.' Luther was nonetheless 'a co-mover of our history', and for that reason, regardless of all differences between the theological and the Marxist-Leninist view, the GDR's commemorative celebrations were relevant to the present. 'The celebration of both the person and the work of Martin Luther in our state reflects the cooperation between the citizens of our country, regardless of their world view and religion.' The interviewer's impression that the GDR was integrating German history 'in order to connect its self-image with positive elements from the tradition' was not fully accepted by Honecker: 'And anyway, we don't need to integrate German history. We come from it, we're standing within it, and we're taking it further.'

The Honecker of the 1980s sounded a good deal more 'nationalist' than the Honecker of the early 1970s. During a speech to a meeting of SED district representatives in Berlin on 15 February 1981, he said something that many people in the west also appreciated:

And if today certain people in the west are talking up 'Greater Germany' and acting as if the reunification of the two German states is closer to their hearts than their wallets, then we would like to say to them: be careful! Socialism will one day come knocking on your door, too! (Strong applause) And when the day comes on which the workers of the Federal Republic take up the socialist transformation of the Federal Republic, then the question of the reunification of the two German states will appear in a totally different light. (Strong applause) What we will decide to do then: that's something about which there can be no doubt. (Long-lasting applause)

In repositioning itself with regard to the national question and the history of Germany, the SED was hoping to increase its legitimacy, badly damaged by the country's economic crisis. For the first time since the theory of the two German nations was established in the years after 1970, German unity was once again declared possible, even desirable—under the condition that West Germany adopted the GDR system. This was a clear admission that the attempt to impose a new national identity on the East Germans had failed. This realignment was accompanied by a reorientation of the official historiography. In order to gain the support of non-Marxists, the SED 'historicized' the past, granting it a certain independence from dogmatic, non-'dialectic' ideas about the 'correct' historical process.

The rehabilitation of Martin Luther was only one example of the new East German politics of history. In 1980 Honecker had Christian Daniel Rauch's equestrian statue of Frederick the Great restored to Unter den Linden street in Berlin. A new biography of the Hohenzollern king had come out the year before. Although its author, Ingrid Mittenzwei, was a staunch Marxist, her study was balanced and nuanced in its judgement, paying tribute to the progressive elements in Frederick's rule. In 1985 another dedicated Marxist, Ernst Engelberg, published the first volume of his Bismarck biography, in which he interpreted the German unification as a 'revolution from above' and ascribed great historical achievements to the founder of the Reich. Prussia now no longer appeared as the incarnation of reaction, but as a political entity with positive and negative sides. Even Hitler's conservative opponents received their due. With regard to the past, or at least parts of the past, the SED of the 1980s was seen as more pluralist and tolerant of 'dissident' opinion than it was in the other areas of its rule.

The party was also at pains to emphasize that its revaluation of German history was not restricted to the territories that had belonged to the GDR since 1949. It saw all of the German past as the history of the *two* German states. Moreover, it claimed that its picture of German history was the only truly scientific one and therefore superior to the 'bourgeois' historiography of the FRG.

Two of the key concepts that framed historical debates in the GDR during this period were 'legacy' and 'tradition'. 'Legacy' included everything that the past had bequeathed to the present, negative as well as positive. 'Tradition' was everything good and worthy of preservation or development. The core of this tradition was the 'revolutionary legacy' of the working class, then the 'progressive humanist legacy' and other 'positive legacies'. 'Negative' legacies also existed, but not in the GDR; their home was 'capitalist' and 'imperialist' West Germany, which had not experienced an 'antifascist-democratic transformation' or the 'construction of socialism' and which therefore did not possess a 'developed socialist society'. These were the terms the SED set for historical discussion in the 1980s. But the emphasis on legacies and traditions could also have an effect quite different from the one intended: it could lead to the rediscovery of German–German commonalities, which could, in turn, undermine the party's claim to sole authority in all matters ideological.

The bulk of German history in the twentieth century—the history of communism, social democracy, and fascism, as well as the entire post-1945 period—was untouched by 'revision'. The central committee's statements on the subject in June 1988, on the occasion of the seventieth anniversary of the KPD, were as doctrinaire as always, to the displeasure of a number of historians at the East German Academy of Sciences and the Karl Marx University in Leipzig. The period of Nazi rule continued to be seen in the light of the old formulas about the open terrorist dictatorship of the most reactionary elements of finance capital. Anti-Semitism and the murder of the European Jews were *not* the focus of the Marxist-Leninist approach to 'fascism'. As late as 1970, histories of the Second World War written in the GDR were still glossing over the fact that the Jews were the main victims of the SS's systematic campaign of human annihilation in Poland.

Ideological narrow-mindedness was one of the reasons East German historians found it difficult to deal with the racial fanaticism of the Nazis and its consequences. Since they deduced politics from economics, they were unable to recognize the profoundly irrational impulses at the heart of National Socialism. Another reason was Stalinist 'anti-Zionism', which remained alive in the GDR into the 1980s. As heir to the anti-fascist KPD and ally of the victorious

Soviet Union, the SED considered itself to be among the 'victors of history'. It saw no reason for self-criticism in reviewing German history between 1933 and 1945.

For this reason, strict limits were placed on the emancipation of history from dogma in the GDR. This was especially true in the schools and universities, where stringent rules continued to apply. In its 1984 'Curriculum for the Subject Area of History in the Field of the Humanities at the Universities and Technical Colleges of the GDR', the ministry of higher education described the 'educational goal' (*Ausbildungs- und Erziehungsziel*) very clearly:

> The students of the subject area of history are given the skills that allow them, on behalf of the working class and their party, to actively and creatively cooperate in solving problems of societal development; to spread the experiences and lessons of history and the insights of Marxist-Leninist historiography; to confront bourgeois and revisionist historical ideology in the spirit of the party; and to contribute to the further development of the study of history . . . The students are empowered to contribute as propagandists toward the formation of socialist consciousness and educated both to understand and perceive their future activity as a political function and to deploy it in keeping with the relevant socio-political requirements and tasks of the party and state authorities.

The SED's monopoly on the interpretation of history was a significant part of its monopoly on truth as a whole. In their *Deutsche Ideologie** of 1845–6, Marx and Engels had written that '[w]e know only one science, the science of history', only to eliminate the paragraph headed by this sentence in the final version. While the central committee's Institute for Marxism-Leninism did not print this statement in its edition of the works of Marx and Engels, it nonetheless acted in keeping with it. The ruling Marxist-Leninists were still firmly convinced that the 'correct consciousness' was, first and foremost, a matter of the correct historical consciousness. And their intent to impose this correct consciousness remained unbroken. The fact that reality did not conform to their wishes was seen as a result of the historical backwardness still prevailing in West Germany, a backwardness striving to regain East Germany for itself. The struggle between the contradictory aspects of the common German legacy was obviously not yet over. But since it could only be won by the one class that had recognized the true nature of the historical process, good Marxist-Leninists could entertain no real doubts about the final outcome.

To those of less steadfast faith, the number of people now applying to leave the country was necessarily very discouraging. In the year 1983, 11,300 exit permits were granted; the numbers for 1984 and 1985 were 40,900 and 24,900. But even this generous emigration policy had its positive side. It removed enemies of the state and thus weakened the opposition within the GDR. The FRG was also prepared to pay handsomely in return, indirectly through loans, the lump sum

---

* Marx and Engels, *The German Ideology*.

for transit visas, and the 'swing' in German–German trade, but also directly, in purchasing the freedom of prisoners. These transfers allowed the GDR to continue presenting itself as a social welfare state. The specialists knew of course that the social services were not paid for by the country's own economy. But for Honecker's circle, what counted was the external effect of East Berlin's western policy, and this effect was to stabilize the system. It was true that the capitalist class enemy thereby became a pillar of socialism, but even that was acceptable, given the proper 'dialectical' perspective.[19]

WEST GERMAN IDENTITY, THE GERMAN NATION, AND THE NAZI PAST

The GDR became steadily less familiar to the citizens of West Germany after the wall went up in Berlin. It was true that the 'Day of German Unity' was celebrated on 17 June every year after 1963, when Heinrich Lübke had declared it the 'National Commemoration Day of the German People' to mark the tenth anniversary of the workers' uprising in East Germany. But already by the mid-1960s the official events had become a perfunctory routine, and during the Grand Coalition there was serious debate about abolishing the official holiday altogether (which never happened). On 17 June 1973, the twentieth anniversary of the uprising, the CDU under its new head Helmut Kohl held a demonstration in Berlin. Brandt's social–liberal government deliberately refrained from official solemnities in order not to provoke the GDR four days before the Basic Treaty was scheduled to go into effect.

Once the eastern treaties had been passed, the left found itself increasingly dominated by the belief that the sovereign German national state was a thing of the past. The right had fought against the *Ostpolitik* with the language of nationalism. By the mid-1970s, therefore, it looked as if the traditional roles, which the Adenauer era had shaken up, were once again restored: the right as nationalist, the left as anti-nationalist. Many Social Democrats, liberals, and intellectuals would have preferred to replace the all-German 17 June national holiday with a different, solely West German state holiday: 23 May, the day the Basic Law was promulgated in 1949. This did not happen, and 17 June remained what it had been since 1963. Still, during the Schmidt era, it was celebrated in a different manner than during the 1950s. Instead of a moment of national longing, it turned into a celebration of 'constitutional patriotism' and pride in liberal democracy—a system developed in the west, but one to which the Germans in the GDR also had a codified right. To the dismay of many conservatives, the 1982 'turn' did nothing to permanently alter this treatment of the 17 June holiday.

The idea of 'constitutional patriotism', *Verfassungspatriotismus*, was not widely discussed until the 1980s. It first appeared in a leading article in the *Frankfurter*

Allgemeine Zeitung on 23 May 1979, the thirtieth anniversary of the Basic Law. The author was Dolf Sternberger, a political scientist and publicist. 'Our national feeling is still wounded; we do not live in a whole Germany,' Sternberg wrote. 'Still, we live in a whole constitution, in a whole constitutional state, and that is also a kind of fatherland.'

Three years later, on 29 June 1982, Sternberg developed this idea further in a speech to the Academy of Political Education in Munich at that institution's twenty-fifth anniversary. Since the German Reich was no more; since the German people, or at least the citizens of the former German Reich, were living in two separate states; and since 'their reunification has receded into a painful and ambiguous future, due to the partition of Europe, the partition of the world'—for these reasons the question had to be asked anew: 'What is the German's Fatherland; that is, which is our *patria* in this divided country and people?' Sternberg's answer: it was the constitutional state of the Basic Law to which the citizens of the FRG owed their allegiance.

Sternberger appealed to the example of Thomas Abbt, Prussian by choice and follower of Frederick the Great, whose 1761 book *Vom Tode für das Vaterland** he quoted: 'The voice of the Fatherland can no longer resound if the air of liberty is taken away.' Sternberg went on to quote another passage from the same source: 'When birth or my free resolution unify me with a country, to whose holy laws I place myself in subjection, laws that take from me no more of my freedom than is necessary for the good of the whole country—at this moment do I call this country my Fatherland.'

According to Sternberger, this statement showed that Abbt had been promoting a 'constitutional idea of the fatherland'. Taken as a whole the text, written at the time of the Seven Years War, proved that patriotism was older than nationalism and the whole nation state-based European order. Switzerland and the United States, two ethnically mixed political entities, were 'unified by nothing more than their constitutions and by the patriotic sentiments these constitutions inspire'.

Sternberger did not claim that other factors apart from the constitution, things like 'the historical tradition, an elaborated linguistic culture, and closer ethnic ties', had no important role to play in the 'patriotic interrelation and cohesion of society'.

We Germans, too, we truly do not need to forget our common national bonds, much less our ties with those who must live in an unfree state . . . But I hope all the more, and for this very reason, that we take our place in this our constitution, holding onto it with tooth and claw, and that we do not throw away the safeguard out of carelessness or softheartedness, or even push it away, believing that we can get hold of liberty itself. It is not to be had other than in this armour! I also hope that we do not succumb to the temptation of departing from our constitution for the sake of the nation and

---

* Abbt, *On Death for the Fatherland.*

its wholeness. And furthermore, I wish that we would demonstrate our attachment to the constitution . . . This, too, is appropriate now: to openly demonstrate our common loyalty to the constitution, citizens as well as parties.

Sternberger was not the first to sound the call for West German patriotism. In the 1960s, liberal-conservative publicists and political scientists like Burghard Freudenfeld and Hans Buchheim, and in 1970 Waldemar Besson, had made similar appeals. In contrast to his 'forerunners', however, Sternberger avoided anything that could be construed as a rejection of all-German patriotism, which would have violated both the spirit and the letter of the Basic Law. Nonetheless, he certainly was trying to help West Germany develop a 'we' sentiment with a constitutional focus as strong as that of the United States. The Basic Law was a western constitution, but not just *any* western constitution; it was a document that reflected the experiences of *German* history, especially those of the Weimar Republic and National Socialism. It contained all of German constitutional history since 1848–9 in 'sublated' form, in Hegel's terminology; that is, in a way that simultaneously preserved and superseded this history.

On one point, however, the ideal of 'constitutional patriotism' was contradicted by the document itself. The creators of the 1949 Basic Law defined what it meant to be 'German' in the same way as the citizenship law of 1913 had done: as the possession of German nationality or German ethnic origin, not as the expression of an act of will. That is, German citizenship was 'objective', based on ethnic heritage or the 'right of blood' (*jus sanguinis*), not 'subjective', based on place of birth or the 'right of soil' (*jus soli*). One of the reasons it was so defined in 1949 was out of consideration for the ethnic Germans who had fled or been expelled from areas outside the 1937 borders of the Reich. But the result was to make naturalization of non-Germans very difficult until the reform of the citizenship law in 1999.

The logic of Sternberger's 'constitutional patriotism' would have dictated that German citizenship be westernized, incorporating elements of *jus soli*, as in France and other western democracies. Sternberger himself did not draw this conclusion. But he also did not limit the 'German nation' to the FRG. In his view, it included the Germans in the GDR. Consequently, while he wanted to move beyond the official provisional status of the West German state, as the Parliamentary Council had formulated it in 1949, he also did not wish to exclude the possibility of extending the constitution's authority to the territory of the GDR. This compromise position was one that most of the West German 'political class' could agree with.

The same could not be said of the views and proposals that Günter Gaus presented to the West German public in January 1981. In an interview for *Die Zeit* the publicist—then just about to leave his post as the FRG's Permanent Representative in East Berlin—lamented that

among ourselves we have not yet internally recognized the GDR . . . We sometimes use the GDR in a very coarse manner, like a big communist party in a domestic dispute, as a sort of replacement KP, which, unlike in France or Italy, we don't have as a serious factor in West Germany . . . We have to put aside our arrogance with regard to the GDR's efforts to develop—however unacceptably to ourselves—their definition of a GDR nation. This arrogance is totally inappropriate. It prevents us from seeing that our idea of the nation is also the product of history and the bourgeois class.

Gaus demanded a 'self-critical review of the simple adaptation of 1870–1' and recommended 'thinking seriously and deeply about *Grossdeutschland* and *Kleindeutschland*, about the real meaning of federalism, and also about what the middle of Europe has represented, for good and for ill'. He called upon the Federal Republic to put an end to 'the superficial debates over restoration of the political unity of the nation, or at least unity of the cultural nation'. 'Must we talk so much about the nation?' he asked rhetorically. The two sentences of the interview that caused the most controversy were the following:

Possibly we must even give up using the concept of nation, since it rapidly puts us at risk of engaging in shadow boxing once more. That is, we give people in the GDR another opportunity to say: 'Here comes that old revanchist who refuses to recognize that there are two German states here, independent of each other and each sovereign.'

Gaus, born in 1929 in Brunswick, was arguing in the Guelf tradition, against Bismarck's Prussian solution to the German question. But there was something prepolitical about his advocacy for *Grossdeutschland* and rejection of *Kleindeutschland*. The idea of the 'cultural nation' represented for him 'a notable improvement in the discussion', even if he did not want to use it himself, out of consideration for the GDR. None of that was 'unpatriotic', but it was 'nationalist' in a way that struck him as archaic. Taking up Ernst Moritz Arndt's statement about the Rhine, Gaus put his own spin on it: 'The Elbe is Germany's river, not Germany's border.' He preferred to see East Germany not as a 'police state', but as 'a German country' that seemed in many ways more German than the FRG. 'It hasn't been melted down and levelled as much. There is a very conscious turn to history here.'

Gaus's recommendations were to 'occupy ourselves with German history, reach out to the Saxons and Mecklenburgers, and develop a relationship with this state, even if we don't like it.' The interviewer asked him if this meant that he wanted West Germans to 'overcome the ahistoricity we are suffering from, not only with regard to the landscapes that today make up the GDR'. Gaus's response: 'Yes, that is what I want. I consider that the prerequisite for us even entering into a serious conversation here about what is possible with regard to a fundamental stabilizing of the European condition, beyond the conclusion of treaties, beyond a little more respect for the citizenship of the GDR.'

The debate provoked by this interview was joined by, among others, two historians. One of them was Hans Mommsen, a professor at the Ruhr-Universität in Bochum and great-grandson of Theodor Mommsen. For him the idea of 'the

German nation', which was 'used in an unreflecting way by West Germans and based, implicitly or explicitly, on Bismarck's nation state', needed to be redefined. For this reason he spoke out against the 'Guidelines for the Treatment of the German Question in the Classroom', adopted by the conference of cultural ministers on 23 November 1978. There was no doubt, Mommsen wrote, that a 'process of bi-nationalization of both parts of Germany' had been going on for some time. In the FRG a 'national identity consciousness' had already arisen, while the GDR had preserved a stronger 'pan-national sentiment'—a fact Mommsen connected to a 'deficit in societal modernization', but which he thought could not last. 'Even apart from the efforts of the GDR leadership to foster the consciousness of a "socialist German nation", a quasi-nationalist, special state identity is alive there, one continually fed by the GDR clichés of the West Germans.'

A 'persistent fixation on the model of the political nation', as Mommsen saw it, ran counter to both 'the general trend of development in eastern central Europe in the medium term and the historical-political consciousness of the middle and younger generations in the Federal Republic'. The formation of Austrian national identity during and after the Second World War was apposite in this context.

Parallel to this development we can observe that national-cultural solidarities are being set free and lastingly strengthened . . . The historical existence of the German nation as a historical-ethnic unity reaches far beyond the two German states and also includes minorities throughout the whole world who are in no way conscious of a political loyalty to divided Germany. This idea of the nation cannot form the basis of German–German relations.

Mommsen conceded that it was 'certainly opportune' to 'stick to constitutional realities that serve concrete Federal German national interests with regard to the GDR'.

'Nor is our solidarity with the Germans on the other side of the wall—a solidarity based in history—open to debate. But the legitimation of these ties is not to be looked for within the tradition of the Bismarck empire, nor in the deformed, *kleindeutsch* constitution of the Paulskirche. Paradoxically, German guilt on account of the horrors of the Holocaust tells us more about German–German solidarity than the projection of elements from pre-Nazi German history.

In Mommsen's view, therefore, the common lament over the 'lost national identity' was not at all justifiable. Those who voiced it overlooked the fact that this identity represented 'only one short episode in German history'.

The citizens of the Federal Republic feel national loyalty towards the Federal Republican nation. They know about their historical ties to the Germans in the GDR. They are participating in the national-cultural community that is developing apart from territorial nationalisms . . . In the long run the Federal Republic cannot afford the luxury of burdening the national solidarity of its citizens with all-German aims that the great majority views as no longer relevant. As Günter Gaus has shown, Germany as a historical and cultural unity only stands to profit from this.

Hans Mommsen's article appeared in *Die Zeit* on 6 February 1981 under the title 'Aus Eins macht Zwei'.* The next issue of the Hamburg weekly carried the response of the Freiburg historian Heinrich August Winkler, entitled 'Nation—ja, Nationalstaat—nein'.†

The claim that the Germans in the GDR want to be a nation for themselves flies in the face of everything we know about their wishes and sentiments. They bear no more guilt for National Socialism than the Federal Germans, yet they are suffering the consequences of the Second World War to a much greater degree than we ourselves. Since from an inner-German perspective the Federal Germans are the victors of 1945, there are far more Germans here who can accept the German status quo than in the GDR, where the losers live . . . A unilateral abandonment of the German nation would be a triumph of Federal German egotism. As long as the consequences of the war are so unequally distributed, as they still are to this day, the Germans in the FRG will lack the moral right to terminate their national solidarity with the Germans in the GDR.

Even Winkler did not deny that the era of the sovereign nation state had come to an end, at least in Europe.

After its experiences with Germany during this century, Europe will not accept the restoration of a German Reich, whatever it would be called. Not even in the borders of 1945. The interests of the two superpowers, the USA and the Soviet Union, also make such a restoration impossible . . . The reunification of Germany as a nation state is therefore not a realistic political goal. What national solidarity with the Germans in the GDR requires of Federal Germans is that they do what they can to help their countrymen across the Elbe *inwardly* accept their own state. The inner recognition of the GDR that Günter Gaus and Hans Mommsen demand of the FRG can only happen if the Germans in the GDR precede us . . . If one day the Germans in the GDR come to accept their own state like the Federal Germans do theirs, then, and only then, will the Germany of 1870–1 be a completed piece of history. At that moment Bismarck's 'Little Germany' will have finally become the episode it may well prove to be . . . As long as this is not the case, the Federal Germans cannot, and must not, release themselves from their special national solidarity with the Germans in the GDR.

The spring 1981 debate shed a bright light on the 'studied ambiguity of the Federal Republic's identity', as the sociologist M. Rainer Lepsius had put it in 1968 in a contribution to the nationality debate started by the Catholic journal *Hochland*. Gaus avoided using the word 'nation' for tactical reasons, but in substance he was arguing for a distinct 'two-state nationalism', just like Bahr and Bender, who backed him up in their own contributions for *Die Zeit*. Mommsen, in linking his own rejection of the *kleindeutsch* nation state embracing

---

* Mommsen, 'From One make Two'.
† Winkler, 'Nation—Yes, Nation State— No'.

East and West Germany to a plea for a greater German or all-German cultural nation, was advocating the coexistence of two irreconcilable ideas of nation: a political one that could apply to West Germany or the GDR or Austria, and a second, linguistic-cultural idea of the nation transcending all political borders. For Winkler, historical and ethical considerations dictated that the idea of *one* German nation within what remained of Bismarck's Reich should be preserved for the time being, but that reunification should no longer be an active political goal. His assumption that the German question would be solved when the Germans in the GDR possessed the same freedom within their state as the West Germans in theirs was in keeping with what West German politicians of all camps had been saying for years. Nonetheless, he was as little able as they to explain why the Soviet Union should favour such a development and why the East Germans should be content with it.

Advocates of 'bi-nationalization' (in addition to Mommsen, this group included the historians Lutz Niethammer and Jürgen C. Hess and the political scientist Gebhard Schweigler) had no difficulty in multiplying examples of West German state consciousness and interpreting them according to their own premises as signs of national consciousness. A high degree of agreement with the political and social system of the FRG was always at the top of the list. With regard to East Germany, the case was much more difficult to prove. Subjective impressions had to stand in for empirical evidence. Even during times of relative peace between the regime and the population, as in the first years after Honecker took over from Ulbricht, the GDR remained a democratically illegitimate party dictatorship. For this reason most West Germans found East Germany repellent, while many if not most East Germans found the FRG attractive. By the early 1980s West Germany lacked only one ingredient of a true *Staatsnation* or political nation: the official consciousness that it was one. In the case of the GDR, the official claim to be a political nation was all there was.

Some years before, in the second half of the 1970s, the problems inherent in the concept of the 'nation' had led one author to declare the matter closed, at least as far as Germany was concerned. In the afterword to the fifth edition of his book *Die deutsche Diktatur** Karl Dietrich Bracher, a political scientist and historian of modern Germany living in Bonn, referred to the FRG as a 'postnational democracy among nation states'. He then gave voice to a hope similar to that expressed by Burghard Freudenfeld in the 1967 essay that had started the *Hochland* debate: 'By relieving the 1949 "provisorium" of the burden of the unfulfilled nation state, we can turn it into something definite and complete: a liberal social democracy, consciously freed from the dilemmas of 1870 and 1918, 1933 and 1945 . . . The unique German path has been refuted and seems to be at an end.'

---

* Bracher, *The German Dictatorship*.

Bracher's views did not receive much attention at the time. That changed when he reiterated them ten years later, in a contribution for the fifth volume of the *Geschichte der Bundesrepublik Deutschland* (1986):*

'Despite the continuing relevance of the German question, the Federal Republic is not a special case, sending the Germans off along unique paths. To dramatize its central geographic position—as is constantly done in the national identity debate—is to repeat the self-pitying lamentations and arrogant ideas of an ultimately failed German past. In reality the Federal Republic's location makes it an open, vital stage for all contemporary trends—and certainly also for fears and dreams that cannot be lived out in the GDR and eastern Europe . . . Overcoming all the turbulence since the mid-1960s, the Federal Republic has shown itself to be a productive, adaptable, stable, and open society . . . The European and Atlantic community gives it the support it needs in order to meet the particular challenge it has faced ever since the end of the German dictatorship: living as a post-national democracy among nation states. Thus the FRG—which already has it far better than the population of the GDR—can bear the consequences of self-imposed dictatorship and resulting partition, while also doing justice to the experiences both of the first, failed democracy and the new, successful one.

By the mid-1980s West German intellectuals had gone very far towards coming to terms with the partition of Germany. The realization that the Germans had brought it on themselves by unleashing the Second World War was not confined to the 'left'; it was part of the basic liberal consensus that formed the foundation of the West German state. The GDR was increasingly lost from view in this process. The fate of those who lived there was lamented, but West Germans did not feel that they could do much about it.

Many East German activists also saw the division of Germany as an atonement for the Nazi period, the last common chapter in German history. This was especially the case in the Evangelical milieu. A statement by two pastors, Martin Gutzeit and Markus Meckel, on the fortieth anniversary of 8 May 1945, put it as follows: 'If today we search for a German identity, it is only to be found in an acceptance of the common culpable past of both German states and in the recognition of the fact of these two states.' In contrast to western intellectuals, however, East Germans were directly and existentially affected by the status quo. They did not have the kind of freedom that made it easy for those in the west to accept the lack of national unity.

The phrase 'post-national democracy among nation states' described a peculiarity of the FRG, perhaps even a new *Sonderweg*. The other members of the European Community, as democratic nation states, represented the norm. This did not prevent some West German intellectuals, especially on the left, from viewing the situation in terms of a positive achievement: West Germany had 'overcome' and 'left behind' the nation and the nation state; in this it was 'ahead' of its partners, having 'passed them without catching up to them', to modify

---

* *History of the Federal Republic of Germany.*

the famous phrase by Walter Ulbricht. In reality, its western neighbours saw little attraction to claims that West Germany represent the model 'post-national community' of the future. But this was hardly noticed. The same was true of the fact—explicitly mentioned by Bracher—that there was a specific German reason for questioning the 'post-national' self-image: the consequences of the shared German past were very unevenly distributed between the Germans in the west and those in the east.[20]

The crimes of National Socialism, above all the murder of the European Jews, had become by the 1980s the central feature of a self-critical consciousness of German identity. The quasi-apologetic attitude towards the Third Reich that had characterized the 1950s was now finally overcome (although it still persisted in certain conservative circles). Many factors had contributed: the rise of new generations who did not have to ask the 'culpability question' of themselves; the scholarly reappraisal and critical incorporation of the history of the concentration camps and the systematic destruction of human masses; the great trials against those who had helped carry out the genocidal policy (including the prosecution of Adolf Eichmann, director of the Jewish Section of the Reich Security Central Office, in Jerusalem in 1960–1; the Auschwitz trial in Frankfurt of 1963–5; and the Treblinka trial in Düsseldorf in 1964–5); plays like Rolf Hochhuth's *Der Stellvertreter* (1963);* the March 1960 made-for-television film based on Hans Scholz's novel *Am grünen Stand der Spree*,† which showed a mass shooting of Jews in occupied Poland; and finally, something that surpassed everything else in its effect on the public: the American television series *The Holocaust*, aired simultaneously by all regional service stations of the ARD public broadcasting consortium on four evenings at the end of January 1979. Over 16 million viewers were counted.

It was only after this television event in 1979 that the term 'Holocaust' (ancient Greek for 'burnt offering') came into widespread use to describe the murder of the Jews. In the ensuing years the word 'Auschwitz' came to symbolize for the Germans the essence of the evil that Hitler's Germany had unleashed upon the world. In the 1980s, scholarly debates over the deeper causes of the German partition did not focus on the murder of the Jews, but on the German political decisions that had led to the two world wars. In the general public consciousness, however, a different view was subliminally at work, one that would not be articulated until later. It saw the partition of Germany not only as a security for the east–west balance of power in Europe and global peace, but also as a punishment and atonement for the German crimes against humanity—for Auschwitz.

When the time came in 1985 to commemorate the fortieth anniversary of the unconditional surrender of the German Reich, chancellor Helmut Kohl chose a form of remembrance that caused heated protest both at home and abroad.

---

* Hochhuth, *The Deputy.*
† Scholz, *On the Green Banks of the Spree.*

Together with the American president Ronald Reagan, who was in Europe for this anniversary, he scheduled a visit to the military cemetery of Bitburg in the Eifel region, intending this as a gesture of reconciliation between the two countries. The cemetery contained the bodies of some 2,000 German soldiers, among them—and this had been missed in Bonn—49 from the Waffen-SS. Once this piece of news made it round the world, Reagan found himself the target of massive attacks, especially from Jewish organizations. Kohl nonetheless insisted on sticking to the schedule for the visit. It took place on 5 May. The retired generals Matthew Ridgeway and Johannes Steinhoff, both veterans from the front, shook hands as a gesture of reconciliation. Had Reagan not subsequently paid a visit to the former concentration camp at Bergen-Belsen, the Bitburg event would have sent a disturbing message: that West Germany and the United States had now agreed to look upon the Second World War as a 'normal' European war.

Three days later, on 8 May, President Richard von Weizsäcker (elected one year previously, on 23 May 1984, by the coalition parties and the Social Democrats) gave a speech in the Bundestag that the left and centre welcomed as a contrast to Kohl's insensitive approach to historical symbols—not to mention the unanimously positive echoes from abroad. Weizsäcker pronounced openly 'what must be said for all of us today: 8 May was a day of liberation. It liberated us all from the National Socialist tyranny and its contempt for human life.' It was true that the liberation would not make anyone forget the sufferings that for many only began on 8 May 1945 and afterwards.

However, we must not think of the end of the war as the cause of the flight, the expulsions, the lack of freedom. This cause lies in the war's beginning and in the beginning of the tyranny that led to the war. We cannot separate 8 May 1945 from 30 January 1933. We truly have no reason to take part in victory celebrations today. But we have every reason to recognize 8 May 1945 as the end of a wrong path in German history, an end that contained the seeds of hope for a better future.

The president commemorated the victims of the German resistance, 'in the bourgeoisie, the military, among people of faith, the resistance among the workers and the unions, the resistance of the communists'. He declared that there was virtually no state with a history free of wrongful entanglement in war and violence. 'Nonetheless', he added,

the genocide against the Jews is without parallel in history. The execution of the crime lay in the hands of a few. It was concealed from the public eye. But every German could see what their Jewish fellow citizens had to go through, from cold indifference to hidden intolerance to open hatred. Who could remain blind to what was going on after the synagogues were burned, after the looting started, after the Jews were stigmatized with the yellow star, after they lost their rights, after the ceaseless violations of human dignity?

Much of what could have been said in connection with 8 May 1945 and 30 January 1933 was left out of this speech, or left unclear. Weizsäcker lamented the nationalist passions that had flamed up anew after the 1919 peace treaties and attached themselves to conditions of social misery. 'Hitler was the driving force on the way to misfortune. He created and used mass hysteria. A weak democracy was unable to stop him. And the European world powers, too, in Churchill's view "guileless, though not guiltless", contributed through their weakness to the catastrophic developments.' But the role the old upper classes and the bourgeoisie had played in destroying the Weimar Republic, in Hitler's success, and in the Second World War—these things were not mentioned by the German president, son of the long-time state secretary of the foreign office, Ernst von Weizsäcker. Nonetheless, his speech had a liberating effect. It showed that a head of state from the Union could deal with conservative interpretations of German history nearly as critically as his Social Democratic predecessor Gustav Heinemann had done a decade and a half before.

But even a president was unable to completely silence conservative apologetics. On 28 February 1986 the *Frankfurter Allgemeine Zeitung* ran a commentary by Friedrich Karl Fromme on a parliamentary debate over anti-Semitism the day before. 'Other nations', wrote Fromm,

might ask if their predilections are to be dictated to them. In the Nazi state the 'destruction of the Jews'—the word belongs in quotation marks—took place in a discreet manner. It was in no way the case that German radio in those days sent out a weekly bulletin announcing that such-and-such a number of Jews had been killed in the past few days . . . How impartial [*unbefangen*] can a German be today? He must remain partial in the sense that the otherwise freely permitted separation of people into those one likes and those one doesn't like is forbidden in the case of the Jews . . . There is much good will towards the Jews among young people and among those who are no longer quite so young. But to a generation that feels itself impartial it must be granted that its patience has a limit. Reason and humanity, two ideas that do not always go together, must be handled with delicacy—by all sides.

Two months later, on 24 April 1986, another writer for the *FAZ*, Ernst-Otto Maetzke, commented on the international controversy surrounding the Austrian presidential elections. The conservative candidate, Kurt Waldheim, had been a member of the SA. He was accused—by the Jewish World Congress and American newspapers, among others—of having participated in or covered up war crimes in the Balkans during the Second World War. Maetzke claimed, perhaps rightly, that the attacks against Waldheim were connected to the Austrian government's policy towards Israel. He then went on: 'But one thing is certain: it is reprehensible and hypocritical to misuse the dead of a past war and a tyranny in the pursuit of current political goals. The fact that this method is widespread in political battles does not make it better. Run-of-the mill corpse-robbers are benign in comparison.'

The *FAZ* caused much more controversy later that spring when it printed, on 6 June 1986, a speech by Ernst Nolte, a historical researcher at the Free University of Berlin (his training had been in philosophy) and author of several important books, including one entitled *Faschismus in seiner Epoche*.* What Nolte had to say to the readers of the 'newspaper for Germany' he had actually planned to say at the 'Römerberg talks' in Frankfurt, but his invitation had been cancelled. The historian attempted to put himself in the position of the Nazi Führer. He described what Hitler knew about the terror of the Bolsheviks, especially the interrogation methods of their secret police. One of these methods, he said, was the threat—ascribed to the 'Chinese Cheka'—of turning a rat that had been starved to the point of madness on a prisoner in order to force a confession.

Nolte then asked a number of rhetorical questions:

Could it be that the National Socialists, that Hitler performed an 'Asiatic' deed only because they saw themselves and people like themselves as potential or actual victims of an 'Asiatic' deed? Did the 'Gulag Archipelago' not exist before Auschwitz? Was Bolshevik 'class murder' not the logical and factual predecessor to the Nazi 'racial murder'? Can Hitler's most secret acts not also be explained by the very fact that he did *not* forget the 'rat cage'? Did Auschwitz not, perhaps, originate in a past that would not pass away?

Not even Nolte was willing to deny that 'despite their comparability, the Nazi campaign of biological destruction differed qualitatively from the Bolshevik campaign of social destruction.' 'But', he continued,

however little a murder, much less a mass murder, can be 'justified' by another murder, it is fundamentally erroneous to fixate on the one murder and the one mass murder and refuse to recognize the other one, even though a causal nexus is likely. Whoever looks at this history not as a mythologem, but considers it in its basic context, will be forced to draw a central conclusion: if this history, in all its darkness and all its horrors, but also in its confusing novelty, which one must make allowances for when judging those who acted in it—if this history has had any meaning for later generations, then it must be in being liberated from the tyranny of collectivist thinking . . . To the extent that the debate over National Socialism is characterized by exactly this kind of collectivist thinking, the matter ought to be considered closed, once and for all.

Nolte's article set off what became known as the *Historikerstreit*, the 'conflict of the historians' over the historical singularity of the Nazi destruction of the Jews. What bothered Nolte was that the whole world recognized only *one* crime as the crime of the century, the Nazi genocide. This was unacceptable to him as a German and as a bourgeois, and, before the century came to an end, he intended to straighten history out, in terms of giving appropriate consideration to the *other*, chronologically earlier crime against humanity, the Bolshevik class murder. Nolte represented the relationship between the two mass murders in such a way that Hitler appeared as the one who was reacting, acting in self-defence or at least in the belief he was doing so. If this view prevailed it meant that Germany, and the European bourgeoisie to the extent it had collaborated with Hitler, would be

---

* Nolte, *Fascism in Historical Context* (tr. as *Three Faces of Fascism*).

partially exonerated. The apologetic effect of Nolte's approach—both in terms of the nation and in terms of social class—was obvious. That was the essence of his attacks against allegedly 'collectivist' assignments of guilt.

The sharpest response to this historical revision came from the Frankfurt philosopher Jürgen Habermas. In an article in *Die Zeit* on 11 July 1986 he accused Nolte and several of his more or less conservative colleagues (he named Andreas Hillgruber, Michael Stürmer, and Klaus Hildebrand) of 'ideological planning' for the purpose of 'reviving German national consciousness'. For Nolte, he wrote, Auschwitz had shrunk 'down to the dimensions of a technological innovation'; it could be explained away by the '"Asiatic" threat of an enemy still standing at our door'. The attempt to '*shake off* the burdens of a happily amoralized past' was dangerous, since it was tantamount to spiritually alienating the country from the west.

The Federal Republic's unreserved opening towards the political culture of the west is the greatest intellectual achievement of our post-war period, something my generation in particular can be proud of. The result will not be made more stable by a quasi-nationalist German nature philosophy...The only kind of patriotism that will not alienate us from the west is a constitutional patriotism. Unfortunately, in the cultural nation of the Germans the allegiance to universal constitutional principles, anchored in convictions, has only been able to establish itself after—and through—Auschwitz. If someone wants to use a bromide like 'guilt obsession'...to drive the blush of shame over this fact from our faces; if someone wants to call the Germans back to a conventional form of their national identity, then he is destroying the only dependable basis of our tie to the west.

The majority of historians who took part in the controversy sided against Nolte. One of them, Heinrich August Winkler, saw a connection between the historiographic 'politics' of Nolte and his publicist allies—including Joachim Fest, co-editor of the *Frankfurter Allgemeine Zeitung*—and the call for German reunification, which the *FAZ* had been energetically sounding for some time.

If the restoration of the German Reich is to be called for today, then history will indeed have to be rewritten. The regime that forfeited Germany's political unity must no longer appear as what it was: the most inhuman in all of history...Considering the part Germany played in the origins of the two world wars, Europe cannot want, and the Germans ought not to want a new German Reich, a sovereign nation state. This is the logic of history, which, as Bismarck said, is more stringent than the Prussian high chamber of accounts...However, our legacy also includes a national solidarity with the Germans in the GDR, who to this day bear the burden of German history to an incomparably greater degree than the citizens of the Federal Republic.

The *Historikerstreit*, though not yielding any new historical knowledge *per se*, was important for the political culture of the FRG. The warding off of Nolte's attempts to exculpate the Germans for their history helped develop what we might call a 'posthumous Adenauer left': the intellectual left, which had once fought passionately against Adenauer's western policy, now began to look upon the alliance with the west as its very own achievement, one that had to be defended against any kind of nationalist 'revisionism', real or imagined. This gave rise to a specifically leftist or left-liberal West German 'constitutional patriotism'. To be sure, Habermas's understanding of that term differed from Dolf Sternberger's, above all in its higher degree of abstraction. The Frankfurt philosopher did not refer to the Basic Law, but to 'universal constitutional principles' of the west in general. It was doubtful whether these alone would be a sufficient basis for West German identity—without even getting into the question of whether a 'universally' oriented West Germany still needed to feel an obligation to the Germans in the GDR, who were not permitted to participate in western values.

The confrontation with Nolte was necessary, and it was successful. No apologetic nationalist revision of German history took place. The self-critical analysis of the German political tradition continued and gathered strength. But the victory had a price: it strengthened the status quo, which, while comfortable for citizens of the FRG, meant the oppression of most East Germans. The awareness of the moral ambivalence of this state of affairs grew increasingly weaker. The idea of the singularity of the Holocaust, while it prevented the relativization of German crimes against humanity, also had other effects: it allowed the relativization of 'leftist' crimes; it placed a taboo on the question of what role the fear of a civil war—a fear deliberately created by the communists—had played in the fascist rise to power; and it obstructed the comparison between different forms of totalitarian rule, including even the use of the term 'totalitarian'. Thus it was not only conservatives like Nolte who were pursuing a particular 'politics of history' (the term *Geschichtspolitik* first appeared in 1986); leftists and left-liberals had their own agenda.

The idea of Auschwitz as a West German 'myth of origin' seems to have first appeared in 1997. Only in the 1980s did the name of the concentration camp acquire this kind of legitimating force, and only then was the argument made that the Holocaust was the only common point of reference within German–German identity. To use the Nazi genocide in this way was to instrumentalize history for political aims. How the murder of the Jews was to be interpreted, and for what or against what it was to be utilized as an argument—this depended on what was being advanced as in the 'German interest'. The shame provoked by the most terrible crime in German history could even mutate into pride, a *Sühnestolz* or 'pride of atonement', fuelling the rise of a negative nationalism, a sentiment with quasi-religious features just like any 'authentic' nationalism. It was true that only parts of the West German left developed these tendencies. But when it did happen, the desire to learn from the German catastrophe took on a pathological character.

In his aforementioned speech President Weizsäcker had thought out loud about 'why, forty years after the end of the war, there are such lively debates over the past. Why are they more lively now than after twenty-five or thirty years?' He answered this question by telling his audience that periods of forty years 'play an important role in human lives and the fates of peoples'. He cited the Old Testament.

Israel was to remain forty years in the desert before a new period in their history would begin with their entrance into the promised land. Forty years were necessary for a complete generational change in leadership . . . Thus forty years always represent a big shift. They have an important effect on human consciousness, whether it means the end of a dark time with hope for a new and good future, or the danger of forgetting and as a warning about the consequences.

Three years after the fortieth anniversary of the German surrender it was time to commemorate the fiftieth anniversary of the *Reichskristallnacht* (9 November 1938). The official speech was given on 10 November 1988 by Philipp Jenninger (CDU), president of the Bundestag. Jenninger attempted to explain the reasons for the popularity of Hitler and the Third Reich between the years 1933 and 1938. Rhetorically this was very awkward, since he reproduced—partly in question form—ideas of the time and Nazi concepts like 'Aryan property' and 'racial disgrace' without making it clear that he was paraphrasing.

At this point numerous Green delegates, as well as some from the SPD and FDP, got up and walked out of the hall, thus missing what Jenninger then said: 'The essentials were known.' It was a phrase used by the late Adolf Arndt, an SPD delegate and 'half Jew' according to the Nuremberg race laws. Jenninger was trying to counter the widespread view that the Germans did not know about the destruction of the Jews during the Second World War. And something else he said he put more forcefully than anyone else had done before parliament up to that time: 'Until the end of all time people will remember Auschwitz as a part of our German history.'

Those who left the hall probably had various reasons for doing so. Many found the speech inappropriate for the occasion; they had good reason. Others thought they detected apologetic intentions behind the speaker's incompetence; they were wrong. Some probably wanted only to show that they were good anti-fascists. The public outrage over the speech was so great that Jenninger resigned from the office of Bundestag president the next day. He was replaced by Rita Süssmuth (CDU), hitherto minister for youth, family, women, and health, on 25 November.[21]

GORBACHEV AND THE NEW PHASE IN EAST–WEST RELATIONS

The history of the two German states seems subject to a strange process of twelve-year cycles. The Berlin wall, one of the most closely guarded political borders in the world, was built twelve years after the founding of the FRG and the GDR. Twelve years later, in 1973, the Basic Treaty entered into effect, putting relations between the two states into a legal form that both sides had agreed upon. Another twelve years after that, in March 1985, a man came to power in Moscow who, by dramatically changing east–west relations, would also dramatically change the relationship between East and West Germany. That man was Mikhail Gorbachev.

The new general secretary of the central committee of the Soviet Communist party did not have a concrete plan for what he wanted to accomplish, either domestically or in foreign policy. He only knew that things could not continue as they were. The necessary internal reforms had been delayed during the long years of 'stagnation' under Brezhnev. Instead, Moscow had become involved in a ruinous arms race and risky foreign ventures like the intervention in Afghanistan. The Soviet economy now found itself in rapid decline. When OPEC fell apart in 1985, bringing down the price of crude oil, the Soviet Union and its allies, including the GDR, lost the temporary advantages that had resulted from the difference between the price for oil on the world market and the price inside COMECON.

In order to deal with all these crises, Gorbachev had to move the USSR in a fundamentally new direction: internally by giving reform-oriented forces more freedom, fostering autonomy and competition among businesses, and promoting private initiative and small private companies; internationally by following what was now the only reasonable course: improving relations with the USA, renewing the détente, and using international disarmament to cut military expenditures.

The key concepts in the process of inner change were *glasnost* ('openness') and *perestroika* ('restructuring'). They stood for transparency and the democratization of decision-making processes. In the conclusion to his speech at the CC plenum assembly on 28 January 1987, Gorbachev pronounced the famous sentence: 'We need democracy like the air we breathe.' He probably was not aware that he was quoting a statement by Friedrich Engels of the year 1865. Engels did not believe a workers' movement was possible without freedom of the press, association, and assembly. 'Without this freedom it [the workers' party, H.A.W.] cannot freely manoeuvre. In this struggle it is fighting for its own life element, for the air it needs to breathe.' Nearly a century and a quarter later, the man at the head of the CPSU reiterated this observation as a goal to be realized. Gorbachev did not apply a rigorous democratic logic in his call for democracy. He had no intention of renouncing the Communist party's claim to leadership, that is, of breaking radically with Leninism. But while democracy in a western sense was not possible in this way, Gorbachev did want to do more than just soften the dictatorship. Under his leadership, individual freedom of expression and diversity in the media were introduced in the Soviet Union.

Gorbachev was helped by the fact that Ronald Reagan, re-elected president of the United States in November 1984, had also begun to rethink his nation's foreign policy. There were two main reasons for this. The Democratic majority in the House of Representatives was pressuring Reagan to work with the Soviets on disarmament. And he was also faced with the necessity of defusing a serious domestic crisis, the so-called 'Iran–Contra affair'. (Members of the National Security Council had sold arms illegally to Iran in exchange for Teheran's release of American hostages; the proceeds were used to help finance the war—covertly supported by the CIA—of the rightist 'Contras' against the leftist Sandinista government in Nicaragua.)

At an October 1986 summit between Reagan and Gorbachev in Reykjavik (their second meeting, preceded by one in Geneva in 1985), the two leaders came close to agreeing to the complete dismantling of Eurostrategic weapons. The accord ultimately failed owing to Reagan's refusal to accept his partner's compromise proposals with regard to the 'SDI' missile defence programme. But the breakthrough came the following year. On 28 February 1987 Gorbachev, internationally weakened by the consequences of the nuclear disaster at Chernobyl in April 1986, withdrew the Soviet demand that negotiations over medium-range missiles be linked to talks on the SDI or antiballistic missiles. Five months later, on 22 July, the Soviets announced their willingness to accept a worldwide 'double zero solution' with regard to medium and short-range nuclear missiles *without* making agreement dependent on American concessions in its defensive and space weapons. This was tantamount to accepting a resolution made by the foreign ministers of the NATO countries at their meeting in Reykjavik that June. Since the USSR had far more medium-range missiles in Europe than America did, it was agreeing to an asymmetric disarmament.

Gorbachev and Reagan signed the INF treaty in Washington on 8 December 1987. At the end of May 1988, two weeks after Moscow began withdrawing its troops from Afghanistan, Reagan visited the Soviet Union and exchanged the ratification documents with Gorbachev. The firmness of the west in the battle over Eurostrategic weapons had paid off. The result surpassed the boldest hopes of those who had supported *both* parts of the 1979 NATO decision. Europe profited from the readiness of the great powers to put confrontation behind them and return to cooperation.

The relationship between the Soviet Union and West Germany was subject to considerable fluctuation after Gorbachev came to power. After a visit to Moscow at the end of July 1986, during which he had the opportunity to speak at length with Gorbachev and Eduard Shevardnadze, the new foreign minister, Hans-Dietrich Genscher, returned with the impression that the Soviet leadership was interested in good relations with Bonn and that Gorbachev, as he put it, even wanted to 'turn over a new leaf' between the two states. That autumn, however, Helmut Kohl was responsible for a serious setback in this process: the American magazine *Newsweek* published a conversation with the German chancellor in which he compared Gorbachev with Hitler's propaganda minister. Gorbachev, Kohl said, was a modern communist leader who understood something about pubic relations, but Goebbels had, too. The Kremlin was outraged, and relations between the two states entered an 'interim ice age'. Not even a personal letter of apology from Kohl could help. When Genscher met Shevardnadze in Vienna on 4 November, he had the greatest difficulty in convincing his Soviet colleague that Kohl had not intended any insult to Gorbachev.

About four months later, on 25 January 1987, elections took place for the eleventh German Bundestag. The Union parties garnered 44.3% of the vote, a loss of 4.5% from 1983 and their worst result since 1949. The Social Democrats, with North Rhine-Westphalian prime minister Johannes Rau as their candidate and 'Conciliation, not conflict' (*Versöhnen statt spalten*) as their electoral slogan, managed 37.0%, a loss of 1.2% from the previous elections. The FDP and the Green party made gains, the former of 2.1% for a total of 9.1% of the vote, the latter of 2.7% for a total of 8.3%. The distribution of seats made it clear that, despite the Union's losses, the current coalition would again control a parliamentary majority: 282 seats over 237 for the SPD and Greens.

Before the election of the chancellor, on 1 February 1987, Foreign Minister Genscher, speaking at the World Economic Forum in Davos, Switzerland, indicated his government's willingness to work with Moscow. (A Soviet delegation was taking part in the conference for the first time.) Humanity, he said, faced a decision: it would either be destroyed by confrontation or survive by cooperation.

Whoever takes Gorbachev's statements at their word must be prepared to cooperate . . . Our maxim can only be: Let us take Gorbachev seriously; let us take him at his word . . . Let us not sit with arms crossed and wait to see what Gorbachev brings us! Rather, let us try to influence, move forward, and shape developments from our side . . . Firmness is necessary, but a policy of strength, of striving for superiority, of each one trying to out-arm the other: these things must be consigned to the mental categories of the past once and for all, in the west, too. This kind of attitude would bring disaster on humanity.

Genscher describes the contradictory response to this speech in his memoirs:

Massive agreement on the one hand, extraordinary scepticism on the other. The by no means friendly word 'Genscherism' was revived. Although originally invented by the German left as a critique against my realistic détente policy, the word now came from America and England, though with a completely different meaning, of course. Now it implied the harbouring of unrealistic expectations with regard to the Soviet Union. There was open and veiled criticism in Germany, too, even in the government.

On 11 March 1987 Helmut Kohl was elected chancellor for the third time (253 to 225 votes, with 3 invalid votes and 6 delegates abstaining). In his inaugural address on 18 March he adopted Genscher's language. 'General Secretary Gorbachev talks about a new kind of thinking in international relations,' Kohl said.

We will take him at his word. If his policy means opportunities for more understanding, more cooperation, and above all for concrete results in disarmament and arms control, we will embrace it. If he is going to further clear the way for cooperation between all west and east European states, then we are resolved to avail ourselves of this to the maximum—within the framework of bilateral relations as well as within the framework of the east–west dialogue as a whole.

The problems in east–west relations did not go unmentioned. Kohl talked about the 'overwhelming Soviet superiority in shorter-range ballistic missiles' and declared it his goal 'to reduce all these systems down to a low level with uniform ceilings'. He called for greater efforts in overcoming the conventional imbalance in Europe and advised the United States (though he did not explicitly mention the country's name) to respond to a dramatic decrease in offensive weapons by examining the 'necessity and the scope of defensive weapons'. The GDR was assured of the chancellor's intention 'of further developing relations between the two states in Germany in a good, open climate' and conducting a 'political dialogue on all levels'. Nonetheless, the FRG was sticking to its goal of 'liberty and unity for all Germans' and would continue to insist on a single German citizenship. And Kohl left no doubt about another issue: 'We will never accept a wall and barbed wire and orders to shoot.'

The year 1987 saw a number of notable east–west encounters. Between 6 and 11 July President Weizsäcker, accompanied by Genscher, was on a state visit in Moscow, the main purpose of which was to overcome the crisis provoked by Kohl's comparison of Gorbachev with Goebbels. In this Weizsäcker was successful. Speaking at a dinner arranged for him by Andrei Gromyko, the Soviet president since July 1986, Weizsäcker asserted that the Germans, though living separately in the east and west, had not stopped and would not stop thinking of themselves as one nation. He then added: 'It is in liberty that the the unity of the nation finds fulfilment.' *Pravda*, the Communist party newspaper, left this and other sensitive passages out of its 'account' of Weizsäcker's talk. The complete speech was not printed until Genscher intervened with his colleague Shevardnadze, and then not in *Pravda*, but, after a delay of a few days, in the government paper *Izvestia*.

Then, in a detailed and at times acrimonious talk with Gorbachev, Weizsäcker returned to the 'open German question', which prompted the Communist party leader to deny at first that such a question even existed. Later in the conversation, however, Gorbachev urged that the resolution of the German question be left to history, since nobody knew 'what the situation would be like in one hundred years'. When Weizsäcker, smirking, asked Gorbachev if he knew what the situation would be like in fifty years, the latter also began to smile. Genscher, who was present, discussed the General Secretary's words with Weizsäcker later on, and drew his own conclusion: Gorbachev was also saying that, in the longer term, the German question was open.

In the following month the cooperation between the SPD and the SED reached its remarkable zenith with the adoption of what both parties agreed to call their *Streitkultur* or 'culture of controversy'. The first meeting had taken place in early summer 1984 on the Scharmützelsee in Brandenburg. Erhard Eppler, head of the SPD's 'basic values commission', led the SPD delegation, and the GDR delegation was headed by Otto Reinhold, director of the East German Academy of Social Sciences. The outcome of arduous negotiations was a paper entitled 'Conflicting Ideologies and Mutual Security' (*Der Streit der Ideologien und die gemeinsame Sicherheit*), published on 27 August 1987. This was followed by a discussion between Eppler, Reinhold, and the text's two main authors, Thomas Meyer for the SPD and Rolf Reissig for the SED, broadcast live on East German television on 1 September.

The so-called *Streitkulturpapier* was the first declaration of common principles ever since the conflict between the Social Democrats and the Communists, the two heirs of the German Marxist workers' movement, began in the wake of the First World War. The differences, especially with regard to the meaning of 'democracy', were stated openly. But the points of agreement were also emphasized:

Neither side may contest the other's right to exist. Our hope cannot be that one system will abolish the other. Rather, it is that both systems are capable of reform and that the competition between the systems strengthens the will to reform on both sides . . . Each system must consider the other peaceable . . . Each societal system must consider the other capable of development and reform . . . The ideological debate is to be conducted in such a way that there is no interference in the internal affairs of either side. Criticism, even sharply worded, may not be rejected as 'interference in the internal affairs' of the other side . . . Open discussion about the competition between the systems, their successes and failures, advantages and disadvantages, must be possible within each system. In fact, real competition requires that this discussion be promoted and lead to practical results.

The *Streitkultur* paper, published in both states, represented a bigger risk for the SED than for the SPD. Anyone who wished to openly discuss the failures and disadvantages of 'real existing socialism' could now appeal to yet another document signed, like the Helsinki Final Act, by the SED itself. And in fact SED officials did have to deal with uncomfortable discussions after August 1987, even inside the party. To that extent the paper was a success for the West German Social Democrats.

But there was another side to the story. The SPD did more than just recognize the *political* existence of the GDR; it expressly confirmed the East German *societal system* in its right to exist. Despite the fact that it had not ceased to be a dictatorship, the Social Democrats were now officially rejecting a fundamental repudiation of the GDR system, and the SED could count this as a success. Since both systems were considered 'capable of development and reform', critics of communism could now be answered by the claim that change would come through 'gradual improvements'. Up to this point the SED had suppressed demands for such improvements. The *Streitkultur* paper contained promises that were flagrantly contradicted by SED practice. The SPD could only hope that its 'partner', in making such promises, would be forced to change accordingly.

Even more spectacular than the SPD–SED statement was an event that formed the ceremonial high point in the history of German–German relations up to that point: the official visit to West Germany of the president of the State Council of the German Democratic Republic and general secretary of the Socialist Unity Party of Germany, Erich Honecker, between 7 and 11 September 1987. Preparations for the occasion had been lengthy. Horst Sindermann, the Volkskammer president, had gone to Bonn in February 1986 in a kind of 'practice run'. The Soviets had given their final agreement probably in July, immediately after Weizsäcker's trip to Moscow. Bonn and East Berlin had negotiated exhaustively over who Honecker would speak with and what he would talk about while in the FRG, including the subjects of after-dinner speeches; over the places he would visit; and over a joint communiqué at the end of the visit. Finally, there had been unofficial articles of greeting, including one from Helmut Schmidt. 'Even with Honecker', the former chancellor wrote in *Die Zeit* on 24 July,

German identity is now in evidence, not merely a bit of homesickness for Wiebelskirchen and the Saarland. Honecker is a German who wishes to do his duty. His duty, such as he feels it incumbent on him to do . . . Even if Erich Honecker and we can never be friends, in terms of party or politics in general, let us receive him honourably. Receive him as one of our brothers!

Honecker received another Social Democratic greeting (and best wishes for his seventy-fifth birthday on 25 August 1987) from his Saarland compatriot Oskar Lafontaine, prime minister of Saarland since 1985 and deputy head of the SPD since 1986. In the 24 August edition of *Der Spiegel*, three days before the publication of the *Streitkulturpapier*, Lafontaine depicted the SED general secretary as a man who, like all natives of Saarland, was capable of 'not taking things too seriously'. Honecker was 'not even unpopular' in his homeland and, even if he did sometimes have all-German dreams, was one thing above all: a realist.

The relative prosperity that the GDR reached during the Honecker era has made it easier for its inhabitants to come to an arrangement with their state. This agreement, which has been increasing among the population since the 1950s and 1960s, has allowed the GDR to open itself towards the outside world somewhat more, even towards the west. . . The recognition of others gives one the self-confidence one needs to stand on one's own. . . Of course, we cannot demand of the German communist Erich Honecker what his ideological convictions and his life experience do not permit him to do . . . It makes little sense to constantly provoke him with our convictions. They are not his own. His values are those of the communist world view . . . And we will not be able to have Erich Honecker as a partner if we cannot respect him as a communist. Considering his difficult youth and his resistance to the fascist tyranny, even staunch opponents of communism should be able to muster this respect.

With a few intentional exceptions, the protocol for this visit was like that for any other foreign head of state or government on an official visit in the FRG. Honecker was received at his arrival in the Cologne-Bonn airport on 7 September by the head of the chancellor's office, Wolfgang Schäuble. He was greeted by Chancellor Kohl in front of the chancellery. The flags of both states were raised; a military band played both national anthems; and together Honecker and Kohl inspected an honour guard. Foreign Minister Genscher did not attend this opening ceremony in order to make it clear that the Federal Republic still did not consider the GDR to be a foreign country. The foreign head of state's ceremonial signing of the Golden Book of the city of Bonn was also omitted, as was Honecker's reception by the diplomatic corps.

Honecker found attentive interlocutors during his visit, some of whom made things easier for him than others. President Weizsäcker avoided controversial subjects. According to the notes made by the East German side, Willy Brandt, now honorary head of the SPD (he had given up the office of head at the end of March), asked Honecker 'if the 1918 line of separation between Social Democrats and Communists is to be permanent, or if, beyond the question of peace, noteworthy commonalities between Social Democrats and Communists cannot be ascertained.' He told Honecker that he had already spoken with János Kádár (the leader of the Hungarian Communist party) on the subject, and that Gorbachev was entertaining similar thoughts.

Another Social Democrat, Johannes Rau, asked Honecker what he thought of Gorbachev's reforms in the USSR, and learned that 'the GDR has already achieved what Gorbachev is trying to do for the Soviet Union.' Hans-Jochen Vogel (SPD fraction leader since 1983 and party head since June 1987), quoting Johannes Hempel, bishop of the Evangelical Church of Saxony, called the situation on the border a 'bleeding wound'; he also insisted that the maximum duration of visits by West Berliners to East Berlin be extended and that former citizens of the GDR living in West Germany be permitted to travel to the east. The head of the CDU/CSU Bundestag fraction, Alfred Dregger, greeted Honecker as a 'German among Germans' (the phrase came from Weizsäcker), but then added: 'though as a German communist'. Dregger's sharpest words were the following: 'The order to shoot violates the dignity of the Germans and the dignity of the German nation.' Petra Kelly asked Honecker in the name of the Green party to permit her friend Bärbel Bohley, a painter, civil rights activist, and one of the founding members of the 'Women for Peace Initiative' (she had been imprisoned for several weeks at the end of 1983 and beginning of 1984), to travel to West Germany for an exhibition of her work. (The request was never granted.) Other Greens, led by Waltraud Schoppe, the speaker of the parliamentary fraction, assured Honecker that they supported the idea of two states, since it was a requirement for lasting peace in Europe. But the Greens were also a pacifist party, Schoppe said, and were therefore on the side of the East

German peace organizations who were being subjected to repression. As a pacifist, she had to ask why there was no alternative to military service in the GDR.

The most important talks, those between Honecker and Kohl, were made easier by prior concessions on both sides. The GDR had been generous in awarding travel permits. Some 3.2 million East Germans had been allowed to visit West Germany in the first eight months of 1987 alone. In addition to the retired, who usually had no trouble obtaining permits, this number included 860,000 people travelling for 'urgent family reasons' (nearly all of whom returned to East Germany). Moreover, the death penalty was abolished by the State Council on 17 June 1987 and a comprehensive amnesty—including political prisoners—was announced for the 7 October, the thirty-eighth anniversary of the GDR. For its part the West German government, at Genscher's urging, had agreed to include the Pershing Ia missiles in the 'double zero solution' recently adopted by the two superpowers. Since these missiles were in the possession of the Bundeswehr, they were not covered by the Geneva accord. Unlike in France and Britain, however, the nuclear warheads in West Germany were under American command. This meant that Bonn's concession was more symbolic than real.

The talks yielded little of actual substance, and positions remained unchanged in most of the disputed issues. For example, Honecker said that the GDR would be willing to negotiate over cleaning up the Elbe only if Bonn was prepared to recognize that the border ran down the middle of the river. He gave the same answer when Kohl asked that Hanover, Hamburg, and Kiel be allowed to participate in 'near border traffic', which enjoyed a privileged status. The chancellor did promise negotiations over the Elbe border in the near future, however, as did Ernst Albrecht (CDU), the prime minister of Lower Saxony. Honecker could look upon this as an accomplishment. When Kohl brought up the matter of the order to shoot at the German–German border, Honecker replied that there was no such order and that the regulations for the use of armed force at the border were in keeping with those in the FRG. Three agreements were signed: one for cooperation in environmental matters, one in the areas of science and technology, and one dealing with radiation protection. All of them had been agreed upon in advance.

On the evening of 7 September, after banqueting at the Godesberg inn La Redoute, both leaders gave speeches that were broadcast live on West and East German television and watched by large audiences in both countries. 'The consciousness of the unity of the nation is as alive as it has always been,' Kohl declared. 'The will to preserve it, unbroken . . . The German question remains open, but its resolution is not on the agenda of world history for the time being, and we will also still need the agreement of our neighbours.' Experience had shown that opposing positions on the fundamentals did not necessarily preclude cooperation on practical matters.

Let us concentrate on what is possible at this time, and let us also agree not to focus on the questions that cannot be solved today . . . The common history that inescapably unites us Germans, both in the good and in the bad, has taught us one important and central lesson: a human being must never be used as a mere means to a political end . . . Every human being must be able to decide his own fate and make his own decisions . . . We wish peace in Germany, and that means that guns must be permanently silenced along the border . . . The people in Germany are suffering from the separation. They are suffering from a wall that is literally blocking their path and repelling them. If we dismantle what separates people, we will be responding to a desire impossible to ignore in Germany: they want to come together because they belong together.

Kohl's speech was a balancing act. The chancellor had to keep in mind that the Germans in both countries were looking to Honecker's visit for practical results. But he also had to think of those for whom the enhanced diplomatic and political status of the GDR was distasteful. The western allies, who had received the text of his speech in advance, could not be forgotten even for a moment or given occasion to doubt West Germany's commitment to its alliances. Kohl mastered this challenge with remarkable skill, showing himself to be both principled and pragmatic, speaking to the national sentiments of the Germans without awakening nationalist illusions. Although he quoted the preamble to the Basic Law, which called upon the entire German people 'to achieve in free self-determination the unity and freedom of Germany', he steered clear of the word 'reunification'. He used plain language, but said what was necessary in a way that did not put his guest in an unduly awkward position. Four months before, when Ronald Reagan had visited West Germany, he had called in a public speech given between the Reichstag building and the Brandenburg Gate: 'Mr Gorbachev, open this gate! Mr Gorbachev, tear down this wall!' (12 June 1987). Kohl did not say anything like this to Erich Honecker, nor would the East German leader have been the proper recipient for such a demand.

In considering his response, Erich Honecker will also have reflected on a powerful ally who expected loyalty from the GDR, and also on the elements within his own party who looked askance at his German–German policy. To have left Kohl's declaration of support for human rights (the chancellor cited the Final Act of Helsinki) unanswered would have exposed him to the charge of ideological weakness. He therefore told his audience that the GDR fulfilled all the necessary requirements. 'In doing so, we ascribe no small significance to humanitarian questions and human rights, which find their daily expression in practical life in the totality of political, civil, economic, and social rights in the German Democratic Republic.'

For the rest, the general secretary knew only one theme: 'Today there is nothing more important than preserving the peace, beyond all differences and world views, ideologies and political goals.' He did not speak of 'Germany' and 'the Germans', only of 'German soil', from which war was never again to arise, only peace. He and Kohl had already agreed to this language in the 'Moscow declaration' of 12 March 1985. There were two reasons why it made sense to repeat it at every opportunity: it had a calming effect on the outside world, and it could also not be denied by those who had a different understanding of human rights and self-determination than that of the SED. To this extent what Honecker said was at least logical.

One West German politician found words of explicit praise for Honecker's speech in La Redoute: Oskar Lafontaine. The two men met in the chancellery in Saarbrücken during Honecker's visit to his native Saarland, where he had not set foot in many decades, and to the house where he was born in Neunkirchen. The notes kept by the East German clerk record the following: 'Referring to the speech by H. Kohl on 7 September, O. Lafontaine said that E. Honecker was well advised to react in such a way. E. Honecker answered that this made it clear that the SED's approach to the political questions was fundamentally different from that of the CDU'. Honecker also told his host that he, Lafontaine, 'could be assured of the support of the GDR in the future as well. A change in the political relations of power in the FRG in favour of the SPD would have great significance for the whole situation in Europe and for relations between the two German states.'

Saarland was the penultimate stop in Honecker's trip. He had already been to Cologne; Düsseldorf; Essen; Wuppertal, where he had seen the Friedrich Engels House; and Trier, where the North Rhine-Westphalian prime minister Bernard Vogel (CDU) had accompanied him on a visit to the house where Karl Marx was born. The final stop was Bavaria. Prime Minister Strauss received Honecker with the highest ceremonial honours: three anthems (that of Bavaria, 'Gott mit dir, du Land der Bayern', along with the West and East German anthems) and a large police escort. During a long conversation, Strauss assured his guest that he in no way supported a kind of policy that would make war seem possible once again. He also expressed a number of wishes: that the May 1986 German–German cultural agreement be implemented, that commerce between Bavaria and the GDR be broadened, and other requests concerning border traffic and transit matters. From Munich Honecker drove to the former concentration camp of Dachau, where, according to the East German records, he met with 'antifascists from the FRG', representatives from the two large Christian denominations, and the Israeli religious community.

His visit to the Federal Republic considerably increased both Honecker's own prestige and that of his state. West German opinion polls noted two phenomena that caused concern in the chancellery in Bonn: Honecker's reputation had clearly gone up among the citizenry, and the tendency to disregard the antinomy between the East and West German political systems was on the increase.

The Ministry for State Security in East Berlin had totally different concerns. On 16 September 1987 its 'Central Evaluation and Information Group' dealt with 'possible negative effects of this visit'. It feared 'ideological rifts' as the 'process of further normalization of GDR–FRG relations' continued. The speeches by Chancellor Kohl and 'other FRG politicians' as well as the final communiqué (which gave the views of both sides) had strengthened 'expectations and speculations'. 'At the present moment we note that expressed expectations have tended to become more concrete and in many cases contain exaggerated, unrealistic notions. The persons expressing themselves in this way represent all classes and strata in the population.'

It seemed that the restrictions in the freedom of movement were drawing more and more criticism.

In this regard workers and employees, staff of state agencies and institutions often expressed the view that a greater freedom of movement in transit traffic would bring about a decrease in illegal departures from the GDR as well as in emigration applications, since GDR citizens could witness the realities in the FRG for themselves and would have a greater appreciation for their secure lives in the GDR. Clandestine agents in the most diverse areas of society, including employees in the research institutes of concerns and factories as well as in transportation and news agencies, declared repeatedly that while people confide in them with regard to their professional activities, this is not the case when it comes to plans to travel to the non-socialist world. They say that this contradiction is incomprehensible and makes them wish to resign as clandestine agents.

All in all, however, the SED found that the benefits of Honecker's visit to West Germany far outweighed the negative aspects. It was ironic that a chancellor from the CDU, the party that had once fought bitterly against the social–liberal *Ostpolitik*, had rolled out the famous 'red carpet' for the leader of the GDR. Now there was no way back. The smaller, democratically illegitimate German state had received what in the circumstances was the highest possible degree of recognition from its larger, democratically legitimate partner.

It was important for the East German leadership that the CDU/CSU had now made rapprochement into its own cause. Equally if not more important was continued progress in the relationship between the SED and the SPD. Much had already been accomplished. The two parties had become partners in a quasi-official security agreement and had initiated an open debate over questions of ideology. The Social Democrats were clearly moving towards an acceptance of several of Honecker's 'Gera demands' of October 1980: the Elbe border solution; the dissolution of the Central Documentation Office in Salzgitter, which documented acts of violence and cases of judicial terror in the GDR; and recognition of GDR citizenship. With regard to the Salzgitter question, Willy Brandt told Honecker when the two men first met on 19 September 1985 that if Gerhard Schröder became prime minister of Lower Saxony, he would 'close down the shop'. After 1985 Saarland, ruled by Oskar Lafontaine, stopped payments to the Central Documentation Office. Under Klaus von Dohnanyi, Hamburg did the same thing in 1987.

On 9 September 1986 Egon Bahr, speaking for Brandt, personally told Honecker that the Social Democrats would 'fully' respect GDR citizenship if they returned to power. There was a condition, however: the GDR was to stop the flow of asylum seekers from the Schönefeld airport in East Berlin to West Berlin and make this concession seem like the result of efforts by Johannes Rau, the SPD candidate for the chancellorship. Honecker thus began to work for the SPD election campaign. On 18 September Rau was able to announce in Düsseldorf that he had 'received the agreement of the GDR leadership that only such persons will be allowed to make the transit who also have a visa for another state.' The West Berlin 'loophole' was now closed. But the Social Democratic victory in the January 1987 elections was not yet won.

On 23 October 1987, a few weeks after Honecker's visit in West Germany, three Social Democratic heads of government met with the SED leader during the ceremonies commemorating the 750th anniversary of the city of Berlin: Oskar Lafontaine, prime minister of Saarland; Klaus von Dohnanyi, First Mayor of the Free and Hanse City of Hamburg; and Klaus Wedemeier, senate president and mayor of the Free Hanse City of Bremen. Dohnanyi turned Honecker's attention to the next Bundestag election, scheduled to take place at the end of 1990. In the interests of peace and social stability, he said, the SPD had to return to the government. Taking up Gorbachev's idea of a 'common European house', Dohnanyi spoke of the task of 'drawing the outlines of a common European house' and showing 'a greater imagination in Germany and foreign policy'.

Lafontaine was more concrete. According to the East German notes of the conversation, the SPD deputy head said that it would be good

if in the near future we could work out common ideas about what agreements an SPD-led government should strive for with the GDR. In view of the fundamental interests of the GDR, along with an absolute recognition of the existence of the two states, I consider it necessary to find out what steps are possible in this regard. It is now the general consensus in the FRG that the existence of the two states is a reality that nobody can get around. Equally desirable, however, are fundamental improvements above all for the people. Therefore, he would like to request that in the year 1988 a consultation take place about what the GDR leadership considers possible and what it considers not possible.

Honecker agreed and mentioned that Hermann Axen, responsible for international relations in the politburo, had been given the job of coming up with proposals. Later in the conversation Lafontaine summarized the expectations of the Social Democrats in explaining 'that we have to link stabilization on the one hand with a maximum amount of liberalization in the relations between the two German states' on the other hand. Concluding the talk, Honecker said that

things can only move forward if progress is made in the core question, the one that concerns all humanity: the prevention of a nuclear catastrophe. For that to happen, it is indispensable that the workers' movement come together. The old mistakes must not be repeated and lessons must be learned of history. For this reason we continue to be interested in a fruitful cooperation with the SPD.

These final words sounded like an echo of what Willy Brandt had said to Honecker about the relationship between Social Democrats and Communists on 8 September in Bonn. Once *glasnost* and *perestroika* began, the honorary head of the SPD seemed to believe that it would one day be possible to reunite the workers' movement. Beginning in the mid-1970s, several western European communist parties, led by the Italians and the Spanish, had renounced Leninism and taken up the cause of civil rights, liberty, and democracy, thus putting themselves on a course towards rapprochement with social democracy. Gorbachev's efforts were also possibly leading in this same 'Eurocommunist' direction. Brandt apparently thought that something similar was possible in Germany, and there is evidence to suggest that he wanted to use Social Democratic self-criticism to move this process forward.

On 11 September 1988, in a talk entitled 'Landmarks in German History' for the 'Berlin Lessons' lecture series, Brandt expressed his belief that the 'landmark of January 1933', Hitler's rise to power, could not be understood unless one grasped what had taken place in Germany at the end of 1918 and beginning of 1919. Brandt called the 'Bolshevist threat' a 'myth' and spoke of the 'Bolshevist bogeyman'. He criticized the Social Democratic leaders for believing

that they had to choose between turmoil and order, and then the choice was not difficult . . . President Friedrich Ebert, who was commendable in other ways and certainly worthy of all honours, allowed himself to be convinced that the young republic would not survive unless it had the support of the monarchist right.

Ebert, Brandt said, had no interest in depriving the old ruling elite, the counter-revolutionary officer corps, of power. The 'reactionary forces' were 'not seriously shaken up, much less broken up'. Moving forward to the end of the Weimar Republic, Brandt claimed that even in the summer of 1932, all had not been lost. 'Nonetheless, for me there is not the slightest doubt that the weaknesses and missed chances of 1918–19 were one of the causes of 1933.'

Such views were in keeping with a widespread, generally leftist interpretation of the history of the Weimar Republic. The honorary head of the SPD overestimated the room for manoeuvre that the Majority Social Democrats possessed in late 1918/early 1919, and he underestimated the risk of a civil war. Brandt, who was well into his seventies by this time, seemed to be returning to his own youth, during which he had been active in the Socialist Workers' Party, a leftist splinter group that dreamed of the reunification of the Marxist proletariat. Six decades later, the divide between Social Democrats and Communists was still unbridgeable. The SED had no intention of becoming a 'Eurocommunist' party or even of taking the path Gorbachev represented. Brandt was not alone; many leading Social Democrats were in danger throughout the 1980s of confusing their political wishes with reality.[22]

THE EXPANSION OF THE EC AND THE DISSOLUTION OF THE 'EASTERN BLOC'

The reality of the 1980s included great advances in the process of west European integration. Greece became the tenth member of the European Community in 1981. Spain and Portugal joined in 1986. In February 1984 the European Parliament passed by a large majority the draft of a treaty to found the 'European Union', which was to form a much closer union than the EC. At the end of June 1984 the European Council, meeting in Fontainebleau, passed a measure reducing inspections at the borders. The Single European Act, passed by the European Council in December 1985 in Luxembourg, went into effect on 1 July 1987. According to this act, the guidelines that the Council would follow in harmonizing national legislation would be established mainly by majority voting until the completion of the single European market on 31 December 1992. The European Parliament gained new powers. It now had an advisory role in decisions of the Council (which retained the final say), and it had a voice in accepting new members and concluding future treaties of association. 'European Political Cooperation', officially begun in October 1970, was to be expanded into a common European foreign policy. EC law was extended to research, technology, and environmental protection.

At their fiftieth summit in Karlsruhe in November 1987, West Germany and France, the FRG's most important European ally, agreed to establish a closer security partnership, work more closely together on arms policy and arms control, and form a German–French brigade, a large unit composed of troops from both armies. Two new bilateral bodies were created in January 1988: a Defence and Security Council and a Finance and Economic Council. One month later the European Council approved a 'package', presented by French Socialist Jacques Delors and supported by Paris and Bonn, containing reform proposals in structural, finance, and agrarian policy. The most significant component concerned the reform of EC finance. From now on, a percentage of each member state's gross domestic product, recalculated every year, would be added as a fourth source of EC revenue, along with agricultural taxes, customs duties, and value-added tax revenues.

At the end of June 1989 in Madrid the European Council, despite continuing resistance from the British, took an important step towards economic and monetary union. The first stage, the integration of all the currencies of the member states into the European Monetary System, was set to begin on 1 July 1990. No schedule was established for the next two stages, the founding of a European central bank and the creation of a single currency. They were to be preceded by an intergovernmental conference, but the date for this was open, too. Mitterrand wanted it to be held in the second half of 1990, Kohl only after the Bundestag elections in December of that year. The German chancellor was also much more interested than the French president in having the European political union keep pace with the monetary union.

The relationship between Paris and Bonn was just as close under Mitterrand and Kohl as it had been under Giscard d'Estaing and Schmidt. Difference in party affiliations did not prevent the two countries' leaders from forming personal friendships. Relations between West Germany and Britain were a great deal more complicated, despite the fact that both countries were currently ruled by conservatives.

Apart from their disagreement over the speed of European integration, London and Bonn had very different ideas about NATO security policy. Margaret Thatcher, prime minister of the United Kingdom from 1979 to 1990, strongly supported the modernization of short-range missiles, in which area the Soviets possessed a massive superiority. Genscher did not want to risk damaging the détente, recently revived by the agreement over medium-range missiles, with a new rearmament. He called for disarmament talks *before* a possible 'modernization' of the obsolete American Lance missiles.

The question of short-range missiles had long divided the coalition in Bonn. Influential voices in the CDU/CSU warned about the 'denuclearization' of western Europe as a consequence of the new missile agreement. This group included Franz Josef Strauss; Manfred Wörner, defence minister between 1982 and 1988 and German NATO secretary general since 1988; and Rupert Scholz, Wörner's successor in the defence ministry. Kohl himself, after a long hesitation, adopted Genscher's position in February 1989 so as not to damage the coalition. For her part, Margaret Thatcher enjoyed the full support first of Ronald Reagan, then of the next American administration after January 1989. The Republican George Bush, secretary of state James A. Baker, and secretary of defence Richard B. Cheney wanted to commit NATO to modernization immediately. Once again, the German foreign minister was seen in Washington as standing for a soft policy towards Moscow ('Genscherism'), one that put the interests of the west at risk.

Genscher found support in Oslo, Copenhagen, Luxembourg, Brussels, Rome, Madrid, Athens, and Paris. The French backing had only symbolic meaning, since France was not a part of the NATO military structure. Genscher's staunchest ally was the Norwegian foreign minister Thorvald Stoltenberg, a Social Democrat, whom Genscher described in his memoirs as 'a personified Harmel report'. (He was referring to the December 1967 document named after the Belgian foreign minister Peter Harmel in which NATO declared defence and détente as equally important goals.)

On 29–30 May 1989, forty years after the founding of the alliance, NATO held an anniversary summit in Brussels. It was here that the decision had to be made. The partners finally agreed to a solution that seemed to represent a compromise between the Anglo-American 'hawks' and the continental 'doves':

at the suggestion of Secretary of State Baker, NATO would adopt a policy of negotiating over short-range missiles with the aim of a 'partial reduction'. The introduction and deployment of a system to replace the Lance missiles would be decided in 1992 in the light of developments in the overall security situation. This new policy was not the double zero solution Genscher had wanted to preserve as an option, but it also did not mean immediate modernization.

Genscher was satisfied. 'The obligation to modernize without simultaneously conducting negotiations has turned into an obligation to negotiate without simultaneous modernization,' he stated after the summit. The Bonn government also had cause to be pleased that NATO wished to work towards 'a new political order of peace in Europe' from the Atlantic to the Urals. The positive assessment of the 'important changes' under way in the USSR and the progress towards democracy being made 'in some countries of Eastern Europe' was also fully in keeping with the thinking in Bonn.

Mikhail Gorbachev's USSR, NATO's main addressee, had reached agreements with the west on more than just medium-range missiles. A Conference on 'Confidence- and Security-building Measures and Disarmament in Europe' was successfully concluded in September 1986 in Stockholm. (It had been planned in 1983 in Madrid at a review conference of the CSCE in 1980, the first round in the Helsinki process after the initial meeting in 1975.) The outcome in Stockholm was a major breakthrough in the areas of announcement and observation of military manoeuvres, including so-called 'surprise inspections'.

The Mutual and Balanced Force Reduction talks in Vienna, in contrast, which dealt with conventional forces and armaments, had got virtually nowhere since they had begun in October 1979. They were concluded on 2 February 1989 with no result once it became clear that another set of talks, also in Vienna, would take up the same task in March: the Negotiations on Conventional Armed Forces in Europe (CFE). In November 1990, under radically altered international conditions, these negotiations led to an agreement to create a balance of power at a reduced level. One year later, in July 1991, the START talks, after nine years, led to the START I Treaty, which obligated both sides to reduce their strategic weapons potential by a third.

When he opposed the immediate modernization of the short-range missiles, Genscher had his eye on the recent dramatic changes in eastern central Europe—changes he wanted to promote and not endanger. In Poland the 'state of war' had been 'suspended' at the end of 1982 and then lifted in July 1983. A comprehensive political amnesty followed in September 1986. A wave of strikes swept over the country in the spring of the following year, concentrated mainly in the areas where Solidarity (which was still outlawed) had been strong in 1980–1. On 31 August 1988, after further strikes throughout that spring and summer (including at the Lenin shipyards once again), the interior minister, General Czeslaw Kiszczak, met with Lech Walesa, the legendary union leader of 1980–1. At this meeting, for which the Catholic Church acted as middleman, 'round table' talks between the government and the opposition were discussed for the first time. Kiszczak was responding here to the idea of a national dialogue first launched by intellectuals at the beginning of the year (the historian Jerzy Holzer, one of the Solidarity circle, in an open letter to Jaruzelski and Walesa, then Bronislaw Geremek in a newspaper interview). On 17 and 18 January 1989 the central committee of the Polish United Workers party let it be known indirectly that it would support the withdrawal of the ban on Solidarity. The Round Table began its discussions on 6 February. Among the leaders of the opposition were the chief thinkers behind Solidarity, among them Mazowiecki and Geremek. Their immediate aim was to work out a 'historic compromise' to lead Poland out of the crisis and onto the path of democracy.

If it was massive pressure from 'below' that catalysed a profound transformation in Poland, in Hungary the changes had all the features of a 'revolution from above'. János Kádár, the long-time Communist party leader, was removed from office in May 1988. His successor Károly Grósz, hitherto prime minister, was a reformer, as was Miklós Németh, Grósz's successor as head of government. In April 1989 the whole politburo resigned. The new elections strengthened the reformist forces around Németh and Imre Pozsgay. In its economic and political liberalization (which a loan from Bonn in October 1987 did more to slow down than accelerate) Hungary was taking advantage of the greater freedom that Gorbachev had given the states of the Warsaw Pact. The 1968 Brezhnev doctrine, which restricted the national sovereignty of the socialist states, had been de facto abolished by Gorbachev in November 1986, if not yet formally renounced. From this point forward, members of the 'socialist state community' could pursue their own views of socialism without having to fear an intervention by their 'brother states'.

While Poland and Hungary saw *glasnost* and *perestroika* as a historic opportunity to free themselves from domination by Moscow, two other central European communist countries felt increasingly threatened by Gorbachev's 'new thinking'. The orthodox leaders of Czechoslovakia continued to be haunted by the trauma of 1968. They also feared the consequences of liberalization for the cohesion of their binational state. The GDR was even more ideologically-oriented than the CSSR. Since there was no true East German nationality, Marxism-Leninism played a greater role as a discourse of identity than it did in any other member of the Warsaw Pact.

Neither in the CSSR nor in the GDR was there a mass opposition like the Catholic-oriented Solidarity movement in Poland. Another difference was the lack of 'Eurocommunists' in the parties in Prague and East Berlin. The Communist party of Czechoslovakia simply had to live with the fact that, for reasons of foreign policy, it could not totally crush the intellectual civil rights movement that had formed in October 1977 under the name of 'Charter 77'. The SED had to deal with diffuse expressions of opposition, mostly from peace and environmental organizations that enjoyed a measure of protection through the

Evangelical church. In retrospect, however, we cannot say that the intellectuals or students as a whole opposed the state. With the exception of small fragments grouped around the houses of Evangelical pastors, the old educated bourgeoisie had all migrated or been deported to the west. Independent spirits had generally found the natural sciences and technological fields to be the most congenial professions. The 'state intelligentsia', on the other hand, consisted mostly of social climbers who owed—or thought they owed—their better education to the 'workers' and peasants' state'. In Poland, a 'civil society' had developed, or revived, under the dictatorship. Nothing similar took place in East Germany. The staunch opponents of the regime were a small minority, and they had much less support in the universities and colleges than their counterparts in the other communist countries.

The SED's response to opposition was repression, a fact Gorbachev's new policies did nothing to change. In June 1987 the police and Stasi took massive action against a group of young people gathered at the Brandenburg Gate to listen to a pop concert on the other side of the wall; some of them had been calling out: 'The wall must come down!' In mid-November 1987 the dissident 'environmental library', established in the Church of Zion in the Mitte district of Berlin in the autumn of the previous year, was searched by the state prosecutor and the Stasi. The strike was directed mainly against the journal *Grenzfall*, the voice of the 'Initiative for Peace and Human Rights' (*Initiative Frieden und Menschenrechte*), also founded in 1986. The arrest of several of the founding members led to protest campaigns in many East German cities. Along with the picketers at the Church of Zion, these demonstrations drew so much international attention that the regime gave in, releasing all imprisoned library workers by 29 November. But it continued criminal investigations.

On 17 January 1988, during the traditional Liebknecht–Luxemburg demonstration in East Berlin, members of independent peace and civil rights organizations carried signs with Rosa Luxemburg's most famous words: 'Freedom is always the freedom of those who think differently.' Many were arrested. A new wave of detentions and deportations followed. Those affected included the theatre director Freya Klier and the political songwriter Stephan Krawczyk, who declared upon their arrival in West Germany on 2 February that they had not left the GDR willingly. On 18 November 1988 the Soviet journal *Sputnik* was banned from circulation in East Germany. Its October issue had mentioned the secret addendum to the 1939 Hitler–Stalin pact settling two signatories' spheres of interest; the text had been published for the first time in the Soviet Union in August 1988.

The banning of *Sputnik* was the GDR's most decisive move against *glasnost* to date. The justification was that anyone denigrating the heroic struggle of the anti-fascists against the Nazis and disparaging socialism had no place 'among us'. This explanation, as well as the measure itself, also set many long-time members of the SED against the party leadership. Employees in the ministry for state security observed that those who supported the journal's prohibition were in the minority. 'The main argument of those persons expressing disbelief and rejection is that this measure takes away the ability of the GDR population to form its own political opinion.' But there was method to the ban. It was fully in keeping with the policy that the chief party ideologist Kurt Hager had explained in an interview with the Hamburg magazine *Stern* at the beginning of April 1987. Asked about the GDR's attitude toward *perestroika*, Hager replied: 'Would you, by the way, if your neighbour puts up new wallpaper, also feel obligated to put up new wallpaper?'

The anti-reform attitude of the SED and its continuing violation of human rights had virtually no effect on German–German relations at first. Chancellor Kohl rarely addressed such things publicly and then only with great reservation. Human rights concerns did not figure prominently in his correspondence with Honecker. He brought them up in a general way in his talks with Gorbachev in Moscow at the end of October 1988, during his official visit to the Soviet Union. He also talked about the right of the Germans to self-determination. But the human rights violations in the GDR do not seem to have been discussed. Dorothee Wilms (CDU), however, minister for German–German relations since March 1987, did protest against the attack on the 'environmental library' and the persecution of dissidents during and after the Luxemburg–Liebknecht demonstration.

The Social Democrats reacted in various ways. Willy Brandt avoided expressing any kind of public solidarity with activists while on visits to communist countries, preferring to bring up particular cases of repression in private conversation with the leadership. While visiting Poland in December 1985 for the fifteenth anniversary of the Warsaw Treaty, for example, he met with Jaruzelski; contrary to the expectations of the opposition, however, he avoided Lech Walesa, leader of the banned Solidarity movement, despite the fact that Walesa was a fellow recipient of the Nobel Peace prize (in the year 1983). Most of the other SPD leaders acted similarly. Their interlocutors in communist countries were the party and state leaders, and no one else. The GDR was no exception. The SPD continued to pursue its 'parallel foreign policy' just as if disagreement over human rights did not exist. On 7 July 1988 Hermann Axen and Egon Bahr presented a proposal, approved by the executives of both parties, for a 'zone of confidence and security in central Europe'.

Some Social Democrats behaved more sensibly than others. Active Protestants like Johannes Rau, Jürgen Schmude, and Erhard Eppler—all three originally from Gustav Heinemann's All-German People's party—visited regional church congresses in the GDR and met with civil rights and peace activists there. In late 1987 Gert Weisskirchen, an SPD Bundestag delegate, established contact with the dissident pastor Rainer Eppelmann and became so active on behalf of the East German civil rights movement that he was refused entry into the country several times. Hans-Jochen Vogel and Erhard Eppler lodged strongly worded protests against the arrests and deportations in January 1988, as did the conference of Social Democratic fraction leaders. In general, however, these voices did little to combat the impression among activists in the GDR and other communist countries that the SPD looked only for changes from 'above' and would, if necessary, subordinate change to security.[23]

NEW REFLECTIONS ON THE GERMAN QUESTION IN WEST GERMANY

One of the effects of Gorbachev's 'new thinking' was to produce new debate over the German question in West Germany. After about the beginning of 1988, those who insisted on the priority of civil liberty over national unity grew in number. This was also the case within the CDU. On 25 January, for example, Dorothee Wilms declared in a speech in Paris that the 'national state for its own sake' was not the goal of the Basic Law, nor was it

in keeping with our political consciousness...It is not a question of seeking a past-oriented solution to the German question, but a forward-looking, liberal answer. It is a question of finding an answer in harmony with the experiences and lessons of history, in harmony with the will and the values of Europe...This excludes a unilateral solution to the German question or one that goes against the will of our neighbours...Since in our view the national question is primarily one of self-determination, we consider the territorial issue to be secondary...The partition of Europe must be overcome if the German partition is to be brought to an end...We know that the end of the German partition is not to be looked for in the near future, for the partition of Europe continues.

One of Wilms's allies was her cabinet colleague Heiner Geissler. The CDU general secretary was currently working together with a commission on a foreign and Germany policy motion for the June 1988 Wiesbaden party congress. Like Kohl in his speeches, Geissler avoided the word 'reunification', and the chancellor initially gave his draft the green light. It ran as follows:

The unity of the German nation continues, despite the fact that today the German people must live against their will in political separation. The Germans are not prepared to accept this as a permanent state of affairs. Consequently, the Germany policy of the CDU continues to be the preservation of national unity. The CDU holds firmly to the goal of creating a stable order of peace in Europe, one in which the German people, freely exercising their right to self-determination, achieve the unity of Germany in freedom. In its pursuit of this goal the CDU observes the following goals: liberty is the prerequisite of unity, not its price; unity can only be achieved by non-violent means; the Germans can only reach their goal of unity in agreement with their neighbours in the west and east.

The work of Geissler and the other members of the commission (the ministers Schäuble and Wilms, the delegates Volker Rühe and Karl Lamers, the political scientists Hans-Peter Schwarz and Werner Weidenfeld, and Horst Teltschik, a department director in the chancellery) was fully in keeping with Kohl's policy. Several politicians on the party right, however, led by Manfred Abelein and Jürgen Todenhöfer, thought of Geissler's and Wilms's qualification of the national state as a sacrilege. Supported by the *Frankfurter Allgemeine Zeitung* and former president Karl Carstens, they managed to convince the chancellor to distance himself from the proposal. The text ultimately adopted by the Wiesbaden party congress, the 'Christian-Democratic Perspectives on Germany, Foreign, Security, European, and Development Policy', contained not only the term 'reunification', but also a pertinent quote from Konrad Adenauer: 'The reunification of Germany in freedom was and is our most urgent political goal.' In actual practice, of course, this had not been Kohl's policy, nor could it have been.

The reappearance of the term 'reunification' provoked sharp criticism from a number of Social Democrats. Several years before, in an address to the Munich Kammerspiele Theatre on 18 November 1984, Willy Brandt had observed that 'Our Sunday rhetoricians often nurse—or are once again nursing—the vital lie of the 1950s. The other six days of the week are dedicated to the western interests of the Federal Republic.' (The text had actually been drafted by Egon Bahr.) On two occasions in early autumn 1988—the first in his 'Berlin lessons' speech on 11 September, then in an address to the Friedrich Ebert Foundation in Bonn three days later—Brandt returned to the idea of the 'vital lie' (*Lebenslüge*), which his political opponents generally reinterpreted as his alleged rejection of the idea of national unity. 'Promoted by the Cold War and its consequences, the hope for *re*-unification became the vital lie of the second German republic' (14 September).

It was primarily the first part of the term 'reunification' to which Brandt took exception. 'As if history and the reality of Europe were keeping a hookup to the Bismarck Reich ready for us,' he remarked in both speeches. 'Or as if the whole problem could be reduced to how the GDR could be and will be annexed to the Federal Republic of Germany.'

At his first meeting with Honecker on 19 September 1985, the East German minutes record that Brandt agreed with his interlocutor's statement that 'the German Reich of Bismarck has gone down in the flames of the Second World War' and that 'daydreams about a restoration of the 1937 borders are dangerous.'

What E. Honecker has said about the German Reich does not provoke his disagreement, W. Brandt said. As he says at home: the re- in 'reunification' will lead nowhere. Nobody knows what the future will bring. If Europe grows closer together in the next century, then there may be opportunity for the question of whether the two German states can enter into a closer relationship.

The term 'vital lie' was first used by the Norwegian dramatist Henrik Ibsen. Among the first to apply it to the idea of German reunification or to the 'provisorium' orthodoxy of the West German state were Fritz René Allemann in 1956 and Burghard Freudenfeld in 1967. Golo Mann used it in 1972 in an essay on the Basic Treaty. He was followed twelve years later by Egon Bahr, who worked it into Brandt's Munich speech in November 1984. Freudenfeld, Mann, Bahr, Brandt: all of these men hoped that the abandonment of German 'vital lies' would have a liberating effect. This was something much different from what Ibsen had meant when he put the term into the mouth of Dr Rilling in his 1885 play *The Wild Duck*: 'When you take away the average man's vital lies, you take away his happiness.' In the West German 1980s, of course, very few 'average' citizens were still staking their happiness on the 'vital lies' of the 1950s.

In a 1988 book with the vaguely Kantian title *Zum europäischen Frieden* (and with the subtitle *Eine Antwort auf Gorbachev*),* Egon Bahr once again turned to the German question. Conventional stability and structural incapacity for aggression were the prerequisites for a dissolution of NATO and the Warsaw Pact and their replacement by a pan-European security system. The new European peace would also 'include the right of the two German states to give up the border between them if they so desire'. Once peace treaties were concluded with the Federal Republic and the GDR—and it could now only be a question of two treaties, Bahr thought—it would then be up to the two German states

to exercise their right to self-determination as they see fit and to the extent they are able, certainly not without consideration for their neighbours, much less their friends . . . Ultimately, peace in Europe depends on the two superpowers withdrawing from the zone that today forms their front against each other. If Europe's security can sustain itself, then both the American and the Soviet troops have fulfilled their tasks of protecting the west from the east and the east from the west.

If the polemically-intended term 'equidistance' was ever justified, then it certainly applied to Bahr's ideas of a European order in the interest of Germany. All the agreements he had worked out with communist parties of the Warsaw Pact throughout the 1980s, especially with the SED, can be seen as fragments of a single grand vision. The architect of the Social Democratic *Ostpolitik* wanted to argue *both* superpowers out of central Europe. For him they were both equally dangerous, and 'the weapons themselves' had become a greater threat than either side's enemy. Bahr did not have the slightest doubt about the final goal, German national unity. He saw the political consolidation of the German partition only as the means to an end—overcoming the partition. With regard to the feasibility of this goal, Willy Brandt was more sceptical than his friend and adviser. Both men opposed a rhetoric of reunification that had no counterpart in practical politics, and both did so for nationalist reasons.

On 1 December 1988 the chancellor delivered his 'report on the state of the divided German nation' to the Bundestag. Kohl spoke again about the 'increased

---

* Bahr, *On European Peace: A Response to Gorbachev*.

consciousness of the unity of the nation', about the 'feeling that we belong together as a nation', and about the 'solidarity of the nation'. He did not use the word 'reunification'. He also emphasized that there was no reason to think that that the solution to the German question was any closer. During the ensuing debate, open disagreement over the goal of political unity was expressed for the first time in West German history. Hans-Jochen Vogel, head of the Social Democratic party and fraction, praised the general secretary of the CDU, Heiner Geissler, for opposing the claim by the Union fraction leader, Alfred Dregger, that 'there must and will be a reconnection to the Bismarck empire and that the whole problem can be reduced to the question of how the annexation of the GDR by the FRG can be brought about and will be brought about.'

Nobody knew, Vogel continued, what answer history had in store for the German question.

The preamble to the Basic Law...certainly also allows for an answer within the framework of a European peace order, an order that makes the borders more porous, overcomes simplistic notions of 'the enemy', strengthens individual and social human rights, and allows Germans, regardless of how they are organized politically, to continue to see themselves as members of one and the same community of history, culture, language, and feeling. That is, as members of one nation—these being the constitutive elements of nationhood—within which different societal systems compete with each other in a peaceful manner.

Vogel was basically arguing for the de-politization of the concept of 'unity'. He could have quoted to this end statements made many years in the past by Konrad Adenauer and Franz Josef Strauss (who had died two months before, on 2 October 1988). Unlike these two Union politicians, however, Vogel did not confront the east with western standards of freedom and democracy. A certain degree of liberalization within the 'socialist' GDR would suffice. The idea of strengthening 'individual and social human rights' was congenial to the GDR to the extent that it primarily emphasized the second of the two and saw itself as far superior to the 'capitalist' states in this regard. Vogel's words could only be understood as an appeal to *mutual* rapprochement between the two systems. As such, it was in line with the SPD/SED *Streitkultur* paper, which he quoted. Vogel's reading of the preamble to the Basic Law was a near-total reinterpretation, a reduction to the 'core of what the Basic Law calls on us to preserve'—or what Vogel took to be the 'core', to be more precise.

Another Social Democratic speaker went even further in the revision of what had been, up to that point, the fundamental consensus on Germany policy, constantly reiterated throughout West German history. Gerhard Heimann, a delegate from Berlin, stated his belief 'that German history has withheld from the Germans the normality of other nations, a normality that means that other nations, especially France, are able to look back on a happy union of state, nation, and democracy.' The movement of 1848, Heimann said, had been unable to fulfil the double task of unity and liberty. While Germany had attained the union of the state and nation under Bismarck, the liberty and democracy it had gained were deficient. Moreover, the Bismarck empire had only lasted seventy-four years. It was also no help to look back on an even more remote part of German history, the Holy Roman Empire, as Alfred Dregger, the fraction leader of the Union, had recently done in a speech in Nuremberg. For the Holy Roman Empire had never been a state in the modern sense. 'We Germans have had to learn, again and again, to live in different configurations of more than one state . . . But why do we always have to place the question of the unity of state and nation, which has never succeeded in German history, in the centre of our discussions?'

While Heimann did wish to preserve the concept of nation, he wanted the plurality of German states to be seen as a 'concrete opportunity'.

The essence of the partition is not the national separation of one state from another. Rather, the partition has been forced upon us as a consequence of the east–west conflict. It is also a consequence of our own doing, of course, since we are the ones who began the Second World War. Whoever wants to overcome the partition must overcome the antagonism of two systems and two alliances. This is only possible from both sides . . . If the two German states cooperate towards this end, then it is not only a disadvantage that these two German states exist; it can turn into an advantage, since a part of the cause can be overcome.

The most radical position in the debate was that of a Green delegate, Helmut Lippelt. Unlike Vogel and Heimann, Lippelt wanted to do away with the concept of a single German nation.

Today . . . we are debating over the state of the nation. Which nation? The political nation of the FRG? The political nation of the GDR? The cultural nation of Germany—since occasionally the distinction is made between a political and a cultural nation? Or the historical nation that came to an end in 1945? Nations are not natural facts. They are not defined in terms of a common language, as are peoples. They are defined in terms of a common history. They arise in a complex historical process, and they can also be forfeited in a historical process. So what counts? Our common history ended in twelve years of fascism, in the destruction of Europe, especially in the destruction of the mixed ethnic coexistence that was once eastern Europe. Or is it the forty years of parallel history that count—here as the Federal Republic, over there as the GDR? Consequently, talking about the state of the nation also means talking about a historical fiction.

Lippelt did not leave his parliamentary colleagues in suspense concerning the results of his meditations. To leave the 'reunification option' open meant, for him, a choice between only two possible scenarios: stabilizing the anti-reform forces in the GDR or waiting for the East German state to collapse. In practical terms, he said, both the Kohl government and its predecessor, the Schmidt government, had opted for the former course. Those who, like Kohl and the delegates Lamers and Rühe, constantly stressed the connection between the creation of a European peace order and the reunification of Germany were obligated to clarify how they would achieve all this without ulterior motives and without banking on the political collapse of eastern Europe.

Is it not more honest to accept that these forty years of the Federal Republic and GDR, fifty since the outbreak of the war, since the attack on Poland, are of a piece with the forfeiture of our national unity? Then, and only then, will we be free to pursue a strong policy of European peace. Within the framework of this policy we will demand and must demand from the GDR, as well as from the other states of eastern Europe, that they release their societies from the grip of the party and the state. We will be free to ask that the GDR leadership cease its repression only when our intentions are completely free of all ulterior speculation on the destabilization of the GDR.

In shying away from this logic, the Green delegate said, the West German government was stabilizing the anti-reform forces in the GDR in their current ascendancy. His conclusion: 'We Greens call for the reunification policy to be ended, since doing so will give us the ability to pursue a necessary European policy, one that goes beyond the abbreviation of the idea of "Europe" to "Western Europe".' The chancellor, Lippelt went on, had repeated the old formula in his speech that day: 'Unity, but not at the price of liberty.' Should the question 'not be exactly the opposite at this point: can liberty and open systems not be achieved at the price of unity? For if you speak openly about Europe, about a peace order for a free Europe, then the Europe you see in your mind's eye must necessarily be a Europe of regions, a Europe of open borders and a Europe of open systems.' Turning to the chancellor, Lippelt concluded: 'You, too, will have to think about what it will really cost to give up this whole illusionary reunification policy, and what it can bring in terms of political freedom of action.'

Never before had a Bundestag delegate so clearly expressed the dilemma of the West German government's attitude toward the GDR. Despite its avowedly 'national' position, the Christian–liberal coalition was pursuing a Germany policy that differed very little in practice from that of its social–liberal predecessors. This policy stabilized the GDR, and not least because the two states were now so closely interconnected that a destabilization of the GDR would have immediately harmed West Germany. Bonn's policy made it easier for the SED to ignore the calls to reform. Paradoxically, the same was true of the West German 'reunification rhetoric', which hampered rather than helped the implementation of *glasnost* and *perestroika* in East Germany. For as long as the SED was able to claim that the larger German state sought to abolish its smaller rival, the Soviet Union would have to look upon the GDR as an imperilled outpost on the frontiers of its empire. As a result, Honecker did not have to deal with massive reform pressure from Gorbachev.

To this extent Lippelt's analysis was irrefutable. But there was no reason to think that abandoning the idea of a single German nation would bring about a change for the better. The responsibility the free Germans bore for their unfree brothers and sisters was a product of their common history. This history had *not* come to an end with the downfall of the German Reich. It lived on, and it did so primarily *because* the burdens of this history after 1945 had been so inequitably distributed. If feelings of special national solidarity with the Germans in the GDR had been successfully done away with in the FRG, West Germans would no longer have had any particular reason to push for the liberalization and democratization of the GDR. For this reason, the status quo could not be overcome by the general appeal to human rights, at least in the way that Lippelt imagined.

One prominent Social Democrat who did not participate in the debate on 1 December 1988 found another way of showing that when it came to expressing 'anti-nationalism', he was not going to be outdone by the Greens. In his 1988 book *Die Gesellschaft der Zukunft*,* Oskar Lafontaine called for the 'overcoming of the nation state'. 'What sense does it make to strive for national unity in the long view,' the deputy head of the SPD asked, 'when it is already clear that within a short period of time the political idea of the national state is going to be practically annulled by the trans-national nature of the problems?'

In Lafontaine's view, the national state 'has already today outlived the rationale of its conception', and the Germans had a particular reason to act on this insight.

The 'belated' German nation, unlike the French, for example, did not arise from a civil war successfully waged by democracy against monarchy, but out of a war between political alliances. Sedan meant not only the capitulation of the Third [*sic!*] Empire of the French, but also the surrender of the German dream of unified democracy. Bismarck's triumph shored up the Prussian monarchy and placed the German nation at its feet. From that moment on the idea of the German nation had very few positive associations left in Germany.

Nonetheless, the evils of German history could, in retrospect, turn out to have a positive effect on the future, Lafontaine thought.

Precisely because we were not granted, and for the foreseeable future will not be granted, the fulfilment of our unity as a nation state; precisely because we Germans have had the most awful experiences imaginable with a perverted nationalism—for these very reasons, it should be easier for us to give up the national state than for other nations who were able—and still are able—to tie to their national histories the development of a democratic social order. The Germans, on the basis of their recent history, are virtually predestined to be the driving force in the supra-national process of European unification.

There was, of course, little indication that this insight had penetrated the minds of the political adversary to the right of the centre.

Instead, we are seeing a kind of renaissance of the idea of the nation state in the neoconservative camp, a desperate search for the better, more appealing roots of the

* Lafontaine, *The Society of the Future.*

German nation in German history. This is a flight from political reality. We see how difficult it is for the neoconservatives to admit to themselves that the Federal Republic also has its roots in Auschwitz. To forget this, or to repress it, would be as dangerous as it would be amoral. For if our Federal German national identity no longer went back to Auschwitz, but only back to the year 1949, we would lose the consciousness of our responsibility for what took place in the decade before that in the name of the German people.

Quoting Jürgen Habermas, Lafontaine demanded that 'the FRG's western integration, which has come to be generally accepted since the Second World War, no longer be called into question.' As for a reunification of Germany, at the present time there was 'neither any realistic prospect', nor did the reunification even seem 'desirable, in the sense of a restoration of a German national state of whatever kind'. What was important was not the recovery of political unity, but the expansion of the 'scope of human liberty'.

At the present time, in Lafontaine's view, there was still every reason to think of the Federal Republic as a provisional entity, albeit of a different kind than that intended by the fathers and mothers of the Basic Law. 'The future is called Europe,' he wrote, much as Walter Scheel had done in the *Hochland* debate twenty years before.

This is now the only greater unity into which it makes any sense for the Federal Republic to be absorbed. We Germans need Europe, since otherwise our cultural identity threatens to gradually disintegrate . . . To give up the national state means neither to give up the idea of the state nor that of the nation. A trans-nationally unified Europe can only have the political form of a democratic state, under whose roof there would be room for a variety of nations. At that point, the concept of nation would no longer be mainly a criterion of political identity, but one of cultural identity—a European identity, which would arise from the productive cultural tension between nation and region, between standard language and dialect. The nation state has no future.

There was nothing specifically 'leftist' about the argument that the national state had become 'inadequate' and that its political institutions could not 'master global problems'. Nor was it new. Adenauer and the other conservative founding fathers of the European project had already been acting on this insight at a time when the Social Democrats under Kurt Schumacher were still in the grips of nationalist thinking. The western integration of the Federal Republic was a Christian-Democratic idea, and it was pushed through against the resistance of the left. It would probably not have survived the 1980s if Oskar Lafontaine—who had demanded that West Germany leave the military organization of NATO during the missile controversy—had had his way. The Germans had ruined *their* nation state; there was no getting around that. But this did not mean that Germany had a new historical mission to liberate the rest of the Europeans from the fetters of their nation states and from national identities that were not only cultural, but also political in nature.

In Lafontaine's logic, the German crime against humanity represented by 'Auschwitz' seemed almost to take on the features of a *felix culpa*, the 'fortunate sin' that, in the view of the Church Father St Ambrose, was necessary for salvation. *Because* the Germans had perverted nationalist sentiment to such extremes, they were now predestined to be the moral leaders of Europe on the road to a trans-national or post-national future. Predestination through perversion: this dialectical sleight of hand was perhaps a fruit of Lafontaine's Catholic upbringing. It was, in any case, an idea that found a strong echo on the West German left throughout the 1980s. It was no coincidence that Lafontaine, when referring to Auschwitz, did not speak of 'German national identity', but of 'Federal German identity' (*bundesdeutsche Identität*). His book was not only a contribution to the 'politics of history' in a general sense. More specifically, it sought to propagate a new myth of origin for the Federal Republic of Germany.

Lafontaine's ideas and those of Brandt and Bahr were worlds apart. The former chancellor and his long-time adviser had experienced pre-1933 Germany. Brandt was 19 years of age when Hitler came to power, Bahr 9. Brandt, who came from Lübeck, and Bahr, who came from Treffurt in Thuringia, had both spent formative years of their lives in the western sector of post-war Berlin. For them, 'Germany' was the remains of the German Reich; it was never the Federal Republic alone. Lafontaine, born in 1943, was 13 years old when the Saarland joined the FRG. He had a close sentimental connection to the whole Saar region on both sides of the German–French border. The 'German nation' meant little to him. He wanted more 'scope for liberty' for the Germans in the GDR—the same thing he wished for all people who did not enjoy liberty's blessings. There was no indication that the 'German question' ever caused him any disquiet.

Lafontaine represented the world view of a whole generation of West Germans. They thought of themselves as citizens of the FRG, as Europeans, and as citizens of the world, but hardly as members of the German nation. This 'posthumous Adenauer left' saw the partition of Germany as having lifted a historical burden from their shoulders, since it seemed to draw a line under the history of the German national state—a history they believed to have failed in its entirety. At the beginning of the twentieth century, the historian Friedrich Meinecke had described the development of cosmopolitanism into nationalism as a historical step forward. For the 'posthumous Adenauer left', it was the reversal of this process that represented historical progress.

Goethe and Schiller wrote in the *Xenien* in 1796:

> Zur Nation euch zu bilden, ihr hoffet es,
> Deutsche, vergebens;
> Bildet, ihr könnt es, dafür freier zu
> Menschen euch aus!*

---

* To make yourself a nation—for this you hope, | Germans, in vain; | make yourselves instead—you can do it! | into men the more free.

These lines were quoted by Günther Grass in a speech to the press club in Bonn on 29 May 1967. The writer considered them relevant to the current situation, since they seemed to confirm his view of the German nation:

Since we, measured by our natural disposition, cannot form a nation; since we, having learned the lessons of history, and conscious of our cultural diversity, should not form a nation, we must finally realize that federalism is our only chance . . . Concord [*Einigkeit*], European as well as German, does not presuppose unity [*Einheit*]. Germany has only ever been forced into unity, and always to its own detriment. For unity is an idea set against humanity. It restricts liberty. Concord requires the free decision of the many. Germany must finally become the free, cooperative, mutually supportive community of Bavarians and Saxons, Swabians and Thuringians, Westphalians and Mecklenburgers. Germany in the singular is a sum that will never work out again, since, to be exact, Germany is in the communicative plural.

German politicians, historians, writers, and intellectuals were not the only ones who had difficulty with the idea of the 'German nation'. The West German citizenry as a whole oscillated between different views of the term in the 1980s. According to one survey in July 1986, 37% of the West German population identified the FRG with the word 'nation', while 35% applied the term to both the FRG and the GDR. Only about a quarter of those polled had a wider sense of 'the German nation': 12% considered it to include the former eastern territories, and for 11% it embraced all German-speaking territories. When asked by another survey in spring 1987 if the Germans in the FRG and those in the GDR constituted one people or two peoples, 78% of respondents said the former, 21% the latter. One-third affirmed and two-thirds denied that they thought of East Germany as a foreign country. Even after the ratification of the eastern treaties, all surveys showed that large majorities—mostly around 80%—supported the goal of reunification. But in mid-1987, only 9% of those asked stated that they believed they would live to see it; 72% thought they would not. When asked if they believed the reunification would take place during the twentieth century, 8% of the same group considered it possible, and 79% thought it impossible.

Taken together, these data seem to speak against the existence of a specifically West German national consciousness. But there are strong generational differences. In 1987, only 65% of respondents between the ages of 14 and 29 (in contrast to 90% of those older than 60) felt themselves to be members of *one* German people; 34% said there were two German peoples. Between 1976 and 1987, an average of 15% of respondents over 60 thought of the GDR as a foreign country; half of the young people polled felt this way. One interpretation of these figures, published in the *Deutschland Archiv* in October 1989, came to the conclusion that the GDR was perceived by a large number of the younger generation as a foreign state with a different social system, no longer part of Germany. 'This is leading to a dismantling of the consciousness of common nationality and a continual increase in alienation.'[24]

REVOLUTION IN POLAND
AND HUNGARY—STANDSTILL IN THE GDR

The changes that took place in eastern central Europe during the first eight months of 1989 meant nothing less than the end of the post-Second World War international order. On 10 February the Hungarian politburo discussed the introduction of a real multi-party system. The barriers along the borders with Austria began to come down on 2 May. On 13 June the leadership in Budapest, following on the Polish example, took up round-table discussions with the opposition. Three days later the remains of Imre Nagy, the martyr of the 1956 revolution, were reburied, this time in a grave of honour. On 27 June the Hungarian foreign minister, Gyula Horn, and his Austrian colleague ceremonially opened the border between their countries by removing a section of barbed wire fence. There was now no longer an 'Iron Curtain' between Austria and Hungary.

The Round Table in Warsaw, which had begun talks on 6 February (there were three main committees, two subcommittees, and ten working groups), presented their results on 5 April in three protocols, one for political reforms, one for economic and social policy, and one for labour union pluralism. In the first protocol, the government and opposition committed themselves to a comprehensive process of liberalization and democratization. For the time being, the principle of free elections was to be rigorously applied only to one of the two houses, the senate. In the other house, the Sejm, there would be a period of transition: during the tenth parliamentary term, 60% of the seats would belong to the bloc parties, 5% to the Catholic groups close to the regime, and 35% would be determined in free elections. Bills rejected by the senate required a two-thirds majority in the Sejm to be made into law. The second protocol dealt with the shift from the planned to a market economy. The third guaranteed equal rights for both 'old', state labour unions and 'new', independent workers' organizations.

'Solidarity' was officially registered again on 17 April. The first round of 'semi-free' parliamentary elections took place on 4 June, the second round—which required only a simple majority—on 18 June. The newly founded 'Solidarity Citizens' Committee' won all available seats in the Sejm and 99 out of the 100 seats in the senate. Not even the erstwhile extra-parliamentary opposition, which had been planning to play the role of parliamentary opposition during the transition phase, had expected a triumph of this kind.

On 19 July General Wojciech Jaruzelski, prime minister during the years of military law and president of the state council since 1985, was elected president of Poland by the Sejm. He received one more than the necessary absolute majority, a 'victory' he owed solely to the fact that a number of Solidarity delegates deliberately cast invalid votes. As for the position of prime minister, Lech Walesa claimed it for the 'Citizens' Committee' on 7 August. After considerable back and forth, Jaruzelski and the newly elected (2 August) Communist prime minister, Czeslaw Kiszczak, relented. The latter resigned on 19 August, and the Sejm elected the Catholic democrat Tadeusz Mazowiecki, Walesa's long-time adviser, prime minister of the Polish government. He formed a cabinet of national concentration in which the Communists had four ministries, including those of the interior and defence. His predecessor, Kiszczak, returned to his former post as minister of the interior. The 'cohabitation' of a Communist head of state with a non-Communist head of government was part of the 'historic compromise' that was to inaugurate a simultaneously radical and carefully regulated process of transformation. Poland, the first post-communist state in Europe, became the pioneer of a revolution that would embrace large parts of the continent—a new type of revolution, the 'peaceful revolution' of 1989.

The reason the authorities in Poland and Hungary gave into the pressure for change was not only because they could no longer count on military support from Moscow. They also wanted to free their countries from dependence on the Soviet Union, but without falling behind Gorbachev's reforms. They had come to realize that, in the long term, economic liberalization and democracy were the only viable alternative to collapse. These kinds of reform could not be forced through against society as a whole, but only in cooperation with it. Cooperation was possible because both sides were interested in reaching an understanding and because a bridge between the regime and society was already in place: national identity. In both Poland and Hungary, the nation and civil society turned out to be the two sides of the same coin. Whether this example would spread to other countries was an open question.

As for the GDR, there was little indication in the first half of 1989 that the regime had recognized the sign of the times. On 6 February, the day the Round Table convened in Poland, border guards shot and killed Chris Gueffroy, a 22-year-old East German, as he was attempting to escape into West Berlin. The international protests were so massive that the border soldiers were instructed on 12 April to cease using armed force. However, this order was kept secret.

Municipal elections took place in the GDR on 7 May. Activists had called for a boycott and in many places made use of their right to be present when the votes were counted. They were able to demonstrate massive fraud. The number of negative votes was reduced by up to 20% in order to yield the desired result. Officially the unified list of the National Front achieved 98.85% of the votes throughout the country, and 98.78% of eligible citizens had cast votes. The protests, which began on the evening of the elections in Leipzig, were suppressed by the police and security forces. But reports in the western media turned them into a political success for the activists.

The activities of the Volkskammer usually drew little public attention. That was not the case on 8 May 1989. Four days previously, the first round of elections had taken place in Poland, and the Chinese army had silenced the student reform and democracy movement of that country with a massacre on Tiananmen Square in Beijing. The Volkskammer delegates lamented the victims, but called the demonstrations in China 'violent, bloody riots by anti-constitutional elements' and unanimously approved the restoration of order and security 'through the use of armed force'. The message was clear: similar developments in the GDR would be dealt with using the 'Chinese solution'.

Four days later Michael Gorbachev arrived for a visit in West Germany. (He was now—since 1 October 1988—also head of the Supreme Soviet and president of the USSR.) Everywhere he made an appearance, in Bonn, Cologne, and Stuttgart, he was received by cheering crowds. He generated even more enthusiasm than the visit of George Bush two weeks before, during which the American president had pronounced the FRG and the United States 'partners in leadership' in a speech in Mainz. Gorbachev, speaking on 12 June in response to a policy address by Kohl, stated: 'We are drawing the line under the post-war period.' In a joint statement, the two leaders declared their support for human rights and for the right of 'all peoples and nations to freely determine their own destiny and to shape their relations with each other as sovereign states on the basis of international law'. Unrestricted respect for the integrity and security of every state was one of the building blocks of a Europe of peace and cooperation. 'Each has the right to freely choose its own political and social system.'

During the concluding press conference on 15 June, Gorbachev also addressed the issue of the Berlin wall. It had arisen 'in a concrete situation', he said. The GDR was a sovereign state. 'The wall can vanish, too, when the conditions that brought it into existence have also disappeared.' When asked about the partition of Germany, the Soviet leader replied: 'The situation we have today in Europe is a reality.' This reality formed the basis of the Helsinki process and other events. One could hope 'that time itself will determine what is to come'.

Gorbachev's foreign policy adviser, Vadim Sagladin, had gone even further a week before. Reunification was not on the agenda at the present time, he said during an interview with *Bild am Sonntag*. Nonetheless 'the Germans, like all other peoples', had 'the right to national self-determination'. The pan-European process was the important thing at the moment, in order to improve relations among all the European states. 'Then we will see how things develop further in Europe.'

The second day after Gorbachev's return to Moscow, 17 June, was the thirty-sixth anniversary of the 1953 workers' uprising in the GDR. By interparty agreement, the task of addressing the Bundestag on the Day of German Unity now fell to a Social Democrat: Erhard Eppler. The former confederate of Gustav Heinemann asked his audience to understand the position of Germany's European neighbours, who heard primarily the 're-' in 'reunification' and never again wanted to witness the rise of an all-German great power. At the same time, Eppler criticized the delegates of the left who wanted to eliminate the subject of German unity from the political agenda altogether. And yet 'unity' was not to be understood as a final status to be attained at some date, he said, but as 'an event, as a process, as an increasing communality in action, in taking responsibility . . . The more sovereign German politics becomes, the less it needs the sovereign national state in order to represent and consolidate the unity of the Germans.'

The most electrifying part of Eppler's speech—continually interrupted by applause from all party fractions—was his warning to the SED. Many people in East Germany, he said, felt

something akin to a GDR consciousness, a feeling, at times almost defiant in nature, of belonging to this small, poorer German state, which they would like to make into something. If I do not deceive myself, this feeling was stronger two years ago than it is today. But there is probably still a majority in the GDR who aspire not to the end, but rather to the reform of their state. Yet if the leadership of the SED insists on remaining as self-satisfied and blind to reality as we have seen it to be in the last few months, then in two more years it could be that this majority will have turned into a minority.

Eppler did not consider this scenario either desirable or inevitable. But he thought that only a radical change would allow the SED to save its state. 'When the ice of the Cold War melts beneath all our feet, the GDR will only be able to survive in the long term if it fulfils a function that makes sense to its own citizens and appears at least interesting to the rest of the Europeans.' Whatever might be imagined in that regard was irreconcilable with the

monopoly on power and truth by a single party . . . Dialogue is only possible among equals. For this reason, it means a renunciation of all privileged doctrines of the state . . . Anyone capable of carrying on a dialogue with the basic values commission of the SPD as with a coequal . . . is certainly also capable of entering into a similar open, taboo-free, critical dialogue with citizens of his own state.

Concerning the conceivable objection that he was interfering in the internal affairs of the GDR, Eppler replied: 'No, I do not want to do that. But I do want the citizens of the GDR to be able to interfere in the internal affairs of their own state.' The minutes record here 'vigorous applause'.

This applause could not disguise the fact that there were also completely different views on the German question to the right of the political centre. Speaking at a meeting of the Territorial Association of Silesia (*Landsmannschaft Schlesien*) in Hanover on 2 July 1989, Theo Waigel (Franz Josef Strauss's successor as head of the CSU and minister of finance as of 21 April) declared that the 'restoration of the political unity of the German people in free self-determination' remained the political goal. The German territories to the east of the Oder and Neisse rivers were also part of the German question, he said. 'The German Reich did not come to an end with the surrender on 8 May 1945.' Ernst Albrecht (CDU), prime minister of Lower Saxony, made similar remarks. The president of the *Landsmannschaft*, Herbert Hupka (a delegate for the SPD in 1969–72 and for the CDU up to 1987), called for 'liberty and unity for the whole of Germany', which, he said, also included Silesia.

Apart from Hupka, the Union politicians who spoke in Hanover were motivated by purely tactical, domestic concerns. Their speeches, padded with legalist rhetoric, were calculated to attract both expellees and conservative voters in general. What Waigel and others like him said was not a real expression of foreign policy revisionism and German nationalism. But the damage such rhetoric did was real. In Poland, just then beginning to open to the west, alarm was widespread, a fact communicated with great emphasis to Helmut Kohl on 7 July by Bronislaw Geremek, head of the Solidarity Citizens' Committee in the Sejm. In western European countries, the tendency of some Germans to continually point to the borders of 1937 strengthened the already widespread feeling that two German states were better than one. The East Berlin leadership considered speeches like those in Hanover as evidence of the threat of the FRG and the indispensability of the GDR. When the Soviet foreign minister, Eduard Shevardnadze, met with Erich Honecker on 9 June, the latter told his guest 'that the FRG continues to propagate the existence of the "German Reich" within the borders of 1937, which also affects the USSR, the People's Republic of Poland, and the CSSR, and is always trying to hold up the example of the Peoples' Republic of Poland and the Hungarian People's Republic to the GDR.'

The conversation with Shevardnadze was part of Honecker's preparations for a visit to Moscow. What the East German leader heard Gorbachev say in the Soviet capital on 28 June was, in part, similar to Eppler's philippic on 17 June. 'Socialism will never be uniform in Europe, but—as we know today—it will become more democratic, or it will cease to be,' Eppler had told the Bundestag, taking up and modifying a statement by Kurt Schumacher, the first post-war head of the SPD, in an April 1946 speech ('In Germany, democracy will be socialist or it will not be at all.') Gorbachev's words to Honecker were closer in spirit to Eppler than to Schumacher. 'At the present time, the Soviet Union is freeing itself from the old system of command and administration,' he said. 'It is through democracy that the main question of socialist democracy must be solved—overcoming the alienation of the workers from production and political power.'

Honecker made it clear that on this point he was not going to follow the old maxim 'Learning from the Soviet Union means learning victory!' 'Comrade Gorbachev surely knows that in the GDR and in the SED the question of the system of command has not played a decisive role,' Honecker said.

The Party has always had a vital political dialogue with the people. Likewise, the preparations for the twelfth party congress in May 1990 will be a matter for the whole people. The focus will be on the continuing development of socialist society and the unity of economic and social policy, which has proven effective and plays a stimulating role. The principle of the unity of continuity and renewal will be taken further . . . Comrade Gorbachev himself has pointed out that a successful social policy plays an enormously important role in strengthening the image and popularity of the party. In this matter, the SED has always placed the solution of the housing question at centre stage.

Thus Gorbachev failed to win Honecker over to his policy of 'openness' and 'restructuring'. As always, the general secretary of the SED played material well-being and social security off against liberty and democracy. Of course, he was careful not to mention that the 'unity of economic and social policy' had only been possible with the help of the 'capitalist FRG'. Gorbachev will not have been surprised at the course and outcome of the talk. In his memoirs he writes that his cautious attempts to convince Honecker 'of the importance of not delaying the start of reforms in the country and the party produced no practical result. It was like coming up against a wall of misunderstanding, every time.'

In summer 1989 the Kremlin grew worried that the reform blockade in the SED could plunge East Germany into a serious crisis. This time, there would be no more help from the Soviet Union in dealing with uprisings. A meeting between the Warsaw Pact members in Bucharest on 7 and 8 August 1989 concluded with a declaration rejecting interference in the internal affairs of the member states. There was 'no universal model of socialism', the text read. Socialism would develop 'according to the conditions, traditions, and requirements of each country'. Relations among the socialist states were 'to be cultivated on the basis of equality, independence, and the right of each country to work out its own course, strategy, and tactics without interference from outside'. This declaration spelled the official end of the Brezhnev doctrine.

This meant that the GDR was permitted to take a different path than the Soviet Union, Poland, or Hungary. And there was even a certain undeniable logic to the SED's rejection of *glasnost* and *perestroika*. As the publicist Hermann Rudolph noted in mid-July 1989, East Germany found itself in a 'state of double siege': by the 'reformist élan' in the Soviet Union, Poland, and Hungary on the one hand, and by the 'west's power to attract and overwhelm' on the other. To take the Polish or Hungarian path and abandon the anti-FRG policy could, its leaders feared, cost the GDR its right to exist as a state. It was left to Otto Reinhold, director of the East German Academy of Social Sciences and Eppler's interlocutor for the *Streitkultur* paper on August 1987, to justify the East German *Sonderweg* (as Rudolph called it). He did so with considerable force in a 'Radio GDR' address on 19 August 1989:

The heart of the matter is . . . what can be called the socialist identity of the GDR. In this matter there is obviously a fundamental difference between the GDR and the other socialist countries. All of them existed as states with a capitalist or semi-feudal order before the process of socialist transformation. That is, their statehood did not depend first and foremost on their social order. The GDR is different. It is only conceivable as an anti-fascist, as a socialist alternative to the FRG. What right would a capitalist GDR have to exist at the side of a capitalist FRG? None, of course. Only by keeping this fact in mind at all times will we realize the importance of a societal strategy uncompromisingly devoted to the consolidation of the socialist order. There is no room here for any casual playing around with socialism, with socialist state power.[25]

5

Unity in Freedom 1989–1990

FLIGHT AND OPPOSITION: THE PROTEST MOVEMENT IN THE GDR

On 8 August 1989 the FRG's Permanent Mission in East Germany took an unusual measure: it closed its building in the Hannoversche Strasse in East Berlin after more than 100 GDR citizens had taken refuge there, hoping to get out of the country. The West German embassies in Budapest and Prague soon—on 10 and 22 August—had to do the same. Some East Germans managed to escape by other means, crossing the border between Hungary and Austria, from which the fortifications had been removed by 27 June. Those who were caught by Hungarian border patrols were sent back to the GDR.

The number of East Germans seeking to leave their country in the first part of 1989 had grown much faster than the number of travel permits. The causes of this refugee wave were obvious: dissatisfaction with the economic situation, and now bitterness over the lack of the kinds of reform that had been introduced in the Soviet Union, Poland, and Hungary. Many citizens were now much less willing to come to terms with the SED regime. The desire to flee was an expression of protest, and for the moment it was the version of protest that gained the most attention both within the GDR and abroad.

On 31 August, those who had taken refuge in the Hannoversche Strasse were finally told by their government that they could apply for a permit to leave the country upon leaving the building. But what the Budapest leadership decided to do in those days of late summer was truly momentous. Meeting secretly with Helmut Kohl and Hans-Dietrich Genscher at Gymnich castle near Bonn, prime minister Miklós Németh and foreign minister Gyula Horn stated their willingness to open the Hungarian–Austrian border for East Germans by mid-September. In return, West Germany offered Hungary generous economic assistance. With this move, the Hungarian leaders unilaterally terminated their Warsaw Pact obligation to extradite refugees to their 'socialist' country of origin. Hungary's membership in the eastern alliance was mere formality after 25 August 1989; it was in the process of joining the west. What was agreed on in Gymnich took place on 11 September: thousands of East German refugees who had been waiting weeks in reception camps poured over the Hungarian–Austrian border. By the end of the month, some 25,000 had fled through Hungary to the FRG.

Those who had taken refuge in the West German embassy in Prague—almost 6,000 in number by the end—were kept in suspense much longer. Their fate was the subject of informal talks conducted on 27 September between Genscher and his colleagues from Moscow and East Berlin, Eduard Shevardnadze and Oskar Fischer, during a UN meeting in New York. Finally, on 30 September, the GDR's Permanent Representative in West Germany, Horst Neubauer, told the head of the chancellor's office, Rudolf Seiters, that the GDR citizens waiting in Prague could travel through East Germany to the Federal Republic. In order to allay the suspicions of the embassy refugees, Genscher and Seiters flew to the Czechoslovak capital that same day. The whole world watched on television as Genscher, speaking from the balcony of the embassy, told his countrymen the happy news. The first of six trains left Prague on the morning of 1 October. East Berlin had insisted on the longer route through the GDR for reasons of prestige; before they reached West Germany, the passengers received documents terminating their GDR citizenship.

More trains soon followed the same route, transporting thousands more East Germans from Prague through Dresden and Leipzig to Hof. The more than 700 who had taken refuge in the FRG's embassy in Warsaw were also permitted to travel through the GDR to West Germany. The East German leadership had good reason to let its citizens leave. On 4 October began the ceremonies in connection with the fortieth anniversary of the GDR's founding. They were not to be tainted by images of people who had no greater desire than to turn their backs on their country. But scenes like those in Prague would also not be repeated. On 3 October East Germany suspended visa-free travel to Czechoslovakia.

Since this also cut off access to Hungary, it was like building another wall. For many of its citizens the GDR now seemed more than ever like a prison, and the MfS records overwhelmingly negative reactions. In 'the most varied circles', the report on 4 October ran, arguments such as the following were heard: the decision was a 'declaration of bankruptcy by the government'; 'now it is not possible to travel anywhere abroad; we are locked in; this is a "fine gift" to receive on the republic's birthday; now the only option left is to leave the country . . . Older citizens expressed the fear that the new travel restrictions might be the cause of tumults, disturbances, and large-scale acts of resistance.' That same day, 4 October, saw serious clashes in Dresden as the trains from Prague were passing through on their way to Hof. The tracks were blocked and people flooded the station, hoping to get aboard. Rocks were thrown, a police car went up in flames, and both demonstrators and policemen were injured.

Among those who left the GDR at the beginning of October were many who had participated in demonstrations—not yet very large—in Leipzig during the previous weeks, where they had shouted: 'We want out!' As more and more people left, another call resounded even more loudly: 'We are staying here!' (It was heard for the first time on Monday 4 September after the prayer for peace in the Church of St Nicholas in Leipzig.) The crisis that prompted the mass exodus also drove into the streets citizens who wanted not to abandon, but to reform their state. From September onwards, more active forms of protest and opposition became increasingly common, spearheaded by groups of civil rights activists. The Stasi estimated their 'total potential' to be some 2,500 persons, organized into 160 'hostile/negative' groups, of which 150 were based in the church.

One of the oldest of these groups, the 'Peace and Human Rights Initiative' (founded in 1986), deliberately kept its distance from the church. A new group, the 'New Forum' (*Neues Forum*), was founded on 9 September. 'Democracy Now' (*Demokratie Jetzt*) followed on 12 September, and the 'Democratic Awakening—Ecological, Social' (*Demokratischer Aufbruch—ökologisch, sozial*, also DA) on 2 October. On 7 October, the fortieth anniversary of the founding of the GDR, opponents of the regime established the 'Social Democratic Party in the GDR' (*Sozialdemokratische Partei in der DDR* or SDP) at the house of the Evangelical minister in Schwante near Berlin. Though altogether only a small number of East Germans were active in these groups, their courage was infectious.

The New Forum was the most visible group in spring 1989. It united intellectuals, scientists, and artists, including the painter Bärbel Bohley; the physicist Sebastian Pflugbeil; the molecular biologist Jens Reich and his wife Eva Reich, a physician; Robert Havemann's wife Katja Havemann; Hans-Jochen Tschiche, an Evangelical minister; and Rolf Henrich, a lawyer. 'In our country the communication between state and society is obviously dysfunctional,' ran the first sentence of the group's manifesto of 9 September.

The dysfunctional relationship between state and society hampers the creative potential of our society and prevents the solution of pressing local and global concerns . . . At the current stage of societal development, it is important that a larger number of people participate in the process of societal reform, that the various activities of individuals and groups be united into one collective action.

The New Forum saw itself as a 'political platform for the entire GDR', whose goal it was to initiate dialogue between the state authorities and society as a whole. Quoting Article 29 of the GDR constitution, which promised freedom of association, the founders made a formal request for official recognition. The interior ministry rejected the application on 21 September. 'The goals and concerns of the proposed association are not in keeping with the constitution of the German Democratic Republic,' the official statement read, 'and represent a platform hostile to the state.'

Among the founders of Democracy Now were Ulrike Poppe, one of the initiators of the group 'Women for Peace' (*Frauen für den Frieden*) along with Bärbel Bohley; the computer scientist Ludwig Mehlhorn, also involved in

'Action Reconciliation' (*Aktion Sühnezeichen*); the church historian Wolfgang Ullmann; and the film director Konrad Weiss. Three days after the New Forum was launched, Democracy Now came out with their manifesto, 'A Call to Interference in Our Own Affairs' (*Aufruf zur Einmischung in eigener Sache*). The 'era of state socialism is at an end,' it announced. Socialism needed a peaceful, democratic renewal. '[It] must find its authentic democratic form if it is not to be lost to history. It must not be lost, for threatened humanity, in search of viable forms of human cohabitation, needs alternatives to western consumer society, whose prosperity is paid for by the rest of the world.' In this spirit, the ensuing 'theses for a democratic transformation of the GDR' contained an invitation to the Germans in the FRG to 'work for a transformation of their own society that could make possible a new unity of the German people within the domestic community of the peoples of Europe. For the sake of unity, both states should reform towards each other. History imposes upon us Germans a particular duty to peace.'

The main leaders of Democratic Awakening were Evangelical ministers: Rainer Eppelmann from Berlin, Friedrich Schorlemmer from Wittenberg, and Edelbert Richter from Erfurt. Their manifesto called for an 'open, responsible, democratic society', an 'honest disclosure of all environmental problems', and a 'new social solidarity in society'. 'All words, platforms, and phrases hitherto in circulation are now used up and empty! We call on you: let us take common steps towards a dignified, worthwhile transformation of society: democratic, ecological, social, anti-fascist, non-violent.'

The New Forum was the group with the strongest appeal, and for two reasons. On the one hand it was the first oppositional organization to go public in September 1989 (at that time, the 'public' meant virtually the same thing as 'the western media', above all the West German television stations ARD and ZDF). On the other hand, its manifesto was the only one all opponents of the SED regime could support. 'In reading the text, one notes the high degree of generality,' writes historian Stefan Wolle, himself an early member of the organization.

There is a declaration of support neither for socialism . . . nor for the market economy, neither for the GDR nor for German unity. It defers all important questions to a future dialogue. Yet this is the very thing that gives it its enormous power. Once it was made public, the telephones of its first signatories rang day and night. More and more people signed the manifesto, and each signature lowered the degree of personal risk. Every day, more and more people crossed that invisible line between fear and involvement they had carefully observed for decades.

The group that announced the founding of the East German Social Democratic party on 12 September was led by the Evangelical pastors Markus Meckel and Martin Gutzeit. Like the civil rights organizations, this group believed that radical change in the direction of pluralism and democracy was needed in the GDR.

By referring to themselves as a 'party' and taking up the name and legacy of classical social democracy, however, the founders of the SDP represented an even greater challenge to the SED than the other groups critical of the regime. Meckel, Gutzeit, and their associates, among them the computer scientist Stephan Hilsberg, the pastor Steffen Reiche, and the biologist Angelika Barbe, denied the SED the right to any appeal to the democratic traditions of the workers' movement. 'Before the necessary democratization of the GDR can begin, the ruling party's claim to truth and authority must first be fundamentally called into question. We need an open philosophical debate over the state of our country and its future course.'

The central demands of the new party were an 'ecologically oriented social democracy', clear separation of the state from society, the rule of law, strict separation of powers, parliamentary democracy, party pluralism, federalization, a social market economy, the democratization of economic life, free labour unions, and the right to strike. These ideas had nothing to do with the SED's version of socialism, but a great deal to do with the Godesberg platform of the SPD. This proximity to a western party, initially quite one-sided, angered many activists, most of whom were very suspicious of political parties in general and believed it too early to start forming them in the GDR. The kind of democracy the New Forum and Democracy Now were interested in was to have the character of a civic movement, not of a party state on the pattern of West Germany.

Nonetheless, in terms of their ideas about what kinds of changes were needed, the civil rights groups and the SDP had so much in common that there was nothing standing in the way of their cooperation. On 4 October—three days before the party was officially founded in Schwante—the New Forum, the Peace and Human Rights Initiative, Democracy Now, Democratic Awakening, the newly founded Group of Democratic Socialists (*Gruppe Demokratischer SozialistInnen*), the Social Democratic Party Initiative in the GDR (*Initiativgruppe Sozialdemokratische Partei in der DDR*), and several peace organizations agreed to a 'Joint Statement', which culminated in the call for free elections with a secret ballot under the observation of the United Nations. The manifesto concluded with the following statement: 'The political transformation of our country requires the participation and the critical thinking of everyone. We call upon all citizens of the GDR to work together for democratic renewal.'

The Ministry for State Security was in general very well informed about the activities of the oppositional groups. Within a short time of the founding of the Peace and Human Rights Initiative in 1986, about half of its members were 'Unofficial Collaborators'. The lawyer Wolfgang Schnur, co-founder and later head of Democratic Awakening, was a Stasi informer, as was Manfred (aka. Ibrahim) Böhme, who belonged to the Social Democratic Party Initiative in the GDR, became the SDP party whip on 7 October, and was elected party head in February 1990.

Why did the MfS not simply destroy the opposition and stop the founding of formal civil rights groups? It provided its own answer. The minutes of a meeting in Department XX/4 on 21 September record the following statement in connection with the plans to establish the SDP: 'It was judged that oppositional efforts have developed to such a point that they can no longer simply be liquidated. In view of the current situation, MfS operative measures with repressive character are not possible. For this reason, political influence/leadership is decisive.'

The East German opposition was on its own. There was no power independent of the party and state to back it up, like the Catholic Church in Poland. In the GDR the Catholic Church was living in the diaspora. While it sought to shield itself from the atheist state, it made no attempt to influence politics. Within the Protestant church the MfS had succeeded in extending its network of Unofficial Collaborators to the highest levels, especially via the group of canon lawyers. Manfred Stolpe, secretary of the Federation of Evangelical churches in the GDR between 1969 and 1982, then consistorial president of the Evangelical church of Berlin-Brandenburg, was listed as an unofficial collaborator under the name *Sekretär* after 1969. He cultivated his Stasi contacts conspiratorially, without the knowledge of his church superiors. While the church did accord a measure of protection to members of the opposition, it also tried to prevent them from challenging the state. Over the years, the 'church within socialism' had developed a certain degree of affinity for socialism, at least as an idea, linking it to German traditions of socially just authoritarian government. It looked with favour on the state's commitment to peace and considered the GDR, at bottom, to be the more 'anti-fascist' of the two German states. In the view of many leading Protestants, these things formed at least partial compensation for what the GDR lacked in terms of democracy.

Accordingly, those Protestants who openly came out against the SED also opposed the diplomatic manoeuvring of many of their church leaders. The civil rights groups were by no means dominated by active Protestants. Nonetheless, there was something very 'Protestant' about the protest movement as a whole, especially the appeal to individual conscience, even against one's own church, and the rationalization of the existence of two German states as an 'atonement' for German guilt. And the reservations of many—though not all—of the activists against the west, including now West Germany, can be seen as 'Protestant' in terms of the political tradition of German Lutheranism.

Not that 'Protestant' and 'western' necessarily had to stand in opposition. On 25 September in Leipzig, before the first great collective Monday demonstration in that city, a prayer for peace was offered at the church of St Nicholas. It began with a request by Pastor Christian Führer that the city council refrain from deploying police forces, as it had done the previous week. The prayer itself was spoken by Pastor Christoph Wonneberger. It would be difficult to think of a clearer pledge of allegiance to the basic values of western democracy.

Whoever arbitrarily robs another of his liberty will himself soon have no route of escape. Whoever takes up the sword will perish by the sword. By this I do not mean to call state power into question. I affirm the state's monopoly on armed force. I see no sensible alternative. However, state power must be effectively controlled—by the courts, by the parliament, and by the public's unrestricted right to form and express its opinion. State power must be effectively limited. Our country is not wealthy enough to afford such a gigantic security apparatus. As the Polish satirist Stanislaw Jerzy wrote twenty years ago: 'The constitution of a state should be such that it does not ruin the constitution of the citizen.' We will just have to amend the constitution.

According to eyewitness accounts, there were some 2,000 people in the church itself and at least the same number assembled in the square in front. Between 8,000 and 10,000 were thought to have participated in the demonstrations, which processed over the Karl-Marx-Platz (formerly Augustusplatz) for the first time since 17 June 1953. The masses were led by the 300 men and women who had been the first to leave the church and had given the signal to start the procession. The demonstrators sang the 'International' and 'We shall overcome', and chanted 'Liberty!' and 'Allow New Forum!'

The police and security forces acted with restraint, by and large. When one member of a riot squad seized the legs of a young man and tried to drag him away, 'onlookers' intervened and prevented him from doing so. When some 800 demonstrators gathered in the west hall of the train station and demanded the official acceptance of the New Forum, the police broke up the unauthorized 'concentration of persons'. Six people were 'brought in' (*zugeführt*), though all but one were released immediately. One protester was threatened with a fine of 1,000 marks. Those wishing to leave the GDR were told by the police that their authorization would be granted. The purpose behind this was obvious. Everything was to be done to prevent the exhibition city of Leipzig from becoming the scene of bloody uprisings just a few days before the festivities in celebration of the GDR's fortieth anniversary.[1]

WEST GERMAN REACTIONS TO THE EVENTS IN EASTERN CENTRAL EUROPE

The first day of September 1989 was the fiftieth anniversary of the German attack on Poland that began the Second World War. The 154th session of the eleventh German Bundestag was devoted to commemorating the 55 million people who had lost their lives in this conflict. Chancellor Kohl spoke first, then the former chancellor and honorary head of the SPD, Willy Brandt. Towards the end of his speech, Brandt turned to the great changes taking place in eastern and eastern central Europe. 'I will openly express my feeling . . . that an era is coming to an end, an era in which the most important thing in our relationship to the other German state was helping, with many small steps, to preserve the unity of separated families, and thus the unity of the nation.'

What Brandt then said made it clear that he saw the day coming when the German question would return to international politics.

What is now being put on the agenda with regard to the democratic awakening in the other part of Europe will entail new risks, if only because our European neighbours and the other, semi-European powers have a strong interest in what becomes of us Germans. This interest is historically founded and has many different aspects, not all of which arose only in connection to the Hitler war. The wish and desire of the Germans for self-determination was confirmed in the western treaties and has not disappeared on account of the eastern treaties. These treaties remain pillars of our policy. What form of state this fact will take in the future is an open question. What matters is that, today and tomorrow, the Germans in both states fulfil their responsibility towards the peace and future of Europe. We are not the guardians of our countrymen in the GDR. We do not give them orders, but we are also not permitted to throw up any obstructions in their way.

What gave Willy Brandt hope was a cause for extreme concern among certain other Social Democrats. 'The ominous coat spreads over Europe,' Günter Gaus warned in an essay in *Der Spiegel* on 4 September, alluding to a famous phrase of Bismarck's. The former director of the FRG's Permanent Representation in East Germany found it disturbing that

a large part of Europe is losing its footing... History, as old custom teaches us, needs its humus, makes its claims, and has its victims. How anaemic reason is by comparison, with its 'however'. Of what use is complicity with the still-ruling repressors for the sake of small treaty advances when we must reach out to whole peoples? Thus do the historicizing feature pages reconquer their place in political consciousness.

Gaus made no secret of the fact that he deeply disapproved of what was happening in Hungary and Poland. He was convinced that history would prove him right and the freedom-hungry peoples wrong.

Cassandra is only popular *after* catastrophes... Hungary is making the interests of a two-thirds society into its reasons of state. How many unemployed people will there be in five years? What will the inflation rate be? Is all this nothing but humus for history?... Perhaps the underprivileged will soon attempt a rebellion there that will cause the western applause for the historical changes to die down. What will happen if Poland takes a detour through anarchy? Just the victims history is entitled to? Everything just a stimulus to put the western public in a historically generous mood? Recognizing the signs—that is, cast down before history. The events in the east are not only justifiable, but *natural*. But no word of concern from the experts about how in the end, after a breather, it always goes as it has always gone? No words of farewell to the modest hopes?

The third prominent Social Democrat who in September 1989 publicly expressed his opinion on the changes in the east was Norbert Gansel, a Bundestag delegate from Kiel and head of the party council. In a speech (subsequently printed by the *Frankfurter Rundschau*) delivered on 11 September at a meeting of the

Berlin party, Gansel took Egon Bahr's old maxim of *Wandel durch Annäherung* ('change through rapprochement') and changed it to *Wandel durch Abstand* (roughly: 'change through keeping our distance'). Unlike Brandt, Gansel did not think it possible that the two German states could reunite. He even called for the FRG to renounce this goal as 'certain to fail' in order to give the Germans in the GDR the 'historical chance for liberty'. But unlike Gaus he also called for pressure to be put on the SED.

If we in the Federal Republic wish to promote these changes, then what is needed is not more rapprochement, but more distance. Nothing needs to be undone at the state level. But we must distance ourselves from the leadership of the GDR . . . Photo opportunities with the reactionary diehards in the SED only do a disservice to the process of inner change in the GDR . . . 'Change through distance' instead of 'change through rapprochement'—this may seem to be a break with the SPD's 25-year-old Germany policy. It is not a break, but it is more than a shift in emphasis. What is important today is not foreign policy, but the process of inner change in the GDR. For this reason, we need to distance ourselves from the opponents of reform in the GDR.

Gansel had only moderate words of criticism for the policies that Volker Rühe, the new general secretary of the CDU, would castigate as *Wandel durch Anbiederung* (roughly: 'change through sycophancy') shortly thereafter, on 25 September. It was true that ever since its return to the parliamentary opposition in 1982 the SPD had consciously been downplaying the socio-political antagonism between West and East Germany and the ideological antagonism between social democrats and communists in order to promote its project of 'mutual security'. But the Social Democrats had no monopoly on 'sycophancy'. No prominent Social Democratic politician had ever supported the communist doctrine of the development of two German nations, whereas already in 1975 a member of the CDU executive, Walther Leisler Kiep, had found it appropriate to make this concession to the 'other side'. As Vadim Sagladin—at that time deputy director of the international department of the Soviet central committee—reported a conversation with him in Moscow on 6 September of that year, Kiep said that he personally did not believe in the practical possibility of reunification:

[Kiep continued] 'This will not happen in the next centuries . . . Two nations are developing in Germany. The GDR is distancing itself from everything all-German. We have recognized its independence in a de facto sense, like Austria.' Furthermore, as Kiep assumes, neither the west nor the east will permit a reunification, neither on a capitalist nor a socialist basis, in order not to be confronted with a powerful Germany numbering 80 million inhabitants.

Volker Rühe had succeeded Heiner Geissler as CDU general secretary. Helmut Kohl had separated himself from his closest associate at the Konrad-Adenauer-Haus because he thought Geissler had become too independent and because Union conservatives had long considered him too progressive. For his part, Geissler—along with other leading Union politicians like Lothar Späth, prime minister of Baden-Württemberg, and Rita Süssmuth, president of the Bundestag—considered it impossible for Kohl to win the federal elections at the end of 1990. Major CDU losses in Berlin in January 1989, in Hesse in March, and in the European elections in June had further decreased Kohl's notoriously low 'market value' in the opinion polls. His adversaries in the Union were plotting a 'putsch': at the party congress in Bremen that September, either Späth or Süssmuth would take over the leadership of the CDU.

But Kohl, who knew his party better than anyone else, had already taken precautions, with the result that the conspirators, who found themselves without backing in most of the regional parties, lost heart even before the federal party congress. On 11 September Helmut Kohl was re-elected head of the federal party by 571 of 738 votes. There was no other candidate. The new general secretary, Volker Rühe, achieved the impressive result of 628 votes. Lothar Späth failed to get re-elected into the executive, gaining only 357 votes. The Bremen congress strengthened Kohl's position in the CDU and permanently weakened his adversaries. But whether he would be re-elected chancellor in 1990 was another question. The only thing that was clear was that he was going to need a great deal of luck.[2]

'HE WHO COMES TOO LATE WILL BE PUNISHED BY LIFE'—HONECKER LEFT BEHIND

Monday, 2 October 1989, was the day the demonstrations in Leipzig took on a new quality—when, in other words, quantity changed into quality. Some 20,000 people now went over to open rebellion against the rule of the SED in the streets and on the squares of the city on the Pleisse river. 'On this Monday in October, those who could not gain entrance to the church of St Nicholas were directed, first by a sign and then by a church spokesman, to go to the Reformed Church on the Tröndlinring,' reported the Leipzig historian Hartmut Zwahr.

On this 2 October, the call of the masses was the main form in which goals and plans were articulated. The core concerns spontaneously broke through in what was yelled out. But something different was being readied on the homemade banners for the next Monday demonstration: mass hegemony . . . *We are staying here! We are staying here! No violence!*, the demonstrators called out, and *Not another China!* Others called out *Gorbi, Gorbi* . . . Two hundred years after the people of Paris stormed the Bastille, the people of Leipzig raised the call for *Liberty, Equality, Fraternity!*

They did so in words well known to the 'party of the working class'.

The demonstrators sang and in singing grew courageous. They sang the Internationale, from music class in the seventh and eighth grades of the Polytechnic Colleges of the GDR. They had learned it and grown sick of it and never willingly sang it again until this moment, when a piece of the refrain, bellowed out at full power, perfectly expressed the protest: *Völker, hört die Signale,* | *auf zum letzten Gefecht!* | *Die Internationale* | *erkämpft das Menschenrecht!** Human rights—how they had been twisted! Now everybody felt the same thing: taking to the streets was a human right. Everything that made up the greatness of the moment sounded together in the cry *Democracy now!* and in the words *auf zum letzten Gefecht!* To take the risk. Now.

The next day the MfS sent the leaders of the party and state a report on the events in Leipzig describing how members of the police had been subjected to 'slanderous abuse' and even 'physical attacks' by groups of young people.

In places, these forces succeeded in breaking through police barriers. At approximately 20.20 some 1,500 persons made another attempt to gather up at the Thomaskirchhof and to march in the direction of the inner city / market. In order to prevent this, and especially to fend off the physical attacks that came from this group and to secure the safety of the police forces, it was necessary to make use of the baton and bring in officers with guard dogs (with muzzles). By 21.25 the concentration of persons had been broken up. A total of 20 persons were brought in, in connection with whom the necessary legal steps will be taken once the facts of individual involvement can be established.

Officers of the party, police, and security forces were as present in Leipzig—the GDR's second largest city—as they were throughout the rest of the country. But the coverage was not as dense there as in the capital. Also, by the late 1980s, the political-ideological pressure was not as great at Leipzig's Karl-Marx-Universität as it was at the Humboldt-Universität in Berlin. On the other hand, 500,000 inhabitants made Leipzig large enough for the mass mobilization of protest. It was no coincidence that the major events began here in the autumn of 1989. Not that Leipzig long remained an island of protest. By 5 October demonstrations were being forcibly broken up in Dresden and Magdeburg, too.

Between 5 and 7 October the eyes of the entire world were on East Berlin and the ceremonies in celebration of the GDR's fortieth anniversary. Many honorary guests attended, including Mikhail Gorbachev. In his official speech on 5 October, the Soviet leader criticized Bonn's call for the restoration of Germany in the borders of 1937. His treatment of the GDR leadership was very cordial. The only hint of criticism was a comment that he did not doubt the SED's ability to work together with all groups in society to find answers to the pressing questions of the day.

Gorbachev was more direct in a confidential talk with Honecker on 7 October. He told Honecker that 'the party could not operate in any other way than by uniting all impulses from society . . . He knows from personal experience, he said, that one must not come too late.' Gorbachev described the policy of

---

* [Translator's note: in order to be correctly understood, Zwahr's comment about 'human rights' requires a literal translation from the German text of the 'Internationale': 'Ye nations, hear the signals: | off to the final battle! | The Internationale | will fight for human rights and win!' In the traditional English version the same lines read: 'So comrades, come rally, | And the last fight let us face. | The Internationale | Unites the human race.']

'restructuring' as a 'revolution in the revolution', which however did not mean 'a negation of the values, ideals, and ideas of October'. 'What is needed is an active party policy. Delay means defeat, since spontaneous and chaotic forces can get out of control, and anti-socialist and anti-social elements can abuse these processes.' Honecker responded by telling Gorbachev, among other things, something Chancellor Kohl had said two days before: 'if the GDR undertakes reforms, then Bonn will provide economic support. We totally rejected that of course; we are not going to let Bonn dictate any conditions to us.'

At an ensuing meeting with the SED politburo, Gorbachev combined criticism of the political stagnation in the GDR with praise for what had been achieved.

What the GDR is today is an excellent culmination of the arduous path to the founding of the workers' and peasants' state on German soil. Of course there were also difficulties, mistakes, and deficiencies. Of course! For only in diagrams does everything go smoothly; in real life things are different . . . We look upon the anniversary of the German Democratic Republic as our common celebration. That does not, of course, release you from the primary responsibility for what occurs in this country. Not that this remark implies any pretensions on our part, not at all. I am only stating reality . . . Courageous times await you, courageous decisions are necessary . . . I consider it very important not to miss the right moment and not to waste any opportunity. The party must have its own view, propose its own approach. If we remain behind, life will punish us immediately.

At a press conference of the Soviet delegation, Gennadi Gerasimov, the spokesman of the foreign ministry, put Gorbachev's warning not to delay necessary reforms into words that immediately became a catchphrase in their German translation: *Wer zu spät kommt, den bestraft das Leben* ('He who comes too late will be punished by life'). Gorbachev himself also said similar things in public, remarking to journalists that only those who did not react to life exposed themselves to dangers. It was perfectly clear to the Soviet leader what the people of the GDR expected from him. When he placed a wreath in the Neue Wache, the monument for the victims of fascism and militarism in Unter den Linden street, a group of young people called out 'Gorbi, help!' In his memoirs he mentions hearing the same thing during the evening torch-lit procession of the FDJ along Unter den Linden, whereupon Mieczyslaw Rakowski, head of the PUWP, came up to him in an agitated state: 'Mikhail Sergeyevich, do you understand what slogans they are calling out?' Then Rakowski translated: 'They are calling "Gorbachev, rescue us!" That is the active of the party! It's the end!'

There were other things that Gorbachev did not see. At about 4.00 in the afternoon, some 200 people, mostly young, gathered at the World Time Clock on the Alexanderplatz. Their chanting grew louder at about 5.20. About 300 people began to move towards the Palast der Republik. They were joined by passers-by.

The police did not intervene until Gorbachev and the other guests of state left the official reception and the crowd, which had grown to about 1,000 people, started to move towards Prenzlauer Berg, passing the building where the General

German Intelligence Agency (*Allgemeiner Deutscher Nachrichtendienst* or ADN) was housed. Here is what followed, as described by the investigating commission in its report on the events of 7 and 8 October:

With unbelievable brutality, individual demonstrators were seized as if at random from the crowd, beaten by up to eight Stasi civil agents, and then forcibly dragged away. Police and Stasi agents beat many of those arrested as they were being transported away, even though no resistance was offered. The women were treated with particular brutality in order to provoke male demonstrators into attempting to use force against the security personnel.

Altogether, 547 people were arrested and temporarily taken into custody on the evening of 7 October. Similar scenes were repeated the next day after the conclusion of a service at the Gethsemane Church in Prenzlauer Berg.

Without a doubt, one of the reasons for the massive use of force in Berlin was to deter the Leipzig demonstrators, who were preparing for a new demonstration on 9 October. But the tactic did not work. Rumours circulated in Leipzig that the security forces were planning the violent suppression of the protest movement, perhaps even to the point of causing a bloodbath like the one in Beijing in June, when the leadership of the Chinese Communist party had ordered the slaughter of the peaceful demonstrators at Tiananmen Square.

By the late afternoon there was a sign of hope: a short appeal to peaceful dialogue was read in four Leipzig churches. It was signed by the director of the Leipzig Gewandhaus Orchestra, Kurt Masur, the cabaret artist Bernd-Lutz Lange of the Akademixer club, the theologian Peter Zimmermann, and—the real sensation—three SED district officials, Roland Wötzel, Jochen Pommert, and Kurt Meyer. 'We need a free exchange of views on the future of socialism in our country,' the appeal read. A dialogue was necessary not only in Leipzig, but also 'with our government'. 'We urgently request that it act in a level-headed manner, so that peaceful dialogue is possible.'

The appeal, read by Masur, was broadcast on city radio at approximately 6.00. But fear was still very much in the air when the demonstration, the largest of its kind thus far, got under way shortly thereafter. Some 70,000 people chanted slogans like 'Stasi out!', 'Gorbi, Gorbi!', 'We are staying here!', 'We are the people!', and, loudest of all, 'No violence!'

And there was none. The police used neither the baton nor guns, and combat groups were not deployed. The decision against the 'Chinese solution' was taken in Leipzig, not East Berlin. An order from Honecker—forwarded by Security Minister Erich Mielke—had gone out from the capital on 8 October: 'Further riots are expected. They are to be stopped before they can begin.' The leaders of the district forces were to determine the 'necessary measures'. This left the local authorities a certain room for manoeuvre. Egon Krenz, a member of the politburo and deputy head of the State Council (since 1984), wanted to avoid a bloodbath, but did not get involved until the early evening. Speaking by telephone to the Leipzig authorities, he stated his support for the 'declaration of the six', thus approving the decision for de-escalation.

This day, 9 October 1989, was the turning point in the crisis. The East German leadership retreated in the face of mass protest. The fact that the Soviet Union could no longer be counted on to intervene militarily had a demoralizing effect on many people in the party and security apparatus. If Honecker and Mielke had had their way, a bloody example would have been set in Leipzig. But there were enough people—not only in Leipzig, but also at the highest levels—who saw the hard line as a policy of catastrophe. The logical consequence was an attempt to remove Honecker and his closest associates, above all Günter Mittag, from office.

Honecker will have been aware of such plans no later than 8 October, when Egon Krenz passed him the outline of an announcement he was to make to the politburo two days later. The text had been worked out with three other politburo members, Günter Schabowski (head of the Berlin SED), Siegfried Lorenz (head of the party in Karl-Marx-Stadt), and Wolfgang Herger (director of the central committee security department). It contained an implicit critique of a commentary by the ADN that Honecker had caused to be published in *Neues Deutschland* on 2 October. The subject was the embassy refugees: 'In acting as they did, they have all treated moral values with contempt and excluded themselves from our society. No tears should be shed for them.' Krenz was of a different opinion. According to his text, the politburo was to declare that socialism needed and had room for everybody. Honecker interpreted this as an attack and reacted with hostility.

That evening, Krenz talked on the telephone to the Soviet ambassador in East Berlin, Vyacheslav Kochemasov, telling him what had happened. Kochemasov supported him. The main issue, he said, was seeing to it that no blood was spilt in Leipzig the next day. Immediately after the conversation with Krenz, Kochemasov exhorted the commander of the western group of the Soviet forces not to intervene in Leipzig under any circumstances. An order to this effect arrived from Moscow the next day.[3]

THE CAPITULATION OF THE SED AND THE FALL OF THE WALL

The politburo session on 10 and 11 October was the beginning of the end for Erich Honecker. The discussion of Krenz's draft, sent to all politburo members and candidates, did not go as Honecker had expected. Most of those present agreed with Krenz. On 12 October, a text taken from the final version of the document was published in *Neues Deutschland*. It read:

Socialism needs everybody. It has room and holds prospects for all. It is the future of the coming generation. For this reason it does not leave us cold when people who have lived and worked here decide to break with our German Democratic Republic . . . Their reasons for doing so may be many. We must and will look for them here too, each in his own place, all of us together.

Between the politburo session and the next meeting of the central committee on 18 October came a meeting of the SED district leaders (12 October) and another Monday demonstration (16 October). The party meeting also did not go well for Honecker. After his introductory speech, in which he made virtually no mention either of the politburo statement or of the general crisis in the country, he was faced with sharp criticism above all from Johannes Chemnitzer (Neubrandenburg), Hans Modrow (Dresden), and Günter Jahn (Potsdam). Jahn all but called for him to resign. The demonstration in Leipzig on 16 October was the largest to date, with some 120,000 people calling for free elections, freedom of movement, freedom of the press, free speech, and the acceptance of the New Forum. They chanted 'We are the people!' and 'No violence!' Large demonstrations also took place in Dresden, Magdeburg, Halle, and Berlin.

Meanwhile the anti-Honecker faction—which Mielke had joined by this time—was making its final preparations to bring down the general secretary. The politburo met again on 17 October. Right at the beginning Willi Stoph, the prime minister, motioned for Honecker to be replaced. Honecker protested fiercely at first, then submitted to the will of the other members, including now even Günter Mittag. On the morning of 18 October the central committee met without Honecker and voted unanimously for 'cadre change'. Stoph proposed that Krenz take Honecker's place. Immediately thereafter the politburo, again at a motion from Stoph, approved a text written by Krenz and Schabowski that Honecker was to read, announcing his resignation as general secretary of the SED, member of the politburo, and secretary of the central committee, for 'reasons of health'.

The CC meeting that afternoon went as the conspirators had planned. Honecker himself proposed Krenz as his successor. Two other members of the politburo, Günter Mittag and Joachim Herrmann, were also removed from their posts. 'They did not meet the demands placed on them,' Stoph explained to a member of the central committee.

That evening the newly elected general secretary of the SED went before the television cameras. His address to the public, which he began with 'dear comrades', was mostly general in nature and formulaic in tone. 'With today's meeting we will usher in a change. Most importantly, we will retake the political and ideological offensive.' This was the main message. Krenz assured the public of the SED's 'firm conviction' that 'there is a political solution to all the problems in our society'. At the same time, he emphasized that the party was resolved to secure the peace and order and not abandon 'socialism on German soil'. He declared the '*perestroika* of the USSR' unavoidable and said that no communist party could isolate itself from processes 'that affect our own movement, the changes in the Soviet Union and in other fraternal countries'. One remark at the end caused a stir: the politburo, Krenz said, had suggested that the government prepare new legislation on foreign travel. This would allow the 'temporarily effected restrictive measures on travel to socialist fraternal countries to be lifted or modified'.

The Honecker era that came to such an abrupt end on 18 October 1989 had, in its latter phase, much in common with the final years of the Ulbricht era. Both men showed increasing stubbornness, and both tended to overestimate their own abilities and importance as the years passed. Just as Ulbricht had done starting in the late 1960s, in the late 1980s Honecker provoked the Soviet Union by claiming that the GDR was a model socialist society ahead of the other Warsaw Pact countries, including the Soviet Union. Unlike Ulbricht, however, Honecker was dealing with a USSR whose leaders had recognized the crisis of 'real existing socialism' while he remained blind to it. Nor was he able to see that the relative prosperity of the GDR was not its own achievement, but the result of financial assistance from West Germany.

After his fall, Honecker saw himself as the victim of an intrigue. As far as the party was concerned, this was an abbreviated but not altogether incorrect perception. 'Moscow' however, which played a role in Ulbricht's removal from power in May 1971, was not involved in Honecker's case. Gorbachev, who had been receiving detailed information on the catastrophic consequences of Honecker's policies from Stoph and others ever since spring 1986, did not intervene. The SED would have to solve its leadership problems on its own.

Egon Krenz, 52 at the time, had been leader of the FDJ for many years, just like his predecessor. He was generally considered a typical representative of the apparatus and party line. The reform activists reacted to his elevation with corresponding scepticism. The Leipzig pastor Christoph Wonneberger pointed out that Krenz had never yet distinguished himself as a proponent of reform. Bärbel Bohley noted that his name was connected to the campaign against the Zion Church in November 1987 and that he had just recently justified the suppression of the Chinese democracy movement in Beijing. Chancellor Kohl's reaction to Krenz was comparatively amicable. With the change in leadership, Kohl said, the SED was seeking to do justice to the desire of the East German population for changes in their state and society. 'The decisive question, however, is whether Krenz will now clear the path for the overdue reforms.'

On 24 October the Volkskammer elected Egon Krenz head of both the State Council and the National Defence Council. For the first time in East German history the custom of unanimity was not observed: 26 delegates voted against Krenz in the State Council ballot. Most of them were from the LDPD and CDU, the 'bourgeois' bloc parties. Another 26 abstained. In the second ballot there were 8 negative votes and 17 abstentions.

Two days later, on 26 October, the new SED leader talked to the West German chancellor on the telephone. Kohl assured Krenz that it was neither in the interest of his government nor in his own interest 'that the developments in the GDR proceed in such a way as to make calm, reasonable developments impossible'. The chancellor spoke of the 'hopes' that Krenz's election had awakened; of the new travel legislation; an amnesty for East Germans who had been condemned for attempting 'flight from the republic'; the release of demonstrators who had been arrested; and a positive solution for embassy refugees who needed documents they had left behind in the GDR. The focus, Kohl said, should not be on the divisive issues, as before, but on cooperation—an 'opinion' Krenz said he 'fully' supported. For his part, Krenz said that of all the expectations he had of the chancellor, one was particularly important: if the GDR passed a generous travel law in the near future, then the West German government should handle a number of practical issues in a manner 'that makes it more clear that citizenship of the GDR is being respected'.

By the end of October, the relations between Bonn and East Berlin were much less tense than those between the new SED leadership and the citizens of the GDR. Krenz's biggest problem turned out to be his lack of credibility. The demonstrations not only continued; they spread all over the country, and Krenz himself became their target. The main accusations were that Krenz was politically responsible for the fraud in the local elections that May in his capacity as central returning officer and for the police excesses against demonstrators in his capacity as secretary of security in the central committee. On 28 and 29 October protest and reform demonstrations as well as mass meetings were reported in Berlin, Neubrandenburg, Magdeburg, Dresden, Leipzig, Erfurt, Jena, Karl-Marx-Stadt, Plauen, Greiz, and Senftenberg. On 30 October (another Monday) Leipzig alone saw 300,000 hit the streets and demonstrate for reforms, free elections, and freedom of travel.

Krenz was in Moscow on 31 October and 1 November. He spent 2 November in Warsaw. That was also a day of resignations in the East German capital. Among those who left their offices were Harry Tisch, head of the Free German Labour Union Association; Gerald Götting, head of the CDU; Heinrich Homann, head of the NDPD; and Erich Honecker's wife Margot Honecker, minister of education. In a televised address the next day, Krenz announced the upcoming replacement of Kurt Hager, Erich Mielke, Hermann Axen, Alfred Neumann, and Erich Mückenberger in the politburo. He also told the public that new legislation on the right to association and a new constitutional court were in the works.

Regardless of what he said and did, Krenz failed to stop events from taking their course. On 4 November an initiative group from the 'Berlin Ensemble' held a rally—officially requested and permitted—on the Berlin Alexanderplatz. More than half a million people participated, and the event was broadcast live on GDR television. The crowd demanded what all such crowds throughout the GDR were demanding: free elections, freedom of expression, an end to the

SED monopoly on power, the resignation of the government, and the official acceptance of opposition groups.

Among the speakers were well-known activists like Jens Reich, Friedrich Schorlemmer, and Marianne Birthler; writers like Christa Wolf, Stefan Heym, Heiner Müller, and Christoph Hein; the actress Steffie Spira, whose cry 'No more flag ceremony!' was hailed with storms of applause; the lawyer Gregor Gysi; the head of the LDPD, Manfred Gerlach; but also Markus Wolf, former chief of espionage; and Günter Schabowski. The last two received more hisses and boos than applause. The presence of the SED, which had exhorted its members to join in, allowed of only one conclusion: the reform-willing wing of the party was trying to ally itself to the civil rights movement in order to preserve as much power as possible in a new multi-party environment and to rescue the political existence of the GDR. For it was now borne in on the belated reformers in the SED that the new East Germany was going to be radically different from the old one, and that it was going to have to do justice to the 'democratic' part of its official name for the first time.

On Monday 6 November, two days after the demonstration, the *Frankfurter Allgemeine Zeitung* came out with the headline 'Mass Flight—Reform Consent—Demands'. Mass flight was made possible after the GDR once again allowed visa-free travel to Czechoslovakia (1 November) and made an agreement with the CSSR (3 November) that opened that country's borders to West Germany for citizens of the GDR, now required to show only their personal identification. The new regulations were to remain in effect until the passage of new travel legislation. This solved the problem of the embassy refugees, which had immediately become a huge problem again after 1 November. Between 3 and 5 November more than 10,000 GDR citizens entered West Germany from Czechoslovakia, arriving on special trains, buses, and in private automobiles.

Only a few participants and observers recognized the massive significance of these new regulations at the time. One of them was the journalist Klaus Hartung. On 6 November he wrote in the West Berlin *tageszeitung*:

Just imagine: a dream is coming true and nobody really even notices. The wall is down. As of 3 November a GDR citizen from Karl-Marx-Stadt can climb into his Trabi and drive to Munich. All that is needed is a personal ID and enough juice in the tank. As of Friday night the situation is not that 'the wall has symbolically come down', as we hear on television. No: it is the reality that has come down, and the symbol is still standing in Berlin.

And in truth, the die was cast on 3 November. What happened six days later and turned 9 November 1989 into a world-historical watershed was, in reality, the ineluctable outcome of the decisions to open the GDR border to Czechoslovakia and the Czechoslovak border to West Germany. There was no going back now. East Germany had to open its borders to West Berlin and the rest of West Germany. Anything else would have been absurd and pointless.

Before that could be done, however, a great number of things happened all at once. On 6 November the GDR government published the draft of a travel law allowing nearly every citizen thirty days of travel abroad per year. But the approval process was so time-consuming and bureaucratic that protests started again immediately—with particular vehemence in Leipzig at the demonstration that evening. The next day the review committee rejected the bill in the Volkskammer, demanding an end to the visa requirement and reasonable regulations regarding access to foreign currency.

That same day, 7 November, the Stoph administration stepped down, followed on the next day by the resignation of the entire politburo. The SED central committee then elected a new, eleven-member politburo, one of whose three new members, Dresden party chief Hans Modrow, considered a reformer, it also proposed as the new prime minister.

The tenth congress of the SED central committee from 8 to 10 November 1989 turned into a general declaration of political bankruptcy. Only now did the CC members learn the details of the deepest crisis in GDR history. Günter Ehrensperger, director of the CC planning and finance department since 1974 and CC member since 1981, traced the fiscal causes of the crisis back to the early 1970s.

If we want to sum up in one sentence why we are in this situation today, then we must say very clearly that we have been living beyond our means every year since at least 1973 and pretending we have not been. Our debts were paid for with new debts. They have risen, and the interest has risen, and it has reached the point where today we have to pay a large part of several billion marks every year in interest. And if we want to get out of this predicament, we will have to work hard for at least fifteen years and consume less than we produce.

The head of the State Planning Commission, Gerhard Schürer (CC member since 1963), had submitted a report to the politburo on 30 October in which he stated that merely to 'stop going into debt' vis-à-vis the 'NSW' (*Nicht-Sozialistisches Wirtschaftsgebiet* or 'Non-Socialist Economic Area', i.e. the capitalist countries) 'would require a lowering of the living standard by 25–30% in the year 1990 and make the GDR ungovernable'. Schürer said that he had been telling Honecker ever since 1976 'that to secure our solvency, changes are necessary in economic policy and also restrictive measures.' But to no avail. In May 1978, he said, Honecker had caused the government to issue a statement that culminated as follows: 'The State Planning Commission is using the balance of payments as the benchmark of economic policy. But the benchmark of economic policy must be the unity of economic and social policy.' At the end of 1982, Schürer went on, Honecker responded to Stoph's call for 'drastic measures to change our economic policy' by saying: 'We never want to hear those words about drastic measures again.'

After these and other revelations Karl Kayser, director of the Leipzig city theatre and also on the central committee since 1963, burst out: 'We have been lied to, the whole time! It's not my fault, really it isn't! . . . I am shaken by what I have heard here. Everything in me is completely broken. My life is in ruins. I believed in the party. I was raised that way from the cradle. I believed in the comrades!'

On the afternoon of 9 November, around 3.50, Egon Krenz interrupted the discussion to speak on a problem 'that is burdening us all', that is, the number of people leaving the GDR.

The Czechoslovak comrades are starting to look upon it as a burden, as the Hungarian comrades did earlier. And regardless of what we do in this situation, we are making a mistake. If we close the borders to the CSSR, we are basically punishing decent GDR citizens, who then won't be able to travel and will exercise their influence on us in this way.

In his capacity as incumbent head of the government, Krenz said, Willi Stoph had proposed an ordinance to be in effect until a new travel law could be passed.

According to this ordinance, the following 'temporary interim' regulations would immediately apply to travel and 'permanent departure' (*ständige Ausreise*) from the GDR: a citizen could apply for permission to take a trip abroad without presenting special reasons or proof of family relations. 'Permits will be speedily granted. Reasons for refusal will only be applied in exceptional cases.' As for those wishing to leave the country permanently, the local police departments in charge were told to grant them visas 'immediately'. 'Permanent departures can proceed over all GDR checkpoints to the FRG or to Berlin (West).' A corresponding press statement was to be published on 10 November. Krenz concluded his announcement with the words: 'I said: however we do it, we're doing it wrong. But this is the only solution that spares us the problems of handling everything through third-party states, which is not good for the international image of the GDR.'

In the short debate that followed, the interior minister, Friedrich Dickel, suggested that the communiqué should not come through his office, but through the government press office, since it concerned an ordinance by the head of the government. Krenz agreed. 'Yes, I would say that the government speaker should take care of that right away, yes.' In other words, there would be no delay until '10 November'. The central committee agreed to drop the words 'temporary' and 'interim' after two speakers said that they would only create feelings of insecurity and pressure.

Schabowski was not in the room while Krenz was explaining the 'proposal'. He had taken responsibility for media issues the previous day and was off to a press conference scheduled for 6.00 at the International Press Centre in the Mohrenstrasse. Before he left, Krenz gave him his copy of the ordinance draft. This text was supposed to go to the government press speaker. Schabowski either did not read or only skimmed it, and he took it out only when, just before the end of the conference (6.53), a member of the Italian press agency ANSA,

Riccardo Ehrman, asked him whether the new travel bill was not a big mistake. The cameras were running.

Schabowski said that it was not and mentioned the new ruling recommended by the politburo. When asked when it was to go into effect, Schabowski recited large sections of the draft and then, in response to other questions, interpreted it to the effect that it was to apply 'immediately, without delay'. When he was asked 'Does this also apply to Berlin?', he answered by quoting the text: 'Permanent departures can proceed over all GDR checkpoints to the FRG or to Berlin-West.' The last question Schabowski permitted, at 7.00, concerned the fate of the Berlin wall. He gave a circuitous answer: disarmament measures on the part of the Federal Republic and NATO would have a positive effect 'in regard to the relations between the GDR and FRG'.

The news agencies reported on Schabowski's statements shortly after 7.00. The Associated Press was the first to mention an 'opening of the border' (7.05). ZDF broadcast parts of the press conference at 7.17 during the news programme 'Heute'. Tom Brokaw, chief correspondent for the American television station NBC, gave his report for the American public while standing in front of the wall at the Brandenburg Gate. 'Good evening. Live from the Berlin wall on the most historic night in this wall's history. What you see behind me is a celebration of this new policy announced today by the East German government that now for the first time since the wall was erected in 1961 people will be able to move through freely.'

Meanwhile, in West Germany, the Bundestag was in session. At 8.20 proceedings were interrupted by the news from Berlin. Rudolf Seiters, minister of the chancellor's office, used the break to call Helmut Kohl, who was on an official visit in Warsaw. Bundestag vice president Annemarie Renger reopened the session at 8.46. Seiters was the first to speak. He called the 'temporary lifting of controls on visits and departures from the GDR' a 'step of enormous significance. It means, practically for the first time, freedom of movement for the Germans in the GDR.' Hans-Jochen Vogel asked the delegates for their understanding if he turned his gaze to Willy Brandt at that moment, 'the Governing Mayor of Berlin on the day, 13 August 1961, when that inhuman construction went up'. Alfred Dregger, CDU/CSU fraction leader, echoed Seiters's and Vogel's appeal to the duty of the Germans in the FRG to show solidarity with their countrymen in the GDR. Helmut Lippelt of the Greens expressed his joy that 'already tonight and certainly tomorrow the festival of free movement will take place in Berlin.'

The last to speak was the FDP fraction leader Wolfgang Mischnick, 68 years old at the time and a native of Dresden. He recalled a long journey:

Those of us who were there when the first comparatively free elections were held, under the occupation, in September 1946 and October 1946; those of us who were there on 17 June 1953 and politically active on 13 August 1961 — today we are filled with a great hope, the happiness of knowing that together we never lost faith in our common nation and that the people in the GDR have today found faith in themselves.

When Mischnick finished, a number of Union delegates stood up and sang the third stanza of the 'Deutschlandlied': 'Unity and right and freedom for our German fatherland'. They were joined by members of the other fractions, Free Democrats, Social Democrats, and even a few Greens. The minutes summarize the unusual event as follows: 'Those present stand up and sing the national anthem.'

Neither Krenz nor Schabowski had anticipated or intended what happened in Berlin in the night of 9 and 10 November. But even if the new travel regulations had not been 'mistakenly' announced on the evening of 9 November, the 'festival of free movement' that Helmut Lippelt spoke about would probably have been delayed by only one day. For the new party leadership did not have the authority to compel obedience to the procedures that the new ordinance required for 'travel' and 'permanent departure' applications.

The opening of the borders *was* the capitulation of the SED. The East Berliners who thronged to the checkpoints on 9 November sensed this. The border soldiers were taken completely off guard. At 9.00 p.m., after the failure of initial attempts to hold back the crowds of people, the checkpoint in the Bornholmer Strasse received a telephone call from Department VI of the security ministry ordering them to stamp the personal IDs of persons who crossed to West Berlin. That meant 'expatriation', but it made no difference, since the will of the citizens prevailed in this matter, too. The vast majority of them did not want to 'emigrate', but only to visit West Berlin and West Germany and then return.

The stamping of IDs ceased after awhile, and thousands crossed the borders of the divided city unchecked—from east to west, but also from west to east. For the East Germans, what had stopped being normal on 13 August 1961 was 'crazy'. They felt suddenly free of decades-long repression. The West Germans and West Berliners rejoiced with their countrymen from the east, with whom they shared so much despite the political separation. In the night of 9–10 November, Berlin became one city again. All Germans celebrated the opening of the wall, and the friends of liberty throughout the whole world celebrated with them.

Since 13 August 1961, 231 people had been killed attempting to cross the Berlin wall to the west. The last was Chris Gueffroy, who died on 6 February 1989. A total of at least 943 people had died along the whole length of the German–German border since 1949, according to a study by the '13 August Association' (*Arbeitsgemeinschaft 13. August*). The fall of the wall ended this dark chapter in German history.

Germans see 9 November as one of their 'days of destiny'. Philipp Scheidemann proclaimed the republic in Berlin on 9 November 1918. Hitler staged his Munich putsch on 9 November 1923. The synagogues burned throughout Germany on the night of 9 November 1938. And in the evening of 9 November 1989 it was already clear that that day, too, would go down in history. The post-war period and the Cold War now finally belonged to the past. Regardless of what was to become of the two German states, the Germans had known no happier day than 9 November 1989 in the whole course of the twentieth century. When Walter Momper, the Social Democrat mayor of Berlin, gave his address as president of the Bundesrat on 10 November in Bonn, he said aloud what all were feeling: 'Last night the German people were the happiest people in the world.'[4]

THE 'PEACEFUL REVOLUTION': ORIGINS AND CAUSES

'The demonstration of the twenty thousand in Leipzig on Monday 2 October was the start of the democratic revolution in the GDR,' writes Hartmut Zwahr. What began on that day was not a revolution of the classic type. There was no fighting in the streets and no storming of the citadels of power in East Germany in autumn 1989. This was a new kind of revolution, one that reined itself in with the slogan 'No violence!' That was not the least of the reasons for its success. The 'peaceful revolution' had conscious and unconscious participants. The conscious ones were the founders of the civil rights organizations and the demonstrators who began to gather into masses on 2 October. The unconscious participants were the masses leaving the GDR. Until late summer 1989 the exodus of so many people dissatisfied with the system had weakened the opposition to it. In late summer and early autumn the stream of refugees grew so massive that the opposition drew from it new moral energy. To many, the demands for reform now seemed like the GDR's last chance.

A successful revolution means the collapse of the old order. In most of the 1989 revolutions, in fact, collapse was the dominant feature. Except in the case of Poland, the masses appeared on the scene only later and helped bring down regimes that had already begun to fall. But not all these revolutions were peaceful. Regimes that did not acquiesce in their inevitable fate, like Ceausescu's Romania, suffered a bloody mixture of *coup d'état* and mass action.

In his 1938 book *The Anatomy of Revolution*, the American historian Crane Brinton summarized the signs of impending revolution:

government deficits, complaints over taxation, governmental favoring of one set of economic interests over another, administrative entanglements, desertion of the intellectuals, loss of self-confidence among many members of the ruling class, conversion of many members of that class to the belief that their privileges are unjust or harmful to society, the intensification of social antagonisms, the stoppage at certain points (usually in the professions, the arts, perhaps the white-collar jobs generally) of the career open to talents, the separation of economic power from political power and social distinction.

Brinton's area of focus was the French Revolution of 1789. Most of the crisis symptoms he found in the French *ancien régime* of the late eighteenth century and then rediscovered in other proto-revolutionary contexts are also present on the eve of the 1989 revolutions in eastern central Europe. In the case of the

GDR, let us begin with the intellectuals, the demoralization of the ruling class, and its reaction to the complaints from 'below'.

Since it had no national identity of its own, the GDR was more dependent on ideology and its intellectual purveyors than any other Warsaw Pact state. The state intelligentsia was mostly the product of the SED and, by and large, long faithful to it. (Writers and artists were a special case. Most did not belong to the state intelligentsia, and they often left for or were deported to West Germany when their opposition went beyond a certain limit.) Then, once the Gorbachev era had begun in the Soviet Union, the relationship between the party and the state intelligentsia began to change. The reformer in the Kremlin embodied and legitimated hopes that many SED intellectuals shared. This was true of members of the East German Academy of Sciences, professors in the universities, and even high cadres, including some in state security. Markus Wolf, for example, director of the MfS General Reconnaissance Administration, voluntarily left office in February 1987 because he considered the GDR's resistance to *glasnost* and *perestroika* a danger to the system.

The criticism articulated by SED intellectuals at the universities was never very radical, not even in the autumn of 1989. The 'party reformers' pushed for a responsible environmental policy, more market and less command economics, the legal codification of decision-making processes, and more democracy within the party. But they did not question the SED's monopoly on power. Their idol was Hans Modrow, who never hid his belief that Gorbachev's policy of reform and transparency could be a model for the GDR. Modrow only made it into the politburo on 8 November 1989. Before October of that year reform-minded SED intellectuals had no ally among the high party leadership.

Stasi documents from September and October 1989 clearly show to what extent the loyalty crisis had taken hold of party members and functionaries. A report on 11 September, for example, describes how large numbers, especially among the older membership, were 'filled with profound worry over the current general mood among the workers, especially in the factories, partly connected with serious fears concerning the preservation of political stability in the GDR'. As to why increasing numbers of people were leaving the SED, the report listed the following reasons: disagreement with the way the party's economic policy was implemented and enforced; lack of confidence in the party leadership; rejection of the party's information policy. Another was that '[m]embers feel that they have no convincing arguments when dealing with people not in the party and that they can therefore no longer represent the party line.' 'University teachers (SED members) said that they feel increasingly uncomfortable during lectures and seminars, since more and more students are bringing up politically sensitive themes and asking questions to which they can give no convincing reply without casting doubt on party fundamentals.'

One month later, on 8 October, 'progressive forces, and SED members in particular', had come to the conclusion that the socialist state and societal order of the GDR is in serious danger... Numerous members of the progressive forces, including many workers, especially younger ones, fear that there will be major disruptions in the country that the party will not be able to control. Already now—so they argue—the GDR finds itself in a situation similar to the one just before the counter-revolutionary events on 17 June 1953.

The 'progressive forces', according to the Stasi, admitted to

becoming increasingly uncertain in their judgement of the situation and possessing no arguments to persuade the workers... During relevant ideological debates in the work collectives, many progressive forces say that they are being confronted with a wide range of discussions concerning the existence of a so-called privileged class in the GDR (meaning party functionaries and directors of state and economic management bodies, from the central down to the district level) as well as with references to the massive expansion of black marketeering and speculation. These discussions, which are very aggressively conducted, contain the argument that the above-mentioned circles of people are the real beneficiaries of socialism. Apparently, it is said, it is no longer fashionable in our society to earn money in an honest way.

At the tenth meeting of the SED central committee on 10 November 1989, Gerhard Schürer described his personal dilemma:

I myself have been living in conflict for many years. How far can I go with my opinion, recognizing it to be the truth, if it does not correspond to the party line? How do I best serve the party—by acquiescing in the decision taken once the problems have been discussed? I have done that, and I believed I had to, because that was the statute. Or would it have been better to go further, to the point of accepting scandal or being thrown out of the party? But how can I serve the party then, and expend my energy helping it discover the truth and work on?

The director of the State Planning Commission was not alone in this conflict. Many GDR technocrats—the 'institutionalized counter-elite', as western observers like Peter Christian Ludz had called them in the 1960s—faced a similar predicament.

Whenever high-level decisions were made in the GDR, it was always a 'strategic clique' (Ludz's term) that had the final say. There was, in fact, no 'institutionalized counter-elite', but only individual experts who, when the chips were down, turned out to be powerless. The GDR was *not* a 'polycratic' state. The institutional concentration of power was greater than in the Third Reich—in which, of course, 'polycratic' structures existed only as long as Hitler desired or tolerated them. In terms of the powers it lay claim to, the 'Marxist-Leninist' SED was a totalitarian organization right up to the end. The institutions of the GDR contained no checks and balances capable of restricting it. Nonetheless, the party was increasingly unable to assert its claim to total power. Western television provided a potent corrective to its monopoly on truth and propaganda. Once the GDR signed the Helsinki Final Act in 1975, it had to rein in the terror. It remained a police and surveillance state, and the surveillance actually increased in intensity and coverage. Still, as a consequence of the intensive communication between the inner opposition and the western public, its repressive potential could not be deployed as massively as before.

The moral erosion of the 'socialist' German state proceeded at the same rate as its growing material dependence on 'capitalism'. The governments in Bonn stabilized the GDR, but they inadvertently stabilized it to death. The 'Germany policy' of the 1970s and 1980s was aimed at bringing about humanitarian relief and avoiding chaos in East Germany. But its stabilization by the west made it easier for the GDR to turn its back on the political reforms of the Gorbachev era—reforms its 'fraternal countries', including the Soviet Union itself, considered unavoidable. In refusing to change, the SED progressively lost the support of its own membership. In the end, a fairly trivial amount of revolutionary mass pressure was sufficient to bring down the regime.

The day after the wall fell, Egon Krenz informed his central committee colleagues that a 'very complicated situation' had arisen. (The CC was scheduled to end its congress on 9 November, but continued into the next day on account of the unresolved problems.)

The situation has come to a head in the capital, in Suhl, and in other cities. Panic and chaos are spreading. Workers are abandoning factories . . . The party workers do not understand the new travel possibilities decided upon. Erfurt is reporting a large onrush at the Wartha checkpoint. There is a great disturbance among the party comrades, since nobody can really predict the economic effects and consequences. The opinion is widespread that the big sell-out is coming.

The 'sell-out' could only mean a handing over of the GDR to West Germany. The Soviet Union, which had politically and militarily guaranteed the existence of the East German state up to this point, was no longer willing to play the protector. The border had been opened with the tacit agreement of Moscow, though the Soviets were not involved in the details. It was highly doubtful that the FRG, which had been sustaining the GDR economically for years, would be willing to guarantee its survival. What Crane Brinton called the separation of economic and political powers had also taken place in the GDR. Honecker's 'unity of economic and social policy' was made possible by the fact that the GDR contented itself with political power and made itself economically dependent on West Germany. For this reason—though it is not the only one—the fate of the GDR depended on the decisions taken in Bonn.

For the East German state, the fall of the Berlin wall on 9 November 1989 represented the same thing as the storming of the Bastille on 14 July 1789 meant for France's old regime: a blow from which there would be no recovery. Symbolically speaking, the Berlin wall enclosed no less a prison than the Bastille. When the symbol fell, the old regime was at its end. The 'peaceful revolution' in the German Democratic Republic had now attained the one goal all of the progressive forces could agree on. Other goals would not easily find such accord.[5]

THE 'NATIONAL DEMOCRATIC REVOLUTION'
AND KOHL'S 'TEN POINTS'

Helmut Kohl was in Warsaw when the wall came down. He ended his visit in Poland early in order to be in Berlin on 10 November. Konrad Adenauer had waited ten days to visit the divided city after the wall was built in August 1961. His political heir had no intention of making a similar error. The first crowd Kohl spoke to, gathered on the John-F.-Kennedy-Platz in front of the Schöneberg city hall, had nothing but hisses and boos for him. This was not surprising, since it was composed mostly of supporters of the SPD and the Alternative List, the two parties forming the Berlin government at the time. CDU supporters gathered shortly thereafter at their own demonstration near the Kaiser Wilhelm Memorial Church on the Breitscheidplatz. There Kohl got the applause he was expecting.

During his Schöneberg speech, which was continually interrupted by catcalls from the crowd, Kohl received a message from Mikhail Gorbachev (it came via telephone from the Soviet ambassador in Bonn, Yuli Kvizinski) asking him to do what he could to calm the masses and help avoid 'chaos' in the GDR. The chancellor did what he could. 'Behaving intelligently means not listening to radical slogans and voices,' he told the crowd. 'At the present moment, behaving intelligently means viewing the whole dimension of international, European, and German developments.' It was important 'to find our way carefully into the future, step by step. For it is our *common* future that is at stake. It is liberty that is at stake—liberty above all for our countrymen and women in the GDR, liberty in all areas of their lives.' The chancellor expressed his 'respect' for Gorbachev, and he also did not fail to thank the FRG's three western allies for their 'support and solidarity', which 'were of vital significance for the liberty of free Berlin in the past decades'.

Kohl did not say anything about the political reunification of Germany. Nor did Hans-Dietrich Genscher, Walter Momper, or Willy Brandt, who also spoke at the same event. Nonetheless: 'We are on your side!', he told the Germans in the east. 'We are and will remain one nation, and we belong together!' He concluded with the following words: 'It's about Germany! It's about unity and right and freedom. Long live a free German fatherland! Long live a free, unified Europe!'

The speech that received the most applause on the John-F.-Kennedy-Platz was Willy Brandt's. 'That Germans pull together: that's what this is about,' the former mayor of Berlin and former chancellor told the crowd.

German togetherness is turning out to be something different from what most people expected. And nobody should act as if he knows exactly what form the relationship between the people in the two states is going to take. That they start a new relationship;

that they find their way to each other in liberty, and develop in liberty—that is what this is all about... It was always my firm belief that the cemented partition and the partition of barbed wire and the death strip were standing against the current of history. And this very summer I put it down in writing: Berlin will live, and the wall will fall... The division of Europe, of Germany, and of Berlin grew out of the war and out of the disunity of the victorious powers. Now we are seeing—and I thank the Lord God I may live to see it—how the divided parts of Europe are growing together.

Contrary to popular opinion, Brandt did not make his famous pronouncement 'Now what belongs together is growing together' (*jetzt wächst zusammen, was zusammengehört*) in this particular address. But he had stated it several times that day, at the Brandenburg Gate, in an interview with *Deutschlandfunk*, and to the *Berliner Morgenpost* during the rally on the John-F.-Kennedy-Platz. Germans now found themselves in a situation where 'what belongs together is growing together again,' the newspaper quoted Brandt as saying in its article the following day. 'The same is true of Europe as a whole.' With this comment, Brandt took up and expanded a statement he had made a quarter century before, when he was mayor of Berlin. 'Germany must be united,' he had said on 12 August 1964, the third anniversary of the building of the wall, 'bringing together what belongs together.'

Despite the differences in what the speakers at the Schöneberg city hall had to say (the youngest of them, Walter Momper, was much less 'patriotic' than Kohl, Genscher, and Brandt), on one thing they were agreed: all of them wanted to counter any kind of nationalist exuberance that could unsettle Germany's neighbours or the rest of the world. Two days before, the Bundestag had held its last debate over the chancellor's report on the 'state of the nation in divided Germany'. It was characterized by the same general reservation concerning the goal of German political unity as in the Schöneberg speeches (though, like these, some voices were more reserved than others). The chancellor was no exception. While he did use the word 'reunification' in his Bundestag speech, he was not talking about an immediate political goal, but describing what he took to be the duty the German constitution imposed on the Germans: 'Free exercise of the right to self-determination by all Germans is the prerequisite to reunification in liberty... The German question is a question of liberty and self-determination.'

The opposition groups in the GDR rejected the idea of German reunification as sharply as did groups within the West German SPD and Greens. In the 'programmatic speech' he gave at the founding of the Social Democratic party in the GDR in Schwante on 7 October, the Evangelical theologian Markus Meckel said that in the light of the European situation, such as it had developed in the forty-five years since 1945, the 'talk of reunification' was 'extremely unproductive and basically backward-looking, since now there will definitely not be a reunification.' Meckel rationalized his acceptance of German partition as follows: 'We recognize the existence of two German states as a consequence of our people's culpable past. Options within the framework of a European peace order are not impossible in the future, but they cannot form the goals of political action at present.'

Democracy Now made similar arguments.

Our special relationship to the Federal Republic of Germany, based in the unity of German history and culture, is highly valued by Democracy Now . . . Nonetheless, Democracy Now assumes the existence of two German states. The long-term political solution to this and related questions can only take place within the framework of a European peace order.

A 1 October manifesto from the New Forum, deliberately quoted by Hans-Jochen Vogel in the Bundestag on 8 November, read: 'Reunification is not on our agenda, since we assume the existence of two German states and do not aspire to a capitalist social order. We want changes in the GDR.'

Once the wall came down, the defenders of the continued existence of two German states were quickly put on the defensive. Hartmut Zwahr has called 9 November 1989 *die Wende in der Wende* ('the turning point within the turning point') and the transition to a new phase of 'peaceful revolution', namely 'national democratic revolution'. Calls like 'Germany!' and 'The wall must come down!' were not frequently heard in October. It was not until 13 November, four days after the wall fell, that the Leipzig crowds began to chant a verse from the GDR national anthem: *Deutschland einig Vaterland!* ('Germany, united Fatherland!'; the words were by Johannes R. Becher, the music by Hans Eisler. After the early 1970s the anthem was only played, not sung). Another chorus at the same demonstration ran: 'Black, red, gold! Saxony a Free State! Free Europe!' At a rally in Auerbach in the Vogtland four days later there was a banner that read 'Vogtland our home, Germany our fatherland, Europe our future'.

Contrary to widespread opinion, the chorus 'We are one people!' was not or only rarely heard. One flyer by three Leipzig 'base groups' for the 9 October demonstration ran: 'We are one people. Violence among us will leave behind eternally bleeding wounds.' But that was an appeal to the authorities, not a statement for German unity. West German stickers with the words 'We are one people' were sold in Leipzig on 20 November. According to Hartmut Zwahr, banners with the words 'Reunification yes! We are *one* people!' did not appear at a Leipzig Monday demonstration until 4 December. The passage from the national anthem, on the other hand, was louder and more enthusiastic and more frequently displayed with each rally. On 20 November it was much more noticeable than the week before, and on 27 November, when 200,000 people hit the streets again, it was seen and heard all over.

The nationalist turn was very troubling to most of the activists. They had the feeling that the protest movement was about to take a new direction, one they did not desire. They were correct. By the middle of November, however, most of the demonstrators were not the same ones who had been on the streets in September and October. Older people got involved in large numbers for the first time. Workers were now more prevalent than intellectuals. The 'silent majority' in the GDR articulated their demand for equal rights with the fortune-favoured West Germans by calling for reunification.[6]

Not all reactions from West Germany were encouraging. The 16 November issue of the *tageszeitung* came out with 'theses for a new Green Germany policy' by Joschka Fischer. This was a draft for the upcoming Green party strategy conference in Saarbrücken. 'Is the threat of reunification real?' Fischer asked rhetorically. 'Has the single Little German national state (that is, without Austria) returned to the agenda of history, as leading Union politicians never weary of asserting?' Fischer disputed that this was the case, and he did not wish it to be, for historical-moral reasons.

Bismarck's German nation state, the German Reich, twice inflicted war on the world, war that caused inconceivable suffering . . . The post-war order set up in Europe after 8 May 1945 had one main goal, which it still has today: feverish fits of violent German nationalism must never again strike fear in the hearts of Europeans, and therefore Germany must never again be allowed to become a belligerent great power . . . We leftists are living and making politics in the country that set up and ran the gas chambers and crematoria of Auschwitz-Birkenau and that followed its Führer Adolf Hitler faithfully, to the point of self-destruction . . . If, forty-five years after Auschwitz, we react with panic to all things nationalist in Germany, then that is not a cause for shame and criticism, but the duty of every democrat for at least another forty-five years, if we wish to survive.

On 17 November, one day after this Green attack on reunification, Hans Modrow, the new prime minister of the GDR, spoke before the Volkskammer. Managing the economic crisis and pushing through democratic reforms were the most important goals of his government, he told the delegates. His suggestion that East and West Germany form a *Vertragsgemeinschaft* ('treaty community' or 'contractual community') caused a great stir. Modrow saw this as an alternative to the 'unrealistic and dangerous speculations over a reunification', which he firmly rejected.

Despite the great differences in their social orders, the two German states look back on centuries of common history. Both sides should realize that herein lies an opportunity to give their relationship a good-neighbourly character, in a qualified sense . . . The government of the GDR is prepared to extend its cooperation with the FRG across the board and to elevate it to a new level . . . We want to undergird the community of responsibility between the two German states with a contractual community, one that goes far beyond the Basic Treaty and the other accords and agreements already concluded between the two states.

In rejecting the reunification, the SED knew that it was still in agreement with most of the opposition. On 26 November a number of prominent intellectuals and artists (including the social scientist Dieter Klein, considered a 'SED reformer'; the writers Stefan Heym, Volker Braun, and Christa Wolf; the Evangelical superintendent Günter Krusche, and civil rights activists Sebastian

Pflugbeil, Ulrike Poppe, Friedrich Schorlemmer, and Konrad Weiss) came out with a manifesto entitled *Für unser Land*.* There were two ways for the GDR to get out of its deep crisis, it said. It could either remain an independent state, developing a 'society of solidarity' that 'guarantees peace and social justice, individual liberty, free movement for all, and environmental protection', or else it would have to face the prospect of being 'appropriated' by the economically powerful Federal Republic. The signatories were for the first option, which represented, in reality, a 'third way' between capitalism and communism. 'We still have a chance to develop a socialist alternative to the Federal Republic as an equal partner in the neighbourhood of European states. We still have time to remember the antifascist and humanist ideals that once guided us. We call upon all citizens who share our hope and our concern to join us in signing this appeal.'

By this time it was clear that the initiators of *Für unser Land* did not speak for a majority of their countrymen and -women. On 18 and 19 November, the second weekend after the opening of the wall, more than 3 million people from the GDR had visited West Germany and West Berlin (according to the ADN). For most, the personal impressions they gained from the west fostered a desire for unity. Between 20 and 23 November, West German pollsters reached the unanimous conclusion that more than 60% of the East German population favoured reunification. The same was true of the West Germans. In its 'Polit-Barometer' programme on 20 November, ZDF reported that 70% of those polled supported reunification, 60% were for a neutral reunified Germany, and 48% believed that unity was possible within ten years.

On the evening of 23 November Chancellor Kohl, after consulting with his closest advisers, decided to take the initiative. The immediate background for this decision was a conversation two days before between Horst Teltschik, director of foreign and Germany policy issues in Department II of the chancellor's office, and Nicolai Portugalov, a member of the department for international relations in the central committee of the Soviet Communist party. Portugalov, elucidating the contents of a handwritten document, told Teltschik that the Kremlin was now 'thinking the practically unthinkable', for example about some kind of German confederation. Teltschik was the author of various speech drafts that then, after the talk with Portugalov, gave rise to Kohl's 'Ten Points', a plan the chancellor delivered to the Bundestag on 28 November. Neither his coalition partner, nor the foreign office, nor any of the FRG's western allies except President Bush were informed in advance about Kohl's move.

In his Bundestag address, the chancellor offered the GDR further cooperation if it resolved and put in motion a thorough and irreversible transformation of its political and economic system. He took up Modrow's idea of a *Vertragsgemeinschaft* and declared his willingness 'to go a decisive step further, namely,

* *For Our Country.*

to work out confederative structures between the two states in Germany with the aim of creating a federation, a federal order in Germany.' Kohl stressed that German–German developments would remain embedded in the pan-European process and east–west relations overall. The future architecture of Germany had to fit into the future architecture of Europe as a whole. Nobody yet knew what a united Germany would look like, he said. 'But that unity will come if the people in Germany want it—of that I am sure.' In his last point the chancellor emphasized again explicitly: 'Reunification, that is, the restoration of Germany's unity as a state, remains the political goal of the Federal German government.'

All fractions except the Greens supported Kohl's Ten Point programme. Hans-Jochen Vogel, who spoke before the chancellor, also emphasized the importance of linking the German to the European process of unification. Common German–German institutions and the creation of a German confederation could, Vogel said, be important steps toward the goal of German unity and liberty, which 'should be completed, at the latest, together with the unity and liberty of Europe in accordance with the Helsinki process'. After Kohl spoke, Karsten Voigt, the SPD foreign and security policy speaker, came out in support of the Ten Points, saying that they agreed with Social Democratic thinking. (He had first consulted with Vogel.) There was one conspicuous gap in Kohl's plan: no mention was made of the inviolability of Poland's western border. Voigt, too, passed over this matter in silence.

The Ten Points represented a major risk for the West German chancellor. One foreign head of government had already firmly rejected the idea of German reunification. The Israeli prime minister Yitzhak Shamir, in an interview with an American television station on 15 November, said that if the Germans once again became 'the strongest nation in Europe and perhaps in the world', they might again use the opportunity to kill millions of Jews. Kohl could safely assume that no other western or eastern statesman would express himself in such an extreme manner. Nonetheless, he was well acquainted with the widespread resistance to the idea of a renascent German national state. In presenting his allies with a fait accompli on 28 November, Kohl could expect them to be very seriously annoyed.

And in truth, François Mitterrand and Margaret Thatcher were both furious. Only George Bush, who received Kohl's advance warning about the Bundestag speech on the morning of 28 November, immediately assured the chancellor of his full support. Bush left it for his secretary of state, James Baker, to make the most important American stipulation clear at a press conference on 29 November: a reunited Germany would have to belong to NATO. Moscow sharply rejected the Ten Points—an unpleasant surprise for Kohl, who was expecting an encouraging response in the light of Teltschik's talk with Portugalov. When Genscher went to Moscow shortly thereafter, Gorbachev told him (5 December) that Kohl's manner of turning to the people in the GDR was 'revanchism incarnate'. Shevardnadze went so far as to say that 'not even Hitler would have permitted himself such a move.'

Gorbachev's meeting with Genscher had been preceded by a Soviet–American summit in Malta on 2 and 3 December, where Bush had made the American position very clear. One could not expect the United States to reject the reunification of Germany, he said, responding to Gorbachev's argument that the existence of two German states was simply the 'product of history'. On the other hand, the United States was determined to uphold the inalterability of the Polish western border.

The Malta talks were followed on 4 December by a meeting between the leaders of the NATO states in Brussels. Kohl sought to calm his allies by telling them that further western integration was a prerequisite for his plan and that the last stage of German reunification, the federation, would not be practicable for years, perhaps five. Bush clearly restated his support for reunification here, too. American policy was guided by four fundamentals, he said. The first was the principle of free self-determination, and none of the possible paths to German unity was to be favoured or excluded in that process. Secondly, a reunified Germany would have to belong to NATO and the EC. Thirdly, reunification would have to take place stepwise and peacefully. Finally, the inviolability of the borders, such as it had been codified in the Helsinki Final Act, would have to be upheld. Margaret Thatcher and the Italian prime minister Giulio Andreotti objected to reunification, but found no support among the rest of the group. One by one, the NATO partners declared their support for Bush's four fundamentals. Kohl had gained an interim victory.

The leaders of the European Community member states met in Strasbourg on 8 and 9 December. Kohl had informed Mitterrand beforehand that he would go a long way towards accommodating France on the question of economic and monetary union. At Strasbourg, the chancellor announced his support for the plan to start a preparatory conference at the end of 1990. Without this concession, it is difficult to imagine that the French president would have agreed to the declaration of support for German reunification that was finally, after long controversial debates, written into the summit's concluding statement. Repeating the classic formula from the 1970 'Letter on German Unity', the European Council declared that it aspired to strengthen 'the condition of peace in Europe in which the German people can regain their unity in free self-determination'.

Kohl was partially responsible for the controversy. He still refused to make a clear declaration on the finality of the Oder–Neisse border, pointing to the fact that a peace treaty had not yet been concluded. Ultimately a compromise was worked out between France and Germany. The final statement tied the recognition of the German right to political unity to the condition that this process 'take place peacefully and democratically, in the context of dialogue and west–east cooperation, in adherence to the relevant agreements and treaties as well as to all principles set forth in the Final Act of Helsinki' and that it be 'embedded in the perspective of European integration'. A week later, on 14 and 15 December in Brussels, the foreign and defence ministers of the NATO states declared their support for the German right to self-determination in exactly the same words.

The French and British misgivings were still far from dispelled. With American support, however, the FRG's position was strong enough to gain the recognition of the fundamental right of the Germans to self-determination and unity. The moment was propitious. It was, in fact, the first time since the founding of the two German states that a real opportunity for unification had arisen. The French president avoided criticizing Kohl's Ten Points as openly as did Margaret Thatcher. Nonetheless, his official visit to the GDR a few days later (20–22 December) made his reservations on the subject unambiguously clear. Mitterrand was the first (and last) western head of state to visit East Germany. American support for reunification was of inestimable importance to the West German government. In December 1989, however, nearly all participants and observers found it difficult to imagine that the Soviet Union would ever agree to the American demand that a reunified Germany belong to NATO.

The *ex post facto* support of the west for his Ten Points was a great personal and political triumph for Helmut Kohl. It was a bold initiative, and there is every reason to believe that the factor of surprise was one of the conditions for its success. If the chancellor had consulted his allies beforehand, then intensive deliberations surely would have followed, and the issue might well have been deliberated to death. Kohl could not afford to take this risk. Once he had publicly committed himself to German reunification and received Washington's support, effective resistance from London, Paris, and Rome was only possible at the price of a serious crisis in the Atlantic alliance and the European Community.

The chancellor was willing to pay a high price for French assent. After December 1989 it became increasingly clear that the European Monetary Union, which was very important to France, would be put in place before the Political Union, which was West Germany's main interest. This meant that the German mark would give way to a new European currency before Europe had found its political identity and transformed itself into a state-like entity. This was a risk Kohl was willing to take, for the sake of German reunification and French support for it. He knew that the only way of dispelling French and European anxieties about a powerful Germany was by giving up the Deutschmark, the symbol par excellence of West German economic might, and adopting a common European currency. This he was willing to do. The tactician of power had become a statesman. When the decisive moment came, Helmut Kohl acted with such purpose, mastery, and sure instinct that the memories of his numerous weaknesses, blunders, and acts of political ineptitude began to fade.

On the domestic political front, too, the *fait accompli* of 28 November turned out to be a clever stratagem. The Social Democrats had no opportunity to consult with the deputy party head, Oskar Lafontaine, who was aspiring to be his party's candidate for the chancellorship in the 1990 federal elections. Hans-Jochen Vogel was as patriotic as the chancellor. Although he had long been more sceptical than Kohl about a nation state solution to the German question, that changed with the fall of the wall. Now Vogel also considered German political unity a realistic option, and he, too, wanted to link German unification to the process of European unification as much as possible. For Lafontaine, on the other hand, the nation state in general and the German nation state in particular were historically obsolete. German reunification was not desirable, and it could be downright dangerous if it happened before and independent of the European process.

The SPD deputy head and prime minister of Saarland was also guided by tactical considerations. Elections were scheduled in his home state on 28 January, and he wished to use them as a plebiscite for his chancellorship candidacy. During his electoral campaign, Lafontaine talked about the continued arrival of immigrants from the GDR, as well as of ethnic German immigrants from throughout eastern Europe (so-called *Volksdeutsche*), primarily in terms of the financial burdens they placed on the West German state. In an interview with the *Süddeutsche Zeitung* on 25 November, for example, he called for radical changes in the citizenship law in order to make it impossible for the immigrants 'to gain access to the social insurance programmes of the Federal Republic' (child benefits, health and unemployment insurance, pensions, etc.). As Lafontaine saw it, this revocation of a single German citizenship was justifiable and necessary because the GDR was in the process of becoming a democracy and because it made more sense for West Germany to provide financial incentives for the East Germans to stay in the GDR rather than for them to leave.

Lafontaine hoped that this populist approach would negate the effects of Kohl's emotional patriotism. When asked about the upcoming SPD party congress in Berlin, which was supposed to work out a new Germany policy platform, Lafontaine, who was also managing director of the platform commission, had the following to say:

For us, the question of reunification has already been answered. The SPD is for a European unity that includes both the GDR and Poland and therefore the territories beyond the Oder and Neisse rivers. The focus now is on the steps towards this goal, and whoever wants European unity cannot reject the political unity of the GDR and FRG as an intermediate step. The question is, within what period of time will it take place, and under what conditions? . . . The nation state of the old type is increasingly unimportant—which can also be seen in the fact that we and the other states of the EC are always handing over powers to the European Community . . . It is obvious that the conservative right wing of the Union is being guided by the old nation state model and is overemphasizing the German nationalist aspect. Today that is out of date, and it also has nothing to do with the current desires and sentiments of the people in the GDR.

After Kohl's speech on 28 November Vogel, in full agreement with Brandt and Voigt, had seen to it that the parliament—all except the Green party delegates—supported the chancellor's Ten Points. Lafontaine was going to do his best to make sure that did not happen again. On 29 November the SPD Bundestag fraction refused to support the inter-party statement (CDU/CSU,

FDP, and SPD) on Germany policy unless three points were added to the chancellor's ten: the inviolability of the Polish western border, the right to self-determination, and the question of short-range missiles. Since the coalition did not agree to this, only the Union and Free Democratic delegates voted for the statement on 1 December.

Two days later, Lafontaine began steering towards a direct confrontation with the chancellor. In a 3 December radio interview he attacked what he called the administration's 'kohl-onialism' of the people in the GDR. Later that day he called the Ten Points a 'huge diplomatic failure'. The Social Democrats now presented themselves to Germany and the world as a Janus-faced party, with the patriotic face of Willy Brandt looking in one direction, and the post-national face of Oskar Lafontaine looking in the other.[7]

THE ROUND TABLE AND THE 'CONTROLLED IMPLOSION' OF THE GDR

Meanwhile, dramatic events were again coming thick and fast in the GDR. On 23 November Günter Mittag, former member of the politburo, was thrown out of the SED and proceedings against Erich Honecker began. On 8 December came the announcement that the state prosecutor of the GDR had begun investigating Honecker, Erich Mielke, Willi Stoph, Werner Krolikowski, Hermann Axen, and Günther Kleiber (another former politburo member) for abuse of office and corruption. All but Honecker and Axen were arrested. Honecker was spared arrest and interrogation for reasons of health, and Axen was in Moscow for an eye operation.

On 1 December the Volkskammer, acting on a petition from all parties, struck from Article 1 of the GDR constitution the passage codifying the 'leadership of the working class and its Marxist-Leninist party'. (The vote was unanimous, with five abstentions.) Two days later the SED central committee convened for a special session. Erich Honecker, Werner Krolikowski, Horst Sindermann, Willi Stoph, Harry Tisch, Alexander Schalck-Golodkowski (who had fled to the west the night before), and other former leading party functionaries were thrown out of the SED.

Thereafter the whole politburo and central committee, led by Egon Krenz, stepped down. This was in response to a demand that Gregor Gysi and other speakers in the name of the 'party base' had made at a demonstration the previous day, to great acclaim. On 4 December the CDU and LDPD announced their departure from the 'Central Democratic Bloc', thus abandoning their traditional self-image as 'bloc parties'. Krenz resigned as head of the State and National Defence Councils on 6 December. He was replaced in the former office by Manfred Gerlach, head of the LDPD, who had been distancing himself from the SED in the weeks before.

Egon Krenz had been in power not even seven weeks. By the end of that period the 'power' he led and represented was a mere shadow of its former self. Krenz was not the only one whose lack of personal credibility undermined his pretension to renew the SED and make it into a 'new kind of party'. The party as a whole, faced with the radically altered conditions of a 'new kind of revolution', could not long continue to be what it still was, according to its structure: a top–down, Leninist cadre party. What would become of it once it had been compelled to give up its 'leading role', and whether it would even survive as a political party: these questions were completely open on the evening of 3 December. Unless it began afresh with new personnel, a new organization, and a new platform, it had no chance in a German Democratic Republic desiring to do justice to its name—and less than no chance in a reunified Germany.

On 7 December, four days after the abdication of the 'old' SED, the Round Table (also called the Central Round Table in order to distinguish it from similar bodies on the local level) convened in Berlin for its first session. Composed of 'new' and 'old' elements in equal proportion, the Round Table was the product of an initiative by a 'contact group' formed on 4 October by seven civil rights organizations, Democracy Now, Democratic Awakening, the Peace and Human Rights Initiative, the New Forum, the United Left (*Vereinigte Linke*), the SDP, and the Green party. The Evangelical and Catholic churches had supported the project and now provided the mediators. The SED and the other 'old' parties got on board at the end of November.

The activists wanted the Round Table to temporarily assume a number of responsibilities that, in democratic countries, are exercised by parliaments. Until free elections for the Volkskammer could be held, the government was to render account to the Round Table concerning the country's ecologic, economic, and fiscal situation; inform it in advance of all important decisions; discuss these with it, and accept its advice and proposals. The Round Table was to work up the draft of a new constitution, a new voting law, and legislation on the organization of parties and other associations. It was to be strictly bound to the principle of the rule of law, provide for the investigation and prosecution of abuse of office and corruption, and, not least, oversee the dissolution of the Office for National Security (the new name of the Ministry for State Security since 17 November). One idea was very far from the minds of the East German 'peaceful revolutionaries': the immediate takeover of political power. They wanted to guarantee a non-violent transition from a democratically illegitimate to a democratically legitimate government, nothing more and nothing less.

For the SED, political wisdom dictated cooperation with the 'contact group'. A Round Table could bring greater political legitimacy to the Modrow government and help channel the protest. Above all, it could help divert the mass pressure for reunification with the FRG. For despite everything that separated the SED from the opposition, for the time being it still had at least one thing in common with the majority of the activists: belief in the political independence of the GDR.

This was explicitly stated at the conclusion of the Round Table's first session on 7 December: 'The members of the Round Table are meeting together out of deep concern for our profoundly crisis-ridden country, for its independence, and for its sustained development.'

There was also agreement on another point: the first free elections for the Volkskammer should take place on 6 May 1990. This was a symbolically important date, calling to mind the notorious municipal elections of 7 May 1989 and the systematic fraud behind their outcome. It also gave the new groups the time they needed to consolidate themselves enough to organize effective campaigns.

The first of the 1989 Round Tables, that in Poland, had been wrested from a regime still strong enough at the time to push through a stepwise transition to democracy, to take place over the course of several years. By the time its Berlin counterpart was in place, the collapse of the old order was already far advanced. The West German political scientist Uwe Thaysen, who participated as an observer at the Round Table meetings, spoke of the 'controlled implosion' of the GDR:

The actors at the Round Table, calculating the consequences of the collapse, saw to it that the fragments of this dangerous process—hardly less dangerous than an explosion—affected as few people as possible. Thus they blocked the kinds of mechanisms that tend to unleash the guillotines in the penultimate phase of revolutions.

Probably one of the reasons for this success lay in the fact that the parity of 'old' and 'new' elements existed only on paper. By this time, the 'old' forces were very different from what they were before the 'peaceful revolution'. The former bloc parties had vital interest in emancipating themselves from the SED, and the SED could only survive if it became a new party.

During the course of an extraordinary party congress, held on 8–9 and 16–17 December, the Socialist Unity Party of Germany transformed itself into the SED/PDS, the second part of the name standing for Party of Democratic Socialism (*Partei des Demokratischen Sozialismus*). This double name revealed the difficulties involved in bringing together reformers and traditionalists. Critics of the SED dictatorship and its Stalinist practices were cheek by jowl with those who openly declared their intent to continue the work of Marx, Engels, and Lenin.

Gregor Gysi gave the opening speech at the congress. He was president of the East Berlin Lawyers' Collegium, head of the Council of Presidents of the Lawyers' Collegia in the GDR, and, after 3 December, director of the interim 'work committee' of the SED. His address was a balancing act. On the one hand he demanded a 'complete break with the failed Stalinist, and by this I mean administrative-centralist socialism in our country' and a commitment to individual liberty and basic rights; democratic separation of powers; free forms of economic, political, and cultural competition; radical democracy; the rule of law, and humanism. On the other hand, he lamented that the democratic achievements of the west were limited by the interests of capitalist monopolies.

We must not gamble away the democratic awakening of the people in the GDR and their right to self-determination. But that is what we would be doing if we allowed a new regime of capitalist magnates to take over where the old regime of polit-bureaucrats left off. The crisis of administrative-centralist socialism in our country can only be solved if the GDR takes a third way, beyond Stalinist socialism and the rule of trans-national monopolies . . . This orientation towards a third way uncovers and takes up the democratic and humanist sources of our traditions in the German and international workers' movement. These include, above all, social democratic, socialist, non-Stalinist communist, anti-fascist, and pacifist traditions. We are not talking about new wallpaper, we are talking about a new party.

Gysi firmly rejected the 'dissolution of the party and its refounding'. In his view, this could only be a 'catastrophe for the party'.

We would be disappointing all the people who have worked so hard throughout the whole country in the past weeks for the renewal of their party. They don't want to rescue just any party, but our party. By what right would we rob ourselves of our political home? Besides, this would create a political vacuum in our country that nobody could fill and that would exacerbate the crisis, with unforeseeable consequences.

There was another reason not to dissolve the SED, one Gysi did not mention: it would have meant losing the party assets. Virtually none of the active members were willing to do this. Gysi also affirmed a commitment to the welfare of members of the old party, state, and security apparatus, something a liquidation of the SED would have made very difficult. In October 1989 the party had numbered some 2.3 million members. By December 1989 it was down to 1.5 million, and by February 1990, when the name was changed to just PDS, the numbers fluctuated between 700,000 and 650,000. The leadership was now dominated by reformers like Gysi, elected party head in December by an overwhelming majority, and two of his three deputies: prime minister Hans Modrow and the mayor of Dresden, Wolfgang Berghofer (who had already left by January 1990, however). The conservative forces were far stronger at the party 'base', especially in the orthodox Communist Platform (*Kommunistische Plattform*), which numbered 3,500 members at the beginning of 1994.

What Gregor Gysi and the other leaders had to say at the congress was seen by many members merely as the tactically unavoidable accommodation to the new situation. Most of them vacillated between critique and apologetics in their attitude towards the GDR and towards the traditions of German and international communism. Their feelings about western-style democracy were correspondingly ambivalent. One of the convictions underlying what Gysi called the 'third way' was that democracy would not reach its full maturity until it was transformed by socialism. 'Capitalist' democracy was seen as only partially worth preserving, and wholly in need of reform.

The parties of the former 'bloc' made a far more radical break with the past. The SED loss of power offered them the opportunity to overcome their satellite status and return to their bourgeois origins. In the CDU, a 'Letter from Weimar' had caused considerable unrest in the party leadership already on 10 September 1989. It was signed by Christine Lieberknecht, a pastor, and Martin Kirchner, a high church official (who would later be exposed as a former IM with the Stasi). Its demands—for the fostering of the public sphere, respect for the political maturity of the citizens, disclosure of the economic problems and travel issues, and a new media policy—were all still considered subversive at the time.

The *Neue Zeit*, mouthpiece of the CDU, reprimanded the letter's four signatories, and the party head Gerald Götting initiated proceedings to have them thrown out. But it was too late. Götting was forced to resign his posts on 2 November. He was replaced on 10 November by Lothar de Maizière, an attorney and member of the Synod of the Federation of Evangelical Churches in the GDR. It was his first party office. Evidence presented at the end of 1990 revealed that de Maizière had been on the list of Unofficial Collaborators with the MfS ever since 1981, under the name 'Czerni'. But it has never been shown that his contacts with the Stasi went beyond what all legal defenders of civil rights activists were compelled to accept.

The CDU's separation from socialism and from a commitment to two German states did not happen immediately, but in several stages. In his first official position statements de Maizière was still declaring his support for socialism. Then, in the 'basic principles' of the CDU of 18 November, it was 'socialism out of Christian responsibility'. On 17 November the new CDU head entered the Modrow cabinet as minister for church issues and deputy prime minister. On 25 November the CDU came out in support of a 'confederation of the two German states within the current borders, a confederation in which the unity of the German nation will be realized.' (The first GDR politician to speak of a 'German confederation' in autumn 1989 was Günter Hartmann, the new head of the National Democratic Party of Germany, in a speech before the Volkskammer on 17 November.) In a first, unofficial talk between de Maizière and the general secretary of the West German CDU, Volker Rühe, on 24 November, differences in economic and social policy were very much in evidence. De Maizière made no secret about his reservations against capitalism and the free market economy.

The contacts between the East and West German parties grew closer in the first part of December. Wolfgang Schäuble, minister of the interior since April 1989, was the driving force on the western side. The departure of the eastern CDU from the Democratic Bloc on 4 December made the rapprochement easier. The extraordinary party congress in Berlin on 15 and 16 December, at which three of the four signatories of the 'Letter from Weimar' made it into the party leadership, also did much to soothe the qualms of the 'sister party' in the west. Speaking at the congress, de Maizière called upon the CDU to make a 'political confession' and admit its co-responsibility for deformations and crises in East

German society. The term 'socialism', he said, was no longer serviceable. The new platform, 'Positions of the CDU for the Present and Future', declared the party's support for a 'market economy with social commitments in ecological responsibility'.

As for the question of German unity, the eastern CDU now moved in the direction that Helmut Kohl had indicated in his Ten Points. As it was put in the 'Positions': 'Unity of the German nation—with a German confederation as a transitional stage—in a free and unified Europe on the basis of the right to national self-determination.' Nonetheless, the platform commission rejected the term 'reunification'. The Germany that the word 'reunification' implied, its speakers stated, had 'died at Auschwitz, completely and irrevocably'.

The Liberal Democratic Party of Germany began its transformation earlier than the CDU. Manfred Gerlach, LDPD head and GDR vice president, was supporting demands like those in the September 'Letter from Weimar' already in April 1989, albeit not yet publicly. In June the LDPD executive openly referred to the party as part of a 'multi-party system'. On 15 November the Liberal Democrats were the first fraction in the Volkskammer to motion that the passage granting the SED the leading role in the state be struck from the constitution. As late as 26 November, however, Gerlach was still supporting 'socialism with a human face', as he told the FDP leadership under Otto Graf Lambsdorff. The final break with socialism did not come until 19 December in a public declaration by the LDPD executive committing the party to a social and ecological market economy. The statement was also clear on the national question: the LDPD supported German unity within the borders of 1989 and, as steps along the way to this goal, a contractual community and confederative structures, possibly even a 'German confederation' with all-German institutions like a federal assembly and confederation president.

Unlike the West German CDU, the Free Democrats had repeatedly sought to maintain contact with their 'sister party' in the east during the years of partition. But the LDPD was not the FDP's only interlocutor during the revolution. The Thomas-Dehler-Haus in Bonn also cultivated contacts with groups like Democratic Awakening, the German Forum Party (*Deutsche Forumspartei*, a splinter group from the New Forum), and the Free Democratic Party in the GDR, founded in January 1990. Democratic Awakening was also being courted by the West German CDU. On 3 December it became the first opposition group to come out for German unity—prompting sharp protest from one of its prominent founding members, the Wittenberg pastor Friedrich Schorlemmer.

Democratic Awakening officially transformed itself into a political party in Leipzig on 16 December. It declared its support for a 'social market economy with high ecological priorities' and for the unity of the German nation within the current borders, a goal to be realized in a stepwise process leading from a confederation to a federal state and in agreement with Germany's neighbours and the Four Powers. One major point of its Germany policy divided the DA from the Bonn coalition: it wanted a neutral and de-militarized Germany. Despite this difference, Schorlemmer found the DA's shift towards Bonn unbearable. In mid-January he called Kohl's Ten Points the 'greatest disaster after the opening of the borders', since it strengthened 'not our self-confidence, but our neediness'. Schorlemmer left the DA and joined the Social Democrats. The Erfurt pastor Edelbert Richter, hitherto speaker of the DA, did the same.

Another civil rights group came out with a completely different version of German unification at about this same time. On 14 December Democracy Now presented a 'three-stage plan' inspired by the belief that a 'reunification' via annexation of the GDR by the FRG was not a viable solution. 'In our view, the time is not yet ripe for a new German political unity—although unity, based on a society in solidarity, also remains our goal.' As the first step in a 'process of mutual rapprochement', Democracy Now proposed thoroughgoing reforms in both German states, with the Federal Republic moving in the direction of more social justice and more eco-friendliness. The second phase was to be a national treaty between East and West Germany, a confederation, and the creation of a 'dual German citizenship'. The third stage would involve the de-militarization of Germany and the withdrawal of the Allied powers, to be followed by a referendum on political unity in the shape of a federation of German *Länder*. United Germany was then given the task of collaborating in the development of a new cooperative world economic order and the realization of a method of production that would protect the environment.

The call for a federation of German *Länder* and the recognition of two German citizenships meant, in essence, that the partition would first be made more profound before, one day perhaps, it could be overcome. The only partners the initiators could hope to gain for such an enterprise were the West German Greens and a few writers and intellectuals in both countries. In neither would it find a majority. By December 1989, proponents of East German independence had practically vanished from the demonstrations in Leipzig and other cities in the GDR. And when they did show up, they were shouted down. The black–red–gold flag *without* the hammer and compass had become the symbol of a mass movement for 'Germany, united Fatherland', a movement that called the status quo radically into question and had no interest in a 'third way' between the systems. Activists who rejected or wished to postpone reunification were fighting for a lost cause. The pioneers of 'peaceful revolution' were now defending an indefensible situation.

The East German Social Democrats recognized earlier than most of the opposition that continuing insistence on two German states was a ticket into isolation and political irrelevance. On 3 December the party executive published a 'declaration on the German question' supporting the 'unity of the German nation', which was to be shaped by both sides but not rushed into. This was somewhat weaker than the statement by Democratic Awakening on that same day, but it went beyond what a number of prominent West German Social Democrats were saying. Relations between the SDP and the SPD were close and cordial by this time. After the SDP's founding at Schwante on 7 October, Egon Bahr had denied it was a political party. After a talk between Hans-Jochen Vogel and Steffen Reiche, one of the SDP founders, on 23 October, the SPD changed its position, moving towards recognition and support.

Markus Meckel, the second representative of the SDP, gave a brief speech at the SPD policy congress in Berlin on 18 October. Meckel now supported German unity, in contrast to his position ten weeks before in Schwante.

The unification of the Germans and the unification of Europe are one and the same process. Everything that disturbs their connection must be excluded. At the same time, there can be different things driving each part forward, at different stages. Now that the German question is everywhere on the table, it must be dealt with and moved forward in such a way that it also promotes European unity. A special German path will not take us forward. We think as you do: a confederation between the two German states would be an important step, and one that could be put in place quickly. I believe it would already find a majority in both states . . . We must guide the process of German and European unity towards the future—guide it and think it and shape it, avoiding any kind of nation state romanticism.

Willy Brandt, honorary head of the SPD, spoke at the congress on the same day—his seventy-sixth birthday. His whole speech focused on the German question. Nothing would be the same as it once was, he said. 'We can help what belongs together grow together . . . There will be no reunification of parts that were never really together, much less a return to the Reich. That, and that alone, was the "vital lie" of the 1950s, in which I, too, participated, but which I did not think it right to cultivate further.'

Even Social Democrats who were less nationally-minded than the speaker could agree with him thus far. But what Brandt then had to say caused difficulties for many in the audience. He cautioned against delaying the solution to the German question until Europe had been unified.

It would be idle for us—on both sides—to engross ourselves with a certain German thoroughness in the question of what kind of common roof we will live under in the future. But if it is true that parts of Europe are growing together, then what could be more natural than that the Germans cooperate more closely together, in the areas where they have more in common than others in Europe? For nowhere is it written that they, the Germans, must wait on a side track until, some day, a pan-European train reaches the station. That is not what embeddedness means, such as I understand the term. Still, I willingly admit that the journeys of both trains, the European and the German, should be sensibly coordinated. Whom would it benefit if they collided on the tracks somewhere?

Shortly hereafter came a passage that was applauded, as the minutes record. But the applause was far from unanimous. Brandt reiterated an idea he had expressed in the Church of St Mary in Rostock on 6 December.

Young Germans—I may be permitted to say this, who have followed the history of this people over a long period of time—the young Germans of today desire peace and liberty just like young people—at least most of them—do in other countries. And who will seriously contradict me if I add: however great be a nation's guilt, an everlastingly ordained partition is not the way to remove it.

Brandt's speech was aimed at certain Social Democrats whom he did not explicitly name. One of them was Günter Grass, who spoke shortly afterwards with a passionate diatribe against reunification. Nobody in his right mind and possessed of memory, Grass said, could ever again permit a concentration of power in the middle of Europe.

Not the great powers, now emphatically 'victorious powers' once again; not the Poles; not the French; not the Dutch; not the Danes. But not we Germans either. For that unitary state, whose changing executioners, within the short space of seventy-five years, wrote suffering, ruination, defeat, millions of refugees, millions of dead, and the burden of unimaginable crimes into the history books, for others and for us—this unitary state needs no new edition and must never again ignite a political will, regardless of how well-meaningly we now know how to behave.

Even though all Germans had lost the Second World War, Grass continued, the Germans in the GDR had borne the greater part of its burden. For this reason, the Germans in the FRG were obligated to render them far-reaching and unconditional compensation.

Only when our countrymen and -women in the GDR—who are exhausted, with the water up to their necks, but fighting for their liberty, piece by piece—only when they receive what they deserve from us, too, will they be able to speak and negotiate with us on equal terms, and we with them, about Germany and Germany, about two states of one history and one cultural nation, about two confederated states in the European house. Self-determination presupposes full independence, and that includes economic independence.

Grass did not think of confederation as a step along the way to political unity, but its alternative.

Unification as incorporation of the GDR would cause losses that could not be compensated. The citizens of the other state, once it was appropriated, would lose their whole identity, born in suffering and won, finally, in exemplary struggle. Their history crushed by the mindless dictate of unity . . . A reunified Germany would be a colossus loaded down with complexes, standing in its own way and the way of European unity. But a confederation, along with the express renunciation of a unitary state, would promote European unity, especially since the latter, like the new German self-image, will be confederative in nature.

Oskar Lafontaine was another Social Democrat who would have felt that Brandt's words were directed at him. He had a chance to respond the next day. The nominal purpose of his address was to explain the new platform, in which the SPD presented itself as the 'party of democratic socialism'. (The platform commission had no way of knowing that the SED would usurp this name shortly before the SPD congress.) But Brandt's speech the day before gave his words a new meaning. Lafontaine was now countering the nationalist fervour of the honorary head of his party—who was also head of the Socialist International.

'The ideas of free social democracy are international,' Lafontaine said. 'We emphasized internationalism. We consciously set it in contrast to what is everywhere visible as the renaissance of nation states and nation state discourse.' The nation state had to be differentiated from the nation. Citing what Grass had said the day before concerning the cultural nation, Lafontaine emphasized that

reference to the same language, to the same history, to the same ideas cannot necessarily lead us to the conclusion that all those who claim allegiance to these things must be unified in one nation state. This was never the case in the history of the Germans, and it will not be so in the future, regardless of how we solve the issue between the GDR and the Federal Republic. For the German nation cannot be defined within the borders of the GDR and the Federal Republic.

Lafontaine pointed to the example of France. The French nation, he said, was defined according to the revolutionary ideas of liberty, equality, and fraternity. The Germans had a different history of ideas, tied to the concept of the cultural nation. They were what many historians called 'the nation that came too late'. Since at the time of the French Revolution the Germans had not managed 'to define a nation state', Lafontaine saw it as patently absurd to aspire to one now. Instead, the 'policy between the Federal Republic and the GDR' was to be embedded in the long-term developmental trends in the world. With the result that

we must hold to the idea of European unity and that European unity is, indeed, already in the process of transforming the nation state more and more. We are, are we not, in the process of transferring the powers of the nation state to the European Community in increasingly stronger form . . . This process cannot be rolled back. It will go on, if we desire to win the future.

Lafontaine did aver that the Social Democrats, too, wanted 'the people in the GDR and the Federal Republic to pull together more closely'. But then he added:

We have never understood the idea of unity as the abstract idea of a state, but as a coming together and a moving together of the people . . . When asked about German unity, I have said again and again: for me the important thing is that my friends in Leipzig, Dresden, and everywhere have it just as good as I do or as my friends in Vienna. This is the decisive project of the future, comrades!

This statement was greeted with vigorous applause from the audience.

The question of political organization was, in comparison, a 'second question'. It was still important when it came to solving the international problems, Lafontaine said.

But the idea of social justice must take precedence over all else for us in the Federal Republic as well. The idea of social justice always takes precedence over the idea of how future states are to be created. For me—and this will be the debate in the coming months, which I urge the party to engage in—for me the important question is how we organize social justice in the GDR and in the Federal Republic in the coming weeks and months. This is precisely where the Achilles' heel of the conservatives is. This is where we can harry them. With this instrument we can resist all the excesses of nationalism that have emerged again and fight against them in our political work. For the Germans in the GDR and the Federal Republic are primarily interested in how well they are doing, whether they need medical attention, are warm in the winter, have enough to eat, have work, and find housing. That interests them far more than the question of what the legal construct will be within which we will perhaps one day realize our ideas.

It would have been difficult for any West German politician to be more clear than Oscar Lafontaine in telling the East Germans that he had no desire to live with them under a common political roof. While he could not prevent the congress from endorsing the goal of federal unity in its 'Berlin declaration', the deputy SPD head received so much applause for his speech that he could be virtually certain of being awarded the candidacy for the chancellorship.

In his book *Die Gesellschaft der Zukunft* of the previous year, Lafontaine had used the Nazi crimes against humanity as an argument against a new German nation state. In discussing the new Berlin platform, he contented himself with the contention that the 'nation' and the 'nation state' had never been the same thing in Germany. When he named Vienna along with Leipzig and Dresden as cities where his 'friends' should have it as good as he did in West Germany, he made it clear—probably not unintentionally—that he was thinking in the categories of the *grossdeutsch* cultural nation.

The idea of Germany as 'the nation that came too late' was borrowed from Helmut Plessner's book *Die verspätete Nation.** In reality the German nation postdated only those of Britain and France. The problem with the Bismarck empire was not that it solved the national question, or even how it did so, but that it deferred the question of individual liberty. Lafontaine saw it differently, of course. For him, Bismarck's *kleindeutsch* nation state was historically illegitimate by its very nature. Thus it was illegitimate to seek to take it up again in 1989. Three German states—the Federal Republic of Germany, the German Democratic Republic, and the Republic of Austria—were for Lafontaine a perfectly valid, indeed desirable, solution to the German question. The only requirement was that all three also had to demonstrate Lafontaine's version of social justice.

Social justice was also a main concern of Günter Grass. But Grass based his appeal for indemnification of the Germans in the GDR on a completely different and morally more credible argument than Lafontaine's—that is, on

---

* Plessner, *The Belated Nation.*

the particular injustice that resided in the fact that the East Germans had suffered far more because of a war they were no more responsible for than the West Germans. Indemnification was indeed overdue, but that was more a reason *for* unification than an argument *against* it. The reason Grass ended up rejecting reunification had to do with his problematic interpretation of history.

What he said at the SPD congress in Berlin he put in even stronger form on 2 February 1990 in an address entitled 'Kurze Rede eines vaterlandslosen Gesellen'* to the Evangelical Academy in Tutzing.

The German unitary state existed in varying size for just seventy-five years: as the German Reich under Prussian hegemony; as the Weimar Republic, endangered from the very start; and finally, until the unconditional surrender, as the Greater German Reich. We should be conscious—and our neighbours are conscious—of how much suffering this unitary state caused, what the dimensions are of the sorrow it brought to others and to us. The crime of genocide symbolized by Auschwitz, a crime not subject to the least bit of qualification, weighs heavily on this unitary state . . . It formed the precondition for Auschwitz, a precondition put in place at an early date . . . The German unitary state helped provide the National Socialist racial ideology with an appallingly serviceable basis. There is no getting past this realization. Anyone who reflects on Germany at the present time and looks for answers to the German question must think Auschwitz, too. That place of horror, named as an example of perennial trauma, makes a future German unitary state impossible.

The problems with this view of history are obvious. The murder of the European Jews had historical roots reaching back far beyond Bismarck's Reich. They go all the way back to the Christian hatred of the Jews, such as it developed between late antiquity and the Reformation era. The founding of the *kleindeutsch* national state—which unlike the French republic was *not* a unitary, but rather a federal state—did not yet mean that the course was set for Hitler's dictatorship.

The idea of the 'cultural nation' (*Kulturnation*), which Grass and Lafontaine ascribed to Herder, had been introduced into the discussion at the beginning of the twentieth century, accompanied by its counterpart, the nation state or 'political nation' (*Staatsnation*). As Friedrich Meinecke showed in his 1907 book *Weltbürgertum und Nationalstaat*,[†] the German cultural nation preceded the Prussian-dominated German political nation and embraced a far greater territory than the latter. Thus it made no sense if applied only to the Germans who had belonged to the *kleindeutsch* state between 1871 and 1945. Besides, what was being debated in 1989–90 was not the classic, sovereign nation state, such as the German Reich represented. A reunified Germany was now only conceivable as a federal state firmly integrated into Europe—that is, as a post-classical national state, like the other members of the European Community.

---

* Grass, 'Short Speech by an Unpatriotic Comrade' (*vaterlandslos* means literally 'fatherlandless').
[†] Meinecke, *Cosmopolitanism and the National State*.

Grass's views on 'thinking Auschwitz' were shared by many people. The 1980s had seen what we might call an unconscious rededication of the Berlin wall. The wall was now regarded by many West German intellectuals not as a symbol of the East Germans' lack of liberty, but as a memorial to the murdered Jews. Germany had not been divided as a result of the Nazi crimes against humanity, but because the Allies could not agree on the solution to the German question. 'National guilt cannot be removed by arbitrarily dividing a nation,' Brandt had said on 6 December in Rostock. To put it another way: German guilt would not go away if the division were ended. German guilt would *never* go away.

Willy Brandt had always believed that the Germans in the FRG were obligated to preserve a specific kind of solidarity with the Germans in the GDR—that is, national solidarity. This had been the basis of his *Ostpolitik*, at a time when a German national state could be at best a distant goal. Once unification became politically possible in 1989, it became for Brandt a moral necessity. His particular objections to the term 'reunification' were not valid. The Germans who had been living in the FRG and the GDR since 1949 had lived in *one* state for three-quarters of a century, from 1871 to 1945. And the territory of a newly unified Germany would not be identical with that of the German Reich prior to its downfall in 1945. All that remained to reunify was what was left over from the Bismarck empire after two world wars.

It was not Oskar Lafontaine who dominated German politics on 19 December 1989, but Helmut Kohl, who was in Dresden at the time. He had gone there to meet with the East German prime minister about a contractual community between the two states. His visit turned into a rally for reunification and a personal triumph for the chancellor. Wherever Kohl went, people cheered and called out 'Helmut! Helmut!' One banner read 'The Federal State of Saxony greets the Federal Chancellor.' The square in front of the ruins of the Frauenkirche, where Kohl gave a short, unplanned speech that afternoon at the behest of the mayor, was like an ocean of black, red, and gold flags. The citizens of Dresden cried out 'Germany! Germany!', 'Unity! Unity!', and 'Germany, united Fatherland!'

It was no easy speech for Kohl to give. He had to take the feelings of the people into account and, at the same time, avoid awakening false hopes. He had to speak to the call for unity while steering clear of everything that could worsen the crisis in the GDR and create suspicions abroad. But the chancellor was more than equal to the task. 'We do not wish to make up anyone's mind for them, and we will not,' he told the crowd.

We will respect what you decide for the future of the country. We will not leave our compatriots in the GDR in the lurch. And we know how difficult this path into the future is. But I also call out to you: together we shall make our way into the German future!... We want people to feel comfortable here. We want them to remain at home and find happiness here. My goal is still the unity of our nation, if the historical hour permits it. And dear friends, I know that we can reach this goal and that that hour will come if we work for it together, if we work with sense and perspicacity and a mind for what is possible . . . The house of Germany, our house, must be built under a European roof. That must be our political goal . . . God bless our German fatherland!

By the time Kohl left Dresden the next day, he was convinced that the East German regime was on the brink of collapse and that there was no alternative to a reunification within the shortest possible time. Among the agreements he had worked out with Modrow were visa-free travel to East Germany and East Berlin for West Germans beginning on Christmas Eve (and not from 1 January 1990 onwards, as previously planned); a currency exchange rate of one West German to three East German marks once the policy of forced exchange was ended; and, most spectacular of all, the opening of the Brandenburg Gate, the symbol par excellence of Germany divided, to pedestrian traffic before Christmas.

The new crossing was opened on 23 December 1989, accompanied by short speeches from Kohl, Modrow, and the two mayors of Berlin, Walter Momper and Erhard Krack. Richard von Weizsäcker (re-elected president of the FRG by an overwhelming majority that May) had said years before: 'The German question will remain open as long as the Brandenburg Gate remains shut.' The Brandenburg Gate was now open, and the German question was open, too. But it was not difficult to foresee that it would not long remain so.[8]

MODROW IN MOSCOW: THE SOVIET POLICY TURN

Stasi in die Produktion! ('Stasi, to the production lines!') was a frequent chant heard at the demonstrations in autumn 1989 in the cities of the GDR. (It was also sung to the melody of the popular hit 'Ja, wir sind mit'm Radl da'.) The security apparatus had no intention of paying heed to this call, at least not in the way it was intended. It was true that the Ministry for State Security had been formally dissolved on 17 November and replaced by the Office for National Security (*Amt für Nationale Sicherheit* or AfNS; demonstrators referred to it as the 'Nasi'). But its director Wolfgang Schwanitz continued Erich Mielke's policy of destroying sensitive files—an activity countenanced by an ordinance from the Modrow government on 7 December. Special care was taken to destroy such things as plans to prepare and increase the number of 'objects' (i.e. prisons) to be used for the purpose of isolating members of the opposition in event of crisis; mobilization plans; and documents dealing with the deployment of biological and chemical weapons. The Nasi considered itself just as much the 'sword and shield' of the party as the Stasi had done. It continued to spy on the opposition. At the same time, with a view to the end of the dictatorship, it worked to secure positions for 'chekists' in the police force, customs, state agencies, and state companies.

The ordinance from the government told the AfNS 'to destroy all wrongfully compiled documents immediately'. The Round Table, meeting that day for the first time, decided just the opposite: the AfNS was to be dissolved under civilian supervision and the destruction of documents and other evidence was to cease. Thereupon the Modrow government resolved to dissolve the agency itself and set up two others in its stead: one for the protection of the constitution, and one for intelligence.

The activists were unwilling to go along with this and caused the Round Table to issue a decision that the office for constitutional protection should not be set up before the Volkskammer elections on 6 May. The reorganization of the former MfS and the destruction of documents continued, however, with the result that another Round Table decision followed on 8 January 1990, this time supported by the former bloc parties and in the tone of an ultimatum: Modrow was to give a report on the situation of domestic security on 15 January. The prime minister responded on 12 January, announcing the dissolution of the AfNS, proposing Round Table supervision of the process, and promising to delay the constitutional agency until after the elections.

This announcement did not have a calming effect. Modrow's rejection of any unification with the FRG in his 11 January policy statement, along with his tactical manoeuvring on the security question, drove masses onto the streets day after day. On 14 January, Magdeburg alone saw tens of thousands of people demonstrate against 'the return of the SED'. Modrow visited the Round Table on the next day, despite stating on 13 January that Interior Minister Lothar Ahrendt (SED/PDS) would be the one to give the security report. The prime minister promised close cooperation and continual consultation with the Round Table. The most important thing, he said, was 'to eliminate once and for all the grounds for the persistent anxieties and to create mutual trust. Without this trust it will be impossible to move forward on the path to democratic renewal.'

The battle over the Modrow government's handling of the security situation continued to escalate. Some 100,000 people, responding to a call by the New Forum, gathered in front of the (former) MfS building in the Normannenstrasse to demonstrate against the Stasi and Nasi. Things soon got out of control. Thousands stormed the building, ransacked many rooms, and destroyed important evidence. There is good reason to think that *agents provocateurs* from the security system were involved. Round Table representatives, along with the prime minister, tried to calm the crowd, and finally succeeded. But the violence could not be undone. It was now very uncertain that the 'peaceful revolution' would remain peaceful.

The events in the Normannenstrasse exposed what Uwe Thaysen has called a 'power vacuum'. The government by now had so little popular support that Modrow found it necessary to accept the Round Table as the central body of supervision and control. He no longer had any choice. He had decided to change the cabinet from an SED/bloc party monopoly into a 'government of national responsibility', and this could not be done without the Round Table.

Resistance to this plan was strongest in the SDP. At a party congress from 12 to 14 January, the party had changed its name to SPD and adopted reunification as its political goal. Participation in the Modrow government, it feared, would harm its electoral chances. The CDU tried to apply pressure on the Social Democrats on 24 January, threatening to withdraw its own ministers unless a Grand Coalition were formed. The CDU ministers in the Modrow cabinet, it said, would act only in a caretaker capacity from 25 January onward. An agreement was finally reached on 28 January, and a 'government of national responsibility' came together on 5 February. All parties and groups at the Round Table sent one minister without portfolio to the new cabinet. The SPD joined only after the Round Table and the government had agreed to schedule the Volkskammer elections for an earlier date, 18 March 1990. The previous date, 6 May, was kept for municipal elections.

The Round Table's decision to join the government was motivated by fears of economic collapse and general chaos. Many people continued to leave the GDR, 119,000 between the opening of the border on 9–10 November and 31 December 1989, and 55,000 more in January. In an interview for *Die Welt* on 25 January, de Maizière spoke of 2 to 3 million Germans 'sitting on packed suitcases'. Modrow gave a very gloomy account of the situation at the Round Table on 28 January. 'The country's economic and social tensions have increased and are already affecting the daily lives of many people. More and more . . . demands are being made that are far beyond the state's ability to handle and, if we give into them, will put the existence of the GDR at risk.' He told the Volkskammer the same thing the next day.

The rescheduling of the Volkskammer elections fitted in well with Helmut Kohl's desire to start negotiating with a democratically legitimate government in the GDR as soon as possible. It was also in the interests of the SED/PDS and SPD. The former was still the best organized political party in the country, and it could assume that its image would be even worse in May than in March. The Social Democrats believed they could emerge from the elections as the strongest party and gain the prime ministership. The massive popularity of Willy Brandt was not the least of reasons for this optimism. As far as the CDU and LDPD were concerned, everything depended on the relationship with the respective 'sister party' in Bonn. They had reason to hope that the earlier election date would help remove remaining doubts in the west. Democratic Awakening, still vacillating between the western CDU and FDP, was now the most 'pro-western' force among the activist groups; the earlier date did not represent a greater risk for it. For those groups without a strong western partner, on the other hand, the situation was very difficult. If all forces working together in the 'contact group' were to campaign in concert, they could expect a good result. But it was increasingly unlikely that the SPD would refrain from entering the race as an independent party; its poll results were simply too good.

On 30 January Modrow went to Moscow for his second visit as prime minister of the GDR. (The first time had been for political talks with the Soviet leadership on 4 December.) He spoke with Gorbachev, and the result was no less than a sensation. The ADN announced that even before meeting Modrow, Gorbachev had said that there was a certain agreement among the Germans and the representatives of the Four Powers that 'the unification of the Germans is not called into question by anybody.' After his meeting with the Soviet leader, Modrow told journalists that 'problems having to do with the unification of the German states' had been discussed in detail. Gorbachev, he said, had agreed to the statement that 'the two German states should strengthen their relations' with a view to 'continuing the rapprochement between the GDR and the FRG along the path of a confederation'.

It was clear that Gorbachev had performed an about-face. This had been foreshadowed by an interview with Nikolai Portugalov in *Bild* on 24 January. 'If the people of the GDR desire reunification,' the international affairs consultant of the Soviet central committee said, 'then it will come. In no circumstances will we go against this decision. We will not interfere.'

Thus by the end of January the Soviet veto against German reunification was removed and the right of the Germans to self-determination fundamentally recognized, including the right of East and West Germany to make themselves into one state. The one snag in Moscow's position change did not become visible until 1 February, when Modrow introduced his plan 'For Germany, united Fatherland—proposal for the path to a unified Germany' at a press conference in East Berlin. The individual steps along this path were to be the conclusion of a treaty on cooperation and good neighbour relations; the formation of a confederation between the German Democratic Republic and the Federal Republic of Germany; the transfer of sovereignty rights to the confederation; and the formation of 'a unified German state in the shape of a German confederation'. The prerequisite for all this, Modrow stated, was the 'military neutrality of the GDR and FRG on the way to federation'.

For the USA, Great Britain, and France, a militarily neutral united Germany was not acceptable. Gorbachev and Modrow knew this. What was less certain was how the political forces in West Germany would react to Modrow's proposal. It was to be expected that the Kohl administration would uphold the American condition that a united Germany be a member of NATO. Oskar Lafontaine, however, had rejected this as 'historical nonsense' at the Berlin congress of the SPD. It seemed likely that West Germany was headed for another controversy.

Unlike during the Stalinist era, however, this time Moscow and East Berlin were not trying to drive a wedge between the West Germans and their allies. The GDR was now so weak that it depended on the prospect of German unity, and the Soviet Union was no longer strong enough to prevent it. Seen in this light, German neutrality was a maximalist demand, just like the full integration of unified Germany into NATO. A compromise was possible only through negotiation.[9]

NATO OR NEUTRALITY?

Bonn's answer to Modrow's plan was monetary union and the introduction of a market economy in the GDR. The Social Democrats were the first to call for a monetary union—Willy Brandt in wildly cheered speeches in Rostock on 6 December and in Magdeburg on 19 December; Ingrid Matthäus-Maier, the parliamentary fraction's spokeswoman on financial policy, in *Die Zeit* on 19 December; and Wolfgang Roth, the fraction's economics spokesman, on 2 February. On 30 January Finance Minister Theo Waigel committed his agency to the position that the Deutschmark was to be made the official method of payment in the GDR as soon as possible. On 6 February Helmut Kohl, after consultation with the FDP head Otto Graf Lambsdorff, went public: he would propose to the cabinet that they offer the GDR negotiations over a 'monetary union with economic reforms'. The cabinet agreed to this the next day, and put a 'German Unity Committee' in place.

There was now no more talk of a confederation (or of 'confederative structures', as Kohl had put it with deliberate caution on 28 November). Modrow, speaking with the chancellor at the World Economic Forum in Davos on 3 February, described the situation in the GDR in such dismal terms that Kohl saw his view confirmed: the East German state was sinking into chaos. Speedy introduction of the DM seemed the only way to stem the tide of migration into the west. Massive economic assistance of the kind Modrow wanted did not promise any improvement, since his government had not shown the strength to push through radical reforms. It was true that the economic problems associated with monetary union were considerable. According to experts, labour productivity in the GDR was only 50 per cent of the West German level. Both the federal bank and an investigating commission set up by the government stated that they considered a rapid introduction of the DM unrealistic. Politically speaking, however, there was every reason to accelerate the unification process and get rid of the main obstacle to economic recovery, widespread lack of confidence in the future of the territory between the Elbe and the Oder. 'Politically' speaking also meant party politics, of course. It seemed likely that the symbol of the Deutschmark would best serve the electoral interests of the new 'Alliance for Germany', founded on 5 February between the CDU, Democratic Awakening, and the German Social Union (*Deutsche Soziale Union* or DSU, set up under the guidance of the Bavarian CSU on 20 January) in order to counter the Social Democrats. Kohl did not want to make monetary union the subject of his talks in the Kremlin, scheduled for 10 February. But he also did not wish to offend Gorbachev by suddenly announcing the plan right after his Moscow visit. One way out of this dilemma was by creating facts before he went to the Soviet Union.

The result of Modrow's talks with Gorbachev had shown that the military status of a reunified Germany would be the most difficult subject under discussion in Moscow. Foreign Minister Genscher, speaking to the Evangelical Academy at Tutzing on 31 January, had proposed that a united Germany belong to the Atlantic alliance but that the territory of the GDR not be integrated into NATO military structures. When Genscher went to Washington on 2 February, both his American colleague James Baker and President Bush stated their support for his idea. Agreement was also reached on another issue: negotiations over reunification should, following a State Department proposal, be conducted according to a 'two-plus-four' formula, that is, between the two German states and the four former occupying powers. Genscher placed great importance on this precise sequence; the impression that the Four Powers were deciding Germany's fate was to be avoided at all costs. This was not an unrealistic fear. A meeting between the ambassadors of the Four Powers in the building of the Allied Control Council in Berlin on 11 December had provoked heated protests from the Bonn government.

Baker preceded Kohl and Genscher to Moscow, where he conducted talks with Shevardnadze and Gorbachev on 7 February. He had already obtained the support of his colleagues in London and Paris, Douglas Hurd and Roland Dumas, for 'two-plus-four' negotiations. Now he got Gorbachev's agreement. The Soviet leader would have preferred a 'four-plus-two' scenario, but did not consider the difference terribly important. He also proved surprisingly conciliatory on the alignment question. He was even willing to entertain the idea of NATO membership for all of Germany if it could be guaranteed that the Atlantic alliance would not extend itself any further eastwards. This did not yet mean Gorbachev actually accepted the American proposals, however, as would be seen shortly.

When Kohl and Genscher met with the Soviet leader three days later, on 10 February, they knew the result of Baker's efforts. Gorbachev confirmed what he had said to Modrow on 30 January: the Germans in the GDR and the FRG knew best what path they wished to take. It was up to them to decide if they wanted unity, as long as the choice was made 'in the context of the realities'. He made no objection to 'two-plus-four' negotiations. ('Nothing without you,' as he told the chancellor.) But when it came to the military status of unified Germany, Gorbachev was more hesitant. Non-alignment after the model of India or China was worth thinking about, he said, and made it clear to his interlocutors that the Soviet Union had no intention of accepting a shift in the balance of power to the detriment of the Warsaw Pact and in favour of NATO.

At the ensuing press conference Kohl said that he believed the open questions could be solved in conjunction with Washington, Paris, and London. The most important message was that Gorbachev and he agreed 'that it is the sole right of the German people to decide whether they wish to live together in one state. General Secretary Gorbachev has told me in no uncertain terms that the Soviet

Union will respect the Germans' decision to live in one state, and that it is the business of the Germans to determine when and how unity will come about.'

The talks in Moscow gave the Bonn government greater self-confidence. On 13 February, at a meeting of NATO and Warsaw Pact foreign ministers in Ottawa (dubbed the 'Open Skies Conference'), the Italian foreign minister Gianni De Michelis and his Dutch colleague Hans van den Broek demanded a role in the negotiations over the unification of the two German states. 'You are not part of the game,' Genscher told them bluntly. And in fact the decision had already been made. After Eduard Shevardnadze agreed to 'two-plus-four' negotiations in Ottawa, all the other states in both blocs had to content themselves with the promise of regular consultations.

That same day, 13 February, Hans Modrow, who had come with a large delegation to Bonn, was forced to confront the fact that the West German government was no longer willing to continue supporting his administration economically and financially. Kohl and Waigel rejected the demand for an immediate 'solidarity contribution' (*Solidarbeitrag*) of 10 to 15 billion marks. They countered by calling for speedy introduction of a social market economy and statutory alignment with the FRG in the central areas of the economic order. The opposition ministers accompanying Modrow protested, but in vain. Round Table participation in a Grand Coalition had lent only ephemeral strength to the GDR prime minister. As the Volkskammer elections approached, it became more and more obvious that neither the GDR government nor the Round Table had any real power. All of it lay in Bonn.

But the United States was even more powerful than West Germany. Even while Baker was in Moscow, the administration in Washington had come to the conclusion that Genscher's Tutzing plan, according to which East Germany would not be integrated into the NATO military structures, amounted to the de-militarization and neutralization of the territory in question. This would compromise NATO's guarantee of protection for all of Germany. At the most, East Germany could be granted a 'special military status' within the alliance. NATO general secretary Manfred Wörner, defence minister Gerhard Stoltenberg (CDU), and Kohl's foreign policy adviser Horst Teltschik all thought similarly.

In order not to endanger his coalition, Kohl first adopted Genscher's point of view and pushed through a joint declaration by the foreign and defence ministers that was largely in keeping with the Tutzing formula (19 February). At the talks between Kohl, Bush, and Baker at Camp David on 24 and 25 February, however, the Americans succeeded in asserting their view. At a joint press conference Bush, with Kohl's agreement, said that both agreed that

a unified Germany should remain a full member of the North Atlantic Treaty Organization, including participation in its military structure. We agreed that US military forces should remain stationed in the united Germany and elsewhere in Europe as a continuing guarantor of stability. The chancellor and I are also in agreement that in a unified state the former territory of the GDR should have a special military status that would take into account the legitimate security interests of all interested countries, including those of the Soviet Union.

By no means had Helmut Kohl always been as unshakably committed to full NATO membership for a united Germany as Bush made him out to be. According to a story by Associated Press, the *Washington Post* had reported on 18 January 1990 that the chancellor had said in an interview that

the developments in eastern Europe have rendered obsolete the American position that German unity can only be achieved in connection with German membership in NATO. Kohl said that there were differences of opinion with Washington on this issue. He thinks, however, that the American view could change if the relationship between NATO and the Warsaw Pact changes.

On 19 February Kohl had supported Genscher against Stoltenberg in the question of East Germany and the NATO military structures. And on 24 February at Camp David the chancellor, to the dismay of Bush, asked if a united Germany could belong to NATO without participating in its military organization, like France.

The American president knew that his uncompromising approach would meet with Soviet resistance. He will also have been aware that for Gorbachev to give in on the question of German NATO membership would weaken his position with regard to his conservative adversaries. Nonetheless, Bush swept such considerations aside at Camp David: 'To hell with that. We prevailed, they didn't. We can't let the Soviets clutch victory from the jaws of defeat.' By the time of the press conference, when Bush announced a special military status for East Germany as the most the west was willing to concede, Kohl, too, had been committed to the new American policy.

In terms of his NATO plans for a united Germany, Genscher was thus taken down a notch. But on another question things developed just as he wished. The recognition of Germany's eastern border had been a matter of conflict between the Bonn coalition partners ever since autumn 1989. In a speech to the UN general assembly on 27 September, the West German foreign minister had stated that Poland should know 'that its right to live within secure borders is not being called into question by us Germans through territorial claims, and will not be in the future . . . The inviolability of the borders is the foundation of peaceful coexistence in Europe.' For his part, Kohl—with an eye on his constituency among the expellees—did not want to give up the possibility of a different settlement on the eastern border in a future peace treaty. He managed to assert his position in a Bundestag resolution on 8 November. The lack of any statement on the Polish western border in Kohl's Ten Point plan was a major factor in the worsening of relations between the coalition parties in winter 1989–90.

The conflict came to a head at the beginning of March. On 1 March Roland Dumas, the French foreign minister, said that it was not sensible to postpone an answer to the border question until a unified German parliament could deal with it. Kohl then tried to bundle recognition of the Oder–Neisse border by both German governments with Polish renunciation of war reparations and a treaty securing the rights of the German minority in Poland. All other parties protested, the FDP hardly less than the SPD and Greens.

The coalition finally reached a compromise on 6 March. In a resolution two days later, passed with the votes of the Union parties and FDP, the Bundestag proposed that as soon as possible after the GDR elections, the two freely elected German parliaments and governments should make identical announcements containing the following message: 'Be it known to the Polish people that their right to live within secure borders is not being called into question by us Germans through territorial claims, and will not be in the future.' After restoration of German unity, the border question was to be worked out in this spirit between the German and Polish governments. Poland's renunciation of reparations, announced 'to Germany' on 23 August 1953, would also apply to reunified Germany, the resolution stated. The same was true of a joint statement by Prime Minister Mazowiecki and Chancellor Kohl on 10 November 1989, which agreed to a treaty codifying the rights of the German minority in Poland.

Five Union delegates abstained from the ballot, and seven, including the expellee politician Herbert Czaja, went on record to the effect that the resolution was not a legally valid decision about the post-war border. The Social Democrats and Greens voted against it because of Kohl's attitude on the border question. The Polish government was dissatisfied, and Paris also did not think the resolution went far enough. But it *was* an important step forward towards final recognition of the Oder–Neisse line. In a letter to Kohl on 7 March, Margaret Thatcher spoke of 'very statesmanlike steps. They will be very useful and help overcome the prevailing uncertainty.'[10]

ACCESSION OR NEW CONSTITUTION?

In his policy speech on 8 March 1990 the chancellor stated that he considered the accession of the GDR to the Federal Republic according to Article 23 of the Basic Law to be the best way to German unity. This article provided for the extension of the Basic Law to 'other parts of Germany . . . on their accession'. Another solution was contained in Article 146: 'This Basic Law shall cease to be in force on the day on which a constitution adopted by a free decision of the German people comes into force.'

A heated controversy broke out over the question of 'accession' or 'new constitution' in the spring of 1990. The positions were anything but a simple partisan affair of government coalition vs. opposition or east vs. west. Article 146 had in its favour the undeniable democratic legitimacy that a referendum would grant to a new German constitution, as well as the integrating effect that could be expected from an exercise of the German people's *pouvoir constituant*.

The 1949 Basic Law, according to its preamble, had been designed to 'give a new order to political life for a transitional period'. It had been passed by the Parliamentary Council, a body composed of delegates from the individual state parliaments, and by the parliaments themselves (except the Bavarian). This was considered sufficient democratic legitimation for a temporary constitution, but the final constitution that would eventually replace it was to receive a higher sanction: from the people themselves.

Article 146 did not contradict Article 23. 'Other parts of Germany' could first enter the jurisdiction of the Basic Law and thereafter participate in a new constitutional process. It was also nowhere stated that the exhortation for the German people to 'achieve in free self-determination the unity and freedom of Germany' would only be fulfilled once a new constitution for unified Germany entered into force. This unity and freedom could also be 'achieved' through accession.

Within the Bonn government, the view that accession was the only viable option prevailed in February 1990, after the monetary union was settled. Article 23 had in its favour the fact that the Basic Law had proven its great worth over the course of more than forty years. The idea of abandoning it now for a new constitution seemed almost sacrilege, or at least very imprudent. But the strongest arguments for rapid unification through accession were *argumenta e contrario*: that is, the reasons militating against the much slower process through Article 146.

There were basically three of these. First, in the spring of 1990 nobody could predict how long Gorbachev and Shevardnadze would be in power and able to continue their realist, compromise-oriented policies. A regime change in the Kremlin was by no means out of the question. If the hard-line adversaries of German reunification won out, it would also mean a windfall for those in the west who were—to greater or lesser degrees—opposed to the project. Secondly, the economic situation in the GDR was growing worse by the day, driving large numbers of people out of the country and increasing the risk of violence. Thirdly, the proponents of an extended unification process obviously had the majority of East Germans against them.

The events of autumn 1989 had put to rest an unwritten law that had determined international politics for four decades: that European stability depended on the partition of Germany to guarantee the relative balance of power between east and west. Now, European stability was being threatened by nothing so much as the danger that the GDR would become a source of continual unrest. This danger could only be dispelled by overcoming the partition of Germany, and doing it quickly. This could be done only through Article 23, since the process through Article 146 would be arduous and fraught with risk. Moreover, the accession of the GDR to the FRG was the logical consequence of combining the monetary union with economic reform. The rapid introduction of a market economy demanded the rapid standardization of the legal system. This would be easier to achieve within one state than through negotiations between two separate countries. In terms of democratic legitimacy, it was true that accession was less ideal than a new constitution, since it rested on the decisions of elected bodies rather than on the direct sanction of the people. But if this was a deficiency, it was one that could be removed by a nationwide constitutional debate and, if necessary, by a constitutional reform and a referendum *after* accession. In spring 1990 the arguments for Article 23 and against Article 146 were compelling.

There were also proponents of accession among the Social Democrats, in both countries. Herta Däubler-Gmelin, head of the SPD fraction's legal affairs committee, was one of them, as was Harald Ringstorff, head of the Rostock district party. At a meeting between the leaders of the eastern and western SPD on 12 February, Ringstorff and his political associates called for the accession of the GDR to the Federal Republic immediately after the Volkskammer elections. They were opposed by Vogel and Brandt. Both men knew what would happen if they supported Ringstorff: Oskar Lafontaine (who was not present at the meeting), the probable SPD nominee for the chancellorship ever since his triumph in the Saar elections on 28 January, would abandon his candidacy.

Lafontaine was indeed the sharpest critic of accession according to Article 23—the very article the Saarland had used in 1956 to enter the Federal Republic. On 20 February, he told Vogel in Saarbrücken that he would accept the nomination only if the SPD accepted his conditions: rejection of rapid reunification, interdiction of migration from the GDR to the limits of the law, and subordination of German to European unification. Lafontaine's speech at the congress of the East German SPD in Leipzig on 23 February was entirely in this spirit.

Similar arguments were made by Peter Glotz, who called accession an '*Anschluss* à la Kohl', and Gerhard Schröder, a member of the party executive. Willy Brandt (after the Leipzig congress honorary head of *both* Social Democratic parties) supported reunification according to Article 146. Working for a new constitution, he thought, would have a positive effect on the relations between East and West Germans. Hans-Jochen Vogel preferred Article 146 but did not want to reject the process through Article 23. On 7 March the party executive officially endorsed a referendum on a new German constitution according to Article 146 before accession under Article 23.

On 25 February the Leipzig congress of the eastern SPD adopted an electoral platform that included a 'road map to German unity'. This 'road map' involved a stepwise process from social to monetary to economic union. Political union was to be handled by a 'council of German unity', a body containing an equal number of delegates from the Bundestag and the freely elected Volkskammer. This council would draft a new German constitution, using the Basic Law as its model. The constitution would then be subject to a referendum after parliamentary elections were held in the five new *Länder* of the former GDR in summer 1990. The referendum, in turn, would be followed by new all-German

Bundestag elections. The fact that the 'council of German unity' was not a *representative* constituent assembly was not a cause for concern.

The Round Table firmly rejected Kohl's plan of accession. On 19 February, after Hans Modrow had reported on his visit to Bonn, it passed a resolution rejecting 'the annexation of the GDR or individual *Länder* by the Federal Republic through an extension of the jurisdiction of the Basic Law of the FRG' according to Article 23. NATO membership was clearly excluded, too. It was, according to another resolution that same day, 'impossible to reconcile with the goal of German unity within the framework of a European peace order'. A unified Germany was to have a de-militarized status.

Once the 'government of national responsibility' was formed on 5 February, the Round Table became part of the executive. Its leading thinker, Wolfgang Ullmann, a church historian and one of the co-founders of Democracy Now, on 12 February made a move towards economic reform that was to have important consequences. As minister without portfolio in the second Modrow cabinet, he proposed the creation of a 'Fiduciary Office for the Supervision of the Public Wealth' (*Treuhänderische Behörde zur Betreuung des Volksvermögens*). This office was to distribute all collective property in the GDR. A quarter was to be granted to the citizens as shares, that is, privatized. A quarter was to be set aside to pay debts and compensations. The greater part of the remaining half was to be transferred to the state and used for infrastructure and environmental protection, and the smaller portion put into a foundation promoting non-commercial projects.

After the Round Table had approved Ullmann's initiative in principle, Economics Minister Christa Luft (SED/PDS) took charge. Once it was worked out and reshaped in a 'socialist' sense, the plan seemed to provide a way to prevent the restoration of the old property relations. After its mid-February visit to Bonn and the start of consultations over the monetary union, the Modrow government considered the roll-back of major 'socialist achievements' to be the real danger of reunification. In order to counter this risk, the government decided on 1 March to found a fiduciary agency (*Treuhandanstalt*, also *Treuhand*) that would deal with most of the national wealth. Not much was left over from Ullmann's original plan by this time. Christa Luft insisted that all assets be evaluated, citizens' claims gathered, and rights to the proceeds established before any distribution took place. The transformation of combines and Publicly Owned Enterprises into joint-stock companies was to have priority.

The arguments against rapid privatization à la Ullmann were justified, but they served above all to secure collective property and keep the state in control of the economy. Western capital was to be kept out of the GDR as much as possible. Among the bills passed by the Volkskammer on 6 and 7 March was one that guaranteed freedom of trade and occupation to GDR citizens but not to western investors. The political will was even more clearly written into a law of 7 March on the sale of public buildings. It granted GDR citizens the right to purchase public properties as long as they could prove prior usufruct. The main beneficiaries of this 'reform' were the old 'nomenclature cadres' of the GDR, who could thereby obtain prize properties at low prices. Before going under, the SED regime wished to demonstrate its gratitude for services faithfully rendered. It acted in the spirit of the French 'citizen king' Louis Philippe's motto *enrichissez-vous!*— 'Get rich!'

The Round Table, several of whose members benefited from this law, could have blocked it. But it preferred to spend this time working to safeguard another kind of vested interest. On 5 March it passed a 'Social Charter', the addressee of which was no longer the Modrow government, but the administration that would be put in place after the Volkskammer elections. In a wider sense it was also aimed at the government in Bonn, with whom the reunification would be negotiated. The 'Social Charter' embraced the rights to employment, free education, free termination of pregnancy services, health care, and housing at state-controlled prices. The right to employment included comprehensive job protection, reduction of work hours at full pay, and a ban on lockouts during industrial action. The Volkskammer approved the 'Social Charter' on 7 March—the same day as it passed the law on the sale of public property. The document was then sent to the Bundestag as a basis for negotiations over a German social policy union.

Meanwhile, work continued on another ambitious project: a new constitution for the GDR. Several West German jurists from the left side of the political spectrum participated in the deliberations. But the Round Table never got the chance to pass its draft. By the time the commission presented it on 4 April, the new Volkskammer had already been elected. The Round Table's self-appointed task was over. The authors' appeals for a maximum of direct democracy and social security had no political effect, and their declaration that compulsory military service had been abolished was ignored.

What remained was a myth. Many former civil rights activists and West German leftist intellectuals believed then and continue to believe that in spring 1990 the GDR was well on its way to becoming an autonomous democracy, superior to the West German representative model in its proximity to the people and commitment to social justice. The reason this democracy never became reality was, according to this interpretation, because the GDR was overwhelmed by the west. And the west only succeeded because it used materialist incentives and political deception.

The Round Table had bridged the hundred days between its first session on 7 December and the first open Volkskammer elections on 18 March. Under the first Modrow cabinet it had functioned as supervisory body, consultant, and veto power. Then, after the 'government of national responsibility' was formed on 5 February, it became the central coordinator, legislator, and co-regent of the GDR. It contributed towards keeping the 'peaceful revolution' peaceful and the collapse of the state under control.

The closer it got to the Modrow government, however, the further away it moved from what the great majority of the people wanted: the rapid introduction of the Deutschmark and reunification with the Federal Republic. The Round Table stood for those who did not want German unity, or not yet, or not under the conditions in question, and who were thus determined to inject as much of the renewed GDR into the new Germany as possible, if reunification could not be prevented. But these were a minority. The Round Table did not have a democratic mandate, and therefore it could not function as the representative body of a post-dictatorial GDR. Only the freely elected Volkskammer could do this. The Volkskammer would represent the people of the GDR as they were, not the idea the Round Table had made of them.[11]

THE VOLKSKAMMER ELECTIONS: PLEBISCITE FOR ACCESSION

Many West German politicians were involved in the electoral campaigns in the GDR, especially Helmut Kohl, Willy Brandt, and Hans-Dietrich Genscher (a native of Halle). All three were wildly cheered almost everywhere they went. Kohl spoke at rallies held by the conservative Alliance for Germany, which campaigned for the rapid introduction of the Deutschmark and rapid reunification by accession according to Article 23 of the Basic Law. It promoted its agenda with stickers that read 'We are one people'. Genscher lent his support to the 'League of Free Democrats' (*Bund Freier Demokraten*), a liberal party alliance formed on 12 February between the LDPD, the eastern FDP, and the German Forum party. Brandt was the most popular of all West German politicians. His disadvantage was that he did not have the whole SPD behind him. Oskar Lafontaine—who only got involved in the East German campaign in three places—made no secret of the fact that he was trying to slow down the process of unification, for economic, financial, and social reasons.

The PDS, which chose Hans Modrow as its prime candidate, was banking on the personal popularity of the prime minister. The party's electoral platform called for the reunification process to take place slowly, in several stages, and for the values and achievements of the GDR to be preserved. Three of the civil rights groups—the New Forum, Democracy Now, and the Peace and Human Rights Initiative—together formed an 'Alliance 90' (*Bündnis 90*), which, however, was unable to decide on a common platform. The Green party (*Grüne Partei*), founded at the end of November, made an alliance with the Independent Women's Association (*Unabhängiger Frauenverband*), but it came apart soon after the election.

Opinion polls showed the SPD far ahead right up to the day of the vote. The Alliance for Germany had begun to catch up in March, but had to deal with a scandal in the final stretch. Wolfgang Schnur, head of Democratic Awakening, was accused—not for the first time—of having been a Stasi informer for years, all the way up to the revolution. He denied everything, but the evidence was overwhelming. He stepped down as party head on 14 March, and the next day he was thrown out of the DA on account of 'actions harmful to the party'. He was replaced by his deputy, Rainer Eppelmann.

For most of the observers the outcome of the first open Volkskammer elections on 18 March 1990 was a surprise. With participation at 93.4% of eligible voters, the Alliance for Germany was the clear winner with 48% of the vote (the CDU gained 40.8%, the DSU 6.3%, and the DA 0.9%). With 21.9% the SPD did far worse than expectations, including their own. The PDS obtained 16.4%, the League of Free Democrats 5.3%, Alliance 90 2.9%, and the Green party 2% of the vote.

This was not only the first open electoral contest in the GDR, but the first on East German territory since the Reichstag elections on 6 November 1932. The results show a near total lack of continuity with voter behaviour during the Weimar Republic. The vast majority of workers voted CDU, even in old SPD strongholds like Saxony and Thuringia. Only in Berlin did the Social Democrats do better than the Alliance for Germany (39.4% vs. 21.6%). They did comparatively well in the districts of Potsdam and Frankfurt an der Oder, where the German Nationalists had once been strong. The liberals took 10% of the vote, their only double-digit result, in the district of Halle, Genscher's home town. The PDS did best in Berlin, with 30.2%. It was strong in administrative centres and, according to studies by Forschungsgruppe Wahlen, drew most of its votes from intellectuals, administrators, salaried employees, university students, and pupils. It had very little support among the workers.

The election was a plebiscite for accession to the Federal Republic of Germany. The outcome allowed of no other interpretation. The majority wanted German unity as soon as possible and through wholesale adoption of the West German economic, social, and constitutional system. Reunification would bring a long-overdue justice, ending the inequitable distribution of the burdens of German history since 1945. A not inconsiderable minority, the constituency of the PDS, felt loyal to at least some of the values of the GDR and wanted to preserve them. The 'heroes' of autumn 1989, however, the civil rights activists, were dealt an outright punishment. To the overwhelming majority of their compatriots, their ideas about a 'third way' were simply out of touch with reality.

The Volkskammer elections on 18 March 1990 mark the end of the 'peaceful revolution' in the GDR. The result represented a radical break with the status quo. It was, in effect, a vote to get rid of the state, one that had never possessed any democratic legitimacy. This was not what the instigators of the 'peaceful revolution', the intellectual activists, had intended. The liquidation of the GDR was the will of the masses, who took control of the demonstrations after the fall of the wall in November 1989 and gave the revolution a nationalist turn.

Within the masses it was, ironically, the workers who most rejected the 'workers' and peasants' state'. The SED, which called itself the 'party of the working class', had basically 'neutralized' the workers after the June 1953 uprising. It was they who were the real target of the 'unity of economic and social policy' that had driven the GDR to financial ruin. This policy was a 'success' to the extent that there was no more significant labour resistance in the GDR, right up to the finish. When the dictatorship began to crumble in autumn 1989, however, it was quickly evident that the working class was no pillar of the regime.

The active role of critical intellectuals, the decisive impact of mass action, the collapse of the old order: these are all characteristics of a successful revolution. But one thing was missing. The leaders of the protest movement had no real leadership strategy of their own. The activists were not themselves interested in power; they wanted to let the people decide. In this they resembled the Majority Social Democrats during the 1918–19 revolution, with the difference that the latter had been able to count on mass support. The reason a revolutionary *Erziehungsdiktatur* or 'educational dictatorship' had no chance in post-First World War Germany was because of the democratic tradition of a codified right to political participation in the form of general equal suffrage. At that time, the only possible result was *more* democracy. Seven decades later, the desire for an end to dictatorship was so strong that no group could contemplate putting itself in the place of the sovereign people for a lengthy period of time. Once again, an important factor for a 'great' or 'classic' revolution was lacking in Germany.

The one thing all parties had agreed on in 1918–19 was prompt elections. This was even more true in 1989–90, since those who opposed elections had already been thrown out of power in October and November 1989 under the combined efforts of activists, masses, and critics within the SED. Once the date for elections was set in December, the only thing that mattered was keeping the progressive collapse of the old order under as much control as possible. Tolerating a transitional government composed of comparatively enlightened representatives of the old regime, who made no resistance to the idea of being replaced through free elections, but instead rescheduled them for an earlier date—this behaviour reflected a general longing to avoid chaos on the way to the new system.

The reason slogans like 'No violence!' had a chance was because the regime decided not to use force. Without the backing of the Soviet Union, none of the dictatorships dependent on it were able to withstand rebellious masses for long. Unlike in 1953, 1956, and 1968, by 1989 political wisdom and economic weakness had made the Soviet leadership unwilling to intervene. Thus the new emancipation movements, beginning in Poland, could assert themselves for the most part without violence. Just a few years before, Moscow would probably not have renounced a strategically important territory like the GDR without a fight. But by 1989 it had lost the battle of the systems on all fields. It could not risk a great confrontation without placing its very existence in jeopardy. Whether it would be able to survive the loss of its eastern European buffer zone was still an open question at this juncture.

For the west, firmness and willingness to cooperate, the hallmarks of the common *Ostpolitik*, had paid off. It is undeniable that West Germany had prevented an earlier collapse of the GDR by granting it financial assistance on a large scale. It was a maxim of Bonn's Germany policy from the era of the social–liberal eastern treaties that such a collapse could quickly turn into a global crisis and so had to be avoided at all costs. In the 1980s, none of the important political parties contested this insight any longer. In 1989–90, it mainly depended on Bonn whether the mishmash of collapse and revolution in the GDR would give rise to a stable or an unstable situation. The FRG could act as a stabilizer, and since it could, it had no legitimate option but to do so. When Bonn acted in accordance with its Basic Law and opened up the door to accession, it confronted the East Germans with the mirror of their own future. The rational expectation that unification stood at the end of the crisis was a decisive factor in defusing the crisis. A policy of delay would only have made it worse.

All this was by no means general knowledge in West Germany at the time. Jürgen Habermas, for example, reacted to the outcome of the Volkskammer elections by warning against 'Deutschmark nationalism'. 'It is difficult not to write satire when faced with the first blossoms of a chubby-cheeked DM nationalism,' he wrote in *Die Zeit* on 30 March. 'The people of the GDR were forced to vote for those in power for forty years. Kohl has made it clear to them that it would be better to vote for the government in power this time, too.' Habermas predicted that this would not remain without consequences for the FRG. The Alliance for Germany, he wrote, might well 'continue its campaign, with minor variations, on the soil of the Federal Republic, demanding from the citizens here collective efforts in the spirit of a nationalist identification with the expansion of the DM empire, from which they have lived quite well up to this point.'

What disturbed Habermas most of all was the return of 'traditional patriotism' via the collapse of the GDR. This was a sentiment that the philosopher had thought long since relegated to the dustbin of history.

The citizens of the Federal Republic *had* developed a non-nationalist self-image and a sober awareness of just how much personal cash or utilitarian value is to be got from the political process. What will become of this disposition under the pressure of a politics that, concealing its insecurity under arrogance, is steering straight for the all-German national state?

For the sake of Europe, the danger of renationalization had to be counteracted.

If we do not free ourselves from the diffuse ideas of the nation state, if we do not rid ourselves of the prepolitical crutches of 'nationality' and 'community of destiny', then we will not be able to *continue* unburdened along our—already well travelled—road to a multicultural society, to a regionally widely-fanned and strongly federal state, and above all to a unified European state of nationalities.

The question of what article of the Basic Law should be used with regard to the GDR was quickly answered by Habermas:.

The path through Article 23 means *subjecting* the citizens to the process of reunification. The path through a Constitutive Council, on the other hand, will prevent a politics of fait accompli. This will, perhaps, grant the GDR citizens some breathing space for self-determination, and it will also allow time for a discussion of the priority of European considerations. Only a referendum on a constitutional draft, with a choice between an all-German federal state and a federation, will give *all* citizens the chance to say no . . . Only when given a free choice will we become conscious of something many younger people among us already feel: that the formation of a single nation of citizens within the current territory of the Federal Republic and GDR is by no means *foreordained* through the prepolitical facts of linguistic commonality, culture, or history. For this reason, we would at least like to be asked.

The Germans in the GDR were holding up to the Germans in the Federal Republic the mirror of their history. But it could easily turn into a magic mirror, changing the citizens of the FRG back into conventional Germans, thus throwing them back culturally. Therefore everything had to be done to prevent reunification into a single German nation, or else to postpone the process until Europe had reached a point where it no longer contained any nation states. This was the direction in which Habermas was thinking, and his ideas provided a theoretical basis for the position that Oskar Lafontaine had been championing for some time (not infrequently with reference to Habermas). German history, as the philosopher viewed it, had been exorcized in West Germany, since the citizens had learned to think of themselves in terms of the civil and the universal, no longer in terms of history and the nation. Now, German national history was returning in the shape of the ruined GDR, threatening everything the Federal Republic had achieved by way of an intellectual disengagement from this very history.

Habermas considered it absurd to bring Auschwitz into the equation as a 'metaphysical culpability', for which the loss of something like East Prussia or Silesia could atone. Nor could Auschwitz serve

to leverage the negative nationalism of a community of destiny . . . Auschwitz can and should remind the Germans—regardless of what state territories they arrange themselves in—of something else: that they cannot depend on the continuity of their history. With that momentous breach of continuity, the Germans lost the chance of basing their political identity on something other than universalist civil principles, by the light of which the national tradition can no longer be indiscriminately absorbed, but only critically and self-critically appropriated. Post-traditional identity loses its substantial, its uninhibited character. It *exists* only in the mode of public, discursive struggle over the interpretation of a constitutional patriotism that must be made concrete according to changing historical conditions.

The partition of Germany was thus not only a *consequence* of the German past, but also the very *precondition* of West Germany's being able to break with that past. Post-traditional identity, as Habermas understood it, meant that Germany was now headed for its most profound identity crisis ever. He campaigned for the option of rejecting the unity and freedom of Germany right at the moment when it was becoming possible to fulfil the preamble to the Basic Law. The breach of historical continuity that was Auschwitz as an argument against the obligation to solidarity that German history imposed; the cultivation of a 'universalist' constitutional patriotism that had never had much to do with the actual constitution and now abandoned it in an important point—what Habermas was calling for here was *not* the product of a critical and self-critical appropriation of the national tradition. It was an almost desperate attempt to defend a particular West German arrangement with history against the claims of those Germans whom history had left in the lurch—an ethically very questionable venture.

Four years before, during the *Historikerstreit* over the uniqueness of the Holocaust, Habermas had written his famous credo: 'The Federal Republic's unreserved opening towards the political culture of the west is the greatest intellectual achievement of our post-war period, something my generation in particular can be proud of.' He now saw this achievement put at risk by the expected 'accession' of the East Germans. The ideal of a 'discourse without dominance' was now being jeopardized by the consequences of a dominance without discourse.

Habermas was not only speaking for himself. In 1989–90 many West German intellectuals believed that the 'western' character of the part of Germany they lived in was under threat. The other part had disappeared from their consciousness, by slow degrees over the course of many years. This, too, could be called repression. Now, for the first time since 1945, there was an opportunity to westernize the east. The theories of Jürgen Habermas were of no help here. Precisely the opposite was called for—the accession of East to West Germany.[12]

UNITY AND ITS PRICE: ECONOMIC AND MONETARY UNION

The process of forming a new East German government proved difficult. As far as parliamentary seats and platforms were concerned, a Christian–liberal coalition like that in Bonn would have been possible. Considering the scope of the problems on the agenda, however, including a number of constitutional amendments, Lothar de Maizière believed that a broader parliamentary basis in the shape of a Grand Coalition was absolutely necessary. The Bonn coalition agreed. Inclusion of the SPD seemed like a good way to thwart Oskar Lafontaine's campaign for the chancellorship, which was calculated to polarize.

Lafontaine had received the unanimous nomination of the SPD on 19 March, the day after the Volkskammer elections. Thus before it even came into existence, the new GDR government was already a problem of West German domestic politics.

The East German Social Democrats were divided on the issue of participation in the government. Ibrahim (Manfred) Böhme, head of the party since the Leipzig congress that past February, opposed it. The most prominent advocates were his deputy Markus Meckel and the Berlin theologian Richard Schröder. Cooperation with the DSU was unanimously rejected, at least outwardly. Böhme, who knew he could count on the support of the Bonn SPD and especially Oskar Lafontaine, was elected fraction leader on 21 March. But he had to resign his party offices only a few days later, on 26 March. Two former members of the MfS had accused him in *Der Spiegel* of having worked as a regular IM for the Stasi. (This was later confirmed.) Meckel temporarily became party head, Schröder fraction leader. This meant that the two most important offices now lay in the hands of politicians who favoured a Grand Coalition. Their position was strengthened by the fact that in the western SPD, too, the popularity of a broad governing coalition in the east was now on the increase. Even Lafontaine finally gave up his resistance.

The SPD conditions for participation in government were generally in keeping with de Maizière's own positions: recognition of the Oder–Neisse line; non-inclusion of the GDR in the NATO military structures; consultation with Germany's eastern and western neighbours in the reunification process; the legal validity of the 1954 land reform; and the protection of property rights in the GDR. There was also agreement on the one-to-one conversion rate for the monetary union. The parties disagreed on the question of accession vs. a referendum on a new constitution. The Alliance and the liberals were for the former, the Social Democrats for the latter. As talks progressed, however, the SPD withdrew its insistence on this point.

By the time the negotiations were concluded on 10 April, the cabinet had also been decided. The CDU's Lothar de Maizière became prime minister. Besides the leadership in general matters, he reserved for himself the right to determine the government's Germany policy. There were eleven further CDU ministers, including Gerhard Pohl for economics and Klaus Reichenbach in the office of the prime minister. Among the seven Social Democrats were Markus Meckel as foreign minister, Walter Romberg as minister of finance, and Regine Hildebrandt as minister of labour. The DSU received the interior ministry, which went to Peter-Michael Diestel (also made deputy prime minister), and a 'Ministry for Economic Cooperation', which went to Hans-Wilhelm Ebeling. Rainer Eppelmann of Democratic Awakening led the 'Ministry of Disarmament and Defence'. Kurt Wünsche became justice minister for the liberals.

The new government received encouragement from the Soviet Union on one particular question, itself not a matter of controversy among the coalition partners. On 28 March—Modrow was still prime minister—Moscow made an official statement to Bonn insisting that

in the process of their rapprochement and unification the two German states proceed from the assumption that economic measures taken by the Soviet military administration in Germany between 1945 and 1949 were lawful. It would be absolutely unacceptable to deny the rights of the current owners of land and other assets in the GDR, which were acquired . . . with the permission or by decision of the Soviet side at the time.

(This text is the one circulated by the Tass news agency.) Thus did the former occupying power declare its land redistribution project untouchable.

The new Volkskammer convened for its constitutive session on 5 April 1990. The CDU delegate Sabine Bergmann-Pohl was elected president. One week later, on 12 April, the Volkskammer passed a 'joint statement' by all fractions. It was underwritten by the will to a new moral beginning.

We, the first freely elected parliamentarians of the GDR, bear witness to the responsibility of the Germans in the GDR for their history and their future and declare with one voice to the world: immeasurable suffering was brought to the peoples of the world by Germans during the time of National Socialism. Nationalism and racial fanaticism led to genocide, especially against the Jews from all European countries, against the peoples of the Soviet Union, against the people of Poland, and against the people of the Sinti and Roma . . . We feel sorrow and shame and take responsibility for this burden of German history . . . We ask the Jews throughout the whole world for forgiveness. We ask the people in Israel to forgive the hypocrisy and hostility of official GDR policy with regard to the state of Israel and for the persecution and degradation of Jewish fellow citizens in our country even after 1945.

What then came was directed at the peoples of the Soviet Union.

We have not forgotten the terrible suffering that Germans caused the peoples in the Soviet Union during the Second World War. In the end, this violence from Germany also struck our own people. We keenly wish to continue the process of reconciliation between our peoples. For this reason it is our intent to integrate Germany into a pan-European security system in such a way as to guarantee peace and security to our peoples. We are aware that the restructuring in our country would not have been possible without the new thinking and the *perestroika* in the Soviet Union. We are grateful to the citizens of the Soviet Union for the encouragement and inspiration we have received from them in this regard.

Turning to Czechoslovakia—which had disposed of its own communist dictatorship during the 'Velvet Revolution' of November and December 1989—the delegates had the following to say:

The Volkskammer of the GDR accepts the partial responsibility of the GDR for the suppression of the 1968 'Prague Spring' by troops of the Warsaw Pact. This unlawful military intervention caused the people in Czechoslovakia great suffering and delayed the democratic process in eastern Europe for twenty years . . . In our fear and lack of courage we failed to stop this violation of international law. The first freely elected parliament in the GDR asks the peoples of Czechoslovakia to forgive this wrong.

In its conclusion the Volkskammer turned its gaze to the future, in which German–Polish relations would be especially important.

We consider it our special responsibility to bring Germany's long historical relationships to the peoples of eastern Europe into the political process. In this regard we once again solemnly declare that we unconditionally accept the post-Second World War German borders with all neighbouring states. The Polish people in particular should know that its right to live within secure borders is not being called into question by us Germans, and will not be in the future. We affirm the inviolability of the Oder–Neisse border with the Republic of Poland as a basis for peaceful coexistence between our peoples in a common European house. A future united German parliament should codify this in a treaty.

The Volkskammer session that passed the joint statement also elected Lothar de Maizière prime minister with 265 of the 303 Grand Coalition votes. The cabinet as a whole, composed of 23 ministers, received 247 votes. De Maizière gave his inaugural speech a week later, on 19 April. He used a quote from Hölderlin's *Hyperion* to draw the balance of four decades of dictatorship: 'The state has always been made a hell by man's wanting to make it his heaven.' He assured the citizens of the GDR that the decision for unity had been made. 'How we will get there is something we will have a decisive say in . . . Unity must come as quickly as *possible*, but the basic conditions must be as good, as sensible, and as sustainable as *necessary*.' Turning to the citizens of the FRG he said: 'The partition can only be overcome through sharing.' Then, to all Germans: 'Germany is our inheritance of historical achievement and historical guilt. If we commit ourselves to Germany, we also commit ourselves to this dual legacy.'

De Maizière then went on to more concrete demands, calling for wages, salaries, retirement pensions, savings, and savings-based insurance programmes to be converted at an exchange rate of one to one. As for property questions, the land reform was not open to debate and transfers of property undertaken in good faith of their lawful validity were to remain legally valid. The prime minister announced the creation of a constitutional court, the stepwise formation of administrative, labour, and social tribunals, and—one of the most important things—a decentralization of power: 'By 1991 there will be individual states again.' State parliamentary elections were to be held already in late autumn 1990. The government knew that it had an arduous path ahead, de Maizière said.

No government can work miracles, but we will strive for what is possible with all our energy. If we recognize what is possible and make it reality, step by step, with prudence and sober minds, then we will lay the basis for a better future for the people in our country. In this we are counting on the support, the courage, and the energy of all citizens.

Five days later, on 24 April, Kohl and de Maizière agreed in Bonn to conduct the negotiations on economic, monetary, and social policy union such that the relevant treaty could enter into force on 1 July. As to the vexed question of the exchange rate, on 23 April the West German government had agreed to a more differentiated solution: one-to-one conversion of wages, salaries, and pensions as well as cash and savings up to 4,000 *Ostmark* per person. Beyond this amount, and for company debts, a two-to-one rate was to be applied. The criteria on which these rates were based were purely political. Economically speaking, the productivity of the GDR was too low to justify them. This did not stop de Maizière from saying that the 4,000 mark limit was too low. On 2 May a compromise was worked out that took the factor of life expectancy into account and treated older people more generously. Persons between 15 and 59 years of age would have a 4,000 mark limit; for children and older people the limits would be 2,000 marks and 6,000 marks, respectively.

The first open municipal elections in the GDR were held four days later, on 6 May. The parties of the Alliance lost votes, the CDU alone 6 per cent. The SPD did not benefit, however, despite the fact that it had campaigned on higher exchange limits for personal savings. Neither did the PDS, which suffered minor losses compared to its Volkskammer result. The winners (relatively speaking) were the liberals, the Democratic Farmers' Party of Germany (*Demokratische Bauernpartei Deutschlands*), and the newly founded Farmers' Association (*Bauernverband*).

In the talks on economic union the GDR committed itself to creating the framework for a social market economy with private property; free competition; free formation of prices; and free movement of labour, capital, goods, and services. Over a transitional period, the FRG would provide structural adjustment assistance to the fiduciary agency for East German enterprises, which was to be newly organized. In agriculture the GDR introduced a price support and protection system in keeping with European Community regulations. The social policy union consisted of the phased introduction of West German labour law, social insurance, and social welfare assistance programmes. The GDR would align its state budget, finances, tariffs, and fiscal administration with the statutes of the FRG and use its public assets primarily for economic reform and rehabilitation of the budget. It would receive budget assistance in 1990–1 in the shape of appropriated funds and start-up financing for pensions and unemployment. The Treaty on the Creation of a Monetary, Economic, and Social Union was signed by the two finance ministers, Theo Waigel and Walter Romberg, on 18 May 1990 in Bonn.

The West German government wanted to finance the reunification through economic growth, not tax increases. Despite high growth rates in the previous two years (a 3.7% GDP increase in 1988 and 3.6% in 1989), despite low rates of inflation and gradually falling unemployment (in 1990 the number of those out of work dipped below 2 million for the first time since 1983), this proposition was nothing short of foolhardy. The old buildings in the GDR were dilapidated. Many city centres were practically in ruins, the consequence of extremely low rents and the single-minded promotion of prefabricated housing complexes in the suburbs and surrounding countryside. In many places the environment had been destroyed and contaminated for decades to come, worst of all at the brown coal mines near Bitterfeld. In May 1990 the GDR ministries estimated that only one-third of East German industries were competitive and could survive without state assistance; a good half were working at a loss but were worth renovating, and 14 per cent were in danger of bankruptcy. This was more realistic than what the Modrow government had told Bonn at the beginning of the year. As was soon to emerge, however, it was still much too optimistic.

The costs of reunification would therefore be gigantic. Anyone who thought soberly on the matter had to come to this conclusion. Nonetheless, Finance Minister Waigel refused to undertake a realistic assessment, and recommendations to this effect from his East German colleague Romberg were brusquely rejected. The Bonn government, led by Helmut Kohl, did not want to face the obvious. It did not want to confront the citizens with the unpleasant realization that the reunification was going to require material sacrifices. After all, 1990 was an election year. It is not certain how the voters would have reacted to the truth, but one thing is certain: in 1990 the hour of truth was merely postponed.

The Bonn government was not the only responsible party. The *Länder*, irrespective of the party composition of their governments, rejected Waigel's attempt to redistribute revenue from the value-added tax in favour of the Federation. They also refused to let the future 'new *Bundesländer*' participate in the inter-state fiscal adjustment programme (the *Länderfinanzausgleich*) right away. Since Waigel persisted in his rejection of tax hikes—arguing that otherwise the growth that was to finance the reunification would be adversely affected—the only other option was increasing state debt.

The 'Special German Unity Fund' (*Sonderfonds Deutsche Einheit*), which the chancellor and prime ministers of the *Länder* agreed to on 16 May 1990, corresponded to this approach. Kept apart from the regular budget, this special fund was to have a duration of four and a half years and provide 115 billion marks by 1994. Savings on the federal level would generate 20 billion, mostly by eliminating now-obsolete 'partition-based' programmes like assistance to Berlin and the regions along the German–German border, the transit subsidy, etc. Loans were to provide 95 billion. Repayment of both principle and interest was to be evenly split between the federal and the state levels and was scheduled for a period of more than twenty years. The start-up financing for the pension and unemployment insurance programmes was borne by the federal budget alone, which was therefore burdened to a far greater extent than the states from the beginning. Then, during the talks on the Unification Treaty in August, the Federation gave up some of its own monies from the Special German Unity Fund so that the new *Länder* could draw on 85% of the fund (instead of 50%, as previously agreed) to cover their general expenses. This cost the 1991 federal budget 12.3 billion marks.

The Special German Unity Fund concealed the true extent of the borrowing, and it was only the first stop on the way down a slippery slope. In August the FRG assumed the entire debt of the GDR, including its foreign debt. The total, more than 600 billion marks, was transferred to a special federal account. Interest payments were split between the Federation and the *Treuhand*. This office, which a law passed by the Volkskammer on 17 June had made into an organization for the privatization of public assets, became a public agency directly under federal control. Its shares in the former Publicly Owned Companies were thus indirectly held by the state, with all attendant risks.

Under Helmut Kohl's chancellorship, new borrowings had grown from 350 billion marks in 1982 to 490 billion by 1989. The fact that the country was living beyond its means was well known to experts. It now assumed the costs of the decades-long mismanagement of the East German economy. The debt reached the 1 trillion mark in the course of 1990. The shadow budgets eased the strain on the Federation (or at least gave that appearance) so that the credit flexibility required by the Basic Law could be formally maintained. But one consequence of this method of financing German unity was already foreseeable in 1990: the borrowings drove up interest rates, and since rising base rates at the federal bank meant rising base rates in the rest of western Europe, the costs of German unity were partially Europeanized without the consent of Germany's neighbours.

The Social Democrats had good reason to be critical. Their candidate was the main opponent of rapid economic and monetary union. On 25 April Oskar Lafontaine was stabbed and seriously injured by a mentally ill woman in Cologne-Mülheim during a campaign event for the North Rhine-Westphalian parliamentary elections. On 13 May the SPD, led by prime minister Johannes Rau (the would-be-assassin's real target, before she turned on Lafontaine) won an absolute majority in North Rhine-Westphalia for the third time in a row. Another Social Democrat, Gerhard Schröder, won the elections in Lower Saxony that same day. On 21 June, at the head of a red–green coalition, Schröder replaced the Union's Ernst Albrecht as prime minister. The SPD now had a majority in the Bundesrat. This meant that the treaty with the GDR could not be signed without their support. The position of Lafontaine, who had begun to recover, was now much stronger than before.

Lafontaine's original plan was to block the treaty. As he had put it on 22 April at a conference of SPD leaders from the east and west, his goal was not the restoration of the national state, but social unity, which could only be realized over the course of years. The sudden introduction of the Deutschmark, he said, would have an adverse effect on many East German companies. And the impact of the currency and economic union on the citizens of the Federal Republic was also unknown.

Lafontaine soon realized that it was too late to stop the monetary union. But it was still possible to make a strong gesture against the politics of Kohl and Waigel. The SPD Bundestag fraction and the *Länder* governed by Social Democrats were to vote against the treaty. If the social–liberal senate in Hamburg voted for it, it would go through. Lafontaine told the party head Hans-Jochen Vogel that, if that were to happen, he would withdraw his candidacy for the chancellorship.

The party executive and the fraction were prepared to compromise. The Social Democrats would reject the treaty in its current form, but vote for it if certain 'improvements' could be reached in further negotiations with the Bonn government. What they wanted were temporary measures to save companies that could be rehabilitated from collapse; improved economic protection; and the use of the assets of the SED, the bloc parties, and mass organizations for general and social policy purposes. But this did not go far enough for Lafontaine. In an interview with *Der Spiegel* on 28 May, he said that there was no compelling reason for the SPD fraction to support a decision that would lead to mass unemployment. In the Bundesrat, however, the party could let the treaty pass. These statements called forth protest from both western and eastern Social Democrats, from Horst Ehmke to Herta Däubler-Gmelin to Richard Schröder. Lafontaine's supporters, politicians like Gerhard Schröder and Reinhard Klimmt, head of the Saarland parliamentary fraction, were in the minority.

On 5 June Lafontaine told the party leadership that he intended to write them a letter announcing his resignation from the candidacy. A group of prominent Social Democrats, led by Willy Brandt and Hans-Jochen Vogel, promptly hurried to Saarbrücken and managed to talk him out of it. He told Vogel on 9 June that he would still run. That same day, the east German Social Democrats called on their western colleagues to vote for the treaty. On 14 June the party executive and council determined that the 'improvements' reached in talks with the government (including a supplementary article to the law governing the treaty's implementation) were sufficient to warrant its passage.

The next day, both German governments made a joint statement on how unresolved property questions would be handled. It said that 'expropriations based on occupation law or occupation sovereignty (1945 to 1949)' were

no longer reversible. The governments of the Soviet Union and the German Democratic Republic see no possibility of revising the decisions taken at that period of time. In the light of the historical developments, the government of the Federal Republic of Germany takes note of this. It is of the view that a final decision on any state compensation payments must be reserved for a future all-German parliament.

On the most controversial property issue, however, the Bonn government did get its way. This meant 'restitution before compensation'. Property expropriated after the founding of the GDR was, as a rule, to be restored to the earlier owner. This did *not* apply to expropriated land and buildings later dedicated to 'general use', incorporated into 'complex housing and settlement construction', or given over to industrial use. If GDR citizens had 'acquired in an honest manner the ownership or usufruct of expropriated real estate', the earlier owners were to be compensated in a socially acceptable way. Since many deeds had been systematically rendered useless, however, it would later prove extraordinarily difficult to determine property rights. This turned the precedence of restitution into a investment hindrance. Another obstacle was the law of 7 March on the sale of publicly owned property, which had been continuing under the new cabinet. The de Maizière administration promised to put a stop to it. In unclear ownership situations, sales concluded after 18 October 1989, the day of Honecker's fall, were to be scrutinized.

The Treaty on the Creation of a Monetary, Economic, and Social Union between the Federal Republic and the GDR was passed by the two parliaments on 21 June 1990. In the Volkskammer 302 delegates voted for and 82 against it, with one abstention. The two-thirds majority necessary to amend the constitution was thus reached. The result in the Bundestag was 444 to 60, again with 1 abstention. The rejections came from 35 Green and 25 SPD delegates. Speaking for the former, Antje Vollmer lamented that West German politicians had 'never thought the citizens of the GDR capable of handling the whole truth about the processes [of unification], and offering them an idea of unity totally fixated on the Deutschmark and economic prosperity.' Peter Glotz, speaking for the SPD minority, stated: 'We are for the unification of the two German states. But we are deeply convinced that the federal government has taken the wrong path to the unification of the two German states.'

The Bundesrat dealt with the treaty on the following day. All *Länder* except the Saarland and Lower Saxony voted for it. The new prime minister of the latter, Gerhard Schröder, reasoned his rejection in a way that recalled Habermas's article on 'Deutschmark nationalism'.

It would certainly have been reasonable—if we want a legitimation for the process of German unity not only in the GDR, but here, too—that we especially involve the people who have been politically socialized in the Federal Republic in deciding the question that will define their future: namely, under what kind of constitution, and in what kind of constitutional reality, they wish to live . . . For this reason, I believe, such a constitution must be presented to the people, and they must be able to vote on it, and this should happen, in my view, before there are all-German elections.

The monetary union and the 'political' exchange rate of one to one were, first and foremost, an attempt to stop the population haemorrhage from the east. Some 38,000 people had left the GDR for West Germany between the Volkskammer elections on 18 March and the end of May. That made a total of 184,000 since the beginning of the year. Speculations over an exchange rate of two to one drove the numbers up again in April. Slogans like the following were frequently heard and carried on signs at demonstrations in the GDR: 'If the Deutschmark comes, we stay. If it doesn't, we'll go to it.' When the monetary union became reality on Sunday 1 July 1990, its effect on the East Germans was as dramatic as the West German monetary reform on 20 June 1948 had been for the citizens of the FRG. There was now only one legal tender in Germany, the

Deutsche Mark. The inspection of personal documents at the German–German border crossings was also terminated that same day. East Germans had every reason for joy. They were now a good deal closer to sharing equal rights with their compatriots in the west. The *Deutsche Mark* had changed from a West German symbol to a symbol of Germany.

A failure of the monetary union, for which Oskar Lafontaine was working as late as April, would have taken Germany to the brink of political catastrophe. The fact that he did not succeed in gaining the support of his party was due to the conscientiousness of Social Democrats like Hans-Jochen Vogel. It was not the monetary union *per se* that provoked massive criticism. The things the experts objected to were, for the most part, politically unavoidable. The real errors were the principle of 'restitution before compensation' and the financing through debt. The Bonn government and coalition were responsible for the first. All political forces in the FRG were responsible for the second.

'The whole discussion in the media and in politics showed how journalists and politicians judged the attitude of the citizens in the Federal Republic to the detriment of unity: German unity, yes, but at no charge, please!', writes the political scientist Dieter Grosser.

The decisions in connection with the German Unity Fund established a pattern according to which the further financing was handled: the precedence of debt financing. Though assailable, this was politically the easiest way to procure funds. The special fund was used as an independent holder of debt whenever possible, in order to keep the impact on the public budgets cosmetically small . . . The use of the funds followed the same trend, which was in evidence already in May 1990: debt-financed expenditures, which economically and constitutionally speaking were only justifiable for financing investments, served primarily to support consumption. Thus the wrong financial course was set towards unity already in May 1990. Politically, however, no other option seemed available at the time.[13]

THE GERMAN QUESTION ON THE INTERNATIONAL STAGE

The Two-Plus-Four negotiations were scheduled to commence in May at the ministerial level. But the Soviet position hardened again suddenly before they could get under way. During a visit by Modrow to Moscow on 5 and 6 March, Shevardnadze told the prime minister that German unification according to Article 23 was unacceptable and illegitimate. Moreover, Gorbachev declared that the Soviet Union could not agree to any kind of NATO membership for a united Germany. Shortly thereafter the French president threw an unexpected obstacle in Kohl's path. During a visit by Prime Minister Mazowiecki in Paris on 9 March, Mitterrand came out in support of Warsaw's position that a German–Polish treaty on the recognition of the Oder–Neisse border should be signed *before* German unification and that Poland should have at least some kind of role in the Two-Plus-Four talks. (As far as the border question was concerned, the last point was not controversial between Bonn and Paris.)

On another disputed question, however, France was firmly in support of the FRG, as was the United States. On 14 March in Bonn, at the first meeting preliminary to the Two-Plus-Four negotiations, both Paris and Washington opposed the Soviet demand for a peace treaty. Forty-five years after the end of the Second World War, the concept of a 'peace treaty' seemed like a relapse into a bygone era and obsolete political categories—not to mention the prospect of conducting talks with the 110 countries officially at war with Germany in May 1945. But Bonn had an even greater worry: peace treaty negotiations could put reparations claims on the agenda again—claims by states of the former eastern bloc, but also by western and neutral countries. (The London Debt Agreement of 27 February 1953, in which the eastern bloc states did not participate, had deferred reparations claims to a final peace treaty.)

On the peace treaty issue, the British government's position during the internal western debate had not differed notably from that of Moscow. In no other western country was the fear of a 'Fourth Reich' so great as in Great Britain. On 31 October 1989, ten days before the fall of the wall, the Irish historian and journalist Conor Cruise O'Brien wrote an article in the London *Times* entitled 'Beware a Reich Resurging'. 'I fear that the Fourth Reich, if it comes,' wrote O'Brien, 'will have a natural tendency to resemble its predecessor.' The Conservative prime minister shared this concern. In an interview with the *Sunday Times* on 25 February 1990 she stated that German reunification meant that Europe was headed for an 'enormous upheaval': 'You cannot just ignore the history of this century as if it did not just happen and say: "We are going to unify and everything else will have to be worked out afterwards." That is not the way.'

One month later, on 24 March 1990, Margaret Thatcher and Foreign Secretary Douglas Hurd met with four prominent historians and two publicist experts on Germany—Gordon Craig (Stanford), Fritz Stern (Columbia University in New York), Hugh Trevor-Roper (Baron Dacre of Glanton; Oxford), Norman Stone (Oxford), Timothy Garton Ash, and George Urban—to discuss the consequences of German reunification. The meeting took place at the prime minister's estate at Chequers. An account written by Thatcher's private secretary Charles Powell, who was present, found its way to the press on 15 July. It revealed that a good deal of the all-day discussion had focused on alleged German character traits like angst, aggressiveness, assertiveness, bullying, egotism, inferiority complexes, and sentimentality.

The 'optimists', according to the report, had pointed out that Germany and the Germans had changed fundamentally and for the better. 'After 1945 there was no longer a sense of historic mission, no ambitions for physical conquest, no more militarism. Education and the writing of history had changed. There was an innocence of mind about the past on the part of the new generation of Germans. We should have no real worries about them.' But even the benevolent participants were not free of worries. 'We could not assume that a united Germany would fit quite so comfortably into Western Europe as the FRG. There would be a growing inclination to resurrect the concept of *Mittel-Europa* with Germany's role being that of broker between East and West.' Still, the final recommendation of the experts was that 'we should be nice to the Germans.'

The German public was outraged at the 'Chequers affair'. One of the reasons was because on 14 July, the day before the *Independent on Sunday* published Powell's notes, Nicholas Ridley, secretary of state for trade and industry, had said in an interview with the *Spectator* that the Germans wanted to take over the whole of Europe. 'You might just as well give it to Adolf Hitler, frankly.' When confronted with the objection that Kohl was certainly preferable to Hitler, Ridley said that Kohl would 'soon be coming here and trying to say that this is what we should do on the banking front and this is what our taxes should be. I mean, he'll soon be trying to take over everything.'

Several of those present at the Chequers seminar immediately contradicted the tenor of Powell's account and its angry German commentators. Good will towards present-day Germany and German unification, they said, far outweighed the criticism of the Germany of Bismarck, Wilhelm II, and Hitler. Nonetheless, Margaret Thatcher's negative attitude towards everything that had been happening in Germany since autumn 1989 could not be overlooked. In September she had tried to commit Gorbachev to rejecting reunification. At the meeting of the European Council in Strasbourg in December, she had campaigned for a Franco-British axis to stop German unity, and she made another attempt in this direction during a meeting with Mitterrand in January 1990. In February she voiced her concerns in a telephone conversation with George Bush.

But all to no avail. Gorbachev began to rethink his position soon after the new year began. Mitterrand shared Thatcher's fears but was unwilling to break with Kohl. Bush was for German reunification, as long as it happened on western conditions. The historians and writers at the Chequers seminar also did not support Thatcher's hard line. It is possible they even managed to soften it a little. In any case, after the end of March Thatcher's resistance to German unification began to wane measurably. She treated Kohl with great courtesy at the German–British 'Königswinter conference' on 29 March in Cambridge, and again at the consultations in London the following day.

Three weeks later, on 21 April in Dublin, the EC foreign ministers agreed to the incorporation of the GDR into the European Community in the process of German unity. The European Commission under Jacques Delors had done preliminary studies, working up a three-stage plan. As far as Germany and France were concerned, the process of European integration was to move forward at the same time. Dumas and Genscher presented their colleagues with an ambitious plan towards this end. It had been the subject of intensive consultations between Bonn and Paris in the weeks before and on 18 April had led to a joint letter from

Mitterrand and Kohl to the president of the European Commission, Charles Haughey, the prime minister of Ireland. The EC, it said, should create a second intergovernmental conference on political union concurrent to the deliberations over monetary union.

In light of far-reaching changes in Europe and in view of the completion of the single market and the realization of economic and monetary union, we consider it necessary to accelerate the political construction of the Europe of the Twelve. We believe that it is time to 'transform relations as a whole among the member states into a European Union . . . and invest this union with the necessary means of action', as envisaged by a Single Act [of 1 July 1987, H.A.W.].

The objective was to 'strengthen the democratic legitimation of the union, render its institutions more efficient, ensure unity and coherence of the union's economic, monetary, and political action', and 'define and implement a common foreign and security policy'. The foreign ministers were to prepare an initial report for the meeting of the European Council in June and a final report for the meeting in December 1990. The two intergovernmental conferences were to be coordinated in such a way as to make the European Union a reality on 1 January 1993.

Mitterrand had complied with Kohl to the extent that the Political Union—or what remained of it—would now be undertaken and completed *together* with the monetary union. But the concept of a 'European Union', which replaced 'Political Union' in the letter, bore all the marks of a dilatory formal compromise. It concealed ongoing differences of opinion between Paris and Bonn over the form and content of the desired union. Bonn wanted to strengthen the European Parliament and Community institutions like the Ministers' Council and the Commission. Instead, the letter spoke only of 'strengthening democratic legitimacy' and making the institutions 'more efficient'. France wanted to neutralize the economic might of a larger Germany as much as possible. The FRG wanted to use the monetary union to leverage the political unification of Europe. The 18 April letter served Paris better than Bonn. Kohl was willing to pay this price for French support of German unity.

When the heads of state and government of the EC countries met again in Dublin on 28 April, the British, Danish, and Portuguese objections to a new intergovernmental conference were so strong that the decision had to be postponed again. By the time of the next meeting in June, the foreign ministers were to examine whether treaty changes were going to be necessary. But there was basic agreement that the European Community should become a European Union by 1 January 1993. To this extent, the Franco-German initiative was a success.

The European Council's official statement on German unity did not betray any of the frictions of the past months between Bonn and London and Bonn and Paris:

The Community warmly welcomes German Unification. It looks forward to the positive and fruitful contribution that all Germans can make following the forthcoming integration of the territory of the German Democratic Republic into the Community. We are confident that German Unification—the result of a freely expressed wish on the part of the German people—will be a positive factor in the development of Europe as a whole and of the Community in particular . . . We are pleased that German Unification is taking place under a European roof. The Community will ensure that the integration of the territory of the German Democratic Republic into the Community is accomplished in a smooth and harmonious way . . . The integration will become effective as soon as reunification is legally established, subject to the necessary transitional arrangements. It will be carried out without revision of the Treaties.

One week later, the first conference of foreign ministers in the framework of the Two-Plus-Four talks took place in Bonn. The date, 5 May 1990, could hardly have been more symbolic. The Federal Republic had become a sovereign state (with certain restrictions) exactly thirty-five years before. Genscher, Meckel, Baker, Shevardnadze, Hurd, and Dumas came to an agreement about the focal points in the work that lay ahead of them. There were to be four of these: borders, political-military matters, Berlin issues, and Germany's status within international law after the termination of the rights and responsibilities of the Four Powers. At first, Shevardnadze had demanded that a further item be put on the agenda, the 'synchronization' of German unification with the pan-European process. Since nobody agreed with him, however, he finally assented to a modification of the description of the second area to 'political-military matters, in view of approaches to suitable security structures in Europe'.

In substance, however, disagreement continued. By 'synchronization' the Soviet foreign minister meant the replacement of the existing alliances with pan-European, cooperative security structures—before German reunification. He rejected NATO membership for a reunified Germany. The western powers, including the FRG, wanted the CSCE process to be expanded while maintaining NATO. The GDR took a middle position: cooperative security structures should be built up after German unification; unified Germany would only temporarily be a member of NATO, which would also have to undergo major changes.

Shevardnadze also made another suggestion that caused a great deal of consternation: Germany's inner unification, he said, should be chronologically separated from its foreign and security policy status. That is, Germany was to become a state before the alliance question was settled. In this scenario, the rights of the Four Powers would have continued in a reunified Germany for an undefined period of time. The country would not have been sovereign. Genscher did not decisively reject this proposal before the first Two-Plus-Four round came to an end, thus giving rise to the impression that the Federal Republic was prepared to accept this kind of 'de-coupling'. But Kohl categorically rejected it, and after Genscher, too, had told the Bundestag on 10 May that unified Germany was not to be burdened down with unresolved questions, Bonn's position was once again clear: the internal and external unification processes were to be simultaneous.

Thus the first round had brought no progress on the alliance question. The most important reason for Shevardnadze's staunch rejection of German NATO membership probably had to do with the Lithuania crisis. The erstwhile Baltic Soviet republic had declared its independence in March, provoking harsh counter-measures from Moscow, including the deployment of KGB troops and a stop to oil and natural gas shipments. Gorbachev (who had been elected president of the Soviet Union on 15 March) was in a difficult position. If he gave the impression of inclining towards the western viewpoint on the military status of Germany, it would give his adversaries in the Communist party yet another grievance against him.

Nothing changed in the Soviet position for three weeks after the first Two-Plus-Four meeting. Baker and Mitterrand both visited Moscow during this time (the former on 18, the latter on 25 May), but neither noticed any softening. In a long conversation with Genscher in Geneva on 23 May, Shevardnadze said that it was psychologically and politically impossible for him and Gorbachev to support a reunified Germany's accession to NATO.

Around this same time, however, there were increasing signs of imminent economic collapse in the Soviet Union. Its calls for western help, especially from the United States and the FRG, could no longer be ignored. American assistance was not to be expected at this time. On 1 May the Senate had passed a measure denying commercial privileges to the Soviet Union until it ended its embargo of Lithuania and started negotiations. For his part, George Bush had no desire to cause trouble for Gorbachev. When Kohl and Mitterrand wrote to the Lithuanian president Vytautas Landsbergis on 26 April, asking him to delay the declaration of independence for the time being, they did so with the express agreement of the American president.

Bush also supported German assistance to the Soviet Union. On 4 May, just before the start of the Two-Plus-Four talks, Shevardnadze had communicated a message from Gorbachev and Nikolai Ryshkov, the Soviet prime minister, asking Kohl for a German loan to secure the solvency of the Soviet Union. Kohl was only too happy to promise support. On 13 May Horst Teltschik, accompanied by two officials from the Deutsche Bank and Dresdner Bank, Hilmar Kopper and Wolfgang Röller, flew to Moscow. Talks with Gorbachev, Shevardnadze, and Ryshkov led to a 5 billion mark loan to the USSR, guaranteed by the FRG. Gorbachev was given very clearly to understand that Bonn viewed this assistance as part of a 'package deal' towards the solution of the German question.

Between Teltschik's visit to Moscow and his own to Washington on 31 May, Gorbachev must have been visited by doubts about whether he would be able to uphold the Soviet rejection of a German NATO membership much longer—at least if he hoped to gain further western assistance. In his talk with Bush at the White House on 31 May, he repeated Shevardnadze's frequent statement that a united Germany could belong either to both alliances or to neither. Then he brought up the idea of the Soviet Union joining NATO, and said that both alliances should be changed into primarily political organizations. When Bush noted that the CSCE Final Act granted every state the right to freely choose its own alliance, Germany included, Gorbachev agreed with him—to the shock of his advisers, Sergei Achromeyev and Valentin Falin. The United States and the USSR, Gorbachev said, should announce that they would allow united Germany to decide what alliance it wished to belong to. He also agreed when Bush proposed another wording: the USA would clearly declare its support for German NATO membership, but it would also tolerate a different decision.

When Bush called him immediately after the first round of talks with Gorbachev, Kohl was at first unable to grasp what he was hearing: the Soviet leader had just admitted that a unified Germany had the right to opt for full membership in the Atlantic alliance. At their joint press conference at the end of the summit on 3 June, Bush made the following announcement, which went uncontradicted by Gorbachev:

On the matter of Germany's external alliances, I believe, as do Chancellor Kohl and members of the alliance, that the united Germany should be a full member of NATO. President Gorbachev, frankly, does not hold that view. But we are in full agreement that the matter of alliance membership is, in accordance with the Helsinki Final Act, a matter for the Germans to decide.

Gorbachev returned to Moscow without the promise of a loan, but he was able to secure a Soviet–American commercial treaty. His concession on the question of Germany's future alliance status did represent a breakthrough. After his obviously improvised remark about Germany's right to decide its own alliance status, Gorbachev could no longer simply return to his former hard line. As long as both the basic conditions and the details had not yet been worked out, however, the USSR was also not committed to an acceptance of full German NATO membership. Much now depended on the manner in which the Atlantic community understood and described its own future role.

The NATO foreign ministers met in Scotland at Turnberry on 7 and 8 June. The result was the 'Message from Turnberry', which was a response to a Warsaw Pact announcement of the previous day stating that the ideologically-driven enmity of the past was over and offering cooperation to the Atlantic alliance. The NATO representatives in turn extended 'to the Soviet Union and to all other European countries the hand of friendship and cooperation'. They spoke of the growing importance of the CSCE process as an instrument for cooperation and security in Europe. This process

should be strengthened and given effective institutional form. We are committed to work for a rapid and successful conclusion of the Vienna negotiations on conventional forces. The arms control process must be vigorously pursued. We are convinced that German unification is a major contribution to stability in Europe. Recognizing the eminently political importance of these tasks, we are ready to do our utmost for their accomplishment.

The Warsaw Pact and NATO conferences were followed by several meetings between Genscher and Shevardnadze. On 11 June they met in Brest in Byelorussia (formerly Brest-Litovsk). The Soviet foreign minister had proposed this location—which in Poland awakened unpleasant memories of the partition of the country in the wake of the Hitler–Stalin pact—for personal reasons. His brother Akaki had fallen and been buried there in June 1941, in the first days of the war between the USSR and the German Reich. Genscher would later refer to this encounter, which involved a joint visit to the grave of Shevardnadze's brother, as 'perhaps the most important German–Soviet meeting prior to the unification'. Shevardnadze, Genscher records, stated in Brest that a German NATO membership 'as we wish it' was possible, if NATO and the Warsaw Pact were to change into *political* alliances and fundamentally reshape their relationship.

The two men saw each other again in Copenhagen on 15 June at the second CSCE conference on the 'human dimension' of the east–west relations. Shevardnadze also had a long exchange with James Baker there. Another meeting between Genscher and Shevardnadze followed on 18 June in Münster. Genscher chose this city for historic reasons. 'The Peace of Westphalia in October 1648 brought the Thirty Years War to an end in Europe,' he wrote in his memoirs. 'Now a war that had lasted more than forty years, the Cold War, was being brought to an end.' The Copenhagen and Münster meetings confirmed the impression that Genscher had gained in Brest: the USSR was in the process of accepting the idea of German NATO membership, as long as the new NATO clearly differed from the old one.

Not all political forces in West Germany were happy about an Atlantic solution to the German question. The SPD security expert Egon Bahr held to his view—by now shared only by a majority of his party—that the two alliances ultimately had to be replaced by a pan-European, collective security system. (Genscher himself had come out for the same idea in a speech to the West European Union on 23 March, to the great displeasure of the chancellor.) On 18 June in Bonn, just before the fifth meeting of ministerial officials in connection with the Two-Plus-Four talks, Bahr warned the advisers of the East German foreign minister that the Bonn government was working with the USSR towards a bilateral agreement on full German NATO membership. As Bahr saw it, the rights of the Four Powers had to be preserved for the time being. 'If the rights of the Four Powers are replaced, there will no longer be a lever for a European security system.' To Bahr's disappointment, Meckel's associates did not fall in with his proposal to defer the restoration of sovereignty to a united Germany—despite the fact that they, like Meckel, shared Bahr's goal of a pan-European security architecture.

On 21 June 1990, the day the Bundestag and Volkskammer ratified the Treaty on Monetary, Economic, and Social Union in third reading, the two parliaments also passed identically worded resolutions on the German–Polish border. It stated that the border would be determined by the treaty between the GDR and the Republic of Poland of 6 July 1950, including the supplementary and implementation agreements, as well as by the Treaty of Warsaw between the FRG and the People's Republic of Poland from 7 December 1970. Furthermore, the delegates declared that the border should be confirmed by a treaty under international law between united Germany and the Republic of Poland. The following language was to be used: 'Both sides confirm the inviolability of the border between them now and in the future and commit themselves to unqualified respect for each other's sovereignty and territorial integrity. Both sides declare that they entertain no territorial claims against each other and will raise no such claims in the future.' The two German governments were exhorted to communicate this resolution to Poland 'as the expression of their own will'.

The preamble to this resolution addressed the history of the German–Polish relationship. The parliaments, it said, were acting

in awareness of the fact that the Polish people has experienced terrible suffering on account of crimes committed by Germans and in the name of Germany; in awareness of the fact that great injustice has been done to millions of Germans who were driven from their ancestral homes; with the wish that, in memory of the tragic and painful sides of history, a united Germany and the Republic of Poland will steadfastly continue the process of understanding and reconciliation between Germans and Poles, shape their relations with a view to the future, and thus provide an example of good neighbourliness.

The Volkskammer passed the resolution against only 6 votes (all from the DSU) and with 18 abstentions. In the Bundestag it passed by 486 votes to 15 with 3 abstentions. The rejections came from the CDU and CSU, the abstentions from one CSU delegate and two Greens.

One day later, on 22 June 1990, the second round of the Two-Plus-Four talks got under way in East Berlin. This day was the forty-ninth anniversary of the German attack on the Soviet Union, something the Soviet foreign minister did not fail to mention. Shevardnadze presented his colleagues with the comprehensive outline of a 'final international settlement with Germany'. It proposed a double membership in NATO and the Warsaw Pact for a transitional period of five years and a total Bundeswehr strength of 200,000 to 250,000 soldiers. All other foreign ministers rejected the idea of double alliance membership. On the question of troop strength, Markus Meckel mostly agreed with Shevardnadze, much to the displeasure of his four western colleagues. Meckel's own suggestion was 300,000 troops. Moreover, the East German foreign minister wanted German unification to mark the beginning of a transition to a European security system. Dumas called on both German governments to immediately begin talks with Poland on a border treaty. This was not only the position of Paris, but also of Warsaw.

All the foreign ministers acknowledged that Poland should have a chance to express its views on the border settlement at the next meeting, scheduled in Paris on 17 July. Everyone also agreed that a unified Germany would include the territory of the FRG and GDR and all of Berlin, would raise no additional territorial claims, and would officially recognize the final status of its borders. In the ensuing discussion Genscher succeeded in convincing Shevardnadze to have the concluding document of the Two-Plus-Four negotiations ready for the CSCE special summit that November. This committed the Soviet Union to a clear unification timetable.

The balance of the Berlin conference was mixed. Shevardnadze had taken positions that seemed far behind what Gorbachev had said in Washington and everything he himself had been telling Genscher and Baker in the weeks thereafter. If NATO changed its character and the CSCE gained in importance, German NATO membership would appear in a completely different light. But it was obvious that Gorbachev and Shevardnadze were biding their time until after the upcoming NATO summit in London on 5–6 July and the twenty-eighth congress of the Soviet Communist party, scheduled to begin on 1 July. If both events went smoothly, the Soviet leadership would again have a greater freedom of action. Shevardnadze himself explained this to Baker in a long talk after the conference.

Three days later the EC heads of state and government met again in Dublin. Lothar de Maizière, prime minister of the GDR, was present as a guest. Together with Helmut Kohl he reported on the preparations for the German monetary union. The two intergovernmental conferences, on economic/monetary and political union, were set to begin work in December. Kohl's and Mitterrand's April agreement had become the new EC policy.

The Dublin summit of the EC was followed nine days later by the NATO summit in London. The decisions taken there were calculated to go a long way towards accommodating Gorbachev. NATO emphasized its defensive nature and its changing *political* role. It would respond to the withdrawal of Soviet troops from central and eastern Europe and a treaty on the limitation of conventional forces in Europe by fundamentally reviewing its own forces and strategy. It would field smaller and restructured active forces and decrease its reliance on nuclear weapons—that is, revise its doctrines of 'forward presence' and 'flexible response'. NATO also underscored its willingness to work for the elimination of all nuclear artillery shells from Europe, including short-range missiles. The Warsaw Pact states were invited to participate in a joint declaration on the renunciation of the threat or use of force and to take up regular diplomatic liaison with NATO. Finally, the Conference on Security and Cooperation in Europe 'should become more prominent in Europe's future, bringing together the countries of Europe and North America.' It was proposed that the CSCE summit in Paris at the end of 1990 sign an agreement on conventional forces in Europe and 'set new standards for the establishment, and preservation, of free societies'.

The news about NATO's 'London Declaration' reached Gorbachev during the CPSU congress in Moscow. Both he and Shevardnadze were having a difficult time. The conservative opposition around Yegor Ligachev accused both men of having lost eastern Europe. The London Declaration strengthened Gorbachev's position. It was one of the main reasons he was reconfirmed in his party office by a clear majority, thus receiving a mandate to continue his reformist course.

The congress came to an end on 13 July after nearly two weeks of deliberations. Two days before, the world economic summit of the seven largest industrial nations had come to an end in Houston. Though he was not present, Gorbachev had been at the centre of attention in Texas, too. Chancellor Kohl was the most vocal proponent of generous economic and financial assistance for the reformer in Moscow, but he did not manage to convince all participants. George Bush and Margaret Thatcher also wanted to help the Soviet Union, but only after careful analysis of its economic problems.

One of the factors militating against western help for Moscow was now no longer an issue. In accordance with the request by Mitterrand and Kohl, Lithuania had suspended its declaration of independence on 29 July, and Gorbachev had lifted the Soviet embargo the next day. For this reason the G7 did not simply reject Kohl's initiative. The International Monetary Fund was asked to conduct a study of the Soviet economic situation and present reform recommendations by the close of the year. An assistance programme would then be decided on this basis.

On 15 July (the same day the account of the Chequers seminar hit the press) Kohl arrived in Moscow with a government delegation. He was responding to an invitation from Gorbachev on 9 June. Much had happened since the two men had last met in February. For Gorbachev, Kohl was the western statesman who had done and continued to do the most for *perestroika*. No other western country was willing to help the USSR as much as West Germany, and only Bonn could prevent a power vacuum from arising in the middle of Europe. The era in which the partition of Germany had guaranteed relative stability in Europe was definitively over. For European stability the pressing need was now German unification.

Had the Soviet Union been stronger it would never have accepted the western condition of full membership in NATO for a united Germany. But since the Warsaw Pact had practically ceased to exist and there was no longer a military balance of power between the east and west, the Kremlin had no alternative. It could not even refute the argument that a Germany firmly integrated into NATO was less of a threat to the USSR than a non-aligned Germany. The London Declaration had made it easier for the Soviets to accept the inevitable, and after the CPSU congress Gorbachev no longer had to worry about resistance from his adversaries for the time being. If economic assistance from Bonn allowed him to survive politically, then Kohl could be granted what could now only be delayed, but no longer prevented—the reunification of Germany and full German membership in the Atlantic alliance.

During the Moscow talks on 15 July no more was said about a transitional phase between the restoration of German political unity and the restoration of sovereignty. The rights of the Four Powers were to come to an end with unification, Gorbachev said. When Kohl asked if that meant Germany would have full sovereignty at that time, he answered: 'Of course'. The only condition was that NATO would not extend its area of operations to the territory of the GDR until the Soviet troops there had been withdrawn, which Gorbachev said would take three to four years. Kohl could agree to this transitional phase. He also stated his willingness to help finance the troop withdrawal. The two leaders also agreed on the future German borders and that Germany would not pursue atomic, biological, or chemical weapons.

What Gorbachev told Kohl represented *his* position. 'Gorbachev had been granted the authority for the decisions he made, neither by the Supreme Soviet nor by the government, neither by the defence or presidential council nor by the federation council, not to mention the politburo or the secretariat of the central committee,' writes one of his sharpest critics, Valentin Falin, at that time director of the international relations department in the central committee, in his memoirs. 'The president had not even told the parliament, the government, or the councils about his plans and intentions. The presidential council, and it alone, was deemed worthy of approving the results achieved in the negotiations with the leaders of the Federal Republic.' For the time being, however, Gorbachev had the power to do what he wanted, and he was resolved to do what he thought was right.

Gorbachev did not want Moscow to be the only place the German–Soviet negotiations were held. He had invited the whole German delegation to his native town in the Caucasus, Archys in the district of Stavropol. This was meant as a personal gesture to the German chancellor. There the two men discussed the future troop strength of the Bundeswehr. Kohl proposed an upper limit of 370,000 troops, which Gorbachev ultimately accepted. (There were 495,000 troops in 1989 and more than 521,000 in 1990, after the incorporation of units from the National People's Army of the GDR.) In order to avoid 'singling Germany out', the reductions were not to begin until the Vienna accord on conventional forces in Europe was in force. Only non-NATO units of the Bundeswehr were to be stationed on former GDR territory until the Soviet troop withdrawal was complete. Kohl also promised that foreign NATO troops would not be moved there after the Soviet soldiers were gone.

The amount of financial assistance the USSR would receive from the FRG was not fixed at this time. Finance Minister Waigel had carefully avoided making concrete promises to his colleague, Stepan Sitaryan. Politically speaking, however, the die was already cast. By agreeing to German NATO membership the Soviet Union had cleared away the largest obstacle to German unity. Kohl and Genscher had every reason to be proud of what they had achieved. The reunification was now within reach.

On 17 July, the day after the conclusion of the German–Soviet talks, the third Two-Plus-Four round was held in Paris. Polish foreign minister Krzysztof Skubiszewski participated in some of the deliberations. Poland was now no longer insisting that the German–Polish border agreement enter into force before the Two-Plus-Four treaty. It was content with the assurance that the border treaty would be signed and ratified as soon as possible after reunification and the restoration of German sovereignty. The Paris round mostly dealt with the current status of the negotiations. Now that the talks in Moscow and Archys had gone so well, the final Two-Plus-Four documents could be drafted. They were to be finished by the next round in Moscow on 12 September, which looked to be the last.

Not all of the participants in Paris were pleased with the outcome. The GDR government, especially the foreign office, was upset that it had not been consulted about Kohl's talks with Gorbachev in Moscow and the Caucasus. Meckel's state secretary Hans-Jürgen Misselwitz told a conference of officials from the six foreign offices on 17 July that the GDR still reserved the right to determine its own position, since it had not been officially informed of the result and still had substantive reservations. For his part, Meckel was not content with Kohl's assurance that Germany would not have ABC weapons. He demanded that no nuclear weapons be stationed on German soil. But this met with no response.

And in fact, Gorbachev's talks with Kohl had taken the ground from beneath the feet of any independent GDR foreign policy. By the summer of 1990, even London and Paris no longer had a decisive role in the negotiations over Germany's future. The politicians upon whom everything depended sat in Washington, Moscow, and Bonn. The events of 1989–90 had changed the post-war hierarchy.[14]

THE PATH TO UNITY: THE UNIFICATION AND TWO-PLUS-FOUR TREATIES

That the GDR would be joined to the Federal Republic was, as far as the popular will was concerned, all but certain after 18 March 1990. On this day the great majority of East Germans voted for parties that favoured accession according to Article 23 of the Basic Law, and the Basic Law obligated the state to make the people's will reality. *When* accession would take place depended primarily on the result of the Two-Plus-Four process. *How* it would take place depended on negotiations between the two German governments. On this Bonn and East Berlin agreed.

Bonn began preparations for the Unification Treaty even before the negotiations on economic, monetary, and social union had been concluded. Interior

Minister Wolfgang Schäuble, who would be leading the unification talks, had a first outline ready by 29 May. He submitted it to his East German partner, Günther Krause, the parliamentary state secretary in the prime minister's office (and also the CDU fraction leader). Haste was necessary; there were forces in the Volkskammer demanding immediate and unconditional accession. On 17 June (the Day of German Unity, which the two parliaments celebrated together) the DSU brought forward a motion to this effect. It was transferred to the committee for legal and constitutional affairs. But new motions could be expected.

Schäuble and Krause settled on 2 December 1990 for the official unification. Since the twelfth German Bundestag was scheduled for election that day, both states could hold elections for a unified German parliament. It was expected that the Two-Plus-Four negotiations would be over by this time. The Unification Treaty would involve amendments to the Basic Law, thus requiring a two-thirds majority in both the Bundestag and Bundesrat. This meant that Schäuble had to get in touch with the *Länder* and the Social Democratic opposition. He sent the now completed second treaty draft to the *Länder* on 26 and 27 June. Several points of friction were already obvious: the restructuring of finances between the federal and state levels, the redistribution of seats in the Bundesrat, and the question of the country's capital city. Everybody knew that the GDR would insist on Berlin as the seat of government and parliament. But this was by no means the unanimous view of the West German *Länder*. North Rhine-Westphalia, massively supported by Rhineland-Palatinate and the Saarland, wanted to keep the government and the Bundestag at Bonn. They prevailed upon Kohl to leave the decision to the institutions themselves—that is, to leave the issue out of the treaty.

Negotiations over unification got started on 6 July—five days after the monetary union went into effect. Schäuble and his GDR interlocutors quickly agreed to keep the constitutional changes to a minimum. The *Länder* governed by the SPD, on the other hand, insisted on new official state goals like environmental protection, responsibility for underdeveloped areas of the earth, the right to work, housing, social security, health care, education, and culture. The issue of abortion dominated the agenda in August. In the GDR there was immunity from prosecution for an abortion within the first twelve weeks of pregnancy. In West Germany abortion was permitted only if considered medically necessary. There was a large majority in the Volkskammer for the preservation of the status quo, and the West German Social Democrats mainly agreed. Ultimately a compromise was worked out: on this particular question Germany would remain divided into two separate zones of law during a two-year period of transition. An abortion would be immune from prosecution if performed within the new *Länder* in the two years after reunification. Thereafter new legislation would be put in place for the whole country.

After mid-July the negotiations came under increasing time pressure. As the economic situation in the GDR got worse, the number of Volkskammer delegates calling for rapid accession increased. Pan-German elections *before* 2 December 1990—the date agreed to by the parliaments' joint 'German Unity Committee' on 26 July—thus became a possibility. A common voting law was urgently needed in any case.

Schäuble and Krause signed one on 3 August. It standardized a 5 per cent exclusion clause for all German elections. The SPD and FDP were the driving forces behind this ruling, since they both believed it would be to their advantage. Parties who were not running against each other in the same *Bundesland* were permitted to form alliances. Thus the DSU could form an alliance with the CSU and thereby enter the federal parliament, whereas the PDS, which had no comparable western partner, would probably not make it past the 5 per cent clause. That this arrangement would find favour with the Federal Constitutional Court was something Schäuble himself doubted—correctly, as it turned out.

The unification negotiations were overshadowed by problems within the East German Grand Coalition. Interior Minister Diestel left the DSU on 30 June, alleging that the party had moved too far to the right for him. He was joined by the party head, Hans-Wilhelm Ebeling, on 2 July. Both men stayed in the cabinet, which meant that the DSU was no longer represented in the government. On 24 July the liberals in the League of Free Democrats also left the de Maizière cabinet, accusing the prime minister of opposing a standardized voting law for all of Germany and rapid accession to the FRG.

Shortly thereafter, the prime minister himself came to the conclusion that the economic situation in the GDR was too bad to allow of any further delay in accession. On 1 August he and Günther Krause flew to the Wolfgangsee, where Helmut Kohl was vacationing, and sought to gain the chancellor's support for earlier elections. They had in mind 14 October, for which day municipal elections were already scheduled in the GDR. If de Maizière could have his way, he also wanted the official restoration of German political unity to take place before the elections and before the forty-first anniversary of the founding of the GDR on 7 October 1990.

The path to pan-German elections before the end of the legislative period in the FRG could be cleared by a vote of confidence with a negative outcome—after the pattern of 17 December 1982. Kohl himself had no problem with this solution, but President von Weizsäcker rejected it for constitutional reasons. The only other way was an amendment to the constitution, and a two-thirds majority was nowhere in sight. Oskar Lafontaine believed that the closer the election date came to that of reunification, the better Kohl's prospects were of winning the election. Conversely, Lafontaine thought his own chances would be better if reunification could be done quickly and the elections held on the scheduled date of 2 December. Towards the end of the year, he believed, the expected enthusiasm over German unity would have faded and yielded to reality. Consequently, Helmut Kohl could not depend on the Social Democrats to hand him a two-thirds majority.

On 8 August, one week after the meeting between Kohl and de Maizière, the Volkskammer rejected the DSU motion to announce the immediate accession of the GDR to the jurisdiction of the Basic Law. Another motion by the SPD to declare accession by 15 September also failed. When the CDU and Democratic Awakening proposed that the FRG open up the possibility of elections and accession on 14 October 1990, however, a majority agreed. Early the next morning, the voting law from 3 August failed the ratification process; too few delegates were present. The Bundestag then took further deliberations over the law off the agenda. A motion by the CDU/CSU and FDP to hold pan-German elections on 14 October failed to gain the necessary two-thirds majority. This meant that the date of 2 October would be kept, which the cabinet announced later that day.

From this moment Bonn and East Berlin were dominated by the electoral campaign. On 15 August de Maizière reshuffled his cabinet. Citing political differences of opinion and the continuing economic crisis, he dismissed the Social Democratic finance minister, Walter Romberg, the non-aligned (but SPD-friendly) minister of agriculture, Peter Pollack, and the economics minister, Gerhard Pohl, who was from his own party. The prime minister accused all three men of not respecting his policy guidelines and not correctly administering funds in support of industry, commerce, and agriculture. He did not appoint new ministers, but transferred the duties of the dismissed cabinet members to the respective state secretaries. He did the same thing after dismissing Kurt Wünsche, the (now non-aligned) justice minister, because of the controversy surrounding his political biography.

The East German Social Democrats interpreted de Maizière's actions as a political declaration of war. Wolfgang Thierse, who had succeeded Ibrahim Böhme as party head, pressed for the Social Democrats to abandon the coalition. He succeeded. All SPD ministers stepped down on 20 August. De Maizière, now head of a CDU/DA minority cabinet, transferred the vacant posts partly to the remaining ministers, partly to state secretaries. He himself assumed the duties of foreign minister. On 21 August Richard Schröder, who had warned against ending the Grand Coalition, resigned as SPD fraction leader and was replaced by Thierse.

The two-thirds majority necessary for the Unification Treaty was now at risk—*if* the Social Democrats chose to oppose it. Another bill requiring a two-thirds majority passed on the second attempt: the voting law, which had failed on 9 August. The PDS, Alliance 90, and the Greens voted against it on account of the 5 per cent clause. The Bundestag passed it the next day against the votes of the Greens. It then went to the Bundesrat, where it easily passed on 24 August.

By this time the day of unification had also been set. In the early morning of 23 August the Volkskammer voted 294 to 62 (with 7 abstentions) for the joint CDU/DA/FDP/SPD motion to declare the accession of the GDR to the jurisdiction of the Basic Law according to Article 23 on 3 October 1990. As the text stated, the Volkskammer was assuming 'that by this date the deliberations on the Unification Treaty will have been completed; the Two-Plus-Four negotiations at a point where the foreign and security policy conditions of German unity will have been set; and the formation of the *Länder* such that elections to the parliaments can be held on 14 October 1990.' The negative votes came from the PDS. When Gregor Gysi angrily remarked that the parliament had 'just done no more nor less than schedule the downfall of the German Democratic Republic for 3 October 1990', the assembly broke out in cheers. Gysi's party had no part in that decision.

A few hours later Helmut Kohl, speaking in the Bundestag, called the 23 August 1990 a 'day of joy for all Germans'. On Wednesday 3 October 1990, he said, Germany would be reunified. 'It will be a great day in the history of our people. After forty years, what the preamble to the Basic Law exhorts the whole German people to do will finally be fulfilled: to achieve in free self-determination the unity and freedom of Germany.' Kohl recalled the historical achievements of Konrad Adenauer and Kurt Schumacher. He thanked the Germans in the GDR, the delegates in the Volkskammer, and the civil rights activists in Poland and Hungary. He also thanked the Hungarian prime minister Miklós Németh, who had opened the border for refugees from the GDR and, in so doing, taken the first stone out of the wall; George Bush; François Mitterrand; and Gorbachev, whose reform policy had made the far-reaching changes in Germany and Europe possible. He did not mention the name of Margaret Thatcher.

Oskar Lafontaine, speaking right after Kohl, also welcomed the decision of the Volkskammer, 'since it represents the basis for the people in the GDR to live out their future lives in freedom'. But political unity, he added, was only the prerequisite for the creation of 'real unity', that is, the 'unity of living conditions for the people in the GDR and the Federal Republic'. Lafontaine once again demanded that the costs of unification be made clear, a constitutional council be set up, and that the people be allowed to decide on their own constitution. He wanted the obsolete idea of the nation founded on biological heritage to be replaced by one like the American, French, or Swiss concept of nationality, based on universal values. Quoting one of the last Bundestag speeches by Carlo Schmidt (from 25 February 1972), Lafontaine called for 'one nation of Europe to be built'. The idea of a 'nation of Europe' had not been invented by the Social Democrat Schmidt, however. For over four decades it was the title (*Nation Europa*) of a radical right-wing journal founded by Arthur Ehrhardt, a former SS commander and expert on 'combat against small bands' in the Führer headquarters. The publication had changed its name to *Nation und Europa* at the beginning of 1990.

On 24 August, the day after the accession announcement, the Volkskammer passed a 'Law on the Security and Use of Personal Data from the Former Ministry for State Security/Office for National Security'. The relevant files were not to be given over to the federal archive, but kept in special archives in the new *Bundesländer* and in a central location in the eastern part of Berlin. Every citizen would have the right to know about any data collected on his or her person. The files were to serve the critical reappraisal of East German history, the investigation of criminal acts, and the rehabilitation of victims.

Interior Minister Schäuble, together with Günther Krause, did everything he could to prevent the new law from being incorporated into the Unification Treaty. He feared not only the abuse of the countless informer reports (in 1989 the MfS had 91,000 employees and 174,000 Unofficial Collaborators), but also the consequences of the fact that the Stasi had extensively tapped and recorded telephone conversations made in the FRG. The treaty draft disregarded the law. The protest from the Volkskammer was so massive (and nearly unanimous) that the draft had to be altered again. The result was the so-called 'Gauck office', named after the Rostock pastor Joachim Gauck, commissioner for Stasi files in the Volkskammer (and later in the German federal government). The East German activists had won their last battle. The recent past would be studied, not suppressed all over again. The victims of the second dictatorship on German soil would be able to learn what they had suffered, and who the perpetrators were.

The Treaty on the Unity of Germany was initialled in the early morning of 31 August 1990. It was approved by the governments in Bonn and East Berlin, then signed by Schäuble and Krause at 1.15 in the afternoon in the Palace of the Crown Prince on Unter den Linden street. Five new *Bundesländer* would be created out of the territory of the former GDR: Brandenburg, Mecklenburg-West Pomerania, Saxony, Saxony-Anhalt, and Thuringia. The two national holidays—in the FRG 17 June and in the GDR 7 October—would be replaced by 3 October as the 'Day of German Unity'. Berlin was designated the 'capital of Germany', but this statement was followed by an addendum that stripped it of any real meaning: 'The location of parliament and government will be decided after the restoration of German unity.'

The Unification Treaty involved the revision of a number of passages in the Basic Law. The new preamble stated the German people's will to a united Europe and to world peace. Article 23 was abolished. Article 146 held open the possibility that the Basic Law, 'which since the achievement of the unity and freedom of Germany applies to the entire German people', would cease to apply 'on the day on which a constitution freely adopted by the German people takes effect'. The legislative bodies of united Germany were urged to make additional changes to the Basic Law within two years, including language on the overarching goals of the state and the 'use of Article 146 of the Basic Law and a referendum within its framework'.

The specific areas the Unification Treaty dealt with were state finance; alignment of legal systems; public administration and law; public assets and debt; labour, social, and family policy; women's issues; health care and environmental protection; culture; education; science; and sports. Based on its composition, the Volkskammer was entitled to send 144 delegates to the eleventh German

Bundestag (elected in 1987). The new *Länder* would participate in the meetings of the Bundesrat in an advisory capacity until their respective authorized representatives (who were responsible for setting up new state government agencies) could elect a prime minister.

Bonn had had its way on several particularly controversial points. The location of the seat of government and parliament was left open, more serious constitutional amendments were postponed, and a number of unresolved property questions—specifically, matters dealing with the expropriations from the period after the founding of the GDR—were settled in its favour. East Berlin managed to push through improvements in the financial arrangements: the new *Länder* would receive 85 per cent of the resources in the German Unity Fund. This made up for the fact that they would be excluded from the financial compensation system between the states until 1994 and temporarily receive a smaller percentage of revenue from the value-added tax (at first 55 per cent, then 70 per cent of the average share until 1994). Moreover, expropriations from the occupation period would be recognized, location would determine how abortion was dealt with, and the Stasi files would be archived in a manner similar to what the Volkskammer delegates had in mind.

The fact that the treaty discussed future amendments to the constitution made it easier for the Social Democrats to vote for it. It passed in both parliaments with the necessary two-thirds majority on 20 September. In the Volkskammer the vote was 299 to 80 with 1 abstention. The negative votes came from the PDS and the delegates of the newly founded Alliance 90/The Greens. The result in the Bundestag was 440 to 47 with 3 abstentions, the rejections coming from Greens and 13 CDU/CSU delegates. The Bundesrat approved the treaty on the following day.

On the Two-Plus-Four front, the Paris conference on 17 July had left things far from settled. The general treaty on future political relations between Bonn and Moscow had yet to be prepared, the consequences of the GDR's economic obligations to the Soviet Union decided, and—hardest of all—the withdrawal and interim location of the Soviet troops in the GDR worked out. The last point was above all a question of funding. At the beginning of September the USSR demanded a total sum of 36 billion marks, far more than the West German government had been planning on paying. There followed arduous negotiations between the finance ministers and two telephone conversations between Kohl and Gorbachev. An agreement was in place by 10 September: Bonn would pay 12 billion marks and grant the Soviet Union 3 billion more in interest-free loans.

The reductions in the German armed forces had already been decided during the talks in the Caucasus in mid-July. On 30 August, during the Vienna negotiations on conventional forces in Europe, Genscher declared that the German armed forces would be reduced to 370,000 troops. The Federal Republic, he said, considered this an important German contribution to the reduction of conventional forces in Europe and was assuming 'that in the talks to follow the other participants will also make their contributions to increasing security and stability in Europe, including measures to limit the number of personnel'.

Lothar de Maizière, speaking as foreign minister of the GDR, endorsed this statement. Germany was now committed to a concession that—despite Genscher's exhortation—did not involve any concomitant obligation on the part of the other powers. However, two factors militated against the impression that Germany was being 'singled out': the nature of the forum in which Genscher and de Maizière spoke, and the voluntary character of the obligation Germany was imposing on itself—something both men were at great pains to emphasize.

The last Two-Plus-Four meeting of foreign ministers took place in Moscow on 12 September. It came close to failure when the British, backed by the Americans, insisted on NATO's right to conduct military manoeuvres on the territory of the former GDR. The Soviets rejected this, quoting Kohl's promise during the Caucasus talks that no foreign NATO troops would be transferred to East Germany. In a late-night meeting, Genscher and Baker were able to work out a compromise that the Soviets accepted: in an 'Agreed Minute', it was stated that all questions having to do with the application of the word 'deployed' were to be 'decided by the government of the united Germany in a reasonable and responsible way taking into account the security interests of each contracting party'.

This cleared away the final obstacle. The 'Treaty on the Final Settlement with Respect to Germany' could now be signed. It ended the rights of the Four Powers, restoring to Germany full sovereignty in its domestic and foreign affairs at the moment of reunification (not upon the conclusion of the ratification process). Western troops would remain on German soil as long as Soviet troops were stationed on the territory of the former GDR and in Berlin. The treaty contained the language worked out on Germany's borders, its renunciation of ABC weapons, its troop reductions, and its right to join alliances with all the accompanying rights and responsibilities.

Included in the documents of 12 September was a joint letter by Genscher and de Maizière informing their four colleagues of the common declaration on the unresolved property questions between the two countries. This gave the 'land reform' additional diplomatic backing, at the express wish of the Soviets. The letter also committed Germany to the care of war graves and monuments commemorating the victims of war and dictatorship; stated that parties and groups hostile to the constitution, including those with Nazi aims, would continue to be banned by the Basic Law; and said that the status of international treaties concluded by the GDR would be worked out in consultation with the relevant treaty partners.

The day after the Moscow meeting, Genscher and Shevardnadze initialled the 'Treaty on Good Neighbour relations, Partnership, and Cooperation between the Federal Republic of Germany and the Union of Soviet Socialist Republics' (usually referred to in English as the German–Soviet friendship treaty). On 24 September the GDR, with the agreement of the USSR, withdrew from the Warsaw Pact. On 27 and 28 September an exchange of notes with the three western powers suspended the 1952 Germany Treaty. (It was formally abolished after the Two-Plus-Four treaty went into effect on 15 March 1991.) On 1 October the Four Powers suspended the exercise of their rights and privileges with regard to Berlin and Germany until the Two-Plus-Four treaty entered into force. This was done during a CSCE conference in New York, where Genscher gave an official report on the results of the Two-Plus-Four negotiations. President Bush presented comprehensive proposals for the institutionalization of the CSCE. He spoke of a 'trans-Atlantic partnership', by which he meant not only the relations between the USA and its western allies, but now also those with all of the CSCE participants, including the USSR.

From 1 October, therefore, the international foundations of German unity were in place. George Bush's statements even went beyond what Bonn had hoped. Domestically things were not so good. An 'accident' (though it was not entirely unexpected) had occurred two days before, when the Federal Constitutional Court handed down its decision on the suit brought against the new voting law by the Republicans (an extreme right-wing party founded in November 1983), the Greens, and the Left List/PDS (*Linke Liste/PDS*, an electoral alliance formed on 5 August 1990). The court declared the treaty partly unconstitutional. The unified 5 per cent exclusion clause, it said, violated the principle of electoral equality, since it put parties and other political organizations of the GDR at a disadvantage under the particular conditions of the first pan-German election. Alliances by way of lists were therefore to be allowed. Separate exclusion clauses applying to one of the two German states were permissible.

This decision prompted the Bonn government to present the Bundestag with a bill on 1 October containing two different exclusion clauses and allowing lists. All parties except the Greens desired to keep the election date of 2 December. By this time they were nearly all organized throughout the whole of Germany. On 5 August the East German Green party and Alliance 90 joined the Greens of the FRG in a common list called 'Alliance 90/The Greens' (*Bündnis 90/Die Grünen*). For the West German Greens, cooperation with the activists of the GDR represented another step on a long path of transformation. They had once been a fundamental opposition, rejecting the state's monopoly of armed force. Now they were well on their way to becoming a pillar of the state under the rule of law. Sociologically speaking, this could also be seen as a process of embourgeoisement. Several far left party members reacted to the new developments by leaving the party. Some joined the Left List/PDS.

The first real party fusion took place among the liberals. On 11 and 12 August the League of Free Democrats (whom the National Democratic party had joined at the end of March) united with the Free Democrats of the FRG in Hanover. The latter's name was kept. The two Green parties united in Magdeburg between

7 and 9 September, and the two SPDs joined forces in Berlin on 26–7 September. The CDU was the last to fuse, on 1–2 October. The East German CDU had first absorbed the Democratic Farmers' party and Democratic Awakening. The new party leaders were, from the western point of view, the old ones: Helmut Kohl, Hans-Jochen Vogel, and Otto Graf Lambsdorff. The two candidates for the chancellorship also stayed the same: Helmut Kohl and Oskar Lafontaine. The latter was confirmed almost unanimously at the party congress in Berlin.

The Volkskammer ended its work on 2 October with a ceremony at the Schauspielhaus. This was intended as a counterbalance to the row that had occurred during the final regular session on 28 September. Vice President Wolfgang Ullmann of the Greens, after incessant tumult and over the protest of the prime minister, had read the names of fifty-six delegates and ministers whom the relevant investigatory committee had identified as Unofficial Collaborators with the Stasi. (The session was closed to the public, but the Berlin *tageszeitung* published numerous names on 1 October. According to its report, thirty-five of the people Ullmann named belonged to the CDU.) There was no more talk of such things at the ceremony. Lothar de Maizière called the passing of the GDR from the world stage 'an hour of great joy' and a 'farewell without tears'. President Bergmann-Pohl (who had refused to read the names on 28 September, citing reasons of conscience) declared: 'We have fulfilled our task of achieving in free self-determination the unity and freedom of Germany.'[15]

FROM 3 OCTOBER TO THE FIRST PAN-GERMAN ELECTIONS

A massive crowd gathered on the Platz der Republik in Berlin on the evening of 2 October. At midnight the 'Liberty Bell', donated to Berlin by American citizens in 1956 as a gesture of solidarity, sounded from the Schöneberg city hall. A large black, red, and gold banner was elevated in front of the main entrance to the Reichstag to the cheers of hundreds of thousands. President Weizsäcker stepped up to the microphone and said: 'The unity of Germany has been achieved. We are conscious of our responsibility before God and humanity. We wish to serve the cause of world peace in a unified Europe.' Then wind soloists and a choir intoned the 'Deutschlandlied', and the crowd sang along. 'Unity and right and freedom for the German fatherland.' Fireworks followed.

Official ceremonies were held in the Berlin Philharmonie on 3 October. The first to speak was Sabine Bergmann-Pohl. (In addition to being president of the Volkskammer she had also been acting head of state in the GDR since 9 April.) She called German unity a gift of history. 'The Christians among us will recognize God's grace at work. But this unity in freedom does not stand against the interests of our neighbours. It will take its place within a greater Europe.' The former citizens of the GDR were not expecting the land of milk and honey, but rather a country in which we can develop our energies, a country, also, of sharing in solidarity . . . Today we have every reason to celebrate the first day of German unity. We also have every reason to see the false paths of German history for what they were. Auschwitz will remain an everlasting warning for us.

It was the president who gave the main address. Weizsäcker placed the reunification in the larger context of German and European history.

For the first time we Germans are not one of the points of contention on the agenda of Europe. Our unity was not imposed upon anybody, but freely agreed upon. It forms part of a pan-European historical process, one that has as its goal the liberty of the peoples and a new peace order on our continent . . . We now have a state we no longer look upon as provisional, whose identity and integrity is no longer contested by our neighbours. On this day the unified German nation takes its recognized place in Europe . . . The unification of Germany is something other than a mere expansion of the Federal Republic. The day has come on which, for the first time in history, the whole of Germany takes its lasting place in the circle of western democracies.

On the next day, 4 October 1990, a pan-German parliament met in the Reichstag for the first time since 9 December 1932. The constitutive session of the expanded Bundestag was convoked by the president, Rita Süssmuth. In keeping with the Unification Treaty, it contained 144 delegates from the Volkskammer. Five members of what had remained of de Maizière's 'bourgeois' coalition, including himself, were appointed and sworn in as ministers without portfolio in the cabinet. On 5 October the Bundestag ratified the Two-Plus-Four treaty and then passed the new version of the voting law, made necessary by the decision of the Federal Constitutional Court on 29 September. The Bundesrat ratified the Two-Plus-Four treaty three days later.

On 14 October the citizens of the five new *Länder*, Mecklenburg-West Pomerania, Brandenburg, Thuringia, Saxony-Anhalt, and Saxony, elected their parliaments. With the exception of Brandenburg, where the Social Democratic candidate Manfred Stolpe took the top spot, the CDU emerged from all races as the strongest party, securing the prime ministerships in Dresden, Erfurt, Magdeburg, and Schwerin. The citizens of former East Berlin had to wait awhile before they could vote, since the voting law had scheduled the elections to the Berlin House of Representatives on 2 December, the date of the first pan-German elections. Until that day the city would have the West Berlin House of Representatives, the East Berlin *Stadtverordnetenversammlung* (a city council freely elected in May), a 'Berlin Unity Committee' put in place by the two bodies and with equal representation, and, on the government level, joint sessions of the West Berlin Senate and the East Berlin Municipality (*Magistrat*).

On 9 November 1990, the first anniversary of the opening of the Berlin wall, Kohl and Gorbachev signed the German–Soviet friendship treaty in Bonn. The German–Polish border treaty was signed in Warsaw on 14 November by Genscher and Skubiszewski. It confirmed what the Two-Plus-Four treaty said: reunited Germany would include the territories of the FRG, the GDR, and all of Berlin. Perhaps the four decades of German partition had been necessary to make the recognition of the Oder–Neisse border more than a mere formality. In any case, the settlement codified in the two treaties was no longer felt to be a 'sacrifice', at least by the overwhelming majority of Germans. Serious disagreement over where Germany lay and what belonged to it was now no longer possible. The same was true of Poland. There was no longer a German question, nor a Polish question, and each resolution presupposed the other.

Five days after Genscher and Skubiszewski met in Warsaw, on 19 November, the CSCE summit got under way in Paris. During this conference the NATO and Warsaw Pact heads of state and government signed the treaty on conventional forces. Among other things, it provided for the 'reduction' via 'destroying' of battle tanks, armoured combat vehicles, artillery pieces, combat aircraft, and attack helicopters. This was conventional disarmament on a considerable scale. Bonn's concessions had not led to Germany being 'singled out', but contributed towards a major arms reduction. Furthermore, the twenty-two leaders signed a declaration committing their countries to renounce the threat or use of force, except in cases of self-defence or in a manner in keeping with the Charter of the United Nations.

The culmination of the CSCE summit was the signing of the 'Charter of Paris' on 21 November 1990. The thirty-four heads of state and government undertook 'to build, consolidate, and strengthen democracy as the only system of government of our nations'. Fifteen years after the Final Act of Helsinki was concluded, at a moment when 'a new era is dawning in Europe', the participants committed themselves to settling disputes by peaceful means and continuing their cooperation on all levels. A council of foreign ministers was to meet at least once per year. A 'Conflict Prevention Centre' was to be set up in Vienna and an 'Office for Free Elections' in Warsaw. Finally, a CSCE parliamentary assembly was also to be created.

The first pan-German Bundestag election was held two weeks later, on 2 December 1990. It was the first free election throughout all of Germany since the Reichstag election on 6 November 1932. The Bonn coalition was the clear victor. Kohl's Union received 43.8% of the vote, Genscher's Free Democrats, 11%. Oskar Lafontaine's SPD managed only 33.5%. With 4.8%, the Greens did not make the 5% hurdle set for the west. In the east, Alliance 90/The Greens received 6% of the vote, which secured them 8 seats. The PDS average throughout the country was only 2.4%. However, the party received 11.1% in the east, which meant 17 seats.

The defeat of the Social Democrats had repercussions within the party executive on the next day. Willy Brandt stressed that he had been moved by reasons of principle, not by tactical considerations, in exhorting the party 'not to let the pan-German theme pass it by'. Without addressing Lafontaine directly, Brandt lamented that the SPD campaign had given rise to the impression that 'we see unity and freedom more as a burden than an opportunity.' He recommended that the party see to it 'that caution and hope are in a humanly meaningful relationship to each other'. Several older Social Democrats agreed with him. Erhard Eppler said it openly: 'Many would not have wanted a united Germany.' Klaus von Dohnanyi called Oskar Lafontaine a great talent. On the Germany question, however, he could not follow him. He could not support someone who made such a huge mistake in this matter unless a change of position was undertaken. Hans Koschnick, a former mayor of Bremen, said that for him 'the national question does not depend on generations.' He was disagreeing with Dieter Spöri from Baden-Württemberg, who had said that the 'Germany theme' was a 'problem based on the generation question'.

Of the younger Social Democrats only Wolfgang Thierse, the last head of the eastern SPD and now one of Vogel's deputies, supported Brandt. The discussion of the costs, he said, had not been understood in the east. '[O]n the national question, the SPD has some catching up to do.' Most younger members of the party executive disagreed with Brandt. Gerhard Schröder, prime minister of Lower Saxony, said, 'I do not believe that the national question, as Willy Brandt sees it, was responsible for the election outcome. I cannot understand this view. The issue has also not been part of my life.' Anke Brunn, minister of economics in North Rhine-Westphalia, said, 'I am not automatically enthused about the Fatherland. It is good that the SPD can admit to having difficulties with the national question.' Heidemarie Wieczorek-Zeul from Hesse called the national debate 'inconsequential'.

Lafontaine himself said that he was 'deeply hurt that the impression could arise—through things said on our side, too—that I am against the people in the GDR and that I have problems with German unity. This is untrue. I simply dealt with the issue differently, approaching the unification process through the social question.' He regretted that he and Brandt did not agree 'on the so-called national question'. Lafontaine rejected Hans-Jochen Vogel's suggestion that he, Lafontaine, take over the leadership of the party and the fraction.

Willy Brandt was also not one to hide his disappointment and bitterness. The important thing was not the national question, he said at the end of the discussion, but the question of self-determination. 'Self-determination has led to unity. That I remind us of this is certainly better than if I had asked to step down as honorary head.' He recalled his electoral slogan of 1972, 'Germans, we can be proud of our country!', and cautioned against pitting European integration against the nation state. 'We really should speak about the subject of the "nation state" again. Europe is, first of all, the unification of states. This cannot simply be thrown over. That is "a pure illusion".'

The clash between Brandt and Lafontaine, between older and younger party members, was an hour of truth for the Social Democrats. The fact that they presented two faces—the patriotic one of Brandt, and the post-national one of Lafontaine—was not the least of reasons they had done so poorly in the election.

For Brandt and many of the older generation, national solidarity with the East Germans was simply obvious. It was a dictate of justice. For this reason it made no sense to pit the social against the national question. For Lafontaine and many younger party members, on the other hand, nothing was politically obvious any longer, least of all a reconnection with the *kleindeutsch* nation state of Bismarck.

On 17 September, two weeks before reunification, Lafontaine had reiterated his position on the theme of German unity in a speech at the Friedrich Ebert Foundation in Bonn. 'It is my goal that the people in Leipzig, Dresden, or another city in the GDR have it just as good as the people in the Federal Republic or Austria.' He lamented the fact that the FRG still had an 'ethnic idea of the nation' instead of following Ernest Renan's understanding of the nation as 'a plebiscite repeated daily'. He regretted that

the government has allowed itself to be guided in the reunification of Germany by a traditional idea of the nation state and a traditional German idea of the nation based on heritage, instead of the idea of European unity. . . Considering the federalist tradition of Germany, a confederation between the two German states would have been an obvious pathway to German unity. . . This would have laid the foundation stone for a future European confederation. This opportunity has passed. . . The founders of the Federal Republic thought of this as a provisional state, destined from the beginning to be absorbed into a greater nation state one day. I still imagine Germany this way: destined, some day in the not-too-distant future, to be absorbed into a greater Europe, into the United States of Europe.

Lafontaine's critique of the ethnic, heritage-based concept of German nationality was justified. A reform of the citizenship law was long overdue. But Brandt's idea of national solidarity had nothing to do with heritage and everything to do with history. Also, Lafontaine did not pose the question of whether the other European nations wished to 'be absorbed' into Europe in the way he envisioned for Germany. To the French, whose concept of nationhood Lafontaine recommended for imitation in Germany, this image of themselves and Europe was just as foreign as it was to all other European countries. They were certainly able to imagine their nations as separate building blocks in a politically unified Europe. The call for the abolition of the nation state, however, will have appeared to them as an attack on their identity and as German presumptuousness.

Lafontaine's reference to Austria, as in his speeches in the previous year, contained a strange contradiction. The *grossdeutsch* idea of a German cultural nation was far more ethnic, indeed *völkisch*, in character than the *kleindeutsch* national idea of the 'enlightened' proponents of German unity. Lafontaine was certainly not alone in harbouring *grossdeutsch* reminiscences. In his September 1990 book *Der Irrweg des Nationalstaates*,* Peter Glotz, one of Lafontaine's close political associates, had the following to say on the subject: 'I cannot. . . forget

---

* Glotz, *The False Path of the Nation State.*

how the Prussian Bismarck kept the Germans of the former Austro-Hungarian monarchy out of his unitary Little German state: through war.' Five years later Heiner Geissler, former CDU general secretary, wrote a book entitled *Der Irrweg des Nationalismus.** Citing Golo Mann (though controvertibly), he claimed that the Bismarck empire had not been 'a real nation state', since 'a considerable portion of the nation was left out, and, according to the will of the founder, rightly so. The first German partition did not take place in 1945, but in 1866.'

The truth is that a *kleindeutsch* solution had been far more tolerable to the rest of Europe than any kind of *grossdeutsch* project. The Two-Plus-Four treaty legitimated the *kleindeutsch* solution within a radically reduced national territory and on a radically altered international basis. Anyone who, consciously or unconsciously, harboured *grossdeutsch* ideas about a German cultural nation was bound to be dissatisfied. The conflict between Willy Brandt and Oskar Lafontaine was about politics *and* history. The Germans had to find their way towards a realistic relationship to their nation state, and to the idea of the nation state in general, before they could hope to play a constructive role in the process of European unification. This was the thrust of Brandt's concluding remarks at the meeting of the SPD executive on 3 December 1990. Lafontaine's utopia of a Europe absorbing its nation states was wishful thinking. If the Social Democrats followed him, they would drift further and further into a political and historical dead end.[16]

THE DEBATE OVER THE CAPITAL, THE MAASTRICHT TREATY, AND CONSTITUTIONAL AMENDMENTS

Only three states had ratified the Two-Plus-Four treaty by the time the year 1990 came to an end. The first was the FRG, where it had passed the Bundestag on 5 October and the Bundesrat on 8 October. The Senate of the United States ratified it on 10 October. The British ratification document was given to the Bonn government on 16 November. France and the Soviet Union followed suit after the new year, the former on 17 January, the latter on 4 March. The treaty entered into force on 15 March 1991.

Another ratification process took more time. The German–Polish border treaty was supposed to be approved at the same time as the treaty on good neighbour relations and cooperation. This latter agreement was initialled on 17 June 1991. Both were ratified by the Bundestag on 17 October 1991 and by the Sejm on the next day. This brought the international phase of German reunification to an end.

The internal matters, the tasks imposed upon the new German legislature by the Unification Treaty, were still far from being resolved. The most dominant

---

* Geissler, *The False Path of Nationalism.*

theme in the first half of 1991 was the question of the capital of newly unified Germany. Everything had been clear before the fall of the wall. The Bundestag resolution of 30 September 1949, continually reiterated, had stated that Berlin was the German capital and that the most important organs of state would be moved there as soon as free elections had been held in all of Berlin and the Soviet zone. Only after the wall came down and reunification became a possibility were voices heard against moving the government and parliament from the Rhine to the Spree—that is, for keeping Bonn the de facto capital.

The arguments for and against both sides went back and forth for more than a year. The proponents of the Rhenish university town said that Bonn was the symbol of the first successful German democracy and that it stood for the western alliance, federalism, and for the new German sobriety and modesty. Many of them, though not all, argued that Berlin represented the bad old German traditions of centralism, Prussian militarism, and nationalist megalomania. There were also those who connected Berlin to the Third Reich in this debate. Moving the government and the parliament to Berlin, it was felt, meant running the risk of a relapse into unfortunate periods of German history. Besides, the move would be expensive, and too harsh a blow for Bonn, its environs, and tens of thousands of Germans.

The friends of Berlin recalled the 1949 resolution, the city's fortitude during the 'Cold War', and its role in establishing friendship between Germany and the United States. They pointed out that since Berlin itself had to grow together as one city again, making it the capital would allow Germany to better help the old and new *Länder* grow together. They emphasized the cultural attractions and the democratic traditions of the former German capital. Bonn seemed unfit to foster the process of inner unification in Germany and the rapprochement between western and eastern Europe. Finally, the move was a dictate of compensatory justice. Since the bastions of the economy, technology, banking, and the media all lay in the west, at least German political life should be centred in the east. Seen in this light, the prospect of a new concentration of power and a weakening of federalism seemed nothing less than absurd. Having lost nearly all large industrial enterprises during the partition, Berlin was now economically too weak ever to regain the kind of dominance it had enjoyed during the German Reich.

Most of the pre-eminent German politicians were for the move. President von Weizsäcker came out for it early, on 29 June 1990, while accepting honorary citizenship in the city he had once governed. Willy Brandt, Hans-Dietrich Genscher, Wolfgang Schäuble, and Hans-Jochen Vogel were all passionate advocates of a return to the old capital. Helmut Kohl was somewhat more reserved, and he took pains to emphasize that his support for Berlin represented his opinion as a delegate and not as the chancellor. Bonn had the votes of most of the important politicians from North Rhine-Westphalia, from Johannes Rau to Otto Graf Lambsdorff to Norbert Blüm; 'post-national' Social Democrats like Oskar Lafontaine and Peter Glotz; and virtually all of the CSU. The highest-ranking advocate of Bonn was Rita Süssmuth, president of the German Bundestag. In order to win majorities, the Bonn supporters were prepared to make Berlin the main location of the federal president's office and the Bundesrat. The friends of Berlin contented themselves with moving the president's office, the Bundestag, the chancellor's office, and only a part of the ministries to the Spree. The remaining ministries, the Bundesrat, and most of the government jobs could remain in Bonn, which would thereby be allowed to retain its role as the administrative centre of Germany.

The roll call vote in the Bundestag on 20 July 1990 was 'free'. Since all parties were divided on the issue, there was no pressure on delegates to vote with their fractions. The outcome was open; the debate had a major influence on the decision. The best speeches were those in favour of the better cause, Berlin. Wolfgang Schäuble, Willy Brandt, Hans-Dietrich Genscher, Wolfgang Thierse, and Wolfgang Ullmann all spoke with a moral persuasiveness that was lacking in the speeches for Bonn. Seen from the west, Berlin was the more uncomfortable solution, Bonn by far the more popular one.

When the Bundestag president reported the result of the ballot shortly before 10.00 p.m., Berlin rejoiced, and Bonn sank into dejection. The motion entitled 'Completion of the Unification' (or 'Berlin motion') had defeated the motion called 'Federal State Solution' (or 'Bonn motion') by 338 to 320 votes. Of the CDU delegates, 146 had voted for Berlin, 124 for Bonn. Since in the CSU it was 8 to 40, the combined fraction actually favoured Bonn (164 to 154). A majority of Social Democrats also favoured Bonn (126 to 110). Most Free Democrats were for Berlin (53 to 26), as were the PDS/Left List (17 to 1) and Alliance 90/The Greens (4 to 2). The delegates from the old *Länder* were more for Bonn than Berlin (291 to 214). The reverse was true of those from the new *Länder*, including Berlin (124 to 29). The politicians from the old *Länder* of the north—Schleswig-Holstein, Hamburg, Bremen, and Lower Saxony—voted mostly for Berlin, as did the delegates from Hesse. Those from Rhineland-Palatinate, North Rhine-Westphalia, Bavaria, Baden-Württemberg, and the Saarland were mostly for Bonn. Catholic delegates favoured Bonn, Protestant and non-denominational delegates, Berlin. Among the members of the cabinet, Berlin was more popular than Bonn (13 to 5).

The parliament's historic decision for Berlin was followed on 5 July by a conditional vote for Bonn on the part of the Bundesrat. The decision was to be revisited later, in the light of the new circumstances. (This would happen on 27 September 1996, with Berlin emerging as the victor, against the votes of North Rhine-Westphalia and Rhineland-Pfalz.) On 11 December 1991 the cabinet decided that the following ministries would accompany the government and the government press office to Berlin: the foreign office, the ministries of the interior, justice, finance, economics, labour, transport, regional planning, the ministry of the family and senior citizens, and the ministry of women and youth affairs. The remaining seven would keep their main offices in Bonn. There were also compensatory measures for the city on the Rhine. The move did not actually take place until 1999, much later than originally planned. When it did, however, the expected pull exercised by the new capital was so strong that the division of responsibilities between the two cities soon became purely fictional.

To a certain extent, the dispute over the capital in 1990–1 was an ersatz debate. Things that had not been said openly during the unification process now came out. Critiques of Berlin, Prussia, and the Bismarck state had been voiced and written already in 1989–90, but they were now much more forcefully articulated. The old Federal Republic appeared in increasingly rosy hues. The 'posthumous Adenauer left' saw the political culture of the west and the unification of Europe in jeopardy if Germany was to be governed from Berlin. As the Social Democrat Peter Glotz put it to the Christian Democrat Helmut Kohl on 20 July 1991: 'With the vote for Berlin you are veering away towards a Europe of fatherlands . . . Preserve the supra-national European idea of Konrad Adenauer. It is the most important legacy of that great politician . . . Bonn is the metaphor for the second German republic. Bonn must remain, and should remain, the seat of government and parliament.'

It was Interior Minister Wolfgang Schäuble (now in a wheelchair, having been paralysed from the waist down after an attempt on his life on 12 October 1990) who stated the case for Berlin most clearly on the day the decision was made. 'We have often said that we must be prepared to share if we want to overcome the partition. Sharing means that we must be ready to bear together the changes that German unity will bring,' he said. Berlin had always been

the symbol for unity and freedom, for democracy and the rule of law in all of Germany, from the airlift to 17 June 1953 to the building of the wall in August 1961 all the way to 9 November 1989 and 3 October of the past year . . . German unity and European unity presuppose each other. For this reason, the decision for Berlin is a decision to overcome the partition of Europe.

The sceptics' fears that German unification could endanger European unification were soon proven wrong. Between 9 and 11 December 1991 the European Council, meeting in Maastricht in Holland, put the European Community on the path to becoming a European Union. The Treaty of Maastricht was signed on 7 February 1992. It represented the most radical amendment and extension of the 1957 Rome Treaties to date. The first pillar of the EU was the economic and monetary union, which was to lead to a new European currency by 1 January 1999 at the latest. The second pillar was a Common Foreign and Security Policy (CFSP). This involved making the West European Union (WEU) into a defence policy component and bridge between the EU and NATO. The third pillar was Justice and Home Affairs. As border controls were dismantled, domestic security issues became increasingly Europeanized.

The European Parliament was granted new powers, including a veto against the European Commission in the drafting of laws in certain areas. These powers fell far short of what Bonn had wanted. A 'Committee of the Regions' with a consultative function was established, mostly at the behest of the German *Länder*. A new EU citizenship would enable citizens of EU countries to vote in and stand for local and European elections in any member state under the same conditions as the nationals of that state. Generally speaking, the principle of 'subsidiarity' would apply: the EU would only act where the action of individual countries was deemed insufficient.

The Treaty of Maastricht involved amendments to the Basic Law. The place and number of the old Article 23, the 'accession article' abolished with the reunification, was taken by a new 'Europe article'. In keeping with the principle of subsidiarity, the Federation could transfer sovereign powers to the European Union by a law with the consent of the Bundesrat. The Bundesrat was to participate in the decision-making process of the Federation 'insofar as it would have been competent to do so in a comparable domestic matter, or insofar as the subject falls within the domestic competence of the *Länder*'. According to the new Paragraph 1a of Article 24, the *Länder*, for their part, could transfer sovereign powers to 'trans-frontier institutions in neighbouring regions' with the consent of the federal government. A new version of Article 50 gave the *Länder* the right to participate through the Bundesrat 'in matters concerning the European Union'. Finally, the amended Article 88 authorized the Federal Bank to transfer responsibilities and powers to the European Central Bank.

These changes meant that very soon after its reunification, the new German national state underwent a twofold qualification, from 'above' and from 'below'. It transferred sovereign rights to the European Union and granted the *Länder*, which did not wish to become 'victims' of the European integration, expanded powers of participation. These powers were so far-reaching that several of the states—especially North Rhine-Westphalia, Bavaria, and Baden-Württemberg—began to compete with the Federation as independent political actors on the European stage, above all in Brussels, the 'capital' of the European Union. This did not mean a regression from a German federal state to a confederation of German states, but the desires of the aforementioned *Länder* did and do seem to move in this direction.

There were further constitutional amendments pursuant to the recommendations in the Unification Treaty. On 29 October 1993 the Joint Constitutional Commission concluded its work. (This body had sixty-four members, half elected by the Bundestag and half appointed by the Bundesrat.) After heated disputes between the Bundestag, Bundesrat, and mediation committee, the amendments entered into force on 15 November 1994.

The section on basic rights obligated the state to work towards the practical realization of equal rights for men and women and towards the removal of persistent disadvantages. Nobody was to be discriminated against because of a disability (Article 3). A new Article 20a made environmental protection an official goal of the state. The individual financial responsibility of the municipalities was guaranteed (Article 28, Paragraph 2), the restructuring of the *Länder* made easier (Article 29, Paragraph 8 and, concerning Berlin and Brandenburg, Article 118a). In the area of competing or 'concurrent' legislation, the Federation accepted a 'necessity clause' that limited its legislative powers. According to the new version of Article 72, it would have the right to legislate in this area 'if and to the extent that the establishment of equal living conditions throughout the federal territory or the maintenance of legal or economic unity renders federal regulation necessary in the national interest'. In the event of disagreements over whether the necessity clause had been fulfilled, the Federal Constitutional Court was to have the final say (Article 93, Paragraph 1, No. 2a).

The constitutional reform fell far short of what erstwhile East German activists, Social Democrats, Greens, and PDS had wanted. But it is questionable whether the introduction of new state goals for things like inclusiveness and community spirit, job and housing creation, social security, defence of minorities, and protection of animals would really have led to a 'better' society. There were good reasons to caution against the normative overburdening of the constitution. It is also doubtful whether plebiscitary elements on the federal level would have strengthened democracy. By weakening the parliament and, with it, the principle of representative democracy, such elements might well have adversely affected democratic political culture as a whole. In the light of the manipulated votes of confidence in 1972 and 1982, on the other hand, it would have been reasonable to grant the Bundestag the power to dissolve itself. But this, too, failed through the resistance of the Union.

Since there was no two-thirds majority for more radical changes to the constitution, the results of the reform debate could only be what a minimal consensus yielded. Still, there was no compelling reason not to make use of the referendum provided for in Article 146 (which, presupposing the political will existed, could have been held on the day of the second pan-German Bundestag election, 16 October 1994). If the parties that voted for the amendments had made the reformed constitution part of their electoral campaigns, the voters certainly would have confirmed it in a constitutional referendum.

The price for not holding a referendum was high. First, it gave critics another opportunity to point to a normative deficit in the unification process. Secondly, it had the paradoxical consequence that the Basic Law, despite the 'eternity clause' of Article 79, Paragraph 3, would still remain provisional in a way that the 1949 Parliamentary Council had *not* intended. Article 146 retained the language it had been given in the Unification Treaty: 'This Basic Law, which since the achievement of the unity and freedom of Germany applies to the entire German people, shall cease to apply on the day on which a constitution freely adopted by the German people takes effect.'

The German public was less interested in the Joint Constitutional Commission than in an amendment that would have been put on the agenda even if the reunification had never happened. The sentence 'Persons persecuted on political grounds shall have the right of asylum' in Article 16, Paragraph 2 reflected the experience of Nazi dictatorship and German emigration after 1933. The fathers and mothers of the Basic Law had not imagined, and could not have imagined, the flood of asylum-seekers and asylum-abusers such as Germany experienced in the late 1980s and early 1990s. In 1992, 438,191 foreigners applied for political asylum in Germany. This was 78 per cent of all asylum-seekers in the whole European Community during this year. Ultimately only about 4.5 per cent were recognized as political refugees, but it was becoming more and more difficult to properly care for, house, and provide counsel for the huge numbers of applicants.

The Union parties had long been pushing for changes in the asylum policy. The FDP and SPD resisted at first. After arduous negotiations and passionate protest from the left and the churches, a compromise finally emerged. It was reflected in Article 16a, which went into effect on 1 July 1993, and in changes to the law governing asylum claims. The individual right to asylum was preserved. However, persons who entered Germany from 'safe' third states could no longer appeal to it. The same was generally true for people who came from a 'safe' country of origin. 'Safe' third states and countries of origin were the member states of the European Community and those specified as 'safe' in terms of human rights and basic freedoms by a law requiring the consent of the Bundesrat. The deportation process in cases where asylum was 'clearly unjustified' was streamlined. Never before had an article of the Basic Law been so freighted with procedural matters. Though this contradicted the basic nature of the constitution, it reflected the difficulties of finding a compromise between extreme positions.

The battle over abortion rights was even more heated than that over asylum. According to Article 31 of the Unification Treaty, by 31 December 1992 the legislature had to come up with regulations that 'ensure better protection of unborn life and provide a better solution in conformity with the Constitution to conflict situations faced by pregnant women—notably through legally guaranteed entitlements for women, first and foremost to counseling and public support—than is the case in either part of Germany at present.'

In June 1992 the Bundestag passed a Maternity and Family Welfare Law (*Schwangeren- und Familienhilfegesetz*) against the votes of most CDU and CSU delegates. It allowed (that is, exempted from punishment) the termination of pregnancy within the first twelve weeks after conception (the *Fristenlösung*) if the woman first provided written confirmation that she had received counselling. This rule was to apply to the whole country. However, on 4 August the Constitutional Court, acting on a motion by 247 CDU/CSU delegates and the Bavarian government, ordered the law not to enter into effect until after its constitutionality had been examined.

The decision, handed down on 28 May 1993, declared the new abortion law unconstitutional. Terminations of pregnancy remained exempt from punishment in the first twelve weeks, but were still considered 'unlawful'. They could only be paid for by the health insurance funds if a criminological, medicinal, or embryo-pathological indication was present—that is, in cases of rape, risk to the mother, or fetal deformation. The counselling session had to take place at least three days before the operation was scheduled and be aimed at preventing the abortion—'completely committed to the protection of the unborn life', in the language of the decision. The court put a transitional regulations in place until a new law could be passed.

That finally happened in June 1995. Abortions would be exempted from punishment within the first twelve weeks of pregnancy, with prior counselling required. Except in a few defined cases they could not be paid for by the health insurance funds. Five years after reunification, Germany had fulfilled the task imposed on it by the Unification Treaty that it unify its legal system.[17]

EAST GERMAN SOCIETY AFTER 1989–1990

In his poem 'Frisches Ei, gutes Ei', Goethe wrote that '[e]nthusiasm is not like pickled herring, which will keep for years.' This was true of the German reunification. The euphoria soon dissipated, even more quickly in the new than in the old *Länder*. The economic situation in east Germany was dismal. Very few companies were competitive, not even in microelectronics, which had been massively subsidized in the latter half of the 1980s. The *Treuhand* was unable to assess the viability of new enterprises, since the joint stock companies into which the old Publicly Owned Enterprises had been transformed lacked both closing and opening balance sheets. One of the factors in the decline of the east German economy was the loss of the eastern markets for state commerce, caused in part by the change to freely convertible currencies at the end of 1990 and beginning of 1991. Another was the strong and continuing predilection of east Germans for west German goods after the monetary reform. 'The change came as a shock, a revolution,' writes Dieter Grosser. 'Almost overnight, the greater part of the east German economy turned out to be hopelessly obsolete, uncompetitive, destined to go under.'

The west German labour unions took care of the rest. In order to gain members from the old FDGB, they forced the barely functional employers' unions in summer 1990 to grant two-digit wage hikes (30% in the metal industry, no less than 60% in construction), shorten the working day, and provide longer-term job protection. According to Grosser, in the third quarter of 1990 contract wages in east Germany were an average of 30% higher than the previous year. A process of de-industrialization began and would continue until 1997, flanked by growing unemployment—especially among women, the great majority of whom had been employed in the GDR. The unemployment rate rose from 2.7% in 1990 to 14.8% in 1992. By 1998 it was 19.5%. It had fallen to 16.5% in June 2000, but this was still twice as high as the figure for the west (7.4%).

The situation in the new *Länder* made it necessary to correct mistakes, most of which had been the fault of the Bonn government. The financial transfers from west to east had to be increased, and they could no longer be financed through new debt. On 8 March 1991 the cabinet passed tax increases, though the main justification used was German participation in the Gulf War. (An international coalition, led by the USA, had driven Iraq out of Kuwait, one of the world's most important oil-producing countries, which Iraq had attacked and annexed in August 1990 on the orders of its president, Saddam Hussein.) On 1 July 1991 taxes on oil and natural gas were raised and a 'solidarity surcharge' (*Solidaritätszuschlag* or *Soli* for short) of 7.5% added to income and corporate taxes.

The decision to increase taxes had been preceded by an agreement on 28 February 1991 between the chancellor and the sixteen prime ministers to grant the new *Länder* 100% of the average share per capita of the value-added tax revenues—contrary to the what the Unification Treaty said. The Federation gave up its 15% share from the German Unity Fund. On 8 March, along with the tax increases, an 'Upswing East Project' (*Gemeinschaftswerk Aufschwung Ost*) was passed, funded at 12 billion marks. It was designed to foster investment in construction; extend and improve the transport network; and promote regional economic structures, shipyards, environmental protection, and job creation projects.

Several other mistakes were also corrected, to the extent that they could be. The principle of 'restitution before compensation' was partially reversed by a 'law to remove impediments' (*Hemmnisbeseitigungsgesetz*) in March 1991 and an 'investment priority law' (*Investitionsvorranggesetz*) in July 1992. In March 1993 the government, the prime ministers, and the leaders of the CDU, CSU, FDP, and SPD concluded a 'solidarity pact' to finance German unity. After 1 January 1995 the new *Länder* and the entire city of Berlin would fully participate in the inter-state financial compensation structure for the first time. The *Treuhand* was granted greater credit for financing the clean-up of ecologically contaminated sites and the preservation and renewal of 'industrial nuclei'. To these things were added a housing construction programme for east Germany, further resources for job creation, a replenishment of the German Unity Fund, and, after the abolition of the solidarity surcharge in June 1992, a new one of 7.5% with an open-ended duration, also from 1 January 1995 onward.

The 'industrial nuclei' that benefited from the 'solidarity pact' included shipyards on the Baltic, a large steelworks in Brandenburg (EKO Steel), a manufacturer of heavy machinery and industrial plant in Saxony-Anhalt (SKET), and mechanical engineering firms in Saxony. The state-supported renovation guaranteed many thousands of jobs, but it could not guarantee the competivity of the companies. On 1 January 1995 the 'solidarity pact' became part of a 'federal consolidation programme'. In the course of the restructuring of the inter-state compensation system the *Länder* received an increased share of the value-added tax: 44%, up from 37%. The Federation created a 'redemption fund for inherited liabilities' (*Erblastentilgungsfonds*). It gathered together all the debts of the *Treuhand* and the credit-processing fund that had accumulated up to the end of 1994, as well as the capped liabilities from the GDR's housing economy, and repaid the total with interest.

The growth that occurred in the east German economy between 1992 and 1995 was driven primarily by construction. No other area had so much catching up to do. But the growth rate in the gross domestic product decreased as the demand levelled out, and after 1997 east German economic growth again fell behind that in the west. Eastern labour productivity grew. In 1991 it was only a third of the western level (excluding Berlin); by 1993 it was more than half. However, this was mostly a result of the dismantling of jobs. Almost everywhere in the east unemployment remained far higher than in the west. Still, there were regional differences. The old industrial zones in Thuringia and Saxony and in the 'bacon belt' around Berlin experienced much greater improvements than Saxony-Anhalt, which had the biggest environmental problems, or rural Mecklenburg-West Pomerania.

Even after reunification, many Germans in the west found east German society difficult to comprehend. Only gradually did Germans on both sides begin to understand what the mass migration to the west and the 'building of socialism' had wrought: a reduction in the reservoir of experts and trained professionals in a whole range of fields, a social structure radically different from that in the west, and far lower standards of qualification and performance. There were very few small and medium-sized private businesses left in the trades, commerce, and freelance professions, and none at all in industry. There were no private farmers and no tenured civil servants. And there was no 'visible' unemployment at first. The GDR had become an undifferentiated labourer society with a highly privileged *Nomenklatura*. The elite had so many characteristics of a 'ruling class' that the concept of a 'classless society' is of only very limited utility in describing the East German state.

After 1989–90 the lack of qualified personnel was especially great in areas where ideological dependability had been the most important career factor. This was especially the case in the party and security apparatus, the higher positions in the military, the judicial system, and in large parts of the education establishment. As a rule, the more 'political' a job had been before the revolution, the smaller was the chance that its holder would have the qualification or opportunity to exercise a similar function in reunified Germany. Loss of position and social prestige was the inevitable result for many people.

Among the most strongly affected were the regular employees in the Ministry for State Security and some of the Unofficial Collaborators who did not succeed in refuting the accusations levelled against them. The true dimensions of the espionage system and the criminal energy of the 'Stasi octopus' became visible only after the revolution. In spying out the civil rights movement, Mielke's ministry had used the 'friends' and closest relatives of the activists as informers. Some opponents of the regime were even exposed to radiation. In June 1990 eight RAF 'drop-outs' were arrested whom the Stasi had helped to acquire 'new identities' in the GDR in the years before. The legislative passed two laws to help the victims of the Stasi and the East German judicial system, one in October 1992 and another in June 1994. They simplified the process of rehabilitation, compensation, and care. In many cases the help was little more than symbolic, but it was nonetheless an important gesture.

The highest leaders of the GDR had long been stripped of power by the time of the reunification. Some of them had been arrested at the end of 1989. In November 1992 criminal proceedings were begun against Erich Honecker, who was charged with responsibility for the deaths at the Berlin wall and the German–German border. The case was called off in January 1993 owing to Honecker's weak state of health (he had liver cancer). Immediately thereafter he left Germany for Chile, where his daughter lived. There he died in May 1995 at the age of 81. Among the first high-ranking defendants to be charged were Heinz Kessler, former minister of defence, and his deputy Fritz Streletz. They were condemned to long-term prison sentences in 1992. The case against former GDR prime minister Willi Stoph was called off in August 1993 for reasons of health and disability (Stoph was then 79 years old). In 1993 Erich Mielke was condemned to six years in prison for the murder of two policemen in August 1931. He gained early release in 1995 and died in May 2000. In November 1999 the Federal Supreme Court upheld an August 1997 decision by the Berlin district court condemning three former politburo members—Egon Krenz, Günter Schabowski, and Günter Kleiber—to prison sentences (Krenz got six and a half years, Schabowski and Kleiber three). All three were found guilty of indirect complicity in homicide, the court basing its judgment on four separate incidents at the Berlin wall. On 7 July 2000 the Berlin district court acquitted three other former politburo members—Hans-Joachim Böhme, Herbert Häber, and Siegfried Lorenz—of the same charge.

In an appeal case in November 1992 the Federal Supreme Court decided that two former border guards had been lawfully convicted for fatal shootings. The shootings represented 'the most grievous violation of human rights' and could not be justified by reference to the GDR border law, since no state law could stand 'in an intolerable opposition to justice'. At the same time, the court emphasized that the Berlin tribunal, as a court of appeal, had imposed only a good behaviour bond. The soldiers, subject to indoctrination by the GDR regime, had also been 'victims' of the exceptional situation at the wall and the German–German border.

Only a few of the top-level GDR functionaries received prison sentences. For most of them, loss of position was the worst punishment they suffered after reunification. This was also true of professors in the subjects that had been most involved in the ideological system: philosophy, history, education and pedagogy, law, and economics. After 1945 there had not been a large academic 'reserve army' available for a significant change in the teaching staff. After 1990 there was. The fact that most of their replacements came from the west was something that filled those affected with great bitterness. It also gave their political representatives in the PDS ongoing cause to castigate the 'colonization' of the east. Without this recourse to western personnel, however, no new beginning would have been possible at the eastern universities.

The same was true of the administrations in the *Länder*, the large cities, the judicial system, and the police forces. The extent of the change in personnel was different from state to state. As far as the renewal of the judicial apparatus was concerned, for example, Berlin was far ahead and Brandenburg far behind. How an individual citizen's earlier activity on behalf of the security system would be evaluated depended on the political colour of the government in question. Brandenburg—the only new state that did not employ a commissioner for the Stasi files—was especially lenient in this regard. Relatively few personnel changes were made in the eastern schools, as opposed to the universities. Western textbooks replaced those from the GDR. How much of the new content (in history or world politics, for example) a given teacher took in and taught to the students was mostly an individual decision.

In areas where 'secondary virtues' played an important role, the transition from the old to the new system was relatively unproblematic. The Bundeswehr was able to integrate parts of the NVA—formally dissolved on 3 October 1990—after a thorough examination of the applicants. In the economic sphere, many former leaders and managers were able to use their expertise and connections to find similar positions within the new order. (Old coteries in the *Treuhand* were often able to assist them.) No small number of those who set up on their own had only been forced out of business during the final wave of socialization at the beginning of the 1970s. Members of the directorial collectives of the Agricultural Cooperatives before 1990 also had a strong chance of finding a good position in the new cooperative or joint-stock agricultural companies. As profound as the break was in 1989–90, there were also continuities.

The continuities that linked the Germans in the east to the time *before* the founding of the GDR had grown weaker in the four decades of political partition, but they had not vanished entirely. The older generation could still remember when the country had not been divided. In fact it is likely that more of the old Germany survived in the east than in the west, which seemed 'Americanized' to many east Germans. Many West German and foreign observers also thought that the GDR was the 'more German' of the two countries. The citizens of the FRG had opened themselves to the political culture of the west, and many had travelled there. They were used to living with non-Germans. Most east Germans have had no experiences of this kind. For this reason, they think on average in more traditionally nationalist ways than the west Germans. Crude xenophobia can be found in both parts of the country. But in the east it is socially acceptable, unlike in the west. The 'critical public sphere' that was able to develop in the west is still hardly to be found in the east.

Not much of the old educated bourgeoisie was left in the new *Länder*. The house of the Evangelical pastor was not sufficient compensation for the emigration of most of the other 'notabilities'. Along with natural scientists (whose profession was less infused with ideology), Protestant theologians had played a very important role in the 'peaceful revolution'. But the societal influence of the church had been steadily on the decrease since 1949. In 1950 more than nine-tenths of the citizens of the GDR belonged to a Christian church (81.3% were Protestant, 11.1% Catholic). By 1990, church membership had shrunk to less than half of the population of the new *Länder* (37.6% Protestants, 7.1% Catholics). It had also decreased in the west, though not as radically as in the GDR: from 95.8% in 1950 (51.5% Protestants, 44.3% Catholics) to 80.3% in 1990 (37.7% Protestants, 42.6% Catholics).

Thus the SED had gone a long way towards reaching one of its goals, the severing of the bonds between the citizens and the church. It was so successful in this that the trend continued even after the party had departed from the scene. By 1997 only 28.7% of east Germans belonged to one of the two main churches (22.9% Protestants, 5.8% Catholics). The west German figure for the same year is 76.7% (35.9% Protestants, 40.8% Catholics). As superficial as the statistical criterion of 'church membership' may be, it nonetheless points to the viability of certain cultural traditions and ties to traditional values. These traditions and ties are much weaker in the east than in the west. The continuing popularity of 'youth dedication' ceremonies sheds light on the same phenomenon from a different angle. But the *Kulturkampf* of the SED also had another effect. It helped create a nihilism that still bears unfortunate fruit in the lives of many east German youth, contributing to their often violent reactions against people who seem foreign to them.

Yet another legacy of the SED is the result of its 'politics of history'. Present-day Germany, though united, is a country with a partitioned historical culture. In the 1950s the old Federal Republic had cultivated the myth of 20 July 1944, reinterpreting the conservative resistance against Hitler in terms of a spiritual-intellectual anticipation of the Basic Law. The founding myth of the GDR was 'anti-fascism'. It connected the GDR with the victorious Soviet Union and permitted the SED to count itself and its state among the victors of history. There was no room for self-critical debates over culpability, such as were conducted among intellectuals in the west. The SED saw itself in the tradition of the only truly revolutionary German party, the Communists, and their monopoly on the interpretation of history allowed it to transform Leninists and Stalinists into freedom fighters. The results were long-lasting. Four years after the reunification, the Berlin PDS was still able to organize a large movement for the preservation of names like Clara-Zetkin-Strasse, Dimitroffstrasse, and Wilhelm-Pieck-Strasse.

In the 1980s, when 'Auschwitz' began to replace '20 July 1944' as the founding myth of the Federal Republic, the GDR was busy appropriating large chunks of German national history, from Luther to Frederick the Great to Bismarck to Stauffenberg. But the history of the democratic movement was virtually ignored. Here, too, the results are still with us today. For the citizens in the west, at least the older ones, the 'experiences of Weimar' have to do with the failure of the first German democracy in the struggle against *two* totalitarian movements, National Socialism and Communism, and with the anti-totalitarian lessons codified in the Basic Law. In the east, much still survives of the old communist view that the Social Democrats betrayed the November revolution, prevented the formation of an anti-fascist united front, and thus allowed monopoly capital to bring the fascists to power. It says a lot about the didactic finesse of the SED experts in historical folklore that some of these notions have also become fixed in the minds of people who were critical of the system of 'real existing socialism' not just after the fact.

It is not only the collective memory of united Germany that is partitioned, but also the party landscape. The Party of Democratic Socialism is an east German regional party. Its 1993 platform states that it is 'against the westernization of the east'. The PDS articulates east German sentiments in more than one way. 'Equality' plays a greater role than 'freedom' in its platforms and propaganda. The call for social justice is an appeal to the citizens of the former GDR who think of themselves as the losers of German reunification. The state the PDS aspires to create would not be a dictatorship, but it would be authoritarian enough to be clearly different from a western-style democracy.

By 1990 the economic situation of the GDR was so miserable that there was no reason to hope it could improve quickly. But the unification process was accompanied by just such hopes, and there was no lack of rhetoric from Bonn to feed them. Disappointment was therefore inevitable, and with the disillusionment came the tendency to see the fallen regime in a milder light. Mass unemployment convinced many people that the job security in the time before the revolution had been a real achievement of the GDR. It was gradually forgotten that this security was itself an illusion, paid for at the price of economic ruin. The 'nostalgic' gaze at the recent past was not shared by all east Germans. In the 1990s, however, the great majority of them would probably have agreed that not everything about the old system was bad and not everything about the new one was good.[18]

GERMANY'S NEW INTERNATIONAL RESPONSIBILITIES

Nostalgia soon spread in the western part of Germany, too, in fact even sooner after the reunification than in the east. The mourning for the old Federal Republic was greatest among the 'posthumous Adenauer left'. When, in September 1990, two members of the Bundestag fraction of the Greens spoke of 'Germany's role as world power', Joschka Fischer responded in the Berlin newspaper *taz* on 14 September:

I cannot see what sense it makes for the Federal Republic when the Greens open up a world power discussion, about the likes of which the CDU/CSU only secretly dares to dream. And I have absolutely no idea why, in the light of 'Germany, united Fatherland' and with the grace of most recent birth, we should now go about disposing the historical waste of Auschwitz.

One week later other Greens, including Marieluise Beck-Oberdorf, Ralf Fücks, Christa Nickels, Bernd Ulrich, and Antje Vollmer, spoke up:

How long can the Green committees, following the maxim 'I am small, my heart is pure', afford to ignore the *de facto great power role of united Germany*? We know of nobody among the Greens who has desired and 'propagated' a German role as a world power. Nonetheless, we consider the slogan 'Never again Germany!' to be simply nationalism in reverse. The important question is how the Republic will be structured and how it will act in Europe and the world. The Greens must intervene in this debate—acknowledging the explosive force of the German nation state throughout history, but also confident that we are not condemned to repeat this history, since the inner and outer conditions have changed.

Germany regained full sovereignty on 3 October 1990, but hardly anyone felt that to be a good thing. As long as the Germany Treaty and the Allied rights and privileges it codified had been in force, the Federal Republic was not sovereign in the classic sense. In a military emergency, when it was a question of war and peace, the country was not able to make independent decisions. Moreover, according to the dominant interpretation of the Basic Law, the Bundeswehr could be deployed only in defence of Federation territory or, under certain conditions, in the case of a domestic emergency.

After Iraq attacked Kuwait on 2 August 1990 and annexed it a week later, it became clear in Germany that this interpretation of the Basic Law, or the text itself, might have to be changed. On 25 August the UN Security Council passed a resolution (665) empowering the naval forces of the member states to take appropriate measures for the implementation of the trade embargo adopted against Iraq. Since the sanctions did not succeed in forcing Saddam Hussein to back down, on 29 November the Security Council issued its first ultimatum since the Korean War. It threatened the use of force unless Iraq cleared out of Kuwait by 15 January 1991 at the latest. When Bagdad ignored this, too, 'Operation Desert Storm' got under way on 17 January. Warplanes of a multinational strike force of twenty-six countries—including the USA, Great Britain, France, Saudi Arabia, and the United Arab Emirates—bombarded Iraq. In response, Iraqi missiles attacked Israel on 18 January.

For the Federal Republic, the timing of the Kuwait conflict was lucky; most of the difficult obstacles to German unification had already been overcome. However, since the Gulf War started before the Supreme Soviet had ratified the Two-Plus-Four treaty, Genscher pressed for extreme caution on the part of Bonn: Germany should provide material assistance to Israel, the USA, and Britain, but send no troops. This drew criticism from Germany's allies. British, American, and Israeli newspapers repeated again and again that the Germans wanted to buy their way out of military engagement.

This impression was not completely unfounded. The pacifist German left attempted to pressure the government with demonstrations in the spirit of 'No blood for oil!' In the major German cities and university towns, opponents of the war hung white sheets out of windows, expressing their will to absolute non-violence. The fact that Saddam Hussein was the aggressor, that the UN legitimated armed force, that Iraqi Scud missiles were coming down on Israel—none of this any effect on the German peace movement, which insisted that Germany had the duty to resist the war of the American 'imperialists'.

Among the staunchest opponents of the Gulf War were prominent Social Democrats and Greens. They generally justified their position with reference to the German genocide during the Second World War. 'As Germans, we deal with our past differently than all other nations deal with theirs, who do not bear "Auschwitz" as their mark of Cain,' wrote Oskar Lafontaine at the beginning of February 1991 in an article for the Zurich *Weltwoche* (reprinted by the *taz*). 'Whoever exhorts the Germans to remain conscious of this burden of guilt must also allow them to acquire a specific attitude from a specific memory. This has less to do with a new separate German path than with the historical singularity of the crime perpetrated by the Nazis in the name of the Germans.'

Peter Glotz, head of the SPD in southern Bavaria, disallowed all comparison between Hitler and Saddam Hussein—a comparison made by the writer Hans Magnus Enzensberger, among others.

The comparison of Saddam to Hitler is unpolitical, demonizing characterology . . . During the *Historikerstreit* the left insisted on the singularity of Adolf Hitler's crimes, even when weighing them against the atrocities of Stalin. Now, during the Gulf War, suddenly Saddam Hussein is 'Satan'. What a glorious justification for the relativizers, who have always considered Hitler a criminal among criminals . . . Communism has fallen apart. How might it be brought about that the theory of the just war falls apart, too?

The former Bundestag delegate Antje Vollmer, writing in the *taz*, connected the Gulf War to the end of the east–west conflict and called for Europe to detach itself from the United States.

The fall of the Iron Curtain weakened the USA as a custodian of the old world order. NATO had lost its reason for existence. The reason it was not dissolved was probably to prevent the weakened status of the USA as a world power from being openly demonstrated. Cruel though it sounds, however, the fall of the wall also meant the loss of a certain amount of global stability and world peace . . . A continuing Intifada [the Palestinian uprising in the Gaza strip and West Bank between 1987 and 1994, H.A.W.] in the humiliated Middle East would be the most wretched of all Pyrrhic victories—with an atomic solution as the apocalyptic version. If the Europeans want another solution, then they no longer have much time to finally draw a clear line of separation between themselves and the Anglo-American strategy.

Unconditional pacifism met with energetic criticism, also from the left. Hans-Ulrich Klose, the treasurer of the SPD, wrote in the *Frankfurter Allgemeine Zeitung* that 'the rhetorically often cleverly disguised attempt by politicians to hide from reality' was unacceptable and embarrassing. The Social Democrats were not the only ones isolated at the present moment, he said, but also the government.

There is a kind of a Hitler-reflex at work, among us, and especially among our neighbours . . . All other western European governments are more decisive (lie less low) when it comes to answering the question of how to deal with Saddam Hussein's violation of international law. Why do the Dutch, the Danes, even the Czech government react so differently than we do? Is it perhaps because they are smaller countries, all of whom know what it is like to be attacked and occupied by a larger country (namely by Germany)? Do we want to separate ourselves from these governments? Is this yet another case of a separate German path?

In the *Süddeutsche Zeitung*, the publicist Cora Stephan accused the German peace movement of thinking that fear was a useful way to begin the pacifist learning process.

It is the apocalyptic vision and its age-old thrill of fear that led, in the first days of the Gulf War, to a massive distortion of perception and to a permanent confusion of cause and effect; that exudes, paradoxically, egotism and hard-heartedness . . . German inwardness has always been a profoundly unpolitical phenomenon. Today, its gestures of defence and denial lead us to conclude that the gift of more than forty years of democracy still has not been sufficient to make the Germans capable of politics . . . Clearly, they still have yet to learn that an increase in sovereignty also means an increase in obligations, and that the slogan 'No German soldiers in the Gulf' can also be interpreted in terms of nationalist self-involvement . . . Whoever does not wish to defend freedom and human rights can fall back into the peaceful beauty sleep of a non-sovereignty secured and guaranteed by others. After all, this condition has done wonders for German prosperity and respectability.

No peace movement revelled in fantasies of death as much as the one in Germany, wrote the liberal Gustav Seibt in the *FAZ*.

Norbert Elias identified a willingness to anticipate one's own downfall as one of the preconditions for the National Socialist excesses. One of the reasons people were able to commit the most extreme acts was because they were no longer imagining an Afterwards. They were gazing not on defeat, but on annihilation . . . For Elias, the massive German romanticism of ruination is a reflection of national history, which turned Germany into a European battlefield for decades . . . And the history of Germany in this century was hardly calculated to liberate us from fantasies of destruction. We remember fields of corpses and cities aflame, and today these memories call forth a longing for peace that is prepared to go to extremes . . . Fear that is celebrated is a great enemy of reason and a symptom of a profound moral weakness.

Jürgen Habermas tried to mediate between the two sides. The Frankfurt philosopher considered the allied intervention justified in principle, but doubted that it would stand up to a scrupulous examination. There were historical reasons for many citizens of the Federal Republic reacting to the Gulf War with such ambivalence, he wrote in mid-February 1991 in *Die Zeit*.

The link between the dictatorship and the destruction of the Jews makes us loyal to Israel. The link between nationalism and wars of conquest makes us sceptical with regard to a power politics that endangers the civil cohabitation of peoples. Almost instinctively, our break with the fascist past expresses itself in two reflexes: never again anti-Semitism and violation of equal civil rights, and never again nationalism and war.

Consequently, Habermas wanted Germany's reservations against the Gulf War to continue.

This hesitation is not the reflection of old *incertitudes allemandes*, and it is not the expression of a consciousness of a new separate German path. At the most, it is the product of a reflection on specifically German experiences. I hope—not least in the interests of our neighbours and Israel—that the policy of reservation is not suffocated by that fearful normality designed to restore to reunited Germany its old forcefulness, and give us our longed-for elixir of forgetfulness . . . Judged by the standards of a civilized political culture, which had seemed to be prevailing in the old Federal Republic, the political union did not exactly give the expanded FRG a new impetus for liberalization—over there the return of old mentalities, here an increase in the chauvinism of a high living standard. If the very notion of world citizenship, which the end of the Cold War seemed to be bringing us closer to, is now once again made ridiculous by the persistent and natural belligerency between states, then the world will again be in order for the advocates of a fetishized normality. Since their administratively executed German policy earned them no laurels, do they now intend to start flexing some international muscle?

Germany was unable to stay completely out of the military operations in the Middle East. It was the centre of American reinforcement operations. It sent troops to its ally Turkey, which was considered to be under military threat. Bundeswehr minesweepers were also sent to the Persian Gulf between the crushing defeat of Saddam Hussein on 27 February and 12 April 1991, when the final armistice took effect. Above all, however, Germany paid, a total of 18 billion marks. The west was *not* impressed. 'Chequebook diplomacy' was one of the more polite terms used to describe Bonn's policy in the Gulf War.

Germany was not prepared for the demands placed on it by its allies just a few short months after reunification, whether militarily or politically or morally. The deployment of armed forces had been absent from the agenda for more than forty years. Now, however, references to constitutional obstacles to an 'out of area' operation legitimated by the UN would be interpreted as excuse-making. During the Gulf War, the appeal to the singularity of the Holocaust made a disgraceful impression, given that the targets of Saddam's missiles were Jews. The pacifist left resisted the 'normalization' foreign policy that now set in. It derived from the Holocaust a German claim to an exceptional status. It transformed the historical singularity of the murder of the Jews into a German right to permanent and comprehensive singularity. This part of the left did not understand that the normalization expected of Germany by the rest of the world had nothing to do with forgetting the German past. On the contrary: it aimed at drawing practical lessons from that past. If Germany took its commitment to human rights and to the principles of international law seriously, it had no alternative.

The year of the Gulf War would also go down in history as the final year of the Soviet Union and the first year of the wars over the break-up of Yugoslavia. On 27 June the Council for Mutual Economic Assistance dissolved itself, and the Warsaw Pact followed suit four days later. On 23 August the 'radical reformer' Boris Yeltsin, made president of the Russian Soviet Federative Socialist Republic by directly popular election in June, banned all activities of the Communist party in Russia. This was a reaction to a failed putsch by conservative cadres a few days before—men whom Gorbachev himself, at the end of 1990, had placed in the key positions from which they were able to attempt their coup. On 24 August Gorbachev resigned as general secretary of the Soviet Communist party.

By this time the breakdown of the USSR was already in full swing. Georgia, following the example of Lithuania, had declared its withdrawal from the Soviet Union in April 1991. Estonia, Latvia, Ukraine, Byelorussia, Moldavia, Azerbaijan, Kyrgyzstan, and Uzbekistan followed in August, Tajikistan, Armenia, and Turkmenistan in September. On 7 December Russia, Byelorussia, and Ukraine formed a Commonwealth of Independent States, which eight non-Slavic republics also joined later that same month. Kazakhstan declared its independence on 16 December. Gorbachev resigned as president of the USSR on 25 December. His farewell speech, broadcast on television, marked the end of the Soviet Union. Seventy-four years after Lenin's October revolution, the state that under Stalin had advanced to become the second most powerful on earth was no more. History's first real totalitarian regime, which had only shed its totalitarianism under Gorbachev, finally departed from the stage of history.

The USSR's loss of power was also Gorbachev's. There can be no doubt that his fall was caused in part by his renunciation of the GDR, his agreement to German reunification, and his acceptance of German NATO membership. But the decline of the Soviet Union could not have been stopped during the 1980s, and the emancipation of eastern Europe and the reunification of Germany were only possible *because* the USSR's economic, political, ideological, and moral collapse was so far advanced by the end of the decade.

Gorbachev was a gifted tactician, but he was no strategist. He was the very embodiment of the 'tragic reformer'. In liquidating the communist dictator-ship—directly in the USSR, indirectly in large parts of Europe—he achieved something other than he had intended: the accelerated collapse of the system he had sought to rescue.

The open disintegration of Yugoslavia began on 25 June 1991 when Slovenia and Croatia declared their independence. The Serbian-dominated federal presidency refused to recognize either move and authorized the Yugoslav army to intervene. In September the population of Macedonia opted for independence in a referendum and was able to gain it without fighting. That same month Kosovo—annexed by Serbia in July 1990 despite a majority Albanian population—also held a secret referendum for independence, which was supported by an overwhelming majority. Thereafter, however, repressive measures from the authoritarian regime of Serbian president Slobodan Milosevic increased. In October the parliament of Bosnia-Herzegovina, with the votes of the Muslim and Croatian delegates and the absent Serbs, voted for sovereignty. Referendums on 29 February and 1 March 1992 gained majorities for independence. Slovenia secured its own after brief fighting. In Croatia and Bosnia-Herzegovina, however, even international recognition and the deployment of UN peacekeeping troops could not prevent a long and bloody war. Europe had a new crisis zone.

Germany was the first country to grant diplomatic recognition to Slovenia and Croatia. It did so on 23 December 1991, after Bonn had tried and failed to get the European Community to adopt a unified stance. The German initiative had no effect on the conflicts in the region. On 2 April 1993 the Bonn government, with the votes of the Union ministers, decided that German soldiers would participate in a mission of NATO surveillance aircraft (of the AWACS type) securing the no-fly zone that the UN had declared over Bosnia-Herzegovina. Never before had a government of the Federal Republic given the Bundeswehr a combat mission. Hurried motions by the SPD and the FDP for an interim injunction to block this decision—the latter for constitutional, the former for political and constitutional reasons—were rejected by the Constitutional Court on 8 April. 'Otherwise there would be an inevitable loss of trust on the part of [the Federal Republic's] alliance partners and European neighbours, and the damage this would cause would be irremediable.'

The final 'out of area' decision was handed down on 12 July 1994. The court decided that the Bundeswehr could undertake humanitarian and/or military missions even outside of NATO territory. Article 24, Paragraph 2 of the Basic Law, it said, subordinated the Federal Republic to a system of collective security. This meant that it could agree to a limitation of its own sovereignty. Article 87a, which regulated the deployment of the Bundeswehr in defensive situations, was not an obstacle. Nonetheless, the government would first—or, in an exceptional situation, afterwards—have to seek the 'constitutive approval' of the Bundestag with a simple majority. The SPD and FDP motions were thus dismissed.

The Bundestag dealt with the Karlsruhe decision in a special session on 22 July. Klaus Kinkel (FDP), the new foreign minister (he had replaced Genscher on 18 May 1992), said that it meant 'in political terms a clear rejection of a separate German path'. Nonetheless, Germany would still stick to its 'tried and tested culture of reserve. We will not push ourselves forward. In foreign and security policy, normality means not playing global policeman, not sending German soldiers everywhere there is a crisis. There will not be anything automatic about German participation.' After the debate an overwhelming majority of the Bundestag retroactively approved the deployments, the purpose of which was to prevent Serbian bomb attacks against Bosnia-Herzegovina.

During the following year the parliament dealt with a Bundeswehr contribution to protect and support the 'rapid reaction force' in Bosnia-Herzegovina, which the cabinet had voted for on 26 June 1995. The coalition parties approved the decision; the majority of the SPD, Greens, and all of the PDS rejected it. It passed on 30 June, by 386 votes to 258, with 11 abstentions. Four delegates from Alliance 90/The Greens voted for the government's motion: Marieluise Beck, Helmut Lippelt, Gerd Poppe, and Waltraud Schoppe. Among the 45 SPD delegates supporting it were Freimut Duve, Norbert Gansel, Stephan Hilsberg, Hans-Ulrich Klose, Ingrid Matthäus-Maier, Markus Meckel, and Karsten Voigt. In the August issue of *Vorwärts*, the party publication, Günter Verheugen, the managing director of the SPD, responded to those who had broken ranks. Verheugen supported a 'basically non-violent foreign policy', for which he gave historical reasons. Even after the great changes in Europe, he wrote, Germany could not 'become a normal country . . . like other countries without such an abnormal history. Those who still do not believe this should ask themselves what the newly opened Holocaust museum in Washington means.'

Three years later—Germany was now governed by a red–green cabinet under Gerhard Schröder as chancellor and Joschka Fischer as foreign minister—a large Bundestag majority approved another Bundeswehr mission in Kosovo. Auschwitz once again played a significant role in the justifications, but this time it was used as a reason *for* the intervention, which was seeking to prevent genocide against the Kosovo Albanians. The references to Nazi crimes against humanity also helped the ruling left get past residual doubts about the efficacy of military power to bring peace to the conflict zone. Unlike in 1995, however, in 1999 the parliamentary left, too, was nearly united in accepting the consequences of German sovereignty. Germany acted as one among other western democracies. Only small minorities continued to insist on a separate German path, pointing to the German past.[19]

ARRIVAL IN THE WEST: THE NEW GERMAN NATION

A survey by the Allensbach Institute for Opinion Research in April 1993 revealed how deep the divide between east and west Germany still was in the third year after reunification. The question on the survey read as follows: 'Do you believe that west and east Germans feel solidarity with each other, that they both feel like Germans [*sich gemeinsam als Deutsche fühlen*], or do they feel like west and east

Germans, with contrary interests?' Only one-fifth (22%) of west Germans and one-tenth of east Germans (11%) responded positively to the first question; 71% of west Germans and 85% of east Germans polled said that they had 'contrary interests'.

The year 1993 seems to mark the nadir in the relationship between the two groups. Six years later, in summer 1999, 48% of west and 63% of east Germans considered the reunification a joyful occasion. The percentages of those who saw it as an occasion for distress were 28% and 19% respectively. When asked if the sentence 'We are one people' was still true, 53% of west and 45% of east Germans said yes—significantly higher numbers than in 1994 (west 50%, east 32%). In June 2000 the Ipos Institute in Mannheim reported that 80% of west Germans and 68% of east Germans regarded themselves first and foremost as Germans and not as east or west Germans. This seemed to indicate that the integration was making progress.

The four decades of separation had alienated the two populations from each other far more then they realized at the time of reunification. The more frequent and intensive their contact, the more they seemed to annoy each other. The clichés of the whining *Ossi* and the arrogant *Wessi* were most prevalent in the early 1990s. Dialectically speaking, of course, these images already represented a certain degree of rapprochement; the Germans in the west and east were at least less indifferent to each other now than when they had little contact.

The feelings of alienation were articulated primarily by intellectuals—in the east by members of the former state intelligentsia, who saw themselves as the losers of the unification and who sought in the PDS a surrogate for the GDR, the political home they had lost; and in the west by the 'posthumous Adenauer left', who felt more homeless than ever in reunified Germany. Before 1989, the need to justify the partition had led Germans on both sides to wrestle with history and find new meaning in it. When unification unexpectedly happened, history itself seemed to lose all meaning, and its interpreters their *raison d'être*. It was very difficult not to quarrel with this fate.

In April 1991, a half a year after the reunification, Peter Glotz saw cause to believe that the Germans were once again in the process 'of becoming a dangerous people—dangerous, because lacking internal balance'. As evidence he cited 'belligerent' voices during the war against Iraq. 'The reawakening of German nervous fever has been most noticeable during the Gulf War. But the real cause lies in the disconcerting expectations concerning Germany's new role in the world.' Glotz believed that 'elitist nationalism' was threatening his own party, too.

The central European revolution of 1989 took from it the philosophy that guided it through a quarter of a century, a peace policy fed by passionate dedication to small steps. Now it lacks a compass. It has also been out of power for a long time. In mass parties, long opposition inevitably gives rise to a deep longing for emotional accord with the majority of one's own people. In any case, we cannot discount the danger that some of this party might forget that the European federalist Adenauer was right and the national-republican centralist Schumacher was wrong.

Three weeks later, on 10 May 1991, the publicist Klaus Hartung wrote a response in *Die Zeit*, the newspaper that had printed Glotz's essay.

Glotz represents the nostalgic West German left, one that took until after 1989 to discover that the Federal Republic was its Golden Age. Federalism, lifestyle, ecology, civil society, western alliance, Perpetual Peace (at least in central Europe) and, of course, high standard of living—this is the rhetoric of desire in the country now being invaded by the greedy, uncultivated, impoverished masses of the east. But the east: that is Glotz's real trauma . . . For Glotz, there has anyway been far too much waving of flags and too much swinging of incense burners in eastern Europe, for too long. *Solidarność* was for him a kind of secularized Catholicism. He, too, participated in a Social Democratic politics that supported Jaruzelski right up to the Round Table, a Social Democratic politics for which the stability of the state was a value in itself. . . The obvious was ignored, and it continues to be ignored: that from Slovenia to the Baltic, the demand for political and social emancipation proceeds via the rediscovery of the nation and through the return to the national religion. The concept of democracy is indissolubly bound up with this process.

In the same issue of *Die Zeit*, Jürgen Habermas once again lamented the manner in which the political unification of Germany had come about. The method of accession had stripped four-fifths of the voting public of the opportunity to make a free decision, he wrote.

They were not even asked. The only thing they could do was confirm the annexation after the fact—in a melancholy Bundestag election with comparatively low voter turnout. The normative deficit lies in the fact that the 'political class', except in absurd campaign rhetoric like 'We are looking forward to Germany!', made no effort to gain the support of the majority of the West German voters—who are far too young to have much of an idea about the fairly alien state of the GDR—for the arduous project of a common nation of citizens. There was a similar deficit on the other side, too. Other than hastily presenting clean bills of health for an 'Alliance for Germany', nobody made an effort to explain to the masses—who no longer have personal memories of the time before 1933—the normative content of the principles of democracy and justice embodied in the Basic Law.

One of the key terms in Habermas's article was *Beziehungslosigkeit*, 'lack of a connection' (literally: 'connectionlessness'). The Frankfurt philosopher, born in Düsseldorf in 1929, described the few occasions on which he had come into contact with the GDR and its citizens. As he correctly noted, this lack of experience was typical for his generation (though it was hardly perceived as a lack).

I mention this history of connectionlessness in order to recall to mind the fact that the likes of us had more in common with the post-war history of Italy or France or the USA than with the GDR. Its history was not our history. That is even more true for my children and the generation of my children. We must be permitted to register this fact, without sentimentality.

The GDR had been for Habermas not only an alien world; he was more convinced than ever that it was also a danger for unified Germany, even posthumously.

In seeking to legitimate itself, the GDR—a 'workers' and peasants' state' only by the grace of its own presumption—availed itself of a political rhetoric that misused progressive ideas. Its inhuman practice made a mockery of them, thereby discrediting them. I fear that this dialectic of devaluation will be more ruinous for the mental hygiene in Germany than the concentrated resentment of five or six generations of anti-enlightenment, anti-Semitic, faux romantic, Teutonizing obscurantists. For me, the devaluation of our best and weakest intellectual traditions is one of the most pernicious aspects of the inheritance that the GDR brings into the Federal Republic. This is a destruction of reason that Lukács had not thought of.

This was a reference to the Hungarian Marxist philosopher Georg Lukács's classic 1953 work *Die Zerstörung der Vernunft,** a critical history of 'reactionary' irrationalism in Germany from Schelling to Nietzsche to Hitler. Accordingly, Habermas's article was entitled 'Die andere Zerstörung der Vernunft'.[†]

Three weeks later the east German theologian Richard Schröder (head of the SPD fraction in the Volkskammer from the end of March to the end of August 1990) responded to Habermas in another article in *Die Zeit*. He defended the accession according to Article 23 of the Basic Law.

The Federal Republic had committed itself. It had decided . . . The objection: But I, I personally, I was not asked if I want to have Article 23 in the constitution. This objection contains a bit too much 'I' . . . In truth, to the credit of the *Wessies* and to the comfort of our belief in humanity, the majority of the citizens welcomed unification even via accession and did not demand that it first had to be tested whether hardness of heart is capable of winning a majority in the Federal Republic . . . There is a certain kind of leftist whose heart bleeds for all the suffering in the world, except when it comes to actual people, whom he finds contemptible. He finds them lacking in—his own point of view.

What Richard Schröder diagnosed in the case of Habermas's article was a normative deficit among those who, like Habermas, criticized the normative deficit of the unification process. It was indeed highly questionable to accuse the 'political class' of the old FRG of not appealing to something that the accuser himself had once been at pains to dispose of: the consciousness of a specific national solidarity with the Germans in the GDR. And it was no less questionable for a west German now to declare solidarity with none other than those east Germans who before 1990 had legitimated the dictatorship.

'It is *always* a catastrophe when a career is suddenly cut short,' Habermas had written in reference to the 'administrative processing' of academies, universities, and museums. Schröder answered:

* Lukács, *The Destruction of Reason*.
† Habermas, 'The Other Destruction of Reason'.

'Processing' is often unavoidable. You cannot simply say to the ML [Marxist-Leninist, H.A.W.] philosophers: OK, reform yourselves! You cannot leave it to them alone to determine who among them will teach philosophy in the future. That would be the wrong time and place for 'self-determination'. If that were permitted, everybody would say that they were important and—a victim of the system. In fact, outside evaluation is a more human thing to do than to play yet one more round of that compulsory game of voluntary 'criticism and self-criticism' . . . A criticism that does not say how it can be done better is nothing but opium for those who only feel good when they see the badness of the world confirmed.

The German–German alienation led after 1990 to a belated attempt on the part of some intellectuals to put themselves in the shoes of 'the other Germans'. Strangely, however, these 'other Germans' were not the former civil rights activists or the many East Germans who had been forced to come to an arrangement with the regime but had not compromised themselves in the process. Rather, most of the empathy was directed at people who had once been involved in or who had supported the East German state—people who were now saying that they were victims of west German 'colonizers' or western 'victor's justice'. This group included no small number of Unofficial Collaborators of the Stasi, to whom west Germans now confessed that they did 'not know how they themselves would have acted in a similar situation'. The *IM* advanced to become, in retrospect, the veritable embodiment of the *Ossi*—a tragic figure, but one perhaps more representative of certain west German intellectuals than the majority of real east Germans.

Consequently, criticism from the 'left' was directed not only at the (typically) mild sentences against former high functionaries of the GDR, but also at the Gauck office. (It was now often forgotten that this agency had been wrested *from* the West *by* the East Germans.) The typical argument was that the examination of the East German past was being undertaken by the west far more rigorously than it had once dealt with its own Nazi past. While this was not incorrect, it amounted to arguing for the repetition of what had long turned out to be a grave error. Those who protested most sharply against such arguments were not West but East Germans, and they prevailed.

In March 1992 the Bundestag, taking up a proposal by the SPD delegate Markus Meckel, set up a 'Commission to Investigate the History and Consequences of the SED Dictatorship in Germany'. It was headed by the CDU delegate Rainer Eppelmann, a former civil rights activist. The commission's studies, in which many scholars participated, were printed in an extensive work of eighteen volumes. A concluding inter-party resolution, passed by the Bundestag on 17 June 1994—the forty-first anniversary of the East German uprising—called the GDR a 'dictatorship'.

The *forms* of domination changed throughout the system's forty-five year existence. The more the apparatus of domination was perfected, the more subtle these could be. In substance, however, the SED state remained what it was designed to be: a totalitarian system in which the ruling party's—or its leadership's—claim to power extended to all areas of political, societal, and economic life and was asserted by all the instruments of control in the state, up to the 'Shield and Sword of the Party', the MfS . . . The main responsibility for the injustices perpetrated by this system lies with the SED.

The PDS was the only party that disagreed with the resolution. It passed by an overwhelming majority.

The term 'totalitarian' remained controversial. As before, the 'leftist' objection was that it conflated 'red' with 'brown', placing the GDR in the same category as the Third Reich and thus vitiating 'Auschwitz'. This was far from what the investigatory commission and the scholars who used the word intended. 'Totalitarian' was and is a term of comparison. To compare does not mean to conflate, but to look for differences and similarities. Both German dictatorships of the twentieth century were totalitarian in their claims on the totality of the human person and in the structures and methods of domination they derived from these claims. Totalitarian systems *might* engage in mass extermination, as under Stalin and Hitler, but they do not do so *automatically*.

The GDR and the other communist regimes of post-war Europe were 'derivative totalitarian systems', to modify a phrase by Richard Löwenthal. They were built on the model of the Soviet Union, such as it had emerged from the mass terror of the 'great purges' during the 1930s. The investigatory commission employed the word 'totalitarian' not in a static, but in an elastic manner. It could be reconciled with the fact that the GDR of the late 1980s was far less totalitarian than the GDR of the early 1950s—that the totalitarian institutions had outlasted the totalitarian dynamic, as Löwenthal put it back in 1965, at the start of the Brezhnev era.

The Nazi dictatorship was infinitely more terrifying than the SED regime. Nothing done by the GDR came even remotely close to the crimes Hitler's Germany committed against the Jews and other peoples of eastern Europe during the Second World War. The Third Reich plunged the world into war. The same could not be said of the GDR—nor the Soviet Union, for that matter. The SED repressed its own population more than the Nazis did, but that was because the latter's rule was more popular, from the beginning to the bitter end. National Socialism appealed to a profoundly irrational view of the world. Communism appealed to a scientific theory it claimed as superior to all other theories. Communism *was* qualitatively superior to National Socialism, and for this reason its power of attraction for intellectuals was far greater.

The Third Reich was destroyed after twelve years. The GDR lasted four decades. When Hitler's rule collapsed, the society it left behind was basically the same as it had been during the Weimar Republic. East German society, in contrast, underwent a profound transformation between 1945 and 1989. Both regimes changed the consciousness of the people over which they ruled, but in very different ways. The mental effects of forty years of 'real existing socialism' were stronger than those of twelve years under National Socialism. The balance is different in the long view: the German dictatorship experienced by all Germans in 1933–45 has had a stronger effect on the collective consciousness than the dictatorship imposed on a part of the population by the Soviet Union after the Second World War and kept in power until 1989.

Despite all the differences between the two systems, the Germans needed to study and come to terms with both of them, and this task continues today. Forty years of authoritarian domination and suppression have left deep marks on the east Germans. Reunification turned this into a problem for the whole country, and it is a problem that can only be overcome by common effort. The investigatory commission did *not* share Habermas's view that the history of the GDR was 'not our history'. (The word choice alone indicates how much the philosopher was still thinking in categories of 'us' and 'them'.) The resolution passed by the Bundestag on 17 June 1994 took the opposite position:

Working up a historically founded judgement of the causes and structures of the second dictatorship in Germany is not only part of coming to terms with the consequences of the SED rule and the partition of Germany. It also represents a fundamental ongoing task in the effort to further develop the democratic political culture of reunited Germany.

The battle over who got the credit for and who had stood in the way of reunification began even before the event actually took place on 3 October 1990. The Christian Democrats saw it as the culmination of the work of Konrad Adenauer. A western solution to the German question had indeed been what the first chancellor, who had rejected a Germany 'between west and east' for good reason, had had in mind. But German unity had not been a strategic goal of Adenauer's policy. Given the conditions at the time, it could not have been.

The Social Democrats emphasized the contribution of Willy Brandt's *Ostpolitik*. Without the 'policy of small steps', they said, the USSR and Germany's eastern neighbours could not have overcome their mistrust of Germany, and the 'peaceful revolution' of 1989 would never have happened. This was also correct, but it did not refute the conservatives' argument that a significant portion of the SPD—not to mention the Greens—had not only rejected the goal of political unity, but had abandoned the very idea of a single German nation. And there could be no talk of Social Democratic support for the liberation movements in eastern central Europe during the 1980s.

The western alliance and the *Ostpolitik* were both part of the foundations of German unification. To this extent both the Union and the SPD were right, as were the liberals in both cases. Those who, in all camps, had held to the idea of a single German citizenship and to the right of self-determination and political unity could, in 1990, justly say that this steadfastness had paid off. The claim to a German nation within the 1937 borders, on the other hand, was calculated to erect barriers against what could be achieved in the real world. This was the other side of the conservative position, though it was rarely mentioned after 1990. Even the opponents of unity helped bring unity about, in a dialectic way.

The insistence that the partition of Germany was the result of German politics was correct and helped delegitimate German nationalism. Germany would never have been offered the Two-Plus-Four treaty if it had been thought that it could relapse into nationalism.

It was above all the Germans in the GDR who desired and expected unification in 1989–90. The West Germans accepted it; to have done otherwise would have put the lie to their political identity and their constitution. The publicist Hermann Rudolph, speaking in Bonn at the conferral of the Karl Herman Flach Award in 1993, described the West German way of thinking at the turn of the past decade in the following way:

At the moment when the opportunity for reunification presented itself, the Federal Republic was simply no longer prepared for this possibility, whether in the sentiments of its citizens or in the ideas of its politicians . . . The Federal Republic's path to itself also involved a turning towards democracy and liberalism and a turning away from the old Germany that had come to an end in megalomania and hubris. This transformation was part and parcel of getting used to life in the Federal Republic, this moving away from the ideality of the nation state in all of political and social life, this opening towards the western world and its values, this orientation to Europe. All of this together finally made it possible for the Federal Republic to prioritize liberty over unity—a unity that could not be achieved.

For Rudolph, the results were ambivalent. On the one hand, 'a different, better Germany' was taking shape in the Federal Republic. This meant that this state would be 'not a mere episode, but an epoch' in German history, 'the most important . . . since the founding of the Reich, if not since the era in which the Germans first entered modern European political life'. On the other hand, the Germans 'no longer really knew what to do with the nation state that had been given to them again'. In overcoming this dilemma the Germans, in Rudolph's view, would be helped neither by those who were pushing for a nationalist revision of German history nor by those who, always warning against a resurgence of German nationalism, had 'run aground on a no-I-will-not-eat-my-soup rejection of the nation state'. The speaker's solution: 'Instead, what is necessary is that we focus on and strengthen what the Germans in the west and the east have in common, and keep the perspective of the unification alive in the minds of the people.' Rudolph concluded with a quote from the first speech by president Theodor Heuss before the Bundesversammlung on 12 September 1949: the Germans were faced with the 'great task of forming a new national consciousness'.

And indeed, after 1990 the task at hand was nothing less than to create the German nation anew. There were still common memories of a common past, but only among the older generation. Furthermore, the common past was so laden with problems and guilt that a national renewal first had to begin with critical self-analysis. Reunited Germany was not a 'post-national democracy among nation states', as Karl Dietrich Bracher had said with a certain justification of the old FRG. It was a nation state, though not of the old kind, like the German

Reich. It was one post-classical democratic nation state among others, firmly integrated into NATO and the European Community, and prepared to yield even more sovereignty to the new European Union. It differed strongly from the old German Reich, but not from the other EC member states.

The second German national state could not return to the authoritarian structures and the power politics of the first. But it could reconnect with other traditions that *had* been present before 1933: the rule of law, the constitution, federalism, and social welfare policies. In part, these traditions predated even the founding of the Reich. This was true of parliamentary culture and general equal suffrage (though at first only for males), first codified in the Reich constitution of 1849, then adopted by Bismarck in the 1867 constitution of the North German Confederation and the 1871 constitution of the German Reich.

The new Germany could also take up national traditions that had formed part of the democratic movement. The Weimar experiences were a chapter in this history—a chapter that lived on in the Basic Law. The experiences of the old Federal Republic also lived on, even if they were specifically west German experiences. Bonn was a 'success story' when compared with Weimar, but it is not a period in German history that is well-suited for idealizing retrospectives. In this area, too, there is much still in need of critical reappraisal. The history of illegal party financing, for example, has been uncovered only in part, and the Germans must live with the fact that the 'chancellor of German unity' who demonstrated such historical greatness in 1989–90 also broke the law and violated his oath of office over the course of many years.

Ten years after reunification, the danger that Germany might become less western than the old FRG is less frequently emphasized than in 1990. As much as still remains to be done in terms of anchoring the political culture of western democracy in the daily life of the new *Länder*, in one major area westernization took a huge step forward after reunification: in the 1999 reform of the citizenship law. This law, a product of a 'traffic light coalition' between the SPD, Greens, and liberals, moved away from the nearly exclusive focus on ethnic heritage and towards the mixture of elements of *ius sanguinis* and *ius soli* characteristic of most western democracies.

The new citizenship law, which took effect on 1 January 2000, modified the German idea of the nation, making it more western. This might help to clear away some of the reservations against the new, post-classical German nation state that still exist among the old west German left. This change is overdue. Europe is not being built against the nation states, but with them and by them. Europe will be supra-national, but it will not be post-national.

In the autumn of 1990, at the time of reunification, Ralf Dahrendorf gave the following verdict:

Whoever gives up the nation state loses what up to this point has been the only effective guarantor of his basic rights. Whoever today considers the nation state dispensable is also—whether he intends to or not—declaring civil rights to be dispensable . . . In doing this the German left, in particular, is running a risk, inasmuch as it is prepared to write off the institutions of the nation state in exchange for the mere hope of a European federal state. Here we see the anti-institutional bent of the sixty-eighter generation at work once again, a new edition of the obscure cultural criticism that fits so well into the nasty history of German cultural pessimism . . . It is a naïve illusion to believe that some international organization, even NATO or the EC, could prevent an unsettled Germany from taking out its frustrations on its neighbours. This is another reason it is important that united Germany consciously take the path towards the nation state of right and freedom.[20]

Ten years later, at the beginning of the new century, there is every reason to believe that the democratic left is in the process of adopting this view of things.

Farewell to Separate Paths: Looking Back and Looking Ahead

Was there or was there not a German *Sonderweg*? Did Germany develop along its own 'unique path' through history? This was the question that we posed at the outset of this study of Germany in the nineteenth and twentieth centuries. Since it is not one that can be answered if we restrict ourselves to the last two centuries, the first volume began much further back in history, examining the three basic phenomena that shaped German history until 1945: the Holy Roman Empire and the German myth of the Reich, the confessional divide of the fifteenth century, and the dualism between the two German great powers, Austria and Prussia.

In comparison to western Europe—and it is only in *this* context that a German *Sonderweg* is debated, among scholars or in the general public—we note a twofold historical belatedness. Germany became a nation state much later than countries like Britain and France, and a democracy later still. The old Reich, the Holy Roman Empire of the German Nation, was not even a real state, much less a nation state. Neither was the German Confederation of 1815–66. The first attempt to create a liberal national state in Germany failed in 1848–9. Liberalism proved unable to achieve unity and liberty at the same time. When the revolution began in spring 1848, most champions of those two goals were still thinking in the categories of a 'greater' Germany, one that would include the German-speaking parts of the Habsburg monarchy, a few non-German territories like Italian Tyrol and Trieste, and, if at all possible, Bohemia and Moravia. A *kleindeutsch* solution without Austria would *perhaps* have been internationally possible at that time, but it was not yet desired. Two years later, the majority of the German national assembly in Frankfurt did desire it. But by this time it was no longer internationally possible.

Bismarck solved the unity question his own way, with Prussian leadership and against Austria. For Europe, the *kleindeutsch* solution was far more tolerable than any kind of *grossdeutsch* project, which would have weighted the European balance of power even more strongly in Germany's favour. The question of unity *had* to be solved; at least that was how German public opinion saw things in the decade prior to 1871. At first, the founding of a German national state brought a certain degree of westernization or normalization. Once they had said farewell to the universalist traditions of the old Reich and to the German Confederation, the Germans differed from the other nation states of Europe less than before.

In another respect, the differences were still deep. Bismarck's 'revolution from above' had solved the question of unity, but not the question of liberty. The German empire was a *constitutional* but not a *parliamentary* monarchy. And it was constitutional only to a limited extent. Absolutism lived on in the supreme military authority of the king of Prussia, who became emperor in 1871. Still, the German empire was not a purely authoritarian state. General equal suffrage for men, which Bismarck had introduced into the North German Confederation in 1867 and adopted for the German Reich in 1871, gave Germany more progressive voting rights than the monarchies of Britain or Belgium gave to their citizens at the time. The social legislation of the 1880s also deserves to be called 'progressive'. The German empire wore a Janus face. It was archaic and modern at the same time, and what it seemed to be in any particular instance depended on one's vantage point.

It has occasionally been argued that the German empire was on the way to a 'silent parliamentarization' before 1914. This is not true. There was no majority in the Reichstag for parliamentary governance. The conservatives were absolutely opposed to it, the National Liberals only partly in favour. The Catholic Centre preferred the status quo, which guaranteed it a key role in the negotiation of compromises, to a parliamentary system in which it would necessarily be in the minority. The Social Democrats, the strongest party, supported parliamentary rule in principle, but the doctrine of class war kept it from entertaining the idea of entering into coalitions with the bourgeois parties.

Parliamentary rule did not come until Germany was defeated in the First World War, the 'seminal catastrophe' of the twentieth century and one for which the German Reich and Austria-Hungary bore the main responsibility. But the new constitution of October 1918 could not prevent revolution from below. Parts of the old elite, including the leadership of the navy, refused to accept the new situation or recognize the constitution. This catalysed the sailors' revolt on the northern coasts, which rapidly turned into a revolutionary mass uprising. The monarchy fell on 9 November 1918. But a large-scale or 'classic' revolution was no longer possible in Germany after the war. The country was economically, socially, and politically too highly developed to make a radical break with its past.

In a country that had known general equal male suffrage for a half a century, the kind of revolutionary 'educational dictatorship' the extreme left aspired to was inconceivable. An attempt in this direction would have led to a general civil war, and the victorious Allies would quickly have intervened. Whatever the Social Democrats could have done differently or better when they unexpectedly found themselves in power in November 1918, what stood on the agenda in those days was *more* democracy: female suffrage; the democratization of the voting laws in the individual states, districts, and municipalities; and parliamentary governance. Elections to a constituent national assembly thus had to happen quickly. If the Social Democrats had not heeded this call, they would have lost all credibility and turned their own supporters against them.

The Social Democrats of 1918 were not what they had been in 1914. They had split over the issue of war credits. The opponents left the party, taking the doctrinaire Marxists with them. The majority party approved the credits to the end of the war. In summer 1917 they joined the parties of the bourgeois centre in calling for a negotiated peace. The split in the Marxist workers' movement would soon prove to be a serious handicap for the Weimar Republic. In a paradoxical way, however, it was also a *precondition* for democracy. If the moderate forces in the working class and bourgeoisie had not been willing to compromise and cooperate, the Weimar Republic would never have existed in the first place.

Another of the young republic's handicaps was everything that linked it to the monarchy: a high degree of continuity among the landowning, industrial, military, bureaucratic, and judicial elites; the legacy of the authoritarian state among the educated bourgeoisie, in the universities and *Gymnasien*; and an unwillingness to deal with the question of war guilt. The success of the campaign against the 'diktat of Versailles' cannot be understood apart from this latter issue. Although the Weimar constitution of 1919 *did* attempt a new beginning, it remained closely tied to the old system. At the head of state was a president directly elected by the people and vested with special powers—a 'surrogate emperor', latently at first, then, after Hindenburg's election in 1925, manifest in reality. Whenever they found themselves unable to compromise, the parties were tempted to shift responsibility for unpopular decisions to the president. Because this mechanism was built into the constitution, the inclination to use it was great from the beginning.

The authoritarian state lived on in the heads not only of the monarchists, but also of many staunch republicans. In November 1926 Paul Levi, a former head of the German Communist party who had returned to the SPD four years before, wrote the following: 'Democracies and republics know only two things: a government that governs, and a parliament to which the government is responsible. . . . The government and the parliament must face each other openly as free and independent institutions. The debate between them—sometimes it is a battle—is the very life of the democratic republic.'[1]

Although Levi used the term 'democratic republic', he was thinking in the categories of constitutional monarchy, where the government and the parliament were independent of each other. In a parliamentary democracy, on the other hand, the government depended on the confidence of a parliamentary majority. It was not the parliament and the government who faced each other, but the governing majority and the parliamentary opposition.

The last majority government of the Weimar Republic broke up in March 1930, unable to reconcile differences over the reform of unemployment insurance. Immediately thereafter the transition to a presidential system began: rule via emergency decrees according to Article 48 of the Weimar constitution. Soon the Reichstag had less power than under the emperors. The parliament's loss of power—we could also view it as a self-deprivation—meant nothing less than the return to a bureaucratic version of the authoritarian state.

But it turned out that the clock could not simply be turned back to the nineteenth century. Authoritarian rule put wind in the sails of the anti-parliamentary parties on the extreme right and left—the National Socialists much more than the Communists, to be sure. Hitler became the main beneficiary of one of the contradictions within the process of Germany's modernization: the early democratization of suffrage and the belated democratization of the governmental system. After 1930 Hitler could appeal to *both* the widespread resentment against the new, allegedly 'un-German' parliamentary democracy, forced on the country by the western victors, *and* to the right of political co-determination in the form of general equal suffrage, which the people had enjoyed for decades—a right that went a long way towards making the presidential governments ineffective.

Hitler did not come to power through electoral victory. But his electoral successes between 1930 and 1932 were the precondition for his elevation to the chancellorship on 30 January 1933. Both factors—the support of the 'nationalist' masses and the decision of the ruling elites—were essential. Given the political will, the power centre around Hindenburg could have prevented Hitler's takeover of the state. It was *not* the inevitable result of the prior developments. But it was also no mere 'accident'. The Junkers, foremost among those pushing for Hitler, at this time had greater access than any other group to the real authority in the state, President Hindenburg. The Junkers' power was not coincidental, but the result of their efforts under Bismarck as well as Bismarck's on behalf of them. Hitler's successes at the polls were also not by chance, as we have seen. What happened on 30 January 1933 had a long prehistory.

Germany was not the only country to suffer as a result of the world economic crisis in 1929. Old democracies like France and (to a lesser extent) Britain also experienced crises in parliamentary rule in the period between the two world wars. But France and Britain were victorious powers, and this fact prevented national resentments from being mobilized there as they were in defeated Germany. As a 'rightist' ideology of integration, nationalism was especially attractive in a country where the confessional divisions were as sharp as class divisions. Nationalism's message of unification answered a broad social need. All of Europe feared civil war after the Bolshevik revolution of 1917. In old democracies, however, the readiness to meet the danger from the left with dictatorial measures was weaker than in new ones. What best served the western democracies were their long democratic traditions and the rootedness of these traditions in both the masses and the elites—in other words, their fundamental democratic consensus. This consensus was strong in Britain and France, and virtually non-existent in Germany.[2]

Nearly all the new European democracies—those formed after 1918—became rightist authoritarian regimes in the 1920s and 1930s. Italy was the first to set up a dictatorship of the new type, a 'fascist' regime (though in Italy's case the term 'young democracy' is of very limited utility). If Hitler's regime had simply been a fascist system like that of Mussolini's Italy, there would probably never have been any discussion of a 'unique German path'. But the 'Third Reich' was not simply 'German fascism', a term still popular on the left to this day. It was the regime that unleashed the Second World War and committed the crime of the century by murdering the European Jews.

Anti-Semitism was a pan-European phenomenon, and it was not limited to Europe. In Germany, bourgeois political culture was saturated with anti-Jewish prejudice well before 1914. But this, too, was true of other countries. In fact, anti-Semitism was far more strongly pronounced in imperial Russia, the Balkans, and Austria-Hungary than in the German Reich. It was also more pronounced in France. It was only after the First World War, in the wake of defeat, revolution, and inflation, that Germany surpassed its western neighbour in Jew-hatred. The Jews now served as scapegoats for everything the radical nationalists detested about the new Germany. The demand to strip the Jews of their equal civil rights was as old as Jewish emancipation. Even the call for the destruction of the Jews can be found in the writings of nineteenth-century German authors like Paul de Lagarde and Eugen Dühring. But it was only with the Nazis that open, radical anti-Semitism turned into a mass movement of millions.[3]

Anti-Semitism was at the very centre of Hitler's world view, but it did not play centre stage during the Nazi agitation of the early 1930s. If it had, the NSDAP would not have achieved such huge successes at the polls. Anti-Semitism was often accompanied by anti-democratic and nationalist attitudes, but the connection was not automatic. What distinguished National Socialism from other 'rightist' movements was the fact that it linked radical anti-Semitism and nationalism to a populist—and popular—hostility to democracy. For some voters, including many academics and students, anti-Semitism was the thing that drew them to the NSDAP. But for most of the party's constituency, it probably would have been more accurate to say that the anti-Semitism of the Nazis did not bother them or that they did not disapprove of it.

The 'educated' among Hitler's supporters, both before and after 1933, were especially fascinated by his dream of a large Germany—the 'Greater German Reich'. All political forces in the country were *grossdeutsch* in attitude after 1918, from the extreme left to the extreme right. The Social Democrats felt most strongly in this regard, since they saw themselves as the heirs of 1848, a time when nationalism was still 'leftist'. The German Nationalists, guardians of the more recent, 'rightist', Prussian-Evangelical nationalism of the Bismarck era, were measurably less enthusiastic. The dissolution of the Habsburg monarchy at the end of 1918 removed an obstacle that had stood in the way of Austria joining the German Reich. But there was no doubt that the Austrians wished to unite with Germany in one state. The veto of the victors was the only thing that prevented that from happening.

Nonetheless, the idea of one great empire included more than simply the addition of Austria to Bismarck's *kleindeutsch* nation. The idea of 'the Reich' struck deep chords in the collective psyche. Protestants (and not only they) would have had the last line of Luther's famous hymn 'A Mighty Fortress is our God' in their minds: *Das Reich muss uns doch bleiben.** (although Luther had not been thinking of the Holy Roman Empire of the German Nation, of course, but of the Kingdom of God). Catholics would have thought of the medieval *Sacrum Imperium*. In both cases the idea of the Reich was theologically loaded, far more so than other analogous ideas, like that of the British world empire, for example, not to mention the purely secular cult of the *Impero* in Fascist Italy. Only the medieval cult of Moscow as the 'Third Rome', the heir of Byzantium and the Rome of antiquity, is comparable to the German idea of the Reich. (It is also still very much alive in Russia today.) Historically and theologically educated Germans liked to remind themselves and others about the old myth according to which the Antichrist would not come to power as long as the Roman empire, transferred to the Germans (i.e. to the Franks) at the crowning of Charlemagne in the year 800, was still standing. In the German view there was only one real Empire, and that was the German one.[4]

'The Reich' was something different and more than a nation state. It was universal in conception. It enjoyed a special status among the peoples of the west. It had a divine mission. There was no other idea capable of providing a similar compensation for the profoundly felt national weakness in the defeated, decimated, and humiliated Germany that emerged from the First World War. The ideologists of the 'conservative revolution' knew this as well as Hitler. Many of them toyed with the idea of the Reich, but none with so much virtuosity and to so great an effect as the Nazi leader.

In 1934 the historian Rudolf Stadelmann meditated upon the historical nature of the German revolutions. The common view of the German as 'not made for revolution' was incorrect, he said. The fact that all German revolutions had failed, from Luther's Reformation to the revolt against Napoleon, had a deeper cause.

It is to be found in the clash between the German revolution and the fact of the Reich. This Reich is there, with its truths and exigencies that transcend states, peoples, even laws. The French and the Roman yokes could be shaken off. The destiny of the Reich cannot be discarded . . . The revolution of 1520 and the revolution of 1810 allowed the Reich to continue on its own way, and for that reason the storm was ensnarled in the statesmanlike cleverness of a Charles V and a Metternich, the conscious statesmen of the universal idea of the Reich. This invisible opponent, the Reich, was not recognized as such, since it was affirmed as a German destiny and a German mission.

The nation, Stadelmann continued, had 'advanced to this great institution, the Reich, only in its desires, not with deeds'—an institution 'that it had not created, but come across as the legacy of history'. However, the state-forming power of the German revolutions only benefited the individual territorial state,

---

* [Translator's note: 'The empire ours remaineth.' The standard English translation of this line is 'The kingdom ours remaineth'. The word *Reich* can mean both 'kingdom' and 'empire'.]

and then only in an ongoing dialectical process that often seemed to contemporaries like a terrible reverse. Wrongly, of course, for the authoritarian state of the sixteenth and the nineteenth centuries rests on Luther and Hegel and is a legitimate fruit of the revolution. But the problem of the Reich remained unsolved nonetheless. Thus did it happen that the Reich, the state, and the nation all went their own ways, each holding back and standing in the way of the other. The tragic result of these frictions was the premature standstill of the German movement in the sixteenth and nineteenth centuries.

The two revolutions in German history that, for Stadelmann, deserved the name, the Reformation and the German uprising against Napoleon, were in his view both 'revolutions of the *Volksgemeinschaft*'. 'The Reformation and the War of Liberation were attempts to solve the question of German destiny via the *Volk*. The history of more recent centuries has also seen attempts to put the fundamental structure of the nation in place via the *state*.' Bismarck had made such an attempt, but his work, too, was ground up in the dualism between Prussia and the Reich. Hitler's 'national revolution' of 1933 would not meet with the same fate as the earlier German revolutions. The historical task of the present was still the same:

To make the *Volk*, the state, and the Reich one and the same by means of a constitution that, in all its dimensions, befits the essence of German destiny. We can already see the outlines of this solution emerging: it is the transformation of the Reich into the *Volk* [*Volkwerdung des Reiches*] . . . We will still have to engage in much contemplation before we really know what *Volk* is and in what manner it is formed out of the four elements: pride of ancestry, discipline of speech, deep security of morals, and ethos of profession. It will still take a great deal of effort for us to grasp the state as a thing constituted by enmity and lordship. And nearly everything still remains for us to do in order that we fathom the meaning of the Reich. For it is the Reich that distinguishes the German from the Englishman and the Frenchman.[5]

The cult of the Reich was the bridge between Hitler and educated Germany. German scholars used it to justify the *Anschluss* of Austria, the Protectorate of Bohemia and Moravia, the subjugation of Poland, the hegemony over northern, western, and southern Europe, and the war against Bolshevist Russia, the allegedly modern embodiment of the Antichrist. And Hitler himself alluded to the Book of Revelation and the medieval interpretation of the Antichrist as a Jew (originally in St Jerome). On 30 January 1942, the ninth anniversary of the Nazi takeover, he prophesied the destruction of the Jews: 'And the hour will come when the most evil enemy of the world throughout all time will be finished, at least for a millennium.'[6]

Both the Reich founded by Bismarck in 1871 and the ancient myth of the Reich came to an end with the downfall of the 'Third Reich' of Adolf Hitler. A few years after the 'collapse', the German historian Karl Bosl wrote: 'The *media aetas*, as the humanists called it, is perhaps more present to the Germans than to any other people in our part of the world. And perhaps no other people has remained so medieval, to our fortune and misfortune.'[7] Whatever Bosl might have meant by 'fortune', it was by far outweighed by the misfortune.

In his *Einleitung zur Kritik der Hegelschen Rechtsphilosophie** (1843–4), Marx wrote that '[i]n Germany emancipation from the *Middle Ages* is possible only as an emancipation from *partial* emancipations from the Middle Ages.'[8] For Marx, Luther's Reformation was one of these 'partial emancipations' from the Middle Ages, and he was right. The list should also include Bismarck's empire, the 'revolution from above' that solved the question of unity but deferred the question of liberty. The final emancipation did not occur until much later, more than 400 years after the Reformation, 100 years after Marx's verdict, and three-quarters of a century after the founding of Bismarck's state. Only with the collapse of the German Reich in 1945 were the Middle Ages over in Germany, once and for all.

There was indeed a German *Sonderweg*. It was a long and late journey from the Middle Ages to modernity. The partial emancipation from the past can also be seen in terms of partial modernization. The medieval stood cheek by jowl with the modern and reshaped it to the point where the old was infused with the new and the new saturated with the old. This was true of the Bismarck empire, and it was true of the 'Third Reich' in a way that can only be described as diabolical. Hitler's regime was the climax of the German rejection of the western world, a world to which Germany had so many cultural and social ties. It is only in the light of the commonalities that it even makes sense to talk of a German *Sonderweg*.

The strongest argument against the existence of a unique German path has always been that there is no such thing as a 'normal' western path of historical development. The British, French, and American paths were all unique. Still, the concept of 'western democracy' does point to one particular characteristic shared by all these states, a characteristic Germany lacked until 1945. Human and civil rights—in the tradition of the British *habeas corpus* acts of 1679, the American Declaration of Independence of 1776, and the declaration of human and civil rights by the French National Assembly on 26 August 1789—were anchored deeply enough in the political culture of the western democracies to make violations a public scandal and to drive forward the struggle for their further development. This tradition was not completely lacking in Germany, but it was weaker than that of the long-lived authoritarian state. To put it another way: the deferment of the question of liberty in the nineteenth century is one of the main chapters in the prehistory of the 'German catastrophe', the years 1933–45.

Before 1945, for German philosophers, historians, and writers to speak of a separate German path meant to contrast German 'culture' with western 'civilization', to historically justify the German authoritarian state, and to reject

---

* Marx, *Contribution to the Critique of Hegel's Philosophy of Right: An Introduction*.

western democracy as irreconcilable with Germanness. After 1945 the concept of a German *Sonderweg* underwent a radical transformation, prepared by German emigrants and catalysed by the experience of Nazi rule. Now the idea stood for the historical deviation from the west that led to the 'German catastrophe'.

One of the German historians who had defended the German *Sonderweg* before 1945 changed his position after the 'collapse'. In 1946 Rudolf Stadelmann wrote an essay entitled 'Deutschland und die westeuropäischen Revolutionen'* (it was originally a lecture given in Ulm, Göttingen, and Freiburg, then published in a volume of essays entitled *Deutschland und Westeuropa*† in 1948, a year of many commemorations and reflections on the 1848 revolution). For a hundred years, Stadelmann wrote, the other nations had

shoved the political will of the German people into the drawer of reaction almost without looking at it and placed on it the label: 'The people without revolution'. The lack of familiarity with the practice and the ideas of the west European revolutions, the lack of experience and education when it came to radically turning away from the absolutist past in recent centuries—this is what has stamped our history with the mark of the pariah for about three generations. The absence of a normal revolutionary crisis of puberty in German history is the first and probably most important root cause of why the German name now stands condemned.

For Stadelmann, the deeper reason for the German immunity to western revolutionary ideas lay in enlightened absolutism.

In a certain way the fate of medieval Germany was repeated. The unique German form of the enlightened princedom, which at first represented a head start, ended up leading into a dead end. In a similar way the great head start, the early creation of the Reich on Carolingian soil, while it brought the German state to the forefront of developments in the west, then burdened it for a thousand years and prevented a closed national state from crystallizing on imperial territory, a state such as the western peoples, England, France, and Spain, achieved beginning in the thirteenth century. Just as the character of the Reich was the pride and the curse of the German Middle Ages, so too enlightened absolutism was the most honourable and unique contribution of the Germans to modern constitutional history and, at the same time, the indelible stamp that excluded the Germans from the community of western European ideals. It is a paradox: it was not the German reaction, but German progress that threw Germany back in comparison to the west.

Habituation to the ideal of the 'revolution from above', a long-lasting legacy of enlightened absolutism, was ultimately the reason the revolution of 1848 failed—the one revolution Stadelmann had not considered as such in his 1934 study.

The failure of the forty-eighter movement was disastrous for the political development of the Germans, all the more so because the setback that inevitably occurs after every

---

* Stadelmann, 'Germany and the Western European Revolutions'.
† *Germany and Western Europe.*

revolution—as in England after 1660 and France after 1814—sharpened and poisoned the internal antagonisms and blocked now once and for all the path of rational reform from above that we have come to know as the most cherished idea of the Germans . . . From 1850 onward the poison of this partial fermentation, this deferred crisis, is circulating in the body of the German people. It was the typical illness of the 'country without revolutions'.[9]

Stadelmann had given a conclusive answer to the question of *why* Germany was unable to look back on a successful revolution. The Germans had been hampered by progress, and not only in 1848–9. The same thing happened seventy years later in the 1918–19 revolution; the country was too highly developed to make the kind of radical break with the past necessary for a new democratic beginning. And yet, after freeing himself from the cult of the Reich, Stadelmann laid the foundations for a new myth: that of the missed revolutionary opportunity. German history would have been different and proceeded more positively if the staunch revolutionaries had won the day in 1848 and 1918. While Stadelmann did not make this particular argument, it was one based on his interpretation of history and read like a continuation of his analysis of the 'mark of the pariah' upon the 'people without revolution'.

This reading of history is as questionable as it is popular. The staunch revolutionaries of 1848–9 wanted a great European war of liberation against tsarist Russia. Some, like Marx and Engels, wanted a world war against both autocratic Russia *and* capitalist Britain. The result would have been a pan-European bloodbath and, most likely, a total victory on the part of the reaction. The same was true in 1918–19; if the most resolute revolutionaries had had their way, they would have begun a civil war in Germany, then looked to revolutionary Russia to help spread it to all of Europe and lead the international proletariat to victory. In fact, no outcome was less likely. The attempt at radical revolution would have plunged Europe into catastrophe and probably brought the right to power everywhere.

Just like 'the Reich', the 'German revolution' did not wish to see itself confined to Germany. As Marx wrote in the introduction to his critique of Hegel: 'The *thorough* Germany cannot make a revolution without making a *thoroughgoing* revolution. The *emancipation of the German* is the *emancipation of the human being*.'[10] Marx did indeed prepare the way for a revolution, but it took place in Russia, not Germany. The 'German revolution' was a revolution against Marxism and against western democracy. It was defeated by powers with different revolutionary origins: the western democracies and the Soviet Union, the latter claiming to be the real heir of Marx. The myth of revolution thus outlived the myth of the Reich.

But the myth of revolution also does not offer access to a real understanding of German history. It is the expression of a backward-looking wishful thinking nourished by an envy of the revolutionary traditions of other peoples. It leads to the construction of a free-floating alternative history, one that regularly neglects to enquire about the costs of the path that 'should have been taken'. It provides false certainly in places where doubt would be more appropriate. And it refuses to recognize that history can sometimes be tragic, that there are situations in which the rational course—or what in retrospect appears as such—is impossible because the realities are more powerful than reason.

After 1945 Germany experienced the kind of profound political, social, and moral rupture that did *not* occur after 1918. In the words of Rainer Lepsius:

The collapse of the National Socialist regime, the unconditional surrender, the crimes committed by Germans in the name of the German nation also shook the validity of German nationalism as a political ideology of integration. The order of the German nation could no longer claim priority as an idea of order and as the ideal order. The Allied occupation of the country and the governmental authority, but also the inner de-legitimation of nationalism, made this impossible.[11]

The early Federal Republic saw a reversal of the political roles played in the Weimar Republic. The moderate left now assumed the nationalist mantle, and the moderate right took up the politics of international integration. Catholic Christian Democrats would sometimes even appeal to the old idea of the Reich. Adolf Süsterhenn, for example, speaking at the sixth session of the Parliamentary Council on 20 October 1948, said that the historical concept of the Reich had been 'improperly used by the Bismarck Reich and the Weimar Republic—I will not even speak about the Third Reich.' He continued:

The concept of the Reich, as it lived for a thousand years in German history, was the concept of an international, of a European entity. It was the term used to designate the Christian occident. And if I were to translate the concept of the Reich into the modern language of contemporary politics, I would have to call what was once called 'the Reich' now 'European Union' or 'European federation'.[12]

During the Adenauer era, the supra-national political practice of the government was accompanied by a rhetoric of the nation state. That changed after the wall went up in 1961; parts of the centre right began to argue that the Federal Republic should cultivate a patriotism devoted exclusively to itself, not to all of Germany. The Social Democrats began their 'policy of small steps' in Berlin, working from the premise that the German national state could only be a distant goal and that, in the meantime, the cohesion of the German nation would require cooperation with the 'other side'. Then, at the time of the social–liberal *Ostpolitik*, the Union opposition once again emphasized their nationalism. The Weimar roles thus seemed to be restored, at least on the surface.

But that, too, turned out to be only an intermezzo. Just as the Social Democrats had to accept Adenauer's policy of western integration before Willy Brandt could become foreign minister and then chancellor, so too the Union had to accept Brandt's eastern treaties before they were in a position to govern Germany again. By the 1980s, the pan-German national idea no longer played much of a role in West German political thinking. Karl Dietrich Bracher's description of the FRG as a 'post-national democracy among nation states' accurately described how most intellectuals and many politicians both right and left of centre felt during this period.[13]

The German Democratic Republic moved away from the idea of one German nation in the early 1950s, replacing it with the theory of two German nations, the old capitalist and the new socialist one. The GDR was the ideological state par excellence among the members of the Warsaw Pact: a state without a national identity and therefore more dependent than all others on 'proletarian internationalism' as a surrogate. In other words, *both* Germanies followed unique paths, the GDR an 'internationalist', the FRG a 'post-national' *Sonderweg*. The former was never anything more than party doctrine, whereas the latter became the feeling of an entire generation.

The GDR saw itself as the heir of the antifascist resistance and born in the spirit of this resistance. This was its own particular myth of origin. In the 1980s, antifascism was supplemented with other national traditions considered to be progressive, including certain aspects of the Prussian legacy. This was a tacit admission that the doctrine of the socialist nation had struck no roots among the people. The Federal Republic's first myth of origin was 20 July 1944. The conservative resistance against Hitler was interpreted as having prepared the way for the post-war West German state under the rule of law. During the 1980s the extermination of the Jews increasingly took centre stage in discussions of the 'Third Reich'. The 'Never Again!' attitude applied above all to genocide. Intellectuals came to see the German partition as a punishment and atonement for the Holocaust. At the beginning of 1997 Hanno Loewy wrote an article in the *tageszeitung* talking about Auschwitz as the 'foundational myth' of a new German national sentiment.[14]

In his 1925 book *The Social Frameworks of Memory*, the French sociologist Maurice Halbwachs wrote 'that memory depends on social environment'. The past does not seem to be history. Rather, there is every reason to believe that it 'is not preserved, but constructed, with the construction proceeding from the present . . . Society imagines the past in different ways, depending on the circumstances and the period of time. It changes its conventions. Since every one of its members bows to these conventions, individual memory moves in the same direction in which collective memory develops.' Halbwachs's conclusion was that 'societal thinking is primarily a memory, one whose content is composed entirely of collective memories, and that the only memories and parts of memories that are preserved in any given era are those that society can reconstruct within the framework of that era.'[15]

Four decades after the German crimes against humanity, a generational shift was clearly well under way. The number of those who remembered the war, among them the surviving perpetrators and victims of the Holocaust, became ever smaller. The younger generations knew of the events only through the stories of older people, written accounts, films, and radio and television programmes.

To use terminology developed from Halbwachs's work by the Egyptologist Jan Assman: 'communicative memory' was being replaced by 'cultural memory', a different form of collective memory. In order to preserve a given memory, cultural memory had to ritualize it. It had to create traditions against forgetting.[16]

This ritualization was necessary, but it had its risks. It was often only a short step from ritualization to instrumentalization. In the foundational myth of 'Auschwitz', for example, the self-image of the Federal Republic came objectively very close to the self-image of the state of Israel. The heirs of the perpetrators usurped—though inadvertently—a myth to which only the surviving victims of the Holocaust and their descendants had a right.

Robert Musil's novel *Der Mann ohne Eigenschaften**contains a passage that speaks of the snares of conscience.

Perhaps we can say, to modify an adage, that a bad conscience sleeps even better in thunder than a quiet one, just as long as it is bad enough! The continuous subliminal work of the mind, aimed at deriving a good personal conscience from all the wrong it is involved in, then comes to a stop, leaving behind an unmeasured independence for the spirit.[17]

In the second half of the 1980s there developed, above all on the left, a kind of 'pride of atonement' with regard to the Holocaust: an attitude that the Nazi crimes were being dealt with and expiated in such an exemplary way as to give the Federal Republic a claim to a higher political morality—higher than countries which had never gone through a comparable crisis of national identity. Predestination through perversion: Oskar Lafontaine's meditations on the nation state in the year 1988 contain the thought of a new German historical mission. The post-national Federal Republic was destined to lead the nation states, still trapped in 'national' thinking, toward the unification of Europe.[18]

The occasions on which Auschwitz was used as an argument resulted—again inadvertently—in its banalization. The murder of the Jews served to justify the rejection of reunification, German participation in the Gulf War, and the sending of 'Tornados' to Bosnia. What was really being rejected in all of these cases was a state of affairs in which Germany would have to decide matters of peace and war in a sovereign manner and thus no longer be able to avoid the possibility of making a mistake—like other nations.[19]

'Sovereign is he who decides on the exception.' Thus reads the famous first sentence of Carl Schmitt's 1922 book *Politische Theologie.*†[20] In 1990 the historical exception of Germany's non-sovereignty came to an end. The habituation to this—in retrospect seemingly comfortable—condition was so strong in the old Federal Republic that it gave rise to a fear of sovereignty. This

---

* Musil, *The Man without Qualities.*
† Schmitt, *Political Theology.*

fear fostered a rejection of the nation state, both in theory and in practice. It would have been remarkable if the reunification had *not* led to a crisis in German identity. The conflict over the lessons of Auschwitz was a symptom of this crisis.

When it came out in 1998, the French *Black Book of Communism* provoked great controversy in Germany. In an article in the *taz*, Stefan Reinecke wrote that several members of the left, including the historian Wolfgang Wippermann, used

the crimes of the Nazis like so many conceptual weapons in this debate. One continually hears that the Holocaust was the catastrophe of the century, in comparison to which all other crimes diminish to second-rate phenomena. 'We should preserve our Holocaust fixation', as Wippermann writes. This argument has a quasi-religious undertone. Thou shalt have no other crimes of the century before me. In this way the destruction of the Jews comes close to being a kind of secular negative theology.[21]

This perceptive observation led Reinecke to a further conclusion: like German nationalism before 1945, certain forms of German anti-nationalism were fraught with religious language and sensibilities.

The appeal to the singularity of the Holocaust in order to qualify or avoid condemning other crimes—especially those of communist or ex-communist regimes—marks the nadir of a pathological learning process. Auschwitz served as a pretext for lowering moral standards of judgement. The upshot of *this* instrumentalization of the Holocaust was a desensitization to the abuse of human rights, from the genocidal campaign of Pol Pot's Khmer Rouge in Cambodia to the 'ethnic cleansing' in former Yugoslavia, regardless of whether it was perpetrated by Serbs, Croats, or others. The 'Holocaust fixation' also had another, no less paradoxical consequence. It led to the narrowing of the historical horizons down to only two fixed points: the negative one of the Holocaust and the positive 'success story of the Federal Republic'. The question of the deeper historical roots of the 'German catastrophe' no longer had an important place in this reading of history. The typical analysis was then simply: 'It was the German nation state that led to Auschwitz.'

In reality the founding of the German national state in the nineteenth century was a paradoxical affair: westernization on the one hand, consolidation of the authoritarian state on the other. It was not the solving of the unity question that stands at the beginning of the road to catastrophe, but the failure to solve the question of liberty. The origins of Germany's self-destruction between 1933 and 1945 lie not with the German nation state, but with the myth of the German Reich, which sought to be different and more than a nation state.

The anti-western *Sonderweg* of the German Reich came to an end in 1945. The post-national *Sonderweg* of the old Federal Republic and the internationalist *Sonderweg* of the GDR came to an end in 1990. The reunited Germany of today is not a 'post-national democracy among nation states', but one democratic, post-classical national state in the company of others. The new Federal Republic is no less sovereign than other members of the European Union, which have also transferred powers to the EU and to another supra-national alliance, NATO. This is a part of the *European* normalization of Germany that led to Bundeswehr participation in an international mission in Kosovo in 1999, under an SPD–Green government. Another part of this process took place that same year: the overdue reform of German citizenship.

On the eve of reunification, Peter Glotz made a few 'Vorschläge zur Identität des grösseren Deutschland'.* The most important element in the idea of education that he wanted to see put in place was as follows:

The Holocaust as the spiritual-intellectual turning point in the modern German nation. Not as the only important one, of course, but as a fact that cannot be circumvented. The role that 1789 plays in the canon of French thought belongs in the German canon to the fascist period. National consciousness means dealing with this history, with the experiences and motivations of the guilty and the innocent.[22]

Glotz hit upon a central point. Whereas nations with old democratic traditions can look back on successful revolutions, Germans who seek the historical origins of their democracy must first confront the memory of the catastrophic failure of their own revolution *against* democracy during the years 1933–45. In retrospect, the Nazi dictatorship became the great *argumentum e contrario* for western-style democracy, for human and civil rights.

In 1985, four decades after the 'collapse', the German Evangelical church discussed the rationale behind its acclaimed memorandum *Evangelische Kirche und freiheitliche Demokratie. Der Staat des Grundgesetzes als Angebot und Aufgabe.*[†] The first reason it gave was the following:

The historical experiences that burden us Germans represent a permanent admonition. Hitler came to power in 1933 not because the National Socialists had been so numerous in the republic of Weimar, but because there were not enough democrats who recognized the inestimable value of the Weimar constitution and were prepared to defend it.[23]

The historical memory of the 'Third Reich' must include more than the years 1933–45 and their immediate prehistory, however. It cannot circumvent the necessity of placing this era in the larger context of German history. Remembrance of the Nazi past also cannot be the only reference point for an enlightened democratic and national consciousness in modern Germany. Liberty and unity, democracy and the nation are all phenomena with a much longer and deeper history. It is a paradoxical history, and it cannot be mastered without critical analysis.

'Willingness to remember and commemorate depends on an individual's relationship to his or her own history, to the history of his or her own people, and

---

* Glotz, 'Proposals for the Identity of the Larger Germany'.
† *Evangelical Church and Liberal Democracy: The State of the Basic Law as a Choice and a Task.*

depends on the degree of identification with this people, state, and nation,' said Salomon Korn in 1996, speaking on Yom ha-Shoa in the Westend synagogue in Frankfurt am Main.

The closer and more firmly we stand to the destinies of our community, the more we will seek to preserve the memory of its history, which is felt to be our own. The more ambivalent, difficult, and fragile the past is of the people to whom we belong, the more effort it takes to deal with its history, which then tends to be denied as our own. Under these conditions, remembering and commemorating become an arduous activity, confronting us with the dark sides of our community and making it more difficult to establish an unbroken identity with it. Then, remembering and commemorating mean being forced to deal with the biographies of our parents, grandparents, and ancestors. The willingness to hold the National Socialist crimes in honest remembrance depends on the willingness of non-Jewish Germans to take up national identity in its historically formed ruptures and discontinuities—to not take refuge in an ostensibly unscathed national identity, which necessarily bends, qualifies, and ultimately falsifies the National Socialist mass murder to fit its own needs.[24]

Germany's road to the west was long, and long stretches of it were a path set apart. And while all of history is a history of separate and unique paths, some lead further afield than others. Germans must recall their past. They must do so not only for their own sake, but also for Europe, a project they share with others.

A European identity will not arise against the nations, but only with and through them. All of them, the European nations on both sides of the former Iron Curtain, have cause to take a good, self-critical look at their histories and their myths, old as well as new. 'It is certainly harder to live without myths and idols,' remarked the Italian publicist Angelo Bolaffi in 1995, 'but it's definitely easier to think.'[25] What the Germans do to overcome their myths is part of a bigger picture.

Notes

CHAPTER 1. THE GERMAN CATASTROPHE 1933–1945

1. Adolf Hitler, *Mein Kampf. Zwei Bände in einem Band* ('711.–715. Auflage') (Munich: F. Eher, 1942), 69–70 (emphasis in the original); Eric Voegelin, *Die politischen Religionen* (Vienna: Bermann-Fischer Verlag, 1938), 3rd edn (Munich: Wilhelm Fink, 1993); *Totalitarismus und Politische Religionen. Konzepte des Diktaturvergleichs*, ed. Hans Maier (Paderborn: Schöningh, 1996), tr. as *Totalitarianism and Political Religions* (London, New York: Routledge, 2004); Philippe Burrin, 'Political Religion: The Relevance of a Concept', *History and Memory*, 9 (1997), 321–49; Michael Ley, *Genozid und Heilserwartung. Zum nationalsozialistischen Mord am europäischen Judentum* (Vienna: Picus, 1993); *Der Nationalsozialismus als politische Religion*, ed. id. and Julius H. Schoeps (Bodenheim: Philo Verlagsgesellschaft, 1997); Klaus Vondung, *Magie und Manipulation. Ideologischer Kult und politische Religion im Nationalsozialismus* (Göttingen: Vandenhoeck & Ruprecht, 1971); Klaus Schreiner, 'Formen und Funktionen von politischem Messianismus in der Weimarer Republik', *Saeculum*, 49/1 (1998), 107–60; Sabine Behrenbeck, *Der Kult der toten Helden. Nationalsozialistische Mythen, Riten und Symbole 1923–1945* (Vierow bei Greifswald: SH-Verlag, 1996), 33 ff.; Ernst Nolte, *Der Faschismus in seiner Epoche. Die Action française. Der italienische Faschismus. Der Nationalsozialismus* (Munich: Piper, 1963), 279 (Mussolini, 1925), tr. as *Three Faces of Fascism* (New York: Holt, Rinehart and Winston, 1966); Hannah Arendt, *Elemente und Ursprünge totaler Herrschaft* (Frankfurt am Main: Europäischer Verlagsanstalt, 1955), orig. *The Origins of Totalitarianism* (New York: Harcourt, Brace, 1951); Carl Joachim Friedrich and Zbigniew K. Brzezinski, *Totalitäre Diktatur* (Stuttgart: W. Kohlhammer, 1957), orig. *Totalitarian Dictatorship and Autocracy* (Cambridge, MA: Harvard University Press, 1956); Raymond Aron, *Demokratie und Totalitarismus* (Hamburg: Christain Wegner, 1970), orig. *Démocratie et totalitarisme* (Paris: Gallimard, 1966); *Totalitarismus. Ein Studien-Reader zur Herrschaftsanalyse moderner Diktaturen*, ed. Manfred Funke (Düsseldorf: Droste, 1978); *Totalitarismus. Eine Ideengeschichte des 20. Jahrhunderts*, ed. Alfons Söllner et al. (Berlin: Akademie Verlag, 1997); Wolfgang Wippermann, *Totalitarismustheorien. Die Entwicklung der Diskussion von den Anfängen bis heute* (Darmstadt: Primus, 1997); *Totalitarismus im 20. Jahrhundert. Eine Bilanz der internationalen Forschung*, ed. Eckhard Jesse (Bonn: Bundeszentrale für Politische Bildung, 1996); Karl Dietrich Bracher, *Zeitgeschichtliche Kontroversen. Um Faschismus, Totalitarismus, Demokratie* (Munich: Piper, 1976); id., *Zeit der Ideologien. Eine Geschichte politischen Denkens im 20. Jahrhundert*, 2nd edn (Stuttgart: Deutsche Verlagsanstalt, 1984).

2. *Hitler. Sämtliche Aufzeichnungen 1905–1924*, ed. Eberhard Jäckel with Axel Kuhn (Stuttgart: Deutsche Verlagsanstalt, 1980), 88–90 (letter to Adolf Gemlich, 16 Sept. 1919); id., *Mein Kampf* (note 1), 738, 742–3; *Hitlers Zweites Buch. Ein Dokument aus dem Jahr 1928* (Stuttgart: Deutsche Verlagsanstalt, 1961); tr. as *Hitler's Second Book: The Unpublished Sequel to Mein Kampf* (New York: Enigma,

2003); Max Domarus, *Hitler. Reden und Proklamationen 1932–1945*, 4 vols., 2nd edn (Munich: Süddeutscher Verlag, 1965); i/1. 203–8 (speech on 10 Feb. 1933), 447–8 (speech on 4 Sept. 1934), i/2. 732 (speech at Nuremberg congress on 19 Sept. 1937, 'The German nation now has its Germanic empire!'); *Hitler. Speeches and Proclamations, 1932–1945*, 3 vols. (Wauconda, IL: Bolchazy-Carducci, 1990); Hans-Dietrich Loock, 'Zur "Grossgermanischen Politik" des Dritten Reiches', *VfZ* 8 (1960), 37–63 (references to 'Greater Germanic Empire of the German Nation' in Hitler's speeches and writings 1921–37: 37); Thilo Vogelsang, *Neue Dokumente zur Geschichte der Reichswehr 1930–1933*, *VfZ* 2 (1954), 397–436 (434–5: Hitler, 3 Feb. 1933); (Arthur) Moeller van den Bruck, *Das dritte Reich*, ed. Hans Schwarz, 3rd edn (Hamburg: Hanseatische Verlagsanstalt, 1931), 158, 244–5; Heinrich August Winkler, *Mittelstand, Demokratie und Nationalsozialismus. Die politische Entwicklung von Handwerk und Kleinhandel in der Weimarer Republik* (Cologne: Kiepenheuer & Witsch, 1972), 275 (*Kampfbund*, Dec. 1932); Fritz Stern, *Kulturpessimismus als politische Gefahr. Eine Analyse nationaler Ideologie in Deutschland* (Bern: Scherz, 1963), 223 ff., orig. *The Politics of Cultural Despair* (Berkeley: University of California Press, 1961); Lothar Kettenacker, 'Der Mythos vom Reich', *Mythos und Moderne. Begriff und Bild einer Rekonstruktion*, ed. Karl-Heinz Bohrer (Frankfurt: Suhrkamp, 1983), 261–89; Herfried Münkler, 'Das Reich als politische Macht und politischer Mythos', in *Reich–Nation–Europa. Modelle politischer Ordnung* (Weinheim: Beltz Athenaeum, 1996), 11–59; Hans Fenske, 'Das "Dritte Reich". Die Perversion der Reichsidee', *Deutschland in Europa. Ein historischer Rückblick*, ed. Bernd Martin (Munich: DTV, 1992), 210–30 (213: order from the party chancellery on 13 June 1939); Jean F. Neurohr, *Der Mythos vom Dritten Reich. Zur Geistesgeschichte des Nationalsozialismus* (Stuttgart: Cotta, 1957); Klaus Breuning, *Die Vision des Reiches. Deutscher Katholizismus zwischen Demokratie und Diktatur (1929–1934)* (Munich: Hueber, 1969), 176 ff.; Ernst Bloch, 'Zur Originalgeschichte des Dritten Reiches (1937)', in *Erbschaft dieser Zeit* (Frankfurt: Suhrkamp 1985), 126–52, tr. as *Heritage of our Times* (Berkeley: University of California Press, 1991); Karl Löwith, *Weltgeschichte und Heilsgeschehen. Die theologischen Voraussetzungen der Geschichtsphilosophie*, 3rd edn (Stuttgart: Kohlhammer, 1953), 136 ff. (Joachim of Fiore); Norman Cohn, *Das Ringen um das Tausendjährige Reich. Revolutionärer Messianismus im Mittelalter und sein Fortleben in den modernen totalitären Bewegungen* (Bern: Francke, 1961), esp. 94 ff., orig. *The Pursuit of the Millenium* (London: Secker & Warburg, 1957); Friedrich Heer, *Der Glaube des Adolf Hitler. Anatomie einer politischen Religiosität* (Munich: Bechtle, 1968); Jost Hermand, *Der alte Traum vom neuen Reich. Völkische Utopien und Nationalsozialismus* (Frankfurt: Athenäum, 1988), tr. as *Old Dreams of a New Reich: Volkish Utopias and National Socialism* (Bloomington: Indiana University Press, 1992); Eberhard Jäckel, *Hitlers Weltanschauung. Entwurf einer Herrschaft* (Tübingen: R. Wunderlich, 1969), tr. as *Hitler's World View: A Blueprint for Power* (Cambridge, MA: Harvard University Press, 1981); Frank-Lothar Kroll, 'Geschichte und Politik im Weltbild Hitlers', *VfZ* 44 (1996), 327–53; id., *Utopie als Ideologie. Geschichtsdenken und politisches Handeln im Dritten Reich* (Paderborn: Schöningh, 1998), 65 ff.; id., 'Die Reichsidee im Nationalsozialismus', *Imperium / Empire / Reich. Ein Konzept politischer Herrschaft im deutsch-britischen*

Vergleich, ed. Franz Bosbach and Hermann Hiery (Munich: K. G. Saur, 1999), 179–96; Kurt Sontheimer, *Antidemokratisches Denken in der Weimarer Republik. Die politischen Ideen des deutschen Nationalismus zwischen 1918 und 1933* (Munich: Nymphenburger Verlagshandlung, 1962), 280 ff. On the history of the term *Volksgemeinschaft* see Norbert Götz, 'Ungleiche Geschwister. Die Konstruktion von nationalsozialistischer Volksgemeinschaft und schwedischem Volksheim', Ph.D. thesis, Humboldt University Berlin, 1999, 87 ff.; for Hegel's adaptation of the 'three empires' idea see Georg Wilhelm Friedrich Hegel, *Vorlesungen über die Philosophie der Geschichte* (*Sämtliche Werke*, xi), 3rd edn (Stuttgart: Fromman, 1949), 440 ff. Luther's version of the Lord's Prayer (Matthew 6: 13) concludes with the words *Denn dein ist das Reich und die Kraft und die Herrlichkeit in Ewigkeit. Amen*: ('For yours is the Kingdom [Empire] and the power and the glory in eternity. Amen'). This passage is not in Matthew, but originated in the second century. *Das Neue Testament. Nach der Übersetzung Martin Luthers* (Stuttgart: Deutsche Bibelgesellschaft, 1984), 18.

3. *Das Deutsche Reich von 1918 bis heute* (1933), ed. Cuno Horkenbach (Berlin: Verlag für Presse, Wirtschaft und Politik), 72 (official announcement on Reichstag fire); *Schulthess' Europäischer Geschichtskalender*, 74 (1933) (Munich: C. H. Beck, 1934), 56–66 ('national revolution'; Hitler's appeal on 10 March 1933; 'day of Potsdam'); Rudolf Diels, *Lucifer ante portas . . . es spricht der erste Chef der Gestapo . . .* (Stuttgart: Deutsche Verlagsanstalt, 1950), 214, 220, 222 (terrorism statistics); Heinrich August Winkler, *Der Weg in die Katastrophe. Arbeiter und Arbeiterbewegung in der Weimarer Republik 1930–1933*, 2nd edn (Bonn: J. H. W. Dietz Nachfolger, 1990), 876 ff.; Fritz Tobias, *Der Reichstagsbrand. Legende und Wirklichkeit* (Rastatt: Grote, 1962); *The Reichstag Fire: Legend and Truth* (London: Secker & Warburg, 1963); Hans Mommsen, 'Der Reichstagsbrand und seine politischen Folgen', *VfZ* 12 (1964), 351–413; Uwe Backes et al., *Reichstagsbrand. Aufklärung einer historischen Legende* (Munich: Piper, 1986); Jürgen Schmädecke et al., 'Der Reichstagsbrandprozess in neuem Licht', *HZ* 269 (1999), 603–51 (criticism of the three previous studies and the argument that van der Lubbe was the sole perpetrator); Henry A. Turner, Jr., *Die Grossunternehmer und der Aufstieg Hitlers* (Berlin: Siedler, 1985), 395 ff. (electoral help for the NSDAP from big business), orig. *German Big Business and the Rise of Hitler* (Oxford: Oxford University Press, 1985); Karl Dietrich Bracher, 'Stufen der Machtergreifung', *Die nationalsozialistische Machtergreifung. Studien zur Errichtung des totalitären Herrschaftssystems in Deutschland 1933/34*, id. et al., 2nd edn (Cologne: Westdeutscher Verlag, 1962), 31–368 (on 'day of Potsdam' and Enabling Act: 144 ff.); Otto Seeber, 'Kriegstheologie und Kriegspredigten in der Evangelischen Kirche Deutschlands im Ersten und Zweiten Weltkrieg', in *Kriegsbegeisterung und mentale Kriegsvorbereitung. Interdisziplinäre* Studien, ed. Marcel van der Linden and Gottfried Mergner (Berlin: Duncker & Humblot, 1991), 233–58 (on Dibelius: 244); Erich Matthias, 'Die Sozialdemokratische Partei Deutschlands', in *Das Ende der Parteien 1933*, ed. id. and Rudolf Morsey (Düsseldorf: Droste, 1960), 101–278 (166 ff.); id., 'Die Deutsche Staatspartei', ibid. 31–97 (68–9); Rudolf Morsey, 'Die Deutsche Zentrumspartei', ibid., 281–453 (353 ff.). On Dryander's sermon on 4 Aug. 1914 compare the first volume of this history, 302.

4. *Die Tagebücher von Joseph Goebbels. Sämtliche Fragmente,* ed. Elke Fröhlich, pt I, *Aufzeichnungen* 1924–1941, ii, 1 Oct. 1931–31 Dec. 1936 (Munich: K. G. Saur, 1987), 400–1. (1–2 Apr. 1933), tr. as *The Goebbels Diaries* (New York: Popular Library, 1948); *Die Weizsäcker-Papiere 1933–1950,* ed. Leonidas E. Hill (Berlin: Propyläen-Verlag, 1974), 71 (22 Apr. 1933); Avraham Barkai, *Vom Boykott zur 'Entjudung'. Der wirtschaftliche Existenzkampf der Juden im Dritten Reich 1933–1943* (Frankfurt: Fischer, 1987), 26 ff., tr. as *From Boycott to Annihilation: The Economic Struggle of German Jews, 1933–43* (Hanover, NH: University Press of New England, 1989); Helmut Genschel, *Die Verdrängung der Juden aus der Wirtschaft im Dritten Reich* (Göttingen: Musterschmidt, 1966), 43 ff.; Uwe Dietrich Adam, *Judenpolitik im Dritten Reich* (Düsseldorf: Droste, 1972), 46 ff.; Saul Friedländer, *Das Dritte Reich und die Juden. Die Jahre der Verfolgung 1933–1939* (Munich: C. H. Beck, 1998), 31 ff., orig. *Nazi Germany and the Jews* (New York: HarperCollins, 1997).

5. Hans Mommsen, *Beamtentum im Dritten Reich. Mit ausgewählten Quellen zur nationalsozialistischen Beamtenpolitik* (Stuttgart: Deutsche Verlagsanstalt, 1966); Martin Broszat, *Der Staat Hitlers. Grundlegung und Entwicklung seiner inneren Verfassung* (Munich: DTV, 1969), 130 ff., tr. as *The Hitler State: The Foundation and Development of the Internal Structure of the Third Reich* (New York: Longman, 1981); Hans-Ulrich Thamer, *Verführung und Gewalt. Deutschland 1933–1945* (Berlin: Siedler, 1986), 303 ff. (book burning); Karl Dietrich Bracher, *Die deutsche Diktatur. Entstehung, Struktur, Folgen des Nationalsozialismus* (Cologne: Kiepenheuer & Witsche, 1969), 270 ff., tr. as *The German Dictatorship: The Origins, Structure, and Effects of National Socialism* (New York: Praeger Publishers, 1970); id., 'Stufen' (note 3), 288 ff. (321: figures for the changes in the teaching staff); Gerhard Schulz, 'Die Anfänge des totalitären Massnahmenstaates', *Machtergreifung* (note 3), 371–682 (esp. 565 ff.; on the reduction of the numbers of Jewish students: 567); Hugo Ott, *Martin Heidegger. Unterwegs zu seiner Biographie* (Frankfurt: Campus, 1988), 138 ff.; Victor Farías, *Heidegger und der Nationalsozialismus* (Frankfurt: Fischer, 1989), 131 ff., orig. *Heidegger et le nazisme* (Paris: Verdier, 1987), tr. as *Heidegger and Nazism* (Philadelphia: Temple University Press, 1989); Günther Gillessen, *Auf verlorenem Posten. Die Frankfurter Zeitung im Dritten Reich* (Berlin: Siedler, 1986).

6. 'An die Mitglieder der Gewerkschaften', *Gewerkschafts-Zeitung,* 16 (22 Apr. 1933); 'Der Bundesausschuss des ADGB zum 1. Mai', ibid.; Domarus, *Hitler* (note 2), i/1. 259–64 (1 May 1933), 266–9 (10 May 1933); Michael Schneider, *Unterm Hakenkreuz. Arbeiter und Arbeiterbewegung 1933–1939* (Bonn: Dietz, 1999), 91 ff.; Winkler, *Weg* (note 3), 907 ff.; id., *Mittelstand* (note 2), 183 ff.; Schulz, 'Anfänge' (note 5), 634 ff.; Reinhard Neebe, *Grossindustrie, Staat und NSDAP 1930–1933. Paul Silverberg und der Reichsverband der Deutschen Industrie in der Krise der Weimarer Republik* (Göttingen: Vandenhoeck & Ruprecht, 1981), 174 ff.; Daniela Münkel, *Nationalsozialistische Agrarpolitik und Bauernalltag* (Frankfurt: Campus, 1996), 93 ff.; J. E. Farquharson, *The Plough and the Swastika: The NSDAP and Agriculture in Germany 1928–1945* (London: Sage, 1976), 43 ff.; Gustavo Corni, *Hitler and the Peasants: Agrarian Policy of the Third Reich 1930–1939* (New York: Berg, 1990); id. and Horst Gies, *Brot, Butter, Kanonen: Die Ernährungswirtschaft in Deutschland unter der Diktatur Hitlers* (Berlin: Akademie-Verlag, 1997).

7. Reichstag deliberations: *Stenographische Bericht über die Verhandlungen des Deutschen Reichstags* (= *Sten. Ber.*), cdlvii, 47–54 (Hitler, 17 May 1933); Matthias, 'Sozialdemokratische Partei' (note 3), 180 ff.; Winkler, *Weg* (note 3), 929 ff.; Schneider, *Hakenkreuz* (note 6), 107 ff.; Bärbel Hebel-Kunze, *SPD und Faschismus. Zur politischen und organisatorischen Entwicklung der SPD 1931–1935* (Frankfurt: Röderberg, 1977), 231–5 (manifesto); *Anpassung oder Widerstand? Aus den Akten des Parteivorstands der deutschen Sozialdemokratie 1932/33*, ed. Hagen Schulze (Bonn: Neue Gesellschaft, 1975), 194–8 (Reich congress on 19 June 1933; emphases in the original); *Schulthess* 1933 (note 3), 159 (Frick's decree on18 June 1933); *Akten der Reichskanzlei* (= *AdR*). *Die Regierung Hitler*, pt I, 1933/34, i (30 Jan.–31 Aug. 1933), ed. Karl-Heinz Minuth (Boppard: H. Boldt, 1983), 575–7 (Frick to the *Länder* on 22 June 1933); Peter Merseburger, *Der schwierige Deutsche. Kurt Schumacher. Eine Biographie* (Stuttgart: Deutsche Verlagsanstalt, 1995), 164 ff.; Winkler, *Weg* (note 3), 929 ff.

8. Friedrich Frhr. Hiller von Gaertringen, 'Die Deutschnationale Volkspartei', in *Ende* (note 3), 543–652 (609 ff.) ed. Matthias/Morsey; eid., 'Die Deutsche Staatspartei', ibid. 31–97 (70 ff.); Hans Booms, 'Die Deutsche Volkspartei', ibid. 523–39 (536 ff.; Dingeldey quotes on 4 July 1933: 537; Hitler on 12 July 1933: 538); Rudolf Morsey, 'Die Deutsche Zentrumspartei', ibid., 281–453 (405 ff.); Karl Schwend, 'Die Bayerische Volkspartei', ibid., 457–519; *Nationalliberalismus in der Weimarer Republik. Die Führungsgremien der Deutschen Volkspartei 1918–1933*, ed. Eberhard Kolb and Ludwig Richter (Düsseldorf: Droste, 1999), ii. 1252–3. (DVP declaration on 1 Apr. 1933), 1253–9 (session of the central executive and Dingeldey's announcement on 23 Apr. 1933), 1259 (statement of dissolution on 4 July 1933); Breuning, *Vision* (note 2), 176 ff. (Köhler quote: 192–3); Ernst-Wolfgang Böckenförde, 'Der deutsche Katholizismus im Jahre 1933', *Von Weimar zu Hitler 1930–1933*, ed. Gotthard Jasper (Cologne: Kiepenheuer & Witsch, 1968), 317–43; Klaus Scholder, *Die Kirchen und das Dritte Reich*, 2 vols., i. *Vorgeschichte und Zeit der Illusionen 1918–1934*, 2nd edn (Frankfurt: Propyläen, 1986), 300 ff; Kurt Meier, *Der evangelische Kirchenkampf. Gesamtdarstellung in drei Bänden*, 2nd edn (Göttingen: Vandenhoeck & Ruprecht, 1984). For the law of 14 July 1933 see *AdR, Kabinett Hitler* (note 7), pt I, i, 659–62 (cabinet session on 14 July 1933).

9. Alfred Rosenberg, *Der Mythus des 20. Jahrhunderts. Eine Wertung der seelisch-geistigen Gestaltenkämpfe unserer Zeit*, 3rd edn (Munich: Hoheneichen-Verlag, 1932); Wilhelm Stapel, *Die Kirche Christi und der Staat Hitlers* (Hamburg: Hanseatische Veragsanstalt, 1933), 29, 88 (emphases in the original); Schulz, 'Anfänge' (note 5), 326 ff. ('German Christians': 330, 334; statistics: 336–7; Rosenberg: 340); Scholder, *Kirchen* (note 8), i. 388 ff.; Thamer, *Verführung* (note 5), 435 ff.; Kurt Nowak, *Geschichte des Christentums in Deutschland. Religion, Politik und Gesellschaft vom Ende der Aufklärung bis zur Mitte des 20. Jahrhunderts* (Munich: C. H. Beck, 1995), 243 ff. On Arndt's efforts towards a German national church see Günther Ott, *Ernst Moritz Arndt. Religion, Christentum und Kirche in der Entwicklung des deutschen Publizisten und Patrioten* (Bonn: Rohrscheid, 1966), 197 ff.; Carl Schmitt, 'Die deutsche Rechtswissenschaft im Kampf gegen den jüdischen Geist. Schlusswort auf der Tagung der Reichsgruppe Hochschullehrer des NSRB

vom 3. and 4. Oktober 1936', *Deutsche Juristen-Zeitung*, 41/20 (1936)(15 Oct.), col. 1, 193–1, 199; Bernd Rüthers, *Carl Schmitt im Dritten Reich. Wissenschaft als Zeitgeist-Verstärkung* (Munich: C. H. Beck, 1990), 96 ff.; Paul Noack, *Carl Schmitt. Eine Biographie* (Berlin: Propyläen, 1993), 164 ff.; Raphael Gross, *Carl Schmitt und die Juden. Eine deutsche Rechtslehre* (Frankfurt: Suhrkamp, 2000); Léon Poliakov and Joseph Wulf, *Das Dritte Reich und seine Denker* (Berlin: Arani, 1959); Matthias von Hellfeld, *Bündische Jugend und Hitlerjugend. Zur Geschichte von Anpassung und Widerstand 1930–1939* (Cologne: Verlag Wissenschaft und Politik, 1987); Bracher, 'Stufen' (note 3), 291 ff. (Reichskulturkammer), 301–2 (expatriations), 312–13 (academic anti-Semitism).

10. Münkel, *Agrarpolitik* (note 6), 129 ff.; Farquharson, *Plough* (note 6), 107 ff.; Tim(othy) W. Mason, 'Zur Entstehung des Gesetzes zur Ordnung der nationalen Arbeit vom 20. Januar 1933: Ein Versuch über das Verhältnis und Momente in der neuesten Geschichte', in *Industrielles System und politische Entwicklung in der Weimarer Republik,* ed. Hans Mommsen et al. (Düsseldorf: Droste, 1974), 303–21; Wolfgang Zollitsch, *Arbeiter zwischen Weltwirtschaftskrise und Nationalsozialismus. Ein Beitrag zur Sozialgeschichte der Jahre 1928 bis 1936* (Göttingen: Vandenhoeck & Ruprecht, 1990), esp. 210 ff.; Dörte Winkler, *Frauenarbeit im 'Dritten Reich'* (Hamburg: Hoffmann und Campe, 1977), 42 ff.; Robert Gellately, *Die Gestapo und die deutsche Gesellschaft. Die Durchsetzung der Rassenpolitik 1933–1945* (Paderborn: Schöningh, 1993), 61 ff. (statistics: 62, 76), orig. *The Gestapo and German Society: Enforcing Racial Policy, 1933–1945* (Oxford: Oxford University Press, 1990); Gisela Diewald-Kerkmann, *Politische Denunziation im NS-Regime oder Die kleine Macht der 'Volksgenossen'* (Bonn: Dietz, 1994); Ian Kershaw, *Der Hitler-Mythos. Volksmeinung und Propaganda im Dritten Reich* (Stuttgart: Deutsche Verlagsanstalt, 1980), Eng. edn *The 'Hitler Myth': Image and Reality in the Third Reich* (Oxford: Oxford University Press, 1987). For the social modernization argument see Ralf Dahrendorf, *Gesellschaft und Demokratie in Deutschland* (Munich: Piper, 1965); David Schoenbaum, *Die braune Revolution. Eine Sozialgeschichte des Dritten Reiches* 2nd edn (Munich: DTV, 1980), orig. *Hitler's Social Revolution: Class and Status in Nazi Germany, 1933–1939* (New York: Norton, 1966); *Nationalsozialismus und Modernisierung*, ed. Michael Prinz and Rainer Zitelmann (Darmstadt: Wissenschaftliche Buchgesellschaft, 1991).

11. Ludolf Herbst, *Das nationalsozialistische Deutschland 1933–1945. Die Entfesselung der Gewalt: Rassismus und Krieg* (Frankfurt: Suhrkamp, 1996), 89 ff. (lowering of unemployment), 99 ff. (foreign policy); Otmar Jung, *Plebiszit und Diktatur: die Volksabstimmungen der Nationalsozialisten. Die Fälle 'Austritt aus dem Völkerbund' (1933), 'Staatsoberhaupt' (1934) and 'Anschluss Österreichs' (1938)* (Tübingen: J. C. B. Mohr, 1995), 35 ff. (statistics: 51–3); Broszat, *Staat* (note 5), 151 ff. (quotes from Frick and Lammers: 151, 153; Broszat: 245–6).

12. *Hitlers Machtergreifung. Dokumente vom Machtantritt Hitlers 30. Januar 1933 bis zur Besiegelung des Einparteienstaates 14. Juli 1933*, ed. Josef and Ruth Becker (Munich: DTV, 1983), 329 (Röhm's June 1933 article; emphases in the original); Domarus, *Hitler* (note 2), i/1. 286–7 (speech on 6 July 1933), 421 (speech on 13 July 1934); 'Die Goebbels-Rede im Sportpalast', *Deutsche Allgemeine Zeitung*, 12 May 1934; *Schulthess' Europäischer Geschichtskalender*, 75 (1934) (Munich: C. H.

Beck, 1935), 131–2 (on Goebbels's speech on 11 May 1934); Immo v. Fallois, *Kalkül und Illusion. Der Machtkampf zwischen Reichswehr und SA während der Röhm-Krise 1934* (Berlin: Duncker & Humblot, 1994), 100 ff. (Hitler's speech on 28 Feb. 1934: 119); Peter Longerich, *Die braunen Bataillone. Geschichte der SA* (Munich: Beck, 1989), 206 ff. (numbers of victims: 219); Heinz Höhne, *Der Orden unter dem Totenkopf. Die Geschichte der SS* (Munich: Bertelsmann, 1984), 90 ff; orig. *The Order of the Death's Head: The Story of Hitler's S.S.* (London: Secker & Warburg, 1969); id., *Mordsache Röhm. Hitlers Durchbruch zur Alleinherrschaft 1933–1934* (Hamburg: Rowohlt, 1984), 207 ff. (number of victims: 319 ff.); Manfred Messerschmidt, *Die Wehrmacht im NS-Staat. Zeit der Indoktrination* (Hamburg: R. v. Decker, 1969), 18 ff.; Klaus-Jürgen Müller, *Das Heer und Hitler. Armee und nationalsozialistisches Regime 1933–1940* (Stuttgart: Deutsche Verlagsanstalt, 1969), 88 ff.; Joachim Petzold, *Franz von Papen. Ein deutsches Verhängnis* (München : Buchverlag Union, 1995), 206 ff. (Marburg speech); Wolfgang Sauer, 'Die Mobilmachung der Gewalt', in Bracher et al., *Machtergreifung* (note 3), 685–966 (829 ff.; SA numbers for 1933: 890). Schmitt quote in Carl Schmitt, 'Der Führer schützt das Recht', in *Positionen und Begriffe im Kampf mit Weimar-Genf-Versailles 1923–1939* (Hamburg: Hanseatische Verlagsanstalt, 1940), 199–203 (200). The law of 3 July 1934 in *RGBl.* (1934), i. 529; report to the SPD leadership in exile in *Deutschland-Berichte der Sozialdemokratischen Partei Deutschlands (Sopade) 1934–1940* (Frankfurt: Verlag Petra Nettelbeck, 1980), 1 (1934), 209.

13. *AdR, Regierung Hitler* (note 7), pt. I, ii (*12 September 1933–27 August 1934*), 1384–5. (ministers' conference on 1 Aug. 1934); Walter Hubatsch, *Hindenburg und der Staat. Aus den Papieren des Generalfeldmarschalls und Reichspräsidenten von 1878 bis 1934* (Göttingen: Musterschmidt, 1966), 380–3 (testament dated 11 May 1934); *Ursachen und Folgen. Vom deutschen Zusammenbruch 1918 und 1945 bis zur Neuordnung Deutschlands in der Gegenwart. Eine Urkunden- und Dokumentensammlung zur Zeitgeschichte*, ed. Herbert Michaelis and Ernst Schraepler (Berlin: Dokumenten-Verlag, 1964), x. 195–6. (Hindenburg to Hitler, 2 July 1934); Goebbels, *Fragmente* (note 4), pt I, ii, 475 (22 Aug. 1934); Horst Mühleisen, 'Das Testament Hindenburgs vom 11. Mai 1934', *VfZ* 44 (1996), 355–71; Thamer, *Verführung* (note 5), 334–5. (oath formula), 338–9 (referendum on 19 Aug. 1934); Jung, *Plebiszit* (note 11), 61–2 (statistics for 19 Aug. 1934).

14. *Programmatische Dokumente der deutschen Sozialdemokratie*, ed. and intr. Dieter Dowe and Kurt Klotzbach (Berlin: Dietz, 1984), 225–38 (Prager Manifest; quotes: 229, 236–7); Heinrich August Winkler, 'Rudolf Hilferding in der Endphase der Weimarer Republik', in *Von der Arbeiterbewegung zum modernen Sozialstaat. Festschrift für Gerhard A. Ritter zum 65. Geburtstag*, ed. Jürgen Kocka et al. (Munich: Saur, 1994), 131–55 (quote from letter to Kautsky: 150); Ursula Langkau-Alex, *Volksfront für Deutschland?*, i. *Vorgeschichte und Gründung des 'Aussschusses zur Vorbereitung einer deutschen Volksfront' 1933–1936* (Frankfurt: Syndikat, 1977), 136 ff. (Hilferding's letter to Hertz, 25 Dec. 1935: 144); Schneider, *Hakenkreuz* (note 6), 783 ff.; Julius Braunthal, *Geschichte der Internationale*, 2 vols. (Hanover: Dietz, 1961–3), ii. 437 ff.; *History of the International* (New York: Praeger, 1967–80); *Widerstand und Verweigerung in Deutschland 1933–1945*, ed. Richard

Löwenthal and Patrik von zur Mühlen (Berlin: Dietz, 1982); *Widerstand und Exil 1933–1945* (Bonn: Bundeszentrale für politische Bildung, 1985); Jan Foitzik, *Zwischen den Fronten. Zur Politik, Organisation und Funktion linker politischer Kleinorganisationen im Widerstand 1933 bis 1939/40* (Bonn: Verlag Neue Gesellschaft, 1986); Horst Duhnke, *Die KPD von 1933–1945* (Cologne: Kiepenheuer & Witsch, 1972).

15. Peter Hoffmann, *Widerstand, Staatsstreich, Attentat. Der Kampf der Opposition gegen Hitler* (Munich: Piper, 1969), 34 ff. (court statistics: 39), tr. as *The History of the German Resistance, 1933–1945* (Cambridge, MA: MIT Press, 1977); Jost Dülffer, *Deutsche Geschichte 1933–1945. Führerglaube und Vernichtungskrieg* (Stuttgart: Kohlhammer, 1992), 144 ff. (statistics for the persecution of the Communists: 149); Ian Kershaw, *Hitlers Macht. Das Profil der NS-Herrschaft* (Munich: DTV, 1992), 88 ff., orig. *Hitler* (Harlow: Longman, 1991); Hans-Günter Hockerts, *Die Sittlichkeitsprozesse gegen katholische Ordensangehörige und Priester 1936/37* (Mainz: Matthias-Grünewald-Verlag, 1971); Matthias Schreiber, *Martin Niemöller* (Reinbek: Rowohlt, 1997), 78 ff.; Merseburger, *Schumacher* (note 7), 166 ff.; Dorothea Beck, *Julius Leber. Sozialdemokrat zwischen Reform und Widerstand* (Berlin: Siedler, 1983), esp. 150 ff.; *Richard Albrecht, Der militante Sozialdemokrat: Carlo Mierendorff 1897 bis 1943. Eine Biographie* (Berlin: Dietz, 1987); Peter Lösche, *Ernst Heilmann. Ein Widerstandskämpfer aus Charlottenburg* (Berlin: Bezirksverordnetenversammlung u. Bezirksamt Charlottenburg, 1981); Thamer, *Verführung* (note 5), 376 ff. (dates for the concentration camps and categories of inmates: 382–3); Enno Georg, *Die wirtschaftlichen Unternehmungen der SS* (Stuttgart: Deutsche Verlags-Anstalt, 1963); Martin Broszat et al., *Anatomie des SS-Staates*, 2 vols. (Olten: Walter-Verlag, 1965), tr. as *Anatomy of the SS State* (New York: Walker, 1968); Eugen Kogon, *Der SS-Staat. Das System der deutschen Konzentrationslager* (Munich: 1979), 1st edn (1947) Ulrich Herbert, *Best. Biographische Studien über Radikalismus, Weltanschauung und Vernunft 1903–1989*, 2nd edn (Bonn: 1996), 147 ff. (inmate statistics in 1935: 169); *Die nationalsozialistischen Konzentrationslager–Entwicklung und Struktur*, 2 vols, ed. id. et al. (Göttingen: Wallstein, 1998); Norbert Frei, *Der Führerstaat: nationalsozialistische Herrschaft 1933 bis 1945*, 6th edn (Munich: DTV, 2001), tr. as *National Socialist Rule in Germany: The Führer State 1933–1945* (Cambridge, MA: Blackwell, 1993); Wolfgang Sofsky, *Die Ordnung des Terrors: Das Konzentrationslager*, 2nd edn (Frankfurt: Fischer, 1993), tr. as *The Order of Terror: the Concentration Camp* (Princeton: Princeton University Press, 1997); Ernst Fraenkel, *Der Doppelstaat. Ein Beitrag zur Theorie der Diktatur* (Frankfurt: Europäische Verlagsanstalt, 1974) (on the relationship between the *Normenstaat* and *Massnahmenstaat*), orig. *The Dual State: A Contribution to the Theory of Dictatorship* (New York: Oxford University Press, 1941).

16. Carl Schmitt, *Völkerrechtliche Grossraumordnung mit Interventionsverbot für raumfremde Mächte* (Berlin: Duncker & Humblot, 1939); Rüthers, *Schmitt* (note 9), 104 ff.; Felix Blindow, *Carl Schmitts Reichsordnung. Strategie für einen europäischen Grossraum* (Berlin: Akademie Verlag, 1999), 56 ff.; Noack, *Schmitt* (note 9), 197 ff.; Ott, *Heidegger* (note 5), 249 ff.; Farías, *Heidegger* (note 5), 261 ff.; Jerry Z. Muller, 'Enttäuschung und Zweideutigkeit. Zur Geschichte rechter Sozialwissenschaftler im "Dritten Reich"', *GG* 12 (1986), 289–316 (esp. on Freyer); Thamer,

Verführung (note 5), 464–5; Herbert, *Best* (note 15), esp. 133 ff.; Martin Broszat, 'Resistenz und Widerstand. Eine Zwischenbilanz des Forschungsprojekts', in *Nach Hitler. Der schwierige Umgang mit unserer Geschichte* (Munich: Oldenbourg, 1986), 68–91; *Dichtung im Dritten Reich? Zur Literatur in Deutschland 1933–1945*, ed. Christiane Caemmerer and Walter Delabar (Opladen: Westdeutscher Verlag, 1996); Jan-Pieter Barbian, *Literaturpolitik im 'Dritten Reich'. Institutionen, Kompetenzen, Betätigungsfelder* (Frankfurt: Buchhändler-Vereinigung, 1993); Friedrich Denk, *Die Zensur der Nachgeborenen. Zur regimekritischen Literatur im Dritten Reich* (Weilheim: Denk-Verlag, 1996).

17. Friedländer, *Drittes Reich* (note 4), 73 ff. (emigration statistics: 75–6; on 9 Nov. 1938: 298); Peter Longerich, *Politik der Vernichtung. Eine Gesamtdarstellung der nationalsozialistischen Judenverfolgung* (Munich: DTV, 1998), 65 ff.; David Bankier, *Die öffentliche Meinung im Hitler-Staat. Die 'Endlösung' und die Deutschen. Eine Berichtigung* (Berlin: A. Spitz, 1995), 105 ff., orig. *The Germans and the Final Solution: Public Opinion under Nazism* (Oxford: Blackwell, 1992); Ian Kershaw, *Hitler 1889–1936* (Stuttgart: Deutsche Verlags-Anstalt, 1998), 663 ff., orig. *Hitler, 1889–1936* (London: Allen Lane, 1998); id., 'Antisemitismus und Volksmeinung. Reaktionen auf die Judenverfolgung', in *Bayern in der NS-Zeit*, II, *Herrschaft und Gesellschaft im Konflikt*, pt. A, ed. Martin Broszat and Elke Fröhlich (Munich: Oldenbourg, 1979), 281–348 (328: Munich, Heilbrunn); Otto Dov Kulka, 'Die Nürnberger Rassengesetze und die deutsche Bevölkerung im Lichte geheimer NS-Lage- und Stimmungsberichte', *VfZ* 32 (1984), 582–624 (quotes: 602); John M. Steiner and Jobst Freiherr v. Cornberg, 'Willkür in der Willkür. Hitler und die Befreiung von den antisemitischen Nürnberger Gesetzen', ibid. 46 (1998), 143–87; Avraham Barkai, 'Etappen der Ausgrenzung und Verfolgung bis 1939', in id. et al., *Aufbruch und Zerstörung* (= *Deutsch-jüdische Geschichte der Neuzeit*, iv) (Munich: C. H. Beck, 1997), 193–224 (205 ff.); id., *Boykott* (note 4), 146 ff. (168: number of Jews in Germany in May and September 1939); *Der Judenpogrom 1938. Von der zum Völkermord*, ed. Walter Pehle (Frankfurt: Fischer, 1988); Adam, *Judenpolitik* (note 4), 177 ff. Hitler on 5 Jan. 1939 in *Akten zur deutschen auswärtigen Politik 1918–1945* (= *ADAP*), series D, 1937–1941 (Baden-Baden: Impr. nationale, 1950–), v. 127–32 (130–1); On 30 January 1939 in Domarus, *Hitler* (note 2), i/2. 1058. On the reports of the SPD agents see *Deutschland-Berichte* (note 12), 2 (1936), 1020–1. (Nuremberg Laws), 5 (1938), 1177 ff. (1204–5). *Geltungsjuden* were 'half Jews' or 'quarter Jews' practising Judaism or with a Jewish spouse.

18. 'Niemals wird Deutschland bolschewistisch!', *Völkischer Beobachter*, 14 Sept. 1936 (Hitler's speech at the party congress on 13 Sept. 1936); Domarus, *Hitler* (note 2), i/2 638 (Hitler on Spanish Civil War, 9 Sept. 1936); Kershaw, *Hitler-Mythos* (note 10), 70–1; Thamer, *Verführung* (note 5), 526 ff.; Dieter Petzina, *Autarkiepolitik im Dritten Reich. Der nationalsozialistische Vierjahresplan* (Stuttgart: Deutsche Verlagsanstalt, 1968), 48 ff., 104 ff.; Wilhelm Treue, 'Hitlers Denkschrift zum Vierjahresplan 1936', *VfZ* 3 (1955), 184–210 (210); Albert Fischer, *Hjalmar Schacht und Deutschlands 'Judenfrage'. Der 'Wirtschaftsdiktator' und die Vertreibung der Juden aus der deutschen Wirtschaft* (Cologne: Böhlau, 1995), 126 ff. The Hossbach protocol in *Internationaler Militärgerichtshof. Der Prozess gegen die*

Hauptkriegsverbrecher (= *IMG*) (Nuremberg, 1947–9; Berlin: Rütten & Loening, 1960), xxv. 403 ff; *Trial of the Major War Criminals before the International Military Tribunal, Nuremberg, 14 November 1945–1 October 1946* (Nuremberg, 1947–9). On Hitler's elucidations on 3 Feb. 1933 see above, p. 10. Blomberg was called 'Reich War Minister' from 5 Feb. 1938. On the electoral manipulations in 1936 see *Deutschland-Berichte* (note 12), 3 (1936), 407 ff.

19. Karl-Heinz Janssen and Fritz Tobias, *Der Sturz der Generäle. Hitler und die Blomberg-Fritsch-Krise* (Munich: C. H. Beck, 1994); Manfred Messerschmid, 'Aussenpolitik und Kriegsvorbereitung', in *Das Deutsche Reich und der Zweite Weltkrieg*, i. *Ursachen und Voraussetzungen der deutschen Kriegspolitik* (Stuttgart: Deutsche Verlagsanstalt, 1979), 535–701 (630 ff.), tr. as *Germany and the Second World War* (Oxford: Oxford University Press, 1990); Klaus Hildebrand, *Das vergangene Reich. Deutsche Aussenpolitik von Bismarck bis Hitler* (Stuttgart: Deutsche Verlagsanstalt, 1995), 618 ff.; Bracher, *Diktatur* (note 5), 330 ff.; Thamer, *Verführung* (note 5), 557 ff.; Müller, *Heer* (note 12), 255 ff.; Kershaw, *Hitler-Mythos* (note 10), 116 (Swabian president, 8 Apr. 1938); *Deutschland-Berichte* (note 12), 5 (1938), 246 (mood after the *Anschluss*), 449 ff. (electoral manipulations); Jung, *Plebiszit* (note 11), 109 ff. Hitler's speech in Vienna on 15 Mar. 1938 in Domarus, *Hitler* (note 2), i/2. 823–4. On the disappearance of the differences between *grossdeutsch* and *kleindeutsch* before 1933 see Stanley Suval, 'Overcoming *Kleindeutschland*: The Politics of Historical Mythmaking in the Weimar Republic', *CEH* 2 (1969), 312–30.

20. *IMG* (note 18), xxv. 415–16 (Hitler's 'Fall Grün' order, 30 May 1938); Domarus, *Hitler* (note 2), i/2. 801–2 (Reichstag speech on 20 Feb. 1938), 903–6 (speech on 12 Sept. 1938), 908–9 (meeting between Hitler and Chamberlain on 15 Sept. 1938), 913–21 (meeting between Hitler and Chamberlain, 22–4 Sept. 1938), 923–32 (Sportpalast speech on 26 Sept. 1938), 960–1 (order on 21 Oct. 1938), 980 (order on 24 Nov. 1938); Ivan Pfaff, 'Stalins Strategie der Sowjetisierung Mitteleuropas 1935–1938. Das Beispiel Tschechoslowakei', *VfZ* 38 (1990), 543–87; Boris Celovsky, *Das Münchner Abkommen 1938* (Stuttgart: Deutsche Verlags-Anstalt, 1958), esp. 151 ff.; Horst Möller, *Europa zwischen den Weltkriegen* (Munich: Oldenbourg, 1998), 191 ff.; Thamer, *Verführung* (note 5), 580 ff. (Hitler's reaction to the attitude of the Berliners on 26 Sept. 1938: 598); Kershaw, *Hitler-Mythos* (note 10), 118 ff.; Hildebrand, *Reich* (note 19), 651 ff.; Hoffmann, *Widerstand* (note 15), 69 ff.; Klaus-Jürgen Müller, *General Ludwig Beck* (Boppard: H. Boldt, 1980), tr. as *Treason was no Crime: Ludwig Beck, Chief of the German General Staff* (London: Kimber, 1976); id., *Armee, Politik und Gesellschaft in Deutschland 1933–1945* (Paderborn: Schöningh, 1979); id., *Heer* (note 12), 345 ff.; Gerhard Ritter, *Carl Goerdeler und die deutsche Widerstandsbewegung* (Stuttgart: Deutsche Verlags-Anstalt, 1954), 151 ff.; *The German Resistance: Carl Goerdeler's Struggle against Tyranny* (Freeport: Books for Libraries Press, 1958); Rainer A. Blasius, *Für Grossdeutschland–gegen den Krieg. Ernst von Weizsäcker in den Krisen um die Tschechoslowakei und Polen* (Cologne: Böhlau, 1981), 29 ff.; Bernd-Jürgen Wendt, *Grossdeutschland. Aussenpolitik und Kriegsvorbereitung des Hitler-Regimes*, 2nd edn (Munich: DTV, 1993). Between 1424 and 1796 the Reich insignia were in the Free Reich City of Nuremberg, thereafter in Vienna.

21. Heinrich Himmler, *Geheimreden 1933–1945 und andere Ansprachen*, ed. Bradley F. Smith and A. F. Petersen (Frankfurt: Propyläen, 1974), 49 (speech on 8 Nov. 1938); Domarus, *Hitler* (note 2), i/2. 974 (speech on 10 Nov. 1938), 960–1 (order on 21 Oct. 1938), 980–1 (order on 24 Nov. 1938), iii. 1075 (talk between Hitler and Tuka on 12 Feb. 1939), 1094 (Hitler–Hacha agreement, 15 Mar. 1939); *ADAP*, series D, v. 127–32 (Hitler–Beck meeting, 5 Jan. 1939); Kershaw, *Hitler-Mythos* (note 10), 123 (president of Unterfranken on 10 Nov. 1939); Jochen Thies, *Architekt der Weltherrschaft. Die 'Endziele' Hitlers*, 2nd edn (Düsseldorf: Droste, 1976), 112–16 (Hitler's speech on 10 Feb. 1939); Klaus Hildebrand, *Vom Reich zum Weltreich. Hitler, NSDAP und koloniale Frage 1919–1945* (Munich: W. Fink, 1969), 176 ff.; id., *Reich* (note 19), 666 ff.; Thamer, *Verführung* (note 5), 470 ff., 600 ff.; Timothy W. Mason, *Arbeiterklasse und Volksgemeinschaft. Dokumente und Materialien zur deutschen Arbeiterpolitik 1936–1939* (Opladen: Westdeutscher Verlag, 1975), 100 ff. On unemployment figures for 1938 see Dietmar Petzina et al., *Sozialgeschichtliches Arbeitsbuch*, iii. *Materialien zur Statistik des Deutschen Reiches 1914–1945* (Munich: C. H. Beck, 1978), 119.

22. Breuning, *Vision* (note 2), 288 (quotes from Hugelmann); Schmitt, *Grossraumordnung* (note 16), 71, 73, 87–8; Herbert, *Best* (note 15), 276–7. (Best); Domarus, *Hitler* (note 2), ii/1. 1173 (Reichstag speech on 28 Apr. 1938); Fritz Fellner, 'Reichsgeschichte und Reichsidee als Problem der österreichischen Historiographie', in *Sacrum Imperium. Das Reich und Österreich 896–1806*, ed. Wilhelm Brauneder and Lothar Höbelt (Vienna: Amalthea, 1996), 361–72; Lothar Gruchmann, *Nationalsozialistische Grossraumordnung. Die Konstruktion einer 'deutschen Monroe-Doktrin'* (Stuttgart: Deutsche Verlags-Anstalt, 1962); Klaus Schwabe, 'Deutsche Hochschullehrer und Hitlers Krieg (1936–1940)', in *Die deutschen Eliten und der Weg in den Zweiten Weltkrieg*, ed. Martin Broszat and Klaus Schwabe (Munich: C. H. Beck, 1989), 291–333; Blasius, *Grossdeutschland* (note 20), 92 ff.; Hans Roos, *Geschichte der polnischen Nation 1916–1960. Von der Staatsgründung im ersten Weltkrieg bis zur Gegenwart* (Stuttgart: Kohlhammer, 1961), 158 ff.; George F. Kennan, *Sowjetische Aussenpolitik unter Lenin und Stalin* (Stuttgart: Steingrüben, 1961), 422 ff., orig. *Russia and the West under Lenin and Stalin* (Boston: Little, Brown, 1961); Manfred Hildermeier, *Geschichte der Sowjetunion 1917–1991. Entstehung und Niedergang des ersten sozialistischen Staates* (Munich: C. H. Beck, 1998), 590 ff.; *1939. An der Schwelle zum Weltkrieg. Die Entfesselung des Zweiten Weltkrieges und das internationale System*, ed. Klaus Hildebrand et al. (Berlin: W. de Gruyter, 1996). On Hitler's 'German Monroe Doctrine' of 1930 see Hitler, *Reden, Schriften, Aufzeichnungen. Februar 1925 bis Januar 1933*, iv. *Von der Reichstagswahl bis zur Reichspräsidentenwahl Oktober 1930–März 1932*, pt I (Oct. 1930–June 1931), ed. and comm. Constantin Goschler (Munich: Saur, 1994), 19–21 (interview on 14 Oct. 1930 with International News Service). The German–Soviet non-agression treaty with the secret supplementary protocol of 23 Aug. 1939 in *ADAP*, series D, vii, 205–7. On the Comintern on 'fascism' see *Komintern und Faschismus. Dokumente zur Geschichte und Theorie des Faschismus*, ed. Theo Pirker (Stuttgart: Deutsche Verlags-Anstalt, 1965), 187.

23. 'Eine kulturpolitische Rede des Führers', *Völkischer Beobachter*, 7 Sept. 1934 (Nuremberg congress, 6 Sept. 1934); Domarus, *Hitler* (note 2), i/2. 557–8.

(interview on 26 Nov. 1935), 730–1 (Nuremberg party congress, 13 Sept. 1937), ii/1. 1310 (euthanasia order on 1 Sept. 1939); Franz Halder, *Kriegstagebuch. Tägliche Aufzeichnungen des Chefs des Generalstabs des Heeres 1938–1942* (Stuttgart: Kohlhammer, 1962–4), i. 38 ('pact with Satan to drive out the devil': Hitler on 28 Aug. 1939); Kershaw, *Hitler-Mythos* (note 10), 125–6 (report of the *Landrats* of Ebermannstadt on 30 June, end of July, 31 Aug. 1939); *Sten. Ber.*, cdlx. 48 (Hitler's speech on 1 Sept. 1939); *Der grossdeutsche Freiheitskampf. Reden Adolf Hitlers*, i (Munich: F. Eher Nachfolger, 1940), 32–3 ('To the German people!', 3 Sept. 1939), 35–6 (appeal to the NSDAP, 3 Sept. 1939); Christian Hartmann and Sergej Slutsch, 'Franz Halder und die Kriegsvorbereitungen im Frühjahr 1939. Eine Ansprache des Generalstabschefs des Heeres', *VfZ* 45 (1997), 467–95; Hans Maier, 'Ideen von 1914–Ideen von 1939? Zweierlei Kriegsanfänge', ibid. 38 (1990), 525–42; Henry Friedlander, *Der Weg zum NS-Genozid. Von der Euthanasie zur Endlösung* (Berlin: Berlin Verlag, 1997), 48 ff. (on Binding and Hoche), orig. *The Origins of Nazi Genocide: From Euthanasia to the Final Solution* (Chapel Hill: University of North Carolina Press, 1995); Hans-Walter Schmuhl, *Rassenhygiene, Nationalsozialismus, Euthanasie. Von der Verhütung zur Vernichtung, 1890–1945* (Göttingen: Vandenhoeck & Ruprecht, 1992); *Eugenik, Sterilisation, Euthanasie. Politische Biologie 1895–1945*, ed. Joachim-Christoph Kaiser et al. (Berlin: Buchverlag Union, 1992); Joachim Fest, *Adolf Hitler. Eine Biographie* (Frankfurt: Büchergilde Gutenberg, 1973), 663 ff., tr. as *Hitler* (New York: Harcourt Brace Jovanovich, 1974); Thamer, *Verführung* (note 5), 607 ff.; Hildebrand, *Reich* (note 19), 689 ff. On Hitler's first speculations about anti-Semitic motives of Stalin during the purges see Goebbels, *Fragmente* (note 4), pt I, iii, 1 Oct. 1937–31 Dec. 1939 (Munich: 1987), 21 (entry on 25 Jan. 1937).

24. Kershaw, *Hitler-Mythos* (note 10), 127 (president of Niederbayern, 8 Sept. 1939), 128 (report from Ebermannstadt on 29 Sept. 1939); Marlis G. Steinert, *Hitlers Krieg und die Deutschen. Stimmung und Haltung der deutschen Bevölkerung im Zweiten Weltkrieg* (Düsseldorf: Econ Verlag, 1970), 91 ff.; Martin Broszat, *Nationalsozialistische Polenpolitik 1939–1945* (Stuttgart: Deutsche Verlags-Anstalt, 1961), 26 ff.; Bogdan Musial, *Deutsche Zivilverwaltung und Judenverfolgung im Generalgouvernement. Eine Fallstudie zum Distrikt Lublin 1939–1944* (Wiesbaden: Harrassowitz, 1999); Angelika Ebbinghaus and Karl Heinz Roth, 'Vorläufer des "Generalplans Ost". Theodor Schieders Polendenkschrift von 7. Oktober 1939', *1999. Zeitschrift für Sozialgeschichte des 20. und 21. Jahrhunderts*, 7 (1992), 62–94 (quotes: 85 ff.); Michael Fahlbusch, *'Wissenschaft im Dienst der nationalsozialistischen Politik? Die 'Volksdeutschen Forschungsgemeinschaften' von 1931–1945* (Baden-Baden: Nomos, 1999); Götz Aly, *'Endlösung'. Völkerverschiebung und der Mord an den europäischen Juden* (Frankfurt: Fischer, 1995), 29 ff.; id. and Susanne Heim, *Vordenker der Vernichtung. Auschwitz und die deutschen Pläne für eine neue europäische Ordnung* (Hamburg: Hoffmann und Campe, 1991), 102 ff.; Christopher Browning, *Der Weg zur 'Endlösung'. Entscheidungen und Täter* (Bonn: Dietz, 1998), 13 ff.; Dieter Rebentisch, *Führerstaat und Verwaltung im Zweiten Weltkrieg. Verfassungsentwicklung und Verwaltungspolitik 1939–1945* (Stuttgart: F. Steiner, 1989). Quotes from Hitler in Domarus, *Hitler* (note 2), ii/1. 1383; quotes

from Himmler in Helmut Krausnick, 'Denkschrift Himmlers über die Behandlung der Fremdvölkischen im Osten', *VfZ* 5 (1957), 194–8 (197–8).

25. Kershaw, *Hitler-Mythos* (note 10), 137 (Swabian president on 9 July 1940; *Kreis* leader of Augsburg-Stadt on 10 July 1940); Friedrich Meinecke, *Werke*, vi. *Ausgewählter Briefwechsel* (Stuttgart: K. F. Koehler, 1962), 364 (letter to S. A. Kaehler, 4 July 1940); Peter Richard Rohden, 'Die Sendung der Mitte', *Das Reich*, no. 9, 21 July 1940; Heinrich Ritter v. Srbik, 'Die Reichsidee und das Werden deutscher Einheit', *HZ* 164 (1941), 457–71 (470); Karl Richard Ganzer, *Das Reich als europäische Ordnungsmacht* (Hamburg: Hanseatische Verlagsanstalt, 1941), 86; Fellner, *Reichsgeschichte* (note 22), 363 ff.; Hans-Erich Volkmann, 'Deutsche Historiker im Umgang mit Drittem Reich und Zweitem Weltkrieg 1939–1949', in *Ende des Dritten Reiches—Ende des Zweiten Weltkrieges. Eine perspektivische Rückschau*, ed. id. (Munich: Piper, 1995), 861–911; id., 'Deutsche Historiker im Banne des Nationalsozialismus', in *Verwandlungspolitik. NS-Eliten in der westdeutschen Nachkriegsgesellschaft*, ed. Wilfried Loth and Bernd A. Rusinek (Frankfurt: Campus, 1998), 285–312; Karen Schönwälder, *Historiker und Politik. Geschichtswissenschaft im Nationalsozialismus* (Frankfurt: Campus, 1992), 171 ff.; *Deutsche Historiker im Nationalsozialismus*, ed. Winfried Schulze and Otto Gerhard Oexle (Frankfurt: Fischer, 1999); Ingo Haar, *Historiker im Nationalsozialismus. Die deutsche Geschichtswissenschaft und der 'Volkstumskampf' im Osten* (Göttingen: Vandenhoeck & Ruprecht, 2000); Eberhard Jäckel, *Die deutsche Frankreichpolitik im Zweiten Weltkrieg* (Stuttgart: Deutsche Verlags-Anstalt, 1966), 32 ff.; Thamer, *Verführung* (note 5), 643 ff.

26. Goebbels, *Fragmente* (note 4), pt I, iii (1 Oct. 1937–31 Dec. 1939), 53 (3 May 1937), 630 (3 Nov. 1939), 633 (7 Nov. 1939), 645 (17 Nov. 1939); *Das politische Tagebuch Alfred Rosenbergs aus den Jahren 1934/35 und 1939/40*, ed. Hans-Günther Seraphim (Göttingen: Musterschmidt, 1956), 104 (Hitler, 9 Apr. 1940); Loock, 'Grossgermanische Politik' (note 2), 37 ff.; Aly, 'Endlösung' (note 24), 147 (Himmler's Burgundy trip); Uwe Mai, ' "Rasse und Raum". Sozial- und Raumplanung ländlicher Gebiete in Deutschland während der NS-Herrschaft' Ph.D. thesis, Technische Universität Berlin, 1997, 354–5. On 'Germania magna' see the first volume of this history, 11, 62.

27. Andreas Hillgruber, *Hitlers Strategie. Politik und Kriegsführung 1940–1941*, 2nd edn (Munich: C. H. Beck, 1982), 207 ff. (first preparations for war in the east: 224–6); *IMG*, xxvi. 47–8. (order for 'Barbarossa Case', 18 Dec. 1940); Helmut Krausnick and Hans-Heinrich Wilhelm, *Die Truppe des Weltanschauungskrieges. Die Einsatzgruppen der Sicherheitspolizei und des SD 1938–1942* (Stuttgart: Deutsche Verlags-Anstalt, 1981), 117 (Hitler's order to Himmler, 3 Mar. 1941; emphases in the original), 217 (Hoepner's order, 2 May 1941); Halder, *Kriegstagebuch* (note 23), ii. 336–7; Domarus, *Hitler* (note 2), ii/2. 1683–4 ('commissar order'), 1730 (proclamation on 22 June 1941), 1732 (Napoleon's proclamation on 22 June 1812); the translation of the June 22 proclamation is that of the *New York Times* of 23 June 1941; 'Dank und Treuegelöbnis', in *Das Evangelische Deutschland. Kirchliche Rundschau für das Gesamtgebiet der Deutschen Evangelischen Kirche*, 27, 6 July 1934 (announcement on 30 June 1941); Guenther Lewy, *Die katholische Kirche und das Dritte Reich* (Munich: Piper, 1965), 254 (Racke, 25 Sept. 1941;

Jäger, 19 Oct. 1941; Kumpfmüller, 21 Sept. 1941), orig. *The Catholic Church and Nazi Germany* (New York: McGraw-Hill, 1964); Bischof Clemens August Graf von Galen, *Akten, Briefe und Predigten 1933–1946*, ii (1939–1946), 2nd edn, ed. Peter Löffler (Paderborn: Schöningh, 1996), 901–4 (letter of 14 Sept. 1941); Heinz Hürten, *Deutsche Katholiken 1918 bis 1945* (Paderborn: Schöningh, 1992), 461 (Catholic bishops on the eastern campaign); Arno J. Mayer, *Der Krieg als Kreuzzug. Das Deutsche Reich, Hitlers Wehrmacht und die 'Endlösung'* (Reinbek: Rowohlt, 1989), 333–4, orig. *Why did the Heavens not Darken?: The 'Final Solution' in History* (New York: Pantheon Books, 1988); Hermann Heimpel, 'Frankreich und das Reich', in *Deutsches Mittelalter* (Leipzig: Koehler & Amelang, 1941), 171–87 (175–6: on 'mission by sword'); id., 'Reich und Staat im deutschen Mittelalter', ibid. 53–78 (56: world revolution and the Kingdom of God; 58: 'God's exhortation', 71: transfer of the Reich); Richard Faber, *Abendland. Ein 'politischer Kampfbegriff'* (Hildesheim: Gerstenberg, 1979), 140 ff.; Schönwälder, *Historiker* (note 25), 245–6. (Maschke), 247 ff. (Grundmann, Rörig), 250–1. (Wittram); *Ursachen* (note 13), ed. Michaelis and Schraepler, xvii. 253–6 (announcement by the *Deutsche diplomatische-politische Information* on 27 June 1941); Kershaw, *Hitler-Mythos* (note 10), 149 ff.; Steinert, *Hitlers Krieg* (note 24), 203 ff. (mood of the population at the start of the eastern war); Hildermeier, *Geschichte* (note 22), 596 ff.; Thamer, *Verführung* (note 5), 649 ff.; Christian Streit, *Keine Kameraden! Die Wehrmacht und die sowjetischen Kriegsgefangenen* (Stuttgart: Deutsche Verlags-Anstalt, 1978), 9 ff.; *Der deutsche Angriff auf die Sowjetunion 1941. Die Kontroverse um die Präventivkriegsthese*, ed. Gerd R. Ueberschär and Lev A. Bezymenskij (Darmstadt: Primus, 1998); *Präventivkrieg? Der deutsche Angriff auf die Sowjetunion*, ed. Bianka Pietrow-Ennker (Frankfurt: Fischer, 2000).

28. Galen, *Akten* (note 27), ii. 907 (letter of 14 Sept. 1941); Friedlander, *Weg* (note 23), 84 ff.; Ernst Klee, *'Euthanasie' im NS-Staat. Die 'Vernichtung lebensunwerten Lebens'* (Frankfurt: Fischer, 1985); *Dokumente zur 'Euthanasie'*, ed id. (Frankfurt: Fischer, 1985); Raul Hilberg, *Die Vernichtung der europäischen Juden*, 3 vols. (Frankfurt: Fischer, 1990), i. 164 ff., iii. 1292 (number of dead in Polish ghettos), orig. *The Destruction of the European Jews* (Chicago: Quadrangle Books, 1961); Longerich, *Politik* (note 17), 227 ff.; Magnus Brechtken, *'Madagaskar für die Juden'. Antisemitische Idee und politische Praxis 1885–1945* (Munich: Oldenbourg, 1997), 226 ff.; Browning, *Weg* (note 24), 13 ff.; Richard Breitman, *Der Architekt der 'Endlösung': Himmler und die Vernichtung der europäischen Juden* (Paderborn: Schöningh, 1996), 191 ff. (201: on Hitler's order to Heydrich), orig. *The Architect of Genocide: Himmler and the Final Solution* (London: Bodley Head, 1991); Aly, *'Endlösung'* (note 24), 268 ff. Dannecker's report in Serge Klarsfeld, *Vichy—Auschwitz. Die Zusammenarbeit der deutschen und französischen Behörden bei der 'Endlösung der Judenfrage'* (Nördlingen: Delphi Politik, 1989), 361–3. On Goebbels–Heydrich talk on 23 Sept. 1941 see *Die Tagebücher von Joseph Goebbels*, ed. Elke Fröhlich, pt II, *Diktate 1941–1945* (Munich: Saur, 1996), i. 480–1.

29. Helmut Heiber, 'Der Generalplan Ost', *VfZ* 6 (1958), 281–325; *Ursachen* (note 13), ed. Michaelis and Schraepler, xxvii. 312 (Hitler, 16 July 1941); Hitler, *Mein Kampf* (note 1), 151–2; Heinrich August Winkler, 'Der entbehrliche Stand: Zur Mittelstandspolitik im "Dritten Reich"', in *Liberalismus und Antiliberalismus.*

Studien zur politischen Sozialgeschichte des 19. und 20. Jahrhunderts (Göttingen: Vandenhoeck und Ruprecht, 1979), 110–44 (140–1: Himmler's letter to *Reichshandwerksmeister* Ferdinand Schramm, 21 Oct. 1941); Josef Ackermann, *Heinrich Himmler als Ideologe* (Göttingen: Musterschmidt, 1970), 273 (Himmler, Aug. 1942); Rolf-Dieter Müller, *Hitlers Ostkrieg und die deutsche Siedlungspolitik. Die Zusammenarbeit von Wehrmacht, Wirtschaft und SS* (Frankfurt: Fischer, 1991); *Die Wehrmacht. Mythos und Realität*, ed. id. and Hans-Erich Volkmann (Munich: Oldenbourg, 1999); Reinhard Otto, *Wehrmacht, Gestapo und sowjetische Kriegsgefangene im deutschen Reichsgebiet 1941/42* (Munich: Oldenbourg, 1998); Streit, *Keine Kameraden* (note 27), 115–16. (Reichenau, Manstein; emphasis in the original); Hilberg, *Vernichtung* (note 28), ii. 309–12 (statistics on Jews murdered by the Special Action Groups); Longerich, *Politik* (note 28), 293 ff.; Krausnick and Wilhelm, *Truppe* (note 27), 107 ff.; Ralf Ogorreck, *Die Einsatzgruppen und die 'Genesis der Endlösung'* (Berlin: Metropol, 1996); Dieter Pohl, *Nationalsozialistische Judenverfolgung in Ostgalizien 1941–1944. Organisation und Durchführung eines staatlichen Massenverbrechens* (Munich: Oldenbourg, 1996), 123 ff.; Thomas Sandkühler, *'Endlösung' in Galizien. Der Judenmord und die Rettungsinitiativen von Berthold Beitz 1941–1944* (Bonn: Dietz, 1996), 63 ff.; Ian Kershaw, 'Improvised Genocide? The Emergence of the "Final Solution" in the Warthegau', in *Transactions of the Royal Historical Society* (1992), 51–78; Alexander Dallin, *Deutsche Herrschaft in Russland 1941–1945* (Düsseldorf: Droste, 1958), 15 ff. (Kube-Rosenberg: 218), orig. *German Rule in Russia, 1941–1945* (New York: St Martin's Press, 1957); Omer Bartov, *Hitlers Wehrmacht. Soldaten, Fanatismus und die Brutalisierung des Krieges* (Reinbek: Rowohlt, 1995), orig. *Hitler's Army: Soldiers, Nazis, and War in the Third Reich* (Oxford: Oxford University Press, 1992), 27 ff.; *Vernichtungskrieg. Verbrechen der Wehrmacht 1941–1944*, ed. Hannes Heer and Klaus Naumann (Hamburg: Hamburger Edition, 1995).

30. *IMG*, xxvi. 11–12 (Goering to Heydrich, 31 July 1941), xiii. 210 ff. (Wannsee conference); Domarus, *Hitler* (note 2), ii/2. 1663 (Reichstag speech 30 Jan. 1941), 1808 (Reichstag speech 11 Dec. 1941), 1828–9. (Sportpalast speech 30 Jan. 1942); 'Unser Glaube und Fanatismus stärker denn je!', *Völkischer Beobachter*, 25 Feb. 1943 (proclamation on 24 Feb. 1943); Adolf Hitler, *Monologe im Führerhauptquartier 1941–1944. Die Aufzeichnungen Heinrich Heims*, ed. Werner Jochmann (Hamburg: A. Knaus, 1980), 91 (17 Oct. 1941); Goebbels, *Tagebücher* (note 29), pt II, i. 250 (entry on 17 Aug. 1941 on the circulation of the weekly *Das Reich*), 265, 269 (19 Aug. 1941), 284 (14 Nov. 1941), 498–9 (13 Dec. 1941); id., 'Die Juden sind schuld!', *Das Reich*, 46, 16 Nov. 1941; id., 'Der Krieg und die Juden', ibid., no. 19, 9 May 1943; L. J. Hartog, *Der Befehl zum Judenmord. Hitler, Amerika und die Juden* (Bodenheim: Syndikat Buchgesellschaft, 1997), 45 ff. (Hitler's order to Heydrich 30 Nov. 1941: 55; Hartog quote: 65–6), orig. *Hoe ontstond de jodenmoord?: Hitler, Amerika en de Endlösung* (Maastricht: Sdu Uitgeverij Koninginnegracht, 1994); *Nationalsozialistische Vernichtungspolitik 1939–1945. Neue Forschungen und Kontroversen*, ed. Ulrich Herbert (Frankfurt: Fischer, 1998), tr. as *National Socialist Extermination Policies: Contemporary German Perspectives and Controversies* (New York: Berghahn Books, 2000); Christian Gerlach, 'Die Wannseekonferenz, das Schicksal der deutschen Juden und Hitlers Grundsatzentscheidung, alle Juden

Europas zu ermorden', *Werkstatt Geschichte*, 18 (1997), 7–44 (Himmler's notes of 18 Dec. 1941: 22; Frank's elucidations of 16 Dec. 1941: 29–30). The English translation of the Wannsee protocol is from the House of the Wannsee Conference Educational and Memorial Site (http://www.ghwk.de/); Christian Gerlach, *Krieg, Ernährung, Völkermord. Forschungen zur deutschen Vernichtungspolitik im Zweiten Weltkrieg* (Hamburg: Hamburger Edition, 1998); id., *Kalkulierte Morde. Die deutsche Wirtschafts- und Vernichtungspolitik in Weissrussland 1941 bis 1944* (Hamburg: Hamburger Edition, 1999); Tobias Jersak, 'Die Interaktion von Kriegsverlauf und Judenvernichtung. Ein Blick auf Hitlers Strategie im Spätsommer 1941', *HZ* 268 (1999), 311–74 (on the significance of the Atlantic Charter); Bankier, *Meinung* (note 17), 159 ff.; Dülffer, *Geschichte* (note 15), 189–90 (statistics on the extermination of the Jews); Christopher Browning, *Ganz normale Männer. Das Reserve-Polizeibataillon 101 und die 'Endlösung' in Polen* (Reinbek: Rowohlt, 1993), orig. *Ordinary Men: Reserve Police Battalion 101 and the Final Solution in Poland* (New York: HarperCollins, 1992); Daniel Jonah Goldhagen, *Hitlers willige Vollstrecker. Ganz gewöhnliche Deutsche und der Holocaust* (Berlin: Siedler, 1996), orig. *Hitler's Willing Executioners: Ordinary Germans and the Holocaust* (New York: Random House, 1996); *Dimension des Völkermords. Die Zahl der jüdischen Opfer des Nationalsozialismus*, ed. Wolfgang Benz (Munich: Oldenbourg, 1991); Leni Yahil, *Die Shoah. Überlebenskampf und Vernichtung der europäischen Juden* (Munich: Luchterhand, 1998), 341 ff.; Eng. edn *The Holocaust: The Fate of European Jewry, 1932–1945* (New York: Oxford University Press, 1990); Hilberg, *Vernichtung* (note 28), iii. 1083 (Lichtenberg); Longerich, *Politik* (note 17), 293 ff. (Himmler to Bradfisch: 372), 419 ff.; Wolf Gruner, *Der geschlossene Arbeitseinsatz deutscher Juden. Zur Zwangsarbeit als Element der Verfolgung 1938–1943* (Berlin: Metropol, 1997), tr. as *Jewish Forced Labor under the Nazis: Economic Needs and Racial Aims, 1938–1944* (New York: Cambridge University Press, 2006); Hans Mommsen, 'Die Realisierung des Utopischen: Die "Endlösung der Judenfrage" im "Dritten Reich"', *Geschichte und Gesellschaft*, 9 (1983), 381–420; *Die Deutschen und die Judenverfolgung im Dritten Reich*, ed. Ursula Büttner (Hamburg: Christians, 1992); Theodore S. Hamerow, *Die Attentäter. Der 20. Juli–von der Kollaboration zum Widerstand* (Munich: 1999), 323 ff. (on Wurm: 329 ff.), orig. *On the Road to the Wolf's Lair: German Resistance to Hitler* (Cambridge, MA: Harvard University Press, 1997); Hans Werner Neulen, *Europa und das 3. Reich. Einigungsbestrebungen im deutschen Machtbereich 1939–1945* (Munich: Beck, 1987); Faber, *Abendland* (note 27), 140 ff. The Atlantic Charter in *Ursachen* (note 13), ed. Michaelis and Schraepler, xvii. 586–7. On Goebbels's August 1932 article see the first volume of this history, 462.

31. *Deutscher Widerstand 1938–1944. Fortschritt oder Reaktion*, ed. Bodo Scheurig (Munich: DTV, 1969) (quotes from Goerdeler's text from the beginning of 1941: 75–7; from 1944: 263); tr. as *German Resistance to Hitler: Count von Moltke and the Kreisau Circle* (New York: Van Nostrand Reinhold Co., 1971); Christof Dipper, 'Der deutsche Widerstand und die Juden', *GG* 9 (1983), 349–80; Ger van Roon, *Neuordnung im Widerstand. Der Kreisauer Kreis innerhalb der deutschen Widerstandsbewegung* (Munich: Oldenbourg, 1967); Hermann Graml, 'Die aussenpolitischen Vorstellungen des deutschen Widerstandes', in *Der deutsche Widerstand gegen Hitler,*

ed. Walter Schmitthenner and Hans Buchheim (Cologne: 1966), 15–72; Hans Mommsen, 'Gesellschaftsbild und Verfassungspläne des deutschen Widerstandes', ibid. 73–167; id., *Alternative zu Hitler. Studien zur Geschichte des deutschen Widerstands* (Munich: Beck, 2000), tr. as *Alternatives to Hitler: German Resistance under the Third Reich* (Princeton: Princeton University Press, 2003); Herbert von Borch, *Obrigkeit und Widerstand. Zur politischen Soziologie des Beamtentums* (Tübingen: Mohr, 1954); Ritter, *Goerdeler* (note 20), 266 ff.; Hans Rothfels, *Die deutsche Opposition gegen Hitler. Eine Würdigung* (Frankfurt: Fischer, 1958), orig. *The German Opposition to Hitler: An Appraisal* (Hinsdale: Henry Regnery, 1948); Joachim Fest, *Staatsstreich. Der lange Weg zum 20. Juli* (Berlin: Siedler, 1994); *Widerstand gegen den Nationalsozialismus*, ed. Peter Steinbach and Johannes Tuchel (Bonn: Piper, 1994); Peter Hoffmann, *Claus Schenk Graf von Stauffenberg und seine Brüder* (Stuttgart: Deutsche Verlags-Anstalt, 1992), 166 ff. (letter, 13–14 Sept. 1939: 189); tr. as *Stauffenberg: A Family History, 1905–1944* (Cambridge: Cambridge University Press, 1995); id., *Widerstand* (note 15), 301 ff. (on the assassination attempts), 349–50. (Popitz–Himmler), 371 ff. (Stauffenberg's attitude at the start of the war; 'brown plague' quote: 375–6), 626 (statements in court), 630–1. (number of executions); Christian Gerlach, 'Männer des 20. Juli und der Krieg gegen die Sowjetunion', in *Vernichtungskrieg* (note 29), ed. Heer and Naumann, 427–46 (Tresckow and the partisan war); *NS-Verbrechen und der militärische Widerstand gegen Hitler*, ed. Gerd R. Ueberschär, (Darmstadt: Primus, 2000); Fabian von Schlabrendorff, *Offiziere gegen Hitler* (Frankfurt: Fischer, 1959), 88 ff. (1st edn 1946), orig. *Revolt against Hitler* (New York: AMS Press, 1948); Hamerow, *Attentäter* (note 30), esp. 233 ff.; Detlef Graf von Schwerin, *'Dann sind's die besten Köpfe, die man henkt'. Die junge Generation im deutschen Widerstand*, 2nd edn (Munich: Piper, 1994); Kershaw, *Hitler-Mythos* (note 10), 187–8 (president of the Nuremberg court, 1 Aug. 1944).

32. Ulrich Herbert, *Fremdarbeiter. Politik und Praxis des 'Ausländer-Einsatzes' in der Kriegswirtschaft des Dritten Reiches* (Bonn: Dietz, 1985); *Europa und der 'Reichseinsatz'. Ausländische Zivilarbeiter, Kriegsgefangene und KZ-Häftlinge in Deutschland 1938–1945*, ed. id. (Essen: Klartext, 1991); *Zur Arbeit gezwungen. Zwangsarbeit in Deutschland 1940–1945*, ed. Rimco Spanier et al. (Bremen: Edition Temmen, 1999); Hans Mommsen with Manfred Grieger, *Das Volkswagenwerk und seine Arbeiter im Dritten Reich* (Düsseldorf: Droste, 1996); Barbara Hopmann et al., *Zwangsarbeit bei Daimler-Benz* (Stuttgart: Franz Steiner, 1994); Corni and Gies, *Brot* (note 6), 411 ff.; Winkler, *Frauenarbeit* (note 10), 102 ff.; Kershaw, *Hitler-Mythos* (note 10), 193 (SD reports); Steinert, *Krieg* (note 24), 554 ff.; Hitler, *Monologe* (note 30), 83–4 (14 Oct. 1941), 91 (17 Oct. 1941: 'executioner' quote), 99 (21 Oct. 1941: Saul–Paul), 412–13 (30 Nov. 1944); *Hitlers Politisches Testament. Die Bormann-Diktate vom Februar und April 1945*, ed. Hugh R. Trevor-Roper and André François-Poncet (Hamburg: A. Knaus, 1981), 68–9 (3 Feb. 1945); Domarus, *Hitler* (note 2), ii/2. 2250 (report of Hitler's death); Paul de Lagarde, *Deutsche Schriften*, 3rd edn (Munich: J. F. Lehmann, 1937), 67–8; Heer, *Glaube* (note 2), 391 ff.; Ernst Nolte, 'Eine frühe Quelle zu Hitlers Antisemitismus', *HZ* 192 (1961), 584–606; Gunnar Heinsohn, *Warum Auschwitz? Hitlers Plan und die Ratlosigkeit der Nachwelt* (Reinbek: Rowohlt,

1995), 129 ff. (difference between anti-Semitism and racism, Old Testament commandment against killing); Michael Zimmermann, *Rassenutopie und Genozid. Die nationalsozialistische 'Lösung der Zigeunerfrage'* (Hamburg: Christians, 1996).

33. Wilhelm Röpke, *Die deutsche Frage* (Erlenbach/Zurich, 1945), 30, 170; tr. as *The Solution of the German Problem* (New York: G. P. Putnam's Sons, 1947); Armin Boyens, 'Das Stuttgarter Schuldbekenntnis vom 19. Oktober 1945–Entstehung und Bedeutung', *VfZ* 19 (1971), 374–97 (347–8: Stuttgart confession, 18–19 Oct. 1945); Clemens Vollnhals, 'Die Evangelische Kirche zwischen Traditionswahrung und Neuorientierung', in *Von Stalingrad zur Währungsreform. Zur Sozialgeschichte des Umbruchs in Deutschland*, ed. Martin Broszat et al. (Munich: Oldenbourg, 1988), 113–67 (esp. 130 ff.); Karl Jaspers, *Die Schuldfrage. Für Völkermord gibt es keine Verjährung* (1st edn 1946)(Munich: Piper, 1979), 55–7, 69–70; Friedrich Meinecke, *Die deutsche Katastrophe. Betrachtungen und Erinnerungen*, 3rd edn (Wiesbaden: E. Brockhaus, 1947), 29, 52–3, 65, 85, 89, 97, 168, 175, 177; Thomas Mann, 'Deutschland und die Deutschen', in *Gesammelte Werke in dreizehn Bänden*, xi (Frankfurt: Fischer, 1990), 1126–48 (1130–1, 1136–8, 1140–1, 1144–6; emphasis in the original). The English text of the original address in the Library of Congress can be found in *Thomas Mann. Death in Venice, Tonio Kröger, and Other Writings*, ed. Frederick A. Lubich (New York: Continuum, 1999), 303–19 (307–8, 310–11, 314, 315, 317–18); id., 'Bruder Hitler', ibid., xii. 845–52; id., *Doktor Faustus*, ibid., vi; Ernst Cassirer, *Der Mythus des Staates. Philosophische Grundlagen politischen Verhaltens* (1st edn 1949; Frankfurt: Fischer, 1985), 364. Control Council law no. 46, 25 Feb. 1947 in *Dokumente des geteilten Deutschland*, ed. Ingo v. Münch (Stuttgart: Kröner, 1976), 54.

CHAPTER 2. DEMOCRACY AND DICTATORSHIP 1945–1961

1. *Dokumente der deutschen Politik und Geschichte*, ed. Klaus Hohlfeld, vi. *Deutschland nach dem Zusammenbruch* (Berlin: Dokumenten-Verlag H. Wendler, 1952), 39–40 (Potsdam agreement, section xiii); Karl Dietrich Erdmann, *Die Zeit der Weltkriege* (= Bruno Gebhardt, *Handbuch der deutschen Geschichte*, iv/2) (Stuttgart: Klett, 1976), 643 ff. (Nuremberg trials); Lutz Niethammer, *Entnazifizierung in Bayern* (Frankfurt: Fischer, 1972); Justus Fürstenau, *Entnazifizierung. Ein Kapitel deutscher Nachkriegspolitik* (Neuwied: Luchterhand, 1969); Clemens Vollnhals, *Evangelische Kirche und Entnazifizierung 1945–1949. Die Last der nationalsozialistischen Vergangenheit* (Munich: Oldenbourg, 1989); *Entnazifizierung. Politische Säuberung und Rehabilitierung in den vier Besatzungszonen 1945–1949*, ed. id. (Munich: DTV, 1991); Jörg Friedrich, *Freispruch für die Nazi-Justiz. Die Urteile gegen NS-Richter seit 1948. Eine Dokumentation* (Frankfurt: Rowohlt, 1983); *Sowjetische Speziallager in Deutschland 1945 bis 1950*, ed. Sergej Mironenko et al. (Berlin: Akademie Verlag, 1998–); Manfred Overesch, *Buchenwald und die DDR oder Die Suche nach Selbstlegitimation* (Göttingen: Vandenhoeck & Ruprecht, 1995); Petra Weber, *Justiz und Diktatur. Justizverwaltung und politische Strafjustiz in Thüringen 1945–1961* (Munich: Oldenbourg, 2000); *Geglückte Integration? Spezifika und Vergleichbarkeiten der Vertriebenen-Eingliederung in der SBZ/DDR*, ed. Dierk Hoffmann and Michael Schwartz (Munich: Oldenbourg, 1999); Hermann Weber, *Die DDR 1945–1990*, 2nd edn (Munich: Oldenbourg, 1993), 10 ff. (on the 'special

camps': 10; on land and industry reform: 12 ff.); Klaus Schroeder with Steffen Alisch, *Der SED-Staat. Geschichte und Strukturen der DDR* (Munich: Bayerische Landeszentrale für Politische Bildungsarbeit, 1998), 68–9 (statistics on the special camps); Dörte Winkler, 'Die amerikanische Sozialisierungspolitik in Deutschland 1945–1948', in *Politische Weichenstellungen im Nachkriegsdeutschland 1945–1953*, ed. Heinrich August Winkler (*GG* special issue 5) (Gottingen: Vandenhoeck und Ruprecht, 1979), 88–110; Udo Wengst, *Beamtentum zwischen Reform und Tradition. Beamtengesetzgebung in der Gründungsphase der Bundesrepublik Deutschland 1948–1953* (Düsseldorf: Droste, 1988); Hermann-Josef Rupieper, *Die Wurzeln der westdeutschen Nachkriegsdemokratie. Der amerikanische Beitrag 1945–1952* (Opladen: Westdeutscher Verlag, 1993); *Von Stalingrad zur Währungsreform. Zur Sozialgeschichte des Umbruchs in Deutschland*, ed. Martin Broszat et al. (Munich: Oldenbourg, 1988); Klaus-Dietmar Henke, *Die amerikanische Besetzung Deutschlands* (Munich: Oldenbourg 1995); Theodor Eschenburg [et al.], *Jahre der Besatzung 1945–1949* (= *Geschichte der Bundesrepublik Deutschland*, i) (Stuttgart: Deutsche Verlags-Anstalt, 1983), 375 ff.; Manfred Görtemaker, *Geschichte der Bundesrepublik Deutschland. Von der Gründung bis zur Gegenwart* (Munich: Beck, 1999), 15 ff. 'Displaced persons' was the term for refugees from eastern Europe (including slave labourers and Jews) who were in occupied Germany after the end of the war and could not or did not wish to return to their home countries. On the origins of the term 'Thirty Years War' for the span of the two world wars see Matthias Waechter, 'De Gaulles 30 jähriger Krieg: Die Résistance und die Erinnerung an 1918', in *Intentionen–Wirklichkeiten. 42. Deutscher Historikertag in Frankfurt am Main, 8. bis 11. September 1998. Berichtband* (Munich: Oldenbourg, 1999), 235–6.

2. Eschenburg [et al.], *Jahre* (note 1), 171 ff.; Hans-Peter Schwarz, *Vom Reich zur Bundesrepublik. Deutschland im Widerstreit der aussenpolitischen Konzeptionen in den Jahren der Besatzungsherrschaft 1945–1949* (Neuwied: Luchterhand, 1966); *'Nach Hitler kommen wir'. Dokumente zur Programmatik der Moskauer KPD-Führung 1944/45 für Nachkriegsdeutschland*, ed. Peter Erler et al. (Berlin: Akademie Verlag, 1994), 168–9. (Ulbricht, 24 Apr. 1944), 394 (appeal the CC of the KPD, 11 June 1945); *Die 'Gruppe Ulbricht' in Berlin April bis Juni 1945. Von den Vorbereitungen im Sommer 1944 bis zur Wiederbegründung der KPD im Juni 1945. Eine Dokumentation*, ed. Gerhard Keiderling (Berlin: A. Spitz, 1993); Norman M. Naimark, *Die Russen in Deutschland. Die sowjetische Besatzungszone 1945 bis 1949* (Berlin: Propyläen, 1997), orig. *The Russians in Germany: A History of the Soviet Zone of Occupation, 1945–1949* (Cambridge, MA: Harvard University Press, 1995); Stefan Creutzberger, *Die sowjetische Besatzungsmacht und das politische System der SBZ* (Weimar: Böhlau, 1996); Jan Foitzik, *Sowjetische Militäradministration in Deutschland (SMAD) 1945–1949. Struktur und Funktion* (Berlin: Akademie Verlag, 1999); Wilfried Loth, *Stalins ungeliebtes Kind. Warum Moskau die DDR nicht wollte* (Berlin: Rowohlt, 1994), tr. as *Stalin's Unwanted Child: The Soviet Union, the German Question, and the Founding of the GDR* (New York: St Martin's Press, 1998); *Sowjetisierung und Eigenständigkeit in der SBZ/DDR (1945–1953)*, ed. Michael Lemke (Cologne: Böhlau, 1999); Andreas Malycha, *Auf dem Weg zur SED. Die Sozialdemokratie und die Bildung einer Einheitspartei in den Ländern der SBZ. Eine Quellenedition* (Bonn: Dietz, 1995); Bernd

Bonwetsch and Gennadij Bordjugov, 'Stalin und die SBZ. Ein Besuch der SED-Führung in Moskau vom 30. Januar bis 7. Februar 1947', *VfZ* 42 (1994), 279–303; Wladimir K. Wolkow, 'Die deutsche Frage aus Stalins Sicht (1947–1952)', *ZfG* 48 (2000), 20–49; *Kurt Schumacher, Reden–Schriften–Korrespondenzen 1945–1952*, ed. Willy Albrecht (Berlin: Dietz, 1983), 254 (First Appeal from the Office of Dr Schumacher, mid-August 1945), 276 ('Political Guidelines', 25 Aug. 1945); Konrad Adenauer, *Briefe 1945–1947*, ed. Hans Peter Mensing, Rhöndorf edition (Berlin: Siedler, 1983), 123–4 (talk with foreign correspondents on 9 Oct. 1945); Hans-Otto Kleinmann, *Geschichte der CDU 1945–1982* (Stuttgart: Deutsche Verlags-Anstalt, 1993); Alf Mintzel, *Die CSU. Anatomie einer konservativen Partei* (Opladen: Westdeutscher Verlag, 1975), 83 ff.; Thomas Schlemmer, *Aufbruch, Krise und Erneuerung. Die Christlich-Soziale Union 1945 bis 1955* (Munich: Oldenbourg, 1998); Wilhelm Mommsen ed., *Deutsche Parteiprogramme* (Munich: Isar, 1960), 576–82 (the CDU's Ahlen economic platform, Feb. 1947). The 'political fundamentals' of the Potsdam agreement in *Dokumente* (note 1), 29–31 (section iii).

3. Eschenburg [et al.], *Jahre* (note 1), 281 ff.; Andrei A. Zhdanov, *Über die internationale Lage* (Berlin: SWA, 1952), 12–13; Adam B. Ulam, *Expansion and Coexistence: The History of Soviet Foreign Policy 1917–1967*, 3rd edn (New York: Praeger, 1969), 378 ff.; Elke Scherstjanoi, 'Die Berlin-Blockade 1948/49 im sowjetischen Kalkül', *ZfG* 46 (1998), 495–509; John Gimbel, *Amerikanische Besatzungspolitik in Deutschland 1945–1949* (Frankfurt: Fischer, 1971), orig. *The American Occupation of Germany: Politics and the Military, 1945–1949* (Stanford, CA: Stanford University Press, 1968); Werner Abelshauser, *Wirtschaft und Westdeutschland 1945–1949* (Stuttgart: Deutsche Verlags-Anstalt, 1975); Rudolf Morsey, *Die Bundesrepublik Deutschland. Entstehung und Entwicklung bis 1969*, 2nd edn (Munich: Oldenbourg, 1990), 9 ff.; Andreas Hillgruber, *Europa in der Weltpolitik der Nachkriegszeit 1945–1963*, 4th edn (Munich: Oldenbourg, 1993), 39 ff.; Friedrich Jerchow, *Deutschland in der Weltwirtschaft 1944–1947. Alliierte Deutschland- und Reparationspolitik und die Anfänge der westdeutschen Aussenwirtschaft* (Düsseldorf: Droste, 1978), esp. 132 ff. On Reuter's campaign for the inclusion of Berlin in the western currency reform see Willy Brandt and Richard Lowenthal (= Löwenthal), *Ernst Reuter. Ein Leben für die Freiheit. Eine politische Biographie* (Munich: Kindler, 1957), 403 ff. (quote: 407); David E. Barclay, *Schaut auf diese Stadt. Der unbekannte Ernst Reuter* (Berlin: Seidler, 2000), 191 ff., 249–50.

4. *Der Parlamentarische Rat 1948–1949. Akten und Protokoll*, i. *Vorgeschichte*, ed. Johannes Volker Wagner (Boppard: Boldt, 1975), 192 (Reuter); ii. *Der Verfassungskonvent auf Herrenchiemsee*, ed. Peter Bucher (Boppard: Boldt, 1981), 516 (forfeiture of basic rights); v/I. *Ausschuss für Grundsatzfragen*, ed. Eberhard Pikart and Wolfram Werner (Boppard: Boldt, 1993), 169–70 (Kaiser [CDU], Schmid [SPD], Heuss [FDP], Mangold [CDU] on 6 Oct. 1948 on the term 'Reich'); ix. *Plenum*, ed. Eberhard Pikart and Wolfram Werner (Boppard: Boldt, 1993), 36 (Schmid), 72 (Menzel), 93 (Schwalber), 182–200 (Schmid [SPD], Süsterhenn [CDU], Heuss [FDP], Seebohm [DP] on official name of the state), 587–90 (flag question); Michael F. Feldkamp, *Der Parlamentarische Rat 1948–1949* (Göttingen: Vandenhoeck & Ruprecht, 1998); Karlheinz Niclauss, *Der Weg zum Grundgesetz. Demokratiegründung in Westdeutschland 1945–1949* (Paderborn: Schöningh,

1998); Eschenburg [et al.], *Jahre* (note 1), 459 ff. (the name 'Federal Republic of Germany', discussion of the 'Reich': 506); Friedrich Karl Fromme, *Von der Weimarer Reichsverfassung zum Bonner Grundgesetz. Die verfassungspolitischen Folgerungen des Parlamentarischen Rates aus Weimarer Republik und nationalsozialistischer Diktatur* (Tübingen: Mohr, 1960); Dirk van Laak, *Gespräche in der Sicherheit des Schweigens. Carl Schmitt in der politischen Geistesgeschichte der frühen Bundesrepublik* (Berlin: Akademie Verlag, 1993), 157 ff.; Hans-Peter Schwarz, *Die Ära Adenauer 1949–1957* (= *Geschichte der Bundesrepublik Deutschland*, ii) (Stuttgart: Deutsche Verlags-Anstalt, 1981), 27 ff. (on the 'high government on the Petersberg': 48); *Die Bundesrepublik Deutschland. Geschichte in drei Bänden*, i. *Politik*, ed. Wolfgang Benz (Frankfurt: Fischer, 1983); Reiner Pommerin, *Von Berlin nach Bonn. Die Alliierten, die Deutschen und die Hauptstadtfrage nach 1945* (Cologne: Böhlau, 1989), 54 ff., 86 ff.; Görtemaker, *Geschichte* (note 1), 44 ff.; Morsey, *Bundesrepublik* (note 3), 18 ff.

5. Anton Ackermann, 'Gibt es einen besonderen deutschen Weg zum Sozialismus?', *Einheit*, 1 (1946) 22–32; *Wilhelm Pieck—Aufzeichnungen zur Deutschlandpolitik 1945–1953*, ed. Rolf Badstübner and Wilfried Loth (Berlin: Akademie Verlag, 1994), 259–63 (Stalin and Pieck, 18 Dec. 1948); *Die Verfassung der Deutschen Demokratischen Republik. Mit einer Einleitung von Dr. Karl Steinhoff, Ministerpräsident der Landesregierung Brandenburg* (Berlin: Heymann, 1949), 17–18. (Article 6); Loth, *Kind* (note 2), 129 ff.; Naimark, *Russen* (note 2), 583 ff.; *Das letzte Jahr der SBZ. Politische Weichenstellungen und Kontinuitäten im Prozess der Gründung der DDR*, ed. Dierk Hoffmann and Hermann Wentker (Munich: Oldenbourg, 2000); Elke Scherstjanoi, ed., *'Provisorium für längstens ein Jahr'. Die Gründung der DDR* (Berlin: Akademie Verlag, 1993); Wolkow, *Frage* (note 2), 26 ff. (Stalin and the NDPD: 29); Weber, *DDR* (note 1), 23 ff. (NDPD, 'Volksrat': 23); Schroeder, *SED-Staat* (note 1), 71 ff. (on the theory of the 'special German path to socialism' and its retraction: 38, 64); Andreas Malycha, *Die SED. Geschichte ihrer Stalinisierung. 1946–1953* (Paderborn: Schöningh, 2000); Gerhard Wettig, *Bereitschaft zu Einheit in Freiheit? Die sowjetische Deutschland-Politik 1945–1990* (Munich: Olzog, 1990), 171 ff.; Christoph Klessmann, *Die doppelte Staatsgründung. Deutsche Geschichte 1945–1955* (Göttingen: Olzog, 1989), 202 ff.; Herfried Münkler, 'Antifaschismus und antifaschistischer Widerstand als politischer Gründungsmythos der DDR', *APZ* 1998, B 45, 16–29; Raina Zimmerling, *Mythen in der Politik der DDR. Ein Beitrag zur Erforschung politischer Mythen* (Opladen: Leske & Budrich, 2000), 37 ff.; id., 'Der Antifa-Mythos der DDR', in *Politische Mythen und Geschichtspolitik. Konstruktion—Inszenierung—Mobilisierung*, ed. Rudolf Speth and Edgar Wolfrum (Berlin: Centre Marc Bloch, 1996), 39–52; Theodor Maunz, *Deutsches Staatsrecht*, 8th edn (Munich: C. H. Beck, 1958), 11 ff. (12: Volkskammer numbers), 302 ff.

6. Fritz René Allemann, *Bonn ist nicht Weimar* (Cologne: Kiepenheuer & Witsch, 1956), 274; *Sten. Ber., 1. Wahlperiode*, i. 524–5. (Schumacher, 24–5 Nov. 1949); Konrad Adenauer, *Erinnerungen 1945–1953* (Stuttgart: Deutsche Verlags-Anstalt, 1965), 350 ff. (talk with the High Commission, 17 Aug. 1950); *Memoirs, 1945–1953* (Chicago: H. Regnery Co., 1966); *Akten zur Auswärtigen Politik* (= *AAP*) *1949–50, September 1949 bis Dezember 1950* (Munich: Oldenbourg, 1997),

322–9 (Adenauer's memorandum on 29 Aug. 1950); *AAP* 1951, *1. Januar bis 31. Dezember 1951* (Munich: Oldenbourg, 1999), 637–43 (draft of the general treaty, 22 Nov. 1951); Josef Müller, *Die Gesamtdeutsche Volkspartei. Entstehung und Politik unter dem Primat nationaler Wiedervereinigung 1950–1957* (Düsseldorf: Droste, 1990); Andreas Meier, *Hermann Ehlers. Leben in Kirche und Politik* (Bonn: Bouvier Verlag, 1991); Thomas Sauer, *Westorientierung im deutschen Protestantismus? Vorstellungen und Tätigkeit des Kronberger Kreises* (Munich: Oldenbourg, 1999); Diether Koch, *Heinemann und die Deutschlandfrage* (Munich: Kaiser, 1972); Matthias Schreiber, *Martin Niemöller* (Reinbek: Rowohlt, 1997), 108–9 (quote, Dec. 1949), 118 (quote, Nov. 1952 on 'practical' pacifism); Ulrich von Hehl ed., *Adenauer und die Kirchen* (Bonn: 1999); Hans-Peter Schwarz, *Adenauer. Der Aufstieg: 1876–1952*, 2nd edn (Stuttgart: Bouvier, 1986), 727 ff.; id., *Ära Adenauer* (note 4), 119 ff.; Erich Kosthorst, *Jakob Kaiser. Bundesminister für gesamtdeutsche Fragen 1949–1957* (Stuttgart: Kohlhammer, 1972), 141 ff.; Anselm Doering-Manteuffel, *Die Bundesrepublik Deutschland in der Ära Adenauer. Aussenpolitik und innere Entwicklung 1949–1963*, 2nd edn (Darmstadt: Wissenschaftliche Buchgesellschaft, 1988), 36 ff.; Morsey, *Bundesrepublik* (note 3), 27 ff.; Adolf M. Birke, *Nation ohne Haus. Deutschland 1945–1961* (Berlin: Siedler, 1989), 280 ff.; *Die Bundesrepublik Deutschland und Frankreich: Dokumente 1949–1963*, 4 vols., ed. Horst Möller and Klaus Hildebrand, i. *Aussenpolitik und Diplomatie*, ed. Ulrich Lappenküper (Munich: Saur, 1997), 55 ff.; Ulrich Lappenküper, 'Der Schumann-Plan. Mühsamer Durchbruch zur deutsch–französischen Verständigung', *VfZ* 42 (1994), 403–45; *Anfänge westdeutscher Sicherheitspolitik 1945–1956*, i. *Von der Kapitulation bis zum Pleven-Plan*, ed. Roland G. Foerster et al. (Munich: Oldenbourg, 1982); Rainer Zitelmann, *Adenauers Gegner. Streiter für die Einheit* (Erlangen: D. Straube, 1991). The quote by Ulbricht in Schroeder, *SED-Staat* (note 1), 97.

7. *Die Bemühungen der Bundesrepublik um Wiederherstellung der Einheit Deutschlands durch gesamtdeutsche Wahlen. Dokumente und Akten. Januar 1954* (Bonn: Deutscher Bundes-Verlag, 1954), 83–6 (Soviet note of 10 Mar. 1952), 86–7 (first western response, 25 Mar. 1952), 87–9 (second Soviet note, 9 Apr. 1952); *AAP*, ii. 1952 (Munich: Oldenbourg, 1990), 27 ff. (minutes of the talks between Adenauer and the High Commission on the Stalin notes); Konrad Adenauer, *Teegespräche 1950–1954*, ed. Rudolf Morsey, Hans-Peter Schwarz, Hanns Jürgen Küsters, Rhöndorf edn (Berlin: Siedler, 1984), 227 ('tea' on 2 Apr. 1952); Paul Sethe, *Zwischen Bonn und Moskau* (Stuttgart: Heinrich Scheffler, 1956), 36 ff.; Wettig, *Bereitschaft* (note 5), 215 ff.; Manfred Kittel, 'Genesis einer Legende. Die Diskussion um die Stalin-Noten in der Bundesrepublik 1952–1958', *VfZ* 41 (1993), 355–89; Hermann Graml, 'Nationalstaat oder westdeutscher Teilstaat? Die sowjetischen Noten vom Jahre 1952 und die öffentliche Meinung in der Bundesrepublik Deutschland', ibid. 25 (1977), 821–64; Markus Kiefer, 'Die Reaktion auf die Stalin-Noten vom Jahre 1952 in der zeitgenössischen deutschen Publizistik. Zur Widerlegung einer Legende', *Deutschland-Archiv* 22 (1989), 56–76; Josef Becker, 'Eine neue Dolchstosslegende? Zu den Kontroversen um die Stalin-Noten von 1952', in *Kontroversen zur Zeitgeschichte. Historisch-politische Themen im Meinungsstreit*, Volker Dotterweich ed. (Munich: E. Vögel, 1998), 181–206; Hans-Peter Schwarz, ed., *Die Legende von der verpassten Gelegenheit. Die*

Stalin-Note vom 10. März 1952 (Stuttgart: Belser, 1982); id., *Aufstieg* (note 6), 906 ff.; Rolf Steininger, *Eine Chance zur Wiedervereinigung? Die Stalin-Note vom 10. März 1952. Eine Darstellung und Dokumentation auf der Grundlage britischer und amerikanischer Akten* (Bonn: Neue Gesellschaft, 1985) ('missed chance' argument); *Adenauer und die Deutsche Frage,* ed. Josef Foschepoth (Göttingen: Vandenhoeck & Ruprecht, 1988); Udo Wengst, *Thomas Dehler 1897–1967. Eine politische Biographie* (Munich: Oldenbourg, 1997); Wolkow, *Frage* (note 2), 42 ff.; Loth, *Kind* (note 2), 175 ff. On expellee statistics see Erdmann, *Zeit* (note 1), iv/2. 808–9. The 1955 opinion survey in *Jahrbuch der öffentlichen Meinung,* iii. 1958–1964 (Allensbach: Verlag für Demoskopie, 1965), 323.

8. *Schumacher* (note 2), 902 (interview with UP, 15 May 1952); Arnulf Baring, *Aussenpolitik in Adenauers Kanzlerdemokratie. Bonns Beitrag zur Europäischen Vertei-digungsgemeinschaft* (Munich: Oldenbourg, 1969), 103 ff., 217 ff. (on the changes to the 'binding clause': 409 ff.); Andreas Hillgruber, *Europa in der Weltpolitik der Nachkriegszeit 1945–1963,* 4th edn (Munich: Oldenbourg, 1993), 56 ff.; Gregor Schöllgen, *Die Aussenpolitik der Bundesrepublik Deutschland. Von den Anfängen bis zur Gegenwart* (Munich: C. H. Beck, 1999), 18 ff.; Morsey, *Bundesrepublik* (note 3), 29 ff.; Görtemaker, *Geschichte* (note 1), 271 ff.; Schwarz, *Ära Adenauer* (note 4), 169 ff.; id., *Aufstieg* (note 6), 925 ff. German text of the Germany treaty of 26 May 1952 in *Die Auswärtige Politik der Bundesrepublik Deutschland,* published by the foreign ministry (Cologne: Verlag Wissenschaft und Politik, 1972), 208–13.

9. Ulrich Mählert, *Kleine Geschichte der DDR* (Munich: C. H. Beck, 1998), 56 ff.; Ehrhart Neubert, *Geschichte der Opposition in der DDR 1949–1989* (Bonn: Bun-deszentrale für politische Bildung, 1997), 80 ff.; Karl Wilhelm Fricke, *Opposition und Widerstand in der DDR. Ein politischer Report* (Cologne: Verlag Wissenschaft und Politik, 1984), 71 ff.; id., *Politik und Justiz in der DDR. Zur Geschichte der politischen Verfolgung 1945–1968. Bericht und Dokumentation,* 2nd edn (Cologne: Verlag Wissenschaft und Politik, 1990); Wolfgang Eisert, *Die Waldheimer Prozesse. Der stalinistische Terror 1950* (Esslingen: Bechtle, 1993); Schroeder, *SED-Staat* (note 1), 71 ff. (109: numbers for the 'Waldheim trials'; 120: numbers of refugees; 124: wave of arrests after 17 June 1953); Weber, *DDR* (note 1), 27 ff. (31: Volkskammer election in 1950; 32–3: purges, show trials; 35: economic figures; 37: quote from Weber; 40–1: statistics for 17 June 1953); Klessmann, *Staatsgründung* (note 5), 261 ff. (on the Young Community: 267); Jeffrey Herf, 'Antisemitismus in der SED. Geheime Dokumente zum Fall Paul Merker aus SED- und MfS-Archiven', *VfZ* 42 (1994), 635–67; id., *Zweierlei Erinnerung. Die NS-Vergangenheit im geteilten Deutschland* (Berlin: Propyläen, 1998), 130 ff., orig. *Divided Memory: The Nazi Past in the Two Germanys* (Cambridge, MA: Harvard University Press, 1997); Ulrich Kluge, 'Die verhinderte Rebellion. Bauern, Genossenschaften und SED im Umfeld der Juni-Krise 1953 in der DDR', in *Demokratie in Deutschland. Festschrift für Heinrich August Winkler zum 60. Geburtstag,* ed. Wolther von Kieseritzky and Klaus-Peter Sick (Munich: C. H. Beck, 1999), 317–35; Martin Jänicke, *Der Dritte Weg. Die antistalinistische Opposition gegen Ulbricht seit 1953* (Cologne: Neuer Deutscher Verlag, 1964); Schwarz, *Ära Adenauer* (note 6), 189 (numbers of refugees); Arnulf Baring, *Der 17. Juni 1953* (Cologne: Kiepenheuer & Witsch, 1965); Armin Mitter and Stefan Wolle, *Untergang auf Raten. Unbekannte*

Kapitel der DDR-Geschichte (Munich: Bertelsmann, 1993), 27 ff.; ed. eid., *Der Tag X–17. Juni 1953* (Berlin: Ch. Links, 1995); Christoph Buchheim, 'Wirtschaftliche Hintergründe des Arbeiteraufstandes vom 17. Juni 1953 in der DDR', *VfZ* 38 (1990), 415–33; 17. Ilko-Sascha Kowalczuk, *Juni 1953—Volksaufstand in der DDR: Ursachen, Abläufe, Folgen* (Bremen: Edition Temmen, 2003).

10. *Sten. Ber., 1. Wahlperiode*, xvii. 13873 (Adenauer, 1 July 1953), 13883 (Brandt, 1 July 1953), 13903 (Max Reimann [KPD], 1 July 1953); Edgar Wolfrum, *Geschichts-politik in der Bundesrepublik Deutschland. Der Weg zur bundesrepublikanischen Erinnerung 1948–1990* (Darmstadt: Wissenschaftliche Buchgesellschaft, 1999), 65 ff. (Adenauer in Berlin, 22 June 1953: 101; 'Kuratorium Unteilbares Deutsch-land': 108 ff.; Hermann memorial, 17 June 1954: 125–6); Schwarz, *Ära Adenauer* (note 4), 104 ff. (quote: 105); Görtemaker, *Geschichte* (note 1), 119 ff.; *Der Boom 1948–1973. Gesellschaftliche und wirtschaftliche Folgen in der Bundesrepublik Deutschland und in Europa*, ed. Hartmut Kaelble (Opladen: Westdeutscher Verlag, 1992); Werner Abelshauser, *Die Langen Fünfziger Jahre. Wirtschaft und Gesellschaft der Bundesrepublik Deutschland 1949–1966* (Düsseldorf: Droste, 1987); *Sozialgeschichte der Bundesrepublik Deutschland. Beiträge zum Kontinuitätsproblem*, ed. Werner Conze and M. Rainer Lepsius (Stuttgart: Klett-Cotta, 1983); M. Rainer Lepsius, *Demokratie in Deutschland. Soziologisch-historische Konstellationsanalysen* (Göttingen: Vandenhoeck & Ruprecht, 1993) (on the 'social-moral milieus', etc.); Paul Nolte, *Die Ordnung der deutschen Gesellschaft. Selbstentwurf und Selbstbeschreibung im 20. Jahrhundert* (Munich: C. H. Beck, 2000), esp. 318 ff.; Axel Schildt, *Moderne Zeiten. Freizeit, Massenmedien und 'Zeitgeist' in der Bundesrepublik der 50er Jahre* (Hamburg: Christians, 1995); id., *Ankunft im Westen. Ein Essay zur Erfolgsgeschichte der Bundesrepublik* (Frankfurt: Fischer, 1999); Hans Günter Hockerts, *Sozialpolitische Entscheidungen im Nachkriegsdeutschland. Alliierte und deutsche Sozialversicherungspolitik 1945–1957* (Stuttgart: Klett-Cotta, 1980); *Drei Wege deutscher Sozialstaatlichkeit. NS-Diktatur, Bundesrepublik und DDR*, ed. id. (Munich: Oldenbourg, 1998); Lutz Wiegand, *Der Lastenausgleich in der Bundesrepublik Deutschland von 1949–1985* (Frankfurt: P. Lang, 1992); Constantin Goschler, *Wiedergutmachung. Westdeutschland und die Verfolgten des Nationalsozialismus 1945–1954* (Munich: Oldenbourg, 1992); *Wiedergutmachung in der Bundesrepublik Deutschland*, ed. Ludolf Herbst and Constantin Goschler (Munich: Oldenbourg, 1989); *Vertriebene in Deutschland. Interdisziplinäre Ergebnisse und Forschungsperspektiven*, ed. Dierk Hoffmann et al. (Munich: 2000); Sven Olaf Berggötz, *Nahostpolitik in der Ära Adenauer. Möglichkeiten und Grenzen 1949–1963* (Düsseldorf: Droste, 1998), 431 ff. (Israel and Middle East policies); Gerhard A. Ritter, *Über Deutschland. Die Bundesrepublik in der deutschen Geschichte* (Munich: Oldenbourg, 1998); Josef Mooser, *Arbeiterleben in Deutschland 1900–1970. Klassenlagen, Kultur und Politik* (Frankfurt: Suhrkamp, 1984); Helmut Schelsky, 'Gesellschaftlicher Wandel', *Offene Welt*, 41 (1956), 62–74.

11. Konrad Adenauer, *Erinnerungen 1953–1955* (Stuttgart: Deutsche Verlags-Anstalt, 1966), 270 ff. (quotes: 289, 304, 347); Henning Köhler, *Adenauer. Eine politische Biographie* (Berlin: Ullstein, 1994), 775 ff.; Hans-Peter Schwarz, *Adenauer. Der Staatsmann: 1952–1967* (Stuttgart: Deutsche Verlags-Anstalt, 1991), 121 ff.; id., *Ära Adenauer* (note 4), 197 ff.; Herbert Elzer, 'Adenauer und die Saarfrage

nach dem Scheitern der EVG 1954', *VfZ* 46 (1998), 667–708; *Bundesrepublik* (note 6), ed. Möller and Hildebrand, i. 285 ff.; Görtemaker, *Geschichte* (note 1), 271 ff.; Baring, *Aussenpolitik* (note 8), 329 ff.; Morsey, *Bundesrepublik* (note 3), 35 ff.; Hillgruber, *Europa* (note 3), 65 ff.; Schöllgen, *Aussenpolitik* (note 8), 34 ff.; Philipp-Christian Wachs, *Der Fall Theodor Oberländer (1905–1998). Ein Lehrstück deutscher Geschichte* (Frankfurt: Campus, 2000), 25 ff.; Franz Neumann, *Der Block der Heimatvertriebenen und Entrechteten 1950–1960. Ein Beitrag zur Geschichte und Struktur einer politischen Interessenpartei* (Meisenheim: Hain, 1968), 91 ff. Adenauer to the national CDU leadership on 11 Oct. 1954 in *Adenauer: 'Wir haben wirklich etwas geschaffen'. Die Protokolle des CDU-Bundesvorstands 1953–1957*, ed. Günter Buchstab (Düsseldorf: Droste, 1990), 258. The German text of the Germany treaty in the version of 23 Oct. 1954 in *BGBl.* 1955 ii, 305 ff.

12. Theodor Heuss, *Die grossen Reden. Der Staatsmann* (Tübingen: Wunderlich, 1965), 86 (8 May 1949), 247–62 (19 July 1954); *Schumacher, Reden* (note 2), 895–8 (letter to Liebmann Hersch, 20 Oct. 1951); Matthias Rensing, *Geschichte und Politik in den Reden der deutschen Bundespräsidenten 1949–1984* (Münster: Waxmann, 1996), 18 ff.; Peter Merseburger, *Der schwierige Deutsche. Kurt Schumacher. Eine Biographie* (Stuttgart: Deutsche Verlags-Anstalt, 1995), 501 ff.; Ulrich Herbert, *Best. Biographische Studien über Radikalismus, Weltanschauung und Vernunft 1903–1989*, 2nd edn (Bonn: Dietz, 1996), 444 ff.; Thomas Alan Schwarz, 'Die Begnadigung deutscher Kriegsverbrecher. John McCloy und die Häftlinge von Landsberg', *VfZ* 38 (1990), 375–414; Adalbert Rückerl, *NS-Verbrechen vor Gericht. Versuch einer Vergangenheitsbewältigung*, 2nd edn (Heidelberg: C. F. Müller, 1984); Peter Steinbach, *Nationalsozialistische Gewaltverbrechen. Die Diskussion in der deutschen Öffentlichkeit nach 1945* (Berlin: Colloquium, 1981); Norbert Frei, *Vergangenheitspolitik. Die Anfänge der Bundesrepublik und die NS-Vergangenheit* (Munich: C. H. Beck, 1996), 25 ff. (Adenauer in Werl: 292–3); Manfred Kittel, *Die Legende von der 'Zweiten Schuld'. Vergangenheitsbewältigung in der Ära Adenauer* (Berlin: Ullstein, 1993), 67 ff.; Ralph Giordano, *Die zweite Schuld oder Von der Last Deutscher zu sein* (Hamburg: Rasch und Röhring, 1987); Hartmut Berghoff, 'Zwischen Verdrängung und Aufarbeitung. Die bundesdeutsche Gesellschaft und ihre nationalsozialistische Vergangenheit in den fünfziger Jahren', *GWU* 49 (1998), 96–114; Jörg Friedrich, *Die kalte Amnestie: NS-Täter in der Bundesrepublik* (Frankfurt: Fischer, 1985); Helmut Dubiel, *Niemand ist frei von der Geschichte. Die nationalsozialistische Herrschaft in den Debatten des Deutschen Bundestages* (Munich: C. Hanser, 1999), 35 ff.; Herf, *Erinnerung* (note 9), 194 ff. Opinion survey results in *Jahrbuch der öffentlichen Meinung* (n. 7), 1 (1947–55), 35 (NS leaders), 138 (20 July 1944); ibid. 3 (1958–64), 256 (flag question); ibid. 5 (1968–73), 201 ('golden years').

13. Hans Freyer, *Weltgeschichte Europas* (Stuttgart: Deutsche Verlags-Anstalt, 1954), 607, 612; Ludwig Dehio, *Gleichgewicht oder Hegemonie. Betrachtungen über ein Grundproblem der neueren Staatengeschichte* (Krefeld: Scherpr, 1948); id., 'Deutsche Politik an der Wegegabel', in *Deutschland und die Weltpolitik im 20. Jahrhundert* (Munich: Oldenbourg, 1955), 143–55 (147, 154–5); Emil Franzel, 'Die deutsche Frage', *Neues Abendland*, 11 (1956), 213–43 (243); Paul Wilhelm Wenger, 'Föderalismus–deutsches Schicksal und europäisches Schicksal', ibid. 245–53 (252–3; emphases in original); id., *Wer gewinnt Deutschland? Kleinpreussische*

Selbstisolierung oder mitteleuropäische Föderation (Stuttgart: Seewald, 1959), 97 (on the *translatio*), 325–60 (speech on 20 Apr. 1958), 360–4 (reactions to speech); Karl Jaspers, *Wahrheit, Freiheit und Friede. Hannah Arendt, Karl Jaspers. Reden zur Verleihung des Friedenspreises des Deutschen Buchhandels 1958* (Munich: Piper, 1958), 9–26 (19–20, 22); id., *Freiheit und Wiedervereinigung. Über Aufgaben deutscher Politik (1960)* (Munich: Piper, 1990); Ralf Kadereit, *Karl Jaspers und die Bundesrepublik Deutschland* (Paderborn: Schöningh, 1999); Wolfrum, *Geschichtspolitik* (note 10), 226 ff. (on the 'Jaspers scandal' of 1960); Richard Faber, *Abendland. Ein 'politischer Kampfbegriff'* (Hildesheim: Gerstenberg, 1979); Helga Grebing, *Konservative gegen die Demokratie in der Bundesrepublik nach 1945* (Frankfurt: Europäische Verlagsanstalt, 1971); Axel Schildt, *Konservatismus in Deutschland. Von den Anfängen im 18. Jahrhundert bis zur Gegenwart* (Munich: C. H. Beck, 1997), 211 ff.; id., *Zwischen Abendland und Amerika. Studien zur westdeutschen Ideenlandschaft der 50er Jahre* (Munich: Oldenbourg, 1999); id., *Ankunft* (note 10), 149 ff.; *Modernisierung im Wiederaufbau. Die westdeutsche Gesellschaft der 50er Jahre*, ed. id. and Arnold Sywottek (Bonn: Dietz, 1993); *Westbindungen. Amerika und die Bundesrepublik*, ed. Heinz Bude and Bernd Greiner (Hamburg: Hamburger Edition, 1999); Anselm Doering-Manteuffel, *Wie westlich sind die Deutschen? Amerikanisierung und Westernisierung im 20. Jahrhundert* (Göttingen: Vandenhoeck & Ruprecht, 1999). For the idea of the post-war period as 'Thermidor' of the 'Third Reich' see David Schoenbaum, *Die braune Revolution. Eine Sozialgeschichte des Dritten Reiches*, 2nd edn (Munich: DTV, 1980), 25, orig. *Hitler's Social Revolution: Class and Status in Nazi Germany, 1933–1939* (New York: Doubleday, 1966). On the 'Franzel case' see Trautl Brandstaller, *Die zerpflügte Furche. Geschichte und Schicksal eines katholischen Blattes* (Vienna: Europa Verlag, 1969), 95 ff. On Gentz see the first volume of this history, 48–9, on Frantz, 207.

14. Hermann Lübbe, 'Der Nationalsozialismus im politischen Bewusstsein der Gegenwart', in *Deutschlands Weg in die Diktatur. Internationale Konferenz zur nationalsozialistischen Machtübernahme im Reichstagsgebäude zu Berlin. Referate und Diskussionen. Ein Protokoll*, ed. Martin Broszat et al. (Berlin: Siedler, 1983), 329–49 (333–4, 335, 341); Walter Dirks, 'Der restaurative Charakter der Epoche', *Frankfurter Hefte* 5 (1950), 942–54 (943–4, 951–2; emphasis in the original); Eugen Kogon, 'Die Aussichten der Restauration. Über die gesellschaftlichen Grundlagen der Zeit', ibid. 7 (1952), 165–77 (177); id., *Der SS-Staat. Das System der deutschen Konzentrationslager* (Munich: K. Alber, 1946); *Verwandlungspolitik. NS-Eliten in der westdeutschen Nachkriegsgesellschaft*, ed. Wilfried Loth and Bernd-A. Rusinek (Frankfurt: Campus, 1998); Hans-Peter Schwarz, *Die Ära Adenauer 1957–1963* (= *Geschichte der Bundesrepublik Deutschland*, iii) (Stuttgart: Deutsche Verlags-Anstalt, 1983), 323 ff.; id., *Ära Adenauer* (note 4), esp. 375 ff.; Christoph Klessmann, *Zwei Staaten, eine Nation. Deutsche Geschichte 1955–1970* (Göttingen: Vandenhoeck & Ruprecht, 1988), 21 ff.; *Vergangenheitsbewältigung durch Strafverfahren? NS-Prozesse in der Bundesrepublik Deutschland*, ed. Jürgen Weber and Peter Steinbach (Munich: G. Olzog, 1984); Frei, *Vergangenheitspolitik* (note 12), 88 ff. (Schlüter affair), 300 ff. (Ulm trial); *Geschichte vor Gericht. Historiker, Richter und die Suche nach Gerechtigkeit*, ed. id. et al. (Munich: Beck, 2000); Schildt, *Ankunft* (note 10), 107 ff.; Herf, *Erinnerung* (note 9), 194 ff.; Ritter, *Deutschland* (note 10), 13 ff.

15. Adenauer, *Erinnerungen* (note 11), 437 ff.; Schwarz, *Ära Adenauer* (note 4), 264 ff. (quote: 335); Morsey, *Bundesrepublik* (note 3), 53 ff.; Hillgruber, *Europa* (note 3), 74 ff.; Schöllgen, *Aussenpolitik* (note 8), 87 ff.; Görtemaker, *Geschichte* (note 1), 328 ff.; Klessmann, *Zwei Staaten* (note 14), 68 ff.; Helga Haftendorn, *Sicherheit und Entspannung. Zur Aussenpolitik der Bundesrepublik Deutschland 1955–1982*, 2nd edn (Baden-Baden: Nomos, 1986), 26 ff.; Bruno Thoss, 'Die Lösung der Saarfrage 1954/55', *VfZ* 38 (1990), 225–88; Hans Günter Hockerts, 'Konrad Adenauer und die Rentenreform 1957', in *Die dynamische Rente in der Ära Adenauer und heute*, ed. Konrad Repgen (Stuttgart: Belser, 1978), 11–29; Werner Abelshauser, 'Erhard oder Bismarck? Die Richtungsentscheidung der deutschen Sozialpolitik am Beispiel der Sozialversicherung in den fünfziger Jahren', *GG* 22 (1996), 376–92; Müller, *Gesamtdeutsche Volkspartei* (note 6), 378 ff.; Patrick Major, The *Death of the KPD: Communism and Anti-Communism in West Germany 1945–1956* (Oxford: Clarendon Press, 1997), 257 ff.; Otto Büsch and Peter Furth, *Rechtsradikalismus im Nachkriegsdeutschland. Studien über die 'Sozialistische Reichspartei'* (Cologne: Westdeutscher Verlag, 1967); Heinrich August Winkler, 'Die konservative Demokratie. Die Parteiverbotsurteile des Bundesverfassungsgerichts in zeitgeschichtlicher Perspektive', *GWU* 12 (1961), 435–44. The quote from Adenauer's policy speech on 22 Sept. 1955 in *Sten. Ber.*, 2. *Wahlperiode*, xxvi. 5647.

16. *Kampf um Freiheit. Dokumente zur Zeit der nationalen Erhebung 1789–1815*, ed. Friedrich Donath and Walter Markov (Berlin: Verlag der Nation, 1954); *Parteiauftrag: Neues Deutschland. Bilder, Rituale und Symbole der frühen DDR*, ed. Dieter Vorsteher (Munich: Koehler & Amelang, 1996); Alexander Abusch, *Der Irrweg einer Nation* (Berlin: Aufbau-Verlag, 1946); Harald Bluhm, 'Befreiungskriege und Preussenrenaissance in der DDR. Eine Skizze', in *Mythen* (note 5), ed. Speth and Wolfrum, 71–95 (Norden quote: 76; emphasis in the original); Schroeder, *SED-Staat* (note 1), 93 ff. (refugee numbers), 131 ff. (Ulbricht quote, 4 Mar. 1956: 133–4; numbers in Hungary: 135; on agricultural collectivization: 145; 'socialist revolution' in culture and education: 147); Weber, *Geschichte* (note 1), 45 ff. (quote: 48–9; skilled trade and retail statistics: 54); Klessmann, *Zwei Staaten* (note 14), 303 ff.; Jänicke, *Dritter Weg* (note 9), 71 ff.; Gerhard A. Ritter, 'Weder Revolution noch Reform. Die DDR im Krisenjahr 1956 und die Intellektuellen', in *Demokratie* (note 9), ed. Kieseritzky and Sick, 336–62; Thomas Klein, 'Reform von oben? Opposition in der SED', in *Zwischen Selbstbehauptung und Anpassung. Formen des Widerstand und der Opposition in der DDR*, ed. Ulrike Poppe et al. (Berlin: Ch. Links, 1995), 125–41; *Entstalinisierung. Der XX. Parteitag der KPdSU und seine Folgen*, ed. Reinhard Crusius and Manfred Wilke (Frankfurt: Suhrkamp, 1977); Carola Stern, *Ulbricht. Eine politische Biographie* (Cologne: Kiepenheuer & Witsch, 1963), 165 ff.; *Sozialgeschichte der DDR*, ed. Hartmut Kaelble et al. (Stuttgart: Klett-Cotta, 1994); Ulrich Mählert, 'Jugendpolitik und Jugendleben 1945–1961', in *Materialien der Enquete-Kommission 'Aufarbeitung von Geschichte und Folgen der SED-Diktatur in Deutschland'*, iii/2. *Ideologie, Integration und Disziplinierung*, (Baden-Baden: Nomos, 1995), 1442–88; Udo Margedant, 'Bildungs- und Erziehungssystem der DDR–Funktion, Inhalte, Instrumentalisierung, Freiräume', iii/3. 1489–1529; Charlotte Schubert, 'Phasen und Zäsuren des Erbe-Verständnisses der DDR', ibid. 1773–1811; Heinrich August Winkler, 'Kein

Bruch mit Lenin. Die Weimarer Republik im Geschichtsbild von SED und PDS', in *Streitfragen der deutschen Geschichte. Essays zum 19. und 20. Jahrhundert* (Munich: C. H. Beck, 1997), 107–22; Gregor Schöllgen, *Geschichte der Weltpolitik von Hitler bis Gorbatschow 1941–1991* (Munich: C. H. Beck, 1996), 107 ff.; Michael Lemke, *Die Berlinkrise 1958 bis 1963. Interessen und Handlungsspielräume der SED im Ost–West-Konflikt* (Berlin: Akademie Verlag, 1995), 96 ff. Ulbricht' speech to the fifth party congress in *ND*, 11 July 1958; Grotewohl's speech ('catch up and surpass'), ibid., 17 July 1958; Ulbricht's speech on 27 Oct. 1958, ibid., 29 Oct. 1958.

17. Konrad Adenauer, *Erinnerungen 1955–1959* (Stuttgart: Deutsche Verlags-Anstalt, 1967), 347 ff. (talk with Smirnov, 19 Mar. 1958: 377); Lemke, *Berlinkrise* (note 16), 731 ff. (Khrushchev's speech on 10 Nov. 1958 and Berlin ultimatum); Schwarz, *Ära Adenauer* (note 14), 19 ff. (plan for 'disengagement' : 42 ff.); Görtemaker, *Geschichte* (note 1), 355 ff.; Hillgruber, *Europa* (note 3), 84 ff.; Morsey, *Bundesrepublik* (note 1), 54 ff.; Schöllgen, *Geschichte* (note 8), 137 ff.; Andreas Wenger, 'Der lange Weg zur Stabilität. Kennedy, Chruschtschow und das gemeinsame Interesse der Supermächte am Status quo in Europa', *VfZ* 46 (1998), 69–99; Klaus Gotto, 'Adenauers Deutschland- und Ostpolitik 1954–1963', in *Adenauer-Studien*, 5 vols., ed. Rudolf Morsey and Konrad Repgen (Mainz: Matthais-Grünewald-Verlag, 1971–), iii. 3–91; Peter Siebenmorgen, *Gezeitenwechsel. Aufbruch zur Entspannungspolitik* (Bonn: Bouvier, 1990), 121 ff.; Gilbert Ziebura, *Die deutsch-französischen Beziehungen seit 1945. Mythen und Realitäten* (Pfullingen: Neske, 1970), 94 ff.; Kurt Klotzbach, *Der Weg zur Staatspartei. Programmatik, praktische Politik und Organisation der deutschen Sozialdemokratie 1945 bis 1965* (Berlin: Dietz, 1982), 467 ff. The text of the Soviet notes of 27 Nov. 1958 in *Dokumente zur Berlin-Frage 1944–1962*, 2nd edn, ed. Wolfgang Heidemeyer and Günter Hindrichs (Munich: Oldenbourg, 1962), 300–35; of 10 Nov. 1959, ibid. 373–5.

18. Adenauer, *Erinnerungen 1955–1959* (note 17), 483 ff.; Heinrich Krone, *Tagebücher*, i. *1945–1961* (Düsseldorf: Droste, 1995), 328–68 (notes of 3 Feb.–1 July 1959); Daniel Koerfer, *Kampf ums Kanzleramt. Erhard und Adenauer* (Stuttgart: Deutsche Verlags-Anstalt, 1987), 227 ff.; *Parteiprogramme* (note 2), ed. Mommsen, 680–98 (SPD Godesberg platform, 1959); *Sten. Ber., 3. Wahlperiode*, xlvi. 7056–7, 7061 (Wehner, 30 June 1960); Klotzbach, *Weg* (note 17), 433 ff.; Petra Weber, *Carlo Schmid 1896–1979. Eine Biographie* (Munich: C. H. Beck, 1996), 631 ff.; Hartmut Soell, *Fritz Erler. Eine Biographie*, 2 vols. (Berlin: Dietz, 1976), i. 413 ff.; Terence Prittie, *Willy Brandt. Biographie* (Frankfurt: Goverts Krüger Stahlberg, 1973), 246 ff.; Schwarz, *Ära Adenauer* (note 14), 177 ff.; id., *Adenauer* (note 11), 502 ff.; Rüdiger Altmann, *Das Erbe Adenauers*, 3rd edn (Stuttgart: Seewald, 1960), 87 ff. On the SPD platform debate in the Weimar Republic see the first volume of this history, 385–6.

19. Konrad Adenauer, *Erinnerungen 1959–1963. Fragmente* (Stuttgart: Deutsche Verlags-Anstalt, 1968), 42 ff.; *Memoirs, 1945–1953* (Chicago: H. Regnery Co., 1966); Schöllgen, *Geschichte* (note 16), 149–50; Schwarz, *Ära Adenauer* (note 14), 103 ff., 141 ff.; Birke, *Nation* (note 6), 475 ff.; Lemke, *Berlinkrise* (note 16), 149 ff.; Hillgruber, *Europa* (note 3), 93 ff.; Schröder, *SED-Staat* (note 1), 162 ff. (Ulbricht, 15 June 1961: 167); Weber, *DDR* (note 1), 53 ff. (refugee numbers for April 1961: 55); Helge Heidemeyer, *Flucht und Zuwanderung aus der SBZ/DDR*

1945/49. Die Flüchtlingspolitik der Bundesrepublik Deutschland bis zum Bau der Berliner Mauer (Düsseldorf: Droste, 1994), 37 ff.; Prittie, *Brandt* (note 18), 246 ff.; Hanns Jürgen Küsters, 'Konrad Adenauer und Willy Brandt in der Berlin-Krise 1958–1963', *VfZ* 40 (1992), 483–542; Walther Stützle, *Kennedy und Adenauer in der Berlin-Krise 1961–1962* (Bonn: Verlag Neue Gesellschaft, 1973), 53 ff.; Robert M. Slusser, *The Berlin Crisis of 1961. Soviet-American Relations and the Struggle for Power in the Kremlin, June–November 1961* (Baltimore: Johns Hopkins University Press, 1973); Honoré M. Catudal, *Kennedy in der Mauer-Krise. Eine Fallstudie zur Entscheidungsfindung in den USA* (Berlin: Berlin-Verlag, 1981); Norman Gelb, *The Berlin Wall* (London: M. Joseph, 1986); Michael R. Beschloss, *The Crisis Years: Kennedy and Khrushchev 1960–1963* (New York: Edward Burlingame Books, 1991); Hope M. Harrison, *Ulbricht and the Concrete 'Rose': New Archival Evidence on the Dynamics of Soviet-East German Relations and the Berlin Crisis, 1958–1961*, Cold War International History Project, Working Paper (Washington, DC: Woodrow Wilson Center, 1993); Bernd Bonwetsch and Alexej Filitow, 'Chruschtschow und der Mauerbau. Die Gipfelkonferenz der Warschauer-Pakt-Staaten vom 3.–5. August 1961', *VfZ* 48 (2000), 155–98.

20. Heinrich Potthoff, *Im Schatten der Mauer. Deutschlandpolitik 1961 bis 1990* (Berlin: Propyläen, 1999), 13 ff.; Richard Löwenthal, 'Vom kalten Krieg zur Ostpolitik', in *Die zweite Republik. 25 Jahre Bundesrepublik Deutschland—eine Bilanz*, ed. id. and Hans-Peter Schwarz (Stuttgart: Seewald Verlag, 1974), 604–99 (659 ff.); Weber, *DDR* (note 1), 53 ff.

CHAPTER 3. TWO STATES, ONE NATION 1961–1973

1. Hans-Peter Schwarz, *Die Ära Adenauer 1957–1963* (= *Geschichte der Bundesrepublik Deutschland*, iii) (Stuttgart: Deutsche Verlags-Anstalt, 1983), 141 ff. (Fechter crisis: 148–9; Adenauer's talk with Smirnov: 145; Regensburg speech: 152, 220; Schröder on Berlin: 241); Richard Löwenthal, 'Vom kalten Krieg zur Ostpolitik', in *Die zweite Republik. 25 Jahre Bundesrepublik Deutschland—eine Bilanz*, ed. id. and Hans-Peter Schwarz (Stuttgart: Seewald Verlag, 1974), 604–99 (665); Michael Lemke, *Die Berlinkrise 1958 bis 1963. Interessen und Handlungsspielräume der SED im Ost–West-Konflikt* (Berlin: Akademie Verlag, 1995), 173 ff.; Gregor Schöllgen, *Geschichte der Weltpolitik von Hitler bis Gorbatschow 1941–1991* (Munich: C. H. Beck, 1996), 162 ff.; Heinrich Potthoff, *Im Schatten der Mauer. Deutschlandpolitik 1961 bis 1990* (Berlin: Propyläen, 1999), 13 ff.; A. James McAdams, *Germany Divided: From the Wall to Reunification* (Princeton: Princeton University Press, 1993), 3 ff.

2. David Schoenbaum, *Ein Abgrund von Landesverrat. Die Affäre um den Spiegel* (Vienna: Molden, 1968) (on reactions in the press, including those of Ritter and Bracher: 159 ff.), orig. *The Spiegel Affair* (Garden City, NJ: Doubleday, 1968); Jürgen Seifert, *Die Spiegel-Affäre* (Frankfurt: Walter-Verlag, 1966); Schwarz, *Ära Adenauer* (note 1), 261 ff.; Hartmut Soell, *Fritz Erler—Eine politische Biographie*, 2 vols. (Berlin: Dietz, 1976), ii. 735 ff.; Gerhard Ritter, 'Blind für die Wirklichkeit' (letter to the editor), *FAZ*, 10 Nov. 1962; Karl Dietrich Bracher, 'Demokratie oder Obrigkeitsstaat' (letter to the editor), ibid. 13 Nov. 1962. Adenauer's statement in the Bundestag, 7 Nov. 1962 in *Sten. Ber., 4. Wahlperiode*, li. 1984.

3. Konrad Adenauer, *Erinnerungen 1959–1963. Fragmente* (Stuttgart: Deutsche Verlags-Anstalt, 1968), 158 ff.; *AAP 1963*, i, *1. Januar bis 31. Mai 1963* (Munich: Oldenbourg, 1994), 111–31, 137–51 (negotiations in Paris, 21–2 Jan. 1963, Franco-German treaty); Hans-Peter Schwarz, *Adenauer. Der Staatsmann: 1952–1967* (Stuttgart: Deutsche Verlags-Anstalt, 1991), 810 ff.; id., *Ära Adenauer* (note 1), 255 ff. (de Gaulle's Germany visit: 259), 288 ff.; *Adenauer und Frankreich. Die deutsch-französischen Beziehungen 1958 bis 1969*, ed. id. (*Rhöndorfer Gespräche*, vii) (Bonn: Bouvier, 1985); Daniel Koerfer, *Der Kampf ums Kanzleramt. Erhard und Adenauer* (Stuttgart: Deutsche Verlags-Anstalt, 1987), 707 ff.; Gilbert Ziebura, *Die deutsch–französischen Beziehungen seit 1945. Mythen und Realitäten* (Pfullingen: Neske, 1970), 94 ff.; Thomas Jansen, 'Die Entstehung des deutsch–französischen Vertrages vom 22. Januar 1963', in *Konrad Adenauer und seine Zeit. Politik und Persönlichkeit des ersten Bundeskanzlers*, ii. *Beiträge der Wissenschaft*, ed. Dieter Blumenwitz et al. (Stuttgart: Deutsche Verlags-Anstalt, 1976), 249–71; *Die Bundesrepublik Deutschland und Frankreich: Dokumente 1949–1963*, 4 vols., ed. Horst Möller and Klaus Hildebrand, i. *Aussenpolitik und Diplomatie*, ed. Ulrich Lappenküper (Munich: Saur, 1997), 698 ff.; Waldemar Besson, *Die Aussenpolitik der Bundesrepublik. Erfahrungen und Massstäbe* (Munich: Piper, 1970), 287 ff.; *Von Adenauer zu Erhard. Studien zur auswärtigen Politik der Bundesrepublik Deutschland 1963*, ed. Rainer A. Blasius (Munich: Oldenbourg, 1994).

4. *Legacy of a President: The Memorable Words of John Fitzgerald Kennedy* (Washington, DC: US Information Agency, n.d.), 23–6 (speech on 10 June 1963); http://millercenter.virginia.edu/scripps/diglibrary/prezspeeches/kennedy/index.html (English text and audio); *Dokumente zur Deutschlandpolitik*, series 4, ix (1963), i. 442–9 (Kennedy in the Paulskirche, 25 June 1963), 460–1 (Kennedy at Schöneberg city hall, 26 June 1963), 463–7 (Kennedy at the Free University of Berlin); ii. 565–75 (Bahr in Tutzing, 15 July 1963); Willy Brandt, *Koexistenz–Zwang zum Wagnis* (Stuttgart: Deutsche Verlags-Anstalt, 1963), 7 ff. (speech at Harvard University, 2 Oct. 1962); id., *Erinnerungen* (Berlin: Propyläen, 1989), 65 ff. (Tutzing speech: 74 ff.); tr. as *My Life in Politics* (New York: Viking, 1992); Egon Bahr, *Zu meiner Zeit* (Munich: Kiepenheuer & Witsch, 1996), 152 ff.; Peter Bender, *Offensive Entspannung. Möglichkeit für Deutschland* (Cologne: 1964), 124–6 (emphasis in the original); Andreas Vogtmeier, *Egon Bahr und die deutsche Frage. Zur Entwicklung der sozialdemokratischen Ost- und Deutschlandpolitik vom Kriegsende bis zur Vereinigung* (Bonn: Dietz, 1990), 59 ff.; Löwenthal, 'Vom kalten Krieg' (note 1), 604 ff., 664–5; Schwarz, *Ära Adenauer* (note 1), 297 ff. (quote: 297); Potthoff, *Schatten* (note 1), 31 ff. The quote from Wilson on 22 Jan. 1917 ('The world must be made safe for democracy') in August Heckscher, *Woodrow Wilson* (New York: 1991), 440.

5. *Sten. Ber.*, *4. Wahlperiode*, liii. 4161–5 (Gerstenmaier, 15 Oct. 1963), 4165–7 (Adenauer, 15 Oct. 1963); Hans-Peter Schwarz, *Die Ära Adenauer 1949–1957* (= *Geschichte der Bundesrepublik Deutschland*, ii) (Stuttgart: Deutsche Verlags-Anstalt, 1981), 368 (1957 electoral campaign); id., *Ära Adenauer* (note 1), 306 ff. (Adenauer to Henkels, 15 Oct. 1963: 318); *Allensbacher Jahrbuch der Demoskopie*, viii. 1978–83 (Munich: Saur, 1983), 187 (1951 and 1963 opinion surveys); Rolf Rytlewskiand Manfred Opp de Hipt, *Die Bundesrepublik Deutschland in Zahlen*

1945/49–1980. Ein sozialgeschichtliches Arbeitsbuch (Munich: C. H. Beck, 1987), 44 (confessional data), 79 (agriculture); Werner Abelshauser, *Die langen Fünfziger Jahre. Wirtschaft und Gesellschaft der Bundesrepublik Deutschland 1949–1966* (Düsseldorf: Droste, 1987).

6. Hermann Weber, *Die DDR 1945–1990* (Munich: 1993), 57 ff. (1964–5 economic data: 61, schools: 64–5); *DDR. Dokumente zur Geschichte der Deutschen Demokratischen Republik 1945–1985*, ed. id. (Munich: DTV, 1986), 264 (Hoffmann, 24 Jan. 1962), 266–71 (SED platform, 18 Jan. 1963), 277–81 (law of 25 Feb. 1965), 283 (Honecker, 15 Dec. 1965); Klaus Schroeder with Steffen Alisch, *Der SED-Staat. Geschichte und Strukturen der DDR* (Munich: Bayerische Landeszentrale für Politische Bildungsarbeit, 1998), 149 ff. ('youth communiqué': 175; Havemann: 176; eleventh plenary session and the FDJ: 178); Christoph Klessmann, *Zwei Staaten, eine Nation. Deutsche Geschichte 1955–1970* (Göttingen: Vandenhoeck & Ruprecht, 1988), 330 ff.; Monika Kaiser, *Machtwechsel von Ulbricht zu Honecker. Funktionsmechanismen der SED-Diktatur in Konfliktsituationen 1962 bis 1972* (Berlin: Akademie Verlag, 1997), 26 ff.; *Kahlschlag. Das 11. Plenum des ZK der SED 1965. Studien und Dokumente*, ed. Günter Agde (Berlin: Aufbau Taschenbuch Verlag, 1991); Erhart Neubert, *Geschichte der Opposition in der DDR 1949–1989* (Bonn: Bundeszentrale für politische Bildung, 1997), 203 ff.; Peter Christian Ludz, 'Entwurf einer soziologischen Theorie totalitär verfasster Gesellschaft', in *Studien und Materialien zur Soziologie der DDR*, ed. id. (*Kölner Zeitschrift für Soziologie und Sozialpsychologie*, special issue 8) (Cologne: Westdeutscher Verlag, 1964), 11–58 (50); id., *Parteielite im Wandel. Funktionsaufbau, Sozialstruktur und Ideologie der SED-Führung. Eine empirisch-systematische Untersuchung* (Opladen: Westdeutscher Verlag, 1968), 37, 324–7; Ernst Richert, *Die neue Gesellschaft in Ost- und West. Analyse einer lautlosen Revolution* (Gütersloh: S. Mohn, 1966), 382; Pitirim A. Sorokin, 'Soziologische und kulturelle Annäherungen zwischen den Vereinigten Staaten und der Sowjetunion', *Zeitschrift für Politik*, NS 7 (1960), 341–70; Jan Tinbergen, 'Do Communist and Free Economies Show a Converging Pattern?', *Soviet Studies* 12 (1961), 333–41; Richard Löwenthal, 'Vom Absterben der Russischen Revolution. Zu Chruschtschows Sturz durch die Parteioligarchie (1965)', in *Weltpolitische Betrachtungen. Essays aus zwei Jahrzehnten* (Göttingen: Vandenhoeck & Ruprecht, 1983), 95–109 (107–9). Text of the 'National Document' in *Das Programm der SED. Das vierte Statut der SED. Das Nationale Dokument*, ed. Stefan Thomas (Cologne: Verlag Wissenschaft und Politik, 1963), 134–60 (quotes: 151); SED platform: 28–109 (quote: 57). On Erich Apel's death see Klaus Wiegrefe, 'Wohin führt das?', *Der Spiegel*, no. 10, 6 March 2000.

7. Klaus Hildebrand, *Von Erhard zur Grossen Koalition 1963–1969* (= *Geschichte der Bundesrepublik Deutschland*, iv) (Stuttgart: Deutsche Verlags-Anstalt, 1984), 92 ff.; Wolfram F. Hanrieder, *Die stabile Krise. Ziele und Entscheidungen der bundesrepublikanischen Aussenpolitik 1949–1969* (Düsseldorf: Droste, 1971), 57 ff., orig. *The Stable Crisis: Two Decades of German Foreign Policy* (New York: Harper & Row, 1970); Kurt Klotzbach, *Der Weg zur Staatspartei. Programmatik, praktische Politik und Organisation der deutschen Sozialdemokratie 1945 bis 1965* (Berlin: Dietz, 1982), 588 ff. (1965 electoral campaign); Schöllgen, *Geschichte* (note 1), 195 ff. (break between Beijing and Moscow); Ziebura, *Beziehungen* (note

3), 119 ff.; Löwenthal, 'Vom kalten Krieg' (note 6), 665 ff.; Rytlewski and Opp de Hipt, *Bundesrepublik* (note 5), 141 (unemployment). Brandt's statements to the SPD leadership committees on 25 Sept. 1965 in *SPD. Pressemitteilungen und Informationen*, no. 584, 25 Sept. 1965.

8. *Sten. Ber.*, *5. Wahlperiode*, lx. 17–33 (Erhard, 10 Nov. 1965), lxiii. 3656–65 (Kiesinger, 13 Dec. 1966); *Dokumente* (note 4), series 4, xi, 869–897 (EKD memorandum, quote: 896), 973–6 (message from the Catholic bishops, quote: 775), xii. 381–5 (government peace note from 25 Mar. 1966), 401 ff. (documents on SPD–SED exchange of speakers); Rudolf Morsey, 'Die Vorbereitung der Grossen Koalition von 1966. Unionspolitiker im Zusammenspiel mit Herbert Wehner seit 1962', in *Von der Arbeiterbewegung zum modernen Sozialstaat. Festschrift für Gerhard A. Ritter*, ed. Jürgen Kocka et al. (Munich: Saur, 1994), 462–78; Klaus Schönhoven, 'Entscheidung für die Grosse Koalition. Die Sozialdemokratie in der Regierungskrise im Herbst 1966', in *Gestaltungskraft des Politischen, Festschrift für Eberhard Kolb*, ed. Wolfram Pytaand Ludwig Richter (Berlin: Duncker & Humblot, 1998), 379–97; *AAP* 1966, ii, *1. Juli bis 31. Dezember 1966* (Munich: 1997), 1242–51, 1263–8 (talks between Johnson and Erhard, 26–7 Sept. 1966); Willy Brandt, *Begegnungen und Einsichten. Die Jahre 1960–1975* (Hamburg: Hoffmann und Campe, 1976), 163 ff.; *People and Politics: The Years 1960–1975* (London: Collins, 1978); id., *Erinnerungen* (note 4), 82–3 (exchange of speakers); Hildebrand, *Von Erhard* (note 7), 160 ff. (1965–6 economic data: 206; chancellorship crisis: 216 ff.; 241 ff.: formation of the Grand Coalition); *Begegnungen mit Kurt Georg Kiesinger. Festgabe zum 80. Geburtstag*, ed. Dieter Oberndörfer (Stuttgart: Deutsche Verlags-Anstalt, 1984), 83 ff. (minutes of 7 Nov. 1944: 127–30); Klessmann, *Zwei Staaten* (note 6), 193 ff. (Grass–Brandt correspondence: 525–6); Alf Mintzel, *Geschichte der CSU. Ein Überblick* (Opladen: Westdeutscher Verlag, 1977), 386 ff. The SPD eight point plan ('Tasks for a new government') of 12 Nov. 1966 in *Jahrbuch der Sozialdemokratischen Partei Deutschlands 1966/67* (Bad Godesberg, Neuer Vorwärts Verlag, 1968), 354–61. On the SPD decision for the Grand Coalition on 27–8 Nov. 1966 see *Die SPD-Fraktion im Deutschen Bundestag. Sitzungsprotokolle 1961–1966*, ed. Heinrich Potthoff (Düsseldorf: Droste, 1993), 1029–70.

9. Franz Josef Strauss, *Entwurf für Europa* (Stuttgart: Seewald, 1966), 50–1, 162–3; Burghard Freudenfeld, 'Das perfekte Provisorium. Auf der Suche nach einem deutschen Staat', *Hochland* 59 (1967), 421–33 (426, 433); Eugen Gerstenmaier, 'Was heisst deutsches Nationalbewusstsein heute?', ibid. 60 (1967/8), 146–50 (149–50); Helmut Schmidt, 'Bundesdeutsches Nationalbewusstsein?', ibid. 558–62 (561–2); Walter Scheel, 'Falsches Demokratieverständnis', ibid. 365–9; M. Rainer Lepsius, 'Die unbestimmte Identität der Bundesrepublik', ibid. 562–9 (567 ff.); Hans Buchheim, *Aktuelle Krisenpunkte des deutschen Nationalbewusstseins* (Mainz: Hase & Koehler, 1967), 31; Waldemar Besson, *Die Aussenpolitik der Bundesrepublik. Erfahrungen und Massstäbe* (Munich: Piper, 1970), 459; Peter Bender, *Zehn Gründe für die Anerkennung der DDR* (Frankfurt: Fischer, 1968), 5–6.

10. Fritz Fischer, *Griff nach der Weltmacht. Die Kriegszielpolitik des kaiserlichen Deutschland* (Düsseldorf: Droste, 1961); *Bericht über die 26. Versammlung deutscher*

Historiker in Berlin. 7. bis 11. Oktober 1964 (Stuttgart: E. Klett Schulbuchverlag, 1965), 42–51 (debate over workers' and soldiers' councils), 63–72 (Fischer controversy); *Der deutsche Widerstand gegen Hitler*, ed. Walter Schmitthenner und Hans Buchheim (Cologne: Kiepenheuer & Witsch, 1966); Ralf Dahrendorf, *Gesellschaft und Demokratie in Deutschland* (Munich: Piper, 1965), 444; Alexander and Margarete Mitscherlich, *Die Unfähigkeit zu trauern. Grundlagen kollektiven Verhaltens* (1st edn 1967) (Munich: Piper, 1991), 13–85 (80); Theodor W. Adorno, 'Was bedeutet: Aufarbeitung der Vergangenheit?' (1959), in *Gesammelte Schriften*, x. *Kulturkritik und Gesellschaft*, pt 2, *Eingriffe, Stichworte, Anhang* (Frankfurt: Suhrkamp, 1977), 555–72.

11. Wolfgang Fritz Haug, *Der hilflose Antifaschismus. Zur Kritik der Vorlesungsreihen über Wissenschaft und NS an deutschen Universitäten* (Frankfurt: Suhrkamp, 1967), esp. 100 (on Horkheimer); Otto Bauer, Herbert Marcuse, Arthur Rosenberg et al., *Faschismus und Kapitalismus. Theorien über die sozialen Ursprünge und die Funktion des Faschismus*, ed. Wolfgang Abendroth, intro. Kurt Kliem, Jörg Kammler, and Rüdiger Griepenburg (Frankfurt: Europäische Verlags-Anstalt, 1967 (Horkheimer quote: 5); Willy Albrecht, *Der Sozialistische Deutsche Studentenbund. Vom parteikonformen Studentenverband zum Repräsentanten der neuen Linken* (Bonn: Dietz, 1994); Tilman Fichter, *SDS und SPD. Parteilichkeit jenseits der Partei* (Opladen: Westdeutscher Verlag, 1988); id. and Siegward Lönnendonker, *Kleine Geschichte des SDS. Der Sozialistische Deutsche Studentenbund von 1946 bis zur Selbstauflösung* (Berlin: Rotbuch-Verlag, 1977); Clemens Albrecht et al., *Die intellektuelle Gründung der Bundesrepublik. Eine Wirkungsgeschichte der Frankfurter Schule* (Frankfurt: Campus, 1999); Klotzbach, *Weg* (note 7), 454 ff. The Marx quote in Karl Marx and Friedrich Engels, *Werke* (Berlin: Institute for Marxism/Leninism, Central Committee of the SED, 1959–), i. 386.

12. Hildebrand, *Von Erhard* (note 7), 352 ff. (Ehmke quote: 272; 1967–8 state elections: 467 ff.); Klessmann, *Zwei Staaten* (note 6), 245 ff. (march on 11 May 1968: 248 ff.); Wolfgang Kraushaar, *1968. Das Jahr, das alles verändert hat*, 2nd edn (Munich: Piper, 1998); *Frankfurter Schule und Studentenbewegung. Von der Flaschenpost zum Molotowcocktail 1946–1995*, 3 vols., ed. id. (Frankfurt am Main: Rogner & Bernhard bei Zweitausendeins, 1998); Ingrid Gilcher-Holtey, *'Die Phantasie and die Macht'. Mai 68 in Frankreich* (Frankfurt: Suhrkamp, 1995) (quote: 473); ed. ead., *1968. Vom Ereignis zum Gegenstand der Geschichtswissenschaft* (*GG* special issue 17)(Göttingen: Vandenhoeck & Ruprecht, 1998); Heinrich August Winkler, 'Die "neue Linke" und der Faschismus: Zur Kritik neomarxistischer Theorien über den Faschismus', in *Revolution, Staat, Faschismus. Zur Revision des Historischen Materialismus* (Göttingen: Vandenhoeck und Ruprecht, 1978), 65–117; Ulrike Ackermann, *Sündenfall der Intellektuellen. Ein deutsch–französischer Streit von 1945 bis heute* (Stuttgart: Klett-Cotta, 2000), 120 ff.; Lutz Niethammer, *Angepasster Faschismus. Politische Praxis der NPD* (Frankfurt: Fischer, 1969). For an example of the APO understanding of fascism see Johannes Agnoli, 'Die Transformation der Demokratie', in id. and Peter Brückner, *Die Transformation der Demokratie* (Frankfurt: Europäische Verlagsanstalt, 1968), 7–87; Manfred Clemenz, *Gesellschaftliche Ursprünge des Faschismus* (Frankfurt: Suhrkamp, 1972); H. C. F. Mansilla, *Faschismus und eindimensionale Gesellschaft*

(Neuwied: Luchterhand, 1971). On Marcuse's term 'repressive tolerance' see Herbert Marcuse, 'Repressive Toleranz', in Robert Paul Wolff, Barrington Moore, and Herbert Marcuse, *Kritik der reinen Toleranz* (Frankfurt: Suhrkamp, 1966), 91–128.

13. Heribert Knorr, *Der parlamentarische Entscheidungsprozess während der Grossen Koalition 1966 bis 1969. Struktur und Einfluss der Koalitionsfraktionen und ihr Verhältnis zur Regierung der Grossen Koalition* (Meisenheim: Hain, 1975), 49 ff.; Andrea H. Schneider, *Die Kunst des Kompromisses. Helmut Schmidt und die Grosse Koalition 1966–1969* (Paderborn: Schöningh, 1999); Hans Georg Lehmann, *Öffnung nach Osten. Die Ostreisen Helmut Schmidts und die Entstehung der Ost- und Entspannungspolitik* (Bonn: Verlag Neue Gesellschaft, 1984), 131 ff.; Dirk Kroegel, *Einen Anfang finden. Kurt Georg Kiesinger in der Aussen- und Deutschlandpolitik der Grossen Koalition* (Munich: Oldenbourg, 1997); Rytlewski and Opp de Hipt, *Bundesrepublik* (note 5), 141 (labour market data); Hildebrand, *Von Erhard* (note 7), 283 ff. (GDP and inflation rate: 296; Kiesinger, Adenauer and Strauss on non-proliferation treaty: 310; *Das Bild* headline on 23 Nov. 1968: 322); Gregor Schöllgen, *Die Aussenpolitik der Bundesrepublik Deutschland. Von den Anfängen bis zur Gegenwart* (Munich: C. H. Beck, 1999), 87 ff.; id., *Geschichte* (note 1), 198 ff. (de Gaulle in the USSR: 199, in Pnom Penh: 208; Vietnam War statistics: 234); Löwenthal, 'Vom Kalten Krieg' (note 1), 664 ff. (quote: 664); Besson, *Aussenpolitik* (note 9), 384 ff.; Brandt, *Erinnerungen* (note 4), 168 ff. (quote: 182); Potthoff, *Schatten* (note 1), 55 ff.; Kaiser, *Machtwechsel* (note 6), 263 ff.; *EA*, series 20 (1966), D 519 (Johnson, 7 Oct. 1966). L. B. Johnson's speech at: http://www.presidency.ucsb.edu/ws/index.php?pid=27908; *Texte zur Deutschlandpolitik* 3 (1970), 254 (FRG government statement on Germany and peace policy, 30 May 1969); *AdG* 38 (1968), 14074–8 (Warsaw Pact ultimatum, 15 July 1968); ibid., 39 (1969), 14555–6. (Budapest appeal, 20 Mar. 1969); ibid., 14613–14. (NATO communiqué, 11 Apr. 1969); *Dokumente* (note 4), series 4, xii (1966), 812–13 (Brandt, 1 June 1966); ibid., series v, i/1 (1968), 2236–41 (Harmel report, 14 Dec. 1967; text in English at: http://www.nato.int/docu/comm/49–95/c671213b.htm); ibid., series 5, ii/1 (1968), 891–4 ('signal from Reykjavik', 24 June 1968); ibid., series 5, ii/2, 1074–84 (Ulbricht, 9 Aug. 1968). Kiesinger–Stoph correspondence: ibid., series 5, i (1966/7), 1115 ff. On the Paris summit on 12–14 Jan. 1967 see *AAP 1967*, i, *1. Januar bis 31. März 1967* (Munich: Oldenbourg, 1998), 64–77, 90–102; on the Soviet memorandum from 5 July 1968: ibid., *1968*, ii, *1. Juli bis 31. Dezember 1968* (Munich: Oldenbourg, 1999), 838–42; talk between Brandt and Zarapkin, 10 Jan. 1969: ibid., *1969*, i, 1. *Januar bis 30. Juni 1969* (Munich: Oldenbourg, 2000), 31–7.

14. Klessmann, *Zwei Staaten* (note 6), 203 ff. (Augstein, Jaspers, Rasch quotes: 204); Hildebrand, *Von Erhard* (note 7), 339 ff. (FDP Germany policy), 352 ff. (DKP founding: 373), 383 ff. (electoral slogans: 387, 401; Weyer quote: 395); Gustav W. Heinemann, *Es gibt schwierige Vaterländer . . . Reden und Aufsätze 1919–1969*, ed. Helmut Lindemann (Frankfurt: Suhrkamp, 1977), 334–5. (television address, 14 Apr. 1968), 339 ff. (Bundestag speech, 10 May 1968), 350 (interview with the *Stuttgarter Zeitung*, 8 Mar. 1968); id., *Allen Bürgern verpflichtet. Reden des Bundespräsidenten 1969–1974* (Frankfurt: Suhrkamp, 1975), 13–20 (speech on

1 July 1969; emphasis in the original), 36–44 (Rastatt speech, 26 June 1974), 45–51 (speech on 17 Jan. 1971); Manfred Rensing, *Geschichte und Politik in den Reden der deutschen Bundespräsidenten 1949–1984* (Munich: Waxmann, 1996), 106 ff.; Edgar Wolfrum, *Geschichtspolitik in der Bundesrepublik Deutschland. Der Weg zur bundesrepublikanischen Erinnerung 1948–1990* (Darmstadt: Wissenschaftliche Buchgesellschaft, 1999), 258 ff. (reactions to Heinemann's speech on 18 Jan. 1971); *Politische Zeittafel 1949–1979. Drei Jahrzehnte Bundesrepublik Deutschland*, 2nd edn (Bonn: Presse- und Informationsamt der Bundesregierung, 1981), 158 (DKP founding), 169 (DM revaluation data); Arnulf Baring and Manfred Görtemaker, *Machtwechsel. Die Ära Brandt-Scheel* (Stuttgart: Deutsche Verlags-Anstalt, 1982), 27 ff.; Wolfgang Jäger, 'Die Innenpolitik der sozial–liberalen Koalition 1969–1974', in Karl Dietrich Bracher and Wolfgang Jäger and Werner Link, *Republik im Wandel 1969–1974. Die Ära Brandt* (= *Geschichte der Bundesrepublik Deutschland*, v/I)(Stuttgart: Deutsche Verlags-Anstalt, 1986), 15–160 (Wehner quote: 16); Knorr, *Entscheidungsprozess* (note 13), 219. On the 'strategy of limited conflict' see Horst Ehmke, *Mittendrin. Von der Grossen Koalition zur Deutschen Einheit* (Berlin: Rowohlt, 1994), 93; Ahlers quote in Klaus Hoff, *Kurt Georg Kiesinger. Die Geschichte seines Lebens* (Frankfurt: Ullstein, 1969), 152.

15. *Protokoll der Verhandlungen des VII. Parteitages der Sozialistischen Einheitspartei Deutschlands, 17. bis 22. April 1967 in der Werner-Seelenbinder-Halle zu Berlin* (Berlin: Dietz, 1967), ii. 308–26 (Ulbricht's concluding address; on 'socialist human community': 323), iv, 261 (CC report: retraction of 'confederation' idea); Walter Ulbricht, 'Die Bedeutung des Werkes "Das Kapital" für die Schaffung des entwickelten gesellschaftlichen Systems des Sozialismus in der DDR und den Kampf gegen das staatsmonopolistische Herrschaftssystem in Westdeutschland', in *Zum ökonomischen System des Sozialismus in der DDR* (Berlin: Dietz, 1968), 530–3 (quote: 530–1); id., *Die Bedeutung und die Lebenskraft der Lehren von Karl Marx für unsere Zeit* (speech on 2 May 1968) (Berlin: Dietz, 1968), 42 ('socialism in a modern, industrially highly developed country'), tr. as *The Significance and Vital Force of the Teachings of Karl Marx for our Era* (Dresden, Verlag Zeit im Bild, 1968); id. '20 Jahre Deutsche Demokratische Republik. Thesen', *ND*, 16 Jan. 1969; Weber, *DDR* (note 6), 67 ff. (Ulbricht's statements on socialism and on the GDR in 1967–68: 74); *DDR* (note 6), ed. id., 156–63 (excerpts from the constitution of 7 Oct. 1949), 297–8. (Ulbricht, 12 Sept. 1967), 298–9 (excerpts from the criminal code of 12 Jan. 1968), 299–303 (excerpts from the constitution of 6 Apr. 1949), 306 (Ulbricht, 22 Mar. 1969); Klessmann, *Zwei Staaten* (note 6), 368 ff. (quote: 369); Schroeder, *SED-Staat* (note 6), 181 ff. (numbers for the 1968 persecution: 187); Kaiser, *Machtwechsel* (note 6), 133 ff. (Ulbricht's plan for a letter to Heinemann: 312); Armin Mitter and Stefan Wolle, *Untergang auf Raten. Unbekannte Kapitel der DDR-Geschichte* (Munich: Bertelsmann, 1993), 367 ff. (party report, 12 Dec. 1968: 463); Falco Werkentin, *Politische Strafjustiz in der Ära Ulbricht* (Berlin: Ch. Links, 1995), 287 ff.; Neubert, *Geschichte* (note 6), 163 ff.; Gerhard Besier, *Der SED-Staat und die Kirche. Der Weg in die Anpassung* (Munich: Bertelsmann, 1993), 421 ff.; id., *Der SED-Staat und die Kirche. Die Vision vom 'Dritten Weg'* (Berlin: Propyläen, 1995), 21 ff.; Ilko-Sascha Kowalczuk, ' "Wer sich in Gefahr begibt . . . " Protestaktionen gegen die Intervention in Prag und die Folgen von 1968 für die DDR-Opposition',

in *Widerstand und Opposition in der DDR*, ed. Klaus-Dietmar Henke et al. (Cologne: Verlag Wissenschaft und Politik, 1999), 257–74; Roger Engelmannand Paul Erker, *Annäherung und Abgrenzung. Aspekte deutsch–deutscher Beziehungen 1956–1969* (Munich: Oldenbourg, 1993). For the talk between Brandt and Gromyko, 22 Sept. 1969: *AAP 1969*, ii. 1. *Juli bis 31. Dezember 1969* (Munich: 2000), 1057–63.

16. *Zeittafel* (note 14), 172 (DM revaluation), 175 (stability programme, 22 Jan. 1970), 185 (stability programme, 9 May 1971), 187 (numbers of students, building of universities/colleges); *Sten. Ber., 6. Wahlperiode*, lxxi. 20–34 (Brandt's inaugural on 28 Oct. 1969); Klessmann, *Zwei Staaten* (note 6), 260 ff. (Picht, Dahrendorf); Brandt, *Begegnungen* (note 8), 293 ff.; id., *Erinnerungen* (note 4), 214–15 ('Warsaw kneeling'), 219 (Prague treaty); *Jahrbuch der öffentlichen Meinung 1968–73* (Allensbach: Verlag für Demoskopie, 1974), 525 (opinion survey on Oder–Neisse border); Detlef Nakath, 'Erfurt, Kassel und die Mächte. Zum Beginn des deutsch-deutschen Dialogs im Frühjahr 1970', *DA* 33 (2000), 216–22; Werner Link, 'Aussen- und Deutschlandpolitik in der Ära Brandt 1969–1974', in Bracher et al., *Republik* (note 14), 163–282 (esp. 163 ff.); Jäger, 'Innenpolitik', ibid. 27 ff.; Baring, *Machtwechsel* (note 14), 197 ff.; Löwenthal, 'Vom kalten Krieg' (note 1), 681 ff. (on the Berlin agreement: 687–8); Bahr, *Zeit* (note 4), 268 ff.; Vogtmeier, *Bahr* (note 4), 118 ff.; Potthoff, *Schatten* (note 1), 73 ff. (on Bahr's secret 'channel': 82–3, 97–8); Kaiser, *Machtwechsel* (note 6), 332 ff.; Peter Bender, *Die 'Neue Ostpolitik' und ihre Folgen. Vom Mauerbau bis zur Vereinigung* (Munich: DTV, 1995), 155 ff.; Benno Zündorf, *Die Ostverträge. Die Verträge von Moskau, Warschau, Prag, das Berlin-Abkommen und die Verträge mit der DDR* (Munich: C. H. Beck, 1979), 17 ff. Ulbricht–Heinemann correspondence: *Texte* (note 13), 4 (1970), 143 ff., Brandt–Stoph correspondence: 277 ff., Erfurt meeting: 327 ff.; Kassel meeting: ibid. 5 (1970), 96 ff.; Moscow treaty: ibid., 6 (1970–1), 74 ff., Warsaw treaty: 215 ff., Brandt's television address on 7 Dec. 1970: 263–5; on 1971 Berlin agreement between the Four Powers: ibid. 8 (1971), 371 ff. The decision of the Federal Constitutional Court on 29 May 1973 in *Entscheidungen des Bundesverfassungsgerichts* (= *BverfGE*), xxxv (Tübingen: Mohr, 1974), 79–170.

17. 'Pionierleistungen für unseren Sieg im Klassenkampf', *ND*, 24 Feb. 1970 (Ulbricht, 23 Feb. 1970); *Texte* (note 13), 4 (1970), 256–74 (Ulbricht, 19 Jan. 1970); ibid. 6, 291–6 (Ulbricht, 17 Dec. 1970); *Protokoll der Verhandlungen des VIII. Parteitages der Sozialistischen Einheitspartei Deutschlands. 15. bis 19. Juni 1971 in der Werner-Seelenbinder-Halle zu Berlin, 1. bis 3. Beratungstag* (Berlin: Dietz, 1971), 34–121 (CC report; on the 'socialist nation': 56; economic policy goals: 62, 64); Peter Przybylski, *Tatort Politbüro*, i. *Die Akte Honecker* (Reinbek: Rowohlt, 1992), 101 ff., 280–8 (Brezhnev and Honecker, 28 July 1970), 289–96 (SED and CPSU delegations, 20 Aug. 1970); ibid., ii, *Honecker, Mittag und Schalck-Golodkowski* (Berlin: Rowohlt, 1992), 20 ff., 340–5 (Brezhnev, 20 Aug. 1970); Kaiser, *Machtwechsel* (note 6), 324 ff. (Honecker's notes on his talk with Brezhnev, 28 July 1970: 379–80; Ulbricht's statements on 21 Aug. 1970: 395); Stefan Wolle, *Die heile Welt der Diktatur. Alltag und Herrschaft in der DDR 1971–1989* (Berlin: Ch. Links, 1998), 40 ff. (quotes: 41, 45); *DDR* (note 6), ed. Weber, 323–5 (Hager, 14 Oct. 1971), 77 ff. (eighth party congress: 77); Schroeder, *SED-Staat* (note 6), 206 ff.

(Ulbricht on the nation question, 1970/1: 207; eighth party congress of 1971: 210–11); Jochen Staadt, 'Walter Ulbrichts letzter Machtkampf', *DA* 29 (1996), 686–700 (Brezhnev's letter to Ulbricht, 21 Oct. 1970: 694); Erich Honecker, *Reden und Aufsätze*, i (Berlin: Dietz, 1975), 431–41 (speech on 6 Jan. 1972; quote: 438); Karl-Heinz Schmidt, *Dialog über Deutschland. Studien zur Deutschlandpolitik von KPdSU und SED (1960–1979)* (Baden-Baden: Nomos, 1998); Alfred Kosing and Walter Schmidt,' Zur Herausbildung der sozialistischen Nation in der DDR', *Einheit*, 29 (1974), 179–88; Jens Hacker, 'SED und nationale Frage', in *Die SED in Geschichte und Gegenwart*, ed. Ute Spittmann (Cologne: Edition Deutschland Archiv, 1987), 43–64; Ulrich Neuhäusser-Wespy, 'Nation neuen Typs. Zur Konstruktion einer sozialistischen Nation in der DDR', *Deutschland-Studien* 32 (1975), 357–65; Gottfried Ziegler, *Die Haltung von SED und DDR zur Einheit Deutschlands* (Cologne: Verlag Wissenschaft und Politik, 1988); Heinrich August Winkler, 'Nationalismus, Nationalstaat und nationale Frage in Deutschland seit 1945', in *Nationalismus, Nationalitäten, Supranationalität. Europa nach 1945*, ed. id. and Hartmut Kaelble (Stuttgart: Klett-Cotta, 1993), 12–33.

18. *Texte* (note 13), 9 (1972), 548–9. (CDU national committee, 24 Jan. 1972); *Sten. Ber., 6. Wahlperiode*, lxxix. 9764 (Barzel, 23 Feb. 1972), 10704–5. (Scheel, 27 Apr. 1972), 10711 (Brandt, 27 Apr. 1972); Brandt, *Begegnungen* (note 8), 560 ff.; id., *Erinnerungen* (note 4), 283 ff.; Bahr, *Zeit* (note 4), 381 ff.; Rainer Barzel, *Auf dem Drahtseil* (Munich: Droemer-Knaur, 1978), 59 ff.; Walter Leisler Kiep, *Was bleibt ist grosse Zuversicht. Erfahrungen eines Unabhängigen. Ein politisches Tagebuch* (Berlin: Philo, 1999), 53–69 (notes of 23 Feb.–17 May 1972); Henry A. Kissinger, *Memoiren 1968–1975* (Munich: Bertelsmann, 1979), 437 ff., orig. *The White House Years* (Boston: Little, Brown, 1979); Markus Wolf, *Spionagechef im geheimen Krieg. Erinnerungen* (Munich: List Verlag, 1997), 261–2; Stephan Fuchs, *'Dreiecksverhältnisse sind immer kompliziert'. Kissinger, Bahr und die Ostpolitik* (Hamburg: Europäische Verlagsanstalt, 1999); Hubertus Knabe, *Die unterwanderte Republik. Stasi im Westen* (Berlin: Propyläen, 1999), 15 ff. (on Steiner and Wienand); Gerd Lotze, *Karl Wienand. Der Drahtzieher* (Cologne: VGS, 1995), 91 ff.; Baring, *Machtwechsel* (note 14), 396 ff., 580 ff.; Link, 'Aussen- und Deutschlandpolitik' (note 16), 206 ff.; Jäger, 'Innenpolitik' (note 14), 67 ff. (text of the joint statement on the eastern treaties on 17 May 1972: 210); Löwenthal, 'Vom kalten Krieg' (note 1), 688 ff. 'Zum Fall Wagner: CSU-Spion enttarnt', *Der Spiegel*, no. 48, 27 Nov. 2000.

19. *Zeittafel* (note 4), 192 (Washington monetary conference 17–18 Dec. 1971), 193 ('Anti-Radical Decree'), 195 ('currency snake'); Bahr, *Zeit* (note 4), 393 ff.; Vogtmeier, *Bahr* (note 4), 152 ff.; Baring, *Machtwechsel* (note 14), 355 ff. ('Löwenthal paper': 358), 373 ff. (terrorism), 494–6 (Basic Treaty), 497 (television discussion on 15 Nov. 1972), 664 ff. (Schiller's letter of resignation: 673–6); Link, 'Aussen- und Deutschlandpolitik' (note 16), 241 ff.; Jäger, 'Innenpolitik' (note 14), 77 ff. (statistics on leftist extremism: 77); Winkler, 'Linke' (note 12), 107 ff.; Potthoff, *Schatten* (note 1), 104 ff.; *Texte* (note 13), 11 (1972), 259 ff. (Basic Treaty materials). The statement by historians and political scientists on the new *Ostpolitik* in *FAZ*, 15 Apr. 1972. On 'corporative' fascism see for example Agnoli, 'Transformation' (note 12), 7 ff.

20. *Sten. Ber.*, *7. Wahlperiode*, lxxxi. 121–34 (Brandt's inaugural, 18 Jan. 1973);
Willy Brandt, *Über den Tag hinaus. Eine Zwischenbilanz* (Hamburg: Hoffmann
und Campe, 1974), 57 ff. ('New Centre'); Klaus Harpprecht, *Im Kanzleramt.
Tagebuch der Jahre mit Willy Brandt* (Reinbek: Rowohlt, 2000), 19 ff.; *BVerfGE*,
xxxvi (Tübingen: Mohr, 1974), 1–36 (decision on 31 July 1973: quotes: 1–2,
26); Link, 'Aussen- und Deutschlandpolitik' (note 16), 83 ff.; Löwenthal, 'Vom
kalten Krieg' (note 1), 690 ff.; Potthoff, *Schatten* (note 1), 104 ff.; Hans Buchheim,
Deutschlandpolitik 1949–1972. Der politisch-diplomatische Prozess (Stuttgart:
Deutsche Verlags-Anstalt, 1984), 163 ff.

CHAPTER 4. RAPPROCHEMENT AND ESTRANGEMENT
1973–1989

1. Willy Brandt, *Begegnungen und Einsichten. Die Jahre 1960–1975* (Hamburg:
Hoffmann und Campe, 1976), 473 ff.; *People and Politics: The Years 1960–1975*
(London: Collins, 1978); Egon Bahr, *Zu meiner Zeit* (Munich: K. Blessing, 1996),
429 ff.; Andreas Vogtmeier, *Egon Bahr und die deutsche Frage. Zur Entwicklung der
sozialdemokratischen Ost- und Deutschlandpolitik vom Kriegsende bis zur Vereinigung*
(Bonn: Dietz, 1996), 180 ff.; Werner Link, 'Aussen- und Deutschlandpolitik in der
Ära Brandt 1969–1974', in Karl Dietrich Bracher, Wolfgang Jäger, and Werner
Link, *Republik im Wandel 1969–1974. Die Ära Brandt* (= *Geschichte der Bundesre-
publik Deutschland*, v/1) (Stuttgart: Deutsche Verlags-Anstalt, 1986), 163–282
(227 ff.; Brandt's letter to Brezhnev on 30 Dec. 1973: 231–2); Heinrich Potthoff,
Im Schatten der Mauer. Deutschlandpolitik 1961 bis 1990 (Berlin: Propyläen,
1999), 121 ff.; Arnulf Baring and Manfred Görtemaker, *Machtwechsel. Die Ära
Brandt-Scheel* (Stuttgart: Deutsche Verlags-Anstalt, 1982), 601 ff. (Wehner's
Moscow trip and Brandt's reaction: 616 ff.); Klaus Wiegrefe and Carsten Tessmer,
'Deutschlandpolitik in der Krise. Herbert Wehners Besuch in der DDR 1973', *DA*
27 (1994), 600–27 (documents on Wehner's GDR visit on 30–31 May 1973:
616–27). 'Was der Regierung fehlt, ist ein Kopf', *Der Spiegel*, no. 4, 8 Oct. 1973.
The communiqué on Brezhnev's visit to the FRG in *Texte zur Deutschlandpolitik*,
12 (1973), 569–75. On the Prague treaty: *AdG* 43 (1973), 17988–90, 18373–4.

2. Willy Brandt, *Über den Tag hinaus. Eine Zwischenbilanz* (Hamburg: Hoffmann
und Campe, 1974), 170 ff.; id., *Erinnerungen* (Frankfurt: Propyläen, 1989), 315 ff.,
tr. as *My Life in Politics* (New York: Viking, 1992); ' "Von zentraler Bedeutung: die
Rolle Herbert Wehners". Die Aufzeichnungen Willy Brandts über die Umstände
seines Rücktritts im Mai 1974', *FAZ*, 26 Jan. 1994; Klaus Harpprecht, *Im
Kanzleramt. Tagebuch der Jahre mit Willy Brandt* (Reinbek: Rowohlt, 2000),
540 ff.; Hans-Dietrich Genscher, *Erinnerungen* (Berlin: Siedler, 1995), 194 ff., tr.
as *Rebuilding a House Divided: A Memoir by the Architect of Germany's Reunification*
(New York: Broadway Books, 1998); Günther Nollau, *Das Amt. 50 Jahre Zeuge
der Geschichte* (Munich: Bertelsmann, 1978), 253 ff.; Wolfgang Jäger, 'Die
Innenpolitik der sozial–liberalen Koalition 1969–1974', in Bracher et al., *Republik*
(note 1), 15–160 (91 ff.; Brandt and the party executive, 9 Sept. 1973: 100; Zundel
quote: 111); Baring, *Machtwechsel* (note 1), 541 ff. ('April theses': 715, 717), 722 ff.
(Guillaume affair; quote from Brandt's letter offering resignation: 754); Manfred
Görtemaker, *Geschichte der Bundesrepublik Deutschland. Von der Gründung bis*

zur Gegenwart (Munich: C. H. Beck, 1999), 475 ff. (quote: 475); Richard
Löwenthal, 'Vom kalten Krieg zur Ostpolitik', in *Die zweite Republik. 25 Jahre
Bundesrepublik Deutschland—eine Bilanz*, ed. id. and Hans-Peter Schwarz (Stuttgart: Seewald, 1974), 604–99 (quote: 604). Brandt's ten-point declaration (etc.)
in *SZ*, 3 Apr. 1974.

3. Hubertus Knabe, *Die unterwanderte Republik. Stasi im Westen* (Berlin: Propyläen,
   1999), 9 ff. (number of 'IMs': 10), 42 ff.; id., *West-Arbeit des MfS. Das Zusammenspiel von 'Aufkärung' und 'Abwehr'* (Berlin: Ch. Links, 1999), 9 ff.; Patrick
   Major, *The Death of the KPD: Communism and Anti-Communism in West Germany,
   1945–1956* (Oxford: Oxford University Press, 1997), 294 ff.; Klaus Schroeder
   and Steffen Alisch, *Der SED-Staat. Geschichte und Strukturen der DDR* (Munich:
   1998), 223 ff.; Hermann Weber, *Die DDR 1945–1990*, 2nd edn (Munich:
   Bayerische Landeszentrale für Politische Bildungsarbeit, 1993), 83 ff.; *DDR.
   Dokumente zur Geschichte der Deutschen Demokratischen Republik 1945–1985*,
   ed. id. (Munich: DTV, 1986), 345–7 (changes to the constitution: 1974); Kurt
   Hager, 'Die Lösung der nationalen Frage im Sozialismus' (15 Mar. 1973), *Texte
   zur Deutschlandpolitik*, 12 (1973), 233–43; id., 'Rede auf der 9. Tagung des ZK
   der SED' (29 May 1973), ibid. 661–4; Hermann Axen, *Zur Entwicklung der
   sozialistischen Nation in der DDR* (Berlin: Dietz, 1973); Alfred Kosing and Walter
   Schmidt, 'Zur Herausbildung der sozialistischen Nation in der DDR', *Einheit*, 29
   (1974), 179–88 (183–4, 187–8); Walter Schmidt, *Das Zwei-Nationen-Konzept
   der SED und sein Scheitern. Nationsdiskussionen in der DDR in den 70er und 80er
   Jahren*, Hefte zur DDR-Geschichte, 38 (Berlin: Gesellschaftswissenschaftliches
   Forum, 1996); Erich Kitzmüller, Heinz Kuby and Lutz Niethammer, 'Der Wandel
   der nationalen Frage in der Bundesrepublik Deutschland', *APZ*, 33 (1973), 3–33;
   APZ 34 (1973), 3–31; Gebhard Schweigler, *Nationalbewusstsein in der BRD
   und der DDR* (Düsseldorf: Droste, 1973) ('bi-nationalization' argument); Ulrich
   Neuheusser-Wespy, 'Nation neuen Typs. Zur Konstruktion einer sozialistischen
   Nation in der DDR', *Deutschland-Studien*, 32 (1975), 357–65; Gottfried Ziegler,
   Die Haltung von SED und DDR zur Einheit Deutschlands (Cologne: Verlag
   Wissenschaft und Politik, 1988). On Ulbricht see above, pp. 267–8 ff.

4. *Reden der deutschen Bundespräsidenten Heuss, Lübke, Heinemann, Scheel*, intro.
   Dolf Sternberger (Munich: C. Hanser, 1979), 190–201 (Heinemann, 24 May
   1974; quotes: 190–3), 209–17 (Scheel, 1 July 1974; quote: 215); *Sten. Ber.,
   7. Wahlperiode*, lxxxviii. 6593–605 (Schmidt, 17 May 1974), xciii, 11782–3.
   (Schmidt, 25 Apr. 1975); *Deutscher Bundestag, 7. Wahlperiode, Drucksache
   7/3885* (motion by the CDU/CSU fraction, 25 July 1975); *Texte zur Deutschlandpolitik*, series 2, 3 (1975), 330–407 (Helsinki Final Act); Helsinki text
   at http://www1.umn.edu/humanrts/osce/basics/finact75.htm; Helmut Schmidt,
   Menschen und Mächte (Berlin: Siedler, 1987), 51 ff. (Moscow visit in Oct. 1974),
   72 ff. (Helsinki), 210 (agreement with Ford), tr. as *Men and Powers: A Political
   Retrospective* (New York: Random House, 1989); id., *Weggefährten. Erinnerungen
   und Reflexionen* (Berlin: Siedler, 1996), 225 ff. (on Giscard d'Estaing); Henry
   A. Kissinger, *Memoiren 1968–1973* (Munich: Bertelsmann, 1979), 779 ff.,
   orig. *The White House Years* (Boston: Little, Brown, 1979); *Politische Zeittafel
   1949–1979. Drei Jahrzehnte Bundesrepublik Deutschland*, 2nd edn (Bonn: Presse-

und Informationsamt der Bundesregierung, 1981), 226–7, 238 (terrorism); *Die Häber-Protokolle. Schlaglichter der SED-Westpolitik 1973–1985*, ed. Detlef Nakath and Gerd-Rüdiger Stephan (Berlin: Dietz, 1999), 96, 98 (Kiep, 26 June 1975); Potthoff, *Schatten* (note 1), 134 ff.; Christian Hacke, *Die Aussenpolitik der Bundesrepublik Deutschland. Weltmacht wider Willen?* (Berlin: Klett-Cotta, 1997), 197 ff.; Gregor Schöllgen, *Geschichte der Weltpolitik von Hitler bis Gorbatschow 1941–1991* (Munich: C. H. Beck, 1996), 309 ff.; Werner Link, 'Aussen- und Deutschlandpolitik in der Ära Schmidt 1974–1982', in Wolfgang Jäger and Werner Link, *Republik im Wandel 1974–1982. Die Ära Schmidt* (= *Geschichte der Bundesrepublik Deutschland*, v/II) (Stuttgart: Deutsche Verlags-Anstalt, 1987), 275–432 (290 ff.); Wolfgang Jäger, 'Die Innenpolitik der sozial–liberalen Koalition 1974–1982', ibid. 9–272 (GDP in 1974–5: 14; Jäger quote: 19; Strauss's Sonthofen speech: 37–8); id., 'Innenpolitik' (note 2), 127 ff. On the 1974–5 economic data: Ralf Rytlewski and Manfred Opp de Hipt, *Die Bundesrepublik Deutschland in Zahlen 1945/49–1980. Ein sozialgeschichtliches Arbeitsbuch* (Munich: C. H. Beck, 1987), 141 (unemployment), 135 (prices). 'Die Sonthofener Rede von Strauss: Aufräumen bis zum Rest dieses Jahrhunderts', *Der Spiegel*. no. 11, 10 Mar. 1975. The 'Watergate' affair began when Nixon associates organized a break-in at the electoral headquarters of the Democratic party in Washington, DC, on 17 June 1972. The president attempted to cover up the fact that he was in the know. He resigned on 9 Aug. 1974 and was pardoned by his successor Gerald Ford. On the *Hochschulrahmengesetz* see above, pp. 258–9.

5. Schroeder, *SED-Staat* (note 3), 219 ff. (economic data: 220–1), 233 ff. (MfS quotes: 236, 240), 474 ff. (church policy, Eisenach synod: 479–80); Weber, *DDR* (note 3), 87 ff.; *In Sachen Biermann. Protokolle, Berichte und Briefe zu den Folgen einer Ausbürgerung*, ed. Roland Berbig et al. (Berlin: Ch. Links, 1994); Karl Wilhelm Fricke, *MfS intern. Macht, Strukturen, Auflösung der DDR-Staatssicherheit* (Cologne: Verlag Wissenschaft und Politik, 1991), 93–136 (MfS Guideline no. 1/76; quotes: 126–7); Stefan Wolle, *Die heile Welt der Diktatur. Alltag und Herrschaft in der DDR 1971–1989* (Berlin: Ch. Links, 1998), 41 ff., 241 ff.; Gerhard Besier, *Der SED-Staat und die Kirche 1969–1990. Die Vision vom 'Dritten Weg'* (Berlin: Propyläen, 1995), 65 ff. On the 'unity of economic and social policy' see *Protokoll der Verhandlungen des IX. Parteitages der Sozialistischen Einheitspartei Deutschlands im Palast der Republik in Berlin, 18. bis 22. Mai 1976* (Berlin: Dietz, 1976), i. 51–69. SED platform: ibid. 209–66 (quotes: 231, 251, 254, 263).

6. *Sten. Ber., 8. Wahlperiode*, c. 31–52 (Schmidt, 16 Dec. 1976), cii. 3756–60 (Schmidt, 20 Oct. 1977); *Bulletin. Presse- und Informationsamt der Bundesregierung*, no. 35, 14 Apr. 1977, 322–3 (Schmidt, 13 Apr. 1977), no. 104, 20 Oct. 1977 (Scheel, 18 Oct. 1977); *Zeittafel* (note 4), 243–8 (terrorism); Jäger, 'Innenpolitik' (note 4), 63 ff. (pension crisis: 64; Mogadishu: 80; statement of Schleyer's kidnappers on 19 Oct. 1977: 81; 'Mescalero' quote : 82); Görtemaker, *Geschichte der Bundesrepublik* (note 2), 584 ff.; Alf Mintzel, *Geschichte der CSU. Ein Überblick* (Opladen: Westdeutscher Verlag, 1977), 402 ff. Strauss's 'Wienerwald' speech: *Der Spiegel*, no. 49, 29 Nov. 1976.

7. Hermann Rudolph, *Die Herausforderung der Politik. Innenansichten der Bundesre-publik* (Stuttgart: Deutsche Verlags-Anstalt, 1985), 209 ff.; Dennis Meadows et al.,

Die Grenzen des Wachstums. Bericht des Club of Rome zur Lage der Menschheit (Stuttgart: Deutsche Verlags-Anstalt, 1972), orig. *The Limits to Growth: A Report for the Club of Rome's Project on the Predicament of Mankind* (New York: Universe Books, 1972); Erhard Eppler, *Ende oder Wende. Von der Machbarkeit des Notwendigen* (Stuttgart: Kohlhammer, 1975); Genscher, *Erinnerungen* (note 2), 403 ff.; Schmidt, *Menschen* (note 4), 222 ff. (quotes: 231–2); Herbert Wehner, 'Deutsche Politik auf dem Prüfstand', *NG* 26/2 (Feb. 1979), 92–4 (93); 'Wehner: Die sowjetische Rüstung ist defensiv. Konflikt mit Schmidt über Mittelstreckenraketen', *FAZ*, 5 Feb. 1979; Vogtmeier, *Bahr* (note 1), 222 ff.; Christian Hacke, *Zur Weltmacht verdammt. Die amerikanische Aussenpolitik von Kennedy bis Clinton* (Berlin: Propyläen, 1997), 213 ff.; Jäger, 'Innenpolitik' (note 4), 89 ff. (Brokdorf: 90 ff.; quote from *Die Zeit* on 19 Nov. 1976: 91; Brandt, 4–5 Sept. 1977: 106; SPD party congress 1979: 113–14; 1979 presidential election: 122; Green platform, Mar. 1986: 156); Link, 'Aussen- und Deutschlandpolitik' (note 4), 310 ff. (Bahr on the neutron bomb: 314; on double-track decision: 318); 'Identität und Zukunft der SPD. Die sechs Thesen Richard Löwenthals', *FAZ*, 7 Dec. 1981; Richard Löwenthal, 'Identität und Zukunft der Sozialdemokratie', *NG* 28 (1981), 1085–9; Lilian Klotzsch and Richard Stöss, 'Die Grünen', in *Parteien-Handbuch. Die Parteien der Bundesrepublik Deutschland 1945–1980,* 2 vols. ed. Richard Stöss (Opladen: Westdeutscher Verlag, 1983–4), ii. 1509–99; *Die Grünen. Personen–Projekte–Programme,* ed. Hans-Werner Lüdke and Olaf Dinné (Stuttgart: Seewald, 1980), 211–44 (Saarbrücken platform, short version), 245–64 (electoral platform, 12 June 1980; on defence policy: 253); Helga Haftendorn, *Sicherheit und Entspannung. Zur Aussenpolitik der Bundesrepublik Deutschland 1955–1982,* 2nd edn (Baden-Baden: Nomos, 1986), 232 ff.; ead., *Sicherheit und Stabilität. Aussenbeziehungen der Bundesrepublik zwischen Ölkrise und NATO-Doppelbeschluss* (Munich: DTV, 1986), 92 ff. (Schmidt in London, 28 Oct. 1977: 25–6); Frank Fischer, *'Im deutschen Interesse'. Die Ostpolitik der SPD von 1969 bis 1989* (Husum: Matthiesen, 2001), 58 ff. (Wehner, Feb. 1979: 74, discussion on 19 May 1979: 75); Herbert Dittgen, *Deutsch–amerikanische Sicherheitsbeziehungen in der Ära Helmut Schmidt. Vorgeschichte und Folgen des NATO-Doppelbeschlusses* (Munich: W. Fink, 1991), 110 ff.; Dan Diner, *Verkehrte Welten. Antiamerikanismus in Deutschland. Ein historischer Essay* (Frankfurt: Eichborn, 1993), tr. as *America in the Eyes of the Germans: An Essay on Anti-Americanism* (Princeton: Markus Wiener Publishers: 1996); Richard Herzinger and Hannes Stein, *Endzeit-Propheten oder die Offensive der Antiwestler. Fundamentalismus, Antiamerikanismus und Neue Rechte* (Reinbek: Rowohlt, 1995); Jeffrey Herf, *War by Other Means: Soviet Power, West German Resistance, and the Battle of the Euromissiles* (New York: Free Press, 1991); David Gress, *Peace and Survival: West Germany, the Peace Movement, and European Security* (Stanford, CA: Hoover Institution Press, 1985). On the discussion in the chancellor's office on 19 May 1979 see Horst Ehmke, *Mittendrin. Von der Grossen Koalition zur Deutschen Einheit* (Berlin: Rowohlt, 1994), 308; Hans Apel, *Der Abstieg. Politisches Tagebuch 1979–1988* (Stuttgart: Deutsche Verlags-Anstalt, 1990), 82–3 (on Bahr). The *Spiegel* interview withSchmidt in *Der Spiegel,* no. 43, 18 Oct. 1976. The text of Schmidt's London address on 28 Oct. 1977 ('Political and Economic Aspects of Western Security') in *Bulletin. Presse- und Informationsamt der Bundesregierung,* no. 112, 8 Nov. 1977. The motion of the SPD executive ('Security

Policy in the Framework of Peace Policy') in *Parteitag der Sozialdemokratischen Partei Deutschlands vom 3. bis 7. Dezember 1979* (Bonn, 1980), ii. 1228–44 (1243). Bahr's 'Conceptions of European Security' of 27 June 1968 in *AAP der Bundesrepublik Deutschland 1968*, i. *1. Januar bis 30. Juni 1968* (Munich: Oldenbourg, 1999), 796–814.

8. Schmidt, *Menschen* (note 4), 99 ff. (120: Carter, 2 July 1980), 235 ff. (240–3: Brzezinski and Carter on the 'punishment' of the USSR; 245–6: talk with Cyrus Vance); Klaus Bölling, *Die fernen Nachbarn. Erfahrungen in der DDR* (Hamburg: Gruner + Jahr, 1983), 122 ff. (Schmidt's cancellation of visit to GDR, Aug. 1980); Hacke, *Aussenpolitik* (note 4), 245 ff. (Giscard–Schmidt statement, 5 Feb. 1980: 246); Heinrich Potthoff, *Bonn und Ost-Berlin 1969–1982. Dialog auf höchster Ebene und vertrauliche Kanäle. Darstellung und Dokumente* (Bonn: Dietz, 1997), 520 ff. (plan for Schmidt to visit GDR, summer 1980); id., *Schatten* (note 1), 168 ff.; Schöllgen, *Geschichte* (note 4), 350 ff.; Link, 'Aussen- und Deutschlandpolitik' (note 4), 321 ff.; Jäger, 'Innenpolitik' (note 4), 166–7 (Union electoral slogan: 168); Richard Löwenthal, 'Die Krise von Entspannung und Gleichgewicht: Können sie gerettet werden?', in *Weltgeschichtliche Betrachtungen. Essays aus zwei Jahrzehnten* (Göttingen: Vandenhoeck & Ruprecht, 1983), 218–34; Jerzy Holzer, *Solidarität. Die Geschichte einer freien Gewerkschaft in Polen* (Munich: C. H. Beck, 1985), 110 ff. (quote from the Gdańsk agreement on 31 Aug. 1980: 129); Hartmut Kuehn, *Das Jahrzehnt der Solidarność. Die politische Geschichte Polens 1980–1990* (Berlin: BasisDruck, 1999), 15 ff. On the Comintern's 'twenty-one conditions' of 1920 see the first volume of this history, 385; on the 'papal revolution' of Gregory VII, ibid. 8.

9. Weber, *DDR* (note 3), 89 ff.; *DDR* (note 3), ed. id., 370–2 (meeting between Honecker and church leadership, 6 Mar. 1978); Schroeder, *SED-Staat* (note 3), 231 (Franke, 3 July 1980), 241 ff. (Havemann, Bahro, Berg), 246 ff. (economic situation), 250 ff. (quotes on Poland crisis); Wolle, *Welt* (note 5), 209–10; Knabe, *Republik* (note 3), 31 ff., 443–4 (Berg case); Link, 'Aussen- und Deutschlandpolitik' (note 4), 353 ff. (German–German commerce: 358–9; travel agreements: 366, 374; Brezhnev, 6 Oct., Honecker, 1 Dec. 1979: 371; Honecker, 13 Dec. 1979: 372); Potthoff, *Schatten* (note 1), 156 ff. (Schmidt in 1980 electoral campaign 1980: 173); id., *Bonn* (note 8), 469 ff. (Schmidt's plans to visit GDR, Nov.–Dec. 1979), 504–15 (Mittag and Schmidt, 17 Apr. 1980), 516–34 (meeting between Schmidt and Honecker in Belgrade, 8 May 1980), 546–7 (Schmidt to Honecker, 5 Oct. 1980), 548–61 (talk between Honecker and Gaus, 3 Nov. 1980); *Von Hubertusstock nach Bonn. Eine dokumentierte Geschichte der deutsch–deutschen Beziehungen auf höchster Ebene 1980–1987*, ed. Detlef Nakath and Gerd-Rüdiger Stephan (Berlin: Dietz, 1995), 22 ff., 43–50 (Mittag's report on 22 Apr. 1980 in the politburo on his talk with Schmidt, evaluation by Stoph and Krolikowski); Monika Tantzscher, ' "Was in Polen geschieht, ist für die DDR eine Lebensfrage!"–Das MfS und die Polnische Krise 1980/81', in *Materialien der Enquete-Kommission 'Aufarbeitung von Geschichte und Folgen der SED-Diktatur in Deutschland', v/3. Deutschlandpolitik, innerdeutsche Beziehungen und internationale Rahmenbedingungen* (Baden-Baden: Nomos, 1995), 2601–760 (Mielke, 2 Oct. 1980: 2625); *'Hart und kompromisslos durchgreifen': Die*

SED contra Polen 1980/81. Geheimakten der SED-Führung über die Unterdrückung der polnischen Demokratiebewegung, ed. Michael Kubina and Manfred Wilke (Berlin: Akademie Verlag, 1995), 83 (analysis of the CC dept. of international relations, September 1980), 97 (Joachim Hermann to Zimyanin, 27 and 31 Oct. 1980), 111 (Honecker–Olszowski talk, 20 Nov. 1980), 122 (Honecker to Brezhnev, 26 Nov. 1980), 197–200 (National Defence Ministry order on 6 Dec. 1980), 204 (Honecker to Hoffmann, 10 Dec. 1980), 204–6 (Honecker's order on 10 Dec. 1980); Peter Przybylski, *Tatort Politbüro*, i. *Die Akte Honecker* (Berlin: Rowohlt, 1991), 340–4 (Krolikowski's note of 16 Dec. 1980), 345–8 (Krolikowski's note of 13 Nov. 1980 about a talk between Stoph and Mielke). 'Zu den Zahlen Frankes: 13 000 DDR-Häftlinge seit 1964 vorzeitig freibekommen', *FAZ*, 4 July 1980. Honecker's Gera speech in Erich Honecker, *Reden und Aufsätze*, vii (Berlin: Dietz, 1982), 430–3.

10. *Sten. Ber.*, 9. *Wahlperiode*, cxvii. 25–41 (Schmidt's inaugural, 24 Nov. 1980); Schmidt, *Menschen* (note 4), 288 ff.; Apel, *Abstieg* (note 7), 180 ff. (church congress in Hamburg); Brandt, *Erinnerungen* (note 2), 353 ff.; Link, 'Aussen- und Deutschlandpolitik' (note 4), 336 ff.; Jäger, 'Innenpolitik' (note 4), 188 ff. (1981 Hamburg church congress: 188; 1980–1 economic data: 194; social statistics, xenophobia: 198; Brandt, 18 May 1981: 205); Rytlewski and Opp de Hipt, *Bundesrepublik* (note 4), 47–8 (foreigner statistics); Schöllgen, *Geschichte* (note 4), 372 (Reagan, Mar. 1983: 374); Hacke, *Weltmacht* (note 7), 283 ff.; Knabe, *Republik* (note 3), 243 ff. (peace movement); Fischer, *Interesse* (note 7), 98 ff. (developments in the SPD; Bielefeld declaration, Dec. 1980: 103; Bonn peace demonstration, 10 Oct. 1981: 111). Brandt's discussion of his Moscow trip in *Der Spiegel*, no. 28, 6 July 1981.

11. Robert Michels, *Zur Soziologie des Parteiwesens in der modernen Demokratie. Untersuchungen über die oligarchischen Tendenzen des Gruppenlebens* (1911), new edn (Stuttgart: A. Kröner, 1957), 342 ff., tr. as *Political Parties: A Sociological Study of the Oligarchical Tendencies of Modern Democracy* (Glencoe: Free Press: 1958); Genscher, *Erinnerungen* (note 2), 445 ff. (on the *Wendebrief* : 446 ff.); Apel, *Abstieg* (note 7), 313–14. (Flick affair); *AdG* 51 (1981), 24977–80 (peace movement, Oct. 1981); Erwin K. and Ute Scheuch, *Cliquen, Klüngel und Karrieren. Über den Verfall der politischen Parteien–eine Studie* (Reinbek: Rowohlt, 1992), 116 ff. (117); Jäger, 'Innenpolitik' (note 4), 208 ff. (SPD fraction meeting, 8 Sept. 1981: 210–11; party donation scandal and Flick affair: 226 ff.; Jäger quote: 229); Rolf Ebbighausen et al., *Die Kosten der Parteiendemokratie. Studien und Materialien zu einer Bilanz staatlicher Parteienfinanzierung* (Opladen: Westdeutscher Verlag, 1996), 15 ff. (on Friedrich-Ebert-Stiftung: 265 ff.); Peter Lösche and Anna Otto-Hallensleben, *Wovon leben die Parteien? Über das Geld in der Politik* (Frankfurt: Fischer, 1984), 38 ff. (party finance since 1949), 53–4 (HS-30 affair). Genschers, *Wendebrief* in Joseph Bücker and Helmut Schlimbach, *Die Wende in Bonn. Deutsche Politik auf dem Prüfstand* (Heidelberg: C. F. Müller, 1983), 14–17. On the size of the payments by the 'Civic Association' see 'Die gepflegte Landschaft', *Der Spiegel*, no. 50, 13 Dec. 1999. On the illegal CDU accounts see 'CDU-Protokolle belasten Kohl schwer', *SZ*, 5–6 Feb. 2000. On the end of the Grand Coalition in 1930 see the first volume of this history, 433–5.

12. Jerzy Holzer, 'Drohte Polen 1980/81 eine sowjetische Intervention? Zur Verkündung des Kriegsrechtes in Polen am 13 Dec. 1981', *Forum für osteuropäische Ideen- und Zeitgeschichte* 1 (1997), 197–230; id., *Solidarität* (note 8), 163 (Solidarność membership), 270–1 (letter from the CC of the CPSU, 5 June 1981), 296–7 (Kania, 20 July 1981), 315 (Solidarność congress in Gdańsk; Geremek: 319), 364 (fourth plenum, 18 Oct. 1981), 391 ff. (sixth plenum, reaction of Solidarność, Glemp's letter); Kubina and Wilke ed., *Hart* (note 9), 38–9 (Brezhnev on his meeting with Kania and Jaruzelski, Aug. 1981), 387–9 (meeting of the Warsaw Pact defence ministers in Moscow, 1–4 Dec. 1981), 389–91 (preparation of martial law in Poland, 4–6 Dec. 1981), 392–3 (Honecker–Jaruzelski telephone call, 16 Dec. 1981); Potthoff, *Schatten* (note 1), 188 ff.; id., *Bonn* (note 8), 621–32 (Schmidt–Honecker telephone call, 30 Oct. 1981), 652–97 (meeting at Werbellinsee and Döllnsee, 11–13 Dec. 1981; quotes: 670, 672–3), 698–714 (Schmidt–Honecker telephone call, 12 Jan. 1982; quote: 698–9); *Hubertusstock* (note 9), ed. Nakath and Stephan, 55 ff.; Helmut Schmidt, *Die Deutschen und ihre Nachbarn. Menschen und Mächte II* (Berlin: Siedler, 1990), 64 ff. (visit to GDR, Dec. 1982); id., *Menschen* (note 4), 315 ('moral dilemma' quote); Bölling, *Nachbarn* (note 8), 126 ff. (quote: 142); Schroeder, *SED-Staat* (note 3), 266–7 (Güstrow); *Sten. Ber., 9. Wahlperiode*, cxx. 4289, 4293 (Schmidt, 18 Dec. 1981), 4295–6 (Kohl, 18 Dec. 1981); 'Schmidt berichtet dem Bundestag', *SZ*, 15 Dec. 1981 (with Strauss's statements); 'Militär unterdrückt Streiks in Warschau und Danzig', *SZ*, 17 Dec. 1981 (number of arrests); 'Historiker greift Schmidt an', *FR*, 14 Oct. 1993; 'Der Angriff gegen mich offensichtlich allein auf SED-Aufzeichnungen gestützt', *FR*, 25 Oct. 1993 (letter to the editor from Helmut Schmidt); 'Entspannungspolitik ohne Kaltschnäuzigkeit (interview with Willy Brandt)', *Die Zeit*, 5 Feb. 1982; Markus Wolf, *Spionagechef im geheimen Krieg. Erinnerungen* (Düsseldorf: Droste, 1997), 214–15, 493–4 (Herbert Wehner's talks with Wolfgang Vogel, 7–10 Aug. 1981; diary entry on 24 Aug. 1981); Egon Bahr, *Was wird aus den Deutschen? Fragen und Antworten* (Reinbek: Rowohlt, 1982), 22–3; Günter Gaus, 'Polen und die westliche Allianz oder Ein Plädoyer für die Entspannungspolitik', in *Verantwortlich für Polen?*, ed. Heinrich Böll et al. (Reinbek: Rowohlt, 1982), 109–18 (113 ff.; emphasis in the original of the *Zeit* article); Peter Bender, 'Da wird Nachdenken zur politischen Pflicht', ibid. 27–42 (41–2); Heinrich August Winkler, 'Die Polenkrise als Prüfstein. Streit um die Ostpolitik oder Sind die Deutschen Nationalisten?' (originally in *Die Zeit*, 29 Jan. 1982), ibid. 204–12; Timothy Garton Ash, *Im Namen Europas. Deutschland und der geteilte Kontinent* (Munich: Carl Hanser, 1993), esp. 457 ff., orig. *In Europe's Name: Germany and the Divided Continent* (London: Random House, 1993). The quote from Schmidt in the television interview with Friedrich Nowottny on 13 Dec. 1981 was provided by ARD (28 Apr. 2000). On the 1555 Augsburg peace see the first volume of this history, 17–18.

13. *SPD-Parteitag, 19.–23. April 1982, München. Dokumente. Beschlüsse zur Aussen-, Friedens- und Sicherheitspolitik* (Bonn: Abt. Presse u. Information, 1982), 3–7; 'Beschlüsse zur Wirtschafts- und Beschäftigungspolitik,' ibid. 3–14; text of the 'Munich declaration' in *SZ*, 24–5 Apr. 1982; Schmidt, *Menschen* (note 4), 302 ff. (Washington visit, Jan. 1982; quote from the *Wall Street Journal* : 304); 'Ostpolitik

or Illusion?', *New York Times*, 28 Dec. 1981; Jäger, 'Innenpolitik' (note 4), 214 ff.; Link, 'Aussen- und Deutschlandpolitik' (note 4), 341 ff.; Schöllgen, *Geschichte* (note 4), 376 ff.; Dittgen, *Sicherheitsbeziehungen* (note 7), 231 ff.; Bücker and Schlimbach, *Wende* (note 11), 22–3 (quotes from the *Neue Zürcher Zeitung* on 29 Apr. 1982: 47; from *Die Zeit* on 30 Apr. 1982: 49); Klaus Bohnsack, 'Die Koalitionskrise 1981/82 und der Regierungswechsel 1982', *Zeitschrift für Parlamentsfragen*, 14 (1983), 5–32.

14. 'Wie will denn die Partei vor sich selbst bestehen?', *FR*, 22 July 1982 (Helmut Schmidt in SPD fraction on 22 and 30 June 1982); 'Mein Sozi für die Zukunft', *Der Stern*, no. 29, 15 July 1982 (Lafontaine's comments); Karl-Heinz Janzen, 'Das Mass an Zumutungen ist voll. Zu den Haushaltsbeschlüssen 1983', *NG* 29 (1982), 775–7 (777); *Sten. Ber.*, *9. Wahlperiode*, cxxii. 6745–61 (Schmidt, 9 Sept. 1982), 7072–7 (Schmidt, 17 Sept. 1982), 7159–66 (Schmidt, 1 Oct. 1982), 7167–8 (Barzel, 1 Oct. 1982), 7181 (Mischnick, 1 Oct. 1982), 7194–5 (Baum, 1 Oct. 1982), 7196 (Hamm-Brücher, 1 Oct. 1982), 7201 (ballot on 1 Oct. 1982), 7202 (swearing in, 1 Oct. 1982); Klaus Bölling, *Die letzten Tage des Kanzlers Helmut Schmidt. Ein Tagebuch* (Hamburg: Rowohlt, 1982), 14 (Schmidt's reference to the end of the Grand Coalition in 1930, 31 Aug. 1982), 107 (FDP fraction, 28 Sept. 1982); Genscher, *Erinnerungen* (note 4), 445 ff.; Peter Glotz, *Kampagne in Deutschland. Politisches Tagebuch 1981–1983* (Hamburg: Hoffmann und Campe, 1986), 212–13 (Brandt, 26 Sept. 1982); Klaus Dreher, *Helmut Kohl. Leben mit der Macht* (Stuttgart: Hoffmann und Campe, 1998), 239 ff.; Jäger, 'Innenpolitik' (note 4), 234 ff. (Breit: 240; FDP fraction and party leadership, 17 Sept. 1982: 252–3; Brandt on 26 Sept.: 257); Bohnsack, 'Koalitionskrise' (note 13), 16 (Genscher, 15 Aug. 1982), 19 (Lambsdorff, 31 Aug. 1982); Bücker and Schlimbach, *Wende* (note 11), 60–70 (Lambsdorff's memorandum on 9 Sept. 1982). On the 'Borm case' see Knabe, *Republik* (note 3), 67 ff.

15. *Sten. Ber.*, *9. Wahlperiode*, cxxii. 7207 (swearing in, 1 Oct. 1982), 7215–29 (inaugural, 13 Oct. 1982), cxxiii. 8938–9 (Kohl, 17 Dec. 1982), 8939–48 (Brandt, 17 Dec. 1982), 8960–2 (Schmidt [Kempten], 17 Dec. 1982), 8962–4 (Schuchardt, 17 Dec. 1982), cxxiv. 56–74 (Kohl, 4 May 1983); Jürgen Busche, *Helmut Kohl. Anatomie eines Erfolgs* (Berlin: Berlin Verlag, 1998), 146 ff. (quote: 149); Jürgen Leinemann and Helmut Kohl, *Die Inszenierung einer Karriere* (Berlin: Aufbau Taschenbuch Verlag, 1998); Alexander Gauland, *Helmut Kohl. Ein Prinzip* (Berlin: Rowohlt, 1994); Karl Carstens, *Erinnerungen und Erfahrungen* (Boppard: Boldt, 1993), 551 ff.; Dreher, *Kohl* (note 14), 272 ff. (Carstens and Kohl, 10 Nov. 1982: 299–300); Bücker and Schlimbach, *Wende* (note 11), 167 ff. (Sommer quote: 175; Carstens's speech on 7 Jan. 1983: 201–3; decision of the *BverfGE* on 16 Feb. 1983 and reactions: 208–21); *Entscheidungen des Bundesverfassungsgerichts*, lxii (Tübingen: Mohr, 1983), 1–116 (decision on 16 Feb. 1983); Hans-Jochen Vogel, *Nachsichten. Meine Bonner und Berliner Jahre* (Munich: Piper, 1996), 151 ff.; Apel, *Abstieg* (note 7), 225 ff. (Schmidt, 26 Oct. 1982: 229; Apel on Vogel: 233); Glotz, *Kampagne* (note 14), 211 ff. (SPD electoral slogan: 278; final CDU slogan: 285; SPD 'missile campaign' poster: 290; Geissler: 291); *AdG* 52 (1982), 26161 (Schmidt's elucidations to the SPD fraction, 26 Oct. 1982), 26162 (Vogel's nomination); *AdG* 53 (1983), 26303–5 (Mitterrand in the Bundestag, 20 Jan. 1983). On the 'Letter on German Unity' compare above, p. 262

16. Eberhard von Brauchitsch, *Der Preis des Schweigens. Erfahrungen eines Unternehmers* (Bonn: Propyläen, 1999), 208 ff. (Kohl, Schily, and Geissler 1985–6: 250 ff.); Walther Leisler Kiep, *Was bleibt ist grosse Zuversicht. Erfahrungen eines Unabhängigen. Ein politisches Tagebuch* (Berlin: Philo, 1999), 311 ff.; *Flick-Zeugen. Protokolle aus dem Untersuchungsausschuss*, ed. Rainer Burchardt and Hans-Jürgen Schlamp (Reinbek: Rowohlt, 1985) (on Brauchitsch: 64 ff., Brauchitsch quote: 72–3); Hans Werner Kilz and Joachim Preuss, *Flick. Die gekaufte Republik* (Reinbek: Rowohlt, 1983); Ebbighausen et al., *Kosten* (note 11), 103 ff. (contribution scandal, amounts from Flick: 104), 141 ff. (legislation and *BverfGE* rulings); Lösche, *Wovon* (note 11), 38 ff., 105 ff.; 'CDU-Protokolle belasten Kohl schwer', *SZ*, 5–6 Feb. 2000; Uwe Lüthje's notes to Kohl (quotes from the originals), ibid.; Hans Leyendecker, 'Lügen für Kohl', ibid. 1–2 July 2000; 'In Gelddingen ist nicht nur Kohl zugeknöpft', *FAZ*, 10 Feb. 2000 (on Nau's 'collective donation'). On party finance through the state after 1982 see Peter Schindler, *Datenhandbuch zur Geschichte des Deutschen Bundestages 1983 bis 1991* (Baden-Baden: Nomos, 1994), 129 ff. On Steiner case compare above, pp. 273–4.

17. *AdG* 53 (1983), 27192–3 (SPD party congress in Cologne); Brandt, *Erinnerungen* (note 2), 367 (Bonn peace demonstration, 22 Oct. 1983); Oskar Lafontaine, *Angst vor den Freunden. Die Atomwaffen-Strategie der Supermächte zerstört die Bündnisse* (Reinbek: Rowohlt, 1983), 81 ff. (quote: 121); *Sten. Ber., 10. Wahlperiode*, cxxvi. 2506, 2509 (Brandt, 22 Nov. 1983); 'Zur Lage und Zukunft der Sozialdemokratie. Zehn Professoren üben Kritik am gegenwärtigen Kurs der Partei', *FAZ*, 28 May 1983; Karl Kaiser, 'Die SPD und ihre Glaubwürdigkeit. Die Diskussion um die Nachrüstung und die Prioritäten sozialdemokratischer Aussen- und Sicherheitspolitik', pt I, *Vorwärts*, no. 41, 6 Oct. 1983; pt II, ibid., no. 42, 13 Oct. 1983; Egon Bahr, 'Die Priorität bleibt der Friede', ibid., no. 43, 20 Oct. 1983; Karl Kaiser, 'National im anti-nuklearen Gewande. Egon Bahr und die Rückkehr zur sicherheitspolitischen Nationalstaatsidee', *Die Zeit*, 30 Mar. 1984; Heinrich August Winkler, 'Wohin treibt die SPD? Die Bundesrepublik braucht eine regierungsfähige Opposition', *Die Zeit*, 11 Nov. 1983; *Wohin treibt die SPD? Wende oder Kontinuität sozialdemokratischer Sicherheitspolitik*, ed. Jürgen Maruhn and Manfred Wilke (Munich: G. Olzog, 1984) (texts by Kaiser, Schwan, Winkler, et al.; Schmidt's speech on 19 Nov. 1983: 129–64; quotes: 162 ff.); Helmut Herles, *Machtverlust oder Das Ende der Ära Brandt* (Stuttgart: Seewald, 1983) (professors' declaration: 148–56); Peter Glotz, 'Das Flügelchen oder Antikommunismus aus Identitätsangst. Über die Kritik der Akademischen Rechten in und an der SPD', *NG* 31 (1984), 266–75; Karsten D. Voigt, 'Schrittweiser Ausstieg aus dem Rüstungswettlauf. Nach dem Berliner Parteitag der SPD', ibid. 27 (1980), 47–51 (quote: 48); Klaus Moseleit, *Die 'Zweite' Phase der Entspannungspolitik der SPD 1983–1989. Eine Analyse ihrer Entstehungsgeschichte, Entwicklung und der konzeptionellen Ansätze* (Frankfurt: P. Lang, 1991), 1 ff. (on Voigt: 1); *Die Ost- und Deutschlandpolitik in der SPD in der Opposition 1982–1989*, ed. Dieter Dowe (Bonn: Forschungsinstitut der Friedrich-Ebert-Stiftung, Historisches Forschungszentrum, 1993); Peter Bender, *Das Ende des ideologischen Zeitalters. Die Europäisierung Europas* (Berlin: Severin & Siedler, 1981), 429 ff.; id., *Deutsche Parallelen. Anmerkungen zu einer gemeinsamen Geschichte zweier getrennter Staaten*

(Berlin: Siedler, 1989), 217 ff.; Marko Martin, *Orwell, Koestler und all die anderen. Melvin J. Lasky und* Der Monat (Asendorf: Mut-Verlag, 1999); Ulrike Ackermann, *Sündenfall der Intellektuellen. Ein deutsch–französischer Streit von 1945 bis heute* (Stuttgart: Klett-Cotta, 2000), 52 ff.; Heinrich Potthoff, *Die 'Koalition der Venunft'. Deutschlandpolitik in den 80er Jahren* (Munich: DTV, 1995), 47 ff.; Vogtmeier, *Bahr* (note 1), 241 ff.; Fischer, *Interesse* (note 7), 169 ff. On the 'Löwenthal paper' of 14 Nov. 1970 compare above, p. 277; on Bahr's ideas for European security, p. 324. The Heine quote from *Heinrich Heines sämtliche Werke in zwölf Bänden* (Berlin: Hesse & Becker, n.d.), ii. 136 (*Deutschland. Ein Wintermärchen. Kaput VI*).

18. *Sten. Ber., 10. Wahlperiode,* cxxiv. 56 (Kohl, 4 May 1983); Potthoff, *Koalition* (note 17), 94–100 (Carstens–Genscher–Honecker talks in Moscow, 14 Nov. 1982), 267–88 (Honecker–H. J. Vogel talks, 14 Mar. 1984; here (278) also Honecker's use of the terms 'security partnership' and 'community of responsibility'); 305–10 (Kohl–Honecker meeting in Moscow, 12 Mar. 1985); Nakath and Stephan eds., *Hubertusstock* (note 9), 144–6, 132–44 (Honecker–Strauss meeting, 24 July 1983; quote: 134–5), 145–6 (Honecker to Kohl, 5 Oct. 1983), 150–5 (Kohl to Honecker, 24 Oct. 1983), 155–9 (Kohl to Honecker, 14 Dec. 1983; quotes: 155, 157), 159–70 (Kohl–Honecker telephone call, 19 Dec. 1983; quotes: 168, 170), 170–5 (Honecker–Kohl meeting in Moscow, 13 Feb. 1984); Franz Josef Strauss, *Die Erinnerungen* (Berlin: Siedler, 1989), 521 ff. (quote: 527–8); Alexander Schalck-Golodkowski, *Deutsch–deutsche Erinnerungen* (Reinbek: Rowohlt, 2000), 284 ff.; *Deutsche Geschichte und politische Bildung. Öffentliche Anhörungen des Ausschusses für innerdeutsche Beziehungen des Deutschen Bundestages 1981* (Bonn: Informationszentrum, 1981), 19 (Thadden); Schroeder, *SED-Staat* (note 3), 269 ff.; Przybylski, *Tatort* (note 9), i. 351 (Krolikowski, 30 Mar. 1983); Dieter Grosser, *Das Wagnis der Währungs-, Wirtschafts- und Sozialunion. Politische Zwänge im Konflikt mit ökonomischen Regeln* (= *Geschichte der deutschen Einheit in vier Bänden*, ii) (Stuttgart: Deutsche Verlags-Anstalt, 1998), esp. 25 ff.; Karl-Rudolf Korte, *Deutschlandpolitik in Helmut Kohls Kanzlerschaft. Regierungsstil und Entscheidungen 1982–1989* (= *Geschichte der deutschen Einheit in vier Bänden*, i) (Stuttgart: Deutsche Verlags-Anstalt, 1998), 161 ff. (on the term 'community of responsibility': 201, 569; Schäuble in East Berlin, 5–6 Dec. 1984: 213 ff.; on the 'Moscow declaration': 219 ff.); Karl Lamers, 'Zivilisationskritik, deutsche Identitätssuche und die Deutschlandpolitik', in *Suche nach Deutschland. Nationale Identität und die Deutschlandpolitik*, ed. id. (Bonn: Europa Union, 1983), 21–59 (Kohl quote, 1983 electoral campaign: 45); Potthoff, *Schatten* (note 1), 202 ff. Bundestag resolution on 9 Feb. 1984 in *Texte zur Deutschlandpolitik*, series 3, ii. 45–7. Text of the 'Moscow declaration' (etc.) in *Innerdeutsche Beziehungen zwischen der Bundesrepublik Deutschland und der Deutschen Demokratischen Republik 1980–1986. Eine Dokumentation* (Bonn: Bundesministerium für Innerdeutsche Beziehungen, 1986), 212.

19. 'Offener Brief zu den Vorsitzenden des Präsidiums des Obersten Sowjet der UdSSR, Leonid Breschnew', *SZ*, 21–2 Nov. 1981; Rainer Eppelmann, *Fremd im eigenen Haus. Mein Leben im anderen Deutschland* (Cologne: Kiepenheuer & Witsch, 1993), 171 ff.; Ehrhart Neubert, *Geschichte der Opposition in der DDR 1949–1989* (Bonn: Ch. Links, 1997), 335 ff. (reactions to Solidarność: 384 ff.; 'Swords

to Ploughshares': 398 ff.; 'Berlin appeal': 408; Jahn case: 433 ff., 486 ff.); Detlef Pollack, *Politischer Protest. Politisch alternative Gruppen in der DDR* (Opladen: Leske + Budrich, 2000), 62 ff.; *Opposition in der DDR von den 70er Jahren bis zum Zusammenbruch der SED-Herrschaft*, ed. Eberhard Kuhrt et al. (Opladen: Leske + Budrich, 1999), 139 ff.; 'Aufruf zum 30. Jahrestag der Gründung der Deutschen Demokratischen Republik (beschlossen vom ZK der SED, Staatsrat und dem Ministerrat der DDR sowie dem Nationalrat der Nationalen Front der DDR)', *ND*, 18 Nov. 1977; 'Interview Erich Honeckers mit der BRD-Zeitschrift *Lutherische Monatshefte*: DDR-Lutherehrung Manifestation der Humanität und des Friedens', *ND*, 6 Oct. 1983; 'Alles zum Wohl des Volkes—dafür leben, dafür arbeiten, dafür kämpfen wir. Aus dem Schlusswort von Erich Honecker auf der Bezirksdelegiertenkonferenz Berlin', *ND*, 16 Feb. 1981; Ingrid Mittenzwei, *Friedrich II. von Preussen* (Berlin: Pahl-Rugenstein, 1979); Ernst Engelberg, *Bismarck. Urpreusse und Reichsgründer* (Berlin: Siedler, 1985); Walter Schmidt, 'Zur Entwicklung des Erbe- und Traditionsverständnisses in der Geschichtsschreibung der DDR', *ZfG* 33 (1985), 195–212; Bernd Riebau, 'Geschichtswissenschaft und Nationale Frage in der Ära Honecker', *DA* 22 (1989), 533–42; Johannes Kuppe, 'Die Geschichtsschreibung der SED im Umbruch', ibid. 18 (1985), 278–94; '70 Jahre Kampf für Sozialismus und Frieden, für das Wohl des Volkes. Thesen des Zentralkomitees der SED zum 70. Jahrestag der Gründung der Kommunistischen Partei Deutschlands. Beschluss der 6. Tagung des Zentralkomitees der Sozialistischen Einheitspartei Deutschlands, 9./10. Juni 1988', *Einheit*, 43 (1988), 586–629; Dietrich Eichholtz, *Geschichte der deutschen Kriegswirtschaft, 1939–1945*, i. *1939–1941*, 2nd edn (Berlin: Akademie Verlag, 1971), 9 (example of the silence about the Jewish victims of the Nazi extermination policy); Raina Zimmerling, *Mythen in der DDR. Ein Beitrag zur Erforschung politischer Mythen* (Opladen: Leske + Budrich, 2000), 169 ff.; Hans-Ulrich Thamer, 'Nationalsozialismus und Faschismus in der DDR-Historiographie', *APZ* 13 (1987), 27–37; Angelika Timm, *Hammer, Zirkel, Davidstern. Das gestörte Verhältnis der DDR zu Zionismus und Staat Israel* (Bonn: Bouvier, 1997); Michael Wolffsohn, *Die Deutschland Akte. Juden und Deutsche in Ost und West. Tatsachen und Legenden*, 2nd edn (Munich: Bruckmann, 1996); *Studienplan für die Fachrichtung Geschichte in der Grundstudienrichtung Geschichtswissenschaften zur Ausbildung an Universitäten und Hochschulen der DDR* (Berlin: Ministerium für Hoch- u. Fachschulwesen, 1984), 5–6; Gerhard Besier, *Der SED-Staat und die Kirche 1983–1991. Höhenflug und Absturz* (Berlin: Propyläen, 1995), 1 ff.; id., *SED-Staat* (note 5), 79 ff. The quote from the *Deutsche Ideologie* in Karl Marx, *Die Frühschriften*, ed. Siegfried Landshut (Stuttgart, 1953), 346. 'Swords to Ploughshares' comes from Micah 4: 3: 'They shall beat their swords into plowshares, and their spears into pruning hooks.' On the 'swing', see above, p. 333.

20. Edgar Wolfrum, *Geschichtspolitik in der Bundesrepublik Deutschland. Der Weg zur bundesrepublikanischen Erinnerung 1948–1990* (Darmstadt: Wissenschaftliche Buchgesellschaft, 1999), 211 ff. (17 June); Dolf Sternberger, 'Verfassungspatriotismus' (1979), in *Verfassungspatriotismus. Schriften*, x (Frankfurt: Insel, 1990), 13–16 (13); id., 'Verfassungspatriotismus. Rede bei der 25-Jahr-Feier der "Akademie für politische Bildung"' (1982), ibid., 17–31 (19, 21–2, 30–1); 'Die Elbe—ein

deutscher Strom, nicht Deutschlands Grenze" ', *Die Zeit*, 30 Jan. 1981 (interview with Günter Gaus; the phrase 'entering into' (*eintreten*) in the last quote has been added by me (H.A.W.); Hans Mommsen, 'Nationalismus und transnationale Integrationsprozesse in der Gegenwart', *APZ* 9 (1980), 3–14; id., 'Aus Eins mach zwei. Die Bi-Nationalisierung Rest-Deutschlands', *Die Zeit*, 6 Feb. 1981; Egon Bahr, 'Gegen die Pharisäer', ibid.; Peter Bender, 'Reden reicht nicht', ibid.; Heinrich August Winkler, 'Nation—ja, Nationalstaat—nein. Die deutschen Gewinner von 1945 stehen in der Schuld der Verlierer', *Die Zeit*, 13 Feb. 1981 (emphases in the original); id., 'Nationalismus, Nationalstaat und nationale Frage in Deutschland seit 1945', in *Nationalismus—Nationalitäten—Supranationalität*, ed. id. and Hartmut Kaelble (Stuttgart: Klett-Cotta, 1993), 12–33; M. Rainer Lepsius, 'Die unbestimmte Identität der Bundesrepublik', *Hochland*, 60 (1967/8), 562–9 (569); Jürgen C. Hess, 'Die Bundesrepublik auf dem Weg zur Nation?', *NPL* 26 (1981), 292–324; Heinrich Best, 'Nationale Verbundenheit und Entfremdung im zweistaatlichen Deutschland. Theoretische Überlegungen und empirische Befunde', *KZSS* 42 (1990), 1–19; Kitzmüller et al., 'Wandel' (note 3), no. 33, 3 ff., no. 34, 3 ff.; Schweigler, *Nationalbewusstsein* (note 3); Karl Dietrich Bracher, *Die deutsche Diktatur. Entstehung, Struktur, Folgen des Nationalsozialismus*, 6th edn (Cologne: Kiepenheuer & Witsch, 1979), 544, tr. as *The German Dictatorship: The Origins, Structure, and Consequences of National Socialism* (Harmondsworth: Penguin University Books: 1985); id., 'Politik und Zeitgeist. Tendenzen der siebziger Jahre', in id. et al., *Republik* (note 1), 285–406 (405–6); Markus Meckel and Martin Gutzeit, *Opposition in der DDR. Zehn Jahre kirchliche Friedensarbeit–kommentierte Quellentexte* (Cologne: Bund-Verlag, 1994), 266–74 ('Der 8. Mai 1945—unsere Verantwortung für den Frieden'., Feb./Apr. 1985; quote: 272); Florian Roth, *Die Idee der Nation im politischen Diskurs. Die Bundesrepublik Deutschland zwischen neuer Ostpolitik und Wiedervereinigung (1969–1990)* (Baden-Baden: Nomos, 1995), 109 ff; 'Der Beschluss der Kultusministerkonferenz vom 23 Nov. 1978: Die Deutsche Frage im Unterricht', *GWU* 30 (1979), 343–56. On the *Hochland* debate see above pp. 224–6ff.; on Ulbricht's slogan 'surpass without catching up' ct. p. 266 above; on Thomas Abbt see the first volume of this history, 30, 43; on the 1913 citizenship law, ibid. 295.

21. Heinz Werner Hübner, 'Holocaust', in *Geschichte im Fernsehen. Ein Handbuch*, ed. Guido Knopp and Siegfried Quandt (Darmstadt: Wissenschaftliche Buchgesellschaft, 1988), 135–8 (number of viewers: 17); Richard von Weizsäcker, 'Der 8. Mai 1945–40 Jahre danach', in *Von Deutschland aus* (Berlin: Siedler, 1985), 11–36 (15–16, 18, 22, 33–4), tr. as *A Voice from Germany* (New York: Weidenfeld & Nicolson, 1987); 'Wortlos reichen sich die Generäle in Bitburg die Hand', *FAZ*, 6 May 1985 (numbers in Bitburg); 'Feingefühl, allerseits', ibid. 28 Feb. 1986; 'Übler als Fledderei', ibid. 24 Apr. 1986; Ernst Nolte, *Der Faschismus in seiner Epoche. Die Action Française. Der italienische Faschismus. Der Nationalismus* (Munich: Piper, 1963), tr. as *Three Faces of Fascism: Action Française Italian Fascism, National Socialism* (New York: Holt, Rinehart and Winston: 1966); id., *Der europäische Bürgerkrieg 1917–1945. Nationalsozialismus und Bolschewismus* (Berlin: Propyläen, 1987); id., 'Vergangenheit, die nicht vergehen will. Eine Rede, die geschrieben, aber nicht gehalten werden konnte', in *'Historikerstreit'. Die Dokumentation der*

Kontroverse um die Einzigartigkeit der nationalsozialistischen Judenvernichtung
(Munich: Piper, 1987), 39–47 (45–6; emphases in the original); Jürgen Habermas,
'Eine Art Schadensabwicklung. Die apologetischen Tendenzen in der deutschen
Zeitgeschichtsschreibung', ibid. 62–76 (71, 73, 75–6; originally in *Die Zeit*, 11
July 1986; emphasis in the original); Christian Meier, 'Eröffnungsrede zur 36.
Versammlung deutscher Historiker in Trier, 8. Oktober 1986', ibid. 204–14 (on
the term *Geschichtspolitik*: 204); Heinrich August Winkler, 'Auf ewig in Hitlers
Schatten? Zum Streit um das Geschichtsbild der Deutschen', ibid. 256–63 (origi-
nally in *FR*, 14 Nov. 1986; term *Geschichtspolitik* and the quoted passages: 262–3);
id., 'Ein europäischer Bürger namens Hitler. Ernst Noltes Entlastungsoffensive
geht weiter', *Die Zeit*, 4 Dec. 1987 (review of Nolte's *Europäischer Bürgerkrieg*);
id., 'Kehrseitenbesichtigung. Zehn Jahre danach: Ein Rückblick auf den deutschen
Historikerstreit', *FR*, 29 Oct. 1996; id., 'Lesarten der Sühne', *Der Spiegel*, no.
35, 24 Aug. 1998; Hans-Ulrich Wehler, *Entsorgung der deutschen Vergangenheit?
Ein polemischer Essay zum 'Historikerstreit'* (Munich: C. H. Beck, 1988); Charles
S. Maier, *Die Gegenwart der Vergangenheit. Geschichte und die nationale Identität
der Deutschen* (Frankfurt: Campus, 1992), orig. *The Unmasterable Past: History,
Holocaust, and German National Identity* (Cambridge, MA: Harvard University
Press, 1988); Richard J. Evans, *In Hitler's Shadow: West German Historians and
the Attempts to Escape from the Nazi Past* (New York: Pantheon Books, 1989);
Herzinger and Stein, *Endzeit-Propheten* (note 7), 63 ff. For Jenninger's speech: *Sten.
Ber.*, *11. Wahlperiode*, cxlvi. 7270–6; 'Eklat im Bundestag bei der speech Jenningers
zum Jahrestag der Pogrom-Nacht', *FAZ*, 11 Nov. 1988; the mildest evaluation:
'Well-meant, but incompetent', ibid. The earliest example of the view of Auschwitz
as a West German 'myth of origin' seems to be Hanno Loewy, 'Auschwitz als
Metapher', *taz*, 25 Jan. 1997. The Bismarck quote (from his memoirs) is as follows:
'In its revisions, the logic of history is even more stringent than our high chamber of
accounts'. Otto von Bismarck, *Die gesammelten Werke*, Friedrichsruh edn (Berlin:
O. Stollberg, 1924–), xv. 393. The term 'posthumous Adenauer left' first used
in Heinrich August Winkler, 'Wollte Adenauer die Wiedervereinigung?', *Die Zeit*,
7 Oct. 1988.

22. Friedrich Engels, 'Die preussische Militärfrage und die deutsche Arbeiterpartei
(1865)', in Karl Marx and Friedrich Engels, *Werke*, xvi (Berlin: Institute for
Marxism/Leninism, Central Committee of the SED, 1962), 37–78 (77); Mikhail
Gorbachev, *Ausgewählte Reden und Aufsätze*, iv. *Juli 1986–April 1987* (Berlin:
Dietz, 1988), 397 (concluding address at the plenum of the CC of the CPSU); id.,
Erinnerungen (Berlin: Siedler, 1995), 700 ff., tr. as *Memoirs* (New York: Doubleday:
1996); Manfred Hildermeier, *Geschichte der Sowjetunion 1917–1991. Entstehung
und Niedergang des ersten sozialistischen Staates* (Munich: C. H. Beck, 1998), 1014 ff.;
Rafael Biermann, *Zwischen Kreml und Kanzleramt. Wie Moskau mit der deutschen
Einheit rang* (Paderborn: Schöningh, 1997) (the idea of the 'common European
house', first used by Brezhnev and after 1985 by Gorbachev: 85 ff.); Hannes
Adomeit, *Imperial Overstretch: Germany in Soviet Policy from Stalin to Gorbachev:
An Analysis Based on New Archival Evidence, Memoirs, and Interviews* (Baden-Baden:
Nomos, 1998), 191 ff.; Grosser, *Wagnis* (note 18), 25 ff.; Schöllgen, *Geschichte*
(note 4), 390 ff.; Hacke, *Weltmacht* (note 7), 305 ff.; Garton Ash, *Namen* (note 12),

160 (Kohl's interview with *Newsweek*); Genscher, *Erinnerungen* (note 2), 493 ff.
(Gorbachev and Genscher, 21 July 1986; speech in Davos and reactions: 526–7; on
the president's Moscow visit, 6–11 July 1987: 543 ff.); *Sten. Ber., 11. Wahlperiode*,
cxli. 51–73 (Kohl's inaugural, 18 Mar. 1987); Richard von Weizsäcker, *Vier
Zeiten. Erinnerungen* (Berlin: Siedler, 1997), 341 ff. (343, 346); 'Der Streit der
Ideologien und die gemeinsame Sicherheit. Das gemeinsame Papier der Grundw-
ertekommission der SPD und der Akademie für Gesellschaftswissenschaften
beim Zentralkomitee der SED', *FAZ* 28 Aug. 1987; *Ost- und Deutschlandpolitik*
(note 17), ed. Dowe, 57 ff. (on '*Streitkultur* paper'); Harald Neubert, *Zum
gemeinsamen Ideologiepapier von SED und SPD aus dem Jahre 1987*, Hefte zur
DDR-Geschichte, 18 (Berlin: Helle Panke, 1994); Helmut Schmidt, 'Einer unserer
Brüder. Zum Besuch Erich Honeckers', *Die Zeit*, 24 July 1987; 'Er lässt auch fünfe
gerade sein'. Der stellvertretende SPD-Vorsitzende Oskar Lafontaine über den
DDR-Staatsratsvorsitzenden', *Der Spiegel*, no. 35, 24 Aug. 1987; Potthoff, *Koalition*
(note 7), 340–59 (Honecker–Brandt talk, 19 Sept. 1985; quote on Salzgitter:
355), 453–9 (Honecker–Bahr talk, 5 Sept. 1986), 564–668 (Honecker's visit
to FRG, 7–11 Sept. 1987; talk with Weizsäcker: 576–81; with Kohl, Schäuble,
et al.: 582–606; with Vogel: 614, 617; with Dregger and Waigel: 620–1; with
Schoppe et al.: 628 ff.; with Kelly and Bastian: 634–5; with Brandt: 637; with
Rau: 640; with Lafontaine: 653–4; with Strauss: 657–61), 662–8 (Honecker's
talk with Dohnanyi, Lafontaine, and Wedemeier, 23 Oct. 1987); id., *Schatten*
(note 1), 243 ff. (Rau quote, 18 Sept. 1986: 256); Schroeder, *SED-Staat* (note 3),
292–3 (Reagan quote, 12 June 1987: 292); Korte, *Deutschlandpolitik* (note 18),
324 ff. (number of visitors: 359–60; opinion survey results on Honecker's visit:
388); *Hubertusstock* (note 9), ed. Nakath and Stephan, 338–44 (MfS evaluation
of the reactions to Honecker's visit, 16 Sept. 1987); Willy Brandt, 'Deutsche
Wegmarken. Berliner Lektion am 11. September 1988', *Berliner Lektionen* (Berlin:
Siedler, 1989), 71–88 (quotes: 73–7); Heiner Sauer and Hans-Otto Plumeyer,
*Der Salzgitter-Report. Die Zentrale Erfassungsstelle berichtet über Verbrechen im
SED-Staat* (Esslingen: Bechtle, 1991). For Weizsäcker's Moscow visit, 6–11 July
1987: *AdG* 57/II (1987), 31236–46; Kohl's und Honecker's dinner speeches on
7 Sept. 1987: ibid. 31408–10; on revolution of 1918/19 see the first volume of
this history, 330–7, on the Socialist Workers' party, ibid. 443.

23. Hans Georg Lehmann, *Deutschland-Chronik 1945 bis 1995* (Bonn: Bouvier, 1996),
320 ff. (European policy); Desmond Dinan, *Ever Closer Union: An Introduction
to the European Community* (London: Macmillan, 1994), 129 ff.; Genscher, *Erinnerungen* (note 2), 381 ff. (quote on Th. Stoltenberg: 592; discussion of Brussels
'Lance' decision: 621); *AdG* 58 (1988), 32679–84 (Kohl's Moscow visit, 24–7
Oct. 1988), 59 (1989), 33465–8 (EC summit in Madrid, 26–7 June 1989); *EA*
44 (1989), documents 237–56 (concluding document of the NATO summit in
Brussels, 29–30 May 1989; quotes: 238, 253); *Texte zur Deutschlandpolitik*, series
3, 6 (1989), 262–3. (communiqué on Axen–Bahr paper, 7 July 1988); Kuehn,
Jahrzehnt (note 8), 365 ff.; Detlef Nakath and Gerd-Rüdiger Stephan, *Countdown
zur deutschen Einheit. Eine dokumentierte Geschichte der deutsch–deutschen Beziehungen 1987–1990* (Berlin: Dietz, 1996), 80–2 (Kohl to Honecker, 4 May 1988),
125–45 (Honecker's talk with A. Bondarenko, 30 Oct. 1988 with report on Kohl's

Moscow visit); *'Vorwärts immer, rückwärts nimmer!' Interne Dokumente zum Zerfall von SED und DDR 1988/89,* ed. Gerd-Rüdiger Stephan and Daniel Küchenmeister (Berlin: Dietz, 1994), 53–7 (MfS report on 30 Nov. 1988 on *Sputnik* ban; quote: 54); 'Der DDR-Ideologe Kurt Hager über Gorbatschows Reformkurs', *Der Stern,* no. 16, 9 Apr. 1987; Werner Weidenfeld, *Aussenpolitik für die deutsche Einheit. Die Entscheidungsjahre 1989/90* (= *Geschichte der deutschen Einheit in vier Bänden,* iv) (Stuttgart: Deutsche Verlags-Anstalt, 1998), 138 ff. (monetary union); Timothy Garton Ash, *Ein Jahrhundert wird abgewählt. Aus den Zentren Mitteleuropas 1980–1990* (Munich: Hanser, 1990), 43 ff., orig. *The Uses of Adversity: Essays on the Fate of Central Europe* (New York: Random House, 1990); id., *Namen* (note 12), esp. 189 ff. (Brandt in Warsaw, 7–8 Dec. 1985: 448); Fred Oldenburg, *Die Implosion des SED-Regimes. Ursachen und Entwicklungsprozesse* (= *Berichte des Bundesinstituts für ostwissenschaftliche und internationale Studien*) (Cologne: Bundesinstitut für Ostwissenschaftliche und Internationale Studien, 1991), no. 10, 22 ff. (pop festival, June 1987: 23); Schöllgen, *Geschichte* (note 4), 402 ff.; Potthoff, *Schatten* (note 1), 272 ff. (West German reactions to the crisis in the GDR); Schroeder, *SED-Staat* (note 3), 288 ff. (*Sputnik* ban: 295); Neubert, *Geschichte* (note 19), 629 ff.; *Opposition* (note 19), ed. Kuhrt et al., 427 ff. On Gorbachev's rejection of the Brezhnev doctrine see Daniel Küchenmeister and Gerd-Rüdiger Stephan, 'Gorbatschows Entfernung von der Breschnew-Doktrin', *ZfG* 42 (1994), 713–21. On the Harmel report see above, p. 241; on the Rosa Luxemburg quote see the first volume of this history, 321.

24. Korte, *Deutschlandpolitik* (note 18), 398 ff. (Wilms, 25 Jan. 1988: 399; Geissler's draft: 401); ' "Wiedervereinigung vor Einheit Europas". Ein Gespräch mit dem CDU-Abgeordneten Todenhöfer', *FAZ,* 16 Mar. 1988: ' "Wiedervereinigung in Freiheit ist das vordringlichste Ziel" '. CDU-Präsidium ändert Entwurf zur Deutschlandpolitik', ibid. 13 Apr. 1988; *Die CDU-Parteiprogramme. Eine Dokumentation der Ziele und Aufgaben,* ed. Peter Hintze (Bonn: Bouvier, 1995), 479–511 (Wiesbaden decision on Germany policy, etc.; quote: 482); Fritz René Allemann, *Bonn ist nicht Weimar* (Cologne: Kiepenheuer & Witsch, 1956), 119; Golo Mann, 'Gedanken zum Grundvertrag', *Neue Rundschau,* 84 (1973), 1–8 (on the term 'vital lie': 3); *Reden über das eigene Land: Deutschland* (Munich: Bertelsmann, 1984), 57–70 (Willy Brandt, 18 Nov. 1984: quote: 63); Brandt, *Wegmarken* (note 22), 81–2; 'Ein Notdach, unter dem der Rechtsstaat sich entwickeln konnte' (excerpts from Brandt's Bonn speech on 14 Sept. 1988), *FR,* 15 Sept. 1988 (emphasis in the original); Vogtmeier, *Bahr* (note 1), 287 ff. ('vital lie'); Potthoff, *Koalition* (note 7), 340–59 (Honecker–Brandt talk, 19 Sept. 1985; quotes: 350, 355); Egon Bahr, *Zum europäischen Frieden. Eine Antwort auf Gorbatschow* (Berlin: Siedler, 1988), 84 ff. (87, 92, 95, 99–100); *Sten. Ber., 11. Wahlperiode,* cxlvii. 8094–100 (Kohl, 1 Dec. 1988), 8100–3 (Vogel, 1 Dec. 1988), 8106–9 (Lippelt, 1 Dec. 1988), 8118–21 (Heimann, 1 Dec. 1988); Oskar Lafontaine, *Die Gesellschaft der Zukunft. Reformpolitik in einer veränderten Welt* (Hamburg: Hoffmann & Campe, 1988), 155 ff. (quotes: 174, 186–93); Friedrich Meinecke, *Weltbürgertum und Nationalstaat* (1st edn Munich 1907), *Werke,* v (Munich: Oldenbourg, 1962), tr. as. *Cosmopolitanism and the National State* (Princeton: Princeton University Press, 1970); Günter Grass, 'Die kommunizierende Mehrzahl', in *Deutscher Lastenausgleich. Wider das*

dumpfe Einheitsgebot. Reden und Gespräche (Berlin: Luchterhand, 1990), 89–107 (104, 106–7); Silke Jansen, 'Zwei deutsche Staaten—zwei deutsche Nationen? Meinungsbilder zur deutschen Frage im Zeitablauf', *DA* 22 (1989), 1132–43 (survey results; quote: 1139); Gerhard Herdegen, 'Perspektiven und Begrenzungen. Eine Bestandsaufnahme der öffentlichen Meinung zur deutschen Frage, pt I: Nation und deutsche Teilung', ibid. 20 (1987), 1259–73; pt II: 'Kleine Schritte und fundamentale Fragen', ibid. 21 (1988), 391–403; Jens Hacker, *Deutsche Irrtümer. Schönfärber und Helfershelfer der SED-Diktatur im Westen* (Berlin: Ullstein, 1992), 352 ff. (on Golo Mann: 382); Winkler, 'Nationalismus' (note 20), 23 ff. The quote from 'Xenien' in 'Deutscher Nationalcharakter (Xenien)', in Johann Wolfgang von Goethe, *Werke*, Weimar edn (Munich: DTV, 1987), v. 218. Compare i. 37 ff. On the *felix culpa* see Ernst Dassmann, 'Ambrosius', in *Theologische Realenzyklopädie*, ii (New York: de Gruyter, 1978), 362–85. On the *felix culpa* idea in post-Second World War German context see Angelo Bolaffi, *Die schrecklichen Deutschen. Eine merkwürdige Liebeserklärung* (Berlin: Siedler, 1995), 33. On Freudenfeld, Scheel, and the 1967–8 *Hochland* debate see above pp. 224–6 ff.; on Kant's *Perpetual Peace* (1795) see the first volume of this history, 39–40. On Plessner ibid. 199–200, 213.

25. 'Der Anfang auf dem Weg zur parlamentarischen Demokratie. Ergebnisse der Verhandlungen am "runden Tisch" in Warschau. Politische Reformen und Gewerkschaftspluralismus', *FAZ*, 11 Apr. 1989; *AdG* 59 (1989), 33207–13, 33386–9, 33465–8, 33577–81, 33690–705, 33776–9 (situation in Poland), 33409–17 (Gorbachev's visit to FRG, 12–15 June 1989; quotes: 33411, 33415); 33518–21 (Warsaw Pact summit in Bucharest, 8 July 1989); *Dokumente zur Deutschlandpolitik. Deutsche Einheit. Sonderedition aus den Akten des Bundeskanzleramtes 1989/90*, ed. Hans Jürgen Küsters and Daniel Hofmann (Munich: Oldenbourg, 1998), 276–99 (Kohl–Genscher talks, 12–13 June 1989), 339–45 (Kohl–Geremek talk, 7 July 1989); *EA* 44 (1989), 257 (quote from the Bush speech in Mainz, 31 May 1989); Kuehn, *Jahrzehnt* (note 8), 399 ff.; Schroeder, *SED-Staat* (note 3), 281 ff. (data on the municipal elections: 284; termination of the order to shoot: 295); Neubert, *Geschichte* (note 19), 810 ff. (municipal elections, May 1989); '"Deutsche haben Recht auf Selbstbestimmung". Gorbatschow-Berater Sagladin verknüpft Wiedervereinigung mit Europa', *SZ*, 5 June 1989; 'Waigel bekundet Willen zur Wiedervereinigung', ibid. 3 July 1989 (speech on 2 July 1989); Hermann Rudolph, 'Die DDR—doppelt belagert', ibid. 18 July 1989; *Sten. Ber.*, *11. Wahlperiode*, cxlix. 11296–301 (Eppler, 17 June 1989); Gorbachev, *Erinnerungen* (note 22), 700 ff. (quote: 711), 928 ff.; *Honecker–Gorbachev. Vieraugengespräche*, ed. Daniel Küchenmeister (Berlin: Dietz, 1993), 208–39 (210, 218, 222, 227); id., 'Wann begann das Zerwürfnis zwischen Honecker und Gorbatschow? Erste Bemerkungen zu den Protokollen ihrer Vier-Augen-Gespräche', *DA* 26 (1993), 30–40; *Vorwärts* (note 23), 75–88 (Honecker–Shevardnadze talk, 9 June 1989; quote: 85); 'Die "sozialistische Identität" der DDR. Überlegungen von Otto Reinhold in einem Beitrag für Radio DDR am 19. August 1989' (excerpt), *Blätter für deutsche und internationale Politik*, 34 (1989), 1175. The quote from Kurt Schumacher's speech 'Politics and the Student' on 4 Sept. 1946 at the SDS founding congress in Hamburg in id., *Reden–Schriften–Korrespondenzen 1945–1952*, ed. Willy Albrecht (Berlin: Dietz, 1985), 463–74 (469).

CHAPTER 5. UNITY IN FREEDOM 1989–1990

1. *Dokumente zur Deutschlandpolitik. Deutsche Einheit. Sonderedition aus den Akten des Bundeskanzleramtes 1989/90*, ed. Hanns Jürgen Küsters and Daniel Hofmann (Munich: Oldenbourg, 1998), 377–82 (Kohl and Genscher–Németh and Horn talks, 25 Aug. 1989); Richard Kiessler and Frank Elbe, *Ein runder Tisch mit scharfen Ecken. Der diplomatische Weg zur deutschen Einheit* (Baden-Baden: Nomos, 1993), 33 ff.; Hans-Dietrich Genscher, *Erinnerungen* (Berlin: Siedler, 1995), 13 ff., 637 ff., tr. as *Rebuilding a House Divided: A Memoir by the Architect of Germany's Reunification* (New York: Broadway Books, 1998); Helmut Kohl, *'Ich wollte Deutschlands Einheit'. Dargestellt von Kai Diekmann and Ralf Georg Reuth* (Berlin: Propyläen, 1996), 65 ff.; Karl-Rudolf Korte, *Deutschlandpolitik in Helmut Kohls Kanzlerschaft. Regierungsstil und Entscheidungen 1982–1989* (= *Geschichte der deutschen Einheit in vier Bänden*, i) (Stuttgart: Deutsche Verlags-Anstalt, 1998), 438 ff. (refugee numbers: 450); Wolfgang Jäger with Michael Walter, *Die Überwindung der Teilung. Der innerdeutsche Prozess der Vereinigung* (= *Geschichte der deutschen Einheit in vier Bänden*, iii) (Stuttgart: Deutsche Verlags-Anstalt, 1998), 252 ff.; Walter Süss, *Staatssicherheit am Ende. Warum es den Mächtigen nicht gelang, 1989 eine Revolution zu verhindern* (Berlin: Ch. Links, 1999), 177 ff.; *Ich liebe euch doch alle! Befehle und Lageberichte des MfS Januar–November 1989*, ed. Armin Mitter and Stefan Wolle (Berlin: BasisDruck, 1990), 46–75 (information, 1 June 1989; numbers: 47), 161–2 (manifesto of the 'Social Democratic Party in the GDR', 12 Sept. 1989), 162–4 ('New Forum' manifesto, 9 Sept. 1989), 165–9 ('Democracy Now!' manifesto, 12 Sept. 1989), 182–3 ('Democratic Awakening' manifesto, 2 Oct. 1989), 212 (SDP founding document, 7 Oct. 1989), 212–13 ('Joint Statement', 4 Oct. 1989); Stefan Wolle, 'Der Weg in den Zusammenbruch: Die DDR vom Januar bis zum Oktober 1989', in *Die Gestaltung der deutschen Einheit. Geschichte–Politik–Gesellschaft*, ed. Eckhard Jesse and Armin Mitter (Bonn: Bouvier, 1992), 73–110 (Wolle quote; rejection of the New Forum: 98–9); Karsten Timmer, *Vom Aufbruch zum Umbruch. Die Bürgerbewegung in der DDR 1989* (Göttingen: Vandenhoeck & Ruprecht, 2000); Klaus Schroeder and Steffen Alisch, *Der SED-Staat. Geschichte und Strukturen der DDR* (Munich: Bayerische Landeszentrale für Politische Bildungsarbeit, 1998), 297 ff. (IMs in the Peace and Human Rights Initiative: 312); Martin Gutzeit, 'Die Stasi—Repression oder Geburtshilfe?', in *Von der Bürgerbewegung zur Partei. Die Gründung der Sozialdemokratie in der DDR*, ed. Dieter Dowe and Rainer Eckert (Bonn: Friedrich-Ebert-Stiftung, 1993), 41–52 (MfS quote: 45); *Auf den Anfang kommt es an. Sozialdemokratischer Neubeginn in der DDR. Interviews und Analysen*, ed. Wolfgang Herzberg and Patrik von zur Mühlen (Bonn: Dietz, 1993); Wolfgang Gröf, *'In der frischen Tradition des Herbstes 1989'. Die SDP/SPD in der DDR: Von der Gründung über die Volkskammerarbeit zur deutschen Einheit*, 2nd edn (Bonn: AdsD der Friedrich-Ebert-Stiftung, 1996), 9 ff.; Gero Neugebauer, 'Die SDP/SPD in der DDR: Zur Geschichte und Entwicklung einer unvollendeten Partei', in *Parteien und Wähler im Umbruch*, ed. Oskar Niedermayer and Richard Stöss (Opladen: Westdeutscher Verlag, 1994), 75–104; Ute Haese, *Katholische Kirche in der DDR. Geschichte einer politischen Abstinenz* (Düsseldorf: Droste, 1998), esp. 40 ff.; Ralf Georg Reuth, *IM 'Sekretär'.*

Die 'Gauck-Recherche' und die Dokumente zum 'Fall Stolpe', 2nd edn (Frankfurt: Ullstein, 1992); Clemens Vollnhals, 'Die kirchenpolitische Abteilung des Ministeriums für Staatssicherheit', in *Die Kirchenpolitik von SED und Staatssicherheit. Eine Zwischenbilanz*, ed. id. (Berlin: C. Links Verlag, 1996), 79–119; Ehrhart Neubert, 'Zur Instrumentalisierung von Theologie und Kirchenrecht durch das MfS', ibid. 329–52; id., *Geschichte der Opposition in der DDR 1949–1989* (Bonn: Ch. Links, 1997), 825 ff.; id., *Vergebung oder Weisswäscherei. Zur Aufarbeitung des Stasi-Problems in den Kirchen* (Freiburg, 1993); id., *Eine protestantische Revolution* (Osnabrück: Kontext, 1990); Beatrice Jansen-de Graaf, 'Eine protestantische Revolution? Die Rolle der ostdeutschen evangelischen Kirchen in der Wende 1989/90', *DA* 32 (1999), 264–70; *Protestantische Revolution? Kirche und Theologie in der DDR: Ekklesiologische Voraussetzungen, politischer Kontext, theologische und historische Kriterien*, ed. Trutz Rendtorff (Göttingen: Vandenhoeck & Ruprecht, 1993); Claudia Lepp, 'Wege des Protestantismus im geteilten Deutschland', *GWU* 51 (2000), 173–91; *Kirchen in der Diktatur. Drittes Reich und SED-Staat*, ed. Günther Heydemann and Lothar Kettenacker (Göttingen: Vandenhoeck & Ruprecht, 1993); Gerhard Besier, *Der SED-Staat und die Kirche 1983–1991. Höhenflug und Absturz* (Berlin: Propyläen, 1995), 360 ff.; Friedrich Wilhelm Graf, 'Eine Ordnungsmacht eigener Art. Theologie und Kirchenpolitik im DDR-Protestantismus', in *Sozialgeschichte der DDR*, ed. Hartmut Kaelble et al. (Stuttgart: Klett-Cotta, 1994), 295–321; Mary Fulbrook, *Anatomy of a Dictatorship: Inside the GDR 1949–1989* (Oxford: Oxford University Press, 1995), 87 ff.; Christian Joppke, *East German Dissidents and the Revolution of 1989. Social Movement in a Leninist Regime* (Houndmills: Macmillan, 1995); *Opposition in der DDR von den 70er Jahren bis zum Zusammenbruch der SED-Herrschaft*, ed. Eberhard Kuhrt et al. (Opladen: Leske + Budrich, 1999), 381 ff.; Hartmut Zwahr, *Ende einer Selbstzerstörung. Leipzig und die Revolution in der DDR* (Göttingen: Vandenhoeck & Ruprecht, 1993), 19 ff. (demonstrations in Leipzig, 4–12 Sept. 1989; Monday prayer on 25 Sept.: 23–4).

2. *Sten. Ber., 11. Wahlperiode*, cl. 11633–7 (Brandt, 1 Sept. 1989; quotes: 11636); Günter Gaus, 'Die Zeichen erkennend', *Der Spiegel*, no. 36, 4 Sept. 1989 (emphases in the original); ' "Wenn alle gehen wollen, weil die Falschen bleiben" '. Norbert Gansel fordert von SPD Umdenken in der Deutschlandpolitik: Statt ' "Wandel durch Annäherung" ' ' "Wandel durch Abstand" ', *FR*, 13 Sept. 1989; Heinrich August Winkler, 'Die Mauer wegdenken. Was die Bundesrepublik für die Demokratisierung der DDR tun kann', *Die Zeit*, 11 Aug. 1989; Jäger, *Überwindung* (note 1), 142–3 (Rühe, 25 Sept. 1989); *Die Häber-Protokolle. Schlaglichter der SED-Westpolitik 1973–1985*, ed. Detlef Nakath and Gerd-Rüdiger Stephan (Berlin: Dietz, 1999), 83–91 (Sagladin–Kiep talk, 6 Feb. 1975; quote: 87–8); Klaus Dreher, *Helmut Kohl. Leben und Macht* (Stuttgart: Deutsche Verlags-Anstalt, 1998), 388 ff. (Bremen party congress: 440); Kohl, *Ich wollte* (note 1), 75 ff.; Korte, *Deutschlandpolitik* (note 1), 463 ff. On Bahr's 'Change through rapprochement' of July 1963 see above pp. 200–1. The Bismarck quote alluded to by Gaus runs: 'We cannot do anything by ourselves. We can only wait until we hear God's footsteps echoing through events, then jump forward and seize the hem of his coat. That is all.' Arnold Oskar Meyer, *Bismarcks Glaube. Nach neuen Quellen aus dem Familienarchiv* (Munich: C. H. Beck, 1933), 7, 63–4.

3. Zwahr, *Ende* (note 2), 39–41 (emphases in the original), 79 ff. (on the Leipzig declaration of the six : 82 ff.); Mitter and Wolle ed., *Ich liebe* (note 1), 190–1 (MfS information of 3 Oct. 1989; street names corrected); *Honecker–Gorbatschow. Vieraugengespräche*, ed. Daniel Küchenmeister and Gerd-Rüdiger Stephan (Berlin: Dietz, 1993), 240–51 (Honecker–Gorbachev talk, 7 Oct. 1989), 252–66 (Gorbachev's meeting with SED politburo, 7 Oct. 1989); Valentin Falin, *Politische Erinnerungen* (Munich: Droemer Knaur, 1993), 484 ff.; Rafael Biermann, *Zwischen Kreml und Kanzleramt. Wie Moskau mit der deutschen Einigung rang* (Paderborn: Schöningh, 1997), 200 ff. (Gorbachev's speech, 5 July 1989: 201–3; internal talks: 204–8; on the catchphrase: 204); 'Eine von Hochgefühl, Stolz und Glück erfasste Bevölkerung. Wie das DDR-Fernsehen die Jubiläums-Feiern zeigte. Von Ralf-Georg Reuth', *FAZ*, 9 Oct. 1989 (Gorbachev to journalists; wreath-laying); 'Den uniformierten Betriebskampfgruppen schallt es entgegen: Arbeiter-Verräter. Über die Demonstrationen in Ost-Berlin berichtet Monika Zimmermann', ibid.; Mikhail Gorbachev, *Erinnerungen* (Berlin: Siedler, 1995), 933–4, tr. as *Memoirs* (New York: Doubleday, 1996); Wolle, *Weg* (note 1), 105 ff. (Berlin events on 7–8 Oct. 1989, report of the investigatory commission: 106; Leipzig demonstration on 9 Oct. 1989: 107); Zwahr, *Ende* (note 1), 61 ff.; *Ich liebe* (note 1), ed. Mitter and Wolle, 200 (Honecker's order on 8 Oct. 1989); Egon Krenz, *Wenn Mauern fallen. Die Friedliche Revolution: Vorgeschichte—Ablauf—Auswirkungen* (Vienna: Neff, 1990), 11 ff., 122 ff.; Vyacheslav Kochemasov, *Meine letzte Mission* (Berlin: Dietz, 1994), 164 ff.; Günter Schabowski, *Das Politbüro. Ende eines Mythos. Eine Befragung*, ed. Frank Sieren and Ludwig Koehne (Reinbek: Rowohlt, 1990), 71 ff.; id., *Der Absturz* (Reinbek: Rowohlt, 1991), 236 ff.; 'Sich selbst aus unserer Gesellschaft ausgegrenzt', *ND*, 2 Oct. 1989; *Die deutsche Vereinigung. Dokumente zu Bürgerbewegung, Annäherung und Beitritt*, ed. Volker Gransow and Konrad Jarausch (Cologne: Verlag Wissenschaft und Politik, 1991), 76–7 (Leipzig declaration of the six on 9 Oct. 1989).

4. *AdG* 59 (1989), 33885–90 (leadership change in SED, Krenz's television address on 18 Oct. 1989; reactions to his election), 33937–46 (situation in the GDR, 24 Oct.–8 Nov. 1989); Krenz, *Mauern* (note 3), 34 ff. (politburo statement on 11 Oct. 1989: 34–5); Schabowski, *Politbüro* (note 3), 87 ff.; *Das Ende der SED. Die letzten Tage des Zentralkomitees*, ed. Hans-Hermann Hertle and Gerd-Rüdiger Stephan (Berlin: Ch. Links, 1997), 49 ff., 103–33 (ninth session of the CC, 18 Oct. 1989), 135–437 (tenth session of the CC, 8–10 Nov. 1989; Kranz on new travel regulations, 9 Nov.: 303–6; Ehrensperger, 9 Nov.: 363–9; Schürer, 10 Nov.: 382–8; Kayser, 10 Nov: 422); Iwan Kusmin, 'Die Verschwörung gegen Moskau', *DA* 28 (1995), 286–90; *Die 'Koalition der Vernunft'. Deutschlandpolitik in den 80er Jahren*, ed. Heinrich Potthoff (Munich: DTV, 1995), 975–81 (Kohl–Krenz telephone call, 26 Oct. 1989); Zwahr, *Ende* (note 1), 103 ff.; id., 'Die Revolution in der DDR im Demonstrationsvergleich. Leipzig und Berlin im Oktober und November 1989', in *Nation und Gesellschaft in Deutschland. Historische Essays. Hans-Ulrich Wehler zum 65. Geburtstag*, ed. Manfred Hettling and Paul Nolte (Munich: C. H. Beck, 1996), 335–50; 'Massenflucht–Reformzusagen–Forderungen', *FAZ*, 6 Nov. 1989; Klaus Hartung, 'Der Fall der Mauer', *taz*, 6 Nov. 1989; 'Schürers Krisen-Analyse', *DA* 25

(1992), 1112–20 (1119); Gerd-Rüdiger Stephan, 'Die letzten Tage des Zentralkomitees der SED 1988/89. Abläufe und Hintergründe', ibid. 26 (1993), 296–325; Hans-Hermann Hertle, 'Der ökonomische Untergang des SED-Staates', ibid. 25 (1992), 1019–39; id., *Der Fall der Mauer. Die unbeabsichtigte Selbstauflösung des SED-Staates* (Opladen: Westdeutscher Verlag,, 1996), 163 ff. (Schabowski's press conference, 9 Nov. 1989, and reactions); id., *Chronik des Mauerfalls. Die dramatischen Ereignisse um den 9. November 1989* (Berlin: Ch. Links, 1996), 75 ff.; *Sten. Ber., 11. Wahlperiode*, cli. 13221–3 (Seiters, Vogel, Dregger, Lippelt, Mischnick, 9 Nov. 1989); Jäger, *Überwindung* (note 1), 43 (Bundestag, 9 Nov. 1989); *Bilanz der Todesopfer des DDR-Grenzregimes. Bilanz der letzten Mauerreste. Text und Zusammenstellung*, Rainer Hildebrandt, 121st press conference of the '13 August Association' on Wednesday 11 Aug. 1999, 11.00, Checkpoint Charlie (manuscript)(Berlin, 1999), 3; Walter Momper, *Grenzfall. Berlin im Brennpunkt deutscher Geschichte*, 2nd edn (Munich: Bertelsmann, 1991), 144 ff.; *Verhandlungen des Bundesrates 1989. Stenographische Berichte von der 597. Sitzung am 10. Februar 1989 bis zur 608. Sitzung on 21. Dezember 1989*, 453 (Momper, 10 Nov. 1989).

5. Zwahr, *Ende* (note 1), 50; Crane Brinton, *Die Revolution und ihre Gesetze* (Frankfurt: Nest, 1959), 99–100, orig. *The Anatomy of Revolution* (New York: W. W. Norton, 1938); Markus Wolf, *Spionagechef im geheimen Krieg. Erinnerungen* (Düsseldorf: Droste, 1997), 423 ff.; Süss, *Staatssicherheit* (note 1), 301 ff.; *Ich liebe* (note 1), ed. Mitter and Wolle, 148–50 (MfS on 11 Sept. 1989), 204–7 (MfS on 8 Oct. 1989); *Ende* (note 4), ed. Hertle and Stephan, 387 (Schürer), 427 (Krenz); Kusmin, 'Verschwörung' (note 4), 288–9. (Stoph–Gorbachev connection); Eckhard Jesse, 'War die DDR totalitär?', *APZ* B 40 (1994), 12–23; Albert O. Hirschmann, 'Exit, Voice, and the Fate of the German Democratic Republic: An Essay in Conceptual History', *World Politics*, 45 (1993), 173–203 (on the dialectic relationship between exodus and opposition); Charles S. Maier, *Das Verschwinden der DDR und der Untergang des Kommunismus* (Frankfurt: Fischer, 1999), 36 ff., orig. *Dissolution: The Crisis of Communism and the End of East Germany* (Princeton: Princeton University Press, 1997); Konrad H. Jarausch, *Die unverhoffte Einheit 1989–1990* (Frankfurt: Suhrkamp, 1995), 29 ff.; Elizabeth Pond, *Beyond the Wall.: Germany's Road to Unification* (Washington: Brookings Institution, 1993), 1 ff.; Klaus-Dieter Opp et al., *Die volkseigene Revolution* (Stuttgart: Klett-Cotta, 1993); *Der Zusammenbruch der DDR*, ed. Hans Joas and Martin Kohli (Frankfurt: Suhrkamp, 1993); Sigrid Meuschel, *Legitimation und Parteiherrschaft. Zum Paradox von Stabilität und Revolution in der DDR 1945–1989* (Frankfurt: Suhrkamp, 1992), 306 ff.; Robert Darnton, *Der letzte Tanz auf der Mauer. Berliner Journal 1989–1990* (Munich: Hauser, 1991), orig. *Berlin Journal, 1989–1990* (New York: W. W. Norton, 1991); Heinrich August Winkler, '1989/90: Die unverhoffte Einheit', in *Wendepunkte deutscher Geschichte 1848–1990*, Carola Stern and Heinrich August Winkler (Frankfurt: Fischer, 1994), 193–226.

6. Helmut Kohl, *Bilanzen und Perspektiven. Regierungspolitik 1989–1991*, i (Bonn: Presse und Informationsamt der Bundesregierung, 1992), 251–3 (speech in front of Schöneberg city hall, 10 Nov. 1989; emphases in the original); id., *Ich wollte* (note 1), 125 ff.; Horst Teltschik, *329 Tage. Innenansichten der Einigung* (Berlin: Siedler,

1991), 11 ff. (Kohl's visits to Poland and Berlin, 9–14 Nov. 1989); 'Gespräch mit Willy Brandt. In der DDR wird nichts mehr so sein, wie es vor Jahren war', *Berliner Morgenpost*, 11 Nov. 1989; Willy Brandt, '. . . *was zusammengehört. Über Deutschland*, 2nd edn (Bonn: Dietz, 1993), 33–8 (speech on 10 Nov. 1989; the sentence 'Now what belongs together is growing together', 36, was added after the fact; Bernd Rother, 'Gilt das gesprochene Wort? Wann und wo sagte Willy Brandt *jetzt wächst zusammen, was zusammengehört?*', *DA* 33 (2000), 90–3 (here the quotes from 10 Nov. 1989 and 12 Aug. 1964); Genscher, *Erinnerungen* (note 1), 657 ff.; Momper, *Grenzfall* (note 4), 156 ff.; Markus Meckel and Martin Gutzeit, *Opposition in der DDR. Zehn Jahre kirchliche Friedensarbeit—kommentierte Quellentexte* (Cologne: Bund-Verlag, 1994), 379–96 (Meckel's address on 7 Oct. 1989; quotes: 394–5); *Sten. Ber.*, cli. 13016–17 (Kohl, 8 Nov. 1989), 13022 (Vogel, 8 Nov. 1989 with the quotes form the manifestos of the New Forum and Democratic Awakening); Hartmut Zwahr, 'Die Revolution in der DDR', in *Revolution in Deutschland? 1789–1989. Sieben Beiträge*, ed. Manfred Hettling (Göttingen: Vandenhoeck & Ruprecht, 1991), 122–43 ('turning point within the turning point': 132 ff.); id., 'Vertragsgemeinschaft, Konföderation oder Vereinigung? Die Übergänge zur nationaldemokratischen Revolution in der DDR im Herbst 1989', in *Landesgeschichte als Herausforderung und Programm. Karlheinz Blaschke zum 70. Geburtstag*, ed. Uwe John and Josef Matzerath (Stuttgart: Franz Steiner, 1997), 709–29 (poster from 4 Dec. 1989: 729); id., *Die friedliche Revolution in Sachsen. Das Ende der DDR und die Wiedergründung des Freistaates* (Dresden: Hannah-Arendt-Institut für Totalitarismusforschung, 1999), 23–58 (demonstration calls in October and November 1989: 35–6); id., *Ende* (note 1), 136 ff.; Bernd Lindner, *Die demokratische Revolution in der DDR 1989/90* (Bonn: Bundeszentrale für politische Bildung, 1990); id., 'Der Herbst '89 in der DDR und die Kommunikationsstrukturen der Strasse', in *Kommunikation und Revolution*, ed. Kurt Imhof and Peter Schulz (Zurich: Seismo, 1998), 435–52; *Ich liebe* (note 1), ed. Mitter and Wolle, 219 (Leipzig flyer from 9 Oct. 1989); Jäger, *Überwindung* (note 1), 60, 539 (reference to *Bild* headline on 11 Nov. 1989: '*Wir sind das Volk* rufen sie heute. *Wir sind ein Volk* rufen sie morgen'); *Neues Forum Leipzig. Jetzt oder nie—Demokratie. Herbst '89. Zeugnisse, Gespräche, Dokumente* (Leipzig: Forum Verlag, 1989), 203 ff.

7. Joschka Fischer, 'Jenseits von Mauer und Wiedervereinigung. Thesen zu einer neuen grünen Deutschlandpolitik. Gekürzter Beitrag für den Strategiekongress der Grünen am Wochenende in Saarbrücken', *taz*, 16 Nov. 1989; 'Diese Regierung wird eine Regierung des Volkes und der Arbeit sein. Erklärung von Hans Modrow', *ND*, 18–19 Nov. 1989; Charles Schüddekopf ed., *'Wir sind das Volk' Flugschriften, Aufrufe und Texte einer deutschen Revolution* (Reinbek: Rowohlt, 1990), 240–1. (appeal on 26 Nov. 1989); *Chronik der Ereignisse in der DDR*, ed. Ilse Spittmann and Gisela Helwig, 4th edn (Cologne: 1990), 26 (ADN announcement on 19 Nov. 1989), 30 (Leipzig demonstration, 27 Nov. 1989); Jäger, *Überwindung* (note 1), 58 ff. (opinion surveys in November 1989: 61, 63; Lafontaine, 3 Dec. 1989: 69, 541); Teltschik, *329 Tage* (note 6), 40 ff. (ZDF survey, 20 Nov. 1989: 41); *Sten. Ber.*, cli. 13479–88 (Vogel, 28 Nov. 1989), 13502–12 (Kohl, 28 Nov. 1989), 13514–16 (Voigt, 28 Nov. 1989); Hans-Jochen Vogel, *Nachsichten. Meine Bonner und Berliner Jahre* (Munich: 1996), 306 ff.; *Dokumente* (note 1), 59 ff., 594–5 (Shamir, 15 Nov.

1989; Kohl to Shamir, 1 Dec. 1989); Werner Weidenfeld with Peter M. Wagner and Elke Bruck, *Aussenpolitik für die deutsche Einheit. Die Entscheidungsjahre 1989/90* (= *Geschichte der deutschen Einheit in vier Bänden*, iv) (Stuttgart: Deutsche Verlags-Anstalt, 1998), 97 ff. (Gorbachev and Shevardnadze quotes, 5 Nov. 1989: 123); Philip Zelikow and Condoleezza Rice, *Sternstunde der Diplomatie. Die deutsche Einheit und das Ende der Spaltung Europas* (Berlin: Propyläen, 1997), 176 ff., orig. *Germany Unified and Europe Transformed: A Study in Statecraft* (Cambridge, MA: Harvard University Press, 1995): James A. Baker, *Drei Jahre, die die Welt veränderten. Erinnerungen* (Berlin: Siedler, 1996), 149 ff., orig. *The Politics of Diplomacy: Revolution, War, and Peace, 1989–1992* (New York: G. P. Putnam's Sons, 1995); Jacques Attali, *Verbatim, iii. Chronique des années 1988–1991* (Paris: Fayard, 1995), 350 ff. (Mitterrand's reaction to Kohl's Ten Points); Genscher, *Erinnerungen* (note 1), 675 ff.; Kohl, *Ich wollte* (note 1), 157 ff.; Michael Mertes, 'Zur Entstehung des Zehn-Punkte-Programms vom 28. November 1989', in *Die DDR in Deutschland. Ein Rückblick auf 50 Jahre*, ed. Heiner Timmermann (Berlin: Duncker & Humblot, 2001), 17–35; Karl Kaiser, *Deutschlands Vereinigung. Die internationalen Aspekte. Mit den wichtigsten Dokumenten*, ed. Klaus Becker (Bergisch Gladbach: Bastei-Lübbe, 1991), 171–3 (statement of the European Council, 8–9 Dec. 1989), 180–1 (statement of the North Atlantic Council, 14–15 Dec. 1989); id., 'Die Einbettung des Vereinigten Deutschland in Europa', in *Die Internationale Politik 1989. Studienausgabe*, ed. Wolfgang Wagner et al. (Munich: Oldenbourg, 1993), 101–91; *SZ* interview with Oskar Lafontaine on the GDR: 'Nicht das Weggehen prämieren, sondern das dableiben', *SZ*, 25–6 Nov. 1989. On the 'Letter on German Unity' see above, p. 262

8. *Ende* (note 4), ed. Hertle and Stephan, 461–81 (twelfth session of the CC of the SED, 3 Dec. 1989); *Vereinigung* (note 3), ed. Gransow and Jarausch, 105–6 (Round Table statement, 7 Dec. 1989), 110–11 (Democracy Now's three-phase plan, 14 Dec. 1989); *Ausserordentlicher Parteitag der SED/PDS. Protokoll der Beratungen on 8./9. und 16./17. Dezember 1989 in Berlin*, ed. Lothar Hornbogen et al. (Berlin: Dietz, 1999), 51–65 (Gysi, 8 Dec. 1989; quotes: 51, 52–3, 61); Uwe Thaysen, *Der Runde Tisch oder: Wo blieb das Volk? Der Weg der DDR in die Demokratie* (Opladen: Westdeutscher Verlag, 1990), 15 ff. (quote: 188); *Der Zentrale Runde Tisch der DDR. Wortprotokoll und Dokumente*, 5 vols, ed. id. (Wiesbaden: Westdeutscher Verlag, 2000), i. viii. 1 ff.; Jäger, *Überwindung* (note 1), 141 ff. ('Berlin declaration' of the SPD: 156 ff.; extraordinary congress of the SED/PDS: 206 ff.; de Maizière's positions in Nov. 1989: 220–2; CDU party congress, 15–16 Dec. 1989: 223; LDPD and Gerlach quote: 232–7; Hartmann's speech, 17 Nov. 1989: 247; Bahr, 9 Oct. 1989: 258; SDP declaration, 3 Dec. 1989: 261; DA and Schorlemmer quote: 272–3); Süss, *Staatssicherheit* (note 1), 579 ff. (de Maizière); Lothar de Maizière, *Anwalt der Einheit* (Berlin: Argon, 1996), 130 ff.; Alexander Schalck-Golodkowski, *Deutsch–deutsche Erinnerungen* (Reinbek: Rowohlt, 2000), 309 ff.; Patrick Moreau and Viola Neu, *Die PDS zwischen Linksextremismus und Linkspopulismus* (Sankt Augustin: Konrad-Adenauer-Stiftung, 1994), 14 (PDS membership), 49 (membership of the Communist Platform); Gero Neugebauer and Richard Stöss, *Die PDS. Geschichte. Organisation. Wähler. Konkurrenten* (Opladen: Westdeutscher Verlag, 1996); *Protokoll vom Programm-Parteitag Berlin. 18.–20*

Dez. 1989 (Bonn: Vorstand der SPD, 1990), 93–4 (Meckel), 127–30 (Brandt), 151–3 (Grass), 246–54 (Lafontaine), 539–45 (Berlin declaration 'The Germans in Europe'); Günter Grass, 'Lastenausgleich', in *Deutscher Lastenausgleich. Wider das dumpfe Einheitsgebot. Reden und Gespräche* (Berlin: Luchterhand, 1990), 7–12 (8–11); id., 'Kurze Rede eines vaterlandslosen Gesellen. Rede in der Evangelischen Akademie in Tutzing', in *Essays und Reden, III. 1980–1997* (= id., *Werkausgabe*, xvi) (Göttingen: Steidl, 1997), 230–4 (233); Willy Brandt, 'Was Erneuerung heissen soll', in id., '. . . was zusammengehört' (note 6), 49–56 (Rostock speech, 6 Dec. 1989; quote: 54); Anke Fuchs, *Mut zur Macht. Selbsterfahrung in der Politik* (Hamburg: Hoffmann & Campe, 1991), 191 ff.; *Dokumente* (note 1), 668–75 (Kohl–Modrow talk, 19 Dec. 1989); Kohl, *Ich wollte* (note 1), 213 ff.; ' "Ziel bleibt die Einheit der Nation". Kohls Ansprache vor der Frauenkirche—Mehrere tausend Teilnehmer', *Der Tagesspiegel*, 20 Dec. 1989. On 8 June 1985, in a speech on 'The Germans and their identity' at the 21st Evangelical congress in Düsseldorf, President Richard von Weizsäcker remarked: 'In Berlin I heard something that everyone can understand: the German question will remain open as long as the Brandenburg Gate is closed.' On the difference between *Kulturnation* and *Staatsnation* see Friedrich Meinecke, *Weltbürgertum und Nationalstaat* (1st edn 1907), *Werke*, v (Munich: Oldenbourg, 1962), 9–26, tr. as *Cosmopolitanism and the National State* (Princeton: Princeton University Press, 1970); on Plessner see the first volume of this history, 199–200, 213. On Lafontaine's 1988 book see above pp. 431–3 ff.

9. Schroeder, *SED-Staat* (note 1), 335 ff. (decision of the GDR government on 7 Dec. 1989: 342); Chronik (note 7), 50 ff. (demonstration in Magdeburg, 14 Jan. 1990: 53; Modrow–Gorbachev meeting, 30 Jan. 1990, Modrow's press conference, 1 Feb. 1990: 60–1); Teltschik, *329 Tage* (note 6), 114 (*Das Bild* interview with Portugalow, 24 Jan. 1990); Thaysen, *Runder Tisch* (note 8), 64 ff. ('power vacuum': 77; Modrow, 15 Jan. 1990: 79–80; de Maizière, 25 Jan. 1990: 84; Modrow, 28 Jan. 1990: 90–1); *Zentraler Runder Tisch* ed. id. (note 8), ii. 408–9 (Berlin events on 15 Jan. 1990); Süss, *Staatssicherheit* (note 1), 465 ff.; Dieter Grosser, *Das Wagnis der Währungs-, Wirtschafts- und Sozialunion. Politische Zwänge im Konflikt mit ökonomischen Regeln* (= *Geschichte der deutschen Einheit in vier Bänden*, ii) (Stuttgart: Deutsche Verlags-Anstalt, 1998), 102 ff. (number of emigrants, 10 Nov.–31 Dec. 1989: 103); Hans Modrow, *Aufbruch und Ende* (Hamburg: Konkret Literatur, 1991), 65 ff.; id., *Die Perestroika, wie ich sie sehe. Erinnerungen und Analysen eines Jahrzehnts, das die Welt veränderte* (Berlin: Edition Ost, 1999); Mikhail Gorbachev, *Wie es war. Die deutsche Wiedervereinigung* (Berlin: Ullstein, 1999); *Protokoll* (note 8), 252 (Lafontaine, 19 Dec. 1989); Weidenfeld, *Aussenpolitik* (note 7), 224 ff. Number of emigrants in 1990 in *Dokumente* (note 1), 796 (Gorbachev–Kohl talk, 10 Feb. 1990).

10. Brandt, *Erneuerung* (note 8), 55 (Rostock speech, 6 Dec. 1989); 'Magdeburg: 65 000 jubelten Willy Brandt zu', *Das Bild*, 20 Dec. 1989; Ingrid Matthäus-Maier, 'Signal zum Bleiben. Eine Währungsunion könnte den Umbau der DDR-Wirtschaft beschleunigen', *Die Zeit*, 19 Jan. 1990; Grosser, *Wagnis* (note 9), 151 ff. (Matthäus-Maier, 19 Jan. 1990: 153; Roth, 2 Feb. 1990: 155; decision for monetary union:

174 ff.); Jäger, *Überwindung* (note 1), 121 ff. (decision for Article 23; GDR delegation in Bonn, 13 Feb. 1990), 228 ff. (founding of 'Alliance for Germany'); *Dokumente* (note 1), 753–6 (Kohl–Modrow meeting in Davos, 3 Feb. 1990), 768–70 (monetary union with economic reform, 7 Feb. 1990; differences in labour productivity), 795–811 (Kohl–Gorbachev talks in Moscow, 10 Feb. 1990; quotes: 801, 805), 812–13 (Kohl's Moscow declaration, 10 Feb. 1990), 814–26 (GDR delegation in Bonn, 13 Feb. 1990), 860–77 (Bush–Kohl talk, 24–5 Feb. 1990), 920–1 (Thatcher's letter to Kohl, 7 Mar. 1990); Genscher, *Erinnerungen* (note 1), 709 ff. (Kohl's interview on 8 Jan. 1990: 713; Tutzing speech: 713 ff.); Kaiser, *Deutschlands Vereinigung* (note 7), 724 ff. (Ottawa; quote from 13 Feb. 1990: 729); Teltschik, *329 Tage* (note 6), 137 ff.; Falin, *Erinnerungen* (note 3), 489 ff.; Eduard Shevardnadze, *Die Zukunft gehört der Freiheit* (Reinbek: Rowohlt, 1991), 233 ff.; Baker, *Drei Jahre* (note 7), 180 ff.; Korte, *Deutschlandpolitik* (note 1), 469–70 (Genscher's speech to UN on 27 Sept. 1989: 469–70); Zelikow and Rice, *Sternstunde* (note 7), 247 ff. (Bush on the Soviet position, 24 Feb. 1990: 302); press conference, 25 Feb. 1990: 303); English text at: http://www.presidency.ucsb.edu/ws/index.php?pid=18188; Weidenfeld, *Aussenpolitik* (note 7), 222 ff. Bundestag decision on 8 Mar. 1990: *AdG* 60 (1990), 34305–6.

11. Jäger, *Überwindung* (note 1), 161 ff. (Glotz quote, 6 Mar. 1990: 163), 261 ff.; 'Beratungen über den Weg zur Einheit', *FAZ*, 14 Feb. 1990 (SPD attitude); 'Sozialdemokraten wollen "Rat der deutschen Einheit" bilden', *FAZ*, 26 Feb. 1990; 'DDR–SPD beschliesst "Fahrplan zur Einheit"', *SZ*, 26 Feb. 1990; 'Der schwierigste Balanceakt steht noch bevor', ibid. (on Leipzig party congress of the eastern SPD); Vogel, *Nachsichten* (note 7), 319 ff.; 'Verfassung der Deutschen Demokratischen Republik' (text of draft of 4 Apr. 1990), *Blätter für deutsche und internationale Politik* 35 (1990), 731–57; Thaysen, *Runder Tisch* (note 8), 138 ff.; *Zentraler Runder Tisch* (note 8), ed. id., iii. 708–9 (Ullmann's fiduciary initiative), 853–5 (rejection of accession); Grosser, *Wagnis* (note 9), 117 ff. (Vogel–Lafontaine meeting, 20 Feb. 1990: 189); *Treuhandanstalt. Das Unmögliche wagen. Forschungsbericht*, ed. Wolfram Fischer et al. (Berlin: Akademie Verlag, 1993), 17 ff.

12. Hans Michael Kloth, *Vom 'Zettelfalten' zum freien Wähler. Die Demokratisierung der DDR 1989/90 und die 'Wahlfrage'* (Berlin: Ch. Links, 2000); Jäger, *Überwindung* (note 1), 213 (PDS electoral campaign), 307–8. (activist groups), 405 ff. (electoral campaign), 413 ff. (election results and analysis); *Die Intellektuellen und die deutsche Einheit*, ed. id. and Ingeborg Villinger (Freiburg: Rombach, 1997); Peter Förster and Günter Roski, *DDR zwischen Wende und Wahl. Meinungsforscher analysieren den Umbruch* (Berlin: LinksDruck, 1990), 138 ff. (surveys in the GDR, Feb.–Mar. 1990); Jürgen Habermas, 'Der DM-Nationalismus. Weshalb es richtig ist, die deutsche Einheit nach Artikel 146 zu vollziehen, also einen Volksentscheid über eine neue Verfassung anzustreben', *Die Zeit*, 30 Mar. 1990 (emphases in the original); id., 'Eine Art Schadensabwicklung', in *'Historikerstreit'. Die Dokumentation der Kontroverse um die Einzigartigkeit der nationalsozialistischen Judenvernichtung* (Munich: Piper, 1987), 62–76 (75); Florian Roth, *Die Idee der Nation im politischen Diskurs. Die Bundesrepublik Deutschland zwischen neuer Ostpolitik und Wiedervereinigung (1969–1990)* (Baden-Baden: Nomos, 1995); Tilman Mayer, *Prinzip Nation. Dimensionen der nationalen Frage am Beispiel Deutschlands*

(Opladen: Leske + Budrich, 1986); Karl-Rudolf Korte, *Der Standort der Deutschen. Akzentverlagerungen der deutschen Frage in der Bundesrepublik Deutschland seit den siebziger Jahren* (Cologne: Verlag Wissenschaft und Politik, 1990); Anne-Marie Le Gloannec, *La Nation orpheline. Les Allemagnes en Europe* (Paris: Calmann-Lévy, 1989), 85 ff.; ead., *Die deutsch–deutsche Nation. Anmerkungen zu einer revolutionären Entwicklung* (Munich: Printul, 1991). On the 1918–19 revolution see the first volume of this history, 330–7 ff. On the *Historikerstreit* see above pp. 401–4 ff.

13. Jäger, *Überwindung* (note 1), 165 ff. (position of the SPD; Lafontaine on 22 Apr. 1990: 166–7, on 20 May 1990: 169), 427 ff. (municipal elections, 6 May 1990), 431 ff.; Grosser, *Wagnis* (note 9), 69 ff. (FRG economic data), 227 ff. (TASS report on 29 Mar. 1990: 238), 296 (estimates of the cost of unity in May 1990), 330 ff. (property questions; statement from 15 May 1990: 336–9), 368 ff. (German Unity Fund; Grosser quote: 372), 373 ff. (unity treaty negotiations); Kaiser, *Deutschlands Vereinigung* (note 7), 205–7 (Volkskammer statement on 12 Apr. 1990); *Volkskammer der Deutschen Demokratischen Republik, 10. Wahlperiode*, xxvi. 41–51 (de Maizière's inaugural, 19 Apr. 1990); *Treuhandanstalt* (note 11), 32 ff.; *Dokumente* (note 1), 1122–5 (Kohl's talk with the *Länder* prime ministers, 16 May 1990), 1182–4 (Schäuble's and Waigel's negotiations with SPD representatives, 6 June 1990); Ulrike Fokken, 'Soll und Haben. Der Finanzminister und sein ehrgeiziges Ziel: Bis 2006 soll die Neuverschuldung Null betragen', *Der Tagesspiegel*, 4 May 2000 (state debt numbers, 1982–90); Vogel, *Nachsichten* (note 7), 331 ff.; Horst Ehmke, *Mittendrin. Von der Grossen Koalition zur Deutschen Einheit* (Berlin: Rowohlt, 1994), 403 ff.; *Sten. Ber.* cliii. 17178 (Vollmer, 21 June 1990), 17219 (Glotz, 21 June 1990); *Verhandlungen des Bundesrates 1990. Stenographische Berichte von der 609. Sitzung on 16. Februar 1990 bis zur 625. Sitzung on 14. Dezember 1990*, 353 (Schröder, 22 June 1990); Förster and Roski, *DDR* (note 12), 78–9. (emigrant numbers); *Mandat für Deutsche Einheit. Die 10. Volkskammer zwischen DDR-Verfassung und Grundgesetz*, ed. Hans-J. Misselwitz and Richard Schröder (Opladen: Westdeutscher Verlag, 2000); Birgit Lahann, *Genosse Judas. Die zwei Leben des Ibrahim Böhme* (Reinbek: Rowohlt, 1992). *Hyperion* quote: Friedrich Hölderlin, *Sämtliche Werke. Kritische Textausgabe*, ed. D. E. Sattler, xi. *Hyperion* (Darmstadt: Luchterhand, 1984), 46.

14. Gransow and Jarausch ed., *Vereinigung* (note 3), 160–2 (Chequers account, 24 Mar. 1990); Timothy Garton Ash, 'Wie es eigentlich war. Ein Teilnehmer der Thatcher-Runde äussert sich', *FAZ*, 18 July 1990; Norman Stone, 'Recht geredet. Was Frau Thatcher fragen musste', ibid., 19 July 1990; Fritz Stern, 'Die zweite Chance. Die Wege der Deutschen', ibid. 26 July 1990; Gordon A. Craig, 'Die Chequers-Affäre von 1990. Beobachtungen zum Thema Presse und internationale Beziehungen', *VfZ* 39 (1991), 611–23 (Ridley quotes, 14 July 1990: 618–19); Günther Heydemann, 'Partner oder Konkurrent? Das britische Deutschlandbild während des Wiedervereinigungsprozesses 1989–1991', in *Feindbilder. Die Darstellung des Gegners in der politischen Publizistik des Mittelalters und der Neuzeit*, ed. Franz Bosbach (Cologne: Böhlau, 1992), 201–34 (O'Brien quote from 31 Oct. 1989 with emphasis in the original:

211); Thatcher's interview with the *Sunday Times* on 25 Feb. 1990 at: http://www.margaretthatcher.org/speeches/displaydocument.asp?docid=107865; Margaret Thatcher, *Downing Street No. 10. Die Erinnerungen* (Düsseldorf: Droste, 1993), 1094 ff., orig. *The Downing Street Years* (London: HarperCollins, 1993); Kohl, *Ich wollte* (note 1), 333 ff. (Dublin summit, 25–6 June 1990: 408 ff.); Hans-Dietrich Genscher, 'Wir wollen ein europäisches Deutschland', in *Unterwegs zur Einheit, Reden und Dokumente aus bewegter Zeit* (Berlin: Siedler, 1991), 257–68 (speech to WEU, 23 Mar. 1990); Teltschik, *329 Tage* (note 6), 147 ff. (Moscow talks on 14 May 1990: 230 ff.); *Dokumente* (note 1), 1084–90 (Kohl–Shevardnadze talk, 4 May 1990), 1090–4 (Two-Plus-Four meeting in Bonn, 5 May 1990), 1114–18 (Gorbachev–Teltschik talk, 14 May 1990), 1178–80 (Bush's letter to Kohl, 4 June 1990), 1249–65 (Two-Plus-Four meeting in Berlin, 22 June 1990), 1309–23 (NATO summit in London, 5–6 July 1990), 1340–67 (Moscow and Archys talks, 15–16 July 1990; Gorbachev quote, 15 July 1990); Falin, *Erinnerungen* (note 3), 493 ff. (quote: 495); Kaiser, *Deutschlands Vereinigung* (note 7), 208–10 (Dublin declaration of the European Council, 28 Apr. 1990), 224–5 (Warsaw Pact statement in Moscow, 7 June 1990), 225–6 ('Message from Turnberry', 8 June 1990), 231–2 (Bundestag and Volkskammer decisions on the German–Polish border, 21 June 1990), 241–6 (NATO London declaration, 5–6 July 1990); Weidenfeld, *Aussenpolitik* (note 7), 312 ff. (Genscher to WEU, 23 Mar. 1990), 445–6 (Bahr, 18 June 1990), 347 ff. (Mitterrand's and Kohl's letter to Haughey, 18 Apr. 1990: 409 ff.); Jäger, *Überwindung* (note 1), 163 ff. (SPD discussion of alliance question); Zelikow and Rice, *Sternstunde* (note 7), 314 ff. (Shevardnadze on Article 23: 315; Lithuanian crisis: 356 ff.; Gorbachev in Washington, 31 May–3 June 1990: 381 ff.; Bush's statement, 3 June 1990: 389), 417 ff. (NATO London summit), 449 ff. (USSR–FRG negotiations), 497 ff. (changing power relations in 1989–90). English versions: of Dublin declaration of the European Council: http://europa.eu.int/rapid/pressReleasesAction.do?reference=DOC/90/1&format=HTML&aged=1&language=EN&guiLanguage=en; of Bush's statement: http://www.presidency.ucsb.edu/ws/index.php?pid=18549; of Mitterrand–Kohl letter at: http://www.ellopos.net/politics/mitterrand-kohl.htm; of NATO's 'Message from Turnberry': http://www.nato.int/docu/comm/49–95/c900608b.htm; of NATO's London Declaration: http://www.nato.int/docu/basictxt/b900706a.htm.

15. Wolfgang Schäuble, *Der Vertrag. Wie ich über die deutsche Einheit verhandelte* (Stuttgart: Deutsche Verlags-Anstalt, 1991), 123 ff., 265 ff. (Stasi documents); *AdG* 60 (1990), 34808–14 (situation in the GDR, 27 July–23 Aug. 1990); *Dokumente* (note 1), 195 ff.; *Vereinigung* (note 3), ed. Gransow and Jarausch, 198–9 (election contract, 3 Aug. 1990); Kaiser, *Deutschlands Vereinigung* (note 7), 252 (Volkskammer decision on 23 Aug. 1990), 253–5 (Genscher, Vienna, 30 Aug. 1990), 258–310 (documents on the foreign policy aspect of reunification, 12 Sept.–1 Oct. 1990); *Sten. Ber., 6. Wahlperiode*, lxxix. 9981–2 (Carlo Schmid, 25 Feb. 1972), *11. Wahlperiode*, cliv. 17439–43 (Kohl, 23 Aug. 1990), 17443–8 (Lafontaine, 23 Aug. 1990); *Volkskammer* (note 13), xxviii. 1382 (Gysi, 23 Aug. 1990); *BVerfGE*, lxxxii (Tübingen: Mohr, 1991), 322–52 (ruling on 29 Sept. 1990 on voting law); Astrid Lange, *Was die Rechten lesen. Fünfzig Zeitschriften. Ziele, Inhalte, Taktik* (Munich: C. H. Beck, 1993), 114 ff. (*Nation und Europa*; Thomas

Assheuer and Hans Sarkowicz, *Rechtsradikale in Deutschland. Die alte und die neue Rechte* (Munich: C. H. Beck, 1992), 65 ff. (*Nation Europa*); Schroeder, *SED-Staat* (note 1), 440 ff. (MfS employees; numbers for 1989: 442); Genscher, *Erinnerungen* (note 1), 854 ff. (Vienna, 30 Aug. 1990: 861 ff.; Genscher and Bush at CSCE, 1 Oct. 1990: 882–4); *Verträge zur deutschen Einheit* (Bonn: Bundeszentrale für politische Bildung, 1991), 41–78 (Unification treaty), 83–90 (Treaty on the Final Settlement with Respect to Germany), 91 (Agreed Minute); 'Hinter den Türen der Volkskammer', *taz*, 1 Oct. 1990 (identification of IMs during the session on 28 Sept. 1990); Hannes Bahrmann and Christoph Links, *Chronik der Wende, 2. Stationen der Einheit. Die letzten Monate der DDR* (Berlin: Ch. Links, 1995), 333 (Volkskammer ceremony, 2 Oct. 1990); Zelikow and Rice, *Sternstunde* (note 7), 486 ff.; Jäger, *Überwindung* (note 1), 471 ff. On abortion law in the FRG see above, pp. 306–7.

16. 'Geschichte erleben—so nah wie möglich', *SZ*, 4 Oct. 1990 (celebration on the Platz der Republik, Weizsäcker's speech, 2–3 Dec. 1990); 'Sie tanzen, singen und trinken auf das vereinigte Deutschland', *FAZ*, 4 Oct. 1990; *Texte zur Deutschlandpolitik*, series 3, viii b (Bonn: Deutscher Bundes-Verlag, 1991), 708–11 (Bergmann-Pohl, 3 Oct. 1990), 717–31 (Weizsäcker, 3 Oct. 1990); Kaiser, *Deutschlands Vereinigung* (note 7), 360–3 (NATO and Warsaw Pact declarations, 19 Nov. 1990), 368–75 (Charter of Paris, 21 Nov. 1990); Text of the Charter of Paris at: http://www.osce.org/documents/mcs/1990/11/4045_en.pdf; Gregor Schöllgen, *Geschichte der Weltpolitik von Hitler bis Gorbatschow 1941–1991* (Munich: C. H. Beck, 1996), 428 ff.; Oskar Lafontaine, *Deutsche Wahrheiten. Die nationale und soziale Frage* (Hamburg: Hoffmann und Campe, 1990), 85 ff.; id., *Das Herz schlägt links* (Munich: Econ, 1999), 31 ff., tr. as *The Heart Beats on the Left* (Malden, MA: Blackwell, 2000); Oskar Lafontaine, *Probleme und Perspektiven der Deutschlandpolitik, 17 Sept. 1990* (Bonn: Friedrich-Ebert-Stiftung, Projektgruppe Deutschlandpolitisches Wiss. Forum); *Sitzung des Parteivorstands der SPD, 3 Dec. 1990* (Willy-Brandt-Archiv, Bestand Unkel, Mappe 230); Vogel, *Nachsichten* (note 7), 539 ff.; Peter Glotz, *Der Irrweg des Nationalstaates. Europäische Reden an ein deutsches Publikum* (Stuttgart: Deutsche Verlags-Anstalt, 1990), 129–30.; Heiner Geissler, *Der Irrweg des Nationalismus* (Weinheim: Beltz Athenäum Verlag, 1995), 34; Golo Mann, *Deutsche Geschichte des XIX. Jahrhunderts* (Frankfurt: Büchergilde Gutenberg, 1958), 358 ff.; Gerald Stourzh, *Vom Reich zur Republik. Studien zum Österreichbewusstsein im 20. Jahrhundert* (Vienna: Atelier, 1990), 10 ff. (criticism of *grossdeutsch* views of West German historians, like Karl Dietrich Erdmann's formula 'Three states, two nations, one people' [1985] and Wolfgang J. Mommsen's of the FRG as 'core state' and 'two other states "of the German nation"', the GDR and Austria [1978]). On Renan see the first volume of this history, 198–9.

17. *Sten. Ber.*, 12. *Wahlperiode*, clvii. 2746–7 (Schäuble, 20 June 1991), 2754–6 (Glotz, 20 June 1991); *Berlin–Bonn. Die Debatte. Alle Bundestagsreden vom 20. Juni 1991* (Cologne: Kiepenheuer & Witsch, 1991); Klaus von Beyme, *Hauptstadtsuche. Hauptstadtfunktionen im Interessenkonflikt zwischen Bonn und Berlin* (Frankfurt: Suhrkamp, 1991); *Historiker betrachten Deutschland. Beiträge zum Vereinigungsprozess und zur Hauptstadtdiskussion*, ed. Udo Wengst (Bonn: Bouvier, 1992); id., 'Wer stimmte für Bonn, wer für Berlin? Die Entscheidung über den

Parlaments- und Regierungssitz im Bundestag am 20. Juni 1991', *Zeitschrift für Parlamentsfragen*, 22 (1991), 339–43; Ralf Sitte, 'Lobbying in der Hauptstadt-Debatte. Form und Möglichkeiten unkoordinierter Interessenvertretung', ibid., 535–54; Hans-Georg Lehmann, *Deutschland-Chronik 1945–1995* (Bonn: Bouvier, 1996), 456 ff. (transformation of the constitution; asylum figures 1992: 456), 480 ff. (European policy), 522–3. (abortion); Helge-Lothar Batt, *Die Grundgesetzreform nach der deutschen Einheit* (Opladen: Westdeutscher Verlag, 1996), 55–6; *Revision des Grundgesetzes? Ergebnisse der Gemeinsamen Verfassungskommission (GVK) des Deutschen Bundestages und des Bundesrates*, ed. Norbert Konegen and Peter Nitschke (Opladen: Westdeutscher Verlag, 1997); Tatiana Paterna, *Volksgesetzgebung. Analyse der Verfassungsdebatte nach der Vereinigung Deutschlands* (Frankfurt: P. Lang, 1995); Heinrich August Winkler, 'Separatismus auf Filzlatschen', *Die Zeit*, 15 Oct. 1998. For criticism of the procedural overloading of the constitution in the case of the asylum regulations see Dieter Grimm, 'Parteiinteressen und Punktsiege. Wie man eine Verfassung verderben kann', *FAZ*, 12 Dec. 1998. The abortion ruling on 28 May 1993 in *BVerfGE*, lxxxviii (Tübingen: Mohr, 1993), 203–366.

18. Grosser, *Wagnis* (note 9), 380 ff. (quote: 435; contract wage decisions in the third quarter of 1990: 457; growth rates: 466; labour productivity: 474; unemployment in 1990: 477); Lehmann, *Deutschland-Chronik* (note 17), 460 ff. (court ruling on 3 Nov. 1992: 464); *AdG* 69 (1999) 43896–7 (court ruling on 8 Nov. 1999); *Sozialgeschichte* (note 1), ed. Kaelble et al.; Theo Pirker et al., *Der Plan als Befehl und Fiktion. Wirtschaftsführung in der DDR. Gespräche und Analysen* (Opladen: Westdeutscher Verlag, 1995); Inga Markovits, *Die Abwicklung. Ein Tagebuch am Ende der DDR-Justiz* (Munich: C. H. Beck, 1993), tr. as *Imperfect Justice: An East–West German Diary* (Oxford: Oxford University Press, 1995); *Programm der Partei des Demokratischen Sozialismus* (Berlin, 1993), 16; Heinrich August Winkler, 'Kein Bruch mit Lenin. Die Weimarer Republik im Geschichtsbild von SED und PDS', in *Streitfragen der deutschen Geschichte. Essays zum 19. und 20. Jahrhundert* (Munich: C. H. Beck, 1997), 107–22; *Gesellschaft ohne Eliten? Führungsgruppen in der DDR*, ed. Arnd Bauernkämper (Berlin: Metropol, 1997); *Doppelte Zeitgeschichte. Deutsch–deutsche Beziehungen 1945–1990*, ed. id. et al. (Bonn: Dietz, 1998); *Geschichte als Herrschaftsdiskurs. Der Umgang mit der Vergangenheit in der DDR*, ed. Martin Sabrow (Cologne: Böhlau, 2000); *Die DDR–Erinnerung an einen untergegangenen Staat*, ed. Heiner Timmermann (Berlin: Duncker & Humblot, 1999); *Die Grenzen der Diktatur. Staat und Gesellschaft in der DDR*, ed. Richard Bessel and Ralph Jessen (Göttingen: Vandenhoeck & Ruprecht, 1996); Antonia Grunenberg, *Antifaschismus—ein deutscher Mythos* (Reinbek: Rowohlt, 1995). On church data: *Statistisches Jahrbuch der Deutschen Demokratischen Republik 1955* (Berlin: Deutscher Zentralverlag, 1956), 33 (GDR in 1950); *Statistisches Jahrbuch 1991 für das vereinte Deutschland* (Wiesbaden: Metzler Poeschel, 1991), 26, 108, and 109 (1990); *Statistisches Jahrbuch 1999 für die Bundesrepublik Deutschland* (Wiesbaden: Metzler Poeschel, 1999), 32–3, 96–7 (1997). On unemployment in 1992 and 1998: ibid. 121. On unemployment in June 2000: 'Niedrigste Arbeitslosigkeit seit November 1995', *SZ*, 7 July 2000. Goethe quote in Johann Wolfgang von Goethe, *Werke*. Weimar edition (Munich: DTV, 1987), ii. 285.

19. 'Grüne grenzen sich ab', *taz*, 12 Sept. 1990; Joschka Fischer, 'Vorwand und Anlass', ibid., 14 Sept. 1990; Marieluise Beck-Oberdorf et al., 'Opposition bis ins Jahr 2000', ibid. 21 Sept. 1990 (emphasis in the original); Oskar Lafontaine, 'Verzweifelte Aussichten', ibid. 9 Feb. 1991; Peter Glotz, 'Der ungerechte Krieg', *Der Spiegel*, no. 9, 25 Feb. 1991; Antje Vollmer, 'Maggies letzte Rache', *taz*, 21 Feb. 1991; Hans-Ulrich Klose, 'Die Deutschen und der Krieg am Golf—eine schwierige Debatte', *FAZ*, 25 Jan. 1991; Cora Stephan, 'Der anständige Deutsche—zum Fürchten', *SZ*, 9–10 Feb. 1991; Jürgen Habermas, 'Wider die Logik des Krieges', *Die Zeit*, 15 Feb. 1991 (emphasis in the original); Hans Magnus Enzensberger, 'Hitlers Wiedergänger', *Der Spiegel*, no. 6, 4 Feb. 1991; Dan Diner, *Der Krieg der Erinnerungen und die Ordnung der Welt* (Berlin: Rotbuch Verlag, 1991); Richard Herzinger and Hannes Stein, *Endzeit-Propheten oder Die Offensive der Antiwestler. Fundamentalismus, Antiamerikanismus und Neue Rechte* (Reinbek: Rowohlt, 1995); *Liebesgrüsse aus Bagdad. Die 'edlen Seelen' der Friedensbewegung und der Krieg am Golf*, ed. Klaus Bittermann (Berlin: Edition Tiamat, 1991); Ulrike Ackermann, *Sündenfall der Intellektuellen. Ein deutsch–französischer Streit von 1945 bis heute* (Stuttgart: Klett-Cotta, 2000), 19 ff.; Günter Verheugen, 'Politik nicht auf Bundeswehreinsätze reduzieren', *Vorwärts*, no. 8, Aug. 1995; Heinrich August Winkler, 'Rücksichtslos gewaltfrei. Der Balkan, die SPD und die politische Moral', *FAZ*, 7 Aug. 1995; Ernst-Otto Czempiel, 'Besinnungslos gewaltsam? Über einen neuerdings erhobenen kriegerischen Ton: Antwort auf Heinrich August Winkler', ibid. 15 Aug. 1995; *Sten. Ber.*, *12. Wahlperiode*, clxxv. 21165–9 (Kinkel, 22 July 1994); *BVerfGE*, lxxxviii (Tübingen: Mohr, 1994), 173–85 (ruling on 8 Apr. 1993; quote: 183); xc (Tübingen: Mohr, 1994), 286–394 (ruling on 12 July 1994); *AdG* 63 (1993), 37740–1 (AWACS deployment); ibid. 65 (1995), 40171–2 (Bosnia deployment); Genscher, *Erinnerungen* (note 1), 899 ff.; Lehmann, *Deutschland-Chronik* (note 17), 472–3; Helmut Hubel, *Der zweite Golfkrieg in der internationalen Politik. Mit ausgewählten Dokumenten* (Bonn: Forschungsinstitut der Deutschen Gesellschaft für Auswärtige Politik, 1991); Lawrence Freedman and Efraim Karsh, *The Gulf Conflict 1990–1991: Diplomacy and War in the New World Order* (Princeton: Princeton University Press, 1995); Marie-Janine Calic, *Krieg und Frieden in Bosnien-Herzegowina* (Frankfurt: Suhrkamp, 1995); Schöllgen, *Geschichte* (note 16), 452 ff.; Manfred Hildermeier, *Geschichte der Sowjetunion 1917–1991. Entstehung und Niedergang des ersten sozialistischen Staates* (Munich: C. H. Beck, 1998), 105 ff. On Norbert Elias: *Norbert Elias über sich selbst* interview with, A. J. Heerma van Voss and A. van Stolk (Frankfurt: Suhrkamp, 1990); Elias, *Studien über die Deutschen. Machtkämpfe und Habitusentwicklung im 19. und 20. Jahrhundert* (Frankfurt: Suhrkamp, 1989).
20. Elisabeth Noelle-Neumann, 'Wird sich jetzt fremd, was zusammengehört?', *FAZ*, 19 May 1993; ead., 'Wir sind ein Volk', ibid. 15 Sept. 1999; 'Steigende Identifikation mit dem vereinten Deutschland', ibid. 16 June 2000 (data from autumn 1999); Peter Glotz, 'Wider den Feuilleton-Nationalismus', *Die Zeit*, 19 Apr. 1991; Klaus Hartung, 'Wider das alte Denken', ibid. 10 May 1991; Jürgen Habermas. 'Die andere Zerstörung der Vernunft', ibid. 10 May 1991 (emphasis in the original); id., 'Bemerkungen zu einer verworrenen Diskussion. Was bedeutet "Aufarbeitung der Vergangenheit" heute', ibid. 3 Apr. 1992; Richard Schröder, 'Es ist doch nicht alles schlecht', ibid. 31 May 1991; Marion Gräfin

Dönhoff et al., *Weil das Land Versöhnung braucht* (Reinbek: Rowohlt, 1993); *Enquete-Kommission 'Aufarbeitung von Geschichte und Folgen der SED-Diktatur in Deutschland'*, i. *Die Enquete-Kommission 'Aufarbeitung von Geschichte und Folgen der SED-Diktatur in Deutschland' im Deutschen Bundestag* (Baden-Baden: Nomos, 1995), 178–778 (report), 779–89 (motion, quotes: 781–2; emphasis in the original); Hermann Rudolph, 'Schwierigkeiten mit einem Glücksfall', *Der Tagesspiegel*, 31 Oct. 1993; Ralf Dahrendorf, 'Die Sache mit der Nation', *Merkur*, 44/500 (1990), 823–34 (827, 833); Dieter Grimm, 'Braucht Europa eine Verfassung?', in *Informationsgesellschaft und Rechtskultur*, ed. Marie-Theres Tinnefeld et al. (Baden-Baden: Nomos, 1995), 211–30; Georg Lukács, *Die Zerstörung der Vernunft*, in *Werke*, ix (Neuwied: Luchterhand, 1962). Heuss's speech on 12 Sept. 1949 in Theodor Heuss, *Die grossen Reden*, ii. *Der Staatsmann* (Tübingen: Wunderlich, 1965, 88–98 (95). On Richard Löwenthal's view of the KPD as a 'derivative totalitarian party' see id., 'Russland und die Bolschewisierung des deutschen Kommunismus', in *Deutsch–russische Beziehungen von Bismarck bis zur Gegenwart*, ed. Werner Markert (Stuttgart: Kohlhammer, 1964), 97–116 (105); On Löwenthal's 1965 argument see above, p. 207. On Bracher's view of the FRG as 'post-national democracy among nation states' see above pp.397–8 ff.

FAREWELL TO SEPARATE PATHS: LOOKING BACK AND LOOKING AHEAD

1. Paul Levi, 'Die "stille" Koalition', *Sozialistische Politik und Wirtschaft*, 4 (1926), no. 46 (19 Nov). On George F. Kennan's view of the First World War as '*the* great seminal catastrophe' of the twentieth century see the first volume of this history, 298.

2. Andreas Wirsching, 'Krisenzeit der "Klassischen Moderne" oder deutscher "Sonderweg"? Überlegungen zum Projekt Faktoren der Stabilität und Instabilität in der Demokratie der Zwischenkriegszeit: Deutschland und Frankreich im Vergleich', in *50 Jahre Institut zur Zeitgeschichte. Eine Bilanz*, ed. Horst Möller and Udo Wengst (Munich: Oldenbourg, 1999), 365–81.

3. Jakob Katz, *Vom Vorurteil bis zur Vernichtung. Der Antisemitismus 1700–1933* (Munich: C. H. Beck, 1989), 21 ff. (on Dühring: 272 ff.), orig. *From Prejudice to Destruction: Anti-Semitism, 1700–1933* (Cambridge, MA: Harvard University Press, 1980). On Dühring, de Lagarde (Paul Anton Böttcher), and German anti-Semitismus after 1871 see the first volume of this history, 204–13.

4. *Imperium, Empire, Reich. Ein Konzept politischer Herrschaft im deutsch–britischen Vergleich*, ed. Franz Bosbach and Hermann Hiery (Munich: Saur, 1999); Emilio Gentile, *Il culto del littorio* (Rome: Laterza, 1993), tr. as *The Sacralization of Politics in Fascist Italy* (Cambridge, MA: Harvard University Press, 1996); Hildegard Schaeder, *Moskau das Dritte Rom. Studien zur Geschichte der politischen Theorien in der slawischen Welt* (1929) 2nd edn (Darmstadt: Wissenschaftliche Buchgesellschaft, 1957).

5. Rudolf Stadelmann, 'Vom geschichtlichen Wesen der deutschen Revolutionen', *Zeitwende* 10 (1934), 109–16 (112–13, 115); id., *Das geschichtliche Selbstbewusstsein der Nation* (Tübingen: Mohr, 1934), 20–1 (emphases in the original). On the 'Reich' idea among the 'conservative revolutionaries' see the first volume of this history, 466, 492.

6. See above pp. 1–3, 62–4, 73–5. On Hitler's speech on 30 Jan. 1942: p. 90.

7. Karl Bosl, *Geschichte des Mittelalters*, 2nd edn (Munich: Lurz, 1956)(1st edn 1951), 190.

8. Karl Marx, 'Zur Kritik der Hegelschen Rechtsphilosophie. Einleitung', in Karl Marx and Friedrich Engels, *Werke* (Berlin: Institute for Marxism/Leninism, Central Committee of the SED, 1959– , i. 378–91 (391; emphases in the original).

9. Rudolf Stadelmann, 'Deutschland und die westeuropäischen Revolutionen', in id., *Deutschland und Westeuropa* (Laupheim: U. Steiner, 1948), 11–33 (14, 27–8, 30–1). See the first volume of this history, 40.

10. Marx, 'Kritik' (note 8), 391 (emphases in the original).

11. M. Rainer Lepsius, 'Das Erbe des Nationalsozialismus und die politische Kultur der Nachfolgestaaten des "Grossdeutschen Reiches" ' (1988), in *Demokratie in Deutschland. Soziologisch-historische Konstellationsanalysen* (Göttingen: Vandenhoeck & Ruprecht, 1993), 229–45 (235).

12. *Der Parlamentarische Rat 1948–1949. Akten und Protokolle*, ix: *Plenum*, ed. *Wolfram Werner* (Munich: Boldt, 1996), 190.

13. See above pp. 397–8.

14. Hanno Loewy, 'Auschwitz als Metapher', *taz*, 25 Jan. 1997.

15. Maurice Halbwachs, *Das Gedächtnis und seine sozialen Bedingungen* (Frankfurt: Luchterhand, 1985), 19, 22, 368, 390, orig. *Les cadres sociaux de la mémoire* (Paris: F. Alcan, 1925).

16. Jan Assmann, *Das kulturelle Gedächtnis. Schrift, Erinnerung und politische Identität in frühen Hochkulturen*, 2nd edn (Munich: 1999), 48 ff.; Moshe Zuckerman, *Zweierlei Holocaust. Der Holocaust in den politischen Kulturen Israels und Deutschlands* (Göttingen: C. H. Beck, 1998); Aleida Assmann and Ute Frevert, *Geschichtsvergessenheit und Geschichtsversessenheit. Vom Umgang mit deutschen Vergangenheiten nach 1945* (Stuttgart: Deutsche Verlags-Anstalt, 1999).

17. Robert Musil, *Der Mann ohne Eigenschaften*, in *Gesammelte Werke in Einzelausgaben*, ed. Adolf Frisé (Hamburg: Rowohlt, 1952), 1122–3.

18. See above 432–3.

19. Jan Ross, 'Unschuld an der Macht', *FAZ*, 18 Feb. 1991.

20. Carl Schmitt, *Politische Theologie. Vier Kapitel zur Lehre von der Souveränität*, 2nd edn (Munich: Duncker & Humblot, 1934), 11.

21. Stéphane Courtois et al., *The Black Book of Communism: Crimes, Terror, Repression* (Cambridge, MA: Harvard University Press, 1999), orig. *Le livre noir du communisme: crimes, terreurs et répression* (Paris: R. Laffont, 1997); Stefan Reinecke, 'Don't touch my Holocaust', *taz*, 25 June 1998; Peter Novick, *The Holocaust and Collective Memory: The American Experience* (London: Bloomsbury, 2000); Zygmunt Bauman, *Modernity and the Holocaust* (Cambridge: Cambridge University Press, 1989); id., *Ist der Holocaust wiederholbar?* (Wiesbaden: Hessische Landeszentrale für politische Bildung, 1994).

22. Peter Glotz, *Der Irrweg des Nationalstaats. Europäische Reden an ein deutsches Publikum* (Stuttgart: Deutsche Verlags-Anstalt, 1990), 151.

23. *Evangelische Kirche und freiheitliche Demokratie. Der Staat des Grundgesetzes als Angebot und Aufgabe. Eine Denkschrift der Evangelischen Kirche in Deutschland* (Gütersloh: G. Mohn, 1985), 9.

24. Salomon Korn, 'Die zweigeteilte und die gemeinsame Erinnerung. Was es in Israel heisst, des Holocaust zu gedenken, und was in Deutschland', in id., *Geteilte Erinnerung. Beiträge zur 'deutsch-jüdischen' Gegenwart* (Berlin: Philo, 1998), 99–108 (105).

25. Angelo Bolaffi, *Die schrecklichen Deutschen. Eine merkwürdige Liebeserklärung* (Berlin: Siedler, 1995), 13.

Index